Y0-CWM-381

PRODUCT SAFETY and LIABILITY
A Desk Reference

PRODUCT SAFETY and LIABILITY

A Desk Reference

JOHN KOLB
Formerly Associate Editor,
Product Engineering

and

STEVEN S. ROSS
Managing Editor,
Boardroom Reports

McGRAW-HILL BOOK COMPANY
New York St. Louis San Francisco Auckland Bogotá
Hamburg Johannesburg London Madrid Mexico
Montreal New Delhi Panama Paris São Paulo
Singapore Sydney Tokyo Toronto

Library of Congress Cataloging in Publication Data

Kolb, John, 1915–1974
   Product safety and liability.

   Bibliography: p.
   Includes index.
   1. Product safety. 2. Product safety—Law and
legislation—United States. 3. Products liability—
United States. 4. Products liability—Chemical
products—United States. 5. Insurance, Products liabili-
ty—United States. l. Ross, Steven S., joint author.
II. Title.
TS175.K64   658.5'6   79-20215
ISBN 0-07-035380-8

Copyright © 1980 by McGraw-Hill, Inc. All rights reserved.
Printed in the United States of America. No part of this
publication may be reproduced, stored in a retrieval system,
or transmitted, in any form or by any means, electronic,
mechanical, photocopying, recording, or otherwise, without
the prior written permission of the publisher.
This copyright does not cover Appendixes C and F, which
were drawn from the Code of Federal Regulations,
or Appendix E, which was adapted from the Consumer
Product Safety Commission's annual report.

1234567890 KPKP 89876543210

The editors for this book were Jeremy Robinson and Ruth Weine,
the designer was Elliot Epstein, and the production supervisor
was Teresa F. Leaden. It was set in Baskerville by University Graphics, Inc.
Printed and bound by The Kingsport Press

To
Sylvia, Larri, Marion,
Heather, and Leah

CONTENTS

Preface   xi

An Appreciation—Raymond Spilman   xv

I WHY PRODUCT SAFETY, AND WHY NOW?

1. Pressures for Safer Product Design   1
2. Evolution in Court Decisions; History of the Restatement (Second) of Torts   6
3. Some Limitations on the Defense: The Evolution of Statutory Law   22
4. Institutional Changes   35
5. What is a "Safe" Product?   37

II THE REGULATORY PROCESS, FEDERAL AND INDUSTRIAL

1. How Regulators Really Regulate   43
2. Industry Standards   53
3. The Federal Regulatory Process   59
4. Your Liability as a Standards-Setter   64

III ORGANIZING AND OPERATING CORPORATE AND DEPARTMENTAL PRODUCT SAFETY SYSTEMS

1. The Policy Statement   73
2. Design Engineer, the Prime Mover of Product Safety   75
3. Who Shall Judge?   78
4. Maintaining an Effective Program   82

5. What Can Subordinates Do if Management Contravenes Safety? ... 83
6. Personal Liability of the Designer ... 85
7. Using the Outside Consultant ... 87
8. Records Retention ... 89
9. Summary ... 93

IV DEVELOPMENT, ENGINEERING, AND DESIGN OF MINIMUM-HAZARD PRODUCTS

1. Product Conception and Development ... 95
2. Checklists: Hard to Compile, Easy to Misuse ... 99
3. The Formal Design Review Process ... 100
4. The Human Factors Interface ... 105
5. Prediction Techniques: Fault Tree Analysis ... 115
6. Prediction Techniques: Failure Modes and Effects Analysis ... 129
7. The Operator-Design Interface ... 147

V PRODUCTION OF MINIMUM-HAZARD PRODUCTS

1. Introduction ... 157
2. Outside Suppliers ... 166
3. Failure Patterns for Complex Products ... 170
4. Designing a Sampling Program ... 176
5. Change Control ... 189

VI MARKETING, DISTRIBUTION, AND SERVICING

1. The Feedback Chain ... 193
2. The Responsibility to Warn ... 202
3. Packaging ... 206
4. The Long-Lived Product ... 210
5. Accident Investigations ... 218
6. Product Recalls ... 221

VII SPECIAL CONSIDERATIONS FOR CHEMICAL PRODUCTS

1. Introduction ... 225
2. Toxicity and Other Acute Effects ... 231
3. Allergic Reactions ... 240
4. Carcinogenicity ... 241

	5. Compatibility	246
	6. Fire Suppression	257
	7. Spills	263
	8. Figuring Concentrations	267

VIII IF ALL ELSE FAILS—GOING TO COURT

1. General Preparation	275
2. Discovery	276
3. Who Should Testify?	278
4. Using the Outside Expert	282
5. Courtroom Exhibits	285

IX INSURANCE: RATES, CLAIMS, AND NEW DIRECTIONS

1. Negotiating Premiums and Coverage	287
2. Loss Control Surveys	313
3. Handling Claims	315
4. "Unconventional" Insurance Programs	316
5. When an Insuror Sues You	322

APPENDIXES

A	Checklists for Designers and Installers	329
B	Toxic Substances	379
C	Hazardous Materials Handling	401
D	American National Standards for Safety and Health	499
E	Index of Consumer Product Safety Commission Standards	525
F	Federal Record-Retention Requirements Related to Product Safety and Liability	547
G	Standards-Setting and Safety-Information Organizations	585
H	Information Sources	623
I	Bibliography	631
J	Useful Terms	641

General Index	663
Index of Standards for Specific Products and Practices (from Standards-Setting Organizations)	684

PREFACE

All through the seventies, product safety has remained in the news. As we put the finishing touches on this book, Pittway recalled 115,000 fire alarms that could themselves cause fires. Mattel began a "Missile Mail-In" aimed at removing a potentially dangerous toy from the hands of small children. The Consumer Product Safety Commision tagged millions of hair dryers—made by more than 100 companies—as containing asbestos insulation that could flake away and lodge in consumers' lungs. Lithium-sulfur batteries were removed from the emergency beacons of 60,000 private aircraft, after it was shown that the batteries can leak, forming sulfurous acid that eats through vital structural components.

The ability of America's 215 million consumers to misuse products was highlighted on December 14, 1978, when the CPSC agreed to help Hercules Chemical keep its industrial drain cleaner out of private customers' hands. Hercules had pleaded with the commission for help, since the drain cleaner is mainly sulfuric acid. CPSC also asked all manufacturers of CB and television antennas to warn consumers that metal antennas and live power lines make a perilous combination. That fact may be obvious, but at least 220 persons were electrocuted in 1975, and 275 more in 1976, while trying to install antennas. The Commerce Department recently presented a model law on product liability, hoping to protect the public from unnecessarily dangerous products and manufacturers from unusually inept consumers. Perhaps predictably, Commerce's effort was denounced by both consumer and industry groups.

Because some of the largest and most sophisticated companies apparently can't stay out of trouble when it comes to product safety and liability, many manufacturers are tempted to give up in despair. If Firestone, the 48th largest company in America, can be forced into merger by a particularly costly recall, what hope is there for improving the smaller manufacturer's chances for success?

This book, in a sense, represents the authors' conviction that there is good cause for hope, and much new expertise to back it up—that even companies with small design staffs, or firms that depend on outside design expertise, *can* take many steps to improve their chances of avoiding product liability hazards. Perhaps our own efforts here can help keep many companies—and consumers—a bit healthier.

We expect this book to be used in two ways. Those who are uninitiated in the management and technology of product safety can profitably read through the book's nine chapters. Those with more experience will probably use the book mainly as a desk reference, dipping into it to help solve specific problems as they arise. The book has been arranged to facilitate locating elusive, but fundamental, pieces of information. After introductory material on the philosophy—and the reality—of product liability law, the chapters follow the general development of a product, from its conception through the design, manufacture, and marketing phases. Much of the material needed for quick reference has been arranged in tabular form, or brought together in the appendixes. There is also an unusually detailed general index as well as a standards index.

In finishing the work John Kolb conceived and started, I have tried to stay as close as possible to his original outline. He deeply believed that a clearer understanding of the reasoning behind current court and regulatory decisions on product liability would lead designers and their managements toward greater commitment and firmer determination to market the safest possible products. Chapter I, especially, is directed to reporting the evolution of thinking in the courts and in Congress toward the goal of product safety. It is a long and complex story, but its implications are well worth pondering.

John Kolb also accurately predicted the eventual evolution of regulatory authority through the seventies—particularly the growth of the Consumer Product Safety Commission. This is all the more amazing, since the CPSC was created only a year before he died. In some areas, the course of events has been catching up with him. This is especially true in the growing concern about chemical products—their manufacture, transport, use, and disposal. Another area of great change in the past few years has been insurance coverage. Ways for companies to reduce the high cost—and even to face the unavailability—of product liability insurance are now important and varied enough to rate a chapter of their own.

In preparing this book, both authors conducted interviews with technical and managerial personnel in companies of all sizes, all over North America, in Europe, and in Japan. Many, especially in smaller firms, asked that we include extensive design checklists. These have been provided in the first appendix, albeit with some trepidation. If these lists are used by designers as a basis for their own specific and carefully considered checklists, we shall have succeeded. If, however, users of this book just blindly follow what is printed in the appendix, our efforts in writing this book will have been in vain.

Another area of possible misuse is our listing of up-to-date safety-related standards, both those in force at the CPSC, and those available through the American National Standards Institute. Every relevent standards-setting organization in the United States—even those of marginal importance—is also listed and discussed in the appendixes. Some design authorities insist, however, that designers should not be "poisoned" by previewing existing standards' concepts of safety, and that they should complete the design of new products before looking at old standards relating to them. While this approach may be valuable for the brightest and most experienced designers, or for design teams with plenty of time, money, and personnel, it can lead to overlooking or missing the advantages of valuable standards-based design information. We are convinced that easy access to the literature of safety standards is of prime importance in the vast majority of product-design assignments. Again, if designers use existing standards as evidence of "enough safety" in a product, and not as a foundation upon which to build even safer designs, our efforts will have been in vain. Whether this literature is consulted before, during, or after the product-conception stage is, of course, a matter of personal choice and organizational circumstance.

The one choice engineers, designers, and their employers no longer have is whether or not to pursue safety goals. To ignore or pay only lip service to safety—especially on the grounds that consumers are hopelessly inept and the courts hopelessly anticorporation—is professionally irresponsible and can jeopardize corporate survival. That this lesson needs repeating now, in light of recent, well-publicized, safety-related predicaments, is evidence enough of the need for continuing vigilance. Nevertheless, every concerned person can find encouragement in the progress made during the past decade in such obvious categories as automobiles, housing fixtures, and toys. We can only hope that the same claim can be made for many additional categories a decade hence.

A book as large as this one is necessarily the product of many people. Thanks go especially to the hundreds of design professionals, insurance experts, and regulators who shared their thoughts and experiences with the authors. Several supplied subchapters of their own, especially in Chapters IV and V. Sylvia Kolb provided the index. Carole Cole and my wife, Larri, helped with typing and fact-checking. Ruth Weine at McGraw-Hill helped shepherd the book through editing and production. Jeremy Robinson had the wisdom to see the need for this book; his support at McGraw-Hill kept John Kolb's project alive and me involved with its fruition. It is hoped that this book now represents the essential purposes, thinking, and values that, as colleagues, both authors shared.

Steven S. Ross

AN APPRECIATION

The pages of this book, "Product Safety and Liability," blow away the years as clouds before the wind. Jack Kolb, in all his enthusiasm and dedication to safe and sane design practices strides from this book, not as another engineering editor writing for engineers, but as an active apostle and crusader for a better and safer consumer world.

To Jack, the providing of a safer world for the consumer was clearly the personal responsibility of every contributor to a product's evolution. Each was not, however, to be a soloist, but a member of a team working together through every phase of product progression—concept, research and development, legal review, marketing, and management—to achieve a safely designed product, a result he rightly recognized as a social and economic necessity that could be accomplished only through teamwork. Jack promoted this theme as a pioneer, a driven believer working against time—as indeed he was.

Good fortune blessed Jack and his dream with a most supportive and agreeable boss, Elmer ("Tange") Tangerman, editor-in-chief of *Product Engineering* magazine (who nowadays is happily whittling chunks of wood into award-winning pieces of sculpture out Long Island way).

Together, with Jack as the driving force, they changed the tenor of a nuts and bolts, editorially vertical engineering magazine into one of the first and the most powerful sixties' voices for cooperation among technical professionals—first, in articles with supporting editorials; then, by Jack originating and Elmer Tangerman backing the creation of the Product Engineering Master Design Award Program that was to run for some ten years. Many will remember Jack scurrying about, rounding up topflight management juries and exciting product entries, and finally emceeing the Award Competition itself, while Tange later presented the awards in the name of the magazine. No product could be judged unless all major contributors, including engineering specialists, industrial designers, human factors specialists, production engineers, and management, were listed along with their contributions to the result. This award program was the class product-design award of its time, and in this designer's mind, has never been topped in quality, scope, and idealism.

I knew Jack intimately as he moved and worked among industrial designers. He was particularly sensitive to young, product-oriented designers whom he considered to be most knowledgeable and concerned about people but not entirely able to translate their ideas into practical hardware. As a result, he spent an inordinate amount of time helping more young practicing industrial designers than any other single person I know. Professor Arthur Pulos, Chairman, Department of Design at Syracuse University, noted, "Most of us soon learned to follow and use his feature articles teaching the use of cross disciplines as published in *Product Engineering* magazine. We of the Industrial Design Society of America owe him much for his support and interest in industrial design and designers." One of the happiest results of the articles referred to by Pulos, was that engineers and designers began speaking to each other as human beings.

From design workshops, to lunch threesomes, to traveling nationwide as a lecturer to the trial lawyers associations, his *modus operandi* was personal contact. Bringing people together was the heart of the game. He would invite his guests, usually individuals with decidedly differing opinions, to explore and learn of one another's thoughts and talents, and then he would suggest that, after all, they might all do better as teammates than as antagonists. (Sounds simple—but it wasn't easy then, and it still isn't.) The result, of course, was to move everyone a bit closer to Jack's objective of providing a way to assure safer and liability-free products for consumers.

I often think that Jack owed his unique ability to bring together proponents of differing disciplines to his wife, Sylvia, a professional writer and editor of outstanding ability. To these attributes she added a deep compassion for the vagaries of all living things—plant and animal alike—a climate supportive of Jack's values and appreciative of his capabilities.

As a journalist (and as a person), Jack was a remarkable listener, hearing viewpoint and intent as clearly as words. And perhaps that is why he could so successfully draw into consonance the differing approaches of proponents of each of the product-development disciplines and weld the various individual contributions into a productive, cohesive, and progressive statement of intent, direction, or agreement among all parties.

Time passes; the solid core of Jack's lifework that prompted this book is here. Steve Ross, now managing editor of *Boardroom Reports* and formerly editor-in-chief of *New Engineer* magazine, has done a splendid and highly professional job of presenting the factual aspects of the draft manuscript and of updating and adding where needed; in the appendixes, he has also devised ingenious ways of providing encyclopedic amounts of data in compact, easy-access form. In sum, this is a "how-to" book that will not only provide knowledge, joy in use, and satisfaction to you, the reader, but will also help assure the safety and pleasure of the legions of consumers who use the products you help into the marketplace.

Raymond Spilman, F-IDSA, HFS, ISCC
Stamford, Connecticut

I
WHY PRODUCT SAFETY, AND WHY NOW?

1. PRESSURES FOR SAFER PRODUCT DESIGN

It is hardly a secret among business people today that the designing, production, and distribution of products have entered an era of increasing emphasis on safety. This shift in emphasis, which has been occurring gradually since World War II, has been profound. For most of the previous hundred years, efficiency of operation had guided the design of industrial machinery, almost to the exclusion of other considerations. This efficiency was reflected in lower operating expenses, and lower per-unit costs for finished products.

Safety wasn't totally ignored. Obvious problems—problems directly impinging on the bottom line—were faced, and many were solved. Perhaps the best example is the development of design standards for boilers, spurred by insurors appalled at the high incidence of exploding industrial boilers back in the 1880s. Private enterprise and design professionals—especially those associated with the emerging American Society of Mechanical Engineers—created those safety standards in the face of government indifference because it was in their best interests to do so.

As the Industrial Revolution matured, new products literally bombarded twentieth-century man with delights that an earlier age would have considered both miraculous and beyond the economic grasp of common people. Often novelty alone sufficed to create consumer market demand for new products. When novelty wore off, or was an insufficient attraction, the persuasions of advertising could spark sales.

Consumers frequently found, however, that advertised "improvements" in the buyer's style of loving or living exceeded the product's capability to deliver. It is one thing for the public to accept a degree of danger from a product it deems necessary—early gaslights, for example. It is quite another to accept a television set that catches fire, even when it is supposed to be turned off. The pill is especially bitter to a public conditioned to insist upon infallibility among design professionals—as if these professionals were somehow more than mortal, and somehow had control of all products from the moment of conception, through manufacturing, distribution, and widely varying conditions of use.

Figure I-1 Rock crusher in gravel pit. Note the lack of rails on the catwalk and the lack of guarding for the nip points on the belt drive. Many other points on this particular machine were guarded correctly, however. *(Gates Rubber Co. photo.)*

In the United States, the climate shifted very abruptly in the midsixties. Of the four dozen federal consumer protection laws now in force, more than half were passed since 1965.

The political, social, and economic pressures that moved Congress to create these consumer safeguards also extended protection to the workplace. Under the Occupational Safety and Health Act of 1970, federal safety regulations expanded to cover almost all workers in private industry, and many in government as well. Previously, federal rules were limited to workers in such special fields as atomic energy, interstate railroad and highway transportation, and federal construction projects.

Industry's voluntary standards of safety and performance and a hodgepodge of state and local regulations, usually based on voluntary standards adopted within the private sector, were overridden by nationwide regulations, theoretically establishing new ways of bringing safety to the marketplace. By now, nearly every man, woman, and child in the United States is protected, in theory, as a worker and as a consumer. Exactly how well protected they are, in fact, depends greatly upon engineers and managers and on federal policy.

The potential effects of these laws, especially those for consumer goods, reach far beyond the shores of the United States. Under the Consumer Product Safety Act of 1972, no foreign-made products can enter the United States unless they meet the safety standards set for domestic products. As yet, however, few standards have actually been set under the Act. Because the United States offers a rich market for overseas producers, few will abandon it totally. Foreign automobile producers moved swiftly to comply with requirements of the National Traffic and Motor Vehicle Safety Act of 1966 and the Clean Air Act of 1970.

It is clear that a host of social, cultural, and economic factors contributed to the so-called "consumer movement." Life itself became more valuable, especially in the developed countries. In these countries advances in birth control accelerated the decline of birth rates. With fewer babies per family, each child became more precious, adding fuel to safety issues that once drew little attention. In addition, the migration of people away from rural areas that accelerated in the 1950s consolidated the status of the United States as an urban nation while population soared past the 200-million mark.

Thus, most of the thousands of new products introduced after World War II found use under much more crowded conditions than products introduced in the first half of the century. And the migration broke down many traditional patterns of help available to victims—neighbors and family. These patterns were replaced by cold, hard cash—money to cope with medical expenses and to compensate for property damage. Thus the courts and government agencies have, for a large percentage of the population, become the places to go when a product hurts the consumer.

The factors that made a mass market possible—overall production growth, world trade, and metropolitan concentrations—also increased the chances of exposure to accidental death and injury for consumers and workers alike. Improved communications among consumers helped spread the word of potentially dangerous situations to wider audiences than ever before. At the same time, companies and marketing arrangements were becoming bigger, more complex, and more remote. Where once it was possible to settle an argument over a cracked casting by hauling the damaged part over to the local foundry, the arena now belongs to a battery of claims adjusters, low-level functionaries, and lawyers.

Distance and the ever-increasing difficulty of fixing blame when complex products fail, has bred distrust among producers and consumers alike. Potentially hazardous product defects can spread almost uniformly across the nation, and products frequently encounter conditions (changes in climate, for example) unfamiliar to designers and manufacturers.

One classic example was the government-ordered recall of 200,000 trouble lights in 1975. The lights, manufactured by a small firm in Brooklyn, New York, had been equipped with handles molded in thin-gauge polyvinyl chloride (PVC), copied from a design meant to be fabricated in more expensive hard rubber. At no time in the design, fabrication, distribution, or sale of these lights

> A nation that annually loses over 100,000 lives in accidents, sustains over 11 million injuries, and permanently impairs over 400,000 must address itself to the gross incompatibilities that obviously exist between man and the technology that he has created. In the past, humanitarian reasons apparently have not been sufficient to cause management to take firm action nor has the knowledge that the carnage costs billions of dollars each year. Thus, the problem is currently being addressed by adversaries in courts of law.
>
> In my opinion, what is needed is an affirmative action program supported by the top managers of government and industry. And by "affirmative action" I do not mean generation of catchy slogans such as "safety is everyone's business" because when something is everyone's business it usually ends up being no one's business.
>
> **Julien M. Christensen,** *professor and chairman,*
> *Department of Industrial Engineering and Operations Research, Wayne State University,* speaking at the American Society for Engineering Education annual meeting, June 1977.

was an engineer ever called in. One result: A Florida man, using one of the lights in a hot attic, was electrocuted. The PVC handle may have been softened by the high temperatures enough to be pulled away from the light itself, exposing live electrical contacts.

And of course, even large companies are not totally immune from design and production errors. For several years in the early 1970s, domestic automobile manufacturers actually recalled more vehicles for correction of defects than they manufactured!

Well over 10,000 American workers lose their lives each year on the job, and the number of disabling injuries is about 2 million annually. The Occupational Safety and Health Administration has calculated the annual wage loss at approximately 2 billion dollars, and the overall cost to the Gross National Product about 10 billion dollars.

On the consumer side, the National Commission on Product Safety reported data that indicated 20 million injuries each year involved a household or other consumer product other than an automobile. The statistics included 110,000 permanent disabilities and 30,000 deaths annually. On the highways, a peak of 22 million accidents occurred in 1971, an increase of 44 percent over 1965. These accidents produced more than 50,000 deaths in 1971, and nearly 5 million injuries. Lower speed limits and safer vehicles reduced the toll to about 30,000 deaths in 1976.

The odds against escaping an injury at home, at work, or at the steering wheel are thus surprisingly low for the average American family of four—an injury every four years or so.

Economic conditions have also contributed to the demand for safer and more reliable products. Although the country retained its affluence through a period of localized war in Southeast Asia and through minor recessions, inflation stripped away most of the gains in income, even before the more serious recession of 1974. The Insurance Information Institute, for example, found that the average car repair claim nearly doubled over the 10-year period from $176 in 1962 to $345 in 1971. The average doubled again in the five years that followed. And as the cost of acquiring and maintaining goods rose faster than the money in their paychecks, Americans became increasingly vocal in expressing discontent with the quality of goods and services.

> **Throughout the late sixties, consumer worries about dangers in toys were the most potent forces for product safety legislation at the federal level. Among the horror stories they unearthed:**
>
> - **A toy metal casting set that developed temperatures of 800°F on its cooking surface and 600° on its sides.**
> - **A bazooka toy that deafened the playmate of a user—taken off the market in 1966. The manufacturer had employed 300 engineers, but hadn't anticipated the problem.**
> - **Crackerballs—small torpedoes that looked so much like candy that youngsters exploded them between their teeth.**
> - **One company offered "200 explosive formulas" for sale to children. Included was a recipe for nitroglycerin.**
> - **Nearly 6 million blowguns were sold before the manufacturer was forced to install a device to keep the blowgun darts from being inhaled by users.**

A young attorney helped catalyze this discontent through a safety issue. Ralph Nader wrote *Unsafe at Any Speed,* a critical look at automobiles, especially the General Motors Corvair.* This rear-engine car, the American car engineers' answer to the Volkswagen challenge, became the focus for the publicity of congressional hearings. At the hearings, the president of General Motors apologized for attempting to discredit Nader's book by having private investigators search Nader's private life for material that would discredit him. The corporate embarassment brought more attention to the book and launched Nader into a series of consumer and public interest ventures. The attempted use of corporate power against a lone, young critic also dramatized consumer dissatisfactions and attracted to Nader a following of young, energetic investigators who gave the consumer movement a focus and a fervor it had lacked.

Businessmen, generally, abetted the consumer movement by a fearful, public overreaction that made Nader their symbol for a devil attacking the country's economic system.

Later, in September 1973, the president of the Chamber of Commerce of the United States, Edward B. Rust, urged the business community to "look with fresh eyes at Ralph Nader and the kind of consumerism he represents. . . . It is only when products do not live up to their advertising and to buyers' expectations that Nader seeks to have them regulated by the government." He also asserted:

---

*Nader's book highlighted what he felt were the unsafe handling characteristics of the Corvair when driven by persons of average skill.

> I believe that it was inevitable that sooner or later someone like Ralph Nader would arise to focus and articulate the dissatisfactions and frustrations that are widespread among American consumers. As businessmen, our focus must always be on the quality of the service or product we offer, simply because this is the first expectation people have of us. The manufacturer that landscapes the factory site but hedges the obligations in his product warranty has a misplaced sense of priorities. . . . The business manager may need instruction in some of the new social roles that are being urged upon him, but he should need no instruction at all in bringing to the marketplace a product or service that meets whatever claims he is willing to make for it. Above all else, he should know how to do that!

Business reaction to Rust's speech caused his organization to issue a statement publicly branding these views as those of Rust alone, and not representative of the Chamber.

The harshest judgment on the state of the country's technology in the early 1970s, however, was passed by Europeans who voted with their newly valuable currencies after the U.S. dollar was devalued. One of the reasons for devaluation was to make U.S. goods more attractive to foreign buyers. The items in highest demand turned out to be U.S. agricultural products. Said Dr. Edward M. Kaitz, dean of business administration at Georgetown University: "There's nothing else these countries want to buy from the U.S."

Considering the enormous amount of overseas business conducted by American companies, such a verdict seems extreme. No one can deny, however, that we have been running large deficits in our balance of payments, and that these deficits predated the 1973 increase in oil prices. In part, the deficits are due to the preference of many Americans for foreign-made goods, especially automobiles.

2. EVOLUTION IN COURT DECISIONS; HISTORY OF THE RESTATEMENT (SECOND) OF TORTS*

Judicial decisions involving product liability cases have changed considerably in the past half-century. In part, this was due to the slow evolution of the court's thinking on consumer protection. Case by case, the courts righted what many felt was wrong in the battle between consumers and corporations. But the liberalizing trend was aided by a second source as well—the writing and rewriting of the definition of a "tort" or wrong by the lawyers themselves to broaden the definition of a wrong caused by a product that fails or is innocently misused. The actual restatement of liability is on page 22.

There may never have been a more fertile field for plaintiffs' attorneys than product liability. Consumer advocate Ralph Nader estimated in Senate testi-

---

*Adapted, with permission, from Jonathan Evan Maslow, Products Liability Comes of Age, *Juris Doctor,* January 1975: pp. 26–31 and February 1975: pp. 23–34. Copyright © 1975, MBA Communications, Inc.

mony in 1976 that there were 50,000 significant consumer-initiated lawsuits annually. Higher estimates have come from the Defense Research Institute (DRI), a legal think tank for defense attorneys funded by corporations anxious for relief from liability suits. DRI estimates that products cases in litigation increased from 100,000 in 1966 to more than half a million a year in the early seventies. That figure, the Institute predicts, will reach 1 million lawsuits by 1980, muscling out auto negligence as the largest area of tort law.

And according to Jury Verdict Research, Inc., a Cleveland firm, jurors have reversed their longstanding suspicion of plaintiffs in personal negligence suits. While juries came in for plaintiffs in product cases 43 percent of the time in 1965, they returned for plaintiffs 54 percent of the time in 1974. Meanwhile the average award surged from $11,644 in 1965 to $79,940 in 1973, and million-dollar awards, inconceivable in the sixties, are far from uncommon.

The publication of the Restatement (second) of Torts in 1964, including a new section on strict liability in tort for manufacturers, signaled both the passing from the legal scene of the old contract rule of "privity"—which barred suits between manufacturers and consumers not in direct contractual relationship—and the fading of traditional negligence as the test for recovery. Indeed, behind the rush of products cases lies more than half a century of strict liability's birth pains and privity's death throes. And behind them both lies an often subdued but always pitched legal battle over who should pay for the casualties of our consumer society.

As long ago as 1842, the Blue Book reports to the English House of Lords stated that "the accidents which occur to the manufacturing population of Birmingham are very severe and numerous.... Many are caused by the improper fencing of machinery and many are caused by loose portions of dress being caught up by the machinery so as to drag the unfortunate sufferers under its power. The shawls of females or their long hair, and the aprons and loose sleeves of boys and men in this way are frequent causes of dreadful mutilations."

Yet, in that year, 1842, the English judge Lord Abinger made it clear that society took a dim view of blaming one party for what happened to another party, even if the one party were a manufacturer and the other party a worker or consumer. "The most absurd and outrageous consequences, to which I can see no limit" would occur, said Lord Abinger, if the law ever restricted the freedom of individuals and entrepreneurs by expanding tort concepts of negligence or contract concepts of liability.

Dean William Prosser, the great doctrinal writer in torts who authored the second Restatement, habitually referred to privity as "the citadel"—the impregnable castle built in the days of Abinger and fortified ever since—that prevented consumers from invading industry and summoning manufacturers into open court to recover for products injuries. Prosser picked up the term from Benjamin Cardozo, who announced from the New York Court of Appeals bench in 1931 that "the assault on the citadel of privity is proceeding in these days apace." Cardozo in fact had hurled one of the first spears against the citadel and eventually led the attack. For, in 1916, Cardozo had turned against legal tradition, limiting liability to contracts in privity by finding the Buick Motor Company liable in a case involving a man named MacPherson, whose car had collapsed due to defective wooden wheels. Buick argued that it was not liable because MacPherson had bought the car from a dealer, not from the manufacturer. But Cardozo rejoined that "if the nature of a thing is such that it is reasonably certain to place life and limb in peril when negligently made, it is a thing of danger."

Now that the automobile has passed from its birth as an interesting contraption, through its golden age as the master of our lives, to its present incarnation as a deadly weapon, calling an automobile a "thing of danger" might not sound very earthshaking. In 1916, it was revolutionary rhetoric. Not only the captains of industry but almost all lawyers were still, consciously or not, attached to Lord Abinger's nineteenth-century view that in order to prosper and expand, industry had to be protected from the public's onslaught.

Holmes had confirmed the philosophy in his Harvard lectures on the common law when he stated that "a general principle of our law is that loss from accident must lie where it falls." Thing of danger or not, Holmes said, "a man acts at his own peril." And since no contract existed between the original manufacturer and the ultimate consumer, there were no grounds for charges between them. Thus, no tort, no privity, no fault, no social responsibility. As Yale professor Grant Gilmore wrote in *The Death of Contract*, "The theory seems to have been dedicated to the proposition that, ideally, no one should be liable to anyone for anything."

But there were already cracks appearing in the citadel walls when Cardozo arrived "wielding a mighty axe," as Prosser once exclaimed exuberantly in a law review article. For one thing, much as in the present, the cost of living had risen so rapidly in the first decade of the century that the country was in an anti-business mood. The trusts, and those men in the legal profession viewed as the protectors and advocates of the trusts, were highly unpopular. Big business was blamed for both the inflation and the awful social residue of the nation's rapid industrialization. The muckrakers seared the public consciousness—Upton Sinclair's portrait of revolting filth and adulteration in the food industry, for example, resulted in protest that forced the passage of the 1906 Pure Food and Drug Act, the first time the state had intervened to regulate products.

With the overwhelming election defeat of the conservatives in 1912, progressives entered the state legislatures, and, in many cases, the judiciary. States began to pass food and drug laws even tougher than the federal statute, and shortly thereafter, state courts began to put privity requirements to rest in food, beverage, and drug cases. Within one year, precedents in Washington, Kansas, and Mississippi ascribed strict liability to food producers whenever their foods proved defective, and 17 other jurisdictions followed suit.

Cardozo is said to have been fascinated with this process of change in the common law, partly because he viewed law as growing out of social reality and facts, not from principles written on stone tablets. But to the legal establishment, turmoil was intolerable, and so, in February 1923, 300 representatives of the profession, led by Elihu Root and William Draper Lewis, met in Washington to form the American Law Institute (ALI) and save law from the impending political chaos.

Practically everyone who mattered in the profession was there—judges, law professors, and senior partners from all the large New York, Boston, and Philadelphia firms. Underwritten by more than 2 million Carnegie dollars, the new Institute's self-appointed task was to begin the restatement of the common law. The problem was two-fold. On the one hand, the unbridled growth of common law precedents made the law seem less clear, less firm, less orderly. To the lawyers, public disaffection with the legal profession was not political in nature, but administrative.

"There is a general dissatisfaction with the administration of justice," said the opening paragraph of the ALI's incorporating document. "The danger from general dissatisfaction is that it breeds disrespect for the law and disrespect is the cornerstone of revolution." The ALI set out to reduce the uncertainty of common law to the manageable proportions of a system of thought or doctrine.

On the other hand, the swift changes that attracted men like Cardozo also produced what one attorney at the meeting called "the itch for ultimate legislative codification" in statutes like the tough food and drug acts. Statutory codes were anathema to the lawyers, extending to Cardozo himself.

One attorney present at the ALI's first meeting summed up the hostility to the legislatures two months later in the *Illinois Law Review*. "The legislature as we have known it in this country is at best fit for making administrative enactments and the bar has seen to it that innovations upon the common law should be rare," the lawyer wrote. "But this great work of restatement will build its own road.... The prosecution of this difficult labor will dignify and integrate the profession and it is not, seemingly, too much to expect that the time will come when the voluntary legislature now created ... [will] preserve the common law from chaos and dissolution."

The likelihood of a credible "voluntary legislature" of lawyers for the nation was nearly as remote as the possibility of pigeonholing common law into doctrine. It was even difficult to get members of the various ALI advisory boards in contracts, torts, and trusts to agree on just what principles actually came out of the digests of case law prepared by the appointed reporters in each field. As a result, the system that was to be based on common law eliminated specific case citations.

In the end, the ALI decided that its own prestige would vouch for the authenticity of the Restatement. "It became clear that it was not necessary to add individual opinion to support the official statements of the Institute," Lewis wrote. "The professional position of the Institute ... permits it to speak with authority on the general law in the United States. The omission of the citation of case or other authority is practicable only because the Institute has attained an influence far greater than at the start of the work was thought possible. The Institute in its Restatement has become like the Courts an agency for the statement of law."

Cardozo's challenge to the citadel of privity in *MacPherson* had gone nearly ignored in the first Restatement. No separate section dealt with a manufacturer's responsibility to remote consumers of dangerous products. Instead, the doctrinalists seem to have bowed to the Bar's greater interest in commercial law, grounding their views in contract warranty doctrine—retaining, on the one hand, the problems of privity, and, on the other, the principles of negligence in tort cases.

The courts appear to have striven for a balance between Cardozo's seminal opinion in *MacPherson* and the warranty doctrine, with the timely Mississippi Supreme Court creation in 1927 of "running" warranties—implied contracts that would follow food and drugs through the channels of commerce, holding manufacturers strictly liable to the ultimate consumer for their defective products. For a brief historical moment, the delaying action of the Restatement seemed to have patched things over and retained a sense of order in the development of case law.

But the Great Depression and the New Deal created a riot of statutes, so the ALI was once more obliged to restate the law, concentrating this time not on preserving the pure case law system, which statutory codes had already made a shambles, but rather upon influencing and clarifying the statutes the ALI had feared.

In the postwar statutory legacy of the New Deal, Dean William Prosser, foe of the citadel, was appointed ALI reporter for the second Restatement of Torts. "Prosser was very hip on the social content of the law," explained Harvard torts professor Morton J. Horwitz in an interview. "The singular characteristic of his legal thought was viewing the law as a political thing, a social struggle. This was the fifties, don't forget, when judges and legal scholars who were students under the legal realists were coming into their own. Like Prosser, they tended to see torts as a means of redistributing wealth—as a question of who could best bear the costs of injury. To them, the negligence system had terrible redistributive effects. As one of the chief publicists of strict liability, Prosser was very hostile to negligence-based liability."

Prosser was no longer a voice in the wilderness when he talked about spiriting products cases away from contract law, depositing them in torts, and introducing the concept of strict liability. As the consumer economy matured, there was a belated, unspoken consensus in the legal community that suing a large corporation for negligence was like throwing marbles at a Sherman tank. Cardozo's standard, picked up by Prosser, had gained a small but influential army.

In California, Supreme Court Chief Justice Roger Traynor had held Coca Cola strictly liable for a bottle of soda that exploded in a waitress's hands, setting down the principle in a 1944 opinion remarkable for its forthright subjectivity. "I believe the manufacturer's negligence should no longer be singled out as the basis of a plaintiff's right to recover in cases like the present one," Traynor wrote in *Escola v. Coca Cola*. "In my opinion it should now be recognized that a manufacturer incurs an absolute liability when an article that he has placed on the market, knowing that it is to be used without inspection, proves to have a defect that causes injury to human beings."

Then, in a 1960 case considered landmark material for the continuity it provided with Cardozo's decision against Buick, New Jersey's Supreme Court Justice John J. Francis found Chrysler strictly liable for a Plymouth in which the steering wheel had suddenly come off in the hands of its astonished driver, a Mrs. Henningson. Justice Traynor in 1963 repeated his strict liability ruling from *Escola* in a case where the lathe attachment to a Yuba power saw had flown out of the machine and cracked the user, a Mr. Greenman, in the skull. But Traynor added succinctly that "the liability is not one governed by the law of contract warranties." Then he offered the clearest reasoning yet for his products opinions in a paragraph that has since become widely quoted in product liability literature. "The purpose of strict liability in tort," wrote Traynor, "is to insure that the costs of injuries resulting from defective products are borne by the manufacturers that put such products on the market rather than by the injured persons who are powerless to protect themselves."

By the early sixties, Prosser and his ALI advisory board, including the laconic but influential and brilliant Justice Traynor, had been gathering in various cities to discuss the new Restatement of Torts twice every year, three days every session, for almost 15 years. Prosser was disovering dilemmas in the project, including the oddly pleasurable problem of having to hold off as court decisions caught up with what he himself had long urged in products law.

Traynor's groundbreaking decisions were having such an influence on other state courts that Prosser couldn't get a draft to his advisory board soon enough before strict liability was extended. In 1961, he had given them a draft including strict liability for food and drinks only. The next year, he rewrote the section to include articles of "intimate bodily use" such as soap, clothes, and cigarettes. Then two years later—with *Greenman* on the books and being often cited by judges—Prosser submitted his final draft with a new section, 402A, setting down the principle of strict liability in tort for any defective product.

Prosser and Traynor had apparently pulled off a clever coup, for it was undoubtedly Traynor's *Greenman* decision that set the precedent for other jurisdictions to impose strict liability, which in turn allowed Prosser to restate it as law. He even admitted, in a comment to section 402A, that judicial progress in common law had not reached as far as it eventually would, but that strict liability "is the law of the immediate future."

The more delicate problem for the dean, however, was that taking product cases away from contract warranties was an apparent contravention of statutes. Both the Uniform Commerical Code and the Uniform Sales Act were clearly pre-emptive in the field of buyer-seller warranties. The Supreme Court of New Hampshire had said so explicity in rejecting a consumer case for lack of privity. The Commercial Code, in fact, had been written expressly to resolve privity problems in law.

Unfortunately, industry had been so opposed to abolishing privity requirements for consumers that the Code's editors had compromised the consumer sections in order to get the rest of the Code approved by ALI. Nevertheless, while most state courts were beginning to follow *Greenman* and *Henningson* by telling the public that common law upheld strict liability in tort without privity, other state courts were looking at the statutes and agreeing with New Hampshire.

But Prosser dispensed with the delicacies of the situation. The kind of warranty defined in his Restatement, he explained in the comments, "is a very different kind of warranty than those usually found in the sales of goods and ... it is not subject to the various contract rules which have grown up to surround such sales," among them the Commercial Code and Uniform Sales Act. Prosser did not explain exactly why it was different. But by his saying so in the august Restatement, it became so, and judges decided cases on the basis of Prosser's doctrine. As a result, the Commercial Code is withering away in consumer products cases. More than 40 states have adopted some form of strict liability, almost all of them citing *Greenman,* the Restatement, or both as their authority. The precedents have filled books.

"Now, whenever you hear two cars colliding at an intersection there'll be at least two products liability suits," says Roy Reardon, a New York defense attorney who represents General Motors in New York liability suits. Reardon's sarcasm reflects a common attitude among defense attorneys. They feel, in short, that with the judges imposing liability according to the liberal standards of the Restatement, the deck has been stacked against the defense. Many judges have interchanged "strict liability" with "absolute liability," as if they meant the same thing. And chief house counsels from even the largest corporations—who would never have countenanced settling a product lawsuit 10 years ago for fear of hurting the company's integrity—are sending orders down to settle any suit that appears well-founded.

But despite the ever-increasing numbers of suits arising from the ever-increasing number of product-related injuries, and despite the liberal law and the goldmine awards, plaintiffs' attorneys are by no means home free in products suits. Even as state bar associations urge their dispirited personal

Table I-1 You May Be Liable If:

- Your product is defective in its design (not suitable for intended use).
- Your product is defective in its manufacture (inadequate testing and inspection).
- Your product is inadequately labeled as to proper use, and possible warnings.
- Your product is packaged in such a way that safety-related shipping and handling damage could result.
- Your product is packaged in such a way that parts can be sold separately, or instructions can become detached before sale, allowing sale in an incomplete and dangerous form.
- You fail to maintain proper records of product sales, distribution, and manufacture.
- You fail to maintain proper records of failures and customer complaints.

injury members to take up products law, only an estimated 2 percent of plaintiffs' attorneys are financially successful in products practice.

There has rarely been a more difficult field to master. Proving a culprit product both defective and at fault is so difficult that the best products attorneys are long-time members of the Bar who have continued arguing manufacturer's negligence as if they had never heard of Dean Prosser. Nor is the defense quite crushed; they are still winning half their cases in an age of unprecedented consumer antipathy to business. And with their near-monopoly of technical expertise, not to mention their comparatively large legal resources, defendant corporations have not succumbed completely.

"Any new area of the law within torts depends upon judges becoming educated to the merits of the suit," says products attorney Paul Rheingold. "Lawyers are encouraged to bring a case only when they see that someone has gone before them and succeeded. And to have that prior success, you need a judge either at the trial level or at the appellate level creating law in an atmosphere that allows cases to go to the jury. Then as lawyers win they go out looking for cases. Clients become better informed when they read about cases in magazines and know about what Ralph Nader's saying, and they realize that they've been injured by a product and they can do something about it. Then you get the snowball effect: more and more people are using more and more products, realizing that they can sue. Lawyers are more willing to take those cases—they don't say 'Well I don't know, how can you sue anyone for that? Forget it.' And judges and juries are more willing to bring in verdicts for people."

Verdicts, Rheingold could have added, involving millions of dollars for both plaintiffs and their lawyers. Not only manufacturers, but parts and component suppliers, wholesalers, retailers, lessors, and bailors have been held liable for defective products, even though a wholesaler, for example, might not have uncrated the product before passing it along.

The extensions of liability have been matched on the plaintiff's side. With the privity requirement abolished the courts have allowed recovery by the family of the products buyer, by other members of the buyer's household or by guests therein, by innocent bystanders hurt by someone else's product, by children who couldn't understand written danger warnings, and even by Hispanics who couldn't understand warnings in English.

What the fall of the "citadel of privity," as Justice Cardozo called it, and the adoption of strict liability should have meant, then, was that the burden of proof had been removed from consumers and placed upon businesses. This should have been, and was meant to be, an advantage to plaintiffs and a warning to manufacturers. For the larger goal all along has been not only to assure justice to victims once the damage is done, but to deter manufacturers from marketing products that maim and kill.

But in fact, as attorney Reardon declared confidently at a Practising Law Institute conference in 1974, "We may be losing all the precedents, but we're still winning juries and that's what counts." Rudolph Janata, of the Defense

Research Institute, argued in a speech to a products conference that year that "although the rules of liability have become liberalized and the number of products suits is increasing, we have not reached the point at which a manufacturer of a product is absolutely liable for any injury or damages associated with product use."

Janata said that "the philosophy of doom" prevalent among defense attorneys, due in part to the belief that "the deck has been stacked against them," is totally unjustified.

Later, Janata pinpointed the reason in an interview: "The burden of proof as the fact of a defect in the product," he said, "still rests with the plaintiff even in states where strict liability in tort has been adopted."

So while they no longer must prove negligence, the plaintiff's attorneys still are required to prove that their client's injury was the result of a defect in the product, its design, or its installation, a prodigious task. It is, in fact, as difficult to prove defect as it used to be to prove negligence, which is one reason why plaintiffs' attorneys favor a "failure to warn" argument above all others. Most attorneys in the field seem to feel that when you really get down to it in the courtroom, there is very little difference between an old-style personal injury case and a new-age products liability suit.

Some attorneys even say that the heart of the plaintiff's case is still negligence on the part of the manufacturer. "The strict liability argument doesn't make much of an impression on a jury," said New York products attorney Alfred Julien. "I prefer to use the old common law negligence, with strict liability as a very remote fallback argument. You've got to make the jurors see who's at fault in the injury, not that the product's no good. Remember, the job of the products liability lawyer is to overcome, in a very short time, in the courtroom, years of people's training to believe in products through advertising." Other attorneys confirm that jurors lose interest or simply do not comprehend the strict liability argument; unless confronted in court with a "basket case" or "walking skull," they are rarely swayed to spread the social responsibility for a product's victims to the defendant company or its insurance company.

After a near brush with a form of liability threatening to approach the absolute, manufacturers and their defense counsel have regrouped to circumvent the intentions of Cardozo, Traynor, and Prosser, winning back in and out of the courtroom what the legal realists had sought to take away in the law books. This has been accomplished by monopolizing technical expertise in proving defects, minimizing damages through insurance policies, developing new defenses to overcome the improved standing of plaintiffs, and making shrewd trade-offs between liability and government regulation.

In almost all cases, proving a product defective requires expert testimony about the product itself (see Chap. VIII). "You always need an expert and the expert wins or loses the case for you," Paul Rheingold explained. "Let's say you have an exploding tire case where you want to prove that the tire was poorly designed. Who knows anything about making tires except the people who work for tire companies?"

In the last few years, being an expert witness in products cases has become a career unto itself, with many engineers making a substantial portion of their living by going from courtroom to courtroom, often testifying on both sides in various cases to avoid being pegged as a biased witness. Still the number of technical "experts" riding around the country is small in comparison to the number of corporation engineers who testify week in and week out that their company's products are designed with utter dedication to the public welfare.

Since no outside expert could possibly have been present during the designing or construction of a product, the plaintiff's expert can only with great difficulty make his testimony against the product sound like more than conjecture. Meanwhile, defense attorneys remind the jury at every available turn that the witness doesn't really know what he's talking about—simultaneously casting aspersions on the expert's credentials, objectivity, and, of course, his highly mercenary profession. Then they put their own technical expert on the stand, who has not only designed, constructed, and followed the company's product with an acute sense of personal devotion, but has usually brought the suspect product home and let his children sleep with it (eat it, wear it) just to demonstrate his confidence in its safety.

A few companies have the expert take the jurors on a walking tour of their factories to show them the quality control programs. And juries are very often impressed.

Though both defense and plaintiff expert witnesses can trot out enough technical jargon to daze or bore even the jurors who subscribe to *Consumer Reports,* defense experts particularly resort to information that can boggle the minds of the jury. They can normally, for example, introduce into evidence all the particulars of the standards used in their industry, as well as detail the sampling system used in their quality control programs, and then spin on to a climax by reciting the evidence discovered in "destructive testing" done on the culprit product.

Of course, no one has any idea what this means, including the attorneys, who, if they are smart, will have found a scientific wizard to explain it to them as the suit moves along, or, if they are not, will spend their evenings staring cross-eyed in despair at technical drawings and statistics. A number of young defense attorneys interviewed for the *Juris Doctor* article confided that they were working for large insurance companies defending manufacturers in order to acquire the technical and trial expertise necessary for going into their own plaintiffs' products practice. Without a specialist's knowledge of products, they said, there would be no hope of ever winning a plaintiff's case. (See page 6.)

What they find working for insurance companies must be sobering, for many large American manufacturers have followed the lead of the auto industry by handling products liability suits through insurance and outside legal counsel, rather than by making a serious commitment to designing safer products. Products policy underwriting has flowered as quickly as health insurance. Some drug companies—a favorite target of products liability lawyers—are said to carry as much as 100 million dollars of product insurance. And the rash of

Table I-2 Miscellaneous Liability Statutory Underwriting Results, 1966–1975

Company	Underwriting profit (loss) ($000)
Aetna Life & Casualty	($187,162)
Travelers	(274,645)
Hartford	(142,612)
Continental	(73,458)
Crum & Foster	(35,587)
Liberty Mutual	(176,273)
CNA	(143,516)
USF&G	(71,855)
St. Paul	(98,606)
Royal-Globe	(62,315)
	($1,266,029)

SOURCE: Company Convention Statements, *Best's Aggregates and Averages.*

products cases filed by women over birth control pills and intrauterine devices can only augur a hunt for even greater protection.

The increase in products underwriting, however, has not been a windfall for the insurance industry. On the contrary, while liability insurance in the past regularly turned in profit margins of 15 percent, products insurance is now just as regularly a loser. One year after the Restatement (second) of Torts the profit margin skidded to 6 percent. It slid to 2 percent loss in 1967. The loss rose to 5 percent in 1968.

Now, with juries in almost all the big industrial states returning immense awards for plaintiffs, products underwriting has become an enormous problem for the insurors. The loss reached 18.6 percent in 1974, before large rate increases took hold (Table 1-3). Some companies have increased products liability premiums as much as sixfold. Others have thrown in the towel, raising the deductibles for certain products to 1 million dollars—in effect refusing to insure these products altogether. And there is some sense in the industry that as "mass disaster" cases, such as airline crashes or oil tanker explosions, become a specialty within the specialty of products practice, insurance companies will say "enough" and force all major corporations to insure themselves the way the aerospace industry does, with what are called "captive companies" (see Chap. IX).

Insurance indemnification rules are changed practically every other day as corporations scramble to stay on top of the situation. General Motors writes into its insurance policies exactly which law firm will represent it in products suits. Insurance Company of North America, with about 500 engineers on its staff as safety consultants, decided against including products liability in prepaid legal services. Some insurors are writing what is called "sistership exclusions" into their contracts—exclusions of products recalls from coverage, thus making products recall insurance a separate field monopolized by four companies.

And although no insurance company has actually gone under because of products suits, warnings and shivers went through the industry in 1974 when the New York State Insurance Department declared Professional Insurance Company illiquid. Professional had been writing medical malpractice policies, a field closely related to products liability (especially for products attorneys, who specialize in drug and hospital equipment cases in which one usually sues the doctor along with the drug or equipment manufacturer). For a time, no company offered to fill the insurance gap left by Professional's bankruptcy. Finally a Midwest company agreed to underwrite doctors at a premium double that of Professional's.

Faced with potential financial disaster, insurance companies are rapidly changing their methods of operation. INA, for example, which underwrites the products of 2,000 companies, has developed a comprehensive analysis program; its safety engineers go into the manufacturer's plants, design studios, and advertising agencies, ferreting out mistakes that might lead to corporate exposure.

At the behest of some defense attorneys, 24-hour claim services are going full tilt in products insurance, with the avowed purpose of reaching the injured consumer before the consumer gets to a products attorney. Claims adjusters try to tape record their conversations with products victims in an effort to have testimony of contributory negligence at least before it has occurred to the injured consumer that he or she might have a case against the manufacturer. Such tapes have been admitted as evidence in a number of jurisdictions.

Jury Verdict Research has concluded through its statistical studies that the

**Table I-3 Liability Insurance Rate Increases—
The Big Jump of 1975 Drove Manufacturers to
Seek Legislative Solutions**

Category	*Average percentage rate increase 1974–1975 vs. 1975–1976*
Manufacturers	320%
Retailers	39%
Wholesalers	29%

SOURCE: Interagency Task Force on Product Liability, 1977.

old resistance of manufacturers to having the integrity of their products sullied by settlements has disappeared, and that now more suits are settled before reaching trial.

Defense attorneys have started to think about cutting their losses, now that their clients are more exposed than they were in decades past. The liability covered in section 402A covers manufacturers who sell "any product in a defective condition unreasonably dangerous to the user." A comment appended to the section defines "unreasonably dangerous" as "dangerous to an

Table I-4 Use of Insurance Deductibles by Industry and Size of Business (Survey by the Interagency Task Force on Product Liability)

	\multicolumn{5}{c}{Number of companies in each category, by size of 1975 deductible}
Target industries	0–$1,000	$1,000–$9,999	$10,000–$24,999	$25,000–$50,000	$50,000 and over
1. Industrial machinery	1	1	—	1	6
2. Industrial grinding and abrasive products	—	—	—	1	2
3. Ferrous and nonferrous metal casting	—	—	—	2	3
4. Industrial chemicals: organic and inorganic	—	3	—	—	3
5. Aircraft components	—	—	—	—	1
6. Automobile components and tires	1	1	—	1	5
7. Medical devices	—	—	—	—	1
8. Pharmaceuticals	—	1	—	—	3
All other industries	58	5	4	4	15
SIZE OF COMPANY					
Small companies	38	2	—	—	—
Large companies	18	5	3	6	23
BUSINESS TYPE					
Manufacturer	32	6	3	6	23
Retailer	15	—	1	—	—
Wholesaler	6	2	—	—	—
Service	4	—	—	—	—

Table I-5 Product Categories Frequently Singled Out for Special Scutiny by Prospective Insurors (According to the Interagency Task Force on Product Liability)

	Products of the eight target industries of Table I-4	*All others*
Industrial products	Acetylene gas	Animal feed
	Airplane wheels	Cranes
	Calcium carbide	Gas equipment
	Carbonic acid	Hydraulic hoses
	Liquefied gas	Ladders
	Organic chemicals	Precision instruments
	Pesticides	Scaffolding
	Polyvinyl chloride	Waterworks
	Pressing machines	
	Pyroxylin	
	Stamping machines	
	Steam turbines	
Consumer products	Ethical drugs	Aerosol containers
	Hair treatment products	Antifreeze
	Intrauterine devices	Awnings
	Medical life-support systems	Baby furniture
	Motorcycle helmets	Boats
	Oral contraceptives	Boat trailers
	Recapped tires	Food
	Surgical instruments	Lawnmowers
	Vaporizers	Plastic handles
		Salad dressing
		Sports equipment
		Sprinklers
		Tents
		Toys
		Trailer homes

extent beyond that which would be contemplated by the ordinary consumer who purchases it, with the ordinary knowledge common to the community as to its characteristics."

This raises a sticky issue: if the unreasonableness of the danger depends upon the ordinary consumer's not realizing it, what should happen when the consumer purchasing the product does know about a potential defect and gets injured anyway? What happens when the ordinary consumer knows about the potential danger but the one who gets injured does not? According to a close reading of the Restatement, knowledge of a "patent" or obvious defect implies an assumption of risk by the consumer. This, in turn, means that someone getting hurt by an obviously dangerous product is denied recovery as a matter of law, while someone getting hurt by a product's "latent" or unforeseen danger can recover—a formula that comes close to rewarding dangerous products and furnishing incentives to gross defects in product design.

Searching back through case law, defense attorneys found that this principle had actually been enunciated in 1957 by the New York State Court of Appeals in what has come to be called the *Campo Doctrine*. Said the court, "The manufacturer is under no duty to render a machine or other article more safe as long as the danger to be avoided is obvious and patent to all." A number of jurisdictions have accepted the Campo Doctrine, and some defense attorneys have seized on it and other forms of contributory negligence by plaintiffs to exonerate their clients. Manufacturers have been expanding written warnings with their products in order to prove the dangers were patent.

The assumption-of-risk argument, however, has not proved a complete solution for the defense. Other courts have refined it, rejected it, ignored it, and evaded it. For although it is a mystery to some why Prosser went easy on patently dangerous products in the Restatement, it is clear that his intention was never to encourage the manufacture of obviously dangerous products. So the more ingenious courts have been adding a bit of sophisticated reasoning to Campo. Michigan's supreme court, for example, said in 1973 that the consumer had to "voluntarily and unreasonably encounter a known risk." The test, the court said, was not how obvious the danger was, but how much the consumer was aware of that danger.

Most producers, from toymakers to mining equipment manufacturers, have maintained that private, voluntary standards developed within each industry were adequate to prevent the dangerously defective product from reaching the public. But voluntary standards, promulgated and paid for by the industry itself and often written by corporation employees, are often minimal at best and self-serving at worst. Since industry-wide acceptance of any standard is basic to a voluntary system, it was almost inevitable, as the National Commission on Product Safety concluded in 1970, that "the need for consensus commonly waters down a proposed standard until it is little more than an affirmation of the status quo."

Some industries were merely trying to buy some liability protection on the cheap, thinking that if every manufacturer in an industry followed the same shoddy standard, the courts would look upon that standard as the customary definition of due care by manufacturers in that industry. Such standards, say the *Lawyer's Desk Reference,* "represent the industry's attempt to maintain and maximize profit" in a trade-off between "formulating and complying with adequate codes . . . and the cost of liability for failure to exercise due care."

The rude awakening about voluntary standards came when courts ruled that they could not be introduced as absolute evidence of due care. Jurisdictions have accepted Judge Learned Hand's 1932 opinion in the T. J. Hooper case that manufacturers ought to make products with "reasonable prudence," somewhere between the poor level customary in industry and the greatest safety level feasible, the so-called "state of the art." But judges regularly allow introduction of voluntary standards as "some evidence" of due care.

The late 1960s and early 1970s saw a great debate over whether government-imposed standards would decrease the number of products suits, and, if so, whether that was worth the price of government regulation. By 1972, the decision was made in favor of government regulation. Testifying before the Senate Commerce Committee, a representative of the National Association of Manufacturers said that "as far as we can determine manufacturers overwhelmingly recognize the legitimate interest of the federal government in the safety of products in national markets." Shortly thereafter, *Forbes* reported that "the business community hopes that if the government does establish products standards, the number of products liability suits will drop. At the very least, the manufacturers who abided by the standards would have a good defense."

Consumers also were calling for the government to come in with standards forcing manufacturers to produce safer products, and manufacturers saw their own best interest served by the government handing them a defense. The result was, in part, passage in 1972 of the Consumer Product Safety Act, which created a new agency—The Consumer Product Safety Commission. Unfortunately for manufacturers, Ralph Nader realized why they were supporting the legislation and helped force into the Act a provision saying that the Commission's standards couldn't be held up as evidence of due care any better than an industry's voluntary standards. (See Sec. 3.)

The Product Safety Commission's standards are also mandatory, not the consensus standards that the national commission had several times criticized.

Most defense attorneys are in favor of government standards, believing that they will afford defendants more evidence of due care. Some plaintiffs' attorneys and experts agree that the standards are also well advised. As they look back over the courtroom experience of the past decade, they see that strict liability in tort has simply not been enough of a deterrent. And they question whether the courts can go any further than providing just remedies once a product has already done its damage. Even if judges started to apply the tougher "state of the art" standards, who but manufacturers themselves would know the state of the art?

For this reason, courses in products law at Georgetown, Fordham, Boston University, and other law schools have moved away from encouraging students to concentrate on tort actions, emphasizing instead the role of federal agencies and statutory codes. "When you get beyond the car with the wheel falling off and you're asking exactly how much like a tank a car has to be, you begin to realize that tort suits are terribly inefficient," said Boston University professor James Henderson. "We've come to the second level of impact in this field. Having dispensed with the legal shackling is now creating problems of its own. The courts can't go much further, so Congress and the public will be seeking legislation."

Defense attorneys tell each other over and over again—in their publications, seminars, and conventions—that a well-designed, safe product can be successfully defended. Of this there is little doubt. In fact, hosts of poorly designed and dangerous products are also successfully defended every day, although at high cost to the defenders.

3. SOME LIMITATIONS ON THE DEFENSE: THE EVOLUTION OF STATUTORY LAW

Most courts accept the definition of product liability approximately as it is set forth in the second *Restatement of Torts* of the American Law Institute, section 402A. For nonlawyers, the best way to describe the "restatement" is that it is a summary of the case law as it is, or as perhaps it should be (see previous section). As issued in 1959, this section reads:

> (1) One who sells any product in a defective condition unreasonably dangerous to the user or consumer or to his property is subject to liability for physical harm thereby caused to the ultimate user or consumer, or to his property, if
> (a) the seller is engaged in the business of selling such a product, and
> (b) it is expected to and does reach the user or consumer without substantial change in the condition in which it is sold.
>
> (2) The rule stated in Subsection (1) applies although
> (a) the seller has exercised all possible care in the preparation and sale of his product, and
> (b) the user or consumer has not bought the product from or entered into any contractual relation with the seller.

The American Law Institute cautioned that it was making no judgment as to whether the rules applied "to persons other than users or consumers." But in recent years, a growing number of courts have placed liability protection around the so-called "innocent bystander," the person who leases or borrows a product, and the user who cannot read or comprehend any written warnings that may be on it.

The passage of time matters little. There is effectively no "statute of limitations" on how long a manufacturer is responsible for his products. There are cases where the makers of a drill press have been held liable for injuries caused by their product, even though the press had been resold many times in its 30-year life, and had been modified extensively by the various owners.

This situation is illustrated, in part, in the first case that removed the requirements for "unreasonable danger" in a court decision. The case, *Cronin v. J.B.E. Olson Corp.*, was brought in California, a state which has been a leader in these matters. Cronin was a driver of a delivery van for a bakery. Olson had designed aluminum bread racks which were installed in the van. Nine years later, Cronin came to a sudden stop. A safety hasp on the tray assembly failed to hold, and the bread racks slammed forward into the driver, causing serious injury.

Although the court refused to instruct the jury on whether or not the hasp posed "unreasonable danger," the jury found that the device was "defective," and that the defect caused the injury. This was enough, the jury felt, to impose strict liability on the defendant. The state's supreme court later agreed.

Statutory law sets more explicit guidelines for the engineer and for management. These laws exist at state, local, and national levels, and they have proliferated in recent years. While the political power of consumers remained weak, industry trade associations favored state and local legislation. In those arenas, industry until recently generally overwhelmed its opposition with political and technical expertise. When consumer safety became a national concern, however, the political victories of state and local consumer groups presented manufacturers and merchandisers alike with a hodgepodge of safety laws. These local regulations ranged from the very lax to unreasonably strict; many contained conflicts, and others represented inept analyses of the problem. So when major consumer safety legislation reached the U.S. Congress, consumer lobbyists frequently received unexpected support from large catalogue merchandisers, for example, and their suppliers.

This assortment of local regulations threatened to disrupt orderly, efficient mass marketing and distribution of goods. Many large companies found themselves ready to accept tougher safety considerations that applied uniformly across the country, instead of risking the loss of efficient production and distribution systems through fragmented markets. Uniform federal safety laws burdened each company and removed safety factors—or the lack of them—from the arena of competition.

First and hardest-fought of the major safety laws was the National Traffic and Motor Vehicle Safety Act of 1966 and its companion, the Highway Safety Act of 1966. This brought under federal regulation all licensed vehicles, including trailers and motorcycles. Enforcement rested on the new Department of Transportation through a handful of nearly autonomous "administrations."

Originally the Federal Highway Administration monitored both vehicle and roadway hazards. Now the Federal Highway Administration, primarily concerned with administering the highway construction budget, claims jurisdiction only for safe design and construction of the roadway and directly related safety issues, such as traffic control devices and pedestrian safety. Standards developed here form the basis for state and local programs dealing with street and highway safety; this influence is exerted through the leverage of federal money that supports local programs directly or indirectly.

Vehicle safety now falls under the National Highway Traffic Safety Administration. The Administration also affects state and local programs through standards and fund control. Because of the linkage between driver and vehicle, the agency claims jurisdiction over driver safety and attempts to reduce accidents resulting from the misuse of alcohol. The agency has set out more than 200 standards affecting vehicles, their systems and subsystems. Its jurisdiction also extends to tires. In addition to setting standards, the agency operates and funds vehicle safety research programs; in recent years these programs have produced a series of experimental safety cars, passenger restraints, and crash-resistant bumpers. Through safety design programs initiated with Japan, Britain, France, Germany and others, the agency affects trends in vehicle design internationally.

Motor vehicle manufacturers have not gone willingly under regulation. Most standards were opposed vigorously when proposed. The agency compromises standards regularly and remains under constant fire, accused of delaying both the development of standards and their implementation. In some big issues, the National Highway Traffic Safety Administration has held firm, only to be overruled by Congress or the parent Department of Transportation. Introduction of fast-deployment air bags to cushion auto passengers and safety interlock ignition systems to prevent cars from starting until all passengers buckled their seat belts are two notable examples.

Responsibility for safety in rail transportation systems also rests in two jurisdictions within the Department of Transportation. The Federal Railroad Administration once monitored such diverse operations as railroads carrying intercity traffic and pipelines carrying oil and other liquid cargo across the country. Its safety functions stem from early laws administered by the Interstate Commerce Commission, updated to protect employees, travelers, and the general public. These narrow regulations, by the way, were among the first laws passed to correct abuses of safety engineering in a special industry. They set a regulatory pattern that persisted until enactment of broad occupational and consumer safety laws in the early 1970s. Railroad employees remain protected, more or less, from occupational hazards through these regulations rather than the newer Occupational Safety and Health Act.

The other component of rail travel, within metropolitan areas, falls to the Urban Mass Transportation Administration. The failure of safety mechanisms on the Bay Area Rapid Transit (BART) system in San Francisco led to new emphasis on overall systems safety design. The safety programs at UMTA hold special interest for engineers because the agency funds research, development, and demonstration programs in mass transit, including such new forms as automated "people mover" systems. In addition, UMTA, through grants to other governmental bodies and agencies, can pay as much as two-thirds of the cost of systems design and technical studies leading toward integrated and coordinated city transportation networks. Because UMTA controls so much

Table I-6 Major Laws with Impact upon Product Liability and Safety Issues

Title and US Code citation	Year passed	Responsible agency	CFR citations
Consumer Product Safety Act, 15 U.S.C. 2051	1972 1976*	CPSC	16 CFR 1009 to 1207
Federal Hazardous Substances Act, 15 U.S.C. 1261–1274	1927 1969* 1976*	CPSC	16 CFR 1500–1512
Flammable Fabrics Act, 15 U.S.C. 1191–1204	1953 1954* 1967* 1976*	CPSC	16 CFR 1602–1632
Poison Prevention Packaging Act, 15 U.S.C. 1471–1476	1970 1972* 1976*	CPSC	16 CFR 1700
Refrigerator Safety Act, 15 U.S.C. 1211–1214	1956	CPSC	16 CFR 1750
Magnuson-Moss Warranty—Federal Trade Commission Improvement Act (Title I), 15 U.S.C. 2301–2312	1975	FTC	16 CFR 700–703
Federal Boat Safety Act, 46 U.S.C. 1451–1489	1971 1976*	DOT/Coast Guard	46 CFR 160–183
Radiation Control for Health and Safety Act, 42 U.S.C. 263	1968	FDA	21 CFR 5, 1000–1040
National Traffic and Motor Vehicle Safety Act, 15 U.S.C. 1391–1431	1966 (four other amendments)	DOT	49 CFR 501–577
Highway Safety Act	1966	DOT	(same as above)
Federal Railroad Safety Act, 45 U.S.C. 433	1970	DOT	
Occupational Safety and Health Act	1970 1974*	DOL	29 CFR 1900–2300
Toxic Substances Control Act	1976	EPA	40 CFR 710–760
Federal Metal and Nonmetallic Mine Safety Act	1966 1975*	OSHA	30 CFR 55–57
Federal Coal Mine Health and Safety Act	1969 1972*	OSHA	30 CFR 70–77
Federal Food, Drug, and Cosmetic Act and medical device statutes	Numerous amendments	FDA	21 CFR 810, etc.

*Years amended

money, it has come under criticism for disbursing these funds without making recipients produce comprehensive plans for operating safety before receiving developmental funds.

Two of the older agencies in the Department of Transportation maintain a watch on the safety of passengers, crew, and equipment in the air and on the sea. These agencies are the Coast Guard and the Federal Aviation Administration. Overall safety in each of these many branches of the Department of Transportation passes under the scrutiny of the National Transportation Safety Board. The Board investigates, determines probable cause, and reports publicly on all aircraft accidents and major surface accidents. Because it functions autonomously and reports independently of the department to Congress and the public, the Board is normally an objective evaluator of how well safety measures worked in the transportation area. It recommends improvements in both legislation and administration.

Obviously, the Department of Transportation's safety functions consist of applying narrow safety laws to broad problems. Only in 1973 did the agency begin moving toward a more unified approach to safety policy. Through its Office of Environment, Safety, and Consumer Affairs—headed by an assistant secretary—the department moved supervision of both liquid and gas pipeline safety to the highest management levels. A systems safety specialist from the National Aeronautics and Space Administration was named to head the office of systems safety.

The legislation creating the heightened safety functions in the Department of Transportation introduced new elements that were later incorporated into other safety laws affecting workers as well as consumers. A significant innovation was the introduction by Congress of the concept of large fines; deliberate violation of vehicle standards, for example, can bring fines up to $400,000. The transportation legislation also introduced the mandatory recall notice to consumers of defective vehicles and the notion that the manufacturers' quality control responsibility extended to providing free recall and replacement. Many recalls have cost auto makers millions of dollars each. The vehicle safety act also established, in writing, that simply meeting a standard set by the U.S. government did not relieve a manufacturer from the possibility of paying for consumer injury when the standard failed to provide sufficient protection from unreasonable risk. The definition of "unreasonable," of course, was left to the courts.

Following the consolidation of safety measures in the Department of Transportation, the Congress passed a new, stronger Occupational Safety and Health Act in 1970. From farm to factory, all industrial jobs not covered by earlier legislation fell under the purview of the Occupational Safety and Health Administration (OSHA), in the Department of Labor. In spite of being labeled as soft on industry, the OSHA inspectors in their first three years of activity issued 55,000 citations for 274,000 safety violations and collected nearly 5 million dollars worth of penalties. According to angry labor union officials, however, the early OSHA experience illustrated how high-level opposition can blunt the effectiveness of safety policy in any organization. The agency, for example, abandoned its original intention to make power press design eliminate the need for a worker to place his hands inside the dies to position work. The expense of converting would have been prohibitive for smaller businesses, industry argued.

Instead, the agency delayed for years the introduction of a new press standard in order to begin the long process of adopting a modified regulation proposed by the American National Standards Institute (ANSI). The ANSI standard uses passive safety designs for worker protection—such as controls that utilize both hands to cycle the press.

Violations of the Act can bring both civil and criminal penalties. Once notified of a violation, a company that refuses to correct the violation can be fined $10,000 for each violation, and up to $1,000 a day can be levied as long as the violation continues. Criminal penalties include fines up to $20,000 and a year in jail. However the necessarily long process of legal appeals written into the legislation and the vagueness of many standards make it unlikely that any but the most negligent employer would face such a penalty.

To resist attempts at setting "sweetheart standards," the development of recommended standards was lodged in a separate department. Under the law, the National Institute for Occupational Safety and Health (NIOSH), a branch of the Department of Health, Education, and Welfare, has this responsibility. Further insulation from pressure was intended by making the NIOSH director's appointment last for six years. These NIOSH recommendations need not bind the Labor administrators, however.

Design engineers should remember that safe equipment design is a secondary goal of the Occupational Safety and Health Administration. The primary goal is a safe work environment. Products meant for industrial use have been the subject of many expensive safety suits in part because injured plaintiffs can collect so little under standard workers' compensation insurance arrangements in most states. The payment for accidental death can be as little as $10,000 under such insurance, and this generally excuses employers from further payment. But in a product case, the original manufacturer of the equipment causing the injury can be liable for hundreds of thousands of dollars in damages—even if the employer fostered workplace rules that made the use of an otherwise innocuous piece of equipment unsafe.

A particularly fertile area for damage suits concerns safety equipment that fails to protect a worker. The Occupational Safety and Health Administration does not approve, certify, or endorse equipment, products, or services. Other government agencies, most notably the National Bureau of Standards, do, however, test safety equipment under work conditions. A sampling of research released in 1976 reveals safety shoes that don't protect against falling objects, and hearing "muffs" that fail to stop harmful noise frequencies.

Nevertheless, much equipment was redesigned after the first round of OSHA regulations was issued in 1971. More redesign has occurred since the agency began expanding upon those initial regulations (which were mainly the products of the voluntary standards-setting organizations), and as the agency has moved to protect worker health from the subtle effects of long-term low exposures to noise, heat stress, and various chemicals.

Substantial use of a consumer product in the work environment may bring regulation by the industrial agency. Conversely, the designer of a product for industrial applications must consider the possibilities of that item being used outside the occupational field for which it was intended. Heavy-duty power tools, certain types of welding equipment, and power hoists—to cite a few examples—frequently move into "consumer" or off-the-job applications. When the National Football League Players Association complained to the Consumer Product Safety Commission that artificial turf produced unnecessary injuries among players, agency officials were tempted to regard this as a hazard encountered at the athletes' place of work, and shunted the problem over to OSHA. However the consumer product regulators assumed jurisdiction on the grounds that synthetic lawn material was not limited to use on athletic fields for professional sports.

Consumer Product Safety Act

The most far-reaching safety legislation established the Consumer Product Safety Commission in 1972. Its broad, general powers cover an estimated 10,000 products. Its regulatory armament includes a wide range of penalties aimed at products plus their manufacturers and distributors.

To enforce consumer product safety, the five-member Consumer Product Safety Commission can order a manufacturer, distributor, or a retailer to repair, replace, or refund the cost of a product determined by the Commission to present a substantial hazard. A "substantial product hazard," as defined by the law, is noncompliance with a standard or ban which creates a substantial risk of death, injury, or serious or frequent illness, or a defect which causes similar risks because of defect, or distribution patterns. CPSC also can ban a product or seize it. Richard O. Simpson, the Commission's first chairman, has said the aim is not to remove all risk, but all unnecessary risk.

Another consumer product safety provision allows the imposition of substantial civil and criminal penalties. Anyone who knowingly violates certain CPSC rules may be fined $2,000 for each violation, and the Commission can impose multiple penalties up to $500,000 for a series of related violations. Criminal penalties include up to a year in jail, a fine of $50,000, or both.

Other pro-consumer language in the Consumer Product Safety Act authorizes any person injured due to a manufacturer's knowing violation of CPSC rules to file a personal injury suit in federal court if at least $10,000 could be awarded to the plaintiff. This authority, however, does not preclude additional state suits under traditional or "common law" provisions.

In addition, consumers can, by petitions or lawsuits, ask the Commission to move against a specific product or a hazardous situation. Consumers who use remedies provided by the Act may be reimbursed for expenses as well as for personal or property injury. The Commission can also call for manufacturers, distributors or retailers to reimburse any other person in the distribution chain for the cost of providing such remedy.

These and many other provisions of the Act resulted from a conscious effort by Congress to remedy inequities in both the common law and the administration of earlier regulatory acts. To unify consumer product regulation, the new Commission also received administrative power over the Hazardous Substances Act (including the Caustic Poisons Act and the Child Protection and Toy Safety Act), the Poison Prevention Packaging Act, the Flammable Fabrics Act, and the Refrigerator Safety Act.

Where these laws do not adequately protect consumers, the Commission has invoked the Consumer Product Safety Act's broader powers.

Several classes of products were exempted from Consumer Product Safety Commission rules. These are motor vehicles and equipment, food, drugs, cosmetics, and medical devices; "economic or agricultural poisons" (pesticides, fungicides, and so forth); aircraft and boats. These are covered by other agencies under separate federal laws.

Another exemption covers hazards controlled by other agencies under the Atomic Energy Act, the Clean Air Act, the Radiation Control for Health and Safety Act or the Occupational Safety and Health Act. The third class of exempt products specified in the Act includes tobacco, tobacco products, firearms, and ammunition.

Even among those products it regulates directly, the Commission has been reluctant to set firm standards or impose outright bans. Although guidelines have been issued for a few products—bicycles, swimming-pool slides, and matchbooks among them—the Commission has been unwilling and unable to set safety requirements for broad classes of consumer products. There are simply too many of them, used under too many different conditions by consumers with varying degrees of responsibility and intelligence. This places both a responsibility and a burden upon design professionals.

Magnuson-Moss Warranty Act

The Federal Trade Commission was given broad powers under the Magnuson-Moss Act to require that written warranties on consumer products actually protect consumer interests. The Act, signed into law on January 4, 1975, applies to written warranties on tangible personal property—property normally used for household, personal, or family purposes.

The law includes property intended to be attached to or installed in real property (a house, for example). The FTC, however, has interpreted the law's language as not applying to devices already attached to real property (the wiring and plumbing in an existing house, for example), but applying to such fixtures as furnaces and lights which might be replaced, removed, or repaired.

Certain representations, such as energy efficiency ratings for electrical appliances, care labeling of wearing apparel, and other product information disclosures may be express warranties under the Uniform Commercial Code. However, these disclosures are not alone written warranties under the Act. Section

101(6) provides that a written affirmation of fact or a written promise of a specified level of performance must relate to a specified period of time in order to be considered a "written warranty." In addition, section 111(d) exempts from the Act any written warranty required by federal law.

Also not considered a written warranty under section 101(6) are certain terms or conditions of sale made by retailers. For example, a seller of consumer products may give customers an unconditional right to revoke acceptance of goods within a certain number of days after delivery, without regard to defects or failure to reach a given level of performance. Or a seller may permit consumers to return products for any reason for credit toward purchase of another item.

Therefore, suppliers should avoid any characterization of such terms of sale as warranties. The FTC says the use of such terms as "free trial period" or "trade-in credit policy" are appropriate, and do not fall under the meaning of the Act, although they may fall under the regulation of commerce subject to section 5 of the Federal Trade Commission Act.

Many consumer products are covered by warranties which are neither intended for, nor enforceable by, consumers. A common example is a warranty given by a component supplier to the manufacturer of a consumer product. Although the manufacturer may in turn warrant those components to the consumer, the component supplier's warranty is generally neither intended to be conveyed to the consumer, nor even brought to the consumer's attention. Such warranties are generally not subject to the Magnuson-Moss Act.

Examples of exceptions—where the component supplier gives the ultimate consumer a warranty—might include the manufacturer of a built-in refrigerator on a boat (the entire boat being considered the product), or the common tire manufacturer's warranty that comes with a new car.

If a warranty is granted by the manufacturer, it is subject to certain restrictions. They must be designated as "full (statement of duration) warranty," or as "limited warranty." Warrantors may include a statement of duration in limited warranties as well. The designation of "full" or "limited" should appear clearly and conspicuously as a caption or prominent title separate from the text of the warranty itself.

Section 104(b)(4) states that the duties of warranty protection extend from the warrantor to "each person who is a consumer with respect to the consumer product." Section 101(3) defines a consumer as "a buyer (other than for purposes of resale) of any consumer product, any person to whom such product is transferred during the duration of an implied or written warranty (or service contract) applicable to the product." Therefore, a full warranty may not expressly restrict the warranty rights of a transferee during its stated duration. However, the warranty can be defined solely in terms of first-purchaser ownership—a muffler or battery "as good as long as you own your car" is a valid warranty under the law—as long as the burden of proof is on the company and not the consumer to prove he is the first purchaser.

A requirement that the consumer return a warranty registration card or a similar notice as a condition of performance under a full warranty is considered an unreasonable duty under the law. Thus, a notice such as "This warranty is void unless the warranty registration card is returned" is not permissible in the full warranty—nor is it permissible to imply such a condition.

This does not, however, prohibit the use of such registration cards where a warrantor suggests that sending the card in is proof of the date on which the product was purchased, as long as the card also states that failure to return the card does not void the warranty. This provision can be counterproductive, in that it might reduce a manufacturer's chance of learning where his products are—necessary if a product recall is required. However, warrantors of large consumer electrical appliances such as televisions report no reductions in the rate of card returns since the law went into effect.

Nor can a warrantor claim that it alone shall determine what is a defect under the agreement. Section 102(c) prohibits conditioning coverage under a written warranty on the consumer's use of an article or service identified by brand, trade, or corporate name, unless that article or service is provided without charge to the consumer. Under limited warranties, the same section of the Magnuson-Moss Act also prohibits companies from forcing consumers to use their service people when the warranty provides only the parts free.

The job of insuring that chances for product failure (and possible resultant liability) are kept to a minimum is also reduced by the prohibition against such provisions as "This warranty is void if service is performed by anyone other than an authorized Zilchco dealer and all replacement parts must be genuine Zilchco parts," when parts and service are not provided free. This does not preclude a warrantor from expressly excluding liability for defects or damage caused by such "unauthorized" articles or service. Nor does it preclude the warrantor from denying liability where the warrantor can demonstrate that the defect or damage was so caused.

"Written warranty" and "service contract" are defined in sections 101(6) and 101(8) of the act, respectively. A written warranty must be "part of the basis of the bargain." This means that it must be conveyed at the time of sale of the consumer product and the consumer must not give any consideration beyond the purchase price of the consumer product in order to benefit from the agreement.

A service contract, on the other hand, calls for some extra consideration in addition to the purchase price of the product, either at the time of purchase or at a future date (typically, after the initial warranty period expires). An agreement which relates only to the performance of maintenance and/or inspection services, and which is not meant to affirm a specified level of performance or that the product is free of defects in materials or workmanship, is also a service contract under the law, even if offered without extra cost to the consumer as an option at time of sale.

Other agreements may meet the definition of a warranty or a service contract under the law, but may be sold and regulated by a specific state as insurance. One example is the automobile breakdown policy sold in many states as part of casualty coverage. The states hold sway in such matters because the McCarran-Ferguson Act precludes jurisdiction under federal law over the "business of insurance" so the Magnuson-Moss Act covers only to the extent such agreements are not considered "insurance" in a particular state.

There is some confusion on the minimum $10 price, excluding taxes, on the products covered by the Magnuson-Moss Act. The FTC has decided to include multiple-packaged items which may individually sell for less than $10, but which have been packaged in such a manner that does not permit breaking the package to purchase an item or items for less than $10. Thus, a written warranty on a dozen items packaged and priced for sale at $12 must be designated as full or limited, even though identical items may be offered in smaller quantities for less than $10.

Likewise, many manufacturers have decided that the full or limited warranties required under the Act preclude implied warranties to the consumer as to, for instance, suitability for use. Implied warranties can be limited in duration to the duration of a written warranty if the written warranty has a "reasonable" duration, and if this limitation "is conscionable and is set forth in clear and unmistakable language and prominently displayed on the front of the warranty." Such warranty provisions—as with all warranties—must be available to the consumer for inspection before sale, either in binders nearby (with signs directing the consumer's attention to the binders' existence), or on tags or labels.

Toxic Substances Control Act

On October 11, 1976, the federal government was given blanket authority for the first time to regulate any substances that "may present an unreasonable risk of injury to health or the environment." Under the Toxic Substances Control Act signed into law that day, the federal Environmental Protection Agency was left to define "unreasonable."

In a strictly technical sense, the law adds little to earlier legislation that already touched upon the issue of toxic chemicals—the various food and drug laws, the Federal Pesticide Control Act (vastly strengthened in 1972 but weakened somewhat in 1978), the Safe Drinking Water Act of 1974, the Occupational Safety and Health Act, the Consumer Product Safety Act, the Federal Hazardous Substances Act, federal water and air pollution laws, and numerous federal, state, and local laws governing solid waste disposal. But the new law's reporting requirements and enforcement provisions are likely to make it a major (if not *the* major) weapon in the government's arsenal. The reporting requirements also may make it easier for firms to gather material to gage whether or not the chemicals they are using are safe enough for their purpose.

Under the law, however, the Environmental Protection Agency must show that a chemical—or a specific use of a chemical—will be unreasonably risky, that it will be produced in large quantities, and that it will be used in such a way that a large number of people could be exposed to it, or in such a way that the environment could be substantially harmed. Otherwise, EPA cannot require premarket testing of the product.

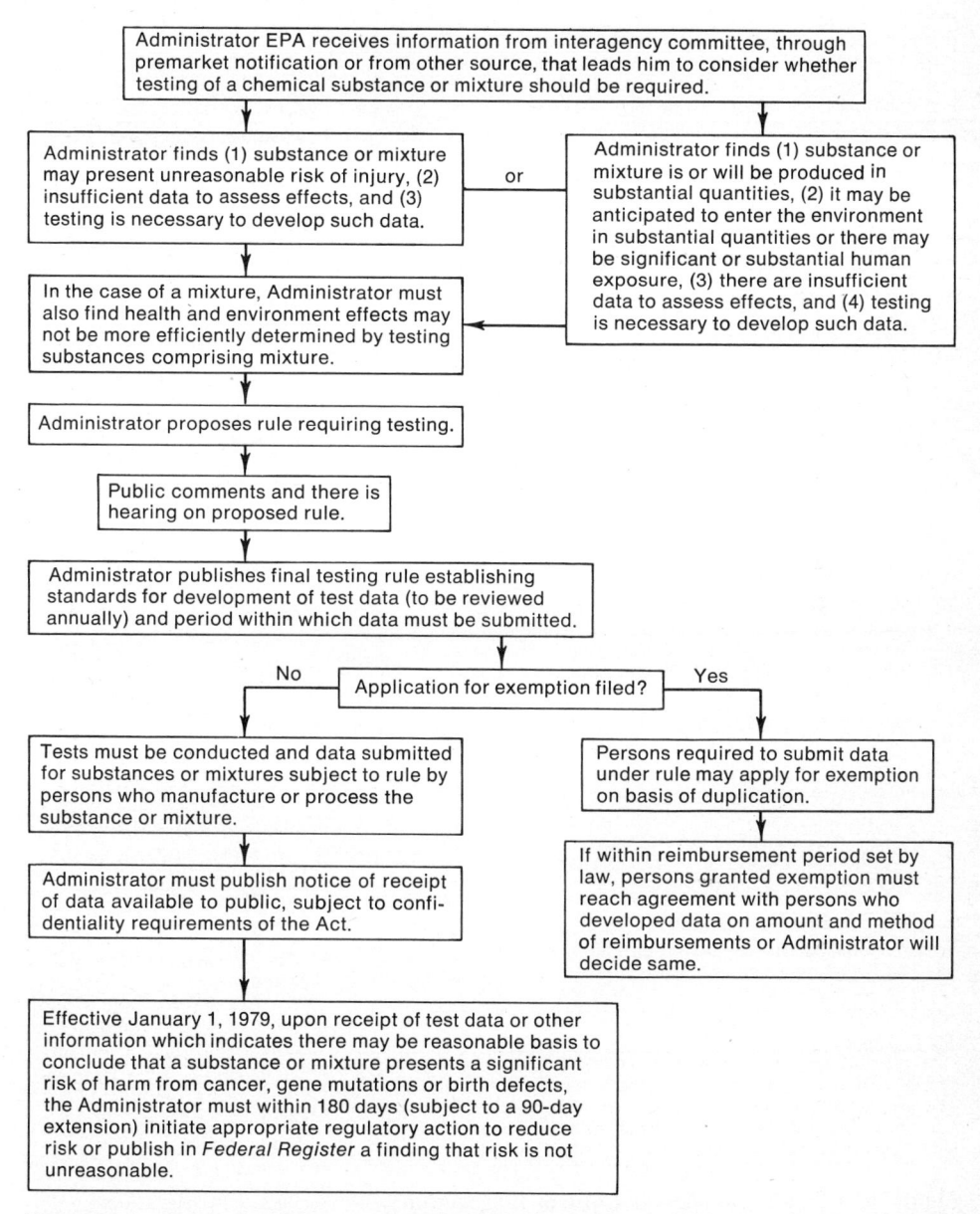

```
┌─────────────────────────────────────────────────────────────┐
│ Administrator EPA receives information from interagency    │
│ committee, through premarket notification or from other    │
│ source, that leads him to consider whether testing of a    │
│ chemical substance or mixture should be required.          │
└─────────────────────────────────────────────────────────────┘
            │                                   │
            ▼                                   ▼
┌──────────────────────────────┐   ┌──────────────────────────────┐
│ Administrator finds (1)      │   │ Administrator finds (1)      │
│ substance or mixture may     │   │ substance or mixture is or   │
│ present unreasonable risk    │or │ will be produced in          │
│ of injury, (2) insufficient  │   │ substantial quantities, (2)  │
│ data to assess effects, and  │   │ it may be anticipated to     │
│ (3) testing is necessary to  │   │ enter the environment in     │
│ develop such data.           │   │ substantial quantities or    │
└──────────────────────────────┘   │ there may be significant or  │
            │                      │ substantial human exposure,  │
            ▼                      │ (3) there are insufficient   │
┌──────────────────────────────┐   │ data to assess effects, and  │
│ In the case of a mixture,    │◄──│ (4) testing is necessary to  │
│ Administrator must also find │   │ develop such data.           │
│ health and environment       │   └──────────────────────────────┘
│ effects may not be more      │
│ efficiently determined by    │
│ testing substances           │
│ comprising mixture.          │
└──────────────────────────────┘
            │
            ▼
┌──────────────────────────────────────────┐
│ Administrator proposes rule requiring    │
│ testing.                                 │
└──────────────────────────────────────────┘
            │
            ▼
┌──────────────────────────────────────────┐
│ Public comments and there is hearing     │
│ on proposed rule.                        │
└──────────────────────────────────────────┘
            │
            ▼
┌──────────────────────────────────────────┐
│ Administrator publishes final testing    │
│ rule establishing standards for          │
│ development of test data (to be reviewed │
│ annually) and period within which data   │
│ must be submitted.                       │
└──────────────────────────────────────────┘
            │
       No   ▼                      Yes
    ┌──── Application for exemption filed? ────┐
    │                                           │
    ▼                                           ▼
┌────────────────────────────┐   ┌──────────────────────────────┐
│ Tests must be conducted    │   │ Persons required to submit   │
│ and data submitted for     │   │ data under rule may apply    │
│ substances or mixtures     │   │ for exemption on basis of    │
│ subject to rule by persons │   │ duplication.                 │
│ who manufacture or process │   └──────────────────────────────┘
│ the substance or mixture.  │                │
└────────────────────────────┘                ▼
            │                   ┌──────────────────────────────┐
            ▼                   │ If within reimbursement      │
┌────────────────────────────┐  │ period set by law, persons   │
│ Administrator must publish │  │ granted exemption must reach │
│ notice of receipt of data  │  │ agreement with persons who   │
│ available to public,       │  │ developed data on amount and │
│ subject to confidentiality │  │ method of reimbursements or  │
│ requirements of the Act.   │  │ Administrator will decide    │
└────────────────────────────┘  │ same.                        │
            │                   └──────────────────────────────┘
            ▼
┌──────────────────────────────────────────────────────────────┐
│ Effective January 1, 1979, upon receipt of test data or     │
│ other information which indicates there may be reasonable   │
│ basis to conclude that a substance or mixture presents a    │
│ significant risk of harm from cancer, gene mutations or     │
│ birth defects, the Administrator must within 180 days       │
│ (subject to a 90-day extension) initiate appropriate        │
│ regulatory action to reduce risk or publish in Federal      │
│ Register a finding that risk is not unreasonable.           │
└──────────────────────────────────────────────────────────────┘
```

Figure I-2 Toxic Substances Control Act Section 4—testing requirements. The flowchart for Section 4 was prepared by Cleary, Gottlieb, Steen & Hamilton, for the Synthetic Organic Chemicals Manufacturers Association; the chart for Section 5 (Figure I-3, next page) is a modification of one prepared by Cleary, Gottlieb, Steen & Hamilton. Flowcharts such as these are meant for guidance only. Because they cannot cover every conceivable case, and because regulatory and court interpretations of the Toxic Substances Control Act may evolve differently from what is shown here, counsel should be consulted before manufacturing or marketing a new chemical substance.

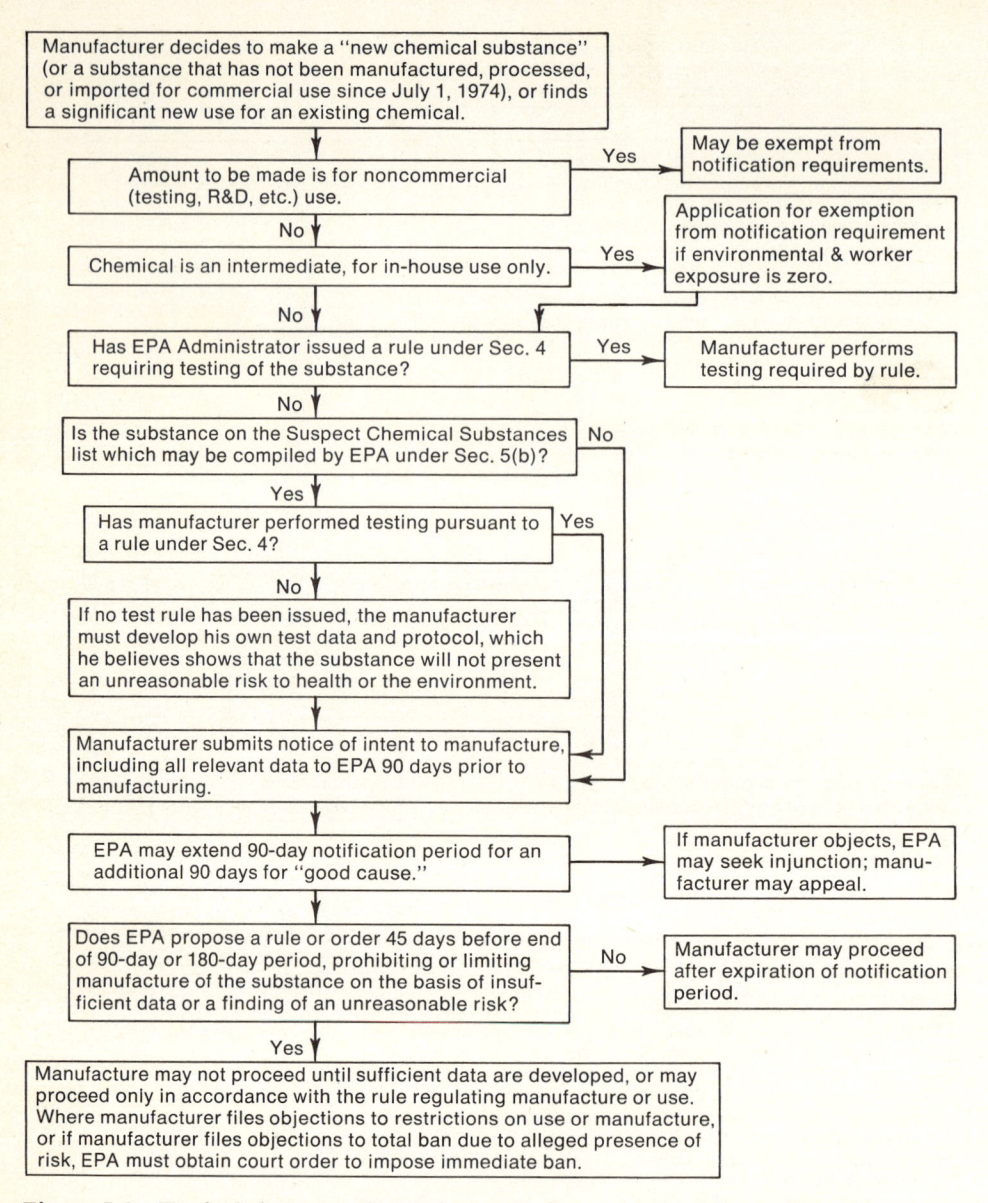

34 PRODUCT SAFETY AND LIABILITY: A DESK REFERENCE

```
┌─────────────────────────────────────────────────────────┐
│ Manufacturer decides to make a "new chemical substance" │
│ (or a substance that has not been manufactured,         │
│ processed, or imported for commercial use since         │
│ July 1, 1974), or finds a significant new use for an    │
│ existing chemical.                                      │
└─────────────────────────────────────────────────────────┘
                    │
                    ▼
        ┌──────────────────────────────┐      Yes   ┌──────────────────────────┐
        │ Amount to be made is for     │──────────▶│ May be exempt from       │
        │ noncommercial (testing, R&D, │           │ notification requirements.│
        │ etc.) use.                   │           └──────────────────────────┘
        └──────────────────────────────┘
                  No │
                    ▼                                 ┌──────────────────────────────┐
        ┌──────────────────────────────────────┐ Yes │ Application for exemption    │
        │ Chemical is an intermediate, for     │────▶│ from notification requirement│
        │ in-house use only.                   │     │ if environmental & worker    │
        └──────────────────────────────────────┘     │ exposure is zero.            │
                  No │                               └──────────────────────────────┘
                    ▼
        ┌──────────────────────────────────────┐  Yes  ┌──────────────────────────┐
        │ Has EPA Administrator issued a rule  │──────▶│ Manufacturer performs    │
        │ under Sec. 4 requiring testing of    │       │ testing required by rule.│
        │ the substance?                       │       └──────────────────────────┘
        └──────────────────────────────────────┘
                  No │
                    ▼
        ┌──────────────────────────────────────────┐  No
        │ Is the substance on the Suspect Chemical │──────┐
        │ Substances list which may be compiled by │      │
        │ EPA under Sec. 5(b)?                     │      │
        └──────────────────────────────────────────┘      │
                  Yes │                                    │
                      ▼                                    │
        ┌──────────────────────────────────────┐  Yes      │
        │ Has manufacturer performed testing   │──────┐    │
        │ pursuant to a rule under Sec. 4?     │      │    │
        └──────────────────────────────────────┘      │    │
                  No │                                 │    │
                    ▼                                  │    │
        ┌───────────────────────────────────────────┐  │    │
        │ If no test rule has been issued, the      │  │    │
        │ manufacturer must develop his own test    │  │    │
        │ data and protocol, which he believes      │  │    │
        │ shows that the substance will not present │  │    │
        │ an unreasonable risk to health or the     │  │    │
        │ environment.                              │  │    │
        └───────────────────────────────────────────┘  │    │
                    │                                   │    │
                    ▼ ◀─────────────────────────────────┘    │
        ┌───────────────────────────────────────────┐        │
        │ Manufacturer submits notice of intent to  │◀───────┘
        │ manufacture, including all relevant data  │
        │ to EPA 90 days prior to manufacturing.    │
        └───────────────────────────────────────────┘
                    │
                    ▼
        ┌──────────────────────────────────────┐     ┌──────────────────────────────┐
        │ EPA may extend 90-day notification   │────▶│ If manufacturer objects, EPA │
        │ period for an additional 90 days for │     │ may seek injunction; manu-   │
        │ "good cause."                        │     │ facturer may appeal.         │
        └──────────────────────────────────────┘     └──────────────────────────────┘
                    │
                    ▼
        ┌──────────────────────────────────────────┐  No   ┌──────────────────────────────┐
        │ Does EPA propose a rule or order 45 days │──────▶│ Manufacturer may proceed     │
        │ before end of 90-day or 180-day period,  │       │ after expiration of          │
        │ prohibiting or limiting manufacture of   │       │ notification period.         │
        │ the substance on the basis of insuf-     │       └──────────────────────────────┘
        │ ficient data or a finding of an          │
        │ unreasonable risk?                       │
        └──────────────────────────────────────────┘
                  Yes │
                    ▼
        ┌────────────────────────────────────────────────────────────┐
        │ Manufacture may not proceed until sufficient data are      │
        │ developed, or may proceed only in accordance with the rule │
        │ regulating manufacture or use. Where manufacturer files    │
        │ objections to restrictions on use or manufacture, or if    │
        │ manufacturer files objections to total ban due to alleged  │
        │ presence of risk, EPA must obtain court order to impose    │
        │ immediate ban.                                             │
        └────────────────────────────────────────────────────────────┘
```

Figure I-3 Toxic Substances Control Act Section 5—premarket notification.

How will EPA know what to worry about? Producers must notify the agency at least 90 days prior to manufacture of a new chemical or mixture of chemicals. If, based on the notification, EPA insists that safety tests be done, the test results must be in hand and fully evaluated before manufacture can actually begin.

Simply changing the proportions of chemicals in a mixture does not constitute a new product under the Act, and such changes do not have to be reported to EPA. However, substantial new uses for existing products will have to be reported in some circumstances. Indeed, the law covers not only the manufacture and use, but also the distribution and disposal of a chemical product.

To aid manufacturers in deciding which products are most likely to raise ire at EPA, the agency published a list of "target" substances in July 1977. The list was reworked and refined by EPA and others all through 1978. The agency also issued a three-volume set listing all chemicals known to be presently manufactured in the United States; chemical companies then reviewed the list and added products they were presently producing.

Any substance not on the list after the review and addition period ended in late 1977 is considered a "new" chemical, subject to all the reporting requirements of the Act (see Figs. I-2 and I-3). Small manufacturers have been exempted from most of the reporting requirements, but not from the testing requirements. Small manufacturers also had to review and report their products for the original EPA listing.

The Toxic Substances Control Act zeroed in on one class of chemicals—polychlorinated biphenyls, or PCBs—and banned their manufacture or importation except for closed-system uses, after January 1, 1978. Manufacture for closed system uses must also end by January 1, 1979, and all use must end in products manufactured after July 1, 1979, except as specifically approved by EPA.

Other substances found by EPA to be unreasonably dangerous can also be banned in extreme circumstances, or their manufacture and distribution can be limited to specific uses. Citizens can bring civil suits against EPA to seek compliance with the Act; the agency can also be petitioned by individuals or environmental groups to initiate rule making or other action against a specific product, class of product, or product use.

EPA can, if necessary, go to federal district court and seek an injunction to block production of a chemical until test results are completed. Civil penalties of up to $25,000 and criminal penalties of up to $25,000 per day of violation (or a year in prison) are possible for violations. The Agency does, however, have to determine the "economic impact" of its actions under the law, including data on plant closings and job losses. Employees reporting to EPA under the law are protected against punitive actions by their employer.

4. INSTITUTIONAL CHANGES

The history of political and economic affairs is studded with the sagas of popular "reform" movements that have flourished and died. The reforms generated in the heat of political emotion generally wind up infiltrated by special interests again, weakened by amendments to the laws, or twisted by easy accommodations between the regulators and the regulated.

Optimists expect that product safety and industrial safety regulations may fare better, for many institutional changes have accompanied the rise of the "consumer movement." One of these institutional changes involves a new attitude on the part of the medical and health services professions. Traditionally, these professions have focused upon the care and treatment of injury and sickness.

Preventive medicine, in the traditional sense, had long been institutionalized in government-run public health programs or in research aimed at specific diseases. However, the medical and health services professions have begun to move slowly away from a treatment-oriented philosophy and toward a "health maintenance" approach. The change is reflected in the small but increasing number of medical partnerships that accept patients on a long-term subscription basis for continuing health checkups and early treatment of signs of deteriorating health. This approach was pioneered decades ago by industrialist Henry J. Kaiser for his employees.

The health services industry was not solely responsible for this change. During the period of intense consumer political activity, 1969 to 1972, physicians' fees increased more than 50 percent, according to figures from the Insurance Information Institute. Daily hospital charges nearly tripled. The increasing cost of medical insurance to pay these treatment charges focused consumer anger on both the medical profession and on the insurance companies. Thus it became more beneficial for the health care industries to support healthy and safe living conditions. One of the more persistent critics of the highway and vehicle programs is the Insurance Institute for Highway Safety, sponsored by insurance companies.

Doctors, especially those associated with hospital poison control centers, became ardent witnesses favoring the Poison Prevention Packaging Act. This forced the redesign of most medicine containers and a great many household chemical dispensers to make them more difficult for children (and adults) to open.

Thus long-term and well-financed institutional support for generally safer products has emerged to lend continuity to product safety interests.

Another institutional change occurred in the labor unions. However much unions may protest the accusation, a large body of case history exists to substantiate some leadership indifference to many unsafe working conditions. Such callousness, often amounting to collusion with company management, resulted in the United Mine Workers throwing out entrenched leadership and securing passage of new, tough legislation governing mine safety and working conditions that contribute to chronic diseases, such as "black lung."

Unions for many years were willing to bargain more for higher wages than for job safety concessions. In the past decade, however, safer working conditions gained new importance. Expressing this interest was made easier by laws allowing a direct appeal by workers and their representatives to government as well as to company management.

The reasons behind this fresh concern for safety lie in the changing nature of union membership. Sar Levitan, director of the George Washington University Center for Manpower Policy Studies, characterizes the new workers as better educated, better paid, and better informed than ever before. "Many are now able to trade marginal boosts in income for increased leisure, a choice that was impossible as long as wages hovered near subsistence levels," declared Levitan.

Along with general dissatisfaction with routine and often meaningless jobs, workers have become even more reluctant to literally risk their lives on the job. With desire for more leisure time came the determination to enjoy this leisure unhampered by job-related injuries. Thus the weight of union personnel and money is increasingly being thrown behind a continuing watch over both industrial and consumer safety.

Another factor that promises to lend continuity to the consumer movement is the emergence of "regulators without portfolio." This includes consumer organizations, Nader-like public interest groups, and other associations. Because such groups have no direct connection with an injured person, courts had generally refused them participation in product injury litigation. Without formal standing in courts, government, or industry, these organizations had limited power.

Courts have now shifted to recognize these groups as having a legitimate interest, and many so-called "class action" suits have been accepted against a broad range of products. Indeed, the new Consumer Product Safety Act formally lists such consumer representatives among those who may initiate product safety actions. Consumer Unions of U.S., for example, now has an attorney in Washington. Other consumer organizations, such as the Consumer Federation of America, located their headquarters in Washington to take advantage of their new access to federal power.

This new influence toward safety from the medical professionals, insurance companies, unions, and organized consumer associations may well provide the long-term effectiveness needed to sustain enforcement of the new safety laws.

5. WHAT IS A "SAFE" PRODUCT?

It is obvious from the previous discussion that designers and manufacturers must meet a moving target when it comes to product safety. In a way, the problem is philosphical: What constitutes a safe society, and what is a "safe" product for that society? The problem may be unique in the nation's regulatory framework—usually, the answer depends on court interpretation at any given time, rather than any regulatory requirement. Likewise, the potential dangers to a company that ignores prudent design practices are greater in civil court actions brought by aggrieved plaintiffs than in actions brought by federal or state regulators.

Overall numbers of casualties may mean little in bringing about the regulation of a product, or of an entire industry. Annual deaths of 50,000 people in automobile-related accidents were sufficient in the mid sixties to produce an intense new look at that product's design. On the other hand, slightly more than 400 deaths a year caused by tractors overturning on hillsides moved OSHA to require rollover protection bars on this equipment.

Historically, risks have been tolerated for many reasons. The accident rate for vehicle miles traveled was once far higher than in the sixties. It was tolerated when driving was more of a "sport" than a necessity, engaged in voluntarily rather than as today, when no other means of transportation exists in many parts of the country. Manly pride slowed acceptance of protective headgear in professional baseball and hockey. But football players, better paid and educated, have shown much more willingness to accept protective equipment. Acceptance by football players has been speeded by the desire of some team owners to protect their "investments" from serious injury. Yet sports equipment remains near the top of the Consumer Product Safety Commission's danger list.

In 1969, Dr. Chauncey Starr took a look at the toleration of hazard in a classic paper read before the National Academy of Engineering. Dr. Starr, who was then dean of engineering and applied science at the University of California at Los Angeles, concluded that the public is willing to accept "voluntary" risks roughly 1000 times greater than "involuntary" exposures, and that the statistical risk of disease appears to be a psychological yardstick for establishing the level of acceptability of other risks.

Starr also noted that "social acceptance of risk is directly influenced by public awareness of the benefits of an activity as determined by advertising, usefulness, and the number of people participating."

Thus it is hardly surprising that the products that cause the most injuries, according to the CPSC, are products the public finds indispensable (stairs, household cleaning compounds, tables), or products used voluntarily by large numbers of Americans (bicycles, sports equipment). This does not mean that changes are impossible in these products. Accidents involving bicycles send nearly 500,000 Americans to hospital emergency rooms each year. CPSC regulations improving bicycle visibility, balance, and quality control are now in effect.

YOUR PRODUCT—IT'S MORE THAN YOU THINK!
  Physical product
  Spare parts
  Installation and/or field assembly
  Service
  Warranty
  Catalog data and sales brochures, advertising
  Instructions for use
  Instructions for user maintenance
  Instructions for factory-supplied service
  Shipping package
  Display package
  Labels, warnings, other on-product messages

There is little question that regulatory authorities can ban an entire class of products, but regulatory action is generally focused on specific products within classes (aerosol cans using fluorocarbon propellents, for example). In short, few (if any) products will be denied access to the market so long as their designers and promoters are aware of safety throughout the process from drawing board to consumer.

Retailers must play an important role, especially for products and activities that are inherently unsafe. Gasoline is an example. No amount of product changes or packaging will make gasoline a totally "safe" product for all its intended purposes.

Prominent warnings or other "labeling" on such a product or its containers may allow such products to be kept on the market. But sales and use may be restricted to keep the product out of the hands of persons who cannot be expected to use it responsibly. Gasoline should not be dispensed in open containers, for instance. And many products may be sold to adults but not to children too young to read. The automobile represents a typically dangerous product licensed for general use if proof of adequte training is shown by the operator.

Certain jobs routinely carry restrictions. To cite one instance, OSHA forbids assigning people over 40 years old to steel mill jobs where heat stress exposure is high and they have had no previous experience. Airline pilots must accept Federal Aviation Administration limits on flight duty when they grow into the years where heart attacks become a significant age-related possibility.

Other products, new and old, will appear on the shelves because producers can demonstrate relative safety, provided the user receives adequate training or instruction. The manufacturer must ensure that such training or instruction actually is delivered by the retailer.

Reliance upon instruction manuals or training to overcome safety hazards and design deficiencies has had less and less standing, however. This is particularly true where regulators may find design changes will not seriously overprice a product, or that safety equipment is available as an optional extra. In fact, extensive training may prove counterproductive by encouraging a false sense of confidence in one's ability to control a dangerous product. An Insurance Institute for Highway Safety study found that drivers qualified as licensed professional racers by the Sports Car Club of America have more highway accidents and traffic violations than noncompetition drivers of similar age and sex.

Another class of products stands "generally recognized as safe" by regulators, although they can be quite dangerous. Most knives, particularly kitchen cutlery, fall into this category. Over thousands of years of use, such products have evolved into cheap, simple, efficient tools of everyday use whose hazards are understood. Although only marginal safety improvements can emerge in most knives—safety locks in pocket knives, for example—other simple items formerly regarded as hazardous have evolved into relatively safe merchandise. Twist-operated manual can openers, with protected rotary knives, have vir-

Figure I-4 No need to worry about the hazard of electrocution here. This impact wrench is driven by compressed air. *(Gates Rubber Co. photo.)*

tually driven out earlier versions that used a sharp, hooked blade and a lever action to puncture and rip open tin cans. Manual can openers and bottle openers rank far down the Consumer Product Safety Commission's list of hazards. And in one of the rare examples of powered equipment being relatively safer than the manual counterpart, electric can openers rate even lower.

Where products fail to evolve safer designs, the designers may find themselves being prodded by the courts or by a regulatory agency. The design of baby cribs, for instance, remained static for generations, before Consumer Product Safety Commission requirements for closer slat spacing, redundant safety catches, and more clear assembly instructions went into effect in 1974.

Style preferences may play a role in maintaining production of another baby product, infant high chairs. A virtually "untippable" chair with a broad-based footing poses no design problems, but does not meet the typical consumer's conception of what such a chair should look like. Thus, government intervention may be necessary to restrict consumer choice. The Consumer Product Safety Act empowers the Commission to publicize the relative merits of various products; the Commission has been reluctant to do so, however.

Plaintiffs are often (but not always) awarded damages for injuries sustained through misuse—even deliberate misuse—of a product. The key questions generally are whether such misuse could have been foreseen, and, if so, could the product have been designed to prevent it? There is a story making the rounds among product designers about the two men who decided to trim a privet hedge by suspending a rotary power lawnmower on two 2- by 4-foot boards and running the machine over the top of the hedge. The story is probably apocryphal. But even if such imaginative use were foreseen, a warning against the practice would have been counterproductive—it would have given the potential users another idea to try.

In short, how safe is safe? As safe as humanly possible, within the bounds of consumer acceptance.

II
THE REGULATORY PROCESS, FEDERAL AND INDUSTRIAL

1. HOW REGULATORS REALLY REGULATE

A small truckline operator, contemptuous of both regulators and his fellow operators, once petitioned the Interstate Commerce Commission for permission to transport "yak butter" across state lines at a specified rate. Nearly a hundred petitions against his request poured into the ICC before anyone caught on to the joke—that there is essentially no trade in the United States in butter from yak's milk, so no one could possibly be damaged by any imagined advantages in freight rates held by any one individual. This reflexive response to "innovation" among the regulated is one reason that many engineers, lawyers, and managers predict that the advent of consumerism will restrict innovation and that the introduction of new products will decline.

In fact, the history of industrial regulation suggests that appearances deceive, for the regulators soon became protectors of the industries they watched. "Federal laws no longer are commands to the few so much as promises to the many," observed Louis M. Kohlmeier, Jr. in opening his series of case studies of regulatory agencies (*The Regulators,* Harper & Row, New York, 1969). Fulfillment of these promises usually begins with the best intentions of the members of the regulatory body to protect the interests of the general public whose members demanded protection from real or imagined abuses.

The Interstate Commerce Commission began in 1887 to protect against overcharging by the railroads. The path followed by the ICC has been repeated endlessly, with variations, by almost every regulatory body chartered in the twentieth century for the United States. Gradually the regulatory agency becomes a captive of the very group it was chartered to command. From the results of the rate schedules filed with the ICC by the railroads, by the small number of regulated barge lines, and by trucking companies, the regulators exercise few of their powers and do little more than umpire disputes between the involved parties.

The result has been a stream of peacemaking decisions that protected existing carriers under the agency's jurisdiction. The broader result has been the decline of railroad passenger and freight service while unregulated modes

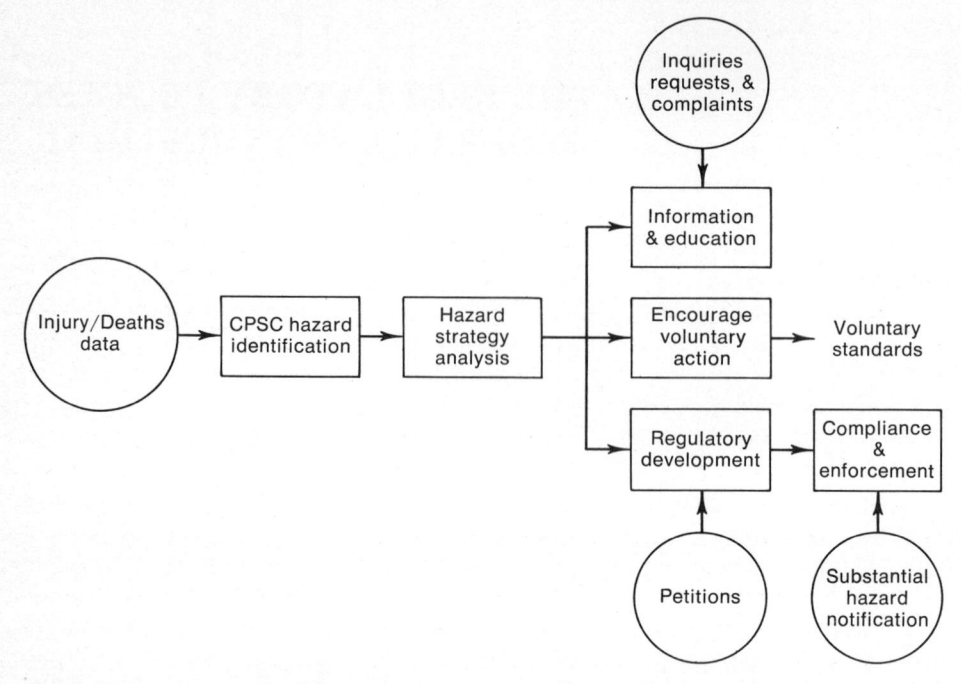

Figure II-1 Consumer Product Safety Commission program structure.

of transportation, such as private autos, grabbed larger and larger shares of the service. Although the interstate trucklines' rates are regulated, many companies have found it less expensive to own and operate their own truck fleets than to pay the posted freight rates approved by the regulators.

Capturing an agency occurs, basically, by several processes working together. One of these processes is cooperation. Early regulatory laws tended to hand the new agency a dual mission—to promote the well-being of the industry and to regulate it. Both the Federal Communications Commission, for example, and the Federal Aviation Administration were chartered to nourish the growth of their new technologies. The regulators thereby became partners with the industry, not adversaries. William C. Jennings, a former FAA regulator, observes in *The Regulators Handbook,* "many agency functionaries compromise their effectiveness by a too-close relationship with the regulated." Often the regulated then will question the regulator's right to make decisions on his own or to protect the public at the expense of the industry. Cooperation is needed between industry and the regulator, says Jennings, but not such close cooperation that both sides regard the arrangement as a partnership. This dual function does not exist in product regulation.

Another way of capturing an agency combines intimidation and reward— the carrot and the stick. In the communications field, for example, a legal or engineering career can be built upon knowledge of the myriad of laws and specifications built into and around the Federal Communications Commission. Both staff and policy-level people know that knowledge of these regulations guarantees a profitable industry career as an alternative to government service—provided the regulator has not shown himself to be too hard upon the members of the commercial community.

Commissioners who have pushed too hard for regulations or reforms opposed by industry seldom have their appointments to the regulatory commissions renewed when their terms expire. In fact, seldom does a man or woman regarded as "anti-industry" ever receive appointment to a regulatory commission. Candidates for these posts have their names circulated among industry leaders, to senators on the committees that must confirm the nominations, and to political party leaders who raise campaign funds. Although occasional mavericks slip through or "reliable" people change their opinions after appointment, seldom does the industry receive any major surprises from an appointee. Even should a maverick appear on a regulatory commission, his or her effect generally is blunted by fellow commissioners.

For these reasons, the most far-reaching changes in industry practice likely will come in the early years of a regulatory body's existence. Once the appointment process begins to cycle through staggered terms, those who have offended an industry tend to disappear. Those with industry support may win re-appointment or go to other jobs in the regulated industry, their places taken by other appointees who have industry's blessings.

The concept of staggered appointments is itself designed to slow the rate of change in regulatory practices except in emergency conditions when public clamor forces the regulators to respond, often hastily. The competent regula-

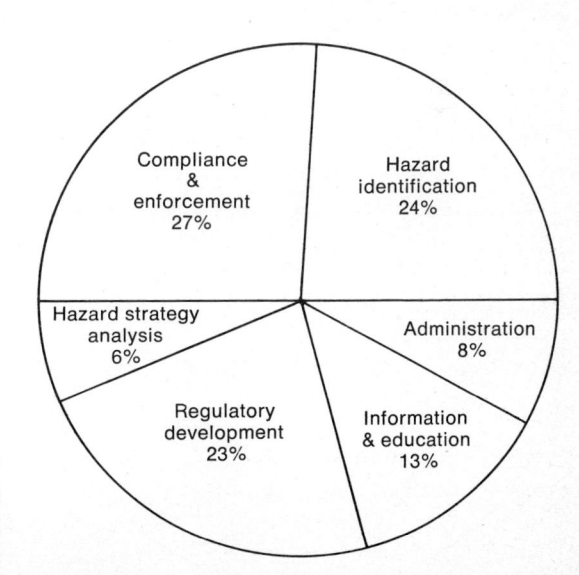

Figure II-2 How the Consumer Product Safety Commission spends its funding. *(From 1979 fiscal year budget request.)*

tor, Jennings advises, must resist such responses, but must operate with an information system that warns of problems early enough to initiate an industry regulation that does not merely react to pressure from one side or another.

To slow the tidal flow of regulators between government and industry, the Consumer Product Safety Act forbids commissioners and high-level members of the agency's staff from taking a job with a regulated manufacturer for a year after leaving CPSC. However, this provision could be tested in court; so many products are regulated by the safety commission that the law may deprive CPSC employees of their right to earn a living except in government.

Regulatory agencies also may set priorities, giving certain cases or types of problems more attention than others. Howard A. Heffron, who analyzed the Food and Drug Administration's enforcement of the Hazardous Substances Act before the HSA was transferred to the Consumer Product Safety Commission, found FDA giving low priority to hazardous substances investigations. The budget for this relatively new act actually was cut back from earlier years so that more money was allocated to traditional drug activities. Field inspectors seldom sought hazardous materials but reported to district and regional offices only the cases they encountered while looking for other things.

As noted earlier, such activities convinced lawmakers to write new protections into the Consumer Product Safety Act. The provisions that allow individuals and consumer groups to petition and sue for enforcement actions potentially enables a nation of citizen activists to enforce the laws. However, as one CPSC commissioner has observed, a regulator does not automatically have to respond to a suit's request for enforcement; he can use the agency's legal staff to fight the lawsuit, forestalling meaningful action.

Another variation on nonregulation by resource allocation may be found in the understaffing of critical analysis sections. Heffron, for example, found the

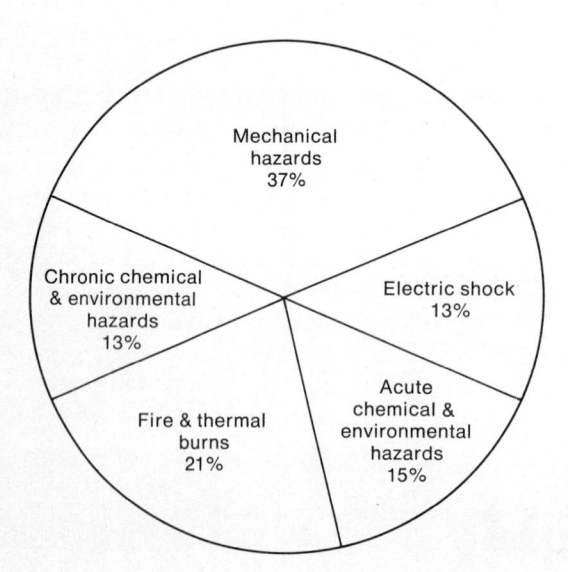

Figure II-3 Consumer Product Safety Commission, spending by hazard areas, fiscal year 1978.

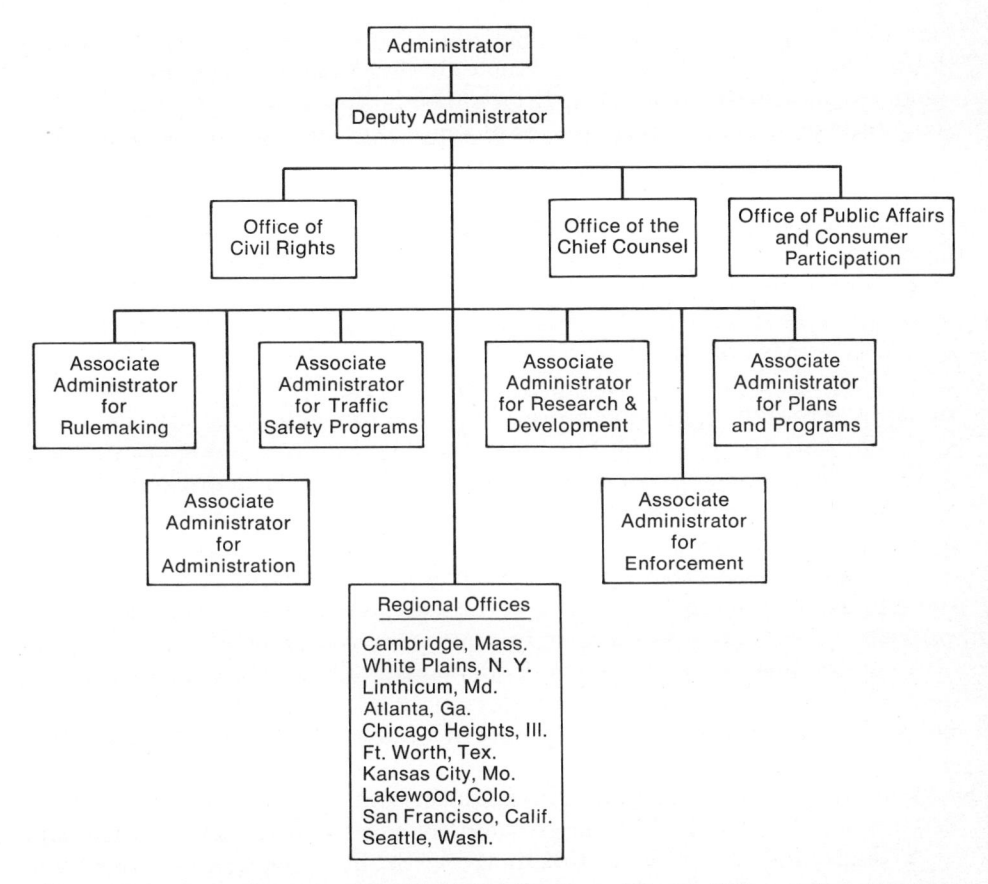

Figure II-4 Organization of the National Highway Traffic Safety Administration, Department of Transportation (effective December, 1977).

FDA using only three people, on a rotating basis, to analyze test reports submitted by manufacturers. Such a staff could never process this pile of reports, much less adequately sift the data for indications of danger.

Most agencies also show a reluctance to bring their most effective weapons to bear swiftly. Publicity, which can kill off the market for a product, is often used sparingly except in cases where "clear and present danger" exists. Even then, the heaviest sanctions may be applied reluctantly. Heffron, for example, cites the case of a product known as X-33, a fast-drying waterproofing paint for use in basements around such appliances as furnaces and water heaters with open flames. The FDA negotiated with the manufacturer for nearly three years over label warnings and other requirements before finally removing the paint from the market. This delay occurred even though the solvent used to achieve rapid drying was mainly gasoline.

Agencies sometimes exhibit an extreme reluctance to disturb their regulated industries. Former regulators Jennings and Heffron both found agencies that almost never publicize their own regulations. New rules are expected to drift down through an industry with a minimum of effort by the agency to educate either the industry or the public. Even today the courts have taken ambiguous stands on the responsibility or liability of a product manufacturer who can claim he was not aware of a particular requirement.

On the other hand, both Heffron and Jennings know of agencies that circulate proposed regulations through industry long before the agency publishes its proposals in the open record. Many agencies discourage public comment, preferring "informal coordination with knowledgeable people," says Jennings. This usually means clearing the regulation with dominant industry and trade association members.

In addition to fear of making powerful people in the regulated industry unhappy, says Jennings, such a procedure also can indicate a lazy regulatory staff. The staff may not want the public record to show conflicting information, or it may not have the personnel or sophistication to define a problem sharply, examine alternative solutions, or make feasibility and economic studies, such as a cost/benefit analysis.

In fairness to regulatory personnel, however, not all agencies indulge in these practices at all times. At least at the start, the newer agencies with their emphasis upon human safety have in some cases moved swiftly.

A considerable body of opinion holds, however, that a smaller company is more likely to feel the whip than a large company or industry, and agencies will move swiftly against minor product lines of a major company before tackling a company's major product.

Thus, the engineer in an innovative smaller company and the engineer for a new and untested product of a large company have to move with more caution.

A rough gauge for the caliber of an agency lies in its willingness to use informal versus formal rulemaking procedures. Informal rulemaking, under the Administrative Procedure Act governing the processes of administrative law, moves much more swiftly than formal rulemaking. The FCC, for example, has built up a tremendous backlog of full-scale hearings by relying on the formal process, which can drag on for years through a complicated procedure. This formal process involves a ritual of notices, the filing of comments, public hearings, counterfilings, and issuance of proposed rules.

Each step may be separated by periods of time, usually 30 to 60 days, allowing all interested parties time to digest and comment upon all that has gone before. The procedure, including agency delays to resolve more pressing matters, may extend for two or three years—sometimes longer. Meanwhile the alleged abuses continue, unless violent events produce an emergency regulation.

Informal rulemaking, varying among different agencies, usually takes less time. Following the public notice of intention to issue a regulation, the agency attempts to take written and perhaps oral arguments from interested parties. Rather than extensive evidentiary procedures and cross-examination, the agency accepts all sides at their face value, adds data from its own expert staff, weighs the merits of the arguments, and then issues the regulation or a proposed regulation. This process can be dragged out, but generally takes much less time than a formal procedure. However it requires the willingness to use expert staff and the willingness of regulatory commissioners to make decisions in the face of often conflicting information.

These daily handicaps, some self-imposed, tempt industry to risk violation of the law—and regulations have the force of law—because the chances of being caught are low. Until recent years, the penalties a regulatory agency could impose—or was willing to impose—were considered low and a part of the cost of doing business. Today, fines can go to $10,000 or more—enough for many to reform their policies.

When the expected profit appears high enough, or competition forces the decision, a company may go to market with a product that has had inadequate or incomplete evaluation. Often the entrepreneur expects his engineers to "safe" the product through on-line production changes. A few company executives, cynically, may calculate on recovering research and development costs before the regulators can halt production.

Congress foresaw, however, the temptation to produce large quantities of a suspect product in anticipation of federal regulation and the selling of such items on the grounds that they were produced before the effective date of the regulation. The Consumer Product Safety Act specifically forbids such stockpiling. The Act also demands immediate reporting of a potential product hazard, in fact buttressing the moral convictions of good designers.

Even the more liberal interpretations of consumer rights have not stripped the effectiveness of lawyers in protecting a company. Formerly the consumer stood little chance of collecting enough damages from a lawsuit to regain his legal expenses. As noted earlier, this has changed somewhat both in case law and statute law decisions that make the odds somewhat better for the injured product user. As demonstrated in automboile injury litigation, however, the company that is sued hardly is helpless. Product liability suits, many lawyers think, may see more of the delaying tactics that encourage plaintiffs to abandon suits, that permit witnesses to scatter, and that see ranks of litigants thinned by death and disease while the company goes on.

How a company assesses the intent and capabilities of an agency to use its regulatory powers may determine its stand on safety and design. The degree of concern with anticipating new safety requirements can become the basis for many interdepartmental conflicts, as engineering, marketing, and production strive to meet immediate goals and deadlines.

Nevertheless, it falls to engineering to prepare testing protocols and to help ensure product reliability at whatever level the law and the courts demand. The problem is critical for technical staffs in smaller firms, which cannot support an independent safety and test engineering unit.

Indeed, most engineers who like precise definitions on the size and scope of a problem are finding themselves treading on marshy ground. The law creating the Consumer Product Safety Commission, for example, asserts that "an unacceptable number of consumer products ... present unreasonable risks of injury." The law provides neither an acceptable level of risk to guide the product designer, nor a definition of unreasonable risk.

This means that engineers designing new products or redesigning old ones move across a terrain that will constantly shift beneath them. Some firm spots will serve as guideposts or stepping stones for determining how "safe" is safe in the years ahead.

First, the Consumer Product Safety Act, in particular, incorporates most of the judicial precedents of the 1960s. And courts have a long record of sustaining rulings proposed by regulatory agencies so long as those rulings take place within the due process of the law. The courts have also been reluctant to take over work delegated by Congress to any particular agency no matter how timidly or boldly the administrators or commissions have interpreted their mandates.

Secondly, it is clear that manufacturers cannot rely solely on warnings against misuse of a product. The law protects the foolish who do not heed these warnings—at least to some extent. The warnings generally cannot cover every situation in which a consumer might find himself or herself. The consumer may not even be able to read—as much as a quarter of all Americans are functionally illiterate, some educators say, not counting the preschool, the blind, and people for whom English is not the native tongue. Nor can warnings, no matter how plainly set forth in an instruction sheet, be expected to last through the useful life of a product, or travel with the product when it is borrowed by the neighbor's teenager. Therefore, safety design must carry most of the burden.

Nevertheless, it is Commission policy to avoid the obvious possibility of pricing a relatively inexpensive item off the market by imposing unduly harsh safety requirements. In 1973, the Commission ordered off the market an inexpensive electrical device that promised to turn any house wiring system into a giant television antenna. The action was taken following a single consumer complaint about the danger of shock.

This particular device, said the Product Safety Commission, contained no safety components that might have reduced the potential for electric shock. Competing devices that used shock-protection components came under investigation but were not ordered off the market immediately.

Although the Commission cannot endorse or issue preproduction approval of a product, the Safety Act and the Commission's policies encourage manufacturers to work with the agency by seeking consultation before launching full production and marketing efforts. Such encouragement, however, must be moderated by the realization that if potential hazards worry the manufacturer enough to seek Commission guidance, the safety aspect of the product may not have received their full consideration at the planning and design stage.

More substantial guidance lies in the established system of industry standards coordinated mainly through the American National Standards Institute in New York. Federal design standards are particularly important and voluminous for vehicles, ships, pipelines, military products, and industrial workplaces.

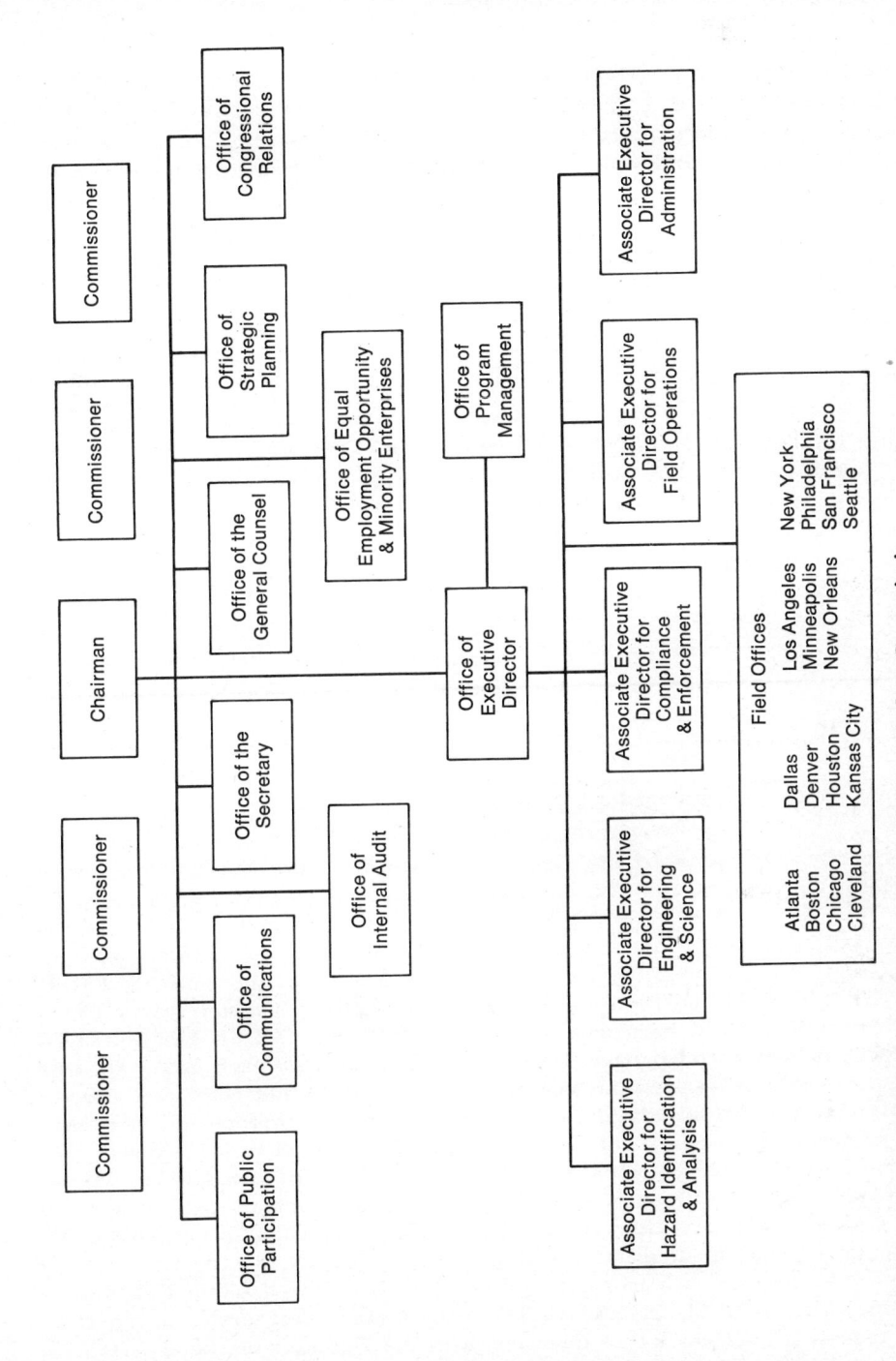

Figure II-5 Organization of the Consumer Product Safety Commission.

Increasingly, however, the courts have demanded that designers and manufacturers go beyond written standards where shown to be inadequate. Justifiably or not, some of these standards are considered the product of "lowest-common-denominator" bargaining among companies in specific industries, or between the regulated and the regulators, as we have already mentioned.

For products in wide use, one yardstick of safety needs is the Consumer Product Safety Commission's National Electronic Injury Surveillance System, best known by its acronym, NEISS (pronounced "nice"). The system, while hardly perfect, corrects a major shortcoming defined by the National Commission on Product Safety. The study groups, whose 1970 report was used as the basis for action that led to the 1972 consumer law, conceded that their estimate of 20 million injuries a year represented little more than an informed guess. Filling another gap, the National Bureau of Standards publishes reports on fire safety, and the National Institute for Occupational Safety and Health reports

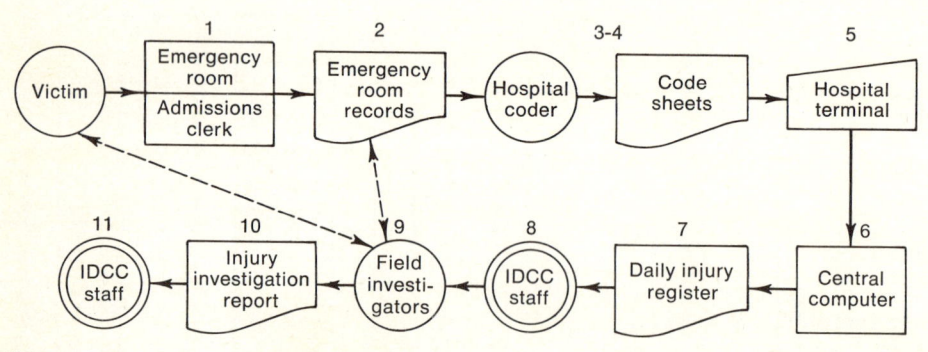

Figure II-6 Operation of the National Electronic Injury Surveillance System (NEISS). When the victim of a consumer product-related injury enters a NEISS hospital emergency room, the NEISS operations are set in motion. (1) The **EMERGENCY ROOM ADMISSIONS CLERK** records information on consumer products associated with the injury, along with answers to routine questions. (2) **EMERGENCY ROOM RECORDS** are completed to show diagnosis, body part affected, and disposition. (3–4) Each day, a trained **HOSPITAL CODER** fills out **CODE SHEETS** in computer language. Data on the code sheet for each injury are date, hospital case number, sex and age of victim, diagnosis and body part affected, disposition, product associated, involvement of a second product, and location or type of accident. (5) The **HOSPITAL TERMINAL** accepts the coder's typed information from the code sheet and stores it on tape ready for transmission. (6) The **CENTRAL COMPUTER** queries all of the 119 hospital terminals each night during hours when line usage is low. (7) A **DAILY INJURY REGISTER** prepared by the computer includes a summary and detailed case printouts. (8) The **IDCC STAFF** reviews the register each morning and determines the need for investigation of specific cases. (9) **FIELD INVESTIGATORS** contact the emergency room concerned and request permission for an interview with the victim or the family. (10) The **INJURY INVESTIGATION REPORT** describes not only the sequence of events but also characteristics of the victim, the environment, and the product, including brand name and product model and serial numbers when available. (11) The **IDCC STAFF** evaluates the report and makes recommendations.

on workplace injuries in a more comprehensive way than was possible through Workers' Compensation records alone.

Of all these activities, NEISS holds center stage. This computerized network links 119 American hospital emergency rooms to the Consumer Product Safety Commission's central data system. Every product-related injury reported at these emergency rooms is fed to the network. The information is coded by what product or products were involved, the affected body part, the injury's severity, and whether or not hospitalization or death occurred. (See Fig. II-6.)

The data are weighted to emphasize the more serious injuries and injuries to young children. Commission officials say they bend over backwards to avoid automatically linking a series of injuries with a product. Injuries involving products are called only "product related" until follow-up investigations by the CPSC staff or outside contractors can establish a direct connection between an injury, a product, and the way the injury occurred. Approximately 1000 product classifications are monitored through NEISS.

The first Consumer Product Hazard Index, based on NEISS data and released in the fall of 1973, fingered bicycles and related equipment as the biggest causers of injury, followed closely by stairs, doors, cleaning agents, and tables. That suggested guidelines for bicycle design deserved high priority. Indeed, the Commission produced such guidelines as one of its first set of standards. Since 1973, stairs and bicycles have been the biggest injury producers, with football equipment, baseball equipment, glass, nails, basketball equipment, tables, and doors also ranking high.

Critics have charged that NEISS is statistically unsound, although the hospital emergency rooms used were chosen because the patients they serve offer a representative sample of the United States population. The Consumer Product Safety Commission responded to the critics in part by sampling injury victims who report directly to doctor's offices without going to hospital emergency rooms, adding a review of death certificates (many victims die before they ever are brought to an emergency room), and changing the reporting technique in 1977.

It seems clear, however, that only the more common consumer products will ever make their statistical weight felt, unless they are so dangerous as to cause injuries among a large percentage of their users. These products—the common and the dangerous—will receive the most government attention in the years ahead.

The emphasis is somewhat different for most standards set by private bodies such as industry trade associations, professional societies, and voluntary standards—setting groups like the American Society for Testing and Materials. Indeed, these bodies vary considerably among themselves.

2. INDUSTRY STANDARDS

The Sub-Council on Product Safety of the National Business Council for Consumer Affairs estimated that more than 60 percent of the standards originate in either trade associations or in professional societies. Trade associations account for more than 300 new standards annually, and professional societies write about 500. Active trade associations include the Aerospace Industries Association of America, the Association of Home Appliance Manufacturers, the Gas Appliance Manufacturers Association, and the National Electrical Manufacturers Association. Representative standards-writing professional societies include the Society of Automotive Engineers, the American Society of Mechanical Engineers, and the Institute of Electrical and Electronic Engineers.

Voluntary standards-writing groups produce another 30 percent of the standards. Most of these groups concern themselves exclusively with standards-setting while the professional societies and trade associations have other interests that may or may not be reflected in the kind and quality of standards writing they undertake. Standards-setting organizations include the American Society for Testing and Materials. The group also includes the Office of Engineering Standards Services, a branch of the federal government's National Bureau of Standards. Besides its acceptance in industry and in the government as a body to initiate standards writing, the American National Standards Institute coordinates the work of other standards makers. This is a vital function required to reach a "consensus standard" that will be accepted throughout the country as an "American National Standard" and for establishing a United States position for negotiations with other countries. Basically this activity aims little at safety and much at making sure that products in international trade can flow easily from country to country.

Most consumer-oriented standards are written by a fourth group of standards-setting organizations. This group includes various types of product-testing and certifying laboratories. Of these, the Underwriters Laboratories, a creation of the insurance companies, is the best known. However, the American Gas Association Laboratories and similar industry-oriented associations also promulgate safety standards.

The quality of these standards, and their ability to protect consumers, varies widely. One of the major battles in consumer protection, for example, was fought over acceptable standards for exposed floor furnaces. The concern grew out of severe burns received by small children who fell upon the hot metal grills of these heating appliances.

Although designers had provided a simple and inexpensive solution to the problem—insulating the metal grills over the furnace heating elements—the industry was reluctant to adopt this solution until forced to do so by the possibility of federal action. The main reason: price competition was heavy in this field, and no single manufacturer felt able to move on safety unless all of the competitors did.

Indeed, most industry-sponsored standards-setting activities were so far removed from safety considerations that the National Business Council for Consumer Affairs was unable to separate out the standards that applied clearly to safety. The situation began to change drastically in the early 1970s, however. The Occupational Safety and Health Administration (OSHA) adopted most of

Director / Deputy Director

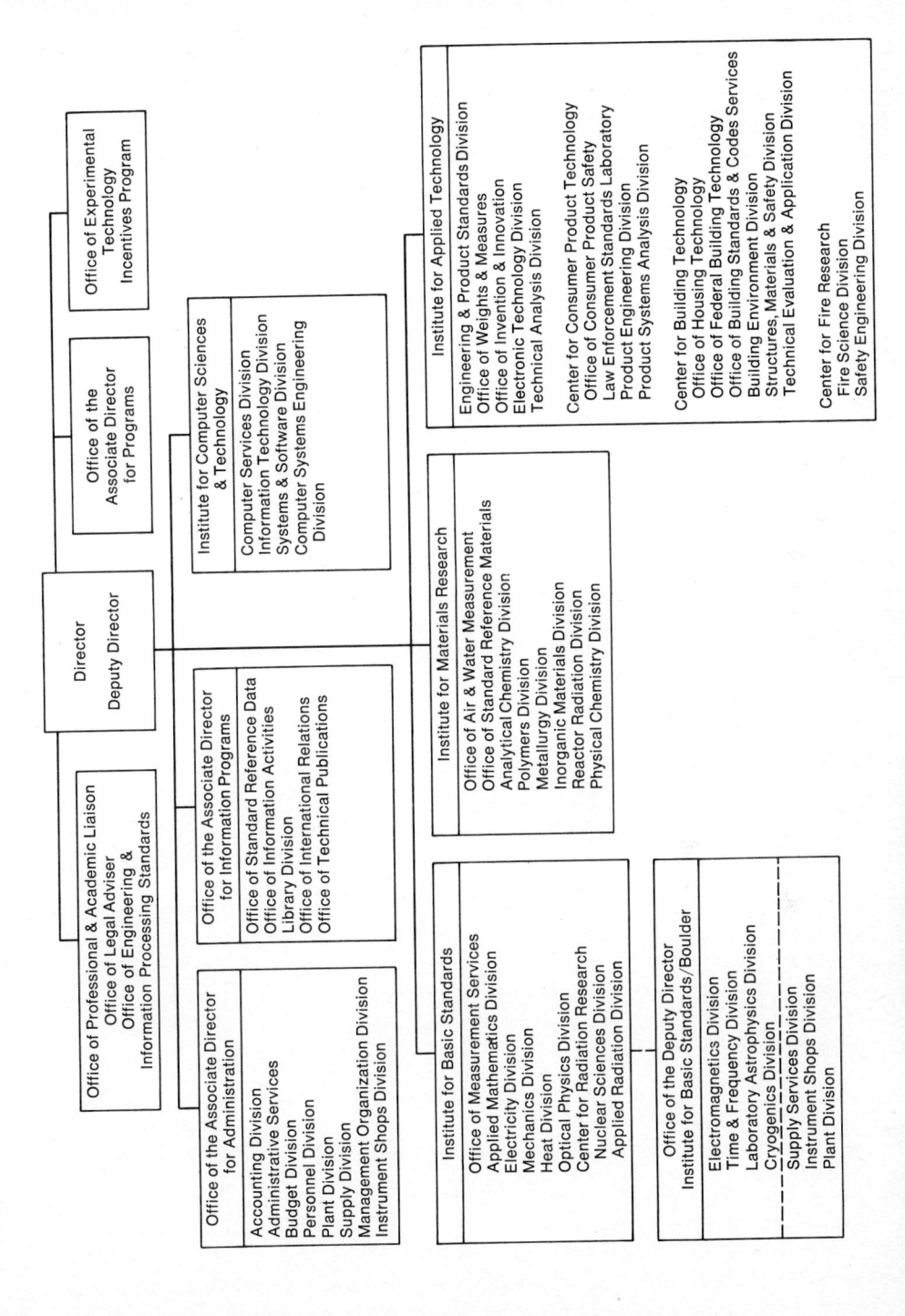

Office of Professional & Academic Liaison
Office of Legal Adviser
Office of Engineering & Information Processing Standards

Office of the Associate Director for Administration
Accounting Division
Administrative Services
Budget Division
Personnel Division
Plant Division
Supply Division
Management Organization Division
Instrument Shops Division

Office of the Associate Director for Information Programs
Office of Standard Reference Data
Office of Information Activities
Library Division
Office of International Relations
Office of Technical Publications

Office of the Associate Director for Programs

Office of Experimental Technology Incentives Program

Institute for Computer Sciences & Technology
Computer Services Division
Information Technology Division
Systems & Software Division
Computer Systems Engineering Division

Institute for Basic Standards
Office of Measurement Services
Applied Mathematics Division
Electricity Division
Mechanics Division
Heat Division
Optical Physics Division
Center for Radiation Research
Nuclear Sciences Division
Applied Radiation Division

Office of the Deputy Director Institute for Basic Standards/Boulder
Electromagnetics Division
Time & Frequency Division
Laboratory Astrophysics Division
Cryogenics Division
Supply Services Division
Instrument Shops Division
Plant Division

Institute for Materials Research
Office of Air & Water Measurement
Office of Standard Reference Materials
Analytical Chemistry Division
Polymers Division
Metallurgy Division
Inorganic Materials Division
Reactor Radiation Division
Physical Chemistry Division

Institute for Applied Technology
Engineering & Product Standards Division
Office of Weights & Measures
Office of Invention & Innovation
Electronic Technology Division
Technical Analysis Division

Center for Consumer Product Technology
Office of Consumer Product Safety
Law Enforcement Standards Laboratory
Product Engineering Division
Product Systems Analysis Division

Center for Building Technology
Office of Housing Technology
Office of Federal Building Technology
Office of Building Standards & Codes Services
Building Environment Division
Structures, Materials & Safety Division
Technical Evaluation & Application Division

Center for Fire Research
Fire Science Division
Safety Engineering Division

Figure II-7 The National Bureau of Standards.

Table II-1 Obligatory Language in American National Standards

SHALL	Means "do it this way."
SHOULD	Means you can do things the way the standard says, but there are other ways, too.
MAY	The way noted in the standard is a "guideline," and entirely different ways could be appropriate. There is no consensus among the "experts" as to what is right, or what is the best way to do the task at hand.

its initial standards from those approved by the American National Standards Institute (ANSI)—and frequently found them to be too vague to enforce. The American Society for Testing and Materials (ASTM), and other large groups, set up specific committees to clear safety-related standards in new fields such as sports equipment, and to tighten up older requirements.

It should be stressed that these new standards have been produced mainly by industry groups, but under the threat of federal action if their standards did not turn out strong enough to protect the public. Because of the many revisions and strengthenings that have taken place since 1975, possession of up-to-date books of standards in your company's field of activity is essential.

With standards becoming more important to each company, more staff and status must flow toward engineers assigned to work with the standards-setting bodies. Most safety and standards experts expect supervision of this process to move higher in the management ranks, even in medium-sized companies.

The process of standards making has also become more public. One of the concessions won by consumer-interest representatives was the admission of public and consumer representatives to formerly closed sessions of technicians. One group whose meetings were always open, ASTM, is now spending thousands of dollars each year to pay the expenses of public representatives at its standards conferences.

Says A. M. Anderson of Hotpoint,

> This is a shift away from the earlier processes applying to technically complex matters in which participation in decision making was limited to those recognized as having technical competence. How this will work out is yet to be determined. In my opinion, this new process will be more raucous, certainly more open to public scrutiny; the balance between idealism and practicality will shift toward idealism; the cost of carrying on the process will increase; and the cost to the consumer of the products themselves will increase.

The rush toward safety has accelerated the use of "performance" standards. These standards set an achievement level for a product or for a product's critical subassemblies. Such standards put a premium on innovation, because they do not tell an engineer or company how to make a product in any detailed way, as do older "specification" standards.

These older standards were useful when nations of artisans moved into the early stages of industrialization. They were—and still are—essential to mass production and marketing, insuring that an electrical device made in one part of the country can be connected to a power supply or outlet box manufactured in another region. For these purposes, specification standards will remain important as new products come onto the market.

Performance standards, however, with stress upon such factors as reliability and mean-time-to-failure, translate more understandably into consumer-oriented language. The protocols for testing so-called child-proof containers for drugs and household chemicals require the closures to survive attempts by a statistically valid number of small children to open the containers.

Another type of standard—the generic standard—is becoming increasingly important. As outlined by the Consumer Product Safety Commission, generic standards would apply to a particular characteristic no matter what kind of product exhibits this characteristic. Any metal surface that is exposed to contact with the human body, for example, may be required to remain below a specified temperature. This temperature requirement would apply uniformly to children's toy stoves (heated by small electric light bulbs), as well as to the oven doors of full-size stoves. Similarly, the CPSC has suggested design guidelines for the sharpness of corners on toys—a source of many childhood injuries. A standard on the readability and understandability of appliance control panels might also be sought.

Pressure from government agencies and consumer groups, as well as from insurors, has speeded up standards setting (although it is of necessity still slow). This will put a premium on participation, even by smaller companies. It also puts a premium on internally generated data about products already in the field (a subject that will be discussed in greater detail later). Even the best corporate complaint systems of a few years ago were geared only to learning what parts of a product failed, and could not provide solid identification of product features or failures that produced injuries.

In standards-setting meetings, there has always existed a reluctance on the part of company representatives to speak too frankly of safety difficulties with products. If a risk element existed, a company representative had problems discussing it in such a way that he or she avoided suggesting a way for competitors to reap commercial advantage. Timetables for improvements tended to be geared to the companies which, for various practical reasons, would have the hardest time making product changes.

Today, consumer representatives at standards-setting meetings often will bring forth the safety data company representatives were too bashful to discuss. And timetables imposed by liability insurors or the government leave less time to institute product changes. There is increasing support, however, for nailing down more firmly the required information before setting new standards in broad areas. The reason: new standards sometimes create more problems than they solve. Pressed to come up with a solution to flammability of children's nightclothes, manufacturers came up with a fireproofing agent that later

Table II-2 Some Common Abbreviation Codes for Standards-Setting Organizations

UNITED STATES	
AAA	Aluminum Association of America
ACI	Alloy Casting Institute (Steel Founders' Society of America)
AGA	American Gas Association
AMS	Aerospace Materials Specifications (of the Society of Automotive Engineers)
ANSI	American National Standards Institute
ASTM	American Society for Testing and Materials
IEEE	Institute of Electrical and Electronics Engineers
MIL	Department of Defense
NEMA	National Electrical Manufacturers' Association
NBS	National Bureau of Standards
QQ-	Federal Supply Service
SA	(also ASME) American Society of Mechanical Engineers
SAE	Society of Automotive Engineers
UL	Underwriters Laboratories
FOREIGN	
AS	Standards Association of Australia
B.S.	British Standards Institution

proved to be carcinogenic: The clothes treated with this agent, (2, 3 dibromopropyl) phosphate (TRIS), were sold for several years, ending in early 1977.

Under most safety laws, companies that think they are being pushed too fast can apply for an exemption to a particular rule. Exemptions are granted to companies that plead their case well. Checker Motors, for instance, received an unpublicized exemption from some Department of Transportation rules because the firm would have been put out of business, and its low volume of production didn't seem to pose too great a threat to the public's safety. Companies should be wary of seeking exemptions, however. The courts have not looked too kindly upon products that hurt, especially when other products in the same class are designed to prevent the specific injury suffered by a plaintiff.

3. THE FEDERAL REGULATORY PROCESS

In some ways, it is easier for smaller firms to participate in the federal regulatory process than in the voluntary standards system. This is because proposals

CSA	Canadian Standards Association
DIN	Deutscher Normenausschuss (West Germany)
DS	Dansk Standardiseringsrad (Denmark)
DTD	Ministry of Technology (Great Britain)
IS	Indian Standards Institution
JIS	Japanese Standards Association
MNC	Metallnormcentralen (Sweden)
NBN	Institut Belge de Normalisation (Belgium)
NF	Association Française de Normalisation (France)
NZSS	Standards Association of New Zealand
ONORM	Osterreichischer Normenausschuss (Austria)
SABS	South African Bureau of Standards
SIS	Sveriges Standardiseringskommission (Sweden)
Wbl	Verein Deutscher Eisenhuttenleute (Germany; Stahl-Eisen-Werkstoffblatt)
UNI	Ente Nazionale Italiano di Unificazione (Italy)
V	Nederlands Normalisatie-Instituut (Netherlands)
VSM	Normenburo des Vereins Schweizerischer Maschinenindustrieller (Switzerland)

for federal action must be published in the *Federal Register* in full, and accompanied by a summary, in plain English, of what the proposal would mean, and what its impact would be. But to participate, firms have to understand the rules of the game.

Under the Constitution, Congress passes bills, which are then signed into law or vetoed by the President. The President is charged under the Constitution with the job of enforcing those laws. This enforcement often is carried out by the regulatory agencies—and that's where the confusion begins.

Congress long has recognized that in this fast-paced and constantly changing world, passing a bill with enough detail for general enforcement is not usually a good idea. Even minor changes in conditions would then require cranking up the entire legislative process to fix things. Therefore, bills that Congress passes usually are vague statements of what should be done. It normally is up to the regulatory agencies to decide how Congress's intent is to be carried out. For consumer products, these agencies include the Food and Drug Administration,

Table II-3 Titles in the Code of Federal Regulations. (Each "title" pertains to a given field of endeavor, and each is updated annually.)

CFR NO.		CFR NO.	
1.	General Provisions.	26.	Internal Revenue.
2.	[Reserved].	27.	Alcohol, Tobacco Products and Firearms.
3.	The President.		
3A.	The President, Appendix.	28.	Judicial Administration.
4.	Accounts.	29.	Labor.
5.	Administrative Personnel.	30.	Mineral Resources.
6.	Economic Stabilization.	31.	Money and Finance: Treasury.
7.	Agriculture.	32.	National Defense.
8.	Aliens and Nationality.	32A.	National Defense, Appendix.
9.	Animals and Animal Products.	33.	Navigation and Navigable Waters.
10.	Energy.	34.	[Reserved].
11.	Federal Elections.	35.	Panama Canal.
12.	Banks and Banking.	36.	Parks, Forests, and Memorials.
13.	Business Credit and Assistance.	37.	Patents, Trademarks, and Copyrights.
14.	Aeronautics and Space.		
15.	Commerce and Foreign Trade.	38.	Pensions, Bonuses, and Veterans' Relief.
16.	Commercial Practices.	39.	Postal Service.
17.	Commodity and Securities Exchanges.	40.	Protection of Environment.
18.	Conservation of Power and Water Resources.	41.	Public Contracts and Property Management.
		42.	Public Health.
19.	Customs Duties.	43.	Public Lands: Interior.
20.	Employees' Benefits.	44.	Public Property and Works.
21.	Food and Drugs.	45.	Public Welfare.
22.	Foreign Relations.	46.	Shipping.
23.	Highways.	47.	Telecommunication.
24.	Housing and Urban Development.	48.	[Reserved].
25.	Indians.	49.	Transportation.
		50.	Wildlife and Fisheries.

the Consumer Product Safety Commission, sometimes the Occupational Safety and Health Administration, and the Department of Transportation. FDA, CPSC, and the Environmental Protection Agency even got together in mid-1977 to jointly announce that they were proposing a ban on fluorocarbon propellants in aerosol cans for most uses, because fluorocarbons affect ozone concentrations high in the earth's atmosphere, and a drop in ozone levels could affect world climate and the incidence of skin cancer.

The regulatory agencies handle the task by issuing regulations in the daily *Federal Register*. Major changes in existing regulations, or any entirely new regulations, must first be issued as "proposals" in the *Register*. In fact, agencies frequently issue "advance notice of proposed rulemaking" (also in the *Federal Register*) to give affected parties as much chance as possible to comment upon proposed rules or rule changes.

When the final regulations appear in the *Federal Register*, they must, by law, include a discussion of all the comments received on the regulation while it was still in the proposal stages. This discussion is published as a "preamble" to each regulation as it is issued.

Once a year, all changes appearing in the *Register* are collated into the *Code of Federal Regulations* (CFR). It should be noted, however, that the preambles and other explanatory material are not republished in the *Code of Federal Regulations*—the CFR includes only the regulations themselves. The vast body of federal regulations is broken down into 50 "titles." Rules issued by the Consumer Product Safety Commission are found in Title 16, Part II; the Federal Trade Commission's are in Title 16, Part I; and the Department of Transportation's are in Titles 23, 46, and 49. You'll find FDA regulations in Title 21, OSHA requirements in Title 29, and EPA rules mainly in Title 40.

The *Federal Register* also contains other things that the CFR does not have. Among these are:

- Presidential proclamations, executive orders, and other presidential documents

- Policy statements by various agencies (sometimes explaining how a particular regulation is intended to be enforced)

- Interpretations of existing regulations, usually in nonlegal, but technical, language

- Notices of proposed rulemaking

- Notices of regulatory guidelines (and sometimes, the entire guideline itself)

- Notice of forthcoming meetings between agency personnel and outside advisory groups, with instructions on how members of the public may attend (and even submit material, sometimes)

- Variances, and other actions taken by regulatory agencies in response to requests by law enforcement officials, corporations, or the public

To make full use of the *Federal Register,* you should not only be able to understand what a regulation says, but also how it is organized internally, and how it, in turn, fits into the CFR. Each of the 50 CFR titles is subdivided into *chapters,* which are numbered consecutively in Roman numerals. A chapter generally is assigned to a single agency. Sometimes a title will have only one chapter, and sometimes the chapters are so long that they have *subchapters* lettered consecutively (A, B, C . . .).

The chapters group together *parts,* which are usually numbered in Arabic numerals running consecutively through a title. They do not begin anew with a different chapter; Chapter I in a title might contain parts 1 to 199, Chapter II might contain parts 200 to 999, and so forth. Frequently, parts are "reserved" for future regulations within a title, so that regulations pertaining to the same class of products can be grouped together as they are written.

A part consists of a unified body of regulations applying to a specific function of the issuing agency (regulations on handling variances, or hearings for instance), or devoted to specific subject matter under control of the issuing agency. For instance, part 1201 of Title 16 refers to Consumer Product Safety Commission regulations on architectural glazing materials. This part would be referred to as 16 CFR 1201.

Parts are in turn divided into *sections* which, according to the Office of the Federal Register, "ideally consist of a short, simple presentation of one principal proposition." Sections are usually just a few paragraphs long, but occasionally run pages. Each section begins with a boldface heading. Sections are numbered consecutively within parts. Thus, the third section in part 1201 would be 1201.3, while the thirteenth would be 1201.13. The Office of the Federal Register calls this a "modified" decimal system. Sections are also subdivided, when necessary, with paragraphs as shown in Fig. II-8. Figure II-8 shows an actual modification to a real regulation.

To aid readers in finding their way around the *Federal Register,* monthly indices are also issued automatically to subscribers. Subscriptions to these indices can also be purchased separately from the U.S. Government Printing Office. One index classifies changes in regulations by subject, and describes notices, guidelines, and so forth as well. The other index lists new regulations (or changes in old ones) by the number of the CFR part they carry.

Indexing is simplified by the use of consecutive page numbering throughout each calendar year (*not* federal fiscal year). In other words, the first issue of the *Federal Register* in January begins with page 1. The last issue in December usually ends with a page close to 60000.

Each daily issue of the *Federal Register* comes with a table of contents, a list of CFR parts affected by changes in that issue, a list of regulations from previous issues that take effect on that date, and a guide to highlights beginning on the front cover.

Labels (left side, with arrows pointing to parts of the regulation):

- Agency identification number → [6355-01]
- Title and name → Title 16—Commercial Practices
- Chapter designation and agency identification → CHAPTER II—CONSUMER PRODUCT SAFETY COMMISSION
- Subchapter number and title → SUBCHAPTER E—POISON PREVENTION PACKAGING ACT OF 1970 REGULATIONS
- Part number and title → PART 1700—POISON PREVENTION PACKAGING
- Descriptive heading → Certain Sodium Fluoride Solutions; Exemption From Child-Resistant Packaging Regulations

PREAMBLE consisting of: Introduction, short summary, name and address of source of further information; Reasons for regulation, resolution of public comments, background, etc.

Regulation text:

AGENCY: Consumer Product Safety Commission.

ACTION: Final rule.

SUMMARY: In this document, the Consumer Product Safety Commission amends provisions of the child-resistant packaging regulations to exempt certain aqueous solutions containing no more than 264 mg. of sodium fluoride. This action is taken because the Commission has found that child-resistant packaging is unnecessary for such preparations to protect young children from serious personal injury or illness.

DATE: The effective date of this amendment is January 11, 1978.

FOR FURTHER INFORMATION CONTACT:
Michael Gidding, Compliance and Enforcement, Consumer Product Safety Commission, Washington, D.C. 20207, 301-492-6617.

SUPPLEMENTARY INFORMATION:

BACKGROUND

In the FEDERAL REGISTER of April 16, 1973 (38 FR 9431), a regulation (16 CFR 1700.14(a)(10)) was issued under the Poison Prevention Packaging Act of 1970 (the "PPPA", 15 U.S.C. 1471–1476) establishing child protection packaging requirements for oral prescription drugs in order to protect children from serious personal injury or serious illness resulting from handling, using, or ingesting these substances.

On February 25, 1974, the Commission received a petition (petition number PP 74-30) from Hoyt Laboratories, Needham, Massachusetts 02194, requesting ...

Labels (right side, with arrows):

- Words of issuance — the language by which the modification of the regulation is tied to the Code of Federal Regulations.

Accordingly, pursuant to provisions of the Poison Prevention Packaging Act of 1970 (secs. 2, 3, 5, Pub. L. 91-601, 84 Stat. 1670, 1671; 15 U.S.C. 1471, 1472, 1474) and under authority vested in the Commission by the Consumer Product Safety Act (sec. 30(a), Pub. L. 92-573, 86 Stat. 1231; 15 U.S.C. 2079(a)), a new subdivision (vii) is added to 16 CFR 1700.14(a)(10) as follows (although un-...

- Section head and number → § 1700.14 Substances requiring special packaging.
- Asterisks (*) denote CFR which sections remain unchanged → (a) * * *

(10) *Prescription drugs.* Any drug for human use that is in a dosage form intended for oral administration and that is required by Federal law to be dispensed only by or upon an oral or written prescription of a practitioner licensed by law to administer such drug shall be packaged in accordance with the provisions of § 1700.15 (a), (b), and (c), except for the following:

- New regulation modification → (vii) Aqueous solutions of sodium fluoride containing no more than 264 milligrams of sodium fluoride per package and containing no other substances subject to this § 1700.14(a)(10).
- "Authority" (a citation of the laws or court decisions which give this agency the right to set the regulations above) → (Secs. 2, 3, 5, Pub. L. 91-601, 84 Stat. 1670-72; (15 U.S.C. 1471, 1472, 1474).)
- Notice of when the regulation will take effect → Effective date: This section becomes effective January 11, 1978.
- Signature → Dated: December 7, 1977.
  RICHARD E. RAPPS,
  Secretary, Consumer Product Safety Commission.
- Date regulation was filed with the FR → [FR Doc.77-35384 Filed 12-9-77;8:45 am]

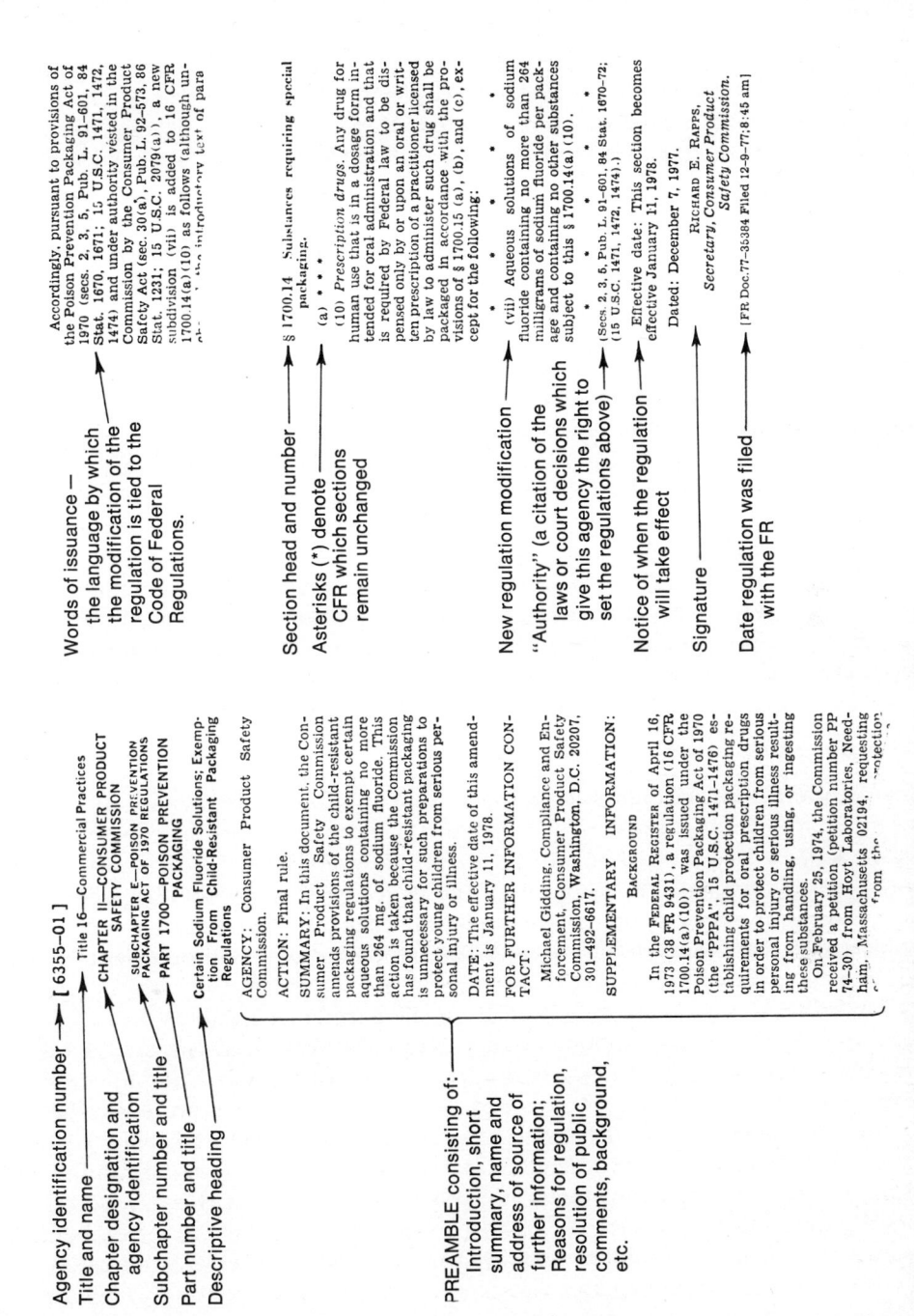

Figure II-8 A typical federal regulation, with its parts labeled.

The language in which regulations are written is not exactly simple English, but it is usually understandable by the people to whom a regulation directly applies. Regulations issued by the Consumer Product Safety Commission are usually quite understandable, and some are well illustrated with line drawings. The Coast Guard's safety regulations are all but impenetrable, however. Highway safety rules lie in between. In any case, if you are not sure a regulation applies to your activities, or if you are uncertain about what a regulation says, you should alert your company's attorney immediately.

The field offices of various regulatory agencies can also help explain the meaning of new regulations or proposals to you (for addresses, see App. A). Keep in mind that the *Federal Register* has become notorious in recent years for misprints and typographical errors—especially in numbers and numerical tables. If a requirement looks like it doesn't make sense to you, it may not make sense to anybody. Also, the *Federal Register* is sometimes not the last word. The Occupational Safety and Health Review Commission, to offer just one example, sometimes overturns regulatory requirements because they are not in keeping with the law upon which OSHA wants to base them.

Bringing a case to the Review Commission or to court is, of course, a job for attorneys. But it is usually up to the technical personnel to tell the attorneys that a specific regulation could affect company operations, or that a regulation appears technically unreasonable.

4. YOUR LIABILITY AS A STANDARDS-SETTER

Some product is being manufactured and sold in accordance to an industry-wide standard. Yet is is involved in a product liability case, and the courts rule that the standard itself is inadequate. What is the liability of the individuals that wrote the standard, and the association that issued it? The question is particularly pressing among designers in the smaller industries—a large proportion of whom may actually be helping to write the standards governing the industry itself.

Many of these standards generated by smaller trade associations eventually are adopted as American National Standards by the American National Standards Institute (ANSI). In 1975, ANSI asked its legal counsel for an opinion on the liability question. The conclusion: Any such claims of liability would probably turn on negligence; strict liability (the basis of most product liability suits today) would probably not be applied to members of standards-writing committees operating under the Institute (a nonprofit corporation, by the way; ANSI is not a government agency). Nor, ANSI counsel said, is it likely that members of standards-writing committees operating under ANSI procedures for assuring consensus, recording negative views, and assuring membership for anyone in the industry or for consumers, will be held liable. Counsel's opinion does not extend to antitrust matters, or to standards-setting committees that operate behind closed doors or in a slipshod manner.

The memorandum notes that no court has ever held a standard approved by a national voluntary standards organization to have been negligently drawn.

Counsel feels this is due to the review and comment procedure national organizations such as ANSI, the American Society for Testing and Materials, and the American Society of Mechanical Engineers require before any new standard is approved. Counsel's memorandum to ANSI is reprinted here.*

I. CAUSES OF ACTION

A. Negligence

A cause of action [a theory of liability] for negligence may be said to require a breach of a duty causing damage (see Prosser, *The Law of Torts* [4th ed.] 143). It is assumed for this discussion that a product manufactured according to an American National Standard has caused injury or damage. To bring a successful claim against standards committee members for negligence, a plaintiff would then have to show that they owed a duty of care to him, that they breached this duty, and that this breach was a proximate cause of the injury.

(1) *Causation.* The simplest of these three elements to deal with is causation. It is clear that the members' duty of care extends only to those acts which they perform, namely, drafting standards intended for approval under ANSI procedures. Thus they and ANSI might be liable for injury caused by a product if negligence on their part in the preparation of the standards approved for the product could be shown. They would not be responsible, however, if injury was caused by a defect in the manufacture of, or the materials used in, a particular item which did not itself meet the standard.

(2) *Existence of Duty.* Assuming that an injury caused by a product can be attributed to the inadequacy of an American National Standard, one must then determine whether a duty of reasonable care is owed to the injured party. Under one or more of several possible theories, it is likely that such a duty would be held to exist.

In *Hall v. E. I. DuPont de Nemours & Co, Inc.*, 345 F. Supp. 353 (E.D.N.Y. 1972), the court held sufficient to state a cause of action a claim of negligence against six explosives manufacturers and their trade association for failure to use a warning label on blasting caps. The court stated that "joint control of risk can exist among actors who are not bound in a profit-sharing joint venture," but noted the following burden on the plaintiff: "To establish that the explosives industry should be held jointly liable on enterprise liability grounds, plaintiffs, pursuant to their pleading, will have to demonstrate defendants' joint awareness of the risks at issue in this case and their joint capacity to reduce or affect those risks" (At 373, 378). The case stands for the proposition that when individual members of an industry choose to delegate the function of safety investigation and design to the industry as a whole and its trade association, then liability for negligence can be placed on the industry as a whole.

*American National Standards Institute, 430 Broadway, New York, N.Y., 10018, "Products Liability of Members of Standards Writing Committees," January, 1975, pp. 4–16. Reprinted with permission.

American National Standards Committee members might be regarded as having similarly assumed at least part of the safety function for an industry[1] that participates in ANSI and uses its standards. It should be noted, however, that potential liability in *Hall* apparently was placed on the industry jointly because it could not be determined which manufacturer produced the explosive that caused the injury. Furthermore, while liability was placed on a group which set standards used by the individual manufacturers, this group was composed entirely of the manufacturers themselves. The participation of interested parties from outside the industry who contribute to American National Standards writing makes the application of this theory of liability more difficult than its application to the trade association in *Hall*.

A second theory of liability for negligence is based on the Restatement of Torts 2d, §311—"Negligent Misrepresentation Involving Risk of Physical Harm."[2] This section was relied on in *Hanberry v. Hearst Corp.*, 276 Cal. App. 2d 680, 81 Cal Rptr. 519, 39 ALR 3d 173 (1969), where the court overruled the defendant's demurrer to a claim that the defendant negligently granted its *Good Housekeeping* Seal of Approval to a shoe which proved to be dangerously slippery.

Section 311 requires a negligent misrepresentation and reasonable reliance thereon. The requirement of reliance seems easily satisfied. Since the reliance need not be by the injured party, the reliance of manufacturers on the challenged standard would seem to suffice, insofar as potential injury to third-party consumers is readily foreseeable. (This theory would not, of course, relieve the manufacturer in any way of his own liability for such an injury.) Further, where American National Standards are incorporated into contracts, there is actual and foreseeable reliance on the standard by the purchaser of the product.

The foregoing reliance must be placed on a negligent misrepresentation of the actor. While the *Good Housekeeping* seal in *Hanberry* certified that products are "good ones," the American National Standards (at least those dealing with safety) make no specific product claims, but rather by implication represent that products manufactured in accordance with the accepted engineering practices incorporated in the standard will not pose unreasonable risks of harm.

The third and, perhaps, the most likely theory of liability for negligence is based on the Restatement of Torts 2d, §324A—"Liability to Third Person

---

[1] Defined as including both producers and users.

[2] **§311**—Negligent Misrepresentation Involving Risk of Physical Harm:
 (1) One who negligently gives false information to another is subject to liability for physical harm caused by action taken by the other in reasonable reliance upon such information, where such harm results.
  (a) to the other, or
  (b) to such third persons as the actor should expect to be put in peril by the action taken
 (2) Such negligence may consist of failure to exercise reasonable care
  (a) in ascertaining the accuracy of the information, or
  (b) in the manner in which it is communicated.

for Negligent Performance of Undertaking." [3] This approach is best illustrated by *Hempstead v. General Fire Extinguisher Corp.,* 269 F. Supp. 109 (D. Del. 1967). A claim was brought against Underwriters' Laboratories, alleging that their negligence in approving the design of a fire extinguisher was a cause of the injury incurred when the instrument exploded. The court reviewed the law of Virginia on the requirement of privity of contract in products liability and denied Underwriters' motion for summary judgment, concluding that the defendant would be liable under §324A if negligence were proved. The court concluded that Underwriters' testing and listing activities amounted to a "tacit" approval of design and was subject to a duty of care. Similarly, the adoption of standards by voluntary standards committees, whether specifying design or performance characteristics, could be held to constitute tacit approval of the safety level of products that meet the standards, particularly where it is foreseeable that manufacturers will rely on the standards.

Plaintiffs alleging negligence in the performance of an undertaking, such as the writing of a safety standard, do not have to prove a misrepresentation as is required under the doctrine reflected in §311. Their burden is rather to show that the standards committee's failure to exercise reasonable care increased the risk of harm.

Thus, under one or more of the above principles, a court would find that standards writers must exercise reasonable care in the establishment of their standards.

(3) *Breach of Duty.* Assuming that an injury was actually caused by a deficiency in the standard itself and that a duty of reasonable care was held to exist, the final element necessary for a successful claim of negligence against members of a standards committee would be a showing that they did actually fail to use reasonable care.

To the extent to which the individuals participating in the process of establishing American National Standards are deemed experts in their fields, their expertise has a two-sided effect on the issue of negligence. First, if an individual "has in fact knowledge, skill, or even intelligence superior to that of the ordinary man, the law will demand of him conduct consistent with it" (Prosser, *The Law of Torts* [4th ed.] 161).

On the other hand, the standard of care exercised by the committee members will be measured at least partly against the custom in the trade and the opinions of experts in the field, including the very individuals compris-

---

[3]§**324A**—Liability to Third Person for Negligent Performance of Undertaking:
One who undertakes, gratuitously or for consideration, to render services to another which he should recognize as necessary for the protection of a third person or his things, is subject to liability to the third person for physical harm resulting from his failure to exercise reasonable care to protect his undertaking, if
    (a) his failure to exercise reasonable care increases the risk of such harm, or
    (b) he has undertaken to perform a duty owed by the other to the third person, or
    (c) the harm is suffered because of reliance of the other or the third person upon the undertaking.

ing the committee. Reliance on custom and usage of the trade, however, does not fully insulate committee participants, since it is well established that custom and usage, while relevant evidence of the appropriate level of care, are not conclusive. "Even an entire industry, by adopting such careless methods to save time, effort or money, cannot be permitted to set its own uncontrolled standard" (Prosser, *The Law of Torts* [4th ed.] 167). At the same time, if a clear preponderance of expert opinion in the field were to agree that a standard reflected a reasonable level of safety, a claim of negligence would be hard to substantiate.

Negligence, however, has been found even where the defendant had relied on a consensus of industry and expert opinion, as illustrated in *Marsh Wood Products Co. v. Babcock & Wilcox Co.*, 207 Wis. 209, 240 N.W. 392 (1932). The defendant was a manufacturer of steel boiler tubes, one of which exploded and caused injury. The plaintiff claimed that the defendant was negligent in failing, *inter alia*, to conduct a microscopic examination of the steel used for the tubes. Two professors of metallurgy testified that such an examination was the only practical way to determine the soundness of the metal. The court held that this testimony was sufficient to support the jury finding of negligence, despite the fact that no manufacturer in the industry generally performed such an examination, that it was not required by the state boiler code, and that it was not incorporated in the specifications of the American Society of Mechanical Engineers. Were such a case brought today, naming the standards writers as defendants in circumstances where microscopic inspection was omitted from the standard, the plaintiff would have good prospects of recovery using one of the modern principles extending the duty of care already discussed.

The *Marsh Wood* case illustrates the need to assure representation on standards committees of the broadest available range of expertise in the field, including experts not employed by the industry involved. Such participation could well be determinative in defending against a claim of negligence.

B. Strict Liability

The doctrine of strict products liability holds a manufacturer or seller liable for an injury caused by a defect in his product without requiring proof of fault or negligence on the part of the manufacturer or seller. To our knowledge, however, no case has extended this doctrine of liability without fault to a voluntary national standards organization or to members of a standards committee. Nor does it seem likely that the thrust of the case law or the policy reasons underlying the doctrine will extend strict liability to them in the foreseeable future.

The factor which seems to govern the reach of the strict liability doctrine is the extent of the connection between the potential defendant and the actual manufacturing and marketing process. While defective design by manufacturers clearly may give rise to strict liability on the part of the manufacturer,[4]

---

[4]See, e.g., *Hoppe v. Midwest Conveyor Company, Inc.*, 485 F.2d 1196 (8th Cir. 1973).

no case has extended the doctrine to apply to design defects in standards prepared by those not employed by, or acting for, the manufacturer or seller.

The effort by the plaintiff to extend strict liability to the certifier (*Good Housekeeping*) in the *Hanberry* case was rejected in the following terms:

> While we have held appellant has stated a cause of action for negligent misrepresentation against Hearst, we reject her contention she may also proceed in warranty or on the theory of strict liability in tort. She has cited no authority, and we have found none, which has extended either theory of recovery to one not directly involved in manufacturing products for, or supplying products to, the consuming public. To invoke either theory of recovery here would subject respondent to liability not warranted by the circumstances.... We believe this kind of liability for individually defective items should be limited to those directly involved in the manufacturing and supplying process, and should not be extended through warranty or strict liability to a general endorser who makes no representation it has examined or tested each item marketed. [At 39 ALR 3d 179, 180]

In *Kasel v. Remington Arms Co., Inc.*, 24 Cal App.3d 711, 101 Cal. Rptr. 314 (1972), the plaintiff was injured by an exploding shell manufactured by a Mexican affiliate of the defendant. The court held that Remington, as a trademark licensor, could be held strictly liable as "an integral part of the composite business enterprise which placed the defective shell in the stream of commerce" (101 Cal. Rptr. at 322). The court's decision was obviously influenced by the fact that the defendant had close ties with the affiliate other than the license agreement, including forty-percent ownership of the affiliate, contracts for the sale of technical information and for technical services, and, as part of the license agreement, the right to inspect and control the quality of all ammunition on which its trademark was used.

Kasel also questions the decision in the *Hanberry* case insofar as the latter case rejects a theory of strict liability of the product certifier and limits such liability to negligence. The court in *Kasel* found *Hanberry* distinguishable because the defendants in *Hanberry* (grantors of the *Good Housekeeping* seal) were not actually part of the manufacturing or supplying enterprise and had no control over the manufacturing process. However, the court's suggestion that the strict liability aspect of the decision in *Hanberry* might be reexamined was based on scholarly writings recommending such liability for trademark licensors and franchisors:

> We recognize that this court in *Hanberry v. Hearst Corp.*, 276 Cal. App.2d 680, 687–688, 81 Cal. Rptr. 519, refused to apply strict liability in tort to a product endorser; however the rationale of that decision was (1) that Hearst, as publisher of *Good Housekeeping* magazine, was not directly involved in manufacturing products for or supplying products to the consuming public and was not a part of the manufacturing and supplying enterprise that produced the defective shoe, and (2) that Hearst, as such, lacked any control over the manufacturing process. The rationale of *Hanberry* is not applicable to *Remington* in the instant case. (The rationale of *Hanberry* may warrant reeval-

uation in the light of the articles heretofore cited. Where it can be established that defendant by its avowed testing was the responsible inducement for the purchase by plaintiff, we see no reason to hold that defendant was not a necessary instrument in the stream of commerce.)

The *Kasel* court's reasons for extending the doctrine to certifiers and trademark licensors do not encompass parties having no control over the manufacturing or labeling of products.

In our view, the strict liability doctrine would not be applied to standards committee members for damages caused by products manufactured according to American National Standards. This view draws support from an examination of reasons set forth in the cases for imposing strict products liability. One such reason is the difficulty of proving negligence in terms of identifying the exact place in the chain of manufacture and supply where the defect came into existence. The committee members have no significant control of events in this chain, except to the extent that their design recommendations were adopted by the manufacturer.

Other reasons used to support strict products liability involve considerations of incentive to reduce product hazards and risk allocation. Since participation in the establishment of an American National Standard is voluntary and unpaid, the imposition of liability without fault for such participation would likely act more as a deterrent than as an incentive to increased product safety. Similarly, holding standards writers strictly liable would not more effectively allocate risk, since they personally do not gain pecuniary advantage from the use of the standards and do not have large resources to expend to lower product risks. Nor are committee members benefitted by lowering safety levels in the standards involved where no single interest group dominates the committee's output.

C. Summary

No case has imposed strict liability on an organization such as ANSI or on voluntary standards committee membership. A claim of negligence, on the other hand, based on failure to adhere to the higher standard of care to which experts are held, would likely be allowed to proceed for a determination on the facts. Proof of such negligence, however, would be difficult in the circumstances. The participation of outside experts on the standards writing committee affords substantial protection against claims of negligent preparation of standards.*

II. PARTIES SUBJECT TO LIABILITY

There are several categories of parties to be considered in determining who might have to respond in damages for injuries caused by a product conforming to an American National Standard. Assuming that the standard in

*Author's note: In a case decided in February 1979 in Federal District Court in Brooklyn, the ASME was held liable for damages to Hydro Level Corp. The company manufactured a device intended to shut off boilers if the water level within them drops too low. Members of an ASME boiler safety code committee (the court said) had falsely stated that the device did not meet the code's intent. The court ruled that the committee members' action destroyed the market for the device. IT&T and the Hartford Steam, Boiler Inspection & Insurance Co.—employers of the committee members—settled out of court in 1978 for $800,000. ASME is appealing a jury award that

question were prepared by an American National Standards Committee, the parties involved would be ANSI itself, the American National Standards Committee, the individual participants on the committee, and the organizations represented by these participants.

A. ANSI and Its Members

Although the American National Standards Committees that formulate standards do not "belong" to ANSI, this fact would almost certainly afford no protection for ANSI itself against a products liability claim. Because ANSI authorizes establishment of the committees, mandates their procedural requirements, and approves the standards which they formulate, the committees would undoubtedly be regarded as agents of ANSI. ANSI would thus bear full responsibility for those acts of the committees which were performed within the scope of ANSI procedures and on ANSI's behalf.

ANSI is potentially liable not only for the negligent conduct of a standards committee, that is, for the actual formulation of the standard, but also for any activities for which ANSI itself has direct responsibility. Such activities would include choosing the members of a committee and assuring itself that the criteria for approval of a standard have been properly met. The danger of a successful claim of negligence in the conduct of these activities, however, is minimal.

B. The American National Standards Committees and Their Members

An American National Standards Committee, since it is legally a voluntary unincorporated association, could be sued directly or through one of its officers under the law of New York[5] and many other states. Notwithstanding the availability of direct suit, the liability of an unincorporated association is based on the liability of its members who can be sued individually.[6]

However, an individual member of an association cannot be held liable for acts of the association or of other members unless these acts were done with the member's participation, knowledge, or approval.[7] Since no case has been found dealing with the liability of a member (whether an individual or an organization) for an act of an association approved by a vote of its members, it is difficult to determine precisely what type of conduct would protect a member from liability. It seems clear that a vote in favor of a standard would constitute approval, while, at the other extreme, withdrawal from a committee in protest would insulate a member from liability. A negative vote should also provide protection, although no case law has been found dealing with this question.[8] Failure to vote is likely to be found insufficient to dissociate a member from the committee's actions.

---

could cost it $9.9 million. The decision, while not directly relevant to this discussion, could signal more court activity in standards setting generally.

[5] See New York's General Association Law, §**13**.

[6] See *Martin v. Curran,* 303 N.Y. 276, 101 N.E.2d 683 (1951).

[7] See, for example, *Feldman v. North British and Mercantile Ins. Co.,* 137 F.2d 266 (4th Cir. 1943).

[8] See *Johnson v. Miller,* 63 Iowa 529, 17 N.W. 34, 50 Am. Rep. 758 (1883) and 69 Iowa 562, 29 N.W. 743 (1886); *Libby v. Perry,* 311A.2d 527 (1973).

III. CONCLUSIONS

We do not believe that members of voluntary standards committees operating under ANSI procedures incur significant risks of products liability for damages based on deficient standards.

The conclusion that a successful products liability claim against participants in such standards committees is unlikely is supported by the fact that there are apparently no reported cases which uphold such a claim or which indicate that such a suit has ever been instituted.

There are two factors that probably contribute to this lack of precedent in the field. One factor is, rather simply, the difficulty a plaintiff would face in winning such a case.

The second factor, which undoubtedly helps to account for the lack of relevant cases, is a practical one. A plaintiff who is injured by a product would normally have no incentive to name as a defendant organizations other than the manufacturer or seller, if they were solvent, particularly where the doctrine of strict liability may be available against these defendants, but not available against parties more removed from the stream of commerce.

Special circumstances might prompt a plaintiff to bring suit against a standards organization. In *Hall v. E. I. DuPont de Nemours,* for instance, the suit was brought against the trade association because the identity of the actual manufacturer was unknown. In *Kasel v. Remington Arms Co., Inc.,* no reason is stated in the opinion, but it may well be that the trademark licensor was sued because the plaintiff would have experienced difficulty in establishing jurisdiction over the Mexican manufacturer.

The fact that product certifiers were named as defendants in the *Hanberry* and *Hempstead* cases may be attributable either to fears that the manufacturer, or the seller, or both, would be financially unable to satisfy a money judgment or simply to the use of a "shotgun" approach, that is, to sue everyone who might possibly be subject to liability in the hope of creating dissension among the defendants. Either of these two reasons could prompt an injured party to include standards writers in a product liability suit.

It should be noted that the plaintiff has the choice of whom to sue and can normally collect the full amount of the judgment from any one of the parties who is found liable. In New York, however, one such party may bring another before the court for an apportionment of the damages based upon the relative fault of the two parties.[9]

These strategic and practical factors tend further to reduce the prospects of products liability claims against participants on standards committees. Even if ANSI were sued, there would seem to be little incentive also to include individual committee members.

---

[9] See *Dole v. Dow Chemical Co.,* 30 N.Y.2d 143, 331 N.Y.S.2d 382, 282 N.E.2d 288 (1972). This rule could presumably be used by a manufacturer against the standards writers and vice versa.

III
ORGANIZING AND OPERATING CORPORATE AND DEPARTMENTAL PRODUCT SAFETY SYSTEMS

1. THE POLICY STATEMENT

Of course, no company intentionally sets out to make a product that by defect or design causes unnecessary injury. Why, then, should management formally put itself on record as supporting product safety? There are several reasons. The first lies in the attitudes that foster the original question. A policy statement should go beyond the vague promise of a "good" product. Unless it does, it is worse than useless, because it can only lull management into a false sense of security.

To be effective, a policy statement must provide a basis for action by operating personnel. What should a supervisor do, if he or she sees a potential danger—a lapse in quality control for instance? What should an assembler do? A packer? Remember, in even a relatively small plant, thousands of items can be packed or even shipped in the hour of confusion between seeing a real danger, and acting upon it.

The statement of policy should also come from a high level in management. Separate policies for design, production, and marketing simply will not do. These groups are, to some extent, mutually antagonistic in their immediate goals—although, of course, they should share the long-term corporate goals of growth, profits, and stability.

To be continually useful, the policy should provide some procedure for getting news of problems down at the plant or on the loading dock back up to the management level that issued the policy in the first place. No news from below is a danger sign that employees feel they can only pay lip service to what should be a firm corporate commitment. This does not mean, in a big organization, that high-level management must make every decision with regard to daily production "crises" affecting quality control. But management must have some idea of what problems subordinates face in this area.

Clearly, effective dissemination is a must. That means that employees must be told, in clear language, what is expected of them. And the message must be refreshed periodically. Suppliers must also understand what is expected of them. Such expectations should go beyond the pious demand for "perfect" materials or subassemblies. It is even dangerous to let the standard contract clause about "notifying the customer of any design or materials changes" carry the ball. If you need a product from an outside vendor that must meet certain temperature, vibration, electrical, chemical, or mechanical specifications, spell them out.

The policy statement should also spell out what actions a supplier should take if your plant's quality control manager calls with a stop order on further shipments until a problem can be ironed out, and your production manager calls the next minute with a demand for more shipments. Which official has the final word? Or whom can the supplier call to resolve the problem?

Strong language is required. Avoid weasel words and phrases such as "depending on the circumstances, product may be shipped." Whoever makes a decision to ship potentially hazardous or defective products should be required to sign off on the matter and investigate before any reach final consumers.

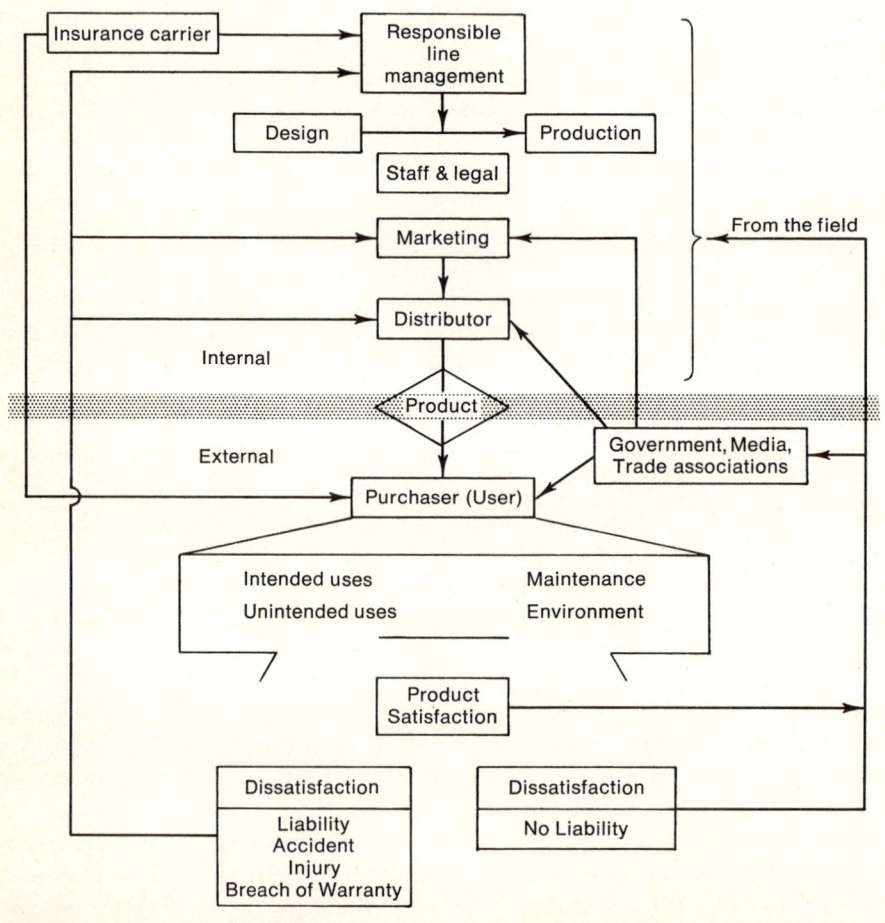

Figure III-1 Information flow in a safety-conscious company. *(After Biancardi.)*

It would also help to cite some of the statutory requirements corporations must live under today with regard to product safety. Of necessity, such a policy statement could run to many pages. It should be structured in such a way that each operating group understands the broad goals of the policy, and its own, more narrow, responsibilities without burdening, let's say, the packing-room supervisor with the designer's responsibilities.

In many cases, it is appropriate to appoint a product safety director to coordinate the effort. This is the high-level management person to whom news of problems should flow. In many companies, this person is directly responsible to the vice-president for engineering, or may well be the head of the engineering design team. This is because, in the implementation of a product safety program, there is no more fundamentally involved group than the design engineering team. As one product safety director put it, "design engineering is product safety from beginning to end and it is there, in design engineering, that the nucleus of the product safety program must be found."

As we shall see, however, companies will have to beware of organizational conflicts if the engineering department has too much authority. And the need for corporate visibility may require an individual of even higher rank than the engineering level.

2. DESIGN ENGINEER, THE PRIME MOVER OF PRODUCT SAFETY

From the first, the design engineer must accept the idea that the only proper design is one that does not offer unreasonable hazard to the consumer or to bystanders. Nor can it force workers into unreasonable danger, or present unacceptable risk to technicians who may have to service it in the field. The designer must be psychologically willing to change a design, to eliminate or reduce risks. Yet he or she must take into account the performance of the product, the seriousness of the potential hazard, and the total cost. If the risk of a significant hazard cannot be eliminated, it is equally the design engineer's responsibility to ensure that the product carries proper warning, and that operators are educated in its use.

Thus, design engineering staffs must:

1. Understand the priorities,
2. Develop systems of hazard identification that assume nothing is safe, and
3. Promulgate countermeasures.

Developing a program based on these mandates is not something that can be accomplished overnight. It requires a great amount of work to acquaint a company's personnel with the nuances that are involved in the review of designs and prototypes for safe features, and in the establishment of a kind of company discipline that assures the end result—a safe product.

This is particularly true today because safe design in the age of regulation requires engineering design, out of necessity, to interface with all other functions in the company.

Product safety has become a matter for specialists. Today's product safety and environmental decisions are not the result of a calculation; rather they usually depend on a consensus of the judgment of those most qualified in a particular field.

Therefore, the product-safety-minded design engineer must communicate with all those departments within a company that are directly involved with product safety. This means that the design engineer must:

1. Have frequent discussions and exchanges on objectives and performance with top management. This exchange should begin with the drafting of the statement of corporate product safety policy or intent. Design engineering has a responsibility to see that management undertakes such a project. The resulting document is important as an indication of top management's support of and participation in all corporate product safety efforts.

2. Establish communication with accounting to help devise systems to measure spending on product safety.

3. Obtain input from advertising as to what claims are being made in ads or product publicity and what safety features are described.

4. Communicate continually with product insurance representatives on claims that have potential personal injury implications, and with legal departments on their methods of handling personal injury litigation and product hazard evaluation.

5. Cooperate with marketing in determining the best ways to describe and promote safety features to generate greater dealer and customer interest.

6. Interface with materials engineering and manufacturing on life and performance measurements of various safety-oriented materials and manufacturing's ability to meet design tolerances.

7. Have on-going programs with purchasing to help suppliers understand and meet company safety requirements on components.

The system for doing all these things must evolve in any organization. There are few in industry who will agree on any one best organization that such systems should take. In this respect the engineer and all others associated with product safety can assume but two things: that the product safety effort and the success of the design engineer can only be assured in a multidisciplinary approach to the problem; and that, to date, there is no accepted "recipe" for the formation of an effective product safety organization.

The form that the product safety organization can or should take in one company varies dramatically from that best suited in another—based on the company size and industry size, the technological sophistication of the product, the production volumes and processes, and the complexity of a product's man-machine relationships.

In just one area, quality control, for example, few people—including manufacturers and engineers—have a full appreciation for the degree of variability that exists in mass-produced products. In many cases, taken from actual test data, the variability between individual units is larger than the average difference between models. Often the real challenge in obtaining a satisfactory product is to be sure that the engineering design is such that the inherent variability of the production process is within the range of acceptable performance.

Since both the variability of the production process and the acceptable level of performance change from product to product and industry to industry, so too must the product safety organization vary to accommodate those differences. The number of people involved in a product safety program, the amount of money spent, and the sophistication of the systems relied upon depend entirely upon the potential hazard level associated with each product. It then becomes the first duty of the engineer to identify all potential product hazards. Only then can a decision be made as to the size and shape the overall company product safety program should take.

Many engineers believe that a good design is by definition a safe design and that there is little need for safety organization and structure as long as engineers of competence are involved. "If product safety becomes a part of the job and not applied to the job, your program will be a success," said one safety engineer. "If a separate product safety group is established to serve as the watchdog and only the watchdog of the various corporate functions then your program is doomed to failure. Hence the importance of designing safely from the beginning."

While some engineers may seize upon this philosophy to fight against the organization of formalized safety programs, sole dependence upon the decentralized design engineering function is not a valid method of assuring product safety, even within the smallest of corporate groups. There are too many regulations, too many potential hazards, and there is too much at stake to depend on the competence of a single person.

The situation becomes even more critical in large companies that are often multimarket, multidivisional, and sometimes multinational. Here the law of growing disorganization, a direct function of the size of a corporation, serves only to confuse the focus of individual safety efforts and blur the true cost (for such things as insurance coverage) of unsafe products. If different divisions in a company all have separate safety programs and all work in different ways, some will perform to excess, some inefficiently, and some not at all.

So, while the design engineer is the prime mover of safety concerns, the basic assumption should be that he or she cannot ensure product safety alone. To prevent the organization, on the other hand, from becoming a mere watchdog of the engineer, more and more companies are building their product safety programs out of systems organization. Such systems approaches were first used by the aeronautical industry in solving complex engineering problems. The same systems concepts enable the design engineer to, in organized fashion, consider each individual design factor and its interrelationship with other factors. The systems cover the ways the design engineer should think about product safety, how he or she can communicate with others in the company, how others can communicate with the design effort, what information he or she should consider as important to the safety effort, and various mechanisms the design engineer can employ or develop to ensure product safety.

3. WHO SHALL JUDGE?

While, because of various prejudices and traditional product goals, design engineers are poor judges of their own product's safety characteristics, their experience and expertise make them naturals to step back from actual design work and coordinate a corporate product safety program. Organizationally, as has been mentioned earlier, some companies put their product safety directors under the direct responsibility of the engineering department. This can be a mistake in that an effective product safety program requires (as we have also said before) the participation of all in the company. The product safety director should have the authority of a vice-president or higher so that all departments in the company can be equally involved and monitored. The product safety effort must draw its authority from a corporate level high enough so that it can also make engineering toe the line.

Other caveats to be aware of in organizing a formalized safety group include keeping product safety responsibility separate from that of the quality control and product assurance functions of manufacturing and separate from the consultation and defense responsibilities of the legal department.

That is not to say, however, that the product safety effort is carried out separately from these groups, for it will be absolutely necessary to have a close liaison with both manufacturing and legal on the greater number of decisions made.

The fact that systems thinking is a relatively new discipline for most of them often leads companies to seek out systems specialists in other industries to serve as safety director. This can be a fatal mistake because to do the safety job required the director of product safety must be intimately familiar with the company's products. Lack of knowledge of the product line will totally frustrate any product safety program. If a company's products have any degree of sophistication it is questionable whether the outside engineer from a nonrelated but systems-organized field can acquire this knowledge.

Above all, avoid the temptation to place former defense aerospace personnel in such positions, unless they can demonstrate the ability to understand profit margins and cost considerations. Knowledge of MIL specs is not enough.

In addition, it is essential that the product safety director have both corpo-

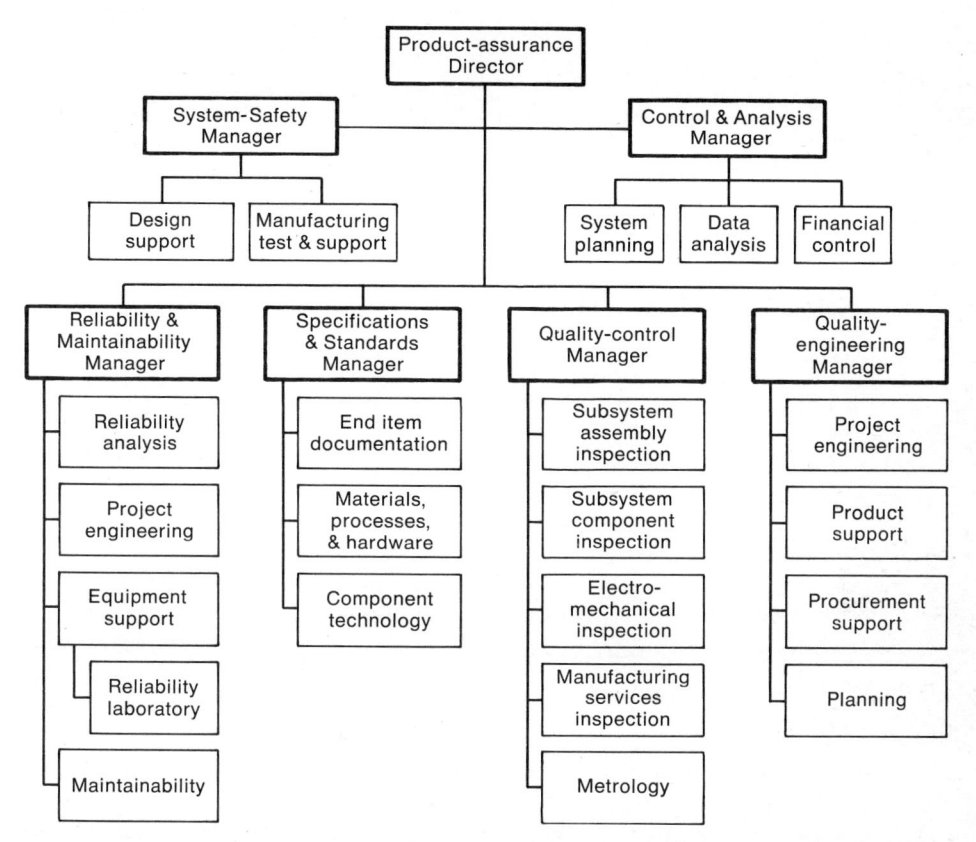

Figure III-2 Organization of product safety team in medium-size company. Typically, the team would include seven individuals, but some of the job titles can be combined or split as company and product needs require.

rate and line engineering experience. Picking the most competent design engineer on the staff is often the best method of selecting a product safety director. Picking an inside person also avoids the psychological slam a product safety program can have on personnel. The throat-cutting or hatchet-man syndrome can be a major difficulty associated with outside systems and safety experts brought into a company.

By his or her very appointment, the product safety director then becomes the seed of a product safety system whether or not a company is accustomed to systems-approach discipline. The scope of the product safety director's responsibility will of its own nature push the company and the program toward greater systems development.

That responsibility includes:

    Ensuring that company safety policies are carried out by all personnel

- Developing guidance in carrying out a safety program from design phase to the repair phase

- Keeping management informed of safety program activities and progress

- Reviewing all safety requirements affecting a company product or future products

- Analyzing the product and its components to ensure that all hazards are eliminated or controlled

- Reviewing histories of product hazards, failures, and mishaps

- Monitoring failure and incident reports to determine discrepancies

- Making safety analyses of work done by associate contractors and suppliers

- Developing safety warning and caution devices where hazards cannot be eliminated

- Disseminating safety information on hazards to interested or affected organizations

- Inviting the participation of boards and committees dealing with product safety

- Developing a plan to respond to and investigate any mishaps involving a company product

- Taking steps to prevent recurrences of mishaps

His or her responsibility further extends to the formation of both corporate and departmental groups and the maintenance of the size of the groups within manageable limits. Generally an engineer in a larger firm will find himself working in a product safety group at the corporate level of from six to ten individuals selected from various disciplines within the company, plus safety representatives at the divisional or departmental level throughout the company.

Within engineering itself, the product design head should serve as the coordinator of the product safety effort of the design team. Depending on how complex the product and how large the design staff, the product engineer can appoint one member of the design team as coordinator of product safety interests at the design team level. However, in all cases at this design team level, safety considerations remain a responsibility of all the design team members involved.

It's openly admitted that a good product safety program probably means the average engineer will have twice the work he or she is accustomed to having.

Table III-1 Roles of Various Segments of the Organization at Various Stages of Product Development. *(After Dodson.)* The numbers refer to the order of response, not the relative importance of each department at each stage of product development.

Source	Birth of an idea	Birth of a prototype	Product	Improved model
Design	2. Feasibility study.	3. Test-check against standards or codes. Make needed design modifications.	3. Evaluate complaints; modify if necessary.	Continuing improvement.
Purchasing	6. How to obtain required materials.	4. Order material and components.	3. Evaluate complaints; correct if necessary.	
Manufacturing	5. Best manufacturing methods.	5. Check design for manufacturing modifications.	3. Evaluate complaints; improve controls.	
Quality Control	7. What controls are needed?	6. Establish controls, tolerances, and limits.	3. Evaluate.	
Marketing	1. Sell at a profit?	1. Get consumer reaction.	3. Consider complaints; appease.	
Legal	3. Patent infringement?	8. Review proposed advertising, literature, warranties.	3. Consider complaints; defensive action.	
Insurance	4. Appraise risk.	9. Obtain coverages.	4. Evaluate complaints.	
Service	8. Potential service problems.	7. Review prototype, notify design and manufacturing about suggestions.	2. Collect complaints	
Consumer		2. Reaction to prototype.	1. Any complaints?	Objective: No Complaints.
Conclusion:	If conclusions of all depts. are "go," develop a prototype or model.	If all conclusions are "go," make a product.	Make any necessary improvements.	Continuing improvement.

81

Much of the extra burden stems from paperwork associated with documentation and communication of data relevant to each product's safety considerations.

This burden is first borne by the product safety coordinators at each level (design team and corporate). These individuals must be ready to prepare an agenda in advance so members of their groups will have time to study the subjects and consider their views. They must ensure that all members of the product safety groups are heard—encouraging reticent members and keeping dominating ones in check, while at the same time preparing a statement of the consensus of the meeting to be sure that all have properly understood it. Lastly, they must see that the minutes of the meetings are distributed for correction and review prior to their release.

The duties of the two principal product safety groups (design team and corporate) include recommending general policy to management, setting goals or objectives for product loss control, ensuring adequate flow of information on such matters as standards, design test results, and the proper application of quality control and service department information.

Within this general framework and with these responsibilities the various departments within a corporation are ready to implement a product safety program.

4. MAINTAINING AN EFFECTIVE PROGRAM

Even the most carefully thought-out systems must be nurtured by management if they are to thrive. To assure that product safety continues to rank high on the list of corporate priorities, the following dictum is necessary:

> **Grant at least as much autonomy and support for the decisions of product designers as is accorded to other corporate decision-making functions, such as finance and marketing.**

Autonomy can't be achieved automatically, simply as a result of a new directive from management. It can only develop out of new management practices, such as issuing a standing requirement that engineering, research, and design staffs should be in on the early stages of new venture development and other substantial product-line changes. Such practices pay off particularly well when technical and design personnel are asked to go beyond their usual functions. In other words, they should not only check out feasibility and costs. They should also evaluate new ventures for potential safety and reliability problems as early in the game as possible.

Depending on the organization, autonomy for engineers and designers should not be limited to "administrators" such as project leaders. If most of the real engineering is done below that level, autonomy should be extended to all who significantly influence the design or selection of the product systems, components, and materials.

Accept the increased costs required to develop less hazardous products.

While the production and other nondesign costs of improving the safety of products may be negligible, fairly often the developmental and engineering costs of arriving at such improvements will prove substantial. This can happen, in particular, when a company finds that it has few guideposts, and must develop product safety standards itself. This is a common situation in industries where safety standards have lagged.

What's more, expenses can soar if a company pioneering a new product field has to develop "human factors" data on how the new device will be used, the effects on product-related tasks it will be required to perform, and the environment in which it will be used. Even as seemingly simple a device as a new type of swivel for office chairs can get a company into trouble. The swivel may be perfect for chairs when someone is sitting on them. But what might happen when the office manager climbs on the chair to change a light bulb? Or a secretary uses the chair as a rolling cart to drag some heavy files out of the back room?

It is penny-wise and pound-foolish to deny design personnel adequate opportunities to get out into the field and investigate for themselves the real-life situations and conditions for which they are expected to devise a product.

Likewise, even smaller firms should be willing to send personnel to refresher courses in design, quality assurance, reliability, and product safety law. In some cases, it may be preferable to arrange for in-plant consulting and training programs, perhaps for attendance by a mix of engineering, production, marketing, and management personnel.

This can be especially useful in industries where the design process has become fragmented among many disciplines. The more varieties of expertise—electrical, mechanical, and chemical, for example—involved in the development of a product, the more complex is the designer's task of synthesizing them into a viable and safe whole.

5. WHAT CAN SUBORDINATES DO IF MANAGEMENT CONTRAVENES SAFETY?

Where safety is concerned, those personnel responsible may discover that some of their recommendations are greeted less than enthusiastically by management. As one product liability lawyer put it, "the engineer's responsibility to implement his safety recommendations often exposes him to virtually limitless explanation, rationalization, and, in certain instances, management harassment." At one memorable product safety panel in Washington, D.C. in 1971, not one of the speakers still worked for the companies or government agencies at which they had raised objections to management safety practices.

In such circumstances, few engineers and designers can look to their professional societies for support. None of them has developed anything like the economic and political "muscle" wielded by physicians' and teachers' groups.

Because of this, the designer's best hope for outside support comes, paradoxically, from government, the courts, and the marketplace itself. Such allies are needed, because too often the product safety effort is initiated without an independent budget line and instead has one engineer working part-time in his or her new assignment.

Positive answers to the following questions indicate weak budget support by management. Are you forced to try to get "free" advice from consultants by telephone-call brain-picking discussions? Has your company resisted the establishment of a small product safety library? Are expenses withheld for trips by designers to outside conferences? Are engineers expected to read all product safety literature "on their own time"?

Even in a well-run program, management and engineering design may occasionally argue over safety-related issues. If the safety and well-being of the potential owners or users of the product are genuinely at stake, what can be done? Confrontation, the issuing of ultimatums, and other such challenges are to be avoided, at least at the beginning. Not only are they counterproductive, but ringing memos based on preliminary design calculations can come back (as we will discuss in greater detail later) to haunt a company in court, even if the product is redesigned but still is involved in an injury.

And, self-serving as it may seem, the engineer or designer should protect himself first. The situation should be carefully documented with formal, written (and witnessed if necessary) statements, backed up by all pertinent data. Some legal experts have argued that such files are time bombs, ticking away until detonated by plaintiff's attorney in a liability suit. But the absence of such information is also a bomb of sorts. It suggests to a jury that the company never even considered safety to be an issue in design, or is trying to hide something.

The written record should show as impartially and as fully as possible the positions of management and the other parties to any disagreement.

If, after all internal avenues of appeal have been exhausted, the designer finds that his or her safety recommendations still are unheeded, the choice of further actions is not inviting. Whether a designer or engineer finds the situation so untenable that resignation is necessary is a decision only the

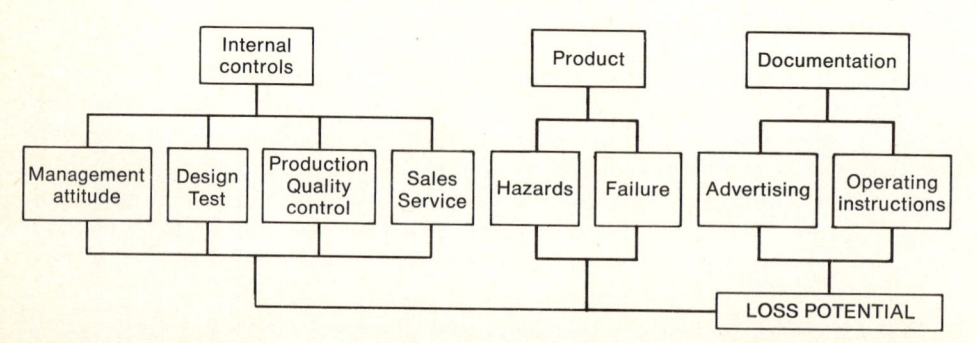

Figure III-3 Management often underestimates the areas for potential for loss due to product liability.

Table III-2 Hierarchy of Faults

1. *Barely perceptible.*   Defects that are unnoticeable or irrelevant to all but 5 or 10 percent of users. Some examples might include minor finish defects in furniture, or a line cord six inches shorter than it should be.

2. *Clearly deficient.*   An automobile that is difficult to start (or that won't run at all); a male electric plug that won't match any receptacle; an electric motor that won't run at specified rpm.

3. *Evident or obvious hazard.*   Corroded structural member; exposed electrical conductor.

4. *Failure and loss.*   Product fails, causing or contributing to accidental injury or property loss. Product either fails in normal or foreseeable use, causing accident, or fails due to extra stress of another product's failure in foreseeable circumstances.

---

professional can make. For management, such a resignation is a firm warning that all is not right with a company's products and design procedures.

6. PERSONAL LIABILITY OF THE DESIGNER

Engineers, designers, and professional people generally are required to exercise a level of care and judgment that is higher than the average nonprofessional's. Nevertheless, society does not demand that technical professionals be perfect in everything they do. The professional can usually be held liable for damages only if he or she performed below the level of expertise in the immediate community. Increasingly, "community" has come to mean the entire inhabited world.

The courts have, however, been more tolerant of the time it takes for technical knowledge to cross disciplinary boundaries. Thus, a designer who specifies a certain finish might be held liable if others know the finish can be flammable under certain circumstances, and it does indeed catch fire and injures someone. But the designer might not be liable if a medical researcher in the university lab just down the street has preliminary evidence that the finish solvent causes bladder cancer.

Likewise, there can be no liability if there is no suit. This generally protects the employed engineer, because the employer usually carries liability insurance, and it is the employer's resources that the plaintiff wants to tap. Nevertheless, individual professional employees are often named as defendants as well. And even if the plaintiffs don't collect a nickel from the employed engineer, the engineer's career can be ruined by the adverse publicity.

The outside consultant is not as well protected. Most consultants are reasonably aware of their responsibilities, however, and carry liability insurance. This is hardly an absolute protection, of course. Insurance does not cover a professional's failure to require or advise a client of the need for his own insurance or bonding. Nor does it cover violation of a patent, copyright, or trademark.

Damages caused by failure to complete drawings or specifications on time are insured only if the failure is due to the error or omission of information by the professional's client or employer. The insured professional is not covered for malicious errors or fraud. Misrepresentation may sometimes be covered, depending on the facts of the case, but many courts consider misrepresentation to be fraud unless proven otherwise.

An interesting case history in this regard is discussed by Lipman Feld* in an article on professional responsibilities. A manufacturer of earthmoving equipment hired a firm of consulting engineers to set up a proper inspection procedure for one model's assembly. An engineer employed by the consulting firm was given supervisory responsibility over the job. Because of the nature of the carburetor design, there was a danger of fire if gas leaked from the bowl. The supervising engineer's inspection procedure was designed to watch for this potential defect, and protect against it (see Table III-2).

Perhaps it would have been more responsible to have insisted on redesign of the system, especially since carburetors could still be assembled by outside service personnel—and thus could not be detected by even a perfect in-plant inspection program. At any rate, the inevitable happened, and a worker operating one of the machines was splattered by gasoline apparently released by an improperly assembled carburetor. A spark of undertermined origin set fire to the gasoline, severely burning the operator.

The injured operator filed suit against the manufacturer, the consulting firm, and the consulting firm's employee. As evidence developed, it was discovered that the manufacturer had decided assembling expenses were too great, and had put pressure on the consulting firm to cut costs. As a result, the procedure was simplified and personnel eliminated. The consulting firm's employee spent less time at the factory, but continued to make the same reports on compliance with his inspection procedures that he had before.

The consultant's insuror claimed that since the engineer had submitted fraudulent reports, it was not liable and would not pay damages. The injured worker's attorney, however, wanted to keep the engineer's insurance company in the picture, because the manufacturer seemed financially shaky. So plaintiff suggested that the consulting engineer had supervised assembly with the same care and skill usually exercised by reputable consultants in the community. In other words, even if the engineer clearly made a mistake for which the insurance firm should cover, he didn't necessarily act in a negligent manner!

Usually, it is far more difficult to pinpoint the responsibility for error of any one person in the design process. It is also difficult to predict what judge or jury will do in any given situation. But because even the cost of defending against an unsuccessful suit can financially ruin an individual, skill tempered by caution is good advice for any designer.

---

*Liability and the Engineer: Responsibility to the Public, *New Engineer* vol. 3, no. 8, p. 35, Sept. 1974.

7. USING THE OUTSIDE CONSULTANT

The outside design consultant has become a permanent fixture on the American industrial scene. Some consultants are experts in certain narrow areas—steel shafting, power transmission, or human factors. Others specialize in certain types of products—lawn mowers, fasteners, or hand tools. Others are mainly stylists, brought in toward the end of the design cycle to wrap an attractive "package" around the product's working parts.

Considering that such consultants—either individuals or large firms—are so common, it is amazing how often they are misused. Frequently, a company will have outside consultants report to corporate legal staff, instead of to engineering. Consultants are often brought into the scene too late in the development cycle, to "pull the chestnuts out of the fire" after corporate staff has been unable to solve a problem satisfactorily.

Consultants are often given tasks that are ill-defined, especially with regard to product safety. Should the consultant have any say? In the previous section's example, a consulting firm was hired to "correct" the problem of a poor carburetor design by specifying better inspection procedures, rather than by redesigning the system. Today, many consultants would refuse that job on the basis of ethical responsibility to ultimate users, and because of potentially large personal liability in case of failure.

Such questions frequently appear in the early negotiating stages. Until the midseventies, most professional engineering societies flatly declared competitive bidding as unethical. Under pressure from the Justice Department, several societies modified their canons of ethics to allow professional engineers to compete on a price basis, and therefore to avoid running afoul of antitrust laws. This does not mean, of course, that companies are forced to solicit bids for professional work. In fact, in product design, the consultant's experience, qualifications, resources, and even personality can be—and usually are—far more important than the consultant's fee.

Before negotiating with a design consultant, the company must first define the task it wants performed. Will testing be required? The consultant must have the proper equipment available to do it. How tight is the product development schedule? The outside professional must have time free to meet it. Who in the company will work with the consultant? When? Only then will a company be able to begin its search for the right consultant or consulting firm. And only then can the consultant estimate what fee he or she will have to charge.

Most companies probably will want to write their requirements into a semiformal document before the search begins. At this stage, the requirements should be capable of modification, either to fit the competence of the outsider actually selected, or to reflect suggestions from the candidates themselves. Nevertheless, it should be as complete as possible in describing the nature of the work to be done—the problem to be solved, and related issues deserving of the outsider's consideration. Rough schedules for completion of each stage of the work, and for payments, should be included. An option for future work on the project also might be spelled out in rough outline at this stage.

From the consultants, firms expect detailed descriptions of facilities available, lists of similar work or related experience for other clients, and thumbnail biographies of the consultant firm's professional personnel. Often these are contained in a "professional brochure" printed ahead of time by the consulting firm or individual. In such brochures, watch especially for unnecessarily flashy layouts, and question the firm carefully about haziness in describing the exact role played by the consultant on projects mentioned.

In the negotiations themselves, don't be afraid to ask hard questions. Money—and even the very survival of a firm—are involved. Likewise, expect hard questions from the consultant. What kind of tooling is available to manufacture the product to be designed? Does the size of the anticipated production run justify new tooling or unusual design work that may have a high first cost but pay for itself in quantity production? How does the consultant expect to approach the problem? How much time will the consultant have to work on it? Is the company negotiating directly with the person or people who will be put on the job? If not, why not? (There are often good reasons, especially in larger consulting firms.)

One especially ticklish issue is that of the consultant's own "suppliers." Specialized testing labs are becoming more common as the cost of some instrumentation climbs, and the skill needed for some tests increases. Computer programming help is often needed today. Or a packaging expert may consult with a specialist in finishes or industrial fasteners. If such organizations must be used, companies hiring consultants should have the right to investigate the organizations' competence as well.

Companies depending on outside expertise for all of their engineering work are at a particular disadvantage. These smaller firms complain about consultants' jargon, and have difficulty defining the scope of the work to be done. In such cases, a two-step procurement program can be helpful. In such a program, a consultant is first picked to define the scope of the work that needs to be done, and to rough out a schedule. Then the company can go ahead on a firmer footing, either using the first consultant to carry the work to completion, or negotiating with others on the company's behalf.

Small companies sometimes enter into time-reimbursable or "cost plus" contracts for outside design help. One advantage, should a product defect cause a liability, is that the outsider must keep careful records in order to document his or her fee. These records can be useful in court. But it is usually preferable to deal with a professional on a "professional" basis, jointly defining the scope of the work to be performed, and the fee for it.

Remember that the consultant's personnel are in your care while doing work for you, especially under your supervision or at your plant. In case of personal injury or death, you may be liable. Investigate insurance and bonding with care, especially if your product development program includes potentially hazardous phases, such as test driving.

Common courtesy dictates that once a consultant has been selected, and has accepted the assignment, other competitors for the work be notified promptly. They should also be requested to return any corporate material in their hands—such as preliminary product specifications, time schedules, and so forth. If you are working on a government contract, documentation of the negotiations almost always is required. This is the government's protection against "rigged" consulting fees, in the absence of competitive bidding. Don't be surprised if one of the "losing" consultants offers to undercut the "winner's" fee. This is becoming increasingly common, even though professional societies consider it unethical. But consumer product safety demands the highest standards of ethical practice. Draw your own conclusions.

Only after negotiations is it time to put everything into legal language. Because of the specialized nature of consulting work, every contract is likely to be a custom-tailored job. But a general outline of things to include is shown in Fig. III-4.

If your contemplated new product might benefit from outside consultation, but you are unaware of qualified consultants in the field, consider contacting relevant societies from among the list in App. G. Some state engineering licensing boards have up-to-date directories of practitioners available. In many states, however, these lists are sadly outdated—even though professional engineers' licensing fees are supposed to pay for their upkeep and publication.

8. RECORDS RETENTION

The answer to the question, "How long should records of my product be kept?" has become deceptively simple in recent years. The answer is "Just about forever." But *which* corporate records are product-related? And, to help control costs, which records should be kept easily accessible, and what can be trundled off to storage?

Requirements under federal regulations are spelled out in the regulations themselves, and listed annually by the Office of the Federal Register. Records retention requirements bearing directly on product safety and liability are listed in App. F as they existed on January 1, 1977 for federal agencies. State and local requirements are not as easy to pin down. For instance, the statute of limitations varies from state to state. But, as a practical matter, since the "limitation" period begins to run only after an accident, after an injury first manifests itself, or (in some states) after the injured party reaches the age of majority, the "forever" warning applies.

As a result, decisions about how records are kept, and for how long, depend on corporate goals and the nature of the product. At a minimum, companies should keep active records to help trace raw materials, suppliers, customers, and design changes. Compliance with regulations on all levels of government is necessary as well. Good record-keeping practices can also help trace the "hidden" costs of product liability—especially those of insurance, employee training and supervision, quality control, and settlements with injured parties.

International Widget Company, a corporation (hereinafter called the "Company") does hereby retain Albert Q. Expert (hereinafter called "Contractor"), whose business address is 931 Balderdash Lane, Confusion, Penn., to furnish consulting services under the following terms and conditions:

1. Description and Limitations

    A. Contractor shall furnish the services as scheduled and described in Attachment A. Except as allowed under Attachments A and B of this agreement, the Contractor will not engage subcontractors, to perform any or all of the work listed herein without written approval of the Company.

    B. Company will provide working space and tools/materials as may be required for completion of this contract, as listed in Attachment C. Unusual equipment and nonstandard tools shall be responsibility of Contractor unless listed in Attachment C.

2. Time to completion; termination provision

    A. The period of service as detailed in Attachment A shall be from _____ to _____. Either party may terminate this agreement at any time upon written notice at least ____ days prior to termination date.

3. Compensation, additional work

    A. Company will pay the following fees for services performed (list schedule of payment, milestones to be reached, etc.).

    B. Work not specified in this agreement, but approved later, shall be paid for under the following conditions: _____

    C. Payment to be made upon submission of Contractor invoices and expense vouchers. Invoices must show Employer Identification Number or Social Security Number in accordance with Internal Revenue Service requirements.

    D. An amount of _____ of monies due Contractor will be withheld pending delivery and acceptance of final report by Company.

    E. Compensation stated herein includes applicable taxes and will not be increased as a result of change in Contractor's tax liabilities, or failure of Contractor to include applicable tax.

4. Company shall have access to directly pertinent records, books, and correspondence related to this agreement or transactions involved with this agreement until ____ years after acceptance of final report.

5. Conflict of interest

    A. Contractor affirms there is no actual or potential conflict of interest, to the best of his/her knowledge, between Contractor, Contractor's family, business, or ownership/financial interest.

    B. In the event of any change in Contractor's status, possible conflicts are to be reported to the Company at earliest practicable date.

    C. Contractor will not hire any Company employee to perform any part of this Agreement.

6. Patents. Inventions or discoveries made or conceived by Contractor in connection with this Agreement shall be the property of the Company. Company will have sole discretion to determine if and when a patent application shall be filed, and by whom. Contractor will, at Company discretion and expense, do all things necessary or proper with respect to patent application(s).

7. In performing services of this Agreement, Contractor shall report to ____.

Figure III-4 Elements of a typical consulting contract. (Such contracts are frequently signed by Company purchasing manager and the Contractor, in the presence of a notary.)

A good record-keeping policy also helps establish that a company is taking reasonable precautions to market safe products. The existence of a questioning memo from a designer concerned with safety aspects of a new product, combined with evidence that the designer's point of view was adequately considered, is probably better in most situations than a "blank record" suggesting that safety-related areas were never considered at all, or that the records have been sanitized to prevent embarrassment in court. In general, records fall into certain broad categories. Here are points to consider in setting up your records-retention program:

Basic Organizational Documents

These records, which include such items as certificates of incorporation, deeds, ledgers, merger agreements, and ownership agreements, can be vital in determining where corporate liability may lie. Victims of a flood caused by the failure of a coal company's dam in heavy rain were able to "pierce the corporate veil" and sue the company's richer corporate parent for damages. Plaintiffs determined that the subsidiary's day-to-day financial affairs were handled by the parent firm—the subsidiary was independent in name only. More complete board meeting minutes can help prevent this from happening in some cases.

Such documents are often kept with corporate counsel, or an outside lawyer on retainer. Other records often kept in the same place include insurance documents, claim records, contracts with customers and suppliers (at least master contracts covering long-term relationships), and, in highly regulated industries, government regulations applicable to the company's business.

Product Safety Policy Documents

The company official to whom product safety responsibility has been delegated should have immediately available copies of the firm's safety policy, directories of responsible employees, recall procedures, and any additional material needed to react to an emergency situation or to routine requests for guidance from others within the company. This official should be able to access all other records relating to current production, and earlier production for a period dependent upon the industry. (For quickly shipped and consumed products, this might be as short as a year; for more durable items, or products likely to move through the distribution chain slowly, much longer times must be considered for records retention.)

Design Data and Design Changes

These would include minutes of design reviews, basic calculations and preliminary designs, drawings, design histories of related products, testing data, records on the establishment of quality control protocols and production specifications, service manuals, installation instructions, correspondence with marketing and production, and field feedback from product users. Many companies leave the collection of such records up to the design department, with little outside supervision or control.

In many cases, this may be a mistake. Although design-related data are profitably located near the design staff, they may best be kept by personnel responsible to the product safety officer. Increasingly, such data are being kept by computer, and are accessible through remote terminals.

Product Records

Such records include design modifications, parts change control, production coding, records to trace the origin of raw materials and subassemblies, test reports, machine maintenance records, inventory, personnel training and time records, job descriptions, accident reports, purchasing control, and invoices. Again, the time such material is kept on active file depends in part on the industry and its products. A good rule of thumb is three years for everything except invoices. The latter should be kept longer in active files—many use seven years as a benchmark to coincide with many state tax requirements.

Marketing and Shipping Records

These records include contracts with distributors, bills of lading, damage claims, installation and servicing reports, advertising (and supporting documentation for advertising), sales records, sales-force training, customer feedback and complaints handled. One particularly pesky item involves locally generated advertising by dealerships and distributors. Such advertising is difficult to document, and often includes claims that can haunt a company in a liability case—claims of roll-over resistance, "easy operation" and durability, for instance.

Obviously, some records must be kept in more than one place—production and marketing, for example. The tendency in recent years is to handle this by coding all documents the same way, company-wide, and using a central record-keeping group (usually computer-aided) to keep track of the large volume of documents. Smaller firms may stick to the "old" way—sending documents only where needed, so that, for instance, summary reports and contracts for particularly large sales are kept with top company officials, and routine or day-to-day records are kept at lower levels within the organization. Or all documentation may be kept with the accounting department (except, perhaps, for purely design matters).

Short of revamping the entire system, safety and liability considerations demand that records necessary for a "quick response" to problems—a recall for instance—*must* be segregated and easily accessible at all times. In particular, smaller organizations using outside computer firms for bookkeeping should make sure that quick-response documentation such as production coding records are available on short notice.

9. SUMMARY

Further on in this book, we will discuss checklists for various phases of product design, manufacture, and marketing. Here's a checklist (adapted in part from one issued in 1976 by the Consumer Product Safety Commission) to help you evaluate your corporate structure with regard to product safety.

1. Is your safety policy widely known within your organization?
2. Is it specific enough so that all key employees know whom to contact in case a safety-related problem develops?
3. Does the policy come from a high enough level in executive management, and is there a specific person upon whom safety responsibility is focused there?
4. Do you have a product safety manager or coordinator? What are this person's responsibilities, and to whom does he or she report?
5. Does an arrangement exist for keeping senior management advised of safety-related product deficiencies?
6. Is documentation standardized and rigorous, to guard against court challenges and employee turnover? Such standardization should include a manual on standard company definitions, another on drafting, and a third on workmanship and tolerances.
7. Are test procedures in line with industry practice, and do they reflect real-world exposures that will be faced by the product? Are they set down in careful, step-by-step manuals?
8. Are internal design changes properly distributed, discussed, documented, and indexed for reference?
9. Who is responsible for informing the Consumer Product Safety Commission of product safety-related defects in accordance with Section 15(b) of the Consumer Product Safety Act?
10. Do you have a formal method for resolving safety-related arguments within your organization?
11. Do you have a formal procedure for periodically reviewing the effectiveness of your safety program?
12. Can you identify costs of safety (extra design time, for instance) and the direct costs of producing unsafe products (higher liability insurance rates, time spent testifying in court, and so forth)?

IV
DEVELOPMENT, ENGINEERING, AND DESIGN OF MINIMUM-HAZARD PRODUCTS

1. PRODUCT CONCEPTION AND DEVELOPMENT

While material was being gathered for this chapter, a score of top product safety experts from manufacturing, consulting, and insurance firms were asked at what point safety should be considered in the development of a new product. Despite their diverse backgrounds, the answer was almost unanimous: at the very beginning. Said Al Tilley of Henry Dreyfuss Associates: "As soon as design work is begun on a client's project—even in the blue sky stage—we incorporate thinking on safety. For 25 years our credo has been to apply five points to every design problem—utility and safety, maintenance, cost, sales appeal, and appearance."

A designer and vice-president for research at a manufacturer of industrial equipment said he tells his staff to satisfy a "six dimensional" design equation—function + structure + cost + environment + safety and health + statutory requirements. Some experts went so far as to note that without a safety analysis, it is nearly impossible to determine whether a market even exists for a product. If it cannot be used with an acceptable degree of risk, the cost of defending liability suits could outweigh the profit.

All this is well and good, but where does it leave the designer? After all, most companies would rather not "play it so safe" as to stop developing new products. If the company has organized a product safety group as discussed in the previous chapter, much of the internal work that will be necessary can be done almost automatically—at least in the initial stages.

The first need is to draw up a hazards control checklist—a hazards analysis—applicable to the product in question (Fig. IV-3). This is a responsibility of the entire design team, and the work should be divided among its members under the supervisory coordination of the product engineer or—in the case of large design teams—the member having the delegated responsibility for safety program coordination.

It is at this point that engineering should have its first meeting with representatives from the other parts of the company that make up the corporate-level safety group. Of most importance in this initial evaluation are the legal, insurance, and service functions. Depending on the sophistication of the prod-

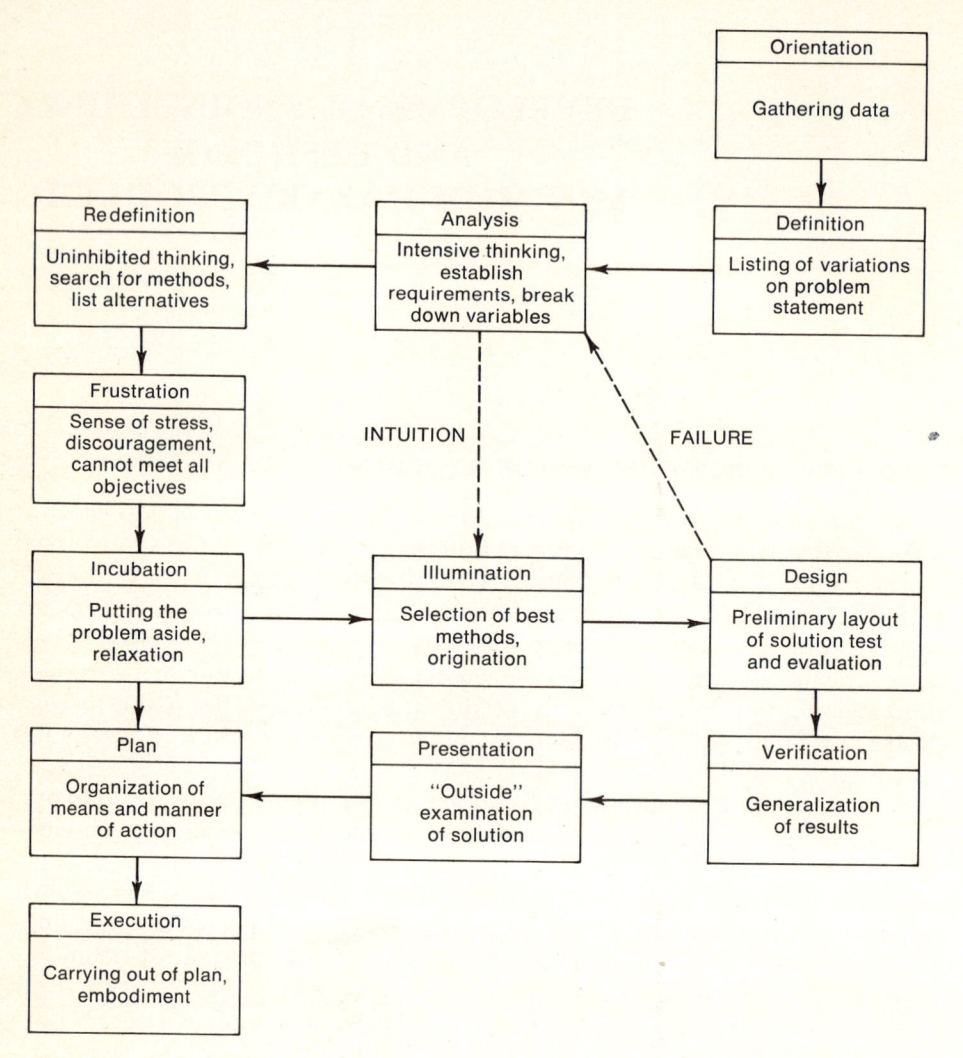

96 PRODUCT SAFETY AND LIABILITY: A DESK REFERENCE

Figure IV-1 The design process.

uct and the potential for hazard, these meetings can be either formal or informal.

At the beginning, the engineer's principal frustration will be that even the experts in the corporate safety group will not have had time to develop any sizable record of information pertinent to the product safety effort. The information, as it develops, will mainly consist of the following:

1. A review of problems known through past experience on similar products or systems, to determine whether they could also be present in the equipment now under consideration.

2. A review of the basic performance requirements, including the environments in which operations will take place.

3. Identification of the obvious hazard areas—sharp edges, electrical wiring, turning blades, and so forth.

4. Identification of secondary hazards, such as noise, which could confuse or benumb an operator to the point where he or she may react poorly.

5. Consideration of alternatives in eliminating these hazards.

6. Considerations of ways to restrict damage in case there is a loss of control of a hazard.

7. An indication of who in the company should take corrective action (such as delaying product development until more safety data is gathered, for instance), or what design changes come immediately to mind, considering that the product is still barely emerged from the conceptual stage.

In this initial stage, feedback from sales personnel who may have observed related products in the field can be extremely useful to the designers. Do the customers defeat safety interlocks? How long do people use an item at a time, between rests? How many are sold to rental establishments, broadening the cross section of the public that might use the product?

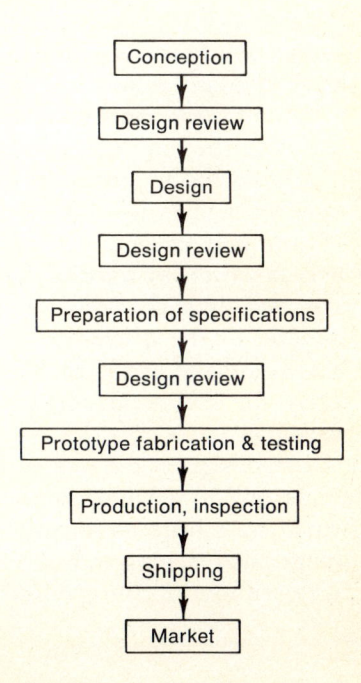

```
Conception
    ↓
Design review
    ↓
Design
    ↓
Design review
    ↓
Preparation of specifications
    ↓
Design review
    ↓
Prototype fabrication & testing
    ↓
Production, inspection
    ↓
Shipping
    ↓
Market
```

Figure IV-2   Evolution of a product.

System: _____ Subsystem: _____	Preliminary Safety Matrix Analysis		Prepared by: _____ Issue Date: _____		Page ___ of ___ Rev _____
1	2	3	4	5	6
Item/Function	Mode	Hazardous aspect	Hazard category	Needed safety provisions	Corrective action priority

Figure IV-3 Preliminary hazard "checklist" format.

As an example, look at the problems a designer faced in developing a new addition to a line of chipper-mulchers. These devices have flails and a whirling blade to chew up small branches. The blade and flails are protected by a long hopper, into which the branches are dumped. The manufacturer wanted to add a model with a removable hopper, so the whole machine could be partially disassembled and loaded into a station wagon for easy transport.

The obvious approach, a safety interlock that would make it impossible for the machine to operate with the hopper removed (by breaking the electrical connection to the ignition switch of the gasoline engine) was discarded after a legal analysis that advised the manufacturer that it would be liable for damages if the interlock connection failed. The company's design consultant suggested installing the interlock, then adding a sign saying that, although the machine was protected by an interlock, for operator safety the hopper should not be removed while the engine is running.

Company lawyers did not want any implication that the machine was fail-safe, however, so warning labels were placed on the machine, but no interlock was used. In a similar decision, a sign warned against removal of a deflector at the end of the discharge chute, although the consulting design team would have preferred an interlock on that as well. If this machine were being designed today, the likelihood is that the interlocks would have been used along with the warnings.

The designers did make the hopper high enough so that the operator would not be able to reach down the throat to unjam it, even though a shorter hopper would have been easier to load. And a warning in Day-Glo orange noted the danger of reaching into the hopper, and described the best way to unjam the blade without reaching inside—by using a stream of water from a garden hose.

2. CHECKLISTS: HARD TO COMPILE, EASY TO MISUSE

Most experts polled were wary of using checklists of hazards. They do have their place, but tend to be leaned upon too heavily. All too often, companies will rely on a checklist compiled from a listing of potential hazards, rather than go through the time and expense of prototype testing to make sure all means of failure have been uncovered in the product at hand. With that warning, let's look in broad outline at what preparation of a good checklist requires. For more detailed advice, consult the publication list in App. I. Some general checklists are given in App. A.

The first step is to list all primary failures the designer and the other company representatives can think of. These should include structural failures in the product, as well as customer actions (such as defeat of an interlock, or tying down of a "dead man's switch").

These primary failures each form branches of a fault tree. Each tree should describe what harmful consequence could happen if the failure occurs, either alone or in combination with other failures. In a very few industries—electronic circuitry, chemical processing, aerospace, and nuclear power, to name the most prominent—the design team can attempt to make a detailed assessment of mean time between failures of a given component or subassembly. In most cases, however, the raw data upon which to make such assessments—the failure rates of the various components—will be sketchy or nonexistent (see Sec. 5 of this chapter). A rough idea of relative hazards can be gained from looking at service records. Does a certain spring have to be repaired frequently? Does the company sell replacement shear pins by the bushelful for a certain machine? The organization of such records for use by the designer is a subject of the next chapter.

Thus, as such analyses are used by most designers and most companies, they are most useful only as an aid in visualizing the relationships that affect product safety. And, they can be useful to others only if the designers record the reasons for setting up the fault trees the way they did. On complex products, the resulting complex models can be coded against supplementary files setting out the reasoning in greater detail.

The design team must avoid the temptation to begin such analyses before consulting other company representatives on matters of reliability, maintainability, operability, supportability, human factors, and production needs. This is important, because in the final review of the product design, the corporate safety group should expect that all these factors have been considered in the analysis.

Many in industry advise that this hazards checklist should be prepared before seeking out the standards and regulations that apply to the product. "In this way you can avoid inhibiting your design intuition through absolute dependence on the standards from the start. It's in no one's interest to re-invent the wheel," said one product safety engineer, "... nor should the engineer rely solely on standards to insure the adequacy of his product safety design."

Once the hazards identification checklist is prepared—in some companies this checklist runs to a dozen pages on moderately sophisticated pieces of equipment like tractors and small trucks—and the standards have been consulted, the engineer should identify areas where no standards exist and then look to company policy for how to proceed.

After the design team has settled on an itemized hazards list, the next priority should be to establish the degrees of hazard caution necessary for each item. The simplest form of caution system is the three-part bruise, bleed, or die evaluation. It will be on those points in the "die" category that engineering must refuse to pass the product on to manufacturing until some more acceptable modification is arrived at.

The final "initial phase" consideration of the design team should be to settle upon countermeasures to the hazards in proportion to the degree of caution warranted in each case.

3. THE FORMAL DESIGN REVIEW PROCESS

After this initial round of meetings and data gathering, most companies agree that the product safety system should become formal (if it isn't already). This helps guard against omission of important information. And, without a formalized process, there is always the risk that some important parts of the company will be bypassed in the rush to get a new product introduced.

This sounds obvious, but beyond the initial data—the function to be performed by the product, projected market and sales volumes, and rough scheduling—many other details must be discussed in the context of product safety. These include:

1. Make or buy consideration
2. Subsystem interfaces
3. Design parameters in order of importance to function
4. Test considerations
5. Continuing documentation
6. Monitoring of parts or subassemblies previously identified as critical
7. Estimates of overall reliability

Depending on the product's complexity, the potential hazards identified, and the difficulty in resolving problems, any number of design review meetings may be held. The process may be as simple as an informal initial get-together, a midcourse review to uncover potential problems, and a final meeting to tie details down for production.

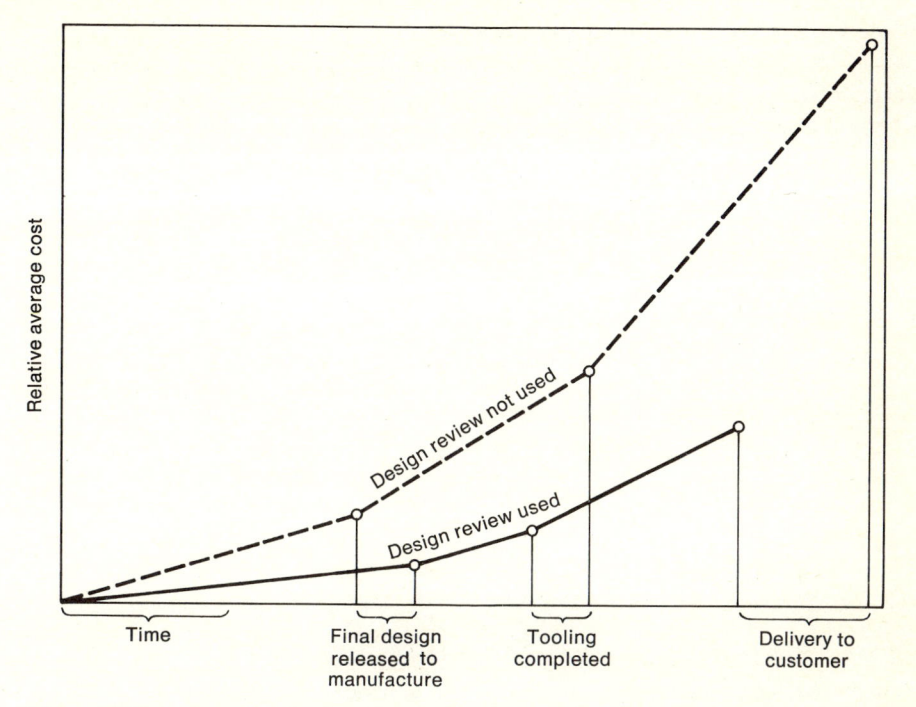

Figure IV-4 On the basis of a study of more than 100 cases, veteran product-safety consultant Richard Jacobs estimates savings of $20 for every dollar spent on design reviews. *(Trial Lawyers Quarterly, Vol. 7, No. 2, 1970.)*

Complex projects, especially those expected to take some time, could require numerous reviews, on a regularly scheduled basis. Ideally, a "data package" on the product's status should be sent to each member of the review team ahead of time, to allow participants to develop constructive questions. All too often, spontaneous negative criticism greets an initial, oral presentation at any technical meeting. But even criticism from a participant playing devil's advocate can rub feelings raw.

There is a sizable difference of opinion among people in industry as to who should chair these formal meetings. In a short handbook published in 1976 (*Handbook & Standard for Manufacturing Safer Consumer Products*), the Consumer Product Safety Commission recommends that the reviews should be chaired "by a designated senior official and representing design, production, quality control, and consumer service." But there is concern among many that having a "senior" official present can deter the free flow of information in such meetings.

Since the chief design engineer has ultimate professional responsibility for designing a safe product, others suggest that this person should be in charge. But it is the very work of this person's team that is being reviewed!

Ideally, if a company's product safety review procedure has evolved successfully, the product safety manager should be in charge of the meeting. But

Table IV-1 Goals of Product Hazard Reviews

PRELIMINARY REVIEW:

Try to identify all risks of using the product as intended

Try to identify all possible misuses, and associated risks

Identify applicable standards

Develop company standards where existing ones are inadequate

Establish testing parameters for critical components

Estimate "how safe" the product will have to be

PROTOTYPE REVIEW (PREPRODUCTION):

Perform required standard tests on completed assembly

From direct and indirect measurement, determine worst-case use environment

Quantify risks in terms of severity, frequency, and potential cost

FINAL REVIEW (PRERELEASE):

Ensure adequacy of advertising, labeling, and associated literature

Test packaging and shipping system with actual product

Obtain certification, if applicable, from Underwriters Laboratories, Canadian Standards Association, etc.

---

depending on personalities, it is often advisable for a lower-level individual to actually chair the meetings (perhaps on a rotating basis), in the presence of the product safety manager. It is management, not the design engineer, which must assure that all relevant parts of the organization are represented—and that no irrelevant or marginal matters clog the proceedings.

Because safety matters are susceptible to long-winded philosophical discussions, and because review sessions should be carefully documented, they should be tightly run and well planned. Each meeting should focus on the hazards checklist, follow-up tests, interfacing problems, and the like. Critiques, when focused in this way, can be handled without making a personal attack on the designer.

Participants will discuss what is probably the most difficult segment of product safety: the design trade-offs. Engineering is frequently pitted against manufacturing, marketing, and sales over the issue of added product cost. "The problem is," according to one product safety expert, "that the direct cost of product liability is not normally associated with the profitability of the product line. This comes about because of the time lapse between the production and the incident of the liability claim. The important argument here should be that lawsuits limit your profit as well. A safe product that has some extra initial safety-related costs can still turn out to be a highly profitable product in the long run."

Marketing personnel would add one warning to that: The product has to be competitive enough to be purchased in numbers justifying design and production in the first place.

In some companies, the work of the design review committee is aided by input from what is called a "test development engineer." These engineers often have the total testing-for-safety responsibility for a product. The test engineer is the antagonist of the designer, for tests are supposed to reflect the user's environment. Therefore, the test engineer looks at each product as a potential user would.

One of the auxiliary tasks often delegated to the design review committee is estimating the failure rates of a product. Failure frequency and severity establish the data needed to determine the warranty term and the estimated cost of providing the warranty. These data then provide management with sufficient

Table IV-2 Agendas for Design Reviews—General

Preliminary review (conceptual stage)	*Intermediate review (design near-finished)*	*Final preproduction review (design completed)*
1. Marketing department explains requirements, which are discussed by all.	1. Product requirements reviewed by chairperson, discussed.	1. Product requirements reviewed by chairperson.
2. Priorities set—is cost most important? Or reliability, appearance, performance, etc.?	2. Mechanical design discussed. Tests, if any, reviewed.	2. Prototype tests reviewed, discussed.
3. Preliminary schedule blocked out.	3. Electrical design (if any) discussed. Tests and outside data, if any, reviewed.	3. Further electrical and mechanical tests reviewed, discussed. Does finish material, lubrication, etc., meet toxic substances standards and OSHA rules, etc.?
4. Meeting summarized.	4. Discuss tooling.	4. Tooling needs reviewed.
	5. Discuss packaging.	5. Packaging reviewed.
	6. Discuss installation.	6. Installation requirements reviewed.
	7. Discuss instructions.	7. Instruction book draft reviewed.
	8. Discuss maintenance.	8. Maintenance manual draft reviewed.
	9. Review and revise schedule.	9. Set "final" schedule.
	10. Summarize meeting.	10. Summarize meeting.

Table IV-3 Management Functions in the Design Review Process

	Preliminary review	Design review	Preproduction review
Chairperson (sometimes the safety coordinator; see text): calls and conducts meetings, evaluates progress and issues reports (especially at end of preproduction review).	X	X	X
Product designer(s): Presents design decisions and supporting test data, calculations, etc.	X	X	X
Reliability manager or consultant: Checks design for reliability. May be aided by designer(s) not involved with this particular product design.	X	X	X
Marketing representative: Checks design process to make sure customer needs with regard to price, performance, etc., are being met. May be aided by sales staff.	X		X
Manufacturing representative: Ensures that production scheduling and costs are realistic. May be aided by procurement personnel for outside suppliers' input.		X	X
Tooling representative: Checks design tolerances needed, materials choice.		X	
Quality control: Ensures that design can be adequately tested in production, estimates test frequency needs from hazard analysis.		X	X
Field engineering: Looks at design's maintainability and installation features.		X	X
Shipping expert: Estimates shipping and packaging costs, package requirements with regard to critical parts damage.		X·	X

basis for deciding what the balance will be between the period of warranty coverage and what has to be set aside in reserve accounts to pay for repair-replacement work. These estimates often prove essential to the design and development of future new products.

Because of their expertise the design engineering members of the review team are normally asked to provide much of the failure-rate information. Failure rates can be determined by first dividing a product into its basic parts on a rough, order-of-magnitude basis. This first reliability assessment is an estimated one based on the parts being considered. Each part should be rated as to expected failure under the stresses assigned to it. (For details see Chap. V.)

After failure rates are assigned to the parts and normalized to a common base to avoid false results obtained by combining extraneous data, the rates assigned to the parts are combined to obtain the failure rate of the equipment. If it is determined that this total rate is too high or reliability too low, the review team should set about determining how reliability can be improved.

Most companies prefer to restrict the activities of their design review committees to old products that are up for normal design reviews or to new products. At least one company, however, decided to perform a total product review as part of a newly instituted product safety program. The firm was able to perform this time-consuming task by relying on several of the company's retired engineers to develop a comprehensive pre-audit to facilitate the review and decisions of the main company review team.

In general, companies believe in making the frequency of their reviews flexible—a function of design change, product liability potential, and other variables.

4. THE HUMAN FACTORS INTERFACE

A very significant contribution of the social sciences to design is the field of human factors engineering.* Early in this century advances in psychology began to provide solutions to industrial problems, but it wasn't until hard data on human performance capabilities evolved that design engineering benefited from psychology's answers.

Out of World War I came an important tool—large-scale psychological testing. Some technique was needed to sort out hundreds of thousands of citizens on the basis of mental ability so the military could select or reject them and then assign draftees to jobs. Psychologists R. M. Yerkes and Arthur Otis developed tests to distinguish the incompetent from the capable, and to rate the capable for general mental ability. This was the birth of the group IQ test, and although such tests have been abused, they served a need.

A second major development was industrial psychologist Elton Mayo's studies of working conditions and productivity at the Hawthorne plant of Western Electric in the 1930s. To his surprise, Mayo discovered that worker productivity not only increased with increased rewards (in the form of more frequent and varied work breaks), but that it increased again when all of these breaks were taken away and the workers had to return to a no-break schedule. What the workers were responding to was the feeling of usefulness that participation in the experiment gave them, as well as the improved treatment from management.

Again in wartime came another part of the foundation for human factors engineering—studies on means of improving personal performance. Heading a team of research psychologists, John Flanagan systematically studied the

---

*Adapted in part from an article by John Dinan in *New Engineer* magazine, December 1977. Copyright © MBA Communications, Inc.

performance of aviation personnel—pilots, bomber crews, and so forth—in an effort to reduce error. The results of this Aviation Psychology Program were documented in a five-foot-high series of volumes that detailed new procedures for improving the manner in which humans use machines.

Flanagan's work leading up to modern human factors engineering resulted from problems with guided missiles. While it was apparent by the latter half of the fifties that the technology was available for developing and flying aerospace hardware, human errors in design, production, and control of these systems were still creating problems—some of which were catastrophic. Air Force studies demonstrated that as many as 60 percent of system failures were attributable to human errors of commission or omission.

Human error is almost inevitable when humans operate machines, and this has produced a need for human factors engineers in three overlapping areas: research, teaching, and application. The association among them can be very close. On many occasions it is necessary for someone in an applied field to design and run an experiment before he or she can come up with design recommendations.

Figure IV-5 Coupling on this truck carrying industrial acid must be pounded open or closed with a mallet. This industry standard could be changed in the interests of safety. *(Gates Rubber Co. photo.)*

Table IV-4 Functional Evaluation of Audio Signals by Operator*

Function	*Type of signal*		
	Tones (periodic)	*Complex sounds (nonperiodic)*	*Speech*
Quantitative indication	*Poor* Maximum of 5 to 6 tones absolutely recognizable.	*Poor* Interpolation between signals inaccurate.	*Good* Minimum time and error in obtaining exact value in terms compatible with response.
Qualitative indication	*Poor-to-fair* Difficult to judge approximate value and direction of deviation from null setting unless presented in close temporal sequence.	*Poor* Difficult to judge approximate deviation from desired value.	*Good* Information concerning displacement, direction, and rate presented in form compatible with required response.
Status indication	*Good* Start and stop timing. Continuous information where rate of change of input is low.	*Good* Especially suitable for irregularly occurring signals (e.g., alarm signals).	*Poor* Inefficient; more easily masked; problem of repeatability.
Tracking	*Fair* Null position easily monitored; problem of signal-response compatibility.	*Poor* Required qualitative indications difficult to provide.	*Good* Meaning intrinsic in signal.
General	Good for automatic communication of limited information. Meaning must be learned. Easily generated.	Some sounds available with common meaning (e.g., fire bell). Easily generated.	Most effective for rapid (but not automatic) communication of complex, multidimensional information. Meaning intrinsic in signal and context when standardized. Minimum of new learning required.

*FROM MIL STD-1472A, May 1970

Table IV-5 Application of Various Types of Displays*

	Scales			Counters	Printers	Flags
Use	Moving pointer	Fixed pointer				
Quantitative information	*Fair* — May be difficult to read while pointer is in motion.	*Fair* — May be difficult to read while scale is in motion.		*Good* — Minimum time and error for exact numerical value.	*Good* — Minimum time and error for exact numerical value. Provides reference records.	Not applicable.
Qualitative information	*Good* — Location of pointer easy. Numbers and scale need not be read. Position change easily detected.	*Poor* — Difficult to judge direction and magnitude of deviation without reading numbers and scale.		*Poor* — Numbers must be read. Position changes not easily detected.	*Poor* — Numbers must be read. Position changes not easily detected.	*Good* — Easily detected. Economical of space.
Setting	*Good* — Simple and direct relation of motion of pointer to motion of setting knob. Position change aids monitoring.	*Fair* — Relation to motion of setting knob may be ambiguous. No pointer position change to aid monitoring. Not readable during rapid setting.		*Good* — Most accurate monitoring of numerical setting. Relation to motion of setting knob less direct than for moving pointer. Not readable during rapid setting.	Not applicable.	Not applicable.

	Good	Fair	Poor		
Tracking	Pointer position readily controlled and monitored. Simplest relation to manual control motion.	No position changes to aid monitoring. Relation to control motion somewhat ambiguous.	No gross position changes to aid monitoring.	Not applicable.	Not applicable.
General	Requires largest exposed and illuminated area on panel. Scale length limited unless multiple pointers used.	Saves panel space. Only small section of scale need be exposed and illuminated. Use of tape allows long scale.	Most economical of space and illumination. Scale length limited only by number of counter drums.	Limited application.	Limited application.

*FROM MIL STD-1472A, May 1970

Take, as an example, a seemingly simple decision by engineering to use three rotary switches with values etched on a panel at roughly the 12 o'clock positions for a task that requires a pilot to make a bearing estimate. Experiments showed that the error rate for reading three digits on rotary switches was greater than 15 percent. An alternative design using three thumbwheel switches (which put the three digits on the same plane and within three inches of each other) produced a near-zero error rate in the experiments.

Or another example: A recent decision to mount light-emitting diodes (LEDs) on printed boards so that the viewer would have to look at the profile of the LED. When measurements were taken with a spot photometer, this design gave a dim reading of less than 10 footcandles (fc). The design was changed when it was shown that the optical axis provided the viewer with a target at 112 fc.

While demonstrations using such lab equipment are necessary, the "human" experiment is still one of our most useful tools. Several years ago a study was conducted to determine the optimum length of trip wires for booby traps—the problem being that wires should be as long as possible while avoiding detection. Common sense suggested that the greater the length of the wire, the more

Washer and Spacer Installation
Possibilities of incorrect installation using washers and spacers

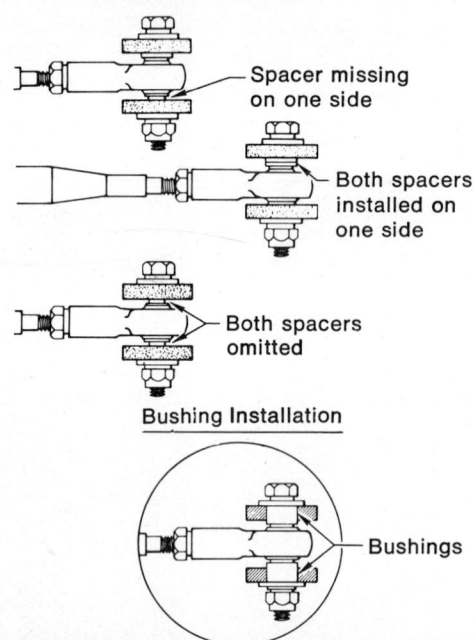

– Spacer missing on one side

– Both spacers installed on one side

– Both spacers omitted

Bushing Installation

– Bushings

By providing the fittings with bushings, omission or misposition of parts is eliminated

Figure IV-6 If parts can be installed incorrectly, sooner or later someone will do so. *(Air Force Systems Command Design Handbook 1-6.)*

easily it could be detected. Not so! Field experimentation with live test subjects and simulated traps showed that there is no direct relationship between the length of the wire and the detection of it.

Much of the human factors work being done today has to do with safety. It is hard to believe, for instance, that a computer manufacturer would require users to open a noninterlocked door for access to an air filter located just over an exposed terminal carrying 480 volts (especially risky when we consider that many individuals wear bracelets or watches with metal bands). But it happened. The experienced human factors engineer knows that users should not be required to enter the cabinet for this task at all—the filter panel should be reachable from the outside. The safety of more knowledgeable technicians who *do* have to poke around inside the cabinet requires proper guarding of the terminal, interlocks on the cabinet doors, and safety labeling to inform the technician of the locations and types of hazards.

As a safety design challenge, the automobile is legend. When the foot is removed quickly from the accelerator of a certain 1975 car, the pedal does not immediately respond to the removal or pressure. A switch in the engine, sensing that the engine is running above a certain level, keeps the accelerator depressed until this lower level is achieved (it takes three or four seconds). The rationale for this was that the catalytic converter is subject to very high engine exhaust temperatures. In an effort to control overtemperatures, the accelerator was rigged to avoid sudden rpm changes. The cars were recalled, but it is hard to believe that this feature went through the normal design review process and into production.

Most problems encountered by the human factors engineer are not as blatant, however. Working as part of the design team, the human factors specialist is called upon to provide guidance on people's basic characteristics. He or she studies basic human sensory capabilities; muscular strength and coordination; body dimensions; susceptibility to electrical, chemical, and mechanical hazards; native skills; optimum workload; and cultural factors influencing performance and judgment.

Most of this work requires some experimentation. While references can and do provide guidelines on human's tolerance for exposure to noise, for example, in any given situation where noise must be considered it is first necessary to measure the existence and severity of the problem. It may then be necessary to redesign the product or add sound-damping materials. Noise measurements must then be repeated to verify the effectiveness of the "fix."

Human factors engineering can require an even deeper understanding of experimental methodology. To obtain performance measures, it is necessary to perform operational suitability tests on products or systems. These tests may employ computer simulation, mockups, field tests, or the use of the item by a sample of ultimate users. Human factors engineers often have major responsibility for such test programs.

The design of training equipment is another specialty. Whether it is a simple device, a moderately complex working model, or a large-scale computer-based

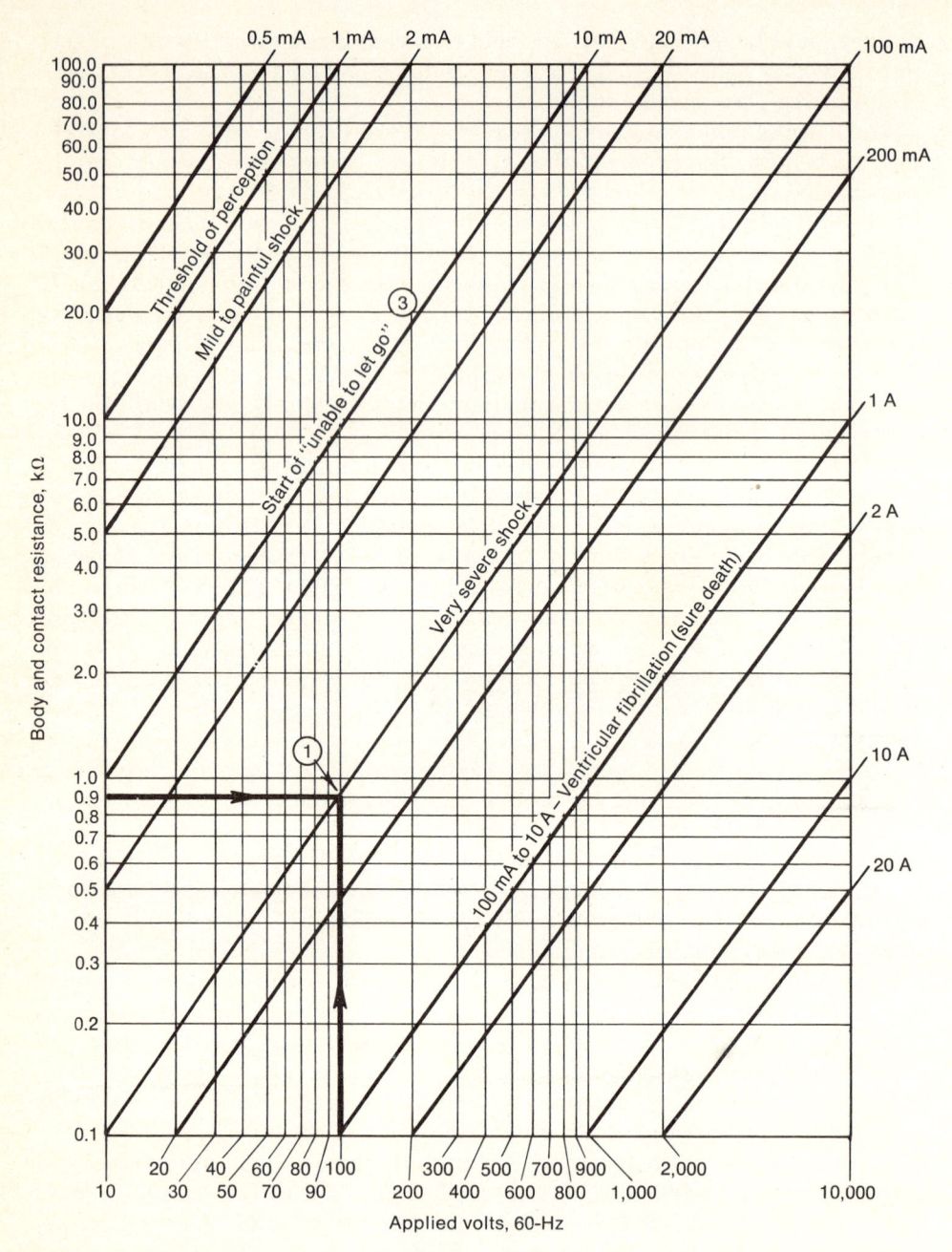

Figure IV-7 Electrical shock hazard to adult males. *(Air Force Systems Command Design Handbook 1-6.)*

① This diagram shows the electric current hazard to adult males as a function of the applied voltage at 60-Hz voltage and the body and contact resistance (e.g., if a person whose body and skin contact resistance is 900 Ω contacts a voltage of 100 V, 100 mA of current would flow through him, assuming a complete circuit).

② An electric current of a given amount affects the body in many different ways, depending on the path of the current. Current paths that include the head or trunk result in more serious injury than those confined to one extremity. Current paths through or near the heart or respiratory system muscles or through the brain are the most critical.

③ Electric currents of only a few milliamperes are sufficient to "freeze" a victim to an electric current. The hazards inherent in electrical equipment must be recognized and precautions taken to prevent electrical shock mishaps.

Resistance of Body Mass (kilohms)

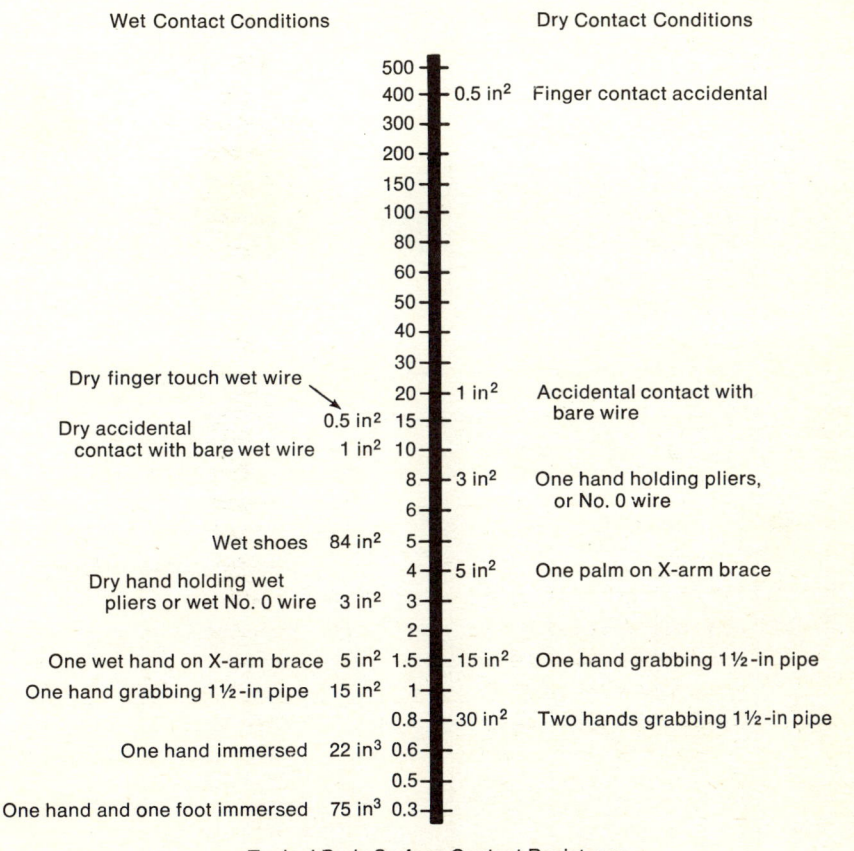

Wet Contact Conditions		Dry Contact Conditions
	500
	400 — 0.5 in^2	Finger contact accidental
	300
	200
	150
	100
	80
	60
	50
	40
	30
Dry finger touch wet wire →	20 — 1 in^2	Accidental contact with bare wire
Dry accidental 0.5 in^2	15
contact with bare wet wire 1 in^2	10
	8 — 3 in^2	One hand holding pliers, or No. 0 wire
	6
Wet shoes 84 in^2	5
	4 — 5 in^2	One palm on X-arm brace
Dry hand holding wet pliers or wet No. 0 wire 3 in^2	3
	2
One wet hand on X-arm brace 5 in^2	1.5 — 15 in^2	One hand grabbing 1½-in pipe
One hand grabbing 1½-in pipe 15 in^2	1
	0.8 — 30 in^2	Two hands grabbing 1½-in pipe
One hand immersed 22 in^3	0.6
	0.5
One hand and one foot immersed 75 in^3	0.3

Typical Body Surface Contact Resistance

system involving dozens of people and millions of dollars worth of equipment, the human factors engineer seeks to design into the training device only those features that will enhance the learning and performance of the tasks being taught. Having first studied the job for which the training device will qualify a student, the human factors engineer draws on knowledge of the principles behind the acquisition of new skills and translates these into working designs, usually in cooperation with a systems specialist and electrical or mechanical engineers.

No single professional group is really responsible for research in human

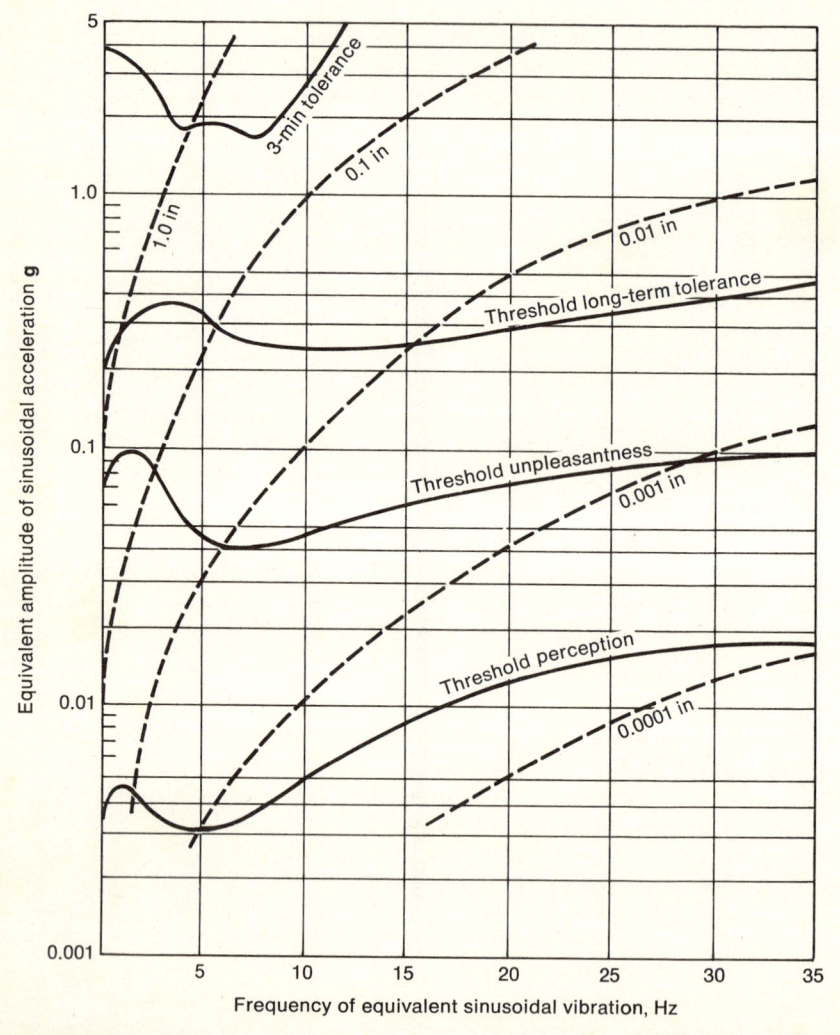

Figure IV-8   Human tolerance to vibration. (*Air Force Systems Command Design Handbook 1-6.*)

factors engineering or the application of human engineering principles to design. Engineers, industrial designers, anthropologists, physicians, physiologists, and psychologists all participate. In a broad sense, everyone concerned with the improvement of devices people use, or the ways in which people use them, is practicing human factors engineering. However, as so often happens in a technical field, a point was reached where every person could no longer be his or her own specialist and the profession of human factors engineering emerged as a distinct one. The majority of human engineering specialists recruited during recent years have been experimental psychologists conversant with some aspects of engineering, or engineers with supplementary training in the behavioral sciences.

While most large companies employ a human factors engineer, others place the burden for providing these services on systems specialists, electrical, or mechanical engineers. A line engineer might be sent to one of the 2- or 4-week courses in human factors like those given at the University of Michigan, Ann Arbor.

5. PREDICTION TECHNIQUES: FAULT TREE ANALYSIS*

Engineering analysts engaged in predicting product behavior have an enormous advantage: They can resolve the determinants of that behavior in substantial detail. The analyst can examine details of design, the characteristics of manufacturing and inspection processes with respect to inducing and revealing flaws, and the effects of the human participants in production and use of the product. The analyst has substantial bodies of data available at this level of detail. The problems lie in the analysis, extrapolation, and combination of such data to yield results useful for prediction purposes.

Thus, the analyst's task is divided into several segments. First, the functional effects of a flawed product performance must be defined. (For convenience in this section, both these effects and the specific malfunctions responsible for them will be referred to as events, faults, or failures.) These functional effect definitions could correspond to potential expected user observations. Examples include "the product won't work," or, preferably, more specific observations such as "there's no picture on my TV set," as well as the more dramatic "the lawn mower cut off my big toe."

The analyst must also be able to identify the physical relationships between specific malfunctions at the subassembly, part, and materials level and the user-observable functional effects. For example, the brakes won't work if the master cylinder fails or the hydraulic lines break. The event probabilities must then be quantified, insofar as possible, by securing data of others or conducting tests on prototype subsystems. We may note that conventional tires wear out in X miles

---

*Adapted in part from Paul Gottfried, Product Risks: Prediction Techniques, *Proceedings of the 1975 Products Liability Prevention Conference,* New Jersey Institute of Technology, pp. 25–36. Copyright © American Society for Quality Control. Reprinted by permission.

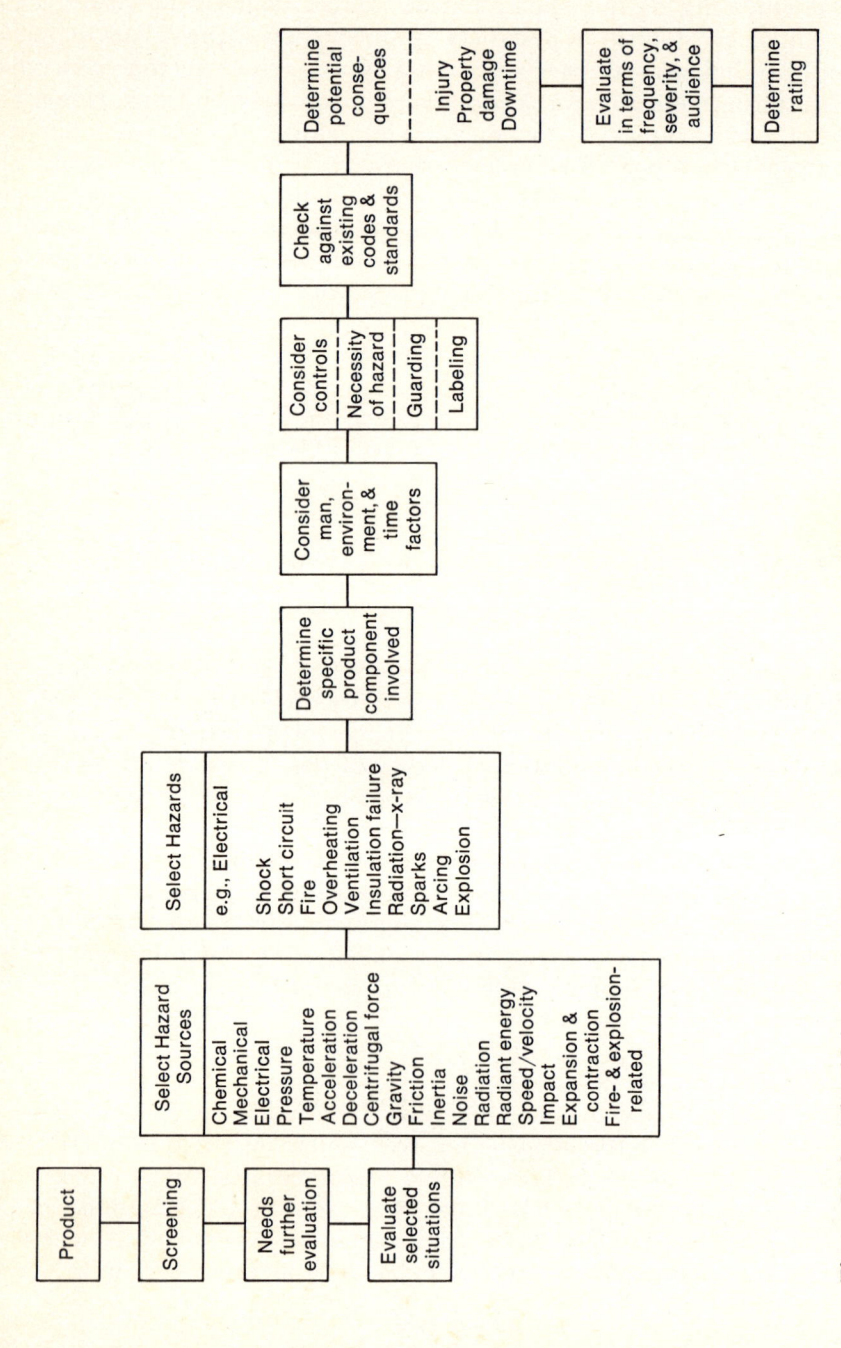

Figure IV-9 Identifying and evaluating product hazards. (*After Biancardi.*)

116

of normal use, project 50 percent longer wear on the basis of laboratory tests of a new formulation, or discover that one out of every Y million soft drink bottles contains a mouse.

Finally, the analyst must determine the time dependencies of event probabilities. It is important to know whether faults of a particular kind are more likely to occur soon after acquisition of the product by the user (perhaps as a result of undetected manufacturing defects) or late in life as a result of deterioration. It is particularly desirable to know how changes in production, design, or materials may affect such trends.

Indeed, for virtually every product it is possible to conceive of a variety of ways in which a flawed performance may be manifested. From the standpoint of product liability, a first-order categorization may group these as follows:

- Faults that are barely perceptible to most users, and cross the tolerance threshold of only a few. One example might be a 10 percent deficiency in engine power output in a large American automobile
- Clearly deficient performance, including total inoperability
- An evident hazard, such as the existence of exposed electrical conductors
- A fullfilled hazard—injury or property damage involving the product as the proximate or contributory cause

These categories, of course, loosely identify the extent of potential liability (and the parties that may be held liable under warranty or tort). The vulnerable parties, including the insuror if there is one, will of course be interested in more detailed characteristics along the following lines: How often will events in each category occur? What is the likelihood that the concerned party will, in fact, be held liable? And finally, what is the cost per event? The probability distribution of costs may also be needed if the potential variability is large, as may be the case for damages caused by "fulfilled" hazards. One very large claim, for example, can destroy a company.

Not all of these questions are within the scope of the engineering analyst. The question of anticipated liability involves legal opinion, or at least an analysis of current court actions and trends. For casualty costs, court actions are also reflected. Costs of warranty-based repairs and replacements can be obtained from within the company.

The engineering analyst must identify the significant possible events with respect to all these questions. The identification must be done in a more detailed way than the categorization described above, however. This is because probability-of-occurrence data usually will be readily extracted for specific physical occurrences and because prospective costs and liability will depend on the specific nature of the event.

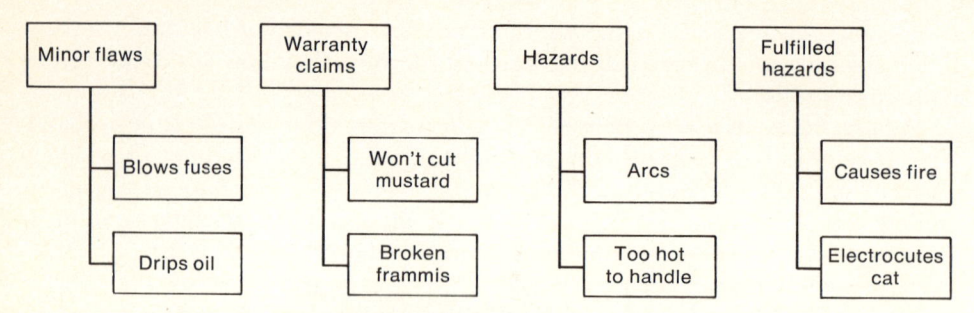

```
Minor flaws          Warranty claims        Hazards              Fulfilled hazards
   │                     │                    │                      │
   ├── Blows fuses       ├── Won't cut        ├── Arcs               ├── Causes fire
   │                     │    mustard         │                      │
   └── Drips oil         └── Broken           └── Too hot            └── Electrocutes
                             frammis              to handle              cat
```

Figure IV-10 Electrical widget functional events.

To aid in tracing the course of the analysis, let us illustrate it with a simple, fictitious device: the electric widget. Figure IV-10 indicates the second level of definition of events in block-diagram form. For most real products, of course, the possible events of interest would be far more diverse. Indeed, the greater the diversity, the more important it becomes to conduct the analysis systematically.

There are two generally established ways of doing this. The first is failure-modes-and-effects analysis (FMEA). The second is called fault tree analysis (FTA) developed at the Bell Laboratories, which became widely used and refined in the space program in the sixties.

FMEA is conducted by considering the failure of individual parts of the product or system, and looking at the possible failure modes one at a time. For each failure mode, the consequences are noted. Multiple failures also are usually taken into account. The approach is thus from the bottom—the lowest level of assembly—upward. The results of the analysis are usually presented in tabular form. In the tables, each part is listed along with its failure modes and functional effects.

Fault tree analysis defines relationships between functional effects and product elements, looking from the top downward. The analyst first defines the functional effects and examines the product to determine, at successive levels of assembly, what physical phenomena could cause those directly observable effects to occur. Figure IV-11 translates the previous block diagrams into fault tree format. The rectangular blocks again identify events, but these blocks are now connected by logic symbols. The arrowhead-shaped symbols in Fig. IV-12 represent OR gates. In this case, if either of the two events indicated under each of the four top-level categories occurs, the corresponding top-level event also occurs. The triangular symbols in the bottom row are merely reference keys allowing continuation of the various branches on separate pages.

Figure IV-12 identifies these and other standard symbols, and Fig. IV-13 indicates possible continuation of two of the branches of the previous tree. This last figure shows how the AND gate is used as a connective—when, in this case, two or more events at a low level must occur in order for the fault to propagate to the higher level—and the conditional event which must be satisfied before

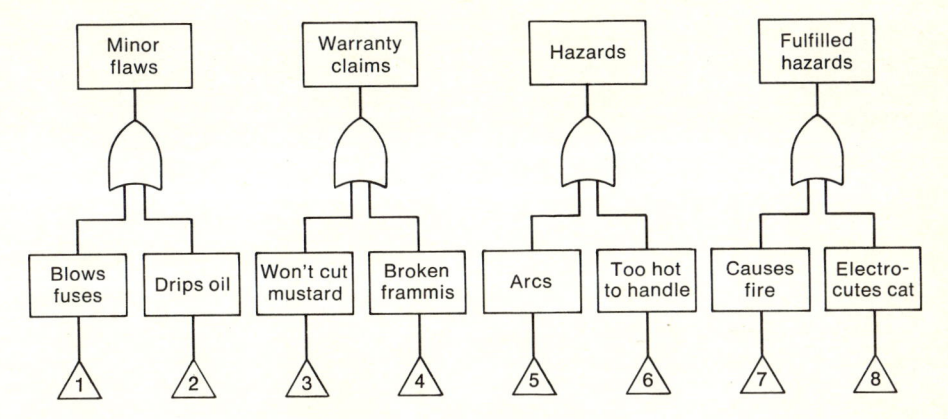

Figure IV-11 Functional events in fault tree form.

the higher-level event can be observed. Note that the "conditional" event is not necessarily a fault in itself.

So far, so good. But the analysis of more complex systems can become extremely time-consuming. The analyst must first define the system to be analysed in detail, both to keep time to a minimum, and to allow the fault tree to fulfill its function of clearly showing potential problems and the relationships among them. As the tree becomes more complex, it becomes harder to use. In

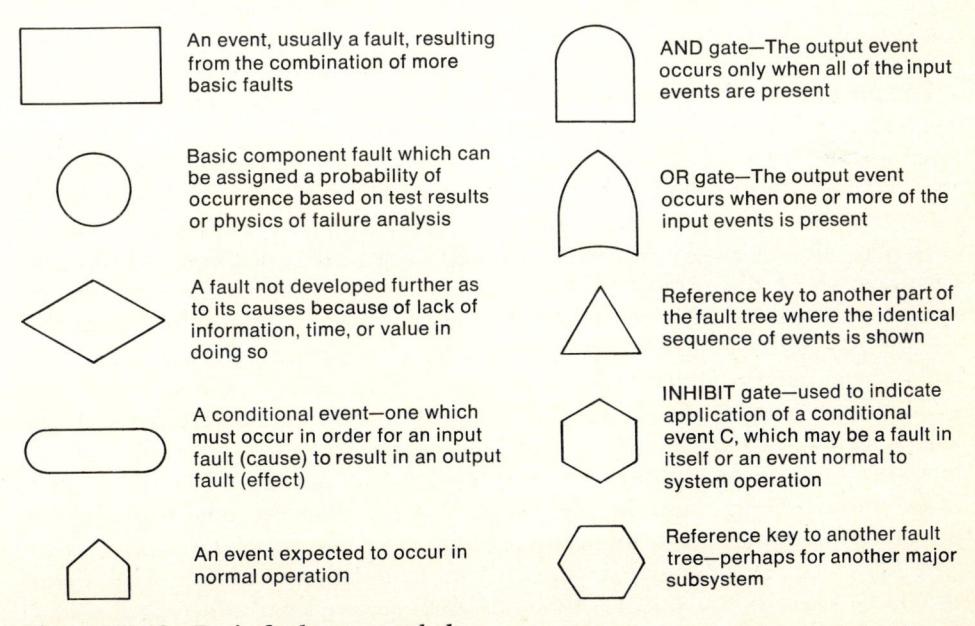

Figure IV-12 Basic fault tree symbols.

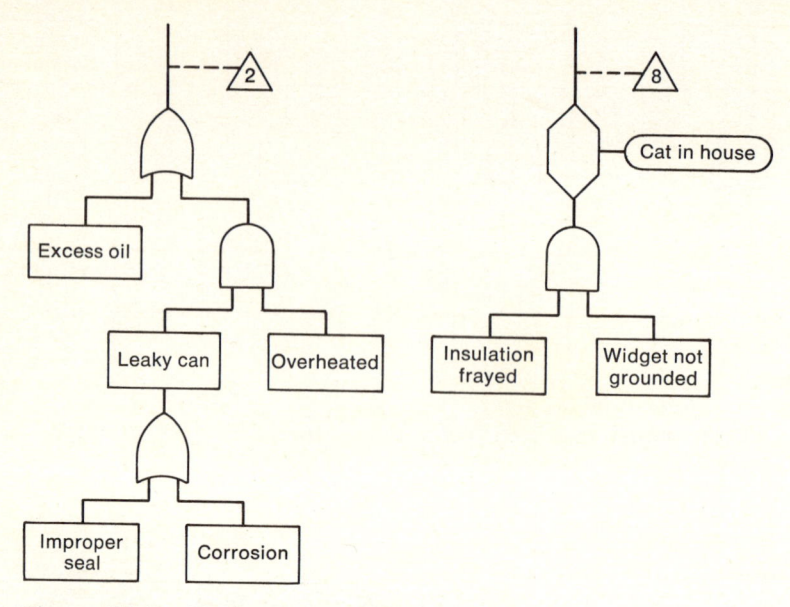

Figure IV-13 Fault tree branch examples.

some cases, tight definition of the system to be analyzed can cut the number of "undesired events" to one or two.

The designer of a fuel pump for an aircraft would not, therefore, define the system as the entire aircraft, or the undesired event as an "aircraft crash." The systems could be reduced to the pump itself, and the undesired events listed as "failure to pump fuel," "reduced flow," "pulsed flow," and so forth. Or if there are many pumps supplying fuel to one engine, or the designer's responsibility extends to fuel pump controls, the system might be the entire engine (undesired events include engine failure, fire, and reduced power)—although only events and causes around the pumps themselves would be subject to detailed analysis. Consequences of such a failure (T1) are shown in Fig. IV-1A.

When fully developed, the fault tree represents the functional and physical relationships of the product. The upper levels tend to represent functional effects common to the given class of products—widgets, aircraft, pumps, or whatever. The lower levels, on the other hand, refer to materials faults and component failures shared by the more-or-less standard parts of which the products are composed. The middle portions of the tree, however, reflect the specifics of the product's design, and can be expected to differ. Analysts tend to concentrate on those middle areas as they gain experience with certain classes of products. The question then becomes: "What is *different* about this product or configuration, and how might the differences cause problems?"

A fault tree can, of course, be drawn after completion of FMEA. The results should be logically equivalent if both analyses are complete and correct. Going directly to the fault tree has some advantage for the experienced designer or for products that are routine modifications of existing models, because the tree need only be developed to the level at which data on reliability and consequences of failure are obtainable. The fault tree can also be begun at an early stage of product development—before design is complete.

FMEA must be carried through from bottom to top before significant results can be obtained. FMEA will be discussed in more detail in the next section. The remainder of this section is devoted to calculating probabilities of occurrences from logic diagrams in fault tree form.

With a knowledge of the fundamentals of combinatorial probability, a set of algebraic expressions relating device faults to functional events may be written by inspection. The expressions may reflect either event probabilities or the complementary no-fault probabilities; examples for the widget are illustrated in Fig. IV-15. As the no-fault probabilities are generally multiplicative, it usually is most convenient to write the expressions in terms of their logarithms so they can be easily summed. Occasionally, an individual event will appear in several branches of the tree; care must be taken to correct for these effects at the first common node.

In the best of all possible worlds (as far as these matters are concerned), all products would be the result of unchanging design and manufacture, used in a stable environment, and documented over a long period of time before analysis is attempted. In that world, the past would be known completely, and the future completely predictable—at least in the aggregate. (We still might not know in advance which particular examples of a product would be doomed to failure during their service life.)

In the real world, however, we live with substantial deviations from the ideal in all these respects. We can and do look for similarity in design, manufacture, and use conditions between products with which we have had experience and those for which we wish to make predictions. We can expect better prediction accuracy when the parts from which the product is made are subject to standardization and when application stresses are known. The farther we venture into the unknown, the more important it becomes that we recognize and quantify prediction uncertainties.

For the moment, however, let's assume that the risk of malfunction associated with a device under fixed conditions may be represented by a single number. This assumption, common in reliability analysis, implies that the risks are independent of the age of the device; a malfunction is as likely to occur in the tenth hour of use as in the hundredth or thousandth hour. The assumption—although it may be intuitively unpalatable—has proven quite acceptable for nonwearing devices and many complex assemblies. The single number is known as the hazard rate (or, loosely, the failure rate) and is often represented by λ. It has the convenient property that the probability of no malfunction in use for time t can be expressed as

$$P_s(t) = e^{-\lambda t}$$

a very tractable mathematical expression known as the exponential distribution.

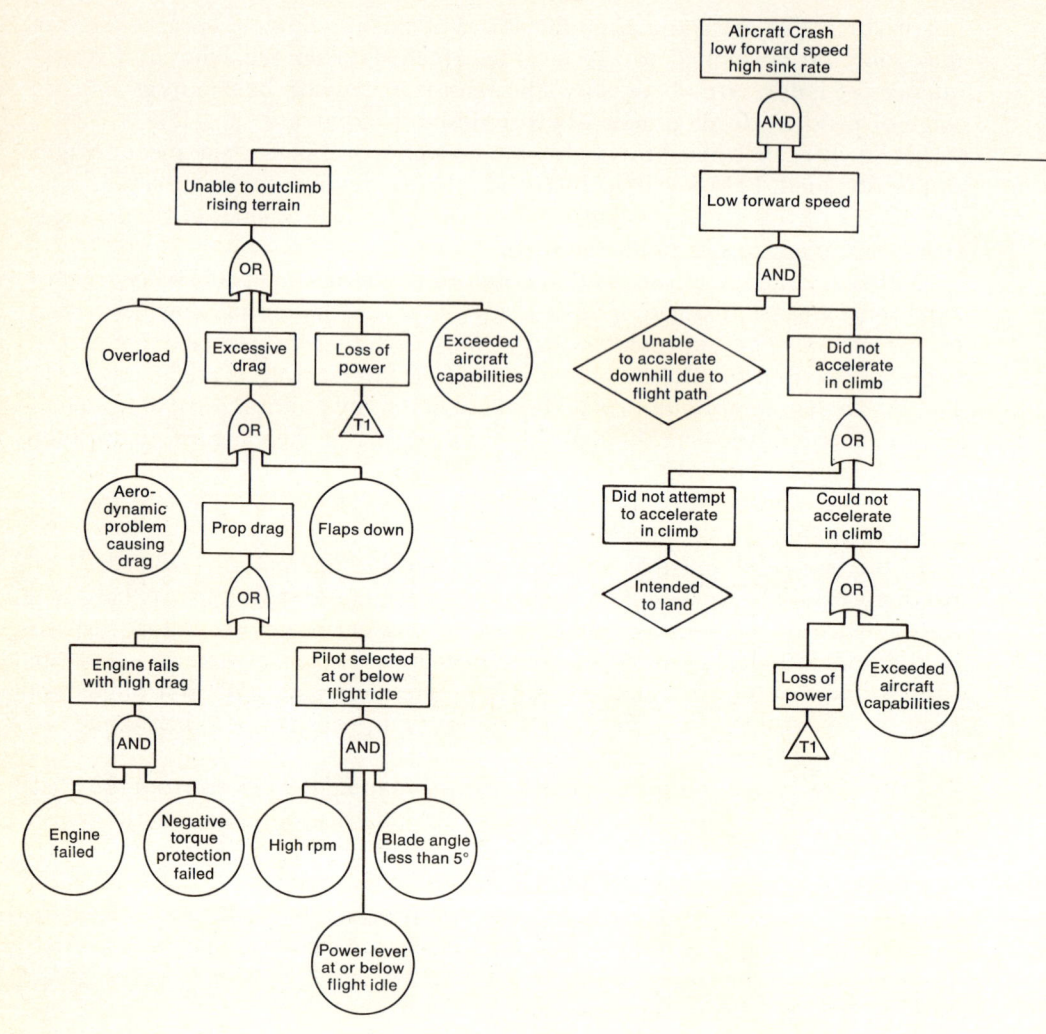

Figure IV-14 A more complex fault tree analysis. *(Air Force Systems Command Design Handbook 1-6.)*

Even when this constant-hazard-rate assumption applies, we expect that the value of the hazard rate will depend on the operating stresses. Figure IV-16 illustrates a possible form of the relationship when operating stress can be represented in one dimension—for instance, when power is the only significant stress variable. In the ideal world, we would simply look up λ for each device in our product (for each failure mode in those devices where the functional effect depends on failure mode), multiply the value by the time interval of interest, and insert the results in the logarithm-of-probability version of our model since λt is simply the (by definition) numerical value of the natural log of $P_s(t)$.

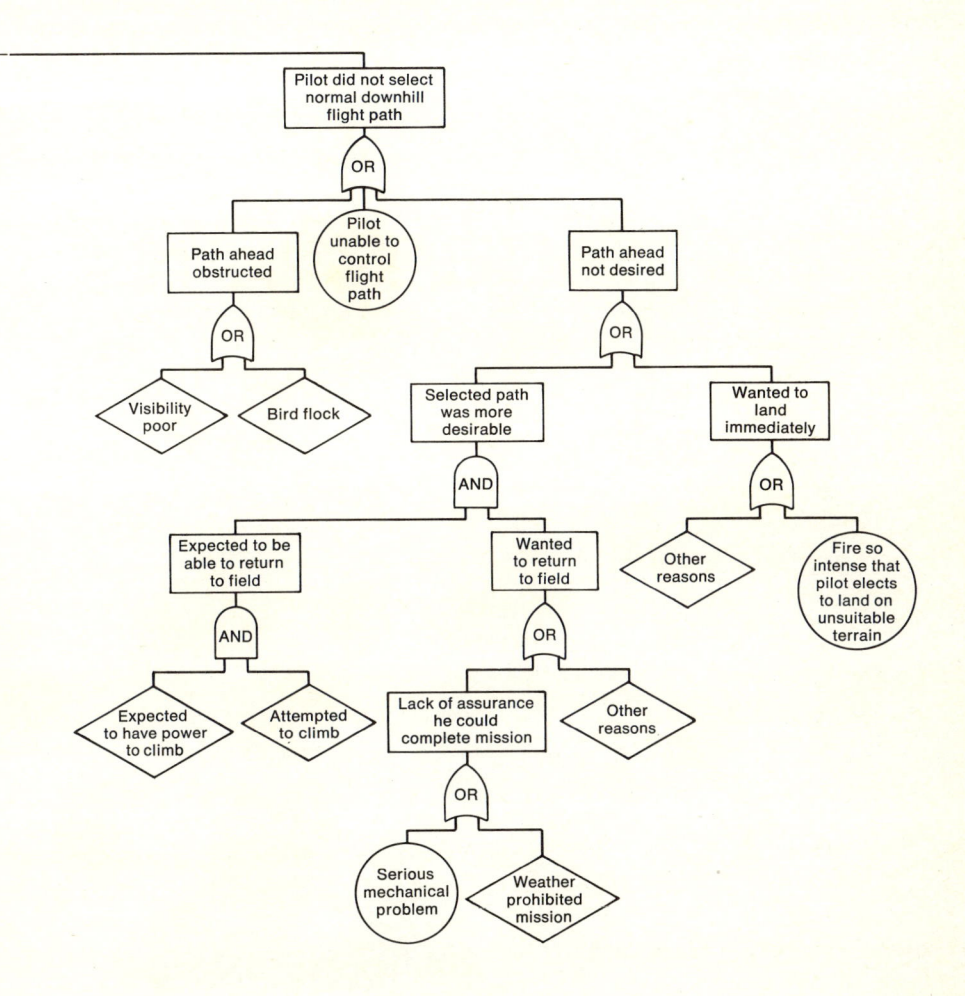

In the real world, there are many tabulations of hazard rates for some device types, and none for others. Where there are many, they often disagree—sometimes for very valid reasons. The simplest (and most common) approach is to pick the tabulation you like best, perhaps because experience and knowledge of the originators has led to confidence, and to make estimates where no tabulated information is available.

There exists a more sophisticated approach, however, that makes it possible to use all available information and, at the same time, to quantify uncertainties concerning the results. That approach involves bayesian statistics. Classical statistics operates on the premise that the sum total of our quantitative knowledge concerning a measure such as hazard rate is derived by inference from experimental data—data obtained from tests or from actual use. The viewpoint is that of "objective" probability—the notion that only the inherent probability (usually with a relative-frequency interpretation) has meaning and that nothing is known about this until experimental data have been obtained.

The bayesian accepts the notion that there is such a thing as *subjective* probability and that it is useful. This recognizes that indirect evidence may be relevant and that arguments based on engineering judgment or physical similarity may have validity. In practical terms, the bayesian is willing in principle to accept the kind of reasoning upon which all of us, for lack of "hard" data, have to make decisions of major importance. It must be emphasized, however, that such "subjective" estimates must be made in as methodical and consistent a way as possible, and that the results be quantified.

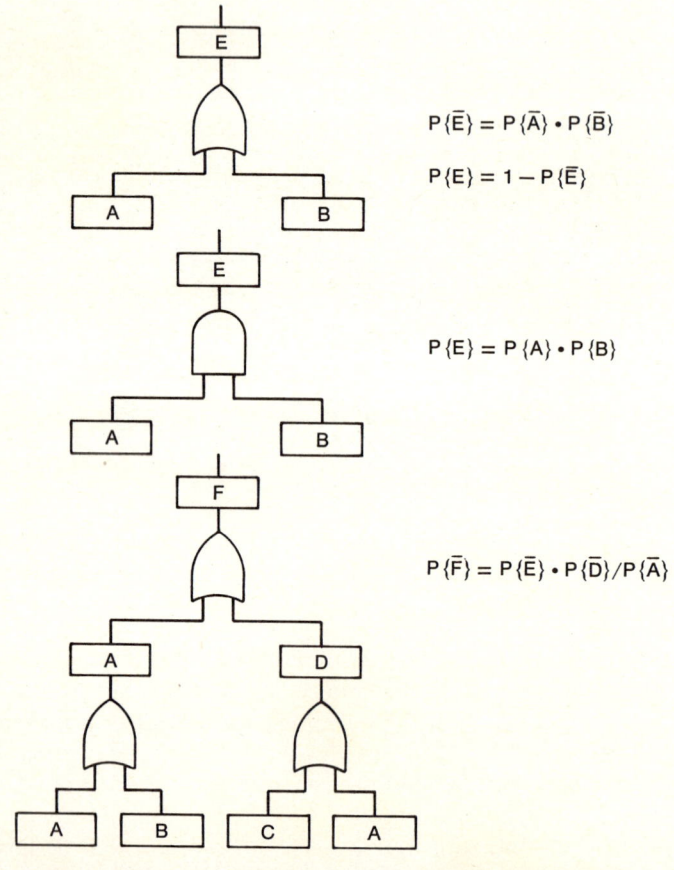

$$P\{\bar{E}\} = P\{\bar{A}\} \cdot P\{\bar{B}\}$$

$$P\{E\} = 1 - P\{\bar{E}\}$$

$$P\{E\} = P\{A\} \cdot P\{B\}$$

$$P\{F\} = P\{E\} \cdot P\{\bar{D}\}/P\{\bar{A}\}$$

Figure IV-15   Fault tree algebraic equivalents.

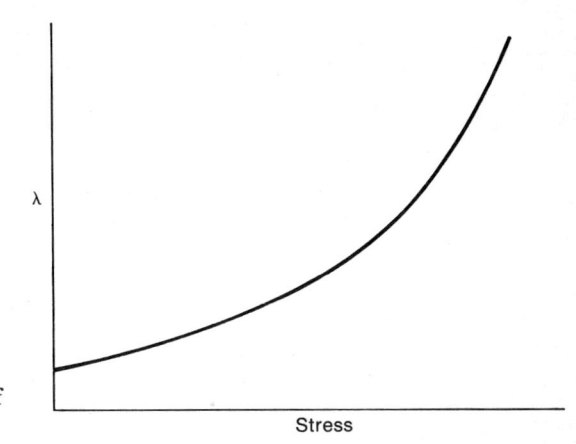

Figure IV-16 Idealized curve of hazard rate λ versus stress.

The most common application of the bayesian approach in fault tree analysis lies in the treatment of differing estimates of the same parameter. Suppose, as illustrated in Table IV-6, that five differing estimates of the hazard rate of a single device (purported to have all been made under identical stress conditions) have been located. You can take the view that all of these estimates are valid and that they represent lot-to-lot and vendor-to-vendor differences in the devices, as well as sampling variation.

If it is not known which vendor or lot yielded what result, or what the sources for your new device will be, it is reasonable to assume that the true hazard rate for that device will be drawn at random from a distribution from which the five estimates are a sample. The mean of that distribution then becomes the expected value of the hazard rate for your own device, and its variance defines the uncertainty about the actual outcome.

In Fig. IV-17 a lognormal distribution has been fitted to the five estimates,

Table IV-6 Differing Hazard Rates Calculated by Various Individuals on the Same Type of Product

	Frammis hazard rates	
	λ	$\log_e \lambda$
Source A	200	5.3
Source B	60	4.1
Source C	135	4.9
Source D	665	6.5
Source E	365	5.9

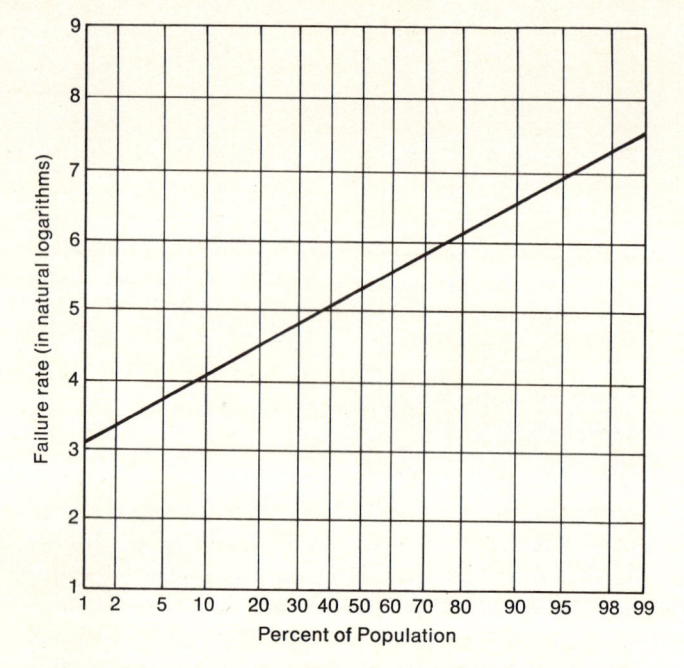

Figure IV-17 Lognormal distribution fitted to five calculations of frammis hazard rates. The following parameters govern:

$$\mu = 5.34$$
$$\sigma = .92$$
$$\text{Median} = e^{\mu} = 209$$
$$\text{Mean} = e^{\mu + 1/2\ \sigma^2} = 317$$
$$\text{Variance} = 135{,}000$$
$$\text{Standard deviation} = 368$$
$$\text{Ratio,}\ \frac{F.95}{F.05} = 27$$

Plotting position:
$$P_i = \frac{i - 0.5}{N} \times 100\%$$

because experience has demonstrated that the *a priori* distribution often takes this form, and it is possible to define both practical and theoretical arguments on its behalf. Bear in mind, however, that this still assumes constancy of the hazard rate, whatever its value may be, over time. The lognormal distribution in this figure describes only the uncertainty concerning the hazard rate's value, and not its behavior in the time domain.

Incidentally, the variances obtained by bayesian statistics or other statistical approaches (depending on what data are available for each branch of the fault tree) may be propagated through the tree "model" to yield uncertainty estimates at the functional event level. By examining the contribution each device makes to the value and uncertainty of the estimates of the product's functional misbehavior probabilities, it may be possible to decide where the maximum payoff potential lies in redesign or testing.

This brings us to testing—the final resort in trying to predict product behavior. It is clear that, short of actual operation in the users' hands, testing under appropriate conditions of simulated use offers the greatest accuracy in characterizing any item. It is also clear, however, that testing can be very expensive and time-consuming, especially when one seeks accurate estimates of what (one hopes) will be very small hazard rates. As a result, intuition is often used in analyzing data. Experimental results and estimates derived from the fault tree or other logical methods are often mixed in either a formal (bayesian) way or informally (sometimes without the analyst even realizing what he or she is doing).

Time-dependent effects, often ignored in logical analysis, play a much greater role in the interpretation of test results, and in some classes of products generally. This problem is discussed more fully in Chap. V, Secs. 3 and 4. For the purposes of this section, we will focus on the "bathtub curve" (so described because of its resemblance to the cross section of a bathtub)—a model of product behavior that has been recognized since the earliest days of reliability analysis (Fig. IV-18). Early after it reaches the user's hands, a product or some of its constituent devices may tend to exhibit a relatively high failure (and maybe hazard) rate. This period is commonly called the "infant mortality" period, and reflects the presence of a subpopulation of inferior devices, perhaps due to latent manufacturing defects that are not evident in final inspection (see Chap. V). Manufacturers of critical electronic equipment often will conduct

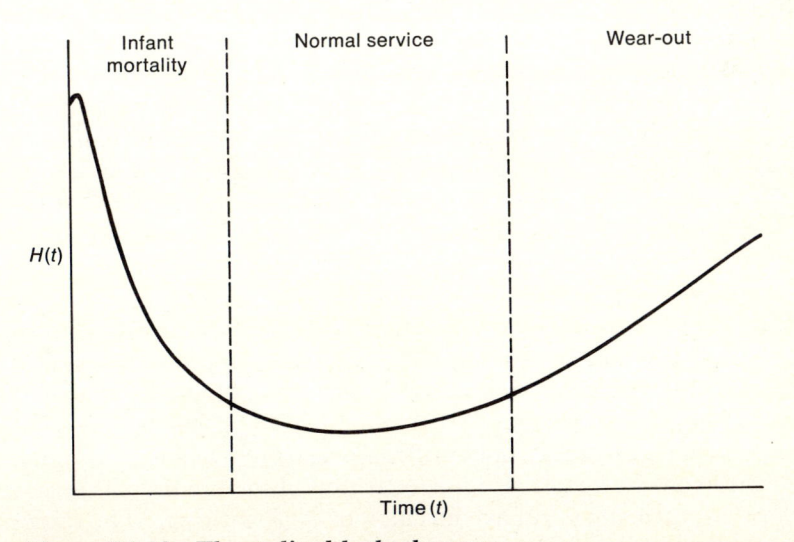

Figure IV-18 **The stylized bathtub curve.**

a "burn in" test of all their products, to catch most of the infant mortality before the items ever leave the plant. Automobile manufacturers acknowledge the phenomenon by allowing, for a brief period after delivery, correction of problems that are not covered by the more extended basic warranty.

After the effects of infant mortality have dissipated, many products enter a period of normal service during which the hazard rate does appear to be essentially constant. Apart from learning-curve effects, one might expect to see this sort of behavior with respect to physical hazards inherent in design.

Finally, the product may enter a period in which wear-out effects predominate. If physical wear or chemical deterioration are present, a rise in hazard rate is to be expected as devices surviving the earlier causes of malfunction reach a critically degraded condition. The more consistent and uniform the product and its use conditions, the more sharply defined the peaking of hazard (failure) rate will be at this stage.

There are several of multiparameter mathematical models in fairly common use to describe nonconstant hazard-rate behavior. The most popular is the Weibull distribution with no-malfunction probability

$$P_s(t) = e^{-t^\beta/\alpha}$$

and hazard rate

$$H(t) = \frac{\beta t^{\beta-1}}{\alpha}$$

where α is a scale parameter and β is a shape parameter. A three-parameter version with location parameter γ also exists; it simply shifts the origin so that malfunction cannot occur before time γ. For β greater than one, the hazard rate increases as a function of time; for β less than one, it decreases. If β equals one, the Weibull distribution reduces to the exponential distribution already discussed (that is, a constant hazard rate). Mixed Weibull distributions, describing distinct subpopulations, are also employed. The Weibull distribution, by the way, is strictly empirical; no theoretical foundation has ever been demonstrated for it.

Another distribution used by many in the hazards-prediction field is the lognormal, describing behavior with time (unlike the use of a lognormal distribution earlier in this section in connection with description of uncertainty about the true hazard rate from consideration of data from different sources). The lognormal distribution applies when the logarithm of the measured characteristic—in this case, malfunction incidence versus time—follows the familiar "normal" gaussian distribution. The no-malfunction probability and the hazard rate are usually expressed in terms of the parameters μ and σ where μ is the mean of the logarithms (and also the logarithm of the median of the measured characteristic) and σ the standard deviation of the logarithms. The choice of the lognormal distribution is supported by substantial evidence in the case of semiconductor devices, and can be supported by theoretical (mathematical) considerations when the factors promoting malfunction interact in a multiplicative sense or when the distribution of manufacturing flaws is normal and their effects follow a power law.

A variety of physical phenomena can also produce nonconstant hazard-rate behavior. Trying to fit these into "standard" distributions can lead to gross errors. Some obvious ones are autocatalytic effects— corrosion products, for example, can either inhibit or accelerate further corrosion, depending on the materials involved. The wear of a mechanical part may affect surface finish or hardness, and thus determine the rate of future wear. Depletion of a material, such as sublimation of tungsten from a light bulb filament, may affect the internal environment of a product.

Ideally, complete knowledge of the significant physical processes and of the distribution of manufacturing tolerances and defects would enable us to predict long-term device behavior from fundamentals (Fig. IV-19). This "physics of failure" approach is still severely limited, especially in areas outside of military and aerospace electronics.

These limitations also inhibit (or should inhibit) the use of multiparameter distributions. When a distribution is used descriptively or for interpolation there is no great problem. Statistical techniques used primarily for smoothing purposes are not likely to produce large errors. A major objective, however, is extrapolation in time—predicting behavior for use periods in excess of those previously observed, or under conditions not previously encountered.

In the first case, the choice of an inappropriate distributional model can lead to gross differences between prediction and reality; the model may zig when reality zags. In the second case, we should expect that a change in conditions will affect more than one parameter of the distribution, even when the same distributional model applies; the number of sample points required to permit independent estimates of the effects for each parameter increases rapidly with the number of parameters. Here the lognormal distribution has an advantage over the Weibull distribution parameters.

6. PREDICTION TECHNIQUES: FAILURE MODES AND EFFECTS ANALYSIS*

Unlike fault tree analysis, in which the analyst starts by postulating an unwanted event and then identifies possible contributing items, failure modes and effects analysis (FMEA) starts with each and every component, investigates the ways in which each component can possibly fail, and enumerates all possible results of such failure. See Table IV-7.

In making a failure modes and effects analysis, it should be remembered that the complete product includes many items in addition to the physical product itself, including advertising, warnings, packing, shipping, installation, and service. These are, at times, more formidable causes for action than what is

*August B. Mundel, P.E., CSI, Inc., Livingston, N.J.

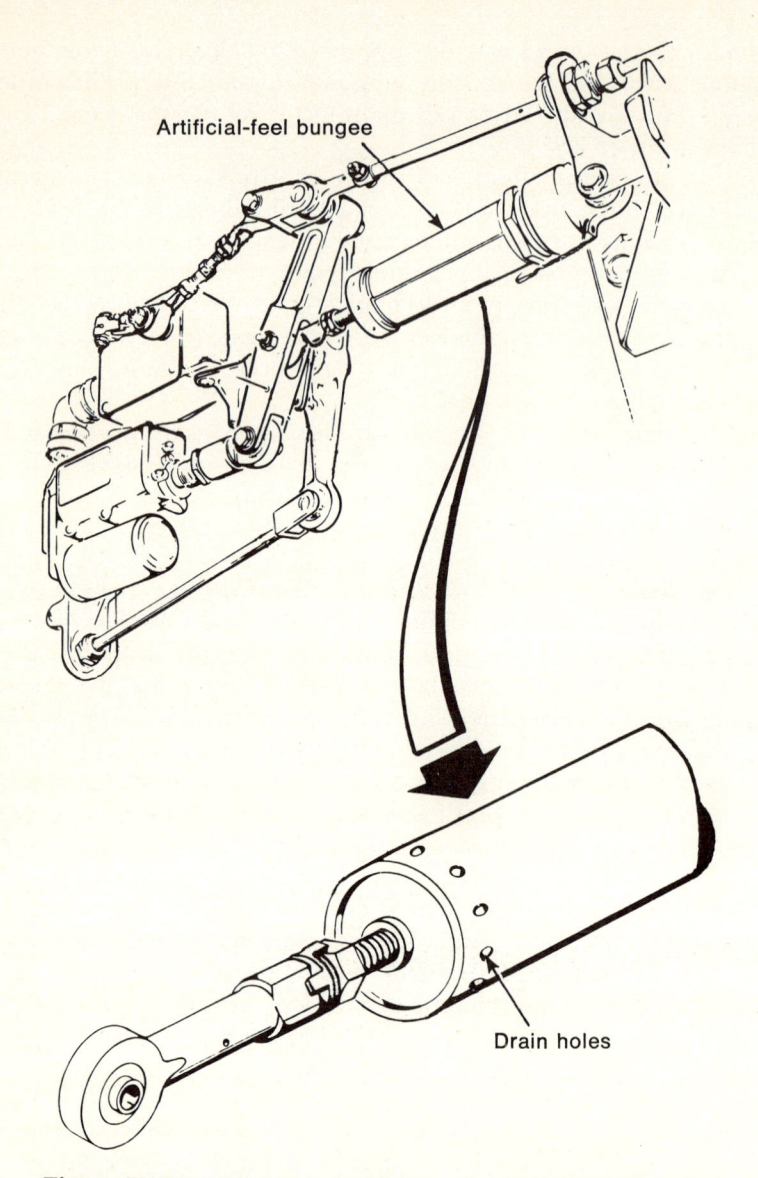

Figure IV-19 The real world is contaminated by dirt and moisture. The designer saw the need for drain holes on the bungee, but the holes weren't made big enough, or placed in the optimal location.

normally thought of as the product. It also helps, of course, to be familiar with what can go wrong. It is therefore frequently advantageous to view the failure modes that can occur with detrimental effects (and the general causes of these) by means of a fault tree analysis before beginning a FMEA. FTA helps to identify the contributing causes and interactions sometimes not so easily identified by the FMEA alone.

Because each component is examined, and because each component can have several different failure modes, FMEA provides information about what must be accomplished to improve performance and to achieve greater freedom from product failure and liability. It identifies the parts that must be improved rather than emphasizing the end results that represent the untoward incidents, as in fault tree analysis.

In practice, FMEA looks very much like an accounting form. Each part is listed and followed by all of the various ways that failure modes can occur, and then by the undesirable performance that should be avoided, if possible. Just as in a parts list, the form is broken down finely with the parts listed toward the left of the FMEA worksheet (Fig. IV-20) by name and part number so as to assure unquestioned identification.

These columns are followed by the failure mode and cause and a method of identifying this failure prior to its occurrence. The next column lists backup

Table IV-7 Steps in Failure Modes and Effects Analysis

1. Define the complete system.
2. Identify each component and each subassembly/component group.
3. List all the possible ways each element identified in the step above can fail or cause ill effect.
4. Describe each possible cause of failure.
5. Describe ways for consumer to identify a failure mode in the product.
6. Define what effects these failure modes may have on product, property, or people in all possible product applications. Remember that multiple effects may require additional analysis numbers under step 3.
7. Classify each effect for severity.
8. Describe backup protection.
9. Estimate and classify frequency of failure.
10. Define and classify the degree of possible imperilment.
11. Plot failure frequency, severity, and imperilment on matrix.
12. Determine corrective action—and warnings, labels, and so forth for items not capable of correction by design.

Analysis number	Part #	Part Name	Failure Mode	Failure Cause	Identification method	Backup protection	Effects; Hazards	Severity	Frequency	Imperilment	Notes
1	2152	fan	stops	bearings	overheating no draft	none	overheat; fire due to contact	III	2 .001	α	improve bearings; install overtemperature switch
2	2152	"	"	coil open or shorted							
4		unit tips over									
14	4286	nut	falls off	loose; too little torque	visual	lockwasher	loose bolt head & bolt shorts on-off switch; turns unit on	II	2 .001 × 10⁶	α or β	Danger can be eliminated by proper insulation of switch terminal.
15	4287	bolt	head off	damaged in mfg; torque too high	visual	bolt thru other unit holds heat coils in place; line fuse blows if short occurs		II	2 .0001 × 10⁶	α or β	
18	5173	heater element	wire opens	overheated or nicked	visual; no glow on one end	none; fuse if broken wire connects to ground	can contact case & cause shock	V	4 10⁶	γ	Can we provide suitable insulation?
19a 19b	5173	heater element	no failure; environmental hazard		???	none	explosion fire	V IV	1 1	ε β	Provide warning.
48	7123	internal lead to switch	opens		fan and heater will not operate	none	external freezeup but adequate warning	I	1 .0001×10⁻⁶	α	No action necessary.

Figure IV-20 FMEA worksheet for electric heater analysis.

132

protection, identifying the provisions for preventing the failure mode from having any serious effects. The next three columns indicate the severity of any injury or damage this failure mght cause, its expected frequency, and its spontaneity (imperilment). Your own operation may require modifying this form. Here are the reasons for each column in Fig. IV-20.

As each failure mode is uncovered, it should be assigned an analysis number for future identification. This is listed in the first column of the form. Many people prefer to issue identification numbers serially, starting with the number 1 as the first item on each program or analysis procedure. Others use a numbering system which can be tied directly to a computer. Still others prefer facilitating future identification with a mnemonic code.

Part number and part name (column 2): The identifiers or descriptors are normally those used in the plant and parts list.

Failure mode and cause (column 3): Where parts are duplicated, one analysis may or may not be sufficient. Each failure mode for each part and application should have its own identification number unless the situation dictates that all are identical, as is, for instance, the situation where five bolts fasten a wheel onto an automobile.

Identification method (column 4): This refers to the method a user, owner, repairer, or other person may use to identify the presence of the failure mode. On some products it is simply "product won't work"—followed by more complex analysis. Other identifications may require either disassembly or complex analytical equipment to diagnose.

Backup protection (column 5): Allow the identification of any device, procedure, or part that is present to prevent the accompanying hazard.

Effect-hazard (column 6): The resulting, often unwanted, event and the result thereof are identified here.

Severity, frequency, imperilment (columns 7, 8, 9): These three columns describe the unwanted accident or event and its effect upon the person or property with regard to severity, frequency, and imperilment. *Severity* can be minimal—a scratch, a minor burn, or some small inconvenience—or it could be death or property destruction. The level is assigned a Roman numeral. The higher the number, the greater the severity. *Frequency* is more readily reduced to a number. The average life or number of times per year or unit of operational time between event occurrences are also numbered, using larger numbers for increased frequency. *Imperilment* is primarily a categorization of the ability of those present to take action to reduce or eliminate deleterious effects when the event occurs. For instance, when brakes fail in the garage, the imperilment may be negligible—evasive action is easy—but on the highway the imperilment is great and evasive action may be difficult or impossible. Imperilment is graded subjectively (the scale is discussed later in this section). An explosion provides no time for evasive action. Therefore, this would represent the highest degree of imperilment. Failure modes resulting in frequent and severe incidents with high imperilment are most objectionable and require major efforts to eliminate.

The last column of the form provides for notes on suggested corrections, changes, and warnings that could aid in preventing untoward events. As a final part of the program, the analysis number is transferred to a display matrix to emphasize the relative importance of the hazards so that the most dangerous and most costly can receive major attention. (See Figs. IV-21 and IV-22.)

The individual items as represented by the analysis numbers are transferred to the *hazard analysis matrix*.

An item at the lowest of frequency, severity and imperilment scales will be placed in box A (Fig. IV-22) and conversely an item at the highest of all of these scales, in box D.

Frequency

There are several methods of categorizing a failure mode on the basis of frequency alone. The simplest method is in terms of failures/unit time. A common unit of time is 10^6 hours (1 million hours). Failure rate information in this form is available from GIDEP and other government-industry data banks (see App. H). Failure rates are a function of application and environment. The

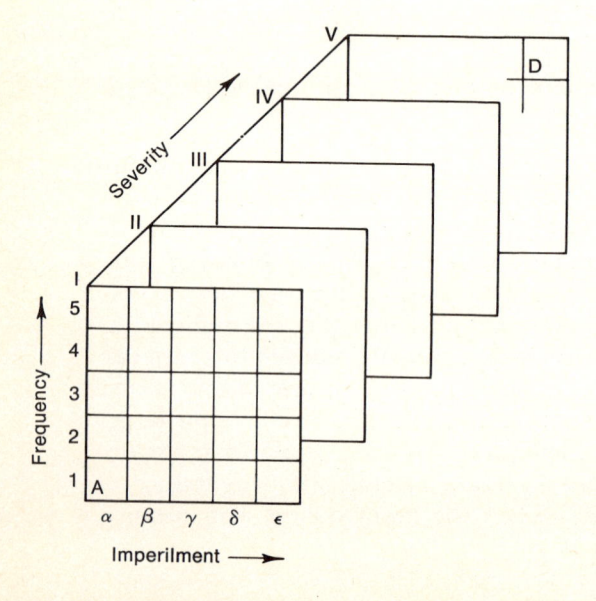

Figure IV-21   Hazard matrix.

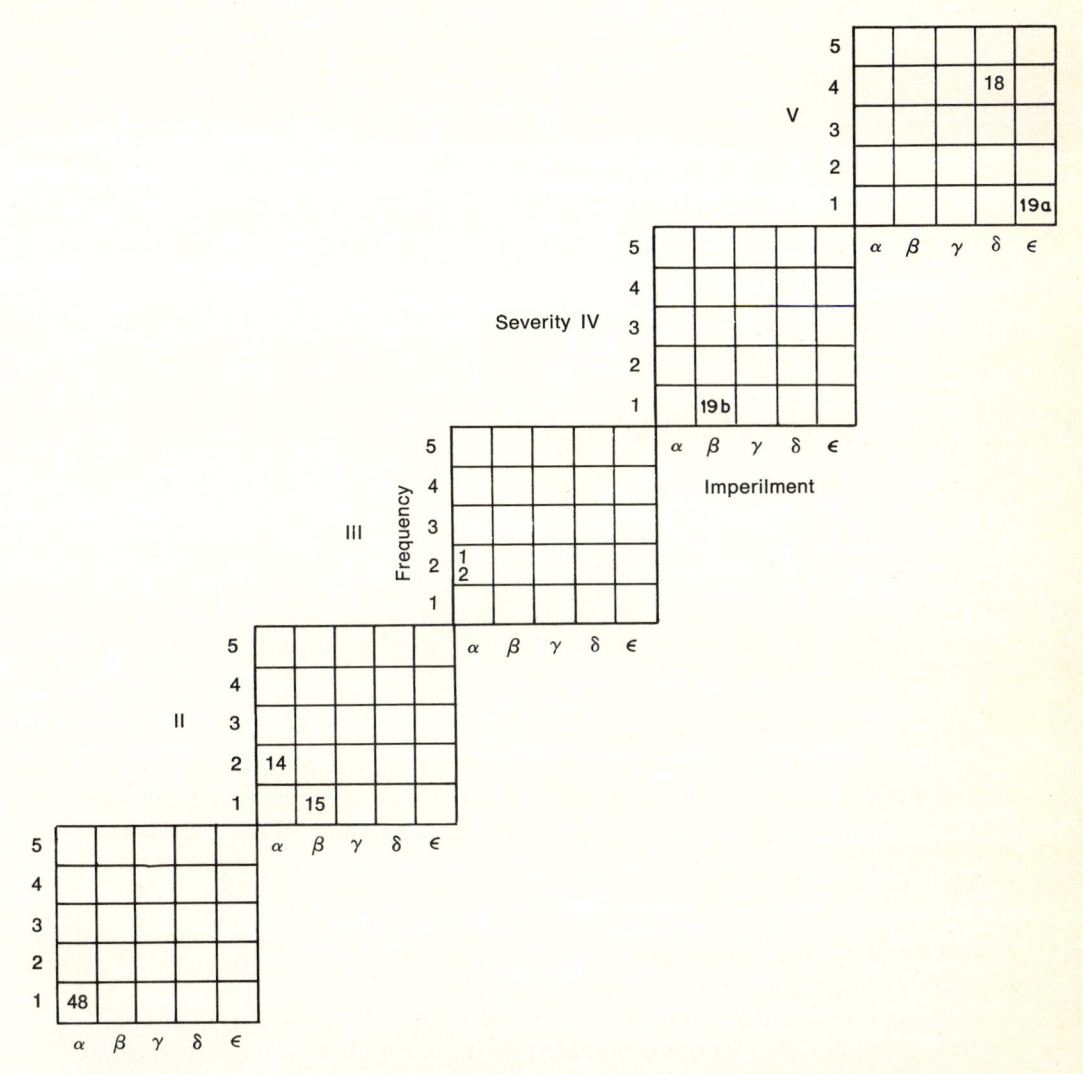

Figure IV-22 Hazard matrix with estimates of effects of failure modes discussed in Fig. IV-20.

application must be properly evaluated. In these data the failure rates may vary from hundreds or thousands per 10^6 hours to 0.0001 per 10^6 hours for specific parts or devices with similar characteristics and functions. A small bolt holding a large mass under conditions of vibration would have a large failure rate. A large bolt with a locking device in a similar application would probably have a low failure rate. In electronic systems a condenser at or near its rated wattage in a shipboard application, operating at 120°C, may exhibit a failure rate of 2 per 10^6 hours, whereas an identical unit at 20°C, used in an ideal laboratory environment, and subjected to less than a tenth its rated wattage, exhibits a failure rate of 0.001 per 10^6 hours.

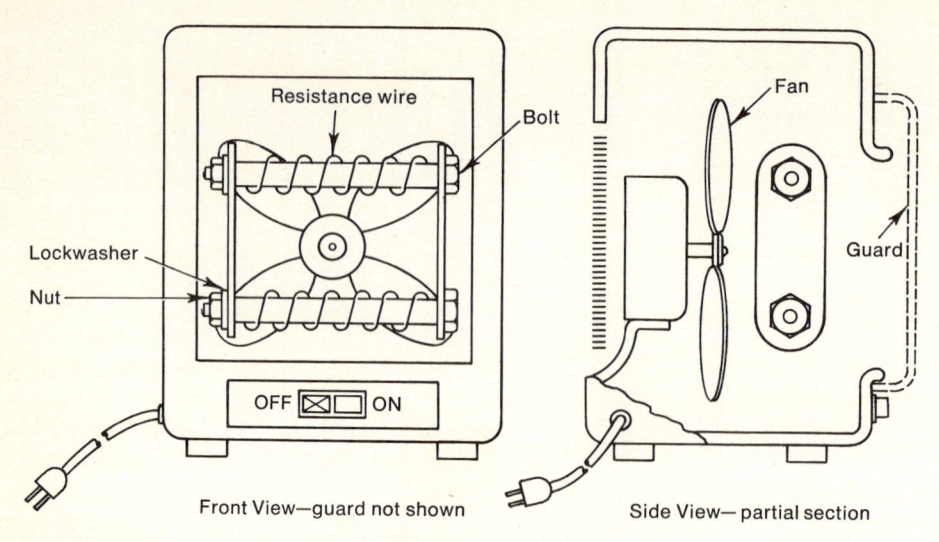

Figure IV-23 Electric heater design under discussion.

Some FMEA failure rate classification systems separate the frequency of occurrence into several groups identified as remote, reasonably probable, or probable. This may be satisfactory for a first pass, but not for an analysis. It may be found that even a "remote" frequency occurs too often to permit its occurrence without safeguards. Numerical values of failure rate are preferable. Where these data are available from a company history or data bank, the appropriate value from the source for frequency of failure should be listed in the FMEA worksheet (as shown for items 14 and 15 in Fig. IV-20). For some applications it is desirable to convert from hours to days, months, or years, using appropriate source data.

As an example of this section, the FMEA procedure will be used to explore the hazards of an electric space heater (Fig. IV-23).

A heater used to provide occasional heat during a heating system failure may see only a few hours of service per year. The unit may in other applications see continuous or off-and-on service over many months or years when used as the sole source of heat in a service station or warehouse. The life cycle may convince the designer that the criteria for failure in different applications warrants special attention or warnings.

In determining failure rates where failure history on similar products cannot be located in data banks, the manufacturer may develop and run a laboratory test and add this to life experience in the field to expand and maintain his knowledge of failure rates as they apply to his product and the application. Categorizing failure rates into groups can also aid in assaying the importance of failure frequencies. These groups should have specific numerical boundaries. Methods by which this can be done are shown in Table IV-8, which shows actual values used in column 4 and failure rates compared to an overall product failure rate in column 5. The groups are numbered in order of increasing frequency of occurrence. Group I would contain the least frequent failure modes and Group V the most frequent.

The total of all failure mode frequencies resulting in warranty, critical, major, or minor events may or may not be the simple sum of the individual values. Whenever each of the failure modes is totally independent of the others, the frequencies of failure are added to find the total failure rate. Conversely, when the failure modes are dependent on other failure modes, or not independent, the frequencies cannot be added in this manner. If there are two nuts, each of which may loosen and fall onto contacts, the frequency may be twice that for an individual nut. On the other hand, where there are two or more fasteners holding parts together and the design is so conceived and executed that either fastener will suffice to maintain the assembly safely operating—and the failure rates of each of these fasteners is independent of the others—the frequency of separation would be much less than the individual fastener failure rates. (In situations of this type, if the frequency of failure for each of two hold-down screws were 0.01 per unit time, the failure rate for part separation—the failure of both hold-down screws—would be 0.01×0.01 per unit time or 0.0001 per unit time.)

When all the failure modes and their frequencies have been collected, each category should be properly combined to determine the total frequency of each classification of failure—critical, major, minor, warranty, and so forth. These total frequencies of failure can then be compared with computed economical

Table IV-8 Common Methods for Classification of Frequency of Occurrence

1	2	3	4. Failure rate	5. Failure rate
Remote	I	Maxima for individual critical modes	<0.0001/unit time	$<0.01 \times f$*
	II	Sum of critical or individual major failure mode	$>0.0001/t$ $<0.001/t$	$>0.01 \times f$ $<0.05 \times f$
Reasonably probable	III	Sum of major or individual minor modes	$>0.001/t$ $<0.01/t$	$>0.05 \times f$ $<0.1 \times f$
	IV	Sum of minor or individual warranty claims	$>0.01/t$ $<0.1/t$	$>0.1 \times f$
Probable	V	Total warranty failures	$>0.1/t$	

*f = Overall failure rate

values. If, for example, the total frequency of failure resulting in warranty service exceeds a specific value, the cost of warranty service will be excessive.

Assume that a warranty exists for a one year period and experience indicates that the average warranty service costs $10.00, and that $1.00 was added to the sales cost for warranty. The failure rate during the year of warranty should not exceed the fraction

$$\text{Max Economic Warranty Use} = \left(\frac{\text{Warranty reserve/unit}}{\text{Warranty cost/unit}}\right) \bigg/ \text{Warranty time}$$

For the example, this would be equivalent to 0.1 failure/unit per year of warranty.

In general the frequency of failure for failure modes which result in repair service, action by the user, or warranty service, can be allowed to add up to the maximum value of Group V (Table IV-8). Any failure mode frequency rate which is greater than Group V would typically result in excessive warranty cost.

Similarly, the failure frequency represented by Group I should be chosen so that it represents the largest frequency that could be tolerated for individual critical failure modes. In some instances it may be wiser to place the sum of the critical failure mode frequencies in this same group. (Note that failure rates of many items that would result in warranty service may also be found in Group I.) Incidents that are likely to cause large monetary losses or serious injury should be reduced, if at all possible, even though their frequency is low (Group I).

It is likely that there will be some failure modes included in this group which result in fail-safe or minimal harm. No critical failure mode can be permitted to have a frequency of occurrence in Groups II, III, IV, V. This grouping is helpful in identifying serious failure modes whose failure rate cannot be tolerated.

From the designer's or manufacturer's viewpoint, there is no safe substitute for numerical boundaries for classifications. In the absence of good data, however, an alternative to using the actual failure rates is to make an arbitrary grouping related to the ratios of the failure rates permissible in each group to the total failure frequency expected or experienced. This is shown in column 5. The classification systems shown in Table IV-8 represent common groupings.

Severity

How does one establish a severity index? Simultaneously discussing severity and frequency can be dangerous, since it may trap the analyst into the belief that a specific failure mode of a component has a sufficiently low probability or frequency of occurrence to be "economically" safe. Such a conclusion is not proper. The courts have repeatedly taken the position that a design which was not sufficiently safe or did not carry adequate warnings may result in the manufacturer being assessed punitive damages as well as actual damages when he is judged to be liable.

Severity scales differ, as do frequency scales, for different applications. Severity scales, in common with frequency scales, should escalate as severity increases. A typical severity scale is shown in Table IV-9. The levels of severity can be labeled alphabetically or with Roman numerals. When entering information on the FMEA worksheet or display, it is sometimes easier to use a different set of notations for the severity, frequency, and other categories by which the hazard is identified.

The four most severe hazards presented by the electric heater are burns, fires, shock, and explosions. Electric heat, unlike heat from fuel burned on-site, can be *delivered* with freedom from explosions. The complete elimination of the possibility of the heater causing harm from heat and shock is probably marginal, however. This device is, after all, an electrical unit designed to deliver heat! It has not yet been possible to completely eliminate these potential hazards without destroying the capability of the heater to perform its primary function.

Although these hazards have existed since heaters were first conceived and marketed, and the number of units in service has increased, the number of injuries may not have increased as rapidly as the product's use. This is the result of the combined efforts of producers, designers, and public and quasi-public agencies to improve the safeguards, the instructions, and warnings and inform the public of the potential for injury.

For each value of property loss, a severity classification might be assigned similar to that used for classifying the severity of injury. (See Table IV-10.)

It is impossible to assign dollar values to levels of severity that will be universally applicable. Property losses for clothes, furniture, furnishings, buildings, cover a wide range. In addition, small losses can be more serious to small companies. A loss of approximately 1 million dollars after a botulism case put Bon Vivant Soups into bankruptcy. An 8 million dollar loss for Campbell's Soup in a similar situation involving a large recall (no injuries or deaths occurred) barely showed up on the profit and loss statement.

The Consumer Product Safety Commission's National Electronic Injury Surveillance System, NEISS (discussed more fully in Chap. II) uses eight severity levels. The more serious the injury, the higher the severity, on the average. These values are estimates of the relative loss incurred at succeeding levels of injury severity. They do not include warranty and service losses.

Table IV-9 Severity Scale, Injuries

I	Warranty service only
II	Minor injury
III	Major injury
IV	Multiple major injuries or death
V	Multiple deaths

Table IV-10 Severity Scale: Property Loss and Corporate Embarrassment

I	No property loss; no embarrassment
II	Minor property loss; often product itself; some embarrassment
III	Large loss; embarrassment in locality of loss
IV	Critical loss; much embarrassment
V	Critical loss; much embarrassment; may threaten corporate survival

Each of the estimated severity categories has a value, geometrically expanded from an arbitrary value of 10 for the lowest level (Category 1). A sprained foot has been placed in Category 1, while an amputation of the foot is placed in Category 6. Each case moves up one severity level as it requires hospitalization. The crude severity values for injuries are shown in Table IV-11. A single Category 8 (fatality) originally had a crude severity value of 34,732, but has since been reassigned a value of 2516. Deaths, however, are treated separately. As discussed in Chap. II, NEISS data indicate that a product was involved in an accident, but not necessarily that the product *caused* the accident or injury.

Imperilment

There are other characteristics of failure that interest the safety and reliability professional. It is common for products to have failure rates that decrease during the early life and then become stable at low frequency per unit time. Some eventually age and wear out. When the wear-out period is encountered, the failure rate increases rapidly.

Table IV-11 NEISS Severity Index

Severity category	Crude severity value	*Trauma*
1	10	Sprain, mild injury in small areas, dermatitis
2	12	Punctures and fractures
3	17	Contusions and scalds
4	31	Internal organ injuries
5	81	Concussion, cell and nerve damage
6	340	Amputation, crushing, anoxia
7	2516	All hospitalized people in category 6
8	2516	Death recorded at same severity level as 7, but analyzed separately

Failure during any short period is usually random. One unit is just as likely or unlikely to fail as another. The failure to perform at any period in life may be a catastrophic event or may be preceded by a degradation of performance. The spontaneity of the failure may be so great that there is no way to avoid injury and harm. Some failures are so obviously progressive that all but the most imprudent would have taken corrective action. Other failures have no serious effect if they are spontaneous or slow and progressive.

Catastrophic failure implies a sudden change from operable to inoperable.

Degradation implies a gradual deterioration of performance. Your car might get you to the gas station but you know it isn't operating well. Your TV isn't right, but you can still watch the big game on it. You will get it repaired next week or next month.

Incandescent light bulbs usually fail spontaneously. The opening of the filament ends their life. Usually there is more than one in a location and no danger is associated with the failure. The failure of an aircraft warning light may present a more serious hazard. The rapidity or spontaneity of a failure can increase the imperilment or the endangerment of individuals. Failures which are of great severity and happen with great spontaneity (explosions) need more attention and greater design effort to preclude their occurrence and to minimize the potential hazard than do failures which give adequate warning.

The degree of imperilment (as with frequency and severity) should be classified in escalating order, as in Table IV-12.

The electric space heater is a mechanical-electric product that may produce serious harm. It is most likely that a serious accident, if it does occur, will occur from overheating of some material in, or adjacent to, the heater. This overheating in turn would cause ignition of some flammable material in the immediate area. If there is a fan, as there is in this particular unit, there can be other mechanical or electrical failures. In the fault tree (Fig. IV-24) some of the occurrences which might result in the ignition of a dangerous nature are shown.

Table IV-12 Categories of Imperilment

Rank	Description of failure
α	Failure either minor, or occurring at innocuous time or over long period, therefore allowing reaction in timely fashion by user(s)
β	Failure with sufficient warning for prudent user(s)
γ	Sufficient warning time so skilled can avoid injury; or failure itself happens in recognizable way for skilled/experienced operators.
δ, ϵ	Failure is instantaneous; no evasive action is possible.

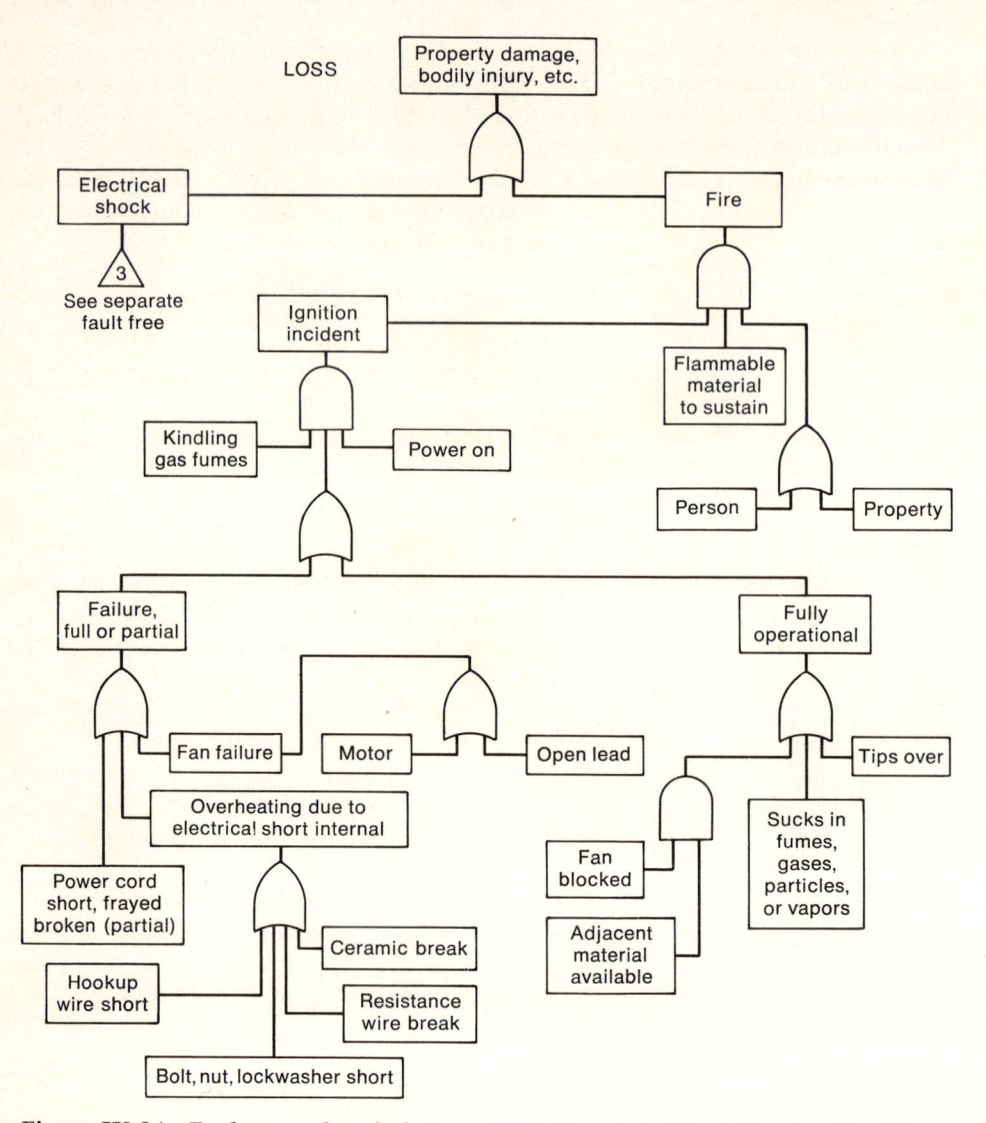

Figure IV-24   Fault tree, electric heater.

Each of the events at the bottom of this fault tree is not equally likely. Nor are they always equally probable in every installation or at all times. A fire resulting from ignition is not always as likely to result in large losses or serious injury when it occurs in the presence of wide-awake young adults. When a similar fire occurs in the presence of an unattended baby or an invalid, the result may be catastrophic. The designer, manufacturer, or analyst making the fault tree analysis would naturally be interested in what can occur, the probability of each event occurring, and how serious the event may be.

Some events or causes are likely to be overlooked in either an FTA or FMEA. Particularly likely to be overlooked are events related to such contingent conditions. In a petroleum-powered heater, for instance, running short of fuel has little consequence and may even be categorized as "fail-safe." Danger of ignition during refilling, due to fuel spilling on a hot manifold, could present a serious problem, however. In the heater of our example, the presence of ignitable gases or fumes in the area may be extremely hazardous, although the device does not use fuel itself directly. Warnings against these conditions are essential. Perhaps there are portions of the design which can be changed to reduce the probability of the ignition of exterior material, and thus provide greater safety. One feature that has been introduced into these heaters is a switch that turns the heater off when it is tipped.

No manufacturer can remove all hazards. Someone could very well connect an electric heater to a power outlet without removing it from its package. Or, having plugged it in, and finding the fan to be nonoperational, a purchaser could wrap it up again while still hot or still connected to a power source. Most of us would consider this to be very careless. Still, it is possible and it is unlikely that anything except a very-low-temperature thermostat would prevent a fire.

Another hazard is the propensity of people to poke fingers or tools into openings. Underwriters Laboratories has a standard probe which must not make contact with live electrical wires when inserted through any opening from the outside of the product. Exposed hot wires or even exposed wires within a perforated enclosure attract grown-ups and children. It is highly improbable that an air heater could be designed to thwart a consumer, exercising great human ingenuity, from inserting a wire and making contact with the electric source. This argument may make some individuals opt for the hot liquid version of the electric heater, with the heating element embedded and insulated from the liquid. Such devices have other problems, however.

In the preliminary FMEA, the fault tree of Fig. IV-24 will be examined. This discusses the possible failure of a resistance element due to breakage of the wire, and its bridging to the other element (thereby causing a reduction of the total resistance), or failure by some bypass of current caused by wires or mechanical parts being displaced.

If the heater is examined, it is evident that the parts involved are the resistor (the heating element), which consists of a special wire wound on a ceramic or refractory spool. A bolt passes through the ceramic and holds it on a metal bracket. The bolt has a head on one end and a lock washer and nut on the other. There are two heating elements, one above the other. They are wired in parallel, both connected to a switch which also feeds the fan.

The task is to identify the most objectionable failure modes in order to provide a "buy basket" or "hit sheet" of priorities for the manufacturer.

Consider the failure of a bolt that holds the ceramic in place, listed as Analysis #15 in Fig. IV-20. The head has come off. This would probably be an uncommon failure mode. It is possible that there would be no record of such an occurrence, and the design might be such that even if one long bolt were removed from the heater, the other heater unit bolt would hold everything in place. The only question would be what happens to the remainder of the assembly and the bolt head. If they drop into safe places, everything will be okay. If they cause a short (or short to ground), consequences could be severe. The analysis in Fig. IV-20 assumes that the adverse results are minimal and extremely unlikely; entries indicate a minimal severity, frequency, and imperilment.

Analysis #18 describes a heater wire opening. The user can readily identify this, since the heater core fails to glow from end to end. The wire may unroll itself from the core and contact the metal frame of the heater. This could cause serious shock or electrical burns to a user. The frequency of this occurring has been classified as medium, but the severity is much greater than in the previous analysis, and the imperilment serious since evasive action is difficult if not impossible. The user would be well advised to disconnect the heater and replace or repair it. It is extremely important that the analyst choose the proper severity and imperilment levels. If it can cause death, the failure mode's effect is certainly Severity IV or greater. The imperilment is certainly γ or δ. A decision is needed to provide for prevention of these hazards.

Analysis #19 represents a situation where the heater wire is glowing in the presence of explosive or flammable vapors. This would unquestionably cause an explosion, which is classified as the maximum in severity and imperilment. Regardless of the frequency, even one such occurrence can be calamitous. The mode and the resulting event ought to be eliminated. The problem for the designer and manufacturer is how to accomplish the improvement.

Analysis items 18 and 19 in Fig. III-20 have different estimates of frequency. Yet there is a greater hazard in an explosion. In one instance there is an indication of the problem. This might result in the prudent individual avoiding the occurrence. This places the imperilment in the category β for Item 19. Item 18 is a situation much less likely to be noticed. If there were any parts of the guard that prevented the heating element from being 100 percent visible, it would only be the skilled who would notice the malfunction. This places imperilment in the γ category. If the open-wire situation occurs as a permanent-open and is infrequent, the warranty cost analysis could be used to evaluate it. If there is danger to people, product liability costs will need to be given serious consideration (Table IV-13).

Keeping the frequency of failure of dangerous failure modes very low does not prevent less critical failure frequencies from being even lower. The design may be completed satisfactorily with the frequency of Item #22 greater than the frequency of Item #48, as for example, it might be determined that

Frequency of Item #22 = 0.00015 per 10^6 hours, and
Frequency of Item #48 = 0.0001 per 10^6 hours,

both quite remote possibilities.

The open resistor (heater) may be found not especially troublesome to the

Table IV-13 Estimating Possible Costs of Future Incidents Involving a Product

Severity	$/Incident (average)	Frequency	Total (5-yr life)	% Frequency
Warranty	$25	800 per year	$100,000	97.3
Minor	$1,000	100/5-yr life	$100,000	2.4
Major	$10,000	10/5-yr life	$100,000	0.24
Critical	$250,000	1/5-yr life	$250,000	0.024
Total			$550,000	100

company. Perhaps there were 10 complaints and requirements to repair heater elements free of charge under warranty last year. Fifty thousand units were sold. Probably some additional unreported incidents occurred. The total cost to the corporation was less than $300. There were no injuries involved. Therefore, even though the failure frequency was 200×10^{-6} per unit per year (10 units per 50,000) there is no cause for alarm. There may be justification to question any major corrective action.

This might lead one to assume that any item with a frequency of failure in the order of 200×10^{-6} per year (10 per 50,000) would not be of major consequence. However, this conclusion does not necessarily follow. The failure rate is too high to be permissible for the bolt failure (Item #15).

Assuming that there were a million units of a product sold in a year, and that the average life of the unit was 5 years, the failure rate must be incredibly low if no serious untoward incidents are to occur during the unit's life, which is much longer than the warranty. One million dollar settlement per year would be the equivalent of adding one dollar ($1.00) to the factory cost, certainly not a very large figure for an automobile, but a very large figure for a toaster or a heater. Moreover, it is unlikely that there would be one large settlement and no smaller settlements resulting from lesser incidents.

Assume, for example, that one was willing to take the risk that all critical incidents involved with this year's product (over the product life span) had a probability of occurrence of .1. This is equivalent to saying that if the product is manufactured year after year, only once in 10 years, on the average, would the product be responsible for a critical incident. On the basis of 1 million products with an average 5-year life (equivalent to 2 hours/week $\times$ 25 weeks $\times$ 5 years = 250 hours) for a heater used occasionally, the maximum permissible failure rate, λ, would be

$$\lambda = 0.1 \text{ failures}/250 \text{ hours} \times 10^6 \text{ units}$$
$$\lambda = 0.0004 \times 10^{-6} \text{ hours}$$

This may be far beyond a prudent risk and too high a failure frequency even if all of the onus could be placed on the user for poor maintenance.

Table IV-14   Precautions in Using FMEA or FTA

1. In estimating failure rates, reliability, or mean time to failure, it is necessary to use data and estimates judiciously, with full knowledge of their real meaning, the conditions under which they apply, and with reference to the physics and chemistry of failure.
2. Failure rates change with product age—the time in the hands of the user—and the severity of service.
3. Designs released on the basis of a fractional incident rate predicted per life cycle (for example, 0.1 failure per life of product) may still fail—values are averages of many repeated occurrences.
4. Therefore, the expected failure rate during a product's useful life must be very low if a low probability of failure is desired.

The average frequency of events for serious, major, and critical failures that is consistent with prudent design may turn out to be fractional. An estimate of 0.01, 0.1, 0.2, or 0.5 events during the entire product life span does not preclude experiencing one or more events. These events follow a Poisson distribution, so some of these life experiences, even though truly averaging only a fractional event, can result in two or more of these failures during a year of product life. A more complete treatment of the Poisson distribution and other statistical matter can be found in Chap. V. In addition, there are other precautions to be observed (Table IV-14).

Thus far, frequency rates and their derivation from warranty, company experience, or the government-industry data banks have been mentioned. Where no data are available, it is essential that complicated structures and devices be subjected to life and fatigue tests to determine how long they will last and how they could fail.

Some companies assiduously follow these practices. One company manufacturing a device used in nuclear power plants has, between in-house and on-site tests, accumulated 1 billion (1×10^9) cycles of service over 5 years with no product failures. (Note that this converts to a failure rate of less than 0.0001 per 10^6 cycles.) It neither says there will be no failures nor does it assure the quality and reliability or freedom from failure of next year's production. The true value of the failure rate is still unknown—it may be smaller or greater than the present indication, although it is obviously low.

In this instance, the costs of life testing are moderate, but the time to accumulate data is long. The cost of an accident is high and the value of a good historical reliability (freedom from failure) is great. This manufacturer considers it worthwhile to regularly review the life history of all units in the field. Reliable field information is available since the installation sites are known on this high-cost item.

Finally, and most importantly, the value of any procedure is not in its doing but in what use is made of its indications. FMEA is a technique for evaluating potential hazards. The correction, elimination, and reduction of these hazards and the potential losses resulting from warranty and product liability claims is the essential purpose of the exercise. There is no value in the exercise unless safety and economics are improved by eliminating unnecessary hazards, and reducing the levels of severity, frequency, and imperilment of those hazards that cannot be eliminated.

7. THE OPERATOR-DESIGN INTERFACE*

The following general principles of design for minimizing errors in production and use were summarized by Dr. Alan D. Swain of Sandia Laboratories in Albuquerque, New Mexico. Swain emphasizes in particular that the number of possible errors in assembly can be much larger than most designers imagine. In one study, of 23,000 production defects detected by inspection, 82 percent resulted from human actions (Table IV-15). Other things being equal, the fewer the opportunities for error in a job, the fewer errors will be made—up to a point. More errors may be committed because of worker or operator boredom—in performing an oversimplified job. As we shall see in later chapters, locating the exact point at which degradation begins to increase is not an easy task.

(a) *Designers should be willing to accept a design which degrades equipment reliability* **if** *the design will result in an overall increase in system reliability through large increases in operator reliability.*

EXAMPLE: A developmental model of an antiaircraft gun for capital ships had a very small variable error when fired from a fixed test stand at a fixed target. But when the gun was mounted on a vessel and used against moving targets by naval gunners, its variable and constant errors were unacceptable. It turned out that the gun's controls and displays did not permit accurate tracking. This degraded the total "man-gun" system even though the weapon itself could lob shells in a very predictable way. Changes were made that actually reduced the accuracy of the gun when fired from the test stand, but that resulted in a highly accurate man-machine system aboard ship.

(b) *Designers should use the users' frame of reference rather than their own when designing operator controls and displays.*

EXAMPLE: A former cow milker who became a designer could not understand why soldiers had trouble disconnecting a particular connector. They did, and

---

*Adapted in large part from Alan D. Swain *Design Techniques for Improving Human Performance in Production,* 1972 (Revised 1977), pp. 127-140. The book, published by InComTec in England, is available in the United States through the author, 712 Sundown Place SE, Albuquerque, NM 87108.

Table IV-15 Production Error Rates for an Electronic Device Based on Errors over a Five-Week Period*

Type of error	Number of observations	Opportunity per device	Error rate	Probability that device fails given the error
Soldering:				
Splash	47,075	596	0.001	0.08
Excess	47,075	596	0.0005	0.00005
Insufficient	47,075	596	0.002	0.0001
Hole	47,075	596	0.07	0.0001
Damage to a component from a solder burn	103,880	213	0.001	0.05
Transposition:				
2 wires reversed	13,083	22	0.0006	1.0
Polarized diode, etc., wired backwards	2,610	27	0.001	1.0
Capacitor wired backwards	2,610	24	0.001	0.5
Wrong value component used	103,880	213	0.0002	1.0
Omissions:				
Solder joint	47,075	596	0.00005	1.0
Component	103,880	213	0.00003	1.0
Small item such as a lockwasher	103,880	73	0.00003	0.00005
Lead left unclipped	33,000	551	0.00003	0.01
Staking on fastener	59,435	48	0.00003	0.0001
Staking on adjustment	59,435	11	0.00003	0.01

*The data upon which these error rates are based was obtained from an analysis of slightly over 23,000 production defects detected in assembly of electronic equipment. The unit is a relatively complex electronic device containing about 20 subminiature vacuum tubes. Almost all interconnections are by means of printed circuits on six printed-circuit boards.

therefore used pliers to effect the disconnection, even though pliers were forbidden. The designer's knob-twisting ability, when tested, placed him in the 100th percentile of the general population—his wrists and hands were so strong that he didn't need pliers.

EXAMPLE: An electric stove was designed with push-button controls numbered from 1 to 5, where 5 was the least warm position because it meant "most resistance" to the designer. The user's frame of reference is that 5 should mean "hottest."

Designers also tend to be above average in attainments. They may easily forget that a good many users will be below median performance in any ability. This also produces a strong tendency to depend too much on the users' presumed training—especially when pressure is strong (due to time or money problems) for shortcutting human factors principles. In the ordinary world (and even in the military), some people will have received a level of training which is clearly inadequate. Designing to meet their level will generally produce a device which can be used even more reliably by properly skilled individuals. In short, one must design for the 95th percentile (or as some say, the 5th percentile) in the intended user population, rather than for the "median" user.

Functional considerations should be put ahead of aesthetic ones, especially where human errors can be costly.

On one missile control panel there were two separate command channels with controls and displays for each. If one channel failed, the operator would have to immediately move to the other. Yet the displays and controls in the two channels were mirror images—ABC versus CBA. Likewise, very important controls such as emergency stop buttons should be set off from the others, even if it leaves the panel looking unbalanced. An automobile dashboard panel was designed so that the displays and controls were beautifully and symmetrically arranged in a neat row across the dashboard. But the oil warning light was placed at the right (passenger) side of the dash, leaving the driver with poor visual access. The design was aesthetic but not very functional.

Figure IV-25 shows the label on one piece of equipment Swain encountered in his work.

(c) *If stress is a consideration, keep the design as simple as possible. Control movements should be in the direction most users expect to produce action.*

North American light switches are wired so that one flips the switch upward to turn on the lights. When a North American goes to England, he finds it difficult to adjust to the British "population stereotype," which is just the opposite—flip the switch down for lights on. Some equipment designed for NATO has toggle

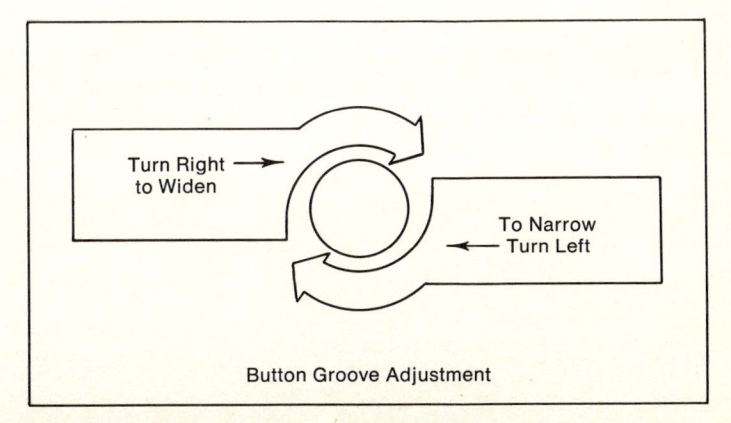

Figure IV-25 A label on a commercial device.

switches placed so they operate sideways. Then everybody is on an equal footing—nobody knows how the switches operate until they're tried.

Occasionally two opposed populational stereotypes coexist, but the contexts are sufficiently different so that errors are not often made. For example, we are used to the idea of a clockwise rotation of an electrical rotary switch to increase some electrical function—the volume control on a radio is a good example. But we are also used to the idea of a counterclockwise rotation of a rotary valve control to increase the flow of some liquid or gas—such as with a water faucet. Many people become upset, in fact, when they visit a hotel where the cold water faucet turns one way and the hot water faucet the other way. This is another case of nonfunctional symmetry.

No matter how well trained or how rational, users tend to revert to the populational stereotype in time of great stress. An automobile driver who for many years has used a car equipped with standard brakes and who then buys one equipped with power brakes will very likely overbrake when traffic conditions require him to stop quickly.

Crane controls frequently consist of off-pivot cranks which require a movement of one's hand to the left to make the crane move to the right (Fig. IV-26). Crane operators evidently get used to this state of affairs sooner or later. Swain wryly relates one incident in which he was the crane operator:

> When suddenly required to reverse the direction of movement of the crane, I instead increased the rate at which a pan of heavy castings was being placed on the bed of a truck. The driver of the truck, who had been giving hand signals to guide the pan, was pinned to the back of his cab. The supervisors decided I was not a suitable crane operator. I still maintain that the incident was clearly a stress-caused error. The truck driver was not especially concerned with the classification of the error.

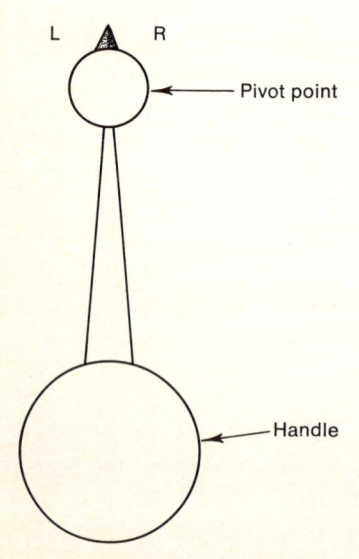

Figure IV-26 Control crank used on crane. Note that hand movement to the right causes crane movement to the left, and vice versa.

Production workers or product users who become fatigued or stressed because of environmental pressures may actually maintain normal accuracy in one or two tasks they consider the most important, while letting accuracy or care degrade on other tasks being done at the same time. This phenomenon is called the "subjective lowered standard" by human factors experts. One implication of this perceptual tunneling for designers is that the most important displays be centrally placed, and that workers and users understand their tasks well enough to know which missteps could cause the most damage—either to themselves or to property.

All this is easy to say, but without special human factors training and a great deal of experience it is difficult for designers to truly put themselves into the shoes of others. A designer's ability to operate an item of equipment in an air-conditioned laboratory is all too often a poor basis on which to judge an operator's ability to use it under the stress of time pressures and adverse industrial environments.

Designers of production equipment and work spaces sometimes find resistance on the part of potential customers to making their workers "too comfortable." The theory is that an uncomfortable operator is an alert operator. All an uncomfortable or stressful design does, however, is make operators more and more aware of their own body movements. This reduces alertness to job signals. The important point is that comfort is not a matter of pleasure—although designers should not make work stations so comfortable that they put operators to sleep—but rather the absence of irrelevant sensation.

Indeed, people tend to settle for a level of job performance which is less than they would normally settle for if the job is considered by them to be unnecessarily difficult or unpleasant. Electronic gear will not be optimally tuned or adjusted if the task requires interacting adjustments so that repeated settings and resettings of controls are required to obtain optimal performance. On one piece of equipment, an electrical adjustment was often improperly made because it required that the operator reach over an exposed high-voltage source.

Sometimes, however, a worker who performs a dangerous task frequently begins to adapt to the element of danger, and safety precautions may be bypassed or ignored. Thus consumers misuse adaptors for three-prong grounded male plugs, because they've determined that the chance of a dangerous short is remote. And people are likely to continue reaching into the discharge chutes of power lawn mowers without turning off the engine—until, that is, they lose a finger or two. In a munitions plant there was a requirement that workers carry only one detonator at a time. Workers who had become used to the idea of working with explosives sometimes ignored the safety rules so they could complete their assembly work more quickly. Dr. Swain says he terminated his observation of one assembly operation when he saw a worker carrying a handful of detonators drop one but catch it on his shoe before it made contact with the cement floor. It is up to designers and employers to reduce such conflicts between safety and getting the job done, for only then is there even a possibility that safety rules will remain in force over long periods.

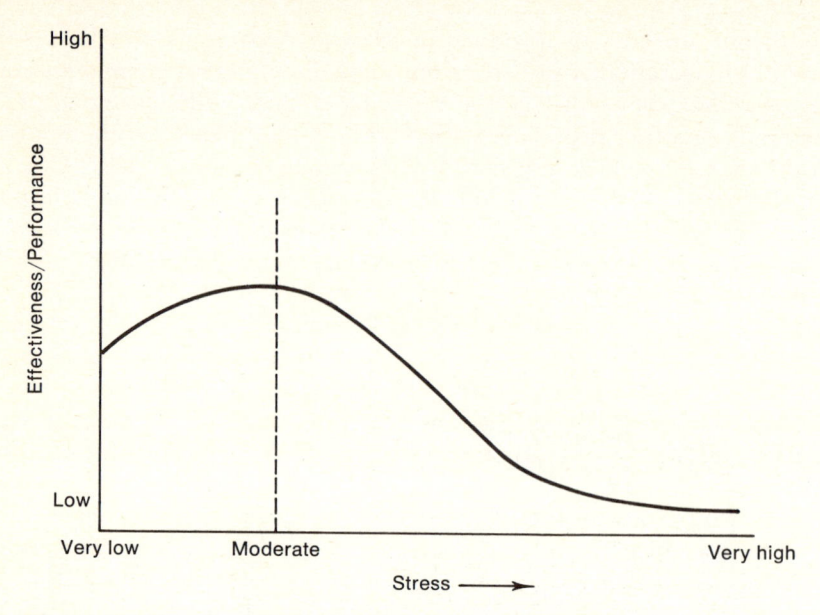

Figure IV-27 Hypothetical relationship between performance and stress. At low stress levels, performance is not necessarily optimal.

Nevertheless, some stress may be desirable. Studies have shown that performance and operator attention are best with some low-to-moderate level of stress, although performance is degraded rapidly as stress increases (Fig. IV-27). It cannot be stated too often that it is undesirable to give the operator a false sense of security. But the exact shape of the stress/performance curve is difficult to determine. It is influenced greatly by the nature of the task and the operator's proficiency. One U.S. Army study of apparently real emergencies[*] showed that experienced soldiers performed better under high stress (i.e., the actual emergency) than under low stress. But the opposite result was obtained with new soldiers. A study of real and simulated aircraft in-flight emergencies[†] showed that of those behaviors critical to coping with the emergencies, 16 percent were ineffective—the behavior did not help to reduce the emergency, or actually made it worse.

A related problem is the rapid falloff in efficiency of individuals in passive monitoring tasks. British and American experiments indicate a half-hour optimum vigilance in such tasks, even for critical jobs where the life of the observer is at stake. This rapid falloff is known as the "vigilance effect" (Fig. IV-28).

---

[*]M. M. Berkun, Performance Decrement Under Psychological Stress, *Human Factors,* 1964, no. 6, p 21.

[†]W. W. Ronan, *Training for Emergency Procedures in Multiengine Aircraft,* AIR-153-53-FR-44, American Institutes for Research, Pittsburgh, Pa., March 1953.

Some inspection tasks in industry show the effect, and some don't. In general, inspection tasks showing the vigilance effect are those in which:

1. The visual or other discriminations are simple
2. The task itself is not very complex or difficult
3. The defect rate being observed is low anyway
4. The task can be classified as "scanning" or "monitoring"; that is, the inspector does not play an active role in the task
5. Inspection is on a continuous basis

Where the average defect rate is low—on the order of 1 percent—a useful estimate is that only 85 percent of the defective units will be detected. However, in tests the detection rate has been shown to vary from 40 percent to over 99 percent among different individuals for the same detection task, and even individual variability has ranged from 45 percent to 100 percent over time.

For critical inspection tasks, therefore, it may sometimes be advisable to provide personnel redundancy. This redundancy must be as independent as possible, however. An "over-the-shoulder" check has relatively little indepen-

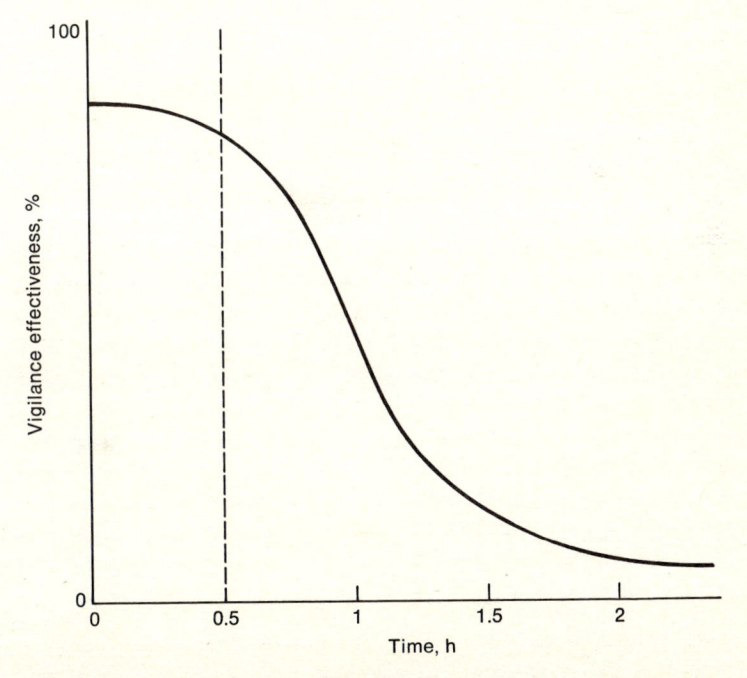

Figure IV-28 Vigilance effect for passive tasks with low signal rate.

dence since it is a monitoring task with all the drawbacks of the vigilance effect described above.

Defect detection rates can sometimes be improved by the use of artificial defects.* If the percentage of expected real defects is less than 1 percent or so, the existence of the artificial defects can serve to keep the inspectors more alert. If they are paid for detecting the artificial defects, and if no attempt is made to fool them with unusual or irrelevant inspection problems, there should be no resentment. Naturally, some independent means of detecting the artificial defects (such as by an invisible dye that fluoresces under ultraviolet light) should be provided to keep them out of the final product stream.

Perhaps the best way to prevent defects from slipping through the inspection process is to redesign the task so that equipment is used to monitor humans, rather than vice versa. The initial design of a fully automatic missile fire control system had displays showing the status of the various fire control functions. But if an operator were not continually following the change in status, it would take him as much as several minutes to determine the status of some functions. This would not be enough time to prevent severe damage to equipment or loss of the missile in some cases. The fire control system had to be redesigned with some manual functions even though these functions could be performed automatically with more speed and greater reliability.

(d) *Instructions for inspection procedures should be carefully written and reinforced with ancillary audiovisual aids wherever they are needed.*

Designers sometimes feel that they will insult the intelligence of assembly and test personnel—or of users—by providing them with detailed information. Designers *will* make these people angry if they provide them with detail for the easy parts of a job, and then gloss over the difficult parts. The same level of detail should *not* be used for all job elements. Consistency in level of written detail is the sign of a lazy manual writer. Don't depend on training as an excuse for avoiding providing detailed instructions for a task. And of course, use plenty of illustrations. For an example of how *not* to write instructions, pick up almost any example of an automobile shop manual. For examples of how to write good instructions, pick up a set of HeathKit instructions for assembling a radio or television set.

The language of potential users or workers must be followed. In one case, the unusual word PAULIN was to be used instead of TARPAULIN to save some money in some manuals. The savings wouldn't begin to pay for the confusion of some users. Had the person making the original suggestion been more clever, however, he would have proposed the shorter, more common, and still correct word TARP. An electronics equipment maintenance manual used

---

*See in particular R. M. McKenzie, On the Accuracy of Inspectors, *Ergonomics*, 1958, no. 1, pp. 258–272, and R. T. Wilkinson, Artificial "Signals" as an Aid to an Inspection Task, *Ergonomics*, 1964, no. 7, pp. 63–72.

exotic color names to describe the desirable hues produced when a large transmitter was properly adjusted. A study was conducted among electronics technicians to see how many of these color names used in the manual they knew: *chartreuse* (yellow green), *cerise* (red), *vermillion* (red), *magenta* (red purple), *turquoise* (light green-blue), *fuchsia* (pink purple), *aqua* (blue green), and *heather* (red purple). No subject knew even a majority of the words. Clearly, color photos would have provided better instructions. Better still, the equipment could have been redesigned with a different method of test readout, to guard against color-blind technicians. This ideal is, unfortunately, often not worthwhile in specialized, few-of-a-kind equipment types.

One manual was rewritten to translate the warning "The batteries in the AN/MSQ-55 could be a lethal source of electrical power under certain conditions" into "LOOK OUT!—This can kill you!"

If job- or use-related information is difficult to find in the written procedures, operators will tend to guess or use "judgment." Studies of maintenance mechanics working on electronic gear show circular behavior—a tendency for them to restrict themselves to three or fewer different hypotheses, usually ones they've tried before. One reason is that trouble-shooting guides have seldom been available (something the military is trying to correct now). In one informal study described by Dr. Swain, operators were given hypothetical troubles and asked to describe the steps needed to correct them. The troubles required the finding of waveforms from maintenance manuals. It took from 30 to 45 minutes to locate such information. Some subjects never did find it (they gave up after an hour).

Likewise, if tolerances for an instrument reading are not stipulated, the operator will assume the tolerances he thinks are reasonable. If a product test calls for 18 volts output, for example, the instructions should provide upper and lower limits. Otherwise, some operators might accept 17 or 19 volts while others might reject any reading below 17.5 or above 18.5 volts. State the nominal value and the range (for example, 18 volts nominal, 16 to 20 acceptable), rather than the conventional (18 $\pm$ 2) because arithmetic errors will be made on even this simple task. You can't get away by only specifying the range (16 to 20 volts) because when the operator has to adjust a tester or tool to some value, some operators will use the lower limit, some the higher limit, and some the midpoint.

It is natural for an operator's mind to wander from the task on repetitious jobs such as the assembly of printed boards. Any operator should be provided with job aids to eliminate the necessity of memorizing the location and orientation of components. On one industrial production line, the error rate for printed board assemblies was reduced 80 percent with the introduction of audio-visual aids which removed the necessity of remembering instructions and also simplified the perceptual aspects of the task. As one supervisor said, "a trained chimpanzee could do the job." Since the task had been boring before the use of the aids, it had been thought that the task would be even more boring after visual aids were introduced. But it turned out that the assemblers preferred the new arrangement because they didn't have to "think" about what they were doing, and could put their minds to more pleasant things like an upcoming weekend trip. In short, in a thinking job, designers have a right to expect judgment and memory (at a certain error rate), but it is not realistic to expect these qualities on a dull, dreary job.

Finally, instructions should not be used in place of good design. A circuit board in which all polar capacitors are placed with polarity band up and one is placed with the band down can only cause grief. Redesign the board so that the bands all face the same way. An electrical junction box with a maze of cables and no handle was built into a large device. When maintenance was required the cables were used as handles, causing subsequent equipment failures. The origin of mysterious footprints on large bombs at one Air Force site was explained when it was discovered that the bombs were being used as workstands for aircraft maintenance. The initial military reaction to the footprints-on-bombs mystery was to paint caution signs on the bombs, warning people not to stand on them. That approach didn't work, nor did direct orders telling the men not to stand on the bombs. A nonmilitary investigator got to the bottom of the matter only by interviewing the workers on a confidential basis. Workstands were provided.

V
PRODUCTION OF MINIMUM-HAZARD PRODUCTS

1. INTRODUCTION

Product safety considerations place increasing burdens on the production process. To put it bluntly, safety considerations change the rules of the game. In most organizations, production departments have evolved various tolerance levels for defects. Operations where mistakes are easy to make tend to be watched more closely than "foolproof" manufacturing steps where errors are occasional.

But what if the product is such that the occasional production error can cause catastrophic failure with a high probability of user injury or property damage? The possibility of having to pay off on a major product liability lawsuit may warp the economics and make mandatory even 100 percent testing of a process step that is *almost* infallible. Alternatively, redesign may be necessary to reduce the consequences of failure of a given part or assembly.

It would be impossible in this book to review all the production techniques and problems of major American industries. But there are a number of things they have in common.

Most importantly, production supervisors should understand what elements of the design are particularly open to production error, from a safety point of view. Excess heat from a welding tool, for instance, could destroy the strength properties of the underlying metal, leaving it open to fatigue after prolonged use—a defect difficult to catch in normal quality-control operations.

In fact, it is good practice to describe all safety-related production steps in writing. This not only alerts the production team to potential problems, it also serves the design function—to be written out, the process has to be thought through. Just think of how many steps there are in even simple tasks, like tying one's shoelace!

Often, the written instructions will require meetings between members of the design and production teams, and direct observation of production on the plant floor. Such written instructions may be in the form of standard work orders, test methods, and schedules, or even as warnings at the top of inspection log sheets or process specification notices.

Table V-1 Production Checklist (suggested by CPSC)

MATERIALS
1. Are material identification procedures adequate to preclude misuse?
2. Are similar but noninterchangeable materials sufficiently segregated?
3. Are materials properly identified?
4. Are sufficient audits and inspections of identification and segregation conducted?

WORK INSTRUCTIONS
1. Are instructions provided when needed?
2. Do they provide necessary and sufficient detail?
3. Are they changed and updated to reflect applicable design and process changes?
4. Are they distributed and utilized as intended?

FACILITIES
1. Are facilities analyzed for adequacy as part of pre-production planning?
2. Are they sufficiently and properly tested to verify capabilities?
3. Are they upgraded or modified concurrent with design or process changes?
4. Are they maintained and checked adequately?
5. Is the work environment (e.g., humidity, temperature and dust limitations) controlled adequately?
6. Do the controls cover all variables affecting product safety?
7. Do the controls adequately cover elements that could distract personnel from proper performance levels?
8. Are audits and inspections performed to verify compliance with federal, state, and local statutes?

PRODUCTION PROCESSES
1. Are adequate work directions provided for "special" production processes?
2. Are personnel sufficiently skilled?
3. Are adequate records maintained?
4. Are the processes sufficiently inspected and controlled?
5. Is adequate action prescribed when "out of control" conditions are detected?

REPAIR AND REWORK ACTIVITIES
1. Are controls provided for original production also implemented for repair operations as applicable?
2. Are adequate work instructions provided for repair items?
3. Are storage and repair activities adequately segregated from other areas?
4. Are records sufficient?
5. Are directions for repair and reporting by distributors, retailers, or third parties adequate?

STORAGE
1. Are adequate protective materials, environmental controls, and facilities provided for handling and storage of parts and assemblies?
2. Do work instructions identify appropriate precautions, including identification of items such as shelf-life limitations?
3. Are audits performed?
4. Is corrective action taken as warranted?

Nevertheless, to produce a safe product, written instructions should not be more detailed than necessary. Long, involved instructions discourage periodic review, and can lead to more attention being paid to the letter of the procedure than to the spirit of the whole operation.

Incoming materials should be carefully logged as to supplier, shipment date, and lot number, if any. This is to help assure traceability in case the material is defective. Where necessary, records of storage conditions should also be kept, or automatically recorded by instrumentation. Some materials for which special care might be required include bulk chemicals, solvents, finishes, electrical equipment carrying high currents or voltages (relays, switches, control panels in particular).

Similar-looking parts with different properties (two springs with the same dimensions and tensioning, but with different surface hardness factors, for example) should be kept strictly segregated, or perhaps given specific color codes (tinted lacquers, painted dots, and so forth). If mix-ups remain frequent, and failure of the part can cause severe safety problems, redesign of one or the other of the similar items could be attempted.

There are numerous standard labeling systems for many types of raw materials. They are especially useful for bulk chemicals, and metals of various finish and strength qualities. These labels are color-coded, and frequently warn

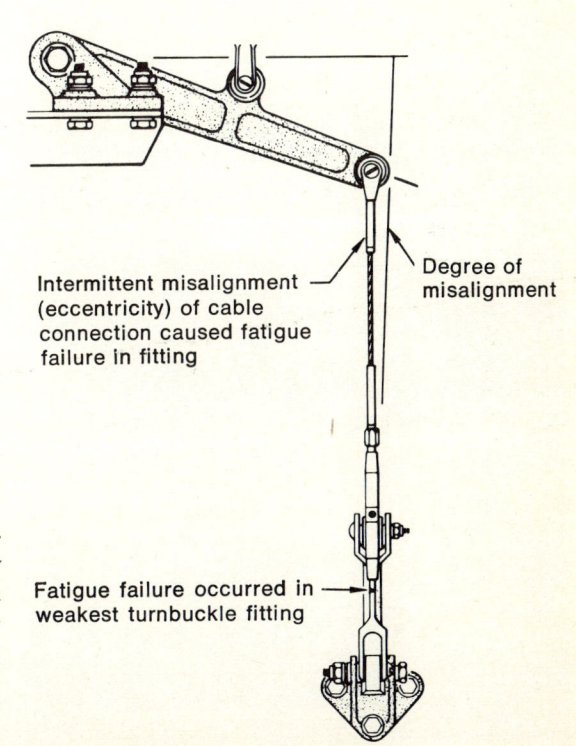

Figure V-1 Subtle assembly errors are difficult to test for—failure occurs in use after many cycles, due to fatigue. Design must prevent these failures, or careful inspection procedures and jigs must be used. (*Air Force Systems Command Design Handbook 1-6.*)

the production work force of potential hazards to health, safety, or the integrity of the raw product itself. Your materials-use system should be established in such a way that critical label warnings remain with the product for as long as possible.

The inspection, storage, and use of critical components from outside vendors is covered in the next section in greater detail, but suffice it to say here that problems imported "from the outside" are at the root of many product liability suits.

Production facilities must be capable of performing at the tolerances required for safety and good product performance. This should be obvious, but is frequently ignored in the rush of production. A good machine is poorly maintained, or simply begins showing signs of wear. A worker begins "playing the odds" against out-of-spec parts, and does not reset his machine as often as the written instructions say. A makeshift machine tool is brought on line to help cope with a production backlog. In short, don't depend on sampling and testing to guard against out-of-spec parts.

Perhaps the biggest problems occur in production processes requiring the application of heat, special adhesives, pressure, and the like. It is difficult, from visual inspection, to pick out a perfect soldered joint from one that will fail after 100 hours of use. It is in such processes especially that money and time spent

Figure V-2 Automatic board-stuffing machine is inserting 78 resistors, one at a time, in 78 separate circuit boards (which will be cut apart after all components have been inserted). The machine is easy to program, making it useful for small runs. (*Avant Guard Devices, Inc.*)

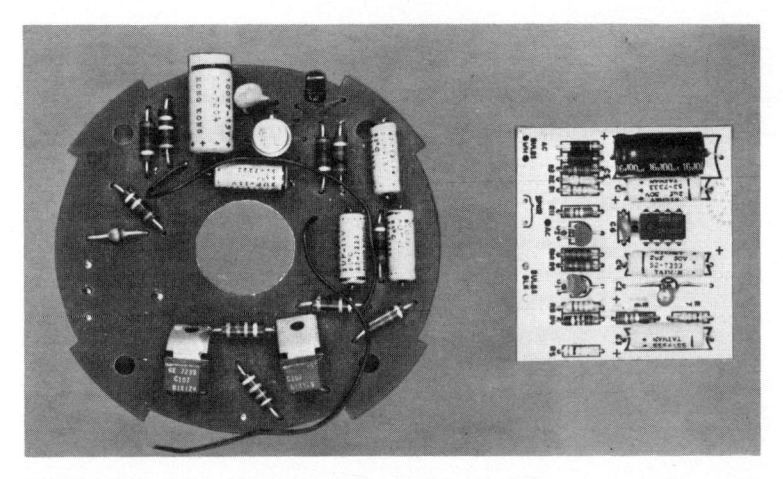

Figure V-3 Because automatic machine can insert components in less space than a human hand needs to work, circuit boards can be designed smaller. Note loose leads and connections in old, round configuration. *(Avant Guard Devices, Inc.)*

assuring quality assembly will help far more than inspection later. And even in cases where this was not so a few years ago, a re-evaluation may be in order now, in light of rising liability costs.

These hard-to-control production processes are often the cause of chronic defects. But the production staff frequently becomes blind to them. Purchasing

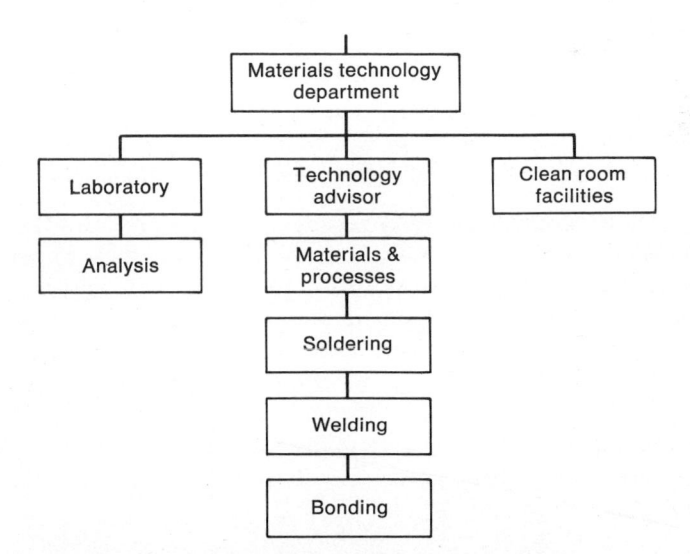

Figure V-4 Materials technology department—one interface between design and production.

knows that 10 percent of scheduled production will be rejected, so it simply orders 10 percent more raw materials and components. Plant managers schedule 10 percent more time than necessary, and so forth. This does not raise problems with higher management, because the defect rate is often budgeted far in advance, year after year.

Rooting out the real cause of such defects can involve real detective work, perhaps even by an outside consultant or a production expert from another division. A spot weld may be failing because of surface contamination, improper temperature, or unforseen stress. A resistor may be blowing because of occasional heat damage caused by inserting an adjacent part, or from transient currents improperly designed for.

Reworked components of finished products are often a source of eventual product failure. The Consumer Product Safety Commission advises that:

1. Material to be repaired or reworked should be carefully tagged to preclude erroneous distribution of rejected products.

2. Products to be reworked should be segregated in storage from acceptable items. It sometimes may be advisable to provide segregated areas for repair operations, especially when special skills or work environments are necessary.

3. Repair procedures should be described in writing, and in detail. One especially troublesome requirement is proper retesting of the repaired product. Do not assume that only the repaired part was cause for rejection in the first place. It is quite possible that the fault hid other problems, or that a new fault was created in fixing the old defect.

4. Reworked and repassed products should be clearly and permanently marked. Sometimes the repair personnel will find a different cause for the defect than was first diagnosed during product testing. Any differences should be clearly noted on worksheets.

5. To facilitate possible product recalls or traces, final product records should note such details as serial numbers, dates of original production, technicians responsible for the repair, and the final inspector. In one case, a batch of home toasters was gathered together and reworked during as much as a month after the batch was made. In that time, a new supplier's switch was phased in. The switch failed in use, and the manufacturer recalled all items from the same batch. Twice as many toasters as expected poured in, because the reworked toasters shared the same lot numbers, although they carried the old switch.

Where repairs or disposal of defective products will be handled by a third party, particular care should go into policing the arrangement. Certification of

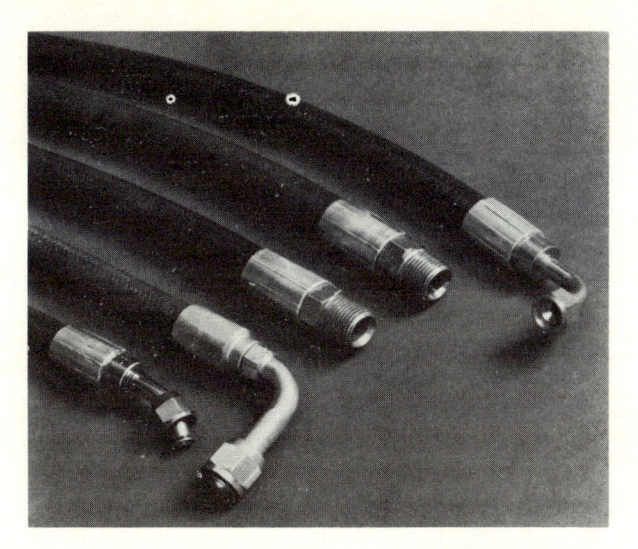

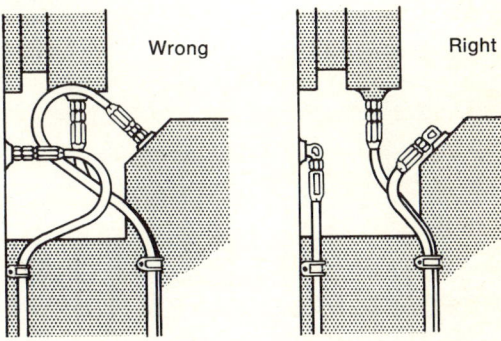

Figure V-5 Specialized fittings for hydraulic hose help prevent kinking and unnecessary flexure. Production supervision must assure that assembly workers have all required fittings on hand—or risk the chance that workers will install the wrong one rather than make a trip to company stores. *(Gates Rubber Co. photo.)*

a repair being made should be required on standardized forms from distributors, and should be checked against shipments before the repaired lot is cleared for sale.

The nation's network of "discount" stores offers a tempting target for fraud. One major consumer goods manufacturer found that out the hard way, when a batch of coffeepots with defective heating elements was handed over to a disposal firm for destruction. Instead, the firm sold the coffeepots to a discount retailer as being in perfect order, but with minor surface imperfections. The manufacturer first realized what happened when customer complaints began flowing in.

Table V-2 The Sometimes Conflicting Duties in the Three Basic Areas of Production Quality Control (Product Assurance Program, Elektronikcentralen.)

Quality assurance	Reliability engineering	Parts and materials
• Prepare, implement, and monitor the product assurance plan	• Perform criticality analyses and maintain critical items list	• Participate in the application review of parts and materials
• Generate quality system directives governing:	• Participate in the review of design, specifications and plans	• Establish and maintain a preferred parts and materials list
• Design and development controls	• Conduct reliability trade-off analyses	• Direct the investigation and analysis of all parts and materials failures
• Identification and traceability	• Conduct failure mode, effect, and criticality analysis	• Participate in parts procurement activities as required by parts procurement plan
• Problem reporting and corrective actions	• Establish reliability models and estimates	
• Co-ordinate training and certification of processes and personnel	• Provide for reliability assessments and apportionments	
• Participate in review of design to establish inspection and test requirements	• Monitor and evaluate effectiveness of co-contractor reliability engineering activities	
• Audit in-house quality activities	• Perform reliability status checks	
• Implement control requirements for procured materials and fabricated articles	• Perform parts applications analysis	
• Prepare inspection and test flow plans		

- Coordinate inspection and test control and the calibration of all measurement and test equipment
- Establish and implement non-conforming material control and review system

SAFETY ASSURANCE

- Prepare, implement and monitor the safety assurance program plan
- Prepare cleanliness, contamination control and handling guidelines
- Analyze and evaluate test data
- Participate in the identification of safety hazards
- Specify reliability requirements in test planning

RELIABILITY CONTROL

- Implement the problem reporting and corrective action system
- Participate in the review of tests program planning
- Perform achieved reliability assessment

2. OUTSIDE SUPPLIERS

The supplier of a tuning assembly changes encapsulating epoxy without telling you. Off-gassing from the new epoxy corrodes a relay contact, causing a short circuit and fire. The manufacturer of the degreasing solvent you buy in bulk changes the formula. Your products begin to fail when inadequately degreased joints give way under stress. Fastening bolts fatigue and fail due to improper heat treatment for your application.

The list is almost endless. What can you do about it? To start with, specify as exactly as possible the performance you want out of the supplier's product. This can be ticklish if you don't want your supplier to know exactly how you are using his product, for competitive reasons. But a good model to follow is one used by most government purchasing agents for their own contracts. Government specifications usually consist of six sections: scope, references, requirements, quality assurance to be provided by supplier, packaging and labeling, and documentation.

The scope is simply a brief description of the item and its function. Usually, any special features of the product are also mentioned in the scope as well. The "function" is usually limited to the part or assembly being supplied ("power supply, input 120 V ac, output 5 V dc"). It does not go into detail about where the part is to be used. A note about "the power supply is to be used in a Z111 combat-rated oscilloscope" is not required.

References can be to the supplier's internal standards, your internal standards, recognized national standards, or a mixture of all three. Avoid the temptation to list all applicable documents, especially if the existing standards are in part contradictory. For example, you may want to specify humidity resistance under a military standard for this class of products, but allow a much greater drift in output voltages than that particular MIL standard specifies. Be aware of differences in testing methodology (look at all the ways to measure output power of home stereo receivers!), and pick tests that will measure parameters the way your design team did in creating the final product design in the first place.

Do not depend on a supplier to tell you that the required referenced standards are contradictory. If you list more than one applying to the same parameter, the supplier will usually be within his rights using the method that's easiest for him to meet. Nevertheless, the requirements section should be as complete as possible. If you know, from other sections of your product, that choice of surface finish, epoxy, or insulating material is critical, tell your supplier—in the contract.

Quality assurance requirements must go beyond the standard instructions for testing so many items in each lot, or so many lots in each production run. They must specify how test records are to be kept by the supplier. In critical chemical work, you may be within your rights to insist upon the type of lab equipment to be used. As an example, dioxin is a stable chemical that often turns up as a byproduct in organo-chlorine compounds. Although it is usually present only in parts-per-billion concentrations (and even parts per trillion), it

Table V-3 Checklist for Use of Outside Suppliers

1. Do you have a standard procedure for assuring safety in items procured from outside suppliers? Is the policy applied to all suppliers?
2. Does the policy allow purchasing agents to pass up low price quotations from suppliers with poor safety records?
3. Are purchase contracts explicit and complete?
4. Are proper sampling and testing procedures followed, both by suppliers and by the manufacturer's receiving department?
5. Are suppliers notified promptly of problems, or are tests made only as production needs the parts?
6. Are suppliers required to report substantial hazards as soon as discovered? To whom?
7. Are critical components easily traceable, through documentation, data codes stamped on them, and so forth?
8. If the part or subassembly conforms to a given government or voluntary standard, is that standard marked on the item?

can cause cancer and death to fetuses in such low concentrations. To measure dioxin at such low levels, sophisticated equipment must be employed in a rigorous manner.

If no existing standard is exactly applicable to the supplier's product, you may even find yourself specifying how his test equipment is to be calibrated.

Packaging and labeling should be specified in any purchase contract. It is ridiculous to insist upon tight testing requirements, and then allow a significant percentage of the product to be damaged on its way from the supplier to your plant. Ideally, the labeling should include standard warnings (poison, flammability, etc.) and mesh with your own inventory requirements.

Finally, documentation should include copies of inspection and test results, changes in design made at the supplier's location, and the standard invoice and shipping documents. Make sure you understand the significance of inspection by a third party. For instance, parts imported from Japan may be inspected by government authorities at the point of export from that country. But the government agency's requirements may not be as tough as those you have set for your supplier.

For critical components, establish a firm chain of documentation from the manufacturer through your plant. Try to avoid purchase through third-party distributors, especially when potential defects are impossible to discern through routine testing. The classic examples continue to be manufacturers of military electronics. They fall prey to "counterfeiters" of high-reliability components such as power transistors and integrated circuits. Usually, the components came off the same assembly lines as the high-quality parts, but were rejected by the

168 PRODUCT SAFETY AND LIABILITY: A DESK REFERENCE

original manufacturer as not suitable for military use. Such components, indistinguishable from high-reliability parts in normal tests, are then given false labels and documentation by shoddy dealers or disposal personnel.

Incoming parts or subassemblies should be tested upon arrival at your plant. This guards against shipping damage and unannounced changes in your supplier's manufacturing process or design, and is a further check upon your supplier's quality control. The tests you plan to impose should also be part of any purchase agreement. What happens when an entire lot turns out bad? Who pays for returning it to the manufacturer? Who pays for costs incurred by you for forced shutdown of the assembly line for lack of raw materials?

There are several ways your purchasing department can help guard against such problems, although none is foolproof. A common testing arrangement, for instance, might call upon your personnel to check incoming subassemblies in lots of 25. Lots that test high are, of course, accepted. Lots that test poorly might be checked one by one for acceptable units, with your supplier paying part of the extra cost (perhaps as a credit against what the return shipping charges would be).

In the electronics industry, which is subject to boom-and-bust cycles and periodic shortages of components, many manufacturers of finished products

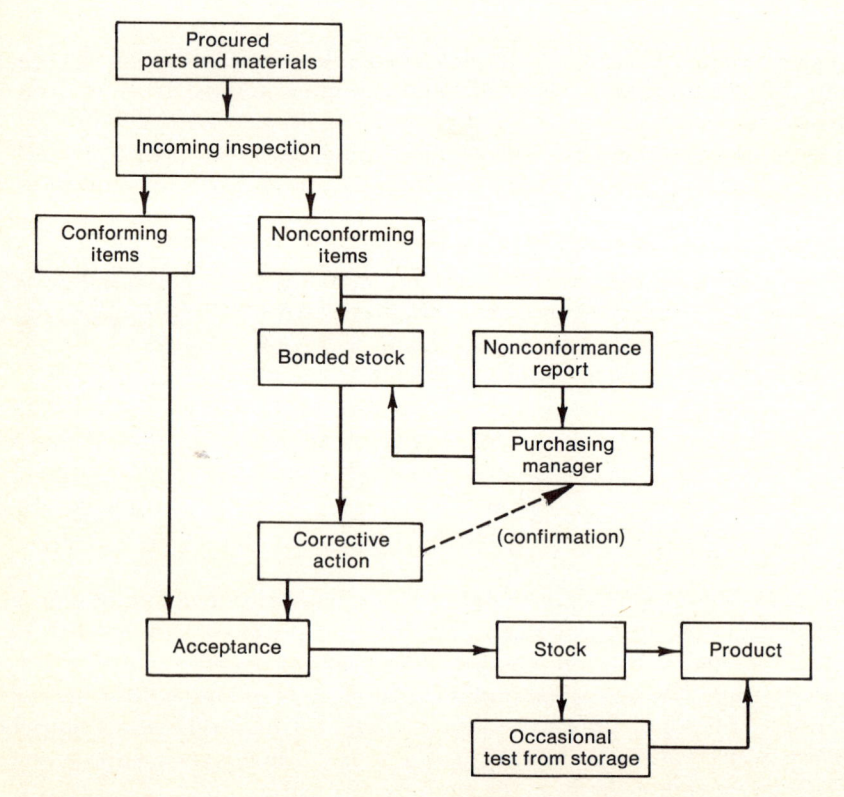

Figure V-6 Flow of materials from outside supplier to stock.

insist on "second-sourcing," that is, buying the same component from two or more manufacturers. Innovative suppliers will sometimes exchange critical data with competitors so there will be a "second source" from which the original equipment manufacturer can buy. This technique can be useful in any industry where an innovative supplier is too small to offer financial indemnity against its own production errors.

For major suppliers, especially suppliers far from your own plant, it can be worthwhile to station your own quality control personnel at the supplier's facility. The American military offers perhaps the best example of this technique, with large resident staffs of officers at major weapons contractors' establishments. This "inspection team" or "quality control team" should be rotated back to your own plant on a regular basis.

In dealing with foreign suppliers, this technique can pay extra benefits. For, despite the existence of the International Standards Organization, national standards often do not travel well across national boundaries. Consider the time frame involved. A standard is developed in the United States by, let's say, the American Society for Testing and Materials. It is then nominated to become an American National Standard. Some two years later, it receives final approval by the American National Standards Institute. It is then passed on to the ISO for consideration, and receives ISO approval three years later.

Meanwhile, ASTM, which by its charter must review each of its standards at least once every five years, has come out with a modification based on better testing equipment! You specify the new standard, without noting the date of issue. Your supplier gets the contract document, finds the equivalent test procedure through the ISO, and happily begins testing, using an outdated method.

To help prevent this sort of thing, you may be advised to append exact copies of the relevant standards to your contract or production agreement. Better yet, send personnel at least to see the supplier's facility, and have them physically turn over the test methodology documents to the proper people there.

Finally, all your suppliers should fully understand and appreciate today's product safety climate, and their responsibilities to notify you and the Consumer Product Safety Commission of any "substantial product hazards" as defined in section 15 of the Consumer Product Safety Act.

In fact, some suppliers have taken the lead in product safety. Dow Chemical, for instance, once refused to sell flexible plastic film bags to a manufacturer who intended to fill them with a caustic drain cleaner. Dow felt the bags were not strong enough for the application, and that the resultant package looked too much like food. A small child, for instance, might be attracted to it, and easily open the package.

Suppliers of various industrial solvents have become more careful about selling them to users with improper ventilation—a care that has grown along with the number of liability suits. Some suppliers insist on a contract clause to the effect that materials supplied "will be used in accordance with applicable Occupational Safety and Health Administration regulations." That's a good first step, but it should be recognized that many OSHA regulations are vague or too weak to protect customer personnel in all circumstances.

3. FAILURE PATTERNS FOR COMPLEX PRODUCTS*

Complex products often follow surprisingly familiar patterns of failure. Consider the data in Table V-4. Assume that one unit was started on test and run

*Adapted from J. M. Juran and F. M. Gryna, Quality Planning and Analysis, McGraw-Hill, 1970.

Table V-4 Failure History for a Unit of Electronic Ground-Support Equipment

Time of failure, infant mortality period		Time of failure, constant failure rate period		Time of failure, wear-out period	
1	7.2	28.1	60.2	100.8	125.8
1.2	7.9	28.2	63.7	102.6	126.6
1.3	8.3	29.0	64.6	103.2	127.7
2.0	8.7	29.9	65.3	104.0	128.4
2.4	9.2	30.6	66.2	104.3	129.2
2.9	9.8	32.4	70.1	105.0	
3.0	10.2	33.0	71.0	105.8	
3.1	10.4	35.3	75.1	106.5	
3.3	11.9	36.1	75.6	110.7	
3.5	13.8	40.1	78.4	112.6	
3.8	14.4	42.8	79.2	113.5	
4.3	15.6	43.7	84.1	114.8	
4.6	16.2	44.5	86.0	115.1	
4.7	17.0	50.4	87.9	117.4	
4.8	17.5	51.2	88.4	118.3	
5.2	19.2	52.0	89.9	119.7	
5.4		53.3	90.8	120.6	
5.9		54.2	91.1	121.0	
6.4		55.6	91.5	122.9	
6.8		56.4	92.1	123.3	
6.9		58.3	97.9	124.5	

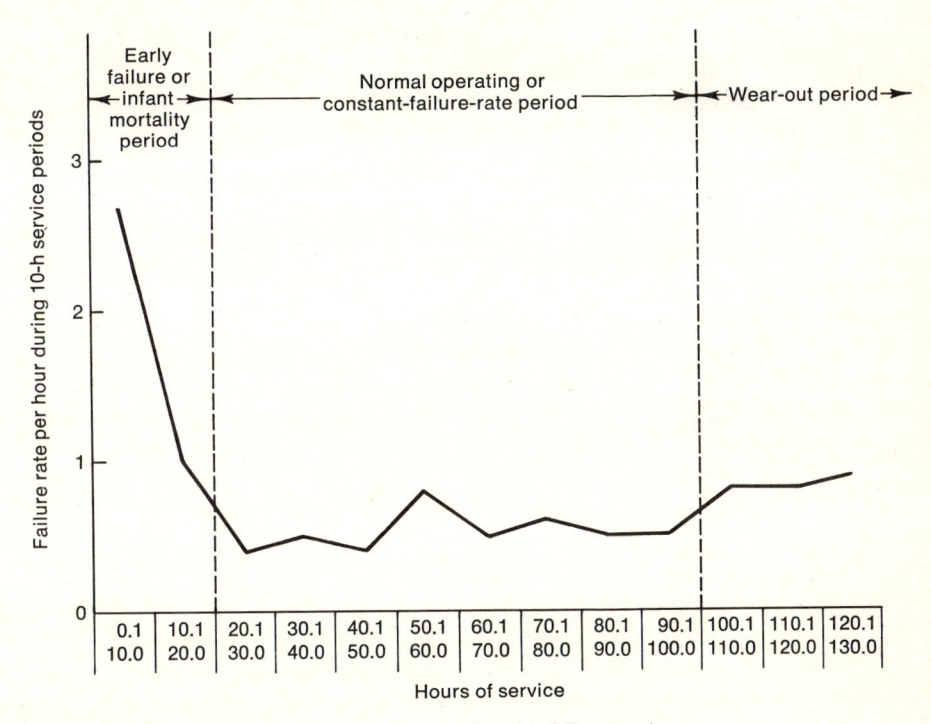

Figure V-7 Failure rate versus time ("bathtub" curve).

until it failed. The time was recorded, the unit repaired, and run again until the next failure. The "failure rate" for the unit can be calculated for equal time intervals as the number of failures per unit time. When the failure rate is plotted against a continuous time scale, the resulting chart (Fig. V-7), known as the "bathtub curve," exhibits three distinct zones:

1. The "infant mortality period." This is characterized by high failure rates which show up early in the product's life. Commonly, they are the result of blunders in manufacture or use of the product, superimposed on the failure that might be expected from design considerations alone.

2. The constant failure rate period. Here the failures result mainly from limitations inherent in the design, in addition to accidents caused by misuse or poor maintenance. A reduction in the basic failure rate usually requires redesign.

3. The "old age" period. These are failures due to simple wearing out—metal becomes embrittled, insulation cracks, and so forth. Reduction or postponement of the failures requires preventive maintenance of these dying components.

For critical applications, it is sometimes possible to "debug" a product by simulated use testing or by overstressing. In electronics, this is known as "burning in." The weak units still fail, but the failure takes place in the test rig rather than in service. Such accelerated testing must reflect actual product use, however. Often such tests produce "hot spots" or fatigue patterns that are not typical of normal use patterns, due to power transients, fast cycling of switches and controls, and the like. This all suggests that statistics is an easy game to play. In fact, however, the game's rules fill many books this size. In this section, the most common errors and pitfalls are described. This is not a game for amateurs!

The users, of course, are concerned with the length of time a product will run without failure. The variation in this time can be studied statistically. In fact, when the failure rate is constant the distribution of time between failures is distributed exponentially. Consider the 42 failure times in the constant failure rate column in Table V-4. The time between failures (TBF) for successive failures can be tallied, and the 41 resulting TBFs can be formed into the frequency distribution shown in Fig. V-8. The distribution is roughly exponential in shape. Note that this applies to the time between failures, and not the *mean* time.

The distribution of time between failures indicates the chance of failure-free operation for the specified time period. The chance of obtaining failure-free operation for a specified period—or longer—can be shown by changing the TBF distribution to a distribution showing the number of intervals equal to or greater than a specified time length (Fig. V-9). If the frequencies are expressed as relative frequencies, they become estimates of the probability of survival. *When the failure rate is constant* (see Chap. IV, Sec. 5 for an expansion of this

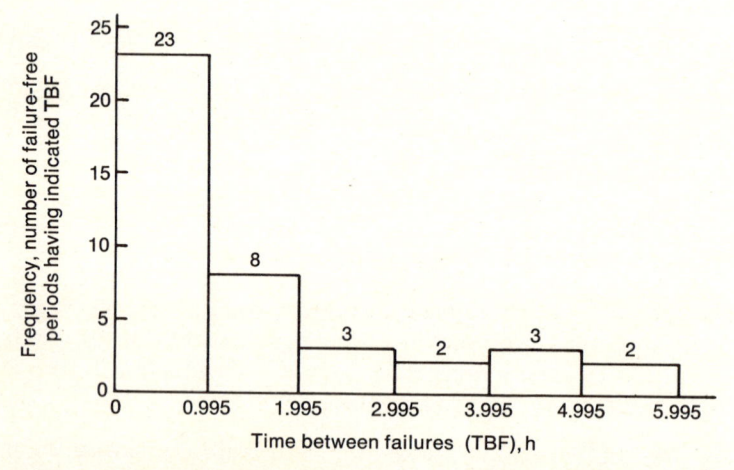

Figure V-8   Histogram of time between failures. *(Data of Fig. V-7.)*

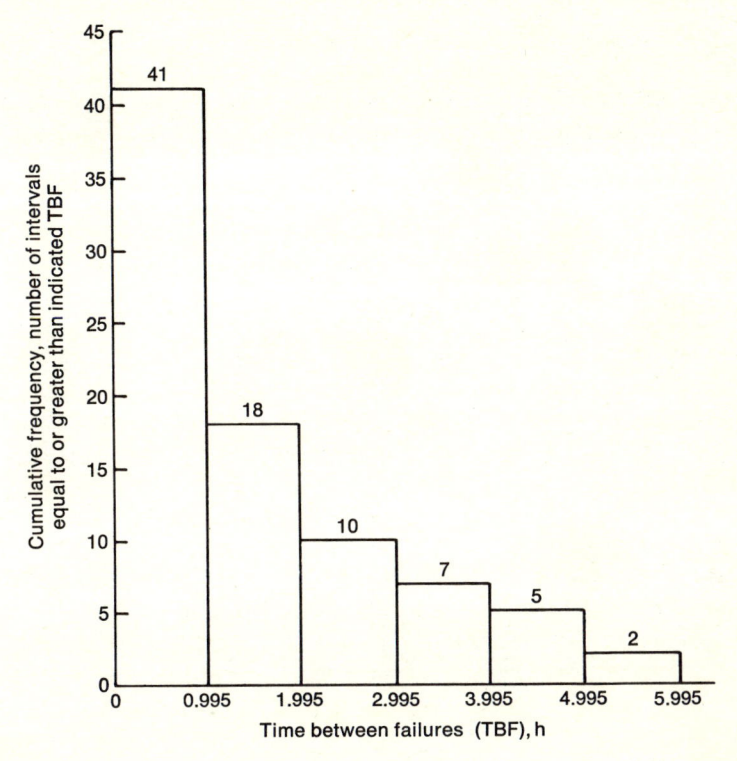

Figure V-9 **Cumulative histogram of time between failures.** *(Data of Fig. V-7.)*

$$P_s = R = e^{-t/u} = e^{-t\lambda}$$

where $P_s = R =$ the probability of failure-free operation for a time period equal to or greater than t
$e = 2.718$
$t =$ a specified period of failure-free operation
$u =$ mean time between failures (the mean or average of the TBF distribution)
$\lambda =$ the failure rate—the reciprocal of u

For example, previous experience shows that the mean time between failures of a radar set is 240 hours. Assuming a constant failure rate, what is the chance of running the set for 24 hours without failure?

$$R = e^{-24/240} = 0.90$$

There is a 90 percent chance of obtaining 24 hours or more of failure-free operation.

The assumption of a constant rate of failure is rightly questioned. However, as published data (Chap. IV, Sec. 5) and the histograms of Figs. V-8 and V-9 suggest, the assumption is a fair one to make in almost any situation.

The "mean time between failure," or MTBF, deserves more attention, however. Many designers and production managers have the intuitive feeling that a product has a 50-50 chance of exceeding an MBTF that has been properly established from test data. The reality is somewhat worse. If the failure rate is constant, the probability that a product will operate without failure for a time equal to or greater than the MTBF is only 37 percent. In the formula, $R = 0.37$ when t equals the MTBF.

Furthermore, the MTBF is not always the most appropriate index for a product. For a product that must operate continuously, for example, the percent of time available for service might be a better measure of performance. In short, the MTBF is not the same as the "operating life" or service life which generally connotes overhaul or replacement time.

Nor does an increase in MTBF result in a proportional increase in reliability (probability of survival). Looking at the formula again, if $t = 1$ hour, the following table can be constructed:

MTBF	R
5	0.82
10	0.90
20	0.95
100	0.99

Thus, a fivefold increase in MTBF from 20 to 100 hours is necessary to increase the reliability by 4 percentage points as compared with a doubling of the MTBF from 5 to 10 hours to get 8 percentage points' increase in reliability. This is important because MTBF is often used as the criterion for making important design and production decisions affecting reliability, whereas the probability of survival for a specified time t may be the more important index.

There are several ways for the statistically naive to partially avoid the MTBF trap. One is to use the reciprocal of MTBF, i.e., the hazard or failure rate. This eliminates confusion with "service life" or "operating life." Another way is to list the reliability over a given service time, instead of as a MTBF.

Reliability of a system (i.e., the probability of survival P_s) is often estimated as the product of the individual reliabilities of the n parts within the system

$$P_s = P_1 P_2 P_3 \ldots P_n$$

PRODUCTION OF MINIMUM-HAZARD PRODUCTS 175

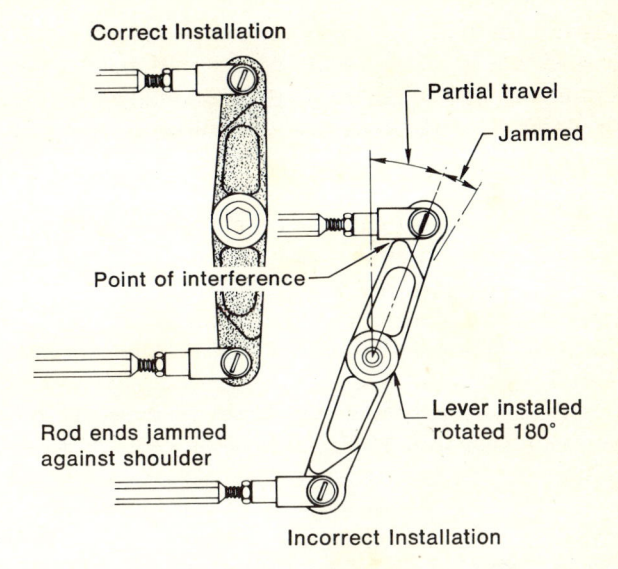

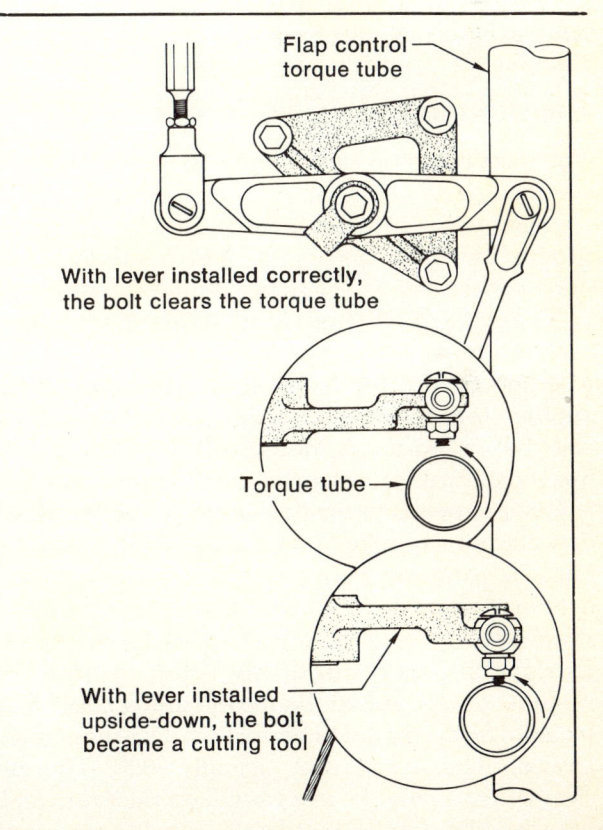

Figure V-10 Incorrect installation of one component (in this case, a bellcrank installed upside-down) can lead to many failures in a complex system. (*Air Force Systems Command Design Handbook 1-6.*)

This is known as the "product rule." It assumes, however, that the failure of any part will cause failure of the system, and, more importantly, for safety considerations, that the reliabilities of the parts are independent of one another—that the failure of one part (say, a cooling fan), is independent of the failure of another (say, an overheated component). Fault tree analyses, when properly done (see Chap. IV), help disentangle the probabilities for designers, but product test personnel often don't get the word.

Aside from these design considerations, there is an irreduceable source of error in any sampling plan that does not look at every item leaving the plant. Historically, the scope of any sampling plan was based on the estimated cost of the plan, versus the estimated cost of repairing or replacing defective products that slip through the quality control department to consumers.

In today's legal climate, however, even one catastrophic failure leading to the death of a consumer can lead to total recall and replacement of the product, as well as to high liability costs. This is not to say that total testing of every item—or even every critical item—is required. It simply means that your sampling philosophy should be adjusted to take into account new sources of risk. Such calculations should be done carefully, for, as we have seen in this chapter, statistics is a tricky business.

4. DESIGNING A SAMPLING PROGRAM

The most common sampling program calls for examination of product lots of specified sizes—15 or 50 or 100 or 1000—for specific attributes such as tensile strength, weight or conductivity. Such attributes should, of course, be related to product reliability and safety. The entire lot is rejected if a certain number of items within it fail to pass the required test.

So far, so good. But manufacturers are loath to discard entire lots on the basis of samples showing inadequacy. Therefore, many manufacturers build in a second chance for "bad" lots. Either the entire lot is passed on the basis of another test of a sample from the lot, or each item in the lot is individually tested for a "go-no go" decision. The individual testing either takes place at the quality control station, or by technicians reworking failed products.

What happens in the first instance, when retesting of a lot is allowed? A well thought out example from the consumers' point of view is provided by David Masselli, formerly a lawyer with the Health Research Group. Under the original regulations for children's sleepwear under the Flammable Fabrics Act, sleepwear was tested in lots of 15. If fewer than four failed any of the various tests, the lot was certified. But if four or more failed, the test series was run again. If the lot passed the second test, it could be certified and sold. If it failed, it had to be destroyed or reworked. The regulators were aiming at a compliance level of about 90 percent (actually 90.3). Therefore, about 10 percent of the sleepwear passing the test would, on the average, be defective. That is, it would not meet the standard set by the regulation as to flammability.

Table V-5 Distinction Between Sporadic and Chronic Quality Problems*

Aspect	Sporadic defects	Chronic defects
Tangible economic loss	Minor	Major
Extent of irritations	Substantial. Sudden problems tend to attract supervisory attention	Small. Continuing nature of trouble leads all concerned to accept it as unavoidable.
Solution required	Restore the status quo	Change the status quo
Data needed	Simple—showing trend of quality with respect to one or two variables such as time or lot number	Complex data, often relating product quality or safety to numerous variables
Data collection plan	Routine—unless potential defect is strongly safety-related	Usually must be specially thought out
Analysis frequency	Very frequent—every hour or every lot	Infrequent. Data often accumulate for months before analysis is made
Data collected	By inspectors, service reps, and so forth, as part of routine work	Often through special experimental procedures
Action by whom?	Usually by line personnel in design or manufacturing	Usually by personnel other than those responsible for meeting the standard.

*After *Quality Planning and Analysis*, by J. M. Juran and Frank M. Gryna, Jr., McGraw-Hill Book Co., 1970.

Juran and Gryna develop the concept of sampling variation using a battery with a 30-hour average desired life as an example. Preliminary data indicate that battery life follows a normal distribution, and the standard deviation is equal to 10 hours. In other words, about two-thirds of the batteries will have a life of from 20 to 40 hours. One sample of four batteries drawn at random from the production run might average 31 hours, but another might average 28, even though all batteries are drawn from the same production process.

The manufacturer, of course, can't continue drawing samples of four. So how reliable is the one four-battery sample upon which the decision must be made to pass or reject the batch? If sampling is continued and averages are calculated for each one, the averages can be compiled into a histogram (Fig. V-11). But this curve of sample averages is narrower than the curve for individual variations, because in calculating the averages, extreme individual values are

Table V-6 Planning Product Tests

1. Determine test requirements and objectives.
2. Review existing data to determine if any existing requirements can be met without tests.
3. Review a preliminary list of planned tests to determine whether economies can be realized by combining individual test requirements.
4. Determine the necessary tests.
5. Allocate time, funds, and effort to perform these tests.
6. Develop test specifications at an appropriate level, or make reference to applicable sections of the system specification to provide direction for later development of test specifications.
7. Assign responsibility for test conduct, monitoring, analysis, and integration.
8. Develop review and approval policies for test reporting procedures and forms.
9. Develop procedures for maintaining test status information throughout the entire program.

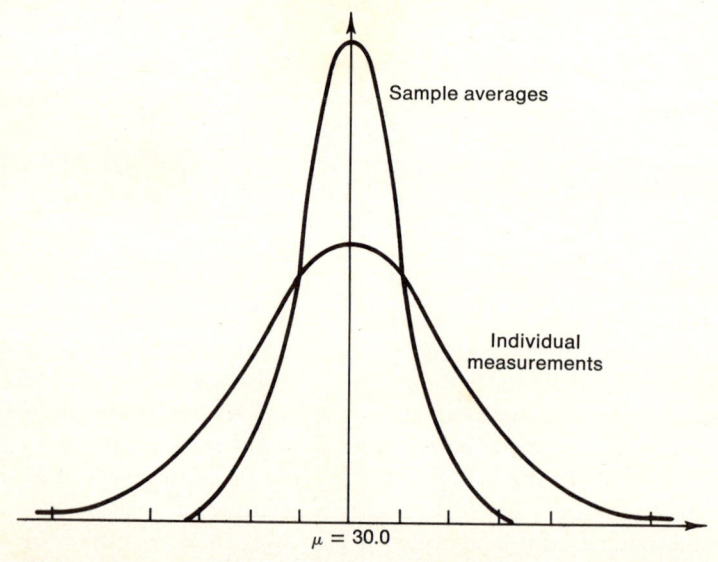

Figure V-11 Distribution of individual and sample averages. *("Continuous" sampling, smoothed curves.)*

offset. It turns out that there is a relationship between the two curves,

$$\overline{SD} = \frac{SD}{\sqrt{n}}$$

Where $\overline{SD}$ = the standard deviation of averages of samples (sometimes called the standard error of the mean)
SD = standard deviation of individual items
n = the number of items in each sample (in this case, four)

If the average exceeds the limits of the individual points, the samples probably are not representative of the entire batch. In practice, one usually hypothesizes an average—in this case 30 hours. If the sample average were different (let's say 36), this could be expressed in standard deviations as follows:

$$\overline{X} = \frac{36 - 30}{10/\sqrt{4}} = 1.2$$

Such errors fall roughly into two classes. If one starts out to evaluate a given hypothesis (the true average is 30.0 hours lifetime), one could reject the hypothesis, even though it happens to be true. Such a "false negative" is called a Type I error. The odds of it happening is the "level of significance," and is often denoted by the Greek lowercase alpha (α).

The second kind of error, Type II, involves accepting a hypothesis that is false. In production work, that means you're passing a product that should have failed the test. It is possible to obtain an acceptable sample result (a Type II error), even if the population has a true average which is not equal to the average stated in the hypothesis. The numerical magnitude of the Type II error (sometimes denoted as Greek uppercase beta, β), depends on the true value of the population average.

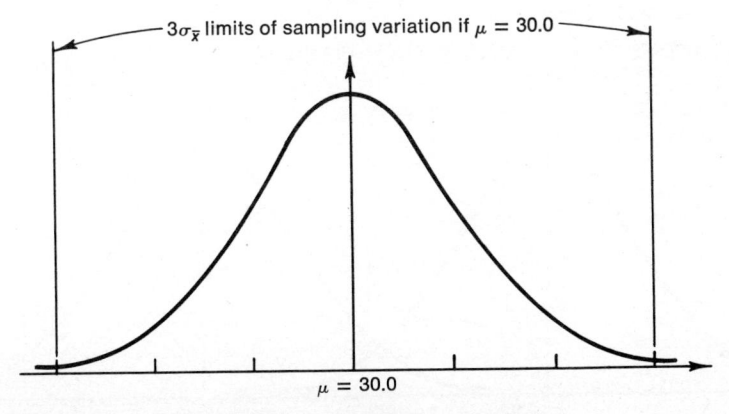

Figure V-12 **Distribution of sample averages.**

This leads to the concept of the operating characteristic curve. Every test of hypothesis has such an OC curve, defining the probability of a Type II error. The Consumer Product Safety Commission has suggested that sampling plans "be examined closely for 'consumer risk' as distinct from 'producer risk' before being specified in an inspection plan. Specifically, it is important to designate the AOQL (Average Outgoing Quality Limit)."

For sampling plans such as described for the batteries, that is, plans that measure certain "attributes" of the product (in this case, service life), a military-developed standard, MIL-STD-105D, is particularly useful. It includes OC curves for both consumer and producer risk for various sampling plans at various probability levels. For sampling plans where only one lot is being tested, it defines consumer risk in terms of a Limiting Quality (LQ). This military standard, titled *Sampling Procedures and Tables for Inspection by Attributes*, is available from the U.S. Government Printing Office (see App. I).

In the battery example, suppose that the Type I error must be 5 percent. The acceptance region can then be obtained by locating values of average battery life which have only a 5 percent chance of being exceeded when the true average life is 30 hours. This acceptance region is shown graphically in Fig. V-15. Remember that the curve represents a population of sample *averages*,

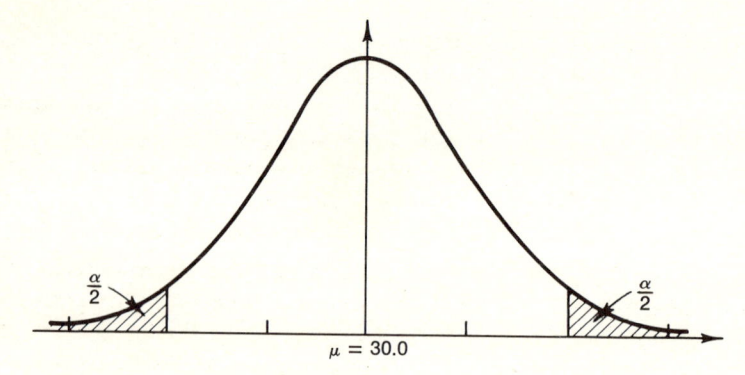

Figure V-13 Type I or alpha (α) error.

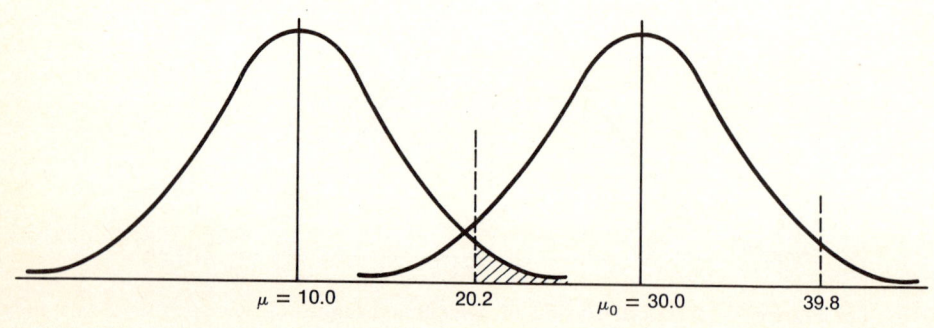

Figure V-14 Type II or beta (β) error.

```
                   ← Acceptance region →
```

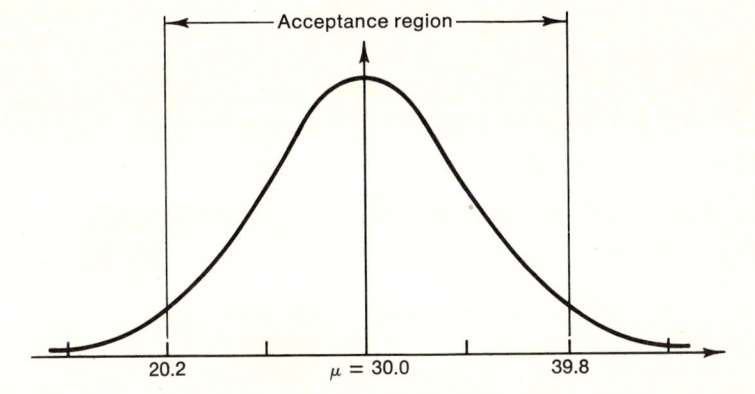

Figure V-15 Acceptance region for battery life 30 hours ($\mu_0 = 30.0$).

because the decision will be made on the basis of a sample average. From a standard table of statistical functions for such "normal" curves, we know that a 2.5 percent area in each tail is at a limit 1.96 standard deviations from 30.0. Thus:

$$\text{Upper limit} = 30 + 1.96 \frac{10}{\sqrt{4}} = 39.8$$

$$\text{Lower limit} = 30 - 1.96 \frac{10}{\sqrt{4}} = 20.2$$

This is close enough to the acceptability range described earlier, of plus or minus 10 hours of service life from the desired 30. If the average of a random sample of four batteries is within this acceptance region, the hypothesis is accepted. If the average falls outside the region, the hypothesis is rejected.

Now construct an OC curve to define the magnitude of the Type II error. Since this error is the probability of accepting the original hypothesis (service life averaging 30 hours) when it is false, the probability of a sample average falling between 20.2 and 39.8 must be found when the true average of the population is equal to something other than 30. Suppose the true average equals 35 hours. Figure V-16 shows the distribution of sample averages and the location of the acceptance region. The Type II error is the shaded area of the figure. It is found by the following calculations:

$$\frac{39.8 - 35}{10/\sqrt{4}} = +0.96 \text{ area greater than } 39.8 = 0.1685$$

$$\frac{20.2 - 35}{10/\sqrt{4}} = -2.96 \text{ area greater than } 20.2 = \frac{0.0015}{0.1700}$$

In other words, if the true average life in the population is 35.0, the probability of selecting a sample of four batteries having an average within the acceptance region is 0.830 (that is, 1 − 0.1700). There is an 83 percent chance of incorrectly accepting the hypothesis that the average service life of the population is 30.

Now suppose the average service life really is 22 hours. Repeating the calculation shows there is a 64 percent chance of incorrectly accepting the hypothesis that the true population average is 30. Repeating the calculations for all possible values of the operating life (let's say from 0 hours to perhaps 60) will form the OC curve shown in Fig. V-17. It is a plot of the probability of accepting the original hypothesis as a function of the true value of the population parameter. Note that for an average equal to the hypothesis (30), the probability of acceptance is 1 − α, or 95 percent, in this example.

The OC curve can be used to set an acceptance region for your product. In the example, the acceptance region was determined by dividing the 5 percent allowable Type I error into two equal parts. The entire 5 percent could have been concentrated at one end of the distribution curve, however. Thus there are three acceptance regions with the same 5 percent error—a two-tailed region, one concentrated in the right tail, and one concentrated in the left tail of the curve. OC curves are different for each.

Sometimes, the manufacturer has some knowledge ahead of time about how the concentration will look. Suppose a new material is being used, of higher average strength than the old. It is reasonable to assume, then, that the average life of the product will be extended, and Type I error will be concentrated at the "high" end of the distribution curve.

As an example (also from Juran and Gryna), a single-cavity molding press has been producing insulators with an average impact strength of 5.15 ft-lb (foot pounds) and with a standard deviation of 0.25 foot-pound. A new lot shows the following data from 12 specimens: 5.02, 4.87, 4.95, 4.88, 5.01, 4.93, 4.91, 5.09, 4.96, 4.89, 5.06, and 4.85 ft-lb. The average strength is 4.95 in this sample of 12.

Assuming a Type I error of 5 percent (0.05), is the new lot significantly different in average impact strength from past lots?

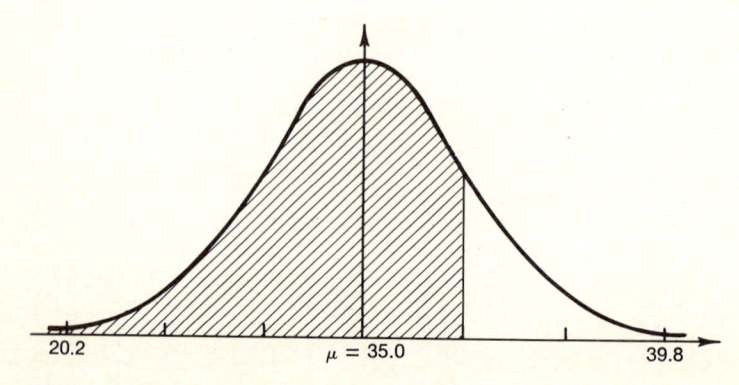

Figure V-16 Acceptance region when $\mu = 35.0$.

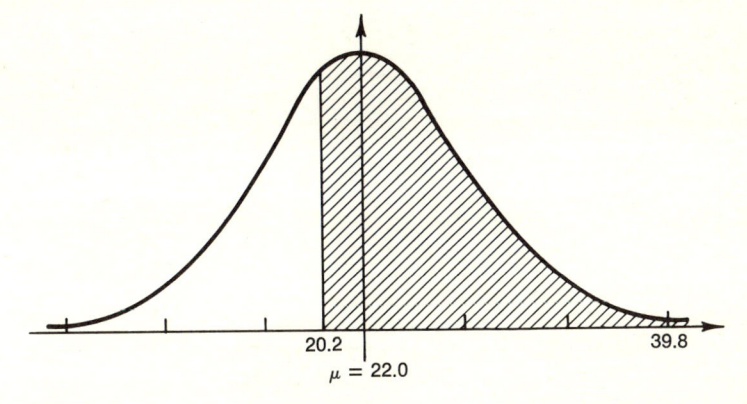

Figure V-17   Acceptance region when $\mu = 22.0$ hours.

With no prior information a two-tail test is applicable. From a table of standard curves, we find that the acceptance region is within 1.96 standard deviations of the average. But the new lot shows:

$$\frac{4.95 - 5.15}{0.25/\sqrt{12}} = -2.75$$

which is outside this limit. Thus the impact strength of the lot is significantly different from previous lots.

Going back to the battery example, note that the acceptance of a hypothesis does not prove that it is correct. It is assumed in such cases that the sample under study represents a population which has not changed from the original population. The sample is simply a piece of evidence used to affirm or deny an assumption. There may have been change, but not of such size that it can be detected with the given sampling technique.

To detect smaller increments, the intuitive remedy—which turns out to be correct in this case—is to increase the sample size. Even if the change is large enough to be observed, the test itself gives only a poor approximation of how big the change actually is. The real amount is more likely to be the observed difference, but it could be smaller or even larger.

Suppose it were important to detect the fact that the average life of the battery cited is 35 hours, and that we want to be 80 percent sure of detecting this change (beta = 0.2). If the true average was 30.0 (as stated in the hypothesis), we want to have only a 5 percent risk of rejecting the hypothesis (alpha = 0.05). Using the OC curve of Fig. V-18, (for a two-tail test that the mean is equal to a specified value),

$$d = \frac{u - u_0}{\text{SD}} = \frac{35 - 30}{10} = 0.5$$

Entering with $d = 0.5$ and beta = 0.2, the curves indicate that a sample size of about 30 is required.

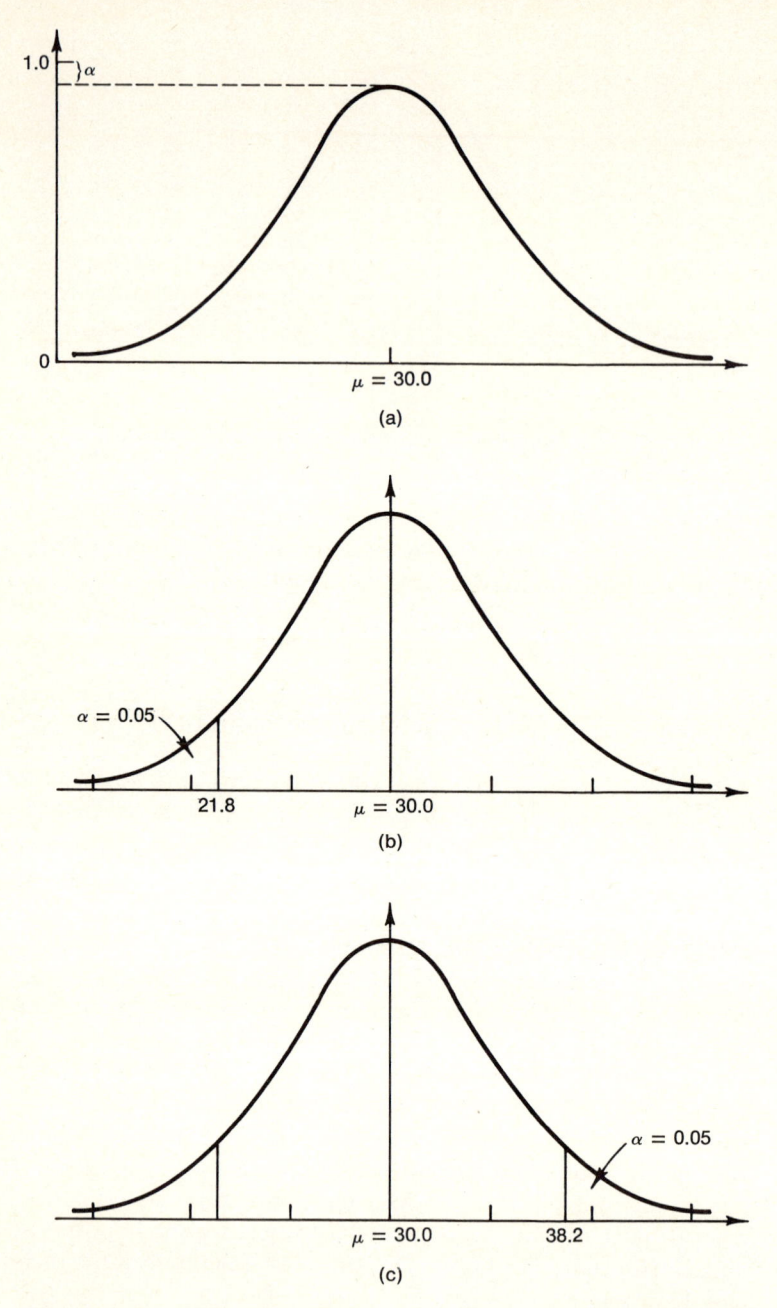

184 PRODUCT SAFETY AND LIABILITY: A DESK REFERENCE

Figure V-18 Operating characteristic curves: (a) normal distribution, (b) entire alpha error on left tail, and (c) entire alpha error on right tail.

One could get by with a smaller sample, but probably at the cost of more sophisticated measuring techniques. For example, there may be a partial link between battery weight, initial voltage, and service life. Therefore, more information can be gleaned from each battery than with the measurement of a single attribute, service life alone.

A particularly useful publication in this regard is MIL-STD-414, *Sampling Procedures for Inspection by Variables for Percent Defective,* also available from the U.S. Government Printing Office (see App. I).

In variables inspection, a certain quality characteristic (weight, length, initial voltage, etc.) is measured for the product. Instead of a "go–no go" decision based on the measurement, the product may fall into a distribution of values ranging around the desired (or nominal) value, as already discussed.

The sampling plan must be carefully designed, and depends strongly on the criticality of the measurements to be made, the extent to which the variability pattern is already known, and the number of specification limits being investigated in each individual item. This can lead the unwary into difficulty using MIL-STD-414, because many complex mathematical functions are reduced to tables of numbers applied mechanically to the problem at hand. The tables are based on the Defense Department's ideas of product acceptability. These may or may not fit the needs of a private manufacturer of consumer products.

To highlight some of the pitfalls, consider an example taken from the standard itself—an example particularly common in industry where production runs can be quite large, the variability in the dimensions to be measured is fairly predictable, and different quality levels are acceptable for the upper and lower specification limits of the variable being examined.

From the manufacturer's point of view, sending sample lots with 10 percent noncomplying items would be self-defeating. For an infinite number of lots, and assuming even distribution, half would fail the test the first time because of unavoidable production variability. The manufacturers must aim higher—or do they?

The test methodology actually set the rejection point between 20 percent (3 of 15) and 27 percent (4 of 15). This was to allow lots with approximately 10 percent defectives to pass 95 percent of the time. As a result, batches of products which are 20 percent defective will actually pass the test 65 percent of the time! The results of the "second chance" are shown below, where p is the probability that a lot has of passing once, and $2p - p^2$ is the probability that the batch will pass one test or the other.

p	$2p - p^2$	*Percentage nonconforming*
.95	0.9975	9.7%
.90	0.99	12
.75	0.938	18
.50	0.75	23
.25	0.4375	32
.10	0.19	39

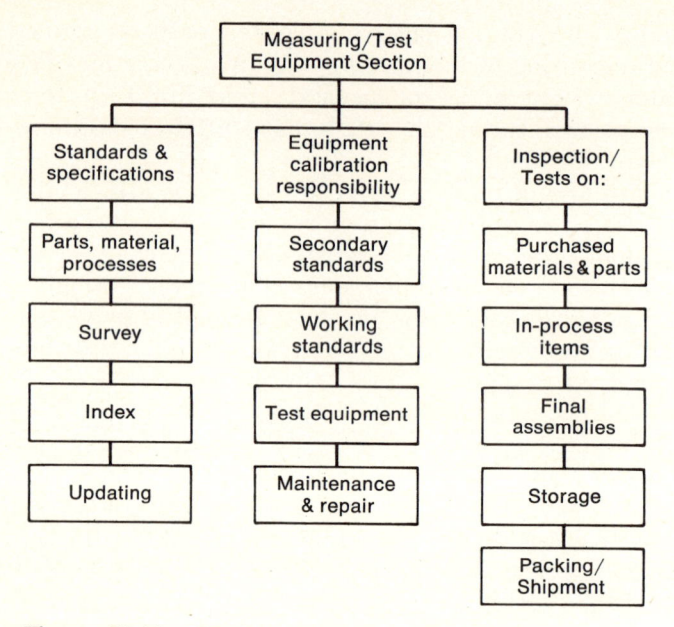

```
                    ┌─────────────────────┐
                    │   Measuring/Test    │
                    │  Equipment Section  │
                    └─────────────────────┘
           ┌──────────────────┼──────────────────┐
    ┌─────────────┐    ┌─────────────┐    ┌─────────────┐
    │ Standards & │    │  Equipment  │    │ Inspection/ │
    │specifications│   │ calibration │    │  Tests on:  │
    │             │    │responsibility│   │             │
    └─────────────┘    └─────────────┘    └─────────────┘
           │                  │                  │
    ┌─────────────┐    ┌─────────────┐    ┌─────────────┐
    │Parts, material,│  │  Secondary  │    │  Purchased  │
    │  processes  │    │  standards  │    │materials & parts│
    └─────────────┘    └─────────────┘    └─────────────┘
           │                  │                  │
    ┌─────────────┐    ┌─────────────┐    ┌─────────────┐
    │   Survey    │    │   Working   │    │  In-process │
    │             │    │  standards  │    │    items    │
    └─────────────┘    └─────────────┘    └─────────────┘
           │                  │                  │
    ┌─────────────┐    ┌─────────────┐    ┌─────────────┐
    │    Index    │    │Test equipment│    │    Final    │
    │             │    │             │    │  assemblies │
    └─────────────┘    └─────────────┘    └─────────────┘
           │                  │                  │
    ┌─────────────┐    ┌─────────────┐    ┌─────────────┐
    │   Updating  │    │ Maintenance │    │   Storage   │
    │             │    │  & repair   │    │             │
    └─────────────┘    └─────────────┘    └─────────────┘
                                                │
                                         ┌─────────────┐
                                         │   Packing/  │
                                         │   Shipment  │
                                         └─────────────┘
```

Figure V-19 Testing departments may have many responsibilities in a large corporation. *(Product Assurance Plan, Elektronikcentralen.)*

The following discussion is not designed to turn readers into statistical experts. It is meant only to show some of the pitfalls of sampling, and the potential effort that may be required to meet safety objectives. See App. I for more detailed references on sampling and testing.

EXAMPLE: The specified maximum and minimum yield points for certain steel castings are 67,000 psi and 58,000 psi respectively. A lot of 500 items is submitted for inspection. Inspection level IV is to be used (this signifies "normal" inspection; it is one of five inspection levels in general Defense Department terminology), with an acceptable quality limit of 1 percent for the upper specification and 2.5 percent for the less critical lower limit. The variability σ, is known to be 3,000 psi. From tables in the standard that relate acceptable quality level, lot size, and confidence level desired (in this case, "normal"), the sample size necessary is determined to be 11. The samples are tested, and the following 11 values are obtained: 62,500; 60,500; 64,000; 59,000; 60,500; 62,000; 61,000; 60,631; 63,000; 62,000; 63,000. The sample mean is

$$\overline{X} = 61,648$$

The variability factor (also from a table) is $v = 1.049$ for this example. From these, and the upper and lower limits desired, two quality indexes are derived (one for each limit):

$$Q_{\text{upper}} = (\text{upper limit} - \overline{X})v/\sigma = 1.87$$
$$Q_{\text{lower}} = (\overline{X} - \text{lower limit})v/\sigma = 1.28$$

For the desired confidence levels and quality limits, these Q values are related in a table to estimated percentages of the lot above the upper limit, and percentages below it, and the percentages are compared with the maximum allowable (gained from another table). In this case, as might be guessed from the sample variability about the mean, the lot does have to be rejected. To be sure, using simple attributes sampling, the sample size would have had to be much larger.

Table V-7 Comparison of Various Sampling Plans: Single, Multiple, Sequential

Characteristic	*Single sampling*	*Multiple sampling*	*Sequential sampling*
Sample size	Known	Average can be computed for various incoming-quality levels. Generally less than single.	Average can be computed for various incoming-quality levels. Generally less than single and multiple.
Decision choices	Accept or reject.	Accept, reject, or take another sample until final sample is selected.	Accept, reject, or test another item.
Predetermined characteristics	Two of the three quantities n, α, and β.	Same as single.	Fix α and β; n is a random variable.
Personnel training	Requires least training.	More trained people required than for single.	Requires most training.
Ease of administration	Easiest. Scheduling can be fairly precise; test-cost estimates can be made.	More difficult than single since the exact number of tests is unknown. Only average test costs can be estimated.	Most difficult in terms of testing, scheduling, and overall administration. Most time-consuming.
Miscellaneous	Best used for testing situations where ease of administration is most important and cost of testing is relatively unimportant.	Has psychological advantage in that supplier is given a "second chance" by taking further samples if first-sample results indicate a marginal lot.	Most efficient test in terms of required sample size. May require approximately 50% of sample size of single sampling plans. Best to use when test costs are most important.

Table V-8 Stratified and Simple Random Sampling Compared *(Air Force Systems Command Design Handbook 1-6)*

Factor	Comparison
Planning of sample	Stratified sampling requires more detailed planning and knowledge of underlying maintenance-task population than does simple random sampling.
Administration of sampling procedure	Stratified sampling includes all administrative aspects of simple random samples plus additional control to meet stratification sample-size criteria.
Analysis of data	Standard analytical methods are based on simple random sampling. Stratified analytical procedures for stratified samples are relatively complex and may not be generally available.
Sampling efficiency	Stratified sampling generally is more efficient than simple random sampling in that variances of sample estimates are lower than for simple random samples.
Sub-hypotheses	Stratified sampling provides a means to test hypotheses on different portions of the system with adequate control. Such control is not generally available for simple random sampling.
Representativeness	Stratified sampling provides assurance that sample observations from each stratum will be observed. Simple random samples can only provide such assurance probabilistically.

Table V-9 Comparison of Attributes Tests with Variables Tests

Factor	Attributes test	Variables test
Type of information yielded	Number or percent of sample that meets some specified characteristic	Observed distribution of some quantitative output
Type of maintainability goal	Median or percentile most commonly used	Mean, median, percentile, and variance are most common
Sample size requirements	Higher than variables test for corresponding plan	Lower than for attributes test for corresponding plan
Ease of application	Data recording and analysis relatively simple	More clerical and analysis costs than for attribute plans
Statistical considerations	Applies to both parametric and nonparametric tests	Requires an assumption on the underlying distribution unless large sample properties are assumed

5. CHANGE CONTROL

Prototypes have been tested, 10,000 units are in the hands of consumers, and your production chief says there's a new surface-finish lacquer that will do the job and save a few cents per item. Does the production chief simply go over to purchasing and order some of the new stuff? Or is the prospective change passed up the line to some central authority? Perhaps the lacquer has an ignition temperature low enough so that excess spilled inside your product's casing can be ignited. Or perhaps its electrical conductivity is high enough so that excess can cause a short circuit.

When it comes to product safety, it seems that no change is small. Large, sophisticated firms follow production changes with computerized record-keeping systems. Small operations often file changes in a single drawer, and in the production chief's head. Many medium-size operations today find themselves awash in a sea of paperwork, change orders bulging out of every nook and corner.

Pratt & Whitney, for example, uses computers, both in batch processing and on-line, to keep track of a common data base for both engineering design, and manufacturing. The data base includes complete engine part design, supporting design information and calculations, supplementary manufacturing information, and inspection criteria. It is unusual among other systems of its nature, in that there are no back-up files. The computerized data base is the official document for everything that happens to an engine, from conception through production.

Lockheed offers a computer graphics system that some firms have already found useful. It links drafting to engineering analysis programs, and can even do the programming for automated machine tools on the assembly line. Com-

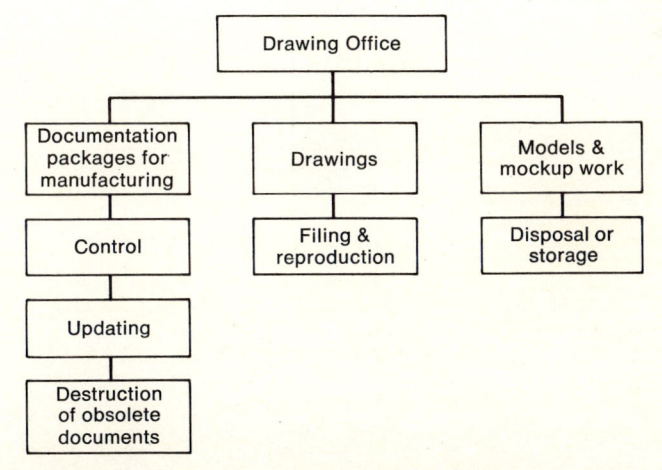

Figure V-20   Typical manual-file drawing and specification office.

puter Aided Manufacturing, Inc., has a simple program designed for batch processing on small machines with as little as 60K memory. It can handle parts classifications in a fairly large matrix, so it should be adaptable to many existing corporate record-keeping systems.

But no matter how sophisticated or simple your system is for keeping track of production changes, the most important thing to remember is that authority to make such changes should be invested in as few people as possible, and that corporate product safety personnel always must be consulted. These key people

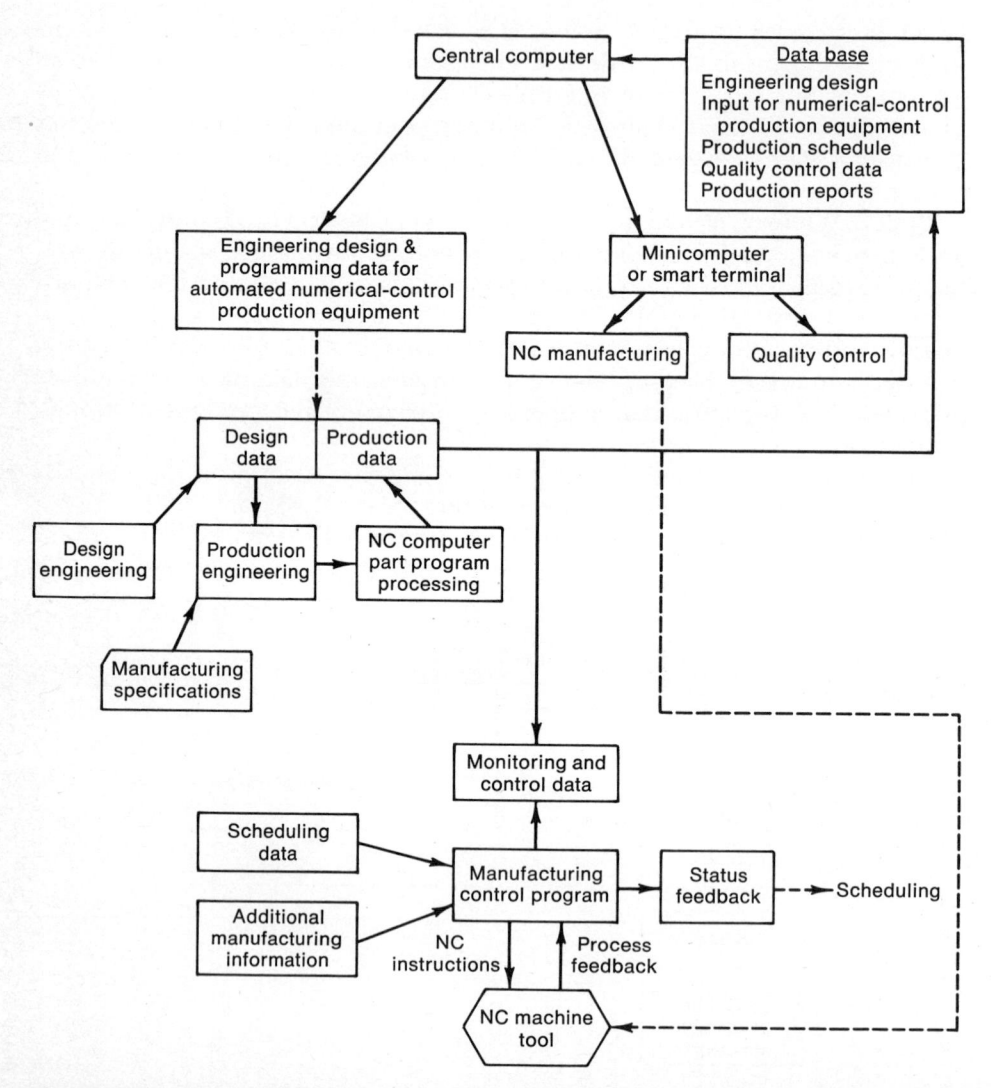

Figure V-21 Recordkeeping and change control as a part of a computer-aided manufacturing operation.

Table V-10 Documentation and Change-Control Checklist (Suggested by CPSC)

1. Is responsibility and authority for safety-related changes clearly assigned?
2. Are safety-related changes clearly delineated and expedited?
3. Is process documentation controlled to assure that it is current with design changes?
4. Do products carry model, part, and serial numbering or other forms of identification that permit traceability?
5. Are arrangements adequate to assure that user manuals, safety instructions, advertising, labeling, and so forth are current with design and production changes?

should also have the responsibility for coordinating changes and transmitting the news to production, purchasing, field service, and even customers if necessary.

Changes made in the heat of a production crisis can come back to haunt management years later. For one year in the mid 1970s, for example, a major refrigerator manufacturer used a circulation-fan motor turning in the opposite direction from models both earlier and later. Replacing that fan motor with one from another year caused the refrigerator to run almost continuously, as warm air was blown directly across the thermostat. Since the refrigerator's exterior did not change much from year to year, mistakes were made frequently by repair personnel.

Although changes from below—that is, due to parts availability or other production and purchasing problems—must be carefully considered, the system should not be so cumbersome that changes from above (especially safety-related changes) cannot be implemented promptly. Many organizations will find it worthwhile to tag "safety related" changes for special attention and prompt action.

To aid traceability and to make sure changes are made only where intended, documents should be carefully coded. One of the easiest codes to administer uses the date of manufacture, maybe followed by the shift or production line number.

Finally, federal, state, and local laws may require that such records be kept for substantial lengths of time. For details, see Appendix F and Chap. II, Sec. 8.

VI
MARKETING, DISTRIBUTION, AND SERVICING

1. THE FEEDBACK CHAIN

Organizing an effective product safety program requires more than formation of "internal" monitoring agents such as the product safety review. It also requires the formation of agents to develop and report information back on your product. This feedback chain should not be considered an afterthought in product development and marketing. It should be a logical outgrowth of the design process. The chain really starts functioning with the preliminary design review, in which corporate management, marketing, production, and purchasing specialists first lay out design requirements. It continues to grow as the design evolves through the preliminary stages and into production.

Both staff and line management groups participate in the chain. In many companies, the focus of the feedback information will be the the product safety director and the director's staff. It is management at that level who must see to it that engineering, production, marketing, field service, and distribution systems all record and get pertinent data on the product back to a central point for analysis, dissemination, and action.

Such a system is called for by the Consumer Product Safety Act of 1972, which states:

> Every person who is a manufacturer, private labeler, or distributor of a consumer product shall establish and maintain such records, make such reports, and provide such information as the Commission may, by rule, reasonably require for the purposes of implementing this Act, or to determine compliance with rules or orders prescribed under this Act. Upon request of an officer or employee duly designated by the Commission, every such manufacturer, private labeler, or distributor shall permit the inspection of appropriate books, records and papers relevant to determining whether such manufacturer, private labeler, or distributor has acted or is acting in compliance with this Act and rules under this Act.

The chain must also operate in both directions. While the design engineer should be able to depend on the corporate-level product safety group to say

Figure VI-1 This installed machine, a hamburger grinder and patty maker, killed a cleaning man when a power switch (arrow) shorted during hosing of the machine with detergent agent. Manufacturer was held partially liable for poor installation. (Irwin Feerst photo.)

how many failures of the washing machine's intake valve have occurred, he or she must also be ready to provide pertinent design safety information to the corporate-level product-safety group.

The design engineer fulfills his or her responsibility to provide the vital "inside" information through careful documentation of his preliminary hazards analysis and all design suggestions or alterations made over the course of the design reviews. All other departments are expected to do the same. For the design engineer, this means that design records must include information on:

1. Interrelationships of primary, initiating, and contributory hazards that may be present, especially in complex systems (Fig. VI-1)

2. Circumstances, conditions, equipment, personnel, and other factors involved in the safety of a product or system

3. Means of avoiding or eliminating specific hazards with better design, procedures, processes, or material selection

4. Controls that may be required for possible hazards (and the best method of incorporating them)

5. The estimated effects of the loss or lack of these controls

6. Safeguards to prevent injury if control of the hazard is lost

If products are sophisticated and the design load heavy, engineering should assign an individual or a team to receive and process records, and to make them available again in times of need.

The corporate task is much harder. There, safety-related material must be collected from diverse sources with varying degrees of sophistication—cus-

Table VI-1 Elements of a Data System*

1. *Organization.* Prior to deciding that data will be collected, a commitment to do something with it—and subsequent analyses—is mandatory. The precise organization of the data collection system can vary widely by industry and product, but whoever has the task of reacting must have as a goal the correction of all product defects as soon as they are confirmed as being caused by or aggravated by the product.

2. *Identification.* A procedure for identifying each end product and its replaceable parts is vital—to take action on an item, you must be able to identify it.

3. *Data sources.* Must be consistent and comprehensive.

4. *Feedback.* Assure that all parties have timely and accurate data (including customers and suppliers). Let others know what's happening.

*After a table in *Data Collection and Reaction,* by H. D. Hulme, Product Liability Prevention Conference, August 1973.

tomer service reports, accident investigations, and internal quality-control documents. Apart from in-plant sources, the product safety group must have safety input from government agencies, voluntary standard-setting organizations, research laboratories, technical and scientific societies, competitors, and knowledgeable people within the industry.

In reviewing this organization periodically for effectiveness, large amounts of potentially useful information can be gleaned. This includes customer satisfaction data, proof of performance of the product for advertising claims, and demand in the market for new products to do similar or related tasks.

In some companies—especially ones making products that have substantial lifetimes and are expected to be maintained and repaired periodically, there can be large dividends from improvements in existing claims and complaint-handling procedures to include product safety feedback. In particular, customer complaints should be fed back to corporate headquarters in a form that can be analyzed for patterns which betray safety-related problems (Fig. VI-2).

To improve and encourage this flow, some companies have found it necessary to have a member of the corporate-level product safety group form or take a position on a committee—normally an offshoot of the product reliability staff—that is charged with getting this data back to management members responsible for product safety. In very large companies, such committees occasionally are composed of a mix of individuals from safety, engineering, manufacturing, and sales, so that products are viewed in total perspective.

To be really effective, this department or committee must work closely with the service department. This is not an easy task—service centers may be geographically remote, and more used to getting data from above than passing it up from below. Nevertheless, the service department has the closest contacts with customers. But seemingly insignificant complaints or claims are often overlooked although they may really indicate a design or production problem.

Take as an example a new model that requires a small spiral spring in a return mechanism. The designers, after due deliberation, rule out existing springs in the company's inventory. Several have the desired shape, strength, and elasticity modulus, but none of the proper size has the surface hardness to stand the slight flexing that will occur as the spring's ends rub against detents in the subassembly's moving parts.

The production department, not having documentation for the choice of the specified spring, grumbles about those "gold-plate designers" and substitutes one from inventory. The substitution goes unnoticed until the new model is in customer hands. Eventually, the springs begin to fail. The service centers replace the springs happily. Cost of the part is small, and the labor costs charged to warranty, if anything, make the service center's financial books look better than ever. The flow of replacement springs is hardly noticed at the corporate level, because although their number is large, the dollar volume is extremely low. Obviously, however, a maintainability problem exists (Fig. VI-3).

Then a product liability claim is filed by a consumer who, seeking to separate

Product	Super Framilator	Serial Number		Period	
Sales		Repairs		Defect ratio	

DEFECT CODE	PERIOD TOTAL	REMARKS
A1 HOUSING		
A2 dents		
A3 finish		
A4 footing adjust		
A5 bell cover weld		
A6 other		
B1 POWER SUPPLY		
B2 exposed conductor		
B3 line cord		
B4 door interlock		
B5 overload resistor		
B6 strain relief housing		
B7 on-off switch		
B8 primary timer		
B9 secondary timer		
B10 thermal cut-out		
B11 fan over-ride		
B12 timer relay protector		
B13 filament		
B14 low-voltage transformer		
B15 high-voltage transformer		
C1 ROTATING PARTS		
C2 shaft		
C3 perambulator 1		
C4 perambulator 2		
C5 frammis cage		
C6 frammis gearing—primary		
C7 frammis gearing—secondary		
C8 main framilator bearing		
C9 framilator bushing		
D1 NO TROUBLE FOUND (contact customer education)		
D2 wrong framilator specified		
D3 insufficient wiring suspected		
D4 low-temperature cycle slow		

PRINCIPAL DEFECT(s)

Code	Repair & cost		symptom and comments
	Total cost		

Figure VI-2   Product defect report for corporate level.

the frozen jaws of the device with his hands, loses three fingers, or has a fragment of broken spring lodge in his eye.

Centralized investigative activity is also necessary because opinions differ within companies as to what claims and complaint information is ultimately valuable. Once management knows from historical data what items are likely to go wrong, it can help refine estimates of the annual cost of having each failure occur—a powerful way of making sure that all levels of management and supervision pay attention to customer and service data.

Some companies are able to calculate these costs monthly and subtract them from the annualized profit being projected. This figure is then an estimate of the amount that will be spent in the coming year due to errors or omissions that occurred in the period preceding the report.

It is vitally important, as most legal departments will indicate, that all documents showing the opportunity for product improvement be accompanied by documents attesting to the fact that the improvement was made. Alternatively, suggestions for potential safety improvements that are preliminary should say so. Decisions not to go ahead with a suggested safety improvement

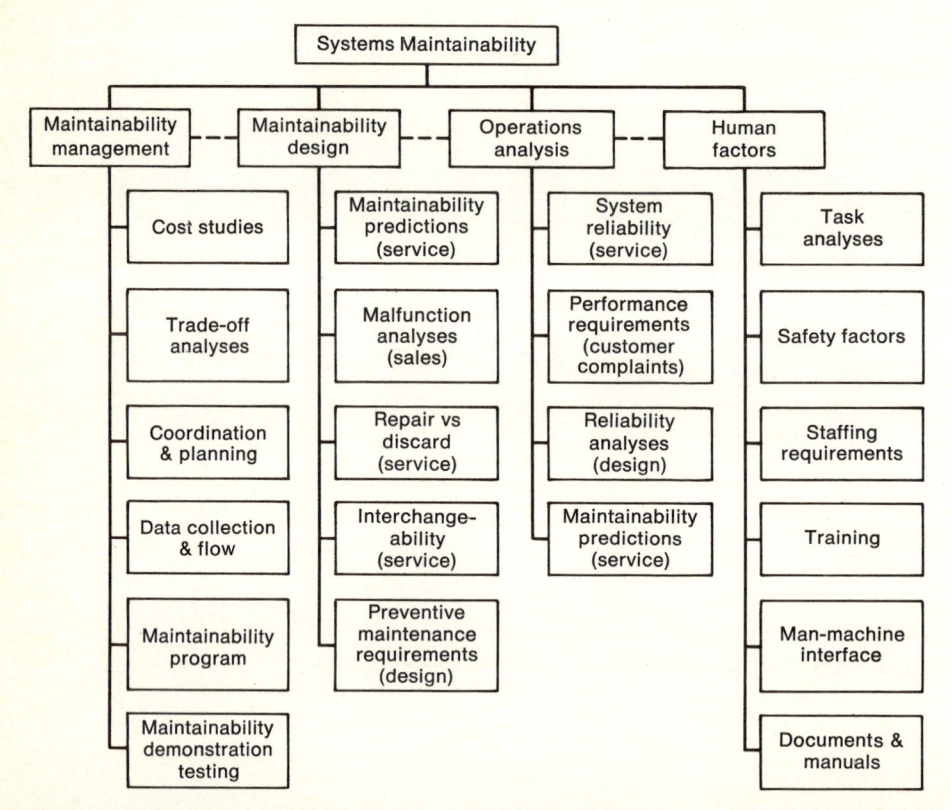

```
                         Systems Maintainability
        ┌──────────────┬──────────┴─────────┬──────────────┐
 Maintainability   Maintainability      Operations        Human
   management         design              analysis        factors

   Cost studies    Maintainability      System          Task
                   predictions          reliability     analyses
                   (service)            (service)

   Trade-off       Malfunction          Performance     Safety factors
   analyses        analyses             requirements
                   (sales)              (customer
                                        complaints)

   Coordination    Repair vs            Reliability     Staffing
   & planning      discard              analyses        requirements
                   (service)            (design)

   Data collection Interchange-         Maintainability Training
   & flow          ability              predictions
                   (service)            (service)

   Maintainability Preventive                           Man-machine
   program         maintenance                          interface
                   requirements
                   (design)

   Maintainability                                      Documents &
   demonstration                                        manuals
   testing
```

Figure VI-3 Maintainability factors interface with other corporate sectors.
(Adapted from Air Force Systems Command Design Handbook 1-6.)

Product ______________ Serial numbers ________ ________ ________

Returned for servicing (month) ________

Final entry (date) ____/____/____ Prepared by ______________

	Serial Number	Repair details	(Office use) Units repaired	Code
ADJUSTMENTS				
ELECTRICAL				
MECHANICAL				

Comments

Total repaired	
No trouble found	
Defect ratio	

Figure VI-4 Product defect report from service center.

should be carefully resolved for the record. Some attorneys and designers faced with product liability problems would rather that all records simply disappear, and all safety-related discussions be handled orally. But dangling solutions indicate that the product safety group is not performing effectively, that design teams are not paying enough attention to safety, and that, in the event of a product liability suit, the company will have little defense.

```
------------------------REPAIR AUTHORIZATION----------03/22/77--
                              NET    UN-
         EQ. CODE      REP    IP     REP    AUTH.       DN         PX        SL
         103A3          0      3     40      17       10( 27)    6( 12)    1(  1)
         103F2          2     10      4       4        1(  1)    1(  1)    2(  2)
         103G4          0      0      1       1        1(  1)    0(  0)    0(  0)
         103G5          0      1      1       1        1(  1)    0(  0)    0(  0)
         113AL1/2       0      6      2       2        0(  0)    1(  1)    1(  1)
         113AL1A        0      3      3       3        2(  2)    0(  0)    1(  1)
         113AL1A/2      0      0      3       3        2(  2)    0(  0)    1(  1)
         113BL1         2      4     21      21        5(  5)   16( 16)    0(  0)
         201AL1A2A36A
         7A             8      3      2       2        2(  2)    0(  0)    0(  0)
         201A3          9      4      6       6        4(  4)    1(  1)    1(  1)
         201CL1/2/3     1      3      1       1        1(  1)    0(  0)    0(  0)
         201CL1/2/3/4   5      7     28      21        9(  9)    9( 16)    3(  3)
         201CL1/2/4/5   0     12     47      47       16( 16)   28( 28)    3(  3)
         201CL1/2/5    19      1      3       3        0(  0)    3(  3)    0(  0)
         202C12         0      0      1       1        1(  1)    0(  0)    0(  0)
         202D2          0      1      1       1        1(  1)    0(  0)    0(  0)
         202D3          4      0      2       2        2(  2)    0(  0)    0(  0)
         202D4          2      1      1       1        1(  1)    0(  0)    0(  0)
         202RL1/2       2      0      1       1        1(  1)    0(  0)    0(  0)
         202SL1         1      0      1       1        1(  1)              0(  0)



         804A3          0      1      6                   6)    1(  1)    1(   )
         804A6          0      1      6       6        6(  6)    0(  0)    0(  0)
         804A8          0      0      1       1        1(  1)    0(  0)    0(  0)
         804TL1/2       0      0      3       3        3(  3)    0(  0)    0(  0)
         806A2          1      1      1       1        1(  1)    0(  0)    0(  0)
         806A3          0      1      2       2        2(  2)    0(  0)    0(  0)
         829AL1         0      9     13      13       13( 13)    0(  0)    0(  0)
         829BL1         0      5     36      36       11( 11)   25( 25)    0(  0)
         829CL1         0     32      4       4        4(  4)    0(  0)    0(  0)

         TOTAL REPAIR QUANTITY:      337
         TOTAL REPAIR COST     :   50582
         CUTOFF INDEX          :    0.500
         ---------------------------END----------------------------------
```

Figure VI-5 Computerized repair data from Bell Systems. *(Copyright © 1977, Bell Telephone Laboratories, Inc.; reproduced with permission from the* Bell Laboratories Record, *July/August 1977, p. 186.)*

Repair recommendation. This output gives the Operating Company equipment code, total repaired (REP), unrepaired (UNREP), and in-repair-process (NET IP) inventory, and total repairs recommended (AUTH) for the entire company. The remainder of the report shows repair allocations at individual service centers. The numbers in parentheses under each service-center code are the center's available unrepaired inventories; the numbers not in parentheses are the repairs recommended. The three service centers in this example are Denver, Phoenix, and Salt Lake City.

Because records retention can become cumbersome, the corporate-level product safety group should standardize the form these records take (Fig. VI-4). Even if the company files such records in a predominantly manual system now, the forms should be set up for eventual keyboarding into a computer. One way to do this is to establish standardized data sheets with identical categories, arrangements, and requests for detail, for distribution to all departments. This will enable the design engineer and others in the company to judge how much detail will be expected of them. It also allows comparability with other departments (Fig. VI-5).

A first step in standardizing such data sheets is to define terms used. The same definition for each product safety term must be used throughout the company. Words like "hazard," "danger," "damage," "safety," and "risk" can be used in different ways by different people (see App. J). What's more, unless definitions are settled upon, there can be no guarantee that one department's records can be related to another's, even if the reporting forms are identical.

Regardless of how the information is stored—manually in files, on computer, or in simple situations, in loose-leaf service and production manuals—it should be divided on a product-by-product basis. Subcategories within each product grouping should be broadly divided into three areas—inherent hazard properties or characteristics of the product, material and human failures, and natural environmental stresses. Documentation of design reviews and design modifications resulting from these reviews could profitably be organized into the same three categories.

Because the records retention and compilation system must be complete and comprehensive, it will add much to corporate expenses in a potentially significant way. Therefore, the wholehearted and continuing backing of management is necessary. Looking ahead, the problem may be getting worse. "Today it is a case of having the records to support products that you have put on the market," said one engineer. "Tomorrow companies will likely have to retain records of product variations that never got to market—and why they didn't."

In the end, the corporate safety data will include:

Customer specifications

Research and product development documentation

Design and standards information

Production requirements and instructions to personnel

Inspection procedures

Standards compliance documentation

Material review records

Reports of process, product, and system audits

Quality control reports

Outside lab examinations and reports

Customer complaints and actions taken

Advertising materials and other information supplied to the consumer

To keep from being overwhelmed, it is imperative that the system be designed to recognize and keep only the most vital information on immediate recall.

2. THE RESPONSIBILITY TO WARN

In spite of all reasonable efforts to design away specific safety hazards, in certain instances some degree of hazard may remain inherent to the product. Therefore, it is an additional task of the design engineer and of the product safety group as a whole to organize a systematic procedure for dealing with hazards inherent to the well-designed product.

This procedure should include safety-caution messages inserted into operator's manuals, safety warning signs on machines, and predelivery, safety-oriented information for all those who come into contact with the product.

Most companies rely on staff groups of technical writers to produce warning and/or advisory information. However, the design engineer has the first responsibility of providing the various elements of the product safety group with recommendations for user-operator warning. Some companies believe so strongly that user warning is a function of design that design engineers with an ability to write clear and concise explanations of safety problems are being recruited for this task. It has been recognized that safety warning is no longer merely a public relations function. Nor is it only legal forethought.

Inscription on the packaging of Ford Motor Company's Autolite spark plugs:

"Contents conform to Federal Motor Vehicle Safety Standards, if any are applicable." (1970)

During the preliminary hazards analysis the design engineer should draw up a list of all individuals who are likely to come into contact with the product from the time it leaves the drawing board to the time it is no longer serviceable. Such a list would include, for example, those who must handle the product in the factory, in delivery, the dealer or retailer, the installer and serviceman, and, of course, the user of the product.

In each case the design engineer should ask himself what sort of warning information is required to protect specific individuals who come into contact with the product. The design engineer should rely on data obtained from the corporate-level product safety group to determine what man-machine problems pose the greatest problem for similar products. Questions that should be asked by the design engineer include:

1. Is information required for the safe starting of the product?
2. Can special adjustment of controls contribute to safe operation of the product?
3. Are there special techniques that can ensure a safe shutdown of the product?
4. Are there special maintenance requirements that can contribute to the safety of the product?
5. Are there recommended procedures for installing and/or hooking up the product?
6. Is special information necessary for safe disassembly and repair?

The next question for the design engineer should be where and how various individuals come into contact with the product. If a serviceman works inside the product, warning instructions on the bottom or top of the product may not be readily apparent. If a manual is used to provide installation instructions, the manual could become separated from the product. Likewise, if operation or maintenance warnings are located on removable panels of the product, warnings can be lost when the panels are discarded or lost.

Once the design engineer has identified the individuals who need warning and the locations for that warning, the next consideration should be the form the warning should take. Again, the design engineer should rely on the product safety group to supply information on the environment of the product—information obtained from service departments. Warnings that are issued with the product must last as long as the product does. This means that they must stand up to high and low temperatures, dirt, grease and oil, and operator abuse. The design engineer must decide what warning medium is best suited for both the man and the machine. Basic considerations should be whether to use manuals or instructions stamped on the product, accompanying manuals, or warning colors.

Most safety engineers agree that the best warning information cannot be separated from the product itself. In some cases where lengthy explanations are necessary, companies have gone so far as to chain manuals to their products to prevent separation and loss of warning instructions. Use of color can be a good warning device but the engineer should make careful review of what warning colors are currently being used in the industry and whether there are any governmental requirements—like OSHA, for example—that stipulate what colors should be used to indicate specific dangers. The design engineer should always remember that the man half of the man-machine interface can be counted upon not to read lengthy and involved warning documents or messages. The design engineer also must always be aware that warning is only second best to the actual elimination of the hazard.

At this preliminary hazards analysis stage, the engineer should consult the legal and advertising departments, either informally or through the product

SECTION A—SAFETY SIGNS

⚠ **DANGER**
Stay clear while beaters are turning

Agricultural

⚠ **WARNING**
Pressure cooling system
Remove cap slowly

Industrial

⚠ **WARNING**
Pressure cooling system
Remove cap slowly

⚠ **CAUTION**
1. Keep all shields in place.
2. Make certain everyone is clear of machine before starting engine or operation.
3. Stop engine, lower implement to ground and shift to "PARK" before dismounting. Wait for all movement to stop before servicing machinery.
4. Keep hands, feet and clothing away from power-driven parts.
5. Keep others off equipment unless observation seat or platform is provided.
6. Reduce speed when turning or applying individual brakes.
7. Couple brake pedals together for road travel and use flashing warning lights on highway unless prohibited by law.

⚠ **CAUTION**
1. Keep all shields in place.
2. Make certain everyone is clear of machine before starting engine or operation.
3. Stop engine, lower implement to ground and shift to "PARK" before dismounting. Wait for all movement to stop before servicing machinery.
4. Keep hands, feet and clothing away from power-driven parts.
5. Keep others off equipment unless observation seat or platform is provided.
6. Reduce speed when turning or applying individual brakes.
7. Couple brake pedals together for road travel and use flashing warning lights on highway unless prohibited by law.

Figure VI-6 Sampling of warning signs by John Deere. The company's design manual includes details on type sizes and styles, the material from which the warning sign is to be made, and details of procedure for clearing finished signs with the company legal department. The originals are printed in bright, Day-Glo colors. (© *John Deere.*)

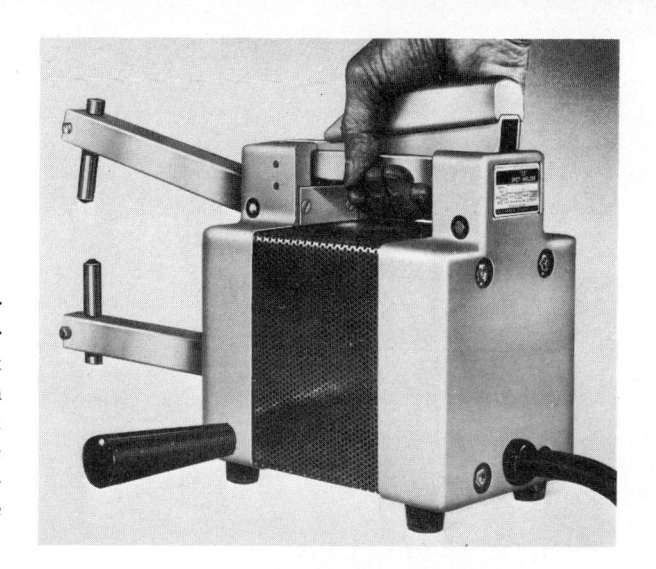

Figure VI-7 Advertising for spot welder for consumer and light-industrial market shows machine being held in unprotected hand and in an unsafe manner (in use, the user's other hand would normally grasp the side handle projecting at left).

Figure VI-8 Warning sign on door of laser laboratory is standardized by Food and Drug Administration regulation. Occupational rules of American National Standards Institute also mandate safety glasses and knocking before entering. Photo shows Sid Charschan of Western Electric, who chaired committee that wrote the rule.

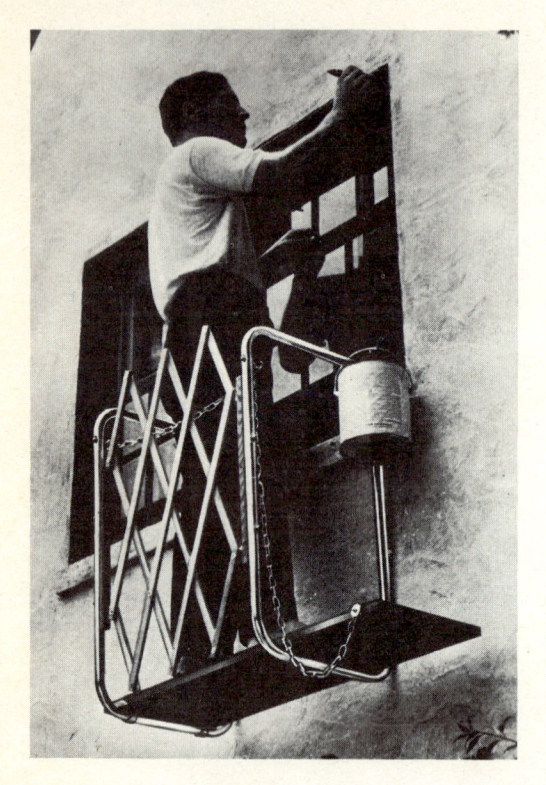

Figure VI-9 Advertising brochure for this portable scaffolding said the device meets OSHA standards; also said it could be used to "wash and paint outside high-level windows in complete safety." In fact, there are no standards for this specific device.

safety group, if that group has such information available, to see whether any implied warranties will be offered with the product. Generally the design engineer should take the position that all implied warranties and superlative statements should be removed from product literature.

Once the product reaches the design review stage, final decisions on hazard warning can be taken by the product safety group based on the preconsiderations of the design engineer. The design engineer should also be ready at this time to advise both the legal and advertising departments on what the machine or product will or will not do, to aid in the removal of implied warranties or superlative and excessive advertising statements.

3. PACKAGING*

In this section, product packaging will be defined as the outer shell of the product itself, as well as the protective layers added to the product to keep it from being damaged during handling and transportation. Therefore, packag-

---

*Adapted from Packaging—Handling and Products Safety, by Richard Jacobs and John Mihalasky, October 1972. Presented at ASME annual winter meeting, 1972. Copyright © ASME. Reprinted with permission.

ing includes the television set's cabinet, and the big cardboard box in which it comes. Unfortunately, most packaging consultants have historically approached the packaging problem from mainly an "architectural" point of view, rather than from an "engineering" standpoint. They study the aesthetics of the design first, and then look at the package's "internal" functions.

Before the Consumer Product Safety Act was passed, Lorna Opatow set the goals for packages in an article for the American Management Association's *Management Review** as:

1. *Functional effectiveness*—is the product easy to handle, open, close, store and use wherever the package protects the contents for some time?
2. *Visual impact*—the relative ability of the package to produce a reaction or describe the design on the package, etc.
3. *Communications effectiveness*—the degree to which the package design succeeds in communicating the idea of the product's function and of its desirable attributes.

---

*Lorna Opatow, Packaging Impact: It's What They Think They See That Counts, *Management Review,* vol. 61, no. 9, pp. 21–27, September 1972.

Table VI-2 Packaging Choice from the Standpoint of Maintenance (Adapted from *Air Force Systems Command Design Handbook 1-6*)

Desirability	*For physical access*	*For visual inspection only*	*For test and service equipment*
Most desirable	Pull-out shelves or drawers	Opening with no cover	Opening with no cover
Desirable	Hinged door (if dirt, moisture, or other foreign materials must be kept out)	Plastic window (if dirt, moisture, or other foreign materials must be kept out)	Spring-loaded sliding cap (if dirt, moisture, or other foreign materials must be kept out)
Less desirable	Removable panel with captive, quick-opening fasteners (if there is not enough room for hinged door)	Break-resistant glass (if plastic will not stand up under physical wear or contact with solvents)	
Least desirable	Removable panel with smallest number of large screws that will meet requirements (if needed for stress, pressure, or safety reasons)	Cover plate with smallest number of large screws that will meet requirements (if needed for stress, pressure, or safety reasons)	Cover plate with smallest number of largest screws that will meet requirements (if needed for stress, pressure, or safety reasons)

Nowhere in these goals is the idea of product safety introduced. Things have begun to change, however. Medicine bottles now must be offered with "child-proof" closures. Games meant for adults, such as a lawn dart game, must be marked by packagers as not to be sold at toy counters. Pictures of children and fatuous statements such as "fun for all the family" are an invitation to Consumer Product Safety Commission action, or to a product liability lawsuit should a dart land in a child's eye.

There are many cases where substantial losses occurred due to faulty containers, or to handling problems arising from improper design. Even the sulfur in kraft board corrugated containers can cause corrosion in some materials, especially if dampness penetrates. But there are a number of ways packaging can help contribute to making products safer. First, each package—both wrapper and protector—should have the following information on it:

1. Product name and model number.
2. Serial and lot number or date of manufacture. Date coding is preferred by safety experts, but often discouraged because of warranty considerations. A good compromise is to transform the date into letters (A for January, C for March, and so forth), or use day and year codes (such as 7123 for the 123rd day of 1977).
3. Manufacturing codes for plant, shift, line, and so forth.
4. The carton sequence.

This information is particularly important should a safety problem arise that calls for product repairs or recall. The proper codes should thus be visible while the product is stored or stacked in a warehouse.

Packing material and the product casing can also carry warning and instruction labels. For materials deemed hazardous, the label should name the product, contain a signal word and symbol indicating the hazard (FIRE, POISON, ACID, etc.), state the precautionary measures to be taken, and the emergency measures to be taken after any exposure to the hazard.

Warnings should not only "warn," but also indicate what the consequences are of disregarding the warning. The warning must be in large enough type to draw attention and be easily read.

Instructions coming with, on, or in packages should cover such areas as safe unpacking procedures, safe stacking procedures, carton disposal, and disposal of internal packing. For example, directions for unpacking should include carton size and weight information, the sequence of steps for unpacking, instructions for tipping and handling of partially uncrated or uncartoned product, and the method of removing securing fasteners. In one case, a transformer manufacturer changed its packing system. A regular customer removed the usual bolts, but the transformer didn't come off the skid. In removing the bolts, the customer actually damaged the transformer instead. The manufacturer sent a new transformer, and paid penalty charges.

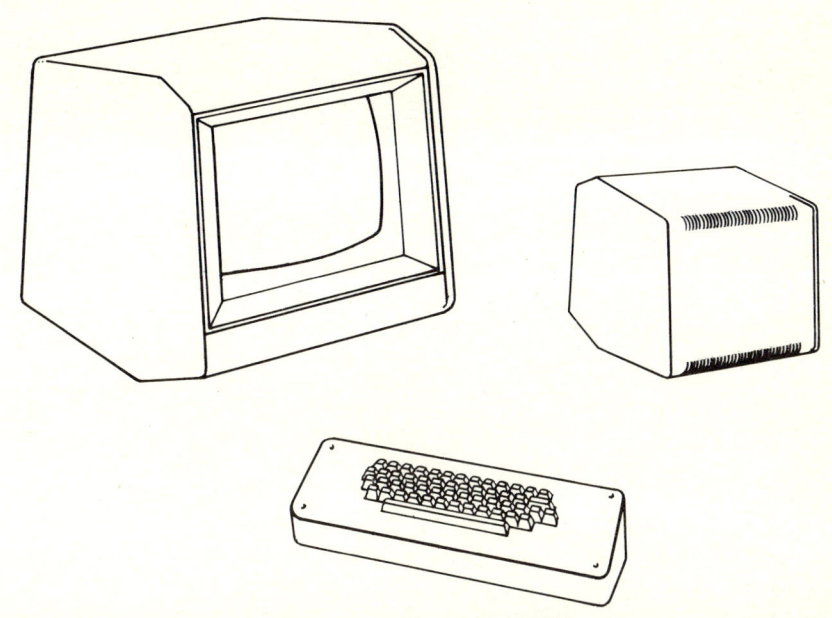

Figure VI-10 If you don't want hot coffee spilled into your electronic equipment, design without a flat horizontal surface. These particular sheet-metal housings are available from Backer-Loring Corp. in numerous standard sizes.

    The product package, to be as safe as possible, should have provisions for handling—such as holes for hand moving, forklift handling, and adequate eyebolts for lifting if necessary.

    Finally, the product's casing can be made tamperproof if necessary, to keep the insides from being exposed to persons unfamiliar with potential hazards. In some cases it might be possible to arrange the parts in such a way that if they are tampered with (to change performance), the item will no longer operate, or can't be re-assembled without special tools. Among the techniques that can be used are tamperproof screw heads, epoxy glues, potted electrical components, spun-tight enclosures, and tear-apart gaskets.

    Many companies use the tamperproofing philosophy to force consumers to have repair work performed only by their organization, to limit the use of replacement parts to only those which are direct factory-approved ones, and to eliminate any confusion over who is responsible for the product's safety and performance characteristics. Even so, maintenance personnel and repair and service businesses—as well as some consumer protection groups—deplore the practice of tamperproof devices because they can be harder to repair, and can hide quality deficiencies.

    Either way, it is clear that such decisions on packaging your product must be addressed at the initial design review, and not as an afterthought when the

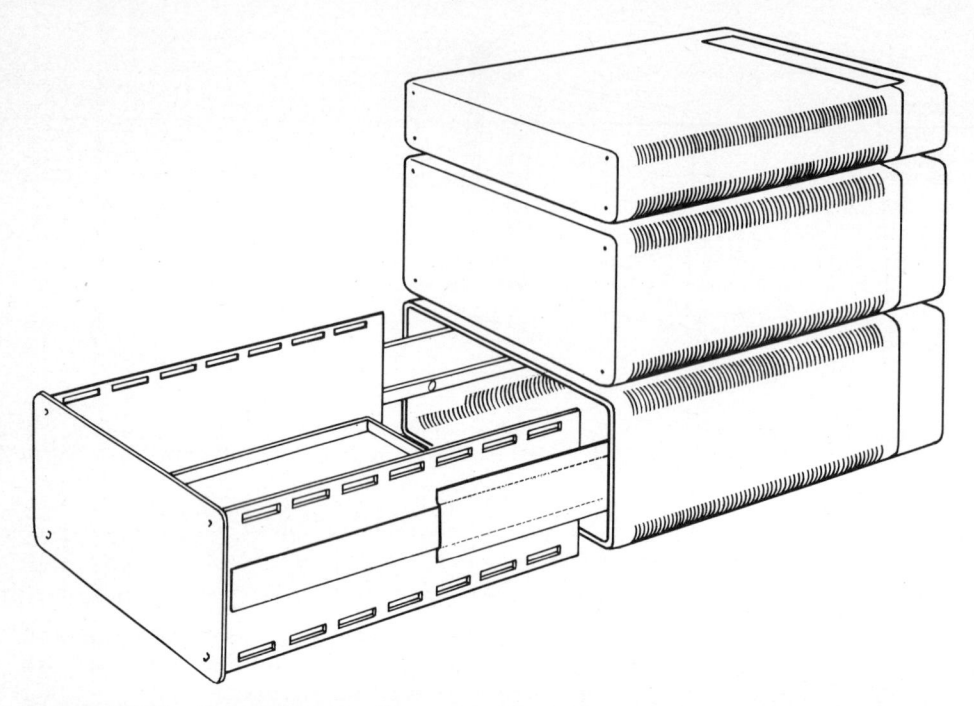

Figure VI-11 Vent holes on these standard sheet-metal housings for electrical equipment are not blocked when equipment is stacked. *(Backer-Loring Corp.)*

product is finished with prototype testing. It will cost considerably more to devise proper packaging after design and tooling are completed for the product—and may even contribute to unsafe and unrepairable conditions.

4. THE LONG-LIVED PRODUCT

Durability can be a curse in product safety matters. There have been numerous cases where workers have been seriously injured using machine tools that are 30, 40, and even 50 years old. Prevented under workers' compensation laws from receiving more than a pittance through their employer's insurance coverage (even death benefits are as low as $10,000 in some states), the workers turn to the only other source of potential cash—the original manufacturer of the machine on which the accident occurred. And even if they don't, the employer's insuror frequently sues the equipment manufacturer to recover its own losses.

The courts have ruled in some cases that it is not enough to provide safety features on a machine tool, such as double switches (so a worker's hands must each be on a switch when parts of a press or knife jaw come together). Such devices cannot be easily removed from the machine, either—because it is clearly foreseeable that some manufacturers, to boost production, will remove such devices if possible.

MARKETING, DISTRIBUTION, AND SERVICING 211

Rivets

Brazing, welding, etc.

Welded seams or molded one-piece engineering plastic

Fasteners requiring special tools to turn

Holes for turning tool

Slants in head allow for easy tightening but not removal

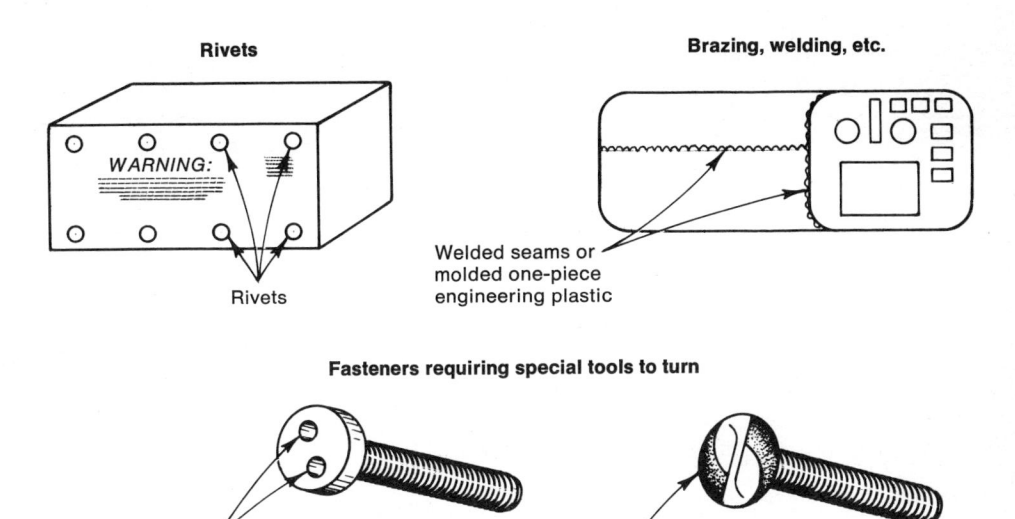

Figure VI-12   Various fasteners can be used to make a product tamperproof. Components that must be accessible to repair personnel but not to users (as in complex household appliances) may also use keyed locks, combinations of ordinary fasteners, and ones requiring special tools, etc.

Figure VI-13   To help guard against the use of small "sponge" for picking up mercury spills, J. T. Baker Chemical Company also has a large kit for spills of up to 5 pounds. Package shown will handle up to 10 grams—more than enough for typical lab spills.

Table VI-3 Guarding of Machinery (Recommendations—almost with the force of regulation—of the Occupational Safety and Health Administration)

INTERLOCKING DEVICES

Enclosure with electrical or mechanical interlock.   Enclosure or barrier shuts off or disengages power and prevents starting of machine when guard is open; prevents opening of the guard while machine is under power or coasting. Should not prevent manual operation or "inching" by remote control.

Barrier with electrical contact or mechanical stop-activating brake.   Barrier quickly stops machine or prevents application of injurious pressure when any part of the operator's body contacts it or approaches danger zone.

Electric eye.   Connected to brake which quickly stops machine or prevents its starting if hands are in the danger zone.

Push-away device with barrier.   A movable barrier, attached to the machine section that will produce pressure, pushes or lifts hands out of the danger zone.

Pull-away device.   Cable attached to moving machine section at one end, and operator's hands on the other, often through a pulley system. Pulls arms back only if they remain in danger zone, otherwise stays slack.

Limitation of stroke.   Machine's plunger travel limited to $3/8$ inch or less; fingers cannot enter between pressure points.

Two-hand trip.   Simultaneous pressure of two hands on switch buttons, air control valves, levers, etc., actuates machine. For multiple-operator machines, each operator should be at a station with such controls, and all must be used simultaneously.

MACHINE FEEDING

Automatic or semiautomatic feed.   Stock is fed by chutes, hoppers, conveyors, movable dies, rotating feed stations, and so forth. Stock passes through enclosure that will not admit any part of body.

Special jigs or feeding devices.   Hand-operated feeding devices of metal or wood to keep operator's hands at a safe distance from danger point. For product liability reasons, such jigs should be permanently attached to machine.

In other cases, tool manufacturers have been held liable for developing new safety devices, and not strongly notifying existing machine users of the new devices.

Products strictly in the consumer realm, such as automobiles and lawn mowers, have also caused unusual product safety hazards and headaches for designers and manufacturers. A disc brake is installed backwards by the gasoline-station mechanic, and it fails in a panic stop. A rusted lawn mower body pulls away from the motor housing. An old chair collapses.

In many such cases, the biggest source of product wear may very well be environmental stress, rather than use. A lawn mower may last 10 years or more, but only be used 50 hours per year to actually cut grass. Sitting in the garage over long winters, it quietly is corroded by water combined with soil or acids from its motor oil. A machine tool bearing is missed in routine maintenance. One day, after years of service, the bearing fails after continuous use on three-shift days for two weeks. Electrical wiring, incorrectly installed, pulls loose from a terminal and starts a fire.

"Any rotating object is dangerous," says the Occupational Safety and Health Administration. "Even smooth, slowly rotating shafts can grip clothing or hair, and through mere skin contact force an arm or hand into a dangerous position." Such accidents are not common, but when they occur, the severity of the injury is often extremely great.

The problem is compounded for manufacturers and designers of such equipment, because often the scale of the machinery is so large, and the design so specialized, that guarding screens and barriers must be specially fabricated and installed for each user location. Purchasers may want to handle the chore themselves. But because of product safety considerations, this is rarely a good idea. The equipment manufacturer should, in most cases, insist on designing and supervising the job.

Product design configurations can help make the task easier. Can a large flywheel be provided with solid or sheet-metal sides, rather than spokes? Can in-running nip points be guarded by a ridge on the machine's casting, rather than a screw-in bar or length of angle stock? Can long shafts and pulley belt systems be kept to a minimum?

Designers and manufacturers must often consider design features on a case-by-case basis. Is it wise to install a "panic bar" to engage the body or forehead of a worker caught in a machine such as a stamping press? Or will the employer and worker, relying on the panic bar, rip out guards or double switches to boost production? The answer may depend on the possible severity of an accident. It is too late to provide a panic bar at eye level, if a worker's arm has already been mangled before the bar is engaged.

A nip-point's guard catches metal shavings, causing a jam. In freeing the machinery, a worker suffers severe burns. The nip point guard might have worked perfectly with a machine used to mill a soft metal such as aluminum, and caused a safety problem while machining steel. How can a manufacturer, knowing that his machine might be used for many different tasks over the years, cope? Any guard that is adjustable can probably be removed. Tamper-resistant fasteners, preferably in awkward locations, must often be used.

Manufacturers of such long-lived devices must, as a matter of policy, centralize all customer records at corporate headquarters. Distributors change, merge, and go out of business. Vital warnings, maintenance instructions, and the manufacturer's name and address should be firmly attached to the machinery—even cast directly into the equipment's frame.

Continuing service contracts with indefinite renewability must be offered at a reasonable price to customers, and proper spare parts must be stocked for immediate shipment to users in need. The original manufacturer cannot trust

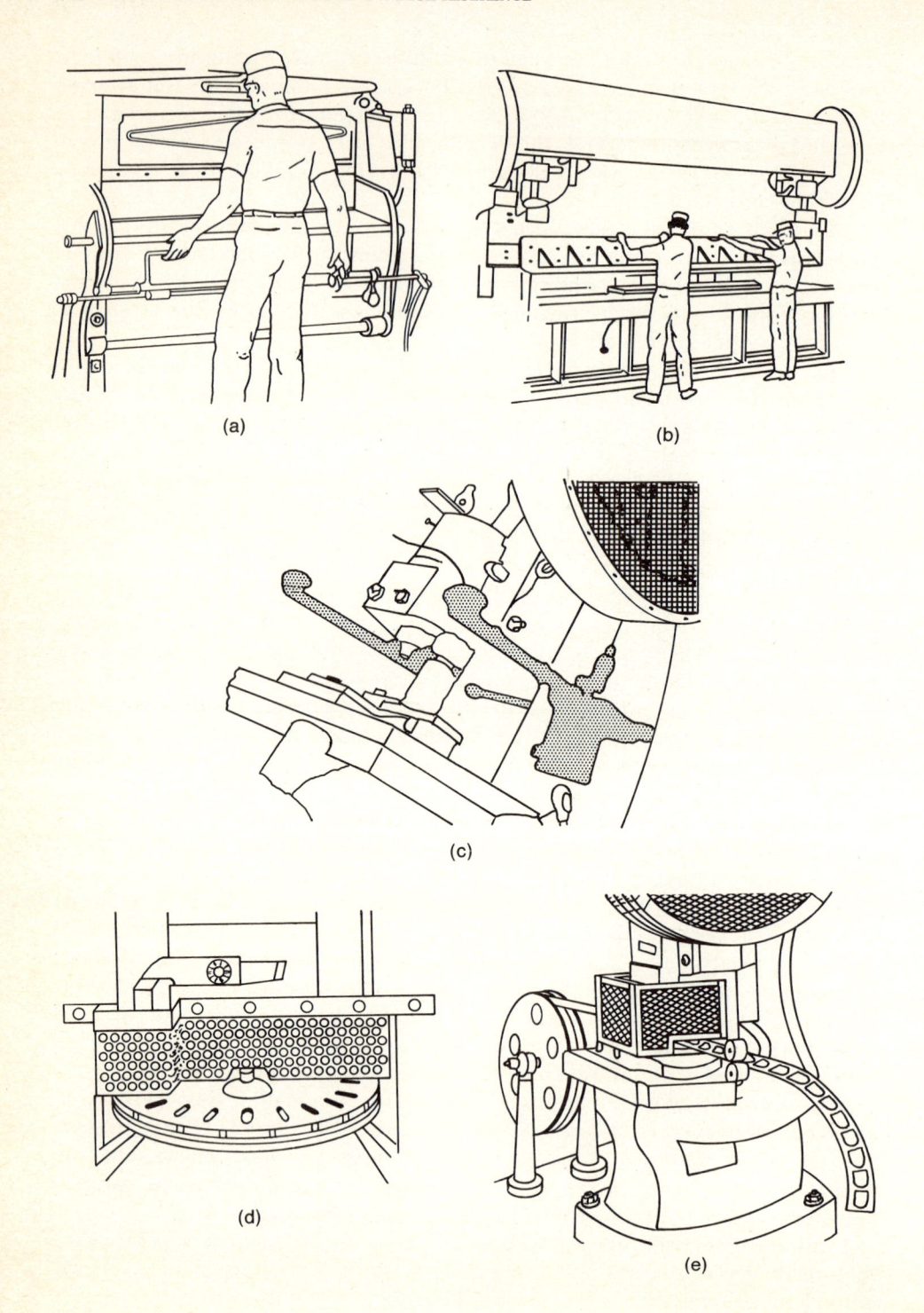

(a)

(b)

(c)

(d)

(e)

(f)

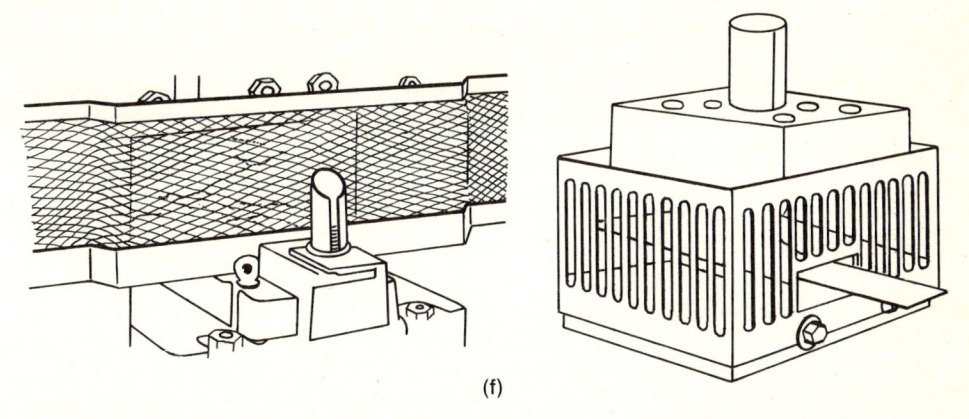

Figure VI-14 Various types of machine guards. (*a*) Two-handed tripping device for paper guillotine shear. (*b*) Two-man operated press with each operator required to activate two switches simultaneously. (*c*) Punch press. Two-handed tripping device requires the simultaneous use of both hands to trip the press. On presses with noninterrupting stroke, device should require continuous pressure on controls so that operator cannot reach into the press. (*d*) Rotating die. Stock is fed manually into rotating die and is carried automatically under the plunger. (*e*) Automatic feed. Stock is fed automatically to plunger, operator required only to restock feeding device. (*f*) Other types of enclosure guards for use with automatic feeding.

outside maintenance of specialized components, or makeshift replacements under the pressure of the user's own production schedules.

Manufacturers of specialized or large-scale equipment must also keep track of the latest in testing and quality assurance techniques. In one case, a manufacturer was not held liable for a steel railroad-car wheel, because no known testing procedure could have detected the flaw that eventually allowed the wheel to fail under extreme stress, and the wheel had been manufactured under customary stringent conditions. But what if a new test procedure is developed? Should all existing wheels in customer's hands be returned in batches for testing? Should customers be notified, in case they want to test the wheels themselves? Should all wheels in distributors' hands be checked? Or should only new production be involved?

A proper decision must depend on the cost of the testing, versus the potential of the threat—the number of possibly defective items outstanding, and the possible consequences of product failure. A good way to start would be to install the new test and see how many extra defects it picks up over old procedures. But that could take time. What if someone is injured in a product failure before then? In such cases, management must go back to the designer for rough estimates of risk, using industry data that only the designer would be expected to have—failure rates, failure modes, and an understanding of the new test's capabilities.

Table VI-4 Various Filler and Frame Materials for Machinery Guards (OSHA)

Filler material*	Clearance from moving part at all points, in	Largest mesh or opening allowable, in	Minimum gage (U.S. standard) or thickness	Minimum height of guard from floor or platform level, feet-inches
Woven wire	Under 2	3/8	No. 16	7–0
	2–4	1/2	No. 16	7–0
	Under 4	1/2	No. 16	7–0
	4–15	2	No. 12	7–0
Expanded metal	Under 4	1/2	No. 18	7–0
	4–15	2	No. 13	7–0
Perforated metal	Under 4	1/2	No. 20	7–0
	4–15	2	No. 14	7–0
Sheet metal	Under 4	——	No. 22	7–0
	4–15	——	No. 22	7–0
Wood or metal strip crossed	Under 4	3/8	Wood 3/4 inch or Metal No. 16	7–0
	4–15	2		
Wood or metal strip not crossed	Under 4	1/2 width		
	4–15	1 width		
Standard rail	Minimum 15 Maximum 20			

*Framework Materials:

1. Minimum dimensions of materials for the framework of all guards except as noted in paragraph 3 shall be angle iron 1 inch × 1 inch × 1/8 inch, metal pipe of 3/4 inch inside diameter or metal construction of equivalent strength.
   All guards shall be rigidly braced every 3 feet or fractional part of their height to some fixed part of machinery or building structure. Where guard is exposed to contact with moving equipment, additional strength may be necessary.

2. The framework for all guards fastened to floor or working platform and without other support or bracing shall consist of 1 1/2 inch × 1 1/2 inch × 1/8 inch angle iron, metal pipe of 1 1/2 inch inside ddameter or metal construction of equivalent strength. All rectangular guards shall have at least four upright frame members each of which shall be carried to the floor and be securely fastened thereto.
   Cylindrical guards shall have at least three supporting members carried to floor.

3. Guards 30 inches or less in height and with a total surface area not in excess of 10 square feet may have a framework of 3/8 inch solid rod, 3/4 inch × 3/4 inch × 1/8 inch angle or metal construction of equivalent strength.

MARKETING, DISTRIBUTION, AND SERVICING   **217**

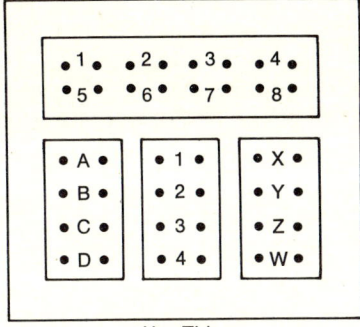

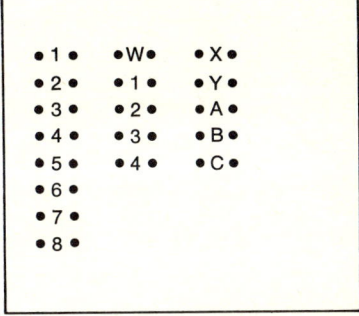

Use This   Do Not Use This

Figure VI-15 Group test points and service points by function. This technique not only helps make service and maintenance easier, it can also help personnel "dope out" points on old machines where no documentation is available.

Table VI-5   Should Test Equipment Be Built In? *(Air Force Systems Command Design Handbook 1-9)*

Advantages	*Disadvantages*
1. Minimizes requirements for external support equipment.	1. Resulting hardware is heavier, larger, and requires more power. Requires compromise on part of designer as to minimum number of types of tests that can be performed without exceeding weight and size limitations.
2. Minimizes downtime required to troubleshoot equipment. Also decreases service-induced failures and possible injury to repair personnel by allowing fault isolation to be performed without needless probing into interior of equipment.	2. Increases complexity of prime equipment, thus increasing development effort, cost, and time. Also increases maintenance to be performed on prime equipment and system.
3. Identifies performance degradation by operating personnel in sufficient time to avoid serious breakdowns.	3. Difficult to calibrate test facilities because of inability to separate these facilities from prime equipment.
4. Increases system confidence through availability of monitoring facilities.	4. Requires additional self-checking features to ensure that degradation of test facilities does not go unnoticed.
5. Assures that modifications of prime equipment are made concurrently with integral test facilities.	5. Requires extreme caution in selection of tests to be performed. Change in procedures of later date requires equipment redesign. Inflexibility in this area is limiting factor.

5. ACCIDENT INVESTIGATIONS

Warning! Accident investigations are fraught with pitfalls that will trap the unwary in two ways. The first mistake that is commonly made is to overreach—to suggest the cause of an accident based on sketchy or incomplete data. The second way is to carefully investigate, but be trapped by too much experience. The investigator who has seen a device fail because of metal fatigue several times before, pronounces the same cause at a new accident scene. In the new case, however, the broken metal was really due to stress fracture from the impact of a foreign body.

Until 1960, for instance, it had been assumed by almost all authorities that fires and explosions of oil-fueled space heaters were due to manufacturing defects, misinstallation, or gross consumer misuse, such as pouring fuel oil directly into the combustion chamber. A careful investigation by the Boston Fire Department showed instead that there was a much more common cause. Heaters generally were fed from a small integral tank filled with oil. Much of the force pushing oil into the heater combustion chamber came from the pressure of the oil itself, as it expanded in the tank.

What happened when a careful user, who stored his fuel oil in a container outside, filled the heater tank only part way with the cold oil, and then capped the tank? Cold air, trapped inside, would expand violently as the heater got warmer, forcing more fuel into the combustion chamber and setting off a fire.

The hypothesis was proven convincingly when Fire Department researchers were able to routinely explode new heaters this way in a test room. The heaters all bore the seal of approval of Underwriters Laboratories, which quickly removed the heaters from its list of approved devices. A conversion device, to allow gravity-feed of the fuel, was on sale within a year. The number of space heater fires in Boston dropped from 159 reported in the 1959–1960 heating season, to only 6 the following year.

Today, a manufacturer often does not have the luxury of being able to compare the common features in a number of accidents involving his product, before having to figure out what went wrong. One serious incident can prompt a demand for a product recall from the Consumer Product Safety Commission.

Table VI-6 Sources of Accident Reports

Customer
Injured parties
Distributors
Retailers
News media
Government agencies
Service centers or repair departments

Table VI-7 Reporting Accidents That Did Cause or Could Have Caused Injury or Property Damage

You need to know:

  Product name, model, serial number

  Customer's name and address

  Location of the accident

  Names and addresses of injured parties

  The nature of injury or damage caused

  Date of the incident

  Names and addresses of witnesses

  Description of the accident: time of day, contributing factors, aftermath (amount of hospitalization, etc.)

But:

  Beware of describing a chain of events or accident cause without expert, reliable information and analysis!

The legal outcome of a single accident settlement can put a manufacturer into the red—or out of business.

What's more, the record of the accident itself is often incomplete. The manufacturer's first eyes on the scene of a serious accident involving his product (but not necessarily caused by the product) frequently belong to a distributor, retailer, or (increasingly) a claims adjustor who may be a full-time employee or an outside "expert" hired by the firm or its insurance carrier.

To keep such people from describing a hypothetical "chain of events" which may prove damaging (though untrue) in court, supply reporting forms that carefully circumscribe what the investigator can say about the occurrence. At first, you need to know exactly what model and serial number of your product was involved, the customer's name and address, circumstances surrounding the accident, all injured parties, the nature of their injuries and the proximate cause of those injuries, and a description of the accident. A correct statement at this stage might be "a sliver of wood lodged in the user's left eye while he was cutting a six-inch log with the model 761 chain saw." An incorrect appraisal might read, "a sliver of wood kicked up by the chain of our model 761 saw lodged in the user's eye while he was cutting a six-inch log." At the preliminary stage, how does an investigator know that the chain drove the wood directly? Perhaps the wind kicked up a sliver, or the user rubbed his eyes with a sawdust-covered arm of his work shirt.

Nor should a manufacturer rely on any "in-depth" report of the accident that may be done by the Consumer Product Safety Commission's staff or consultants. The Commission in 1975 admitted it paid anywhere from $300 to

To: ________________ Customer–Name: ________________
Location: ________________

Product: ________________ Customer order # ________________
Installation date: ________________

Style ________________ Hours/service ________________
Mfg. date ________________
Serial # ________________ Use ________________

1. CUSTOMER COMPLAINT (to be filled in by sales engineer)
Action desired (use separate sheet if necessary) ________________
Date of trouble or failure ________ In warranty? ☐ A ☐ B ☐ C Claim? Yes ☐ No ☐
Shipping damage? Yes ☐ No ☐ Terms: FOB ☐ Factory ☐ Shipper ________
Charge repair to customer Yes ☐ No ☐ / Parts & labor? ☐ Parts ☐ Labor ☐
Repair authorized by ________________ Date ________
Credit approval: Yes ☐ No ☐ Signed ________________ Date ________

2. INVESTIGATING OFFICER'S REPORT Date filed ________ Signed ________
Date called ________ Date on job ________ Date finished ________
Environmental conditions hot ☐ cold ☐/wet ☐ dry☐/temp. max ____ °C
Other environmental factors ________________

Problem ________________

Action needed ________________

3. RELIABILITY REVIEW
Corporate or division reliability officer analysis: ________________

Signed ________________ Date ________
Could product failure of this type cause injury? ________________

ACCOUNTING USE:	division	war.	cust.	remarks
charge:				
Total cost				Approved: Date:

Figure VI-16 Field reliability check for major products or installations (normally to be used by field sales, maintenance, or sales engineers).

$600 for typical reports. That kind of money is adequate for simple reports that will be compared with one another to deduce patterns of problems with specific products. But each report standing alone will often prove inadequate and possibly wrong.

Often, the best evidence will be derived from attempts to duplicate the failure under similar conditions to the accident. Such attempts should be made, ideally, with a sample of the product from the same lot as the item involved in the original accident. This sort of duplication tends to uncover design defects—stresses not accounted for—and manufacturing problems such as spot welds that fail repeatedly, or poor heat treatment. Simulating failures may uncover hidden defects that improved quality control procedures could catch—flaws in castings, for example. The cost of such procedures or of redesign must, of course, be weighed against the cost of more product failures.

At this stage of an accident investigation, management often decides to "fix" the product by adding a warning. For instance, a portable circular saw "kicked back" on a user who was sawing from near the top of a 15-foot ladder. The user fell backward and was severely injured. The manufacturer added a warning never to use the saw from the top of a ladder. Since that warning would probably be ignored by a typical consumer who had to handle a job 15 feet off the ground, and since no thought was given to improving the saw blade's guard to cut the incidence of kickbacks (other saws in the industry had units that tended to work better in this regard), the courts would probably rule, in a future incident, that the warning is insufficient.

But what if the saw was already as "safe" as any that have evolved in the field? Then a court might very well rule in the manufacturer's favor—especially since a circular saw is known by all to have a potential for being dangerous, simply by virtue of its function.

Finally, management may have to review original medical records of the accident to determine possible proximate causes. An x-ray of a broken arm, for instance, can help determine whether the arm was broken by a kicked-back flying object from the product, or in the resulting fall. Unfortunately, such records are usually privileged—between a doctor and his or her patient. They tend to be produced mainly at trials—by which time it is often too late.

In short, despite tremendous advances in the field in the past decade, accident investigation still is an evolving science, with some element of art involved. There is plenty of room for "experts" to disagree on the causes of an accident (as will be seen in the chapter on trials). Investigations deserve the attention of top management, because they may uncover problems requiring immediate action by diverse sections of the company—design and production, marketing or product testing.

6. PRODUCT RECALLS

The product safety group should prepare itself to respond quickly to the discovery of a safety problem. For most organizations, this means preparation of an "emergency response" document detailing the steps that will have to be taken, or might have to be taken, to deal with a safety-related problem. Based on the needs expressed in that document, subsidiary departments—design, production, marketing, and so forth—must formulate their own actions, and pass them back to the product safety coordinator for approval.

In some companies, standard forms are used to indicate safety-related problems that are discovered. These "action sheets" then are passed through

Table VI-8 Costs of a Product Recall

- *Communications:* Press releases, paid advertising, registered and certified mail, Mailgrams, visits by employees to distributors, major retailers, and so forth. Locating customers and items in the supply chain inventory.
- *Disposition:* Packaging, removal from customer property, inventory, inspection, repair or replacement, disposal, refunds, compensation for loss of use, new customer instructions and explanations of defect, warehousing.
- *Documentation:* Invoicing, labeling, work authorizations, orders for replacements, tallying of number of product items returned, authorizations for shipping costs, customer reimbursements, communications costs.
- *Compensation for injury:* Medical bills, salary compensation, legal fees, judgments.
- *Management overhead:* Investigative time, testimony and depositions, coordination, interface with regulatory agencies.
- *Long-term intangibles:* Loss of sales, attitude changes on the part of design, production, and test personnel.

---

the chain of command. Some consultants in the field say the department first noticing the problem should recommend whether or not the problem is serious enough to warrant a production stoppage, design change, or recall. Others say that such documents can prove embarrassing, if, for example, marketing urgently requests a design change when in reality a minor quality-control adjustment would solve the problem. If the document ends up in court, it could prove damaging even if ill-founded.

The same caveat applies to whether or not the issuing department should be allowed to label a problem as, for example, one that should be taken up at the next design review, or one that needs immediate attention. Here a company treads the thin line between being so alarmist that when real problems crop up they are ignored, and reacting too slowly to potentially disastrous problems. Each individual firm's solution will probably depend on the type of product produced, industry practice, and the abilities of personnel in various departments.

Some companies can "turn a problem around" and meet on an hour's notice in response to such a call for action. The matter remains open until the description of the problem is approved by the product safety director and distributed back to the individual departments with an explanation of what happened and what corrective action, if any, will be taken. In high-hazard industries, emergency response documents take precedence over all other activities.

To react that quickly, the response team must know immediately how many potentially defective products were produced, and where they are—with customers, retailers, distributors, in transit, warehoused, or in production. There must be a means of notifying your company's shipping department immediately, to stop shipments of potentially defective products that may still be on hand. Arrangements should be made ahead of time with large customers (major retailers and private-brand labelers, for example) as to how recalls should be handled. Does the manufacturer or the private labeler assume responsibility for recalls? How well is that responsibility discharged in an actual incident?

If the item is a consumer product which could cause a "substantial" hazard, the Consumer Product Safety Commission must be notified immediately under the Consumer Product Safety Act, section 15(b). Other agencies have differing requirements in this regard, but "immediate" notification appears to be the best policy in the absence of firm requirement—perhaps before the response team meets, or immediately after if you have an organization with a quick (one hour or so) mechanism for considering problems.

Most large retailers have been evolving response mechanisms of their own. It will often be most efficient to notify the corporate headquarters of a firm about a problem, rather than individual stores, even though corporate buying might be mainly the responsibility of local purchasing agents. When in doubt, notify both headquarters and local stores. But try to avoid the confusion by arranging ahead of time who should be notified.

After notification passes to the distribution and sales chain, the next step is to prepare to receive recalled products. Surprisingly, recalls often are not too "successful," especially for inexpensive items for which no record is made of the ultimate purchaser. In 1974, for instance, after the Consumer Product Safety Commission ordered a recall of trouble lights manufactured by A. K. Electric, only about 5 percent of the lights were actually returned. In that case, by the way, the manufacturer ended up accepting large numbers of trouble lights of similar design made by others.

The Commission may require that a manufacturer purchase paid advertising in local newspapers to spread the word of the recall. In the trouble light case, the Federal District Court in Washington ruled this to be unnecessary, in part because the recall already had received wide publicity on network television.

In the 1960 oil heater situation described in the previous section, the Boston Fire Department prevailed upon radio, television, and newspapers to carry detailed instructions for safely filling heaters with oil. Pamphlets were prepared at public expense and distributed through schools, fuel-oil dealers, kerosene peddlers, hardware stores, and neighborhood committees.

To get the word out quickly, product safety groups should prepare the skeletons of transmittal letters in advance, ready to fill in the last few lines with details about the specific model and the specific hazard, along with advice to customers on using the product before the defect is corrected. For motor vehicle equipment, the form the letter takes is actually specified by Department of Transportation regulation.

Of course, corporate public affairs personnel must be brought into the picture early, both to handle press enquiries, and to help notify media in the area affected by the product being recalled. Here, too, management treads a thin line between wanting to notify all customers of the hazard, lest resultant suits put the company out of business, and reassuring other users of the firm's products that everything is fine. Surprisingly, the existence of recalls and defect notices does not always diminish a firm's standing among customers and the public at large. There seems to be a realization among many that, in today's world, mistakes will occur. The company that can stand behind its products and correct problems before they cause accidents often is described by regulatory personnel and consumerists alike as a good corporate citizen.

To Report a Product Hazard or a Product-Related Injury:

Write the Consumer Product Safety Commission, Washington, DC 20207 or call (800)638-2666.

Maryland residents, call (800)492-2937.

Alaska, Hawaii, Puerto Rico, or Virgin Islands residents call (800)638-8333.

A teletype for the deaf is available from 8:30 A.M. to 5 P.M. Eastern Time, for people who call the hot line.

VII
SPECIAL CONSIDERATIONS FOR CHEMICAL PRODUCTS

1. INTRODUCTION

Polybrominated biphenyls are useful as flame retardants in a wide variety of applications. In 1974, workers at a chemical company in Michigan mistook bags of a polybrominated biphenyl (PBB) mix (trade-named Firemaster) for a similarly packaged feed supplement (trade-named Nutremaster). They blended the PBB into cattle feed sold to hundreds of farmers. In the next few years, thousands of contaminated cattle had to be slaughtered. Hundreds of farm families fell victim to disorders of the nervous system. And the company, Michigan Chemical, had to be sold. After-effects of the mistake will probably be felt well into the 21st century, for not only are PBBs known poisons, they may cause cancer as well—and the cancer might not show up for another generation.

In 1971, several chemical companies made multimillion dollar investments in facilities to produce nitrilotriacetic acid (NTA) as a replacement for phosphates in detergent. For most, the investments came to naught as NTA's properties as a chelating agent—ability to remove metals from plumbing and deposit them in the nearest waterway—became generally known.

The Apollo Project to put Americans on the moon was held back for a year, after three astronauts lost their lives in a fire during a ground test. Supposedly "nonflammable" material inside the Apollo command module caught fire and burned readily in the capsule's pure oxygen atmosphere.

In all three of these examples, the potential dangers were well known. No company in the business of preparing human food would handle a poison in the same area as a food additive, but animal feed preparation had not evolved the proper safety standards. NTA's properties were common knowledge in the chemical industry, and one firm was—and still is—making hundreds of millions of pounds of it every year. But nobody stopped to think of the consequences of scaling up its use 100-fold as a consumer product for every home in the nation. Grade-school children learn that many things burn in pure oxygen, although they would be absolutely safe in normal atmospheres.

Where, then, did the designers go wrong? Most importantly, they did not fully understand the potential dangers in the materials they were working with.

Figure VII-1 Some of the 80 exhaust vents on the roof of MIT's Chemical Engineering Building (plastic covers were used to keep out water during construction).

Nor did they take into account all possible conditions under which the materials would be used. In Apollo, for example, the spacecraft enroute to the moon would be filled with pure oxygen, but at reduced pressure, giving about the same oxygen density as on Earth. But in the testing phase, pure oxygen was used at much higher pressures to fulfill some of the test requirements. Design criteria did not adequately note the test requirements.

Compared to the potential for harm in mechanical devices, chemicals can pose truly staggering liabilities to a manufacturer, transporter, or product fabricator. A few pounds of dioxin—an impurity created in the manufacture of many chlorinated hydrocarbons—contaminated many square miles of the Italian countryside after a plant mishap released a cloud of it.

Unfortunately, designers are at serious disadvantage in getting—and understanding—the data they need to make decisions on matters of chemistry. Chemical engineers can help with questions on materials compatability and, sometimes, toxicity and flammability. Chemists have deeper actual knowledge of potential problems, but frequently don't work well with engineering teams. The Manufacturing Chemists Association in Washington, and some other trade groups, maintain data sheets on many chemicals. But so many compounds are proprietary that the composition of a supplier's product is often unknown. The supplier's own health and safety tests, if any, may have been done on outdated equipment, or under very different conditions than occur as part of the manufacturer's finished product.

To help, the federal Environmental Protection Agency was authorized to set up a data bank of all known chemicals manufactured or imported into the United States. The data file, established under the Toxic Substances Control

Act, was basically complete by mid-1978. Also useful is TOXLINE, a computer-accessed data bank run by the National Institutes of Health, and available through many technical libraries on surprisingly short notice. Unfortunately, its coverage of health data published before 1970 is rather sketchy. Other sources of information are listed in the Appendixes.

The larger chemical companies have been forced by product liability considerations to vastly expand their safety efforts. Such efforts must go far beyond simply having health data available to a few favored individuals high in management, because the potential for harm rests at many levels within the organization. In the early 1970s, Dow Chemical began an unusually comprehensive program called "product stewardship," with a 10-year timetable to educate its employees, and the management of its industrial customers.

Under the program, Dow's research and development staff must consider new products or new applications for old products in light of requirements for

Table VII-1 Chemical Hazards Checklist

1. Name of chemical

2. What is its physical state?

3. Is it toxic?
    acute?
    chronic?
    by ingestion?
    by inhalation?
    by absorption?
    can its toxicity level be readily determined?
    threshold-limit value

4. What is its:
    vapor density?
    vapor pressure?
    freezing point?
    specific gravity?
    miscibility in water?

5. What is its incompatibility?

6. Is it flammable, highly flammable?
    What is its:
        flash point?
        explosive limits?
        ignition temperature?

7. What type of fire appliance should be used?

8. What type of protective clothing should be used?

9. Other special safeguards

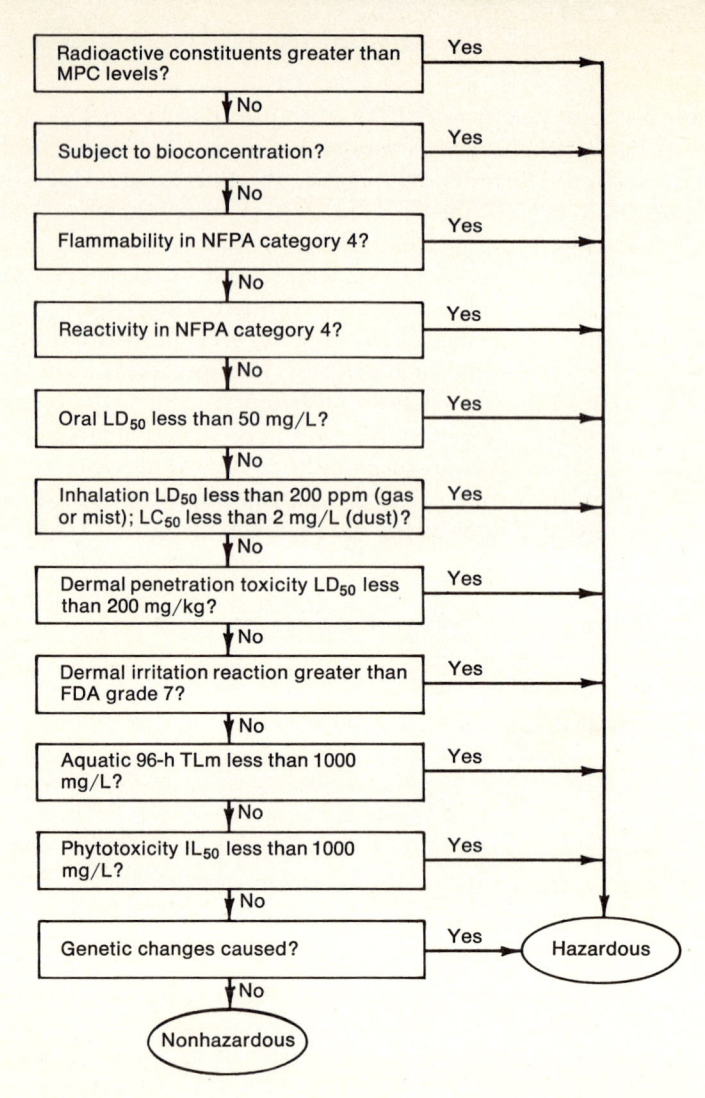

```
┌─────────────────────────────────────┐  Yes
│ Radioactive constituents greater than│──────┐
│ MPC levels?                         │      │
└─────────────────────────────────────┘      │
              │ No                           │
              ▼                              │
┌─────────────────────────────────────┐  Yes │
│ Subject to bioconcentration?        │──────┤
└─────────────────────────────────────┘      │
              │ No                           │
              ▼                              │
┌─────────────────────────────────────┐  Yes │
│ Flammability in NFPA category 4?    │──────┤
└─────────────────────────────────────┘      │
              │ No                           │
              ▼                              │
┌─────────────────────────────────────┐  Yes │
│ Reactivity in NFPA category 4?      │──────┤
└─────────────────────────────────────┘      │
              │ No                           │
              ▼                              │
┌─────────────────────────────────────┐  Yes │
│ Oral LD₅₀ less than 50 mg/L?        │──────┤
└─────────────────────────────────────┘      │
              │ No                           │
              ▼                              │
┌─────────────────────────────────────┐  Yes │
│ Inhalation LD₅₀ less than 200 ppm   │──────┤
│ (gas or mist); LC₅₀ less than       │      │
│ 2 mg/L (dust)?                      │      │
└─────────────────────────────────────┘      │
              │ No                           │
              ▼                              │
┌─────────────────────────────────────┐  Yes │
│ Dermal penetration toxicity LD₅₀    │──────┤
│ less than 200 mg/kg?                │      │
└─────────────────────────────────────┘      │
              │ No                           │
              ▼                              │
┌─────────────────────────────────────┐  Yes │
│ Dermal irritation reaction greater  │──────┤
│ than FDA grade 7?                   │      │
└─────────────────────────────────────┘      │
              │ No                           │
              ▼                              │
┌─────────────────────────────────────┐  Yes │
│ Aquatic 96-h TLm less than          │──────┤
│ 1000 mg/L?                          │      │
└─────────────────────────────────────┘      │
              │ No                           │
              ▼                              │
┌─────────────────────────────────────┐  Yes │
│ Phytotoxicity IL₅₀ less than        │──────┤
│ 1000 mg/L?                          │      │
└─────────────────────────────────────┘      │
              │ No                           │
              ▼                              ▼
┌─────────────────────────────────────┐ Yes ╭──────────╮
│ Genetic changes caused?             │────▶│Hazardous │
└─────────────────────────────────────┘     ╰──────────╯
              │ No
              ▼
        ╭────────────╮
        │Nonhazardous│
        ╰────────────╯
```

Figure VII-2 Decision algorithm for determining chemical or radiological hazard. *(Battelle Northwest, Program for the Management of Hazardous Wastes, EPA Contract 68-01-0762, July 1973.)*

Term	Equivalent
MPC	NRC maximum permissible level
NFPA	National Fire Protection Association
LD_{50}	Lethal dosage (mg/L) for 50% of large test animal population.
TLm	Lethal threshold for 50% of fish and other aquatic organisms for constant 96-hour exposure.
IL_{50}	Inhibiting limit reducing test culture to 50% control in biomass, cell count, or photosynthesis after 14 days.

Table VII-2 Representative Hazardous Substances within Industrial Waste Streams (Environmental Protection Agency, *Report to Congress on Hazardous Waste Disposal, June 30, 1973*)

Industry	Arsenic	Cadmium	Chlorinated hydrocarbons*	Chromium	Copper	Cyanides	Lead	Mercury	Miscellaneous organics†	Selenium	Zinc
Mining & metallurgy	X	X		X	X	X	X	X	X	X	X
Paint & dye		X		X	X	X	X	X		X	
Pesticide	X		X				X	X	X		X
Electrical & electronic			X		X	X	X	X		X	
Printing & duplicating	X			X	X		X		X	X	
Electroplating & metal finishing		X		X	X	X	X				X
Chemical manufacturing			X	X	X			X	X		
Explosives	X				X		X	X	X		
Rubber & plastics			X			X		X	X		X
Battery		X					X	X			X
Pharmaceuticals	X							X	X		
Textile				X	X		X		X		
Petroleum & coal	X		X				X				
Pulp & paper								X	X		
Leather				X					X		

*Includes polychlorinated biphenyls.
†For example, acrolein, chloropicrin, dimethyl sulfate, dinitrobenzene, dinitrophenol, nitroaniline, and pentachlorophenol.

229

safe handling, use, and disposal. Product testing is conducted at each stage of product development to uncover potential long-term and short-term environmental effects. Certain classes of products are looked at especially carefully. For instance, a product known to be fat-soluble but insoluble in water would tend to bioconcentrate—that is, it will tend to be taken up into the life chain, and concentrate mainly in the higher forms of life. Since those higher forms include humans, and human food, Dow requires that such products be examined for possible carcinogenicity or mutagenicity. Likewise, a chemical's breakdown products must also be checked carefully.

The research and development staff must also develop data for Dow's production and marketing personnel so that proper safety procedures are followed.

Manufacturing staff is told, as a matter of highest company policy, to exhaustively review product specification or process changes "which may alter product properties, utility, or quality, including product impurities." Shipment of slightly off-spec material as a courtesy to customers in time of shortages was discontinued by the company as part of the stewardship program.

Marketing personnel are given materials and the training to inform customers of applicable limitations upon the use of Dow products, and to alert corporate officials to potential safety problems at a customer facility. In one case, a glass company purchased a tank car that had been leased to Dow. The tank car was to serve as a storage tank for Dow-supplied liquid caustic soda to be used in producing glass. The glass company asked Dow for the car's calibrations. The data were supplied by Dow's Boston sales office, which also asked that Dow personnel be allowed to visit the installation. The Dow safety people found a hazardous situation—the car tracks lay between the employees' parking lot and the walkway into the building. Any malfunction, either in filling the tank with caustic soda or unloading it for use in the plant could have sprayed caustic on personnel walking in the area, or on parked cars 12 feet away. Alarmed, Dow's Boston sales personnel, with the backing of the company, refused to supply the caustic soda until the situation was corrected.

The glass firm could have purchased caustic soda from another supplier—it is a common chemical. Instead, it saw the merit in Dow's advice, and built a 12-foot reinforced fiberglass enclosure wall around the tank car and pumping area. The glass firm even asked Dow personnel to inspect other areas of the plant where caustic soda was in use, and took Dow's advice for corrective action.

Essentially, the needs of both companies coincided. For the glass firm, Dow provided free safety inspection. For Dow, a chance was seized upon to make sure its product was being used in accordance with good safety practices. Otherwise, Dow might have been more exposed to liablity in case of disabling accidents at the glass plant than the glass manufacturer. The glassmaker is at least shielded from very high liability claims by worker's compensation laws.

This type of service does not come cheaply, of course. The number of worker hours of industrial hygiene services provided to customers by Dow shot from 100 per quarter in 1971 to 600 per quarter only three years later before leveling off.

Nor does it always show good results. Dow has been nervous about exposure to methyl chloride by employees of fabricators using Styrofoam. Methyl chloride is the blowing agent used in molding this plastic. The company had been pressuring its customers to watch for methyl chloride since the 1950s, with only mixed success. Then, in the early 1970s, better health data on the chemical, and the interest of the federal Occupational Safety and Health Administration, stiffened Dow's resolve. All customers received Dow inspections over a two-year period, and fabricators out of compliance with OSHA standards were cut from Dow's distribution list in January 1975.

2. TOXICITY AND OTHER ACUTE EFFECTS

Despite the large amount of publicity given to incidents of long-term, low exposure to certain compounds producing cancer in some of those people exposed, the biggest chemical hazards are still due to toxic effects. This is, in a sense, surprising, because toxicity data is much more complete than data on carcinogenicity or mutagenicity.

Part of the problem is that toxicological studies generally have been based on industrial situations. For instance, the typical Threshold Limit Values of the American Council of Governmental Industrial Hygienists are listed as allowable exposure concentrations for eight hours per day, five days per week. Most are applicable to white males only, because only recently have large numbers of women entered the industrial work force. Women—particularly pregnant women and their fetuses—are extra sensitive to a wide range of industrial products. Furthermore, because of the vast number of compounds used in most industrial situations, millions of potential combinations of exposures are possible. The synergism among these compounds is not particularly well understood.

Thus, the very definition of a "toxic" or "dangerous" substance has never been agreed upon. Various private and governmental groups generally agree that acute toxicity is grounds for including a compound on a "danger list." Acute toxicity tests are more clear-cut than chronic effects—death versus some level of physical impairment. Likewise, organizations—both inside government and outside—define substances as "flammable" or "hazardous" according to their own needs and perceptions. The Occupational Safety and Health Administration, the Department of Transportation, the Alcohol, Tobacco and Firearms Division of the Treasury Department, and the Pentagon each have valid definitions for "explosives." Manufacturers must be careful in using such data, to make sure their definitions coincide with the data sources' meanings. (See Table VII-3.)

Tests for acute toxicity include lethal doses of a substance administered to test animals orally, through the skin, or by inhalation. They are often listed in toxicology books as the LD_{50} (oral, etc.) in a specific test animal such as the rat. "LD_{50}" is the "lethal dose" at which half the test animals died. A substance that can be eaten with little chance of harm (because it is broken down in the digestive system) might be deadly if inhaled or absorbed through the skin in

Table VII-3 Levels of Hazard Defined (J. L. Buckley and S. A. Wiener, "Documentation and Analysis of Historical Spill Data to Determine Hazardous Material Spill Prevention Research Priorities," in *Proceedings,* 1974 National Conference on Control of Hazardous Material Spills, AIChE, New York, pp. 85–89)

A. Relationship of Relative Hazard to Toxicity Range.

Relative hazard level	Toxicity range for LD_{50} (mg/kg)*
1	$LD_{50} > 5000$
2	$1000 < LD_{50} \leq 5000$
3	$100 < LD_{50} \leq 1000$
4	$10 < LD_{50} \leq 100$
5	$LD_{50} \leq 10$

*LD_{50} level is that dosage at which 50% of test organisms succumb to the agent administered. Lethal dosages for humans are typically lower than the LD_{50} dosage.

B. Hazard Potential Categorization Table.

	\multicolumn{5}{c}{Quantity of material spilled (liter or kg)}				
Hazard potential	\multicolumn{5}{c}{Relative hazard level}				
	1	2	3	4	5
1	7,640	2,550	510	50	5
2	19,100	6,370	1,270	130	13
3	38,200	12,700	2,550	255	26
4	76,400	25,500	5,100	510	51
5	152,800	50,900	10,200	1,020	102
6	382,100	127,400	25,500	2,550	255
7	764,200	254,700	50,900	5,100	510
8	1,528,400	509,500	101,900	10,190	1,019
9	3,821,100	1,273,700	254,700	25,470	2,547
10	>3,821,100	>1,273,700	>254,700	>25,470	>2,547

C. Hazard Potential Category Ranges.

Hazard potential category	Theoretical spill concentration as percentage of reference LD_{50}
1	TSC < 1% RLD
2	1% RLD ≤ TSC < 2.5% RLD
3	2.5% RLD ≤ TSC < 5% RLD
4	5% RLD ≤ TSC < 10% RLD
5	10% RLD ≤ TSC < 20% RLD
6	20% RLD ≤ TSC < 50% RLD
7	50% RLD ≤ TSC < 100% RLD
8	100% RLD ≤ TSC < 200% RLD
9	200% RLD ≤ TSC < 500% RLD
10	TSC ≥ 500% RLD

minute quantities, so the method of dose is vitally important. Typically, this kind of toxicity data is recorded as doses in milligrams per kilogram of body weight. Rats and humans aren't entirely the same, but they react closely enough for a simple scaling up of the rat's weight to a human's weight to be a good rough guess of toxicity in humans.

Other tests that are not as easily evaluated are the concentration of a substance lethal to certain kinds of aquatic life, or substances causing a decrease in the amount or diversity of aquatic flora.

Flammability data are extremely difficult to evaluate. Substances that burn poorly or not at all at low temperatures may flame wildly at elevated ones—temperatures well within the range of a typical structure fire, but higher than those produced in many standard flammability tests. Poisonous gases can be given off from such innocuous substances as polyurethane. Sometimes compounds are exempted from certain labeling requirements or toxicity warnings because they have been used in amounts too small to attract attention—certain specialized finishes for bearings or reflective surfaces, for instance. A manufacturer can be lulled into a false sense of security by this, as he prepares an application using much larger amounts on his product, or gathers large amounts together for the manufacturing process itself.

The National Institute for Occupational Safety and Health periodically publishes a listing of toxic substances. NIOSH also cooperated with the Environmental Protection Agency to compile a chemical substances list under provisions of the Toxic Substances Control Act of 1976. NIOSH, in its work, differentiates relatively toxic and nontoxic substances according to route of administration to experimental animals.

NIOSH prefers testing by oral dose, because that is the basis upon which most existing standards have been set, and upon which most existing data have been collected. The agency realizes, however, that the oral route may not be the dominant one in most workplace or product-related situations. Inhalation data are used if oral data are unavailable, and skin absorption data are the third choice.

NIOSH recognizes that the best data on toxic effects come from controlled studies of humans. Next in preference are data from (in order) rats, mice, dogs, monkeys, cats, rabbits, pigs, guinea pigs, and hamsters. Limiting dosages for substances administered by any route other than inhalation may be:

1. LDLo: Lethal Dose Low—the lowest dose of a substance (other than LD_{50}) introduced over any given period of time, and reported to have caused death in humans, or the lowest single dose introduced in one or more divided portions and reported to have caused death in animals, or

2. LD_{50}: Lethal Dose 50—as already mentioned, the dose of a substance expected to cause death of 50 percent of an entire population of an experimental animal species, as determined from the exposure to the substance of a significant number of animals.

Other "lethal dose" rates (LD_{10}, LD_{30} especially) are used as well, if they are available.

Typically, limiting doses for substances administered by inhalation are given in terms of continuous or 24-hour exposures. Unless otherwise indicated, LCLo is the lowest *concentration* of a substance, other than an LC_{50} in air, which has been reported to have caused death in animals when they have been exposed for 24 hours or less; the LC_{50} is the concentration of a substance, in air, at which exposure for 24 hours or less would cause death in 50 percent of the population of an experimental animal species.

Inhalation doses are particularly subject to synergism. An early guinea pig study of sulfur dioxide concentrations showed that sulfur dioxide in otherwise pure air was good for the animals—the higher the concentration, even up to 100 parts per million, the longer the animals lived. This dose, which is 5000 times the federal clean air standard for this substance, was prolonging life by killing potentially dangerous throat bacteria in the test animals. Likewise, guinea pigs exposed to large doses of soot in their air showed only minor ill effects. But soot and sulfur dioxide together killed the test animals at very low concentration levels—concentrations close to the actual ambient air levels in many American cities. Reason: the soot particles—each a tiny activated charcoal filter—combined with the sulfur dioxide and moisture to produce acids and sulfates far more harmful to health than the sulfur dioxide alone.

The NIOSH toxic substances list also includes substances reported to have produced any toxic effect in humans at fairly low doses (even common table salt is toxic at high doses). Aside from the obvious high doses, however, there are no qualifying limitations as to duration of exposure, concentration, or circumstances. The list includes "carcinogenic materials" as well; these will be discussed in the next section.

NIOSH also has a "priority list" of substances for which occupational safety and health standards should be written as soon as possible. The list is made up of chemicals of varying toxicity and varying use. Chemicals on the list had to meet a certain overall "rating," obtained by multiplying the number of workers at risk by a severity factor. The factor was derived from the (sometimes subjective) severity rankings of 50 industrial hygienists polled by NIOSH. In short, many dangerous substances are not on the list. NIOSH has developed "criteria documents" and suggested standards for many of these, for action by the Occupational Safety and Health Administration. There is almost always a long delay between the time NIOSH proposes a standard and when one is finally adopted by OSHA, because of the hearings and fact finding that OSHA must do first, as required by the Occupational Safety and Health Act.

As a result, companies will usually receive more guidance about the current thinking of the technical community by turning to the professional organizations' own hazard lists—especially the authoritative but relatively short Threshold Limit Value list of the American Council of Governmental Industrial Hygienists (App. B).

Table VII-4 Hazardous Chemicals—Available Treatment Processes (Environmental Protection Agency, *Report to Congress on Hazardous Waste Disposal*, June 30, 1973)

Process	Functions performed	Applicable to Waste Types* 1	2	3	4	5	6	7	8	Forms† S	L	G	Resource recovery capability
A. PHYSICAL TREATMENT:													
Carbon sorption	Vol. reduc./separ.	X	X	X	X	X					X	X	Yes
Dialysis	Vol. reduc./separ.	X	X	X	X						X		Yes
Electrodialysis	Vol. reduc./separ.	X	X	X	X		X				X		Yes
Evaporation	Vol. reduc./separ.	X	X			X					X		Yes
Filtration	Vol. reduc./separ.	X	X	X	X	X					X		Yes
Flocculation-settling	Vol. reduc./separ.	X	X	X	X	X					X		Yes
Reverse osmosis	Vol. reduc./separ.	X	X	X	X		X				X		Yes
Stripping-ammonia	Vol. reduc./separ.	X	X	X	X						X		Yes
B. CHEMICAL TREATMENT:													
Calcination	Vol. reduction	X	X			X					X		
Ion exchange	Vol. reduc./separ., detoxification	X	X	X	X	X					X		Yes
Neutralization	Detoxification	X	X	X	X						X		Yes
Oxidation	Detoxification	X	X	X	X						X		
Precipitation	Vol. reduc./separ.	X	X	X	X	X					X	X	Yes
Reduction	Detoxification	X	X								X		

236

		1	2	3	4	5	6	7	8				
C. THERMAL TREATMENT:													
Pyrolysis	Vol. reduc./detox.			X	X		X			X	X	X	Yes
Incineration	Detox./disposal		X	X	X	X		X	X	X	X	X	Yes
D. BIOLOGICAL TREATMENT:													
Activated sludges	Detoxification	X			X					X			No
Aerated lagoons	Detoxification	X								X			No
Waste stabilization ponds	Detoxification	X								X			No
Trickling filters	Detoxification	X								X			No
E. DISPOSAL/STORAGE:													
Deep-well injection	Disposal	X	X		X		X			X			No
Detonation	Disposal			X				X	X	X	X	X	No
Engineered storage	Storage	X	X	X	X	X	X	X	X	X	X	X	Yes
Land burial	Disposal	X	X	X	X		X			X	X		No
Ocean dumping	Disposal	X	X	X			X			X	X	X	No

SOURCE: EPA Contract Nos. 68-03-0089, 68-01-0762 and 68-01-0556.

*Waste type: (1) inorganic chemical w/o heavy metals, (2) inorganic chemical w/heavy metals, (3) organic chemical w/o heavy metals, (4) organic chemical w/heavy metals, (5) radiological, (6) biological, (7) flammable, (8) explosive.

†Waste form: S, solid; L, liquid; G, gas.

NAME _Aniline_   MOLECULAR FORMULA _C₆H₅NH₂_   MOLECULAR WT. _93.12_

MATERIAL DATA

I. IDENTIFICATION
A. Other Names
  Phenylamine
  Aminobenzene
  Aniline Oil
B. Code Numbers
  1) CAS No. _000062533_
  2) C-G Code No. _____
  3) WLN _ZR_
C. Structural Formula

  NH₂
  ⬡

D. Emergency Phone Numbers
  1) Corp. SH&E
  2) Supplier
  3) User (site)

II. PHYSICAL PROPERTIES
A. liquid ☒ gas ☐ solid ☐ polymorphic ☐
B. melting point _(−)6.2_ °C C. boiling point _184_ °C
D. flow point _6.2_ °C   E. vapor density _3.22_
F. specific gravity _1.018@20_ G. % volatile _____
H. vapor pressure _51mmHg 77_°C I. flash point _168_°_FCC TAG_
J. solubility in water _slightly miscible_ mg/mL
K. soluble in other solvents _alcohol, ether, chloroform_
L. appearance _Colorless oily liquid_
M. odor _Characteristic odor_
N. auto ignition temperature _537.7_ °C

III. HAZARDOUS PROPERTIES
	Yes	No
A. Flammable	☐	☒
B. Combustible	☒	☐
C. Corrosive	☐	☒
D. Explosive	☐	☒
E. Oxydizing Agent	☐	☒
F. Radioactive	☐	☒

G. Flammability limits _1.3_ % to _not available_
H. Evaporation rate _____

*IV. TOXICITY DATA:
A. Acute Oral LD₅₀ _440_ mg/kg
   Species _rat_
B. Dermal LD₅₀ _820_ mg/kg
   Species _rabbit_
C. Inhalation LCLo _250 ppm/4H_
   Species _rat_
D. Toxicity rating _2-Moderately Hazardous_
E. Toxic Substances List Entry
   _BW 66500_

V. HEALTH EFFECTS
A. Acute Symptoms: The most important aspect is conversion of hemoglobin to methemoglobin causing bluish discoloration of lips, ear lobe, fingernail beds (cyanosis). Headache, weakness, irritability, collapse. Cyanosis may not be noticed until a few hours after exposure.
B. Chronic Symptoms: Palpitation, dizziness, drowsiness, shortness of breath, unconsciousness collapse, red cells may show Heinz bodies and aminophenol may appear in urine.

VI. FIRST AID:
General: Remove patient from contaminated area immediately. Clear airway, give oxygen and artificial respiration if necessary. Consult a physician immediately.
In Case of Contact: Remove contaminated wearing apparel including shoes; wash clothing before reuse (discard contaminated shoes). Immediately flush eyes with plenty of water for at least 15 minutes.
Flood contaminated skin with water (may remove clothing under safety shower), make sure that fingernails and hair are decontaminated.
If ingested and patient is conscious: induce vomiting.

Figure VII-3 Material data folder for hazardous chemicals handled by XYZ company. (*After Chemical Engineering, April 11, 1977.*)

Medical Data Sheet

Notice To The Physician: This medical data sheet is intended to provide information on the known properties of the chemical. It is only meant to furnish guidance to the physician in the event of an emergency. The attending physician must make his own diagnosis of the illness and prescribe the specific treatment to be administered.

ANILINE   Chemical Formula: $C_6H_5NH_2$

General Information
Aniline is a colorless, oily liquid which darkens after exposure to light in presence of air. The odor threshold is 1 ppm. The threshold limit value (TLV) is 5 ppm.

Toxicity
Aniline is an irritant to the eye and mildly irritating to the skin. Toxic concentrations of aniline may be absorbed by inhalation, ingestion or skin absorption. The toxicity is due to conversion of hemoglobin to methemoglobin with resulting loss of oxygen transport. Hemolysis with anemia and mild renal involvement may occur. Due to shifting of the oxyhemoglobin dissociation curve, hypoxia is relatively greater than would be caused by equivalent anemia. The oral LD_{50} in rats is 440 mg/kg. The mean lethal oral dose is probably between 15 and 30 gm for an adult human, although lesser amounts (1 gm) have been reported to be fatal.

Clinical Signs and Symptoms
The symptoms correlate with blood methemoglobin concentration and develop insidiously if the exposure is not massive. Cyanosis (bluish discoloration of lips, ears, fingernail beds, cheeks) is usually apparent with 15% methemoglobin. Variation in skin pigmentation may alter evaluation of cyanosis. At times there is a feeling of well-being (euphoria) although there may be no symptoms until 30-40% methemoglobin. Above 40% methemoglobin symptoms include headache, weakness, dizziness, ataxia, irritability, drowsiness, shortness of breath, confusion, nausea, vomiting, tinnitus, and finally coma

Medical Treatment
(Suggestions depending on clinical course)
- Administer oxygen.
- Make sure skin decontamination is adequate (vinegar or 5% acetic acid wash may be used).
- Order serial blood methemoglobin concentration determinations.
- Use analgesic (aspirin, codeine, etc. — but no acetanilid or acetophenetidin) for headache.
  The following measures are indicated if methemoglobin concentration reaches above 40%:
- Administer methylene blue (1% solution) 1-2 mg/kg intravenously over a 5-10 minute period. This may be repeated in 1-2 hours. Avoid perivascular infiltration which results in tissue necrosis. Methylene blue does not benefit patients with glucose-6-phosphate dehydrogenase deficiency.
- If methylene blue is not effective consider exchange transfusion or hemodialysis.
- Avoid alcohol (delays recovery from methamoglobinemia).

If Ingested:
- Perform gastric lavage with large amounts of water (no more than 250 ml at one time). Leave 30 gm of sodium sulfate in 250 ml water in the stomach after lavage.
- Consider gastroenterostomy.

In Case of Eye Contact:
The injured eye requires thorough irrigation with water, and immediate attention of an ophthalmologist. The use of agents such as anticollagenases, steroids, antibiotics and drugs to prevent iritis require careful and continuing evaluation of the clinical status of the patient. Substances to neutralize the injurious material should not be put into the eye.

Figure VII-4   Medical data sheet. *(Chemical Engineering.)*

3. ALLERGIC REACTIONS

There are no national statistics on the extent of the population that suffers from allergic reactions of any kind. The National Institute of Allergy and Infectious Diseases estimates that about a tenth of all Americans suffer from various allergies, and that most of those are hay fever or asthma. The Institute suggests that perhaps only 3 percent of the population is allergic to substances found in consumer products or in an occupational setting. The Institute does not consider substances that affect a large percentage of the population as allergic, however. Thus, cigarette smoke may cause adverse reactions in a quarter of the population, but those individuals are not considered "allergic" to the smoke unless the reaction is particularly severe. A small reaction is considered "normal" by medical authorities.

There is also an "under-reporting" problem in the field. A 1958 survey of nearly 3000 American dermatologists* uncovered 15,000 cases of reactions that year to permanent waves, hair dyes, lipstick, and nail polish. But from 1956 to 1960 the number of reported products liability claims for drugs, pharmaceuticals, and cosmetics was fewer than 6000 (of which more than 4500 were for cosmetics alone).

Although careful premarket testing of a new product can determine the percentage of the population likely to suffer allergic reaction to it (leading to reformulation of the product or warnings on the packaging and in advertising), the consumer's view is often that the reaction is unpredictable. Whether an individual will react adversely to a product depends in part on heredity, in part on the extent of the exposure, and maybe partially on other stresses the individual has suffered (stress can upset the body's system of antibodies and antigens).

Furthermore, an individual usually does not suffer an allergic reaction to a substance until at least the second exposure. The first exposure mobilizes the body's antigen-antibody system and sensitizes the individual to subsequent exposures. If an individual is susceptible, but only slightly susceptible, to a given substance, hundreds of exposures might be necessary to produce a serious reaction. This is usually the cause of those "cute" newspaper stories about lawyers suddenly allergic to paper and ink, bankers allergic to money, or bakers allergic to flour. The reaction—which can range from mild blistering to runny nose, to congestive heart failure and death—may occur after a stressful incident on the job, heightening an employer's view that the problem is psychosomatic.

Despite the uncertainties facing manufacturers, they are generally held strictly liable for allergic reactions to their products—especially in the area of cosmetics, where the presumed "benefits" to society from use are close to zero. Thus manufacturers in the drug and cosmetics industries conduct broad-based testing programs among large numbers of individuals over long periods of time (to account for hereditary differences and sensitizing periods).

---

*Discussed in P. D. Rheingold and Sheila L. Birnbaum, *Product Liability: Law, Practice, Science*, pp. 413–443; Practising Law Institute, N.Y.

Even so, many products slip through the tests and into the market, and cause harm. Problems commonly occur when suppliers of raw materials change their formulations slightly without telling the manufacturer of the final product. A new solvent or different kind of vegetable oil can make a whole series of tests useless. In *Carter v. Yardley & Co* (decided in the Supreme Judicial Court of Massachusetts in 1946), plaintiff suffered second-degree burns after using Yardley perfume. Testimony revealed others who suffered the same reaction. Defendant admitted it did not even know all the ingredients in the perfume, or their proportions. Plaintiff won on the basis of simple negligence.

The court record on awards to plaintiffs allergic to substances considered harmless by the great bulk of the population has been mixed. Procter & Gamble won a case in 1963, against a plaintiff allergic to the stannous fluoride in Crest toothpaste—the courts ruled that too few people were allergic to it. Other jurisdictions might decide the case differently today (the case was based on failure to warn of the potential danger).

The courts—worried about long lists of potential warnings covering exceedingly small segments of the population—have tended to limit the requirement to warn in such cases. But recognizing that the manufacturer is better able to stand the burden of covering damages for widely used products that are harmful to a few, the courts usually award damages in strict liability to injured consumers.

4. CARCINOGENICITY

Companies, consumers, and politicians react in diverse ways to news that a substance may be carcinogenic. The reactions depend on the amount of the suspect substance in use, its perceived value to society, and the number of jobs that may be lost in its manufacture. Rarely do the reactions have much to do with the actual strength of the evidence against a substance.

In part, this is due to the uncertainties in the tests themselves, and in their interpretation. Based on the same data, the United States has banned the use of the food dye Red 2, while Canadian scientists have allowed it. But in part the diversity of reactions is due to the long terms over which cancer can develop. Who's worrying about the effects of a substance on a small percentage of the population 20 years from now?

Indeed, it may be difficult to hold manufacturers liable for "mistakes" made long ago. Women—the daughters of mothers treated with diethylstilbestrol (DES) some 20 years ago—have developed cancers in their reproductive organs at an extremely high rate. Medically, the link between DES and the cancers is beyond dispute. But as of this writing, no court has awarded damages to the sufferers. Why? Because hospital records are not accurate enough to determine exactly which manufacturer of DES was responsible for which case, and courts at the federal district level have ruled that the victims cannot sue the drug manufacturers as a group. How, then, can a victim of bladder cancer attribute the disease to any particular cause, when many substances are known to cause it?

Nevertheless, manufacturers can often suffer large losses when a federal agency determines that a substance is dangerous, and bans its use. The cost of destroying or reworking inventory can be disastrous, as we shall see later in this section, in a discussion of the TRIS* case. Thus, it behooves manufacturers to stay current with the technical literature and with notices from federal agencies—especially the National Institutes of Health and the Food and Drug Administration—that any substances are being investigated for potential problems. Manufacturers must also understand the significance of the carcinogenicity tests most often used today.

The most "certain" tests are those that involve humans. Because there are so many potential sources of cancer in the environment, evidence of carcinogenicity in humans has been confined to a relatively few substances that are particularly strong carcinogens (they cause enough cases to be noticed above the "background"), or substances that have been used in the workplace for a long time.

Perhaps the best known are certain coal tar products. In 1775 Percival Potts first linked cancer of the scrotum in English chimney sweeps to the soot and tar picked up in their work. By the end of the nineteenth century, his observations had been confirmed in controlled statistical samples of workers in the coal tar chemical industry. More recently, animal studies beginning in 1962 of such relatively "mild" or "weak" carcinogens as vinyl chloride, led researchers to look more carefully at exposed human populations and confirm the link between the chemical and the cancer.

Although animal tests have been roundly criticized—especially by manufacturers who stand to lose money on the test results—they remain the most accepted way of determining carcinogenicity. In a typical "animal bioassay" large numbers of test animals are given large doses of the suspect chemical over a relatively short period—rarely more than two years. The doses are normally fed to the animals, but they may be injected, inhaled, or painted on the skin instead. The animals almost always are pure strains that have been standardized and bred to be as genetically alike as possible, thus reducing the chance that genetic variability in susceptability to cancer will mask the results being sought. Normally, medical authorities insist that cancer be shown to occur in at least two species of test animal before a substance is declared dangerous to humans.

Although these tests have never been shown to produce a "false alarm"—that is, every substance fingered in animal tests as being carcinogenic has eventually been shown to cause cancer in humans as well, and many substances have passed the animal tests—the criticism that they are not "realistic" is frequently heard.

For instance, supporters of saccharin deride Canadian tests on the substance by saying that a "human would have to drink 800 bottles of diet soda a day to get cancer from saccharin," based on the weight difference between man and mouse. Strictly speaking, this is not entirely true, because a rat's lifespan is only a thirtieth of a human's. Furthermore, the higher dose over a short period to

---

*(2,3 dibromopropyl) phosphate.

produce a cancer in a large proportion of the test animals is thought by most medical authorities to be directly related to long-term, low-dose exposure in the much larger human population.

Nevertheless, it is extremely expensive and time-consuming to do animal bioassays. Authorities put the cost at $100,000 or more per chemical. What's more, the results are only as good as the laboratory that performs the test. The Food and Drug Administration has been investigating charges of sloppy lab work, and has been looking into the possibility of outright fraud.

As with studies of toxicity, researchers try to determine a substance's potential carcinogenicity from its molecular structure—and the structure's relation with known problem-causing chemicals. Success has been limited.

One quick screening test has come into fairly wide use since the mid-1970s, however. This is the so-called Ames Test, named after its chief developer, Dr. Bruce Ames, a biochemist at the University of California at Berkeley. This test uses various strains of *Salmonella* bacteria, upon which suspect chemicals act. Once a lab has been set up to do the test, the screening of a suspect chemical can be done in a few days for only a few hundred dollars.

The test does not measure carcinogenicity—the potential for causing a tumor—directly. Instead, it measures the mutagenicity of a chemical—that is, its ability to produce a genetic change. Almost all known carcinogens turn out to be mutagenic as well, although the reverse is not necessarily true. Among the chemicals registering positive in the Ames test are known carcinogens such as the nitrosamines, aromatic amines, direct alkylating agents, polycyclic hydrocarbons, certain fungal toxins, nitrofurans, a number of antibiotic carcinogens such as adriamycin, daunomycin, and mitomycin C, and even some drugs used to fight cancer itself.

All known human carcinogens that have been tested show positive. These include beta-naphthylamine, benzidine, cigarette smoke condensates, *bis*-dichloromethyl ether, aflatoxin, vinyl chloride, and 4-amino biphenyl.

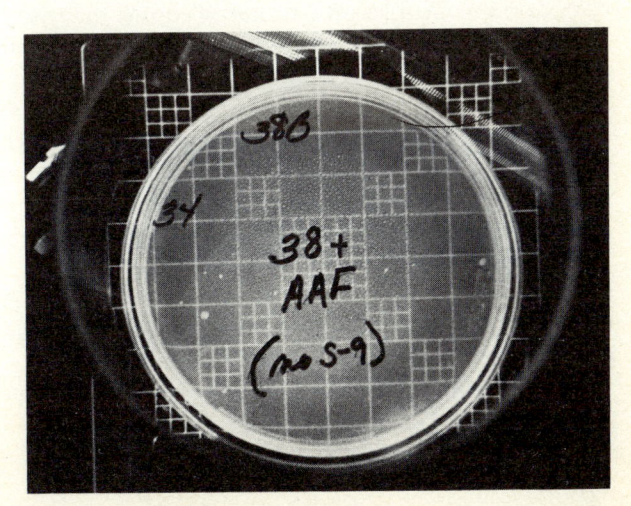

Figure VII-5 Ames test culture dish. (*Aileen Smith photo.*)

The test can substitute for the more complicated biological systems of animals and humans because mutations occur through alteration of deoxyribonucleic acid (DNA), and DNA is basically the same in all living organisms. Thus, a substance that causes mutations in *Salmonella* bacteria is likely to do the same in an animal, unless the animal's metabolic system can change the substance into something that is less harmful before it can affect the DNA.

In the Ames test, the chemical being investigated is added to the bacteria on a petri dish and incubated. If the chemical is a mutagen it will mutate the bacteria. Normally, the mutated bacteria would be undetectable in the growth of normal bacteria, so the Ames test is actually a "reverse mutation test." Ames and his co-workers have developed strains of *Salmonella* that already have various kinds of mutations in the genes that govern their ability to make histidine (a substance needed by the bacteria to grow). After two days incubation, the colonies of *Salmonella* that have been mutated back to producing histidine have grown enough to be seen. If the chemical being tested is not a mutagen, the petri dish will at best contain only a few isolated colonies (from spontaneous mutations).

Ames and his co-workers screened hundreds of known mutants of *Salmonella typhimurium* bacteria before finding a few appropriate ones. Each of the tester strains is sensitive to a particular type of mutation. One strain detects what are called "base-pair" substitutions, another detects various kinds of "frame shift" mutagens. Therefore, the test can be focused on the type of mutation a chemical is suspected of causing, greatly increasing the test's accuracy. Because some chemicals are not carcinogenic when they enter the body—they're activated only when exposed to other chemicals there—Ames has devised a way to make his *Salmonella* bacteria mimic mammalian activation mechanisms. The trick—adding a liver homogenate to the petri dish—is still controversial.

Nevertheless, at least 50 chemical and drug companies were using the test by late 1976 to perform routine screening of new compounds at an early stage of development. American Cyanamid found that one positive reaction by a promising new chemical was due to a mutagenic impurity. Manufacturing procedures were tightened to eliminate the problem.

Unfortunately, a few classes of chemicals containing known and suspected carcinogens have proved difficult to pick up in the Ames test. In particular, carbon tetrachloride and dieldrin have registered negative. This may be a serious defect, because both are in the chlorinated hydrocarbon family, an extremely important source of new and useful chemical products. Ames has voiced confidence that new bacterial strains will be developed to test these, too.

One shortcoming that probably always will be present is the inability of the test to provide quantitative answers about the potency of substances that register as mutagens. It may be that at low doses the human body can handle a "weak" carcinogen by metabolizing it to a harmless substance. Vinyl chloride may be one such chemical. The Ames test may unfairly point to such compounds as bigger problems than they really are.

The argument over TRIS, a chemical that has been exhaustively tested using the Ames method and animal bioassay, offers some insight into problems business (and the consumer) faces. TRIS—the actual chemical name is (2,3-dibromopropyl) phosphate—was used by manufacturers of children's clothing to meet requirements for flame-resistance set by the Consumer Product Safety Commission. TRIS was not the only chemical available for the task, but it was one of the few that did not cause allergic reactions in a significant number of test subjects and consumers, and its price was reasonable to most manufacturers. Some fibers do not need any flame-retarding chemicals on them to meet the CPSC standards for the clothing in which it was mandatory—up to size 14 sleepwear. But most polyester, acetate, and triacetate fabric blends cannot meet the standards without some extra chemical treatment.

Soon after TRIS came into wide use, it was suspected of being potentially harmful; animal bioassay tests began at the National Cancer Institute early in 1974, using rats and mice. By 1976, the animal bioassays were not quite finished, but TRIS had been subjected to the Ames test, and caused mutations both with and without the liver homogenate added.

Citing the unfavorable Ames test results, the Environmental Defense Fund petitioned the Commission to force TRIS off the market, at least in fabrics with a surface concentration of more than 100 parts per million of the substance. The CPSC stalled until the bioassays were completed. When they, too, showed positive (both the rats and the mice developed tumors in the kidneys, and the mice also developed tumors in the liver, lungs, and stomach), the Commission ordered all TRIS-containing fabric off the market on April 8, 1977. All such material still in the stores, or bought by consumers before that date and still unwashed, was to be returned to the manufacturers.

The clothing manufacturers, alarmed by the Environmental Defense Fund's first petition a year earlier, had begun to switch to other flame retardants. Even so, the Commission's Bureau of Economic Analysis estimated that 18 million garments—more than a third of the spring 1977 production of children's sleepwear—contained TRIS. The manufacturers sued, claiming that a recall would be ruinous financially. The federal district court in Washington, D.C., agreed, and stayed the ban until the CPSC could come up with a more equitable recall procedure.

Even given the fact that TRIS tested positive as a carcinogen, the risks and benefits to the consumer were a subject of some debate. CPSC's own Bureau of Epidemiology said that it detected a decrease in the average severity of children's burns since the original rule on flame-resistance as put into effect. The Commission's Bureau of Biomedical Science projected cancer incidence rates of approximately 300 kidney cancers per million males in the affected population, and about 60 cancers per million females. The estimates were based on both the National Cancer Institute results and upon the estimated actual exposure that children would incur, either wearing affected clothing or chewing on it.

This is considered the best estimate, but the Bureau also obtained estimates of lifetime cancer incidence ranging as high as 5,100 cases per million males.

These estimates were also generated with acceptable calculation procedures, and produce a clearly unacceptable incidence rate—about one in 200. The Environmental Defense Fund, also using the same data, estimated the incidence at 6,000 per million. Ames and his co-workers went further, suggesting that 17,000 per million (close to one child in 60) would eventually develop cancer from wearing clothes treated with TRIS.

Only time will tell who was right.

5. COMPATIBILITY

On November 3, 1974, a Pan American World Airways 707 jet freighter crashed in Boston en route from New York to Scotland. Among other things, the aircraft was carrying 16,000 pounds of chemicals, including acids. Some containers of nitric acid had been placed on their sides in the cargo hold, and were leaking. The inner packing around the acid containers was sawdust, rather than an inert, noncombustible material. The leaking acid, reacting with the packaging, caused a fire.

According to Dow Chemical, which investigated the crash although none of its own products was involved, more than half a dozen firms including the shipper, the broker, the packer, the freight forwarder, and the airline itself all contributed to the disaster. Violations of existing Department of Transportation regulations included improper packing, improper packaging markings, and careless documentation. The shipper described the acid as "chemicals." The forwarder described them to the airline as "electrical parts." The plane's sensors correctly detected a fire in flight, but because Pan Am personnel failed to advise the pilot that hazardous materials were on board, he believed he had an electrical fire.

Because electrical fires are common and usually not serious, the pilot passed over several airports where he could have landed safely. Nevertheless, the prime cause of the accident was the incompatability of the packing material with the product being shipped—it protected the acid containers from cracking, but contributed to the danger of common spilling.

Such failures due to incompatibilities of chemicals are not common, because most designers understand the limitations of the materials they work with, and design accordingly for normal situations. The incompatibilities lead to great danger when *uncommon* occurrences turn up—fire, abnormally high temperatures, abnormally low temperatures, electrical discharges, the presence of impurities, or extremely poor maintenance procedures. An O-ring of improper material is inserted in a fluid line. The line fails. The wrong hydraulic fluid is used to refill a line; its lower tolerance to extreme temperatures leads to a fire. The gas released by an automatic fire suppression system feeds the fire instead.

Designers of equipment for specific industries often try to head off incompatibility problems by sticking to certain standard materials for all applications, even if other products might be better in a given application. Thus, maintenance personnel for earth-moving equipment have only a limited range of hydraulic fluids, gasket materials, and flexible hose materials to choose from while working on a wide variety of vehicles.

The aerospace industry and civilian hospitals offer good examples of techniques for segregating incompatible materials. Gas tanks used in hospitals, for instance, are color-coded and carefully labeled. To ensure that, for instance, a tank of nitrogen oxide is not connected to a valve meant for an oxygen line (a mistake that might be common in an emergency), the tank's threads don't match the valve's. Various combinations of right-hand and left-hand threads are used, as are various line diameters. Thread widths and profiles are not counted upon, because of the chance a strong individual (perhaps using tools) could force-fit fittings with nonidentical but similar threadings.

In aerospace designs, the problems are more difficult. Not only are weight and vibration resistance complicating factors, but often two "incompatible" materials are meant to be carried, kept separate until needed, then jammed together and ignited in a combustion chamber. The *Air Force Systems Safety Design Handbook 1-6* calls for separating incompatible materials such as fuels and oxidizers so that in case of simultaneous ruptures, one cannot spill upon the other. Fluid lines are to be isolated with sleeves, barriers, or bulkheads, and adjacent incompatible system connectors are to be keyed or sized to avoid interconnections (see Fig. VII-6).

The Air Force, as well as commercial fabricators of large tanks to hold combustible material, calls for nonabsorbent insulation. If absorbent insulation (such as polyurethane) must be used, designers try to seal it with impermeable materials.

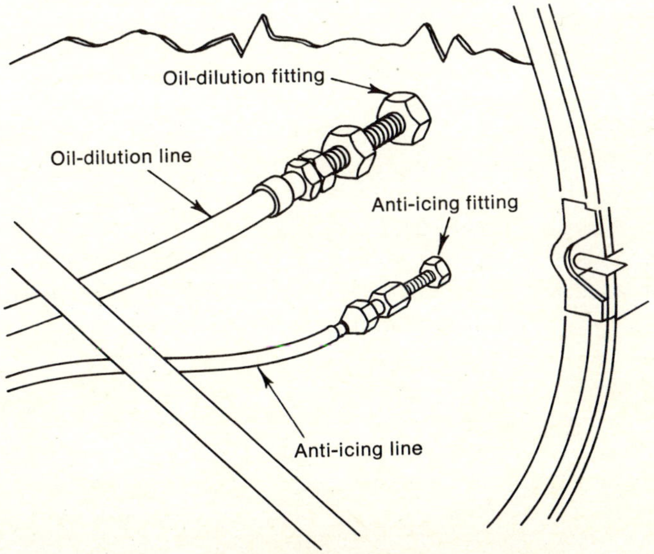

Figure VII-6 Lines and fittings of different sizes prevent interconnection of incompatible systems (*Air Force Systems Safety Design Handbook 1-6.*)

Cleaning agents are a problem, both for the Air Force and for makers of instrumentation using complex organic chemicals in their operation. The Air Force has fingered nitrogen tetroxide as particularly sensitive in combination with many common cleaning and degreasing agents (see Table VII-5).

Easily worked materials such as galvanized pipe and copper tubing are rejected for many applications; the galvanized finish can flake, and copper reacts with many substances. Stainless steel and aluminum alloy are preferred, especially by the aerospace industry (see Table VII-6). Teflon has become increasingly preferred for a wide range of applications requiring flexible couplings, because of its resistance to high and low temperatures (typically $-100°F$ to $+500°$), chemical inertness, and ability to withstand high pressures. It is subject to fatigue in flexing, however, and special attention must be paid to fittings at either end of a run of Teflon hose. The Air Force says failures most commonly occur at fittings.

Teflon is also used in a wide range of seals, O-rings, and even some gaskets. Even the Air Force has found, however, that old standbys such as leather, cork, and natural rubber are useful in many applications, especially for petroleum-based fluids.

Neoprene is a commonly used gasket material, although both the Air Force and chemical industry sources say workers frequently—and mistakenly—use pipe dope or gasket seal compounds with neoprene or nitrile-butadiene. Some chemical companies won't let field repair crews out of the shop with such sealing materials if they are working with neoprene gasket materials.

Table VII-5 Explosive Reaction of Various Commercial Solvents with Nitrogen Tetroxide (*Air Force System Safety Design Handbook, 1-6*)

Solvent mixed with N_2O_4	*Result when exposed to shock*
Trichloroethylene	Violent explosion*
Methylene chloride	Violent explosion
Chloroform	Moderate explosion
Carbon tetrachloride	Very moderate explosion
Dichloroethylene	Violent explosion
Unsymmetrical tetrachloroethane	Violent explosion
Perchloroethylene	Violent explosion
Symmetrical tetrachloroethane	No explosion
Freon MF	No explosion
Freon TF	No explosion

*Violent explosions from solvent N_2O_4 mixtures in open cups containing one liter of 50–50 mix will produce a hole in ¾-inch armor plate approximating the shape of the bottom of the container.

Table VII:-6 Compatibility of Various Common Fluids with Aluminum and Its Alloys *(Air Force Systems Safety Design Handbook 1-6)*

	Cast					Wrought							
Service	40E	356	5052	5056	5086	6061	2014	2024	2219	7075	1060	1100	3003
CRYOGENIC													
Fluorine (Liquid)			L			S		L				S	U
Hydrogen (Liquid)	U		S					S				S	
Hydrogen (Gaseous)	U		S					S				S	
Nitrogen (Liquid)	U	U	S	U	U	U	U	U	U		U	U	U
Nitrogen (Gaseous)	U	U	S	U	U	U	U	U	U		U	U	U
Oxygen (Liquid)			S			L		L		U		S	U
Oxygen (Gaseous)		S	S			S		S		S		S	S
Helium	U	U	S	U	U	U	U	U	U	U	U	U	U
OXIDIZER													
Chlorine trifluoride		S	S			S		S				S	S
Fluorine (Gas)			S			S		S				S	S
Hydrogen peroxide	U	L	L	L	L	L					L		L
Nitric acid (Fuming)											S		
Nitrogen Tetroxide		S_3	S_3			S_3	S	S_3		S_3		S	S_3
FUELS													
Ammonia	Limited use above room temperature												
Hydrazine	L	S	S		L	S	S	S	L	L		S	S
UDMH	L	S	S		L	S	S	S	L	L		S	S
MMH & 50-50 Mixture	U	S	S		L	S	S	S	L	U		L	L
Kerosene (RP-1), JP-4, JP-7, and thermally stable fuels	No limitation												
Pentaborane		S	S			S		S		S		S	S

S = Satisfactory   U = Unsatisfactory S_1 = At below boiling point of fluid
L = Limited use   Blank = Undetermined S_2 = Limited to a maximum of 400 psig
    S_3 = Less than 0.1% water

Table VII-7 Compatibility of Various Common Fluids with Metals (Non-aluminum) and Certain Materials Used in Flexible Lines and Gaskets *(Air Force Systems Safety Design Handbook 1-6)*

Service	Bronze	Aluminum	Carbon Steel	Carbon Moly Steel	3½% Ni Steel	4–6% Chr Moly Steel	304 Stainless Steel	316 Stainless Steel	347 Stainless Steel	400 Series Stainless Steel
CRYOGENIC										
Fluorine (Liquid)	S	*	U	S	S	S	S	S	S	L
Hydrogen (Liquid)	S	*	U	S	S	S	S	S	S	S
Nitrogen (Liquid)	S	*	U				S	S	S	S
Oxygen (Liquid)	S	*	U				S	S	S	S
OXIDIZER										
Chlorine trichloride	S	*					S	S	L	S
Fluorine (Gas)	S	*	S_2	U	U	U	S	S	S	S
Hydrogen peroxide	U	*	U	U	U	U	L	L	L	L
Nitric acid (Fuming)	U	*	U	U	U	U	S	S	S	U
Nitrogen tetroxide	U	*	L	U	U	U	S	S	S	L
FUELS										
Ammonia	U	*	L		L		S	S	S	S
Gasoline	S	*	S	S	S	S	S	S	S	S
Hydrazine	U	*	U				S_1	S_1	S_1	S
UDMH	U	*	U				S_1	S_1	S_1	S
Kerosene RP-1, JP-4	U	*	U	S	S	S	S	S	S	S
JP-7, and thermally stable fuels	U	*	U	S	S	S	S	S	S	S
Alcohol	S	*	S	S	S	S	S	S	S	S
Pentaborane	S	*	S				L	L	L	L
OTHERS										
Ethylene oxide	U	*	S				S	S	S	S

*See Table VII-6   S = Satisfactory   L = Limited use   U = Unsatisfactory   Blank = Undetermined

	Monel	Nickel	Copper	Neoprene	Viton	Teflon	Kel-F	Zytel-Nylon	Asbestos	Buna-N
				\multicolumn{7}{c	}{*Nonmetals*}
	S	S	S	U	U	U	U	U	U	U
	S	S	S	U	U	S	S	S	S	U
	S		S	U	U	S	S	U	S	U
	S	S	S							
	S	S	S	U	U	S	S	U	U	U
	S	S	S	U	S_2	S_2	S_2	U	U	U
	U	U	U		L	S	S	U		U
	U	U	U	U	U	S	S	U	U	U
		L	U			S	S		S	
	S	L	U			S	S		S	
		S	S	S						
		U			U	S	S		S	
	S	U			U	S	S			
	S	U		S		S	S		L	S
	S	S	U	S	S	S	S	S	U	U
	S	S	S	S	L	S	S	U	S	L
	S	S	L		S		S			
			U			S	S	S		S

S_1 = At below boiling point of fluid S_2 = Limited to a maximum of 400 psig

Table VII-8 Hydraulic Fluid Selection Chart (*Air Force Systems Safety Design Handbook 1-6*)

Property or quality	Petroleum oil	Phosphate ester	Phosphate ester base	Chlorinated hydrocarbon	Silicone base	Water/glycol	Soluble oil in water	Water in oil emulsion
Specific gravity	0.85 to 0.90	1.15	1.08 to 1.35	1.30 to 1.45	1.25 to 1.30	1.10	1.0	0.90 to 0.95
Viscosity range	Low to very high	Low to high	Low to high	Low to high	Low	Low to high	Low	Low
Viscosity index	High	Low to high	Low to high	Low to high	Very high	Very high	Very high	High
Temperature limits	0 to 130°F	Below 0 to 130°F	15 to 130°F	45 to 130°F	From −65 to 500°F	Below 0 to 120°F	50 to 120°F	50 to 120°F
Fire resistance								
Open flame	Poor	Good	Good	Good	Fair	Very good	Excellent	Fair
Hot surface	Poor	Very good	Very good	Very good	Fair to good	Good	Excellent	Fair
Auto-ignition temperature	700°F	1100°F	1100°F	1200°F	850 to 900°F	—	—	—
Stability (Oxidation resistance)	Very good	Excellent	Excellent	Excellent	Excellent	Excellent	Excellent	Good

Lubricity	Excellent	Excellent	Excellent	Excellent	Excellent	Limited to good	Very good	Limited	Good
Corrosion protection	Very good	Very good	Very good	Very good	Very good	Good	Good	Fair	Good
Compatibility	Excellent	Very good except coatings and water-absorbing materials	Very good except coatings; need special packings	Very good except coatings; need special packings	Very good except coatings; need special packings	Generally very good; special packings for high and low temperature	Very good except coatings and water-absorbing materials	Very good except coatings and water-absorbing materials	Very good except coatings and water-absorbing materials
Pump wear									
Balanced vane	Excellent	Excellent	Excellent	Excellent	Excellent	Fair to good	Very good	Very poor	Good
Gear pump with bushings	Excellent	Excellent	Excellent	Excellent	Excellent	Fair to good	Excellent	Very poor	Excellent

253

Table VII-9 Suggested Materials for Use with Various Propellants and Oxidizing Chemicals (*Air Force Systems Safety Design Handbook 1-6*)

Substance	Packing and gasket	Service Lubricants	Metals
Ammonia	Neoprene, Teflon, Kel-F, asbestos.	Silicones, graphite.	Any except copper-containing alloys. Also no nickel or Monel.
Aviation gasoline 115/145	Nylon, Kel-F, Trithene, Fluorothene A, polyvinyl alcohol, Teflon, Buna N (linear compound MJ-70), Parker PS-10-13N, plastic rubber compound N209-70. Butyl rubber, Vinylite, polyethylene at ambient temperature.	Molykote, Fluorolubes (Hooker's or Union Carbide's), Nordcoseal 147-S, MIL-G-6032 grease, and electrofilm graphite coating.	Stainless steel, carbon steels, aluminum and magnesium alloys.
Dimethyl hydrazine	Teflon Fluorothene A	Fluorolube—Fs. Fluorolube—S	Stainless steel Aluminum alloys, AISI 4130 low alloy steel.
Ethylene oxide	Teflon Kel-F, nylon, polyvinyl alcohol	Fluorinated hydrocarbon, Teflon grease	Mild steel, stainless steel types 304, 316, 321.
Hydrogen peroxide (up to 90% concentration)	Polyethylene, Teflon, pure tin (treated with HCl and rinsed with H_2O), Koroseal, Kel-F, Trithene, aluminum 1100, degreased Fiberglas, Saran, Vinylite, glass cloth impregnated with Teflon or Kel-F.	Fluorolube 10214, Fluorolube 10213, Kel-Flo Perfluorolube oils.	99.6% pure aluminum and certain aluminum alloys.
Kerosene (RP-1), JP-4	Nylon, Kel-F, Trithene, Fluorothene A, Vinylite, Teflon, Buna N (linear compound MJ-70), polyethylene at ambient temperature.	Molykote, Fluorolubes, MIL-G-6032 grease, and electro-film graphite coating.	Stainless steels and aluminum alloys.

254

JP-7 and thermally stable fuels	Nylon, Kel-F, Trithene, Fluorothene A, Vinylite, Teflon, polyethylene at ambient temperature.	Molykote, Fluorolubes, MIL-G-6032 grease, and electro-film graphite coating	Stainless steels and aluminum alloys.
Liquid fluorine	Use packless valves, copper gasket and seats.	None.	Nickel, 18-8 SS, copper.
Liquid oxygen	Kel-F, Trithene, Fluorothene A, Teflon, asbestos, soft copper, aluminum, and Johns-Manville No. 61-S bonded asbestos sheet.	Molykote, electrofilm graphite coating, Parker Oxyseal for pipe joints.	Any austenitic stainless steel, aluminum, Monel, nickel, Inconel, and copper base alloys.
Nitromethane	Neoprene, Teflon, Kel-F, Trithene, Fluorothene A, Nylon, Saran, polyethylene, Vinylite VE 5901, Perbunan.	Silicones, graphite.	Stainless steel or mild steel with protective plastic to reduce rust formation, aluminum alloys.
Propyl nitrate	Nylon, Dacron, Bakelite, polyethylene, Kel-F, Teflon.	Graphite	Stainless steel, aluminum, wrought or cast magnesium.
Water alcohol	Nylon, polyethylene, Neoprene, AN "O" rings, asbestos, Graphitar, Kel-F, Teflon, Johns-Manville No. 61-S bonded asbestos sheet, Tygon, cork, Saran, Vinylite.	Molykote, silicone greases, Nordcoseal No. 234-S, Parker's Alcolube.	Stainless steel, aluminum, and mild steel. Any copper alloy, any nickel alloy.
White fuming nitric acid and Red fuming nitric acid	Teflon, Kel-F, Trithene, Union Carbide's CF-3, Fluorothene A, Laminates of Fiberglas with Teflon, Kel-F, Trithene, Norbide, polyethylene for ambient temperature.	Kel-Flo, Hooker's and Union Carbide's Fluorolubes, Desco lubricant, Halo-carbon oils of series 13-21 and 8-25 HV.	Worthite, 304 stainless steel (nonwelded), 345 SS (welded), Haynes alloy No. 25. 100, 5052, 5005, 6061, aluminum alloys. Noble metals such as gold, platinum rhodium.
Anhydrous hydrazine	Teflon, ethylene-propylene, Butyl, Kel-F.	MIL-G-27617 grease	Aluminum and alloys 356, 2114, 2020, 2024, 4043, 5052, 6061, 6066, B356, tens-50; corrosion-resistant steels AISI 304, AISI 345; gold, tantalum, titanium 6A1-4V.

Table VII-9 (*Continued*)

Substance	Packing and gasket	Service Lubricants	Metals
Nitrogen tetroxide	Teflon, carboxy-nitroso, Kel-F	MIL-G-27617 grease	Aluminum and alloys 1100, 2014, corrosion-resistant steels AISI 300 series (except 301), AISI 347 unwelded, 17-4PH, PH-15-7MO cond A, AM 350, Inconel, titanium and alloys.
Monomethyl-hydrazine	Teflon, ethylene-propylene, Butyl, Kel-F	MIL-G-27617 grease	Aluminum and alloys 356, 2014, 2020, 2024, 4043, 5052, 6061, 6066, B356, tens-50; corrosion-resistant steels AISI 304, AISI 347; gold tantalum, titanium 6A1-4V.
Unsymmetrical dimethyl hydrazine	Teflon, ethylene-propylene, Butyl, Kel-F	MIL-G-27617 grease	Aluminum and alloys 356, 2014, 2020, 2024, 4043, 5052, 6061, 6066, B356, tens-50; corrosion-resistant steels AISI 304, AISI 347; gold tantalum, titanium 6A1-4V.
Hydrogen (liquid and gaseous)	Teflon, Kel-F	MIL-G-27617 grease	Aluminum and alloys 1100, 1700-T, 2024-T, 4043, 5052; corrosion-resistant steels AISI 300 series, AISI 410; nickel, Monel, Inconel, brass, bronze, copper, molybdenum, titanium, Haynes 21.

Increasingly, nonflammable hydraulic fluids are being developed to replace plain or fortified petroleum oils. Remember that some fluids that are difficult to burn may roar into flame if they are atomized finely—as in the failure of a high-pressure fitting. Fitting points in critical areas can be shielded to prevent sprays from touching exhausts or hot surfaces.

Normally noncorrosive materials can severely pit surfaces with which they are in contact—especially at high pressures, high temperatures, or high flow speeds (Table VII-8). Designers often provide oversize lines and fittings to cut flow speeds in certain critical hydraulic applications, even if it means moving or inventorying larger amounts of fluid.

6. FIRE SUPPRESSION

Fire needs three things—heat, fuel, and oxygen. Remove any one of the three, and the fire stops—at least that's what the manuals say. But fire detection and suppression has become a far more complicated problem since the mid-1960s, with the rise in use of special finishes, structural plastics, cushioning foams, and energy-conserving insulation. This section is not meant to cover the field exhaustively, but mainly to give manufacturers and designers a glimpse of the problems they face. Fire detection and suppression has become a discipline all its own.

Energy considerations have put a premium on correctly sizing a motor to its load. Doing this, without creating overload conditions that overheat the windings and trigger the motor's heat sensors, has led to new refinements in load and cycle prediction. Does the designer expect an air filter to be replaced frequently, or not at all? What about voltage reductions or frequency fluctuations? All can lead to unusual internal temperature patterns. Temperature sensors may have to be placed elsewhere in a motor compartment than in the motor windings themselves.

Temperature sensors remain the most compact and probably the most reliable of all detection devices, both to trigger mechanisms that reduce the chance of dangerous heating (shutting off a motor or turning on a cooling fan, for instance), and to detect fires while they are still small. To work best, they have to be close to critical points where overheating is most likely to occur. Devices that detect ionized gases have become popular in homes and for certain "areawide" protective uses in industry—especially in some forms of warehousing. Cost, as well as the presence of ionized gases such as ozone from motor commutators, has prevented their use inside most equipment. Smoke sensors, which usually detect the presence of smoke particles 0.4 micron and larger as they interrupt a beam of light going to a photosensing device, are still used in many applications. Remote sensing of heat through infrared radiation is also useful.

The choice of a sensing device depends on many factors. Foremost among them, the design team must come up with realistic scenarios of the product in use. Depending on the circumstances, an open fire may be visible before its heat reaches the sensing device. Enclosed, out-of-sight regions around electrical

Table VII-10 OSHA Standards for Fire Extinguishers for Use on Mobile Equipment (National Association of Fire Equipment Distributors)

Vehicle	Standard
LPG INDUSTRIAL TRUCKS USED IN AREAS OF STORAGE & HANDLING OF LPG	One B:C—no rating indicated.
INDUSTRIAL TRUCKS (all types) USED IN INDOOR GENERAL STORAGE AREAS	As above.
OVERHEAD CRANES (cab-operated)	Carbon dioxide or dry chemical (no rating specified).
CRAWLER LOCOMOTIVES; TRUCK CRANES	Carbon dioxide or dry chemical (no rating specified).
WELDING CARTS	"Suitable fire extinguishing equipment shall be maintained in a state of readiness for instant use."
MOBILE LPG COOK UNITS	One 10-B:C (old 8-B:C acceptable)
TRUCKS TRANSPORTING EXPLOSIVES	Two (2) extinguishers required, each rated not less than 10-B:C.
TRUCKS TRANSPORTING OTHER HAZARDOUS MATERIALS	One 10-B:C (carbon dioxide is NOT acceptable).
TRUCKS TRANSPORTING NON-HAZARDOUS MATERIALS	One 5-B:C (two old 4-B:C acceptable).
TANK VEHICLE TRANSPORTING ANY FLAMMABLE LIQUID	One 20-B:C (old 12-B:C acceptable) or two 10-B:C (old 6-B:C acceptable).

cables or junction boxes may allow heat buildup without convection. The designer must also establish the optimum detection level—false alarms caused by oversensitive sensing devices can flood delicate equipment with water or other fire-fighting agents, or cause expensive downtime. A typical example of design selection is shown in Fig. VII-7, adapted from Air Force calculations. The curve is based on the minimum damage area allowable (0.8 inch, the diameter of a match flame), to total loss (in this case, a spacecraft, assumed radius of 65 feet). The system designer then draws the upper curve—maintaining the actual designed equipment capability for fighting the fires at two orders of magnitude greater than the incidence of fires expected. The fire extinguishing system includes both the sensing devices and the extinguishing agent.

In civilian systems, fire protection devices are built into buildings housing the equipment to be protected. Good engineering practice dictates that the system be planned for the maximum expected fire hazard for the space to be protected. This route is normally followed in sprinkler systems in conventional office or commercial space. It is not always followed for equipment spaces such as computer facilities and industrial fabrication. The manufacturer of a certain type of foundry equipment, for instance, may insist on a certain capacity sprinkler system and certain types of sensors. The equipment is installed and all goes well—until a second machine, or materials storage, or new ductwork is added to the area around it.

For "routine" applications, typical local codes now insist on enough "overdesign" in fire protection systems to provide an engineering cushion of safety. There are many blind spots, however. Fire spread in one skyscraper in Balti-

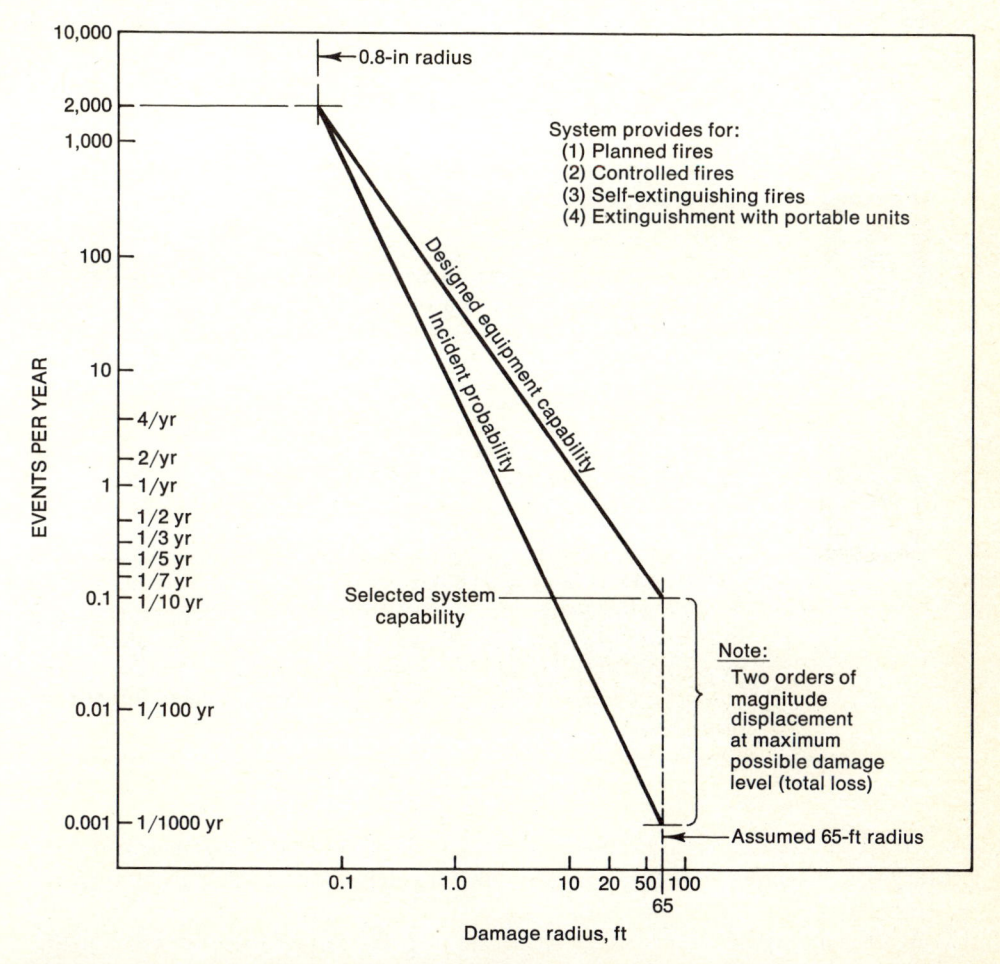

Figure VII-7 Selection of fire extinguishing system. The example given is for a space station; the minimum radius is of a match flame. (*Air Force Systems Safety Design Handbook 1-6.*)

Table VII-11 Extinguisher Classifications and Ratings (National Association of Fire Equipment Distributors)

A (triangle)	**CLASS A FIRES**—are those in ordinary combustible materials such as wood, cloth, paper, rubber, and many plastics. **For extinguishers rated on Class A fires,** the rating **NUMERAL** preceding the letter "A" indicates the size of fire expected to be extinguished. These designations are based upon specific fire tests by Underwriters Laboratories (UL), involving wood and excelsior.
A (triangle, outlined)	**For extinguishers containing multipurpose dry chemical (ABC)** —but NOT rated for Class A fires—a special SHAPE SYMBOL for the A is used. These are small extinguishers charged with ABC dry chemical (typically in 1- or 2-lb size) but have insufficient effectiveness to earn the minimum 1-A rating, even though they have some value in extinguishing small Class A fires. (They are rated, however, for Class B and C fires.)
B (square)	**CLASS B FIRES**—are those involving flammable liquids, gases, and greases. **For extinguishers rated on Class B fires,** the rating **NUMERAL** preceding the letter "B" is a proportionate indication of the square foot area of burning flammable liquid, of appreciable depth (over ¼ inch), that is expected to be extinguished by a **TRAINED** operator.
C (circle)	**CLASS C FIRES**—are those which involve energized electrical equipment where the electrical nonconductivity of the extinguishing agent is of importance. **For extinguishers classified for use on Class C fires,** no **NUMERAL** is used since Class C fires are essentially either Class A or B fires involving energized electrical wiring and equipment. The size of the different suitable extinguishers installed should be commensurate with the size and extent of the Class A and/or Class B components of the electrical hazard or containing equipment being protected.

more after energy-saving measures reduced or stopped circulation in the building's air ducts at night. The fire sensing devices had been located in the ductwork!

Air Force experience is useful in designing fire-suppression systems, especially where electrical or electronic equipment is present. Among the extinguishing agents used are bromochloromethane and dibromodifluoromethane (see MIL-B-4394 and MIL-D-4540, respectively). Where toxicity could cause

CLASS D FIRES—are those involving combustible metals, such as magnesium, titanium, zirconium, sodium, and potassium.

For extinguishers classified for use on Class D fires, no **NUMERAL** is used. The relative effectiveness of these extinguishers, or approved compounds in pails, for use on specific combustible metal fires is detailed on the extinguisher nameplate.

CLASSIFICATION of an *extinguisher* consists of a **LETTER** which indicates the class of fire on which an extinguisher has been found to be effective, preceded by a rating **NUMERAL** (Class A and B only) which indicates the relative extinguishing effectiveness. These "letters" and "numerals" are shown on the extinguisher nameplate.

Many extinguishers have *multiple* fire classifications. On newer models the nameplate indicates multiple classifications by illustrating more than one Classification Shape Symbol. Multiple-rated extinguishers include the following classifications: A, B or B, C or A, B, C.

RATING SYSTEM USED PRIOR TO 1955

These extinguishers are identified by the **LETTER** *preceding* the **NUMERAL** instead of the opposite for the more current extinguishers. **EXAMPLE:** A 10# carbon dioxide extinguisher manufactured prior to 1955 will show on its nameplate the rating of "B-2, C-1.".

The big difference involves Class B extinguishers in that the *discharge rate* usually determines the rating numeral. In short, pre-1955 discharge rates were slow as opposed to rapid discharge rates for newer extinguishers. Result: The fast discharging extinguishers are able to extinguish much larger fires. **This means that pre-1955 rated Class B extinguishers have limited acceptability—no matter how large—as compared with current units.**

---

problems—for civilian fire departments answering the fire alarm, or large numbers of unprotected workers in the vicinity, for instance—bromotrifluoromethane (trade named Halon 1301, MIL-B-12218) or carbon dioxide are often the agents of choice. Tables VII-12 and VII-13 summarize some of the important data on such substances.

To protect areas where an automatic system might be actuated in the presence of large numbers of personnel, Freon FE 1301 has been used.

Table VII-12 Physical Properties of Extinguishing Agents (*Air Force Systems Safety Design Handbook 1-6*)

Extinguishing agent	Molecular weight	Specific gravity liquid 70°F	Boiling point °F	Freezing point °F	Liquid density lb/gal at 70°F	Corrosion resistance Steel‡	Corrosion resistance Brass‡	Corrosion resistance Alum.‡
Carbon dioxide (CO_2)	44.0	0.76	−109.0	−110.0	6.3			
Bromochloromethane, Halon 1011 (CH_2BrCl)	129.4	1.93	156.0	−123.7	16.1	27.0* 280.0	200.0* 2,620.0	1,500.0* 1,500.0
Dibromodifluoromethane, Halon 1202 (CF_2Br_2)	209.8	2.27	76.1	−229.9	19.0	0.8* 62.0	0.7* 375.0	0.7 55.0
Bromotrifluoromethane, Halon 1301 (CF_3Br)	148.9	1.57	−57.9	−270.4	13.1	0.9* −91.0†	1.5* −35.0†	0.7 59.0
1,2-Dibromotetrafluoroethane, Halon 2402 (CF_2BrCF_2Br)	259.8	2.15	117.5	−166.8	18.0	1.5* 140.0*	5.7* 385.0*	0.4 50.0
Bromochlorodifluoromethane, Halon 1211 (CF_2BrCl)	165.0	1.83	25.0	−257.0	15.27	1.1* 82.0*	6.0 435.0	0.8 54.0

*Average penetration (inch/month) × 10^{-6} (upper figures, dry; lower figures, wet).
†The minus sign indicates tightly bound scale forming in layers on the metal test strip rather than corrosion or penetration.
‡Corrosion resistance is high.

Depending on the type and amount of combustible material present, as little as 3 to 5 percent concentration by volume will render a normal-air atmosphere inert. It is low in toxicity, and at typical inerting concentrations does not restrict breathing. Nor does Freon FE 1301 inhibit evacuation, like another fairly popular extinguishing agent, detergent-based expandable foam. The foam restricts vision, and is extremely slippery.

Conventional sprinkler systems are so popular—and effective—because they are simple to design and reliable in operation. Where sensing mechanisms other than heat directly on the sprinkler head are desired, however, complexity can increase greatly. This affects both cost and reliability. Electrical control systems for the extinguishing system must be kept independent of other electrical systems in the structure, and away from the space being protected. Mechanical relays should be avoided. If necessary, two independent relay systems in parallel can be used. The circuits should be parallel all the way to the discharge-triggering device (squib or solenoid). Circuits around the discharge area should be able to withstand expected heat from possible fires—the Air Force, as a matter of routine, uses a fire rating of 2000°F for 5 minutes. A common malfunction that causes unnecessary damage away from the actual fire area is the accidental grounding of the firing circuit through a discharged squib or shorted solenoid. Firing circuits should be designed to anticipate and avoid this.

There is some question among manufacturers of equipment needing "outside" fire protection as to whether they should supply it as a mandatory part of doing business with the equipment purchaser, whether the purchaser can be assumed to have the knowledge to install proper protective devices after being warned of the hazards, or whether the responsibility should be a joint one, between the manufacturer, his customer, and perhaps the outside contractor installing the protective equipment. Many companies have no standard policy, fitting the proper action to the availability of local expertise and the perceived knowledge and experience of the customer.

7. SPILLS

It is hardly a secret that spills are a common occurrence in the American transportation system. Railroad roadbeds are often in deplorable condition. Trucks are subject to tight schedules and severe traffic conditions in many parts of the country. In the past, companies have tended to regard the carriers' legal responsibilities as sufficient protection. But the common transportation of chemicals offering subtle dangers—liquid-based herbicides, for example—and the sheer number of accidents have caused many larger companies to take a second look. Dow Chemical, for instance, estimates that it suffers three spills per working day. Although most of these are quite minor, Dow catalogs all of them. In New Jersey alone, there were 2,000 spills in 1977.

Dow polices its carriers (and its customers' suppliers' carriers) rigorously. Plant-gate inspections of highway carriers help ensure that proper equipment and placarding is used. The drumming of hazardous materials directly from tanktrucks is not allowed. Proper weight limitations are insisted upon. Dow, as one of the largest chemical companies, owns more than 5000 rail cars. It keeps track of incidents involving them on all railroads, and has enough economic clout to force railroads to better their safety performance. Although the railroads are supposedly responsible for inspecting running gear, Dow itself inspects all rail cars handling its products at all plants, even if the cars don't belong to Dow. The company insists that this is good business, because it sells consumer products as well as industrial intermediates, and is particularly vulnerable to bad publicity due to a spill. Dow also has figured that its insurance costs have been cut substantially.

Since the crash of the Pan Am 707 in 1974 exposed the chances of improper labeling of chemicals in air shipments, Dow also insists that all requests for air shipment be approved by its Distribution Services office.

If a spill does occur, quick action and delicate instrumentation are necessary to detect the affected area and contain it. Dow stencils the commodity name and its emergency response number on all its tank cars to help public emergency personnel identify potential hazards and get supporting help quickly. Most public fire departments, for instance, are mainly poorly trained volunteers, even in urbanized states like New Jersey.

Most companies do not have extensive response mechanisms. Instead, they depend on the National Oil and Hazardous Substances Pollution Contingency Plan, developed under the 1972 Federal Water Pollution Control Act. Typically, the first contact a company has with the Contingency Plan is after a major spill. The plan is run jointly by the federal Environmental Protection Agency and the Coast Guard, following the organizational chart in Fig. VII-8.

Most of the cleanup work is done by a "National Strike Force" of Coast Guard personnel. The Force includes three 18-person teams, one each at bases on the Atlantic, Pacific, and Gulf coasts. The teams can respond to spills almost anywhere in the United States on two hours' notice, and can move to contain major spills (usually oil) within 24 hours. Each person on the Strike Force must carry a large amount of cash or traveler's checks and a signal beeper. They even carry official papers, passport, and open orders allowing them to fly anywhere in the world on short notice.

If the federal government must clean a spill, funds are drawn from a 35 million dollar contingency fund. The fund is filled by imposing fines (up to $10,000) and a flat fee of $100 per gross ton of spill material removed. In the past, any money spent by the spiller was not deductible from what would have to be paid to the government. Quick response by a company would therefore help to keep the total spill damage to a minimum, but penalizes a company twice—first for its own costs, and then for the government's. A change in this rule was pending as this book went to press.

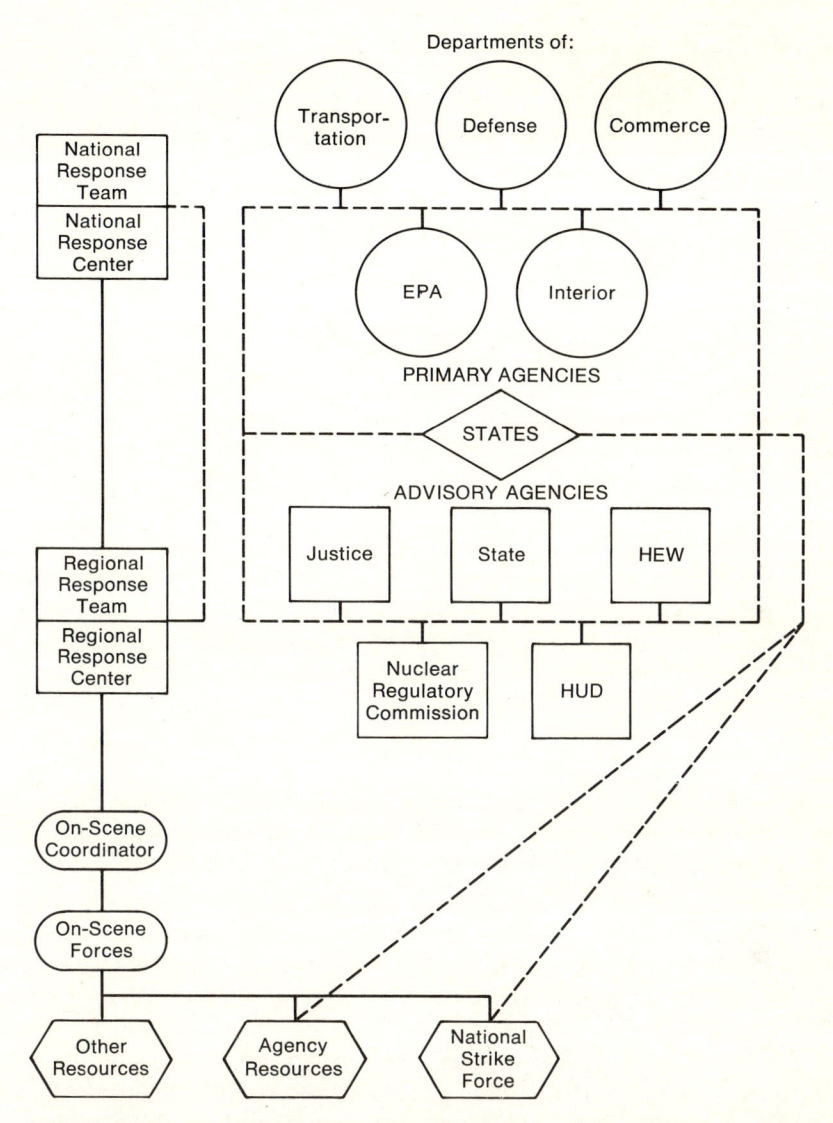

Figure VII-8 Organization of the National Contingency Plan for taking action against spills of petroleum or other hazardous materials.

Various companies concentrated at certain locations—busy harbors for instance—have often set up spill cooperatives to minimize product damage. The oil companies have taken the lead in this, because of the large volumes they ship. Some private companies also handle spill work. One that predates the 1972 water law is the Western Environmental Services Division of Western-Willamette Corporation.

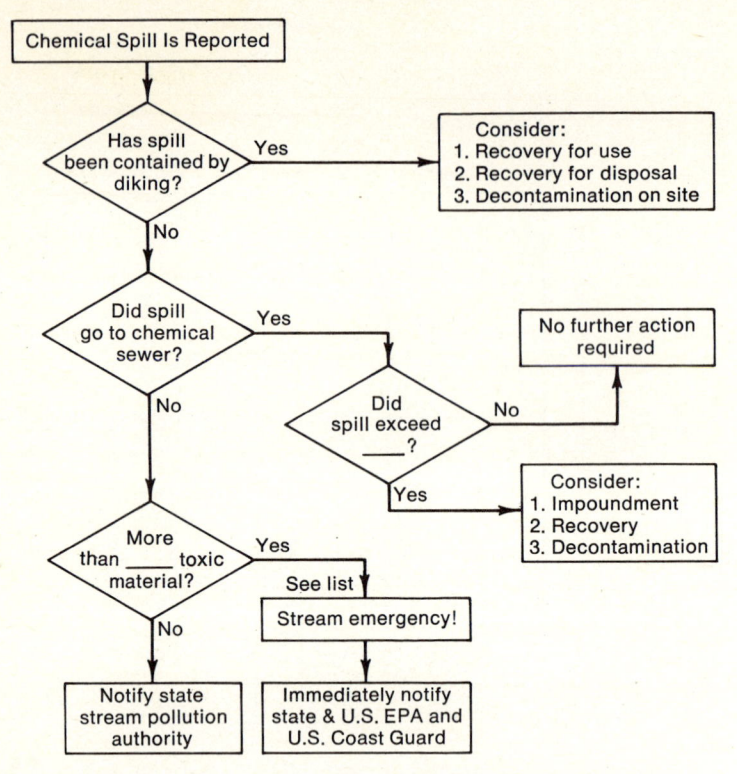

```
                    ┌──────────────────────────┐
                    │ Chemical Spill Is Reported│
                    └──────────────────────────┘
                                 │
                                 ▼
                          ╱ Has spill ╲     Yes         ┌──────────────────────────┐
                         ╱ been contained by╲──────────▶│ Consider:                │
                         ╲    diking?       ╱            │ 1. Recovery for use      │
                          ╲               ╱              │ 2. Recovery for disposal │
                           │ No                          │ 3. Decontamination on site│
                           ▼                             └──────────────────────────┘
                          ╱ Did spill ╲    Yes
                         ╱ go to chemical╲─────────┐
                         ╲    sewer?     ╱         │
                          ╲             ╱          ▼
                           │ No              ╱ Did  ╲    No      ┌────────────────┐
                           ▼                ╱ spill exceed╲─────▶│ No further action│
                                            ╲    ___?    ╱       │    required     │
                          ╱ More  ╲           ╲         ╱        └────────────────┘
                         ╱ than___ toxic╲ Yes  │ Yes
                         ╲  material?   ╱──┐   ▼                 ┌────────────────┐
                          ╲            ╱   │                     │ Consider:       │
                           │ No            │                     │ 1. Impoundment  │
                           ▼          See list                   │ 2. Recovery     │
                                           ▼                     │ 3. Decontamination│
                                    ┌──────────────┐             └────────────────┘
                                    │Stream emergency!│
                                    └──────────────┘
                    ┌────────────────┐  ┌──────────────────────┐
                    │ Notify state   │  │ Immediately notify    │
                    │stream pollution│  │ state & U.S. EPA and  │
                    │   authority    │  │ U.S. Coast Guard      │
                    └────────────────┘  └──────────────────────┘
```

Figure VII-9 What to do when a chemical spill is reported. Blanks would indicate precalculated critical amounts of the chemical for your situation *(Ralph A. Jensen, Rohm & Haas.)*

Particularly hazardous substances are often difficult to sweep up. Calgon once drained an entire lake through activated charcoal filters to protect a drinking water supply and recreational area from another company's pesticide spill. Once material is picked up, it is difficult to dispose of. Dow, for instance, inventories open-head drums around the country, into which damaged containers can be packed. All material picked up after spills is returned to Dow facilities for recycle or disposal. Material can be burned in a high-temperature incinerator or kiln if need be. Contaminated truck floors are decontaminated or replaced with new wood, and the old boards are incinerated.

Needless to say, this kind of vigilance costs money, but may be well worth it in dollars to producers of particularly hazardous materials. Investment in supersafe packaging, record-keeping systems to keep track of shipments, and inspection programs can pay off in public relations, avoidance of fines, and avoidance of high liability in the event of a serious spill in a populated area.

Department of Transportation rules for moving and packaging hazardous materials are summarized in App. C.

8. FIGURING CONCENTRATIONS

One question that commonly arises among manufacturers trying to adhere to published concentration limits for various hazardous substances is the way to figure allowable concentrations of *mixtures* of those substances. In guarding against fire hazards, in mixtures of vapors where there is no known synergistic effect (that is, the components of the vapor themselves will not self-ignite in a chemical reaction with each other), it is normally acceptable to monitor each vapor concentration separately. If any one approaches the danger zone, the workplace or product-use area is unsafe.

For vapors hazardous to health at low concentrations, the method normally employed for figuring concentrations is described by the Occupational Safety and Health Administration at 29 CFR 1910.1000 and following. Again, the calculation method is to be used only where there are no known synergistic effects—such as one chemical being an agent that increases the potency of another agent in the human body. As listed in App. B, exposure limits are given in parts per million (for vapors), or milligrams per cubic meter (for mists), and sometimes both ways. These limits are for a typical 8-hour shift, and 40-hour week.

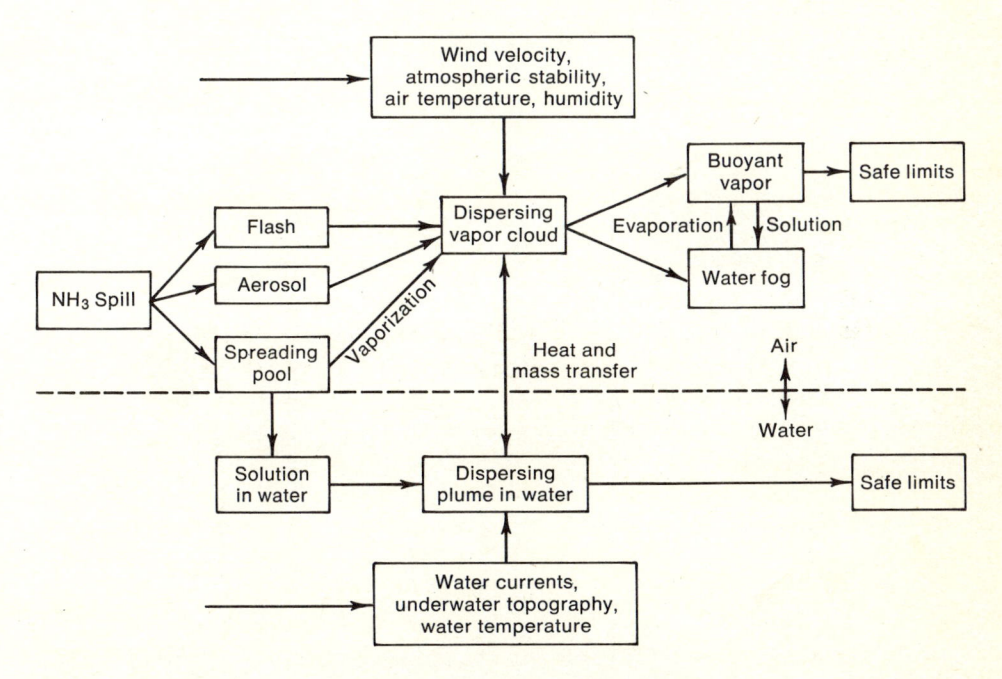

Figure VII-10 Possible airborne problems of a hazardous chemical spill (in this case, ammonia). *(From P. P. K. Raj, and J. H. Hagopian, "Hazards Presented by the Release of Anhydrous Ammonia on Water," proceedings of the 1974 National Conference on Control of Hazardous Material Spills, AIChE, New York, 1974, pp. 179–187.)*

Table VII-13 Physiological Properties of Various Extinguishing Agents (*Air Force Systems Safety Design Handbook 1-6*)

Extinguishing agent	Approximate lethal concentration–ppm volume 15-min exposure rate — Natural vapor	Approximate lethal concentration–ppm volume 15-min exposure rate — Vapor heated to 1470°F	Warning of presence of toxic vapors by smell, irritation, coughing, and lachrymation — Natural vapor	Heated vapor
Carbon dioxide, CO_2	658,000	658,000	Odorless at low concentration; acrid at high concentration	Odorless at low concentration; acrid at high concentration
Bromochloromethane, CH_2BrCl (Halon 1011)	29,000	4,000	Sweet odor	Decomposition products are exceedingly irritating
Dibromodifluoromethane, CF_2Br_2 (Halon 1202)	54,000	1,850	Heavy, ethereal	Decomposition products are extremely painful to inhale
Bromotrifluoromethane, CF_3Br (Halon 1301)	800,000	14,000	Slight, ethereal	Acrid, irritating
1,2-Dibromotetrafluoroethane, CF_2BrCF_2Br (Halon 2402)	126,000	1,600	Slight, ethereal	Acrid, irritating
Bromochlorodifluoromethane, CF_2ClBr (Halon 1211)	324,000	7,650	Slight, ethereal	Acrid, irritating

The cumulative exposure for an 8-hour work shift is computed as:

$$E = \frac{C_a T_a + C_b T_b + \ldots + C_n T_n}{8}$$

where

E = equivalent exposure for the working shift
C = concentration for any period T where the concentration remains constant
T = the duration (in hours in this case) of the exposure at concentration C

The value of E is not to exceed the 8-hour time-weighted average limit in tables of App. B.

To illustrate, note that isoamyl acetate has an OSHA time-weighted average limit of 100 ppm. Assume that an employee is subject to the following exposure: 2 hours at 150 ppm, 2 hours at 75 ppm, and 4 hours at 50 ppm. Substitute these data into the formula:

$$E = \frac{2 \times 150 + 2 \times 75 + 4 \times 50}{8} = 81.25 \text{ ppm}$$

Thus, the exposure is acceptable.

In the case of a mixture of air contaminants, the equivalent exposure is computed as follows:

$$E_m = \frac{C_1}{L_1} + \frac{C_2}{L_2} + \ldots + \frac{C_n}{L_n}$$

where

E_m = equivalent exposure for the mixture
C = concentration of a particular contaminant
L = is the exposure limit for that contaminant

The value of E_m must always be unity or less. To illustrate: Consider the data

Table VII-14 Impacts and Impact Values, Various Chemicals and Transportation Modes (A. S. Kalelkar, L. J. Partridge, and R. E. Brooks, "Decision Analysis in Hazardous Material Transportation," Proceedings of the 1974 National Conference on Control of Hazardous Material Spills, AIChE, New York, pp. 336–344)

	Annual* accident frequency	Relative exposure (urban/rural)	Expected deaths per accident (urban/rural)	$1,000 property damage per accident (urban/rural)	Envir. effect (rural)	Area (acres) fraction of 32 acres	U (urban/rural)	U*f (× 1000)
RAIL								
Acrylonitrile	0.068	0.27/0.73	8.3/0.3	132.0/5.0	10	3.30	−0.49	−125
Impact value			−0.49/−0.07	−0.43/−0.06	−0.46	0.103	−0.07	
Methanol	0.42	0.16/0.84	9.0/0.4	144.4/5.4	11	3.61	−0.49	−612
Impact value			−0.495/−0.08	−0.45/−0.07	−0.56	0.111	−0.08	
Styrene	0.36	0.17/0.83	11.6/0.5	186.0/7.0	11	4.65	−0.54	−599
Impact value			−0.54/−0.09	−0.52/−0.08	−0.56	0.145	−0.09	
Anhydrous ammonia	0.045	0.11/0.89	24.8/0.99	—	6	9.9	−0.74	−101
Impact value			−0.74/−0.16	—	−0.23	0.309	−0.16	
Chlorine	0.004	0.13/0.87	957.5/38.3†	—	6	383	−957.5	−6,310.0†
Impact value			—	—	−0.23	11.94	−38.3	
Sulfuric acid	0.0017	Urban only	1.95	31.2	12	0.78	−0.23	−3.9
Impact value			−0.24	−0.18	−0.84	0.024	—	
Caustic soda	0.065	0.30/0.70	1.95/0.08	31.2/1.2	12	0.78	−0.23	−45
Impact value			−0.24/−0.0	−0.18/0	−0.84	0.024	−0.00	

270

Benzene	0.009	Urban only	13.5	216.4	12	5.41	−0.58	−53
Impact value			−0.58	−0.56	−0.84	0.168	—	
Ethylene glycol	0.055	0.06/0.94	1.95/0.078	31.2/1.2	10	0.78	−0.24	−7.9
Impact value			−0.24/0.0	−0.18/0.0	−0.46	0.024	−0.00	
BARGE								
Acrylonitrile	0.0035	0.08/0.92	28.2/1.2	200.0/7.5	4	11.53	−0.79	−7.4
Impact value			−0.79/−0.16	−0.54/−0.08	−0.19	0.360	−0.16	
Methanol	0.0140	0.15/0.85	28.8/1.2	159.2/6.0	4	11.53	−0.79	−36
Impact value			−0.79/−0.16	−0.48/−0.07	−0.19	0.360	−0.16	
Styrene	0.0087	0.13/0.87	24.8/1.0	396.0/14.9	4	9.9	−0.75	−21
Impact value			−0.75/−0.16	−0.84/−0.13	−0.19	0.309	−0.16	
Anhydrous ammonia	0.0065	0.15/0.85	17.4/0.70	—	6	6.95	−0.64	−13
Impact value			−0.64/−0.12	—	−0.23	0.217	−0.12	
Chlorine	0.0005	0.09/0.91	29,750/1,190.0†	—	6	11,900	−29,750	−18,800
Impact value			—		−0.23	361	−1,190	
Sulfuric acid	0.00003	All urban	8.6/0.3	137.2/5.1	9	3.43	−0.49	0
Impact value			−0.49/−0.06	40.44/−0.05	−0.43	0.107	−0.06	
Caustic soda	0.009	0.26/0.74	5.5/0.2	88.4/3.3	9	2.21	−0.38	−12
Impact value			−0.38/−0.04	−0.34/−0.04	−0.43	0.069	−0.04	

*Includes a factor to account for ignition probability in cases where major hazard is fire.

†Chlorine has expected deaths well beyond the limit of the assessment. Because the number of deaths is large and the decision making became risk-neutral for large numbers of deaths, one can assume that a linear approximation using expected number of deaths is valid in this regime. This means that these numbers are not comparable to those for the other chemicals.

Table VII-14 (Continued)

	Annual* accident frequency	Relative exposure (urban/rural)	Expected deaths per accident (urban/rural)	$1,000 property damage per accident (urban/rural)	Envir. effect (rural)	Area (acres) fraction of 32 acres	U (urban/rural)	U*(× 1000)
Benzene	0.0003	All	36.5	584	4	14.6	−0.85	−2.6
Impact value		urban	−0.85	−1.13‡	−0.19	0.457	—	
Ethylene glycol	0.0018	0.16/0.84	—	—	8	0.04	−0.00	0
Impact value			—	—	−0.37	0.0013	−0.00	
TRUCK								
Acrylonitrile	0.0158	0.23/0.77	2.8/0.0	44.0/1.7	10	1.10	−0.26	−15
Impact value			−0.26/−0.0	−0.23/−0.02	−0.46	0.034	−0.00	
Methanol	0.1083	0.21/0.79	3.0/0.1	47.2/1.8	11	1.18	−0.27	−62
Impact value			−0.27/−0.0	−0.24/−0.02	−0.56	0.038	−0.00	
Styrene	0.0553	0.24/0.76	3.3/0.1	53.2/2.0	11	1.33	−0.28	−37
Impact value			−0.28/−0.0	−0.26/−0.03	−0.56	0.042	−0.00	
Anhydrous ammonia	0.071	0.23/0.77	7.3/0.29	—	6	2.9	−0.45	−95
Impact value			−0.45/−0.04	—	−0.23	0.091	−0.04	

Chlorine	0.004	0.10/0.90	380/15.2†	—	6	152	−380	−2,067†
Sulfuric acid	0.0006	All	—	8.8	12	4.75	−15.2	0
		urban	0.55	−0.08	−0.84	0.22	−0.0	
Impact value			−0.0			0.007	—	
Caustic soda	0.025	0.27/0.73	0.55/0.02	8.8/0.3	12	0.22	−0.0	0
Impact value			−0.0/−0.0	−0.08/0.0	−0.84	0.007	−0.0	
Benzene	0.005	All	3.9	62.4	12	1.56	−0.33	−1.7
		urban	−0.33	−0.29	−0.84	0.048		
Impact value							—	
Ethylene glycol	0.014	0.16/0.84	0.55/0.02	8.8/0.3	10	0.22	−0.0	0
Impact value			−0.0/−0.0	−0.08/−0.0	−0.46	0.007	−0.0	

*Includes a factor to account for ignition probability in cases where major hazard is fire.

†Chlorine has expected deaths well beyond the limit of the assessment. Because the number of deaths is large and the decision making became risk-neutral for large numbers of deaths, one can assume that a linear approximation using expected number of deaths is valid in this regime. This means that these numbers are not comparable to those for the other chemicals.

from the workplace or product-use area, and compare it with the data from App. B. A table may be constructed:

	8-hour time-weighted limit	Observed 8-hour exposure
Acetone	1000 ppm	500 ppm
2-Butanone	200 ppm	45 ppm
Toluene	200 ppm	40 ppm

substituting into the formula we have:

$$E_m = \frac{500}{1,000} + \frac{45}{200} + \frac{40}{200}$$
$$= 0.5 + 0.225 + 0.2$$
$$= 0.925$$

Since E_m is less than unity, the exposure to the combination of vapors is within safe health limits. It must be emphasized again, however, that this approach is to be used only when no synergistic health or safety effects are known. If such effects do become known, specific formulae will have to be used for each suspect combination. The formulae (or more likely, a family of curves) will be highly nonlinear, judging from cases in animal experimentation.

Exposure standards for humans do not take such effects into account, as of this writing. But some documentation does exist for various hazardous materials in the technical literature—waiting for the sharp-eyed plaintiff's attorney to find it. Clearly, the relevant literature should be scanned for such effects before committing oneself to a particular chemical. One useful service for doing such scanning is TOXLINE, a computerized data base available at low cost through many libraries. It is subsidized by the National Institutes of Health (see App. H).

VIII
IF ALL ELSE FAILS—GOING TO COURT

1. GENERAL PREPARATION

No matter how carefully a company designs, manufactures, and markets its products, the odds are fairly good that some consumer or bystander—somewhere—will be injured and that the product will be somehow involved in the injury. It is up to the company, of course, to determine the possible frequency and cost of such injuries and resulting lawsuits, and spend at least an equal sum—and preferably much more—to protect against them.

But when an actual case—an actual injury—appears, corporate action must shift from the abstract to the concrete. One of the biggest barriers to correct corporate action in such cases is the "rational" opinion of management that the product was grievously abused and misused before it caused injury. The best advice: create an action plan beforehand, and stick to it.

The first step in the action plan is to "get the facts." Prompt attention to a consumer's problem can pay off for a company in terms of goodwill with a potential plaintiff. Promptness also helps uncover real problems that need immediate attention, lest the company face damage suits from other users of the product.

The next step is to consider compensation for injury and property damages. Insurance carriers emphasize that quick work in this regard can help foreclose bigger problems later—after the injured party gets to thinking about how he has been abused by a thoughtless, heartless company, and after the relatives describe in glowing terms the settlement that can be obtained through the use of a sharp lawyer.

For such coordination to work, the company and its insuror must agree beforehand on possible courses of action in the event of an injury (see Chap. IX).

If the injury is serious enough to indicate the potential for a large damage award, or if the accident exposed a potentially widespread defect in your company's products, ample justification exists for full-blown meetings of design, production, marketing, and legal staffs under the aegis of the product safety coordinator, as described in a previous chapter. But such meetings cannot be allowed to paralyze corporate action in the immediate case at hand.

The decision about whether to go to court depends, of course, on a large number of variables. Does the company think the injury could have been prevented if it had acted with greater care? Does legal counsel think the case can be won? How much will it cost to fight the case, even if the chance of winning is high? What is the insuror's position? Faced with such questions, defendants often caved in and settled in recent years. But by the mid-1970s, the resolve of many manufacturers and insurors began to stiffen against what many saw as unfair claims.

2. DISCOVERY

Most design engineers have only a hazy appreciation for the work that must go into a successful defense against product liability claims. The ordeal begins long before those short periods spent on the witness stand. In fact, most cases are settled out of court. The settlement might not take place, however, until after months—and even years—of pretrial proceedings.

First, the plaintiff's counsel may require the engineer for the defendant manufacturer to submit to an "interrogatory." Under the legal power of subpoena, each decision-maker on the technical team must answer a sometimes long and involved questionnaire. This usually is done in the team's offices, and requires detailed searching through records of the product's design and development for answers in writing. Pertinent data must be noted, in complete detail.

This procedure may not sound bad to most engineers, as it might seem analogous to an "open book" quiz. But the engineer who thinks he or she can pick and choose the facts to be divulged may be in for a rude surprise. Chances are that the plaintiff's lawyer had an expert's analysis of the product's engineering design and manufacturing methods at hand when the interrogatory was drawn up. And the lawyer is sure to have expert help in evaluating the product engineer's answers. Thus, if the first answers aren't satisfying, the engineer may very well face another questionnaire, even more detailed and more probing.

At about the same time, the company's technical staff may find itself teaching its own lawyers as well. Especially when defense counsel is from an outside firm, and not particularly well acquainted with a manufacturer's operations, detailed briefings and explanations are vital. Furthermore, the technical staff and company management must be willing to tell all—good and bad—and trust the attorneys to make a case.

One prominent New York attorney specializing in defense of a variety of engineered products, finds that sometimes his client's engineers don't fully trust him. "If I am to devise a suitable defense," he notes, "I must know the worst aspects of a product's design before litigation begins. However, I've had men responsible for the engineering of a product at issue in a suit who couldn't bring themselves to admit to a noncolleague that there might be questionable factors in the engineering."

Mistrust—and coordination problems—can be intensified by geographical distance. Increasingly, plaintiffs can bring suit where they live, even if the company that manufactured the product alleged to have caused the injury maintains no office, staff, or authorized distributors there. This increases the chances that an "outside" attorney will be needed, even for large manufacturers with in-house legal staffs.

Distance can also be an enemy of the manufacturer's technical team in the next stage of discovery—the deposition. Members of the team are required to submit to questioning by opposing counsel at a time and place of the lawyer's choosing. This can be in the engineer's own office, but it is frequently at opposing counsel's offices—which may be on the other side of the country. Why should plaintiff's attorney suffer the expense of a long trip? And why should the attorney attempt to make a technical specialist secure in familiar surroundings?

The engineers and management people with knowledge of the product's design and development must appear with all records, and testify on the basis of them. All testimony is recorded for the court record. A skilled lawyer can make the taking of a deposition a grueling experience for an engineer, probing not merely into the written record of an engineering project, but also into the designer's command of current technology, and the motivations and philosophy that he brings to work. Such sessions to take depositions can go on for days, with recesses for the engineers or managers to dig more deeply into records they may or may not have brought with them the first time.

In all discovery procedures, as in the courtroom, the engineer is entitled to personal company counsel or even a personal scientific or engineering consultant.

Much of the way a nonlawyer will react to hostile questioning depends on personality. One lawyer, representing families of several victims of airplane

Table VIII-1   Defenses Against Consumer Pleading Negligence on the Part of the Manufacturer

Contributory negligence.   Consumer voluntarily and knowingly used product in defective condition.

State of the art in design.   The product is designed as safely as it can be; no one else has ever thought of a way to make it safer.

Undetectable defect.   No way exists to test for defect that caused failure and injury; manufacturer, knowing this, mitigated with overdesign, etc. Manufacturer took due care in designing and marketing product.

Compliance with applicable standards.   Juries are often swayed by information that product complies—or does not comply—with applicable standards, government regulations, etc. Strictly speaking, compliance is evidence of "reasonable" care on the part of manufacturer, and not absolute defense (see Consumer Product Safety Act, Section 25).

Statute of limitations.   When did the accident occur? Or when did the accident's damages manifest themselves?

crashes, recalled the contrasting attitudes of two engineers responsible for designing components of an American jet airliner that had crashed in Europe. One was frank about his own work and his company's policies and engineering practices. He gave his employer the benefit of the doubt whenever he could, but he conceded inadequacies in component design when they could be technically substantiated. The other engineer, who was on the managerial level, fought every question the families' lawyer asked, admitting as little as possible.

"I consider these men to have been equally loyal to their company's interests," the attorney said. "And they believed equally in the policies and practices by which its engineering staff operated. Also, as it turned out, the man who was so recalcitrant ended up having to yield as significant evidence as his more reasonable colleague did."

Another attorney specializing in the victims' side said he looks for signs that the truth is being hidden or distorted. "Just so long as a witness persists in keeping back some of the facts, he is open to continued attack," the attorney noted.

In any event, it is not wise for engineers to underestimate the technical ability of lawyers. They have proved over and over again—both in deposition-taking and in the courtroom—that they can learn and retain a startling amount of unfamiliar and complex knowledge, at least for short periods.

3. WHO SHOULD TESTIFY?

Lawyers who have made a career of defending manufacturers against product liability suits, prefer to have the product designer or leader of the design team testify—if he or she can express himself clearly and effectively. Says one attorney, "I have found that when it appears that the engineer has tried to make a product as safe and dependable as he could, it pays to have him describe the alternative ways he might have designed the product, and then explain why

Table VIII-2 Defenses Against Consumer Pleading Strict Liability in Tort, or Breach of Warranty

- *Assumption of risk.*   Consumer knowingly and unreasonably used a product that is dangerous—power saw with a frayed cord, grinding wheel with the guard removed, and so forth.
- *Misuse.*   In most jurisdictions, the misuse must have been unforeseeable. Manufacturers should foresee that chairs will be used as step stools, screwdrivers as prying and cutting tools, and so forth.
- *Statute of limitations.*   Varies from state to state, both in the length of time it runs, and as to the starting point. In almost all jurisdictions, the statute of limitations begins running at the time of the injury, not at time of sale of the product.

Table VIII-3   Defenses That Have Little or No Chance of Success

Disclaimer.   Manufacturer cannot disclaim responsibility for use of product.

Warning on product.   Manufacturer must prove, at a minimum, that no practical way exists to protect against danger by design and manufacture, and that warning was the only option.

---

he made the choices he did—complete with results of any tests he made. Judge and jury are more likely to believe the designer did his best."

What happens, though, when an engineer, who has helped to design a product, but believes it to have been unreasonably faulty, is asked to testify about that product—especially if the engineer stated this belief but was overruled by management during development? For the good of the employer, the engineer should, if possible, refuse to testify, say some experts. Others, however, note that if the designer cannot have some control over his or her own creativity, engineering can hardly be dignified as a "profession."

According to the ethics codes of the National Society of Professional Engineers, and the employment guidelines of Engineers Joint Council, an engineer cannot ethically perform any professional function for which his remuneration depends on the acceptability of the information he develops. This holds for the engineering employee of a manufacturer, and for the "expert witness" who might be called to testify in support of either the plaintiff or the defendant.

The chances of an employee being able to hide qualms about a design or production procedure are slim anyway, says William I. Stieglitz, a veteran expert witness and safety consultant who resigned as head of the then National Highway Safety Agency after a dispute over auto design standards in the Agency's early days. He goes further than the professional ethics codes: "The only possible role for the engineer in litigation is as a technical expert. He must remain objective even about his own work when testifying. As soon as he starts thinking in terms of their side and our side, he makes himself a party to the adversary system on which our courts are based," Stieglitz says.

It doesn't seem to work out that way in practice, however. Arnold Elkind, the New York attorney who chaired the National Commission on Product Safety (the work of which helped lead to the Consumer Product Safety Act of 1972) observes that every engineer is the sum of his or her education, experience, attitudes, opinions, and associations. It is unlikely that he or she can be totally objective. In short, "It is important to know who pays his salary," in Elkind's words.

Background plays a particularly important role in complex issues, as one might expect. But what is a judge or jury to think in a case like the following, from the late sixties. The suit involved an explosion in a petroleum processing plant, allegedly because of negligence on the part of a maintenance company in performing cleaning chores. The key issue became whether a defective light bulb had set off the explosion, and this in turn depended on the bulb's wattage.

An expert witness for the maintenance company testified that, judging from the leads remaining in one of the broken bulbs, the wattage could not have been more than 100. An expert witness for the process plant owners testified that he, too, had measured the leads and had compared them with leads from new bulbs ranging from below 100 watts to above 200. He concluded that the bulb in question had been 200 watts. The judge suggested the witness from the process plant side go out and buy a selection of bulbs, break them in court, and measure their leads. The expert did so—50 bulbs of each wattage. His measurements of the leads confirmed his testimony. But the opposing expert witness, in his turn in front of the judge read data from his micrometer that supported his own testimony.

The judge settled matters by stepping down from the bench, taking the micrometer, and doing the measuring himself for a third time. His measurements agreed with those of the process plant's expert witness, and the court awarded damages to the plant owners.

Attorneys on both sides are concerned about the impression an engineer will make on the judge and jury (many product liability cases are not heard with a jury). They agree that the technical witness should be neat, but not overdressed or flashy; personable, but not necessarily handsome; believable, but not overbearing; convinced he or she is in the right, but not locked in by bias; patient and calm, but not easily riled by opposing counsel. Stanley Mosk, associate justice of the California Supreme Court and a former state attorney general, once compared the engineer's role in the courtroom to that of a doctor, but harder. "People seem to be more informed about medicine than they are about engineering," Mosk said, "also, doctors work with people all the time, so they can more easily relate to a jury."

Perhaps the best advice for engineers not equipped with the proper physical appearance or personality is to behave in court as if he or she were discussing a technical matter with colleagues. Leave it to the lawyer to ask what something means if the witness retreats into jargon. Some lawyers recommend sticking to "yes" and "no" answers, and never volunteering information that isn't asked for; extra information could open a door that the opposing lawyer didn't know existed.

Alfred Julien, the colorful plaintiffs' attorney from New York, recalled a case in point. An engineer who persisted in ending his replies with "becauses" inadvertently revealed he had no practical first-hand knowledge of the subject on which he had been testifying—he had been coached by colleagues who had done the actual design work.

Out of the mouth of another engineer came the admission that held his company liable for the injury of a worker operating a machine the firm made. The worker was crushed when a foundry drum tumbling machine was accidently turned on during unloading. The unit had no safety interlock to prevent operation of the drum while it was open. (In fact, at the time, such interlocking devices were uncommon; no tumbling machines actually came equipped with them.)

The actuating switch, made by another of the defendants, had no ring guard around its push button. An engineer for that company testified that the guard had not been provided because of its possible detrimental effect in another application of the same switch—in a chemical process. The following exchange then took place:

LAWYER: Was your company more interested in guarding and protecting the process because of possible financial loss, rather than the human being?

ENGINEER: We never forget the human being. In this particular case, that was the lesser of two evils.

LAWYER: Which was the lesser?

ENGINEER: The personal injury.

LAWYER: The personal injury did not merit the concern that the damage to the chemical process merited?

ENGINEER: That is correct.

There are exceptions. One engineer who had been called to the stand on behalf of his employer reminded the firm's attorney that he had forgotten to include a vital part of a hypothetical question they had prepared before the trial. The engineer did this by gently asking the attorney to rephrase the question for understanding. Ronald Pawlak, an attorney who defended Chrysler against many product liability claims, suggested in the October 1968 issue of the *Defense Research Institute Newsletter* that engineer-witnesses should watch for opportunities during cross-examination to catch the opposing attorney off-base on technical matters. Nevertheless, most attorneys surveyed warned technical and managerial personnel not to try to assume the functions of the lawyer—on either side.

Engineer and managers must also understand that in a trial they can testify only to what they know from direct observation and experience—and not what they have been told by others. Therefore, it is usually a good idea for the person or people who helped design a product to take part in investigating its role in any accident.

Engineers, nevertheless, often feel constrained by the court's rules of evidence. The engineer may not be allowed to introduce certain proved data, perhaps because the way that the data were obtained seems too abstract to the court. Testimony on how heavy a certain object is might not be allowed, although without this information, certain energy calculations would be impossible.

Likewise, when an engineer says something is probable, that usually means 98 percent sure. In court, "probable" means something closer to 51 percent, or "maybe a strong possibility." It is impossible for engineers to fight the rules, though. Not only are judges and attorneys convinced that their way is the only way to conduct a trial—in court, their way prevails despite what any engineer might argue.

The favorite device of lawyers on both sides may well prove the most troubling problem for engineers to deal with. That is the hypothetical question, often long and rambling. The typical hypothetical question is one in which the lawyer describes a set of circumstances and then asks the technical witness if he or she has an opinion as to why the product failed. For example, a witness might be asked, "If a tire is 50 percent worn, how many miles could it have run?"

The witness can truthfully answer that question in only two ways. He or she can state that it is impossible to make such an estimate, since there are too many unknown factors such as the speed at which the tires are driven, size and make of the car, loads carried, inflation pressure, and so forth. If the lawyer insists on an estimate, a wide range must be given—say, 1000 to 20,000 miles. This would almost certainly be a meaningless response in the trial's context.

It is somewhat comforting that even hypothetical questions are supposed to be limited to those elements already accepted as evidence. But this won't stop the opposition from seizing on one element from a hypothetical question already answered and trying to get witnesses to alter their opinions or contradict themselves. Under court rules, such methods are a legitimate means of examining witnesses.

4. USING THE OUTSIDE EXPERT

Engineering experts are something special in court trials. Ordinarily, such testimony would be considered "hearsay," and therefore inadmissible. But the testimony of technical and medical experts is permitted when it seems likely to provide what the courts call "probative" evidence—a means of testing or proving a fact. Nevertheless, the expert's testimony is welcomed only for its value in helping a judge and jury to better understand the issues—a critically important fact for attorneys and outside experts to remember.

Many of these outside experts are full-time or part-time expert witnesses. They can play many roles in the preparation or trial of a product liability case. Some of these witnesses, who often call themselves consultants, say a substantial number of their cases go no further than tests and analyses, and the reports they make of their findings. Often such reports determine a plaintiff counsel's decision that a case is not worth pursuing, or that a defendant settle out of court.

Lawyer-engineer George Peters, in his book, *Product Liability and Safety*, advises other lawyers: "When you first present a case to the expert, permit *him* to discover for himself the presence or absence of a defect or pertinent causal factor. If you lead or suggest answers to the expert, how can you be sure that your adversary cannot do the same thing at a later date?"

He also warns that

> "The reputable expert is offended by and will avoid those who shop for cut rate prices and quickie opinions as to the presence or absence of defect. For example, it doesn't require too much time or effort for someone to state that

the product "looks okay" and that any problem must have been caused by misuse, carelessness, or abuse. This might be enough if the other party bears a burden of proving a standard of due care or to create an inference of contributory negligence. But it is not enough when the issues have been sharpened technically by knowledgeable preparation and discovery, when incisive cross-examination and strict liability prevails, and when the trier-of-fact is both critical and perceptive."

Peters is among the founders of the System Safety Society. He coined the term "forensic engineering," in part to help describe what technical experts do in product safety investigations.

The investigatory procedure followed by Gordon River, a mechanical engineering professor, is typical of methods used by experienced expert witnesses.

"When I get a new case," River says, "I like to tear the product down. Then I look at the drawings to see if specs are correct. Next I examine each part, first to see if any are broken and then to see if all have been made to the applicable specifications. Finally, I look at the product the way a layman would—I try to operate it the way he would. I also study competitive devices after I have found what seems to be the faulty element. And if, in the course of studying such competitive products, I find what seems to be a flaw, I feel obligated to advise the other manufacturer, too."

Although there are now many full-time "experts," River makes it plain that he got involved in such matters out of his concern for safety, and because it made him a better teacher. Another expert was badgered by the opposing attorney because he testified about many different products. The judge came to his rescue, noting that he was not claiming to be an expert in design, but only in testing.

Some attorneys use the outside expert to buttress the planned testimony of the product's actual designer, and to probe for potential weak spots in the design in a way that the designer alone usually could not do.

There are no firm guidelines about what backgrounds produce the best outside experts. Some attorneys prefer practicing engineers as expert witnesses, and others prefer scientists or college teachers. Sometimes retired practicing engineers—even with design backgrounds—are available and competent. Lengthy lists of such specialists are maintained by the Defense Research Institute, Inc., and the American Trial Lawyers Association (see App. G for addresses).

Sometimes a plaintiff's team, strapped for cash to pay expenses, and finding no obviously qualified experts available, will resort to the use of high-school science teachers, or maintenance experts who might not have a degree at all. Clearly, plaintiff's attorney—and the jury—must be able to believe in such a person's expertise. "I've seen a lift-truck mechanic testify as effectively as an expert," says one attorney, but he warns that all concerned should not try to exaggerate such a person's qualifications.

Impact failure   Internal pressure failure

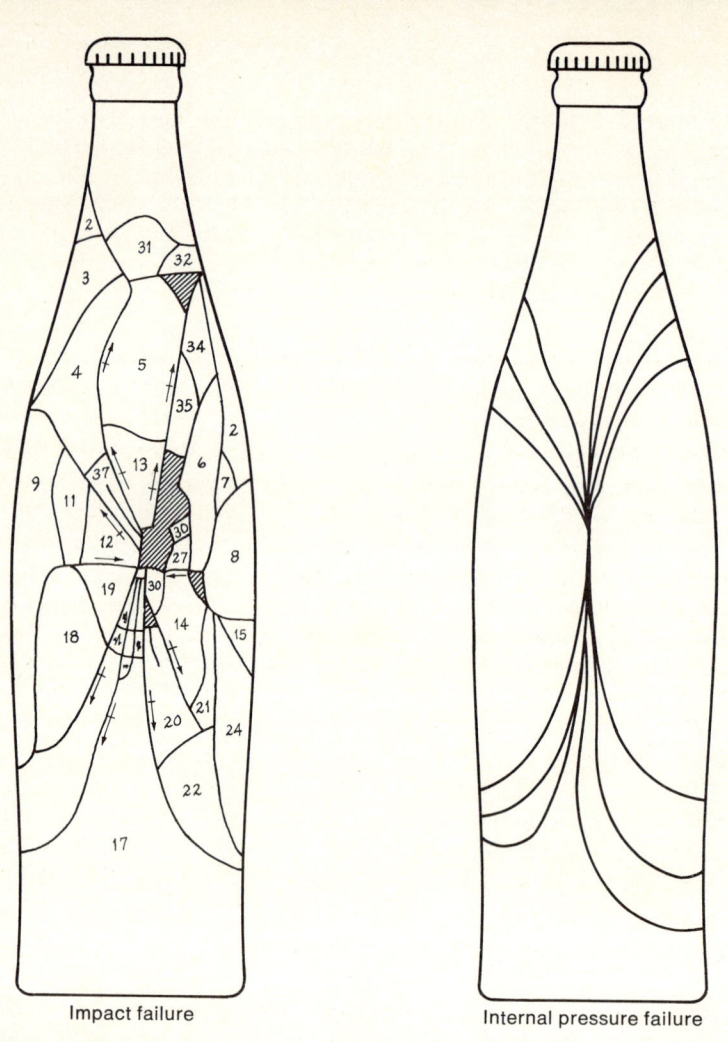

Figure VIII-1 Bits and pieces prove a bottle case. *(Product Engineering, April 21, 1969, p. 6.)* Anyone who has ever dropped a glass bottle on the floor and then tried to gather up the pieces can appreciate what William Harper, a forensic physicist, was up against in gathering proof of why a bottle failed. Worse yet, he had to put the fragments through a number of painstaking analytical steps before he could draw the conclusions that often decide whether his attorney-client (he works most often for defense counsel) should take the case to trial or try to settle out of court.

First the fragments must be cleaned, so the fracture edges can be clearly seen. Then, like working a jig-saw puzzle, Harper assembles the pieces back into the original shape of the bottle, numbering them as he goes and using Scotch tape to hold them together. This reassembly enables him to identify the fragments in the fracture pattern drawings, which differ with each cause of bottle failure—impact, thermal shock, or internal pressure.

Next, Harper makes a "crack map," tracing the directions of the cracks and the sequence (identified by color) in which they formed when the bottle broke. The edges of the fragments along the crack lines must be examined to determine whether the leading edges are on the inside or outside. The crack maps then form the basis of the expert witness's discussions with attorneys, as well as of the exhibits he uses in court.

5. COURTROOM EXHIBITS

Diagrams, working models, even color movies have their place in technical testimony, although there is a backlash in some quarters about unnecessarily flashy and expensive exhibits, especially by the defense. Most technical experts agree that a simple, well-rehearsed narrative is most effective generally. Perhaps this would be accompanied by photographs of the accident scene and of the part or parts—if any—that failed in the product.

Sometimes, however, some rather abstract technical terms must be conveyed to the jury. In one case, a propeller newly installed on a private plane tore loose in flight. Passengers were injured. They sued the propeller manufacturer, charging that the washers used had not been strong enough to protect the bolt assemblies. Admittedly, the washers did not meet Federal Aviation Administration specifications, but it looked to investigators as though the bolts had bent back and forth, a condition not likely to develop merely from failure of washers.

A theoretical analysis by Frank Arnold, expert witness who was formerly an engineering professor at Stanford, supported the conclusion that the fault lay elsewhere than in the washers. Sure enough, under questioning, the mechanic who had installed the propeller admitted he had tightened the bolts by "feel" rather than using a torque wrench as specified.

The problem then was to convince the jury that even carefully hand-tightened bolts might not provide secure enough connections. The effect of various torque levels can be a rather abstract concept for individuals without technical training to grasp. To demonstrate the difference between tightening bolts by feel and by torque wrench, Arnold constructed a working model (Fig. VIII-2) made up of common hardware items—eyebolts, nuts, sections of an I-beam and an angle iron, and a couple of ordinary spring scales of the kind anyone might find around the home.

Using the model, Arnold then told the jury: "The flange with the wire handle welded to it represents the propeller flange on the engine crankshaft, and the 15-pound pressure you see registered on the center spring scale is analogous to the amount of torque that should have been put on the bolts holding the propeller in place."

Hooking a second scale through the handle on the flange, Arnold then pulled back and forth on it, maintaining readings between zero and ten pounds. Arnold then told the jury, "Note that the pointer on the central scale

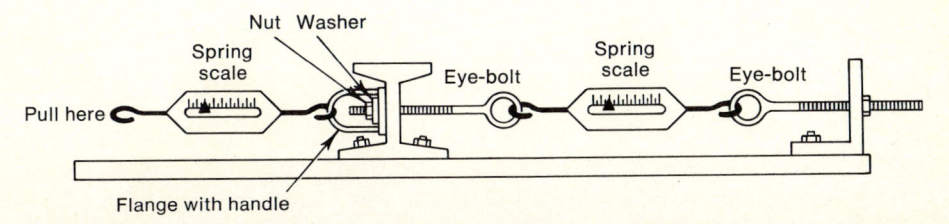

Figure VIII-2 Court exhibit to show importance of torque wrenching. *(Product Engineering, April 21, 1969, p. 5.)*

has not moved, even though the amount of pressure with which I've been pulling on this second scale is analogous to that put on the propeller bolts during normal in-flight engine power fluctuations."

Next, Arnold adjusted one of the eyebolts so the central spring scale read only about seven pounds, and then pulled back and forth on the outer scale, keeping the pressures within the same zero- to ten-pound range as before. Now the pointer on the central scale moved back and forth, as the two scales' springs exerted pressure on the eyebolts in alternating directions. "This variation in pressure which you now see being imposed on the model's eyebolts is analogous to what happened to the propeller," said Arnold, "because the mechanic tightened the bolts by feel rather than with a torque wrench, as he was supposed to have done."

Arnold and the manufacturer also produced the results of ground tests to back up the demonstration and to show that the hypothesized cause of the accident could have actually created the hazard in an actual aircraft. These tests had been conducted with a propeller, engine, washers, and other components identical to those involved in the crash. The jury decided in favor of the defendant, ruling that the fault lay with improper maintenance rather than with inadequate washers.

Said another expert witness, "When you are talking to a jury, it is much like teaching a class. You have to win their confidence. You have to adjust to them." Yet, you lose points by talking down to a jury, mumbling about "things beyond a layman's capacity to understand," and so forth.

An engineer with major responsibilities in product litigation for a leading industrial-equipment maker describes the best engineering witness he has ever seen in action:

> He is slow, deliberate, gives off an aura of confidence. He is consistently polite to both attorneys, and no matter how long he is on the stand or how much the opposition is trying to incite him, he never forgets his manners. He even excuses himself when he steps down to make use of a visual aid. And when he shows such pictures to the jury, he displays them to each member, not just those at his end of the box. Best of all, his answers are always brief and always in terms understandable to the layman.

IX
INSURANCE: RATES, CLAIMS, AND NEW DIRECTIONS

To put it bluntly, manufacturers and their insurors do not have identical interests in the outcome of a typical product liability case. Manufacturers are (or should be) mainly concerned about their business reputation, and the reputation of their products. Companies have been known to incur large legal costs fighting even small claims, in order to uphold their reputation or their view of what liability law "should be." This attitude has been waning—legal costs have grown too high in many instances, and court precedents have been unnerving to manufacturer-defendants. But insurors have always been thought to be more dispassionate—coolly weighing their legal costs and the tying up of capital as they decide whether to defend a suit.

The interests of insurors and manufacturers do coincide on one point, however—the desirability of remaining in business and turning a profit. Upon that point, a surprisingly large number of alternatives revolve.

1. NEGOTIATING PREMIUMS AND COVERAGE

Despite the horror stories circulating about the plight of certain industries—especially the machine-tool industry—with respect to obtaining product liability insurance at affordable rates, most manufacturers—and even ones who have suffered major product liability losses—have not been pinched too badly by the insurance industry.* It is certainly true that liability rates as a percentage of company sales remained just about constant from 1962 to 1975, then jumped dramatically in 1976—an 83 percent increase overall in the rate manual compiled by the Insurance Services Office (the industry's most important rate-making and statistical group).

For some industries, the increases were even more dramatic—bodily injury rates were up 550 percent in the industrial dies, jigs, and fixtures industry, rose 377 percent for dry ice manufacturers, and were up 690 percent for tire manufacturers (who also suffered a 300 percent increase in rates for property damage).

*McKinsey & Company, Interagency Task Force on Product Liability, U.S. Dept. of Commerce, March 1977.

Table IX-1 Total Premium Volume and Miscellaneous Liability Premium Volume of Major Types of Property and Liability Insurors

Type	1954 $ Millions	1954 Percent of total volume	1964 $ Millions	1964 Percent of total volume	1974 $ Millions	1974 Percent of total volume
STOCK						
Miscellaneous liability	$ 461,295	6.5%	$ 874,335	6.9%	$ 2,509,995	7.8%
Total volume	7,143,593	—	12,647,613	—	32,070,729	—
MUTUAL						
Miscellaneous liability	110,427	4.8	236,423	5.0	425,998	4.1
Total volume	2,278,133	—	4,766,940	—	10,459,186	—
RECIPROCAL						
Miscellaneous liability	—	—	NA*	—	53,843	2.6
Total volume	—	—	668,091	—	2,101,403	—
LLOYDS ASSOCIATION						
Miscellaneous liability	—	—	NA	—	NA	NA
Total volume	—	—	23,987	—	25,473	—

SOURCE: Property-Liability, 1975, Best's Aggregates and Averages.
*NA = Not Available

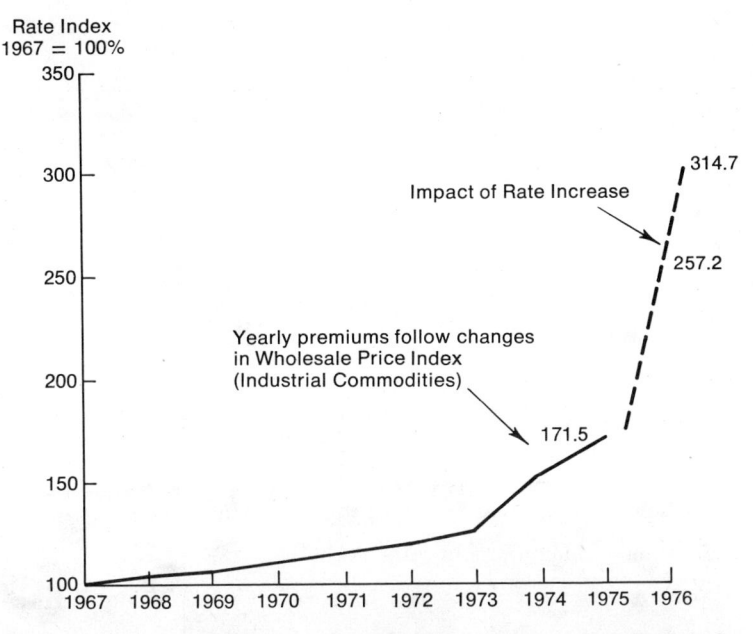

Figure IX-1 Estimated product liability costs indexed to inflation. Based on analysis of 1975 and 1976 basic limits product liability rate filings. Analysis does not include (a) rated products and does not reflect impact of experience or schedule modifications or use of special rating plans. (SOURCES: *ISO Rate Activity Bulletins; U.S. Department of Labor, Bureau of Labor Statistics as presented by Interagency Task Force on Product Liability, 1977*)

Rate increases, however, are not directly indicative of total premiums (which vary with sales of the insured, liability coverage, and the insured's own loss history). And the increases also fell more heavily upon larger companies. The average rate increase from 1974–75 to 1975–76 was 510 percent for companies with more than 2.5 million dollars in 1975 sales; for companies with sales less than that, the increases averaged "only" 39 percent in these high-risk industries. For most product categories, insurance rates amount to less than 2 percent of sales for primary coverage of $500,000, the Interagency Task Force on Product Liability found.

All this is not too surprising, when one considers that insurance is, mainly, a method of spreading risks over a broad societal base. In addition, liability insurance is almost always part of a larger commercial package covering all forms of liability and injury, and perhaps insuring the manufacturer's property as well. Finally, a lack of basic data on injury and liability rates in many industries (or a small industry producing so few products that the number of claims is statistically insignificant) can lead to great variations in the premiums companies pay.

Table IX-2a Product Liability Rate Revisions in Target Product Classifications 1974–1976 (Interagency Task Force on Product Liability, 1977)

	Manual or (a) rate	*Percentage increase in Basic Limits Rates 1974–1976 for manual rates and commentary from underwriters on application of (a) rates*	
		Bodily injury	Property damage
1. INDUSTRIAL MACHINERY			
Tools—dies, jigs and fixtures (Mfg)	Manual	550%	8%
Metal-working machinery and equipment (Mfg)	(a)		
Hand tools—powered	(a)		
Const., mining, and material handling equipment	(a)	"Rates up substantially for these eight categories—no estimates available."	
Industrial machinery and equipment (Mfg. NOC*)	(a)		
Machinery (Mfg)	(a)		
Electrical generating equipment (Mfg. NOC)	(a)		
Electrical equipment	(a)		
Engines and turbines	(a)		
2. INDUSTRIAL GRINDING AND ABRASIVE PRODUCTS			
Abrasive wheels	(a)	"*Very* wide variation in increases depending on the individual risk. The better risks would have only moderate increases, but many would be up several fold."	
Abrasive (Mfg. NOC)	(a)		
3. FERROUS AND NONFERROUS METAL CASTINGS			
Metals—smelting or refining (Mfg)	(a)	"Rates have been increased, but not as much as for risks in the industrial machinery classification."	
Structural iron and steel—excluding erection (Mfg)	(a)		
Metals—process—no. fab. metal prod. manufactured (Mfg)	(a)		

*Not otherwise classified.

	Manual or (a) rate	Percentage increase in Basic Limits Rates 1974–1976 for manual rates and commentary from underwriters on application of (a) rates	
		Bodily injury	Property damage

4. INDUSTRIAL CHEMICALS: ORGANIC AND INORGANIC

Chemicals—industrial use (Mfg, NOC)	(a)	⎫
Chemicals (Mfg, NOC)	(a)	⎪ "Wide variation in (a)
Chemicals—herbicides (Mfg)	(a)	⎬ rate application, but most rates not up as
Chemicals—pesticides (Mfg)	(a)	⎪ high as the one
Gases—in drums (Mfg, NOC)	(a)	⎪ manual classification
Gases—in steel cylinders (Mfg, NOC)	(a)	⎪ listed."
Gases—in tank cars (Mfg, NOC)	(a)	⎭
Dry ice (Mfg)	Manual	377% 33%

5. AIRCRAFT COMPONENTS

Airplane wheels	(a)	⎫
Aircraft (Mfg)	(a)	⎪
Aircraft engines	(a)	⎪ "Products in the eight
Electrical components	(a)	⎬ (a) rated categories are written primarily
Control instruments	(a)	⎪ by the aircraft pools;
Instruments (NOC)	(a)	⎪ these rates have declined."
Computers	(a)	⎪
TV picture tubes	(a)	⎭
Radio, TV, sound systems*	Manual	42% 0
Household TV*	Manual	42 0

6. AUTOMOBILE COMPONENTS AND TIRES

Auto, bus, truck accessories, not operating parts (Mfg)	Manual	285% 7%

---

*This classification is used for certain aircraft instrument components.

Table IX-2a *(Continued)*

	Manual or (a) rate	Percentage increase in Basic Limits Rates 1974–1976 for manual rates and commentary from underwriters on application of (a) rates	
		Bodily injury	Property damage
Auto, bus, truck inner tubes (Mfg)	Manual	35%	300%
Safety belts	Manual	N/A	N/A
Auto accessory supplies	Manual	600	43
Batteries—storage (Mfg)	Manual	367	45
Batteries—dry (Mfg)	Manual	400	50
Tires—auto, bus, truck	Manual	690	300
Tires—recap	Manual	281	51
Autos, buses, trucks (Mfg)	(a)		
Auto bodies—excluding trail. (Mfg)	(a)		
Auto, bus, truck brake lining (Mfg)	(a)	"Increases used for (a) rated products track closely with increases shown for manual rates in this category. (a) rate increases of 300–500 percent not uncommon."	
Camper and trailer bodies	(a)		
Bus bodies	(a)		
Trailers—mobile homes (Mfg)	(a)		
Truck bodies	(a)		
Auto parts (NOC)	(a)		
Motor vehicles—personal (Mfg)	(a)		
Engines and turbines	(a)		

Liability insurance is normally purchased in several layers of coverage. The first layer, so-called "primary" coverage, can be purchased in two ways: as part of a Comprehensive General Liability Policy (CGL), which covers a variety of exposures, including on-premises operations, consultants and independent contractors working for you, and product liability; or as part of "package policies," covering liability and the manufacturer's property as well.

The Task Force survey revealed that in 1975, 52 percent of all primary policies providing product liability coverage were CGLs, and the remainder were package policies. In general, package policies are meant for smaller

| | Manual or (a) rate | Percentage increase in Basic Limits Rates 1974–1976 for manual rates and commentary from underwriters on application of (a) rates ||
		Bodily injury	Property damage
7. MEDICAL DEVICES			
Electrical equipment—direct and indirect application to body (Mfg, NOC)	Manual	432%	32%
Medical, dental, hospital, surgical instruments excluding equipment and diagnostic, treatment machinery (Mfg)	(a)		
Medical, dental, hospital, surgical, equipment—non-expendable (Mfg)	(a)		
Medical, dental, hospital, surgical supplies—expendable (Mfg)	(a)	No commentary available for (a) rate practices.	
Medical, dental, surgical, diagnostic or treatment machinery or devices (Mfg)	(a)		
Instruments—analyzing, calibrating, measuring, testing or recording (Mfg)	(a)		
8. PHARMACEUTICALS			
Drugs, medicines, pharmaceutical products (Mfg) animal use only (NOC)	(a)		
Drugs, medicines, pharmaceutical products (Mfg, NOC)	(a)	"Substantial increases in (a) rates."	
Drugs—ground products (Mfg)	(a)		

companies; 85 percent of the package-policy holders had 1975 sales volumes of less than 2.5 million dollars.

Both types of primary coverage include minimum limits of $25,000 per occurrence for bodily injury damages (including loss of services) and $5,000 per occurrence for property damage. In some policies, these per-occurrence limits are supplemented with annual aggregate limits of $50,000 for bodily injury and $25,000 for property damage.

Most manufacturers purchase more than the basic limits, of course. The Task Force survey of 3000 policies in effect in 1975 showed that the most fre-

Table IX-2b Product Liability Rates for Target Product Categories Calculations reflect basic limits rates and increased limits factors up to a limit of liability of $500,000 for both bodily injury and property damage. Rates *do not reflect* application of experience or schedule modifications.

	ISO product code	Estimated average rate as a percentage of sales*
1. INDUSTRIAL MACHINERY		
Tools—dies, jigs and fixtures (Mfg)	35401	.52%
Metal-working machinery and equipment (Mfg)	35402 (a)	3.12
Hand tools—powered	35202 (a)	2.70
Construction, mining and material handling	35302 (a)	1.70
Industrial machinery and equipment (NOC)	35500 (a)	2.90
Machinery (Mfg)	35992 (a)	2.90
Electrical generating equipment (Mfg, NOC)	36102 (a)	1.10
Electrical equipment	36202 (a)	1.73
Engines and turbines	35100 (a)	1.10
2. INDUSTRIAL GRINDING AND ABRASIVE PRODUCTS		
Abrasive wheels	32902 (a)	1.42
Abrasives (Mfg, NOC)	32908 (a)	.30
3. FERROUS AND NONFERROUS METAL CASTINGS		
Metals—smelting or refining (Mfg)	33300 (a)	.17
Structural iron and steel—excluding erection (Mfg)	33101 (a)	.39
Metals—proc.—no fab. metal prod. manufactured (Mfg)	34702 (a)	.37
4. INDUSTRIAL CHEMICALS: ORGANIC AND INORGANIC		
Chemicals—industrial use (Mfg, NOC)	28105 (a)	1.35
Chemicals (Mfg, NOC)	28905 (a)	.73
Chemicals—Herbicides (Mfg)	28703 (a)	1.58

*(a) Rates shown on this list are based on the results of Task Force underwriting file analysis supplemented by underwriters' estimates of average rates.

	ISO product code	Estimated average rate as a percentage of sales*
Chemicals—Pesticides (Mfg)	28702 (a)	1.58
Gases—in drums (Mfg, NOC)	28102 (a)	(1.88 per number of fillings)
Gases—in steel—cylinders (Mfg, NOC)	28107 (a)	(.48 per number of fillings)
Gases—in tank cars (Mfg, NOC)	28108 (a)	(6.18 per number of fillings)
Dry ice (Mfg)	28103	.13

5. AIRCRAFT COMPONENTS

Airplane wheels	37201 (a)	N/A
Aircraft (Mfg)	37202 (a)	N/A
Aircraft engines	37203 (a)	N/A
Radio, TV, sound systems	36511	.06
Electrical components	36703 (a)	↑
Control instruments	38200 (a)	Insufficient data
Instruments (NOC)	38110 (a)	
Computers	35701 (a)	↓
TV picture tubes	36701	.44
Household TV	36512	.06

6. AUTOMOBILE COMPONENTS AND TIRES

Auto, bus, truck accessories; not operating parts (Mfg)	37105	.42
Autos, buses, trucks (Mfg)	37101 (a)	.66/8.56
Auto bodies—excluding trailers (Mfg)	37102 (a)	.92
Auto, bus, truck brake lining (Mfg)	37103 (a)	1.24
Auto, bus, truck inner tubes (Mfg)	30112	(.87 per number tubes)
Camper and trailer bodies	37113 (a)	1.14
Safety belts	37116	.44

Table IX-2b (*Continued*)

	ISO product code	Estimated average rate as a percentage of sales*
Auto accessory supplies	59351	.17
Bus bodies	37112 (a)	1.84
Auto accessory stores—wholesale	50121	.17
Trailers—mobile homes (Mfg)	37990 (a)	1.30
Truck bodies	37114 (a)	1.40
Auto parts (NOC)	37115 (a)	2.10
Batteries—storage (Mfg)	36902	.23
Batteries—dry (Mfg)	36901	.55
Motor vehicles (personal) (Mfg)	37111 (a)	1.44
Tires—auto, bus, truck	30111	(.52 per number tires)
Tires—recap	75301	(18.11 per number tires)
Engines and turbines	35100 (a)	.90
7. MEDICAL DEVICES		
Medical, dental, hospital, surgical instruments, excluding equipment and diagnostic, treatment machinery (Mfg)	38401 (a)	.47
Medical, dental, hospital, surgical equipment nonexpendable (Mfg)	38402 (a)	1.39
Medical, dental, hospital, surgical supplies—expendable (Mfg)	38403 (a)	.25
Medical, dental, or surgical diagnostic or treatment machinery or devices (Mfg)	38404 (a)	1.79
Electrical equipment—direct and indirect application to body (Mfg, NOC)	36402	1.41
Instruments—analyzing, calibrating, measuring, testing or recording (Mfg)	36101 (a)	.72
8. PHARMACEUTICALS		
Drugs, medicines, pharmaceutical products (Mfg) animal use only (NOC)	28301 (a)	2.35
Drugs, medicines, pharmaceutical products (Mfg, NOC)	28302 (a)	.87
Drugs—ground products (Mfg)	28303 (a)	.48

quently purchased aggregate limit was $500,000, and companies generally purchased insurance for limits of $250,000 to 1 million dollars. Per-occurrence limits were either for the same amount or less. In the larger policies offered by some insurors, aggregate limits may make no distinction between bodily injury and property damage. Under these policies, the insuror agrees to become legally obligated (with some qualifications) to pay damages and settlements up

Table IX-3 Product Liability Coverage and Rating Plans

Size of insured	Insurance program characteristics
I. SMALL*	
Average sales under $2.5 million	• Purchase primary product coverage as part of Mono-line (CGL) policy written on a guaranteed cost basis
	• Product rates are usually based on industry class averages as policy is too small to qualify for experience rating (manual rates)
	• Excess coverage is usually provided by an "umbrella" policy
II. MEDIUM*	
Average sales $2.5 million to $50 million	• Purchase primary product coverage as part of package policy with the liability portion written on a guaranteed cost basis
	• Product rates are usually based on underwriter's judgment (i.e., (a) rated)
	• Policy premium is often large enough to qualify for the application of experience and schedule rating plans
	• Excess coverage is usually provided by an "umbrella" policy
III. LARGE	
Average sales over $50 million	• Purchase primary product coverage as part of Mono-line (CGL) policy written on a retrospective rating plan
	• Product rates are usually based on underwriter's judgment or on (a) rate or composite/loss-rated basis; experience and schedule rating plans are applied
	• Several layers of excess coverage are purchased from many different companies both in the United States and the United Kingdom

*Programs similar to those purchased by large companies are purchased by small and medium companies if they manufacture high-hazard products and can afford the premium.

to the limit of liability stated in the policy, plus any legal costs involved in defending against a liability suit.

Normally in policies available today, the insurance underwriter agrees to pay damages arising from all products—those already sold, those that are in distributors' hands, items not yet off the assembly line, and even items not yet out of the design stage—occurring during the policy period. Thus, the underwriter may have to pay for damages resulting from a product made 10 or 20 years ago.

In most jurisdictions, the statute of limitations does not begin to run until the product causes an injury. The biggest single exception as of this writing is Connecticut, which in 1976 enacted an 8-year statute of limitations that begins when the product first "enters the stream of commerce."

Deductibles are also uncommon in this type of insurance, in primary coverage. Only 3 percent of the 3,000 files examined by the Task Force included deductibles. Only four of the policies excluded any of a company's products from coverage, and for three of those, separate policies had been written to cover the exclusions. In all but a handful of cases, the deductibles applied to the entire liability policy, and not to products liability only.

Policyholders who want more coverage than that which the primary layer can provide purchase additional insurance in "umbrella" or "excess" policies. Umbrella policies assume losses only after primary coverage has been exhausted, or in areas not covered by primary insurance. Typically, umbrella policies offer wider coverage (with fewer exclusions) than primary policies. These extensions are subject to deductibles, however (usually in the $10,000 to $25,000 range). Typical of these extensions is coverage for damage to property in the hands of the insured, such as a large truck sent back to its manufacturer for modification or repair.

Such excess policies may involve limits of 100 million dollars or more. Since single insurors will rarely write a policy for more than 10 million dollars or so, several insurance companies may be used to "fill out the line." Brokers or independent agents handling such large lines will try to obtain uniform pricing and coverage from all the participating insurors, but this may not be possible in every case.

The insurance companies, on the other hand, will almost always spread their risk by "reinsurance" to other insurors. A 5 million-dollar policy usually has 80 to 90 percent of its liability limit insured with other companies. The policyholder has no part in reinsurance transactions—if a loss occurs under the policy, the insuror will pay the claim and then go to the reinsuror(s) for recovery of the portion the reinsuror has agreed to cover.

Whether an insurance company will agree to write a policy depends on the company's underwriters. To help them decide, each company has an underwriting manual with guidelines reflecting the insurance company's experience with various types of insureds.

Most insurance companies' guidelines identify certain product classifications for which the company will not offer insurance, or for which insurance will be

Table IX-4 Frequent Product Liability Underwriting Restrictions Reported by Agents

Frequent underwriting restrictions	Proportion of response	Total	IIAA	NAMIA
Underwriters unwilling to quote on some products/industries	80.6%	441	331	110
Particularly stringent underwriting for small businesses with modest premiums	47.5	260	193	67
Underwriting decisions made only at home office	43.0	235	182	53
Difficulty in obtaining increased limits	41.9	229	177	52
"Unaffordable" premium increases	41.9	229	174	55
Increased minimum premiums	38.8	212	155	57
Refusal to renew coverage	38.6	211	165	46
Deductibles added to policies	21.2	116	94	22
Coverage provided for only a portion of insureds' operations	17.4	95	81	14
Decreases in limits of liability	13.3	74	53	21
Addition of special exclusions	13.3	74	55	19
Changes in policy form	12.4	68	57	11

SOURCES: IIAA and NAMIA 1976 "Products Liability Questionnaire" responses—total responses 547; IIAA (418) and NAMIA (129).

offered only on an extraordinary basis (high premium, low-loss history for the particular manufacturer, or the manufacturer's other insurance business are typical reasons). Such high-risk industries include, according to the Task Force survey:

- Aircraft products (these are excluded in reinsurance treaties, making it almost impossible for an insuror to spread risk, and a well-organized specialized insurance pool exists to cover these products anyway)

- Pharmaceuticals
- Certain industrial machinery
- Certain chemicals
- Medical devices
- Ammunition and explosives
- Control equipment, hoists, motors, and other products capable of causing major claims when put to use as components of larger systems.

In fact, risk can vary dramatically by a product's use. A manufacturer of screws who sells mainly to the wood furniture industry is exposed to less liability than the manufacturer who sells his screws for use in machine tools. No matter what your broker or agent says, most decisions on whether to accept or reject a chance to write a policy are made locally, at an insurance company's branch or field offices. Only policies with particularly large loss potential are referred to the home office. However, a few companies insist that all underwriting decisions for industries with products not included in the Insurance Services Office Manual be referred upward to headquarters.

Table IX-5   Rate Increases in (a) Rated Products of Industries Tabulated Below
(Interagency Task Force on Product Liability, 1977.)

Product classification	Number of companies having data available	Low range	Percent of increase average 1974–1975 vs. 1975–1976	High range
Industrial machinery	27	<0%	244%	350–400%
Industrial grinding and abrasive products	1	——	insufficient data	——
Ferrous and nonferrous metal castings	13	0–50	19	100–150
Industrial chemicals: organic and inorganic	4	0–50	78	100–150
Aircraft components	——	——	insufficient data	——
Automobile components	3	200–250	568	800–850
Medical devices	2	<0	35	0–50
Pharmaceuticals	2	150–200	219	2500–300
All other product categories	765	<0	251	900–950

In deciding whether to accept or reject the business, and in deciding rates and premiums to be set, underwriters consider the following:

- Loss control measures practiced by the manufacturer
- Prior losses, manufacturer's financial stability, and physical plant
- The industry's general exposure to liability
- Limits and coverages requested
- Size of the overall account, and number of years with the insuror
- Overall record of the producer or insurance agent with the insurance carrier.

Premiums charged for product liability coverage are determined by using either of two types of rating plans. The first is a "prospective," or "guaranteed cost" plan; the second is called "retrospective," because it is designed to take into account the actual losses incurred in the new policy period in calculating the final premium to be charged. Although 90 percent of the cases reviewed by the Interagency Task Force were rated prospectively, they probably account for only about 10 percent of the product liability premiums, since the very largest accounts are generally written retrospectively.

There are three distinct ways in which final rates to determine premiums are developed. They are:

- The *traditional method,* which begins with a specific rate for an individual product's "basic limits" coverage and is then modified in various ways to develop a final rate;
- The *composite rating method,* which begins with the same individual product basic limits rates, but then combines them with rates for all other coverages offered so that the final rate is an aggregate rate for the entire policy;
- The *loss rating method,* which begins not with the product basic limits rates, but with an overall estimate of expected losses and expenses, and is then developed into a final rate applicable to the entire policy (with all coverages, not only product liability, included).

Note that in the second and third methods, there is no final rate or premium directly applicable to products liability coverage.

In the traditional method, the calculation begins with the selection of the appropriate "basic limits" rate or rates for the class or classes of products to be covered. (Later in this chapter, we will describe how these rates are developed.)

The term "basic limits" is used to indicate that these rates reflect a standard limit of liability (per-occurence limits of $25,000 and $5,000 for bodily injury and property damage, respectively, and annual aggregates of $50,000 for bodily injury and $25,000 for property damage). If higher limits are desired, these rates must be increased through the use of "increased limits factors" which correspond to the limits desired.

The rate is then usually modified in two additional ways: (1) to reflect the overall liability experience of the policyholder during the prior 3 to 5 years in comparison with the expected experience (referred to as the "experience modification"); and (2) by a series of subjective credits or debits that reflect the quality of the insured's overall operation (referred to as the "schedule modification"). Since these two modifications can have a significant impact on the premium, they are discussed in more detail below. Further, if coverage is provided as part of a package policy, a discount may be applied to the premium. This discount, which generally ranges from 5 to 20 percent, is intended to reflect the insuror's expense savings arising from the replacement of several policies with one master policy. After the final rate is determined, it is multiplied by some measure of exposure, usually sales volume, to determine the premium applicable to the product liability coverage (see Fig. IX-2.)

The purpose of an experience rating plan is to reflect the insured's own loss experience in the determination of the premium. As rates are based on "averages," it follows that these rates may be too high for some risks and too low for others. These plans limit the amount of any one loss included in the calculations to mitigate the effect of a "shock loss." Thus, these plans are far more sensitive to loss frequency than loss severity.

Experience modifications are used if the exposure is of sufficient magnitude for the past loss experience to have some credibility. Although experience rating plans vary among insurance companies, generally if the Comprehensive General Liability premium at basic limits exceeds the company's threshold for experience rating, which is usually $1,000 to $2,500 in annual premiums, an experience modification will be calculated as shown in Tables IX-6 and IX-7. The product liability premium through this process is affected by the liability experience on the insured's entire policy—not merely the product liability losses. Thus, the premium charged is based, in part, on actual as well as anticipated experience.

Schedule Modification

Schedule modification plans are used to further raise or lower the premium level based on less tangible risk characteristics. Underwriters surveyed by the Task Force indicated that schedule modifications were most often used on CGL policies without product coverage to lower the premium to a more "competitive" level. Most underwriters indicated that, although this practice is not usually followed for policies containing product coverage at present, it may have applied during intensely competitive periods in the past. The standards

Description of hazards	Code no.	Premium basis	Basic limits rate B.I.	Basic limits rate P.D.	Increased limits factor Bodily injury	Increased limits factor Property damage	Rate modification Experience mod	Rate modification Scheduled mod	Final rate B.I.	Final rate P.D.	Advance premiums Bodily injury	Advance premiums Property damage
Premises operations											$5,432	$1,583
Independent contractors											467	234
Completed operations											150	75
Products Automobile parts mfg.— not operating parts	37105	$1,000,000 (Sales)	.39	.16	4.52	5.50	1.0769	1.10	2.088	1.043	2,088	1,043
							Total Advance B.I. and P.D. Premiums				$8,137	$2,935
Automobile 1. Owned automobile — premium basis — per auto											2,542	854
2. Hired automobile — premium basis — cost of hire											230	95
3. Non-owned automobile — premium basis — No. of employees											160	42
							Total Automobile Advance B.I. and P.D. Premiums				$2,932	$ 991
							Total Policy Advance B.I. and P.D. Premiums				$11,069	$3,926

Figure IX-2 Sample worksheet for developing a comprehensive general liability policy premium using the traditional rating method.

Steps in Developing the Product Hazard Premium

Step 1: Determine the most appropriate product classification.

Step 2: Use classification code number to determine basic limits rate from manual or develop rate if classification has an (a) rate.

Step 3: Determine increased limits factors from ISO tables in manual [factors used in example are from bodily injury (B.I.) $1,000,000/1,000,000 and property damage (P.D.) $500,000/500,000]. Basic limits rates are for B.I. limits of $25,000 per occurrence, $50,000 aggregate and P.D. limits of $5,000 per occurrence, $25,000 for all damages.

Step 4: Apply rate modifications determined in accordance with experience and schedule rating plans. Note: Experience rating plans differ from company to company. Hence, final rates for the same exposure could differ.

Step 5: Determine from the policyholder the number of exposure units to be multiplied by the final rate. The premium bases most frequently used for products liability coverage are: (1) receipts (the rate applies per $1,000 of receipts). (2) sales (rates are applied per $1,000 of sales) and: (3) units (number of products manufactured).

used for applying a schedule modification are highly judgmental. And while many underwriting files contain justification for their use on an individual risk, underwriters have indicated that it is entirely possible that two underwriters could come to different conclusions as to the need for (or amount of) schedule modifications. These plans vary among companies but typically permit credits

Table IX-6 Sample Experience Rating Plan[a]

STEP 1

$$\frac{\text{Losses[b] incurred in 3- to 5-year period plus loss adjustment expenses} \times \text{Loss trend and development factors[c]}}{\text{Basic limits premium over 3- to 5-year period[d]}} = \text{Actual policy loss ratio}$$

STEP 2

$$\frac{\text{Experience}}{\text{modification}} = \frac{\text{Actual policy loss ratio} - \text{expected loss ratio}}{\text{Expected loss ratio[e]}}$$

STEP 3

$$\frac{\text{Experience}}{\text{modification}} \times \frac{\text{Credibility[f]}}{\text{factor}} = \frac{\text{Final experience}}{\text{modification}}$$

STEP 4

$$\text{Modification} \times \text{Basic rate} = \text{Final rate}$$

[a]Plans vary somewhat among insurors.

[b]Losses = Losses paid on behalf of the insured or incurred by the insured under a comprehensive general liability policy (products and operation losses). Individual losses are often limited to an amount related to premium size to reduce the effect of large losses.

[c]Trend and development factors = Loss estimates (reserves) are increased to reflect the fact that inflation and other forces will increase the ultimate loss payouts.

[d]Experience period = Losses included in the calculation can usually reflect the previous 3 to 5 years.

[e]Expected loss ratio = That percentage of the premium allocated to pay losses. It is determined by subtracting the expense ratio from 100 percent. It is also known as the "permissible" loss ratio.

[f]Credibility factor = Actuarial estimate of the reliability of the insured's losses to predict its actual loss-producing potential, i.e., large policyholders have more credibility than small ones.

Example: Assume an actual loss ratio of 70 percent and an expected loss ratio of 65 percent. The rate modification produced would be a debit of 7.69 percent, if full credibility is assumed. In most plans, the premium would have to exceed $75,000 to approach full credibility.

$$\text{Experience modification} = \frac{70\% - 65\%}{65\%} + 100\%$$
$$= 7.69\% + 100\%$$
$$= 107.69\%$$

If greater than 100 percent, the experience modification is a debit and raises the rate level. If less than 100 percent, the modification is a credit and represents a rate reduction.

Table IX-7 Example of Application of Typical Experience Rating Plan

Model steps	Example

STEP I: CALCULATE ACTUAL POLICY LOSS RATIO

A. Total basic limits premium (without rate modifications) for experience period $10,000

B. Determine ratable losses

    1. Determine basic limits losses $3,000

        Losses to be included cannot exceed the basic limits—e.g., $25,000 BI and $5,000 paid per occurrence; $50,000 BI and $25,000 paid in the aggregate

        The amount of any single loss to be included cannot exceed the maximum single loss amount specified in the "maximum single loss" table. NOTE: This amount varies with premium size and among insurors—e.g., the maximum single loss for $10,000 premium may be $5,000

    2. Determine allocated loss expense   500

    3. Add basic limit loss and allocated loss expense to determine ratable losses   3,500

C. Divide total ratable losses* by total basic limits premium to determine actual policy loss ratio $0.35 = \dfrac{3,500}{10,000}$ or 35%

STEP II: DETERMINE EXPERIENCE DEBIT OR CREDIT

Subtract expected loss ratio (from experience rating plan) from actual loss ratio and divide by expected loss ratio to determine experience debit or credit. NOTE: If result is negative, policy experience has produced a credit, i.e., experience was better than expected

$$(0.30) = \dfrac{0.35 - 0.50}{0.50}$$

STEP III: DETERMINE FINAL EXPERIENCE RATING MODIFICATION

A. Multiply experience credit or debit by the credibility factor (from experience rating plan, factor varies with premium size) to determine adjusted experience credit or debit. In example, $10,000 premium could be considered 29 percent "credible"

(0.087) = (0.30) × 0.29
(Adjusted experience credit) = (Experience credit) (Credibility factor)

B. Add adjusted experience credit or debit to 1.00 to determine final experience rating modification

0.913 = (0.087) + 1.00
(Final experience rating modification) (Adjusted experience credit)

---

*Example assumes ratable losses have been adjusted to reflect loss development and trend.

and debits generally ranging from 5 to 25 percent. Typical plans reflect nonratable risk characteristics such as managerial cooperation with the insuror; employee training; selection and motivation of employees; the condition of the insured's equipment, steps that the insured has taken or has failed to take to prevent losses; and other factors such as product quality assurance programs, which are often verified by the insuror's loss control engineers and documented by the underwriter in his rating files.

Composite Rating Method

Composite rating procedures vary among companies, but most often they begin with the determination of "basic limits" rates in the manner previously described to arrive at a premium figure for the entire policy, including the products hazard, and then divide this premium by one overall measure of exposure—usually sales or payroll—to determine a *composite* rate for the policy. The advantages of this system are said to be twofold. First, from a marketing point of view, only the final composite rates are known, making it difficult for competitors to determine what factors were used to develop them. Thus, it is theoretically more difficult for competitors to bid on accounts written in this manner. Second, since the advance premium paid at the beginning of the policy year is only a provisional premium (advance premium is based on *estimated* exposures—sales or payroll—and the final premium is based on the *actual* figures), the use of a composite rate facilitates the final determination of the policy premium for all risks. This is done by allowing the underwriter to apply one rate, the composite rate, to the actual exposures which are determined by the premium auditor from the insured's records at the end of the policy term.

The disadvantage of this method from a rate-making point of view is that the underlying rates that apply to the individual coverages in the policy are not preserved or made available for statistical purposes. Hence, no actual rate or premium for product liability coverage is available from policies rated by this method.

Loss Rating Method

Loss rating techniques also vary among insurors, but the concept involves dividing the expected losses and expenses by some measure of exposure such as sales, number of units produced, payroll, miles driven, number of employees, etc., to determine how much to charge per unit of exposure. At the end of the policy term, the number of these "exposure units" is determined by audit and a premium adjustment is made. An estimated premium is billed at the inception of the policy term. This approach to rate development is usually used only for insureds the underwriter feels have "full credibility"—i.e., when the losses incurred by the insured provide a sound estimate of all the losses to be expected from this type of risk. This size account is said to be "self-rating." There is no agreement among insurors regarding how large an account must be before it becomes self-rating. However, according to Rule 9 of ISO's Composite Rating Plan, loss rating may be used if the policy develops at least $200,000 of losses during a period of three years at specified limits. For rate-making purposes, this approach has the same disadvantage as does composite rating—the individual rates and premiums applicable to product liability coverage are not available.

Prospective and Retrospective Rating Plans

The term "prospective" rating refers to the fact that the premium charged by the underwriter is calculated at the beginning of the policy term and is not changed to respond to the actual losses incurred during the policy period (although it will vary if the units of exposure—i.e., sales volume—change during the year). With very few exceptions, the traditional method of determining final rates is used in prospective rating plans.

Retrospective rating plans, unlike prospective rating plans, provide for the adjustment of the current policy premium to reflect the losses incurred during the policy term. Under this rating procedure, the insured does not know his actual premium until well after the close of the policy year. In fact, some plans are kept "open" by the underwriter for certain "long-tail" risks for five years or more. Composite and loss rating methods are frequently used in determining rates used in retro plans.

In most retro plans, the premium is capped by a predetermined maximum. That is, at the beginning of the policy term, the insuror and policyholder will agree upon a minimum and a maximum premium, as well as all the factors and coverages to be included. An additional feature of retro plans is the use of a "loss limitation" factor, which specifies the maximum amount of any one loss to be included in the retro formula. Table IX-8a illustrates the retro formula.

Many larger policyholders write all of their liability insurance on a retrospective rating plan referred to as "Plan D." This plan permits the inclusion of all casualty coverage (e.g., automobile, worker's compensation, and general liability, including product liability).

Most "tough" product risks for large manufacturers are written on a retrospective rating basis. This arrangement permits a high degree of flexibility because the key factors that determine the final premium are negotiable. For example, a retro plan can be designed to permit the insured to pay a high proportion of his losses. This can be accomplished by eliminating the loss limitation and eliminating the maximum cap on the retro premium, or by setting it at a very high level. The plan can simultaneously be used to give the insured a greater incentive to produce safe products by specifying a low premium level that will apply if the loss experience is favorable. The variations in between are limited only by the imagination of the contracting parties and their willingness to negotiate.

Table IX-8a The Retrospective Rating Formula*

$$RP = [(SP \times BF) + (LFC \times IL) + PC]TM - DIV$$

Where *RP* = Retrospective Premium payable for the year or years agreed upon, subject usually to a minimum (e.g., 0.65) or a maximum (e.g., 1.75) of the standard premium

SP = Standard Premium (dollars), the premium determined on a prospective guaranteed cost basis, including the experience rating modification

BF = Basic Factor, a negotiated factor applied to the standard premium to determine how much the insuror will use to cover fixed costs in handling the account—e.g., broker commission, etc.

LCF = Loss Conversion Factor, designed to cover the insuror's variable loss experience—e.g., claim adjustment expenses

IL = Incurred Losses paid and reserved for all liability claims, including product liability for limits subject to the plan

PC = Premium charge; the losses to be included in the IL component can be limited to $10,000, $25,000, $150,000, or some agreed-upon amount. Losses above this threshold are "insured" and the premium charge is for this excess coverage. It is determined by multiplying the Standard Premium by an "excess loss premium factor." This premium is often included in the basic premium charge

TM = Tax Multiplier, to make provision for state premium taxes

DIV = Dividend, a return premium, reflecting a participation by the policyholder in the insuror's overall earnings. Dividends are only included on "participation" type retrospective rating plans

*This model reflects the features of a "Plan D" retro. These plans permit the inclusion of all casualty coverages—e.g., Worker's Compensation, commercial automobile, and general liability.

Determining Excess Policy Premium

Umbrella and form-following excess policy premiums are determined by multiplying a factor times the underlying, or primary, policy premium. These factors vary from 10 to 50 percent of the primary premium or higher, depending upon the excess underwriter's judgment concerning the probability that he will be required to pay a loss. Umbrella underwriters charge additional loadings for the coverage extensions provided in those policies. Because excess policies are used to insure infrequent catastrophies, excess underwriters, like reinsurors, price their policies to reflect the fact that they expect to pay very few losses. They try to achieve this by requiring substantial underlying or primary limits as a condition to writing coverage. When this is not practical and excess coverage is written over relatively low primary limits of liability (a layer sometimes referred to as "working excess"), the underwriter will often use a loss rating approach to develop the excess premium.

Establishing "Basic Limits" Rates

Determining the appropriate basic limits rates for product liability exposures involves some difficult problems of credibility. Although a universally acceptable definition of credibility has not been established, there is general agreement that a need exists for a large sample of loss events on which to base conclusions to reflect credibility in rate-making. For example, well over a million automobile policies can be used in a given state to estimate the losses incurred for this group. The group would be large enough so no one incident could distort the outcome. For product liability rates, having credible data becomes problematic—a result of the relatively small number of manufacturers of each type of product, and the large variety of products for a given manufacturer.

Because of the need for large numbers to provide a credible statistical basis for rate making, most product liability carriers have chosen to report their monoline* premium and loss data to the Insurance Services Office (ISO), which aggregates the data from all subscribing carriers and publishes suggested rates based on their aggregate country-wide experience. As of December 31, 1975, some 783, or 89 percent, of the major U.S. underwriters of general liability coverage were ISO members and subscribers or service purchasers and, as such, reported their experience data for rate-making purposes.†

Product liability insurance, as described earlier in this section, is offered through several types of policies. This fact has created additional problems in rate making. Because of the manner in which data are recorded by insurors, only the experience from monoline, manually rated, comprehensive general liability (CGL) policies have been reported in sufficient detail for rate-making purposes. Industry and ISO representatives have estimated that only 10 to 20 percent of the actual product experience has been used for rate making, because of the difficulties in gathering the data from policies other than monoline general liability.

In view of the limited data available, the Insurance Services Office has developed rates in two distinct categories: "manual" rates and (a) rates. The distinction between these two groups is important.

"Manual" Rates

Manually rated classifications (i.e., product classifications for which rates are published by ISO in a manual) consist of those categories of products for which a sufficient volume of detailed experience data (e.g., premiums, losses, and exposures) has been reported to ISO for rates to be determined actuarially. These rates are filed for approval according to individual state regulations. Of

---

*The term monoline is used to identify a liability policy which includes coverage for a variety of liability exposures, including products liability. It is usually used to refer to products coverage provided through the comprehensive general liability policy.

†Best's *Aggregate and Averages 1975*; listing of 882 insurance companies writing comprehensive general liability insurance in a majority of the states. They estimate that there are an additional 1000 small, local, or regional companies who offer such coverage.

Table IX-8b Application of the Formula to a Retrospective Rating Plan

Model steps	Example
STEP 1. DETERMINE THE STANDARD PREMIUM	$500,000 (Standard premium)
This retro formula component is developed just as it would be under a "guaranteed cost" (prospective) rating plan for the included coverages, e.g., worker's compensation, automobile, general liability (including products).	
STEP 2. APPLY THE BASIC FACTOR	$500,000 × 0.20 = $100,000 (Standard premium) × (Basic factor) = (Basic premium charge)
This factor reflects the insuror's overhead, e.g., producer commission (e.g., 10 percent) and a profit factor (e.g., 5 percent). This factor is assumed to be 20 percent for the example.	
STEP 3. DETERMINE LOSSES AND APPLY LOSS CONVERSION FACTOR (LCF):	
The losses incurred during the policy term are multiplied by this factor. The factor, 14 percent in the example, reflects the variable costs associated with handling the losses. The losses are valued at various periods following the expiration of the policy. A typical retro plan will require valuation at 18 months, 24 months, and 36 months after the inception of the policy term. This time period is required for the losses to develop their ultimate value.	

- 18 months
- 24 months
- 36 months

$$100,000 \times 1.14 = 114,000$$
$$250,000 \times 1.14 = 285,000$$
$$300,000 \times 1.14 = 342,000$$
(Incurred losses) × (LCF) = (Converted losses)

The individual incurred losses may be limited to a prearranged amount—e.g., $10,000 to $25,000. Losses above this point are insured on an excess-of-loss basis for a premium.

STEP 4. DETERMINE THE PREMIUM CHARGE AND EXCESS LOSS PREMIUM FACTOR

The premium charge is the cost of insurance above the loss limitation. It reflects the expected cost of losses above this point. This charge is assumed to be 6 percent in this example, and it is applied to the standard premium.

$$\underset{\text{(Standard premium)}}{\$500,000} \times \underset{\text{(Excess premium factor)}}{0.06} = \underset{\text{(Premium charge)*}}{\$30,000}$$

STEP 5. APPLY THE TAX MULTIPLIER

This factor reflects the state premium tax. It is applied to the entire retro premium, Steps 2 to 4. It is 3 percent in this example.

$$\underset{\text{(Basic charge)}}{\$100,000} + \underset{\text{(Converted losses)}}{\$342,000} + \$30,000 = \underset{\text{(Premium charge)}}{\$472,000}$$

$$\underset{\text{(Premium charge)}}{\$472,000} \times \underset{\text{(Tax multiplier)}}{1.03} = \underset{\text{("Retro" premium)}}{\$486,160\dagger}$$

SOURCE: Insurance Services Office, *Casualty Individual Risk Rating Plans*, p. 46.

*The retro premium could be limited to a predetermined minimum of, say, 65 percent of the standard premium ($350,000 in the example) or a maximum of, say, 175 percent ($875,000). These factors are negotiated along with the others at the outset of the policy term.

311

the 418 product classifications listed in the manual, 287, or 67 percent, are manually rated. ISO representatives have estimated that these manually rated classifications account for 25 percent of the product liability exposures written on a monoline basis.

Product classifications included in manual classes can be generally described as relatively low-hazard. The classification does *not* include such products as industrial chemicals, industrial grinding and abrasive products, pharmaceuticals, or many industrial machinery classifications.

(a) Rates

For those classifications of products for which insufficient data are reported to calculate a rate through actuarial techniques, or when a high degree of variability in experience exists within a product class, the alternative is to use a rate that is based primarily on judgment. These rates are called "(a) rates." For the most part, records of premiums and losses attributable to products in the (a) rate category have not been kept separately, because many of these products are written in commercial package policies or policies rated on a composite basis. Although ISO has been unable to develop statistically sound rates for these classifications of products, the Office has developed, on a judgmental basis, a series of suggested basic limits rates to provide some guidance for subscribers who can then vary their own rates as they feel appropriate.

ISO's procedure is to send these (a) rates to the chief executives of subscribing companies for individual consideration. Individual insurance carriers are expected to modify the rates in this category in determining what rates to use for a specific risk.

To accommodate practical reality for (a) rated product classifications, most state regulators have permitted insurors to charge rates based upon their own judgment. These judgmental (a) rates can be used for the 131 product classifications for which ISO has developed no manual rates. In addition, (a) rating can be used for risks that: (1) produce product liability premiums (at basic limits manual rates) in excess of $1000; (2) produce increased limits premiums of $2500 or more; or (3) produce policy manual basic limits premiums of $100,-000 or more. Additionally, premiums for limits in excess rates or surcharges can be applied for any reason with the insured's consent. Depending upon the state involved, these (a) rates may not have to be filed with the insurance commissioner but should be documented in the underwriter's file and made available to state examiners during rate examinations.

Considerations in Determining Basic Limits Rates. In determining (a) rates to use (and occasionally in selecting the appropriate manual rate), the underwriter takes the following factors into consideration:

1. Geographical differences in risk potential—although rates are made on a countrywide basis;

2. Presence of outstanding products for which no premium has been developed but on which claims may arise;

3. Variation in risk potential based on ultimate use;

4. Exposure base (sales) which may not be an accurate measure of risk potential.

These factors are taken into consideration in a number of ways. In some companies, the existence of a large number of outstanding products for which no premium is directly charged influences the underwriter to use another rating classification under which a higher rate may be charged. In another example, the use of a potentially high-hazard product under carefully controlled circumstances has been cited as the rationale for applying a product classification which carries a lower rate.

2. LOSS CONTROL SURVEYS

When your company's risks are uncertain, an insuror sometimes will order a loss control survey. Such surveys have been done mainly for larger firms (with potentially higher coverages wanted), but insurance industry sources confirm that more and more smaller firms are being surveyed now. In part, this reflects corporate product liability programs that have been put into effect among larger companies. Surveys are not normally handled directly by an underwriter; instead, a surveyor (often a full-time employee of the insuror) is engaged.

These surveyors usually are not particularly expert in the processes of a particular manufacturer. Like many inspectors for the federal Occupational Safety and Health Administration, they tend to be generalists who can recognize poor housekeeping practices, fire hazards, and distractions that can lead to employee mistakes. Typically, they will want to review corporate safety policies, quality assurance programs, and testing procedures both for incoming subassemblies and finished product. Surveyors usually will try to evaluate the commitment to safety among designers, production staff, distributors, and marketing personnel. Companies that can trace their liability costs carefully, and show that they are aware of potential problems, often will receive high marks, insurance sources say.

Some insurance companies—and all the major casualty and liability insurors—supplement the generalists with specialists in many fields. Usually, specialists do not actually visit a plant site, but they frequently are used to review the field surveys that are done. Several firms have their own laboratories, and can test a manufacturer's products directly, to help establish potential hazards.

Most small manufacturers tend to leave their insurance needs in the hands of legal staff or outside counsel. Even firms with their own insurance departments often find it difficult to coordinate loss control surveys. Several of the larger casualty insurors have been campaigning to broaden the expertise available in

Table IX-9 Percentage of Cases with Loss Control Surveys Commenting Specifically on Product Liability Exposures (Interagency Task Force on Product Liability, 1977.)

Target industries	Total	Yes	No	N.A.*	Percentage with surveys (N.A. excluded)
1. Industrial machinery	72	46	17	9	73%
2. Industrial grinding and abrasive products	15	12	2	1	86
3. Ferrous and nonferrous metal casting	64	34	10	20	77
4. Industrial chemicals: organic and inorganic	23	14	1	8	93
5. Aircraft components	7	4	2	1	67
6. Automobile components and tires	43	23	6	14	79
7. Medical devices	21	9	6	6	60
8. Pharmaceuticals	19	12	2	5	86
All other industries	2776	927	817	1032	53
Total Product Lines Identified	3040	1081	863	1096	56
SIZE OF COMPANY					
Small companies (Under $2.5 million)	1868	631	552	685	53
Large companies (Over $2.5 million)	740	312	180	248	63
Not reported	347	81	121	145	40
Total Underwriting Files Reviewed	2955	1024	853	1078	55
BUSINESS TYPE					
Manufacturer	1740	717	530	493	57
Retailer	573	142	155	276	48
Wholesaler	335	108	118	109	48
Service	120	26	30	64	46
Not reported	187	31	20	136	61
Total Underwriting Files Reviewed	2955	1024	853	1078	55

Column headers: Number of companies receiving product liability loss control surveys (Total, Yes, No, N.A.*)

*Reflects the frequency of loss control surveys made *specifically* to assess product liability exposures based on comments in survey reports in the underwriting files. Survey reports that did not comment on product exposures are not included as receiving loss control services. Where the files were not set up so that the survey reports were available, they were not included in the reporting base.

such departments beyond simply buying insurance and reporting claims. In part, this can make good sense. The insurance industry is the source of many of the surveys on product liability costs; corporate insurance departments are the closest to this information within any given company. Insurance departments can also prepare cost studies showing the true cost of product liability insurance to manufacturers. This can help garner management support for more extensive safety programs.

3. HANDLING CLAIMS

The reporting and investigation of claims within a company is discussed in detail in Chap. VI. Once a claim is sent to the manufacturer's insuror, it is usually handled with special attention. The Interagency Task Force on Product Liability commissioned a survey of claims-handling procedures in 1975. All 12 insurors in the sample said they assigned product liability claims to senior personnel. All too often, the companies said they received word of the claim through the filing of suit papers, rather than from the insured directly or through the agent or broker handling the account.

Routine data desired by claims handlers are:

- The exact identity of the product, including lot number, serial number, batch codes, and so forth
- A trace of the history of the product after initial purchase
- Conditions under which the accident occurred
- Supporting information—pictures, witnesses' statements, and so forth
- The product that caused the damage (for testing and analysis)
- Any additional information necessary to support or refute the claim

All 12 companies in the Task Force survey said they used outside attorneys to supplement their own staffs in handling product liability claims. The responsibilities of these attorneys can vary widely—some are experts in a given industry's problems, others simply are adept at product liability cases generally.

Once a claim is judged to have potential merit, insurors will set aside a "case reserve" estimating the ultimate dollar cost of the claim to the insuror. Methods for doing this vary among insurors, but field offices generally have their own individual reserve limits. Amounts over those limits require approval from regional or home offices. The "ultimate" cost is cut by some percentage reflecting the insuror's judgment of the chances a plaintiff has of winning the case. Most insurors also review the reserve as a case progresses.

When enough experience on a given product or class of products is available, insurors will also set aside reserves for unknown—but expected—future claims.

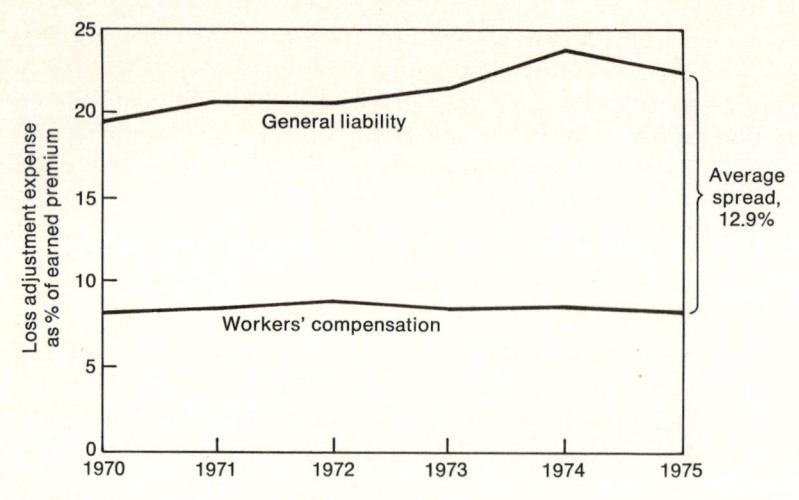

Figure IX-3 Loss adjustment expenses 1970–1975. *(A.M. Best Co. data for the total (stock and mutual) property liability insurance industry.)*

According to the Task Force survey, these are always done in a way that lumps product liability problems in with general liability claim expectations for a given company or industry. This may have begun to change since the survey was made in 1975, however, because companies have been reporting product-related claims separately since then to the Insurance Services Office. Because all such reserves increase the future premiums insurors feel justified in asking, the methods used to calculate reserve losses have come under close scrutiny since the midseventies.

4. "UNCONVENTIONAL" INSURANCE PROGRAMS

Since the midseventies, an increasingly large number of companies have changed their insurance coverage—either because they could not obtain insurance at all, because they could not obtain it at a reasonable price, or they found other techniques to be cheaper. Such "unconventional" (but increasingly common) forms of insurance generally fall into three categories—self-insurance, captive insurance companies, and dealings with "nonadmitted" insurors specializing in high-risk or unusual-hazard policies.

Self-Insurance

The simplest form of self-insurance is a large deductible. The manufacturer agrees to pay the first $1,000, $5,000, or $50,000 of claims arising from an incident or occurring in a given policy period. The most common are per-occurrence deductibles. Of approximately 3000 primary insurance files surveyed in 1975 by the Task Force, only about 100 included deductibles. Among those, it was fairly common (about 40 cases) for companies with sales under 2.5 million dollars per year to have deductibles of $1000 or less. Fewer than 20 companies with over 2.5 million dollars in sales had deductibles in that range, but about 30 of the policies for these larger companies had deductibles of $25,000 or more per occurrence.

Deductibles that large are difficult to get in normal primary insurance coverage. It would therefore become simpler for some manufacturers to forgo primary policies entirely, and obtain extra product liability coverage through umbrella policies. Unfortunately, writers of umbrella policies are not normally equipped to process claims—that's a task usually left to the primary insurors. Some companies will not write policies under such conditions. Others will, but only if professional claims handling by a third party is provided as well.

Table IX-10 Trade Association Survey Summaries (1971–1975) of Members without Coverage (Self-Insurance)

Association	Number surveyed	Number of responses	Without coverage
Machinery and Allied Products Institute (MAPI)	NA	188	8
American Textile Machinery Association	121	49	0
Automotive Parts and Accessories Association, Inc.	1,100	182	10
Water and Wastewater Equipment Manufacturers	260	43	3
Grinding Wheel Institute	NA	NA	NA
National Machine Tool Builders Association	NA	60	NA
Woodworking Machinery Manufacturers Association	NA	88	5
Machinery Dealers National Association	365	247	67
Massachusetts Area Council of Independent Testing Labs, Inc.	NA	7	"Most of the 7"
Farm and Industrial Equipment Institute	NA	NA	"10 companies up against the wall"
Health Industry Manufacturers Association	160	48	0
Railway Progress Institute	86	11	NA

Can a company withstand the risk of self-insurance? Three rough rules of thumb are commonly used: 1 percent of net working capital can be risked annually in a self-insurance plan, or 1 percent of current surplus plus 1 percent of the average earnings over the past five years, or 0.1 percent of net sales. Per-occurrence limits are typically set at a tenth of these levels. Each company should consider its overall financial health, of course, before embarking on this course.

Nevertheless, the number of companies taking the self-insurance road is increasing. A 1973 *Fortune* market research survey* reported that 14 percent of the top 500 companies retain 25 percent or more of total risk, and most planned to increase their retention levels.

Captive Insurance Companies

There are two types of captive insurance companies—those that deal with outside insureds as well at their "parent" company, and those that are organized specifically by a business or group of businesses to insure the risks of that business or group only. The purest "captives" are those that are organized as wholly owned subsidiaries to insure only the risks of their parent. Such operations can insure hard-to-place or uninsurable risks, save money in premiums and taxes, and generate profits both from direct insurance and reinsurance. Because companies are penalized in their federal tax bill for retaining earnings for a loss fund to cover self-insured or retained risks, the use of such captives has been growing as an alternative. The Internal Revenue Service has said, however, in Ruling 77-316 that under some circumstances companies should not be allowed to deduct premiums paid to their captives. A bill clarifying the point and allowing such deductions was introduced in Congress in 1978. Even if this bill does not pass, some captives will still pass IRS muster; competent legal help is a must, however.

Perhaps the best known of the captives are companies organized offshore, especially in Bermuda. The location is favored by companies doing large amounts of business overseas, and because Bermuda allows insurance companies to operate with as little as $120,000 in paid-up capital. This is adequate for small manufacturers, but most captives are far larger. Our own Internal Revenue Service insists that the amount of capital bear a proper relationship to the business being conducted.†

Captives can be tailored precisely to a company's business, and would be expected to defend a company more knowledgeably than would an "outside" insuror. The parent-subsidiary relationship between insuror and insured may also stimulate loss-control plans by manufacturers.

---

*Fortune Market Research; How Major Industrial Corporations View Property-Liability Insurance, p. 21, Oct. 1973.

†See Research Group, Inc., Interagency Task Force on Product Liability, Legal Study, Vol. VII, U.S. Dept. of Commerce, from which some of this discussion was adopted.

The Colorado Captive Insurance Company Act of 1973 also allows captives to be established there. Under the Colorado Act, a pure captive is defined as:

> Any domestic insurance company licensed ... for the purpose of making insurance and reinsurance.... Said insurance shall be limited to the risks, hazards and liabilities of its parent, associated and affiliated companies.

Association captives are also allowed. However, the association setting up the captive insuror must have been in existence for a year. Members of the association must own or control all of the outstanding securities of the captive. A corporation or association wishing to establish a captive in Colorado must show that adequate insurance is not available from other sources, is available only at excessive rates or with unreasonable deductibles, and that the total insurance coverage necessary to insure all risks would develop gross annual premiums of at least 500,000 dollars for a pure captive and 1 million dollars for an association captive.

In Colorado, to protect other insurors and their agents, captives are flatly prohibited from selling insurance to the general public. Captives garner substantial savings by not having to participate in any "assigned risk" pools, plans, or guaranty funds. Captives in Colorado are allowed to reinsure all of their risks with any reinsuror approved by the state insurance commissioner, with full credit allowed on reserves for ceded risks. The commissioner is supposed to watch captives especially closely to make sure that rate-setting is done at arm's length. Captives must have actual capital of $400,000 and an accumulated surplus of $350,000 with enough additional cash to cover operating expenses.

Few captives are organized specifically to handle product liability claims, however. As a practical matter, most companies will want to spread the operating overhead of the captive over as large a premium dollar as possible. And the handling of various insurance lines aside from product liability also offers more financial stability for the captive. Such overhead can cover a surprisingly large amount of the premium dollar, and still be competitive with outside insurors. According to the task force report by McKinsey & Co., only half of the premium dollar is used for settling claims and paying jury awards.

Surplus Lines Insurors

Surplus lines insurors and reinsurors are "not admitted" to write regular insurance—at least not in the state where the prospective policyholder is located, although they may do business as normal insurors elsewhere. They are available to write coverage that "admitted" companies don't want to absorb. Surplus lines laws in each state generally require that coverage first be refused by an admitted insuror. Sometimes, admitted insurors will take over an area of business after surplus lines insurors pioneer it.

Manufacturers forced into the surplus lines market must choose their broker with extra special care. In most states, such brokers doing business with surplus

Table IX-11 Use of Facultative Reinsurance, 1975–76 (Interagency Task Force on Product Liability, 1977.)

Target industries	Companies using facultative reinsurance	Number reporting	Percent using facultative reinsurance
1. Industrial machinery	12	72	17%
2. Industrial grinding and abrasive products	—	15	—
3. Ferrous and nonferrous metal castings	6	64	9
4. Industrial chemicals: organic and inorganic	2	23	9
5. Aircraft components	1	7	14
6. Automobile components	1	43	2
7. Medical devices	3	21	14
8. Pharmaceuticals	1	19	5
All other industries	127	2776	5
Total Product Lines Identified	153	3040	5
SIZE OF COMPANY			
Small companies (under $2.5 million)	39	1868	2
Large companies (over $2.5 million)	89	740	12
Not reported	20	347	6
Total Underwriting Files Reviewed	148	2955	5
BUSINESS TYPE			
Manufacturer	124	1740	7
Retailer	9	573	2
Wholesaler	4	335	1
Service	3	120	3
Not reported	8	187	4
Total Underwriting Files Reviewed	148	2955	5

lines insurors must have a special license. Because such brokers are responsible for payment of the state premium tax—a duty normally performed by the admitted insuror—they usually have to post bond guaranteeing payment.

Non-U.S. surplus lines insurors (perhaps the most famous of which is Lloyds of London) must meet specific trust requirements in many states, and must be "approved" to do surplus lines work by the state insurance commissioner. Surplus lines brokers must file affidavits soon after procuring coverage, stating that the placement was not made for a lower rate than available from admitted insurors, and that a diligent effort was made to find and use an admitted insuror first.

Business tends to flow to the surplus lines market when normal insurors cut back their underwriting. In 1975, for instance, the surplus lines insurors absorbed enormous amounts of medical malpractice insurance. At any one time, the total amount of surplus lines insurance in force runs about half a billion dollars, of which about 50 million is in product liability. This business may increase greatly in the years ahead, thanks to a 1978 law making New York City a "free trade zone" for it. The law allows insurors to join forces more easily to underwrite unusual risks.

Joint Underwriting Associations

Basically, a JUA is a pool of all insurors writing a certain kind of insurance. They are normally organized on a state-by-state basis, at the behest of state insurance authorities to underwrite specific kinds of insurance that would otherwise be unobtainable. Each company is forced to take part of the business, although typically only a small group (and sometimes only one) acts as so-called "servicing carriers," marketing and coordinating coverage. JUAs have become very common in such lines as automobile insurance and medical malpractice coverage. Connecticut is the first state to consider setting up a JUA for product liability specifically.

If a manufacturer is unable to obtain insurance through the regular market, he applies to the "servicing carrier" through an agent or broker. Acceptance in various JUAs is not necessarily automatic—certain (relatively low) eligibility requirements have been set in some state plans. Plans in use for other types of insurance aside from product liability use various rate-setting techniques.

It should be noted that JUAs are not the same as "assigned risk" pools. JUAs pool premiums to spread loss. Assigned risk plans (as for auto insurance) pool insureds of a given class (i.e., the accident prone, etc., in auto insurance) to try to spread risks "equitably" throughout the private insurance industry. Loss is not itself spread through assigned risk plans. Therefore, in a JUA, insurance companies can participate (or be forced to participate) in insuring lines they have never insured before—only the servicing carriers must be competent in the field.

5. WHEN AN INSUROR SUES YOU

A significant proportion of all products liability cases (some commentators put the proportion as high as 80 percent, but it is probably closer to 50) involve an employer and/or a workers' compensation insuror suing the manufacturer of the equipment that the employee injured himself upon. Often the employee joins in the suit, because recovery under workers' compensation laws is sharply limited. In fact, employers have little incentive (aside from sporadic enforcement by occupational safety and health authorities) under existing workers' compensation laws to run a safe plant—employers can modify equipment to increase production and sacrifice safety without exposing themselves to potentially large liabilities. Courts have frequently ruled that manufacturers of the equipment that was modified may be held liable, however.

HOLD HARMLESS CLAUSES

A surprisingly common—but almost totally unenforceable—provision in contracts between employers and manufacturers is the "hold harmless clause." Such clauses state that if the manufacturer is sued as a third party, the employer will reimburse the manufacturer for any losses. The employer, in effect, "holds the manufacturer harmless."

The courts have traditionally felt that such clauses leave the unsophisticated purchaser at the mercy of the manufacturer, however. Such clauses have been held valid only when the two parties entering into the contract are both shown to be sophisticated, knowledgeable, and dealing from positions of equal strength.

Nevertheless, workers' compensation laws, although subject to modification, appear here to stay. Such laws themselves were first enacted among the states at the turn of the century to provide surer and faster compensation for worker injuries than was (and is) possible under common law. Such compensation laws generally provide automatic benefits to workers for injuries suffered in the course of employment. These benefits include payment of a percentage of lost wages (generally half or two-thirds of the average weekly wage or salary at the time of the accident), plus all medical and rehabilitation expenses. In exchange, the employee forfeits common law right to sue the employer for the injury. (Nor can the employer sue the employee—the concept of fault is irrelevant.) Workers' compensation laws are normally overseen by state authorities, and sometimes the insurance is done through a statewide pool. More often, however, the employer is simply required to carry enough insurance to cover his liability under the state's law.

The insuror is liable to pay for wages and so forth according to the "percentage" of disability incurred by the employee in the accident. Typically, minor injuries are overcompensated and major injuries or death are grossly under-compensated. This increases the temptation (and often the need) for employees to sue manufacturers of the equipment involved in the accident, or suppliers of consumables involved. There are cases where suppliers of certain innocuous oils were held liable for injuries suffered by their customers' employees through improper in-plant storage or handling.

Things can be even more inequitable for manufacturers in states where employers or employers' compensation carrier can be subrogated to the employee's claim. The employer (and his insurance carrier, if any), having paid the amounts specified under their state workers' compensation law, then "step into the employee's shoes" and attempt to recover their losses from the manufacturer. Because of the immunity granted by workers' compensation, the manufacturer cannot turn around and sue the employer to shift part of the loss. The employee, however, can be sued by the manufacturer in many states, through the common law remedy of "contribution" or "contributory negligence." (Or, more common, the award from a manufacturer is reduced by that percentage of the damages that were caused by employee negligence.)

Sometimes (although rarely), manufacturers have been allowed to pass the liability for damages on to a third party. This procedure, called "indemnity," is almost never allowed in workers' compensation cases, however. The reason is that indemnity is allowed only against one who has breached a duty owed to a tortfeasor (a person or entity liable in tort). The courts generally say, however, that an employer does not owe any duty of proper care or maintenance to the manufacturer or supplier of a product it buys.

In New York, a quirk of civil procedure limited contribution to defendants sued jointly by the original plaintiff.* A defendant could not seek contribution from those not sued by the plaintiff in the first place. Those parties not sued were sometimes the most at fault—but managed to settle with the plaintiff beforehand. Often, therefore, defendants were left only with indemnity to spread the loss. Since indemnity, as a matter of common law, shifts the entire loss, the courts faced an all-or-nothing choice. Partly as a response to this quirk in New York, and partly as a result of trends in tort law generally, the Court of Appeals there adopted a new common law rule in deciding a 1972 case, *Dole v. Dow Chemical.* As the courts stated the rule,

> [Where] a third party is found to have been responsible for a part, but not all, of the negligence for which a defendant is cast in damages, the responsibility for that part is recoverable by the prime defendant against the third party. To reach that end there must necessarily be an apportionment of responsibility in negligence between those parties.... The adjudication is one of fact and may be sought in a separate action or as a separate and distinguishable issue by bringing in the third party in the prime action.

---

*Discussed in The Research Group, Product Liability, Legal Study, Interagency Task Force on Product Liability, Vol. VI, 1977, pages 24–25.

The "Dole" rule was later codified by legislative law in New York to read,

> The amount of contribution to which a person is entitled shall be the excess paid by him over and above his equitable share of the judgment recovered by the injured party; but no person shall be required to contribute an amount greater than his equitable share. The equitable shares shall be determined in accordance with the relative culpability of each person liable for contribution.

The legislature in New York specifically protected those who settle with original plaintiffs from increases in their settlements—so that settlements would be encouraged, or at least not deterred by the possibility of suits later for contribution from co-defendants.

One unfortunate outcome of the original court decision and the later legislative action has been the use of cumbersome trials. In New York, liability is normally tried first, a second trial fixes the amount of the damages, and a third apportions them. The trials typically are held as separate sessions of one proceeding, all before the same judge and/or jury. And, of course, the whole thing is a cumbersome, unsure way to live with what manufacturers and suppliers see as the greater injustice—the total immunity of the employer for accidents that are suffered by employees.

Several legal remedies for this were researched by the Interagency Task Force. They include permitting "contribution" against employers, irrespective of any "immunity" conferred by workers' compensation laws; allowing indemnity; restricting employer subrogation; and validating hold-harmless clauses, especially in machine-tool sales contracts between manufacturers and employers.

Other possibilities include making workers' compensation the exclusive remedy in work-related product cases, and raising current low levels of compensation for severe incapacitating injuries under workers' compensation, by federal statute if necessary.

In general, these proposals tend to increase employer exposures for ignoring safety standards. This is considered by most commentators to be a desirable thing—especially since employers are often proved to have removed or defeated safety devices, or refused to buy new devices developed for existing machines. For some classes of products, however, the manufacturer may actually be in a better position to define potential dangers. Suppliers of industrial chemical mixtures, the contents of which are proprietary, may (for instance) know far more about the dangers of the mixtures' use, and what equipment and other precautions should be used by the employer.

The results of adopting some changes and grafting them on to the existing legal system can produce unfairness. The federal courts, for instance, have adopted the Dole rule for compensation of claims under the Longshoremen's and Harbor Workers' Compensation Act. But although the adaptation provides that manufacturers can only be liable for their share of the blame for an accident, the employer's liability is limited by the Act itself (a form of workers' compensation). As a result, losses suffered by the employee but not caused by the manufacturer go completely uncompensated beyond the Act's insurance limits.

In light of this, legislators are moving rather slowly to redress the imbalance manufacturers see. Therefore, it seems more useful to examine some remedies—at least partial remedies—that have evolved in the courts, for these remedies may spread more quickly than legislative fiat as one's state courts copy another's. The Interagency Task Force noted several examples of this evolution. Florida, for instance, is like most states at this writing, in that it does not permit the manufacturer to obtain contribution from the employer for damages arising out of an accident. But in 1975, the Florida Supreme Court, in *Sunspan Engineering & Construction Co. v. Spring-Lock Scaffolding,* declared invalid a section of the state's workers' compensation law which would have kept third-party tortfeasors (such as manufacturers) from suing employers in negligence actions.

In the case, an employee of Sunspan suffered injuries when a scaffold manufactured by Spring-Lock failed. The employee sued the manufacturer, who, in turn, sued the employer. The trial court denied the employer's motion to dismiss founded on the amendment. The Florida Supreme Court, on appeal, held that the amendment denied access to the state courts by third-party tortfeasors, as mandated by the state's constitution for "redress of injury," and also violated the United States Constitution by denying equal protection under the law. Because employers could sue manufacturers, yet manufacturers couldn't return the favor, the statute granted negligent employers windfall relief from third-party actions initiated by their employees.

Pennsylvania also has taken a different view. The Commonwealth's courts look beyond the strict legalism of the term "joint liability" among tortfeasors—the idea that, since employers are not *liable* in tort for injuries subject to workers' compensation, they are not liable for a contribution to the costs of injury beyond what the insurance for workers' compensation will pay. Thus third-party actions can be taken against the employer in contribution. Even so, the employer is limited in the amount of contribution it must pay—limited to the liability limits of workers' compensation itself!

In discussing the situation for the Interagency Task Force, The Research Group, Inc., describes the limitation as a

> Highly pragmatic compromise. A rule allowing full contribution would have required employers in many cases to pay amounts far greater than the amount they would pay if they had acted solely to cause the employee's injury because, where the employer is solely at fault, the manufacturer is never involved and the employer's liability is limited to the workers' compensation award. On the other hand, this compromise does not force the third party to bear the entire burden of loss merely because the other tortfeasor happened to be the injured party's employer.

A 1968 case involving the Federal Tort Claims Act cited the Pennsylvania approach, although the case was brought in Rhode Island (*Newport Air Park v. U.S.*). Although the case was overturned on appeal the following year—on the grounds that the matter was governed by federal law, not state court precedent—the affair illustrates how legal precedents move from state to state.

The Pennsylvania system works this way: First, the employer (or employer's insuror) pays workers' compensation benefits to the employee. The employee then sues the manufacturer. The manufacturer, in turn, can have the employer joined in the defense as a joint tortfeasor. (Remember, under workers' compensation, the employee himself could not directly sue the employer first.) If the employee's actual damages are found to exceed twice the amount of the employer's maximum liability under workers' compensation, the employer will be held liable only to the extent of his liability under the Compensation Act, and the manufacturer will bear the total remaining liability. If, however, the employee's damages are found equal to or less than twice the amount of employer's maximum workers' compensation liability, the employer and the manufacturer each bear half of the actual damages.

California has adopted the basic Pennsylvania idea, but in a less cumbersome fashion. "Instead of treating it as a rule which creates a right of contribution," in the words of the Interagency Task Force, "California accomplishes the same result by holding that a third-party tortfeasor may invoke the negligence of the employer as a partial defense to prevent the employer from being reimbursed for his workers' compensation outlay."

In California, the system holds if the third-party action is brought only by the employee, or by the employee and the employer seeking subrogation. The idea is to make a negligent employer bear some of the loss (but no more than he would be liable for under workers' compensation), rather than having the loss partially or entirely reimbursed by the manufacturer or supplier. Thus, in theory, the employer should not profit from his wrong. California has not, however, applied the Pennsylvania rule to cases where the third party is a manufacturer held strictly liable. No matter what contributory circumstances exist, in California the manufacturer bears the entire loss for injury due to defective products. Thus manufacturers get little help, unless it can be shown that the employer was fully aware of the danger, but unreasonably used the product anyway.

Another precedent that helps get manufacturers off the hook (but often at the expense of the employee) was set in 1975, in *Frasca v. Prudential-Grace Lines, Inc.,* brought under the Longshoremen's and Harbor Workers' Compensation Act. It was normal practice in the United States for stevedore foremen to employ longshoremen. Under the Act before 1972, injured longshoremen recovered fixed benefits from the stevedore, but they could also sue the shipowners. If the injury was due to shipboard conditions, the shipowner would be held liable, as a violator of its warranty of seaworthiness, for all damages. The longshoreman would then reimburse his employer (the stevedore) for compensation benefits. According to the Interagency Task Force, "faced with the inequity of having the entire burden fall on the shipowner, and forbidden to require contribution from the stevedore, the federal courts allowed the shipowners to recover full indemnity from stevedores who had violated their 'implied warranty of workmanlike performance.' The entire loss then fell on the stevedore."

The Act was amended in 1972 to preclude such indemnification. The courts got around the problem in *Frasca v. Prudential-Grace* by allowing "equitable credit." In effect, the third party can assert employee negligence (that is, the longshoreman) of the stevedore as a partial defense. Typically, the employee takes the money recovered from the third party, reimburses the stevedore (the employer) for any compensation benefits that were paid, and keeps the rest. The reimbursement can be reduced in proportion to any negligence on the part of the employer.

Thus, the employer pays no more than required under workers' compensation. Nor does the third party pay any more than its share in contributory negligence. But, as already noted, the employee can be left holding the bag.

APPENDIX A
CHECKLISTS FOR DESIGNERS AND INSTALLERS

The use of checklists is frequently frowned upon—they are too easy to use as a crutch. It is strongly recommended that designers familiarize themselves with Chap. IV, Sec. 2 before using the ones printed here. Generally, although these lists are as exhaustive as possible, designers should find it necessary to modify these lists for their own situation. Checklists in this section were drawn from military and industry sources, in particular the *Air Force Systems Command Design Handbook 1-X, Checklist of General Design Criteria*. Lists were condensed and combined, and explanatory material was added. They cover the following:

1. General
   Standards and standardization; Basic considerations
2. Human Factors
   General; Displays; Controls
3. Maintainability
4. Instructions
5. Packaging
   General; Environmental factors; Transportability; Identification and marking
6. Structural Materials
   Metals; Nonmetals
7. Fittings
   General; Castings; Universal joints
8. Fasteners
   General; Rivets; Bolts, nuts, and washers; Screws; Pins
9. Welding, etc.
10. Corrosion
11. Hazard Detection
    General; Fire detection; Combustible vapor detection; Explosion detection; Toxic vapor detection; Auditory and visual warning signals
12. Fire Extinguishing and Suppression Systems
13. Electrical/Electronic Equipment and Systems
    General; Installation and maintenance; Electromagnetic compatibility; Spurious responses; Spurious resonances; Shielding; Interference-free components; Shielding between systems; Enclosures; Cables; Low-frequency coupling; High-frequency coupling; Cable measurements; Transmission lines; Connectors; Connector shielding; Bonding and grounding; Corrosion involving dissimilar metals; Grounding considerations; Filtering; Test equipment; Static charges; Discrete components; Relays; Power supplies; Component testing

14. Hydraulic Equipment and Systems
    General; Component and fluid selection; Contamination control; Temperature and pressure considerations in the overall system
15. Pressurization and Pneumatic Equipment and Systems
    General; High-pressure oxygen; Pressure vessels; Pneumatic systems; Pressurization systems
16. Fuel and Storage Systems
    Fluid compatibility; Component selection; Fabrication
17. Material Handling Equipment
    General; Lifting and positioning equipment

GENERAL

Standards and Standardization

1. Have appropriate standards been checked?
2. Are any design parts nonstandard; if so, can they be replaced with standard parts?
3. If nonstandard parts are absolutely necessary, have they been tested under appropriate conditions?
4. Are parts ratings, catalog descriptions, and so forth adequate to describe the functions of all parts in this application? Consider such factors as temperature, electric currents, shock loadings, vibration, corrosion-resistance, anticipated reliability needs.
5. Have anticipated testing needs been budgeted for?
6. Have critical tolerances been identified?
7. Have critical assembly procedures been identified?

Basic Considerations

1. Design systems to permit ready access for operating, testing, repairing, and replacing components without interfering with other components or assemblies.
2. Incorporate characteristics in the design of each component, equipment end item, or system which will permit it to function in harmony with other equipment with a minimum of adapters, extensions, transformers, or other equalizer units.
3. Select components which have withstood previous testing and have established a high level of reliability.
4. When possible, incorporate functional and physical characteristics which allow substitution of one item for another without physical or electrical modification, irrespective of the application.
5. Design to permit personnel of average skill to perform required maintenance under all anticipated conditions.
6. Design systems and equipment taking into consideration the capabilities and limitations of operators.
7. Provide adequate protection for all components, with minimum special shipping, storing, and handling requirements.
8. Design components and assemblies so that they are incapable of being reversed or of being installed in the opposite position from the correct one, especially where reverse installation could cause malfunction.
9. Design the system so that routine servicing (i.e., cleaning, charging, lubricating, replenishing, etc.) will require a minimum of specialized skills and of extra or specialized equipment, and which will allow simple and accurate GO/NO GO testing without requiring special skills.
10. Design systems and system components to function satisfactorily in any environment in which operations are anticipated.

11. Anticipate increasing demands that may be made on a system's capabilities during its design life and provide sufficient growth capacity.
12. Design systems to minimize supporting commodities.
13. Where increased reliability is necessary, provide an alternate part, circuit, or component which can take over if the primary element should fail.
14. Incorporate self-testing and self-adjusting features where applicable.
15. Keep the design as simple as possible consistent with the functions desired so as to increase effectiveness by reducing supply and maintenance problems and turnaround time.

HUMAN FACTORS

General

1. Is activity space adequate?
2. Is distance of the console cabinets from the operator satisfactory?
3. Have differences in sizes of operators been adequately considered?
4. Does overall console height interfere with the operator's direct line of sight?
5. Do working positions permit good posture?
6. Is the seat or operating position readily accessible?
7. Is overall lighting plan adequate?
8. Does glare reflected from other sources make reading instruments and panels difficult?
9. Are console and/or panel lights much brighter than the displays?
10. Is compartment noise loud or distracting?
11. Is compartment heat adjustment adequate to ensure comfort?
12. Is compartment humidity control adequate to ensure comfort?
13. Is compartment ventilation control adequate to ensure comfort?

Displays

1. Is information displayed to the specificity and accuracy required for operator action or decision?
2. Is interpretability of the display satisfactory?
3. How is interpretability compared with similar equipment?
4. Is internal illumination within the instrument(s) satisfactory?
5. Is ability to adjust lighting properly on the equipment satisfactory?
6. Are signals and warning lights bright enough and properly situated to attract attention?
7. Are indicator lights used for maintenance and adjustment readily accessible and visible when required?
8. Can dial numbers and/or markings be read easily?
9. Are scale values and their respective indexes consistent in direction of increase or decrease?
10. Is optimal dial size presented based on best figure, index size, and spacing?
11. Are labels as brief as possible?
12. Are labels readily seen for operation or maintenance?

Controls

1. Are controls distributed so that no limb is overburdened?
2. Are controls requiring rapid, precise settings assigned to the hands?
3. Do control movements conform with control display?
4. Are hand and foot push buttons and toggle switches used for two discrete settings?
5. Are controls needing fine adjustments well placed?
6. Are controls used most frequently the handiest to reach?
7. Does activation of controls obscure visual displays or control markings?
8. Is every control labeled properly according to function?
9. Are controls which have similar functions located in relatively the same positions?
10. Are control shapes standard and easily discernible?
11. Is protection of the instrument from accidental activation satisfactory?
12. Is the same pictorial relationship used on the same panel for combined instruments?
13. Is maximum simplicity maintained commensurate with informational requirements?
14. Is maximum precision and accuracy consistent with display?
15. Is information presented up-to-date in relation to need?
16. Are controls well placed to avoid misidentification?
17. Are controls spaced properly for the most efficient and optimum use?
18. Is location of this instrument for best performance in relation to the importance of the instrument?

MAINTAINABILITY

1. Are components mounted so that they do not interfere with other components or with servicing?
2. Are blind adjustments (done by feel) necessary?
3. Are delicate components located or guarded so that they will not be damaged while the unit is being handled or worked on?
4. Are sensitive adjustments located or guarded so that they will not be accidentally disturbed?
5. Are required maintenance and assembly jobs usually easy?
6. Are there chances of an easy insertion or installation of the wrong components, connector, etc.?
7. Can covers be readily removed and replaced properly?
8. Are access doors hinged at the bottom?
9. Are handles provided where necessary, and are they recessed?
10. Is the type of lubrication required and frequency of use specified on a label near the lubricating point?
11. Are replaceable components of the plug-in type?
12. Can components be replaced easily and rapidly?
13. Were component accesses designed with consideration given to frequency of use?
14. Is it physically impossible to install a wrong unit?
15. Do access to units maintained by one technician require removal of equipment by a second higher skilled operator?
16. Are components located and mounted so that access to them may be achieved without danger to personnel?

17. Can test points, meter jacks, probe points, connectors, etc., be more conveniently located?
18. Are access points well labeled?
19. Are access doors either removable or self-supporting?
20. Unless a component is completely self-checking, has provision been made for checking operation of that unit under operating conditions without the use of special rigs and harnesses?
21. Are conductors bound into cables and held by twine or other acceptable means?
22. Are cables long enough so that they do not interfere with other operations or equipment?
23. Are cables, if routed through holes, etc., well protected from damage?
24. Are cables readily accessible for repairs?
25. Are cables coded for proper identification?
26. Are quick-disconnect plugs used wherever possible?
27. Are connectors located properly for easy access and maintenance?
28. Are aligning pins provided wherever required?
29. Are plugs designed to eliminate inserting wrong plugs in a receptacle?
30. Are all required labels positioned properly?
31. Is color coding adequate and consistent?
32. Are fuses and circuit breakers adequately identified and located for easy and quick replacement or repair?
33. Are tools and test equipment available?
34. Is the variety of tools required at a minimum?
35. Are required tools adequately insulated for safety?
36. Are tools of dull finish adequate to avoid glare?
37. Are fire extinguishers easily accessible and operable?
38. Are shields or covers properly installed to prevent accidental contact with voltages?
39. Do doors, covers, and plates have interlocks to remove electrical potentials?
40. Is overall illumination level in equipment spaces constant and maintained at an appropriate level?
41. Is compartment noise with regard to maintenance distracting?
42. Are functional groups outlined by a line inscribed upon the test panel?
43. Are test points obstructed by cables, components, etc.?
44. Do contacts at test points have sufficient strength to prevent bending?
45. Are test points appropriately labeled by symbol or name?
46. Are test points clearly identified for easy location in the assembly by a contrasting color?
47. Are job instructions coded to test points provided when it is not feasible to provide full or detailed information at the test points?
48. Are appropriate test points provided when a component is not completely self-checking?
49. Are primary test points located and coded so that they are readily distinguished from secondary (maintenance) test points?
50. When feasible, are primary test points grouped in a line or matrix to reflect the sequence of tests to be made?
51. Are primary test points used for component adjustment located close to the controls and displays also used in adjustment?

INSTRUCTIONS

1. Are instructions for safe unpacking included on carton or other outer packaging?
2. Are safe stacking and handling instructions noted clearly on outer packaging?
3. Are instructions for proper storage (temperature and humidity limits, for instance) noted on outer packaging?
4. Does carton and other outer packaging (if any) include product identification, brand name, model number, serial number, and any other information of necessity to identify stored product in case of recall? Does information appear even when cartons are stacked?
5. Does carton or other outer packaging include instructions for disposal, or necessary warnings (to keep plastic liners out of the hands of children, for instance, or to remove staples before pulling product from box)?
6. Are instructions for installation included? Do they detail all possible requirements for the product's use and power supplies?
7. Is equipment needed for installation included with product, or commonly available?
8. Are warnings of the consequences of incorrect installation or improper operation prominently noted?
9. Installation instructions must note proper sequence of operations, must be logical, and must be understood.
10. Do operation instructions cover even such "obvious" items as filling, loading?
11. Do operating instructions note any special skills that may be helpful or necessary to install or operate the product?
12. For most complex products, a checklist for the customer/installer to use in case the product does not work when first installed, is a useful addition to instructions.
13. Are warnings of improper actions permanently attached to product, in prominent locations?
14. Are warnings of improper operation—in high heat, with frayed line cord, in hard-water areas, in low-voltage situations, etc.—also permanently attached to product?
15. Are proper cleaning instructions given, and are they attached to product (in cases of critical concern, such as microwave ovens, etc.)?
16. Are instructions for emergency action properly given and attached to product? Emergency situations could arise in case of fire, unbalanced load, insulation failure, plumbing failure, etc.
17. Are all electrical, mechanical, temperature, and radiation hazards contained or warned against?
18. Are instructions permanently attached to product to cover such situations as rapid restarting, rapid cycling, extremely heavy use, interruption of use cycle, etc.?
19. Are service instructions clearly given and (if at all possible) attached to the product permanently?
20. Are servicing manuals up to date and available to all service personnel?
21. Are schematics attached to product?
22. Are color codes attached to product?
23. Are test points clearly labeled?
24. Are improper parts substitutions warned against?

PACKAGING

General

1. Arrange and locate component parts in such a manner as to provide maximum protection and freedom from damage.
2. Ensure that interior mounting and installation hardware, brackets, securing devices, etc. are of

sufficient strength and of proper design to withstand stress, strain, or impact shocks encountered during handling.

3. Consider the application of inherent shock mounts or individual suspension systems for components which are extremely delicate and highly susceptible to shock or vibration damage.
4. When necessary, incorporate into the design suitable damping features for assemblies or individual items that possess natural vibration frequencies in the same range as those likely to be encountered during transportation.
5. Design inner frameworks and outer shells to furnish the necessary support and protection from external forces.
6. Provide suitable caging, immobilizing, or movement-limiting facilities for free-moving components and assemblies (gyros, gimbal mounted equipment, instruments, balance devices, etc.).
7. Provide proper support and load-bearing provisions for integral parts operating within precise dimensional tolerance or on vertical bearings.
8. When large, bulky multisectioned end items, or items which exceed standard transportability limitations are involved, design for ease of disassembly whenever possible for packaging and delivery.
9. Avoid irregular shapes and abnormal exterior configurations except as dictated by the functional requirements of the equipment involved.
10. Provide heavy, or irregularly contoured items with suitable bases and mounting provisions or devices to facilitate securing to crate bases, pallets, or mounting platforms.
11. When adequate mounting facilities cannot be provided, ensure that inner frameworks and supporting structures are of sufficient strength to withstand the tensions and stresses encountered with strapping hold-down techniques.
12. Avoid delicate, fragile, easily broken exterior projections or protrusions.
13. For protruding parts as well as exterior components or surfaces made of glass or other easily damaged materials, provide appropriate shields, caps, covers, protective devices, and/or recess to prevent damage.
14. Keep centers of gravity as low as possible.
15. Locate large, heavy, dense interior components as near to the base or bottom of the item as practical.
16. If functional needs dictate a relatively tall structure with a corresponding narrow or small base, incorporate features in the design which permit the equipment to be positioned horizontally for packaging and transit purposes.
17. Utilize moisture- and fungus-resistant materials whenever possible and practical.
18. Treat critical surfaces with permanent or semipermanent finishes (paint, plating, anodizing, etc.).
19. When appropriate, apply fungus-proofing and water-proofing compounds.
20. Where item design contains critical parts dictating a protective enclosure against dust or vapors, fabricate the case or outer shell to be entirely water-vaporproof.
21. Avoid the use of dissimilar metals in contact or in close proximity to each other or without adequate protective barrier or insulation to prevent damage and deterioration from electrolytic action.
22. Avoid design or use of electronic components which are susceptible to damage from electromagnetic, electrostatic, or magnetic energy fields which may be encountered in packaging, storage, or transit.
23. When practicable, design external components to be easily removed and replaced to prevent damage during handling or shipping.
24. When external components cannot be removed, provide substantial guards for protection of components or other cargo during handling and shipment.

25. Make provisions in the design of heavy and cumbersome equipment for the inclusion of integral lifting eyes to permit slinging.
26. Position the lifting eyes to permit attachment of sling legs to a single hook when lifting.
27. Consider tie-down devices for securement in transit.
28. When practicable, lifting eyes and tie-down devices may be combined.
29. Consider sectionalized construction to facilitate packaging, handling, transportation, and storage; sectionalized construction of equipment should allow ready assembly and disassembly in the field without the need of special tools.
30. Ensure that in preservation and packaging methods and designs, the established reliability levels of the equipment being packaged are maintained.
31. Prepare dangerous materials to be shipped in accordance with applicable commercial regulations and tariffs in effect at the time of shipment.
32. Avoid flammable materials whenever practicable, while recognizing that certain essential packaging materials (e.g., wood, paint, plastic films, and flexible barriers) are inherently combustible or flammable.
33. As a minimum, use combustible container materials that are either nonburning or self-extinguishing by the following ASTM tests: textiles, D-626; paper and paperboard, D-777; and plastic fibers and foams, D-1692.
34. Ensure that all container materials are nontoxic to humans on contact, and when exposed to flames, will not release poisonous fumes of such a nature as to preclude protection by using conventional fire-fighters' masks.
35. Design to prevent buildup of static electricity on (a) containers for explosive-loaded components and (b) containers for the protection of solid-state devices (diodes, transistors, integrated circuits, and electronic modules) as well as equipment containing such items. The basic design should function to bleed off all static charges through a conducting path to ground in one second or less or to prevent excessive buildup in the first instance.
36. Ensure that items suspended in a shock-mounted cradle are electrically bonded to the container structure. If the container structure is nonmetallic, bond to a through bolt providing a clearly identified external grounding connection.
37. Ensure that maximum resistance of the ground path is 10 ohms or less; structural plastic foam in contact with the contents should be conductive or treated to reduce surface buildup.

Environmental Factors

1. Analyze each system or components thereof to determine the possible ranges and combinations of environments that the system may be subjected to during the transportation, handling, and storage periods.
2. Consider the range of vibration frequencies to which the equipment will be tested or exposed.
3. It should be possible to operate the equipment immediately after removal from its packaging without tuning, electrical alignment, or calibration.
4. Analyze the transit and storage conditions which will be encountered and consider them as prerequisite to packaging design.
5. Apply adequate preservation/packaging measures to ensure there is no degradation of equipment reliability through transportation or storage.
6. If the item fragility (g factor) is known and the height of anticipated drop has been determined, design an adequate shock-damping system to allow proper deceleration/movement/duration of the dropped item to prevent breakage.
7. Since nearly all forms of transportation produce vibration forces, consider these forces when designing protective packaging.
8. Many items of equipment contain components that may be susceptible to damage from steady-

state vibration at a particular frequency. Note that these component parts may have their own natural frequencies and consider them when providing for protection against vibrations.
9. For packaging items that must have a controlled thermal environment, select an adequate thermal insulation material and other thermal control devices that will be required.
10. Mark packages and shipping containers in accordance with any special instruction specified in the contract or applicable equipment/system specification.
11. Consider as a design prerequisite the ease of removal of the equipment from its packaging.
12. Design reusable containers to be used, saved, and reused as a complete system, except for possibly the wrap or moisture barrier. Design opening/closing features to function without impairing the container reusability. In reusable containers, attach cushioning assemblies to the container interior so that it remains integral with the container. But ensure that the cushioning attachment is not so permanent, unless continuous molding technique is used, as to prevent refurbishing of the container interior when necessary.

Transportability
1. Consider the limitations of the particular mode of transportation selected in determining the weight, size, and characteristics of items to be shipped.
2. Identify design requirements that inhibit the transportability of a system or its components, so that solutions may be proposed by the contractor prior to "design freeze."
3. Make personnel safety an essential transportability objective during the design effort.
4. Incorporate handling, tie-down and slinging points in the design of material as needed to optimize transportability and complement maintenance, warehousing, and other handling requirements.
5. Ensure that packaging is lightweight—yet ensures adequate protection to the items being shipped and that the packages can be consolidated into unit loads or pallets, each unit to remain intact until it reaches the user.

Identification and Marking
1. Select words and symbols that are short and to the point and are familiar to the general public.
2. Where it is necessary to use technical words and symbols which are not familiar to the general public, select those commonly applied and well understood by the technical personnel likely to operate the equipment.
3. If the item or the areas to which the symbol is to be applied will not accommodate a symbol of the desired size, identify the item with the largest symbol possible.
4. Unless otherwise specified, make symbols (a) black for aluminum, white, or yellow surfaces, (b) red for black finishes, and (c) yellow for other colored finishes.
5. Provide markings which will remain distinct and readable for the expected life of the item.
6. Whenever possible, locate markings where they will be visible after installation or assembly.
7. Permanently mark or engrave part numbers on all parts or on a metal plate attached to each item.
8. Use appropriate nomenclature to identify all apertures, including maintenance doors, covers, and fuel openings, by means of stencils, decals, etc.
9. Use special markings (and color coding, if applicable) to mark apertures where maintenance personnel may accidentally mix dangerous fluids, but don't depend entirely on color coding—color blindness is common.
10. Use proper electrical symbols (ANSI Y32.9-1972) and the reference designations for electrical and electronic parts and equipment in ANSI Y32.16-1975.
11. Comply with ANSI Y32.3-1969 for welding symbols and AWS A3.0-69 for welding terms and definitions.

12. Comply with AWS A2.2-58 for nondestructive testing symbols.
13. Furnish nameplates and data plates showing wiring and schematic diagrams, lubricating and operating instructions, safety notices, lists of tools, lists of contents, and similar information.
14. Apply markings by reverse etching, machine engraving, die-stamping, lithographing, printing, or silk screening on aluminum, brass, or copper plates.
15. For all letters and symbols, use vertical type with a minimum height of $3/64$ inch and where space permits, provide a border of $1/4$ inch or more on each edge.
16. Design plates that will remain legible for the service life of the equipment on which they are mounted.
17. Affix plates securely and permanently with screws or rivets that will not stain under service conditions.
18. Attach plates in a protected area where they will not become defaced but will be accessible without dismantling part of the equipment.
19. In addition to the identification and marking requirements specified in military specifications and standards, affix these plates to the equipment in a manner to prevent their becoming detached and entering intake ducts or damaging any part of the vehicle or its components.
20. Do not use wire-on metal tags as data plates, since they tend to work loose and foul equipment.
21. Mark each part individually with the applicable part identification number, except when parts do not have a suitable surface or when they are commonly known and present no identification problem.
22. Part numbers of subcontracted or purchased items should be assigned by the original design facility.
23. Mark special parts which are similar to standard parts with part numbers conforming with detail specifications or other warning symbols.
24. Apply the markings by steel-stamping, acid or electric etching, engraving, branding, embossing, casting, or molding directly onto part surfaces.
25. When these methods are not practical, use rubber-stamping, stenciling, decals, or metal or paper tagging.
26. Apply markings either directly to the component or to tags and labels which can be securely fastened to it.
27. Do not die-stamp part numbers on highly stressed components.
28. Mark components which are furnished as uninstalled spares with nomenclature, stock number, manufacturer's identification, and part number.
29. Provide legible, durable markings to identify servicing points and to provide necessary instructions for operating personnel.
30. In readily visible locations, indicate the type of fuel to be used and location of fuel fillers, oil fillers, coolant fillers, and lubrication points, as applicable.
31. Provide gear-shifting diagrams and identification of all operating controls adjacent to such controls.
32. Denote operating limits and place brief operating instructions in a conspicuous place.
33. Attach permanent warning plates outlining necessary precautionary measures in a prominent place.
34. Provide servicing instructions for hydraulic systems, pneumatic systems, etc., on instruction plates or in a permanent, legible form adjacent to charging points and test connections.
35. Clearly and permanently mark all transparent assemblies as to manufacturer and identification.
36. Place the identification markings and initials of the manufacturer so they can be read internally without disassembly after installation.

STRUCTURAL MATERIALS

Metals

1. The spectrum of operational requirements to be considered includes load patterns and magnitudes, operating temperatures, environments including the presence of corrosive and abrasive elements, moisture, ultraviolet radiation, acoustic excitation, the reliability desired, and the life expectancy.
2. Consider the service history of established materials in similar applications.
3. In the design selection of materials, the existence of a crack below detectable size must be assumed.
4. Limit the candidate materials to those which can tolerate slow crack growth throughout the anticipated service life of the part before reaching critical size, or can tolerate the growth from a crack of minimum size detectable by nondestructive inspection techniques during the period between inspections (overhaul). The design function must strike a balance between the crack growth rate and the critical crack size; however, the critical crack size must be large enough to cover the maximum size which may escape detection on inspection plus crack growth during the intervening service to the next inspection.
5. As a precautionary measure, consider including a selection of alternate and more corrosion-resistant materials.
6. In critical applications, run tensile coupons, preferably from the same heat of material as the part being produced, concurrently with each intermediate step in the heat-treating cycle to assure that these properties are obtained for the final part.
7. Do not use quenched-and-tempered parts in applications which require exposure for an extended time to temperatures higher than 100°F below the respective tempering temperature.
8. In heat treatment and in use avoid the application of temperature in the temper brittle range for respective compositions.
9. Select sufficient hardenability to ensure transformation on quenching to not less than 95 percent martensite at the center of maximum cross section (ferrous metals).
10. Avoid use of compositions that result in excessive hardenability.
11. Select compositions which have ductile-to-brittle transition temperatures, measured by impact, that are below any temperature which the part is likely to experience in service.
12. Do not expose components, for which the properties are developed as the result of any cold-working methods, to operating temperatures which during design lifetime would lead to softening that would be detected by a hardness test.
13. Unstabilized austenitic steels may be used up to 700°F.
14. Do not use welded assemblies thereof unless they have been given a solution heat treatment after welding except for the stabilized grades 321 and 347, ELC 304, and ELC 316.
15. Do not use cold-rolled stainless steels at temperatures higher than 50°F below the recovery temperature.
16. Age-harden 17-4PH and 17-7PH steels at temperatures not less than 1000°F in all applications.
17. Minimize surface decarburization of fully hardened steel parts so that the difference in equivalent hardness between Rockwell superficial 15N or Knoop hardness tests on hardened surfaces, and Rockwell C readings on the same surfaces do not exceed 2 points Rockwell C.
18. Do not use aluminum alloy 2020-T6 or aluminum alloy 7178-T6 for structural applications.
19. Make maximum use of alloys, heat treatments, and claddings which minimize susceptibility to pitting and intergranular and stress corrosion.
20. In applications exposed to moisture or weather, protect surfaces against corrosion.
21. Do not use beryllium in applications which will be subjected to high stresses or impact loads.

22. Use magnesium alloys only in areas where low exposure to corrosive environments can be expected and protection systems can be maintained with ease and high reliability.
23. Use the values listed in Table t of MIL-T-9047 for the selection of alloys and the design of titanium parts.
24. Avoid silver brazing of titanium parts.
25. Ensure that cleaning fluids and other chemicals used on titanium are not detrimental to its performance. Contaminants of titanium which can produce stress corrosion include hydrochloric acid, trichloroethylene, carbon tetrachloride, all chlorides, cadmium, silver, and chlorinated cutting oils.
26. For titanium forgings, sheet, and plate, comply with MIL-T-9046, MIL-T-9047, and MIL-F-83142, respectively.
27. Where fretting is suspected, at interfaces between titanium alloys or titanium and other base metal parts, make provisions for antifretting coatings or inserts and conduct tests to assure that life expectancy is not compromised.
28. Machine or chemically mill the surfaces of titanium parts to eliminate all contaminated zones formed during processing.
29. In the design of titanium components, consider the rapid-crack propagation phenomena and the notch sensitivity of the material, with provisions for rounded edges, gradual section changes, optimum grain flow, and special handling to prevent surface damage during manufacture and assembly.
30. Do not use any mercury-containing devices on installed equipment or during production in the presence of aluminum and titanium alloys.

Nonmetals

1. Ensure that elastomeric components have adequate resistance to aging, low temperature, ozone, heat aging, polymer reversion, working fluids, lubricants, etc.
2. Do not use foamed plastics for metal skin stabilization or as a sandwich core material in structural components, other than all plastic sandwich parts, low density filler putties, or hollow glass bead (syntactic) foam.
3. Avoid using these components unless rigorous vibration, sonic fatigue, and all life and environmental exposure tests can amply demonstrate a durable product.
4. Completely seal all components to preclude contact of fluids with core.
5. Base use of glass fiber reinforced plastic upon weight saving, strength, maintainability, adequacy of manufacturing methods, and temperature-strength relationship.
6. Base use of ceramic and cermet materials upon strength capability, maintainability, adequacy of manufacturing methods, and temperature-strength analysis. Use these materials only when an overriding need for their desirable physical properties is encountered.

FITTINGS

General

1. Single-piece designs are preferable to built-up fittings. Design all fittings with a minimum of constituent parts for ease of assembly, disassembly, removability, and replaceability.
2. Avoid eccentric loadings in the design of fittings.
3. Design to eliminate or minimize points of stress concentration caused by holes, sharp corners, or notches in fittings which may be subjected to repeated loadings with resulting fatigue problems.
4. Provide generous fillets, radii, and flanges to minimize stress concentrations and fatigue loadings.
5. Avoid discontinuities and provide adequate web thickness.

6. Do not use welding of any type, including spot welding.
7. Do not weld, braze, or solder washers onto lugs or other parts of the fitting.
8. Ensure that countersunk depths are no greater than one-half the material thickness.
9. Design heavy-duty fittings as an integral part of the member. Otherwise, design the fittings to be a single unit joined to the member by bolted, threaded, or riveted connections.
10. When aluminum alloy is used for fitting stock and if machining to a considerable depth (one inch or more) is required, remove most of the surplus metal prior to heat treatment.
11. When aluminum alloy is used for fitting stock and when a fitting is to contain pressed-in bushings or inserts and the fitting stock is one inch or greater in each principal direction, heat-treat the stock in as near its final size as practicable.
12. If spot-facing or counterboring is unavoidable, provide bosses or extra material on surfaces to be spot-faced.
13. For spot-faces or counterbores with diameters up to 1.25 in., provide a corner radius of not less than 0.062 in.
14. For spot-faces or counterbores with a diameter greater than 1.25 in., provide a corner radius of at least 0.093 in.
15. To protect parts made of soft material that must accommodate threaded fasteners subjected to repeated assembly and disassembly, use inserts.

Castings

1. Ensure that the grain size, density, and wall thickness of castings are adequate for their intended use.
2. Provide adequate fillets at all section junctions.
3. Ensure that all castings are free from sharp corners, discontinuities of contour, or thin webs, both in the rough castings and in the final machined part.
4. Ensure that the minimum radius of any point on the finished part will not be less than 0.062 inch.
5. Do not use castings for wire pull lugs.

Universal Joints

1. Do not operate universal joints at an angle greater than 30° when measured between the axes of the hubs. When used in power-driven systems at speeds of 175 rpm or more, the angle must not exceed 15°.
2. When joints are to be operated at 1000 rpm or higher in power drives, enclose them in a housing and run them in an oil bath.
3. Do not use plain bearing universal joints in power drives where the speed exceeds 2000 rpm.
4. Provide for removal of torque shafts in which universal joints are installed without disassembly or removal of pins from the joints.
5. When two or more joints are used in a shaft, install the joints with the small or corresponding pins parallel.
6. For applications involving speeds greater than 2000 rpm, use antifriction universal joints in accordance with MIL-U-3963.

FASTENERS

General

1. Choose fasteners to resist vibration and acoustic forces.
2. Use the minimum number of sizes, styles, and types of fasteners essential to the system.

3. Do not use fasteners of the same diameter having the same grip length but different shank length, or those having the same shank length but different grip length, in the same bolt circle or in proximity where they could be inadvertently interchanged.

4. When an envelope dimension is given on a drawing for a fastener, design for the maximum envelope dimensions.

5. Protect fasteners from corrosion.

6. Avoid using dissimilar metals.

7. Install all structural fasteners which will be permanent with appropriate primer or sealant.

8. Install fasteners subject to frequent removal during normal operation, inspection, and maintenance by priming the hole and letting the primer dry prior to installation.

9. Do not use cadmium-plated or coated steel fasteners where temperatures may exceed 232°C (450°F).

10. Do not use cadmium-plated or coated steel fasteners in titanium.

11. Conform with AMS 2411 for silver plating of fasteners.

12. To minimize the potential for corrosion when metallic fasteners penetrate graphite epoxy components, use titanium alloy, AMS 5758, or other materials which have been shown by test to resist corrosion when in contact with graphite epoxy.

Rivets

1. Restrict use of rivets to shear applications.

2. Locate rivets so that the edge distance is not less than $1.5 \times D$ (D = fastener shank diameter) or greater than 2.5D in a lap joint.

3. For joints having edge distances less than 2D, substantiate the load allowables with test data.

4. Ensure that the head angle of the countersunk rivets is $100° \pm 1°$ (included angle); where an angle of less than 100° is needed, test-substantiate.

5. Ensure that the rivet heads upset at installation are within the structure and are properly formed.

6. If tubular rivets with solid cross sections for a portion of the length are used, and the strength of the rivets is computed as that of the solid rivets, ensure that the bottom of the cavity is at least 25 percent of the rivet diameter from the plane of shear as measured toward the tubular end.

Bolts, Nuts, and Washers

1. Control of preload is necessary to extend the fastener assembly (bolt or screw and nut) fatigue life and prevent it from being stressed beyond the yield strength. For a bolt or screw that is to be loaded in shear, tighten the fastener assembly to a preload value of 30 percent of the externally threaded component minimum axial yield strength at maximum usage temperature.

2. For a bolt or screw that is to be loaded in tension, tighten the fastener assembly to a preload value of 80 percent of the externally threaded component minimum axial yield strength at maximum usage temperature.

3. Ensure that all fasteners of the same diameter and strength in the same pattern are tightened to the same nominal preload.

4. Consider residual torsional sheer stress and do not exceed the minimum axial yield strength while tightening the assembly.

5. Do not subject the installed fastener to fully rated tensile and shear loads simultaneously, as the combined stresses may exceed the allowable design stresses of the fastener material.

6. Provide all structural threaded fasteners loaded in shear with sufficient shank length so that no threads are in bearing in sheet or fittings having a thickness equal to or less than 0.093 inch.

7. In thicker sheet or fittings, a maximum of two threads, including thread runout, is permitted in bearing when based on the maximum joint thickness and minimum fastener grip.

8. Ensure that no more than 25 percent of the minimum thickness of the sheet or fitting have threads in bearing.
9. To prevent galling and seizing and to reduce the torque values for a given tension, use nondry film lubricant on threaded fasteners. But ensure that the nondry film lubricant is removable with cleaning fluid.
10. Do not consider platings and coatings, such as cadmium or silver, as lubricants.
11. Design hexagon bolts and nuts to conform with the sizes and limits for across-flat dimensions.
12. Design twelve-point or double-hexagon nuts and bolts to conform to all requirements of SAE AS-870.
13. Do not use twelve-point or double-hexagon bolts or nuts in materials with an ultimate tensile strength of 180 kpsi or more. Use spline drive bolts and nuts conforming to MS33787.
14. Ensure that all external wrenching fasteners having an ultimate tensile strength of 150 kpsi or more conform to MS33787.
15. Ensure that all external wrenching fasteners using metric module sizing conform to MS33787 for spline drive fasteners.
16. For other metric external wrenching features use a hexagon drive.
17. Use self-locking, externally threaded fasteners (bolts, screws, and studs) that conform with MIL-F-18240 for 121°C (250°F) applications.
18. Ensure that all these fasteners conform with the design requirements and usage limitations. Use inserts in castings and forgings to increase thread strength and resist stripping, seizing, wearing, and corrosion.
19. Do not use inserts in any primary structure.
20. Do not use self-tapping inserts.
21. To allow for replacement when an insert is used, consider providing sufficient edge distance to permit drilling and tapping for the next larger standard size screw thread. Provide for failure of the installed bolt or screw before failure of the insert.
22. Use self-retaining bolts in all "critical" linkage joints.
23. In selecting bolts which may be subjected to high temperatures, consider the suitability of the metal or alloy and any coating or plating used thereon.
24. Incorporate in the surrounding parts means for lubrication of bolts used to connect members having relative motion; do not drill these bolts.
25. Install bolts loaded in shear and subject to reversals of load in close-tolerance holes with no perceptible play.
26. Install all bolts with heads uppermost or in such direction that loss of bolt due to loss of the nut is minimized.
27. Install bolts with the heads forward or in a direction that allows easy removal for maintenance.
28. Ensure that tension nuts are capable of developing 110 percent of the mating bolt's minimum axial yield strength at maximum usage temperature.
29. Ensure that shear nuts are capable of developing 55 percent of the mating bolt's minimum axial yield strength at maximum use temperature.
30. Do not exceed 0.2 percent offset compressive yield stress of the joint material and/or washer (plane and spacer washers).
31. Use either castellated nuts to be locked with cotter pins or self-locking nuts in structures that may require removal, where strength requirements permit.
32. Select the nuts and pins on the basis of intended use and temperature limits.
33. Use tension nuts on tension bolts where possible, and do not exceed the mechanical properties of the nut during usage.

34. Place the part number on all drawings, parts lists, and bills of material.
35. Use plain (flat) washers under nuts to protect the surface from injury while tightening the fastener and to reduce the stress of the joint by increasing the bearing area.
36. Use spacer washers (one or more plain washers) under nuts where necessary to prevent threads in bearing.
37. Consider use of lock washers carefully, since they damage finish systems, setting up paths of corrosion.
38. The preferred methods of preventing rotation and loss of nuts, bolts, or screws are (*a*) use of castellated nuts with cotter pins, (*b*) use of drilled head screws or bolts with safety wire, and (*c*) use of self-locking screws, bolts, nuts, and inserts.
39. Preload-indicating washers may be used to gauge bolt preloads. But use a new preload-indicating washer assembly each time the bolt or nut is installed.

Screws

1. Ensure that all structural screws conform with the design allowable loads.
2. If these loads are not specified, substantiate them by supporting test data.
3. Carefully consider use of zinc-plated screws.
4. Use screw threads for structural fasteners which conform with MIL-S-7742 or MIL-S-8879.
5. Comply with the preferred or recommended diameter-pitch selection when possible.
6. Use MIL-S-7742 threads for electrical connectors.
7. Whenever possible, eliminate galling and seizing by lubrication.
8. When screw threads are used in components other than bolts, nuts, or screws, consider gaging additional thread elements beyond those required by specs.
9. Use panhead screws in place of brazier, truss, round, binding, or undrilled fillister head machine screws.
10. In countersunk applications, use screws having a head angle of 100° (including angle) whenever possible; otherwise use screws with a head angle of 60°.
11. Use hexagon sockets for headless setscrews (AN565), cap screws, and structural panel fasteners only.
12. Do not use slotted drives except for instrument screws.
13. Tapping screws may be used to a limited extent in lieu of bolts or rivets in applications where the use of the latter is not practicable.
14. Follow standard design handbooks and manufacturer's fastener specifications when using setscrews for flywheels, pulleys, etc.

Pins

1. Clevis pins may be used in tie rods and in secondary controls that are not subjected to continuous operation and where the reversal of stresses and chances of loosening are negligible.
2. Mount clevis pin heads up and safety with standard cotter pins.
3. Use taper pins in all permanent connections that are seldom broken and where absence of play is essential.
4. Put the small end of the pin through the connected parts into a spacer washer, permitting the nut to draw it up tight.
5. Comply with MS 33547 design limitations on the use of spring pins.
6. Conform with design limitations on the use of swaged-collar-headed straight pins and collars.

WELDING, ETC.

1. Heat-treat steel parts in accordance with MIL-H-6875 or industry practice.
2. When steel parts have been cold straightened after hardening to a tensile strength below 1.4×10^9 Pa (200,000 psi), follow with stress-relieving heat treatment and re-inspect parts.
3. Straighten parts hardened to tensile strengths of 1.4×10^9 Pa (200,000 psi) and above at a temperature within the range from the tempering temperature to 37.79°C (100°F) below the tempering temperature.
4. Limit maximum metal removal after final treatment to 3.175 mm (0.125 in.).
5. Heat-treat aluminum parts according to MIL-H-6088.
6. Do not hot straighten or joggle aluminum after aging.
7. Cold straighten or form heat-treated 2000 and 7000 aluminum alloys within two hours after quenching unless refrigerated.
8. Limit maximum metal removal after final heat treatment to 0.150 in.
9. Heat-treat titanium parts according to MIL-H-81200.
10. In adhesive bonding comply with MIL-A-83377, using materials conforming to MIL-A-25463, *Fed Spec* MMM-A-132, and *Fed Spec* MMM-A-134.
11. Perform simulated service tests to demonstrate desired service life adequacy.
12. In choosing materials to be welded, consider weldability, weld efficiency, weld effects on material density, ductility, and stress corrosion of both weld and heat affected zones.
13. Design joints to transmit loads primarily in shear and compression and to minimize tensile loads.
14. Select welding procedures and supplies to provide the required weld quality and to minimize energy input.
15. Protect the weld pool from contaminants.
16. When welds are located in areas in which peak working stresses may reach 40 percent or more of the base metal yield strength, or when a single failure of a weld would endanger the safety of personnel, ensure that weld joints develop 90 percent of base metal fatigue strength and meet requirements below.
17. Accomplish welding operations with automatic or semi-automatic equipment, using established techniques, by operators certified in compliance with MIL-C-5021.
18. When the use of such equipment (no. 17) is impractical, manual gas tungsten arc welding methods may be used.
19. Employ butt welds wherever practical and ensure that they have 100 percent root penetration.
20. Ensure that drop through does not exceed 15 percent of the section thickness.
21. Undercutting is permitted provided the minimum transverse radius of curvature is not less than 0.060 in and the maximum depth of the undercut does not exceed 10 percent of the thickness of the material joined, or 0.005 in, whichever is less.
22. Ensure that joint mismatch does not exceed 10 percent of the thickness of the thinner section joined.
23. Crater cracks are cause for rejection.
24. Ensure that defects do not exceed 0.04 inch in maximum dimension and the cumulative length of defects per inch of weld does not exceed 0.08 in, or 0.24 in per foot of weld.
25. Permit repair welding only in areas and locations indicated by design documentation and ensure that it meets the defect limits specified herein.
26. Do not assume that design properties of welded joints in materials heat-treated subsequently in welding exceed 90 percent of the heat-treated, wrought metal properties.

27. Ensure that the strength of the welded joint is not assumed to exceed 90 percent of the annealed wrought metal properties.
28. Visually inspect welded joints for the presence of undercut, mismatch, penetration, drop through, and crater cracks or other shrinkage cracks open to the surface.
29. Inspect surfaces by penetrant techniques for the presence of surface cracks and voids.
30. Inspect welded joints by radiographic techniques for the presence of internal defects.
31. Limit weld repair to the repair by welding of defects in the production weld revealed by inspection.
32. Ensure that weld repair does not include the correction of dimensional deficiencies by weld buildup or "buttering" of parts in areas where the designer did not provide a welded joint.
33. Braze in accordance with MIL-B-7883.
34. Do not braze critical parts.
35. Prohibit subsequent fusion welding operations in the vicinity of brazed joints or other operations involving high temperatures which may affect the joints.
36. Do not depend upon brazed joints in tension for any calculated strength.
37. Whenever possible, design brazed joints for shear loading.
38. Conform to the allowable shear strength specified in MIL-HDBK-5.
39. Radiograph brazed pressure fittings and structured joints to determine the degree of flow of the brazing material.
40. Do not braze titanium.
41. Accomplish brazing using techniques whose suitability, reproducibility, and properties including fatigue and creep-rupture have been established by statistical analyses of test data.
42. Ensure that aggregate void area does not exceed 10 percent of the joint interface area.
43. For soldering materials and processes comply with MIL-STS-454 and *Fed Spec* QQ-S-571.
44. Do not use soldering as a sole means of securing any structural part.
45. For metal treatment and plating materials and processes, comply with MIL-S-5002.
46. Whenever practicable avoid drilling of holes, beveling, and spot facing in martensitic steel after hardening to stress levels of 180,000 psi and above.
47. When such practices are unavoidable, use techniques necessary to avoid formation of any untempered martensite.
48. Use microhardness and metallurgical examinations to determine the depth of disturbed metal resulting from either drilling or grinding.
49. Ensure that the documents generated to define these techniques are approved by the procuring activity prior to use.
50. Debur both ends of the holes by a method which has been demonstrated not to result in untempered martensite.
51. Comply with MIL-C-6021 for welding of castings.
52. Comply with MIL-A-21180 for structural aluminum castings modified to permit use of CH-70 and KO1 alloys.
53. Classify and inspect all castings according to MIL-C-6021.
54. Strength test to destruction the least acceptable casting (established by radiographic standards) of each lot of Class I castings.
55. Verify by the static tests that the calculated margins of safety using "A" values of MIL-HDBK-5 are not less than 0.33 for limit and ultimate calculations.

56. Design forgings for welded assemblies in accordance with MIL-F-7190 (steel), MIL-A-22771 (aluminum), *Fed Spec* AA-A-367 (aluminum), and MIL-F-83142 (titanium).
57. After the forging technique, including degree of working is established, section and etch the first production forgings to show the grain-flow structure and to determine mechanical properties at critical areas.
58. Repeat this sectioning procedure after any major change in the forging technique.
59. When all surfaces of all structural aluminum forgings have undergone final machining and heat treatment, shot peen them 100 percent or place them in compression by other suitable methods for selected overaged aluminum alloys and for areas requiring lapped, honed, or polished surfaces for functioning engineering requirements.
60. Ensure that aluminum forgings and extrusions used in corrosive environments have essentially no residual surface tensile stresses in the final heat-treated and machined condition.
61. For primary structural aluminum forgings, subject one preproduction forging plus one sample part machined from extruded stock to a standard 5% salt solution alternate immersion test for 2000 cycles (except for those aluminum and overaged aluminum alloys and steels which are not inherently subject to stress corrosion).
62. Ensure that this test consists of 10 minutes total immersion followed by 50 minutes in air that completely dries the part in the first 5-10 minutes of the drying cycle.
63. Inspect for cracks after 250, 500, 750, 1000, 1500, and 2000 cycles.
64. Reject any design that shows any cracks during the first 1000 cycles.
65. Repeat test on redesigns.
66. If cracking occurs after 1000 cycles, attempt to relieve the residual stresses causing the crackings.
67. For crack tests, use Class AA ultrasonic test conforming to MIL-I-8950.
68. Conduct this test using a part that has been machined and heat-treated according to the processes to be used for the production part.
69. Do not use any protective finishes or anodizing and do not apply any external loads.
70. When considering the purpose of the test, determine if the magnitude of residual tensile is sufficiently high to cause stress corrosion cracking.
71. Ensure that pressure cylinders are hollow-forged without flash formation.
72. Use forging stock of such size and dimensions that the work accomplished in forming to finished shape results in approximately uniform grain size throughout.
73. Employ forging techniques that produce an internal grain-flow pattern so that the direction of flow in highly stressed areas is essentially parallel to the principal stresses.
74. Ensure that the grain-flow pattern is essentially free from re-entrant and sharply folded flow lines.
75. Ensure that the angle of grain direction at the surface does not exceed 30°.
76. In sandwich assemblies, preclude the accumulation and entrapment of water or other contaminants within the core structure by providing edge sealing.
77. Avoid perforated or other core configurations which allow moisture transfer.
78. Choose MIL-S-9041 for sandwich construction using plastic honeycomb core and facings, and MIL-S-25392 for sandwich construction using foamed-in-place core and facings.
79. Use core materials which conform to MIL-C-7438, MIL-C-8073, MIL-C-8087, or MIL-C-21275.
80. Select parts of high-strength aluminum alloys, precipitation-hardening steels, and alloy steel heat-treated to tensile strengths above 220,000 psi so that sustained/residual surface tensile stresses in these materials do not exceed the limitations indicated in DH 1-2, DN 7B1, SN12(1).

81. For other metals, develop and use similar threshold levels using 3.5% salt solution in the 2000 cycle altitude immersion test.

CORROSION

1. Suitably finish all system parts, including spares, to provide protection from corrosion.
2. In the use of all finishes and coatings, comply with the requirements of MIL-S-5002, MIL-F-7179, and the following.
3. For the protective finishes and finish schemes of all ground equipment, comply with the requirements of MIL-STD-808.
4. Ensure that the protective finishes of modifications or additions to existing equipment are commensurate with the original requirements of that equipment.
5. Apply all applicable corrosion prevention and control considerations and assure they are properly integrated during system definition, engineering development, and operational phases, in consonance with the designated life cycle of the system and mission objectives.
6. See TO-1-1-2 for additional information on corrosion prevention.
7. Use organic finishes or finish systems that provide the necessary corrosion resistance for the metal being protected and for all materials used in areas subjected to severe corrosive environments.
8. Ensure that all exterior paints and colors are consistent with thermal design requirements.
9. Ensure that marking is in accordance with MIL-M-25047 and TO-1-1-4.
10. Use coatings conforming to MIL-C-7439, MIL-C-27315, or MIL-C-83231 on exterior plastic parts subject to rain or sand erosion.
11. Use chemical finishes that provide adequate corrosion resistance and that are in accordance with MIL-S-5002.
12. Provide chemical finishing to ensure maximum corrosion resistance for those parts or surfaces of parts located in corrosion susceptible areas or which form exterior surfaces of the system.
13. Sulfuric acid anodize all parts made of 2000 and 7000 series high-strength aluminum alloys according to MIL-A-8625, Type II.
14. Shot peen (either completely or in specific areas, as required) those aluminum alloy parts which are determined to be fatigue critical, and ensure that the anodic coating is of a thickness to assure no loss in fatigue strength.
15. Type I anodizing of MIL-A-8625 may be used for adhesively bonded parts where the integrity of the bond line would be adversely affected by Type II anodizing; however, make maximum use of Type II whenever possible.
16. Provide suitable cathodic protection by a process which has been proved to be nonembrittling to high-strength steels for all parts (including fasteners) made of low-alloy, high-strength steels.
17. Ensure that cadmium plating thickness at least equals Type II, Class 2, of *Fed Spec* QQ-P-416.
18. Qualify the bath used for plating of production parts, using production materials, to the requirements of MIL-S-5002.
19. Give magnesium alloys a pretreatment conforming to MIL-M-3171 or MIL-M-45202.
20. In addition to the required finish, provide two coats of exterior paint in accordance with MIL-F-7179 to internal magnesium alloy parts.
21. Process and adequately clean surfaces.
22. Avoid contamination or deterioration prior to or during sealing.
23. Sealants containing 3 percent magnesium chromate may be used provided the minimum physical properties of MIL-S-8802 are complied with.

24. Other sealants covered by military specifications may be used where temperatures exceed those permitted for MIL-S-8802.
25. Seal removable panels and access doors in exterior locations, either by mechanical seals or by separable fay surface sealing.
26. Wet install all nonremovable fasteners that penetrate exterior surfaces with a corrosion-inhibiting primer as specified in *Fed Spec* TT-P-1757, or equal, or with MIL-S-8802 sealant where temperature limitations permit.
27. In high temperature areas up to 176.7°C (350°F) use MIL-P-23377 epoxy primer.
28. If the inhibiting sealant meets the minimum physical properties of MIL-S-8802, a corrosion-inhibiting sealant must be used instead of *Fed Spec* TT-P-1757 or MIL-S-8802.
29. Install fasteners in integral fuel tanks with wet sealant as specified in MIL-S-8802.
30. Design and install quick-release fasteners and removable fasteners penetrating exterior surfaces so as to provide a seal to prevent moisture or fluids from entering.
31. Prime holes for these fasteners and allow them to dry prior to installing the fastener.
32. Provide drain holes as required to prevent collection and entrapment of water.
33. Design exterior surfaces to prevent the entrance of water.
34. Do not use dissimilar metals, as defined in MIL-STD-889, in direct contact unless the mating surfaces are adequately insulated.
35. Except in hermetically sealed assemblies and in such treated parts as paper capacitors and transformers, select materials for use in aerospace system equipment that are not nutrients for fungi.
36. In the event fungi-nutrient materials must be selected to perform the required function, treat such materials so as to render the surfaces fungi-resistant.
37. Select materials which do not degrade in the presence of moisture and do not have tendencies to absorb and retain water.
38. Use the test methods of MIL-STD-810 to verify fungi and moisture resistance.

HAZARD DETECTION

General

1. Include failure-detection or hazard-control systems as an integrated component of the structural design.
2. Consider the overall use of redundancy in the detection and protection systems of all potential extreme hazard conditions.
3. Ensure that response time requirements of the detection and protection system are compatible with the magnitude, rate of burning, and degree of toxic hazards present.
4. Ensure that the detection system selected employs a unique characteristic of the hazard which it protects against. The aim is to avoid triggering the detection system with a similar nonhazardous characteristic or normally expected environmental variance.
5. Design so that detection and warning recycle capability is available to all critical protection areas.
6. Identify all potential fire zones and hazardous areas, and provide fire detection devices for all potential fire zones.
7. Consider automatic explosion detection and suppression devices whenever the triggering of an explosion can occur too swiftly for personnel reaction.
8. Locate warning and caution indicator lights so that they are readily visible to personnel working in hazardous areas and/or to area monitor personnel.

9. Supply emergency power to any area where loss of protective capability would allow an undetected hazard to personnel or equipment to develop.
10. Ensure that interfaces between control systems and other systems cannot cause detection system failure.
11. Include redundancy where relays are used in the detection control system.
12. Ensure that a complete fire hazard analysis has been made whenever oxygen-enriched atmospheres in excess of 30 percent at normal pressures are to be used.
13. Ensure that the ignition temperature, propagation rate, and burning temperature of materials used in environmental chambers are known when oxygen-enriched atmospheres above 30 percent are present at normal pressures.
14. Design and locate system actuating or detection controls to minimize inadvertent activation.
15. Ensure that emergency controls are readily visible and accessible.
16. Specify portable units for surveillance of areas where it is not practical to install fixed sensors.
17. Provide circuitry to allow convenient periodic calibration and test of electrical measuring, display, and alarm circuits.
18. Allow access to permit injection of known gas samples in gas, smoke, or vapor detectors.
19. Ensure that labels or placards are plainly legible under both day and night conditions.
20. Secure and protect the various interconnecting wires and cables to avoid inadvertent contact, chafing, or stresses.
21. Do not use components containing mercury unless it is essential. If it becomes necessary, design to minimize the probability of damage which would result from mercury spillage.

Fire Detection

1. Design and locate fire and overheat detection systems to alert personnel to hazardous or failure conditions.
2. Base selection of a fire detection system upon the anticipated occurrence of fire and the potential costs of false initiations and undetected fires.
3. Use rate-consumption fixed-temperature structural tube-type detectors whenever normal protection requirements must be met or when ambient heat sources or light preclude the use of radiation detection devices.
4. Do not use rate-of-rise devices for area protection where the nominal environmental temperature variations exceed 15° to 20° per minute; under this condition consider other methods.
5. Ensure that areas which may contain smoldering or slow-burning materials are not exclusively protected by rate-of-rise devices. Use fixed-temperature, rate-compensation, or other methods sensitive to products of combustion.
6. Evaluate protection requirements and sensor locations of thermal detection devices to obtain maximum effectiveness by use of either spot or continuous line types.
7. Evaluate carefully applications of infrared devices to avoid stray radiation pickup. Use filters or flame flicker recognition, or select the solar-blind region of the spectrum if avoidance of stray sunlight or high radiation environments cannot be assured.
8. Employ ultraviolet radiation detectors whenever the fire zone requiring protection contains materials that burn with flame outside the visual spectrum.
9. Multiple detection using combinations of ultraviolet and infrared systems are recommended where each system individually cannot be relied upon to provide reliable false-alarm-free coverage of a volume.
10. Avoid the use of dual wavelength discrimination methods when the possibility of one of the two detection methods becoming saturated would place final discrimination of a hazard on a single method.

11. Employ overheat detection in all major equipment installations.
12. Consider using thermoelectric, Curie point, and continuous detectors, as well as fixed-temperature, rate-of-rise, combination rate-of-rise/fixed temperature, and rate compensation devices.
13. Use visual warnings as a minimum plus auditory warning devices in all critical or high-hazard producing equipment or processes.
14. Consider the possible effects (of temperature variations) on the selectivity and sensitivity of a photodetector.
15. Ensure that requirements given for thermal sensing devices used as the overall protection method have included their locations, temperature ratings, and sensitivities based upon nominal ambient temperatures. Consider both constant and anticipated temperature fluctuations.
16. Install thermal sensing devices in locations where they will operate promptly in the presence of fire or heat.

Combustible Vapor Detection

1. Consider combustible vapor detection as a protective requirement in any area where combustible vapors may form or accumulate beyond the lower explosive limit.
2. If ventilation systems cannot prevent the accumulation of flammable vapors, and the hazard presented by these vapors warrants additional protection, then consider using a vapor detection system.
3. Provide special calibrations for meter movements of vapor detectors which will be required to conduct analysis of gases possessing low or high heat of combustion characteristics.
4. Require that special caution be given to detection systems using the catalytic combustion principle of operation in the presence of leaded gasoline vapors. The presence of tetraethyl lead will reduce the effective catalytic activity due to the formation of lead oxide on the filament.
5. Provide flame arrestors on all filament chambers of catalytic combustion detectors to prevent the possibility of flashback.
6. Ensure that the sensitized gas used in nondispersive infrared analysis devices possesses the specific absorption spectra required for the area to be protected.
7. Install a combustion gas-smoke detector in compliance with the National Fire Code (NFPA). If an alternate method is selected which is not identified by the Code, it is to be fully qualified by field testing prior to use.
8. Determine ambient air currents and flow patterns prior to selection of combustion gas or smoke detectors as the protection technique.
9. Consider using mass spectrometry instruments for analyzing complex mixtures of gases or vapors.
10. Employ combustion gas or smoke detectors when the primary protection is by one-shot complete flooding or deluge-type suppression.
11. Use a correlation spectrometer to remotely monitor large areas and to measure the combustion products which precede actual ignition.

Explosion Detection

1. Ensure that explosion detection devices possess sufficient sensitivity to protect against a predetermined rate of pressure rise or static pressure point well below the explosive pressure level of the protected area.
2. Consider an explosion detection system for all hazardous applications, i.e., fuel or propellant tanks, vent stacks, hazardous handling processes, or hazardous area personnel protection.
3. Ensure that the explosion detection devices and suppression agents used in making up the protective system are properly suited to provide maximum protection.

Toxic Vapor Detection

1. Provide that the toxic vapor detection devices display the concentration in parts per million. Ensure that there is a separate display for each type of vapor sampled on a single device.
2. Ensure that any toxic vapor detector designed for a specific gas which may also develop explosive concentrations will indicate both scales on the same meter face. The indication will be ppm and percentage of explosive levels. Also provide the lower explosive limit.
3. Determine that the vapor detection device is compatible with all gases and vapors to be sampled. Also ensure that it is compatible with all other gases normally present in the environment.
4. Ensure that other nonhazardous gases or vapors present will not cause erroneous indications, inhibit, or interfere with detector readings of the toxic or hazardous gases.
5. Design the detector to indicate only specific gases and not a general class of gases.
6. Design the detector so that the reaction time to sense the toxic hazard and initiate alarms is 1 minute or less.
7. Ensure that recovery time is 1 minute or less following removal of the hazardous concentration.

Auditory And Visual Warning Signals

1. Design auditory warning devices to meet the requirements specified in the National Fire Codes (NFPA).
2. Specify visual warning devices in accordance with considerations and requirements outlined in National Fire Codes (NFPA).
3. Ensure that the types and characteristics of auditory and warning devices are suitable for providing the discrimination necessary under all operating conditions.
4. Specify that the brightness of the translucent area of light indicators is at least 150 ft-L in the bright mode.
5. Provide audible alarms where indicator lights may go unnoticed or system status is not monitored.
6. Design displays to minimize reading error.

FIRE EXTINGUISHING AND SUPPRESSION SYSTEMS

1. Identify potential fire zones.
2. Isolate potential fire zones with fire barriers or firewalls.
3. Ensure that firewalls are not stressed by mounted equipment.
4. Use materials on the protected side of firewalls that will not burn as a result of high temperature in the fire zones.
5. Do not use titanium structurally where it may contact molten metal.
6. Ensure that firewalls are as liquid- and vapor-proof as possible.
7. Do not install access doors in firewalls; if necessary, protect them properly and install automatic closing devices.
8. Fabricate air ducts passing through fire zones to ensure fire containment.
9. Ensure that air ducts originating in fire zones can be closed to stop airflow.
10. Provide shutoff valves on flammable fluid lines which flow into or through a fire zone.
11. Design shutoff valves or control circuits so that fire will have no effect on their operation.
12. Specify that flammable fluid lines in fire zones be made of stainless steel or the equivalent.

13. Provide fire detection for all potential fire zones.
14. Provide fire extinguishing systems for all potential fire zones.
15. Select the most effective extinguishing agent consistent with both safety and design goals.
16. Consider effects of toxicity where it is possible for fumes to enter inhabited areas.
17. Locate pressure gages so they are readily accessible for inspection and maintenance.
18. Provide safety relief for extinguishing agent containers.
19. Provide visual indication that safety relief has occurred.
20. Design squib-actuated discharge valves so that electrical connection cannot be made unless the squib is installed.
21. Do not route control wiring through potential fire zones unless it can withstand at least 2000°F for 5 minutes without system degradation.
22. Ensure that interfaces between control systems and other systems cannot cause extinguishing system failure.
23. Provide separate initiation circuits and dual squibs for each container.
24. Provide redundancy where relays are used in the control system.
25. Consider using automatic explosion suppression devices wherever an explosion can be triggered too swiftly for crew reaction.
26. Ensure that suppression system status is provided to indicate system has actuated.
27. Ensure that hazardous quantities of smoke, flames, or extinguishing agents are not allowed to enter inhabited areas.

ELECTRICAL/ELECTRONIC EQUIPMENT AND SYSTEMS

General

1. Ensure that flammable materials are not specified for use in the system.
2. Select materials that will not liberate gases or fumes which are toxic, corrosive, flammable, or explosive under any combination of specified service conditions.
3. Do not use dissimilar metals in intimate contact unless suitable corrosion protection is provided.
4. Do not use glass fiber materials where they may cause skin irritation.
5. Use insulating and jacketing compounds in cordage and cabling that exhibit long life without degradation of performance under the anticipated service conditions.
6. Derate power cordage and cable when operating ambient temperatures exceed 30°C.
7. Hold wiring termination points to a minimum.
8. To prevent accidental body contact, cover or protect high-voltage terminals located near components which are frequently worked on.
9. Protect terminal points from shorting by foreign objects and debris, and from possible circuit degradation by dirt, moisture, or other contaminants.
10. Space terminals to which wires are soldered far enough apart so that work on one terminal contact does not damage another.
11. Ensure that the moisture-excluding property of potted parts is not degraded by normal soldering operations on terminals.
12. Provide adequate spacing or barriers to prevent corona breakdown or low-leakage resistance under specified service conditions.
13. Ensure that wiring terminals are sufficiently strong to support the wires attached and to ensure necessary fabrication and maintenance operations.

14. Avoid connectors with unkeyed symmetrical pin arrangements.
15. Provide alignment pins, keyway arrangements, or similar features on adjacent connectors to prevent cross-connection.
16. Furnish articles of equipment likely to require future additional circuits with connectors having spare contacts in accordance with MIL-STD-454.
17. Terminate connectors so that receptacle pins are "hot" and plug pins are "cold."
18. Furnish caps or covers to keep unmated connectors from contamination.
19. Use connectors for connection terminations where practicable.
20. Ensure that layout and spacing of connectors permit ease of connection and disconnection when using appropriate tools.
21. Include assembly instructions in the design for connectors which require special tools or processes.
22. Color-code chassis wiring.
23. Identify equipment assemblies and parts.
24. Ground inactive wires installed in long lines (conduit or cable) to allow for stray or static electricity discharge.
25. On plug and convenience outlets for portable tools and equipment, include provisions for automatically grounding the case of such equipment when the plug is mated to the receptacle.
26. Do not use shields, excepting coaxial cables, as a current-carrying ground connection.
27. Design and construct the equipment to ensure that all external parts, surfaces, and shields, exclusive of antenna and transmission-line terminals, are at ground potential at all times during normal operation.
28. Ensure that the design considers ground faults and voltage limits established on a basis of hazardous location.
29. Specify that the ground connection to the chassis or frame provides a corrosion-resistant connection.
30. Terminate shielding a sufficient distance from exposed conductors to prevent shorting or arcing between the conductor and the shielding.
31. Secure shielding adequately to prevent contact with exposed current-carrying parts.
32. Provide primary circuits and cables with overload devices to protect against damage by fire, explosion, or overheat due to electrical overload.
33. Furnish fuses that can be replaced without the use of tools.
34. Attach at least one spare fuse of each type and rating to applicable units of the set.
35. Locate fuses at a convenient, serviceable point so they may be readily replaced.
36. Use blown-fuse indicators where practicable.
37. Ascertain that normal performance characteristics of the source or load are not altered by the use of protective devices.
38. Ensure that circuit breaker restoring features are readily accessible to the operator, and a visual indication is given when the breaker is tripped.
39. Protect personnel from accidental contact with voltages exceeding 30 volts rms or dc while operating a complete piece of equipment.
40. Protect personnel from voltage hazards by the use of electrical interlocks in accordance with MIL-STD-454 or industry practice.
41. Provide grounding rods in all portable transmitting equipment of sufficient size where voltages are in excess of 70 volts rms.

42. Provide ground studs to accommodate a portable grounding rod for transmitters of smaller physical size where voltages exceed 70 volts rms or dc.
43. Provide personnel barriers or guards on all contacts or terminals exhibiting voltages between 70 and 500 volts rms or dc with respect to ground.
44. Holes in the barrier may be provided for maintenance and testing.
45. Completely enclose assemblies operating at potentials in excess of 500 volts rms or dc from the remainder of the assembly.
46. Mark clearly the voltage present on contacts and terminals exceeding 500 volts rms or dc.
47. Furnish voltage dividers or other means to allow the safe measurement of potential in excess of 1000 volts peak.
48. Design equipment exhibiting a radiation hazard (e.g., microwave or x-ray) within the limits of MIL-R-9673 or FDA standards.
49. Provide discharging devices to discharge high-voltage circuits and capacitors unless they discharge to 30 volts dc within 2 seconds or less.
50. Ensure that these protective devices are positive acting, highly reliable, and actuate automatically when the case or rack is opened.
51. Ensure that shorting bars are actuated either by mechanical release or by an electrical solenoid when the door or cover is open.
52. When resistive bleeder networks are used to discharge capacitors, ensure that the bleeder network consists of at least two equal-valued resistors in parallel.
53. The particular discharging device that is chosen must insure that the capacitor is discharged to 30 volts dc within 2 seconds.
54. Ground or insulate controls, control shafts, knobs, or levers to prevent shock or burns to personnel.
55. Ascertain that the temperature of front panels and operating controls does not exceed 43°C at an ambient temperature of 25°C.
56. Ensure that the temperature of exposed parts and equipment enclosures which may be contacted by operating personnel does not exceed 60°C at an ambient temperature of 25°C.
57. Locate, recess, or guard critical switches, breakers, and similar controls in a manner to prevent accidental displacement or activation.
58. Design mechanical linkage, instrument leads, and electrical connections to positively prevent inadvertent reversing or cross-connection.
59. Avoid sharp projections, corners, or edges on cabinets, doors, hinged covers, and similar parts of equipment.
60. Guard or protect all moving mechanical parts such as gears, fans, and bolts when the equipment is complete and operating.
61. Protect personnel from possible injury from implosion of cathode-ray tubes.
62. In the event of meter failure, assure that meters possess overload bypass or alternate features to eliminate high-voltage potential at the meter terminals.
63. Do not specify metal ladders for use around electrical/electronic equipment and facilities.
64. Provide adequate equipment cooling for performance under any combination of service conditions.
65. Locate or configure ventilation holes so that foreign objects cannot be inserted inadvertently to contact high-voltage sources.
66. Design equipment to withstand any probable combination of environmental conditions without mechanical or electrical malfunction.

67. Use inherently safe (e.g., explosion-proof, dustproof, moisture-proof) equipment in all hazardous environments.

Installation and Maintenance

1. Provide proper equipment accesses to all points, units, and components which may require testing, adjustment, maintenance, or repair.
2. Locate accesses away from dangerous mechanical or electrical components where possible; otherwise, placard such accesses as to the potential hazard.
3. Furnish accesses with internal fillets, or with rubber, fiber, or plastic if they might injure the operator's hands or arms.
4. Provide screwdriver guides to adjustment points which must be operated near high voltages.
5. Position equipment components and wiring to prevent damage from opening and closing the assembly.
6. Ensure that units are small and light enough for one person to carry and handle, whenever this is feasible.
7. Provide convenient handles on units to assist in removal, replacement, or carrying.
8. Provide rests, stands, or other protectors to prevent damage to delicate parts when elements of the equipment are removed for repair.
9. Furnish limit-stops (with overrides) on all pullout racks and drawers.
10. Provide guide pins on subassemblies for alignment during mounting.
11. Locate components so there is sufficient space to use test probes, soldering irons, and similar tools without difficulty.
12. Do not use resistors, capacitors, and wiring that interfere with tube replacement.
13. Locate tubes so they can be replaced without removing assemblies and subassemblies.
14. Locate cables so they cannot be abraded, chafed, or used for handholds.
15. Locate cables so they are not bent and unbent sharply when they are connected and disconnected.
16. Route cables so they cannot be pinched by doors, lids, or covers.
17. Provide delicate conductors such as wave guides and high-frequency cables with guards, protective routing, or similar protection.
18. Incorporate failsafe features into equipment designs and installations where the failure or malfunction of the equipment may injure the operator or damage the equipment or adjacent equipment.
19. Do not use components containing mercury unless it is essential. If it becomes necessary, design to minimize the probability of damage which would result from mercury spillage.
20. Ensure that system verification test circuits do not indicate the command; rather, that they indicate the system's actual response.
21. Design system monitors and test circuits so that no hazard to the crew is presented.
22. Provide that power application will not actuate critical circuits as a result of function switches which may be cycled without indicating the on-off position during a power-off phase (i.e., push on/push off switches).
23. Provide continuous monitoring for tests requiring judgments rather than standards.

Electromagnetic Compatibility

1. Use filters with the following EMI-producing circuits: choppers, converters, inverters, relays, dc motors, switches, and clocks or timing circuits with fast rise time or high repetition circuits.
2. Filter transformer-rectifier outputs.

3. Electrostatically shield the transformer.
4. Where applicable, use components with inherent shielding (such as cupreous tuning inductors).
5. Use bandpass filtering on transmitter outputs and receiver inputs.
6. Ensure that the shielding material is suitable for the type of field and for the frequency range involved.
7. Use decoupling capacitors on internal power connections.
8. Use feed-through capacitors for internal connections of circuits and as bulkhead-mounted headers.
9. Use shielded subassemblies in the equipment, where appropriate.
10. Use RF chokes and inductors to confine the RF energy to desired circuits.
11. Where applicable, use parts of internal chassis to obtain shielding.
12. Use waveguide-below-cutoff techniques for chassis openings (such as tuning adjustments or air cooling).
13. Ensure that low-level or susceptible circuits are physically separated from EMI-producing circuits within an enclosure.
14. Use toroids to minimize the leakage fields of inductors.
15. Ensure that inductors have been cross-oriented to minimize coupling.

Spurious Responses

1. If possible, operate components in linear rather than nonlinear regions.
2. Use crystal-controlled circuits.
3. Make the best possible choice of multiplier stages.
4. Use crystal filters, bandpass filters, tank circuits, tuned stages, and other narrow-band devices.
5. Use radio frequency (RF) trap circuits for known or expected spurious outputs or responses.
6. Ensure that circuits are used which inherently discriminate against creation or passage of certain harmonics (such as push-pull outputs of amplifiers, balanced mixer-ring coupler combinations, or other hybrid circuits of a similar nature).
7. Use circuits of balanced or symmetrical design.
8. Use diodes or other biasing devices to establish definite minimum or maximum actuation levels for circuits.
9. Where applicable, use coincidence circuits, time-delay circuits, or similar logic circuits.
10. Where applicable, use circuits utilizing coded inputs and outputs.
11. Ensure that filtering is accomplished at subsystem levels, especially multiplier stages.
12. Decouple RF circuits from power supplies.
13. Use short-lead lengths in RF circuits.
14. Ensure that internal wire routing has been controlled.
15. Ensure physical and electrical isolation of circuits potentially capable of producing or of being susceptible to spurious energy.
16. Ensure that internal subassemblies are shielded and filtered to prevent undesired modulation.
17. Choose components and devices that will minimize frequency drift or random modulation due to temperature, aging, vibration, etc.
18. Ensure that potentially susceptible circuits are sufficiently shielded against external RF fields, including low-frequency magnetic fields.
19. Take special precautions to prevent responses at receiver image frequencies.

20. Use shielded antenna inputs.
21. Choose operating frequencies that will not conflict with known existing frequencies or their harmonics.
22. Ensure that the proper power levels of generated frequencies are used in critical places, such as at the local oscillator stages of receivers or at multiplier and output stages of transmitters.
23. Control circuitry (other than RF) of receivers and transmitters (such as power connections, telemetry connections, and monitoring points) to prevent RF coupling to other circuits.
24. Use special methods (such as klystrons and oscillators) to avoid spurious modes of operation of circuit elements.

Spurious Resonances

1. Use short-lead lengths for all components, especially capacitors in RF circuits.
2. Use damping components to minimize oscillation.
3. Use feed-through capacitors for interstage coupling and isolation and for power input connections to RF circuitry.
4. Use waveguide-below-cutoff techniques for all required openings in enclosures.
5. Minimize the number of enclosures and openings.
6. Avoid critical dimensions. Consider the enclosure or subenclosure as an RF cavity.
7. Use tuning methods which minimize nodes or harmonic generation.
8. Design all feedback loops to prevent oscillation under worst-case conditions.
9. Isolate the high-power and low-power stages of units.
10. Ensure that the enclosure bonding is adequate for the known critical radio frequencies.
11. Control component tolerances to prevent frequency drift, mode switching, etc., due to temperature, aging, etc.
12. Use RF components throughout RF stages; i.e., use components that are not self-resonant in the intended frequency range.
13. Use circuits which discriminate against spurious resonance.

Methods of Obtaining Continuous Shielding on Equipment Using Pressure or Hermetic Seals

1. Mechanically design the enclosure to assure sufficient bonding pressure between mating parts.
2. Design the chassis to minimize the number of openings.
3. Analyze each opening in the enclosure to determine the need for RF gaskets, waveguide-below-cutoff techniques, screening, etc.
4. Evaluate the minimum attenuation needed by the enclosure.
5. Ensure that the mating surface pressure, area, finish, or tolerance do not degrade the expected attenuation of the enclosure seams.
6. Avoid using dissimilar metals in the enclosure and ensure that metals are compatible with the expected environment.
7. If RF gaskets are used, ensure that the design is adequate to optimum pressure, class of joint or seam, choice of gasket mounting, size of gasket, attenuation of gasket, etc.
8. Ensure that subenclosures are properly attached to the main enclosure.
9. Ensure that the thickness of case material is adequate to attenuate the expected fields to a tolerable level.
10. Ensure that the estimated added attenuation is provided by shielded subenclosures.

11. Ensure that composite shielding is provided by the enclosure, subenclosure, waveguide-below-cutoff openings, gasket seams, screened openings, or normal mating surfaces.
12. Ensure that associated external cabling does not degrade the required attenuation levels.

Interference-Free Components

1. Use diodes and other suppression components across relay coils.
2. Use RC circuits across switch and relay contacts.
3. Use solid state switches instead of mechanical switches.
4. Ensure that capacitors are being used directly across DC motor brushes.
5. Use electrostatically shielded transformers.
6. Use matched diodes in balanced mixers.
7. Use toroids or other low-leakage field inductors, where applicable.
8. Use nonself-resonant components such as feed-through capacitors.
9. Use bulkhead-mounted components.
10. Use crystal filters.
11. Use twisted pair, twisted triad, or shielded wire.
12. Use balanced-circuit designs.
13. Use diodes or other bias devices to establish definite maximum or minimum actuation levels.
14. Use connectors as inherent parts of filters.
15. Use separate connectors for sensitive and EMI-producing circuits.
16. Use crystals as frequency sources.
17. Use selective waveguide or coaxial components, such as diplexers.
18. Use lossy line techniques to attenuate harmonics.
19. Use temperature-compensated components to minimize drift, etc.
20. Use DC blocks when applicable.

Shielding between Systems

1. Design shielded wires and enclosures to provide maximum shielding efficiency.
2. Use a minimum number of joints, seams, gasket seals, and openings.
3. Use conductive material for gasket seals.
4. Compress all RF gaskets.
5. Use a minimum number of inspection plates, adjustment holes, and screened ventilation ports.
6. Check equipment enclosure for RF leaks through meters, toggle switches, indicator lamps, fuse holders, handles, access doors, and any other openings.
7. Electrically bond screens and honeycomb material to its frame.
8. Whenever possible, electrically bond all discontinuities.
9. Ensure that shielding interfaces with other EMC design considerations.
10. Through good bonding, ensure that seams are electromagnetically tight.
11. Ensure that the RF impedance of the seam does not differ appreciably from that of the materials being joined.
12. Specify that all mating surfaces be cleaned before bonding.
13. Ensure that all protective coatings having a conductivity less than that of the metals being

bonded are removed from the contact areas of the two mating surfaces before the bond connection is made.

14. When protective coatings are necessary, design them so that they can be easily removed from the mating surfaces.
15. To avoid oxidation, require that mating surfaces be bonded immediately after protective coatings are removed.
16. When pressure bonds are required, specify that the surfaces be clean and dry before mating and that they be held together under pressure.
17. Insert RF gasket material (if used) between the mating surfaces and maintain a high pressure against the seam.
18. Ensure that mating surfaces are cleaned thoroughly before the gasket material is inserted.
19. When woven material is used for shielding, perform necessary measurements to validate the material's shielding effectiveness and the configuration intended for use in the system.

Enclosures

1. Design lead entry and exit to:
   a. Isolate leads likely to be noisy (such as power leads) from other leads, or if connectors are used employ separate connectors.
   b. Avoid grounding a power return lead internally if the total system follows the wired power return concept.
   c. Ensure that a system or subsystem having balanced symmetrical input circuits does not use a sensing device or transducer that uses the shield for a signal return.
2. Maintain strict control of the bonding of doors and access cover plates.
3. To prevent compromises of skin conductivity in the area of the antenna:
   a. Ensure that there are no doors or access holes in the antenna area.
   b. Ensure that the skin and fairings are made of highly conductive material such as aluminum.
   c. Ensure that the skin and fairing joints, laps, and seals have a clean, bare metal-to-metal contact.
   d. Ensure that antenna leads are coaxial or waveguide.
   e. Ensure that coaxial shields are at ground potential at point of exit.

Cables

1. Prevent capacitive coupling at low frequency by shielding.
2. When routing wires and cables between subsystems, ensure coordination between engineering factions involved.
3. Analyze cabling for both inductive and capacitive coupling.
4. Separate power wires from signal wires and input lines from output lines.
5. Route susceptible wires away from power supplies, transformers, and other high-power devices.
6. Use twisted pairs instead of shielding power cables.
7. Select and mate coaxial cables with RF connectors according to MIL-HDBK-216.
8. Ensure that cables (wires) interface with other EMC design considerations (shielding, filtering, and bonding).

Low-Frequency Coupling

1. Filter the source of interfering signals.
2. Reduce inductive coupling by reducing the physical area enclosed by the pickup loop and the source loop.
3. Restrict the loop area in the bypass capacitor's grounding return.

4. Reduce coupling by separating power wires from signal wires and input lines from output lines (do not install in same wire bundle or connector).
5. Use shielding to minimize RF coupling.
6. To prevent coupling, avoid passing cables near a magnetic circuit.
7. Ensure that interference is not introduced by magnetic coupling.

High-Frequency Coupling

1. Ensure that filters are properly wired to prevent inductive coupling.
2. At high frequencies, direct grounding concepts toward massive multiple grounding practices.
3. Ensure that all connectors are electromagnetically tight to reduce RF currents external to the shield.
4. Provide a massive ground plane between equipments connected to the cable, and locate the cable close to the ground plane.
5. Avoid RF currents to the external surface of the cable shield.
6. Ensure that open-end wires are not pickup points for RF.
7. Insulate shielded cable sheaths at high frequencies so that they cannot make contact and form common return connections with other shielded cables.

Cable Measurements

1. Make capacitive coupling measurements with the load end of the source interference cable open-circuited.
2. Make inductive coupling measurements with the load end of the source interference cable short-circuited.

Transmission Lines

1. Make a good bond between the cable shield and the shell of the connector.
2. Eliminate all air gaps in the connector.
3. Use connectors built to close mechanical tolerances.
4. Cap all panel mounted connectors not in use.
5. Reduce transmission line interference by matching of the line characteristic impedance to the load impedance.
6. Use triple-shielded coax where pulse generators are separate from the transmitter or other load.

Connectors

1. Select electrical and electronic connectors in accordance with MIL-HDBK-216 and MIL-STD-454 (Requirement 10) where necessary. If necessary to design your own connectors:
2. Design connectors to have negligible resistance.
3. Design connectors to have surfaces which will not corrode, tarnish, oxidize, or be attacked by organic or inorganic contamination.
4. Design connectors to have surfaces which will not gouge or be gouged during mating.
5. Design connectors to permit foolproof alignment under field conditions without pin bending.
6. Design connectors to transmit and maintain adequate force to the contact surfaces for the life of the connector.
7. Design connectors to have surface coefficients of friction low enough so that withdrawal-insertion abrasion will not cause contact resistance to exceed acceptable values.

8. Design connectors to minimize the accumulation of dirt, moisture, fumes, and other contaminants between mating halves, or in pin areas.
9. Design the physical configuration of the connector to minimize damage and deterioration due to use.
10. Ensure that the connector shell has a conductive finish.
11. Route signal and power circuits in separate connectors.
12. Route input and output signal circuits in separate connectors.
13. Provide for termination of shields.
14. When shielded wires are used, provide for peripheral termination.
15. Design shielding termination so that maintenance will not degrade the shielding characteristics.
16. Consider the use of filter pins in the connector.
17. Provide for the use of shielded (coaxial) pins for circuits which must have isolated continuous circuits.
18. Ensure that electrical continuity through the shell is adequate by performing vibration tests.
19. Ensure that chassis- or bulkhead-mounted connectors are mounted by methods that ensure good electrical connections.
20. When testing connectors, use the highest frequency to which the loads are susceptible.
21. When testing connectors, use a safety factor of 10 to measure ac impedance.
22. Submit the connector to low-level, low-impedance test, then submit it to an environmental test of mechanical forces, wear, and corrosion to detect and isolate high impedance contacts.
23. Ensure adequate contact floating to permit insertion without binding, and prevent wedging by correct pin layout.
24. Properly place guide pins to reduce bending, gouging, and abrasion due to misalignment.
25. Provide guides to help in the alignment of connectors.
26. Ensure that the male pins are protected to reduce pin damage.
27. Provide inexpensive protective plastic caps for use during handling and storage of the connectors.
28. Design connectors to prevent entry of moisture, fumes, contaminants, and foreign objects by potting or other means.
29. Use clamps to prevent wires from being pulled and twisted from their contacts.
30. Ensure good contact pressure over a long time by using low-fatigue, high-resilience spring materials.
31. Allow for impedance buildup during system life in the initial design and production phases.
32. Build in tolerable design safety factors to allow for intercabling deterioration during the operational life of the system.
33. Check limits to ensure that the intercabling between the checkout equipment and the system will not cause significant voltage drops.
34. Systems/subsystems engineering personnel must ensure compatibility of cable connectors between subsystems.

Connector Shielding
1. Ensure that the shielding effectiveness of the mated connector equals or exceeds that of an equal length of the cable utilized in the circuit.
2. For shielding effectiveness, properly terminate cable shields.
3. Ground the entire periphery of the shield to a low-impedance reference. Do not use epoxy or other synthetic conducting material for bonding this ground.

4. Individually terminate all shields for connectors that are routed through multipin coaxial connectors.
5. Ensure that there is no break in the shield through the connector and cable which would allow RF energy to leak into the power circuit.
6. Ensure that the connector can withstand environmental conditions (vibration, high and low temperatures, corrosion, etc.) without degradation of the shielding characteristics of the connector.
7. Ensure that the connector's shield at the interface of the two connector halves makes positive contact before the two power contacts mate, and maintains this contact until after the power contacts break.
8. Isolate contacts in the connector's mating sections to preclude the possibility of field personnel accidentally getting a shock by touching the socket (mate) contacts with either their fingers of the mating connector shell while taking the connectors apart.

Bonding and Grounding

1. A uniform grounding philosophy is mandatory to avoid conductive coupling, low impedance ground loops, and hazardous operating conditions.
2. Clean all bare metal mating surfaces.
3. Weld all mating surfaces, when possible.
4. Where protective films are absolutely required, ensure that the film material is a good conductor. Some suitable protective films are silver or gold plating or other plated metals of good conductivity (Oakite #36, Alodine #1000, Iridite #14, and Iridite #18P).
5. Ensure that the fastening method exerts sufficient pressure to hold the surfaces in contact in the presence of deforming stresses, shock, and vibrations associated with the equipment and its environment.
6. If the surfaces are not inert in their storage and operating environments, provide surface protection according to Item 4 or take other suitable measures to ensure the maintenance of the bond for the service life of the equipment.
7. Do not use paint to establish an electrical or RF bond.
8. Do not use threads of screws or bolts to establish RF bonds.
9. Do not use ohmmeters to evaluate RF bonds or RF gaskets.
10. Compress all RF gaskets.
11. Check for impedance coupling.
12. Check for ground loops and floating grounds.
13. Ensure good electrical bonding practices for ground terminations.
14. To achieve the lowest resistance between surfaces:
    a. Do not use films or layers of material between the surfaces unless the film material is a better conductor than the material being bonded.
    b. Ensure that the mating surfaces are smooth and contoured so that maximum surface area is in actual contact.
15. When the bonding application requires good shielding effectiveness to RF, determine the bonding impedance at 1 MHz as well as the direct current.
16. Prepare aluminum and aluminum alloy surfaces for bonding according to MIL-A-5002 and MIL-C-5541.
17. Prepare magnesium alloy surfaces for bonding according to MIL-M-3171. However do not use magnesium as power returns.
18. Clean copper, brass, bronze, nickel, and silver for bonding by degreasing and then slightly etching the surface.
19. Provide a protective finish for all surfaces used for bonding.

20. Treat all exposed metal surfaces so as to be wear-resistant.
21. Use indirect bonding methods when items are subject to shock and vibration or when sections are removable.
22. Provide a means of achieving flanging pressure up to 68.95 kPa (10 psi) to fully realize the low resistivity of the conductive paste.
23. Design gaskets to (*a*) Ensure that the gasket will compensate for the surface discontinuities of the joint. (*b*) Provide correct height and pressure. (*c*) Contain adequate resiliency.

Corrosion Involving Dissimilar Metals

1. To avoid dissimilar metal corrosion, adhere to the requirements of MIL-STD-889.
2. To reduce galvanic reaction, insert a third metal (intermediate in the electromotive series) in the bond between the dissimilar metals.
3. Specify additional finishes, such as paint or plating, with caution. Finishing of the anodic material alone may produce severe corrosion at any finish imperfection.
4. When dissimilar metals are in contact, do not cover the surface of the anodic material alone; cover the surface of both metals or just the cathodic metal.
5. If dissimilar metals cannot be avoided, minimize corrosion by moisture-proofing the bonded areas.
6. Use MIL-STD-889 for selection of suitable sealant materials.

Grounding Considerations

1. Ensure that conduits will prevent shock hazard and carry lightning current.
2. Ensure that conduits do not become a source of interference.
3. To make an RF-tight conduit, ensure that connections are properly bonded.
4. Keep current off conduits to prevent ground loops and conductive coupling.
5. Weld or solder completely shielded (RF) enclosures directly to the equipment chassis with one continuous seam around the base for the best grounding.
6. Terminate shielded and coaxial cables by a continuous weld around the periphery of the opening in the enclosure.
7. Attach shielded and coaxial cables to the enclosure through RF-type connectors.
8. If long wire grounds are necessary, use large diameter, 6.35 mm ($\frac{1}{4}$ in) or larger, copper bus or stranded wire between equipment and ground termination.
9. To reduce RF coupling, make ground leads direct and short as possible and also observe any resonant frequency effects.
10. To reduce conductive coupling, keep ground leads away from conduits, magnetic and RF fields, and other noise-producing wires.
11. To reduce the potential explosion hazard, ensure that an adequate bond exists between the equipment's mounting flange and the basic structure.

Filtering

1. Filter the interference source.
2. Suppress all spurious signals.
3. Design nonsusceptible circuits.
4. Ensure that the filter elements interface with other EMC suppression measures.
5. Use the following methods to reduce the spurious outputs of a transmitter:
    a. Reduce the level of spurious outputs by operating the various components in the transmitter in a more linear operating region.
    b. Incorporate shielding between circuits to eliminate undesirable coupling of signals.

6. Choose the elements of the filter so that the impedance network matches the line into which it is inserted.
7. Ensure that the filter's voltage ratings are sufficient to provide reliable operation under the extreme conditions shown in MIL-STD-704.
8. Determine the maximum allowable voltage drop through the filter and design accordingly.
9. Ensure that the voltage drop caused by a filter does not exceed the total drop permitted by MIL-W-5088.
10. Ensure that the current rating is for the maximum allowable continuous operation of the filter.
11. Ensure that the safety factors used in rating filters are consistent with those used for other circuit components.
12. Ensure that ground leads on capacitors and filter enclosures are short as possible for RF interference filtering.

Test Equipment

1. If barriers must be replaced, serviced, or recharged periodically, it is useful that the front panel has a place to record the next servicing date and action.
2. If rechargeable batteries are used, consider providing an indicator to show the operating time available for use until recharging is required.
3. Provide for semiautomatic operation of all instruments intended for laboratory use.

Static Charges

1. Install static dischargers at the points of static charge accumulation.
2. Do not place dischargers closer than 304.8 mm (12 in) apart due to mutual shielding.
3. Ensure that the surface preparation and treatment is compatible with the operational environment.

Discrete Components

1. Determine operating temperatures, voltages, currents, humidity, etc.
2. Determine tolerance limits for operation.
3. Determine allowable tolerance buildup in circuit (i.e., how much total variability in resistors, etc., will be allowed; include variability due to inherent manufacture of component, aging, temperature, and so forth).
4. In critical applications—where component must work close to temperature limits—have wattage ratings been adjusted to account for possible short leads, component density, etc.?
5. Have surge voltages, other transients, and possible ac ripple been taken into consideration?
6. Secure all components heavier than ½ ounce to circuit boards.
7. For amplification devices such as transistors, ensure that the catalog description is proper for your circuit application.
8. Consider substitutions when any rating of transistors, capacitors, etc., is approached in circuit.
9. For transistors, operational amplifiers, etc., consider the consequences of drift, changing power gain, noise, leakage current and beta (for transistors).
10. For diodes (as rectifiers) consider consequences of inverse voltage and inverse current.
11. For Zeners, what reference voltage is expected?
12. Are transformers, chokes, and coils adequately shielded?
13. Is the highest operating frequency of the choke or coil above the resonant frequency? (Avoid this condition.)
14. Are selected chokes, etc., adequate to handle possible deviations in current and voltage beyond normal circuit operations?

Relays

1. Have the number of actuations per product lifetime been calculated?
2. Have the number of actuations per critical short period of time been calculated?
3. Do catalog specifications include all possible relay orientations?
4. Do catalog specifications take acceptable ripple and voltage drift into account?
5. Does your circuit depend on critical parameters for relay opening or closing time?
6. Has the coil's predictable increase in resistance with age or with temperature buildup been taken into account in circuit design?
7. Has relay arcing on opening been accounted for and protected against? Possible consequences include electromagnetic interference and explosion.

Power Supplies

1. Are expected variations in input voltage and frequency designed for?
2. Is the circuit protected against excessive drops in line voltage, or variations in line frequency?
3. Especially for dc supplies, is ripple within tolerances?
4. What voltages and currents can be expected due to failure of critical components in the power supply?
5. Has power supply waveform shape been taken into consideration?
6. What variations in input and output impedance can be tolerated, and what are expected in normal use?
7. Are all severe impedance mismatches protected against by fusing or circuit breakers?
8. What cable lengths are assumed on input and output terminals?
9. Have feedback loops been checked for phase margin, coupling, decoupling, etc.?
10. Do adjustments have to be made in another part of the circuit when a power supply (or a major component of a power supply) is replaced?
11. Are parasitic oscillations possible? Have they been tested for? Improved manufacturing techniques are producing solid-state devices that often react to high-frequency oscillations, even when the same devices did not exhibit such reactions in earlier years.

Component Testing

1. Are production and preproduction tests reflective of the actual use environment?
2. Have measures been taken to trace parts with excessive failure rates in the field?
3. Are critical components traceable back to the manufacturer?
4. Have estimated mean lives of circuit segments been calculated from available data?
5. Have random failure-rate data been consulted for critical parts (ones that carry high currents and/or voltages, for example)?

HYDRAULIC EQUIPMENT AND SYSTEMS

General

1. Ensure that the system hydrostatic proof pressure rating (the pressure at which the system is tested) is a minimum of 1.5 times the operating pressure.
2. Comply with MIL-T-83431 when designing hazardous equipment, utilizing MIL-C-7024, Type II test fluid and nonhazardous jet engine component test equipment.
3. Design the systems to operate within the 0 to 15,000 psig range ideally.

4. Limit temperatures for petroleum base hydraulic fluid to a maximum of 135°F. Limit synthetic fluid to a maximum of 140°F.
5. Comply with MIL-T-83431 requirements for test stands utilized in a hazardous area.

Component and Fluid Selection

1. Check all materials for fluid compatibility.
2. Ensure that the system fluid requirements will not exceed two-thirds the capacity of the reservoir.
3. Install a positive pressure indicating device on the reservoir.
4. Install a drain plug at the lowest point in the reservoir.
5. Vent the reservoir in such a manner that it will not create a hazardous condition to personnel or equipment.
6. Locate the reservoir where there is free circulation of air.
7. Install a fluid level gage on the reservoir.
8. Provide a pressure regulator where a power pump is used.
9. Ensure that no possibility exists for interconnecting pressure and return systems.
10. Design a component so that it cannot be installed incorrectly.
11. Ensure that the downstream structural limits cannot be exceeded.
12. Ensure that the pump is driven by the proper rated horsepower.
13. Ensure the pump is unloaded during the idle cycle.
14. Identify all piping in accordance with MIL-STD-1247.
15. Ensure that the minimum bend radius is 2.5 to 3 times the inside diameter of the tubing.
16. Provide sufficient tube and pipe supports.
17. Ensure that flexible hose is 5 to 8 percent of the total hose length allocated for slack.
18. Protect all transfer lines from chafing.
19. Provide backup rings where pressures can cause O-ring extrusion.
20. Eliminate sharp corners to reduce O-ring installation damage.
21. Specify the use of nonflammable hydraulic fluid.
22. Design emergency systems to be completely independent of primary systems.
23. Design system routing to bypass inhabited areas or provide alternate protective measures.
24. Provide a filter for the pump's suction line.
25. Use high-pressure fittings with extra heavy or double heavy pipe.
26. Ensure that internal surfaces of components and tubing have rounded corners and do not invite fatigue failure.

Contamination Control

1. Ensure that the filter does not create an excessive pressure drop.
2. Design filter cases to the minimum system safety factor.

Temperature and Pressure Considerations in the Overall System

1. Normally limit hydraulic system pressure to 3000 psi (pressures up to 10,000 psi are being evaluated).
2. Avoid operating temperatures in excess of those specified in MIL-H-5400 (with fluid specified).

3. Provide sufficient coolers to maintain temperatures compatible with the fluid and seals.
4. Specify burst and proof pressures as detailed in MIL-H-5440, MIL-H-8891, or MIL-H-25475.

PRESSURIZATION AND PNEUMATIC EQUIPMENT AND SYSTEMS

General

1. Ensure that lubricants and other materials are acceptable for use with the system gas.
2. Identify all lines by contents, pressure, and direction of flow.
3. Ensure that provisions are made to prevent installation of components in reverse.
4. Key or size adjacent or incompatible pressure connectors so that it is physically impossible to connect the wrong unit or pressure level.
5. Avoid routing high-pressure gas lines through inhabited areas.
6. Provide a positive pressure monitoring device between all isolation control valves.
7. Install bleed valves wherever entrapment of gases can occur.
8. Ensure that remote-control valves have a positive position indicator at the operator's station.
9. Identify hand valves to indicate function and sequence of operation.
10. Avoid locating manual control valves so that an operator must change his position to adjust and monitor the pressure.
11. Provide pressure regulation whenever the source pressure can exceed the system's proof pressure or the desired working pressure.
12. Provide system protection so that a regulator malfunction will not cause downstream system failure.
13. Ensure that the system working pressure is not greater than 75 percent of the maximum regulator capacity.
14. Ensure that regulator bypass capabilities do not exist where system downstream components will not meet full upstream pressure requirements.
15. Provide pressure readout to ensure that pressure is below hazard levels.
16. Locate a pressure readout device as close as practical to the pressure regulator.
17. Specify separate pressurization sources downstream of primary regulation when pressurizing noncompatible commodities.
18. Equip all direct pressure readout gages with a shutterproof safety glass, or a plastic shield installed over the face, and a blowout plug, disk, or vent installed in the case.
19. Locate safety relief valves on the low-pressure side of each pressure regulator where the components or piping cannot meet the requirements of full upstream pressure.
20. Ensure that there are no obstructions downstream of the relief valve or burst disk outlet.
21. Ensure that shutoff valves are not used for maintenance purposes, unless a means for monitoring and bleeding trapped pressure is provided, and the requirements of ASME Code for unfired pressure vessels Appendix M, Paragraph UA354 are met.
22. Provide a means for locking these valves in the open position when the system is pressurized.
23. Install pressure relief valves as close as possible to the pressure regulators.
24. Install relief ports so that escaping gases or vapors will not be hazardous to personnel or equipment.
25. Provide separate lines for vent relief and vessel pressurization.
26. Ensure that relief valves will not permit the system pressure to exceed 110 percent of the allowable working pressure or exceed the downstream structural limits in the event of an upstream regulator failure.

27. Size relief valves to exceed the maximum flow capacity of the pressure source.
28. Install bleed valves and pressure-indicating devices between the relief valve and burst disk to indicate burst disk leakage and allow system pressure bleed.
29. Ensure that fragments from the burst disk will in no way render the relief valve inoperative.
30. If the use of high-pressure flexible hose cannot be avoided, use rubber, Teflon, high-density polyethylene, and metal where possible.
31. Specify periodic proof-pressure tests prior to installation.
32. Avoid using hose connections of the same type and size where inadvertent connection can be made to a higher rated working pressure or a different service commodity.
33. Identify all hose as to rated working pressure and date of certification.
34. Provide a means of plugging or capping the hose when not in use.
35. Design restraining devices to contain at least 150 percent of the maximum calculated open line force pressure of the hose.
36. Use of sandbags or shotbags is undesirable and should not be depended upon.
37. Provide protection where lines or components can be damaged.
38. Do not use components containing mercury unless it is essential. If it becomes necessary, design to minimize the probability of damage which would result from mercury spillage.

High-Pressure Oxygen

1. Provide remote operation for high-pressure oxygen systems.
2. Use nonrotating poppets, slow-closing valves, and nonchattering regulators and relief valves to reduce the possibility of generating impact ignition energy.
3. Ensure that components and systems are qualified and acceptable for use in the intended environment.
4. Specify rigid cleaning and filtration requirements.
5. Ensure that contaminants are not introduced into the system from improper use of materials or lubricants.
6. Continuously ground piping and equipment to reduce triboelectric ignition potential.

Pressure Vessels

1. Ensure that proper proof checks are specified.
2. Equip pressure vessels with a positive pressure indicating device.
3. Provide reservoirs and storage vessels with isolation valves for maintenance.
4. Ensure that storage pressure can be bled off to allow replacement of components.
5. Ensure that burst disk fragments or fluid from a burst part do not foul other equipment or flame.

Pneumatic Systems

1. When possible select fire- and combustion-resistant compressor lubricating oil.
2. Equip all hoses with couplings which automatically lock whenever pressure is applied.
3. Where possible, select high-speed rotating equipment that is capable of containing a disintegrated rotor.
4. Specify speed-limiting devices that will prevent compressor overspeed.
5. Ensure that compressor equipment is supported so that unbalance vibration due to component failure will not cause failure of the supports.
6. Use relief valves, blowout disks, or equally effective devices to relieve overpressures.

7. Ensure that relief devices discharge away from personnel and that blown disk particles are contained so that they do not cause additional damage to equipment or injury to personnel.
8. Ensure that the compressor is automatically shut down whenever the inlet pressure drops below minimum established suction pressure.
9. Provide a sufficient number of bleed valves so that all receivers, lines, and components can be bled down to zero pressure prior to maintenance operations.
10. Select pressure tanks and reservoirs that are comparable with the system's working range.
11. Locate check valves to prevent critical air loss.
12. Ensure that selection of compressors has minimized explosion hazard.
13. Consider explosion hazards when selecting compressors.
14. Provide relatively cool compressor inlet air.
15. Design all pressure tanks and reservoirs in accordance with applicable codes snd standards.
16. Select pressure tanks and reservoirs that are comparable with the system working range.

Pressurization Systems

1. Ensure that inert gases cannot be introduced into inhabited areas.
2. Support all components on structural members.
3. Specify pressure relief where source pressure can exceed the design levels of the system.
4. Ensure that storage pressure can be read and bled off to allow replacement of components.
5. Include provisions for bleeding trapped gas from between components.
6. Equip all Bourdon tube (direct pressure readout) gages with shatterproof glass and blowout plugs.

FUEL AND STORAGE SYSTEMS

Fluid Compatibility

1. Design incompatible systems so that it is impossible to interconnect them.
2. Separate incompatible fluid systems to prevent inadvertent mixing.
3. Use sleeves or barriers to isolate exposed fluid lines.
4. Use components that are qualified for use with the system fluid.
5. Select fluid line insulation that cannot react chemically with the system fluid.
6. Select nonabsorbent fluid line insulation.
7. Use compatible cleaning agents.
8. Establish procedures to purge cleaning agents from the fluid system.
9. Provide overpressure relief where fluid lines or components may be exposed to fire.
10. Ensure that any single failure will not allow tank pressure to exceed the tank's structural limitations.
11. Provide underpressure relief during defueling operations.
12. Use electrical equipment that is approved for operation with the specific fuel or propellant.
13. Locate fluid components and systems so that danger of ignition in hazard areas is minimized.
14. Omit all possible connectors from inhabited areas.
15. Protect fuel lines from cargo movement.
16. Route fuel, propellant, and oxidizer lines as much as possible within their own tank to minimize the effects of leakage.

17. Ensure that components are mounted on structure and not supported by attached tubing.
18. Ensure that tubing is adequately supported to prevent vibration-induced fatigue failures.
19. Do not use fuel, propellant, or oxidizer lines for the support of other lines or components.
20. Provide heat-resistant lines in potential fire areas.
21. Protect reference pressure lines from freezing.
22. Protect the fuel system's electrical controls from short circuits.
23. Make provisions to stop flow of propellants in case of line rupture.
24. Minimize the effects of fuel leakage in the proximity of electrical components.
25. Do not allow several critical fuel system electrical components to be protected by a single fuse or circuit breaker.
26. Provide protection from static electricity.
27. Locate fuel tanks and vents to minimize effects of lightning strikes.
28. Ensure that all access covers into fuel tanks are lightning safe.
29. Design the pressure fuel inlets in tanks to prevent buildup of static charge during the filling process. Ensure that all fuel tube-ins and hose assemblies are bonded and electrically conductive. Provide a ground receptacle at all fuel and defuel locations.
30. Locate fuel tanks for maximum crash protection.
31. Locate propellant tanks below and away from potential ignition sources.
32. Do not use integral tank walls as a boundary for crew, cargo, or engine areas or fire zones.
33. When the location of fuel or propellant tanks adjacent to these areas cannot be avoided, use bladder cells in a sealed and drained compartment.
34. Provide ventilation and drainage where leakage into confined areas is possible.
35. Do not locate fuel tanks in engine compartments.
36. When it is impossible to avoid locating fuel tanks above engine compartments, make provisions to prevent fuel leakage into the engine compartment.
37. Provide sufficient protection to prevent ignition of fuel vapor within the tank in case of an engine compartment fire, bleed-air-line rupture, or other engine failure.
38. Ensure that a single failure of a tank pressurization system will not exceed tank structural limits.
39. Design vent systems to safely dispose of hazardous vapors.
40. Route fuel lines to avoid inhabited areas.
41. Provide closed-loop venting where a toxic hazard is presented.
42. For particularly critical work, consider tank inerting to prevent or limit explosions.
43. Locate filler openings on fuel tanks so that fuel coming from a leaking, loose, or unfastened cap will not drain into the engine compartment, an inhabited compartment, or any area where fuel liquid or vapor will present a hazard.
44. Identify fluid systems by function, commodity, pressure, and direction of flow.

Component Selection

1. Where tubes or hose pass through a bulkhead, use bulkhead fittings or a grommet.
2. Do not use grommets as a line support.
3. Whenever rigid tubing is inadvisable due to relative movement or installation tolerances, use flexible couplings or flexible hose assemblies.
4. Ensure that lubricants used in threaded fittings and on the seals are compatible with the fluids and materials of the system.

5. Incorporate a shear section on shafts of engine-driven pumps to prevent engine damage in case of pump seizure.
6. Ensure that electric pumps are explosion-proof and incorporate adequate pump shaft seal drains and motor housing vents.
7. Incorporate provisions in pumps operating inside of fuel tanks to prevent any portion of the outer surface from being heated up to the self-ignition temperature of the fuel.
8. Select centrifugal-type pumps instead of positive displacement pumps because the hazard of building up excessive pressure is less.
9. Design components' seal drains to prevent any impingement or accumulation in the vicinity of a potential ignition source.
10. Ensure that the inlet and outlet faces of valves are not identical and that any electrical connection is configured to prevent incorrect installation.
11. Ensure that components possess positive identification features to prevent installation of an incorrect assembly.
12. Provide installation and check-out procedures to assure that check and relief valves cannot be installed in reverse.
13. Avoid couplings which can be damaged by overtightening.
14. If you incorporate a bypass feature in fuel strainers and filters, incorporate an indicator to show that the bypass has been actuated. Ensure that it is necessary to remove and inspect the filtering unit in order to reset the indicator.
15. Ensure that "fuel valve closed" lights indicate the actual position of the valve and not the operation of the valve-closing mechanism.

Fabrication

1. Where routing and location can be critical, ensure that fabrication and system modification instructions clearly identify and specify this fact.
2. Beaded tubing with either flexible couplings or hose and clamps are unacceptable for new designs in fuel and propellant systems.
3. In potential fire zones use the minimum number of fuel-line connectors consistent with system design goals.
4. Design the routing as short as possible while remaining as far as is practical from systems which can provide an ignition source.
5. Do not install mechanical linkage close enough to a fuel line to cause abrasion or wear under the most extreme conditions.
6. Design metal bellows installations so that minimum stresses are imposed by the installation.
7. Eliminate sharp corners around seals and O-ring installations.

MATERIAL HANDLING EQUIPMENT

General

1. Design lifting/hoisting slings for a specific operation. Provide all slings with rings, links, hooks, or eyes so they can be safely suspended from hooks.
2. Prohibit the use of open hooks on slings or any other equipment used in handling operations.
3. Where cable or rope slings are employed in conjunction with hoists or cranes, provide sling cables of sufficient length to ensure that the angle formed by the sling cables at the hoist-attaching points does not exceed 45°.
4. Specify that hooks for hoisting apparatus are to be fabricated from forged steel, wrought iron, or built-up steel plates. Ensure that hooks are fitted with safety latches, or other safety devices, and shaped to prevent loads from slipping off.

5. Specify wire rope be made of corrosion-resistant material when there is a possibility it will be used in a corrosive environment.
6. Specify fiber rope of high-grade manila hemp with a minimum tensile strength of 11 400 psi.
7. Specify permanently attached safety chains for vehicles that must be towed, with the capacity to hold the truck or dolly to the tractor in the event of towbar failure or disconnection.
8. Provide grounding connections in the design of all trucks and dollies.
9. Incorporate shock-mounting, nonresetting G-meters, desiccants, and other protective devices on trucks and dollies used for moving sensitive equipment.
10. Provide positive cradling (support devices and tie-downs that conform to the shape, size, weight, and contour of the load to be transported).
11. Enclose all electric wiring in chafe-resistant protective material and clamped clear of sharp edges and moving parts.
12. Provide tie-downs or locking devices to secure pallets and platforms to the loader during movement of the loader.
13. Provide a mechanical safety locking device to prevent inadvertent lowering of the load in the event of a system failure.
14. Design jacks with mechanical adjustable stops to ensure even lifting when several jacks are being used.
15. Specify tension and torque requirements for tie-down straps.
16. Provide hinged-type towbars with a positive latch to hold the towbar in the raised position with a stop to prevent contact with the equipment.
17. Provide grounding straps on all auxiliary equipment.
18. Design wheel chocks to conform to the wheel size and load of the mobile handling equipment.
19. Specify that towbars are fabricated from material of sufficient strength to resist permanent deformation under operating loads.
20. Discourage the use of nonconductive materials in the design of shelters or protective covers that can generate or hold a static charge.
21. Provide electrical bonding to maintain a uniform ground potential on separable sections of portable metal shelters that are separated by insulating or nonconductive materials.
22. Ensure that portable shelters and protective covers are conspicuously marked for STEP, NO-STEP, HOISTING POINT, LIFTING POINT, CENTER OF GRAVITY, THIS SIDE UP, FOLD LINE, and other markings as required.

Lifting and Positioning Equipment

1. Provide a braking system capable of braking, lowering, and safely holding a minimum of 150 percent of rated load.
2. Provide grounding in accordance with ANSI C1 or NFPA 70.
3. Encase all electrical controls, switches, and other sparking devices in a vapor-tight or explosion-proof enclosure when the equipment is intended for use in a corrosive or potentially explosive atmosphere. Refer to the National Electrical Code Article 500 (ANSI C1 or NFPA 70).
4. Incorporate an automatic braking or stop feature on the cable drum in the event of a power failure or mechanical failure in the hoisting mechanism.
5. Design permanent mechanical stops into the equipment to prevent operation in a dangerous mode or position.
6. Specify spark arresters for the exhausts of all engines on mobile equipment.
7. Provide electrical bonding to maintain a uniform ground potential on all structural framework separated by insulating materials.

8. Design the cable length to permit at least four full wrappings around the drum when the equipment is at the maximum extended position.
9. Provide safety guards for critical or emergency controls and switches to prevent inadvertent operation.
10. Provide separate and independent mechanical and electrical brakes for the lifting mechanisms on all electrically powered equipment.
11. Design electrical control, junction, and switch boxes to exclude the entry of water or other undesired and incompatible substances.
12. Design mobile equipment with grounding provisions that are readily accessible.
13. Require a minimum one-hour fire-resistive rating for hoistway enclosures, doors, and door assemblies including the top and bottom of the hoistway.
14. Provide a means of venting smoke and hot gases from the hoistway to atmosphere in case of fire.
15. Ensure that hoistway enclosures have substantially flush surfaces.
16. Provide fire-resistive enclosures for machinery and control equipment.
17. Require a permanent, safe, and convenient means of access to elevator machine rooms and overhead machinery spaces.
18. Ensure that only the electrical wiring, cables, pipes, or ducts used directly in connection with the elevator are installed in the hoistway.
19. Locate counterweights only in the hoistway of the elevator which they serve.
20. Install unperforated metal guards in the pit on the open side or sides of all counterweights where buffers are used.
21. Provide a vertical clearance of not less than two feet between the pit floor and lowest structural or mechanical part installed beneath the car platform when the car rests on its fully compressed buffer.
22. Ensure the elevator cannot leave a level unless the doors are closed.
23. Equip elevator and hoistway doors with interlocks.
24. Provide power-operated car doors or gates with a reopening device which will function to stop and reopen a car door or gate and the adjacent hoistway door in the event that the car door or gate is obstructed while closing. Ensure that the obstruction of either door panel when closing will cause the reopening device to function.
25. Ensure that elevator design and layout drawings indicate bracket spacing, the estimated maximum vertical forces on the guide rails on application of the safety devices, the estimated horizontal forces on the guide rail faces during loading and unloading, and the size and weight per foot of any rail reinforcements where provided.
26. Ensure that elevators suspended by wire ropes are provided with one or more safety braking devices attached to the car frame. Mount all car safeties on a single car frame operated on only one pair of guide rails between which the frame is located.
27. Where two safeties are provided, ensure that the lower safety device is capable of developing not less than one-half of the force required to stop the entire car with rated load. Arrange duplexed safety devices so as to function simultaneously and/or independently.
28. Provide car safeties and counterweight safeties that are actuated by separate speed governors set to trip at overspeeds of not less than 115 percent of rated speed.
29. Ensure that parts of safeties have a safety factor of not less than 3.5:1 and the materials used have an elongation of not more than 15 percent in a length of two inches.
30. Design passenger and freight elevators to safely lower, stop, and hold the car with an additional load up to 25 percent in excess of the rated load.
31. Provide upper and lower terminal stopping devices arranged to slow down and stop the elevator

car automatically at or near the top and bottom terminal landings with any load up to and including rated load in the car and from any speed attained in normal operation.

32. For elevators having polyphase alternating-current power supply, provide a means to prevent the starting of the elevator motor if the phase rotation is in the wrong direction or there is a failure of any phase causing the elevator driving-machine motor to operate in the wrong direction.

33. Provide elevators which are operated at any time without a designated operator with a minimum of one emergency signal device operable from within the car, such as an alarm bell located inside the building or a telephone connected to a central telephone exchange system.

34. Ensure that minimum factors of safety for intermediate wire-rope speeds are based on the actual rope speed corresponding to the rated speed of the car.

35. For elevators suspended by wire ropes ensure that wire ropes of drum-type machines have not less than one turn of the rope on the drum when the car is resting on its fully compressed buffers.

36. Equip elevators with a mechanical blocking device to be used during maintenance periods. It must be impossible to operate the elevator drive with the blocking device engaged. In case of a power failure, ensure that the device will automatically become engaged.

37. Equip elevators with normal and final limit stops to prevent overtravel.

38. Placard the elevator car conspicuously to indicate the rated load capacity.

39. Equip elevator cars with an emergency escape hatch in the ceiling to allow access to the elevator shaft that can only be opened from the exterior.

40. Equip enclosed elevator shafts with emergency ladders.

41. Provide emergency lights inside enclosed elevator cars that will operate automatically in case of a power failure.

42. Where hydraulic elevators are used, ensure that hydraulic driving machines are the direct-plunger type.

43. Where the plunger is subjected to eccentric loading, design the plunger connection to the car to transmit the full eccentric moment to the plunger with a safety factor of not less than 4:1 and so that the total vertical deflection of the loading edge of the car platform due to eccentric loading of the car does not exceed $3/4$ inch.

44. Provide plungers with solid metal stops or other means to prevent the plunger from traveling beyond the limits of the cylinder.

45. Provide a means to open the power circuit to the pump motor.

46. Provide clearance at the bottom of the cylinder so that the bottom of the plunger will not strike the bottom head of the cylinder when the car is resting on its fully compressed buffer.

47. Ensure that flexible connections that are installed on high-pressure lines have a bursting strength of not less than three times the working pressures.

48. Provide a check valve on hydraulic elevators installed in such a way that it will hold the elevator car with rated load at any point when the pump stops or the maintained pressure drops below the minimum operating pressure.

49. Provide every hydraulic elevator with an anti-creep leveling device that will maintain the car within three inches of the landing from any point within the interlock zone irrespective of the position of the hoistway door.

50. Provide electro-hydraulic elevators with a switch so that in an emergency, power can be removed from the pump motor and control valve solenoids.

51. Ensure that the failure of any single magnetically operated switch contactor or relay to release in the intended manner or the occurrence of a single accidental ground will not permit the car to start or run if (*a*) any hoisting door interlock is unlocked, or (*b*) any hoistway-door or car-door or gate contact is in the open position.

52. Ensure that all line parts of electrical apparatus, located in or on elevator cars or in their hoistways, are suitably enclosed to protect against accidental contact.
53. Ensure that electric driving machines have electrically released brakes applied automatically by compression springs or by gravity when the power is removed from the motor.
54. Determine the number of suspension ropes or chains required by multiplying the static load by a safety factor not less than 4.5:1 and dividing the result by the manufacturer's rated ultimate strength of one of the ropes or chains of the size and construction to be used.
55. Provide a slack-rope switch on dumbwaiters equipped with winding-drum machines which will remove the power from the motor and brake if the car is obstructed in its descent.
56. Protect floor openings for escalators against the passage of flame, smoke, or gases in the event of fire when accredited as a required means of egress.
57. Enclose the sides and undersides of escalator trusses and machinery spaces with fire-resistive materials and provide a means of adequate ventilation for the driving machine and control spaces.
58. Provide a solid guard in the intersecting angle of the outside balustrade and the ceiling or soffit. Ensure that the exposed edge of the guard is rounded to eliminate shear hazard.
59. Provide hand and finger guards at the point where the handrail enters the balustrades.
60. Ensure that the design safety factors, based on the static loads, are at least 5:1 for trusses and structural members, and 10:1 for driving machine parts and power transmission members.
61. Provide each escalator with an electrically released, mechanically applied brake capable of stopping the moving escalator with any load up to the applied load when any of the safety devices are actuated.
62. Ensure that emergency stop buttons or other type of manually operated switches having red buttons or handles are accessibly located at or near the top and bottom landings of each escalator and protected against accidental operation.
63. Provide a speed governor, the operation of which will cause the interruption of power to the driving machine should the speed of the stops exceed a predetermined value or more than 40 percent above the rated speed.
64. Provide broken step-chain and drive-chain devices that will cause the interruption of power to the driving machine if either chain breaks.
65. Design the belt-type treadway with a safety factor of 5:1, based on ultimate strength.
66. Ensure that connecting chains and other connecting devices have a safety factor of not less than 10:1, based on ultimate strength.
67. Ensure that the maximum speed of the treadway does not exceed 180 fpm for a slope of from 0° to 3° at point of exit or entrance.
68. Provide each moving walk with an electrically released mechanically applied brake capable of stopping and holding the treadway with any load up to the load rating. Ensure that the treadway will stop automatically upon failure of power or when any of the safety devices operate.
69. Accessibly locate emergency stop buttons or other types of manually operated switches at every entrance to and exit from a moving walk. Protect buttons or switches from accidental operation.
70. Provide a device which will cause the application of a brake if the drive chain breaks.
71. Ensure that all manlift floor openings are uniform in size, approximately circular, each aligned vertically, and centered on the belt run. Keep floor space adjacent to the floor openings free from obstructions and provide landing surfaces with materials that will ensure safe footing.
72. Floor landings or emergency landings should be provided for each 25 ft of manlift travel. Ensure that these landings are (*a*) accessible from both runs, (*b*) completely enclosed, and (*c*) equipped with emergency exit ladders.
73. Ensure that floor openings affording access to the manlift are guarded by staggered railings or handrails equipped with self-closing gates.

74. Provide the motor shaft with a mechanically applied, electrically released brake capable of stopping and holding the manlift when the descending side is loaded with 250 lb on each step.
75. Ensure that the system is designed and constructed so as to catch and hold the driving pulley in event of shaft failure.
76. Ensure that handholds are provided so that they are not less than 4 ft nor more than 4 ft 8 in above the step tread. Locate these handholds to be available on both the up and down runs of the belt.
77. Provide two separate automatic stop devices to cut off power and apply the brake when a loaded step passes the upper-terminal landing.
78. Provide an emergency stop device located within easy reach of ascending and descending runs of the belt.
79. Ensure that all parts have a safety factor of 6:1 based on a load of 200 lb on each horizontal step on the up and down runs.
80. Mark guidelines on cradles designed to carry particular loads to match guidelines on equipment being carried. Locate guidelines to be visible after the equipment is loaded.
81. Shape cradles to fit the equipment to be carried.
82. Ensure that cradle has sufficient bearing area to support the load when the equipment must remain on the cradle without supporting bands or hoists.
83. Provide straps of sufficient strength material to attach the equipment to the cradle during positioning procedures. Equip restraining straps with quick-disconnect, easily accessible fasteners. Encase metal straps with nonabrading material to prevent damage to the equipment.

APPENDIX B
TOXIC SUBSTANCES

This appendix contains two lists of exposure limits for toxic substances—the 1977 Threshold Limit Values of the American Conference of Governmental Industrial Hygienists (ACGIH)* and a list of the sixteen compounds for which the Occupational Safety and Health Administration (OSHA) has set its own exposure standards (Appendix B-7). The 1968 ACGIH list was incorporated into the OSHA standards directly in 1971. Since then, the ACGIH has tightened some of its limits, but OSHA has not, except for the aforementioned sixteen, followed suit.

Manufacturers of chemical products should be most concerned about the exposure levels of employees working in customer facilities. Because of the employers' limited liability for workplace accidents in most states, chemical suppliers may find themselves holding the bag.

Threshold limit values refer to airborne concentrations of substances and represent conditions under which it is believed that nearly all workers may be repeatedly exposed day after day without adverse effect. Because of wide variation in individual susceptibility, however, a small percentage of workers may experience discomfort from some substances at concentrations at or below the threshold limit; a smaller percentage may be affected more seriously by aggravation of a pre-existing condition or by development of an occupational illness.

Tests are available (*J. Occup. Med.* 15:564, 1973; *Ann. N.Y. Acad. Sci.*, no. 151, Art. 2: 968, 1968) that may be used to detect those individuals hypersusceptible to a variety of industrial chemicals (respiratory irritants, hemolytic chemicals, organic isocyanates, carbon disulfide).

Three categories of Threshold Limit Values (TLVs) are specified herein, as follows:

    a. Threshold Limit Value-Time Weighted Average (TLV-TWA)—the time-weighted average concentration for a normal 8-hour workday or 40-hour workweek, to which nearly all workers may be repeatedly exposed, day after day, without adverse effect.

    b. Threshold Limit Value-Short Term Exposure Limit (TLV-STEL)—the maximal concentration to which workers can be exposed for a period up to 15 minutes continuously without suffering from 1) irritation, 2) chronic or irreversible tissue change, or 3) narcosis of sufficient degree to increase accident proneness, impair self-rescue, or materially reduce work efficiency, provided that no more than four excursions per day are permitted, with at least 60 minutes between exposure

*Copyright 1977, ACGIH, Inc., P. O. Box 1937, Cincinnati, OH 45201. Reproduced and adapted with permission.

periods, and provided that the daily TLV-TWA also is not exceeded. The STEL should be considered a maximal allowable concentration, or absolute ceiling, not to be exceeded at any time during the 15-minute excursion period. STELs are based on one or more of the following criteria: (1) Adopted TLVs including those with a

b. "C" or "ceiling" limit. (2) TWA-TLV Excursion Factors listed in App. B4. (3) Pennsylvania Short-Term Limits for Exposure to Airborne Contaminants (Penna. Dept. of Hlth., Chapter 4, Art. 432, Rev. Jan. 25, 1968). (4) OSHA Occupational Safety and Health Standards, *Fed. Reg.* Vol. 36, No. 105, May 29, 1971. The TWA-STEL should not be used as engineering design criterion or considered as an emergency exposure level (EEL).

c. Threshold Limit Value-Ceiling (TLV-C)—the concentration that should not be exceeded even instantaneously.

For some substances, e.g., irritant gases, only one category, the TLV-Ceiling, may be relevant. For other substances, either two or three categories may be relevant, depending upon their physiologic action. It is important to observe that if any one of these three TLVs is exceeded, a potential hazard from that substance is presumed to exist.

The TLV-TWA should be used as guides in the control of health hazards and should not be used as fine lines between safe and dangerous concentrations.

Time-weighted averages permit excursions above the limit provided they are compensated by equivalent excursions below the limit during the workday. In some instances it may be permissible to calculate the average concentration for a workweek rather than for a workday. The degree of permissible excursion is related to the magnitude of the threshold limit value of a particular substance as given in App. B4. The relationship between threshold limit and permissible excursion is a rule of thumb and in certain cases may not apply. The amount by which threshold limits may be exceeded for short periods without injury to health depends upon a number of factors such as the nature of the contaminant, whether very high concentrations—even for short periods—produce acute poisoning, whether the effects are cumulative, the frequency with which high concentrations occur, and the duration of such periods. All factors must be taken into consideration in arriving at a decision as to whether a hazardous condition exists.

Threshold limits are based on the best available information from industrial experience, from experimental human and animal studies, and, when possible, from a combination of the three. The basis on which the values are established may differ from substance to substance; protection against impairment of health may be a guiding factor for some, whereas reasonable freedom from irritation, narcosis, nuisance or other forms of stress may form the basis for others.

The Committee holds to the opinion that limits based on physical irritation should be considered no less binding than those based on physical impairment. There is increasing evidence that physical irritation may initiate, promote or accelerate physical impairment through interaction with other chemical or biologic agents.

In spite of the fact that serious injury is not believed likely as a result of exposure to the threshold limit concentrations, the best practice is to maintain concentrations of all atmospheric contaminants as low as is practical.

These limits are intended for use in the practice of industrial hygiene and should be interpreted and applied only by a person trained in this discipline. They are not intended for use, or for modification for use, (1) as a relative index of hazard or toxicity, (2) in the evaluation or control of community air pollution nuisances, (3) in estimating the toxic potential of continuous, uninterrupted exposures or other extended work periods, (4) as proof or disproof of an existing disease or physical condition, or (5) for adoption by countries whose working conditions differ from those in the United States of America and where substances and processes differ.

Ceiling vs. Time-Weighted Average Limits. Although the time-weighted average concentration provides the most satisfactory, practical way of monitoring airborne agents for compliance with the limits, there are certain substances for which it is inappropriate. In the latter group are substances which are predominantly fast acting and whose threshold limit is more appropriately based on this particular response. Substances with this type of response are best controlled by a ceiling "C" limit that should not be exceeded. It is implicit in these definitions that the manner of sampling to determine noncompliance with the limits for each group must differ; a single brief sample, that is applicable to a "C" limit, is not appropriate to the time-weighted limit; here, a sufficient number of samples are needed to permit a time-weighted average concentration throughout a complete cycle of operations or throughout the work shift.

Whereas the ceiling limit places a definite boundary which concentrations should not be permitted to exceed, the time-weighted average limit requires an explicit limit to the excursions that are permissible above the listed values. The magnitude of these excursions may be pegged to the magnitude of the threshold limit by an appropriate factor shown in App. B4. It should be noted that the same factors are used by the Committee in determining the magnitude of the value of the STELs, or whether to include or exclude a substance for a "C" listing.

"Skin" Notation. Listed substances followed by the designation "Skin" refer to the potential contribution to the overall exposure by the cutaneous route including mucous membranes and eye, either by airborne, or more particularly, by direct contact with the substance. Vehicles can alter skin absorption. This attention-calling designation is intended to suggest appropriate measures for the prevention of cutaneous absorption so that the threshold limit is not invalidated.

Mixtures. Special consideration should be given also to the application of the TLVs in assessing the health hazards which may be associated with exposure to mixtures of two or more substances. A brief discussion of basic considerations involved in developing threshold limit values for mixtures, and methods for their development, amplified by specific examples are given in Chapter VII.

Nuisance Particulates. In contrast to fibrogenic dusts which cause scar tissue to be formed in lungs when inhaled in excessive amounts, so-called "nuisance" dusts have a long history of little adverse effect on lungs and do not produce significant organic disease or toxic effect when exposures are kept under reasonable control. The nuisance dusts have also been called (biologically) "inert" dusts, but the latter term is inappropriate to the extent that there is no dust which does not evoke some cellular response in the lung when inhaled in sufficient amount. However, the lung-tissue reaction caused by inhalation of nuisance dusts has the following characteristics: (1) The architecture of the air spaces remains intact. (2) Collagen (scar tissue) is not formed to a significant extent. (3) The tissue reaction is potentially reversible.

Excessive concentrations of nuisance dusts in the workroom air may seriously reduce visibility, may cause unpleasant deposits in the eyes, ears and nasal passages (Portland Cement dust), or cause injury to the skin or mucous membranes by chemical or mechanical action per se or by the rigorous skin cleansing procedures necessary for their removal.

A threshold limit of 10 mg/m^3, or 30 mppcf, of total dust $< 1\%$ quartz, is recommended for substances in these categories and for which no specific threshold limits have been assigned. This limit, for a normal workday, does not apply to brief exposures at higher concentrations. Neither does it apply to those substances which may cause physiologic impairment at lower concentrations but for which a threshold limit has not yet been adopted. Some nuisance particulates are given in App. B3.

Simple Asphyxiants—"Inert" Gases or Vapors. A number of gases and vapors, when present in high concentrations in air, act primarily as simple asphyxiants without other significant physiologic effects. A TLV may not be recommended for each simple asphyxiant because the limiting factor is the available oxygen. The minimal oxygen content should be 18 percent by volume under normal atmospheric pressure (equivalent to a partial pressure, pO_2, of 135 mm Hg). Atmospheres deficient in O_2 do not provide adequate warning and most simple asphyxiants are odorless. Several simple asphyxiants present an explosion hazard. Account should be taken of this factor in limiting the concentration of the asphyxiant.

Physical Factors. It is recognized that such physical factors as heat, ultraviolet and ionizing radiation, humidity, abnormal pressure (altitude) and the like may place added stress on the body so that the effects from exposure at a threshold limit may be altered. Most of these stresses act adversely to increase the toxic response of a substance. Although most threshold limits have built-in safety factors to guard against adverse effects to moderate deviations from normal environments, the safety factors of most substances are not of such a magnitude as to take care of gross deviations. For example, continuous work at temperatures above 90°F, or overtime extending the workweek more than 25 percent, might be considered gross deviations. In such instances judgment must be exercised in the proper adjustments of the Threshold Limit Values.

APPENDIX B1

Substance	Adopted values TWA ppm*	Adopted values TWA mg/m³ †	Tentative values STEL ppm*	Tentative values STEL mg/m³ †
Abate	—	10	—	20
Acetaldehyde	100	180	150	270
Acetic acid	10	25	15	37
Acetic anhydride	5	20	—	—
Acetone	1000	2400	1250	3000
Acetonitrile	40	70	60	105
Acetylene	—	—	—	—
Acetylene dichloride, see 1,2-Dichloroethylene	200	790	250	1000
Acetylene tetrabromide	1	14	1.25	17.5
Acrolein	0.1	0.25	0.3	0.75
Acrylamide—Skin	—	0.3	—	0.6
Acrylonitrile—Skin	20	45	30	68
Aldrin—Skin	—	0.25	—	0.75
Allyl alcohol—Skin	2	5	4	10
Allyl chloride	1	3	2	6
Allyl glycidyl ether (AGE)—Skin	5	22	10	44
Allyl propyl disulfide	2	12	3	18
Alundum (Al$_2$O$_3$)	—	B3	—	20
4-Aminodiphenyl—Skin	—	B2	—	B2
2-Aminoethanol, see Ethanolamine	3	6	6	12
2-Aminopyridine	0.5	2	1.5	6
Ammonia	25	18	35	27
Ammonium chloride—fume	—	10	—	20
Ammonium sulfamate (Ammate)	—	10	—	20
n-Amyl acetate	100	525	150	790
sec-Amyl acetate	125	650	150	810
Aniline—Skin	5	19	—	—
Anisidine (o-, p-isomers)—Skin	0.1	0.5	—	—
Antimony and Compounds (as Sb)	—	(0.5)	—	—
ANTU (α-Naphthyl thiourea)	—	0.3	—	0.9
Argon	B6	—	B6	B6
Arsenic and compounds (as As)	—	(0.5)	—	—
Arsine	0.05	0.2	—	—
Asbestos (all forms)	—	B2, B7	—	B2, B7
Asphalt (petroleum) fumes	—	5	—	10
Azinphos methyl—Skin	—	0.2	—	0.6
Baygon (propoxur)	—	0.5	—	1.5
Barium (soluble compounds)	—	0.5	—	—
Benzene—Skin	10, B2	30, B2	—	—
Benzidine production—Skin	—	B2, B7	—	B2, B7
p-Benzoquinone, see Quinone	0.1	0.4	0.3	1.2
Benzoyl peroxide	—	5	—	—
Benz(a)pyrene	—	B2, B7	—	B2, B7
Benzyl chloride	1	5	—	—
Beryllium	—	0.002	—	0.025
Biphenyl	0.2	1	—	—
Bismuth telluride	—	10	—	20
Bismuth telluride, Se-doped	—	5	—	10
Borates, tetra, sodium salts, Anhydrous	—	1	—	—
Decahydrate	—	5	—	—
Pentahydrate	—	1	—	—

NOTE: Reference marks are explained on p. 394

APPENDIX B1

Substance	Adopted values TWA ppm*	Adopted values TWA mg/m³ †	Tentative values STEL ppm*	Tentative values STEL mg/m³ †
Boron oxide	—	10	—	20
Boron tribomide	1	10	3	30
Boron trifluoride	1	3	—	—
Bromine	0.1	0.7	0.3	2
Bromine pentafluoride	0.1	0.7	0.3	2
Bromochloromethane	200	1050	250	1300
Bromoform—Skin	0.5	5	—	—
Butadiene (1, 3-butadiene)	1000	2200	1250	2750
Butane	600	1400	750	1610
Butanethiol, see Butyl mercaptan	0.5	1.5	—	—
2-Butanone	200	590	300	885
2-Butoxy ethanol (Butyl Cellosolve)—Skin	50	240	150	720
n-Butyl acetate	150	710	200	950
sec-Butyl acetate	200	950	250	1190
tert-Butyl acetate	200	950	250	1190
n-Butyl alcohol—Skin	50	150	—	—
sec-Butyl alcohol	150	450	—	—
tert-Butyl alcohol	100	300	150	450
Butylamine—Skin	5	15	—	—
tert-Butyl chromate (as CrO₃)—Skin	—	0.1	—	—
n-Butyl glycidyl ether (BGE)	50	270	—	—
n-Butyl lactate	5	25	—	—
Butyl mercaptan	0.5	1.5	—	—
p-tert-Butyl toluene	10	60	20	120
Cadmium, dust and salts (as Cd)	—	0.05	—	0.15
Cadmium oxide fume (as Cd)	—	0.05	—	—
Calcium carbonate	—	B3	—	20
Calcium arsenate (as As)	—	1	—	—
Calcium cyanamide	—	0.5	—	1
Calcium hydroxide	—	5	—	—
Calcium oxide	—	(5)	—	—
Camphor, synthetic	2	12	3	18
Caprolactam				
Dust	—	1	—	3
Vapor	5	20	10	40
Captafol (Difolatan®)—Skin	—	0.1	—	—
Captan	—	5	—	15
Carbaryl (Sevin®)	—	5	—	10
Carbofuran (Furadan®)	—	0.1	—	—
Carbon black	—	3.5	—	7
Carbon dioxide	5000	9000	15000	18000
Carbon disulfide—Skin	20	60	30	90
Carbon monoxide	50	55	400	440
Carbon tetrabromide	0.1	1.4	0.3	4.2
Carbon tetrachloride—Skin	10	65	25	160
Catechol (Pyrocatechol)	5	20	—	—
Cellulose (paper fiber)	—	B3	—	20
Cesium hydroxide	—	2	—	—
Chlordane—Skin	—	0.5	—	2
Chlorinated camphene—Skin	—	0.5	—	1
Chlorinated diphenyl oxide	—	0.5	—	1.5
Chlorine	1	3	3	9

APPENDIX B1

Substance	Adopted values TWA ppm*	Adopted values TWA mg/m³ †	Tentative values STEL ppm*	Tentative values STEL mg/m³ †
Chlorine dioxide	0.1	0.3	0.3	0.9
Chlorine trifluoride	0.1	0.4	—	—
Chloroacetaldehyde	1	3	—	—
α-Chloroacetophenone (Phenacyl chloride)	0.05	0.3	—	—
Chlorobenzene (Monochlorobenzene)	75	350	—	—
o-Chlorobenzylidene malonoitrile—Skin	0.05	0.4	—	—
Chlorobromomethane	200	1050	250	1300
2-Chloro-1, 3-butadiene, see β-Chloroprene	25	90	35	135
Chlorodifluoromethane	1000	3500	1250	4375
Chlorodiphenyl (42% Chlorine)—Skin	—	1	—	—
Chlorodiphenyl (54% Chlorine)—Skin	—	0.5	—	1
1-Chloro, 2, 3-epoxy-propane (Epichlorohydrin)	5	20	10	40
2-Chloroethanol (Ethylene chlorohydrin)	1	3	—	—
Chloroethylene (Vinyl chloride)	B2	—	B2	—
Chloroform (Trichloromethane)	(25)	(120)	—	—
bis-(Chloromethyl) ether	0.001	B2, B7	—	B2, B7
1-Chloro-1-nitro-propane	20	100	—	—
Chloropicrin	0.1	0.7	—	—
β-Chloroprene—Skin	25	90	35	135
Chlorpyrifos (Dursban®)—Skin	—	0.2	—	0.6
o-Chlorostyrene	50	285	75	430
o-Chlorotoluene—Skin	50	250	75	375
2-Chloro-6-(trichloromethyl pyridine (N-Serve®)	—	10	—	20
Chromates, certain insoluble forms	—	0.05 B2	—	B2
Chromic acid and Chromates, (as Cr.)	—	0.05	—	—
Chromium, Sol. chromic, chromous salts (as Cr)	—	0.5	—	—
Clopidol (Coyden®)	—	10	—	20
Coal tar pitch volatiles (See Particulate polyclic aromatic hydrocarbons)	—	B2	—	B2
Cobalt metal, dust and fume	—	(0.1)	—	—
Copper fume	—	0.2	—	—
Dusts and Mists	—	1	—	2
Corundum (Al₂O₃)	—	B3	—	B3
Cotton dust, raw	—	0.2	—	0.6
Crag® herbicide	—	10	—	20
Cresol, all isomers—Skin	5	22	—	—
Crotonaldehyde	2	6	6	18
Crufomate®	—	5	—	20
Cumene—Skin	50	245	75	365
Cyanamide	—	2	—	—
Cyanide, as CN—Skin	—	5	—	—
Cyanogen	10	20	—	—
Cyclohexane	300	1050	375	1300
Cyclohexanol	50	200	—	—
Cyclohexanone	50	200	—	—
Cyclohexene	300	1015	—	—
Cyclohexylamine—Skin	10	40	—	—
Cyclopentadiene	75	200	150	400

APPENDIX B1

Substance	Adopted values TWA ppm*	Adopted values TWA mg/m³ †	Tentative values STEL ppm*	Tentative values STEL mg/m³ †
2, 4-D (2, 4-Diphenoxy-acetic acid)	—	10	—	20
DDT (Dichlorodiphenyltrichloroethane)	—	1	—	3
DDVP, See Dichlorvos................	0.1	1	0.3	3
Decaborane—Skin	0.05	0.3	0.15	0.9
Demeton®—Skin	0.01	0.1	0.03	0.3
Diacetone alcohol (4-hydroxy-4-methyl—2-pentanone)	50	240	75	360
1, 2-Diaminoethane, see Ethylenediamine	10	25	—	—
Diazinon—Skin	—	0.1	—	0.3
Diazomethane	0.2	0.4	—	—
Diborane	0.1	0.1	—	—
1, 2-Dibromoethane (Ethylene dibromide)—Skin	20	145	30	220
Dibrom®	—	3	—	6
2-N-Dibutylaminoethanol—Skin	2	14	4	28
Dibutyl phosphate	1	5	2	10
Dibutyl phthalate	—	5	—	10
Dichloracetylene	0.1	0.4	—	—
o-Dichlorobenzene	50	300	—	—
p-Dichlorobenzene	75	450	110	675
Dichlorobenzidine—Skin	—	B2, B7	—	B2, B7
Dichlorodifluoromethane	1000	4950	1250	6200
1, 3-Dichloro-5, 5-dimethyl hydantoin ..	—	0.2	—	0.4
1, 1-Dichloroethane	200	820	250	1025
1, 2-Dichloroethane	50	200	75	300
1, 2-Dichloroethylene	200	790	250	1000
Dichloroethyl ether—Skin	5	30	10	60
Dichloromethane, see Methylene chloride	200	720	250	900
Dichloromonofluoromethane	(1000)	(4200)	—	—
1, 1-Dichloro-1-nitroethane	10	60	—	—
1, 2-Dichloropropane, see Propylene dichloride	75	350	110	525
Dichlorotetrafluoroethane	1000	7000	1250	8750
Dichlorvos (DDVP)—Skin	0.1	1	0.3	3
Dicrotophos (Bidrin®)—Skin	—	0.25	—	—
Dicyclopentadiene	5	30	—	—
Dicyclopentadienyl iron	—	10	—	20
Dieldrin—Skin	—	0.25	—	0.75
Diethylamine........................	25	75	—	—
Diethylaminoethanol—Skin	10	50	—	—
Diethylene triamine—Skin	1	4	—	—
Diethyl ether, see Ethyl ether	400	1200	500	1500
Diethyl phthalate	—	5	—	10
Difluorodibromomethane.............	100	860	150	1290
Diglycidyl ether (DGE)	0.5	2.8	—	—
Dihydroxybenzene, see Hydroquinone .	—	2	—	3
Diisobutyl ketone	25	150	—	—
Diisopropylamine—Skin	5	20	—	—
Dimethoxymethane, see Methylal	1000	3100	1250	3875
Dimethyl acetamide—Skin	10	35	15	50
Dimethylamine	10	18	—	—
Dimethylaminobenzene, see Xylidene ..	5	25	10	50

APPENDIX B1

Substance	Adopted values TWA ppm*	Adopted values TWA mg/m³ †	Tentative values STEL ppm*	Tentative values STEL mg/m³ †
Dimethylaniline (N-Dimethylaniline)—Skin	5	25	10	50
Dimethylbenzene, see Xylene	100	435	150	650
Dimethyl-1, 2-dibromo-2-dichloroethyl phosphate, see Dibrom	—	3	—	6
Dimethylformamide—Skin	10	30	20	60
2, 6-Dimethylheptanone, see Diisobutyl ketone	25	150	—	—
1, 1-Dimethylhydrazine—Skin	0.5	1	1	2
Dimethylphthalate	—	5	—	10
Dimethyl sulfate—Skin	0.1, B2	0.5, B2	—	—
Dinitrobenzene (all isomers)—Skin	0.15	1	0.5	3
Dinitro-o-cresol—Skin	—	0.2	—	0.6
3, 5-Dinitro-o-toluamide (Zoalene®)	—	5	—	10
Dinitrotoluene—Skin	—	1.5	—	5
Dioxane, tech. grade—Skin	50	180	—	—
Dioxathion (Delnav®)	—	0.2	—	—
Diphenyl, see Biphenyl	0.2	1	0.6	3
Diphenylamine	—	10	—	20
Diphenylmethane diisocyanate, see Methylene bisphenyl isocyanate (MD)	0.02	0.2	0.02	0.2
Dipropylene glycol methyl ether—Skin	100	600	150	900
Diquat	—	0.5	—	1
Di-sec, octyl phthalate (Di-2-ethylhexylphthalate)	—	5	—	10
Disulfuram	—	2	—	5
Disyston—Skin	—	0.1	—	0.3
2, 6-Ditert. butyl-p-cresol	—	10	—	20
Diuron	—	10	—	—
Dyfonate	—	0.1	—	—
Emery	—	B3	—	20
Endosulfan (Thiodan®)—Skin	—	0.1	—	0.3
Endrin—Skin	—	0.1	—	0.3
Epichlorhydrin—Skin	5	20	10	40
EPN—Skin	—	0.5	—	1.5
1, 2-Epoxypropane, see Propylene oxide	100	240	150	360
2, 3-Epoxy-1-propanol, see Glycidol	50	150	65	190
Ethane	B6	—	B6	—
Ethanethiol, see Ethyl mercaptan	0.5	1	1.5	3
Ethanolamine	3	6	6	12
Ethion (Nialate®)—Skin	—	0.4	—	—
2-Ethoxyethanol—Skin	100	370	150	560
2-Ethoxyethyl acetate (Cellosolve acetate)—Skin	100	540	150	810
Ethyl acetate	400	1400	—	—
Ethyl acrylate—Skin	25	100	—	—
Ethyl alcohol (Ethanol)	1000	1900	—	—
Ethylamine	10	18	—	—
Ethyl sec-amyl ketone (4-Methyl-3-heptanone)	25	130	—	—
Ethyl benzene	100	435	125	545
Ethyl bromide	200	890	250	1110
Ethyl butyl ketone (3-Heptanone)	50	230	75	345
Ethyl chloride	1000	2600	1250	3250

NOTE: Reference marks are explained on p. 394

APPENDIX B1

Substance	Adopted values TWA ppm*	Adopted values TWA mg/m³ †	Tentative values STEL ppm*	Tentative values STEL mg/m³ †
Ethyl ether	400	1200	500	1500
Ethyl formate	100	300	150	450
Ethyl mercaptan	0.5	1	—	—
Ethyl silicate	(100)	(850)	—	—
Ethylene	B6	—	B6	—
Ethylene chlorohydrin—Skin	1	3	—	—
Ethylene diamine	10	25	—	—
Ethylene dibromide, see 1, 2-Dibromoethane	20	145	30	220
Ethylene dichloride, see 1, 2-Dichloroethane	50	200	75	300
Ethylene glycol, Particulate	—	10	—	20
Vapor	100	260	125	325
Ethylene glycol dinitrate and/or Nitroglycerin—Skin	0.2§	—	—	—
Ethylene glycol monomethyl ether acetate (Methyl cellosolve acetate)—Skin	25	120	40	180
Ethylene oxide	50	90	75	135
Ethylenimine—Skin	0.5	1	—	—
Ethylidene chloride, see 1, 1-Dichloroethane	200	320	250	400
Ethylidene norbornene	5	25	—	—
N-Ethylmorpholine—Skin	20	94	20	94
Fensulfothion (Dasanit)	—	0.1	—	—
Ferbam	—	10	—	20
Ferrovanadium dust	—	1	—	0.3
Fluoride (as F)	—	2.5	—	—
Fluorine	1	2	2	4
Fluorotrichloromethane	1000	5600	1250	7000
Formaldehyde	2	3	—	—
Formamide	20	30	30	45
Formic acid	5	9	5	9
Furfural—Skin	5	20	15	60
Furfuryl alcohol—Skin	5	20	10	40
Gasoline	—	B5	—	B5
Germanium tetrahydride	0.2	0.6	0.6	1.8
Glass, fibrous ¶ or dust	—	—	—	—
Glutaraldehyde, activated or unactivated	—	(0.25)	—	—
Glycerin mist	—	B3	—	B3
Glycidol (2, 3-Epoxy-1-propanol)	50	150	75	225
Glycol monoethyl ether, see 2-Ethoxyethanol	100	370	150	560
Graphite (Synthetic)	—	B3	—	—
Guthion®, see Azinphos-methyl	—	0.2	—	0.6
Gypsum	—	B3	—	20
Hafnium	—	0.5	—	1.5
Helium	B6	—	B6	—
Heptachlor—Skin	—	0.5	—	1.5
Heptane (n-Heptane)	400	1600	500	2000
Hexachlorocyclopentadiene	0.01	0.11	0.03	0.33
Hexachloroethane—Skin	1	10	3	30
Hexachloronaphthalene—Skin	—	0.2	—	0.6

APPENDIX B1

Substance	Adopted values TWA ppm*	Adopted values TWA mg/m³ †	Tentative values STEL ppm*	Tentative values STEL mg/m³ †
Hexafluoroacetone	0.1	0.7	0.3	2.1
Hexane (n-hexane)	100	360	125	450
2-Hexanone, see Methyl butyl ketone—Skin	25	100	40	150
Hexone (Methyl isobutyl ketone)—Skin	100	410	125	510
sec-Hexyl acetate	50	300	—	—
Hexylene glycol	25	125	—	—
Hydrazine—Skin	0.1	0.1	—	—
Hydrogen	B6	—	B6	—
Hydrogenated terphenyls	0.5	5	—	—
Hydrogen bromide	3	10	—	—
Hydrogen chloride	5	7	—	—
Hydrogen cyanide—Skin	10	11	15	16
Hydrogen fluoride	3	2	—	—
Hydrogen peroxide	1	1.4	2	2.8
Hydrogen selenide	0.05	0.2	—	—
Hydrogen sulfide	10	15	15	27
Hydroquinone	—	2	—	4
Indene	10	45	15	27
Indium and Compounds (as In)	—	0.1	—	0.3
Iodine	0.1	1	—	—
Iodoform	0.2	3	0.4	0.6
Iron oxide fume	B5	5	—	10
Iron pentacarbonyl	0.01	0.08	—	—
Iron salts, soluble (as Fe)	—	1	—	2
Isoamyl acetate	100	525	125	655
Isoamyl alcohol	100	360	125	450
Isobutyl acetate	150	700	187	875
Isobutyl alcohol	50	150	75	225
Isophorone	5	25	—	—
Isophorone diisocyanate—Skin	0.01	0.06	—	—
Isopropyl acetate	250	950	310	1185
Isopropyl alcohol—Skin	400	980	500	1225
Isopropylamine	5	12	10	24
Isopropyl ether	250	1050	310	1320
Isopropyl glycidyl ether (IGE)	50	240	75	360
Kaolin	—	B-3	—	20
Ketene	0.5	0.9	1.5	2.7
Lead, inorg., fumes and dusts (as Pb)	—	0.15	—	0.45
Lead arsenate (as Pb)	—	0.15	—	0.45
Lead Chromate (as Cr)	—	0.05, B2	—	—
Limestone	—	B3	—	20
Lindane—Skin	—	0.5	—	1.5
Lithium hydride	—	0.025	—	—
L.P.G. (Liquefied petroleum gas)	1000	1800	1250	2250
Magnesite	—	B3	—	20
Magnesium oxide fume	—	10	—	—
Malathion—Skin	—	10	—	—
Maleic anhydride	0.25	1	—	—
Manganese and Compounds (as Mn)	—	5	—	—
Manganese cyclopentadienyl tricarbonyl (as Mn)—Skin	—	0.1	—	0.3
Marble	—	B3	—	20
Mercury)Alkyl compounds)—Skin, (as Hg)	0.001	0.01	0.003	0.03

NOTE: Reference marks are explained on p. 394

APPENDIX B1

Substance	Adopted values TWA ppm*	Adopted values TWA mg/m³ †	Tentative values STEL ppm*	Tentative values STEL mg/m³ †
Mercury (All forms except alkyl) as Hg	—	0.05	—	0.15
Mesityl oxide	25	100	—	—
Methane	B6	—	B6	—
Methanethiol, see Methyl mercaptan	0.5	1	—	—
Methomyl (Lannate®)—Skin	—	2.5	—	—
Methoxychlor	—	10	—	—
2-Methoxyethanol—Skin (Methyl Cellosolve)	25	80	35	120
Methyl acetate	200	610	250	760
Methyl acetylene (propyne)	1000	1650	1250	2060
Methyl acetylene-propadiene mixture (MAPP)	1000	1800	1250	2250
Methyl acrylate—Skin	10	35	—	—
Methyl acrylonitrile—Skin	1	3	2	6
Methylal (dimethoxymethane)	1000	3100	1250	3875
Methyl alcohol (methanol)—Skin	200	260	250	325
Methylamine	10	12	—	—
Methyl amyl alcohol, see Methyl isobutyl carbinol	25	100	40	150
Methyl 2-cyanoacrylate	2	8	4	16
Methyl isoamyl ketone	100	475	150	710
Methyl n-amyl ketone (2-Heptanone)	100	465	150	710
Methyl bromide—Skin	15	60	—	—
Methyl butyl ketone, see 2-Hexanone	25	100	40	150
Methyl Cellosolve—Skin, see 2-Methoxyethanol	25	80	35	120
Methyl Cellosolve Acetate —Skin, see Ethylene glycol monomethyl ether acetate	25	120	35	150
Methyl chloride	100	210	125	260
Methyl chloroform	350	1900	450	2375
Methylcyclohexene	400	1600	500	2000
Methylcyclohexanol	50	235	75	350
o-Methylcyclohexanone—Skin	50	230	75	345
Methylcyclopentadienyl manganese tricarbonyl (as Mn)—Skin	0.1	0.2	0.3	0.6
Methyl demeton—Skin	—	0.5	—	1.5
Methylene bisphenyl isocyanate (MDI)	0.02	0.2	—	—
Methylene chloride (dichloromethane)	200	720	250	900
4, 4'-Methylene bis (2-chloraniline)—Skin	0.02, B2	—	B2	—
Methylene bis (4-cyclohexylisocyanate)	0.01	0.11	—	—
Methyl ethyl ketone (MEK), see 2-Butanone	200	590	250	740
Methyl ethyl ketone peroxide	0.2	1.5	—	—
Methyl formate	100	250	150	375
Methyl iodide—Skin	5	28	10	56
Methyl isobutyl carbinol—Skin	25	100	40	150
Methyl isobutyl ketone, see Hexone	100	410	125	510
Methyl isocyanate—Skin	0.02	0.05	—	—
Methyl mercaptan	0.5	1	—	—
Methyl methacrylate	100	410	125	510
Methyl parathion—Skin	—	0.2	—	0.6
Methyl propyl ketone, see 2-Pentanone	200	700	250	875
Methyl silicate	5	30	—	—

APPENDIX B1

Substance	Adopted values TWA ppm*	TWA mg/m³ †	Tentative values STEL ppm*	STEL mg/m³ †
α-Methyl styrene	100	480	—	—
Molybdenum (as Mo)				
Soluble compounds	—	5	—	10
Insoluble compounds	—	10	—	20
Monocrotophos (Azodrin®)	—	0.25	—	—
Monomethyl aniline—Skin	2	9	4	18
Monomethyl hydrazine—Skin	0.2	0.35	—	—
Morpholine—Skin	20	70	30	105
Naphthalene	10	50	15	75
beta-Naphthylamine	—	B2, B7	—	B2, B7
Neon	B6	—	B6	—
Nickel carbonyl	0.05	0.35	—	—
Nickel metal	—	1	—	—
Nickel, soluble compounds (as Ni)	—	0.1	—	0.3
Nicotine—Skin	—	0.5	—	1.5
Nitric acid	2	5	4	10
Nitric oxide	25	30	35	45
p-Nitroaniline—Skin	1	6	2	12
Nitrobenzene—Skin	1	5	2	10
p-Nitrochlorobenzene—Skin	—	1	—	2
4-Nitrodiphenyl	—	B2, B7	—	B2, B7
Nitroethane	100	310	150	465
Nitrogen dioxide	5	9	—	—
Nitrogen trifluoride	10	29	15	45
Nitroglycerin‡—Skin	0.2	2	—	—
Nitromethane	100	250	150	375
1-Nitropropane	25	90	35	135
2-Nitropropane	25	90	—	—
N-Nitrosodimethylamine (dimethylnitrosoamine)—Skin	—	B2, B7	—	B2, B7
Nitrotoluene—Skin	5	30	10	60
Nitrotrichloromethane, see Chloropicrin	0.1	0.7	0.3	2
Nonane	200	1050	250	1300
Octachloronaphthalene—Skin	—	0.1	—	0.3
Octane	300	1450	375	1800
Oil mist	—	5**	—	10
Osmium tetroxide (as Os)	0.0002	0.0002	0.0006	0.006
Oxalic acid	—	1	—	2
Oxygen difluoride	0.05	0.1	0.15	0.3
Ozone	0.1	0.2	0.3	0.6
Paraffin wax fume	—	2	—	6
Paraquat—Skin	—	(0.5)	—	—
Parathion—Skin	—	0.1	—	0.3
Particulate polycyclic aromatic hydrocarbons (PPAH) as benzene solubles	—	0.2, B2	—	B2
Pentaborane	0.005	0.01	0.015	0.03
Pentachloronaphthalene	—	0.5	—	1.5
Pentachlorophenol—Skin	—	0.5	—	1.5
Pentaerythritol	—	B3	—	20
Pentane	600	1800	750	2250
2-Pentanone	200	700	250	875
Perchloroethylene—Skin	100	670	150	1000
Perchloromethyl mercaptan	0.1	0.8	—	—
Perchloryl fluoride	3	14	6	28

NOTE: Reference marks are explained on p. 394

APPENDIX B1

Substance	Adopted values TWA ppm*	Adopted values TWA mg/m³ †	Tentative values STEL ppm*	Tentative values STEL mg/m³ †
Petroleum distillates (naphtha)	B5‡	—	B-5	—
Phenol—Skin	5	19	10	38
Phenothiazine—Skin	—	5	—	10
p-Phenylene diamine—Skin	—	0.1	—	—
Phenyl ether (vapor)	1	7	2	14
Phenyl ether-Diphenyl mixture (vapor)	1	7	2	14
Phenylethylene, see Styrene	100	420	125	525
Phenyl glycidyl ether (PGE)	10	60	15	90
Phenylhydrazine—Skin	5	22	10	44
Phenylphosphine	0.05	0.25	—	—
Phorate (Thimet®)—Skin	—	0.05	—	0.15
Phosdrin (Mevinphos®)—Skin	0.01	0.1	0.03	0.3
Phosgene (carbonyl chloride)	0.10	0.4	—	—
Phosphine	0.3	0.4	1	1
Phosphoric acid	—	1	—	3
Phosphorus (yellow)	—	0.1	—	0.3
Phosphorus pentachloride	—	1	—	3
Phosphorus pentasulfide	—	1	—	3
Phosphorus trichloride	0.5	3	—	—
Phthalic anhydride	1	6	4	24
m-Phthalodinitrile	—	5	—	—
Picloram (Tordon®)	—	10	—	20
Picric acid—Skin	—	0.1	—	0.3
Pival® (2-Pivalyl-1, 3-indandione)	—	0.1	—	0.3
Plaster of Paris	—	B3	—	20
Platinum (Soluble salts) as Pt	—	0.002	—	—
Polychlorobiphenyls, see Chlorodiphenyls	—	—	—	—
Polytetrafluoroethylene decomposition products	—	B5	—	B5
Potassium hydroxide	—	2	—	—
Propane	B6	—	B6	—
beta-Propiolactone	—	B2	—	B2
Propargyl alcohol—Skin	1	2	3	6
n-Propyl acetate	200	840	250	1050
Propyl alcohol—Skin	200	500	250	625
n-Propyl nitrate	25	110	40	140
Propylene	B6	—	B6	—
Propylene dichloride (1, 2-Dichloropropane)	75	350	115	525
Propylene glycol monomethyl ether	100	360	150	450
Propylene imine—Skin	2	5	—	—
Propylene oxide	100	240	150	360
Propyne, see Methyl-acetylene	1000	1650	1250	2050
Pyrethrum	—	5	—	10
Pyridine	5	15	10	30
Quinone	0.1	0.4	0.3	1
RDX—Skin	—	1.5	—	3
Resorcinol	10	45	20	90
Rhodium, Metal fume and dusts (as Rh)	—	0.1	—	0.3
Soluble salts	—	0.001	—	0.003
Ronnel	—	10	—	—
Rosin core solder pyrolysis products (as formaldehyde)	—	0.1	—	0.3

APPENDIX B1

Substance	Adopted values TWA ppm*	Adopted values TWA mg/m³ †	Tentative values STEL ppm*	Tentative values STEL mg/m³ †
Rotenone (commercial)	—	5	—	10
Rouge	—	B3	—	20
Rubber solvent	400	1600	—	—
Selenium compounds (as Se)	—	0.2	—	—
Selenium hexafluoride, as Se	0.05	0.4	0.05	0.4
Sevin® (see Carbaryl)	—	5	—	10
Silane (see Silicon tetrahydride)	0.5	7	—	—
Silicon	—	B3	—	20
Silicon carbide	—	B3	—	20
Silicon tetrahydride (Silane)	0.5	0.7	1	1.5
Silver, metal and soluble compounds, as Ag	—	0.01	—	0.03
Sodium azide	0.1	0.3	—	—
Sodium fluoroacetate (1080)—Skin	—	0.05	—	0.15
Sodium hydroxide	—	2	—	—
Starch	—	B3	—	20
Stibine	0.1	0.5	0.3	1.5
Stoddard solvent	100	575	150	720
Strychnine	—	0.15	—	0.45
Styrene, monomer (Phenylethylene)	100	420	125	525
Subtilisins (Proteolytic enzymes as 100% pure crystalline enzyme)	—	0.00006	—	—
Succinaldehyde (see Glutaraldehyde)	—	(0.25)	—	—
Sucrose	—	B3	—	20
Sulfur dioxide	5	13	—	—
Sulfur hexafluoride	1000	6000	1250	7500
Sulfuric acid	—	1	—	—
Sulfur monochloride	1	6	3	18
Sulfur pentafluoride	0.025	0.25	0.075	0.75
Sulfur tetrafluoride	0.1	0.4	0.3	1
Sulfuryl fluoride	5	20	10	40
Systox, see Demeton®	0.01	0.1	0.03	0.3
2, 4, 5-T	—	10	—	20
Tantalum	—	5	—	10
TEDP—Skin	—	0.2	—	0.6
Teflon® decomposition products	—	B5	—	B5
Tellurium	—	0.1	—	—
Tellurium hexafluoride, as Te	0.02	0.2	—	—
TEPP—Skin	0.004	0.05	0.012	0.15
Terphenyls	1	9	—	—
1, 1, 1, 2-Tetrachloro-2, 2-difluoroethane	500	4170	625	5210
1, 1, 2, 2-Tetrachloro-1, 2-difluoroethane	500	4170	625	5210
1, 1, 2, 2-Tetrachloroethane—Skin	5	35	10	70
Tetrachloroethylene, see Perchloroethylene	100	670	150	1000
Tetrachloromethane, see Carbon tetrachloride	10	65	20	130
Tetrachloronaphthalene	—	2	—	4
Tetraethyl lead (as Pb)—Skin	—	0.100‡‡	—	0.3
Tetrahydrofuran	200	590	250	700
Tetramethyl lead (as Pb)—Skin	—	0.150‡‡	—	0.45
Tetramethyl succinonitrile—Skin	0.5	3	1.5	9

NOTE: Reference marks are explained on p. 394

APPENDIX B1

Substance	Adopted values TWA ppm*	Adopted values TWA mg/m³ †	Tentative values STEL ppm*	Tentative values STEL mg/m³ †
Tetranitromethane	1	8	—	—
Tetryl (2, 4, 6-trinitrophenylmethylnitramine)—Skin	—	1.5	—	3.0
Thallium, soluble compounds (as Tl)—Skin	—	0.1	—	—
4, 4'-Thiobis (6-tert butyl-m-cresol)	—	10	—	20
Thiram®	—	5	—	10
Tin, inorganic compounds, except SnH_4 and SnO_2, (as Sn)	—	2	—	4
Tin, organic compounds (as Sn)—Skin	—	0.1	—	0.2
Tin oxide	—	B3	—	20
Titanium dioxide	—	B3	—	20
Toluene (toluol)—Skin	100	375	150	560
Toluene-2, 4-diisocyanate (TDI)	0.02	0.14	—	—
o-Toluidine	5	22	10	44
Toxaphene, see Chlorinated camphene	—	0.5	—	1.5
Tributyl phosphate	—	5	—	5
1, 1, 1-Trichloroethane, see Methyl chloroform	350	1900	440	2380
1, 1, 2-Trichloroethane—Skin	10	45	20	90
Trichloroethylene	100	535	150	800
Trichloromethane, see Chloroform	(25)	(120)	—	—
Trichloronaphthalene	—	5	—	10
1, 2, 3-Trichloropropane	50	300	150	450
1, 1, 2-Trichloro 1, 2, 2-trifluoroethane	1000	7600	1250	9500
Triethylamine	25	100	40	150
Tricyclohexyltin hydroxide (Plictran®)	—	5	—	10
Trifluoromonobromomethane	1000	6100	1200	7625
Trimethyl benzene	25	120	35	180
2, 4, 6-Trinitrophenol, see Picric acid	—	0.1	—	0.3
2, 4, 6-Trinitrophenylmethylnitramine, see Tetryl	—	1.5	—	3.0
Trinitrotoluene (TNT)—Skin	—	(1.5)	—	—
Triorthocresyl phosphate	—	0.1	—	0.3
Triphenyl phosphate	—	3	—	6
Tungsten and Compounds, as W Soluble	—	1	—	3
Insoluble	—	5	—	10
Turpentine	100	560	150	840
Uranium (natural) soluble and insoluble compounds, as U	—	0.2	—	0.6
Vanadium (V_2O_5), as V Dust	—	0.5	—	1.5
Fume	—	0.05	—	—
Vinyl acetate	10	30	20	60
Vinyl benzene, see Styrene	100	420	150	630
Vinyl bromide	(250)	(1100)	—	—
Vinyl chloride	(200)	(510)	—	—
Vinyl cyanide, see Acrylonitrile	20	45	30	70
Vinyl cyclohexene dioxide	10	60	—	—
Vinylidene chloride	10	40	20	80
Vinyl toluene	100	480	150	720
Warfarin	—	0.1	—	0.3

APPENDIX B1

Substance	Adopted values TWA ppm*	Adopted values TWA mg/m³ †	Tentative values STEL ppm*	Tentative values STEL mg/m³ †
Welding fumes (Total particulate)	—	5, B5	—	B5
Wood dust (nonallergenic)	—	5	—	10
Xylene (o-, m-, p-isomers)—Skin	100	435	150	655
m-Xylene α, α'-diamine	—	0.1	—	—
Xylidene—Skin	5	25	10	50
Yttrium	—	1	—	3
Zinc chloride fume	—	1	—	2
Zinc chromate (as Cr)	—	0.05, B2	—	—
Zinc oxide fume	—	5	—	10
Zinc stearate	—	B3	—	20
Zirconium compounds (as Zr)	—	5	—	10

*Parts of vapor or gas per million parts of contaminated air by volume at 25°C and 760 mm Hg pressure.
†Approximate milligrams of substance per cubic meter of air.
‡An atmospheric concentration of not more than 0.02 ppm, or personal protection may be necessary to avoid headache for intermittent exposure.
§< 7 μm in diameter.
¶As sampled by method that does not collect vapor.
**According to analytically determined composition.
††For control of general room air, biologic monitoring is essential for personnel control.

Biologic Limit Values (BLVs). Other means exist and may be necessary for monitoring worker exposure other than reliance on the Threshold Limit Values for industrial air, namely, the Biologic Limit Values. These values represent limiting amounts of substances (or their effects) to which the worker may be exposed without hazard to health or well-being as determined in his tissues and fluids or in his exhaled breath. The biologic measurements on which the BLVs are based can furnish two kinds of information useful in the control of worker exposure: (1) measure of the individual worker's over-all exposure; (2) measure of the worker's individual and characteristic response. Measurements of response furnish a superior estimate of the physiologic status of the worker, and may be made of (a) changes in amount of some critical biochemical constituent, (b) changes in activity of a critical enzyme, (c) changes in some physiologic function. Measurement of exposure may be made by (1) determining in blood, urine, hair, nails, in body tissues and fluids, the amount of substance to which the worker was exposed; (2) determination of the amount of the metabolite(s) of the substance in tissues and fluids; (3) determination of the amount of the substance in the exhaled breath. The biologic limits may be used as an adjunct to the TLVs for air, or in place of them. The BLVs, and their associated procedures for determining compliance with them, should thus be regarded as an effective means of providing health surveillance of the worker.

Unlisted Substances. Many substances present or handled in industrial processes do not appear on the TLV list. In a number of instances the material is rarely present as a particulate, vapor or other airborne contaminant, and a TLV is not necessary. In other cases sufficient information to warrant development of a TLV, even on a tentative basis, is not available to the Committee.

NOTICE OF INTENDED CHANGES (FOR 1977)

These substances, with their corresponding values, comprise those for which either a limit has been proposed for the first time, or for which a change in the "Adopted" listing has been proposed. In both cases, the proposed limits should be considered trial limits that will remain in the listing for a period of at least two years. If, after two years no evidence comes to light that questions the appropriateness of the values herein, the values will be reconsidered for the "Adopted" list. Documentation is available for each of these substances.

APPENDIX B TOXIC SUBSTANCES **395**

Substance	ppm*	mg/m³†
Aliphatic solvent "140 Flash"	25	150
Aluminum metal and oxide	—	10
Aluminum pyro powders	—	5
Aluminum welding fumes	—	5
Aluminum, soluble salts	—	2
Aluminum alkyls (NOC)*	—	2
3-Amino 1, 2, 4-triazole	B2-2	—
Antimony, soluble salts (as Sb)	—	2
Antimony trioxide, handling & use (as Sb)	—	0.5
Antimony trioxide production (as Sb)	—	0.05, B2-2
Arsenic trioxide production (as As)	—	0.05, B2-1a
Atrazine	—	10
Benomyl	—	10
Bromacil	—	10
Butyl acrylate	10	55
Cadmium oxide production (as Cd)	—	0.05, B2-2
Calcium hydroxide	—	5
Calcium oxide	—	2
Carbonyl fluoride	5	15
Chloroform	10, B2-2	50
Chloromethyl methyl ether	B2-1b, B7	B2-1b, B7
Chromite ore processing (chromate), as Cr	—	0.05, B2-1a
Cobalt metal, dust & fume (as Co)	—	0.05
Cyclopentane	300	850
Dichloromonofluoromethane	500	2100
Dimethyl carbamyl chloride	B2-2	B2-2
Ethyl silicate	10	85
Glutaraldehyde	0.2	0.8
Hexachlorobutadiene	B2-2	B2-2
Hexamethyl phosphoramide—Skin	B2-2	B2-2
Lead chromate (as Cr)	—	0.05, B2-2
Manganese fume (as Mn)	—	1
Manganese tetroxide	—	1
4, 4'-Methylene dianiline	—	B2-2
N, Methyl-2-pyrrolidone	100	400
Nickel sulfide roasting (as Ni)	—	1, B2-1a
Paraquat, respirable sizes	—	0.1
Phenyl-beta-aphthylamine	B2-2	B2-2
Phenyl mercaptan	0.5	2
Phosgene	0.1	0.4
m-Phthalodinitrile	—	5
Propylene glycol dinitrate-Skin	0.2	2
Thioglycolic acid	1	5
1, 2, 4-Trichlorobenzene	5	40
Trimethyl phosphite	0.5	2.6
2, 4, 6-Trinitrotoluene (TNT)	—	0.5
Valeraldehyde	50	175
Vinyl bromide	5	22
Vinyl chloride	Pending, B2-1c, B7	—
VM & P Naphtha	300	1350

*Parts of vapor or gas, per million parts of contaminated air by volume at 25°C and 760 mm Hg pressure.

†Approximate number of milligrams per cubic meter of air.

APPENDIX B2 CARCINOGENS

The Committee lists below those substances in industrial use that have proven carcinogenic in man, or have induced cancer in animals under appropriate experimental conditions. Present listing of those substances carcinogenic for man takes three forms: Those for which a TLV has been assigned **(1a)**, those for which environmental conditions have not been sufficiently defined to assign a TLV **(1b)**, and **(1c)**, those whose reassignment of a TLV is awaiting more definitive data, and hence should be treated as a **1b** carcinogen.

1. Human carcinogens

a Processes, substances associated with industrial processes, recognized to have carcinogenic or cocarcinogenic potential, with an assigned TLV:

Process or Substance	TLV
Arsenic trioxide production	As_2O_3, 0.05 mg/m^3 as As
	SO_2, C 5.0 ppm
	Sb_2O_3, 0.5 mg/m^3 (as Sb)
Asbestos, all forms*	5 fibers/cm^3 > 5 μm in length
bis (Chloromethyl) ether	0.001 ppm
Chromite ore processing (chromate)	0.05 mg/m^3 (as Cr)
Nickel sulfide roasting, fume & dust	1.0 mg/m^3 (as Ni)
Particulate polycyclic aromatic hydrocarbons (PPAH)	0.2 mg/m^3, as benzene solubles

*Cigarette smoking can enhance the incidence of bronchogenic carcinoma from this and others of these substances or processes. See also B7.

b Processes, or substances associated with industrial processes, recognized to have carcinogenic potential without an assigned TLV:

4-Aminodiphenyl (*p*-Xenylamine)
Benzidine production
beta-Naphthylamine
4-Nitrodiphenyl

c Substances with recognized carcinogenic potential awaiting reassignment of TLV pending further data acquisition:

Vinyl chloride (see B7 for OSHA standard)

For the substances in **1b** no exposure or contact by any route—respiratory, skin or oral, as detected by the most sensitive methods—shall be permitted.

"No exposure or contact" means sealing the process or operation by the best practicable engineering methods. The worker should be properly equipped to insure virtually no contact with the carcinogen.

2. Industrial substances suspect of carcinogenic potential for man.

Chemical processes or substances associated with industrial processes, which are suspect of inducing cancer, based on either (1) limited epidemiologic evidence, exclusive of clinical reports of single cases, or (2) demonstration of carcinogenesis in one or more animal species by appropriate methods. For the above, worker exposure by all routes should be carefully controlled to levels consistent with the animal and human experience data, including those substances with a listed TLV.

APPENDIX B TOXIC SUBSTANCES

Process or Substance	TLV
Antimony trioxide production*	0.05 mg/m^3
Benzene—Skin	10 ppm
Benz(a)pyrene	—
Beryllium	2.0 μg/m^3
Cadmium oxide production	0.05 mg/m^3
Chloroform	10 ppm
Chromates of lead and zinc (as Cr)	0.05 mg/m^3
3, 3′-Dichlorobenzidine	—
Dimethylcarbamyl chloride	—
1, 1-Dimethyl hydrazine	0.5 ppm
Dimethyl sulfate	1 ppm
Epichlorhydrin	5 ppm
Hexamethyl phosphoramide—Skin	—
Hydrazine	0.1 ppm
4, 4′-Methylene bis (2-chloroaniline)—Skin	0.02 ppm
4,4′-Methylene dianiline	—
Monomethyl hydrazine	0.2 ppm
Nitrosamines	—
Propane sulfone	—
beta-Propiolactone	—
Vinyl cyclohexene dioxide	10 ppm

*Cigarette smoking can enhance the incidence of respiratory cancers from this or others of these substances or processes.

APPENDIX B3 SOME NUISANCE PARTICULATES TLV, 30 million particles per cubic foot of air or 10 mg/m^3

Alundum (Al$_2$O$_3$)	Kaolin
Calcium carbonate	Limestone
Calcium silicate	Magnesite
Cellulose (paper fiber)	Marble
Portland cement	Mineral wool fiber
Corundum (Al$_2$O$_3$)	Pentaerythritol
Emery	Plaster of Paris
Glass, fibrous or dust	Rouge
Glycerin mist	Silicon
Graphite (synthetic)	Silicon carbide
Gypsum	Starch
Vegetable oil mists	Sucrose
(except castor, cashew	Tin oxide
nut, or similar irritant	Titanium dioxide
oils)	Zinc stearate
	Zinc oxide dust

APPENDIX B4 PERMISSIBLE EXCURSIONS FOR TIME-WEIGHTED AVERAGE (TWA) LIMITS

The Excursion TLV Factor in the table automatically defines the magnitude of the permissible excursion above the limit for those substances not given a C designation; i.e., the TWA limits. Examples in the Table show that nitrobenzene, the TLV for which is 1 ppm, should never be allowed to exceed 3 ppm. Similarly, carbon tetrachloride, TLV = 10 ppm, should never be allowed to exceed 20 ppm. By contrast, those substances with a C designation are not subject to the excursion factor and must be kept at or below the TLV ceiling.

These limiting excursions are to be considered to provide a "rule-of-thumb" guidance for listed substances generally, and may not provide the most appropriate excursion for a particular substance e.g., the permissible excursion for CO is 400 ppm for 15 minutes.

For appropriate excursions for 142 substances consult *Pa. Rules & Regs.*, Chap. 4, Art. 432, and "Acceptable Concentrations," ANSI.

Substance	TLV, ppm	Excursion factor	Max. conc. permitted for short time, ppm
Nitrobenzene	1	3	3
Carbon tetrachloride	10	2	20
Trimethyl benzene	25	1.5	40
Acetone	1000	1.25	1250
Boron trifluoride	C 1	—	1
Butylamine	C 5	—	5

Excursion factors for all substances not bearing C notation:

TLV ppm or mg/m^3	Excursion factor
> 0 to 1	3
> 1 to 10	2
> 10 to 100	1.5
> 100 to 1000	1.25

The number of times the excursion above the TLV is permitted is governed by conformity with the Time-Weighted Average TLV.

APPENDIX B5 SUBSTANCES OF VARIABLE COMPOSITION

1. Polytetrafluoroethylene* decomposition products.

Thermal decomposition of the fluorocarbon chain in air leads to the formation of oxidized products containing carbon, fluorine and oxygen. Because these products decompose in part by hydrolysis in alkaline solution, they can be quantitatively determined in air as fluoride to provide an index of exposure. No TLV is recommended pending determination of the toxicity of the products, but air concentrations should be minimal.

2. Gasoline.

The composition of gasoline varies greatly and thus a single TLV for all types of these materials is no longer applicable. In general, the aromatic hydrocarbon content will determine what TLV applies. Consequently the content of benzene, other aromatics and additives should be determined to arrive at the appropriate TLV (Elkins, et al. A.I.H.A.J. *24*:99, 1963); Runion, ibid. *36*, 338, 1975).

3. Welding fumes—total particulate (NOC)† TLV, 5 mg/m^3

Welding fumes cannot be classified simply. The composition and quantity of both are dependent on the alloy being welded and the process and electrodes used. Reliable analysis of fumes cannot be made without considering the nature of the welding process and system being examined; reactive metals and alloys such as aluminum and titanium are arc-welded in a protective, inert atmosphere

*Trade Names: Algoflon, Fluon, Halon, Teflon, Tetran.

†Not otherwise classified.

such as argon. These arcs create relatively little fume, but an intense radiation which can produce ozone. Similar processes are used to arc-weld steels, also creating a relatively low level of fumes. Ferrous alloys also are arc-welded in oxidizing environments which generate considerable fume, and can produce carbon monoxide instead of ozone. Such fumes generally are composed of discreet particles of amorphous slags containing iron, manganese, silicon and other metallic constituents depending on the alloy system involved. Chromium and nickel compounds are found in fumes when stainless steels are arc-welded. Some coated and flux-cored electrodes are formulated with fluorides and the fumes associated with them can contain significantly more fluorides than oxides. Because of the above factors, arc-welding fumes frequently must be tested for individual constituents which are likely to be present to determine whether specific TLV's are exceeded. Conclusions based on total fume concentration are generally adequate if no toxic elements are present in welding rod, metal, or metal coating and conditions are not conducive to the formation of toxic gases.

Most welding, even with primitive ventilation, does not produce exposures inside the welding helmet above 5 mg/m^3. That which does, should be controlled.

APPENDIX B6 SOME SIMPLE ASPHYXIANTS

Acetylene
Argon
Butane
Ethane
Ethylene
Helium
Hydrogen
Methane
Neon
Propane
Propylene

APPENDIX B7 SUBSTANCES FOR WHICH SPECIFIC STANDARDS HAVE BEEN SET BY OSHA

"Zero" tolerance is meant as goal, not absolute limit.

Substance	Limit 8 hours	ceiling conc.	Precautions
asbestos (fibers longer than 5 micrometers)	2 fibers/cc	10 fibers/cm^3	Ventilation, work practices, personal protection, warning signs.
4-nitrobiphenyl (0.1% solutions or greater)	"zero" (as low as practicable)	—	Decontamination areas, protective clothing and respirators, ventilation.
alpha-naphthylamine (1% solutions or greater conc.)	"zero"	—	Same as above
methyl chloromethyl ether (0.1% conc. or greater)	"zero"	—	Same as above
3,3'-dichlorobenzidine and its salts, 1%	"zero"	—	Same as above
bis-(chloromethyl) ether 0.1%	"zero"	—	Same as above
beta-naphthylamine 0.1%	"zero"	—	Same as above
benzidine, 0.1%	"zero"	—	Same as above
4-aminodiphenyl 0.1%	"zero"	—	Same as above
ethyleneimine, 1%	"zero"	—	Same as above
beta-propiolactone 1%	"zero"	—	Same as above
2-acetylaminofluorene, 1%	"zero"	—	Same as above
4-dimethylaminoazobenzene 1%	"zero"	—	Same as above
N-nitrosodimethylamine, 1%	"zero"	—	Same as above
Vinyl chloride	0.5 ppm	action level	(monitoring required)
	1 ppm	5 ppm/15 min	Various respirators
Coke oven emissions	150 μg/m^3*	—	Respirators, engineering controls

*Benzene-soluble fraction

APPENDIX C
HAZARDOUS MATERIALS HANDLING

The table is based on Department of Transportation regulations current to July, 1978.

PURPOSE AND USE OF THE TABLE.

(a) The table designates materials listed as hazardous for purposes of transportation. In addition, it classifies requirements set forth elsewhere pertaining to the labeling, packaging and transportation of those materials.

(b) Column 1 contains three symbols: *, A, and W.

   (1) *: An asterisk before a proper shipping name means that the material described in column 2 may or may not be regulated under the class shown depending on whether or not the commodity meets the definition of the hazard class listed for that entry. If the commodity does not meet the definition of the class stated, the shipper shall determine whether or not the material meets the definition of any other hazard class, and shall prepare the material for shipment in compliance with the requirements of that class. A material meeting the description of an asterisk entry does not meet the definition of a hazardous material under DOT rules.

   (2) A: The symbol "A" before the shipping name means that the material described in column 2 is subject to the requirements only for transportation by aircraft.

   (3) W: The symbol "W" before the shipping name means that the material described in column 2 is subject to the requirements only for transportation by vessel.

(c) Column 2 lists the proper shipping name of those materials which are designated as hazardous materials. Proper shipping names are limited to those shown in Roman type (not italics). In the selection of a proper shipping name to describe a particular material, if the correct technical name of that material is not shown, or is not appropriate, selection must be made from the general descriptions or n.o.s. entries corresponding to the specific hazard class of the material being shipped. The name that more appropriately describes the commodity must be used, i.e., an alcohol must be shipped as an alcohol n.o.s. rather than a flammable liquid n.o.s. unless the technical name of the alcohol is listed (methyl alcohol). Some mixtures may be more aptly described by their application such as: "Compound, cleaning" or "Compound, rust removing," rather than "Corrosive liquid n.o.s." For materials that meet the definition of more than one hazard class, the hazard class must be determined by using the precedence given in 49 CFR 173.2 of the DOT regulations. If it is believed that an adequate description of a material is not given here, the Office of Hazardous Materials Operations should be contacted for clarification.

   (1) Shipping names may be used in the singular or plural in either capital or lower case letters.

   (2) The words in italics are not part of the proper shipping name but may be used in addition to the proper shipping name. The word "or" in italics indicates that any terms in the sequence may be used as the proper shipping name as appropriate.

(3) The abbreviation "n.o.i." which means "not otherwise indexed" or "n.o.i.b.n." which means "not otherwise indexed by name" may be used interchangeably with "n.o.s."

(4) When qualifying words are used as part of the proper shipping name, their sequence on package markings and shipping paper descriptions is optional.

(5) When one entry references another entry by use of a *"see,"* if both names are in Roman type, either name may be used as a proper shipping name (e.g. Isopropanol *see* Alcohol, n.o.s.).

(6) When a shipping name includes a concentration range as part of the shipping description, the actual concentration being shipped, if it is within the range stated, may be used in place of the concentration range. For example: Hydrogen peroxide solution (8% to 40% peroxide) may be shipped described as "Hydrogen peroxide solution, 30% peroxide." or "30% Hydrogen peroxide solution."

(7) The use of the prefix "mono" is optional in any shipping name. Thus monoethanolamine may be used interchangeably with ethanolamine. In the word "trichloromonofluoromethane" the term "mono" is considered as a prefix to the term "fluoromethane".

(d) Column 3 contains a designation of the hazard class corresponding to each proper shipping name or the word "Forbidden." A material for which the class entry is "Forbidden" must not be offered or accepted for transportation. When re-evaluation of test data or new test data indicates a need to modify the hazard class or labels specified for a material specifically identified in § 172.101, these data should be reported to the Office of Hazardous Materials Operations.

(e) Column 4 specifies the labels required to be applied to each outside packaging, subject to the additional labeling requirements in 49 CFR 127.402.

(f) Column 5 references the applicable packaging section of 49 CFR 173. Exceptions from some of the requirements of this subchapter are noted in column 5(a). References to specific packaging requirements and exceptions other than those specified in 5(a) are noted in column 5(b).

(g) Column 6 indicates the maximum net quantity in one package for air transportation or passenger railcar;

(1) Column 6(a) specifies the maximum net quantity permitted in one package for passenger-carrying aircraft or passenger railcar. For air transportation, any material forbidden on passenger-carrying aircraft but permitted on cargo aircraft, or which exceeds the maximum quantity authorized on passenger-carrying aircraft, must be shipped by cargo-only aircraft and bear the CARGO AIRCRAFT ONLY label as described in 49 CFR 172.448.

(2) Column 6(b) lists the maximum net quantity for one outside package on cargo aircraft. Packaging must bear the CARGO AIRCRAFT ONLY label when the quantity of hazardous material exceeds that authorized on passenger-carrying aircraft, or is forbidden on passenger-carrying aircraft.

(3) For a flammable liquid identified by a n.o.s. entry, the net quantity limitation for carriage aboard a passenger-carrying aircraft or railcar is one gallon per package, and for cargo-only aircraft is 55 gallons per package, if:

(i) The material has a flash point of 73°F. or higher;

(ii) The material does not meet the definition of any other hazard class as defined in this part, and

(iii) The flash point, or an indication that the flash point is 73°F. or higher, is marked on the outside package.

(h) Column 7 specified each of the authorized locations on board cargo vessels and passenger vessels and certain additional requirements for shipments of each listed hazardous material. Section 49 CFR 176.63 sets forth the physical requirements for each of the authorized locations listed in Column 7. (For bulk shipments by water see 46 CFR Parts 30 to 40, 48, 64, 70, 98, 148, 151, and 154.)

(1) "1" means the material may be stowed "on deck" subject to the requirements of 49 CFR 176.63(b). When both "on deck" and "under deck" are authorized, "under deck" should be used if it is available.

(2) "2" means the material may be stowed "under deck" in a compartment or hold subject to the requirements of 49 CFR 176.63(c). When both "on deck" and "under deck" are authorized, "under deck" should be used if it is available.

(3) "3" means the material may be stowed "under deck away from heat" in a ventilated compartment or hold subject to the requirements of 49 CFR 176.63(d).

(4) "4" means the material is authorized to be transported in only the limited quantities specified in the CFR section listed in Column 5 and is subject to the stowage requirements specified for a cargo vessel for the same material.

(5) "5" means the material is forbidden and may not be offered or accepted for transportation.

(6) "6" means the material is authorized to be transported in a magazine subject to the requirements of 49 CFR 176.135 through 176.144.

Hazardous Materials Table

(1)	(2) Hazardous materials descriptions and proper shipping names	(3) Hazard class	(4) Label(s) required (if not excepted)	(5) Packaging (a) Exceptions	(5) Packaging (b) Specific requirements	(6) Maximum net quantity in one package (a) Passenger carrying aircraft or railcar	(6) (b) Cargo only aircraft	(7) Water shipments (a) Cargo vessel	(7) (b) Passenger vessel	(7) (c) Other requirements
	Accumulator, pressurized (pneumatic or hydraulic), containing nonflammable gas	Nonflammable gas	Nonflammable gas	173.306		No limit	No limit	1,2	1,2	
	Acetal	Flammable liquid	Flammable liquid	173.118	173.119	1 quart	10 gallons	1,3	4	
	Acetaldehyde (ethyl aldehyde)	Flammable liquid	Flammable liquid	None	173.119	Forbidden	10 gallons	1,3	5	
A	Acetaldehyde ammonia	ORM-A	None	173.505	173.510	No limit	No limit			
•	Acetic acid (aqueous solution)	Corrosive material	Corrosive	173.244	173.245	1 quart	10 gallons	1,2	1,2	Stow separate from nitric acid or oxidizing materials
	Acetic acid, glacial	Corrosive material	Corrosive	173.244	173.245	1 quart	10 gallons	1,2	1,2	Stow separate from nitric acid or oxidizing materials. Segregation same as for flammable liquids
	Acetic anhydride	Corrosive material	Corrosive	173.244	173.119	1 quart	1 gallon	1,2	1,2	
	Acetone	Flammable liquid	Flammable liquid	173.118		1 quart	10 gallons	1,3	4	
	Acetone cyanohydrin	Poison B	Poison	None	173.346	Forbidden	55 gallons	1	5	Shade from radiant heat. Stow away from corrosive materials
	Acetone oil	Flammable liquid	Flammable liquid	173.118	173.119	1 quart	10 gallons	1,2	1	
	Acetonitrile	Flammable liquid	Flammable liquid	173.118	173.119	1 quart	10 gallons	1	4	Shade from radiant heat
	Acetyl benzoyl peroxide, solid	Forbidden								
	Acetyl benzoyl peroxide solution, not over 40% peroxide	Organic peroxide	Organic peroxide	None	173.222	Forbidden	1 quart	1,2	1	
	Acetyl bromide	Corrosive material	Corrosive	173.244	173.247	1 quart	1 gallon	1	1	Keep dry. Glass carboys not permitted on passenger vessels

Hazardous Materials Table (cont'd)

(1) */W/A	(2) Hazardous materials descriptions and proper shipping names	(3) Hazard class	(4) Label(s) required (if not excepted)	(5) Packaging (a) Exceptions	(5) Packaging (b) Specific requirements	(6) Maximum net quantity in one package (a) Passenger carrying aircraft or railcar	(6) Maximum net quantity in one package (b) Cargo only aircraft	(7) Water shipments (a) Cargo vessel	(7) Water shipments (b) Passenger vessel	(7) Water shipments (c) Other requirements
	Acetyl chloride	Flammable liquid	Flammable liquid	173.244	173.247	1 quart	1 gallon	1	1	Stow away from alcohols. Keep cool and dry. Separate longitudinally by an intervening complete compartment or hold from explosives
	Acetylene	Flammable gas	Flammable gas	None	173.303	Forbidden	300 pounds	1	1	Shade from radiant heat
A	Acetylene tetrabromide	ORM-A	None	173.505	173.510	10 gallons	55 gallons	1	1	
	Acetyl iodide	Corrosive material	Corrosive	173.244	173.247	1 quart	1 gallon	1	1	Keep dry. Glass carboys not permitted on passenger vessels
	Acetyl peroxide solution, *not over 25% peroxide*	Organic peroxide	Organic peroxide	173.153	173.222	Forbidden	1 quart	1,2	1	
	Acid butyl phosphate	Corrosive material	Corrosive	173.244	173.245	1 quart	5 gallons	1,2	1,2	Glass carboys in hampers not permitted under deck
	Acid carboy empty. *See Carboy, empty*									
•	Acid, liquid, n.o.s.	Corrosive material	Corrosive	173.244	173.245	1 quart	5 pints	1	4	Keep cool
•	Acid, sludge	Corrosive material	Corrosive	None	173.248	Forbidden	1 quart	1,2	1	
	Acrolein, inhibited	Flammable liquid	Flammable liquid and Poison	None	173.122	Forbidden	1 quart	1,2	5	Keep cool. Stow away from living quarters
	Acrylic acid	Corrosive material	Corrosive	173.244	173.245	1 quart	5 pints	1	1	
	Acrylonitrile	Flammable liquid	Flammable liquid and Poison	None	173.119	Forbidden	1 quart	1,2	5	Keep cool

	Actuating cartridge, explosive (fire extinguisher, or valve)	Class C explosive	Explosive C	173.114		50 pounds	150 pounds	1,2	1,2	Keep cool and dry
•	Adhesive, n.o.s. See Cement, liquid, n.o.s.								
	Aerosol product, each aerosol container exceeding 50 cubic inches capacity. See Compressed gas, n.o.s.								
•	Air, compressed	Nonflammable gas	Nonflammable gas	173.306	173.302	150 pounds	300 pounds	1,2	1,2
	Aircraft rocket engine (Commercial)	Flammable solid	Flammable solid	None	173.238	Forbidden	550 pounds	1,3	5
	Aircraft rocket engine igniter (Commercial)	Flammable solid	Flammable solid	None	173.238	Forbidden	25 pounds	1,3	5
	Airplane flare. See Fireworks, special								
•	Alcohol, n.o.s.	Flammable liquid	Flammable liquid	173.118	173.125	1 quart	10 gallons	1,2	1
	Alcohol, n.o.s.	Combustible liquid	None	173.118a	None	No limit	No limit	1,2	1,2
	Aldrin	Poison B	Poison	173.364	173.376	50 pounds	200 pounds	1,2	1,2
A	Aldrin, cast solid	ORM-A	None	173.505	173.510	No limit	No limit	1,2	1,2
	Aldrin mixture, dry (with more than 65% aldrin)	Poison B	Poison	173.364	173.376	50 pounds	200 pounds	1,2	1,2
A	Aldrin mixture, dry, with 65% or less aldrin	ORM-A	None	173.505	173.510	No limit	No limit	1,2	1,2
	Aldrin mixture, liquid (with more than 60% aldrin)	Poison B	Poison	173.345	173.361	1 quart	55 gallons	1,2	1,2
A	Aldrin mixture, liquid, with 60% or less aldrin	ORM-A	None	173.505	173.510	No limit	No limit	1,2	1,2	If flash point less than 141 DEG F, segregation same as for flammable liquids
	Alkaline corrosive battery fluid	Corrosive material	Corrosive	173.244	173.249 173.257	1 quart	5 gallons	1,2	1,2
	Alkaline corrosive battery fluid with empty storage battery	Corrosive material	Corrosive	None	173.258	Forbidden	5 pints	1,2	1,2
	Alkaline corrosive liquid, n.o.s.	Corrosive material	Corrosive	173.244	173.249	1 quart	5 gallons	1,2	1,2
•	Alkaline liquid, n.o.s.	Corrosive material	Corrosive	173.244	173.249	1 quart	5 gallons	1,2	1,2
	Alkanesulfonic acid	Corrosive material	Corrosive	173.244	173.245	5 pints	1 gallon	1,2	1

407

Hazardous Materials Table (cont'd)

(1)	(2)	(3)	(4)	(5) Packaging		(6) Maximum net quantity in one package		(7) Water shipments		
	Hazardous materials descriptions and proper shipping names	Hazard class	Label(s) required (if not excepted)	(a) Exceptions	(b) Specific requirements	(a) Passenger carrying aircraft or railcar	(b) Cargo only aircraft	(a) Cargo vessel	(b) Passenger vessel	(c) Other requirements
	Allyl aluminum halides. See Pyrophoric liquid, n.o.s.									
A	Allethrin	ORM-A	None	173.505	173.510	No limit	No limit			
	Allyl alcohol	Flammable liquid	Flammable liquid and Poison	173.118	173.119	1 quart	10 gallons	1,2	1	
	Allyl bromide	Flammable liquid	Flammable liquid	173.118	173.119	Forbidden	10 gallons	1,2	1	
	Allyl chloride	Flammable liquid	Flammable liquid	None	173.119	Forbidden	10 gallons	1,3	5	
	Allyl chlorocarbonate	Flammable liquid	Flammable liquid	None	173.288	Forbidden	5 pints	1	5	Keep dry. Separate longitudinally by an intervening complete hold or compartment from explosives Segregation same as for corrosive materials
	Allyl chloroformate. See Allyl chlorocarbonate									
	Allyl trichlorosilane	Corrosive material	Corrosive	None	173.280	Forbidden	10 gallons	1	1	Keep dry
	Aluminum alkyls. See Pyrophoric liquid, n.o.s.									
	Aluminum bromide, anhydrous	Corrosive material	Corrosive	173.244	173.245b	25 pounds	100 pounds	1,2	1,2	Keep dry
	Aluminum dross, wet or hot. See Sec. 173.173									
	Aluminum hydride	Flammable solid	Flammable solid and Dangerous when wet	None	173.206	Forbidden	25 pounds	1,2	5	Segregation same as for flammable solid labeled Dangerous When Wet

• Aluminum, liquid or paint. See Paint, enamel, lacquer stain, shellac, varnish, etc.							
• Aluminum, metallic, powder	Flammable solid	Flammable solid	173.232	173.232	25 pounds	100 pounds	1,2	1,2	Keep dry. Segregation same as for flammable solids labeled dangerous when wet
Aluminum nitrate	Oxidizer	Oxidizer	173.153	173.182	25 pounds	100 pounds	1,2	1,2	
• Aluminum phosphate solution	Corrosive material	Corrosive	173.244	173.245	1 quart	10 gallons	1,2	1,2	Stow away from acids and oxidizing materials
Aluminum phosphide	Flammable solid	Flammable solid and Dangerous when wet	None	173.154	Forbidden	25 pounds	1,2	1,2	
Amatol. See High explosive								
2-(2-Aminoethoxy) ethanol	Corrosive material	Corrosive	173.244	173.245	1 quart	10 gallons	1,2	1,2	
N-Aminoethylpiperazine	Corrosive material	Corrosive	173.244	173.245	1 quart	10 gallons	1,2	1,2	
Aminopropyldiethanolamine	Corrosive material	Corrosive	173.244	173.245	1 quart	10 gallons	1,2	1,2	
n-Aminopropylmorpholine	Corrosive material	Corrosive	173.244	173.245	1 quart	10 gallons	1,2	1,2	
bis (Aminopropyl) piperazine	Corrosive material	Corrosive	173.244	173.245	1 quart	10 gallons	1,2	1,2	
Ammonia, anhydrous	Nonflammable gas	Nonflammable gas	173.306	173.304 173.314 173.315	Forbidden	300 pounds	1,2	4	Stow in well ventilated space
Ammonia solution (containing more than 44% ammonia)	Nonflammable gas	Nonflammable gas	173.306	173.304 173.314 173.315	Forbidden	300 pounds	1,2	4	Stow in well ventilated space
Ammonia solution (containing 44% or less ammonia in water). See Ammonium hydroxide								
Ammonium arsenate, solid	Poison B	Poison	173.364	173.365	50 pounds	200 pounds	1,2	1,2	Stow away from alkaline corrosives
Ammonium bifluoride. See Ammonium hydrogen fluoride								
Ammonium chlorate	Forbidden							
Ammonium dichromate (ammonium bichromate)	Oxidizer	Oxidizer	173.153	173.154 173.235	25 pounds	100 pounds	1,2	1,2	

Hazardous Materials Table (cont'd)

(1)	(2) Hazardous materials descriptions and proper shipping names	(3) Hazard class	(4) Label(s) required (if not excepted)	(5) Packaging (a) Exceptions	(5) Packaging (b) Specific requirements	(6) Maximum net quantity in one package (a) Passenger carrying aircraft or railcar	(6) (b) Cargo only aircraft	(7) Water shipments (a) Cargo vessel	(7) (b) Passenger vessel	(7) (c) Other requirements
A	Ammonium fluoride	ORM-B	None	173.505	173.510 173.800	25 pounds	100 pounds			
•	Ammonium hydrogen fluoride solution	Corrosive material	Corrosive	173.244	173.245	1 quart	5 gallons	1,2	1,2	Keep dry
A	Ammonium hydrogen sulfate	ORM-B	None	173.505	173.510 173.800	25 pounds	100 pounds			
A	Ammonium hydrosulfide solution	ORM-A	None	173.505	173.510 173.605	10 gallons	55 gallons			
•	Ammonium hydroxide (*containing not more than 44% ammonia*)	Corrosive material	Corrosive	173.244	173.245	2 gallons	2 gallons	1	4	
	Ammonium nitrate (no organic coating)	Oxidizer	Oxidizer	173.153	173.182	25 pounds	100 pounds	1,2	1,2	
	Ammonium nitrate (organic coating)	Oxidizer	Oxidizer	173.153	173.182	25 pounds	100 pounds	1,2	1,2	
	Ammonium nitrate-carbonate mixture	Oxidizer	Oxidizer	173.153	173.182	25 pounds	100 pounds	1,2	1,2	
	Ammonium nitrate fertilizer, containing no more than 0.2% carbon									
	Ammonium nitrate-fuel oil mixture. See Nitro carbonitrate or Explosive, Class A or B									
•	Ammonium nitrate mixed fertilizer	Oxidizer	Oxidizer	173.153	173.182	25 pounds	100 pounds	1,2	1,2	
•	Ammonium nitrate-phosphate	Oxidizer	Oxidizer	173.153	173.182	25 pounds	100 pounds	1,2	1,2	
•	Ammonium perchlorate	Oxidizer	Oxidizer	173.153	173.154 173.239a	25 pounds	100 pounds	1,2	4	Stow away from powdered metals
•	*Ammonium perchlorate. See High explosives*									

Ammonium permanganate	Oxidizer	Oxidizer	None	173.154	Forbidden	Forbidden	1.2	1.2	Separate from ammonium compounds and hydrogen peroxide. This material may be forbidden in water transportation by certain countries
Ammonium picrate. See High explosive									
Ammonium picrate, wet (with 10% or more water)	Flammable solid	Flammable solid	173.192		1 pound	1 pound	1	4	Stow away from heavy metals and their compounds
A Ammonium polysulfide solution	ORM-A	None	173.505	173.510 173.605	10 gallons	55 gallons			
W Ammonium sulfate nitrate	ORM-C	None	173.505	172.910					Must not be accepted for transportation while hot. Separate by an intervening hold or compartment from Class A explosives. Separate from other explosives, corrosive materials, flammable solids, liquids, or gases, oxidizing materials, organic peroxides, or organic materials
• Ammonium sulfide solution	Flammable liquid	Flammable liquid	173.118	173.119	1 quart	10 gallons	1.2	1.2	
Ammunition, chemical (containing a Poison A liquid or gas). See Chemical ammunition (containing a Poison A material)									
Ammunition, chemical (containing a Poison B material). See Chemical ammunition (containing a Poison B material)									
Ammunition, chemical (containing an irritating liquid or solid). See Chemical ammunition (containing an irritating material)									
Ammunition, chemical, explosive, with Poison A material	Class A explosive	Explosive A and Poison gas	None	173.59	Forbidden	Forbidden	6	5	No other cargo may be stowed in the same hold with these items
Ammunition, chemical, explosive, with Poison B material	Class A explosive	Explosive A and Poison	None	173.59	Forbidden	Forbidden	6	5	No other cargo may be stowed in the same hold with these items
Ammunition, chemical, explosive, with irritant	Class A explosive	Explosive A and Irritant	None	173.59	Forbidden	Forbidden	6	5	No other cargo may be stowed in the same hold with these items
Ammunition for cannon with empty projectile	Class B explosive	Explosive B	None	173.89	Forbidden	Forbidden	1.2	5	
Ammunition for cannon with explosive projectile	Class A explosive	Explosive A	None	173.54	Forbidden	Forbidden	6	5	
Ammunition for cannon with gas projectile	Class A explosive	Explosive A	None	173.54	Forbidden	Forbidden	6	5	
Ammunition for cannon with illuminating projectile	Class A explosive	Explosive A	None	173.54	Forbidden	Forbidden	6	5	
Ammunition for cannon with incendiary projectile	Class A explosive	Explosive A	None	173.54	Forbidden	Forbidden	6	5	
Ammunition for cannon with inert loaded projectile	Class B explosive	Explosive B	None	173.89	Forbidden	Forbidden	1.2	5	

Hazardous Materials Table (cont'd)

(1) */W/A	(2) Hazardous materials descriptions and proper shipping names	(3) Hazard class	(4) Label(s) required (if not excepted)	(5) Packaging (a) Exceptions	(5) Packaging (b) Specific requirements	(6) Maximum net quantity in one package (a) Passenger carrying aircraft or railcar	(6) Maximum net quantity in one package (b) Cargo only aircraft	(7) Water shipments (a) Cargo vessel	(7) Water shipments (b) Passenger vessel	(7) Water shipments (c) Other requirements
	Ammunition for cannon with smoke projectile	Class A explosive	Explosive A	None	173.54	Forbidden	Forbidden	6	5	
	Ammunition for cannon with solid projectile	Class B explosive	Explosive B	None	173.89	Forbidden	Forbidden	1,2	5	
	Ammunition for cannon without projectile	Class B explosive	Explosive B	None	173.89	Forbidden	Forbidden	1,2	5	
	Ammunition, non-explosive			173.55						
	Ammunition for small-arms with explosive projectile	Class A explosive	Explosive A	None	173.58	Forbidden	Forbidden	6	5	
	Ammunition for small-arms with incendiary projectile	Class A explosive	Explosive A	None	173.58	Forbidden	Forbidden	6	5	
	Ammunition, rocket. See Rocket ammunition									
	Ammunition, small-arms. See Small-arms ammunition									
	Amyl acetate	Flammable liquid	Flammable liquid	173.118	173.119	1 quart	10 gallons	1,2	1,2	
	Amyl acid phosphate	Corrosive material	Corrosive	173.244	173.245	1 quart	10 gallons	1,2	1,2	
	Amylamine	Flammable liquid	Flammable liquid	173.118	173.119	1 quart	10 gallons	1,2	1	
	Amyl chloride	Flammable liquid	Flammable liquid	173.118	173.119	1 quart	10 gallons	1,2	1	
	Amylene, normal	Flammable liquid	Flammable liquid	173.118	173.119	1 quart	10 gallons	1,3	1,3	
	Amyl formate	Flammable liquid	Flammable liquid	173.118	173.119	1 quart	10 gallons	1,2	1	
	Amyl mercaptan	Flammable liquid	Flammable liquid	None	173.141	Forbidden	10 gallons	1,2	1	
	Amyl nitrite	Flammable liquid	Flammable liquid	173.118	173.119	1 quart	10 gallons	1,3	4	
	Amyl trichlorosilane	Corrosive material	Corrosive	None	173.280	Forbidden	10 gallons	1	5	Keep dry

Anhydrous ammonia. *See* Ammonia, anhydrous								
Anhydrous hydrazine. *See* Hydrazine, anhydrous								
Anhydrous, hydrofluoric acid. *See* Hydrogen fluoride								
Aniline oil drum, empty *See* 173.347(d)	Poison B					1,2	1	Do not accept unless returnable package notice is on drum and the instructions thereon have been carried out
Aniline oil, liquid	Poison B	Poison	None	173.347	Forbidden	55 gallons	1,2	1,2	Stow away from oxidizing materials and acids
Anisoyl chloride	Corrosive material	Corrosive	173.244	173.279	1 quart	1 quart	1,2	1	Keep dry
Antifreeze compound, liquid	Flammable liquid	Flammable liquid	173.118	173.119	1 quart	10 gallons	1,2	1	
Antifreeze compound, liquid	Combustible liquid	None	173.118a	173.119	No limit	No limit	1,2	1,2	
Antifreeze preparation, liquid	Flammable liquid	Flammable liquid	173.118	173.119	1 quart	10 gallons	1,2	1	
Antifreeze preparation, liquid	Combustible liquid	None	173.118a	None	No limit	No limit	1,2	1,2	
Antimonous chloride. *See* Antimony trichloride								
Antimony lactate, solid	ORM-A	None	173.505	173.510	No limit	No limit		1	Keep dry Glass carboys not permitted on passenger vessels
Antimony pentachloride	Corrosive material	Corrosive	None	173.247	1 quart	1 quart		1	
Antimony pentachloride solution	Corrosive material	Corrosive	173.244	173.245	1 quart	5 pints		1	Keep dry Glass carboys not permitted on passenger vessels
Antimony pentafluoride	Corrosive material	Corrosive	None	173.246	Forbidden	25 pounds	1	5	Keep dry
Antimony potassium tartrate solid	ORM-A	None	173.505	173.510	No limit	No Limit			
Antimony sulfide, solid	ORM-A	None	173.505	173.510	25 pounds	100 pounds	1,2	1,2	Keep dry
Antimony trichloride, solid	Corrosive material	Corrosive	173.244	173.245b	25 pounds	5 pints	1	1	Keep dry.
Antimony trichloride solution	Corrosive material	Corrosive	173.244	173.245	1 quart				
Aqua ammonia solution (*containing 44% or less ammonia*). *See* Ammonium hydroxide								
Argon	Nonflammable gas	Nonflammable gas	173.306	173.302 173.114	150 pounds	300 pounds	1,3	1,3	
Argon, liquid pressurized	Nonflammable gas	Nonflammable gas	None	173.304	Forbidden	300 pounds	1,3	1,3	
Arsenic acid, solid	Poison B	Poison	173.364	173.366	50 pounds	200 pounds	1,2	1,2	
Arsenic acid solution	Poison B	Poison	173.345	173.348	1 quart	55 gallons	1,2	1,2	

413

Hazardous Materials Table (cont'd)

(1)	(2) Hazardous materials descriptions and proper shipping names	(3) Hazard class	(4) Label(s) required (if not excepted)	(5) Packaging (a) Exceptions	(5) Packaging (b) Specific requirements	(6) Maximum net quantity in one package (a) Passenger carrying aircraft or railcar	(6) Maximum net quantity in one package (b) Cargo only aircraft	(7) Water shipments (a) Cargo vessel	(7) Water shipments (b) Passenger vessel	(7) Water shipments (c) Other requirements
• W/A	Arsenical compound n.o.s., liquid, or arsenical mixture, n.o.s. liquid	Poison B	Poison	173.345	173.346	1 quart	55 gallons	1,2	1,2	
•	Arsenical compound n.o.s., solid, or arsenical mixture, n.o.s. solid	Poison B	Poison	173.364	173.367	50 pounds	200 pounds	1,2	1,2	Keep dry
	Arsenical dip, liquid (sheep dip)	Poison B	Poison	173.345	173.346	1 quart	55 gallons	1,2	1,2	
	Arsenical dust	Poison B	Poison	173.364	173.368	50 pounds	200 pounds	1,2	1,2	
	Arsenical flue dust	Poison B	Poison	173.364	173.368	50 pounds	200 pounds	1,2	1,2	
	Arsenic bromide, solid	Poison B	Poison	173.364	173.365	50 pounds	200 pounds	1,2	1,2	
	Arsenic chloride (arsenious) liquid. See Arsenic trichloride									
	Arsenic iodide, solid	Poison B	Poison	173.364	173.365	50 pounds	200 pounds	1,2	1,2	
	Arsenic pentoxide, solid	Poison B	Poison	173.364	173.365	50 pounds	200 pounds	1,2	1,2	
	Arsenic, solid	Poison B	Poison	173.364	173.366	50 pounds	200 pounds	1,2	1,2	
	Arsenic sulfide, solid	Poison B	Poison	173.364	173.365	50 pounds	200 pounds	1,2	1,2	
	Arsenic trichloride, liquid	Poison B	Poison	173.345	173.346	1 quart	55 gallons	1,2	1,2	Keep dry
	Arsenic trioxide, solid	Poison B	Poison	173.364	173.366, 173.368	50 pounds	200 pounds	1,2	1,2	
	Arsenic, white, solid. See Arsenic trioxide, solid									
	Arsenious acid, solid. See Arsenic trioxide, solid									
	Arsenious and mercuric iodide solution	Poison B	Poison	173.345	173.346	1 quart	55 gallons	1,2	1,2	
•	Arsine	Poison A	Poison gas and Flammable gas	None	173.328	Forbidden	Forbidden	1	5	

		ORM-C				Forbid-den		1	5	When applicable, no fire or residue thereof may be present in the furnace heating the substance while the vehicle is on board a cargo vessel
W	Asphalt, at or above its flashpoint									
•	Asphalt, cut back	Flammable liquid	Flammable liquid	None	173.118	173.131	1 quart	10 gallons	1,2	1	
•	Asphalt, cut back	Combustible liquid	None	173.118a	None	No limit	No limit	1,2	1,2		
	Automobile, motorcycle, tractor, or other self-propelled vehicle See Motor Vehicle									
	Automobile, motorcycle, tractor, or other self-propelled vehicle, engine, or other mechanical apparatus, with charged electric storage battery, wet See Motor Vehicle									
	1-Aziridinyl phosphine oxide (tris). See Tris-(1-aziridinyl) phosphine oxide									
	Bags, burlap, used, must be classed for the hazardous material previously contained in bag. See 173.28, 173.29									
	Bags, sodium nitrate, empty and unwashed	Flammable solid	Flammable solid	None	None	173.155	Forbid-den	25 pounds	1,2	1,2	Separate from flammable gases or liquids, oxidizing materials, or organic peroxides
•	Barium azide, wet, 50% or more water	Flammable solid	Flammable solid	None	None	173.239	Forbid-den	1 pound	1,2	1,2	Stow away from heavy metals
	Barium chlorate	Oxidizer	Oxidizer	173.153	173.163	25 pounds	100 pounds	1,2	1,2	Separate from ammonium compounds. Stow away from powdered metals	
•	Barium chlorate, wet	Oxidizer	Oxidizer	173.153	173.163	25 pounds	200 pounds	1,2	1,2	Separate from ammonium compounds. Stow away from powdered metals
	Barium cyanide, solid	Poison B	Poison	173.370	173.370	25 pounds	200 pounds	1,2	1,2	Stow away from acids
	Barium nitrate	Oxidizer	Oxidizer	173.153	173.182	25 pounds	100 pounds	1,2	1,2	
A	Barium oxide	ORM-B	None	173.505	173.510 173.800	25 pounds	100 pounds	1,2	1,2		
	Barium perchlorate	Oxidizer	Oxidizer	173.153	173.154	25 pounds	100 pounds	1,2	1,2	Stow away from, powdered metals
	Barium permanganate	Oxidizer	Oxidizer	173.153	173.154	25 pounds	100 pounds	1,2	1,2	Separate from ammonium compounds and hydrogen peroxide
	Barium peroxide (binoxide, dioxide)	Oxidizer	Oxidizer	173.153	173.156	25 pounds	100 pounds	1,2	1,2	Keep dry
	Barrel, empty. See Drum, empty									
	Battery charger with electrolyte (acid or alkaline battery fluid)	Corrosive material	Corrosive	None	173.259	Forbid-den	5 pints	1,2	1,2		
	Battery, dry. Not subject to Parts 170-189 of this subchapter									
	Battery, electric storage, wet	Corrosive material	Corrosive	173.260		Forbid-den	No limit	1,2	1,2		

415

Hazardous Materials Table (cont'd)

(1)	(2)	(3)	(4)	(5)		(6)				(7)	
				Packaging		Maximum net quantity in one package				Water shipments	
			Label(s)	(a)	(b)	(a)	(b)	(a)	(b)		
*/W/A	Hazardous materials descriptions and proper shipping names	Hazard class	required (if not excepted)	Exceptions	Specific requirements	Passenger carrying aircraft or railcar	Cargo only aircraft	Cargo vessel	Passenger vessel	Other requirements	
	Battery, electric storage, wet, with automobile, auto parts, engine (*or other specifically named mechanical apparatus*)	Corrosive material	Corrosive	173.250	173.260	No limit	No limit	1,2	1,2	Keep dry	
	Battery, electric storage, wet with containers of corrosive battery fluid *Battery fluid. See Electrolyte (acid) or Alkaline battery fluid*	Corrosive material	Corrosive	None	173.258	Forbidden	2 gallons	1,2	1,2		
W	Battery parts (*plates, grids, etc., unwashed, exhausted*)	ORM-C	None	173.505	173.915						
	Benzaldehyde	Combustible liquid	None	173.118a	None	No limit	No limit	1,2	4		
	Benzene (*benzol*)	Flammable liquid	Flammable liquid	173.118	173.119	1 quart	10 gallons	1,2	1		
	Benzene phosphorus dichloride	Corrosive material	Corrosive	None	173.250a	Forbidden	5 pints	1	5		
	Benzene phosphorus thiodichloride	Corrosive material	Corrosive	None	173.250a	Forbidden	5 pints	1	5		
	Benzine	Flammable liquid	Flammable liquid	173.118	173.119	1 quart	10 gallons	1,2	1		
	Benzoyl chloride	Corrosive material	Corrosive	173.244	173.247	1 quart	1 quart	1,2	1	Keep dry. Glass carboys not permitted on passenger vessels	
	Benzoyl peroxide	Organic peroxide	Organic peroxide	None	173.157 173.158	Forbidden	25 pounds	1,2	1		
	Benzyl bromide (*bromotoluene, alpha*)	Corrosive material	Corrosive	None	173.281	Forbidden	5 pints	1	5	Keep dry	
	Benzyl chloride	Corrosive material	Corrosive	173.244	173.295	Forbidden	1 quart	1	4	Keep dry	
	Benzyl chloroformate (*or Benzyl chlorocarbonate*)	Corrosive material	Corrosive	None	173.288	Forbidden	5 pints	1	5	Keep dry	
•	Beryllium compound, n.o.s.	Poison B	Poison	173.364	173.365	50 pounds	200 pounds	1,2	1,2		
•	Black powder	Class A explosive	Explosive A	None	173.60	Forbidden	Forbidden	6	5		

416

Black powder igniter with empty cartridge bag	Class C explosive	Explosive C	None	173.106	50 pounds	150 pounds	1.3	1.3	Portable magazine or metal locker. Do not stow blasting caps with any high explosive. Do not handle blasting caps at the same time high explosives are being loaded
Blasting caps—(1,000 or less) (Show actual number)	Class C explosive	Explosive C	None	173.103	Forbidden	Forbidden	1.2	5	Do not stow blasting caps with any high explosive. Do not handle blasting caps at the same time high explosives are being loaded
Blasting caps—(more than 1,000) (Show actual number)	Class A explosive	Explosive A	None	173.66	Forbidden	Forbidden	6	5	Portable magazine or metal locker. Do not stow blasting caps with any high explosive. Do not handle blasting caps at the same time high explosives are being loaded
Blasting caps—electric (1,000 or less) (Show actual number)	Class C explosive	Explosive C	None	173.103	Forbidden	Forbidden	1.2	5	Portable magazine or metal locker. Do not stow blasting caps with any high explosive. Do not handle blasting caps at the same time high explosives are being loaded
Blasting caps—electric (more than 1,000) (Show actual number)	Class A explosive	Explosive A	None	173.66	Forbidden	Forbidden	6	5	Magazine. Do not stow blasting caps with any high explosives. Do not handle blasting caps at the same time high explosives are being loaded
Blasting caps with metal clad mild detonating fuse—(1,000 or less) (Show actual number)	Class C explosive	Explosive C	None	173.103	Forbidden	Forbidden	1.2	5	Portable magazine or metal locker. Do not stow blasting caps with any high explosive. Do not handle blasting caps at the same time high explosives are being loaded
Blasting caps with metal clad mild detonating fuse—(more than 1,000) (Show actual number)	Class A explosive	Explosive A	None	173.66 173.67	Forbidden	Forbidden	6	5	Do not stow blasting caps with any high explosive. Do not handle blasting caps at the same time high explosives are being loaded
Blasting caps with safety fuse—(1,000 or less) (Show actual number)	Class C explosive	Explosive C	None	173.103	Forbidden	Forbidden	1.2	5	Portable magazine or metal locker. Do not stow blasting caps with any high explosive. Do not handle blasting caps at the same time high explosives are being loaded
Blasting caps with safety fuse—(more than 1,000) (Show actual number)	Class A explosive	Explosive A	None	173.66 173.67	Forbidden	Forbidden	6	5	Do not stow blasting caps with any high explosive. Do not handle blasting caps at the same time high explosives are being loaded
Blasting gelatin. See High explosive									
Blasting powder. See Black powder									
W Bleaching powder, containing 39% or less available chlorine	ORM-C	None	173.505	173.920			1.2	1.2	Keep dry. Stow separate from flammable liquids and acids. (Stow away from oils, grease, and similar organic materials.)
Bleaching powder, over 39% available chlorine	Oxidizer	Oxidizer	173.153	173.217	50 pounds	100 pounds	1.2	1.2	Keep cool and dry
• Boiler compound, liquid	Corrosive material	Corrosive	173.244	173.249	1 quart	10 gallons	1.2	1.2	
Bomb, explosive. See Explosive bomb									

Hazardous Materials Table (cont'd)

(1)	(2) Hazardous materials descriptions and proper shipping names	(3) Hazard class	(4) Label(s) required (if not excepted)	(5) Packaging (a) Exceptions	(5) Packaging (b) Specific requirements	(6) Maximum net quantity in one package (a) Passenger carrying aircraft or railcar	(6) (b) Cargo only aircraft	(6) (a) Cargo vessel	(6) (b) Passenger vessel	(7) Water shipments (c) Other requirements
	Bomb, explosive with gas, smoke, or incendiary material. See Explosive bomb									
	Bomb, fireworks. See Fireworks, special									
	Bomb, gas, smoke, or incendiary, non-explosive. See Chemical ammunition									
	Bomb, incendiary, or smoke without bursting charge. See Fireworks, special									
	Bomb, practice, with electric primer or electric squib (non-explosive)									
	Bomb, sand-loaded or empty (non-explosive)									
A	Bone oil	ORM-A	None	173.55						
	Booster, explosive	Class A explosive	Explosive A	173.55						
				173.505	173.510	No limit	No limit			
				None	173.69	Forbidden	Forbidden	6	5	
*	Bordeaux arsenite, liquid	Poison B	Poison	173.345	173.346	1 quart	55 gallons	1,2	1,2	
*	Bordeaux arsenite, solid	Poison B	Poison	173.364	173.365	50 pounds	200 pounds	1,2	1,2	
	Boron tribromide	Corrosive material	Corrosive	None	173.251	Forbidden	1 quart	1	5	
	Boron trichloride	Corrosive material	Corrosive	None	173.251	Forbidden	1 quart	1,2	5	Stow in well ventilated space. Shade from radiant heat. Segregation same as for nonflammable gases
	Boron trifluoride	Nonflammable gas	Nonflammable gas and Poison	None	173.302	Forbidden	Forbidden	1	5	Stow away from living quarters and foodstuffs
	Boron trifluoride-acetic acid complex	Corrosive material	Corrosive	173.244	173.247	1 quart	1 gallon	1,2	1,2	
	Bottles, having previously contained a hazardous material and not cleaned. See 173.29									
W*	Box toe board (nitrocellulose base)	ORM-C	None	173.505	173.925			1,3	1,3	Provide cool stowage in a compartment having a temperature not exceeding 130 DEG F., well away from any sources of heat, and in position to protect or move, even to jettison in event of fire. Separate from explosives, flammable liquids or gases, oxidizing materials, organic peroxides, or corrosive liquids.

•	Box toe gum	Combustible liquid	None	173.118a	None	No limit	No limit	1.2	1.2
•	Box toe gum	Flammable liquid	Flammable liquid	173.118	173.119	1 quart	10 gallons	1.2	1
	Bromine	Corrosive material	Corrosive	None	173.252	Forbidden	1 quart	1	5	Keep cool
	Bromine pentafluoride	Oxidizer	Oxidizer	None	173.246	Forbidden	100 pounds	1	5	Shade from radiant heat. Segregation same as for corrosives
	Bromine trifluoride	Oxidizer	Oxidizer and Poison	None	173.246	Forbidden	100 pounds	1	5	Shade from radiant heat. Segregation same as for corrosives
	Bromoacetic acid, solid	Corrosive material	Corrosive	173.244	173.245b	25 pounds	100 pounds	1.2	1.2	Keep dry
•	Bromoacetic acid solution	Corrosive material	Corrosive	173.244	173.245	1 quart	1 quart	1.2	1.2	Glass carboys in hampers not permitted under deck
	Bromoacetone, liquid	Poison A	Poison gas	None	173.329	Forbidden	Forbidden	1	5	Segregation same as for flammable liquids
	Bromobenzene	Combustible liquid	None	173.118a	None	No limit	No limit	1.2	1.2	
	Bromotoluene, alpha. See Benzyl bromide									
	Brucine, solid (dimethoxy strychnine)	Poison B	Poison	173.364	173.365	50 pounds	200 pounds	1.2	1.2	
W	Burlap bags, cleaned (vacuum cleaned, wheel cleaned, or otherwise mechanically brushed). See Burlap cloth									
W	Burlap bags, new. See Burlap cloth									
AW	Burlap bags, used and unwashed, or not cleaned	ORM-C	None	173.930		No limit	No limit	1	1	Keep cool
W	Burlap cloth (hessian)	ORM-C	None	173.931				1.2	1.2	Keep dry. Stow away from organic liquids
	Burnt cotton, not repicked	Flammable solid	Flammable solid	None	173.159	Forbidden	Forbidden	1	5	Separate from flammable gases or liquids, oxidizing materials, or organic peroxides
	Burnt fiber	Flammable solid	Flammable solid	None	173.169	Forbidden	Forbidden	1.2	1.2	Separate from flammable gases or liquids, oxidizing materials, or organic peroxides
	Burster, explosive	Class A explosive	Explosive A	None	173.69	Forbidden	Forbidden	6	5	
	Butadiene, inhibited	Flammable gas	Flammable gas	173.306	173.304 173.314 173.315	Forbidden	300 pounds	1.2	1	Stow away from living quarters
	Butane or Liquefied petroleum gas. See Liquefied petroleum gas									

Hazardous Materials Table (cont'd)

(1)	(2) Hazardous materials descriptions and proper shipping names	(3) Hazard class	(4) Label(s) required (if not excepted)	(5) Packaging (a) Exceptions	(5) Packaging (b) Specific requirements	(6) Maximum net quantity in one package (a) Passenger carrying aircraft or railcar	(6) (b) Cargo only aircraft	(a) Cargo vessel	(b) Passenger vessel	(7) Water shipments (c) Other requirements
	Butyl acetate	Flammable liquid	Flammable liquid	173.118	173.119	1 quart	10 gallons	1,2	1	
	n-Butyl acid phosphate. See Acid butyl phosphate									
•	Butyl alcohol. See Alcohol, n.o.s.									
	Butylamine	Flammable liquid	Flammable liquid	173.118	173.119	1 quart	10 gallons	1,2	1	
	Butyl bromide, normal	Flammable liquid	Flammable liquid	173.118	173.119	1 quart	10 gallons	1,2	1	
	Butyl chloride	Flammable liquid	Flammable liquid	173.118	173.119	1 quart	10 gallons	1,2	1	
	Butyl ether	Flammable liquid	Flammable liquid	173.118	173.119	1 quart	10 gallons	1,2	1,2	
	Butyl formate	Flammable liquid	Flammable liquid	173.118	173.119	1 quart	10 gallons	1,2	1	
	n-Butyl isocyanate	Flammable liquid	Flammable liquid and Poison	173.118	173.119	1 quart	10 gallons	1,2	1	
	Butyl mercaptan	Flammable liquid	Flammable liquid	None	173.141	Forbidden	10 gallons	1,3	5	
	Butyl phosphoric acid. See Acid-butyl phosphate									
	Butyl trichlorosilane	Corrosive material	Corrosive	None	173.280	Forbidden	10 gallons	1	1	Keep dry
	Butyraldehyde	Flammable liquid	Flammable liquid	173.118	173.119	1 quart	10 gallons	1,2	1	
	Butyric acid	Corrosive material	Corrosive	173.244	173.245	1 quart	10 gallons	1,2	1,2	
	Calcium arsenate, solid	Poison B	Poison	173.364	173.367 173.368	50 pounds	200 pounds	1,2	1,2	
	Calcium arsenite, solid	Poison B	Poison	173.364	173.365	50 pounds	200 pounds	1,2	1,2	
•	Calcium bisulfite solution. See *Calcium hydrogen sulfite solution									

420

	Name								
	Calcium carbide	Flammable solid	Flammable solid and dangerous when wet	None	173.178	Forbidden	25 pounds	1.2	Keep dry. Stow away from copper, its alloys, and salts
	Calcium chlorate	Oxidizer	Oxidizer	173.153	173.163	25 pounds	100 pounds	1.2	1.2	Separate from ammonium compounds. Stow away from powdered metals and cyanide
	Calcium chlorite	Oxidizer	Oxidizer	None	173.160	Forbidden	100 pounds	1.2	1.2	Separate from ammonium compounds powdered materials, and cyanides
AW	Calcium cyanamide, not hydrated, containing more than 0.1% calcium carbide	ORM-C	None	None	173.945	25 pounds	200 pounds	1.2	1.2	Segregation same as for flammable solids labeled Dangerous When Wet
*	Calcium cyanide, solid or Calcium cyanide mixture, solid	Poison B	Poison	173.370		25 pounds	200 pounds	1.2	1.2	Stow away from corrosive liquids. Keep dry
*	Calcium hydrogen sulfite solution	Corrosive material	Corrosive	173.244	173.245	1 quart	5 gallons	1.2	1.2	
	Calcium hypochlorite mixture, dry, (containing more than 39% available chlorine)	Oxidizer	Oxidizer	173.153	173.217	50 pounds	100 pounds	1.2	1.2	Keep cool and dry
	Calcium, metal	Flammable solid	Flammable solid and Dangerous when wet	173.153	173.154	25 pounds	100 pounds	1.2	4	Keep cool and dry. Segregation same as for flammable solids labeled Dangerous When Wet
	Calcium, metal, crystalline	Flammable solid	Flammable solid and Dangerous when wet	None	173.231	Forbidden	25 pounds	1.2	5	Keep cool and dry. Segregation same as for flammable solids labeled Dangerous When Wet
*	Calcium nitrate (See Sec. 173.182 Note)	Oxidizer	Oxidizer	173.153	173.182	25 pounds	100 pounds	1.2	1.2	
AW	Calcium oxide	ORM-B	None	173.505	173.850	25 pounds	100 pounds	1.2	1.2	Keep dry. Stow away from explosives, acids, combustible materials, and ammonium salts
	Calcium permanganate	Oxidizer	Oxidizer	173.153	173.154	25 pounds	100 pounds	1.2	1.2	Separate from ammonium compounds and hydrogen peroxide
	Calcium peroxide	Oxidizer	Oxidizer	173.153	173.156	25 pounds	100 pounds	1.2	1.2	Keep dry
	Calcium phosphide	Flammable solid	Flammable solid and Dangerous when wet	None	173.161	Forbidden	25 pounds	1	5	Keep cool and dry. Segregation same as for flammable solids labeled Dangerous When Wet
	Calcium resinate	Flammable solid	Flammable solid	None	173.166	Forbidden	125 pounds	1	5	
	Calcium resinate, fused	Flammable solid	Flammable solid	None	173.166	Forbidden	125 pounds		5	
AW	Camphene	ORM-A	None	173.505	173.610	No limit	No limit	1.3	1.3	Stow away from foodstuffs and living quarters
	Camphor oil	Combustible liquid	None	173.118a	None	No limit	No limit	1.2	1.2	

Hazardous Materials Table (cont'd)

(1)	(2) Hazardous materials descriptions and proper shipping names	(3) Hazard class	(4) Label(s) required (if not excepted)	(5) Packaging (a) Exceptions	(5) Packaging (b) Specific requirements	(6) Maximum net quantity in one package (a) Passenger carrying aircraft or railcar	(6) (b) Cargo only aircraft	(7) Water shipments (a) Cargo vessel	(7) (b) Passenger vessel	(7) (c) Other requirements
	Cannon primers	Class C explosive	Explosive C	None	173.107	50 pounds	150 pounds	1,3	5	
	Caprylyl peroxide solution	Organic peroxide	Organic peroxide	173.153	173.221	1 quart	1 quart	1,2	4	Keep cool. Stow separate from combustible materials, explosives, or acids
	Caps, blasting. See Blasting caps									
	Caps, toy. See Toy caps									
A	Carbaryl	ORM-A	None	173.505	173.510	No limit	No limit	1,2	1,2	
	Carbolic acid, liquid or Phenol, liquid (liquid tar acid containing over 50% benzophenol)	Poison B	Poison	173.345	173.349	1 quart	55 gallons	1,2	4	
	Carbolic acid, or Phenol	Poison B	Poison	173.364	173.369	50 pounds	250 pounds	1,2	1,2	
	Carbon bisulfide, or Carbon disulfide	Flammable liquid	Flammable liquid	None	173.121	Forbidden	Forbidden	1	5	Keep cool. Not permitted on any vessel transporting explosives
•	Carbon dioxide, liquefied	Nonflammable gas	Nonflammable gas	173.306	173.304 173.314 173.315	150 pounds	300 pounds	1,2	1,2	
•	Carbon dioxide-nitrous oxide mixture	Nonflammable gas	Nonflammable gas	173.306	173.304	150 pounds	300 pounds	1,2	1,2	
•	Carbon dioxide-oxygen mixture	Nonflammable gas	Nonflammable gas	173.306	173.304	150 pounds	300 pounds	1,2	1,2	
AW	Carbon dioxide, solid, or Dry ice, or Carbonice	ORM-A	None	None	173.615	440 pounds	440 pounds	1	1	Stow away from open ventilators. Stow away from cyanides or cyanide mixtures, liquid or dry
	Carbon monoxide	Flammable gas	Flammable gas	173.306	173.302	Forbidden	150 pounds	1	4	
•	Carbon remover, liquid	Flammable liquid	Flammable liquid	173.118	173.119	1 quart	10 gallons	1,2	1	
AW	Carbon tetrachloride	ORM-A	None	173.505	173.620	1 quart	55 gallons	1,2	1,2	Stow away from living quarters
	Carbonyl chloride. See Phosgene									
	Carboys, empty, must be classed for the hazardous material previously contained in carboy. See 173.29									

	Cartridge bags, empty, with black powder igniter	Class C explosive	Explosive C	None	173.106	50 pounds	150 pounds	1,3	1,3
	Cartridge cases, empty, primed	Class C explosive	Explosive C	None	173.107	50 pounds	150 pounds	1,3	1,3
	Cartridge, practice ammunition	Class C explosive	Explosive C	None	173.101a	50 pounds	150 pounds	1,2	1,2
	Case oil. See Gasoline or Naphtha								
	Casinghead gasoline. See Gasoline								
W	Castor beans	ORM-C	None	173.505	173.952			1,2	1,2	Stow away from living quarters and foodstuffs. Bulk shipments permitted in tight vans or containers only on cargo vessels (Castor beans only)
W	Castor pomace. See Castor beans								
	Caustic potash, dry, solid, flake, bead, or granular. See Potassium hydroxide, dry, etc.								
•	Caustic potash, liquid or solution. See Potassium hydroxide solution								
	Caustic soda, dry, solid, flake, bead, or granular. See Sodium hydroxide, dry, etc.								
•	Caustic soda, liquid or solution. See Sodium hydroxide solution								
W	Cellosolve. See Ethylene glycol monoethyl ether								
W	Cellosolve acetate. See Ethylene glycol monoethyl ether acetate								
•	Cement, adhesive, n.o.s. See Cement, liquid, n.o.s.								
•	Cement, container, linoleum, tile, or wallboard, liquid	Flammable liquid	Flammable liquid	173.118	173.132	1 quart	15 gallons	1,2	1
•	Cement, leather	Flammable liquid	Flammable liquid	173.118	173.119	1 quart	10 gallons	1,2	1
	Cement, liquid, n.o.s.	Combustible liquid	None	173.118a	None	No limit	No limit	1,2	1,2
•	Cement, liquid, n.o.s.	Flammable liquid	Flammable liquid	173.118	173.132	1 quart	10 gallons	1,2	1
•	Cement, pyroxylin	Flammable liquid	Flammable liquid	173.118	173.132	1 quart	15 gallons	1,2	1
•	Cement, roofing, liquid	Flammable liquid	Flammable liquid	173.118	173.119	1 quart	10 gallons	1,2	1
•	Cement, rubber	Flammable liquid	Flammable liquid	173.118	173.132	1 quart	15 gallons	1,2	1
	Cesium metal	Flammable solid	Flammable solid and dangerous when wet	None	173.206	Forbidden	25 pounds	1,2	5	Segregation same as for flammable solids labeled Dangerous When Wet

Hazardous Materials Table (cont'd)

(1) °/W/A	(2) Hazardous materials descriptions and proper shipping names	(3) Hazard class	(4) Label(s) required (if not excepted)	(5) Packaging (a) Exceptions	(5) Packaging (b) Specific requirements	(6) Maximum net quantity in one package (a) Passenger carrying aircraft or railcar	(6) Maximum net quantity in one package (b) Cargo only aircraft	(7) Water shipments (a) Cargo vessel	(7) Water shipments (b) Passenger vessel	(7) Water shipments (c) Other requirements
*	Charcoal, activated	Flammable solid	Flammable solid	173.162	173.162	25 pounds	200 pounds	1,3	1,3	
	Charcoal briquettes or briquets	Flammable solid	Flammable solid	173.162	173.162	50 pounds	50 pounds	1,2	1,2	
	Charcoal screenings, made from "pinon" wood	Flammable solid	Flammable solid	173.162	173.162	25 pounds	200 pounds	1,2	1,2	
	Charcoal screenings, wet	Forbidden								
	Charcoal, shell	Flammable solid	Flammable solid	173.162	173.162	25 pounds	200 pounds	1,2	1,2	
	Charcoal, wet	Forbidden								
	Charcoal, wood, ground, crushed, granulated, or pulverized	Flammable solid	Flammable solid	173.162	173.162	25 pounds	200 pounds	1,2	1,2	
	Charcoal, wood, lump	Flammable solid	Flammable solid	173.162	173.162	50 pounds	50 pounds	1,2	1,2	
	Charcoal wood screenings, other than "pinon" wood screenings	Flammable solid	Flammable solid	None	173.162	Forbidden	Forbidden	1	1	
	Charged oil well jet perforating gun (total explosive contents in guns 20 pounds or more per motor vehicle)	Class A explosive	Explosive A	None	173.53 173.80	Forbidden	Forbidden			Forbidden
	Charged oil well jet perforating gun (total explosive contents in guns not exceeding 20 pounds per motor vehicle) See Ammunition, chemical, explosive	Class C explosive	Explosive C	None	173.53 173.110	Forbidden	Forbidden			Forbidden
	Chemical ammunition explosive. See Ammunition, chemical, explosive									
	Chemical ammunition, nonexplosive (containing a Poison B material)	Poison B	Poison	173.345	173.350	Forbidden	55 gallons			See correct shipping name of applicable Poison B material for stowage, special handling, and special segregation requirements
	Chemical ammunition, nonexplosive (containing an irritating material)	Irritating material	Irritant	None	173.383	Forbidden	20 pounds			See correct shipping name of applicable Irritant material for stowage, special handling, and special segregation requirements
	Chemical ammunition, nonexplosive (containing a poison A material)	Poison A	Poison gas	None	173.330	Forbidden	Forbidden			See correct shipping name of applicable Poison A material for stowage, special handling, and special segregation requirements

• Chemical kit	Corrosive material	Corrosive	173.286	1 quart	1 quart	1,3	1,3
Chlorate and borate mixture (containing more than 28% chlorate)	Oxidizer	Oxidizer	173.153	25 pounds	100 pounds	1,2	4	Stow away from ammonium compounds and away from powdered metals
Chlorate and magnesium chloride mixture (containing more than 28% chlorate)	Oxidizer	Oxidizer	173.153	25 pounds	100 pounds	1,2	4	Stow away from ammonium compounds, and away from powdered metals
Chlorate explosive, dry. See High explosive							
Chlorate, n.o.s.	Oxidizer	Oxidizer	173.153	25 pounds	100 pounds	1,2	4	Stow away from ammonium compounds and away from powdered metals
• Chlorate, n.o.s. wet	Oxidizer	Oxidizer	173.153	25 pounds	200 pounds	1,2	4	Stow away from ammonium compounds and away from powdered metals
Chlorate of potash. See Potassium chlorate							
Chlorate of soda. See Sodium chlorate							
Chlorate powder. See High explosive							
• Chlordane, liquid	Combustible liquid	None	173.118a	No limit	No limit	1,2	1,2
Chloric acid. (see chlorine dioxide hydrate)							
Chloride of phosphorus. See Phosphorus trichloride							
Chloride of sulfur. See Sulfur chloride							
W Chlorinated lime (chloride of lime.) See Bleaching powder							
Chlorine	Nonflammable gas	Nonflammable gas and Poison	None 173.304 173.314 173.315	Forbidden	Forbidden	1,2	5	Stow in a well-ventilated space. Stow away from organic materials
Chlorine dioxide hydrate, frozen	Oxidizer	Oxidizer and Poison	None 173.237	Forbidden	Forbidden	1	5	Forbidden
Chlorine trifluoride	Oxidizer	Oxidizer and Poison	None 173.246	Forbidden	100 pounds	1,3	5	Stow in well ventilated area away from organic material
Chloroacetic acid, solid	Corrosive material	Corrosive	173.244 173.245b	25 pounds	100 pounds	1,2	1,2	Keep dry
• Chloroacetic acid, liquid or solution. See Monochloroacetic acid, liquid or solution							
Chloroacetophenone, gas, liquid, or solid (CN)	Irritating material	Irritant	None 173.382	Forbidden	75 pounds	1	5
Chloroacetyl chloride	Corrosive material	Corrosive	None 173.253	Forbidden	1 quart	1	5	Keep dry
Chlorobenzene. See Chlorobenzol							
Chlorobenzol	Flammable liquid	Flammable liquid	173.118 173.119	1 quart	10 gallons	1,2	1,2

425

Hazardous Materials Table (cont'd)

(1)	(2)	(3)	(4)	(5) Packaging		(6) Maximum net quantity in one package			(7) Water shipments	
°/W/A	Hazardous materials descriptions and proper shipping names	Hazard class	Label(s) required (if not excepted)	(a) Exceptions	(b) Specific requirements	(a) Passenger carrying aircraft or railcar	(b) Cargo only aircraft	(a) Cargo vessel	(b) Passenger vessel	(c) Other requirements
	p-Chlorobenzoyl peroxide	Organic peroxide	Organic peroxide	None	173.157 173.158	Forbidden	25 pounds	1	1	
	Chlorodinitrobenzene. See Dinitrochlorobenzene									
	Chlorodinitrobenzol. See Dinitrochlorobenzol, solid									
AW	Chloroform	ORM-A	None	173.505	173.630	10 gallons	55 gallons	1,2	1,2	Stow away from living quarters and foodstuffs
	4-Chloro-o-toluidine hydrochloride	Poison B	Poison	None	173.362	Forbidden	1 quart	1,2	1,2	Keep dry
	Chlorophenyltrichlorosilane	Corrosive material	Corrosive	None	173.280	Forbidden	10 gallons	1	1	Keep cool
	Chloropicrin, absorbed	Poison B	Poison	None	173.357	Forbidden	Forbidden	1	5	Keep cool
	Chloropicrin and methyl chloride mixture	Poison A	Flammable gas and Poison gas	None	173.329	Forbidden	Forbidden	1	5	Keep cool
	Chloropicrin and nonflammable, nonliquefied compressed gas mixture	Poison A	Nonflammable gas and Poison gas	None	173.329	Forbidden	Forbidden	1	5	Keep cool
	Chloropicrin, liquid	Poison B	Poison	None	173.357	Forbidden	Forbidden	1	5	Keep cool
	Chloropicrin mixture *(containing no compressed gas or poison A liquid)*	Poison B	Poison	None	173.357	Forbidden	Forbidden	1	5	Keep cool
A	Chloroplatinic acid, solid	ORM-B	None	173.505	173.510 173.800	25 pounds	100 pounds			
	2-Chloropropene	Flammable liquid	Flammable liquid	None	173.119	Forbidden	10 gallons	1,2	5	
	Chlorosulfonic acid	Corrosive material	Corrosive	173.244	173.254	1 quart	1 quart	1	1	Keep dry. Glass carboys not permitted on passenger vessels
	Chlorosulfonic acid-sulfur trioxide mixture	Corrosive material	Corrosive	173.244	173.254	1 quart	1 quart	1	1	Keep dry. Glass carboys not permitted on passenger vessels
	Chromic acid mixture, dry	Oxidizer	Oxidizer	173.153	173.164	25 pounds	100 pounds	1,2	1,2	Stow away from foodstuffs

426

• Chromic acid, solid	Oxidizer	Oxidizer	173.153	173.164	25 pounds	100 pounds	1,2	1,2	Stow away from foodstuffs. Stow separate from flammable liquids and solids
Chromic acid solution	Corrosive material	Corrosive	173.244	173.287	1 quart	1 gallon	1	1	
Chromic anhydride. See Chromic acid, solid									
Chromic fluoride, solid	Corrosive material	Corrosive	173.244	173.245b	25 pounds	100 pounds	1,2	1,2	
Chromic fluoride solution	Corrosive material	Corrosive	173.244	173.245	1 quart	1 gallon	1,2	1,2	
Chromic trioxide. See Chromic acid, solid									
Chromium oxychloride or Chromyl chloride	Corrosive material	Corrosive	None	173.247	Forbidden	1 gallon	1	1	Keep dry. Glass carboys not permitted on passenger vessels
Cigar and cigarette lighter fluid. See Lighter fluid									
• Cigarette lighter (or other similar ignition device)	Flammable gas	Flammable gas	173.21	173.308	21 ounces	25 pounds	1	1	Not permitted in nonventilated container
• Cigarette lighter (or other similar ignition device)	Flammable liquid	Flammable liquid	173.21	173.118	Forbidden	Forbidden	1	1	Not permitted in nonventilated container
Cigarette load	Class C explosive	Explosive C	None	173.111	50 pounds	150 pounds	1,2	1,2	
Cloud gas cylinder. See Chemical ammunition									
Coal briquettes, hot	Forbidden								
Coal facings. See Coal ground bituminous, etc.									
Coal gas. See Hydrocarbon gas, nonliquefied									
Coal, ground bituminous, sea coal; coal facings; etc.	Flammable solid	Flammable solid	173.165		Forbidden	Forbidden	1	1	Separate from flammable gases or liquids, oxidizing materials, or organic peroxides
Coal oil (export shipment only). See Kerosene									
• Coal tar distillate	Combustible liquid	None	173.118a	None	No limit	No limit	1,2	1,2	
• Coal tar distillate	Flammable liquid	Flammable liquid	173.118	173.119	1 quart	10 gallons	1,2	1	
Coal tar dye, liquid (not otherwise specifically named in Sec. 172.101)	Corrosive material	Corrosive	173.244	173.245 173.249a	1 quart	10 gallons	1,2	1,2	
• Coal tar light oil	Combustible liquid	None	173.118a	None	No limit	No limit	1,2	1,2	
Coal tar light oil	Flammable liquid	Flammable liquid	173.118	173.119	1 quart	10 gallons	1,2	1	
• Coal tar naphtha	Combustible liquid	None	173.118a	None	No limit	No limit	1,2	1,2	

Hazardous Materials Table (cont'd)

(1)	(2)	(3)	(4)	(5) Packaging		(6) Maximum net quantity in one package		(7) Water shipments		
*/W/A	Hazardous materials descriptions and proper shipping names	Hazard class	Label(s) required (if not excepted)	(a) Exceptions	(b) Specific requirements	(a) Passenger carrying aircraft or railcar	(b) Cargo only aircraft	(a) Cargo vessel	(b) Passenger vessel	(c) Other requirements
*	Coal tar naphtha	Flammable liquid	Flammable liquid	173.118	173.119	1 quart	10 gallons	1,2	1	
*	Coal tar oil	Combustible liquid	None	173.118a	None	No limit	No limit	1,2	1,2	
*	Coal tar oil	Flammable liquid	Flammable liquid	173.118	173.119	1 quart	10 gallons	1,2	1,2	
*	Coating solution	Flammable liquid	Flammable liquid	173.118	173.132	1 quart	15 gallons	1,2	1	
	Cobalt resinate, precipitated	Flammable solid	Flammable solid	None	173.166	Forbidden	125 pounds	1,2	1,2	
	Cocculus, solid (fishberry)	Poison B	Poison	173.364	173.365	50 pounds	200 pounds	1,2	1,2	
W*	Coconut meal pellets containing at least 6% and not more than 13% moisture and not more than 10% residual fat content	ORM-C	None	173.505	173.955			1,2	4	Keep dry
	Coir. See Fibers									
	Coke, hot	Forbidden								
	Collodion	Flammable liquid	Flammable liquid	173.118	173.119	1 quart	10 gallons	1,2	1	
	Collodium cotton, wet. See Nitrocellulose, wet									
	Cologne spirits (alcohol)	Flammable liquid	Flammable liquid	173.118	173.125	1 quart	10 gallons	1,2	1	
	Columbian spirits (wood alcohol)	Flammable liquid	Flammable liquid	173.118	173.125	1 quart	10 gallons	1,2	1	
	Combination fuze	Class C explosive	Explosive C	None	173.105	50 pounds	150 pounds	1,3	1,3	
	Combination primer	Class C explosive	Explosive C	None	173.107	50 pounds	150 pounds	1,3	5	
	Combustible liquid, n.o.s.	Combustible liquid	None	173.118a	None	No limit	No limit	1,2	1,2	
	Commercial shaped charge. See High explosive									

428

Common fireworks. *See* Fireworks, common						
• Compound, cleaning, liquid	Combustible liquid	None	173.118a	None	No limit	No limit	1,2	1,2
• Compound, cleaning, liquid	Corrosive material	Corrosive	173.244	173.245	1 quart	1 quart	1,2	1,2
• Compound, cleaning, liquid	Flammable liquid	Flammable liquid	173.118	173.119	1 quart	10 gallons	1,2	1
• Compound, cleaning, liquid (containing hydrochloric (muriatic) acid)	Corrosive material	Corrosive	173.244	173.263	1 quart	1 gallon	1	1
• Compound, cleaning, liquid (containing hydrofluoric acid)	Corrosive material	Corrosive	173.244	173.256	1 quart	1 gallon	1	4
Compound, cleaning liquid (*containing phosphoric acid, acetic acid, sodium or potassium hydroxide*)	Corrosive material	Corrosive	173.244	173.245 173.249a	1 quart	1 quart	1,2	1,2
• Compound, enamel	Flammable liquid	Flammable liquid	173.118	173.128	1 quart	55 gallons	1,2	1
• Compound, lacquer, paint, *or* varnish removing, liquid	Corrosive material	Corrosive	173.244	173.245	1 quart	1 gallon	1,2	1,2
• Compound, lacquer, paint, *or* varnish, removing, reducing, *or* thinning, liquid	Combustible liquid	None	173.118a				1,2	1,2
• Compound, lacquer, paint, *or* varnish, removing, reducing, *or* thinning, liquid	Flammable liquid	Flammable liquid	173.118	173.128	1 quart	55 gallons	1,2	1
• Compound, polishing, liquid	Flammable liquid	Flammable liquid	173.118	173.129	1 quart	55 gallons	1,2	1
• Compound, rust preventing *or* Compound, rust removing	Corrosive material	Corrosive	173.244	173.245	1 quart	1 gallon	1,2	1,2
• Compound, tree *or* weed killing, liquid	Combustible liquid	None	173.118a	None	No limit	No limit	1,2	1,2
• Compound, tree *or* weed killing, liquid	Corrosive material	Corrosive	173.244	173.245	1 quart	1 quart	1,2	1,2
• Compound, tree *or* weed killing, liquid	Flammable liquid	Flammable liquid	173.118	173.119	1 quart	10 gallons	1,2	1
• Compound, tree *or* weed killing, liquid	Poison B	Poison	173.345	173.346	1 quart	55 gallons	1,2	1,2
• Compound, tree *or* weed killing, solid	Oxidizer	Oxidizer	173.153	173.154 173.229	25 pounds	100 pounds	1,2	1,2
• Compound, vulcanizing, liquid	Corrosive material	Corrosive	173.244	173.245	1 quart	1 quart	1,2	1,2
• Compound, vulcanizing, liquid	Flammable liquid	Flammable liquid	173.118	173.119	1 quart	10 gallons	1,2	1
• Compound, water treatment, liquid. *See* Water treatment, liquid								
Compressed gas, n.o.s.	Flammable gas	Flammable gas	173.306	173.302 173.304 173.305	Forbidden	300 pounds	1	4

429

Hazardous Materials Table (cont'd)

(1)	(2) Hazardous materials descriptions and proper shipping names	(3) Hazard class	(4) Label(s) required (if not excepted)	(5) Packaging (a) Exceptions	(5) Packaging (b) Specific requirements	(6) Maximum net quantity in one package (a) Passenger carrying aircraft or railcar	(6) (b) Cargo only aircraft	(7) Water shipments (a) Cargo vessel	(7) (b) Passenger vessel	(7) (c) Other requirements
	Compressed gas, n.o.s.	Nonflammable gas	Nonflammable gas	173.306	173.302 173.304 173.305	150 pounds	300 pounds	1,2	1,2	
	Consumer commodity	ORM-D	None	None	173.510 173.1200	65 pounds gross	65 pounds gross			Not subject to requirements of Part 176
	Container, reused or empty, must be classed for the hazardous material previously contained. See 173.28, 173.29									
	Copper acetoarsenite, solid (emerald green, imperial green, King's green, moss green, meadow green, mitis green, parrot green, Vienna green)	Poison B	Poison	173.364	173.367	50 pounds	200 pounds	1,2	1,2	
	Copper arsenite, solid (Scheeles green, cupric green, copper orthoarsenite, Swedish green)	Poison B	Poison	173.364	173.365	50 pounds	200 pounds	1,2	1,2	
A	Copper chloride	ORM-B	None	173.505	173.510 173.800	25 pounds	100 pounds	1,2	1,2	
	Copper cyanide	Poison B	Poison	173.370		25 pounds	200 pounds	1,2	1,2	Stow away from acids
W	Copra	ORM-C	None	173.505	173.960	50 pounds	300 pounds	1,2	1,2	Segregation same as for flammable solids. Separate from flammable gases or liquids, oxidizing materials, or organic peroxides
	Copra pellets. See Coconut meal pellets									
	Cordeau detonant fuse	Class C explosive	Explosive C	None	173.104	1 quart	1 quart	1,2	1,2	
	Corrosive battery fluid. See Electrolyte (acid), or Alkaline Corrosive battery fluid									
	Corrosive liquid, n.o.s.	Corrosive material	Corrosive	173.244	173.245 173.245a	1 quart	1 quart	1	4	
	Corrosive solid, n.o.s.	Corrosive material	Corrosive	173.244	173.245b	25 pounds	100 pounds	1	4	
•	Cosmetics, n.o.s.	Combustible liquid	None	173.118a	None	No limit	No limit	1,2	1,2	

430

•	Cosmetics, n.o.s.	Flammable liquid	Flammable liquid	173.118	173.119	1 quart	10 gallons	1,2	1
•	Cosmetics, n.o.s.	Flammable solid	Flammable solid	173.153	173.154	25 pounds	100 pounds	1,2	1,2
•	Cosmetics, n.o.s.	Oxidizer	Oxidizer	173.153	173.154	25 pounds	100 pounds	1,2	1,2
•	Cosmetics, n.o.s., liquid	Corrosive material	Corrosive	173.244	173.245	1 quart	1 quart	1,2	1,2
•	Cosmetics, n.o.s., solid	Corrosive material	Corrosive	173.244	173.245b	25 pounds	100 pounds	1,2	1,2	Keep dry
W	Cotton	ORM-C	None	173.505	173.965			1,2	1,2	Segregation same as for flammable solids. See 176.900 to 176.904
W	Cotton batting	ORM-C	None	173.505	173.970			1,2	1,2	Keep dry. Stow away from vegetable or animal oils. See 176.900 to 176.904
W	Cotton batting dross. See Cotton batting									
	Cotton, burnt. See Burnt cotton									
W	Cotton seed hull fiber or shavings, pulp, or cut linters. See Cotton batting									
W	Cotton sweepings. See Cotton waste									
W	Cotton wadding. See Cotton batting									
W	Cotton waste	ORM-C	None	173.505	173.975			1,2	1,2	Keep dry. Stow away from vegetable or animal oils. See 176.900 to 176.904
	Cotton waste, oily (with more than 5% of animal or vegetable oil)	Flammable solid	Flammable solid	None	173.167	Forbidden	Forbidden	1,2	1,2	Separate from flammable gases or liquids, oxidizing materials, or organic peroxides
	Creosote, coal tar	Combustible liquid	None	173.118a	None	No limit	No limit	1,2	1,2	
	Creosote oil. See Creosote coal tar									
	Crotonaldehyde	Flammable liquid	Flammable liquid and Poison	173.118	173.119	1 quart	1 gallon	1,2	1
	Crotonic acid	Corrosive material	Corrosive	173.244	173.245	1 quart	10 gallons	1,2	1,2
	Crotonylene	Flammable liquid	Flammable liquid	173.118	173.119	1 quart	10 gallons	1,3	4
	Crude nitrogen (fertilizer solution (more than 25.3 p.s.i.g.)	Nonflammable gas	Nonflammable gas	173.306	173.304 173.314	Forbidden	300 pounds	1,3	1,3
•	Crude oil, petroleum	Combustible liquid	None	173.118a	None	No limit	No limit	1,2	1,2
•	Crude oil, petroleum	Flammable liquid	Flammable liquid	173.118	173.119	1 quart	10 gallons	1,2	1
	Cumene hydroperoxide	Organic peroxide	Organic peroxide	173.153	173.224	1 quart	1 quart	1,2	4
	Cupric cyanide. See Copper cyanide									

431

Hazardous Materials Table (cont'd)

(1) °/W/A	(2) Hazardous materials descriptions and proper shipping names	(3) Hazard class	(4) Label(s) required (if not excepted)	(5) Packaging (a) Exceptions	(5) Packaging (b) Specific requirements	(6) Maximum net quantity in one package (a) Passenger carrying aircraft or railcar	(6) (b) Cargo only aircraft	(7) Water shipments (a) Cargo vessel	(7) (b) Passenger vessel	(7) (c) Other requirements
•	Cupriethylene-diamine solution	Corrosive material	Corrosive	173.244	173.249	1 quart	1 gallon	1,2	1,2	
•	Cyanide or cyanide mixture, dry	Poison B	Poison	173.364	173.370	25 pounds	200 pounds	1,2	1,2	Keep dry. Stow away from acids
	Cyanogen bromide	Poison B	Poison	None	173.379	Forbidden	25 pounds	1	5	Shade from radiant heat. Segregation same as for corrosive materials
	Cyanogen chloride containing less than 0.9% water	Poison A	Nonflammable gas and Poison Gas	None	173.328	Forbidden	Forbidden	1	5	Shade from radiant heat
	Cyanogen gas	Poison A	Flammable gas and Poison Gas	None	173.328	Forbidden	Forbidden	1	5	
	Cyclohexane	Flammable liquid	Flammable liquid	173.118	173.119	1 quart	10 gallons	1,3	4	
	Cyclohexanone peroxide, 50 to 85% peroxide	Organic peroxide	Organic peroxide	173.157	173.158	Forbidden	25 pounds	1	1	
	Cyclohexanone peroxide, not over 50% peroxide	Organic peroxide	Organic peroxide	173.153	173.154	2 pounds	25 pounds	1,2	1,2	
	Cyclohexanone peroxide and bis (1-hydroxy cyclohexyl) peroxide mixture. See appropriate cyclohexanone peroxide entry immediately preceding									
	Cyclohexenyl trichlorosilane	Corrosive material	Corrosive	None	173.280	Forbidden	10 gallons	1	1	Keep dry
	Cyclohexyl trichlorosilane	Corrosive material	Corrosive	None	173.280	Forbidden	10 gallons	1	1	Keep dry
	Cyclopentane	Flammable liquid	Flammable liquid	173.118	173.119	1 quart	10 gallons	1,3	4	
	Cyclopentane, methyl	Flammable liquid	Flammable liquid	173.118	173.119	1 quart	10 gallons	1,3	4	
	Cyclopropane	Flammable gas	Flammable gas	None	173.306	Forbidden	300 pounds	1,2	1	

432

Cyclotrimethylenetrinitramine, desensitized. *See* High explosive							
Cyclotrimethylenetrinitramine, wet with not less than 10% water. *See* High explosive							
Cylinder, empty, including ton tanks, must be classed for the hazardous material previously contained in cylinder. See 173.29							
2,4-D. *See* 2,4-Dichlorophenoxyacetic acid							
▲ DDT or Dichlorodiphenyltrichloroethane	ORM-A	None	173.505	173.510	No limit	No limit	
Dead oil. See Creosote, coal tar							
Decaborane	Flammable solid	Flammable solid and Poison	None	173.236	Forbidden	25 pounds	1.2 1.2
Decahydronaphthalene	Combustible liquid	None	173.118a	None	No limit	No limit	1.2 1.2
Decalin. See Decahydronaphthalene							
Delay electric igniter	Class C explosive	Explosive C	None	173.106	50 pounds	150 pounds	1.3 1.3
Denatured alcohol. *See* Alcohol, n.o.s.							
Depth bomb. See Explosive bomb							
Detonating fuze, Class A explosive, with or without radioactive components	Class A explosive	Explosive A	None	173.69	Forbidden	Forbidden	6 5
Detonating fuze, Class C explosive	Class C explosive	Explosive C	None	173.113	50 pounds	150 pounds	1.3 1.3
Detonating primer	Class A explosive	Explosive A	None	173.68	Forbidden	Forbidden	6 5
• Diacetone alcohol	Flammable liquid	Flammable liquid	173.118	173.119	1 quart	10 gallons	1.2 1
Diacetyl	Flammable liquid	Flammable liquid	173.118	173.119	1 quart	10 gallons	1.2 1
▲ Diazinon	ORM-A	None	173.505	173.510	No limit	No limit	
Diazodinitrophenol. *See* Initiating explosive							
▲ Dibromodifluoromethane	ORM-A	None	173.505	173.516 173.605	10 gallons	55 gallons	1.2 1.2
W 1,2-Dibromoethane. *See* Ethylene dibromide							
Dichloroacetic acid	Corrosive material	Corrosive	173.244	173.245	1 quart	1 quart	1 1.2 Glass carboy in hampers not permitted under deck Keep dry
Dichloroacetyl chloride	Corrosive material	Corrosive	173.244	173.247	1 quart	1 gallon	1 4
▲ Dichlorobenzene, ortho, liquid	ORM-A	None	173.505	173.510	No limit	No limit	
▲ Dichlorobenzene, para, solid	ORM-A	None	173.505	173.510	No limit	No limit	

433

Hazardous Materials Table (cont'd)

(1)	(2) Hazardous materials descriptions and proper shipping names	(3) Hazard class	(4) Label(s) required (if not excepted)	(5) Packaging (a) Exceptions	(5) Packaging (b) Specific requirements	(6) Maximum net quantity in one package (a) Passenger carrying aircraft or railcar	(6) (b) Cargo only aircraft	(7) Water shipments (a) Cargo vessel	(7) (b) Passenger vessel	(7) (c) Other requirements
A	Dichlorobutene	Flammable liquid	Flammable liquid	173.118	173.119	1 quart	10 gallons	1,2	1,2	
	Dichlorodifluoroethylene	ORM-A	None	173.505	173.510 173.605	10 gallons	55 gallons	1,2	1,2	
	Dichlorodifluoromethane	Nonflammable gas	Nonflammable gas	173.306	173.304 173.314 173.315	150 pounds	300 pounds	1,2	1,2	
	Dichlorodifluoromethane and difluoroethane mixture (constant boiling mixture)	Nonflammable gas	Nonflammable gas	173.306	173.304 173.314 173.315	150 pounds	300 pounds	1,2	1,2	
	Dichlorodifluoromethane-dichlorotetrafluoroethane mixture	Nonflammable gas	Nonflammable gas	173.306	173.304 173.314 173.315	150 pounds	300 pounds	1,2	1,2	
	Dichlorodifluoromethane-monochlorodifluoromethane mixture	Nonflammable gas	Nonflammable gas	173.306	173.304 173.314 173.315	150 pounds	300 pounds	1,2	1,2	
•	Dichlorodifluoromethane-trichloromonofluoromethane mixture	Nonflammable gas	Nonflammable gas	173.306	173.304 173.314 173.315	150 pounds	300 pounds	1,2	1,2	
	Dichlorodifluoromethane-trichloromonofluoromethane-monochlorodifluoromethane mixture	Nonflammable gas	Nonflammable gas	173.306	173.304 173.314 173.315	150 pounds	300 pounds	1,2	1,2	
	Dichlorodifluoromethane-trichlorotrifluoroethane mixture	Nonflammable gas	Nonflammable gas	173.306	173.304 173.314 173.315	150 pounds	300 pounds	1,2	1,2	
	Dichlorodiphenyltrichloroethane. See DDT									
	Dichloroethylene	Flammable liquid	Flammable liquid	173.118	173.119	1 quart	10 gallons	1,2	1	
	Dichloroisopropyl ether	Corrosive material	Corrosive	173.244	173.245	1 quart	10 gallons	1,2	1,2	
A	Dichloromethane or methylene chloride	ORM-A	None	173.505	173.510 173.605	10 gallons	55 gallons	1,2	1,2	
•	Dichloropentane	Flammable liquid	Flammable liquid	173.118	173.119	1 quart	10 gallons	1,2	1,2	

▲	2,4-Dichlorophenoxyacetic acid	ORM-A	None	173.505	173.510	Forbidden	10 gallons	1	1	
	Dichlorophenyltrichlorosilane	Corrosive material	Corrosive	None	173.280	1 quart	10 gallons	1,2	1,2	Keep dry
	Dichloropropene and propylene dichloride mixture	Corrosive material	Corrosive	173.244	173.245	1 quart	1 quart	1,2	4	
	Dicumyl peroxide 50% solution	Organic peroxide	Organic peroxide	173.153	173.224	2 pounds	25 pounds	1,2	1,2	
	Dicumyl peroxide, dry	Organic peroxide	Organic peroxide	173.153	173.154	No limit	No limit	1,2	1,2	
▲	Dieldrin	ORM-A	None	173.505	173.510	Forbidden	5 pints	1,3	4	
	Diesel Fuel See Fuel oil									
	Diethylamine	Flammable liquid	Flammable liquid	173.118	173.119					
	Diethyl cellosolve. See Ethylene glycol diethyl ether									
	Diethyl dichlorosilane	Flammable liquid	Flammable liquid	None	173.135	Forbidden	10 gallons	1	1	Keep dry. Segregation same as for corrosives
	Diethylene glycol dinitrate See 173.51	Forbidden								
	Di-(2-ethylhexyl) phosphoric acid	Corrosive material	Corrosive	173.244	173.245	1 quart	10 gallons	1,2	1,2	
	Diethyl ketone	Flammable liquid	Flammable liquid	173.118	173.119	1 quart	10 gallons	1,2	1	
	1,1-Difluoro 1-chloroethane. See Difluoromomochlorethane									
	Difluoroethane	Flammable gas	Flammable gas	173.306	173.304 173.314 173.315	Forbidden	300 pounds	1,2	1	
	Difluoromonochloroethane (1,1-difluoro 1-chloroethane)	Flammable gas	Flammable gas	173.306	173.304 173.314 173.315	Forbidden	300 pounds	1,2	1	
	Difluorophosphoric acid, anhydrous	Corrosive material	Corrosive	None	173.275	Forbidden	1 gallon	1,2	1,2	
	Dihydropyran	Flammable liquid	Flammable liquid	173.118	173.119	1 quart	10 gallons	1,2	4	
	Diisobutyl ketone	Combustible liquid	None	173.118a	None	No limit	No limit	1,2	1,2	
	Diisooctyl acid phosphate	Corrosive material	Corrosive	173.244	173.296	1 quart	1 quart	1,2	1,2	Glass carboys in hampers not permitted under deck
	Diisopropylamine	Flammable liquid	Flammable liquid	173.118	173.119	1 quart	10 gallons	1,2	1	
	Diisopropylbenzene hydroperoxide solution, not over 60% peroxide	Organic peroxide	Organic peroxide	173.153	173.224	1 quart	1 quart	1,2	4	
	Diisopropylethanolamine	Corrosive material	Corrosive	173.244	173.245	1 quart	10 gallons	1,2	1,2	
	Diisopropylether	Flammable liquid	Flammable liquid	173.118	173.119	1 quart	10 gallons	1,3	4	

Hazardous Materials Table (cont'd)

(1) +/W/A	(2) Hazardous materials descriptions and proper shipping names	(3) Hazard class	(4) Label(s) required (if not excepted)	(5) Packaging (a) Exceptions	(5) Packaging (b) Specific requirements	(6) Maximum net quantity in one package (a) Passenger carrying aircraft or railcar	(6) (b) Cargo only aircraft	(7) Water shipments (a) Cargo vessel	(7) (b) Passenger vessel	(7) (c) Other requirements
	Dimethylamine, anhydrous	Flammable gas	Flammable gas	173.306	173.304 173.314 173.315	Forbidden	300 pounds	1,2	4	
*	Dimethylamine, aqueous solution	Flammable liquid	Flammable liquid	173.118	173.119	1 quart	10 gallons	1,2	1	
	2,3-Dimethylbutane	Flammable liquid	Flammable liquid	173.118	173.119	1 quart	10 gallons	1,3	4	
	Dimethyl carbonate	Flammable liquid	Flammable liquid	173.118	173.119	1 quart	10 gallons	1,2	1	
	1,4-Dimethylcyclohexane	Flammable liquid	Flammable liquid	173.118	173.119	1 quart	10 gallons	1,2	1	
	Dimethyldichlorosilane	Flammable liquid	Flammable liquid	None	173.135	Forbidden	5 pints	1,2	1	
	Dimethyl ether	Flammable gas	Flammable gas	173.306	173.304 173.314 173.315	Forbidden	300 pounds	1,2	1	
	Dimethylhexane dihydroperoxide, dry	Forbidden								
	Dimethylhexane dihydroperoxide, (with 30% or more water)	Organic peroxide	Organic peroxide	None	173.157	Forbidden	25 pounds	1	1	Keep dry. Separate from corrosive and oxidizing materials, and organic peroxides
	Dimethylhydrazine, unsymmetrical (UDMH)	Flammable liquid	Flammable liquid and Poison	None	173.145	Forbidden	5 pints	1,2	1	Keep cool
	Dimethyl sulfate	Corrosive material	Corrosive	None	173.255	Forbidden	1 quart	1	5	
	Dimethyl sulfide	Flammable liquid	Flammable liquid	None	173.119	Forbidden	10 gallons	1,2	5	
	Dinitrobenzene, solid, or dinitrobenzol, solid	Poison B	Poison	173.364	173.371	50 pounds	200 pounds	1,2	1,2	
*	Dinitrobenzene solution	Poison B	Poison	173.345	173.346	1 quart	55 gallons	1,2	1,2	
	Dinitrochlorobenzol, solid or Dinitro chlorobenzene	Poison B	Poison	173.364	173.365	50 pounds	200 pounds	1,2	1,2	
A	Dinitrocyclohexylphenol	ORM-A	None	173.505	173.510	No limit	No limit			
*	Dinitrophenol solution	Poison B	Poison	173.345	173.362a	1 quart	65 pounds	1,2	1,2	Stow away from heavy metals and their compounds. If flash point is 141 DEG F or less segregation same as for flammable liquids

436

Dioxane	Flammable liquid	Flammable liquid	173.118	173.119	1 quart	10 gallons	1,2	1
Dioxolane	Flammable liquid	Flammable liquid	173.118	173.119	1 quart	10 gallons	1,2	1
Diphenylaminechlororarsine (DM)	Irritating material	Irritant	None	173.382	Forbidden	75 pounds	1	5
Diphenyl dichlorosilane	Corrosive material	Corrosive	None	173.280	Forbidden	10 gallons	1	1	Keep dry
Diphenyl methyl bromide, solid	Corrosive material	Corrosive	173.244	173.245b	25 pounds	100 pounds	1	4
Diphenyl methyl bromide solution	Corrosive material	Corrosive	173.244	173.247	1 quart	1 gallon	1,2	1,2
Diphosgene. See Phosgene								
• Disinfectant, liquid, n.o.s.	Combustible liquid	None	173.118a	None	No limit	No limit	1,2	1,2
• Disinfectant, liquid	Corrosive material	Corrosive	173.244	173.245	1 quart	10 gallons	1	4
• Disinfectant, liquid	Poison B	Poison	173.345	173.346	1 quart	55 gallons	1,2	1
• Disinfectant, solid	Poison B	Poison	173.364	173.365	50	200 pounds	1,2	1
Dispersant Gas *or* Refrigerant Gas *See* 173.314 NOTE 13 and 173.315 NOTE 9								
• Distillate *(petroleum or coal tar)*	Flammable liquid	Flammable liquid	173.118	173.119	1 quart	10 gallons	1,2	1
Divinyl ether	Flammable liquid	Flammable liquid	None	173.119	Forbidden	10 gallons	1,3	5
Dodecyl trichlorosilane	Corrosive material	Corrosive	None	173.280	Forbidden	10 gallons	1	1	Keep dry
• Dressing, leather	Combustible liquid	None	173.118a	None	No limit	No limit	1,2	1,2
• Dressing, leather	Flammable liquid	Flammable liquid	173.118	173.119	1 quart	10 gallons	1,2	1
Drier. See Paint drier, liquid								
Drill cartridge			173.55 173.118a					
• Drugs, n.o.s.	Combustible liquid	None	173.118	173.119	No limit	No limit	1,2	1,2
• Drugs, n.o.s.	Flammable liquid	Flammable liquid	173.153	173.153	1 quart	10 gallons	1,2	1
• Drugs, n.o.s.	Flammable solid	Flammable solid	173.153	173.153	25 pounds	100 pounds	1,2	1,2
• Drugs, r.o.s.	Oxidizer	Oxidizer	173.153	173.154	25 pounds	100 pounds	1,2	1,2
• Drugs, n.o.s., liquid	Corrosive material	Corrosive	173.244	173.245	1 quart	1 quart	1,2	1,2

437

Hazardous Materials Table (cont'd)

(1)	(2) Hazardous materials descriptions and proper shipping names	(3) Hazard class	(4) Label(s) required (if not excepted)	(5) Packaging (a) Exceptions	(5) Packaging (b) Specific requirements	(6) Maximum net quantity in one package (a) Passenger carrying aircraft or railcar	(6) (b) Cargo only aircraft	(7) Water shipments (a) Cargo vessel	(7) (b) Passenger vessel	(7) (c) Other requirements
•	Drugs, n.o.s., liquid	Poison B	Poison	173.345	173.346	1 quart	55 gallons	1.3	1	
•	Drugs, n.o.s., solid	Corrosive material	Corrosive	173.244	173.245b	25 pounds	100 pounds	1.2	1.2	
•	Drugs, n.o.s., solid	Poison B	Poison	173.364	173.365	50 pounds	200 pounds	1.3	1.3	Keep dry
	Drums, empty, must be classed for the hazardous material previously contained in drum. See 173.29									
	Dry ice. See Carbon dioxide, solid									
	Dusts, by-product, poisonous. See Arsenical dust									
•	Dye intermediate, liquid	Corrosive material	Corrosive	173.244	173.245 173.249a	1 quart	10 gallons	1.2	1.2	Stow away from foodstuffs and living quarters
	Dynamite. See High explosive									
	Electric blasting caps. See Blasting caps, electric									
	Electric squib	Class C explosive	Explosive C	None	173.106	50 pounds	150 pounds	1.3	1.3	
	Electric storage battery, wet. See Battery, electric storage, wet									
	Electrolyte (acid), battery fluid (not over 47% acid)	Corrosive material	Corrosive	173.244	173.257	1 quart	5 gallons	1.2	1.2	Glass carboys in hampers not permitted under deck
	Electrolyte (acid), or alkaline (corrosive) battery fluid packed with battery charger, radio current supply device, or electronic equipment and actuating device	Corrosive material	Corrosive	None	173.259	Forbidden	5 pints	1.2	1.2	
	Electrolyte (acid), or alkaline (corrosive) battery fluid packed with dry-storage battery	Corrosive material	Corrosive	None	173.258	Forbidden	5 pints	1.2	1.2	
	Empty cartridge bag with black powder igniter	Class C explosive	Explosive C	None	173.106	50 pounds	150 pounds	1.3	1.3	
	Empty cartridge case, primed	Class C explosive	Explosive C	None	173.107	50 pounds	150 pounds	1.3	1.3	
•	Enamel. See *Paint, enamel, lacquer, etc.									

Engine, internal combustion	Flammable gas	Flammable gas	173.120	173.304	Forbidden	60 pounds	1,2	1,2	Not permitted in unventilated containers
Engine starting fluid	Flammable liquid	Flammable gas	None	173.119	1 quart	10 gallons	1,2	5	
Eradicator, paint or grease, liquid	Corrosive material	Flammable liquid	173.118	173.299	Forbidden	10 pounds	1	1	
Etching acid, liquid, n.o.s.	Corrosive material	Corrosive	None	173.304	Forbidden	300 pounds	1,2	5	
Ethane	Flammable gas	Flammable gas	173.306	173.119	Forbidden	10 gallons	1,3	4	
Ether (ethyl)	Flammable liquid	Flammable liquid	None					5	
Ether, Ethyl. See Ether									
Ethyl acetate	Flammable liquid	Flammable liquid	173.118	173.119	1 quart	10 gallons	1,2	1	
Ethyl acrylate, inhibited	Flammable liquid	Flammable liquid	173.118	173.119	1 quart	10 gallons	1,2	1	
Ethyl alcohol. See Alcohol, n.o.s.									
Ethyl aldehyde. See Acetaldehyde									
Ethyl benzene	Flammable liquid	Flammable liquid	173.118	173.119	1 quart	10 gallons	1,2	1	
Ethyl borate	Flammable liquid	Flammable liquid	173.118	173.119	1 quart	10 gallons	1,2	1	Keep dry
Ethyl butyl acetate	Combustible liquid	None	173.118a	None	No limit	No limit	1,2	1,2	
Ethyl butyl ether	Flammable liquid	Flammable liquid	173.118	173.119	1 quart	10 gallons	1,2	1	
Ethyl butyraldehyde	Flammable liquid	Flammable liquid	173.118	173.119	1 quart	10 gallons	1,2	1	
Ethyl butyrate	Flammable liquid	Flammable liquid	173.118	173.119	1 quart	10 gallons	1,2	1	
Ethyl chloride	Flammable liquid	Flammable liquid	None	173.123	Forbidden	173.123	1,2	1	Segregation same as for flammable gases
Ethyl chloroacetate	Combustible liquid	None	173.118a	None	No limit	No limit	1,2	1,2	
Ethyl chloroformate (chlorocarbonate)	Flammable liquid	Flammable liquid and Poison	None	173.288	Forbidden	5 pints	1,2	1	
Ethyl chlorothioformate	Corrosive material	Corrosive	173.244	173.245 173.245a	1 quart	1 quart	1,2	1	
Ethyl crotonate	Flammable liquid	Flammable liquid	173.118	173.119	1 quart	10 gallons	1,2	1	
Ethyl dichlorosilane	Flammable liquid	Flammable liquid	None	173.135	Forbidden	5 pints	1,2	1	

439

Hazardous Materials Table (cont'd)

(1)	(2) Hazardous materials descriptions and proper shipping names	(3) Hazard class	(4) Label(s) required (if not excepted)	(5) Packaging (a) Exceptions	(5) Packaging (b) Specific requirements	(6) Maximum net quantity in one package (a) Passenger carrying aircraft or railcar	(6) (b) Cargo only aircraft	(7) Water shipments (a) Cargo vessel	(7) (b) Passenger vessel	(7) (c) Other requirements
	Ethylene	Flammable gas	Flammable gas	173.306	173.304	Forbidden	300 pounds	1,2	4	
	Ethylene chlorohydrin	Poison B	Poison	173.345	173.346	1 quart	55 gallons	1,2	1	Segregation same as for flammable liquids
	Ethylene dibromide (1,2-dibromethane)	ORM-A	None	173.505	173.620	1 quart	55 gallons	1,2	1,2	Stow away from living quarters
	Ethylene dichloride	Flammable liquid	Flammable liquid	173.118	173.119	1 quart	10 gallons	1,2	1,2	
	Ethylene glycol diethyl ether (*diethyl "Cellosolve"*)	Combustible liquid	None	173.118a	None	No limit	No limit	1,2	1,2	
	Ethylene glycol monoethyl ether (*"Cellosolve"*)	Combustible liquid	None	173.118a	None	No limit	No limit	1,2	1,2	
	Ethylene glycol monoethyl ether acetate (*"Cellosolve acetate"*)	Combustible liquid	None	173.118a	None	No limit	No limit	1,2	1,2	
	Ethylene glycol monomethyl ether (*methyl "Cellosolve"*)	Combustible liquid	None	173.118a	None	No limit	No limit	1,2	1,2	
	Ethylene glycol monomethyl ether acetate (*methyl "Cellosolve acetate"*)	Combustible liquid	None	173.118a	None	No limit	No limit	1,2	1,2	
	Ethylene imine, inhibited	Flammable liquid	Flammable liquid and Poison	None	173.139	Forbidden	5 pints	1,2	1	Segregation same as for flammable gases
AW	Ethylene oxide	Flammable liquid	Flammable liquid	None	173.124	Forbidden	173.124	1,2	1	
	Ethyl ether. See Ether									
	Ethyl formate	Flammable liquid	Flammable liquid	173.118	173.119	1 quart	10 gallons	1,3	4	
	Ethylhexaldehyde	Combustible liquid	None	173.118a	Non.	No limit	No limit	1,2	1,2	
	Ethyl lactate	Combustible liquid	None	173.118a	None	No limit	No limit	1,2	1,2	
	Ethyl mercaptan	Flammable liquid	Flammable liquid	None	173.141	Forbidden	10 gallons	1,2	1	
	Ethyl methyl ether	Flammable liquid	Flammable liquid	None	173.119	Forbidden	10 gallons	1,3	1	Segregation same as for flammable gases

Ethyl methyl ketone	Flammable liquid	Flammable liquid	173.118	173.119	1 quart	10 gallons	1,2	1
Ethyl nitrate (*nitric ether*)	Flammable liquid	Flammable liquid	173.118	173.119	Forbidden	Forbidden	1,2	1
Ethyl nitrite (*nitrous ether*)	Flammable liquid	Flammable liquid	None	173.119	Forbidden	Forbidden	1,3	5
Ethyl phenyl dichlorosilane	Corrosive material	Corrosive	None	173.280	Forbidden	10 gallons	1	5
Ethyl phosphonothioic dichloride, anhydrous	Corrosive material	Corrosive	173.244	173.245 173.245a	1 quart	1 quart	1	4
Ethyl phosphonous dichloride, anhydrous	Corrosive material	Corrosive	173.244	173.245 173.245a	1 quart	1 quart	1	4
Ethyl phosphorodichloridate	Corrosive material	Corrosive	173.244	173.245 173.245a	1 quart	1 quart	1	4
Ethyl propionate	Flammable liquid	Flammable liquid	173.118	173.119	1 quart	10 gallons	1,2	1
Ethyl silicate (*tetra ethyl ortho silicate*)	Combustible liquid	None	173.118a	None	No limit	No limit	1,2	1,2
Ethyl trichlorosilane	Flammable liquid	Flammable liquid	None	173.135	Forbidden	5 pints	1,2	1
Etiologic agent, n.o.s.	Etiologic agent	Etiologic agent	173.386	173.387	173.386	4 liters		
W Excelsior (shredded wood) when dry, clear, and free from oil	ORM-C	None	173.505	173.980			1,3	1,3
W Exothermic ferrochrome	ORM-C	None	173.505	173.985			1	1
W Exothermic ferromanganese. *See* Exothermic ferrochrome								
W Exothermic silicon chrome. *See* Exothermic ferrochrome								
Explosive auto alarm	Class C explosive	Explosive C	None	173.111	50 pounds	150 pounds	1,2	1,2
Explosive bomb	Class A explosive	Explosive A	None	173.56	Forbidden	Forbidden	1,2	5	Magazine stowage authorized. No other cargo may be stowed in the same hold with these items:
Explosive cable cutter	Class C explosive	Explosive C	None	173.102	50 pounds	150 pounds	1,3	1,3
Explosive mine	Class A explosive	Explosive A	None	173.56	Forbidden	Forbidden	1,2	5	Magazine stowage authorized. No other cargo may be stowed in the same hold with this material
Explosive, new approval, and evaluation See 173.86								
Explosive power device, Class B	Class B explosive	Explosive B	None	173.94	Forbidden	150 pounds	1,2	5
Explosive power device, Class C	Class C explosive	Explosive C	None	173.102	50 pounds	150 pounds	1,3	1,3

Notes in right column:
- Etiologic agent row: "Not permitted except under specific conditions approved by the Department"
- ORM-C row: "Stow away from organic, corrosive, or oxidizing materials"

Hazardous Materials Table (cont'd)

(1)	(2)	(3)	(4)	(5) Packaging		(6) Maximum net quantity in one package			(7) Water shipments		
				(a)	(b)	(a)	(b)	(a)	(b)		
*/W/A	Hazardous materials descriptions and proper shipping names	Hazard class	Label(s) required (if not excepted)	Exceptions	Specific requirements	Passenger carrying aircraft or railcar	Cargo only aircraft	Cargo vessel	Passenger vessel	Other requirements	
	Explosive projectile	Class A explosive	Explosive A	None	173.56	Forbidden	Forbidden	1,2	5	Magazine stowage authorized. No other cargo may be stowed in the same hold with this material	
	Explosive release device	Class C explosive	Explosive C	None	173.102	50 pounds	150 pounds	1,3	1,3		
	Explosive rivet	Class C explosive	Explosive C	None	173.100	50 pounds	150 pounds	1,2	1,2		
	Explosive, sample for laboratory examination			173.86		Forbidden	173.86				
	Explosive torpedo	Class A explosive	Explosive A	None	173.56	Forbidden	Forbidden	1,2	5	Magazine stowage authorized. No other cargo may be stowed in the same hold with this material	
•	Extract, liquid, flavoring	Flammable liquid	Flammable liquid	173.118	173.119	1 quart	10 gallons	1,2	1		
	Fabric with animal or vegetable oil. See Fibers or fabric containing not more than 5% animal or vegetable fat										
AW	Feed, wet, mixed	ORM-C	None	173.505	173.990	Forbidden	Forbidden	3	3	Stow in cool, dry, well ventilated compartment. Do not stow bags over ten tiers high without flooring off. Do not overstow	
	Felt, waste. See Cotton waste										
W	Felt, waste, wet. See Waste wool, wet										
	Ferric arsenate, solid	Poison B	Poison	173.364	173.365	50 pounds	200 pounds	1,2	1,2		
	Ferric arsenite, solid	Poison B	Poison	173.364	173.365	50 pounds	200 pounds	1,2	1,2		
A	Ferric chloride, solid, *anhydrous*	ORM-B	None	173.505	173.510	25 pounds	100 pounds	1,2	1,2		
•	Ferric chloride solution	Corrosive material	Corrosive	173.244	173.245 173.245a	1 quart	10 quarts	1,2	1,2		
W	Ferrophosphorus	ORM-A	None	173.505	173.635			1,2	1,2	Keep dry. Stow away from living quarters	

442

AW	Ferrosilicon, containing 30% or more but not more than 70% silicon	ORM-A	None	173.505	173.510 173.645	Forbidden	25 pounds	1,2	1,2	Keep dry. Stow away from living quarters. Segregation same as for flammable solids labeled Dangerous When Wet
	Ferrous arsenate (iron arsenate), solid	Poison B	Poison	173.364	173.365	50 pounds	200 pounds	1,2	1,2	
	Fertilizer ammoniating solution containing free ammonia (more than 25.3 p.s.i.g.)	Nonflammable gas	Nonflammable gas	173.306	173.304 173.314	Forbidden	300 pounds	1,2	4	
W	Fertilizer, tankage. See Garbage, tankage									
	Fibers (jute, hemp, flax, sisal, coir, kapok, and similar vegetable fibers)	ORM-C	None	173.505	173.965			1,2	1,2	Stow away from animal or vegetable oils. Segregation same as for flammable solids
	Fibers, burnt	Flammable solid	Flammable solid	None	173.169	Forbidden	Forbidden	1,2	1,2	Separate from flammable gases or liquids, oxidizing materials, or organic peroxides
	Fibers or fabric, containing not more than 5% animal or vegetable oil	Flammable solid	Flammable solid	None	173.170	Forbidden	Forbidden	1,2	1,2	Separate from flammable gases or liquids, oxidizing materials, or organic peroxides
	Film (nitrocellulose)	Flammable solid	Flammable solid	None	173.177	50 pounds	200 pounds	1,3	1,3	Stow away from other flammable cargo or substances
	Film, photographic, (including scrap film), safety, nonflammable, or slow burning. Not subject to requirements of this subchapter									
	Firecracker. See Fireworks, common or special									
	Fire extinguisher	Nonflammable gas	Nonflammable gas	173.306		150 pounds	300 pounds	1,2	1,2	
•	Fire extinguisher charge containing not more than 50 grains of propellant explosive per unit. Not subject to requirements of this subchapter									
	Fire extinguisher charge containing sulfuric acid	Corrosive material	Corrosive	173.261		1 quart	1 gallon	1,2	1,2	
	Fireworks, common	Class C explosive	Explosive C	None	173.100 173.106	50 pounds	200 pounds	1,3	1,3	Passenger vessels in metal lockers only
	Fireworks, exhibition display piece. See Fireworks, special									
	Fireworks, special	Class B explosive	Explosive B	None	173.88 173.91	Forbidden	200 pounds	3	3	Passenger vessels in metal lockers only. Toy torpedoes must not be packed with other special fireworks

Hazardous Materials Table (cont'd)

(1)	(2) Hazardous materials descriptions and proper shipping names	(3) Hazard class	(4) Label(s) required (if not excepted)	(5) Packaging (a) Exceptions	(5) (b) Specific requirements	(6) Maximum net quantity in one package (a) Passenger carrying aircraft or railcar	(6) (b) Cargo only aircraft	(7) Water shipments (a) Cargo vessel	(7) (b) Passenger vessel	(7) (c) Other requirements
W	Fish meal *or* fish scrap containing 6% to 12% water	ORM-C	None	173.505	173.995			1,2	1,2	Segregation same as for flammable solids. Separate from flammable gases or liquids, oxidizing materials, or organic peroxides. *Use double strip stowage* for cargo 6-12 percent moisture containing not more than 12 percent fat. *Use single strip stowage* for cargo 6-12 percent moisture containing 12-15 percent fat
	Fish meal *or* fish scrap containing less than 6% or more than 12% water	Flammable solid	Flammable solid	None	173.171	Forbidden	Forbidden	1,2	1,2	Separate from flammable gases or liquids, oxidizing materials, or organic peroxides
	Fissile radioactive material. *See* Radioactive material, fissile									
•	Flame retardant compound liquid	Corrosive material	Corrosive	173.244	173.291	1 quart	10 gallons	1,2	1,2	
	Flammable Gas n.o.s. *See* Compressed gas, n.o.s.									
	Flammable liquid, n.o.s.	Flammable liquid	Flammable liquid	173.118	173.119	1 quart	10 gallons	1,2	1	
	Flammable solid, n.o.s.	Flammable solid	Flammable solid	173.153	173.154	25 pounds	25 pounds	1,2	1,2	
	Flare. *See* Fireworks, common									
	Flare, airplane. *See* Fireworks, special									
	Flash cartridge. *See* Fireworks, special *or* Low explosives									
	Flash cracker. *See* Fireworks, common *or* special									
	Flash powder. *See* Fireworks, special *or* Low explosives									
	Flax. *See* Fibers									
	Flexible linear shaped charge, metal clad	Class C explosive	Explosive C	None	173.104	50 pounds	300 pounds	1,3	1,3	
	Flowers of sulfur. *See* Sulfur									

	Article					50 pounds	200 pounds			
	Flue dust, poisonous	Poison B	Poison	173.364	173.368			1,2	1,2	
	Fluoboric acid	Corrosive material	Corrosive	173.244	173.283	1 quart	1 gallon	1,2	1,2	
	Fluoric acid. See Hydrofluoric acid									
	Fluorine	Nonflammable gas	Poison and Oxidizer	None	173.302	Forbidden	Forbidden	1	5	Stow in well ventilated space away from organic materials
	Fluorophosphoric acid, anhydrous. See Monofluorophosphoric acid, anhydrous									
	Fluorosilicic acid. See Hydrofluosilicic acid									
	Fluorosulfonic acid or Fluosulfonic acid	Corrosive material	Corrosive	None	173.274	Forbidden	1 gallon	1	5	Keep dry
AW	Formaldehyde, or formalin solution (in containers of 110 gallons or less)	ORM-A	None	173.505	173.510	10 gallons	55 gallons	1,2	4	
	Formaldehyde, or formalin solution (in containers over 110 gallons)	Combustible liquid	None	173.118a	None	10 gallons	55 gallons	1,2	1,2	
	Formalin. See Formaldehyde solution									
	Formic acid	Corrosive material	Corrosive	173.244	173.245 173.289	1 quart	5 gallons	1,2	1,2	Glass carboys in hampers not permitted under deck
•	Formic acid solution	Corrosive material	Corrosive	173.244	173.245 173.289	1 quart	5 gallons	1,2	1,2	
	Fuel, aviation, turbine engine	Flammable liquid	Flammable liquid	173.118	173.119	1 quart	10 gallons	1,2	1	
•	Fuel oil	Combustible liquid	None	173.118a	None	No limit	No limit	1,2	1,2	
	Fuel oil, Diesel. See Fuel oil									
	Fuel oil, No. 1, 2, 4, 5 or 6	Combustible liquid	None	173.118a	None	No limit	No limit	1,2	1,2	
	Fulminate of mercury, dry	Forbidden								
	Fulminate of mercury, wet. See Initiating explosive									
	Fumaryl chloride	Corrosive material	Corrosive	173.244	173.245 173.152	1 quart	1 quart	1	1	Glass carboys not permitted
•	Fumigant	Combustible liquid	None	173.118a	None	No limit	No limit	1,2	1	
•	Furfural	Flammable solid	Flammable solid	None	173.154a	50 pounds	200 pounds	1,3	1,3	
	Fusee (railway or highway)	Class C explosive	Explosive C	None	173.106	50 pounds	150 pounds	1,3	1,3	
	Fuse igniter	Class C explosive	Explosive C	173.100		50 pounds	150 pounds	1,2	1,2	
	Fuse, instantaneous	Class C explosive	Explosive C	None	173.106	50 pounds	150 pounds	1,3	1,3	
	Fuse lighter									

Hazardous Materials Table (cont'd)

(1)	(2) Hazardous materials descriptions and proper shipping names	(3) Hazard class	(4) Label(s) required (if not excepted)	(5) Packaging (a) Exceptions	(5) Packaging (b) Specific requirements	(6) Maximum net quantity in one package (a) Passenger carrying aircraft or railcar	(6) (b) Cargo only aircraft	(7) Water shipments (a) Cargo vessel	(7) (b) Passenger vessel	(7) (c) Other requirements
	Fusel oil	Combustible liquid	None	173.118a	None	No limit	No limit	1,2	1,2	
	Fuse, mild detonating, metal clad	Class C explosive	Explosive C	None	173.104	50 pounds	300 pounds	1,2	1,2	
	Fuse, safety	Class C explosive	Explosive C	173.100	None	50 pounds	300 pounds	1,2	1,2	
	Fuze, combination	Class C explosive	Explosive C	None	173.105	50 pounds	150 pounds	1,3	1,3	
	Fuze, detonating	Class A explosive	Explosive A	None	173.69	Forbidden	Forbidden	6	5	
	Fuze, detonating, Class C explosive	Class C explosive	Explosive C	None	173.113	50 pounds	150 pounds	1,3	1,3	
	Fuze, detonating, radioactive	Class A explosive	Explosive A	None	173.69	Forbidden	Forbidden	6	5	
	Fuze, percussion	Class C explosive	Explosive C	None	173.105	50 pounds	150 pounds	1,3	1,3	
	Fuze, time	Class C explosive	Explosive C	None	173.105	50 pounds	150 pounds	1,3	1,3	
	Fuze, tracer	Class C explosive	Explosive C	None	173.105	50 pounds	150 pounds	1,3	1,3	
	Gallium metal, liquid	ORM-B	None	None	173.861	Forbidden	Forbidden	1	5	None
	Gallium metal, solid	ORM-B	None	None	173.862	40 pounds	40 pounds	1,3	1	Shade from radient heat
W	Garbage tankage containing 8% or more water	ORM-C	None	173.505	173.1000	Forbidden	Forbidden	1,2	1,2	
	Garbage tankage, containing less than 8% water	Flammable solid	Flammable solid	None	173.209	Forbidden	Forbidden	1	1	Separate from flammable gases or liquids, oxidizing materials, or organic peroxides
	Gas cylinder, empty. See Cylinder, empty									
*	Gas drips, hydrocarbon	Combustible liquid	None	173.118a	None	No limit	No limit	1,2	1,2	

446

					1 quart	10 gallons		
• Gas drips, hydrocarbon	Flammable liquid	Flammable liquid	173.118	173.119	Forbidden	Forbidden	1,2	1
• Gas identification set	Poison A	Poison gas	None	173.331	Forbidden	Forbidden	1	5
• Gas identification set	Irritating material	Irritant	None	173.331	Forbidden	Forbidden	1	5
Gas mine. See Explosive mine								
Gas oil. See Fuel oil								
Gasoline (including casing-head and natural)	Flammable liquid	Flammable liquid	173.118	173.119	1 quart	10 gallons	1,2	4
Gelatine Dynamite. See High explosive								
Germane	Poison A	Poison gas and Flammable gas	None	173.328	Forbidden	Forbidden	1	5
Grenade, empty, primed	Class C explosive	Explosive C	None	173.107	50 pounds	150 pounds	1,3	1,3
Grenade, hand or rifle, explosive (with or without gas, smoke, or incendiary material)	Class A explosive	Explosive A	None	173.56	Forbidden	Forbidden	1,2	5
Grenade, tear gas	Irritating material	Irritant	None	173.385	Forbidden	75 pounds	1,2	1
Grenade without bursting charge: With incendiary material (Special fireworks)	Class B explosive	Explosive B	173.91		Forbidden	Forbidden	3	3
Grenade without bursting charge: With smoke charge (Smoke grenade)	Class C explosive	Explosive C	173.108		50 pounds	150 pounds	1,3	1,3
Grenade without bursting charge: With Poison A gas charge	Poison A	Poison gas	173.330		Forbidden	Forbidden		
Grenade without bursting charge: With Poison B charge	Poison B	Poison	173.350		Forbidden	Forbidden		
Guanidine nitrate	Oxidizer	Oxidizer	173.153	173.182	25 pounds	100 pounds	1,2	1,2
Guanyl nitrosamino guanylidene hydrazine. See Initiating explosive								
Guanyl nitrosamino guanyl tetrazene. See Initiating explosive								
Guided missile, without warhead. See Rocket motor, Class A explosive or Rocket motor, class B explosive								
Guided missile with warhead. See Rocket ammunition with explosive, illuminating, gas, incendiary, or smoke projectile								
Guncotton. See High explosive								

Notes:
- No other cargo may be stowed in the same hold with these items
- Passenger vessels in metal lockers only
- See correct shipping name of applicable Poison A material for stowage, special handling, and special segregation requirements
- See correct shipping name of applicable Poison B material for stowage, special handling, and special segregation requirements
- Separate from nitro-compounds, chlorates, and acids

Hazardous Materials Table (cont'd)

(1)	(2) Hazardous materials descriptions and proper shipping names	(3) Hazard class	(4) Label(s) required (if not excepted)	(5) Packaging (a) Exceptions	(5) Packaging (b) Specific requirements	(6) Maximum net quantity in one package (a) Passenger carrying aircraft or railcar	(6) (b) Cargo only aircraft	(7) Water shipments (a) Cargo vessel	(7) (b) Passenger vessel	(7) (c) Other requirements
	Hafnium metal, dry (*See Note 3, Sec. 173.214*)	Flammable solid	Flammable solid	None	173.214	Forbidden	75 pounds	1	5	
	Hafnium metal, wet	Flammable solid	Flammable solid	None	173.214	Forbidden	150 pounds	1,2	5	
	Hair, wet	Flammable solid	Flammable solid	None	173.172	Forbidden	Forbidden	1,2	5	Separate from flammable gases or liquids, oxidizing materials, or organic peroxides
	Hand signal device	Class C explosive	Explosive C	None	173.108	50 pounds	200 pounds	1,2	1,2	
W	Hay	ORM-C	None	173.505	173.1005			1,2	1,2	Segregation same as for flammable solids. Stow away from animal or vegetable oils
W	Hay or straw (*loose, wet, or damp*)									Forbidden for water shipment
	Heater for refrigerator car., liquid fuel type (*containing fuel*)	Flammable liquid	Flammable liquid	173.146		Forbidden	Forbidden	1,2	1	
*	Helium	Nonflammable gas	Nonflammable gas	173.306	173.302	150 pounds	300 pounds	1,2	1,2	
*	Helium-oxygen mixture	Nonflammable gas	Nonflammable gas	173.306	173.314	150 pounds	300 pounds	1,2	1,2	
	Heptane	Flammable liquid	Flammable liquid	173.118	173.119	1 quart	10 gallons	1,2	1	
W	*Hessian. See Burlap cloth*									
W	Hexachloroethane	ORM-A	None	173.505	173.650	Forbidden	10 gallons	1,2	1,2	
	Hexadecyltrichlorosilane	Corrosive material	Corrosive	None	173.280	Forbidden	10 gallons	1	1	Keep dry
	Hexadiene	Flammable liquid	Flammable liquid	None	173.119	Forbidden	10 gallons	1,2	5	
	Hexaethyl tetraphosphate and compressed gas mixture	Poison A	Poison gas	None	173.334	Forbidden	Forbidden	1	5	Shade from radiant heat
	Hexaethyl tetraphosphate, liquid	Poison B	Poison	None	173.358	Forbidden	1 quart	1	4	
	Hexaethyl tetraphosphate mixture, dry (*containing more than 2% hexaethyl tetraphosphate*)	Poison B	Poison	None	173.377	Forbidden	200 pounds	1,2	5	

448

Hexaethyl tetraphosphate mixture, dry (containing not more than 2% hexaethyl tetraphosphate)	Poison B	Poison	173.377	173.377	50 pounds	200 pounds	1,2	4	
Hexaethyl tetraphosphate mixture, liquid (*containing more than 25% hexaethyl tetraphosphate*)	Poison B	Poison	None	173.359	Forbidden	1 quart	1,2	5	
Hexaethyl tetraphosphate mixture, liquid (containing not more than 25% hexaethyl tetraphosphate)	Poison B	Poison	173.359	173.359	1 quart	1 gallon	1,2	4	
Hexafluorophosphoric acid	Corrosive material	Corrosive	None	173.275	Forbidden	1 gallon	1,2	1,2	
Hexafluoropropylene	Nonflammable gas	Nonflammable gas	173.306	173.304 173.314 173.315	150 pounds	300 pounds	1	4	
Hexafluoropropylene oxide	Nonflammable gas	Nonflammable gas	173.306	173.304 173.314	150	300	1,2	1,2	
Hexaldehyde	Flammable liquid	Flammable liquid	173.118	173.119	1 quart	10 gallons	1,2	1,2	
Hexamethylene diamine, solid	Corrosive material	Corrosive	173.244	173.245b	25 pounds	100 pounds	1,2	1,2	
Hexamethylene diamine solution	Corrosive material	Corrosive	173.244	173.292	1 quart	10 gallons	1,2	1,2	
Hexamethylene imine	Corrosive material	Corrosive	173.244	173.245	1 quart	10 gallons	1,2	1,2	
Hexane	Flammable liquid	Flammable liquid	173.118	173.119	1 quart	10 gallons	1,3	4	
Hexanoic acid	Corrosive material	Corrosive	173.244	173.245	1 quart	10 gallons	1,2	1,2	
Hexyltrichlorosilane	Corrosive material	Corrosive	None	173.280	Forbidden	10 gallons	1	1	Keep dry
High explosive	Class A explosive	Explosive A	173.65	173.61 to 173.87	Forbidden	Forbidden	6	5	
High explosive, liquid	Class A explosive	Explosive A	None	173.62	Forbidden	Forbidden	6	5	
Hydraulic accumulator. *See* Accumulator, pressurized									
Hydrazine, anhydrous	Flammable liquid	Flammable liquid and Poison	None	173.276	Forbidden	5 pints	1	5	Segregation same as for corrosives
Hydrazine, aqueous solution	Corrosive material	Corrosive	None	173.276	Forbidden	5 pints	1	5	Glass carboys not permitted on passenger vessel
Hydriodic acid	Corrosive material	Corrosive	173.244	173.245	1 quart	1 gallon	1	1	
Hydrobromic acid, anhydrous. *See* Hydrogen bromide									
Hydrobromic acid, *more than 49% strength*	Corrosive material	Corrosive	None	173.262	Forbidden	Forbidden	1	1	Glass carboys not permitted on passenger vessel
Hydrobromic acid not more than 49% strength	Corrosive material	Corrosive	173.244	173.262	1 quart	1 gallon	1	1	Glass carboys not permitted on passenger vessel

449

Hazardous Materials Table (cont'd)

(1)	(2)	(3)	(4)	(5) Packaging		(6) Maximum net quantity in one package		(7) Water shipments		
*/W/A	Hazardous materials descriptions and proper shipping names	Hazard class	Label(s) required (if not excepted)	(a) Exceptions	(b) Specific requirements	(a) Passenger carrying aircraft or railcar	(b) Cargo only aircraft	(a) Cargo vessel	(b) Passenger vessel	(c) Other requirements
	Hydrocarbon gas, liquefied	Flammable gas	Flammable gas	173.306	173.304 173.314	Forbidden	300 pounds	1,2	1	
*	Hydrocarbon gas, nonliquefied	Flammable gas	Flammable gas	173.306	173.302	Forbidden	300 pounds	1,2	1	
	Hydrochloric (*muriatic*) acid	Corrosive material	Corrosive	173.244	173.263	1 quart	1 gallon	1	1	Glass carboys not permitted on passenger vessel
	Hydrochloric acid, anhydrous. *See* Hydrogen chloride									
*	Hydrochloric acid mixture	Corrosive material	Corrosive	173.244	173.263	1 quart	1 gallon	1	1	Glass carboys not permitted on passenger vessel
*	Hydrochloric acid solution, inhibited	Corrosive material	Corrosive	173.244	173.263	1 quart	1 gallon	1	1	Glass carboys not permitted on passenger vessel
	Hydrocyanic acid, liquefied	Poison A	Flammable gas and Poison gas	None	173.332	Forbidden	Forbidden	1	5	
	Hydrocyanic acid (*prussic*) solution (5% or more hydrocyanic acid)	Poison A	Flammable gas and Poison gas	None	173.332	Forbidden	Forbidden	1	5	Shade from radiant heat. Aqueous solutions containing more than 20 percent hydrogen cyanide are not permitted in transportation by water
	Hydrocyanic acid (*prussic*), unstabilized	Forbidden								
	Hydrocyanic acid solution, less than 5% hydrocyanic acid	Poison B	Poison	None	173.351	Forbidden	25 pounds	1	5	Shade from radiant heat
	Hydrofluoric acid, anhydrous. *See* Hydrogen fluoride									
*	Hydrofluoric acid solution	Corrosive material	Corrosive	173.244	173.264	1 quart	1 gallon	1	4	
*	Hydrofluoric and sulfuric acids, mixture	Corrosive material	Corrosive	None	173.290	Forbidden	1 gallon	1	5	
	Hydrofluoroboric acid. *See* Fluoboric acid									
	Hydrofluorosilicic acid	Corrosive material	Corrosive	None	173.265	1 quart	1 gallon	1,2	1,2	
	Hydrogen	Flammable gas	Flammable gas	173.306	173.302 173.314	Forbidden	300 pounds	1,2	4	

450

Hydrogen, Liquified	Flammable gas	Flammable gas	None	173.316	Forbidden	Forbidden		Forbidden
Hydrogen bromide	Nonflammable gas	Nonflammable gas	173.306	173.304	Forbidden	300 pounds	1	4
Hydrogen chloride	Nonflammable gas	Nonflammable gas	173.306	173.304	Forbidden	300 pounds	1	4
Hydrogen fluoride	Corrosive material	Corrosive	None	173.264	Forbidden	110 pounds	1	5	Segregation same as for nonflammable gases
Hydrogen iodide solution See Hydriodic acid								
Hydrogen peroxide solution (8% to 40% peroxide)	Oxidizer	Oxidizer	173.244	173.266	1 quart	1 gallon	1,2	1	Shade from radiant heat. Separate from permanganates. Keep away from powdered metals
Hydrogen peroxide solution (40% to 52% peroxide)	Oxidizer	Oxidizer	173.244	173.266	Forbidden	Forbidden	1	4	Shade from radiant heat. Separate from permanganates. Keep away from powdered metals
Hydrogen peroxide solution (over 52% peroxide)	Oxidizer	Oxidizer	None	173.266	Forbidden	Forbidden	1	5	Shade from radiant heat. Separate from permanganates. Keep away from powdered metals. Concentrations greater than 60% hydrogen peroxide not permitted on any vessel except under conditions approved by the Department
Hydrogen selenide	Flammable gas	Flammable gas and Poison	None	173.328	Forbidden	Forbidden	1	5
Hydrogen sulfate. See Sulfuric acid								
Hydrogen sulfide	Flammable gas	Flammable gas and Poison	None	173.304 173.314	Forbidden	300 pounds	1	5
Hydrosilicofluoric acid. See Hydrofluorosilicic acid								
Hypochlorite solution containing more than 7% available chlorine by weight	Corrosive material	Corrosive	173.244	173.277	1 quart	4 gallons	1,2	1	Glass carboys in hampers not permitted under deck
A° Hypochlorite solution containing not more than 7% available chlorine by weight	ORM-B	None	173.505	173.510	No limit	No limit		
Igniter	Class C explosive	Explosive C	None	173.106	50 pounds	150 pounds	1,3	1,3
Igniter cord	Class C explosive	Explosive C	None	173.100	50 pounds	150 pounds	1,3	1,3
Igniter fuse, metal clad	Class C explosive	Explosive C	None	173.106	50 pounds	150 pounds	1,3	1,3
• Igniter, jet thrust (jato)	Class A explosive	Explosive A	None	173.79	Forbidden	Forbidden	6	5
• Igniter, jet-thrust (jato)	Class B explosive	Explosive B	None	173.92	Forbidden	550 pounds	1,3	5
• Igniter, rocket motor	Class A explosive	Explosive A	None	173.79	Forbidden	Forbidden	6	5

451

Hazardous Materials Table (cont'd)

(1)	(2) Hazardous materials descriptions and proper shipping names	(3) Hazard class	(4) Label(s) required (if not excepted)	(5) Packaging (a) Exceptions	(5) Packaging (b) Specific requirements	(6) Maximum net quantity in one package (a) Passenger carrying aircraft or railcar	(6) (b) Cargo only aircraft	(7) Water shipments (a) Cargo vessel	(7) (b) Passenger vessel	(7) (c) Other requirements
•	Igniter, rocket motor	Class B explosive	Explosive B	None	173.92	Forbidden	550 pounds	1,3	5	
	Illuminating projectile. See Fireworks, special									
	Iminobispropylamine	Corrosive material	Corrosive	173.244	173.245	1 quart	10 gallons	1,2	1,2	
	Initiating explosive *Diazodinitrophenol*	Class A explosive	Explosive A	None	173.70	Forbidden	Forbidden	6	5	
	Initiating explosive *Fulminate of mercury*	Class A explosive	Explosive A	None	173.71	Forbidden	Forbidden	6	5	
	Initiating explosive *Guanyl nitrosamino guanylidene hydrazine*	Class A explosive	Explosive A	None	173.72	Forbidden	Forbidden	6	5	
	Initiating explosive *Lead azide, dextrinated type only*	Class A explosive	Explosive A	None	173.73	Forbidden	Forbidden	6	5	
	Initiating explosive *Lead mononitroresorcinate*	Class A explosive	Explosive A	None	173.70	Forbidden	Forbidden	6	5	
	Initiating explosive Lead styphnate (*lead trinitroresorcinate*)	Class A explosive	Explosive A	None	173.74	Forbidden	Forbidden	6	5	
	Initiating explosive *Nitro mannite*	Class A explosive	Explosive A	None	173.75	Forbidden	Forbidden	6	5	
	Initiating explosive *Nitrosoguanidine*	Class A explosive	Explosive A	None	173.76	Forbidden	Forbidden	6	5	
	Initiating explosive *Pentaerythrite tetranitrate*	Class A explosive	Explosive A	None	173.77	Forbidden	Forbidden	6	5	
	Initiating explosive Tetrazene (*guanyl nitrosamine guanyl tetrazene*)	Class A explosive	Explosive A	None	173.78	Forbidden	Forbidden	6	5	
	Ink	Combustible liquid	None	173.118a	None	No limit	No limit	1,2	1,2	
	Ink	Flammable liquid	Flammable liquid	173.118	173.144	1 quart	10 gallons	1,2	1	
•	Insecticide, dry, n.o.s.	Poison B	Poison	173.364	173.365	50 pounds	200 pounds	1,2	1,2	
•	Insecticide, liquefied gas (*containing no Poison A or B material*)	Nonflammable gas	Nonflammable gas	173.306	173.304	150 pounds	300 pounds	1,3	1,3	

452

Insecticide, liquefied gas, containing Poison A material or Poison B material	Poison A	Poison gas	None	173.329 173.334	Forbidden	Forbidden	1	5	Shade from radiant heat
• Insecticide, liquid, n.o.s.	Combustible liquid	None	173.118a	None	No limit	No limit	1.2	1.2	
• Insecticide, liquid, n.o.s.	Flammable liquid	Flammable liquid	173.118	173.119	1 quart	10 gallons	1.2	1	
• Insecticide, liquid, n.o.s.	Poison B	Poison	173.345	173.346	1 quart	55 gallons	1.2	1	
W Insulation tape (varnished cloth type). See Oiled material									
Iodine monochloride	Corrosive material	Corrosive	None	173.293	Forbidden	1 quart	1	5	Keep dry
Iodine pentafluoride	Oxidizer	Oxidizer and Poison	None	173.246	Forbidden	100 pounds	1	1	Keep dry
Iron chloride, solid. See Ferric chloride, solid									
Iron mass or sponge, not properly oxidized	Flammable solid	Flammable solid	None	173.174	Forbidden	Forbidden	1.2	5	Separate from flammable gases, or liquids, oxidizing materials, or organic peroxides
Iron mass or sponge spent	Flammable solid	Flammable solid	None	173.174	Forbidden	Forbidden	1.2	5	Separate from flammable gases, or liquids, oxidizing materials, or organic peroxides
A Iron, oxide, spent					Forbidden	Forbidden			
Iron sesquichloride, solid. See Ferric chloride									
Irritating agent, n.o.s.	Irritating material	Irritant	173.382		Forbidden	75 pounds	1	1	Stow away from living quarters
Isobutane or Liquefied petroleum gas. See Liquefied petroleum gas									
Isobutyl acetate	Flammable liquid	Flammable liquid	173.118	173.119	1 quart	10 gallons	1.2	1	
Isobutylamine	Flammable liquid	Flammable liquid	173.118	173.119	1 quart	10 gallons	1.2	1	
Isobutylene or Liquefied petroleum gas. See Liquefied petroleum gas									
Isobutyric acid	Corrosive material	Corrosive	173.244	173.245	1 quart	10 gallons	1.2	1.2	
Isobutyric anhydride	Corrosive material	Corrosive	173.244	173.245	1 quart	10 gallons	1.2	1.2	
Isooctane	Flammable liquid	Flammable liquid	173.118	173.119	1 quart	10 gallons	1.2	1	
Isooctene	Flammable liquid	Flammable liquid	173.118	173.119	1 quart	10 gallons	1.3	4	
Isopentane	Flammable liquid	Flammable liquid	173.118	173.119	Forbidden	10 gallons	1.3	4	

453

Hazardous Materials Table (cont'd)

(1)	(2) Hazardous materials descriptions and proper shipping names	(3) Hazard class	(4) Label(s) required (if not excepted)	(5) Packaging (a) Exceptions	(5) Packaging (b) Specific requirements	(6) Maximum net quantity in one package (a) Passenger carrying aircraft or railcar	(6) (b) Cargo only aircraft	(7) Water shipments (a) Cargo vessel	(7) (b) Passenger vessel	(7) (c) Other requirements
	Isopentanoic acid	Corrosive material	Corrosive	173.244	173.245	1 quart	10 gallons	1.2	1.2	
	Isoprene	Flammable liquid	Flammable liquid	173.118	173.119	Forbidden	10 gallons	1.3	4	
	Isopropanol. See Alcohol, n.o.s.									
	Isopropyl acetate	Flammable liquid	Flammable liquid	173.118	173.119	1 quart	10 gallons	1.2	1	
	Isopropyl acid phosphate solid	Corrosive material	Corrosive	173.244	173.245b	25 pounds	100 pounds	1.2	1.2	
	Isopropylamine	Flammable liquid	Flammable liquid	None	173.119	Forbidden	10 gallons	1.3	5	
	Isopropyl mercaptan	Flammable liquid	Flammable liquid	None	173.141	Forbidden	10 gallons	1.3	5	
	Isopropyl nitrate	Flammable liquid	Flammable liquid	173.118	173.119	1 quart	10 gallons	1.2	1	
	Isopropyl percarborate, stabilized	Organic peroxide	Organic peroxide	None	173.282	Forbidden	Forbidden	5	5	
	Isopropylpercarbonate, unstabilized	Organic peroxide	Organic peroxide	None	173.218	Forbidden	Forbidden	5	5	
	Isopropyl phosphoric acid, solid. See Isopropyl acid phosphate, solid									
	Jet thrust igniter. See Igniter, jet thrust									
•	Jet thrust unit (jato)	Class A explosive	Explosive A	None	173.79	Forbidden	Forbidden	6	5	
•	Jet thrust unit (jato)	Class B explosive	Explosive B	None	173.92	Forbidden	550 pounds	1.3	5	
W	Jute. See Fibers									
W	Kapok. See Fibers									
	Kerosene	Combustible liquid	None	173.118a	None	No limit	No limit	1.2	1.2	
•	Lacquer. See •Paint, enamel, lacquer, stain, etc.									
•	Lacquer base, liquid. See •Paint, enamel, lacquer, stain, etc.									

454

•	Lacquer base, or lacquer chips, dry	Flammable solid	173.153	173.175	25 pounds	100 pounds	1	1	
•	Lacquer base or lacquer chips, plastic (wet with alcohol or solvent)	Flammable liquid	173.118	173.127	1 quart	25 pounds	1,2	1	
•	Lacquer removing, reducing, or thinning compound. See Compound, lacquer, paint, or varnish, etc., removing, reducing or thinning liquid								
	Lauroyl peroxide	Organic peroxide	173.153	173.157 173.158	2 pounds	25 pounds	1,2	1	
	Lead arsenate, solid	Poison B	173.364	173.367	50 pounds	200 pounds	1,2	1,2	
	Lead arsenite, solid	Poison B	173.364	173.365	50 pounds	200 pounds	1,2	1,2	
	Lead azide. See Initiating explosive								
A	Lead chloride	ORM-B	173.505	173.510 173.800	25 pounds	100 pounds	1,2	1,2	
	Lead cyanide	Poison B	173.370		25 pounds	No limit	1,2	1,2	Stow away from acids
W	Lead dross	ORM-C	173.505	173.1010					Segregation same as for corrosive materials
	Lead mononitroresorcinate. See Initiating explosive								
	Lead nitrate	Oxidizer	173.153	173.182	25 pounds	100 pounds	1,2	1,2	Stow away from foodstuffs
	Lead peroxide	Oxidizer	173.153	173.154	25 pounds	100 pounds	1,2	1,2	Stow away from foodstuffs
W	Lead scrap. See Lead dross								
	Lead styphnate (lead trinitroresorcinate). See Initiating explosive								
	Lead sulfate, solid (containing more than 3% free acid)	Corrosive material	173.244	173.245b	25 pounds	100 pounds	1,2	1,2	
•	Leather bleach or dressing	Flammable liquid	173.118	173.119	1 quart	10 gallons	1,2	1	
•	Leather bleach or dressing	Combustible liquid	173.118a	None	No limit	No limit	1,2	1,2	
	Lighter fluid	Flammable liquid	173.118	173.119	1 quart	10 gallons	1,2	1	
	Lime-nitrogen. See Calcium cyanamide, not hydrated, etc.								
	Lime, unslaked. See Calcium oxide								
A	Lindane	ORM-A	173.505	173.510	No limit	No limit		1	
	Liquefied hydrocarbon gas. See Hydrocarbon gas, liquefied								

Hazardous Materials Table (cont'd)

(1)	(2) Hazardous materials descriptions and proper shipping names	(3) Hazard class	(4) Label(s) required (if not excepted)	(5) Packaging (a) Exceptions	(5) Packaging (b) Specific requirements	(6) Maximum net quantity in one package (a) Passenger carrying aircraft or railcar	(6) (b) Cargo only aircraft	(6) (a) Cargo vessel	(6) (b) Passenger vessel	(7) Water shipments (c) Other requirements
	Liquefied nonflammable gas (*charged with nitrogen, carbon dioxide, or air*)	Nonflammable gas	Nonflammable gas	173.306	173.304	300 pounds	300 pounds	1.2	1.2	
W/	Liquefied petroleum gas	Flammable gas	Flammable gas	173.306	173.304 173.314 173.315	Forbidden	300 pounds	1.2	1	
A	*Liquid other than one classed as flammable, corrosive, poison or irritant, charged with nitrogen, carbon dioxide, or air. See Compressed gas n.o.s.*									
•	Lithium acetylide-ethylene diamine complex	Flammable solid	Flammable solid and Dangerous when wet	None	173.206	Forbidden	25 pounds	1.2	5	Segregation same as for flammable solid labeled Dangerous When Wet
	Lithium aluminum hydride	Flammable solid	Flammable solid and Dangerous when wet	None	173.206	Forbidden	25 pounds	1.2	5	Segregation same as for flammable solid labeled Dangerous When Wet
	Lithium aluminum hydride, ethereal	Flammable liquid	Flammable liquid	None	173.137	Forbidden	1 quart	1	5	Segregation same as for flammable solids labeled Dangerous When Wet
	Lithium amide, powdered	Flammable solid	Flammable solid	173.153	173.168	25 pounds	100 pounds	1.2	4	Segregation same as for flammable solids labeled Dangerous When Wet
	Lithium borohydride	Flammable solid	Flammable solid and Dangerous when wet	None	173.206	Forbidden	25 pounds	1.2	5	Segregation same as for flammable solids labeled Dangerous When Wet
	Lithium ferro silicon	Flammable solid	Flammable solid and Dangerous when wet	None	173.206	Forbidden	25 pounds	1.2	5	Segregation same as for flammable solids labeled Dangerous When Wet
	Lithium hydride	Flammable solid	Flammable solid and Dangerous when wet	None	173.206	Forbidden	25 pounds	1.2	5	Segregation same as for flammable solids labeled Dangerous When Wet

Lithium hydride in fused solid form	Flammable solid	Flammable solid and Dangerous when wet	None	173.206	Forbidden	100 pounds	1,2	5	Segregation same as for flammable solids labeled Dangerous When Wet
Lithium hypochlorite compound, dry (containing more than 39% available chlorine)	Oxidizer	Oxidizer	173.153	173.217	50 pounds	100 pounds	1,2	1,2	
Lithium metal	Flammable solid	Flammable solid and Dangerous when wet	None	173.206	Forbidden	25 pounds	1,2	5	Segregation same as for flammable solids labeled Dangerous When Wet
Lithium metal, in cartridges	Flammable solid	Flammable solid and Dangerous when wet	173.206		1 pound	25 pounds	1,2	4	Segregation same as for flammable solids labeled Dangerous When Wet
Lithium nitride	Flammable solid	Flammable solid and Dangerous when wet	None	173.206	Forbidden	25 pounds	1,2	5	Segregation same as for flammable solids labeled Dangerous When Wet
Lithium peroxide	Oxidizer	Oxidizer	173.153	173.154	25 pounds	100 pounds	1,2	1,2	Keep dry
Lithium silicon	Flammable solid	Flammable solid and Dangerous when wet	None	173.206	Forbidden	25 pounds	1,2	1,2	Segregation same as for flammable solids labeled Dangerous When Wet
London purple, solid	Poison B	Poison	173.364	173.365	50 pounds	200 pounds	1,2	1,2	
Low blasting explosive. See Low explosive									
Low explosive	Class A Explosive	Explosive A	None	173.60	Forbidden	Forbidden	6	5	
Lye. See Sodium hydroxide, solid									
Magnesium aluminum phosphide	Flammable solid	Flammable solid and Dangerous when wet	None	173.206	Forbidden	25 pounds	1,2	1,2	Segregation same as for flammable solids labeled Dangerous When Wet
Magnesium arsenate, solid	Poison B	Poison	173.364	173.367	50 pounds	200 pounds	1,2	1,2	
Magnesium dross, wet or hot	Forbidden		173.173						
Magnesium, metal (powdered, pellets, turnings, or ribbons)	Flammable solid	Flammable solid and Dangerous when wet	173.153	173.220	25 pounds	100 pounds	1,2	1,2	Segregation same as for flammable solids labeled Dangerous When Wet
Magnesium nitrate	Oxidizer	Oxidizer	173.153	173.182	25 pounds	100 pounds	1,2	1,2	Stow away from powdered metals
Magnesium perchlorate	Oxidizer	Oxidizer	173.153	173.154	25 pounds	100 pounds	1,3	1,3	
Magnesium peroxide, solid	Oxidizer	Oxidizer	173.153	173.154	25 pounds	100 pounds	1,2	1,2	Keep dry

Hazardous Materials Table (cont'd)

(1)	(2) Hazardous materials descriptions and proper shipping names	(3) Hazard class	(4) Label(s) required (if not excepted)	(5) Packaging (a) Exceptions	(5) Packaging (b) Specific requirements	(6) Maximum net quantity in one package (a) Passenger carrying aircraft or railcar	(6) (b) Cargo only aircraft	(7) Water shipments (a) Cargo vessel	(7) (b) Passenger vessel	(7) (c) Other requirements
*/W/A										
*	Magnesium scrap (borings, clippings, shavings, sheet, turnings, or scalpings)	Flammable solid	Flammable solid and Dangerous when wet	173.153	173.220	Forbidden	Forbidden	1,2	1,2	Segregation same as for flammable solids labeled Dangerous When Wet
A	Magnetized material	ORM-C	Magnetized material	None	173.1020	No limit	No limit			
A	Malathion	ORM-A	None	173.505	173.510	No limit	No limit			
A	Manganese dioxide	ORM-B	None	173.505	173.510	No limit	No limit			
	Matches, block. See Matches, strike anywhere									
	Matches, safety, book, card, or strike-on-box	Flammable solid	Flammable solid	173.176	173.176	50 pounds	50 pounds	1,2	1	
	Matches, strike anywhere	Flammable solid	Flammable solid	None	173.176	Forbidden	Forbidden	1,2	1	
	Matting acid. See Sulfuric acid									
*	Medicines, n.o.s.	Combustible liquid	None	173.118a	None	No limit	No limit	1,2	1,2	
*	Medicines, n.o.s.	Flammable liquid	Flammable liquid	173.118	173.119	1 quart	10 gallons	1,2	1	
*	Medicines, n.o.s.	Flammable solid	Flammable solid	173.153	173.154	25 pounds	100 pounds	1,2	1,2	
*	Medicines, n.o.s.	Oxidizer	Oxidizer	173.153	173.154	25 pounds	100 pounds	1,2	1,2	
*	Medicines, n.o.s. liquid	Corrosive material	Corrosive	173.244	173.245	1 quart	1 quart	1,2	1,2	
*	Medicines, n.o.s. liquid	Poison B	Poison	173.345	173.346	1 quart	55 gallons	1,3	1	Keep dry
*	Medicines, n.o.s. solid	Corrosive material	Corrosive	173.244	173.245b	25 pounds	100 pounds	1,2	1,2	
*	Medicines, n.o.s. solid	Poison B	Poison	173.364	173.365	50 pounds	200 pounds	1,3	1,3	
*	Memtetrahydro phthalic anhydride	Corrosive material	Corrosive	None	173.298	Forbidden	1 quart	1,2	1	
*	Mercaptan mixture, aliphatic (in containers over 110 gallons)	Combustible liquid	None	173.118a	None	Forbidden	10 gallons	1,2	1,2	

458

		ORM-A	None	173.505	173.510	Forbidden	10 gallons	1,3	5	Stow in well ventilated space away from living quarters
AW	Mercaptan mixture, aliphatic (in containers of 110 gallons or less) see 173.141(h)									
•	Mercaptan mixture, aliphatic	Flammable liquid	Flammable liquid	None	173.141	Forbidden	10 gallons	1,3	5	
	Mercuric acetate	Poison B	Poison	173.364	173.365	50 pounds	200 pounds	1,2	1,2	
	Mercuric-ammonium chloride, solid	Poison B	Poison	173.364	173.365	50 pounds	200 pounds	1,2	1,2	
	Mercuric benzoate, solid	Poison B	Poison	173.364	173.365	50 pounds	200 pounds	1,2	1,2	
	Mercuric bromide, solid	Poison B	Poison	173.364	173.365	Forbidden	25 pounds	1,2	1,2	
	Mercuric chloride, solid	Poison B	Poison	173.364	173.372	Forbidden	25 pounds	1,2	1,2	
	Mercuric cyanide, solid	Poison B	Poison	173.370		25 pounds	200 pounds	1,2	1,2	Stow away from acids
	Mercuric iodide, solid	Poison B	Poison	173.364	173.365	50 pounds	200 pounds	1,2	1,2	
•	Mercuric iodide solution	Poison B	Poison	173.345	173.346	1 quart	55 gallons	1,2	1,2	
	Mercuric oleate, solid	Poison B	Poison	173.364	173.365	50 pounds	200 pounds	1,2	1,2	
	Mercuric oxide, solid	Poison B	Poison	173.364	173.365	50 pounds	200 pounds	1,2	1,2	
	Mercuric oxycyanide, solid	Poison B	Poison	173.364	173.365	25 pounds	200 pounds	1,2	1,2	Stow away from acids
	Mercuric-potassium cyanide, solid	Poison B	Poison	173.364	173.365 173.370	25 pounds	200 pounds	1,2	1,2	Stow away from acids
	Mercuric-potassium iodide, solid	Poison B	Poison	173.364	173.365	50 pounds	200 pounds	1,2	1,2	
	Mercuric salicylate solid	Poison B	Poison	173.364	173.365	50 pounds	200 pounds	1,2	1,2	
	Mercuric subsulfate, solid	Poison B	Poison	173.364	173.365	50 pounds	200 pounds	1,2	1,2	
	Mercuric sulfate, solid	Poison B	Poison	173.364	173.365	50 pounds	200 pounds	1,2	1,2	
	Mercuric sulfo cyanate, solid or mercuric thiocyanate, solid	Poison B	Poison	173.364	173.365	50 pounds	200 pounds	1,2	1,2	
	Mercurol, or mercury nucleate, solid	Poison B	Poison	173.364	173.365	50 pounds	200 pounds	1,2	1,2	
	Mercurous acetate, solid	Poison B	Poison	173.364	173.365	50 pounds	200 pounds	1,2	1,2	
	Mercurous bromide, solid	Poison B	Poison	173.364	173.365	50 pounds	200 pounds	1,2	1,2	
	Mercurous gluconate, solid	Poison B	Poison	173.364	173.365	50 pounds	200 pounds	1,2	1,2	

Hazardous Materials Table (cont'd)

(1) +/W/A	(2) Hazardous materials descriptions and proper shipping names	(3) Hazard class	(4) Label(s) required (if not excepted)	(5) Packaging (a) Exceptions	(5) Packaging (b) Specific requirements	(6) Maximum net quantity in one package (a) Passenger carrying aircraft or railcar	(6) (b) Cargo only aircraft	(6) (a) Cargo vessel	(6) (b) Passenger vessel	(7) Water shipments (c) Other requirements
	Mercurous iodide, solid	Poison B	Poison	173.364	173.365	50 pounds	200 pounds	1,2	1,2	
	Mercurous nitrate, solid	Oxidizer	Oxidizer	173.153	173.154	50 pounds	100 pounds	1,2	1,2	
	Mercurous oxide, black, solid	Poison B	Poison	173.364	173.365	50 pounds	200 pounds	1,2	1,2	
	Mercurous sulfate, solid	Poison B	Poison	173.364	173.365	50 pounds	200 pounds	1,2	1,2	
•	Mercury compound, n.o.s., solid									
	Mercury fulminate. See Initiating explosive									
A	Mercury, metallic	ORM-B	None	None	173.860	173.860	173.860	1,2	1,2	
	Mesityl oxide	Flammable liquid	Flammable liquid	None	173.119	1 quart	10 gallons			
W	Metal borings, shavings, turnings, or cuttings	ORM-C	None	173.505	173.1025			1,2	1,2	Keep dry. Not permitted if temperature of material is at or above 1300DEG0 F
	Methane	Flammable gas	Flammable gas	173.306	173.302	Forbidden	300 pounds	1,2	4	
	Methanol. See Methyl alcohol									
	Methyl acetate	Flammable liquid	Flammable liquid	173.118	173.119	1 quart	10 gallons	1,2	1	
	Methyl acetone	Flammable liquid	Flammable liquid	173.118	173.119	1 quart	10 gallons	1,2	1	
	Methylacetylene-propadiene, stabilized	Flammable gas	Flammable gas	173.306	173.304 173.314 173.315	Forbidden	300 pounds	1,2	1	
	Methyl acrylate, inhibited	Flammable liquid	Flammable liquid	173.118	173.119	1 quart	10 gallons	1,2	1	
	Methylal	Flammable liquid	Flammable liquid	None	173.119	Forbidden	10 gallons	1,3	5	
	Methyl alcohol	Flammable liquid	Flammable liquid	173.118	173.119	1 quart	10 gallons	1,2	1	

Methylamine, anhydrous or Monomethylamine	Flammable gas	Flammable gas	173.306	173.304 173.314 173.315	Forbidden	300 pounds	1	4
Methyl amyl acetate	Flammable liquid	Flammable liquid	173.118	173.119	1 quart	10 gallons	1,2	1,2
Methyl amyl ketone	Combustible liquid	None	173.118a	None	No limit	No limit	1,2	1,2
Methyl bromide and ethylene dibromide mixture, liquid	Poison B	Poison	None	173.353	Forbidden	55 gallons	1	1
Methyl bromide and more than 2% chloropicrin mixture, liquid	Poison B	Poison	None	173.353	Forbidden	Forbidden	1	5	Shade from radiant heat
Methyl bromide and nonflammable, nonliquefied compressed gas mixture, liquid (including up to 2% chloropicrin)	Poison B	Poison	None	173.353a	Forbidden	300 pounds	1	5	Stow away from living quarters
Methyl bromide, liquid (bromomethane) (including up to 2% chloropicrin)	Poison B	Poison	None	173.353	Forbidden	55 gallons	1	5	Stow away from living quarters. Segregation same as for nonflammable gas
Methyl butene	Flammable liquid	Flammable liquid	None	173.119	Forbidden	10 gallons	1,2	5
Methyl butyrate	Flammable liquid	Flammable liquid	173.118	173.119	1 quart	10 gallons	1,2	1
Methyl cellosolve. See Ethylene glycol monomethyl ether								
Methyl cellosolve acetate. See Ethylene glycol monomethyl ether acetate								
Methyl chloride	Flammable gas	Flammable gas	173.306	173.304 173.314 173.315	Forbidden	300 pounds	1,2	4
Methyl chloride-methylene chloride mixture	Flammable gas	Flammable gas	173.306	173.304 173.314	Forbidden	300 pounds	1,2	4
Methyl chlorocarbonate. See Methyl chloroformate								
Methyl chloroform	ORM-A	None	173.505	173.510 173.605	10 gallons	55 gallons	1	
Methyl chloroformate	Flammable liquid	Flammable liquid and Poison	None	173.288	Forbidden	5 pints	1,2	1
Methylchloromethyl ether, anhydrous	Flammable liquid	Flammable liquid and Poison	None	173.143	Forbidden	Forbidden	1	5	Shade from radiant heat
Methylcyclohexane	Flammable liquid	Flammable liquid	173.118	173.119	1 quart	10 gallons	1,2	1
Methylcyclopentane	Flammable liquid	Flammable liquid	173.118	173.115	1 quart	10 gallons	1,3	4
Methyl dichloroacetate	Corrosive material	Corrosive	173.244	173.245	1 quart	1 quart	1,2	1,2
Methyldichloroarsine	Poison A	Poison gas	None	173.328	Forbidden	Forbidden	1	5	Shade from radiant heat

461

Hazardous Materials Table (cont'd)

(1)	(2) Hazardous materials descriptions and proper shipping names	(3) Hazard class	(4) Label(s) required (if not excepted)	(5) Packaging (a) Exceptions	(5) Packaging (b) Specific requirements	(6) Maximum net quantity in one package (a) Passenger carrying aircraft or railcar	(6) (b) Cargo only aircraft	(7) Water shipments (a) Cargo vessel	(7) (b) Passenger vessel	(7) (c) Other requirements
°/W/A	Methyl dichlorosilane	Flammable liquid	Flammable liquid	None	173.136	Forbidden	5 pints	1,2	1	
	Methylene chloride. See Dichloromethane									
	Methyl ethyl ether. See Ethyl methyl ether									
	Methyl ethyl ketone	Flammable liquid	Flammable liquid	173.118	173.119	1 quart	10 gallons	1,2	1	
	Methyl ethyl pyridine	Corrosive material	Corrosive	173.244	173.245	1 quart	10 gallons	1,2	1,2	
	Methyl formate	Flammable liquid	Flammable liquid	173.118	173.119	Forbidden	10 gallons	1,3	4	
	Methylfuran	Flammable liquid	Flammable liquid	173.118	173.119	1 quart	10 gallons	1,3	4	
	Methylhydrazine	Flammable liquid	Flammable liquid and Poison	None	173.145	Forbidden	5 pints	1,2	1	Stow separate from oxidizing materials and corrosives
	Methyl isopropenyl ketone, inhibited	Flammable liquid	Flammable liquid	173.118	173.119	1 quart	10 gallons	1,2	1	
	Methyl magnesium bromide in ethyl ether not over 40% concentration	Flammable liquid	Flammable liquid	None	173.149	Forbidden	Forbidden	1	1	Segregation same as for flammable solids. Separate from flammable gases or liquids, oxidizing materials or organic peroxides
	Methyl mercaptan	Flammable gas	Flammable gas	173.306	173.304 173.314 173.315	Forbidden	300 pounds	1,2	1	
	Methyl methacrylate monomer, inhibited	Flammable liquid	Flammable liquid	173.118	173.19	1 quart	10 gallons	1,2	1	
	Methyl methacrylate monomer, uninhibited (high-purity, if acceptable under Sec. 173.21 of this subchapter)	Flammable liquid	Flammable liquid	173.118	173.119	Forbidden	Forbidden	1,2	1	
	Methyl norbornene dicarboxylic anhydride. See Memtetrahydro phthalic anhydride									

Methyl parathion, liquid	Poison B	Poison	None	173.358	Forbidden	1 quart	1,3	1,3
Methyl parathion mixture, dry	Poison B	Poison	173.377	173.377	50 pounds	200 pounds	1,2	1,2
Methyl parathion mixture, liquid, (containing 25% or less methyl parathion)	Poison B	Poison	None	173.359	1/2 pint	1 quart	1,2	1,2
Methyl parathion mixture, liquid, (containing over 25% methyl parathion)	Poison B	Poison	None	173.359	Forbidden	1 quart	1,2	1,2
Methylpentadiene	Flammable liquid	Flammable liquid	173.118	173.119	1 quart	10 gallons	1,2	1
Methyl pentane	Flammable liquid	Flammable liquid	173.118	173.119	1 quart	10 gallons	1,2	1
Methyl phosphonothioic dichloride, anhydrous	Corrosive material	Corrosive	173.244	173.245 173.245a	1 quart	1 quart	1	4
Methyl phosphonous dicnloride	Corrosive material	Corrosive	173.214	173.245 173.245a	1 quart	1 quart	1	4
Methyl propionate	Flammable liquid	Flammable liquid	173.118	173.119	1 quart	10 gallons	1,2	1
Methyl propyl ketone	Flammable liquid	Flammable liquid	173.118	173.119	1 quart	10 gallons	1,2	1
Methyl sulfate. See Dimethyl sulfate								
Methyl sulfide. See Dimethyl sulfide								
Methyltrichlorosilane	Flammable liquid	Flammable liquid	None	173.135	Forbidden	10 gallons	1,2	1
Methyl vinyl ketone, inhibited	Flammable liquid	Flammable liquid	173.147	173.147	4 ounces	10 gallons	1,2	1
Mild detonating fuse, metal clad. See Fuse, mild detonating, metal clad								
Mine, empty See 172.55								
Mine, explosive, with gas material. See Explosive mine								
Mine rescue equipment containing carbon dioxide	Nonflammable gas	Nonflammable gas	173.306	173.245	150 pounds	300 pounds	1,2	1,2
Mining reagent, liquid (containing 20% or more cresylic acid)	Corrosive material	Corrosive	173.244	173.249a	1 quart	10 gallons	1,2	1,2
Mipafox	ORM-A	None	173.505	173.510	No limit	No limit		
Mixed acid. See Nitrating (mixed) acid								
Molybdenum pentachloride	ORM-B	None	173.505	173.510 173.800	25 pounds	100 pounds		
Monobromotrifluoromethane	Nonflammable gas	Nonflammable gas	173.306	173.304 173.314	150 pounds	300 pounds	1,2	1,2
Monochloroacetic acid, liquid or solution	Corrosive material	Corrosive	173.244	173.294	1 quart	1 quart	1,2	1,2	Glass carboys in hampers not permitted under deck
Monochloroacetone	Forbidden							

463

Hazardous Materials Table (cont'd)

(1)	(2)	(3)	(4)	(5) Packaging		(6) Maximum net quantity in one package			(7) Water shipments		
%/ W/ A	Hazardous materials descriptions and proper shipping names	Hazard class	Label(s) required (if not excepted)	(a) Exceptions	(b) Specific requirements	(a) Passenger carrying aircraft or railcar	(b) Cargo only aircraft	(a) Cargo vessel	(b) Passenger vessel	(c) Other requirements	
	Monochloroacetone, stabilized or inhibited	Irritating material	Irritant	None	173.384	Forbidden	5 gallons	1	1	Stow away from living quarters	
	Monochlorodifluoromethane	Nonflammable gas	Nonflammable gas	173.306	173.304 173.314 173.315	150 pounds	300 pounds	1,2	1,2		
	Monochloroethylene. See Vinyl chloride										
	Monochloropentafluoroethane	Nonflammable gas	Nonflammable gas	173.306	173.304	150 pounds	300 pounds	1,2	1,2		
	Monochlorotetrafluoroethane	Nonflammable gas	Nonflammable gas	173.306	173.304 173.314	150 pounds	300 pounds	1,2	1,2		
	Monochlorotrifluoromethane	Nonflammable gas	Nonflammable gas	173.306	173.304	150 pounds	300 pounds	1,2	1,2		
	Monoethanolamine	Corrosive material	Corrosive	173.244	173.245	1 quart	10 gallons	1,2	1,2		
*	Monoethanolamine solution	Corrosive material	Corrosive	173.244	173.245	1 quart	10 gallons	1,2	1,2		
	Monoethylamine	Flammable liquid	Flammable liquid	None	173.148	Forbidden	5 pints	1,2	5	Segregation same as for flammable gas	
	Monofluorophosphoric acid, anhydrous	Corrosive material	Corrosive	None	173.275	Forbidden	1 gallon	1,2	1,2	Keep dry	
	Monomethylamine, anhydrous	Flammable gas	Flammable gas	173.306	173.304 173.314 173.315	Forbidden	300 pounds	1,2	4		
*	Monomethylamine, aqueous solution	Flammable liquid	Flammable liquid	173.118	173.315	1 quart	10 gallons	1,3	4	Stow away from mercury and its compounds	
	Mortar stain, liquid	Combustible liquid	None	173.118a	None	No limit	No limit	1,2	1,2		
*	Mortar stain, liquid	Flammable liquid	Flammable liquid	173.118	173.128	1 quart	55 gallons	1,2	1		
	Moth balls. See Naphthalene										
	Motion picture film. See Film										

Motor fuel antiknock compound *or* antiknock compound	Poison B	Poison	None	173.354	Forbidden	55 gallons	1	5	If flashpoint less than 141 deg F segregation same as for flammable liquids
• Motor fuel n.o.s.	Combustible liquid	None	173.118a	None	No limit	No limit	1,2	1,2	
• Motor fuel n.o.s.	Flammable liquid	Flammable liquid	173.118	173.119	1 quart	10 gallons	1,2	1	
Motor, internal combustion	ORM-C	None	173.120						Not permitted in nonvented container
Motor vehicle, *etc., including automobile, motorcycle, truck, tractor, and other self-propelled vehicle or equipment powered by internal combustion engine, when offered new or used for transportation and which contain fuel in the engine or fuel tank or the electric storage battery is connected to either terminal of the electrical system*			173.120 173.250 173.120 173.306 173.250 173.257 173.306 175.305 176.905				1,2	1,2	
Muriatic acid. *See* Hydrochloric (muriatic) acid									
• Naphtha	Combustible liquid	None	173.118a	None	No limit	No limit	1,2	1,2	
• Naphtha	Flammable liquid	Flammable liquid	173.118	173.119	1 quart	10 gallons	1,2	1	
• Naphtha distillate	Combustible liquid	None	173.118a	None	No limit	No limit	1,2	1,2	
• Naphtha distillate	Flammable liquid	Flammable liquid	173.118	173.119	1 quart	10 gallons	1,2	1	
AW Naphthalene *or* Naphthalin	ORM-A	None	173.505	173.655	25 pounds	300 pounds	1,2	1,2	Segregation same as for flammable solids
Naphtha petroleum. See •Petroleum naphtha									
• Naphtha, solvent	Combustible liquid	None	173.118a	None	No limit	No limit	1,2	1,2	
• Naphtha, solvent	Flammable liquid	Flammable liquid	173.118	173.119	1 quart	10 gallons	1,2	1	
Natural gasoline. See Gasoline									
Neohexane	Flammable liquid	Flammable liquid	173.118	173.119	1 quart	10 gallons	1,3	4	
• Neon	Nonflammable gas	Nonflammable gas	173.306	173.302	150 pounds	300 pounds	1,2	1,2	
New explosive or explosive device									
Nickel carbonyl	Flammable liquid	Flammable liquid and Poison	173.51 None	173.86 173.126	Forbidden	Forbidden	1	5	Not permitted on a vessel carrying explosives. Shade from radiant heat. Segregation same as for flammable liquids 1a.*
Nickel catalyst, wet, *finely divided, activated, or spent. With not less than 40% water or other suitable liquid*	Flammable solid	Flammable solid	None	173.233	100 pounds	100 pounds	1,2	1	Separate from flammable gases or liquids, oxidizing materials, or organic peroxides
Nickel cyanide, solid	Poison B	Poison	173.370		25 pounds	200 pounds	1,2	1,2	Stow away from acids

465

Hazardous Materials Table (cont'd)

(1) ‡/W/A	(2) Hazardous materials descriptions and proper shipping names	(3) Hazard class	(4) Label(s) required (if not excepted)	(5) Packaging (a) Exceptions	(5) Packaging (b) Specific requirements	(6) Maximum net quantity in one package (a) Passenger carrying aircraft or railcar	(6) (b) Cargo only aircraft	(7) Water shipments (a) Cargo vessel	(7) (b) Passenger vessel	(7) (c) Other requirements
	Nicotine hydrochloride	Poison B	Poison	173.345	173.346	1 quart	55 gallons	1,2	1,2	
	Nicotine, liquid	Poison B	Poison	None	173.358	Forbidden	55 gallons	1,2	1,2	
	Nicotine salicylate	Poison B	Poison	173.364	173.365	50 pounds	200 pounds	1,2	1,2	
•	Nicotine sulfate, liquid	Poison B	Poison	173.345	173.346	1 quart	55 gallons	1,2	1,2	
	Nicotine sulfate, solid	Poison B	Poison	173.364	173.365	50 pounds	200 pounds	1,2	1,2	
	Nicotine tartrate	Poison B	Poison	173.364	173.365	50 pounds	200 pounds	1,2	1,2	
	Nitrate of ammonia explosives. See High explosive									
	Nitrate, n.o.s.	Oxidizer	Oxidizer	173.153	173.182	25 pounds	100 pounds	1,2	1,2	
	Nitrating (*mixed*) acid	Oxidizer	Oxidizer	None	173.267	Forbidden	1 quart	1	5	Segregation same as for corrosive materials
	Nitrating (*mixed*) acid, spent	Corrosive material	Corrosive	None	173.248	Forbidden	1 quart	1	5	Segregation same as for corrosive materials. Stow away from hydrazine, separate from diethylenetriamine
	Nitric acid (*over 40%*)	Oxidizer	Oxidizer and Corrosive	None	173.268	Forbidden	5 pints	1	5	Segregation same as for corrosive materials. Stow away from hydrazine, separate from diethylenetriamine
	Nitric acid, fuming	Oxidizer	Oxidizer and Poison	None	173.268	Forbidden	5 pints	1	5	Stow away from hydrazine, separate from diethylenetriamine
	Nitric acid, 40% or less	Corrosive material	Corrosive	None	173.268	Forbidden	Forbidden	1	5	
	Nitric ether. See Ethyl nitrate									
	Nitric oxide	Poison A	Poison gas	None	173.337	Forbidden	Forbidden	1	5	
	Nitroaniline	Poison B	Poison	173.364	173.373	50 pounds	200 pounds	1,2	1,2	
	p-Nitroaniline. See Nitroaniline									
	Nitrobenzol, liquid (*oil of mirbane, nitrobenzene*)	Poison B	Poison	173.345	173.346	1 quart	55 gallons	1,2	1,2	

Nitro carbo nitrate	Oxidizer	Oxidizer	173.153	173.182	25 pounds	100 pounds	1,2	1,2	
Nitrocellulose, colloided, granular or flake, wet with not less than 20% alcohol or solvent, or block, wet with not less than 25% alcohol	Flammable liquid	Flammable liquid	173.118	173.127	1 quart	25 pounds	1,3	1	
Nitrocellulose, colloided, granular or flake, wet with not less than 20% water	Flammable solid	Flammable solid	173.153	173.184	25 pounds	100 pounds	1,3	1	
Nitrocellulose, dry. See High explosive									
Nitrocellulose flakes, wet with not less than 20% alcohol *or* solvent	Flammable liquid	Flammable liquid	173.118	173.127	1 quart	25 pounds	1,3	1	
Nitrocellulose, wet with not less than 30% alcohol *or* solvent	Flammable liquid	Flammable liquid	173.118	173.127	1 quart	25 pounds	1,3	1	
Nitrocellulose, wet with not less than 20% water	Flammable solid	Flammable solid	173.153	173.184	25 pounds	100 pounds	1,3	1	
Nitrochlorobenzene, ortho, liquid	Poison B	Poison	173.345	173.346	1 quart	55 gallons	1,2	1,2	
Nitrochlorobenzene, meta *or* para, solid	Poison B	Poison	173.364	173.374	50 pounds	200 pounds	1,2	1,2	
Nitrogen	Nonflammable gas	Nonflammable gas	173.306	173.302 173.314	150 pounds	300 pounds	1,2	1,2	
Nitrogen, pressurized Liquid	Nonflammable gas	Nonflammable gas	None	173.304	150 pounds	300 pounds	1,3	1,3	Segregation same as for nonflammable gases. Stow away from organic materials
Nitrogen dioxide, liquid	Poison A	Oxidizer and Poison gas	None	173.336	Forbidden	Forbidden	1	5	
Nitrogen fertilizer solution	Nonflammable gas	Nonflammable gas	173.306	173.304 173.314	150 pounds	300 pounds	1,3	1,3	
Nitrogen peroxide, liquid	Poison A	Oxidizer and Poison gas	None	173.336	Forbidden	Forbidden	1	5	Segregation same as for nonflammable gas. Stow away from organic materials
Nitrogen tetroxide, liquid	Poison A	Oxidizer and Poison gas	None	173.336	Forbidden	Forbidden	1	5	Segregation same as for nonflammable gases. Stow away from organic materials
Nitroglycerin, liquid, desensitized. See High explosive, liquid	Forbidden								
Nitroglycerin, liquid, undesensitized See 173.51									
Nitroglycerin, spirits of. See Spirits of nitroglycerin									
Nitroguanidine, dry. See High explosive									
Nitroguanidine, wet with not less than 20% water	Flammable solid	Flammable solid	173.153	173.184	25 pounds	100 pounds	1,2	4	
Nitrohydrochloric acid	Corrosive material	Corrosive	None	173.278	Forbidden	5 pints	1	5	
Nitrohydrochloric acid, diluted	Corrosive material	Corrosive	None	173.278	Forbidden	5 pints	1	5	
Nitromannite. See High explosive									

467

Hazardous Materials Table (cont'd)

(1) °/W/A	(2) Hazardous materials descriptions and proper shipping names	(3) Hazard class	(4) Label(s) required (if not excepted)	(5) Packaging (a) Exceptions	(5) Packaging (b) Specific requirements	(6) Maximum net quantity in one package (a) Passenger carrying aircraft or railcar	(6) Maximum net quantity in one package (b) Cargo only aircraft	(7) (a) Cargo vessel	(7) (b) Passenger vessel	(7) Water shipments (c) Other requirements
	Nitromethane	Flammable liquid	Flammable liquid	173.118	173.149a	1 quart	10 gallons	1,2	1,2	
	Nitromuriatic acid. *See* Nitrohydrochloric acid									
	Nitrosoguanidine. *See* Initiating explosive									
	Nitrostarch, dry. *See* High explosive									
	Nitrostarch, wet with not less than 30% alcohol *or* solvent	Flammable liquid	Flammable liquid	173.118	173.127	1 quart	25 pounds	1,2	1	
	Nitrostarch, wet with not less than 20% water	Flammable solid	Flammable solid	173.153	173.184	25 pounds	100 pounds	1	4	
	Nitrosyl chloride	Nonflammable gas	Nonflammable gas	173.306	173.304 173.314	Forbidden	300 pounds	1	4	
	Nitrourea. See High explosive									
	Nitrous oxide	Nonflammable gas	Nonflammable gas	173.306	173.304 173.315	150 pounds	300 pounds	1,2	1,2	Under deck stowage must be in well-ventilated space
	Nitroxylol	Poison B	Poison	173.345	173.346	1 quart	55 gallons	1,2	1	
	Nonflammable gas n.o.s. *See* Compressed Gas, n.o.s.									
	Nonliquefied hydrocarbon gas	Flammable gas	Flammable gas	173.306	173.302	Forbidden	300 pounds	1,2	1	
	Nonyl trichlorosilane	Corrosive material	Corrosive	None	173.280	Forbidden	10 gallons	1	1	Keep dry
	Nordhausen acid. *See* Sulfuric acid									
W	Oakum	ORM-C	None	173.505	173.1030	Forbidden		1,2	1,2	
	Octadecyltrichlorosilane	Corrosive material	Corrosive	None	173.280	Forbidden	10 gallons	1	1	Keep dry
	Octane	Flammable liquid	Flammable liquid	173.118	173.119	1 quart	10 gallons	1,2	1	
	Octyl trichlorosilane	Corrosive material	Corrosive	None	173.280	Forbidden	10 gallons	1	1	Keep dry
•	Oil, *described as oil*, n.o.s., petroleum oil, *or* petroleum oil, n.o.s.	Combustible liquid	None	173.118a	None	No limit	No limit	1,2	1,2	

468

	Oil, *described as oil*, oil, n.o.s., petroleum oil, *or* petroleum oil, n.o.s.	Flammable liquid	Flammable liquid	173.118	173.119	1 quart	10 gallons	1,2	1
	Oiled clothing (*manufactured article properly dried to prevent spontaneous heating*). *See* Oiled material								
AW	Oiled material (*manufactured article properly dried to prevent spontaneous heating*)	ORM-C	None	173.505	173.1035	No limit	No limit	1,3	1,3
	Oiled paper (*manufactured article properly dried to prevent spontaneous heating*). *See* Oiled material								
	Oil of mirbane. See Nitrobenzol, liquid								
	Oil of vitriol. See Sulfuric acid								
	Oil well cartridge	Class C explosive	Class C explosive	None	173.112	50 pounds	150 pounds	1,3	1,3
	Oleum (*sulfuric acid (fuming)*)	Corrosive material	Corrosive	None	173.272	Forbidden	5 pints	1,2	1	Under deck stowage must be in metal drums only. Keep dry
•	Organic peroxide, liquid, *or* solution, n.o.s.	Organic peroxide	Organic peroxide	173.153	173.221	Forbidden	1 quart	1,2	1,2	Stow separate from combustible materials, explosives, or acids.
•	Organic peroxide, solid, n.o.s.	Organic peroxide	Organic peroxide	173.153	173.154	Forbidden	25 pounds	1,2	1,2	Stow separate from combustible materials, explosives, or acids.
•	Organic Peroxide liquid *or* solution, n.o.s.	Flammable liquid	Organic peroxide and flammable liquid	None	173.119	Forbidden	1 quart	1,2	5	Stow separate from combustible materials, explosives, or acids
•	Organic phosphate, organic phosphate compound, *or* organic phosphorus compound; mixed with compressed gas	Poison A	Poison gas	None	173.334	Forbidden	Forbidden	1	5	Shade from radiant heat
•	Organic phosphate, organic phosphate compound, *or* organic phosphorus compound; liquid	Poison B	Poison	None	173.358	Forbidden	1 quart	1,2	5
•	Organic phosphate, organic phosphate compound, *or* organic phosphorus compound; solid *or* dry	Poison B	Poison	None	173.377	Forbidden	200 pounds	1,2	4
•	Organic phosphate mixture, organic phosphate compound mixture, *or* organic phosphorus compound mixture; liquid	Poison B	Poison	173.359	173.359	1/2 pint	1 quart	1,2	5
•	Organic phosphate mixture, organic phosphate compound mixture, *or* organic phosphorus compound mixture, solid *or* dry	Poison B	Poison	173.377	173.377	50 pounds	200 pounds	1,2	4
A	ORM-A-n.o.s.	ORM-A	None	173.505	173.510	No limit	No limit		
A	ORM-B-n.o.s.	ORM-B	None	173.505	173.510	No limit	No limit		
	ORM-C. See 173.500 & 176.900								
	Orthonitroaniline. *See* Nitroaniline								

469

Hazardous Materials Table (cont'd)

(1)	(2) Hazardous materials descriptions and proper shipping names	(3) Hazard class	(4) Label(s) required (if not excepted)	(5) Packaging (a) Exceptions	(5) Packaging (b) Specific requirements	(6) Maximum net quantity in one package (a) Passenger carrying aircraft or railcar	(6) (b) Cargo only aircraft	(7) Water shipments (a) Cargo vessel	(7) (b) Passenger vessel	(7) (c) Other requirements
	Oxidizer, or Oxidizing material, n.o.s.	Oxidizer	Oxidizer	173.153	173.154	25 pounds	25 pounds	1,2	1,2	
	Oxidizer material packed with other articles See 173.152									
•	Oxygen	Nonflammable gas	Oxidizer	173.306	173.302 173.314	150 pounds	300 pounds	1,2	1,2	Under deck stowage must be in well ventilated space
•	Oxygen, pressurized liquid	Nonflammable gas	Oxidizer	None	173.304	Forbidden	Forbidden	1,3	1,3	Stow separate from acetylene. Do not overstow with other cargo
•	Paint drier, liquid	Combustible liquid	None	173.118a	None	No limit	No limit	1,2	1,2	
•	Paint drier, liquid	Flammable liquid	Flammable liquid	173.118	173.128	1 quart	55 gallons	1,2	1	
•	Paint, enamel, lacquer, stain, shellac, or varnish; aluminum, bronze, gold, wood filler, liquid or lacquer base, liquid	Combustible liquid	None	173.118a	None	No limit	No limit	1,2	1,2	
•	Paint, enamel, lacquer, stain, shellac, or varnish; aluminum, bronze, gold, wood filler, liquid, or lacquer base, liquid	Flammable liquid	Flammable liquid	173.118	173.128	1 quart	55 gallons	1,2	1	
•	Paint, reducing or thinning compound See *Compound, lacquer, paint, or varnish, reducing or thinning liquid, etc.									
•	Paper caps. See Toy caps									
W	Paper scrap (when dry, clean, and free from oil)	ORM-C	None	173.505	173.1075	Forbidden	Forbidden	1,2	1,2	
	Paper stock, wet	Flammable solid	Flammable solid	None	173.185	Forbidden	Forbidden	1,2	1,2	Separate from flammable gases or liquids, oxidizing materials, or organic peroxides
	Paper waste (when dry, clean, and free from oil). See Paper scrap									
	Paper waste, wet. See Waste paper, wet									
	Paramenthane hydroperoxide	Organic peroxide	Organic peroxide	173.153	173.224	1 quart	1 quart	1,2	4	
	Paranitroaniline, solid. See Nitroaniline									
	Parathion and compressed gas mixture	Poison A	Poison gas	None	173.334	Forbidden	Forbidden	1,3	5	

Parathion, liquid	Poison B	Poison	None	173.358	Forbidden	1 quart	1.3	
Parathion mixture, dry	Poison B	Poison	173.377	173.377	50 pounds	200 pounds	1.3	
Parathion mixture, liquid	Poison B	Poison	None	173.359	Forbidden	1 quart	1.3	
Paris green, solid. *See* Copper acetoarsenite, solid								
Pentaborane	Flammable liquid	Poison and flammable liquid	None	173.138	Forbidden	1	5	Segregation same as for flammable solids. Separate from flammable gases or liquids, oxidizing materials, or organic peroxides
Pentaerythrite tetranitrate. See Initiating explosive								
Pentaerythrite tetranitrate, desensitized, wet. See High explosive								
Pentane	Flammable liquid	Flammable liquid	173.118	173.119	Forbidden	10 gallons	1.3	Shade from radiant heat
Pentolite, dry. See High explosive								
Peracetic acid solution, *not over 40% peracetic acid and not over 6% hydrogen peroxide*	Organic peroxide	Organic peroxide	173.223	173.223	1 pint	5 pints	4	
Perchlorate, n.o.s.	Oxidizer	Oxidizer	173.153	173.154	25 pounds	100 pounds	1.3	Stow away from powdered metals
Perchloric acid, exceeding 50% but not exceeding 72% strength	Oxidizer	Oxidizer	None	173.269	Forbidden	5 pints	5	Segregation same as for corrosive materials. Stow away from hydrazine
Perchloric acid exceeding 72% strength	Forbidden							
Perchloric acid, not over 50% acid	Oxidizer	Oxidizer	173.244	173.269	Forbidden	5 pints	1	Segregation same as for corrosive materials. Stow away from hydrazine
Perchloro-methyl-mercaptan	Poison B	Poison	173.345	173.360	Forbidden	10 pounds	4	
Percussion cap	Class C explosive	Explosive C	None	173.107	50 pounds	150 pounds	1.3	
Percussion fuze	Class C explosive	Explosive C	None	173.105	50 pounds	150 pounds	1.3	
Perfluoro-2-butene	ORM-A	None	173.505	173.510 / 173.605	10 gallons	55 gallons		
Permanganate, n.o.s.	Oxidizer	Oxidizer	173.153	173.154	25 pounds	100 pounds	1.2	Separate from ammonium compounds, hydrogen peroxide, and acids
Permanganate of potash. See Potassium permanganate								
Peroxide, organic See Organic Peroxide								
Pesticide, water reactive, including but not limited to fungicides, and herbicides, etc., which contain manganese ethylenebisdithio carbamate	ORM-C	None	173.505	173.1040		2	2	Keep dry

Hazardous Materials Table (cont'd)

(1)	(2)	(3)	(4)	(5) Packaging		(6) Maximum net quantity in one package			(7) Water shipments	
	Hazardous materials descriptions and proper shipping names	Hazard class	Label(s) required (if not excepted)	(a) Exceptions	(b) Specific requirements	(a) Passenger carrying aircraft or railcar	(b) Cargo only aircraft	(a) Cargo vessel	(b) Passenger vessel	(c) Other requirements
W	Petroleum coke (uncalcined)	ORM-C	None	173.505	173.1045			1,2	1,2	Not permitted if temperature of material is at or above 130 deg F
	Petroleum crude. See Crude oil									
*	Petroleum distillate	Combustible liquid	None	173.118a	None	No limit	No limit	1,2	1,2	
*	Petroleum distillate	Flammable liquid	Flammable liquid	173.118	173.119	1 quart	10 gallons	1,3	4	
	Petroleum ether	Flammable liquid	Flammable liquid	173.118	173.119	1 quart	10 gallons	1,3	4	
	Petroleum gas, liquefied. See Liquefied petroleum gas									
*	Petroleum naphtha	Combustible liquid	None	173.118a	None	No limit	No limit	1,2	1,2	
*	Petroleum naphtha	Flammable liquid	Flammable liquid	173.118	173.119	1 quart	10 gallons	1,2	1	
A	Phencapton	ORM-A	None	173.505	173.510	No limit	No limit			
	Phenol. See Carbolic acid									
	Phenyl dichloro arsine	Poison B	Poison	None	173.355	Forbidden	30 gallons	1	5	
A	Phenylenediamine, meta or para, solid	ORM-A	None	173.505	173.510	No limit	No limit	1	1	Keep dry
	Phenyl trichlorosilane	Corrosive material	Corrosive	None	173.280	Forbidden	10 gallons	1	5	
	Phosgene (diphosgene)	Poison A	Poison gas	None	173.333	Forbidden	Forbidden	1	5	
	Phosphine	Poison A	Flammable gas and Poison gas	None	173.328	Forbidden	Forbidden	1	5	
*	Phosphoric acid or Phosphoric Acid Solution	Corrosive material	Corrosive	173.244	173.245	1 quart	10 gallons	1,2	1,2	Glass carboys in hampers not permitted under deck
	Phosphoric acid triethyleneimine. See Tris-(1-aziridinyl phosphine oxide)									

472

Name							
Phosphoric anhydride (*phosphorus pentoxide*)	Corrosive material	Corrosive	None		Forbidden	100 pounds	1,2	1,2	Keep dry. Glass bottles not permitted under deck
Phosphorus, amorphous, red	Flammable solid	Flammable solid	None	173.188	Forbidden	11 pounds	1,2	1,2	
Phosphorus bromide. *See* Phosphorus tribromide				173.189				1,2	
Phosphorus chloride. *See* Phosphorus trichloride									
Phosphorus heptasulfide	Flammable solid	Flammable solid	None	173.225	Forbidden	10 pounds	1,2	1	Separate from oxidizing materials
Phosphorus oxybromide	Corrosive material	Corrosive	None	173.271	Forbidden	1 quart	1	1	Keep dry. Glass carboys not permitted on passenger vessels
Phosphorus oxychloride	Corrosive material	Corrosive	None	173.271	Forbidden	1 quart	1	1	Keep dry. Glass carboys not permitted on passenger vessels
Phosphorus pentachloride, solid	Corrosive material	Corrosive	None	173.191	Forbidden	5 pounds	1	1	Keep dry
Phosphorus pentasulfide	Flammable solid	Flammable solid, and Dangerous when wet	None	173.225	Forbidden	11 pounds	1,2	1,2	Separate from oxidizing material
Phosphorus sesquisulfide	Flammable solid	Flammable solid, and Dangerous when wet	None	173.225	Forbidden	11 pounds	1,2	1	Separate from oxidizing materials
Phosphorus tribromide	Corrosive material	Corrosive	None	173.270	Forbidden	1 quart	1	1	Keep dry. Glass carboys not permitted on passenger vessels
Phosphorus trichloride	Corrosive material	Corrosive	None	173.271	Forbidden	1 quart	1	1	Keep dry. Glass carboys not permitted on passenger vessels
Phosphorus trisulfide	Flammable solid	Flammable solid	None	173.225	Forbidden	10 pounds	1,2	1	Separate from oxidizing materials
Phosphorus, white or yellow, dry	Flammable solid	Flammable solid and Poison	None	173.190	Forbidden	Forbidden	1,2	5	Separate from flammable gases or liquids, oxidizing materials, or organic peroxides
Phosphorus, white or yellow, in water	Flammable solid	Flammable solid and Poison	None	173.190	Forbidden	25 pounds	1,2	5	Separate from flammable gases or liquids, oxidizing materials, or organic peroxides
Phosphoryl chloride. *See* Phosphorus oxychloride									
Photographic film. See Film									
Photographic flash powder. See Fireworks, special or Low explosives									
Picrate, dry. See High explosive									
Picrate of ammonia. See High explosive									
Picric acid, dry. See High explosive									
Picric acid, wet, with not less than 10% water	Flammable solid	Flammable solid	None	173.192 173.193	1 pound	25 pounds	1	5	Under deck stowage permitted on cargo vessels if wet with more than 30% water. Stow away from heavy metals and their compounds

473

Hazardous Materials Table (cont'd)

(1)	(2) Hazardous materials descriptions and proper shipping names	(3) Hazard class	(4) Label(s) required (if not excepted)	(5) Packaging (a) Exceptions	(5) Packaging (b) Specific requirements	(6) Maximum net quantity in one package (a) Passenger carrying aircraft or railcar	(6) (b) Cargo only aircraft	(7) Water shipments (a) Cargo vessel	(7) (b) Passenger vessel	(7) (c) Other requirements
	Picric acid, wet with not less than 10% water, over 25 pounds. See High explosive									
	Pine oil	Combustible liquid	None	173.118a	None	No limit	No limit	1,2	1,2	
	Pinwheels. *See* Fireworks, common									
	Pivaloyl chloride. *See* Trimethyl acetylchloride									
•	Plastic solvent, n.o.s.	Combustible liquid	None	173.118a	None	No limit	No limit	1,2	1,2	
•	Plastic solvent, n.o.s.	Flammable liquid	Flammable liquid	173.118	173.119	1 quart	10 gallons	1,2	1	
•	Plutoniumnitrate solution	Radioactive material	Radioactive (See Sec. 172.403)	173.393	173.396			1,2	1,2	
	Poisonous liquid, n.o.s. *or* Poison B, liquid, n.o.s.	Poison B	Poison	173.345	173.346	1 quart	55 gallons	1,2	1	
	Poisonous liquid *or* gas, n.o.s.	Poison A	Poison gas	None	173.328	Forbidden	Forbidden	1	5	
	Poisonous solid, n.o.s. *or* Poison B, solid, n.o.s.	Poison B	Poison	173.364	173.365	50 pounds	200 pounds	1,2	1	
•	Polish, metal, stove, furniture *or* wood, liquid	Combustible liquid	None	173.118a	None	No limit	No limit	1,2	1,2	
•	Polish, metal, stove, furniture *or* wood, liquid	Flammable liquid	Flammable liquid	173.118	173.129	1 quart	55 gallons	1,2	1	
	Polymerizable material			173.21						
	Potassium arsenate, solid	Poison B	Poison	173.364	173.365	50 pounds	200 pounds	1,2	1,2	
	Potassium arsenite, solid	Poison B	Poison	173.364	173.365	50 pounds	200 pounds	1,2	1,2	
•	Potassium bifluoride solution. *See* *Potassium hydrogen fluoride solution									

474

Potassium bromate	Oxidizer	Oxidizer	173.153	173.154	25 pounds	100 pounds	1,2	Separate from ammonium compounds. Stow away from powdered metals
Potassium chlorate (potash chlorate)	Oxidizer	Oxidizer	173.153	173.163	25 pounds	100 pounds	1,2	Separate from ammonium compounds. Stow away from powdered metals
Potassium cyanide, solid	Poison B	Poison	173.370		25 pounds	200 pounds	1,2	Stow away from acids
Potassium cyanide solution	Poison B	Poison	173.345	173.352	1 quart	55 gallons	1,2	Stow away from acids
Potassium dichloro isocyanurate. See Potassium dichloro-s-triazinetrione								
Potassium dichloro-s-triazinetrione, dry (containing more than 39% available chlorine)	Oxidizer	Oxidizer	173.153	173.217	50 pounds	100 pounds	1,2	
A Potassium dichromate	ORM-A	None	173.505	173.510	No limit	No limit	1,2	
A Potassium fluoride	ORM-B	None	173.505	173.510	No limit	No limit	1,2	
• Potassium fluoride solution	Corrosive material	Corrosive	173.244	173.249	1 quart	5 gallons	1,2	
Potassium hydrate. See Potassium hydroxide								
• Potassium hydrogen fluoride solution	Corrosive material	Corrosive	173.244	173.249	1 quart	5 gallons	1,2	
A Potassium hydrogen sulfate, solid	ORM-B	None	173.505	173.510 173.800	25 pounds	100 pounds	1,2	
Potassium hydroxide, dry solid, flake, bead, or granular	Corrosive material	Corrosive	173.244	173.245b	25 pounds	100 pounds	1,2	Keep dry. Do not stow with metals or alloys such as brass, copper, tin, zinc, aluminum, solder, or lead
• Potassium hydroxide, liquid or solution	Corrosive material	Corrosive	173.244	173.249	1 quart	10 gallons	1,2	
• Potassium hypochlorite solution. See Hypochlorite solutions containing more than 7% available chlorine by weight								
A Potassium metabisulfite	ORM-B	None	173.505	173.510	No limit	No limit	1,2	
Potassium, metal	Flammable solid	Flammable solid and Dangerous when wet	None	173.206	Forbidden	25 pounds	5	Segregation same as for flammable solids labeled Dangerous When Wet
Potassium, metal liquid alloy	Flammable solid	Flammable solid and Dangerous when wet	None	173.202	Forbidden	1 pound	5	Segregation same as for flammable solids labeled Dangerous When Wet
Potassium nitrate	Oxidizer	Oxidizer	173.153	173.182	25 pounds	100 pounds	1,2	Separate from ammonium compounds and cyanides. Stow away from foodstuffs
Potassium nitrite	Oxidizer	Oxidizer	173.153	173.154	25 pounds	100 pounds	1,2	Separate from ammonium compounds and cyanides. Stow away from foodstuffs
Potassium nitrate mixed (fused) with sodium nitrite	Oxidizer	Oxidizer	173.153	173.183	25 pounds	100 pounds	1,2	Separate from ammonium compounds and cyanides. Stow away from foodstuffs
Potassium perchlorate	Oxidizer	Oxidizer	173.153	173.219	25 pounds	100 pounds	1,3	Stow away from powdered metals

Hazardous Materials Table (cont'd)

(1)	(2) Hazardous materials descriptions and proper shipping names	(3) Hazard class	(4) Label(s) required (if not excepted)	(5) Packaging (a) Exceptions	(5) Packaging (b) Specific requirements	(6) Maximum net quantity in one package (a) Passenger carrying aircraft or railcar	(6) (b) Cargo only aircraft	(7) Water shipments (a) Cargo vessel	(7) (b) Passenger vessel	(7) (c) Other requirements
	Potassium permanganate	Oxidizer	Oxidizer	173.153	173.154	25 pounds	100 pounds	1,2	1,2	Separate from ammonium compounds and hydrogen peroxide
	Potassium peroxide	Oxidizer	Oxidizer	None	173.194	Forbidden	100 pounds	1,2	1,2	Keep dry
	Potassium sulfide	Flammable solid	Flammable solid	173.153	173.207	25 pounds	300 pounds	1,2	1,2	Separate from liquid acids, flammable gases or liquids, oxidizing materials, or organic peroxides
	Pressurized product. See Compressed gas, n.o.s.									
	Primer. See Cannon primer, combination primer, or small-arm primer									
	Primer, detonating. See Detonating primer									
	Projectile, explosive. See Explosive projectile									
	Projectile, gas, nonexplosive. See Chemical ammunition, containing Poison or Irritating Material									
	Projectile, gas, smoke, or incendiary, with burster or booster with or without detonating fuze. See Explosive projectile									
	Projectile, illuminating, incendiary or smoke, with expelling charge but without bursting charge. See Fireworks, special									
	Projectile, sand-loaded, empty or solid See 173.55									
	Propane or Liquefied petroleum gas. See Liquefied petroleum gas									
•	Propellant explosive	Class A explosive	Explosive A	None	173.64	Forbidden	Forbidden	6	5	
	Propellant explosive (solid, Class B, and small-arms primer) See *Propellant explosive, solid									
	Propellant explosive in water (Smokeless powder)	Class B explosive	Explosive B	None	173.93	Forbidden	Forbidden	1,3	5	Magazine stowage authorized

Propellant explosive in water, unstable, condemned, or deteriorated (smokeless powder)	Class B explosive	Explosive B	None	173.93	Forbidden	10 pounds	1,3	5	Magazine stowage authorized
• Propellant explosive, liquid	Class B explosive	Explosive B	None	173.93	Forbidden	10 pounds	1,2	5	Magazine stowage authorized
• Propellant explosive, solid	Class B explosive	Explosive B	None	173.93	Forbidden	10 pounds	1,3	5	Magazine stowage authorized
Propionaldehyde	Flammable liquid	Flammable liquid	173.118	173.119	1 quart	10 gallons	1,2	1	
Propionic acid	Corrosive material	Corrosive	173.244	173.245	1 quart	5 gallons	1,2	1,2	Separated by a complete compartment or hold from organic peroxides
• Propionic acid solution	Corrosive material	Corrosive	173.244	173.245	1 quart	10 gallons	1,2	1,2	Separated by a complete compartment or hold from organic peroxides
Propionic anhydride	Corrosive material	Corrosive	173.244	173.245	1 quart	1 quart	1,2	1	Keep dry
Propyl acetate	Flammable liquid	Flammable liquid	173.118	173.119	1 quart	10 gallons	1,2	1	
Propyl alcohol. See Alcohol, n.o.s.									
Propylamine	Flammable liquid	Flammable liquid	None	173.119	Forbidden	10 gallons	1,3	5	
Propyl chloride	Flammable liquid	Flammable liquid	None	173.119	Forbidden	10 gallons	1,3	5	
Propylene diamine	Flammable liquid	Flammable liquid	173.118	173.119	1 quart	10 gallons	1,2	1	
Propylene dichloride	Flammable liquid	Flammable liquid	173.118	173.119	1 quart	10 gallons	1,2	1	
Propylene imine, inhibited	Flammable liquid	Flammable liquid	None	173.139	Forbidden	5 pints	1,2	1	
Propylene or Liquefied petroleum gas. See Liquefied petroleum gas									
Propylene oxide	Flammable liquid	Flammable liquid	173.118	173.119	Forbidden	1 gallon	1,3	4	
Propyl formate	Flammable liquid	Flammable liquid	173.118	173.119	1 quart	10 gallons	1,2	1	
Propyl mercaptan	Flammable liquid	Flammable liquid	None	173.141	Forbidden	10 gallons	1,2	5	
Propyl trichlorosilane	Corrosive material	Corrosive	None	175.280	Forbidden	10 gallons	1	1	Keep dry
Prussic acid. See Hydrocyanic acid (prussic), liquid or unstabilized									
Pyridine	Flammable liquid	Flammable liquid	173.118	173.119	1 quart	10 gallons	1,2	1	
Pyrophoric liquid, or Pyroforic liquids, n.o.s.	Flammable liquid	Flammable liquid	None	173.134	Forbidden	Forbidden	1	5	Shade from radiant heat Separate from flammable gases or liquids, oxidizing materials, or organic peroxides

477

Hazardous Materials Table (cont'd)

(1) */W/A	(2) Hazardous materials descriptions and proper shipping names	(3) Hazard class	(4) Label(s) required (if not excepted)	(5) Packaging (a) Exceptions	(5) Packaging (b) Specific requirements	(6) Maximum net quantity in one package (a) Passenger carrying aircraft or railcar	(6) (b) Cargo only aircraft	(7) Water shipments (a) Cargo vessel	(7) (b) Passenger vessel	(7) (c) Other requirements
	Pyro sulfuryl chloride	Corrosive material	Corrosive	173.244	173.247	1 quart	1 quart	1	4	Keep dry. Glass carbuoys not permitted on passenger vessels
	Pyroxylin plastic scrap	Flammable solid	Flammable solid	None	173.195	Forbidden	Forbidden	1	5	Shade from radiant heat
	Pyroxylin plastics, rods, sheets, rolls, or tubes	Flammable solid	Flammable solid	173.197	None	50 pounds	350 pounds	1,3	1	
	Pyroxylin solution	Combustible liquid	None	173.118a	None	No limit	No limit	1,2	1,2	
*	Pyroxylin solution	Flammable liquid	Flammable liquid	173.118	173.119	1 quart	10 gallons	1,2	1	
*	Pyroxylin solvent, n.o.s.	Combustible liquid	None	173.118a	None	No limit	No limit	1,2	1,2	
*	Pyroxylin solvent, n.o.s.	Flammable liquid	Flammable liquid	173.118	173.119	1 quart	10 gallons	1,2	1	
	Pyrrolidine	Flammable liquid	Flammable liquid	173.18	173.119	Forbidden	10 gallons	1,2	1,2	
	Quicklime. See Calcium oxide									
	Radioactive device, n.o.s.	Radioactive material	None	173.391				1,2	1,2	
*	Radioactive material, fissile, n.o.s.	Radioactive material	Radioactive	173.393	173.396			1,2	1,2	
*	Radioactive material, low specific activity or LSA, n.o.s.	Radioactive material	Radioactive	173.392	173.393			1,2	1,2	
*	Radioactive material, n.o.s.	Radioactive material	Radioactive	173.393	173.395			1,2	1,2	
*	Radioactive material, limited quantity, n.o.s.	Radioactive material	None	173.391				1,2	1,2	
*	Radioactive material, special form, n.o.s.	Radioactive material	Radioactive	173.393	173.394			1,2	1,2	
	Rags, oily	Flammable solid	Flammable solid	None	173.199	Forbidden	Forbidden	1,2	1,2	Keep dry. Separate from flammable gases or liquids, oxidizing materials, or organic peroxides
	Rags, wet	Flammable solid	Flammable solid	None	173.200	Forbidden	Forbidden	1,2	1	Separate from flammable gases or liquids, oxidizing materials, or organic peroxides

Railway Fusee. *See* Fusee					
Railway torpedo. *See* Torpedo, railway					
Range oil. *See* Fuel oil					
Reducing compound, paint, varnish, lacquer, etc. See "Compound, lacquer, paint, *or* varnish, etc., removing, reducing, *or* thinning, liquid					
Refrigerant gas. *See* Dispersant Gas					
• Refrigerating machine	Nonflammable gas	Nonflammable gas	173.306		No limit	No limit	1.3	1.3
• Refrigerating machine	Flammable gas	Flammable gas	173.306		No limit	No limit	1.3	1.3
• Refrigerating machine	Flammable liquid	Flammable liquid	173.130	173.306	No limit	No limit	1.2	1
Removing compound, paint, varnish, lacquer, etc.. See "Compound, lacquer, paint, *or* varnish, etc., removing, reducing, *or* thinning, liquid					
• Resin solution (*resin compound, liquid*)	Combustible liquid	None	173.118a	None	No limit	No limit	1.2	1.2
Resin solution (*resin compound, liquid*)	Flammable liquid	Flammable liquid	173.118	173.119	1 quart	55 gallons	1.2	1
Rifle grenade. See Grenade, hand or rifle, explosive					
Rifle powder. See "Propellant explosive, or Black powder					
Road asphalt or tar (when heated to or above its flash point). See Asphalt					
Road asphalt or tar, liquid. See Asphalt, cut back					
• Road oil	Combustible liquid	None	173.118a	None	No limit	No limit	1.2	1.2
Rocket ammunition with empty projectile	Class B explosive	Explosive B	None	173.90	Forbidden	Forbidden	1.3	5
Rocket ammunition with explosive projectile	Class A explosive	Explosive A	None	173.57	Forbidden	Forbidden	6	5
Rocket ammunition with gas projectile	Class A explosive	Explosive A	None	173.57	Forbidden	Forbidden	6	5
Rocket ammunition with illuminating projectile	Class A explosive	Explosive A	None	173.57	Forbidden	Forbidder:	6	5
Rocket ammunition with incendiary projectile	Class A explosive	Explosive A	None	173.57	Forbidden	Forbidden	6	5
Rocket ammunition with inert loaded projectile	Class B explosive	Explosive B	None	173.90	Forbidden	Forbidden	1.3	5

Hazardous Materials Table (cont'd)

(1)	(2) Hazardous materials descriptions and proper shipping names	(3) Hazard class	(4) Label(s) required (if not excepted)	(5) Packaging (a) Exceptions	(5) Packaging (b) Specific requirements	(6) Maximum net quantity in one package (a) Passenger carrying aircraft or railcar	(6) (b) Cargo only aircraft	(7) Water shipments (a) Cargo vessel	(7) (b) Passenger vessel	(7) (c) Other requirements
*/ W/ A	Rocket ammunition with smoke projectile	Class A explosive	Explosive A	None	173.57	Forbidden	Forbidden	6	5	
	Rocket ammunition with solid projectile	Class B explosive	Explosive B	None	173.90	Forbidden	Forbidden	1,3	5	
	Rocket body, with electric primer or electric squib. See 173.55									
	Rocket engine, liquid	Class B explosive	Explosive B	None	173.95	Forbidden	Forbidden	1,2	5	Magazine stowage authorized
	Rocket fireworks. See Fireworks, common									
	Rocket head. See Explosive projectile									
*	Rocket motor	Class A explosive	Explosive A	None	173.79	Forbidden	Forbidden	6	5	
*	Rocket motor	Class B explosive	Explosive B	None	173.92	Forbidden	Forbidden	1,3	5	
	Roman candle. See Fireworks, common									
W	Rosin (colophony) or Resin	ORM-C	None	173.505	173.1060	Forbidden	Forbidden	1,2	1,2	
*	Rough ammoniate tankage (less than 7% moisture content)	Flammable solid	Flammable solid	None	173.210	Forbidden	55() pounds	1	5	
W	Rough ammoniate tankage 7% or more moisture content	Flammable solid	Flammable solid	None	173.210	Forbidden	Forbidden	1,2	1,2	Separate from flammable gases or liquids, oxidizing materials, or organic peroxides. Temperature of tankage must not exceed 100 deg F.
W	Rubber curing compound (solid)	ORM-C	None	173.505	173.1065	10 pounds	10 pounds	1,2	1,2	
	Rubber scrap or rubber buffings	Flammable solid	Flammable solid	173.153	173.201	10 pounds	10 pounds	1,2	1,2	
	Rubber shoddy, regenerated rubber, or reclaimed	Flammable solid	Flammable solid	173.153	173.201	10 pounds	10 pounds	1,2	1,2	
*	Rubidium metal	Flammable solid	Flammable solid and Dangerous when wet	None	173.206	Forbidden	25 pounds	1,2	5	Segregation same as for flammable solid labeled Dangerous when wet

Rubidium metal, in cartridges	Flammable solid	Flammable solid and Dangerous when wet	173.206		1 pound	25 pounds	1,2	4	Segregation same as for flammable solid labeled Dangerous when wet
Rum, denatured	Flammable liquid	Flammable liquid	173.118	173.119	1 quart	10 gallons	1,2	1	
Rust preventive coating	Combustible liquid	None	173.118a	None	No limit	No limit	1,2	1,2	
Safety fuse. *See* Fuse, safety									
Safety squib	Class C explosive	Explosive C	None	173.106	50 pounds	150 pounds	1,3	1,3	
Salute. See Fireworks common *or* special									
Sand acid. See Hydrofluorosilicic acid									
Sawdust (*when dry, clean, and free from oil*)	ORM-C	None	173.505	173.1070	50 pounds	150 pounds	1,2	1,2	Keep dry
Selenic acid, liquid	Corrosive material	Corrosive	None	173.245	Forbidden	5 pints	1,2	1,2	
Self-lighting cigarette	Flammable solid	Flammable solid	173.21		Forbidden	Forbidden	1,2	1,2	Keep dry
Self propelled vehicle *See* Motor vehicle									
Shaped charge, commercial. *See* High explosive 173.65(h)									
Shellac. See "Paint, enamel, lacquer, stain, shellac, varnish, etc.									
Shell, fireworks. *See* Fireworks, common *or* special									
Ship, distress signal. See Fireworks, special									
Signal flare	Class C explosive	Explosive C	None	173.108	50 pounds	200 pounds	1,2	1,2	
Silicofluoric acid. *See* Hydrofluorosilicic acid									
Silicon chloride *or* silicon tetrachloride	Corrosive material	Corrosive	173.244	173.247	1 quart	1 gallon	1	1	Keep dry. Glass carboys not permitted on passenger vessels
Silicon chrome, exothermic. See Exothermic silicon chrome									
Silicon tetrafluoride	Nonflammable gas	Nonflammable gas	173.306	173.302	Forbidden	300 pounds	1	4	Stow away from foodstuffs
Silver cyanide	Poison B	Poison	173.370		25 pounds	200 pounds	1,2	1,2	Stow away from acids
Silver nitrate	Oxidizer	Oxidizer	173.153	173.182	25 pounds	100 pounds	1,2	1,2	Stow away from foodstuffs
Sisal. See Fibers									
Sludge acid. See Acid, sludge									
Small arms ammunition	Class C explosive	None	173.101		50 pounds	150 pounds	1,3	1,3	
Small arms ammunition, irritating (*tear gas*) cartridge	Class C explosive	Irritant	None	173.101	Forbidden	150 pounds	1,3	1,3	

481

Hazardous Materials Table (cont'd)

(1)	(2) Hazardous materials descriptions and proper shipping names	(3) Hazard class	(4) Label(s) required (if not excepted)	(5) Packaging (a) Exceptions	(5) Packaging (b) Specific requirements	(6) Maximum net quantity in one package (a) Passenger carrying aircraft or railcar	(6) (b) Cargo only aircraft	(7) Water shipments (a) Cargo vessel	(7) (b) Passenger vessel	(7) (c) Other requirements
	Small arms primer	Class C explosive	Explosive C	None	173.107	50 pounds	150 pounds	1,3	1,3	
	Smoke candle	Class C explosive	Explosive C	None	173.108	50 pounds	200 pounds	1,3	1,3	
	Smoke generator. See *Chemical ammunition, Poison A or B Material*									
	Smoke grenade	Class C explosive	Explosive C	None	173.108	50 pounds	150 pounds	1,3	1,3	
	Smokeless powder for cannon or small arms. See *Propellant explosive, Class A or B*									
W/A	Smokeless powder for small arms (*100 pounds or less*)	Flammable solid	Flammable solid	173.88	173.197a	Forbidden	Forbidden	1,3	1,3	Segregation same as for explosives
	Smoke pot	Class C explosive	Explosive C	None	173.108	50 pounds	200 pounds	1,3	1,3	
	Smoke projectile with bursting charge. See *Explosive projectile*									
	Smoke projectile with expelling charge but without bursting charge. See *Fireworks, special*									
	Smoke signal	Class C explosive	Explosive C	None	173.108	50 pounds	200 pounds	1,3	1,3	
	Soda amatol. See *High explosive*									
	Soda lime, solid	Corrosive material	Corrosive	173.244	173.245b	25 pounds	100 pounds	1,2	1,2	Keep dry
A	Sodium aluminate, solid	ORM-B	None	173.505	173.510 173.800	25 pounds	100 pounds			
•	Sodium aluminate solution	Corrosive material	Corrosive	173.244	173.249	1 quart	5 gallons	1,2	1,2	
	Sodium aluminum hydride	Flammable solid	Flammable solid and Dangerous when wet	None	173.206	Forbidden	25 pounds	1,2	5	Segregation same as for flammable solids labeled Dangerous When Wet

Sodium amide	Flammable solid	Flammable solid and Dangerous When Wet	None	173.206	Forbidden	25 pounds	1,2	5	Segregation same as for flammable solid labeled Dangerous When Wet
Sodium arsenate	Poison B	Poison	173.364	173.365 173.368	50 pounds	200 pounds	1,2	1,2	Stow away from heavy metals, especially lead and its compounds. Stow separate from acids
Sodium arsenite (*solution*) liquid	Poison B	Poison	173.345	173.346	1 quart	55 gallons	1,2	1,2	
Sodium azide	Poison B	Poison	173.364	173.375	50 pounds	100 pounds	1,2	1,2	
Sodium bisulfate, solid *or* solution. *See appropriate* Sodium hydrogen sulfate entry									
Sodium bisulfite, solid. *See* Sodium hydrogen sulfite, solid									
Sodium bromate	Oxidizer	Oxidizer	173.153	173.154	25 pounds	100 pounds	1,2	1,2	Stow separate from ammonium compounds. Stow away from powdered metals
Sodium chlorate (*soda chlorate*)	Oxidizer	Oxidizer	173.153	173.163	25 pounds	100 pounds	1,2	1,2	Stow separate from ammonium compounds. Stow away from powdered metals
Sodium chlorite	Oxidizer	Oxidizer	None	173.160	Forbidden	100 pounds	1,2	1,2	Stow separate from ammonium compounds. Stow away from powdered metals
• Sodium chlorite solution (*not exceeding 42% sodium chlorite*)	Corrosive material	Corrosive	173.244	173.263	1 quart	4 gallons	1,2	1	Glass carboys in hampers not permitted under deck
Sodium cyanide, solid	Poison B	Poison	173.370		25 pounds	200 pounds	1,2	1,2	Stow away from acids
• Sodium cyanide solution	Poison B	Poison	173.345	173.352	1 quart	55 gallons	1,2	1,2	Stow away from acids
Sodium dichloro isocyanurate. *See* Sodium dichloro-s-triazinetrione									
Sodium dichloro-s-triazinetrione (*dry, containing more than 39% available chlorine*)	Oxidizer	Oxidizer	173.153	173.217	50 pounds	100 pounds	1,2	1,2	
A Sodium dichromate	ORM-A	None	173.505	173.510	No limit	No limit	1,2	1,2	
A Sodium fluoride, solid	ORM-B	None	173.505	173.510	No limit	No limit			
• Sodium fluoride solution	Corrosive material	Corrosive	173.244	173.245	1 quart	5 gallons	1,2	1,2	Stow away from acids
Sodium hydrate. *See* Sodium hydroxide									
Sodium hydride	Flammable solid	Flammable solid and Dangerous when wet	None	173.198	Forbidden	25 pounds	1,2	5	Segregation same as for flammable solids labeled Dangerous When Wet
A Sodium hydrogen sulfate, solid	ORM-B	None	173.505	173.510 173.800	25 pounds	100 pounds	1,2	1,2	
• Sodium hydrogen sulfate solution	Corrosive material	Corrosive	173.244	173.245	1 quart	1 gallon	1,2	1,2	

Hazardous Materials Table (cont'd)

(1) */W/A	(2) Hazardous materials descriptions and proper shipping names	(3) Hazard class	(4) Label(s) required (if not excepted)	(5) Packaging (a) Exceptions	(5) Packaging (b) Specific requirements	(6) Maximum net quantity in one package (a) Passenger carrying aircraft or railcar	(6) Maximum net quantity in one package (b) Cargo only aircraft	(7) Water shipments (a) Cargo vessel	(7) Water shipments (b) Passenger vessel	(7) Water shipments (c) Other requirements
A	Sodium hydrogen sulfite, solid	ORM-B	None	173.505	173.800	25 pounds	100 pounds	1,2	1,2	
	Sodium hydrosulfite (*sodium dithionite*)	Flammable solid	Flammable solid	173.153	173.204	25 pounds	100 pounds	1,2	1,2	Keep dry. Below deck stowage in metal drums only. Separate from flammable gases, liquids, oxidizing materials, or organic peroxides
	Sodium hydroxide, dry solid, flake, bead, or granular	Corrosive material	Corrosive	173.244	173.245b	25 pounds	200 pounds	1,2	1,2	Keep dry
	Sodium hydroxide, liquid or solution	Corrosive material	Corrosive	173.244	173.249	1 quart	5 gallons	1,2	1,2	
A	Sodium metabisulfite	ORM-B	None	173.505	173.510	No limit	No limit			
	Sodium, metal or metallic	Flammable solid	Flammable solid and Dangerous when wet	None	173.206	Forbidden	25 pounds	1,2	5	Segregation same as for flammable solids labeled Dangerous When Wet
	Sodium, metal dispersion in organic solvent	Flammable solid	Flammable solid and Dangerous when wet	None	173.230	Forbidden	10 pounds	1,2	5	Segregation same as for flammable solids labeled Dangerous When Wet
	Sodium, metal liquid alloy	Flammable solid	Flammable solid and Dangerous when wet	None	173.202	Forbidden	1 pound	1,2	5	Segregation same as for flammable solids labeled Dangerous When Wet
*	Sodium methylate, alcohol mixture	Combustible liquid	None	173.118a	None	No limit	No limit	1,2	1,2	
*	Sodium methylate, alcohol mixture	Flammable liquid	Flammable liquid	173.118	173.119	1 quart	10 gallons	1,2	1	
*	Sodium methylate, alcohol mixture	Corrosive material	Corrosive	173.244	173.245	1 quart	1 quart	1,2	1,2	
	Sodium methylate, dry	Flammable solid	Flammable solid	173.153	173.154	25 pounds	100 pounds	1,2	1	
	Sodium monoxide, solid	Corrosive material	Corrosive	173.244	173.245b	25 pounds	100 pounds	1,2	1,2	Segregation same as for flammable solids labeled Dangerous When Wet
	Sodium nitrate	Oxidizer	Oxidizer	173.153	173.182	25 pounds	100 pounds	1,2	1,2	Keep dry

484

Sodium nitrate bags. See Bags, sodium nitrate, empty and unwashed							
Sodium nitrite	Oxidizer	Oxidizer	173.153	173.154 173.234	25 pounds	100 pounds	1,2	1,2	Stow separate from ammonium compounds and cyanides. Bagged material not permitted on passenger vessels
Sodium nitrite mixed (fused) with potassium nitrate	Oxidizer	Oxidizer	173.153	173.183	25 pounds	100 pounds	1,2	1,2	Stow separate from ammonium compounds and cyanides.
Sodium nitrite mixture (sodium nitrate, sodium nitrite, and potassium nitrate)	Oxidizer	Oxidizer	173.153	173.234	25 pounds	100 pounds	1,2	1,2	Stow separate from ammonium compounds and cyanides.
Sodium pentachlorophenate	ORM-A	None	173.505	173.510	No limit	No limit	1,3	1,3	Stow away from powdered metals
Sodium perchlorate	Oxidizer	Oxidizer	173.153	173.154	25 pounds	100 pounds	1,2	1,2	Separate from ammonium compounds and hydrogen peroxide
Sodium permanganate	Oxidizer	Oxidizer	173.153	173.154	25 pounds	100 pounds	1,2	1,2	
Sodium peroxide	Oxidizer	Oxidizer	None	173.187	Forbidden	100 pounds	1,2	1	Keep dry. Stow away from powdered metals, permanganates, combustible packing of other cargo, and combustible foodstuffs
Sodium phenolate, solid	Corrosive material	Corrosive	173.244	173.245h	25 pounds	100 pounds	1,2	1,2	
Sodium phosphide	Flammable solid	Flammable solid and Dangerous when wet	None	173.154	Forbidden	25 pounds	1	5	Stow away from heavy metals, especially lead, and its compounds
Sodium picramate, wet (with at least 20% water)	Flammable solid	Flammable solid	None	173.205	Forbidden	25 pounds	1,2	5	Under deck stowage must be readily accessible. Segregation same as for flammable solids labeled Dangerous When Wet
Sodium potassium alloy	Flammable solid	Flammable solid and Dangerous when wet	None	173.206	Forbidden	25 pounds	1,2	5	
Sodium sulfate, acid. See appropriate Sodium hydrogen sulfate entry								
Sodium sulfide, anhydrous	Flammable solid	Flammable solid	173.153	173.207	25 pounds	300 pounds	1,2	1,2	Stow separate from liquid acids. Separate from flammable gases or liquids, oxidizing materials or organic peroxides
Solvent, n.o.s.	Combustible liquid	None	173.118a	None	No limit	No limit	1,2	1,2	
Solvent, n.o.s.	Flammable liquid	Flammable liquid	173.118	173.119	1 quart	10 gallons	1,2	1	
Sparklers. See Fireworks, common								
Spent iron mass. See Iron mass, spent								
Spent iron sponge. See Iron sponge, spent								
Spent mixed acid. See Nitrating acid								
Spent sulfuric acid. See sulfuric acid, spent								

485

Hazardous Materials Table (cont'd)

(1)	(2) Hazardous materials descriptions and proper shipping names	(3) Hazard class	(4) Label(s) required (if not excepted)	(5) Packaging (a) Exceptions	(5) Packaging (b) Specific requirements	(6) Maximum net quantity in one package (a) Passenger carrying aircraft or railcar	(6) (b) Cargo only aircraft	(7) Water shipments (a) Cargo vessel	(7) (b) Passenger vessel	(7) (c) Other requirements
	Spirits of nitroglycerin, (1 to 10%)	Flammable liquid	Flammable liquid	None	173.133	Forbidden	6 quarts	1,2	5	Segregation same as for explosives
*/W/A	Spirits of nitroglycerin, not exceeding 1% nitroglycerin by weight	Flammable liquid	Flammable liquid	173.118	173.133	1 quart	6 quarts	1,2	1	
	Spirits of salt. See Hydrochloric acid									
	Sporting powder. See Black powder or Propellant explosive, solid. Class B explosive									
	Spray starting fluid. See Engine starting fluid									
	Spreader cartridge. See Fireworks, special									
	Squib, electric or safety. See Electric squib or Safety squib									
	Stain. See *Paint, enamel, lacquer, stain, shellac, varnish, etc.									
•	Stannic phosphide	Flammable solid	Flammable solid and Dangerous when wet	None	173.154	Forbidden	25 pounds	1	5	Segregation same as for flammable solid labeled Dangerous When Wet
A	Stannous chloride, solid	ORM-B	None	173.505	173.510	No limit	No limit	1,3	5	
•	Starter cartridge	Class B explosive	Explosive B	None	173.92	Forbidden	200 pounds	1,3	1,3	
•	Starter cartridge	Class C explosive	Explosive C	None	173.102	50 pounds	150 pounds	1,3	1,3	
	Storage battery wet. See Battery, electric storage, wet									
	Straw. See Hay									
	Strontium arsenite, solid	Poison B	Poison	173.364	173.365	50 pounds	200 pounds	1,2	1,2	
	Strontium chlorate	Oxidizer	Oxidizer	173.153	173.163	25 pounds	100 pounds	1,2	1,2	Stow separate from ammonium compounds. Stow away from powdered metals
•	Strontium chlorate, wet	Oxidizer	Oxidizer	173.153	173.163	25 pounds	200 pounds	1,2	1,2	Stow separate from ammonium compounds. Stow away from powdered metals

Strontium nitrate	Oxidizer	Oxidizer	173.153	173.182	25 pounds	100 pounds	1,2	1,2	
Strontium peroxide	Oxidizer	Oxidizer	173.153	173.154	25 pounds	100 pounds	1,2	1,2	Keep dry
Strychnine salt, solid	Poison B	Poison	173.364	173.365	50 pounds	200 pounds	1,2	1,2	
Strychnine, solid	Poison B	Poison	None	173.377	Forbidden	200 pounds	1,2	1,2	
Styphnate of lead. See Initiating explosive									
Styrene monomer, inhibited	Flammable liquid	Flammable liquid	173.118	173.119	1 quart	10 gallons	1,2	1,2	
Succinic acid peroxide	Organic peroxide	Organic peroxide	173.153	173.157 173.158	Forbidden	25 pounds	1	1	
Sulfur chloride (*mono and di*)	Corrosive material	Corrosive	None	173.247	Forbidden	1 gallon	1	1	Keep dry. Glass carboys not permitted on passenger vessels
Sulfur dioxide	Nonflammable gas	Nonflammable gas	173.306	173.304 173.314 173.315	Forbidden	300 pounds	1,2	4	Stow away from living quarters
Sulfur flower. See Sulfur									
Sulfur hexafluoride	Nonflammable gas	Nonflammable gas	173.306	173.304	150 pounds	300 pounds	1,2	1,2	
Sulfuric acid (*For fuming sulfuric acid, see Oleum*)	Corrosive material	Corrosive	173.244	173.272	1 quart	1 gallon	1	1	Keep dry. Under deck stowage is permitted on cargo vessels only in metal drums
Sulfuric acid, spent	Corrosive material	Corrosive	None	173.248	Forbidden	1 quart	1	1	Under deck stowage is permitted on cargo vessels only in metal drums
Sulfuric anhydride. See Sulfur trioxide, stabilized									
*Sulfurous acid	Corrosive material	Corrosive	173.244	173.245	2 gallons	2 gallons	1,2	1	Glass carboys in hampers not permitted under deck
W Sulfur, solid	ORM-C	None	173.505	173.1080			1,2	1,2	Protect from sparks and open flame. Stow separate from oxidizing materials. Segregation same as for flammable solids
Sulfur trioxide, stabilized	Corrosive material	Corrosive	173.244	173.273	Forbidden	1 gallon	1,2	1,2	Keep dry. Glass bottles not permitted under deck
Sulfuryl chloride	Corrosive material	Corrosive	173.244	173.247	1 quart	1 quart	1	1	Keep dry. Glass carboys not permitted on passenger vessels
Sulfuryl fluoride	Nonflammable gas	Nonflammable gas	173.306	173.304 173.314	150 pounds	300 pounds	1,3	1	
Sulphur. See Sulfur									
Supplementary charge (explosive)	Class A explosive	Explosive A	None	173.69	Forbidden	Forbidden	6	5	
Tankage. See Garbage tankage									

487

Hazardous Materials Table (cont'd)

(1) */W/A	(2) Hazardous materials descriptions and proper shipping names	(3) Hazard class	(4) Label(s) required (if not excepted)	(5) Packaging (a) Exceptions	(5) Packaging (b) Specific requirements	(6) Maximum net quantity in one package (a) Passenger carrying aircraft or railcar	(6) Maximum net quantity in one package (b) Cargo only aircraft	(7) Water shipments (a) Cargo vessel	(7) Water shipments (b) Passenger vessel	(7) Water shipments (c) Other requirements
*	Tankage fertilizer	Flammable solid	Flammable solid	None	173.209	Forbidden	Forbidden	1	5	Keep dry. Separate from flammable gases or liquids, oxidizing materials, or organic peroxides
*	Tankage, rough ammoniate	Flammable solid	Flammable solid	None	173.210	Forbidden	Forbidden	1	5	Keep dry. Separate from flammable gases or liquids, oxidizing materials, or organic peroxides
	Tank car, containing residual phosphorus and filled with water or inert gas. See 173.190									
	Tank car, empty (previously used for a hazardous material). See 173.29									
	Tank car, empty (previously used for a Poison A material). See 172.510 and 173.29									
	Tank, portable, empty (previously used for a hazardous material). See 172.510, 173.29, and 172.514									
	Tank truck, empty. See 172.510, 172.514 and 173.29.									
*	Tar, liquid	Combustible liquid	None	173.118a	None	No limit	No limit	1,2	1,2	
*	Tar, liquid	Flammable liquid	Flammable liquid	173.118	173.131	1 quart	10 gallons	1,2	1	
	Tear gas ammunition. See Chemical ammunition (containing an irritant material)									
	Tear gas candle	Irritating material	Irritant	None	173.385	Forbidden	75 pounds	1	5	Stow away from living quarters
	Tear gas cartridge. See Small arms ammunition irritating (tear gas) cartridge									
	Tear gas grenade. See Grenade, tear gas									
	Tertiary alcohol. See Alcohol, n.o.s.									

	Name	Class	Class label	§ 172.101	§ 172.102	Passenger	Cargo	Label	Stowage	Notes
	Tertiary butyl isopropyl benzene hydroperoxide	Organic peroxide	Organic peroxide	173.153	173.224	1 quart	1 quart	1.2	4	
AW	Tetrachloroethane	ORM-A	None	173.505	173.620	1 quart	10 gallons	1.2	1.2	
A	Tetrachloroethylene or Perchloroethylene	ORM-A	None	173.505	173.510 173.605	10 gallons	55 gallons	1	5	
	Tetraethyl dithio pyrophosphate and compressed gas mixture	Poison A	Poison gas	None	173.334	Forbidden	Forbidden	1	5	Shade from radiant heat. Stow away from living quarters. Segregation same as for nonflammable gases
	Tetraethyl dithio pyrophosphate, liquid	Poison B	Poison	None	173.358	Forbidden	1 quart	1	5	
	Tetraethyl dithio pyrophosphate mixture, dry	Poison B	Poison	None	173.377	Forbidden	200 pounds	1	5	
	Tetraethyl dithio pyrophosphate mixture, liquid	Poison B	Poison	None	173.359	Forbidden	1 quart	1	5	
	Tetraethyl lead, liquid (including flash point for export shipment by water)	Poison B	Poison	None	173.354	Forbidden	55 gallons	1	5	If flash point is 141 deg F or less, segregation must be the same as for flammable liquids
	Tetraethyl pyrophosphate and compressed gas mixture	Poison A	Poison gas	None	173.334	Forbidden	Forbidden	1	5	Shade from radiant heat. Stow away from living quarters. Segregation same as for nonflammable gases
	Tetraethyl pyrophosphate, liquid	Poison B	Poison	None	173.358	Forbidden	1 quart	1	5	
	Tetraethyl pyrophosphate mixture, dry	Poison B	Poison	None	173.377	Forbidden	200 pounds	1.2	5	
	Tetraethyl pyrophosphate mixture, liquid	Poison B	Poison	None	173.359	Forbidden	1 quart	1.2	5	
	Tetrafluoroethylene, inhibited	Flammable gas	Flammable gas	173.306	173.304	Forbidden	300 pounds	1.2	1.2	Stow away from living quarters
	1,2,3,6-Tetrahydrobenzaldehyde	Corrosive material	Corrosive	173.244	173.245	1 quart	10 gallons	1.2	1.2	
	Tetrahydrofuran	Flammable liquid	Flammable liquid	None	173.119	Forbidden	10 gallons	1.3	5	
	Tetramethyl ammonium hydroxide, liquid	Corrosive material	Corrosive	173.244	173.245	1 quart	10 gallons	1.2	1.2	
A	Tetramethyl methylene diamine	ORM-A	None	173.505	173.510	No limit	No limit		1.2	
	Tetranitromethane	Oxidizer	Oxidizer	None	173.203	Forbidden	Forbidden	1	5	Shade from radiant heat. Stow away from foodstuffs
	Tetrazene (guanyl nitrosamino guanyltetrazene). See Initiating explosive									
	Tetryl. See High explosive									
	Textile treating compound mixture, liquid	Corrosive material	Corrosive	173.244	173.245 173.249a	1 quart	10 gallons	1.2	1.2	
•	Textile waste. *See Cotton waste*									
	Textile waste, wet	Flammable solid	Flammable solid	None	173.211	Forbidden	Forbidden	1.2	1.2	Separate from flammable gases or liquids, oxidizing materials, or organic peroxides
•	Thallium salt, solid, n.o.s.	Poison B	Poison	173.364	173.365	50 pounds	200 pounds	1.2	1.2	

Hazardous Materials Table (cont'd)

(1)	(2) Hazardous materials descriptions and proper shipping names	(3) Hazard class	(4) Label(s) required (if not excepted)	(5) Packaging (a) Exceptions	(5) Packaging (b) Specific requirements	(6) Maximum net quantity in one package (a) Passenger carrying aircraft or railcar	(6) (b) Cargo only aircraft	(7) Water shipments (a) Cargo vessel	(7) (b) Passenger vessel	(7) (c) Other requirements
*/W/A	Thallium sulfate, solid	Poison B	Poison	173.364	173.365	50 pounds	200 pounds	1,2	1,2	
	Thinner for rust preventive coating. *See* *Rust preventive coating									
	Thinning compound, paint, varnish, lacquer, etc. See *Paint, enamel, lacquer, stain, shellac, varnish, etc.									
	Thiocarbonyl-chloride. See Thiophosgene									
	Thioglycolic acid	Corrosive material	Corrosive	173.244	173.245	1 quart	1 gallon	1,2	1,2	Glass carboys in hampers not permitted under deck
	Thionyl chloride	Corrosive material	Corrosive	None	173.247	Forbidden	1 gallon	1	1	Keep dry. Glass carboys not permitted on passenger vessels
	Thiophosgene	Poison B	Poison	None	173.356	Forbidden	1 gallon	1	5	Shade from radiant heat
	Thiophosphoryl chloride	Corrosive material	Corrosive	None	173.271	Forbidden	1 quart	1	1	Keep dry. Glass carboys not permitted on passenger vessels
A	Thiram	ORM-A	None	173.505 173.226	173.510 173.226	No limit	No limit	1,2	1,2	
	Thorium metal, pyrophoric	Radioactive material	Radioactive and Flammable solid							
	Thorium nitrate	Radioactive material	Radioactive and Oxidizer	173.392	173.393			1,2	1,2	Separate longitudinally by a complete hold or compartment from explosives
	Time fuze. See Fuze, time, non-detonating									
*	Tin chloride, fuming. *See* Tin tetrachloride, anhydrous									
	Tinning flux. *See* *Zinc chloride solution									
	Tin perchloride. *See* Tin tetrachloride, anhydrous									

Name	Classification		Packaging		Max qty passenger	Max qty cargo			Notes
Tin tetrachloride, anhydrous	Corrosive material	Corrosive	173.244	173.247	1 quart	1 quart	1	1	Keep dry. Glass carboys not permitted on passenger vessels
Titanium metal powder, dry or wet with less than 20% water	Flammable solid	Flammable solid	None	173.208	Forbidden	75 pounds	1.2	5	
Titanium metal powder, wet with 20% or more water	Flammable solid	Flammable solid	None	173.208	Forbidden	150 pounds	1.2	5	
Titanium sulfate solution containing not more than 45% sulfuric acid	Corrosive material	Corrosive	173.244	173.297	1 quart	1 gallon	1	4	Shade from radiant heat. Keep dry
Titanium tetrachloride	Corrosive material	Corrosive	173.244	173.247	1 quart	10 gallons	1	1	Keep dry. Glass carboys not permitted on passenger vessels
Toluene (*toluol*)	Flammable liquid	Flammable liquid	173.118	173.119	1 quart	10 gallons	1.2	1	
A Toluenediamine	ORM-A	None	173.505	173.510	No limit	No limit			
Toluene diisocyanate	Poison B	Poison	173.345	173.346	Forbidden	55 gallons	1.3	1.3	Shade from radiant heat
Toluene sulfonic acid, liquid	Corrosive material	Corrosive	173.244	173.245	1 quart	10 gallons	1.2	1.2	
Torch. See Fireworks, common									
Torpedo, railway	Class B explosive	Explosive B	None	173.91	Forbidden	200 pounds	1.2	1.2	Passenger vessels in metal lockers only
Toy caps	Class C explosive	Explosive C	None	173.100 173.109	50 pounds	150 pounds	1.3	1.3	
Toy propellant device	Class C explosive	Explosive C	None	173.111	50 pounds	150 pounds	1.3	1.3	
Toy smoke device	Class C explosive	Explosive C	None	173.111	50 pounds	150 pounds	1.3	1.3	
Toy torpedo. See Fireworks, special									
Tracer	Class C explosive	Explosive C	None	173.105	50 pounds	150 pounds	1.3	1.3	
Tracer fuze	Class C explosive	Explosive C	None	173.105	50 pounds	150 pounds	1.3	1.3	
Tractor *See* Motor vehicle									
Trailer or truck body with refrigeration or heating equipment *See* Motor vehicle									
Treated paper (*manufactured article properly dried to prevent spontaneous heating*). *See* Oiled material									
Treated textile (*manufactured article properly dried to prevent spontaneous heating*). *See* Oiled material									
Trichloroacetic acid, solid	Corrosive material	Corrosive	173.244	173.245h	25 pounds	100 pounds	1.2	1	
• Trichloroacetic acid solution	Corrosive material	Corrosive	173.244	173.245	1 quart	1 quart	1.2	1.2	Glass carboys in hampers not permitted under deck
A Trichloroethylene	ORM-A	None	173.505	173.510 173.605	10 gallons	55 gallons			
Trichlorosilane	Flammable liquid	Flammable liquid	None	173.136	Forbidden	10 gallons	1	5	Segregation same as for flammable solids labeled Dangerous When Wet
Trichloro-s-triazinetrione (*dry, containing over 39% available chlorine*)	Oxidizer	Oxidizer	173.153	173.217	50 pounds	100 pounds	1.3	1.3	Keep dry

491

Hazardous Materials Table (cont'd)

(1)	(2) Hazardous materials descriptions and proper shipping names	(3) Hazard class	(4) Label(s) required (if not excepted)	(5) Packaging (a) Exceptions	(5) Packaging (b) Specific requirements	(6) Maximum net quantity in one package (a) Passenger carrying aircraft or railcar	(6) (b) Cargo only aircraft	(7) Water shipments (a) Cargo vessel	(7) (b) Passenger vessel	(7) (c) Other requirements
•/W/A	(mono-(Trichloro) tetra-(monopotassium dichloro)-penta-s-tri azinetrione, dry *(containing over 39% available chlorine)*	Oxidizer	Oxidizer	173.153	173.217	50 pounds	100 pounds	1.3	1.3	Keep dry
	Trick matches	Class C explosive	Explosive C	None	173.111	Forbidden	Forbidden	1.3	1.3	
	Trick noise maker, explosive	Class C explosive	Explosive C	None	173.111	50 pounds	150 pounds	1.3	1.3	
	Triethylamine	Flammable liquid	Flammable liquid	173.118	173.119	1 quart	10 gallons	1.2	1	
	Trifluorochlorethylene	Flammable gas	Flammable gas	173.306	173.304 173.314	Forbidden	10 gallons	1.2	1	
	Trimethyl acetyl chloride	Corrosive material	Corrosive	173.244	173.247	1 quart	1 quart	1.2	1.2	
	Trimethylamine, anhydrous	Flammable gas	Flammable gas	173.306	173.304 173.314 173.315	Forbidden	300 pounds	1	4	
	Trimethylamine, aqueous solution	Flammable liquid	Flammable liquid	173.118	173.119	1 quart	10 gallons	1.2	1	
	Trimethylchlorosilane	Flammable liquid	Flammable liquid	None	173.135	Forbidden	10 gallons	1.2	1	
	Trinitrobenzene, dry *See* High explosive									
•	Trinitrobenzene, wet containing at least 10% water	Flammable solid	Flammable solid	173.212		1 pound	1 pound	1	4	Stow away from heavy metals and their compounds
	Trinitrobenzoic acid, dry. *See* High explosive									
•	Trinitrobenzoic acid, wet, containing at least 10% water	Flammable solid	Flammable solid	None	173.192 173.193	1 pound	25 pounds	1	5	Stow away from mercury and mercury compounds
	Trinitrobenzoic acid, wet, containing at least 10% water, over 25 pounds in one outside packaging *See* High explosive									
	Trinitroresorcinol. *See* High explosive									
•	Trinitrotoluene, dry. *See* High explosive									Stow away from heavy metals and their compounds

Trinitrotoluene, wet containing at least 10% water	Flammable solid	Flammable solid	173.212		1 pound	1 pound	1	4	Stow away from heavy metals and their compounds
Tris-(1-aziridinyl) phosphine oxide	Corrosive material	Corrosive	173.244	173.299a	1 quart	1 gallon	1	1	Keep dry. Glass carboys not permitted on passenger vessels
• Turpentine	Combustible liquid	None	173.118a	None	No limit	No limit	1,2	1,2	
• Turpentine	Flammable liquid	Flammable liquid	173.118	173.119	1 quart	10 gallons	1,2	1,2	
• Turpentine substitute	Combustible liquid	None	173.118a	None	No limit	No limit	1,2	1,2	
• Turpentine substitute	Flammable liquid	Flammable liquid	173.118	173.119	1 quart	10 gallons	1,2	1	
W Twisted jute packing (rope) (treated or untreated). See Oakum									
Uranium hexafluoride, fissile (containing more than 0.7% U-235)	Radioactive material	Radioactive and corrosive	173.393	173.396			1,2	1,2	
Uranium hexafluoride, low specific activity (containing 0.7% or less U-235)	Radioactive material	Radioactive and corrosive	173.392	173.393			1,2	1,2	
Uranium metal, pyrophoric	Radioactive material	Radioactive and Flammable solid	173.392	173.393 173.396			1,2	1,2	
Uranyl nitrate hexahydrate solution	Radioactive material	Radioactive and corrosive	173.392	173.393 173.395 173.396			1,2	1,2	
Uranyl nitrate, solid	Radioactive material	Radioactive and oxidizer	173.392	173.393 173.396			1,2	1,2	Separate longitudinally by an intervening hold or compartment from explosives
Urea nitrate, dry. See High explosive									
• Urea nitrate, wet with 10% or more water	Flammable solid	Flammable solid	None	173.192 173.193	1 pound	25 pounds	1	1,2	
Urea nitrate, wet with 10% or more water, over 25 pounds in one outside packaging. See High explosive									
Urea peroxide	Organic peroxide	Organic peroxide	173.153	173.227	2 pounds	25 pounds	1	4	Keep dry. Shade from radiant heat
Valeric acid	Corrosive material	Corrosive	173.244	173.245	1 quart	10 gallons	1,2	1,2	
Valeryl chloride	Corrosive material	Corrosive	173.244	173.245	1 quart	1 gallon	1,2	1,2	
Vanadium oxytrichloride	Corrosive material	Corrosive	173.244	173.247a	Forbidden	1 quart	1	4	Shade from radiant heat
Vanadium tetrachloride	Corrosive material	Corrosive	173.244	173.247a	Forbidden	1 quart	1	4	Shade from radiant heat
Varnish. See *Paint, enamel, lacquer, stain, shellac, varnish, etc.									
Varnish drier. See *Paint drier, liquid									

Hazardous Materials Table (cont'd)

(1)	(2) Hazardous materials descriptions and proper shipping names	(3) Hazard class	(4) Label(s) required (if not excepted)	(5) Packaging (a) Exceptions	(5) Packaging (b) Specific requirements	(6) Maximum net quantity in one package (a) Passenger carrying aircraft or railcar	(6) (b) Cargo only aircraft	(7) Water shipments (a) Cargo vessel	(7) (b) Passenger vessel	(7) (c) Other requirements
	Varnish remover or reducer. See *Compound, lacquer, paint or varnish removing, reducing, or thinning liquid*									
	Varnish thinning compound. See *Compound, lacquer, paint, or varnish removing, reducing, or thinning liquid*									
°/W/A	Very signal cartridge	Class C explosive	Explosive C	None	173.108	50 pounds	200 pounds	1,3	1,3	
	Vinyl acetate	Flammable liquid	Flammable liquid	173.118	173.119	1 quart	10 gallons	1,2	1	
	Vinyl chloride	Flammable gas	Flammable gas	173.306	173.304 173.314 173.315	Forbidden	300 pounds	1,2	4	Stow away from living quarters
	Vinyl ethyl ether, inhibited	Flammable liquid	Flammable liquid	None	173.119	Forbidden	1 gallon	1,3	5	
	Vinyl fluoride, inhibited	Flammable gas	Flammable gas	173.306	173.304 173.314 173.315	Forbidden	300 pounds	1	4	
	Vinylidene chloride, inhibited	Flammable liquid	Flammable liquid	173.118	173.119	1 quart	10 gallons	1,3	4	
	Vinyl isobutyl ether	Flammable liquid	Flammable liquid	173.118	173.119	1 quart	10 gallons	1,2	1	
	Vinyl methyl ether	Flammable gas	Flammable gas	173.306	173.304 173.314	Forbidden	20 pounds	1,2	1	Stow away from living quarters
	Vinyl trichlorosilane	Flammable liquid	Flammable liquid	None	173.135	Forbidden	10 gallons	1,2	1	
	Vitriol, oil of. See *Sulfuric acid*									
	War head. See *Explosive projectile*									
	Waste paper, wet	Flammable solid	Flammable solid	None	173.186	Forbidden	Forbidden	1,2	1,2	Separate from flammable gas or liquids, oxidizing materials, or organic peroxides
	Waste textile, wet	Flammable solid	Flammable solid	None	173.211	Forbidden	Forbidden	1,2	1,2	Separate from flammable gases or liquids, oxidizing materials, or organic peroxides

Waste wool, wet	Flammable solid	Flammable solid	None	173 213	Forbidden	Forbidden	1.2	Separate from flammable gases or liquids, oxidizing materials, or organic peroxides
Water reactive solid, n.o.s.	Flammable solid	Flammable solid and Dangerous When Wet	173 153	173 152	Forbidden	25 pounds	1.2	Segregation same as for flammable solids labeled Dangerous When Wet
Water treatment compounds, liquid	Corrosive	Corrosive	173 244	173 224	1 quart	10 gallons	1.2	
Wax, liquid	Combustible liquid	None	173 118a	None	No limit	No limit	1.2	
Wet hair See Hair, wet								
Wet textile waste See Waste textile, wet								
White acid (ammonium bifluoride and hydrochloric acid mixture)	Corrosive material	Corrosive	173 244	173 262	1 quart	1 gallon	1.2	
Wood filler See Paint, varnish, lacquer, stain, shellac enamel, etc								
Wood shavings (when dry, clean and free from oil) See Sawdust								
Wool waste See Cotton waste								
Wool waste, wet See Waste wool, wet								
Xenon	Nonflammable gas	Nonflammable gas	173 306	173 302	150 pounds	300 pounds	1.2	
X ray film See Film								
Xylene (xylol)	Flammable liquid	Flammable liquid	173 118	173 119	1 quart	10 gallons	1.2	Stow away from living quarters
Xylyl bromide	Irritating material	Irritant	None	173 382	Forbidden	75 pounds	1	
Yeast, active, in liquid or pressed form	ORM-C	None	None	173 1085	N, limit	No limit	1.3	This material may be forbidden in water transportation by certain countries
Zinc ammonium nitrite	Oxidizer	Oxidizer	None	173 228	25 pounds	100 pounds	1.2	
Zinc arsenate	Poison B	Poison	173 364	173 365	50 pounds	200 pounds	1.2	
Zinc arsenite, solid	Poison B	Poison	173 364	173 365	50 pounds	200 pounds	1.2	
Zinc chlorate	Oxidizer	Oxidizer	173 153	173 163	25 pounds	100 pounds	1.2	Stow separate from ammonium compounds and away from powdered metals
Zinc chloride solution	Corrosive material	Corrosive	173 244	173 245	1 quart	1 quart	1.2	Stow away from acids
Zinc cyanide	Poison B	Poison	173 370		25 pounds	200 pounds	1.2	
Zinc ethyl See Pyrophoric liquids, n.o.s.								
Zinc muriate solution See Zinc chloride solution								
Zinc nitrate See Nitrates, n.o.s.								

Hazardous Materials Table (cont'd)

(1)	(2) Hazardous materials descriptions and proper shipping names	(3) Hazard class	(4) Label(s) required (if not excepted)	(5) Packaging (a) Exceptions	(5) Packaging (b) Specific requirements	(6) Maximum net quantity in one package (a) Passenger carrying aircraft or railcar	(6) (b) Cargo only aircraft	(7) Water shipments (a) Cargo vessel	(7) (b) Passenger vessel	(7) (c) Other requirements
	Zinc permanganate	Oxidizer	Oxidizer	173.153	173.154	25 pounds	100 pounds	1,2	1,2	Separate from ammonium compounds and hydrogen peroxide
	Zinc peroxide	Oxidizer	Oxidizer	173.153	173.154	25 pounds	100 pounds	1,2	1,2	Keep dry
	Zirconium hydride	Flammable solid	Flammable solid and Dangerous when wet	None	173.206	Forbidden	150 pounds	1,2	5	Segregation same as for flammable solids labeled Dangerous When Wet
	Zirconium metal, dry, chemically produced, finer than 20 mesh particle size	Flammable solid	Flammable solid	None	173.214	Forbidden	75 pounds	1	5	Separate from flammable gases or liquids, oxidizing materials or organic peroxides
	Zirconium metal, dry, mechanically produced, finer than 270 mesh particle size	Flammable solid	Flammable solid	None	173.214	Forbidden	75 pounds	1	5	Separate from flammable gases or liquids, oxidizing materials or organic peroxides
•	Zirconium, metal, liquid, suspensions	Flammable liquid	Flammable liquid	None	173.140	Forbidden	5 gallons	1	5	
	Zirconium metal, wet, chemically produced, finer than 20 mesh particle size	Flammable solid	Flammable solid	None	173.214	Forbidden	150 pounds	1,2	5	
	Zirconium metal, wet mechanically produced, finer than 270 mesh particle size	Flammable solid	Flammable solid	None	173.214	Forbidden	150 pounds	1,2	5	
	Zirconium picramate, wet with at least 20% of water	Flammable solid	Flammable solid	None	173.216	Forbidden	25 pounds	1	1	Stow away from heavy metals and their salts
•	Zirconium-scrap (borings, clippings, shavings, sheets, or turnings)	Flammable solid	Flammable solid	173.153	173.220	Forbidden	Forbidden	1	4	Separate from flammable gases of liquids, oxidizing materials, or organic peroxides
	Zirconium tetrachloride, solid	Corrosive material	Corrosive	173.244	173.245b	25 pounds	100 pounds	1,2	1,2	

496

Hazardous Materials Table (addition, December 4, 1978)

(1)	(2) Hazardous materials descriptions and proper shipping names	(3) Hazard class	(4) Labels(s) required (if not excepted)	(5) Packaging (a) Exception	(5) Packaging (b) Specific requirements	(6) Maximum net quantity in one package (a) Passenger carrying aircraft or railcar	(6) (b) Cargo only aircraft	(7) Water shipments (a) Cargo vessel	(7) (b) Passenger vessel	(7) (c) Other requirement
*/ W/	(Add)									
*	Asbestos	ORM-C	None	173.1090 (c)	173.1090 (d)	No Limit	No Limit	1, 2	1, 2	Stow and handle to avoid airborne particles.

497

APPENDIX D
AMERICAN NATIONAL STANDARDS FOR SAFETY AND HEALTH

Complete copies of the listed standards are available for a nominal price from the American National Standards Institute, 1430 Broadway, New York, NY 10018. Since it typically takes a year or more for a trade association standard to be named an American National Standard, check with the separate associations themselves in your industry (App. G) for the latest standards.

In the following listing, this code is used:

- A   Standard is up-to-date.
- B   Draft standard or revision was in committee at the end of 1977.
- C   Formal submittal by outside organization was being processed by ANSI.
- D   Standard was approved in 1977.
- E   Standard needs updating or reaffirmation.
- N   Standard has been proposed.
- P   Standard-writing project is under way; no standard by end of 1977.
- W   Standard project was withdrawn or discontinued; data may still be available.
- O   Adopted or referenced by OSHA in whole or in part; year indicates if an earlier version of the standard was used.

A10   **Standard for Safety in the Construction Industry**

Scope: Standards relating to the protection of employees and of the public from hazards arising out of or associated with construction and demolition operations.

Secretariats: National Safety Council
                 American Road Builders Association

A10.2-1944	Building Construction, Safety Standard for	W O
A10.3-1972	Explosive-Actuated Fastening Tools, Safety Requirements for	B O
A10.4-1975	Workmen's Hoists, Safety Requirements for	A O-1963
A10.5-1975	Material Hoists, Safety Requirements for	A O-1969
A10.6-1969	Demolition, Safety Requirements for	B
A10.7-1970	Transportation, Storage, Handling and Use of Commercial Explosives and Blasting Agents in the Construction Industry, Safety Requirements for	C
A10.8-1969	Scaffolding, Safety Requirements for	C O
A10.9-1970	Concrete Construction and Masonry Work, Safety Requirements for	B O
A10.10-1970	Temporary and Portable Space Heating Devices and Equipment Used in the Construction Industry, Safety Requirements for	B
A10.11-1971	Safety Nets, Minimum Requirements for	B
A10.12	Excavation	B
A10.13-1972	Steel Erection	A
A10.14-1975	Safety Belts	A
A10.15-1973	Marine Dredging	A
A10.16	Construction of Tunnels, Shafts and Caissons	B
A10.17-1975	Asphalt Paving Operations	A
A10.18	Temporary Floor and Wall Openings, Railings, and Toe Boards	D
A10.19	Pile Driving	B
A10.20	Marble, Ceramic and Mosaic Tile Work	D
A10.21-1975	Safeguarding Bldg. Construction and Demolition Operations	A
A10.22	Rope Guided and Non-Rope Guided Workmen's Hoists	C
A10.23	Earth Moving and Grading	B
A10-24	Roofing	B
A10.25	Temporary Wiring	B
A10.26	Crane Supported Platforms	P

A11   **Standard for Lighting Factories, Mills, and Other Work Places**

Scope: Standards for illumination for different classes of work in factories, mills, and other work places; standards for illumination required for safety in traversed places during the time of use or while work is in progress, and for the avoidance of glare; and recommendations for emergency lighting.

Secretariat: Illuminating Engineering Society

A11.1-1973	Industrial Lighting, Practice for	B O-1965

A12   **Safety Standard for Floor and Wall Openings, Railings, and Toe Boards**

Scope: Standards for guarding of floor and wall openings and holes; open-sided floors, platforms and runways, and the construction and installation of railings and toe boards, including railings used on stairways other than those used exclusively for fire exit purposes. These standards apply to all places of employment and construction operations.

Secretariat: National Safety Council

A12.1-1973	Floor and Wall Openings, Railings, and Toe Boards, Safety Requirements for	A O-1967

A13   **Scheme for the Identification of Piping Systems**

Scope: Identification of piping systems in industrial and power plants which are not buried in the ground; with special reference to personal hazards in time of accident at a plant,

APPENDIX D AMERICAN NATIONAL STANDARDS FOR SAFETY AND HEALTH **501**

including conduits for the transport of gases, liquid, semi-liquids, or plastics, but not including conduits filled with solids.

Secretariats: American Society of Mechanical Engineers
National Safety Council

A13.1-1975	Identification of Piping Systems, Scheme for the	A O-1956

A14 **Safety Standards for the Construction, Care, and Use of Ladders**

Scope: Rules governing the safe construction and use of ladders of various types, including fixed, portable extension, fire, step, trolley, sectional, and trestle, but excluding ladders for mines.

Secretariats: American Mutual Insurance Alliance
American Ladder Institute

A14.1-1974	Portable Wood Ladders, Safety Standard for	A O-1968*
A14.2-1972	Portable Metal Ladders, Safety Requirements for	B O-1956
A14.3-1974	Fixed Ladders, Safety Standard for	B O-1956
A14.4-1973	Job Made Ladders	A
A14.5-1974	Fiberglass Ladders	A
A14.6	Classification of Ladders in Electrical Environment	P
A14.7-1976	Fire Department Ground Ladders (NFPA 193A-1975)	A

A17 **Safety Code for Elevators, Dumbwaiters, Escalators, and Moving Walks**

Scope: This code of safety standards covers the design, construction, installation, operation, inspection, testing, maintenance, alteration, and repair of elevators, dumbwaiters, escalators, private residence elevators and inclined lifts, moving walks, material lifts equipped with permanently mounted automatic load-transferring devices, and inclined elevators and their hoistways.

Secretariats: American Institute of Architects
American Society of Mechanical Engineers

A17.1-1971	Elevators, Dumbwaiters and Moving Walks, Safety Code for	B O-1965
A17.1a-1972	Supplement to A17.1-1971	B
A17.1b-1973	Supplement to A17.1-1971	B
A17.1c-1974	Supplement to A17.1-1971	B
A17.1d-1975	Supplement to A17.1-1971	B
A17.1e-1975	Supplement to A17.1-1971	B
A17.1f-1975	Supplement to A17.1-1971	B
A17.2-1973	Elevators, Practice for the Inspection of	B O-1960

A23 **School Lighting**

Scope: Rules for intensity of illumination required, avoidance of glare, distribution of artificial light, color and finish of interior, location of switching and controlling apparatus, exit and emergency lighting, inspection and maintenance, blackboard lighting. Excluding subject of fire hazard from illumination sources.

Secretariats: Illuminating Engineering Society
Council of Educational Facility Planners

A23.1-1962 (R1970)	School Lighting, Guide for	C

*OSHA simplified these requirements in 1978.

A54   **Systems for Fire Protection**

Proprietary Sponsors: National Fire Protection Association
Underwriters Laboratories

A54.1-1977	Carbon Dioxide Extinguishing Systems (NFPA #12)	D
A54.2-1977	Water Spray Fixed Systems for Fire Protection (NFPA #12)	D
A54.3-1977	Sprinkler Systems (NFPA #13)	D
A54.4-1977	Halogenated Extinguishing Agent Systems-Halon 1301 (NFPA #12a-73)	D
A54.5-1977	Halogenated Fire Extinguishing Agent Systems-Halon 1211 (NFPA #12b)	D
A54.6	Automatic Sprinkler for Fire Protection Service (UL 199)	W
A54.7	Sprinkler Systems in 1 and 2 Family Dwellings & Mobile Homes (NFPA #130)	W
A54.8-1976	Automatic Fire Apparatus	A

A64   **Safety Standards for Fixed General Industrial Stairs**

Scope: Standards for the safe design and construction of fixed general industrial stairs. This classification includes interior and exterior stairs around machinery, tanks, and other equipment, and stairs leading to or from floors, platforms, or pits. These standards do not apply to stairs used for fire exit purposes, to construction operations, to private residences, or to articulated stairs, such as may be installed on floating roof tanks or on dock facilities, the angle of which changes with the rise and fall of the base support.

Secretariat: National Safety Council

A64.1-1968	Fixed Industrial Stairs, Requirements for	B O

A90   **Safety Standard for Manlifts**

Scope: This standard applies to the construction, maintenance, inspection, and operation of manlifts in relation to accident hazards to employees. Manlifts covered by this scope consist of platforms or brackets mounted on, or attached to an endless belt, cables, chains, and such a belt, cables, or chains operating in a substantially vertical direction and being supported by, and driven through pulleys, sheaves, or sprockets at the top and bottom. These manlifts are intended for the conveyance of persons only. It is not intended that this scope cover moving stairways, elevators with enclosed platforms ("Paternoster" elevators), gravity lifts, nor conveyors used only for conveying materials.

Secretariat: American Society of Mechanical Engineers

A90.1-1976	Manlifts, Safety Standard for	A O-1976

A92   **Mobile Scaffolds, Towers, and Platforms**

Scope: Standards relating to the prevention of accidents of employees and to the public arising out of the construction and use of:

(1) Manually propelled mobile scaffolds
(2) Mobile towers
(3) Telescoping work platforms
(4) Truck-mounted elevating or rotating types of work platforms

Fire-fighting equipment and the operation of motor vehicles are not to be included.

Secretariat: American Mutual Insurance Alliance

APPENDIX D AMERICAN NATIONAL STANDARDS FOR SAFETY AND HEALTH **503**

A92.1-1971	Mobile Ladder Standards and Scaffolds (Towers), Manually Propelled	C O
A92.2-1969	Vehicle Mounted Elevating and Rotating Work Platforms	B O
A92.3-1973	Telescoping Work Platforms	A
A92.4-1976	Fire Department Aerial Ladders	A

A113 **Safety Standard for Mechanized Parking Garage Equipment**

Scope: The rules of this standard cover requirements for equipment used exclusively for the parking of automobiles in buildings or structures where during the parking process, each automobile is moved either under its own power, or by means of a power-driven transfer device, onto and off an elevator, operating in either a stationary or a horizontally moving hoistway, directly into parking spaces or cubicles in line with the elevator, and where no persons are normally stationed on any level except the receiving level and/or the discharging level. Elevators in buildings or structures where the automobile, after being unloaded from the elevator, can be driven under its own power across any floor of the structure into any unoccupied space not in line with the elevator are considered power freight elevators subject to the rules of the A17.1 Elevator Code.

Secretariat: American Society of Mechanical Engineers

A113.1-1964 (R1971)   Mechanized Parking Garage Equipment, Safety Standard for   W

A120 **Safety Standards for Powered Operated Platforms and Equipment Used for Exterior and Interior Building Maintenance**

Scope: Safety standards for the design, construction, installation, operation, inspection, testing, maintenance, alteration, and repair of power-operated platforms and equipment used for exterior building maintenance which are hereafter referred to as power-operated equipment, designed for and installed on a specific building or structure to position a suspended working platform carrying one or more workers or operators, or both, to any desired location on the face of the building or structure.

Secretariat National Safety Council
American Society of Mechanical Engineers

A120.1-1970   Powered Platforms for Exterior Building Maintenance, Safety Standard for   B O

A196 **Elevator Door Locking Devices and Contacts**

Proprietary Sponsor: Underwriters Laboratories

A196.1   Elevator Door Locking Devices and Contacts   W

B7 **Use, Care, and Protection of Abrasive Wheels**

Scope: Specifications for safety in the use of bonded, coated and loose abrasives, excluding natural sandstones; including safety requirements for abrasive products, abrasive machines and accessories, and requirements for the proper storage, handling, and mounting of abrasive products.

Secretariats: Grinding Wheel Institute
International Association of Governmental Labor Officials

B7.1-1970	Use, Care and Protection of Abrasive Wheels, Safety Standard for	C O
B7.1a-1973	Errata Sheet for B7.1-1970	A
B7.1b-1975	Supplement	A
B7.3	Construction, Care & Use of Electric Powered, Hand-Held, Portable Abrasive Machines	P
B7.4	Construction, Care & Use of Pneumatic Powered, Hand-Held, Portable Abrasive Machines	P
B7.5	Construction, Use, & Care of Gasoline-Powered, Hand-Held, Portable Abrasive Cutting-Off Machines	P
B7.6	Construction, Care, and Use of Bench & Pedestal Grinders	P
B7.7	Use, Care, and Protection of Coated Abrasives	P
B7.8	Construction, Care, and Use of Masonry and Concrete Abrasive Machines	P
B7.9	Construction, Care, and Use of Machines Using Loose Abrasives	P
B7.10	Construction, Care, and Use of Lapidary Machines	P

B11 Safety Standards for Machine Tools

Scope: Safety requirements applicable to the design, construction, installation, maintenance and use of power-driven machines, not portable by hand, used to shape or form metal or other materials by cutting, impact, pressure, electrical techniques, or a combination of these processes.

Secretariat: National Machine Tool Builders Association

B11.1-1971	Power Presses, Safety Requirements for the Construction, Care, and Use of	B O-1971
B11.2	Hydraulic Power Presses	C
B11.3-1973	Power Press Brakes	A
B11.4-1973	Shears	A
B11.5-1975	Ironworkers	A
B11.6-1975	Lathes	A
B11.7-1974	Cold Headers and Cold Formers	A
B11.8-1974	Drilling, Milling, & Boring Machines	A
B11.9-1975	Grinding Machines	A
B11.10-1974	Sawing Machines	A
B11.11	Gear Cutting and Finishing Machines	W
B11.12	Roll Forming and Roll Bending Machines	C
B11.13-1975	Automatic Screw/Bar and Chucking Machines	A
B11.14	Coil Systems Equipment (Metal Working)	B
B11.15	Pipe, Tube and/or Shape Bending Machines	C
B11.16	Metal Powder Compacting Presses	B
B11.17	Metal Extrusion Equipment	P

B15 Safety Standards for Mechanical Power Transmission Apparatus

Scope: Protection of people from the hazards associated with equipment used in the mechanical transmission of power, which equipment has been installed and is operating in the intended use. The entire power train is included comprising the sources of mechanical power, the associated and intermediate equipment, and the driven machines up to but excluding the point(s) of operation of locomotion. Units in such power trains include, but are not limited to, engines, motors, reducers, shafts, belts, sheaves, pulleys, gears, chains, sprockets, cables, clutches, cams, pistons, cranks, fly-wheels, counterweights and other revolving, oscillating, reciprocating, or other moving parts.

	Secretariats: International Association of Governmental Labor Officials	
	American Society of Mechanical Engineers	
B15.1-1972	Safety Code for Mechanical Power-Transmission Apparatus	B O-1958
B19	**Safety Standards for Compressor Systems**	

Scope: Safety regulations for the construction, installation, operation, and maintenance of air and gas compression equipment except compressors used in refrigeration systems.

Secretariat: American Society of Mechanical Engineers

B19.1	Safety Standard for Air Compressor Systems	C O
B19.3-1972	Compressors for Process Industries, Safety Standard for	A
B20	**Safety Standard for Conveyor and Related Equipment**	

Scope: This standard applies to the design, construction, installation, maintenance, inspection, and operation of conveyors and conveying systems in relation to accident hazards. Conveyors covered by this code include such items as power conveyors, gravity conveyors, pneumatic tubes, skip hoists, vertical reciprocating conveyors, and power unloading scoops, except as provided in the following paragraph: This standard does not apply to industrial power trucks, tiering machines, cranes, derricks, hoists, power and hand shovels, bucket drag lines, moving stairways, dumbwaiters, manlifts, and platform elevators designed to carry passengers or the elevator operator.

Secretariat: American Society of Mechanical Engineers

B20.1-1976	Conveyors and Related Equipment, Safety Standard for	D O-1957
B24	**Safety Standards for Forging and Hot Metal Forming**	

Scope: Drop forging and other hammer forging; includes hazards peculiar to the forging industry and associated with such machines, and whether or not they occur at the point of operation, but does not include cold extrusion of nonferrous metals, or hydraulic presses, except as the standards committee may find it desirable to include small types of the latter. The inclusion of hot pressing and bulldozing, and also of other forging machines, such as bolt-heading and rivet-making machines shall be left to the discretion of the standards committee.

Secretariats: Forging Industry Association
National Safety Council

B24.1-1971(R1975)	Forging, Safety Requirements for	A O-1963
B28	**Safety Standards for Rubber Machinery**	

Scope: The mechanical hazards encountered in the manufacture of rubberized fabrics, rubber tires, fire and garden hose, footwear, molded rubber goods, rubber belting, reclaimed rubber, rubber solution and products made therefrom, and miscellaneous rubber materials; covers the machines used in breaking down, washing, milling, cutting, molding, and vulcanizing of rubber, together with calenders, spreaders, coaters and dryers, and other machinery used in the manufacture of rubber sheeting; special machines used in the manufacture of rubber tires included, but spinning and weaving of fabrics excluded.

Secretariat: National Safety Council

B28.1-1967(R1972)	Mills and Calenders in the Rubber and Plastics Industries, Safety Specifications for	B O-1967
B28.2-1976	Construction Care & Use of Tire & Tube Curing Presses and Post Cure Inflators	D
B28.3	Safety Standard for Tire Building Machines	C

B30   **Safety Standards for Cableways, Cranes, Derricks, Hoists, Hooks, Jacks, and Slings**

Scope: These standards apply to the construction, installation, operation, inspection and maintenance of jacks, power and manually operated cranes, monorails and crane runways; power and manually operated derricks and hoists; lifting hooks and slings; and cableways.

These standards do not apply to track and automotive jacks, railway or automobile-wrecking cranes, shipboard cranes, shipboard cargo-handling equipment, well-drilling derricks, skip hoists, mine hoists, truck-body hoists, car or barge pullers, lever-operated pulling devices, conveyors, excavating equipment, nor to equipment coming within the scope of the following American National Standards Committees: A10, A17, A90, A92, A113, A120, B56, and B77.

Secretariats: American Society of Mechanical Engineers
U.S. Department of the Navy - Naval Ship Engineering Center

B30.1-1975	Jacks, Safety Code for	A O-1943
B30.2.0-1976	Overhead and Gantry Cranes	D O-1967
B30.3-1975	Hammerhead Tower Cranes	A
B30.4-1973	Portal, Tower, and Pillar Cranes	A
B30.5-1968	Crawler, Locomotive, and Truck Cranes	B O-1968
B30.6-1969	Derricks, Safety Code for	B O
B30.7-1971	Base Mounted Drum Hoists	B
B30.8-1971	Floating Cranes and Derricks, Safety Code for	B
B30.9-1971	Slings, Safety Code for	B
B30.10-1975	Hooks	A
B30.11-1973	Monorail Systems & Underhung Cranes	A
B30.12-1975	Hanging Loads Suspended from Rotorcraft	A
B30.13-1977	Stacker Cranes (Controlled Mechanical Storage Cranes)	D
B30.14	Side Boom Cranes	B
B30.15-1973	Mobile Hydraulic Cranes (will be incorporated into B30.5 Rev)	A
B30.16-1973	Overhead Hoists	B
B30.17	Single Girder Top Running Cranes	C
B30.18	Overhead Stacker Cranes	B
B30.19	Cableways	B
B30.20	Below the Hook Lifting Devices	B

B56   **Safety Standard for Powered Industrial Trucks**

Scope: Safety requirements relating to the elements of design, operation, and maintenance of powered industrial trucks—not including vehicles intended primarily for earth-moving or over-the-road hauling.

Secretariat: American Society of Mechanical Engineers

B56.1-1975	Powered Industrial Trucks, Safety Standard for	A O

B56.2-1975	Type Designations, Areas of Use, Maintenance and Operations of Powered Industrial Trucks (NFPA 505-1973)	A
B56.3	Standard for Safety: Electric-Battery-Powered Industrial Trucks (UL 583)	D
B56.4	Standard for Safety: Internal Combustion Engine-Powered Industrial Trucks (UL 558)	D
B56.5	Guided Tow Tractors and Associated Trailers	B
B56.6	Rough Terrain Powered Industrial Trucks	B
B56.7	Safety Standard for Industrial Truck Cranes	P
B56.8	Personnel and Burden Carriers	B

B65   **Safety Standard for Signaling Devices and Controls for Graphic Arts Equipment**

Scope: Covers the design, arrangement, designation, color scheme, and safety interlocking features of controls and signaling devices associated with the main drive for web-fed printing presses, to safeguard personnel operating such presses.

Secretariats: National Safety Council
Printing Industry of America

B65.1-1972	Controls and Signaling Devices for Printing Presses, Safety Specifications for	A

B71   **Safety Standards for Lawn Mowers, Snow Throwers, Power Edgers and Trimmers, Garden Tractors and Related Equipment and Attachments**

Scope: Safety requirements and specifications for real or rotary-type lawn mowers; snow throwers; power edgers and trimmers, garden tractors; and related equipment and attachments; operated by hand, internal combustion engine, or electric motor.

Secretariat: Outdoor Power Equipment Institute

B71.1-1972	Power Lawn Mowers, Lawn and Garden Tractors, & Lawn Tractors, Safety Specifications for	A O-1968
B71.1a-1974	Supplement to B71.1-1972	A
B71.1b-1977	Supplement to B71.1-1972	D
B71.3-1975	Safety Specifications for Snow Throwers	A
B71.4	Safety Specifications for Commercial Turf Care Equipment	P
B71.5	Sound Levels for Outdoor Power Equipment	C
B71.6	Safety Specifications for Shredders and Grinders	B

B77   **Aerial Passenger Tramways**

Scope: The standard covers safety requirements for recreational transportation, including serial cable cars (and similar tramways), chair lifts, T-bar lifts, J-bar lifts, platter lifts (and similar devices) and fiber-rope tows, but excluding equipment, such as cog railways, cable cars running on rails, and material-handling equipment.

Secretariat: National Ski Areas Association

B77.1-1976	Aerial Passenger Tramways, Safety Requirements for	D

B110   **Inside Steel Tanks for Oil Burner Fuel**

Proprietary Sponsor: Underwirters Laboratories

B110.1-1974	Inside Steel Tanks for Oil Burner Fuel (UL 80)	A

B151   **Horizontal Injection Molding Machines**

Proprietary Sponsor: Society of the Plastics Industry

B151.1-1976   Horizontal Injection Molding Machines, Safety Requirements for the Construction, Care and Use of   D

B152   **Die Casting Machines**

Proprietary Sponsor: American Die Casting Institute

B152.1-1973   Die Casting Machines, Safety Standard for Construction, Care and Use of   A

B153   **Automotive Lifts**

Proprietary Sponsor: Automotive Lift Institute, Inc.

B153.1-1974   Automotive Lifts, Safety Standard for the Construction, Care and Use of   A

B154   **Rivet Setting**

Proprietary Sponsor: Tubular and Split Rivet Council

B154.1-1974   Rivet Setting Equipment, Safety Requirements for the Construction, Care and Use of   A

B155   **Packaging Machinery**

Proprietary Sponsor: Packaging Machinery Manufacturers Institute

B155.1-1973   Packaging and Packaging-Related Converting Equipment, Safety Standards for the Construction, Care and Use of   A

B157   **Scales and Weighing Machines**

Proprietary Sponsor: Scale Manufacturers Association

B157.1-1974   Scales and Weighing Machines, Safety Standard for   A

B165   **Brushing Tools**

Proprietary Sponsor: Society of Manufacturing Engineers

B165.1-1977   Safety Code for the Use, Care, and Protection of Power Driven Brushing Tools   D

B169   **Envelope Manufacturing Equipment**

Proprietary Sponsor: Envelope Manufacturing Association

B169.1-1975   Safety Standard for Envelope Manufacturing Equipment   A

B173   **Nail Hammers**

Proprietary Sponsor: Hand Tools Institute

B173.1-1975   Safety Requirements for Nail Hammers   A
B173.2   Safety Requirements for Ball Pein Hammers   C

B174   **Wire and Cable Process Machinery**

Proprietary Sponsor: Wire Machinery Builders Association

B174.1   Safety Requirements for Wire and Cable Process Machinery   B
B174.3   Safety Requirements for Construction, Care & Use of Extrusion Equipment   B

APPENDIX D   AMERICAN NATIONAL STANDARDS FOR SAFETY AND HEALTH   **509**

B175	**Gasoline-Powered Chain Saws**	
	Proprietary Sponsor: Power Saw Manufacturers Association	
B175.1	Safety Specifications for Gasoline-Powered Chain Saws	B
B177	**3-Roller Printing Ink Mills**	
	Proprietary Sponsor: National Association of Printing Ink Manufacturing	
B177.1-1975	Safety Standard for 3-Roller Printing Ink Mills	A
B177.2	Safety Standard for Printing Ink Vertical Post Mixers	D
B186	**Portable Air Tools**	
	Proprietary Sponsor: Compressed Air & Gas Institute	
B186.1-1975	Safety Standard for Portable Air Tools	A
B189	**Safety Standard for Metalworking Fluids**	
	Proprietary Sponsor: Society of Manufacturing Engineers	
B189.1	Water Miscible Cutting and Grinding Fluids	C
D7	**Inspection Requirements for Motor Vehicles**	

Scope: Performance requirements and methods of testing with relation to the safe operation of motor vehicles on the highways of those parts and equipment such as braking systems, steering mechanism, lighting systems, frames, wheels, tires, other parts and equipment, the proper performance of which bears a distinct relationship to the safe operation of the motor vehicle.

Secretariat: American Association of Motor Vehicle Administrators

D7.1-1973	Inspection Requirements for Motor Vehicles, Trailers and Semi-Trailers Operated on Public Highways	A
D7.3-1974	Station Requirements for Inspection of Motor Vehicles, Trailers and Semi-Trailers in Stations Appointed and Licensed by Authority	A
D7.4-1972	Inspection Requirements for School Buses	A
D7.5-1974	Inspection Procedures for Motorcycles	A
D7.6	Inspection Procedures for Intercity Buses	P
F1	**Meat Industry Safety Standard**	
	Proprietary Sponsor: American Meat Institute	
F1.1	Safety Requirements for Circular Saws for Meat Processing	C
F2	**Food, Drug and Beverage Equipment**	
	Proprietary Sponsor: American Society of Mechanical Engineers	
F2.1-1975	Food, Drug and Beverage Equipment	A
F2.1a-1976	Supplement to F2.1-1975	A D
J6	**Rubber Protective Equipment for Electrical Workers (To be redesignated by ASTM)**	

Scope: Specifications for rubber protective equipment for electrical workers, including leather protectors for electrical rubber gloves, necessary to provide protection to electrical workers for their particular occupational hazards; detailed construction requirements for such equipment and specifications for all of the significant materials used therein; recommendations for proper nomenclature and method of designation of such equipment and for such labeling and marking requirements as are deemed necessary.

Proprietary Sponsor: American Society for Testing and Materials

J6.1-1950(R1971)	Rubber Insulating Line Hose	W O
J6.2-1950(R1971)	Rubber Insulator Hoods	W O
J6.4-1971	Rubber Insulating Blankets	W O
J6.5-1971	Rubber Insulating Sleeves	W O
J6.6-1971	Rubber Insulating Gloves, Specification for	W O
J6.7-1935(R1971)	Rubber Matting for Use Around Electric Apparatus	W O

K13   **Identification of Air-Purifying Cartridges and Canisters**

Scope: Applies to the identification of all air-purifying respirator canisters and cartridges used to afford respiratory protection against harmful gases, vapors, or particles, whether in industrial plants, in mines, in connection with public utility operations, in rescue work, or in any other similar endeavor. The requirements do not apply to military air-purifying respirator canisters or cartridges.

Secretariat: Mining Enforcement and Safety Administration

K13.1-1973   Identification of Air-Purifying Canisters and Cartridges   A O-1967

K61   **Storage and Handling of Anhydrous Ammonia**

Scope: Safety standards pertaining to the design, construction, location, installation, and operation of anhydrous ammonia systems, and transportation and storage of anhydrous ammonia, but not pertaining to ammonia manufacturing plants, refrigerating or air conditioning systems.

Secretariats: Compressed Gas Association
The Fertilizer Institute

K61.1-1972   Storage and Handling of Anydrous Ammonia, Safety Requirements for the   A O-1966

K68   **Safety Requirements for Epoxy Resins**

Scope: Standards to provide producers and users of epoxies employed in industrial application with a set of criteria and labeling recommendations so that they can better: (1) define the hazard category into which their specific products fall by use of the classification principles set forth, and (2) design labels which will adequately warn of such hazards according to the degree of care in handling required.

Secretariat: Society of the Plastics Industry

K68.1-1971   Guides for Classifying and Labeling Epoxy Products According to Their Hazard Potentialities   E

L1   **Safety Requirements in the Textile Industry**

Scope: Requirements of this standard for textile safety apply to the design, installation, processes, operation, and maintenance of textile machinery equipment and other plant facilities in all plants engaged in the processing of fibers and the formation and finishing of textiles except those processes used exclusively in the chemical manufacture of man-made fibers.

Secretariat: National Safety Council

L1.1-1972	Textile Industry, Safety Requirements for the	A O-1956

L18   **Protective Occupational Clothing**

Scope: Standards for occupational wearing apparel which provide protection against environmental hazards. This scope excludes linemen's rubber protective equipment, protection of head, eyes, hearing, and respiratory organs and footwear.

Secretariat: American Petroleum Institute

L18.1-1976	Protective Clothing for Structural Fire Fighting (NFPA 19A)	D

M11   **Wire Rope for Mines**

Scope: Specifications for wire rope and cables for use in mines together with the recommendations for safe practice.

Secretariats: American Mining Congress Wire Rope Technical Board

M11.1-1960	Specifications for and Use of Wire Ropes for Mines	B

MH9   **Marine Terminal Operations**

Scope: To formulate safety recommendation for facilities and equipment used in the transfer of cargo in marine terminal operations, including transfer to and from means of land transportation, in order to provide a reasonably safe work place and to prevent injuries to employees involved, as well as to the public.

These recommendations, which will in no way conflict with existing regulations administered by federal, state and local authorities, shall be applicable to all requirements for the prevention of injuries or accidents in the marine terminal operations.

Secretariat: National Safety Council

MH9.1-1972	Marine Terminal Operations, Safety Requirements for	A

O1   **Safety Standard for Woodworking Machinery**

Scope: Standards for the safe installation, operation, and maintenance of woodworking machinery and accessory equipment, including cooperage and veneering operations.

Secretariats: American Insurance Association
International Association of Governmental Labor Officials

	Woodworking Machinery, Safety Standard for	A O-1954

O2   **Safety Requirements for Saw Mills**

Scope: Safety requirements for all sawmill operations, including, but not limited to handling, sawing, trimming, slashing, waste disposal, operation of dry kilns, yards, and yard equipment; and for all power tools and affiliated equipment used in connection with such operations but excluding the manufacture of plywood, cooperage, and veneering.

Secretariat: National Safety Council

| O2.1-1969 | Sawmills, Safety Requirements for | B O-1969 |

O15   **Veneer, Plywood, Hardboards, and Particle-board Manufacturing Plants**

Scope: Safety requirements for plants manufacturing veneer, plywood, hardboard and particle board, including, but not limited to, log handling at the plant, chip production, handling, and storage, veneer peeling, veneer stacking and drying, panel layup, panel finishing, speciality panel processing, panel storage, shipping and affiliated equipment used in such operations.

Secretariat: Forest Industries Council

| O15.1 | Veneer, Plywood, Hardboard and Particleboard Manufacturing Plants, Safety Requirements for | B |

P1   **Safety Standard for Pulp and Paper Mills**

Scope: Safety rules for establishments where paper and/or pulp are manufactured.

Secretariat: American Paper Institute

| P1.1-1969 | Safety Standard for Pulp, Paper and Paperboard Mills | E O |

Z4   **Safety Standard for Industrial Sanitation**

Scope: General standards for sanitation in places of employment including standards for sanitation in the housing of the employees and their families as provided by the employer.

Secretariat: American Conference of Governmental Industrial Hygienists

Z4.1-1968	Sanitation in Places of Employment, Requirements for	B O
Z4.3-1970	Non-Water Carriage Disposal Systems, Minimum Requirements for	B O
Z4.4	Sanitation in Temporary Labor Camps, Minimum Requirements for	D O-1968
Z4.5	Minimum Requirements for Sanitation in the Operation of Food Vending Machines	N

Z8   **Safety Standard for Laundry and Dry Cleaning Equipment**

Scope: Safety provisions for machines and equipment used in commercial/industrial laundry and dry cleaning establishments with special reference to mechanical and health hazards. Equipment available to the public, such as coin-operated machines.

Secretariats: Laundry and Cleaners Allied Trades Association
Institute of Industrial Launderers

| Z8.1-1972 | Laundry Machinery and Operations, Safety Standard for | A |
| Z8.2-1975 | Safety Standard for Drycleaning Machinery and Operations (NFPA 32) | A |

Z9	**Safety Standard for Exhaust Systems**	

Scope: Standards for the design, operation and maintenance of equipment to provide a safe atmosphere in industrial, manufacturing or construction operations by removing harmful substances by either local exhaust or general ventilation and by safely disposing of such substances; and such supplementary standards on personal protection as may be necessary to prescribe methods for the protection of workers.

Secretariats: American Industrial Hygiene Association
American Society of Heating, Refrigerating and Air-Conditioning Engineers

Z9.1-1977	Ventilation and Operation of Open-Surface Tanks, Practices for	D
Z9.2-1971	Design and Operation of Local Exhaust Systems, Fundamentals Governing the	B
Z9.3-1964(R1971)	Design, Construction, and Ventilation of Spray Finishing Operations, Safety Standard for the	B
Z9.3a	Airless Spray Painting Equipment	C
Z9.4-1968	Ventilation and Safe Practices of Abrasives Blasting Operations	B
Z9.5	Asbestos Processing	N
Z9.6	Solid Material Handling	W
Z9.7	Foundry Operation	B
Z9.8	Local Ventilation for Laboratories	W
Z9.9	Molten Metals, Excluding Foundry	W
Z9.10	Recirculation and Contaminate Discharge	B
Z9.11	Textile Plants	B
Z9.12	Woodworking	W
Z9.13	Chemical Manufacturing	W
Z9.14	Printing	W
Z9.15	Pharmaceutical Manufacturing	W
Z9.16	Garage and Powered Lift Truck Operators	W
Z12	**Safety Standard for the Prevention of Dust Explosions**	

Scope: The prevention of dust explosions in connection with processes and industries producing combustible or explosive dusts, including measures for the prevention of ignition, restriction of potential damage by proper construction and arrangement of buildings, restriction of the production and escape of dust through the control of dust-producing processes and equipment, extinguishing methods and related features. Fire prevention and extinguishing are included since dust explosions may result from fires. This project covers both safety to life and protection of property.

Secretariat: National Fire Protection Association

Z12.1-1974	Installation and Operation of Pulverized-Fuel Systems, Standard for the (NFPA 60)	A
Z12.2-1974	Starch Factories, Standard for the Prevention of Dust Explosions in (NFPA 61A)	A
Z12.3-1974	Flour and Feed Mills, Standard for the Prevention of Dust Explosions in (NFPA 61C)	A
Z12.4-1974	Grain Elevators & Buik Grain Handling Facilities, Prevention of Fire and Dust Explosions in (NFPA No61B)	A
Z12.5-1974	Agricultural Commodities for Human Consumption, Prevention of Fire & Dust Explosion in the Milling of (NFPA 610-1973)	A

Z12.6-1959(R1970)	Pulverized Sugar and Cocoa, Standard for the Prevention of Dust Explosions in the Production, Packaging and Handling of (NFPA 62)	W
Z12.7-1959(R1969)	Coal Preparation Plants, Standard for the Prevention of Dust Explosions in (NFPA 653)	E
Z12.9-1959(R1969)	Spice Grinding Plants, Standard for the Prevention of Dust Ignitions in (NFPA 656)	E
Z12.11-1974	Manufacture of Aluminum Powder, Standard for the Prevention of Dust Explosions in the (NFPA 651)	A
Z12.12-1972	Sulfur Fires and Explosions, Prevention of (NFPA 655)	B O-1968
Z12.15-1968	Magnesium Powder or Dust, Standard for Explosion and Fire Protection in the Milling of	W
Z12.16-1971	Plastic Industry, Prevention of Dust Explosions in the (NFPA 654)	E
Z12.18-1959(R1970)	Confectionery Manufacturing Plants, Standard for the Prevention of Dust Explosions in (NFPA 657)	W
Z12.19-1975	Aluminum, Processing and Finishing of (NFPA 65)	A
Z12.20-1962(R1969)	Woodworking and Wood Flour Manufacturing Plants, Standard for the Prevention of Dust Explosion (NFPA 664)	E O
Z12.21-1975	Prevention of Dust Explosions in Industrial Plants, Fundamental Principles for the (NFPA 63)	A
Z12.22-1974	Pneumatic Conveying Systems for Handling Feed, Flour, Grain and Other Agricultural Products (NFPA 66)	A

Z16   **Standardization of Methods of Recording and Compiling Accident Statistics**

Scope: To develop standard statistical methods for recording, measuring, and analyzing the accident and injury experience of workers, both on and off the job; and to maintain a procedure for providing the interpretation of these methods as needed.

Secretariats: National Safety Council
American Insurance Association

Z16.1-1967(R1973)	Recording and Measuring Work Injury Experience, Method of	A
Z16.2-1962(R1969)	Method of Recording Basic Facts Relating to Nature and Occurence of Work Injuries	B
Z16.3-1972	Recording and Measuring off-the-job Disabling Accidental Injury Experience of Employees, Method of	A
Z16.4	Uniform Record Keeping for Occupational Injuries and Illnesses	D

Z26   **Specifications and Methods of Test for Safety Glazing Material**

Scope: Specifications and methods of test for safety glazing material (glazing material designed to promote safety and reduce or minimize the likelihood of personal injury from flying glazing material when the glazing material is broken) as used for windshields, windows and partitions of land and marine vehicles and aircraft.

Secretariat: Society of Automotive Engineers

Z26.1-1977	Safety Glazing Materials for Glazing Motor Vehicles Operating on Land Highways (including Z26.1a-1969)	D

Z35   **Specifications for Accident Prevention Signs**

Scope: Design, application and use of warning signs or symbols (other than slogans) intended to indicate, and in so far as

APPENDIX D AMERICAN NATIONAL STANDARDS FOR SAFETY AND HEALTH

possible, to define specific hazards of a nature such that failure to so designate them may cause, or tend to cause, accidental injury to workers, or the public, or both.

Secretariat: National Safety Council

Z35.1-1972	Accident Prevention Signs, Specifications for	A O-1968
Z35.2-1968(R1974)	Accident Prevention Tags, Specifications for	E O-1968
Z35.4-1973	Specifications for Informational Signs Complementary to ANSI Z35.1-1972	A
Z35.5-1974	Biological Hazard Warning Symbols	A
Z35.6	Hazard Pictographs (submitted by the Inter-Industry Advisory Committee on Product Information)	N

Z41 **Performance Requirements for Protective Occupational Footwear**

Scope: Performance requirements and methods of test for protective features of occupational footwear including resistance to impact or pressure, puncture, oil, acid, other chemicals and heat; resistance to slipping; electrial conductivity; and adaption to special exposures. Specifications and methods of test for sandals, creepers, clogs, footguards, outside toe caps and similar protective devices, but not including devices for the protection of the leg.

Secretariat: National Safety Council

Z41(1976 edition)	Safety Toe Footwear (The 4 following standards in one booklet)	
Z41.1-1967(R1972)	Men's Safety-Toe Footwear	A O
Z41.2-1976	Metatarsal Safety-Toe Footwear	D
Z41.3-1976	Conductive Safety Footwear	D
Z41.4-1976	Electrical Hazard Safety-Toe Footwear	D

Z43 **Grinding, Polishing and Buffing Equipment**

Scope: Sanitation in the grinding, polishing, and buffing operations of all ferrous and nonferrous metals.

Proprietary Sponsor: American Foundrymen's Society

Z43.1-1966	Ventilation Control of Grinding, Polishing and Buffing Operations	E O

Z48 **Marking of Compressed Gas Cylinders to Identify Content**

Scope: Specifications for marking portable compressed gas cylinders so that their content may be readily identified to the extent necessary to prevent the probability of explosions or accidents from their misuse.

Secretariat: Compressed Gas Association

Z48.1-1954(R1971)	Portable Compressed Gas Containers to Identify the Material Contained, Method of Marking (CGA 04-54)	C O-1954

Z49 **Safety Welding and Cutting**

Scope: Safety in welding with respect to protection of workers from accidents, occupational diseases and fires arising out of the installation, operation and maintenance of arc and gas welding and cutting equipment.

Secretariat: American Welding Society

Z49.1-1973	Welding and Cutting, Safety in	A O-1967
Z49.2-1975	Cutting and Welding Processes (NFPA 51B)	A

Z50   **Safety Standard for Bakery Equipment**

Scope: Standards for the design, construction, installation, safe operation, and maintenance of bakery machinery, and equipment used within the bakery.

Secretariat: American Society of Bakery Engineers

Z50.1-1971	Bakery Equipment, Safety Requirements for	C O-1971
Z50.1a-1973	Supplement to Z50.1-1971	A

Z53   **Safety Color Code for Marking Physical Hazards**

Scope: Safety color code for defining the application of colors to specific purposes in connection with accident prevention and recommending the colors to be used for such purposes as marking physical hazards, the location of safety equipment and to identify fire and other protective equipment, etc. This code may include standard shapes for colored symbols.

Secretariat: National Safety Council

Z53.1-1971	Marking Physical Hazards and the Identification of Certain Equipment, Safety Color Code for	C O-1967

Z66   **Prevention or Control of Hazards to Children**

Scope: Specifications, tests, and procedures to minimize home hazards to children which might result in physical injury or poisoning.

Secretariat: National Paint and Coatings Association

Z66.1-1964(R1972)	Paints and Coatings Accessible to Children, to Minimize Dry Film Toxicity, Specifications for	A

Z86   **Underwater Safety**

Scope: Standards for safety in skin and SCUBA (self-contained underwater breathing apparatus) diving including breathing apparatus, air containers, air purity, air pumps, float equipment, land equipment, methods of recording accidents, methods of teaching and certifying participants.

Secretariat: Council on National Cooperation in Aquatics

Z86.1-1972	Commodity Specification for Air (GGA G-7.1)	A
Z86.2-1973	Underwater Accident Report Form	A
Z86.3-1972	Minimum Course Content for Safe Scuba Diving Instructions	B
Z86.4-1976	Skin and Scuba Diving Hand Signals	D
Z86.5	Certification of Scuba Sport Diver Instructors	P
Z86.6	Safe Equipment Standards for Scuba Sport Divers	P
Z86.7	Scuba Sport Dive Boat Carrier Standards	B
Z86.8	Scuba Sport Diver's Flag	B

Z87   **Safety Standard for Eye Protection**

Scope: Safety requirements for the protection of faces and eyes of persons exposed to hazards of flying particles, dusts, splashing liquids, molten metals, vapors, and harmful radiation.

Secretariat: National Society for the Prevention of Blindness

Z87.1-1968	Occupational and Education Eye and Face Protection, Practice for	B O

APPENDIX D AMERICAN NATIONAL STANDARDS FOR SAFETY AND HEALTH **517**

Z88 **Safety Standard for Respiratory Protection**

Scope: Safe practices and requirements for using respirators for the protection of the respiratory system from the inhalation of particulate matter, noxious gases and vapors, and from oxygen deficiencies, excluded are:

(1) Underwater Protection
(2) High-altitude aircraft oxygen systems
(3) Protection against military munitions

Although engineered protective measures (for example, ventilation) are not covered, exposure control shall be accomplished as far as is feasible by accepted engineering methods before considering or instituting use of respirators.

Secretariat: Mining Enforcement and Safety Administration

Z88.1-1969	Respiratory Protection Against Radon Daughters, Safety Guide for	E
Z88.2-1969	Practices for Respiratory Protection	B O
Z88.3	Pesticide Respirators	P
Z88.4-1972	Respiratory Protection Against Coal Mine Dust, Safety Guide for	A
Z88.5-1973	Respiratory Protection for the Fire Service	A

Z89 **Safety Standard for Industrial Head Protection**

Scope: Safety requirements for the protection of the heads of occupational workers from impact and electrical shock.

Secretariat: National Constructors Association

Z89.1-1969	Industrial Head Protection, Safety Requirements for	B O
Z89.2-1971	Industrial Protective Helmets for Electrical Workers, Class B, Safety Requirements for	A O
Z89.4	Fire Fighters Head Protection	P

Z90 **Vehicular Head Protection**

Scope: Safety requirements for head protection for automobile drivers engaged in high-hazard activities or occupations, and for motorcyclists.

Secretariat: Snell Memorial Foundation

Z90.1-1971	Protective Headgear for Vehicular Users, Specifications for	B
Z90.1a-1973	Supplement to Z90.1-1971	A
Z90.2-1976	Protective Headgear for Football, Test for Shock Attenuation Characteristics of (ASTM F 429)	D
Z90.3-1977	Safety Standard for Riot Helmets	D

Z97 **Safety Requirements for Architectural Glazing Material**

Scope: Specifications and methods of test for safety glazing material (glazing material designed to promote safety and to reduce or minimize the likelihood of personal injury from flying glazing material when the glazing material is broken) as used for all general construction and architectural purposes.

Secretariat: National Safety Council

Z97.1-1975	Safety Glazing Material Used in Buildings, Performance Specifications and Methods of Test for	A
Z97.2	Safety Glazing Materials Used in Doors in Buildings	N

Z105 **Air and Gas Cleaning Equipment**

Scope: Standards relating to the performance, maintenance, and application of air and gas cleaning equipment or devices used for the treatment of process effluent.

Secretariat: American Industrial Hygiene Association

No American National Standards

Z108 **Method of Recording and Measuring Patron Accident Statistics**

Scope: To develop standard statistical methods for recording, measuring and analyzing the accident and injury experience of patrons (excluding employees) in places of public accommodations.

Secretariat: National Safety Council

Z108.1-1971	Measuring and Recording Patrol and Non-Employee Injury Statistics, Method of	B

Z112 **Installation, Maintenance, and Use of Portable Fire Extinguishers**

Scope: Standards for the installation of portable fire extinguishers and equipment and recommended practices for the maintenance and use of these devices. Does not apply to permanently installed fire extinguishing systems even though portions of those systems are portable, such as hose and nozzles which may be attached to a fixed supply to extinguishing agent.

Proprietary Sponsor: National Fire Protection Association

Z112.1-1976	Portable Fire Extinguishers, Installation of (NFPA 10)	A
Z112.3-1974	Aircraft Hand Fire Extinguishers (NFPA 408)	A
Z112.4-1974	Good Practice for the Maintenance and Use of Portable Fire Extinguishers (NFPA 10A)	A

Z119 **Aircraft Fuel**

Proprietary Sponsor: National Fire Protection Association

Z119.1-1976	Aircraft Fuel Service (NFPA 407)	D
Z119.2-1972	Aircraft Fuel Systems Maintenance (NFPA 410C)	A

Z120 **Fire Protection Standard for Motor Craft (Pleasure and Commerical)**

Proprietary Sponsors: National Fire Protection Association
Underwriters Laboratory

Z120.1-1974	Motor Craft (Pleasure and Commercial) (NFPA 302)	A
Z120.2	Nonintegral Marine Full Tanks (UL 1102)	W

Z129 **Informative Labeling of Hazardous Substances**

Scope: Prepare standard procedures for informative labeling of hazardous substances.

Secretariat: Manufacturing Chemists' Association

Z129.1-1976	Precautionary Labeling of Hazardous Industrial Chemicals	A

APPENDIX D AMERICAN NATIONAL STANDARDS FOR SAFETY AND HEALTH **519**

Z135	**Safety in Professional and Commercial Diving Operations**	

Scope: Standards for safety in professional and commercial diving operations and equipment including but not limited to personnel medical requirements, qualifications and training; techniques, procedures, and practices; and performance requirements, inspection, testing and maintenance of equipment.

Secretariat: Marine Technology Society's Committee on Man's Underwater Activity

Z135.1	Requirements for Commercial Diver Qualifications	B
Z135.2	Specifications for Medical Certification of Diving Personnel	B
Z135.3	Diving Procedures	B
Z135.4	Diving Equipment	B
Z136	**Safe Use of Lasers**	

Scope: Protection against hazards which are created by the use of lasers.

Secretariat: The Telephone Group

Z136.1-1976	Safe Use of Lasers	A
Z137	**Hearing Protection**	

Scope: Performance standards for wearable personal hearing protectors including use, selection, testing, care and maintenance.

Secretariat: National Safety Council

Z137.1	Standard for Occupational and Educational Personal Hearing Protective Devices	B
Z171	**Soda-Acid Fire Extinguishers**	

Proprietary Sponsor: Underwriters Laboratories

Z171.1-1969	Soda-Acid Fire Extinguishers, Safety Standard for (UL 7)	W
Z211	**Classification and Rating of Fire Extinguishers**	

Proprietary Sponsor: Underwriters Laboratories

Z211.1-1973	Safety Standard for the Classification, Rating and Fire Testing of Class A, B, C Fire Extinguishers (UL 71)	A
Z213	**Aircraft Rescue and Fire Fighting Services at Airports, Practice for**	

Proprietary Sponsor: National Fire Protection Association

Z213.1-1976	Aircraft Rescue and Fire Fighting Services at Airports and Heliports (NFPA 403)	D
Z215	**Airport Ramp Fire Hazards Classifications and Precautions**	

Proprietary Sponsor: National Fire Protection Association

Z215.1-1972	Airport Ramp Fire Hazard Classifications and Precautions (NFPA 411)	W

Z216	**Power-Operated Dispensing Devices for Flammable Liquids**	
	Proprietary Sponsor: Underwriters Laboratories	
Z216.1-1975	Power-Operated Dispensing for Flammable Liquids (UL 87)	A
Z218	**Metal Safety Cans**	
	Proprietary Sponsor: Underwriters Laboratories	
Z218.1-1977	Metal Safety Cans (UL 30)	D
Z220	**Fire Detection Thermostats**	
	Proprietary Sponsor: Underwriters Laboratories	
Z220.1-1971	Fire Detection Thermostats, Safety Standard for (UL 52)	E
Z221	**Metal Waste Cans**	
	Proprietary Sponsor: Underwriters Laboratories	
Z221.1-1971(R1976)	Metal Waste Cans (UL 32)	A
Z222	**Flame Arresters**	
	Proprietary Sponsor: Underwriters Laboratories	
Z222.1-1973	Flame Arresters (UL 525)	A
Z226	**Gas Burning Appliances**	
	Proprietary Sponsor: Underwriters Laboratories	
Z226.1-1973	Primary Safety Controls for Gas and Oil-Fired Appliances (UL 372)	D
Z227	**Aircraft Breathing Systems**	
	Proprietary Sponsor: National Fire Protection Association	
Z227.1-1972	Aircraft Breathing Oxygen Systems Maintenance Operations (NFPA 410B)	C
Z229	**Steel Plate Shops**	
	Proprietary Sponsor: American Institute of Steel Construction	
Z229.1-1973	Safety Requirements for Fabricated Structural and Steel Plate Shops	A
Z238	**Water Type Fire Extinguishers**	
	Proprietary Sponsor: Underwriters Laboratories	
Z238.1	Standard for 1 1/2 Gallon Stored-Pressure Water Type Fire Extinguishers (UL 626)	B
Z239	**Cartridge-Operated Water Type Fire Extinguisher**	
	Proprietary Sponsor: Underwriters Laboratories	
Z239.1	Standard for 1 1/2 Gallon Cartridge-Operated Water Type Fire Extinguishers (UL 715)	B
Z240	**Sweeping Compounds**	
	Proprietary Sponsor: Underwriters Laboratories	
Z240.1-1973	Tests for Combustibility of Sweeping Compounds (UL 41)	A

Z241 — Foundry Operations

Proprietary Sponsor: American Foundrymens' Society

Z241.1-1975	Safety Requirements for Sand Preparation, Molding and Core Making in the Sand Foundry Industry	A
Z241.2	Safety Requirements for Melting & Pouring of Metals in the Foundry Industry	B

Z243 — Water Safety Buoyant Devices

Proprietary Sponsor: Underwriters Laboratories

Z243.1-1972	Marine Special Purpose Water Safety Buoyant Devices (UL 1123)	A
Z243.2-1976	Safety Standard for Buoyant Cushions	D

Z244 — Lockout Protection

Scope: Establishes requirements for lockout devices and lockout procedures of all industrial power sources including auxiliary, single and multiple power sources.

Secretariat: National Safety Council

Z244.1	Safety Standard for the Lockout/Tagout of Energy Sources	C

Z245 — Refuse Collection

Scope: Safety requirements for refuse collection operations, including, but not limited to, pickup, handling, loading, unloading, the use of personal protective equipment, and the design of refuse collection equipment including automotive trucks, hand tools, and garbage cans.

Secretariat: Institute for Solid Wastes

Z245.1-1975	Refuse Collection Vehicles	A
Z245.2-1976	Refuse Containers	D

Z247 — Comparative Flammability of Liquids

Proprietary Sponsor: Underwriters Laboratories

Z247.1	Tests for Comparative Flammability of Liquids (UL 340)	B

Z254 — Marine Through-Hull Fittings and Sea Valves

Proprietary Sponsor: Underwriters Laboratories

Z254.1-1973	Safety Standard for Marine Through-Hull Fitting and Sea Valves (UL 1121)	A

Z259 — Paper Bags and Sacks

Proprietary Sponsors: Paper Shipping Sack Manufacturers' Associations
Paper Bag Institute

Z259.1-1974	Minimum Safety and Health Requirements for Paper Bag and Sack Manufacturers	A

Z268 — Metal and Paper Scrap Processing Equipment

Proprietary Sponsor: Institute of Scrap Iron and Steel

Z268.1-1974	Design, Use and Maintenance of Metal Scrap Processing Equipment	A
Z268.1a-1975	Supplement to Z268.1-1974	A

Z271	**Explosive Materials**	
	Proprietary Sponsor: National Fire Protection Association	
Z271.1-1973	Manufacture, Transportation, Storage and Use of Explosive Materials (NFPA 495)	C
Z273	**Standpipe and Hose Systems**	
	Proprietary Sponsor: National Fire Protection Association	
Z273.1-1974	Standpipe and Hose Systems (NFPA 14)	C
Z274	**Foam Water Sprinkler and Spray Systems**	
	Proprietary Sponsor: National Fire Protection Association	
Z274.1-1974	Foam-Water Sprinkler and Spray Systems (NFPA 16)	A
Z275	**Dry Chemical Extinguishing Systems**	
	Proprietary Sponsor: National Fire Protection Association	
Z275.1-1976	Dry Chemical Extinguishing Systems (NFPA 17)	D
Z276	**Wetting Agents**	
	Proprietary Sponsor: National Fire Protection Association	
Z276.1-1974	Standard for Wetting Agents (NFPA 18)	A
Z277	**Centrifugal Fire Pumps**	
	Proprietary Sponsor: National Fire Protection Association	
Z277.1-1976	Standard for Centrifugal Fire Pumps (NFPA 20)	D
Z278	**Water Tanks**	
	Proprietary Sponsor: National Fire Protection Association	
Z278.1-1976	Water Tanks for Private Fire Protection (NFPA 22)	D
Z279	**Spray Application**	
	Proprietary Sponsor: National Fire Protection Association	
Z279.1-1974	Standard for Spray Application (NFPA 33)	A
Z280	**Organic Coatings Manufacture**	
	Proprietary Sponsor: National Fire Protection Association	
Z280.1-1976	Standard for Organic Coatings Manufacture (NFPA 35)	D
Z281	**Solvent Extraction Plants**	
	Proprietary Sponsor: National Fire Protection Association	
Z281.1	Standard for Solvent Extraction Plants (NFPA 36)	C
Z282	**Fireworks**	
	Proprietary Sponsor: National Fire Protection Association	
Z282.1-1975	Manufacture, Transportation, and Store of Fireworks (NFPA 44A)	A
Z283	**Acetylene Cylinder Charging Plants**	
	Proprietary Sponsor: National Fire Protection Association	
Z283.1	Standard for Acetylene Cylinder Charging Plants (NFPA 51A)	C

APPENDIX D AMERICAN NATIONAL STANDARDS FOR SAFETY AND HEALTH **523**

Z284	**Fumigation**	
	Proprietary Sponsor: National Fire Protection Association	
Z284.1-1974	Standard for Fumigation (NFPA 57)	A
Z285	**Explosion Prevention Systems**	
	Proprietary Sponsor: National Fire Protection Association	
Z285.1-1974	Explosion Prevention Systems (NFPA 69)	A
Z286	**Foam Extinguishing Systems**	
	Proprietary Sponsor: National Fire Protection Association	
Z286.1-1976	Foam Extinguishing Systems (NFPA 11)	D
Z286.2-1976	High Expansion Foam Systems (NFPA 11A)	D
Z286.3-1974	Synthetic Foam and Combined Agent Systems (NFPA 11B)	C
Z304	**Home Playground Equipment**	
	Proprietary Sponsor: National Bureau of Standards	
Z304.1-1976	Safety Requirements for Home Playground Equipment	D
Z306	**Football Helmets**	
	Proprietary Sponsor: National Operating Committee for Standards in Athletic Equipment	
Z306.1	Safety Standard for Football Helmets	P
Z307	**Toy Safety**	
	Proprietary Sponsor: National Bureau of Standards	
Z307.1-1977	Toy Safety	D
Z308	**Unit-Type First Aid Kits**	
	Proprietary Sponsor: Industrial Safety Equipment Association	
Z308.1	Minimum Requirements for Unit-Type First Aid Kits	C
Z315	**Tricycles**	
	Proprietary Sponsor: Toy Manufacturers of America	
Z315.1-1976	Safety Standard for Tricycles	D

APPENDIX E
INDEX OF CONSUMER PRODUCT SAFETY COMMISSION STANDARDS
(REGULATIONS IN EFFECT AS OF SEPTEMBER 30, 1977)

Index of Consumer Product Safety Commission (PSC) Standards
(Regulations in effect as of September 30, 1977)

Product	Act*	Type of Regulation	Reference Source Title 16 CFR Part Number
Accompanying literature	HSA	labeling requirements	1500.125
Acetic acid	HSA	labeling	1500.129(g)
Adhesives, contact	HSA	labeling	1500.133
containing methyl alcohol	HSA	exemption from labeling	1500.83(a)(34)
nitrocellulose base	HSA	exemption from labeling	1500.83(a)(10)
floor covering	HSA	exemption from labeling	1500.83(a)(13)
Ammonia, ammonia water (household), ammonia hydroxide	HSA	labeling	1500.129(1)
Ammunition, small-arms	HSA	exemption from labeling	1500.83(a)(6)
Antifreeze, ethylene glycol-base	HSA	labeling	1500.132
	PPPA	special packaging	1700.14(a)(8) and (11)

* HSA Federal Hazardous Substances Act
PPPA Poison Prevention Packaging Act
CPSA Consumer Product Safety Act
FFA Flammable Fabrics Act

APPENDIX E   INDEX OF CONSUMER PRODUCT SAFETY COMMISSION STANDARDS

Antiquing kits	HSA	exemption from labeling	1500.83(a)(25)
Architectural Glazing Materials	CPSA	safety standard	1201
Art materials	HSA	exemption from ban	1500.85(a)(4)
Artists' paints	HSA	exemption from lead limit	1500.17(a)(6)
Asbestos-containing garments for general use	HSA	ban	1500.17(a)(7)
Aspirin products	PPPA	special packaging effervescent tablet exemption powders exemption	1700.14(a)(1) 1700.14(a)(1)(i) 1700.14(a)(1)(ii)
Aspirin and controlled drugs	PPPA	exemption for veterinary drugs and non-oral drugs	1700.14(a)(1,4)
Baby bouncers and walkers	HSA	standard and ban exemption from banning	1500.18(a)(6) 1500.86(a)(4)
Balloons, plastic mixtures	HSA	exemption from banning	1500.85(a)(6)
Batteries, storage, wet-cell	PPPA	exemption from special packaging	1700.14(a)(9)
Benzene (benzol)	HSA	labeling special labeling	1500.14(a)(3) 1500.14(b)(3)(i)

Index of Consumer Product Safety Commission (PSC) Standards *(continued)*

Product	Act	Type of Regulation	Reference Source Title 16 CFR Part Number
Benzene (paint solvents)	PPPA	special packaging	1700.14(a)(15)
Bergamot oil	HSA	labeling	1500.13(e)
Bicycles	HSA	ban	1500.18(a)(12)
		establishment of safety requirements	1512
Biological specimens, preserved	HSA	exemption from ban	1500.85(a)(4)
Blasting caps	HSA	exemption from labeling	1500.83(a)(35)
Butane in cigarette lighters	HSA	exemption from labeling	1500.83(a)(29)
Carbolic acid (Phenol)	HSA	labeling	1500.129(d)
Carbon tetrachloride	HSA	ban	1500.17(a)(2)
Carpets and rugs			
Large	FFA	standard (FF 1-70) regulations	1630.1
Hide rugs		alternate washing procedure	1630.31 – .32
Flokati rugs		alternate washing procedure	1630.61
General		washing procedure	1630.62
Small		standard (FF 2-70) regulations	1630.63
			1631.1
Hide rugs		alternate washing procedure	1631.31 – .34
Flokati rugs		alternate washing procedure	1631.61
			1631.62

APPENDIX E INDEX OF CONSUMER PRODUCT SAFETY COMMISSION STANDARDS 529

Caustic poisons	HSA	labeling	1500.129
potash	HSA/PPPA	labeling/special packaging	1500.129(i)/1700.14(a)(5)
soda	HSA/PPPA	labeling/special packaging	1500.129(i)/1700.14(a)(5)
Cellulose sponges	HSA	exemption from labeling	1500.83(a)(15)
Charcoal briquettes	HSA	special labeling	1500.14(b)(6)
Chemistry sets	HSA	exemption from labeling	1500.83(a)(23)
		exemption from banning	1500.85(a)(1)
Cigarette lighters	HSA	exemption from labeling	1500.83(a)(29)
		exemption from labeling	1500.83(a)(20)
Cleaning products	HSA	exemption from labeling	1500.83(a)(11)
Comment, informal	HSA	proposed labeling	1500.128
Condensation of label information	HSA	labeling	1500.123
Containers, customer owned (portable)	HSA	exemption from labeling	1500.83(a)(14)
fuel (portable)	HSA	exemption from labeling	1500.81(b)
pressurized	HSA	exemption from naming contents, extremely flammable and flammable substances defined	1500.83(a)(1) 1500.3(b)(10),(c)(6)(v),(vi)
		testing method	1500.45

Index of Consumer Product Safety Commission (PSC) Standards *(continued)*

Product	Act	Type of Regulation	Reference Source Title 16 CFR Part Number
self-pressurized	HSA	exemption from labeling	1500.83(a)(1)
		testing method for extremely flammable contents	1500.45,46
		warning statements required	1500.130
size may determine labeling	HSA	exemption from labeling	1500.82
unlabeled	HSA	exemption from labeling	1500.84
Corrosive substances	HSA	definition	1500.3(b)(7),(c)(3)
Cosmetics	HSA	exemption	1500.81(d)
Cribs (full-size)	HSA	ban	1500.18(a)(13)
		establishment of safety requirements	1508
Cribs (non full-size)	HSA	ban	1500.18(a)(14)
		establishment of safety requirements	1509
Cyanide salts	HSA	ban	1500.17(a)(5)
Dietary supplements, Iron containing	PPPA	special packaging	1700.14(a)(13)
Diethylene glycol	HSA	labeling	1500.14(a)(1)
		special labeling	1500.14(b)(1)
		exemption from labeling	1500.83(a)(15)

APPENDIX E   INDEX OF CONSUMER PRODUCT SAFETY COMMISSION STANDARDS   531

Diethylenetriamine	HSA	labeling	1500.13(c)
Diglycidyl ethers	HSA	labeling	1500.13(c)
Disclaimer, deceptive use	HSA	misbranded	1500.122
Drain cleaners, liquid	HSA	ban	1500.17(a)(4)
	PPPA	special packaging	1700.14(a)(5)(9)
Drugs, controlled	PPPA	special packaging	1700.14(a)(14)
oral prescription	PPPA	special packaging	1700.14(1)(10)
aspirin	PPPA	special packaging	1700.14(a)(1)
	HSA	exemption	1500.81(a)
prescription		special packaging	1700.14(a)(10)
Drugs, Iron containing	PPPA	special packaging	1700.14(a)(12)
Dry-cleaning solvents	HSA	exemption from labeling	1500.83(a)(18)
Epoxy resins	HSA	labeling	1500.13(c)
Ethylenediamine	HSA	labeling	1500.13(c)
Ethylene glycol, in felt pads	HSA	exemption from labeling	1500.83(a)(28)
		special labeling	1500.14(b)(4)
		labeling	1500.14(a)(2)

Index of Consumer Product Safety Commission (PSC) Standards *(continued)*

Product	Act	Type of Regulation	Reference Source Title 16 CFR Part Number
Ethylene glycol antifreeze	HSA PPPA HSA	labeling special packaging labeling	1500.14(a)(2),(b)(2) 1700.14(a)(11) 1500.132
Exemption, request for	HSA	labeling, ban	1500.82
Explosives	HSA	pressure-generating substances	1500.3(c)(7)(i)
Extremely flammable contents of pressurized containers	HSA	definition flashpoint testing method	1500.3(i) 1500.46 1500.45
Extremely flammable and flammable solids	HSA	testing method	1500.44
Extremely flammable and flammable substances	HSA	definition testing method	1500.3(g)(3),(j) 1500.41
Eye irritants	HSA	testing method definition	1500.3(b)(8),(c)(4) 1500.42
Felt-tip marking devices	HSA	exemption	1500.83(a)(9)
Ferrous oxalate	HSA	exemption from labeling	1500.83(a)(17)
Fertilizers, dry granular	HSA	exemption from labeling	1500.83(a)(21)

APPENDIX E INDEX OF CONSUMER PRODUCT SAFETY COMMISSION STANDARDS   533

Fire extinguishers	HSA	exemption from labeling	1500.83(a)(24)
		labeling, warning	1500.15(a),(b)
Fireworks	HSA	ban (more than 2 grains pyrotechnic material and audible report)	1500.17(a)(3)
			1500.83(a)(27)
		exemption from labeling	1500.17(a)(3)
		agricultural exemption	1500.85(a)(2)
		exemption from classification	1500.14(b)(7)
		special labeling	
		ban (firecrackers more than 50 mg.)	1500.17(a)8 and 9
		safety requirements	1507
Flammable solids	HSA	testing method	1500.44
		definition	1500.3(k)(2)
Flammable substances	HSA	labeling in self-pressurized containers, exemption	1500.83(a)(1)
		pressurized containers, testing of	1500.45
		testing method	1500.44
volatile	HSA	flashpoint testing method	1500.43
Flashpoint	HSA	testing method	1500.43,46
Food	HSA	exemption from specific labeling	1500.81(a)
Formaldehyde	HSA	labeling	1500.13(d)
Fuel	HSA	exemptions	1500.81(b)

Index of Consumer Product Safety Commission (PSC) Standards *(continued)*

Product	Act	Type of Regulation	Reference Source Title 16 CFR Part Number
Fuel kits with difluorodichloromethane	PPPA	exemption from banning special packaging	1500.85(a)(5) 1700.14(a)(7)
	HSA	exemption from banning warning labels	1500.85(a)(12)(13)
Fuel pellets and ignition fuses	HSA	exemption from banning	1500.85(a)(11)
Furniture polish, liquid	PPPA	special packaging	1700.14(a)(2)
Furniture polish, paste	HSA	exemption from labeling	1500.83(a)(8)
Gasoline	HSA	exemption from labeling special labeling labeling	1500.83(a)(14) 1500.14(b)(3) 1500.14(a)(3)
Glazing compounds	HSA	exemption from labeling	1500.83(a)(13)
Highly toxic substance	HSA	definition testing method labeling	1500.3(e) 1500.40 1500.121
Household substances	HSA	defined	1500.3(c)(10)(i)
Hydrochloric acid	HSA	labeling	1500.129(a)

APPENDIX E INDEX OF CONSUMER PRODUCT SAFETY COMMISSION STANDARDS 535

Hypochlorous acid	HSA	labeling	1500.129(h)
Hartshorn	HSA	labeling	1500.129(i)
Imports	HSA	various	1500.265–272
Industrial supplies	HSA	exemption	1500.3(c)(10)(i)
Ink, cartridges	HSA	exemption from labeling	1500.83(a)(7)
dry concentrate containers	HSA	exemption from labeling	1500.83(a)(12)
Ink-marking devices	HSA	exemption	1500.83(a)(9)
Iron Preparations	PPPA	special packaging	1700.14(a)(12),(13)
Irritant substances	HSA	definition	1500.3(g)
		testing method	1500.3(g)(3)
Isobutane in cigarette lighters	HSA	exemption from labeling	1500.83(a)(29)
Kerosene	HSA	labeling	1500.14(a)(4)
		special labeling	1500.14(b)(3)
		exemption from labeling	1500.83(a)(14)
Kindling and illuminating preparations	PPPA	special packaging	1700.14(a)(7)
		labeling	1500.12(a)(1)
Labels	HSA	requirements	1500.121
		condensation	1500.123

536 PRODUCT SAFETY AND LIABILITY: A DESK REFERENCE

Index of Consumer Product Safety Commission (PSC) Standards *(continued)*

Product	Act	Type of Regulation	Reference Source Title 16 CFR Part Number
Laboratory chemical, educational research or investigational		informal comment on exemption from labeling	1500.83(a)(5)
Lacquers	HSA	exemption from banning and labeling	1500.85(a)(4) 1500.83(a)(5)
Lawn darts	HSA	exemption from labeling	1500.83(a)(13)
Lead in paint	HSA	ban criteria for exemption from banning	1500.18(a)(4) 1500.86(a)(3)
	HSA	ban, over 0.5% limit ban, over .06% limit	1500.17(a)(6)(i)(B) 1500.17(a)(6)(i)(A)
Lighter fluid, etc.	PPPA	special packaging	1700.14(a)(7)
Literature, accompanying	HSA	labeling requirements	1500.125
Lunar caustic (silver nitrate)	HSA	labeling	1500.129(k)
Lye	HSA PPPA	labeling special packaging	1500.129(j) 1700.14(a)(5)
Matches	HSA	exemption from labeling	1500.83(a)(2)

APPENDIX E INDEX OF CONSUMER PRODUCT SAFETY COMMISSION STANDARDS 537

Mattresses	FFA	standard (FF 4-72), as amended		1632.1
		alternate sampling plan	1	1632.11
			2	1632.12
			4	1632.13
			5	1632.14
			6	1632.15
		regulations		1632.31
		tape edge verification procedure		1632.61
		muslin sheets		1632.62
		renovation of mattresses		1632.63
Methyl alcohol (methanol)	HSA	exemption from labeling		1500.83(a)(10)
		labeling		1500.14(a)(4),(b)(4)
		exemption from labeling		1500.83(a)(19)
		exemption from labeling		1500.83(a)(34)
	PPPA	special packaging		1700.14(a)(8)
Methyl salicylate	PPPA	special packaging		1700.14(a)(3)
Mineral oil (in toys)	HSA	exemption from labeling		1500.83(a)(33)
Mineral seal oil	HSA	labeling		1500.14(a)(3)
		special labeling		1500.14(b)(3)
	PPPA	special packaging		1700.14(a)(2)
Mineral spirits	HSA	labeling		1500.14(a)(3)
		special labeling		1500.14(b)(3)
Minor hazards	HSA	exemption		1500.82,83
Mixtures of hazardous substances	HSA			1500.5

Index of Consumer Product Safety Commission (PSC) Standards *(continued)*

Product	Act	Type of Regulation	Reference Source Title 16 CFR Part Number
Multiple hazard, substances with	HSA	labeling	1500.127
Naphtha	HSA	labeling special labeling	1500.14(a)(3) 1500.14(b)(3)
Nitric acid	HSA	labeling	1500.129(c)
Nitroglycerine, prescription, sublingual dosage	PPPA	exemption from special packaging	1700.14(a)(10)
Orris root, powdered	HSA	labeling	1500.13(b)
Oxalic acid and salts of	HSA	labeling	1500.129(e)(f)
Packages, sample	PPPA	submission	1700.14(b)
Paint, lead in	HSA	ban, over 0.5% limit ban, over 0.06% limit	1500.17(a)(6)(i)(B) 1500.17(a)(6)(i)(A)
varnish, adhesive thinner viscous	HSA HSA HSA	exemption from labeling special labeling exemption from labeling	1500.83(a)(13) 1500.14(a)(4) 1500.83(a)(13)
Paint and similar surface coating solvents	PPPA	special packaging	1700.14(a)(15)

APPENDIX E INDEX OF CONSUMER PRODUCT SAFETY COMMISSION STANDARDS **539**

Painting kits	HSA	exemption	1500.83(a)(25)
Paper items	HSA	exemption from labeling; list	1500.83(a)(3)
Paraphenylenediamine	HSA	labeling	1500.13(a)
Perchlorethylene in visual novelties	HSA	exemption from labeling	1500.83(a)(31)
Percussion explosives	HSA	definition	1500.3(c)(7)(i)(A)
Petroleum distillates	HSA	labeling	1500.14(a)(3)
		special labeling	1500.14(b)(3)
		exemption from labeling	1500.83(a)(8),(9),(11),(13),(14),(20)
	PPPA		1700.14(a)(7),(2),(15)
Phenol (carbolic acid)	HSA	labeling	1500.129(d)
Photodynamic sensitizer	HSA	definition	1500.3(b)(9)
Photographic color processing kits	HSA	exemption from labeling	1500.83(a)(25)
Plant foods, dry granular	HSA	exemption from labeling	1500.83(a)(21)
"Poisons," caustic	HSA	labeling requirements	1500.129
Polishing products	HSA	exemption from labeling	1500.83(a)(11)
Potash, caustic	HSA	labeling	1500.129(i)
	PPPA	special packaging	1700.14(a)(5)

Index of Consumer Product Safety Commission (PSC) Standards (continued)

Product	Act	Type of Regulation	Reference Source Title 16 CFR Part Number
Potassium hydroxide	HSA	labeling	1500.129(i)
	PPPA	special packaging	1700.14(a)(5)
Pressure generating substances	HSA	definition	1500.3(c)(7)(i)
Primary irritant	HSA	definition	1500.3(g)(2)
		testing method	1500.41
Propellant devices for model rockets	HSA	exemption from banning	1500.85(a)(8),(9),(12),(13)
Radiator cleaners	HSA	as household substance	1500.3(c)(10)(i)
Radioactive substances	HSA	defined exemption	1500.3(b)(11),(c)(8)
Refrigerator, doors	RSA	standard to permit opening from inside	1750
Roof coatings	HSA	exemption from labeling	1500.83(a)(13),(34)
Rugs (see carpets)			
Rubber vulcanizing preparations	HSA	exemption from labeling	1500.83(a)(13)
Salt (sodium chloride)	HSA	exemption from labeling	1500.83(a)(16)

APPENDIX E INDEX OF CONSUMER PRODUCT SAFETY COMMISSION STANDARDS **541**

Self pressurized containers	HSA	exemptions from labeling	1500.83(a)(1)
Sensitizers	HSA	definitions	1500.3(b)(9),(c)(5)
Signal words	HSA	labeling requirements	1500.121
Silver Nitrate (lunar caustic)	HSA	labeling	1500.129(k)
Sleepwear, children's sizes 0–6X	FFA	standard (FF 3–71), as amended regulations interpretations and policies	1615.1 1615.31 1615.61 – .63
sizes 7-14		standard (FF 5–74) regulations interpretations and policies	1616.1 1616.31 1616.61 – .64
Sodium arsenite	HSA	labeling	1500.132(b)
Sodium hydroxide	HSA	labeling	1500.129(j)
Sodium/potassium hydroxide	PPPA	special packaging	1700.14(a)(5)
Solder kit	HSA	exemption from labeling	1500.83(a)(30)
Solder paste	HSA	exemption from labeling	1500.83(a)(22)
Special hazards	HSA	additional labeling special labeling	1500.126 1500.14(b)

Index of Consumer Product Safety Commission (PSC) Standards *(continued)*

Product	Act	Type of Regulation	Reference Source Title 16 CFR Part Number
Special packaging	PPPA	standards re-use prohibited test procedure restricted flow requirement	1700.15 1700.15(c) 1700.20 1700.15(d)
Spot removers, single-use	HSA	exemption from labeling	1500.83(a)(18),(19),(26)
Spot removing kits	HSA	exemption from labeling	1500.83(a)(25)
Sponges, cellulose	HSA	exemption from labeling	1500.83(d)(15)
Stoddard solvent	HSA	labeling special labeling	1500.14(a)(4) 1500.14(b)(3)(ii)
Strong sensitizers	HSA	definition	1500.3(i)
Sulfuric acid	HSA PPPA	labeling special packaging list of	1500.129(b) 1700.14(a)(9) 1500.13
Swimming pool slides	CPSA	safety standard	1207
Tank coatings	HSA	exemption from labeling	1500.83(a)(34)

APPENDIX E INDEX OF CONSUMER PRODUCT SAFETY COMMISSION STANDARDS 543

Thread, string, twine, etc.	HSA	exemption from labeling	1500.93(a)(4)
Toluene (toluol)	HSA	labeling	1500.14(a)(3)
		special labeling	1500.14(b)(3)(ii),(iii)
		exemption from labeling	1500.83(a)(8),(9),(11),(9),(11),(13)
			1500.3(b)(5),(c)(2)
Toluene (paint solvents)	PPPA	special packaging	1700.14(a)(15)
Toxic substances	HSA	definition, labeling, testing method	1500.3(f) .129,.121
Toys			
caps and toy guns producing impulse-type sound	HSA	ban	1500.18(a)(5)
		testing method	1500.47
		exemption from banning	1500.85(a)(2), .86(a)(6)
clacker balls	HSA	ban	1500.18(a)(7)
		exemption from banning	1500.86(a)(5)
dolls presenting laceration hazards	HSA	ban	1500.18(a)(3)
		exemption from banning	1500.86(a)(2)
electrically operated toys and children's articles	HSA	ban	1500.18(b)
		requirements	1505
		labeling	1505.3
		performance	1505.6
games	HSA	exemption from banning	1500.85(a)(7)
hollow plastic toys with mineral oil	HSA	exemption from labeling	1500.83(a)(32)
mechanical hazards (various)	HSA	ban	1500.18(a)

Index of Consumer Product Safety Commission (PSC) Standards *(continued)*

Product	Act	Type of Regulation	Reference Source Title 16 CFR Part Number
noisemaking	HSA	ban	1500.18(a)(2)
painted	HSA	ban, over 0.5% lead limit	1500.17(a)(6)(ii)(B)
		ban, over 0.06% lead limit	1500.17(a)(6)(ii)(A)
rattles	HSA	ban	1500.18(a)(1)
		criteria for exemption from banning	1500.86(a)(1)
model rockets	HSA	exemption from labeling	1500.83(a)(36)
model rockets propellant devices	HSA	exemption from banning	1500.85(a)(8)(9), (10),(11),(12),(13)
sewing machines	HSA	requirements	1505.4(h)(3)
stuffed animals with laceration hazards	HSA	ban	1500.18(a)(3)
train smoke	HSA	exemption from labeling	1500.83(a)(33)
Turpentine (gum, gum spirits of, wood)	HSA	special labeling	1500.14(b)(5)
		labeling	1500.14(a)(5)
		exemption	1500.83(a)(8)
	PPPA	special packaging	1700.14(a)(6)
Tubes, collapsible metal	HSA	labeling	1500.121(e)
Unpackaged hazardous substances	HSA	labeling requirements	1500.121(f)
Varnish	HSA	exemption from labeling	1500.83(a)(13)
Vienna paste	HSA	labeling	1500,129(i)
Vinyl plastic film	FFA	standard regulations	1611.1 – .4 1611.31 – .39

APPENDIX E   INDEX OF CONSUMER PRODUCT SAFETY COMMISSION STANDARDS   545

Visual novelty devices containing perchloroethylene	exemption	HSA	1500.83(a)(31)
Volatile flammable materials	flashpoint testing method	HSA	1500.43
Walker-jumper	ban exemption from classification	HSA	1500.18(a)(6) 1500.86(a)(4)
Water-repellant mixtures, masonry	ban	HSA	1500.17(a)(1)
Wax containers	exemption from labeling	HSA	1500.83(a)(8)
Waxes, paste for autos, furniture, floors, shoes	exemption from labeling	HSA	1500.83(a)(8)

Wearing apparel	standard
	  CS 191–53
	  regulations
	clarification of standard
	  CS 191–53
	  standard
	  CS 192–53
	  regulations
		FFA	1610.1
			1610.31 – .39
			
			1610.61
			
			1611.1 – .4
			1611.31 – .39

Xylene (xylol)	Labeling special labeling exemption from labeling	HSA	1500.14(a)(3) 1500.14(b)(3)(ii),(iii) 1500.83(a)(8), (9),(11),(13)
Xylene (paint solvents)	special packaging	PPPA	1700.14(a)(15)

APPENDIX F
FEDERAL RECORD-RETENTION REQUIREMENTS RELATED TO PRODUCT SAFETY AND LIABILITY

The material in this appendix is based on federal regulations in force January 1, 1977, as compiled in the "Guide to Retention Requirements" published in the *Federal Register* of June 7, 1977. For the purposes of this book, two types of retention requirements were listed: (1) direct safety-related regulations, such as records of suppliers of safety equipment or critical subassemblies; and (2) federally required records for certain types of accidents, inspections, and manufacturing operations. The latter records should prove useful to companies directly involved in litigation (to determine, for instance, existing industry practice and accident rates) or, in some cases, to designers trying to calculate costs and benefits of various design changes.

The list is arranged alphabetically by name of the federal agency responsible for the regulation. The Occupational Safety and Health Administration, for instance, would be listed under the Labor Department.

See Chap. III, Sec. 8, for more details on state and local requirements.

DEPARTMENT OF AGRICULTURE

Animal and Plant Health Inspection Service

Research investigators or research sponsors administering experimental biological products to animals.

To maintain adequate records relative to the disposition of each animal administered experimental biological products. Such records include name and address of owner, pertinent data about animals and their location, and, if sold, name and address of purchaser.

Retention period: At least 2 years from the date that an experimental product was administered to such animal. 9 CFR 103.2

Research facilities, exhibitors, operators of auction sales, and dealers engaged in transportation, sale, and handling of certain warm-blooded animals used for research, exhibition, or pet purposes.

To keep records with respect to the purchase, sale, transportation, identification, and previous ownership.

Retention period: 2 years or longer as may be required by any Federal, State, or local law. 9 CFR 2.75–2.78 (retention: 2.79)

DEPARTMENT OF COMMERCE

Economic Development Administration

Technical assistance and research contractors and subcontractors.

To maintain (a) progress control records reflecting acquisition, work progress, expenditures and commitments indicating relationship to established costs and schedules; and (b) written financial records establishing compliance to requirement of the act and terms and conditions of contract or subcontract.

Retention period: At least 3 years after final payment. 13 CFR 307.17

Recipients of financial assistance (including contractors and subcontractors).

To maintain financial records of amount and disposition of funds, total cost of project or undertaking, amount and nature of portion of cost supplied by other sources; and such other records as will facilitate an effective audit.

Retention period: 3 years after date of final expenditure or, for projects renewed annually, after date of submission of annual expenditure report except (a) until audit findings are resolved; (b) 3 years after final disposition of nonexpendable personal property; (c) 3 year retention requirement is not applicable if records are transferred to or maintained by EDA. 13 CFR 305.96, 390.9

National Oceanic and Atmospheric Administration

Persons with permits to engage in activities involving the endangered wildlife species.

To maintain records of any taking, possession, transportation, sale, purchase, barter, exportation, or importation, including names and addresses of persons involved in such transaction, date of transaction, and such other information as may be required.

Retention period: 5 years. 50 CFR 220.46

DEPARTMENT OF DEFENSE

Department of the Air Force

Persons needing further information about listed record retention requirements should contact the following:

Mr. H. Hughes, Headquarters United States Air Force/LGPM, Washington, D.C. 20330. Telephone: 202-695-6969.

DEPARTMENT OF ENERGY

Cost-type contractors.

To keep justifications in support of subcontracts and purchase orders adequate to reflect the procurement practices and procedures used and the circumstances supporting particular transactions.

Retention period: Not specified, 41 CFR 9-55.204

Contractors whose contract contains the safety, health, and fire protection clause prescribed in 41 CFR 9-7.-5004-12. [Amended]

To maintain individual occupational radiation exposure records generated in performance of contract work.

Retention period: Until disposal is specifically authorized by the Administration; or at the option of the contractor delivered to the Administration upon completion or termination of the contract. 41 CFR 9-7.5006-60

Cost-type contractors and subcontractors.

To maintain records in accordance with the provisions of their contract or subcontract.

Retention period: Various. 41 CFR 9-7.5006-1 (ERDA Manual Chapter Appendix 0230 contains established retention periods for more than 900 record items of cost-type contractors and subcontractors.)

DEPARTMENT OF HEALTH, EDUCATION, AND WELFARE

Food and Drug Administration

Persons introducing shipment or delivery of unlabeled food, drugs and devices, and cosmetics into interstate commerce and operators of establishments processing, labeling, and repacking.

To keep written agreements containing such specifications as will insure that such food, drugs and devices, and cosmetics will not be adulterated or misbranded upon completion of such processing, labeling, or repacking.

Retention period: 2 years after final shipment or delivery of such commodities from such establishment. 21 CFR 201.-150, 701.9, 801.150

Commercial processors manufacturing, processing, or packing low-acid foods. [*Amended*]

To maintain (a) complete records covering all aspects of the establishment of the process and associated incubation tests; and (b) processing and production records as specified in sections cited.

Retention period: (a) Permanent; (b) not less than 1 year at the processing plant; and at the processing plant or other accessible location for 2 more years. 21 CFR 507.83, 507.110, 508.35

Distributors of veterinary drugs.

To maintain records of each shipment and other delivery (including exports) of each certified batch or part thereof, showing date and quantity of each shipment or delivery, and name and address of person to whom shipped or delivered.

Retention period: 3 years. 21 CFR 510.350

Suppliers of food flavor certifications. [*Amended*]

To maintain certificates relating to food flavor labeling.

Retention period: At least 3 years. 21 CFR 501.22

Packers of processed shrimp and canned oysters operating under the seafood inspection service.

To keep shipping records covering shipments from each lot of inspected seafood.

Retention period: At least 2 years. 21 CFR 85.9, 85.24

Sponsors, investigators, and shippers of new drugs and antibiotic drugs for investigational use; and investigational review committees.

To maintain records of (a) each shipment and delivery and disposition of each new or antibiotic drug; and (b) documents relating to membership, study discussions, resolutions, etc. of review committees.

Retention period: (a) 2 years after shipment and delivery; (b) 3 years after completion or discontinuance of study. 21 CFR 312.1, 312.9, 312.10, 433.17, 511.1

Persons introducing shipment or delivery of antibiotic drugs into interstate commerce; operators of establishments processing, labeling, storing, repacking, and manufacturing antibiotic drugs; and persons requesting certification of antibiotic drugs.

(a) To keep complete records of all shipments and deliveries of each batch or part thereof.

Retention period: 3 years from date of shipment or delivery and/or receipt of same. 21 CFR 431.61, 433.12–433.16

Photostatic or other permanent reproductions may be used as substitutes for records identified in this section after the first 2 years of retention. 21 CFR 431.62, 433.30

Persons petitioning for exemption from certification for antibiotic drugs intended for local or topical use.

To keep records of all laboratory tests and assays required as a condition for certification on each batch produced and of all shipments and deliveries of each batch or part thereof.

Retention period: 3 years after date of shipment or delivery. 21 CFR 433.1

Photostatic or other permanent reproduction may be substituted for such records after the first 2 years of the holding period. 21 CFR 433.30

Insulin distributors to whom certifications have been issued by the Food and Drug Administration.

To keep records of shipments and deliveries.
    Retention period: 2 years after disposal of all the batch covered by the certificate. 21 CFR 429.60

Dairy farms and plants at which any milk or cream is pasteurized for shipment or transportation into the United States.

To keep all thermograph charts.
    Retention period: 2 years, unless within that period the charts are examined and released by authorized agent of the Secretary. 21 CFR 1210.15

Persons manufacturing, processing, packing, or holding finished pharmaceuticals.

To maintain batch production and control records for each batch of drugs; data concerning laboratory tests performed; records of the distribution of each batch of drug in a manner that will facilitate its recall if necessary; and written and oral complaints regarding the drug.
    Retention period: 2 years after the distribution of the drug has been completed or 1 year after the expiration of the drug, whichever is longer. 21 CFR 211.58, 211.101, 211.110, 211.115

Persons to whom color-additive certificates have been issued by the Food and Drug Administration.

To keep complete and separate records showing the disposal of all the color additive from the batch covered by such certificates.
    Retention period: At least 2 years after disposal of all such color additive. 21 CFR 8.26

Persons delivering for introduction or introducing into interstate commerce a color additive or a food, drug, or cosmetic containing such an additive, for investigational use.

To maintain complete records of each shipment and delivery.
    Retention period: 2 years after such shipment and delivery. 21 CFR 8.33

Manufacturers or distributors shipping new drug substances intended for hypersensitivity testing.

To maintain records of all shipments for this purpose.
    Retention period: 2 years after shipment. 21 CFR 310.103

Persons treating food with low dose electron beam radiation.

To keep a record of the radiation intensity and power used by means of recorders coupled to the electron accelerator. The record shall identify the food that has been subjected to the radiation.
    Retention period: Permanent; 1 year for Food and Drug Administration inspection. 21 CFR 121.3007

Manufacturers, packers, distributors, and shippers of antibiotic drugs for human release.

To maintain such records as specified in section cited to facilitate determination whether such certificate or release should be rescinded or whether any regulations should be amended or repealed.
    Retention period: Not specified. 21 CFR 431.60

Persons holding approved new-drug applications.

To maintain records necessary to facilitate a determination whether there may be grounds for invoking section 505(e) of the Federal Food, Drug, and Cosmetic Act (21 U.S.C. 355(e)) to suspend or withdraw approval of the application.
    Retention period: Not specified. 21 CFR 310.300, 310.303

Manufacturers, processors, packers, and holders of medicated feeds. [Amended]

To maintain (a) receipt and inventory records of drug components; (b) production records; (c) Master Record File; (d) laboratory control records on results of assays; (e) records of action taken when results of assays indicate a problem; (f) proofread labels; (g) distribution records; and (h) records of complaints and action taken and, for certain feeds, records and reports of clinical and other experience with the drug.
    Retention period: (a)–(d) 1 year; (e) not specified; (f) 1 year; (g) 1 year; (h) not specified. 21 CFR 225.42, 225.58, 225.80, 225.102, 225.110, 225.115

APPENDIX F FEDERAL RECORD-RETENTION REQUIREMENTS 551

Manufacturers, processors, packers, and holders of smoked and smoke-flavored fish.

To maintain records providing positive identification of the process procedures used for the manufacture of hot-process smoked or hot-process smoke-flavored fish and of the distribution of the finished product.
Retention period: Not specified. 21 CFR 128a.7(e)(5)

Manufacturers, processors, packers, and holders of medicated premixes for use in the manufacture of medicated feeds.

To maintain receipt and inventory records of any drug components used; batch production and control records; results of assays; distribution records; and oral and written complaints concerning safety and efficacy of each premix.
Retention period: 2 years. 21 CFR 226.42, 226.58, 226.102, 226.110, 226.115

Manufacturers, processors, packers, and repackers of human foods.

To maintain records of coding of food products.
Retention period: The shelf life of the product, except not longer than 2 years. 21 CFR 128.7(i)

Commercial processors manufacturing, processing, or packing cacao products and confectionary.

To maintain records of results of examinations of raw materials, packaging materials, and finished products; suppliers' guarantees; processing and production records; initial distribution records.
Retention period: Exceed shelf life of finished product, except that records need not be retained more than 2 years. 21 CFR 128c.8

Manufacturers, bottled drinking water.

To maintain records of government agency approval of water source; sampling and analysis performed by plant; physical inspection of water treatment equipment, mechanical washers, and sanitizing operations.
Retention period: 2 years. 21 CFR 128d.5, 18-28d.7

Manufacturers of impact-resistant lenses for glasses and sunglasses.

To maintain records of sale, distribution, and results of tests conducted on impact-resistant lenses.
Retention period: 3 years. 21 CFR 201.410

Licensed domestic and foreign manufacturing establishments of biological products.

To keep records concurrently with performance of each step in the manufacture and distribution of each lot; complete records of recall from distribution; sterilization records including date, duration, temperature, and other conditions relating to each sterilization, so as to identify the particular process to which the sterilization relates; animal necropsy records; and records by each establishment participating in manufacture of a product showing degree of individual responsibility with manufacturer preparing product in final form to retain complete records of all manufacturing operations.
Retention period: 5 years after the records of manufacture have been completed or 6 months after the latest expiration date, whichever is later.
Suspension of retention requirements: If a summary is retained, authorization may be granted to suspend retention of records of a manufacturing step upon a showing that such records no longer serve the purpose for which they were made. 21 CFR 600.12

Food manufacturers and processors of mislabeled food products sold to institutions operated by Federal, State or local governments. [Amended]

To retain signed statements of purchasers that acknowledge nature and extent of mislabeling.
Retention period: 2 years after date of shipment. 21 CFR 501.105

Manufacturers of certain electronic products.

To maintain (a) description of the quality control procedures with respect to electronic product radiation safety; (b) record of the results of tests for electronic product radiation safety; (c) for products that display aging effects which may increase radiation emission, records of the results of tests for durability of the product, and the basis for selecting the tests; (d) copies of all pertinent written communications; (e) records of the manufacturer's distribution of products; and (f) records received from dealers or distributors pursuant to § 1002.41.

Retention period: 5 years from the date of the record. 21 CFR 1002.30 (retention: 1002.31)

Dealers and distributors of certain electronic products.

To maintain, for products for which the retail price is not less than $50.00, information as necessary to permit tracing of specific products to specific purchasers.

Retention period: 5 years from the date of sale, award, or lease of such product. 21 CFR 1002.40, 1002.41

Manufacturers, packers, distributors, and retailers promoting retail sales promotions.

To maintain invoices and other records relating to "cents-off" coupons or other savings representations and to package size savings.

Retention period: 1 year subsequent to end of year in which promotion occurs. 21 CFR 1.1d, 1.1e

Hospitals and other authorized dispensers of methadone.

To maintain clinical record for each patient showing dates, quantity, and batch or code mark of drug dispensed.

Retention period: 3 years. 21 CFR 310.505

Manufacturers of methadone.

To maintain signed invoices of methadone delivered to licensed practitioner.

Retention period: Not specified. 21 CFR 310.505

Persons introducing or moving food shipments into interstate commerce who are not the original processors or packers. [Amended]

To keep records of agreements with operators of food processing establishments, signed by and containing the post office addresses of such persons and such operators, and containing specifications for the processing, labeling, or repacking to insure that such food will not be adulterated or misbranded upon completion of such processing, labeling, or repacking.

Retention period: 2 years after date of final shipment or delivery from the establishment. 21 CFR 501.100

Manufacturers or persons employing food additive amino acids to improve the protein value of food.

To keep and maintain records of tests of effectiveness.

Retention period: During period of use of the additive(s) and for 3 years thereafter. 21 CFR 121.1002

Sponsors of approved new animal drug applications.

To maintain full reports of information pertinent to the safety or effectiveness of new animal drugs not previously submitted as part of approved applications.

Retention period: Not specified. 21 CFR 510.300, 510.301

Manufacturers, packers, and distributors of cosmetic products.

To maintain all correspondence and records pertaining to alleged cosmetic product injuries.

Retention period: 3 years. 21 CFR 730.4

Collectors and processors of whole blood (human) collected from human donors for transfusion to human recipients.

To maintain a manual of standard procedures and methods to be followed by employees to determine suitability of donors, and to maintain records of names and qualifications of persons in charge of employees who determine the suitability of donors when a physician is not present.

Retention period: Not specified. 21 CFR 600.12, 640.3

Manufacturers of source plasma (human).

To keep separate and complete records for donors of all initial and periodic examinations, tests, laboratory data, interviews, etc., including donors' written consent for participation in the plasmapheresis program and certifications of good health.
   Retention period: Not specified. 21 CFR 600.12, 640.69

Collectors and processors of whole blood (human) collected from human donors and processed for transfusion or further manufacturing.

To maintain records on compatibility testing, adverse reactions, collection, processing, storage and distribution of each unit as specified in sections cited.
   Retention period: 5 years after records of processing have been completed or 6 months after latest expiration date for individual product, whichever is later. When there is no expiration date, records shall be retained indefinitely. 21 CFR 606.151, 606.160, 606.165, 606.170

Establishments licensed for Source Plasma (Human). [Added]

To maintain results of certain laboratory tests for review by a licensed physician or by an authorized representative of the Food and Drug Administration.
   Retention period: Not specified. 21 CFR 640.71(b)(1)

Plasmapheresis centers. [Added]

To maintain records documenting shipping temperatures for source plasma (human) intended for manufacture into injectable products; maintain records concerning donors; maintain distribution records of plasma found reactive to a serologic test for syphilis.
   Retention period: Not specified. 21 CFR 640.72

Plasma derivative manufacturer. [Added]

To maintain records of source plasma (human) that has been stored or shipped at unacceptable temperatures. Records shall identify the units involved, their disposition, and shall explain the conditions that caused the accidental temperature exposure.
   Retention period: Not specified. 21 CFR 640.76

Manufacturers of cholera vaccine. [Added]

To maintain records of the results of potency testing of the vaccine in mice.
   Retention period: Not specified. 21 CFR 620.33(d)

Persons needing further information about listed record retention requirements should contact the following:
John A. Richards, Federal Register Writer, (HFC–11), 5600 Fishers Lane, Rockville, MD 20857. Telephone: 301–443–2994.

Public Health Service*

Importers of nonhuman primates.

To maintain records relating to number of primates imported, countries of origin, species, dates of importation, dates of shipment to other persons or organizations, disease incidence, and such other information as may be requested by the Director, Center for Disease Control.
   Retention period: Not specified. 42 CFR 71.185

DEPARTMENT OF HOUSING AND URBAN DEVELOPMENT

Office of the Secretary

Agencies designing, constructing or altering publicly-owned residential structures.

To maintain records relating to each contract, grant, or loan involving such publicly-owned residential structures.
   Retention period: Not specified. 24 CFR 40.6

*For Food, Drug and Cosmetic Act regulations applicable to products licensed under the Public Health Service Act, see Food and Drug Administration.

Developers of new communities.

To maintain records of costs incurred for the project, including those of contractors and subcontractors.
    Retention period: Not specified. 24 CFR 710.22

Office of Assistant Secretary for Policy Development and Research

Contractors and subcontractors with research and development contracts.

To maintain books, records, documents and other supporting evidence relating to the contract and such other records as specified in 41 CFR 1-20.301–1-20.301-3.
    Retention period: Various. 41 CFR Part 1-20

DEPARTMENT OF THE INTERIOR

Fish and Wildlife Service

Persons engaged in wildlife activities.

To maintain records of any taking, possession, transportation, sale, purchase, barter, exportation, or importation of wildlife pursuant to permit. Records to include date, names and addresses of persons involved in such transaction, and such other information as may be required.
    Retention period: 5 years from date of issuance of permit. 50 CFR 13.46

Mining Enforcement and Safety Administration*

Operators of metal and nonmetal mines.

To maintain records of instruction on fire alarms signals and procedures.
    Retention period: 2 years. 30 CFR 55.4, 56.4, 57.4

Operators of metal and nonmetal mines.

To maintain written records of investigations of accidents and a copy of report relating thereto.
    Retention period: 3 years from date of accident, 30 CFR 58.23, 58.31

Operators of underground coal mines. [Amended]

To maintain records of tests, examinations, and inspections required by mandatory safety standards.
    Retention period: Not specified. 30 CFR 75.1800–75.1808

Operators of underground coal mines. [Amended]

To maintain a list of all certified and qualified persons designated to perform duties under 30 CFR Parts 75 and 77.
    Retention period: Not specified. CFR 75.159, 77.106

Operators of coal mines.

To maintain (a) written records of investigations of accidents and (b) a copy of report relating thereto.
    Retention period: (a) 5 years from date of the accident, 30 CFR 80.22, 80.23; (b) 5 years from date of occurrence, 30 CFR 80.31

Bureau of Mines

State agencies, organizations, institutions (public and private), or individuals receiving Federal grants for solid waste disposal projects, health and safety programs in coal mines, and research. [Amended]

(a) To maintain books of account and supporting papers of financial transactions involving Federal grants and those financed with matching funds from other sources.

---

*Enforcement of the Mine Safety Act has been transferred to the Occupational Safety and Health Administration in the Department of Labor.

(b) To maintain accountability record of all property items with expected life of more than 1 year and acquisition cost of $100 or more.
Retention period: (a) 3 years after last payment to grantee; (b) not specified. 30 CFR 651.8

Persons needing further information about listed record retention requirements should contact the following:
Victor E. Traver, Bureau of Mines, 2401 E Street N.W., Washington, DC 20241. Telephone 202–634–1571.

DEPARTMENT OF JUSTICE

Manufacturers, distributors, dispensers, researchers, importers, exporters, and chemical analysts subject to the Controlled Substances Import and Export Act.

To maintain records and inventories of each substance manufactured, imported, received, sold, delivered, exported, or disposed of in accordance with Part 1304.
Retention period: 2 years. 21 CFR 1304.03, 1304.11–1304.29, 1308.24 (retention: 1304.04)

DEPARTMENT OF LABOR
Employment Standards Administration

Physicians and hospitals treating Federal employees covered by the Federal Employees' Compensation Act.

To keep records of all injury cases treated by them sufficient to supply the Office of Federal Employees' Compensation with a history of the employee's accident, the exact description, nature, location and extent of injury, the degree of disability arising therefrom, the X-ray findings if X-ray examination has been made, the nature of the treatment rendered, and the degree of disability arising from the injury.
Retention period: Not specified. 20 CFR 10.410

Employers subject to the provisions of the Longshoremen's and Harbor Workers' Compensation Act, as extended by the Defense Base Act, the District of Columbia Workmen's Compensation Act, the Outer Continental Shelf Lands Act, and the Nonappropriated Fund Instrumentalities Act.

To keep records in respect to any injury to an employee, including information of disease, other disability, or death.
Retention period: Not specified. 20 CFR 702.111

Insurance carriers and self-insured employers subject to Longshoremen's and Harbor Workers' Compensation Act, as extended by the District of Columbia Workmen's Compensation Act, the Defense Base Act, the Outer Continental Shelf Lands Act, and the Nonappropriated Fund Instrumentalities Act.

To make, keep, and preserve such records as the Secretary deems necessary or appropriate to carry out his responsibilities under section 44.
Retention period: Not specified. 20 CFR 702.148

Operators subject to Part C of Title IV, Federal Coal Mine Health and Safety Act, as amended.

To keep receipts for payments made to disabled miners, or in case of death, his dependents or personal representative.
Retention period: Not specified. 20 CFR 725.336

Persons needing further information about the above listed record retention requirements should contact the following:
Helen F. Hettick, Administrative Officer, Office of Workers' Compensation Programs, NDOL–S–3524, Washington, D.C. 20210. Telephone: 202–523–7511.

Public agencies engaged in fire protection or law enforcement activities.

To maintain records as indicated in 29 CFR Part 516.
Retention period: Various. 29 CFR 553.21 (retention: Part 516)

Occupational Safety and Health Administration

Persons accredited for vessel cargo gear certification.

To maintain records of all work performed on gear certification, including tests, proof loads, and heat treatment; of the status of the certification of each vessel issued a register by such accredited person.
    Retention period: Permanent. 29 CFR 1919.10, 1919.11

Operators or officers of vessels.

To keep vessel's register and certificates relating to cargo gear.
    Retention period: 4 years after date of the latest entry except for nonrecurring test certificates concerning gear which is kept in use for a longer period, in which case certificates are retained as long as that gear is in use. 29 CFR 1919.12

Employers of maritime employees under the Longshoremen's and Harbor Workers' Compensation Act.

(a) To maintain records of tests of strength of stevedoring gear.
    Retention period: As long as such gear is in use. 29 CFR 1918.61
    (b) To keep records of the dates, times, and locations of tests for carbon monoxide made when internal combustion engines exhaust into the hold or intermediate deck.
    Retention period: 30 days after the work is completed. 29 CFR 1918.93
    (c) To keep records relating to tests and inspections for the existence of hazardous flammable, explosive, or toxic liquids and gases.
    Retention period: 3 months from the date of the completion of the job. 29 CFR 1915.10, 1916.10, 1917.10

Contractors subject to Public Contracts Act (contracts with U.S. agencies or District of Columbia).

To keep an annual summary of occupational illnesses and accidents.
    Retention period: 5 years after date of entry. 29 CFR 1904; 41 CFR 50–201.502

Contractors subject to Public Contracts Act (contracts with U.S. agencies or District of Columbia).

To maintain records of radiation exposure of all employees for whom personnel monitoring is required.
    Retention period: Not specified. 41 CFR 50–204.32

State agencies receiving development and planning grants for occupational safety and health.

To maintain records consistent with pertinent instructions.
    Retention period: Not specified. 29 CFR 1950.11

Employers, except small employers as provided in 29 CFR 1904.15, subject to the Occupational Safety and Health Act of 1970.*

To maintain records for each occupational injury and illness, including an annual summary, and also a supplemental record in detail according to OSHA Form 101 and such other records as specified in sections cited.
    Retention period: 5 years. 29 CFR 1904.2, 1904.4–1904.6, 1952.4

Employers subject to the asbestos standard.

To maintain records of (a) any personal or environmental monitoring required by section cited, and (b) all employee medical examinations.
    Retention period: (a) 3 years, (b) 20 years. 29 CFR 1910.1001

Employers subject to the ionizing radiation standard.

To maintain records of radiation exposure of all employees who are personally monitored.
    Retention period: Indefinite. 29 CFR 1910.96

---

*Any employer with no more than 10 employees during calendar year 1973 need not comply with any requirements of Part 1904 (except for 1904.8) for any funds appropriated under Pub. L. 93–517. 40 FR 7094.

State agencies receiving grants implementing approved State plans in the occupational health and safety program.

To maintain financial records, supporting documents, statistical records, and all other records pertinent to the grant program.

Retention period: 3 years, or longer if audit findings not resolved; for nonexpendable property, 3 years after final disposition. Microfilm copies may be substituted for the originals. 29 CFR 1951.47

Employers subject to vinyl chloride standards.

To maintain (a) monitoring and measuring records; (b) authorized personnel rosters; and (c) medical records.

Retention period: (a) Not less than 30 years; (b) not less than 30 years; and (c) duration of employment plus 20 years, or 30 years, whichever is longer. 29 CFR 1910.1071

Employers subject to mechanical power presses standard.

To maintain records of periodic and regular inspections of power presses and of the maintenance work performed.

Retention period: Not specified. 29 CFR 1910.217(e)

Employers subject to industrial slings standards.

To maintain record of most recent month in which each alloy steel chain sling was thoroughly inspected and proof test certificates for each new, repaired or reconditioned sling; also, to attach permanent tag or mark, or keep a record in order to indicate date and nature of repairs to metal mesh slings.

Retention period: Not specified. 29 CFR 1910.184

Employers, telecommunications.

To maintain (a) written description of training programs and record of employees who have received such training; (b) records of inspections of derricks and associated equipment.

Retention period: (a) Duration of employee's employment; (b) not specified. 29 CFR 1910.268

Employers subject to carcinogen standards.

To maintain records of (a) authorized personnel rosters; and (b) medical records.

Retention period: (a) At least 20 years; (b) duration of employee's employment. 29 CFR 1910.1003–1910.1016

Employers subject to coke oven emissions standard.

To maintain records of (a) all measurements taken to monitor employee exposure required by section cited, and (b) employee medical surveillance programs required by section cited.

Retention period: At least 40 years or the duration of employment plus 20 years, whichever is longer. 29 CFR 1910.1029

Employers subject to ground-fault protection standards.

To maintain records of testing of equipment required by section cited.

Retention period: Until replaced by a more current record. 29 CFR 1910.309(c), 1926.400(h)

Persons needing further information about listed record retention requirements should contact the following:
Flo H. Ryer, NDOL–N–3663, Washington, DC 20210. Telephone: 202–523–7174.

DEPARTMENT OF TRANSPORTATION

Federal Aviation Administration

Aircraft and related products manufacturers.

To maintain records of inspection identified with the completed product and records of Materials Review Board action applying to materials, parts, assemblies, and the completed product.

Retention period: At least 2 years. 14 CFR 21.125

Aircraft and related products manufacturers.

To maintain records of inspection applying to the manufacture of replacement or modification parts and identifiable with the completed part.
  Retention period: At least 2 years. 14 CFR 21.303

Certificated air carriers and commercial operators.

To keep (a) all the records necessary to show that all requirements for the issuance of an airworthiness release under 14 CFR 121.709 or 127.319 have been met and (b) records of total time in service of airframe; current status of life limited parts of each airframe, engine, propeller, rotor, and appliance; time since last overhaul of all items required to be overhauled on a specified time basis; identification of current inspection status of aircraft, including time since last inspection required by inspection program under which aircraft and its appliances are maintained; current status of applicable airworthiness directives, including method of compliance; and a list of current major alterations to each airframe, engine, propeller, rotor, and appliance.
  Retention period: (a) Until work is repeated or superseded by other work or for 1 year after work is performed, except for records of last complete overhaul of each airframe, engine, propeller, rotor, or appliance which are retained until work is superseded by work of equivalent scope and detail; (b) transferred with the aircraft at the time the aircraft is sold. 14 CFR 121.380, 127.141

Certificated repair stations or airframe, powerplant, propeller, or appliance manufacturers.

To maintain a duplicate copy of the customer's work order, when accepted in lieu of the Major Repair and Alteration Form (FAA-337 or equivalent).
  Retention period: At least 2 years. 14 CFR Part 43, App. B

Domestic, flag, and supplemental air carriers and commerical operators of large aircraft.

To retain information taped by flight recorders.
  Retention period: Until the airplane has been operated for at least 25 hours of the operating time specified in §121.359 (a) but no more than 60 days, or for a longer period if requested by a representative of the Federal Aviation Administration or the National Transportation Safety Board. 14 CFR 121.343

Registered owners or operators of civil aircraft.

To keep (a) records of maintenance, alterations, 100-hour, annual, and progressive inspections, and other required or approved inspections for each aircraft, and for each airframe, engine, propeller, rotor, and appliance of an aircraft including a description of the work performed, the date the work was completed, and signature and certificate number of the persons approving the aircraft for return to service and (b) records of total time in service of airframe; current status of life limited parts of each airframe, engine, propeller, rotor, and appliance; time since last overhaul of all items required to be overhauled on a specified time basis; identification of current inspection status of aircraft, including time since last inspection required by inspection program under which aircraft and its applicances are maintained, current status of applicable airworthiness directives, including method of compliance; and a list of current major alterations to each airframe, engine, propeller, rotor, and appliance.
  Retention period: (a) Until the work is repeated or superseded by other work or for 1 year after the work is performed; (b) transferred with the aircraft at the time the aircraft is sold. 14 CFR 91.173

Air carriers (utilizing helicopters in scheduled interstate air transportation).

To keep a maintenance log of all action taken in the case of a reported or observed failure or malfunction of an airframe, engine, rotor, or appliance that is critical to the safety of flight.
  Retention period: Not specified. 14 CFR 127.311

Certificated parachute riggers.

To keep a record of the packing, maintenance, and alteration of parachutes performed or supervised by him.
  Retention period: At least 2 years after the date record is made. 14 CFR 65.131

APPENDIX F   FEDERAL RECORD-RETENTION REQUIREMENTS   559

Certificated domestic repair stations and applicants for a domestic repair station certificate and rating.

To maintain a roster of its supervisory and inspection personnel, and a summary of the employment of each person whose name is on the roster containing enough information to show compliance with experience requirements.
   Retention period: Not specified. 14 CFR 145.43

Certificated domestic repair stations.

To maintain adequate records of work performed, naming the certificated mechanic or repairman who performed or supervised the work, and the inspector of that work.
   Retention period: At least 2 years. 14 CFR 145.61

Certificated foreign repair stations.

To keep a record of the maintenance and alteration performed on United States registered aircraft.
   Retention period: Not specified. 14 CFR 145.79

Holders of parachute loft certificates.

To maintain records of work performed, including names of persons doing the work.
   Retention period: At least 2 years. 14 CFR 149.15

Manufacturers of aircraft.

To maintain at factory, for each product type certificated under the delegation option procedures, current records containing the following: (a) technical data file including type design drawings, reports on tests, and original type inspection report and amendments; (b) data (including amendments) required with original application for each production certificate; (c) record of all rebuilding and alteration performed; (d) complete inspection record for each product manufactured; (e) record of reported service difficulties.
   Retention period: (a), (b), and (c) for the duration of the manufacturing operation under the delegation option authorization; (d) and (e), 2 years. 14 CFR 21.293

Designated alteration stations.

To maintain current records of technical data (including drawings, photographs, specifications, instructions, and reports) for each product for which it has issued a supplemental type certificate; list of products by make, model, manufacturer's serial number, etc.; and a file of information on alteration difficulties of products altered.
   Retention period: For duration of the operation under the DAS authorization. 14 CFR 21.493

Domestic, flag, and supplemental air carriers, and commercial operators of large aircraft.

To keep, in the event of an accident or occurrence requiring immediate notification of the National Transportation Safety Board under Part 430 of its regulations, the information recorded on cockpit voice recorders.
   Retention period: At least 60 days or longer if requested by the Administrator or the Board. 14 CFR 121.359

Aircraft and related products manufacturers holding Technical Standard Order Authorizations.

To keep records pertaining to each article manufactured including (a) a complete and current technical data file, design drawings, and specifications, and (b) complete and current inspection records.
   Retention period: (a) Until the TSO article is no longer produced by the manufacturer; (b) and at least 2 years. 14 CFR 37.13

Aircraft and related products manufacturers—production under type certificate only.

To maintain at the place of manufacture the technical data and drawing necessary for the Administrator to determine whether the product and its parts conform to the type design.
   Retention period: Not specified. 14 CFR 21.123

Owners of non-Federal Simplified Directional Facilities (SDF); non-Federal Distance Measuring Equipment (DME) Facilities; and non-Federal VHF Marker Beacon Facilities.

To maintain: (a) record of meter readings and adjustments (Form FAA-198) reflecting an accurate record of facility operation and adjustment and must be revised after any major repair, modification, or retuning; (b) a facility maintenance log (FAA Form 6030–1), consisting of a permanent record of all equipment malfunctioning met in maintaining the facility, including information on the kind of work and adjustments made, equipment failures, causes (if determined), and corrective action taken; (c) a radio equipment operation record (Form FAA–418) containing a complete record of meter readings, recorded on each scheduled visit to the facility.
   Retention period: (a) Permanent; (b) and (c) not specified. 14 CFR 171.117, 171.163, 171.213

Persons needing further information about listed record retention requirements should contact the following:
Dewey R. Roark, Jr., Office of the Chief Counsel (AGC–20), Federal Aviation Administration, Washington, DC 20591. Telephone: 202–426–3235.

Federal Highway Administration

All common, contract, and private motor carriers operating in interstate or foreign commerce, except private carriers of persons.

To maintain records of inspection and maintenance for each motor vehicle for the period the motor vehicle is controlled by the carrier as set out in the section cited.
   Retention period: Varies. 49 CFR 396.2

All common, contract, and private motor carriers operating in interstate or foreign commerce, except private carriers of persons.

To maintain daily driver reports on the condition of motor vehicles as set out in the section cited.
   Retention period: 3 months from date of the report. 49 CFR 396.7

State highway agencies. State legal expenses in contract claims. [Added]

To maintain records and accounts evidencing the State control over costs or expenses for reimbursement of administrative settlement costs, and other legal expenses in contract claims on Federal-aid projects.
   Retention period: Not specified. 23 CFR 140.504(b)

State highway agencies, research and development property management. [Added]

To maintain an inventory record for each piece of nonexpendable equipment purchased or built under the Federal-aid research and development program.
   Retention period: Not specified. 23 CFR 522.9

State highway agencies, research and development program. [Added]

To maintain internal reports to control R&D portion of the Highway Planning and Research (HP&R) work program, and fiscal accounting records for Federal-aid R&D program.
   Retention period: Not specified. 23 CFR 524.7(c) (3) and (4)

Persons needing further information about listed record retention requirements should contact the following:
Durward E. Timmons, Jr. (HCC–10), Office of the Chief Counsel, Federal Highway Administration, Washington, DC 20590. Telephone: 202–426–0761.

United States Coast Guard

Certificates or documents issued to the public by Coast Guard.

To maintain certificates or documents, as required by laws, rules, or regulations, for the applicable period of time.
   Retention period: If the certificate or document (a) specifies a definite period of time for which it is valid, it shall be retained for so long as it is valid unless it is required to be surrendered; (b) does

APPENDIX F   FEDERAL RECORD-RETENTION REQUIREMENTS   **561**

not specify a definite period of time for which it is valid, it shall be retained for that period of time such certificate or document is required for operation of the vessel; or, (c) is evidence of a person's qualifications, it shall be retained for so long as it is valid unless it is required to be surrendered. 46 CFR 2.95–1

Owners, masters or persons in charge of vessels required to have cargo gear certificates and/or registers, and records regarding such gear.

To keep on board the current, valid cargo gear certificate and/or register, and records regarding such gear, such as inspections and tests or examinations, original or certified copies of certificates of manufacturers and/or testing laboratories, companies, or organizations for loose cargo gear, wire rope, or the annealing of gear, and records of all tests and examinations conducted by or under the supervision of surveyors of organizations or associations approved by the Commandant.

Retention period: The cargo gear certificate and/or register shall be retained for so long as it is valid unless it is required to be surrendered, and in addition until the next Coast Guard inspection for certification of the vessel. The certificates of manufacturers and/or testing laboratories, companies, or organizations shall be maintained so long as the gear described in such certificates is on board the vessel. The records of inspections by ship's officers shall be maintained on the vessel for that period of time which agrees with the period covered by the current Coast Guard certificate of inspection issued to the vessel. 46 CFR 31.10–16, 31.37–75, 71.25–25, 71.47–75, 91.25–25, 91.37–75 (retention: 2.95–5)

Owners, masters, or persons in charge of vessels required to have performed tests and inspections of all firefighting equipment.

To keep on board records of required tests and inspections of all firefighting equipment.

Retention period: For the period of validity of the current Coast Guard certificate of inspection for the vessel. 46 CFR 31.10–18, 78.17–80, 97.15–60, 196.15–60

Owners, masters or persons in charge of new vessels having cargo gear described in approved plans.

To keep on board a set of approved plans of cargo gear showing a stress diagram with the principal details of the gear and a diagram showing arrangement and safe working loads.

Retention period: During period such cargo gear is on board vessel. 46 CFR 31.37–15, 31.37–20, 31.37–23, 71.47–15, 71.47–20, 71.47–23, 91.37–15, 91.37–20, 91.37–23 (retention: 31.37–75, 71.47–75, 91.37–75)

Masters of tank vessels or vessels towing tank barges transporting flammable or combustible cargo.

To keep on board a bill of lading manifest or shipping document giving name of consignee and the delivery point, the kind, grades, and approximate quantity of each kind and grade of cargo, and for whose account the cargo is being handled.
Retention period: Not specified. 46 CFR 35.01–10

Masters or persons in charge of vessels required to conduct fire and lifeboat drills.

To make entries in the ship's logs relating to the fire and lifeboat drills and examinations of emergency equipment.

Retention period: Until official log book is required to be surrendered to the Coast Guard, or for a vessel not required to use the official log book such logs shall be kept for a period of one year after date entries were made. 46 CFR 35.10–5, 78.17–50, 97.15–35, 167.65–1, 196.15–35

Owners, agents, masters, or persons in charge of vessels involved in marine casualties.

To keep such voyage records of the vessel as are maintained by the vessel, such as both rough and smooth deck and engineroom logs, bell books, navigation charts, navigation work books, compass deviation cards, gyro compass records, stowage plans, records of draft aids to mariners, radiograms sent and received, the radio logs, crew and passenger lists, articles of shipment, official logs, and other material which might be of assistance in investigating and determining the cause of the casualty.

Retention period: Until notification of completion of investigation is received from Coast Guard. 46 CFR 35.15–1, 78.07–15, 97.07–15, 167.65–65, 196.07–15

Masters or senior deck officer of tank ships in charge of transfer of flammable and combustible cargo.

To keep on board copy of Declaration of Inspection Prior to Bulk Cargo Transfer.
    Retention period: 1 month. 33 CFR 156.150 (e) and (f)

Manufacturers or contractors responsible for welding and brazing procedures.

To maintain records of test results obtained in welding procedure, welder's performance qualifications, and identification data.
    Retention period: Not specified. 46 CFR 57.02–3

Owners, masters, or persons in charge of nuclear vessels required to have "Operating Manuals."

To keep on board a copy of the approved "Operating Manual," which shall be kept up to date.
    Retention period: At all times vessel has a nuclear reactor on board. 46 CFR 79.20–1, 99.20–1

Owners, operators, and masters of vessels.

To maintain (a) official logbooks or (b) for those not required to have such a logbook, logs and records as prescribed by regulations.
    Retention period: (a) Until filed with Officer in Charge, Maritime Inspection; (b) other, 1 year. 46 CFR 35.07–5, 35.07–10, 46.10–55, 78.37–3, 78.37–5, 97.35–3, 97.35–5

Persons holding certificates or documents of other public agencies or private organizations.

To maintain such certificates or documents which are accepted as prima facie evidence of compliance with Coast Guard requirements.
    Retention period: If the certificate or document (a) specifies a definite period of time for which it is valid, it shall be retained for so long as it is valid unless it is required to be surrendered; (b) does not specify a definite period of time for which it is valid, it shall be retained for the period of time such certificate or document is required for operation of the vessel; or (3) is evidence of a person's qualifications, it shall be retained for so long as it is valid unless it is required to be surrendered. 46 CFR 2.95–5

Owners, their agents, or persons in charge of Outer Continental Shelf artificial or fixed structures involved in marine casualties.

To maintain records concerning loss of life, injury, damage incurred, and need for emergency equipment as indicated in sections cited.
    Retention period: Not specified. 33 CFR 146.01–20; 46 CFR 4.05–15

Owners of manned platforms.

To maintain report records of all emergency drills. Retention period: 1 year. 33 CFR 146.05–25

Masters of vessels storing explosives for a period exceeding 24 hours (other than barges, magazine vessels, and oceanographic vessels). [Amended]

To make an entry in the vessel's log book for each inspection of the storage of the explosives.
    Retention period: 1 year for vessels. 46 CFR 146.02–22

Carriers shipping explosives or other dangerous articles. [Amended]

To keep shipping orders, manifests, or other shipping documents, cargo lists, cargo stowage plans, reports, papers, and records as required to be prepared.
    Retention period: 1 year. 46 CFR 146.02–22

Owners, agents, masters, and operators of vessels involved in a marine casualty.

To maintain voyage records such as logs, charts, books, lists, and such other material as may be related to the casualty.
    Retention period: Not specified. 46 CFR 4.05–15

APPENDIX F FEDERAL RECORD-RETENTION REQUIREMENTS

Masters of vessels subject to load line requirements.

To maintain on board a copy of the load line survey report which shall be made available for inspectors and surveyors when carrying out subsequent load line surveys.
   Retention period: For period of current certificate (5 years). 46 CFR 42.09-1, 43.01-40

Masters of towing vessels towing barges transporting or storing explosives or other dangerous articles or substances, and combustible liquids, as cargo.

To keep on board dangerous cargo manifests, lists, bills of lading, or shipping documents.
   Retention period: During the period of transportation or storage. 46 CFR 151.45-7

Manufacturers of equipment or material which must be approved or found satisfactory for use.

To keep the required drawings, plans, blueprints, specifications, production models (if any), qualification tests, and related correspondence containing evidence that the Coast Guard has found such equipment satisfactory, during the period of time the approval or listing is valid.
   Retention period: Not specified. Most of the specifications containing detailed descriptions of records to be retained are contained in 46 CFR Parts 160-164. 46 CFR 2.95-10

Each voluntary association holding a Certification of Authorization under the Great Lakes Pilotage Uniform Accounting System.

To keep all books, records and memoranda and file them in such a manner to readily permit the audit and examination thereof by representatives of the U.S. Coast Guard. Also, the records must be housed or stored in such a manner as to afford protection from loss, theft or damage by fire, flood, or otherwise.
   Retention period: 10 years unless otherwise authorized by the Commandant. 46 CFR Part 403

Masters or operators of vessels subject to Oil Pollution Act of 1961, as amended.

To keep on board an Oil Record Book as prescribed by 33 CFR 151.35.
   Retention period: As specified in 33 CFR 151.35(h)

Owners, operators, and/or masters of oceanographic vessels.

(a) To keep official logbook, or (b) for vessels not required to have such a logbook, to keep their own logs or records as prescribed by regulations.
   Retention period: (a) 1 year or for period of validity of vessel's current certificate of inspection, whichever is longer; (b) 1 year, except for separate records of tests and inspections of firefighting equipment, which shall be maintained for the period of validity of the vessel's certificate of inspection. 46 CFR 196.35-3, 196.35-5

Masters of ships subject to International Convention on Load Lines, 1966. [Amended]

To enter in the ships' logs, before departure from loading port, the data required by 46 U.S.C. 86g(b) and 88e, including statements of load line marks applicable to the voyage, position of load line marks, and actual drafts of the vessel.
   Retention period: Until official logbook is surrendered to Coast Guard, or 1 year for ships not required to use official logbook. 46 CFR 42.07-20

Manufacturers of marine sanitation devices.

To maintain records required to determine compliance with the act.
   Retention period: Not specified. 33 U.S.C. 1322(g)(3)

Nonprofit firms or associations designated to certify containers for international transport under Customs seal.

To maintain copy of each Certificate of Approval by design type issued, together with copy of plans and applications to which approval refers, and records of manufacturer's serial number assigned to containers manufactured under each approval and such other records as indicated in section cited.
   Retention period: Not specified. 49 CFR 421.30

Operators of oil transfer facilities.

To maintain (a) letter of intent, name of person in charge of transfer, operations, equipment, tests and inspections, hose, information, facility inspection record, and (b) signed copy of each declaration of inspection for facility.

    Retention period: (a) Not specified; (b) 1 month from date of signature. 33 CFR 154.740, 156.150

Owners and operators of vessels engaged in oil transfer operations.

To maintain (a) name of person in charge of transfer operations, date and results of tests, hose information, and valve inspection data; and (b) signed copy of each declaration of inspection for such vessel-to-vessel transfer.

    Retention period: (a) Not specified; (b) 1 month from date of signature. 33 CFR 155.820, 156.150

Licensees, deepwater ports.

(a) To maintain documentation of the designation and qualifications of key deepwater port personnel.

(b) To maintain a record of all machinery, both fixed and portable, such as generators, cargo pumps, fire pumps, and discharge containment and removal systems; and a record of all fire fighting, lifesaving, and other emergency equipment.

(c) To maintain a record of the name, nationality, and owner of vessels discharging crude oil at deepwater ports; the country of origin of crude oil; and the total quantity of oil transferred.

(d) To maintain signed copies of the declaration of inspection of the deep water port form.

    Retention period: (a) Duration of each individual's employment at the deepwater port by the licensee; (b) 1 year for each monthly emergency drill required, 3 years for test and inspection performed by port personnel; (c) 3 years; (d) 1 month from date of signature. 33 CFR 150.753, 150.755, 150.757, 150.759

Persons needing further information about listed record retention requirements should contact the following:
Stanley M. Colby, Office of the Chief Counsel (G–LRA/81), United States Coast Guard, Washington, DC 20590. Telephone: 202–426–1534.

Federal Railroad Administration [Revised]

Railroad companies.

To keep records as prescribed by the following sections:

(a) To keep a record of each inspection of track, switch, and track crossing. Retention period: 1 year after the inspection covered by the record. 49 CFR 213.241

(b) To retain a record or copy of information cards attached to or removed from defective railroad cars. Retention period: 90 days. 49 CFR 215.9

(c) To keep a record of the date and place of each operational test and inspection. Retention period: 1 year. 49 CFR 217.9(d)

(d) To keep a record of each notification to the operator of remotely controlled switches that work is to be performed and that each remotely controlled switch has been lined against movement to that track and locked as prescribed by 49 CFR 218.29(a). Retention period: 30 days. 49 CFR 218.29(a) (effective 1/11/77)

(e) To maintain logs, supplementary records, and annual summaries relating to railroad accidents. Retention period: 5 years after end of calendar year to which they relate. 49 CFR 225.25, 225.27(a).

(f) To retain duplicates of all forms submitted to Federal Railroad Administration relating to railroad accidents. Retention period: 2 years after end of calendar year to which they relate. 49 CFR 225.27(b)

Persons needing further information about listed record retention requirements should contact the following:
Rufus S. Watson, Jr. (RCC), Office of the Chief Counsel, Federal Railroad Administration, Washington, DC 20590. Telephone: 202–426–7710.

Materials Transportation Bureau

Welders of steel materials to be used in pipelines.

To keep records of welding procedures that have been qualified under either section IX of the ASME Boiler and Pressure Vessel Code or section 2 of API Standard 1104.
  Retention period: As long as procedure is used. 49 CFR 192.225(c)

Operators of natural gas pipelines.

Records must be retained showing by milepost, engineering station, or by geographic feature, the number of girth welds made, the number nondestructively tested, the number rejected and the disposition of the rejects whenever nondestructive testing is required under 192.241(b).
  Retention period: Life of the pipeline. 49 CFR 192.243(f)

Operators of natural gas pipelines.

To keep records of safety tests required with names of those involved, methods used, and results of the tests.
  Retention period: Duration of pipeline's use. 49 CFR 192.517

Operators of natural gas pipelines.

To retain records of each segment of pipeline that has been uprated showing each investigation required by the subpart, all work performed and each pressure test conducted in connection with the uprating.
  Retention period: Life of the segment of pipeline. 49 CFR 192.553(b)

Operators of natural gas pipelines.

To keep records necessary to administer the operating and maintenance plan established for each segment of pipeline.
  Retention period: Not specified. 49 CFR 192.603(b)

Operators of natural gas transmission lines.

To keep records governing each leak discovered, repair made, transmission line break, leakage survey, line patrol and inspection.
  Retention period: As long as the segment of transmission line involved remains in service. 49 CFR 192.709

Operators of liquid pipelines.

To retain records of the nondestructive testing of welds, including (if radiography is used) the developed film, with so far as practicable, the location of the weld.
  Retention period: 3 years following the placement of the line in operation. 49 CFR 195.234(g)

Operators of liquid pipelines.

To maintain records showing the total number of girth welds and the number nondestructively tested, including the number rejected and the disposition of each rejected; the amount, location, and cover of each size of pipe installed; the location of each crossing of another pipeline; the location of each buried utility crossing; the location of each overhead crossing; the location of each valve, weighted pipe, corrosion test station, or other item connected to the pipe.
  Retention period: Life of each facility. 49 CFR 195.266

Operators of liquid pipelines.

To retain records of each hydrostatic test including the recording gauge charts, deadweight tester data, and the reasons for any failure during a test. Where elevation differences in the section under test exceed 100 feet, a profile of the pipeline that shows the elevation and test sites over the entire length of the test section must also be included.
  Retention period: As long as the facility tested is in use. 49 CFR 195.310

Operators of liquid pipelines.

To maintain daily operating records that indicate the discharge pressures at each pump station and any unusual operations of a facility.
    Retention period: At least 3 years. 49 CFR 195.404(b)

Operators of liquid pipelines.

To maintain records that indicate the date, location and description of each repair made to its pipeline systems as well as a record of each inspection and test required by the subpart.
    Retention period: Useful life of the part of the pipeline system to which the record relates. 49 CFR 195.404(c)

Operators of liquid pipelines.

To maintain, at the principal place of business, a copy of each accident report required to be filed with the Director, Office of Pipeline Safety.
    Retention period: Not specified. 49 CFR 195.54

Manufacturers of compressed gas cylinders.

To maintain data sheets recording the results of visual inspections of certain compressed gas cylinders.
    Retention period: Permanent. 49 CFR 173.34(e)(10)

Owners of compressed gas cylinders.

To maintain records showing results of reinspection and retest of such cylinders.
    Retention period: Until expiration of retest period, or until cylinder is reinspected and retested, whichever occurs first. 49 CFR 173.34(e)(5)

Owners of tank motor vehicles transporting flammable liquids.

To maintain records of inspection as required in section cited.
    Retention period: 2 years after date of inspection. 49 CFR 177.824(b)

Manufacturers of cylinders and tanks.

To maintain (a) inspector's report on specification DOT–39 cylinders, and (b) test samples on specification DOT–56 and 57 portable tanks.
    Retention period: (a) 3 years; (b) 1 year. 49 CFR 178.65–15(a), 178.251–5(a)

Motor carriers operating cargo tanks.

To maintain manufacturer's data report and certificate of compliance and related papers on specification MC331 cargo tanks; and manufacturer's certificate of compliance on specifications MC 306, 307, and 312 cargo tanks.
    Retention period: During time of use of tank plus 1 year thereafter. 49 CFR 178.337–18(b), 178.340–10(c)

Cargo tank manufacturers.

To maintain sketch of location of plate in specification MC331 cargo tank and records of welder qualification in fabrication of such cargo tanks.
    Retention period: 5 years. 49 CFR 178.337–2(a)(3), 178.337–4(b)

Owners of portable tanks carrying hazardous materials.

To maintain records (a) of manufacturer's data report and (b) date and results of all required tests.
    Retention period: (a) During time used, and (b) until satisfactory completion of next retest. 49 CFR 173.32 (a) and (e)(4)

Shippers of hazardous materials offered by or consigned to the Department of Defense. [Amended]

To maintain duplicate certification of each shipment.
    Retention period: Not less than 1 year. 49 CFR 173.7(a)(1), 177.806(a)(1)

Owners of foreign containers.

To maintain records showing results of retests of foreign containers.
   Retention period: Until the next scheduled retest date. 49 CFR 173.301(j)

Shippers subject to cargo security advisory standards.

To maintain records as specified in section cited.
   Retention period: Various. 49 CFR 85.33 and Appendix, secs. 85–1.19, 85–1.33, 85–1.35, 85–1.41, 85–2.49, 85–3.13, 85–3.71

Owners of tank cars.

To maintain record of (a) reports of latest tests and (b) inspection results of DOT 106A and DOT 106A–W tank cars.
   Retention period: (a) Until next test has been accomplished and recorded; (b) permanently. 49 CFR 173.31(c)(8), (d)(8) and (d)(9)

Shippers of special form radioactive material.

To maintain complete certificate and supporting safety analysis to indicate compliance with requirements of sections cited.
   Retention period: 1 year after latest shipment. 49 CFR 173.394(a)(1), 173.395(a)(1), 173.398(a)(4) Note 1

Motor carriers using cargo tank vehicles.

To maintain manufacturing and testing certificate and any other data furnished.
   Retention period: For length of time cargo tank is used and for 1 year thereafter. 49 CFR 177.814(a)

Manufacturers of shipping containers.

To maintain (a) test results of spec 34 containers; (b) inspectors report on spec 3T cylinders; (c) tests and results of spec 33A polystyrene cases; (d) report of tests results on spec 23H fiberboard boxes; and (e) records of qualification of spec 51 portable tanks.
   Retention period: (a) Not specified; (b) as long as cylinders are authorized for use by regulations; (c) and (d) 1 year; (e) 5 years. 49 CFR 178.19–7(d), 178.45–18(a), 178.150–6b, 178.219–14, 178.245–1(a)

Persons needing further information about listed record retention requirements should contact the following:
Louise Mills, Chief, Docket Section (MTH–11), Materials Transportation Bureau, Washington, DC 20590. Telephone: 202–426–2077.

National Highway Traffic Safety Administration

States participating in the National Highway Safety Program.

To maintain records described in Highway Safety Program Standards 1, 2, 5, 10, and 14.
   Retention period: Not specified. 23 CFR 204.4

Manufacturers of complete or incomplete motor vehicles.

To maintain list of names and addresses of first purchasers or subsequent purchasers to whom a warranty has been transferred and vehicle identification number involved in each safety defect notification campaign.
   Retention period: 5 years after defect information report is submitted to the Administrator. 49 CFR 573.6

Manufacturers, brand name owners, distributors, and dealers of new and retreaded tires.

To maintain records of name and address of tire purchaser and tire seller, and the tire identification number. Retention period: 3 years from date the tire manufacturer records the information is submitted. 49 CFR 574.7, 574.8

Tire manufacturers.

To maintain records of each distributor or dealer purchasing tires directly from him and selling them to purchasers, number of tires purchased, and number of tires for which reports have been received from distributor or dealer.
    Retention period: 3 years from date the tire manufacturer records the information is submitted. 49 CFR 574.7

Manufacturers of motor vehicles.

To maintain records of tires on or in each vehicle shipped to a distributor or dealer, and the name and address of the first purchaser.
    Retention period: 3 years from date of sale of vehicle to first purchaser. 49 CFR 574.10

Manufacturers of motor vehicles and tires.

To maintain records of names and addresses of first purchasers of motor vehicles and tires produced.
    Retention period: Not specified. 15 U.S.C. 1418(b)

Motor vehicle manufacturers.

To maintain records containing information concerning malfunctions that may be related to motor vehicle safety.
    Retention period: 5 years. 49 CFR 576.6 (retention: 576.5)

Persons needing further information about listed record retention requirements should contact the following:
Roger Tilton, Office of the Chief Counsel (N40–3–), National Highway Traffic Safety Administration, Washington, DC 20590. Telephone: 202–426–2077.

DEPARTMENT OF THE TREASURY

Comptroller of the Currency

Security devices required in national banks.

To maintain records showing the name(s) and title(s) of law enforcement officer(s) who advises bank on installation, maintenance, and operation of appropriate security devices.
    Retention period: Not specified. 12 CFR 21.5(b)

United States Customs Service

Owners, importers, consignees, and agents handling merchandise for repairs, alterations, or processing.

To maintain certificates of registration as indicated in sections cited.
    Retention period: 2 years from date of final liquidation of final quantity covered by certificate of registration. 19 CFR 10.8, 10.9

Vessels withdrawing, delivering, or receiving fuel oil.

To maintain all pertinent records, including financial records relating to the withdrawal, delivery, or receipt of such fuel oil.
    Retention period: Not specified. 19 CFR 10.62

Importers and manufacturers of master records and metal matrices.

To maintain plant and account records relating to such records and matrices.
    Retention period: Not specified. 19 CFR 10.90

Manufacturers or producers of articles manufactured or produced in the United States with the use of imported duty-paid merchandise and intended for exportation with benefit of drawback under section 313(a), Tariff Act of 1930.*

To keep records showing the date or inclusive dates of manufacture or production of the articles, the quantity and identity of the imported duty-paid merchandise used or appearing in the exported

---

*These records are required to be kept by manufacturers or producers, proprietors of bonded smelting and/or refining warehouses operating under section 312, Tariff Act of 1930, and importers.

articles, the quantity and description of finished product obtained, and, if valuable waste is incurred in manufacture and claim is not based on the quantity of imported merchandise appearing in the exported articles, the value of the imported merchandise used in manufacture and the quantity and value of the waste incurred, and, in cases where two or more products are obtained, the values thereof at the time of separation.

Retention period: At least 3 years after payment of drawback claims. 19 CFR 22.4, 22.6 (retention: 22.45)

Manufacturers or producers of articles manufactured or produced in the United States with the use, in certain cases, of substituted merchandise in lieu of imported duty-paid merchandise and intended for exportation with benefit of drawback under section 313(b), Tariff Act of 1930, as amended.*

To keep detailed records pertaining to duty-paid merchandise or other articles manufactured or produced under drawback regulations with the use of such merchandise designated as the basis for the allowance of drawback on the exported articles.

Retention period: At least 3 years after payment of drawback claims. 19 CFR 22.5, 22.6 (retention: 22.46)

Importers of merchandise subject to actual use provisions.

To maintain records showing use or disposition of imported merchandise.
Retention period: 3 years from date of liquidation of entry. 19 CFR 10.137

Importers of metal articles to be used in remanufacture by melting.

To maintain plant and import records relating to such remanufacture.
Retention period: Not specified. 19 CFR 54.6

Importers and assemblers, articles assembled abroad with U.S. components.

To maintain records of U.S. components showing quantities, sources, costs, dates shipped abroad and other necessary information in order to waive certain entry requirements.
Retention period: Not specified. 19 CFR 10.24

Persons needing further information about listed record retention requirements should contact the following:
All items except 3.2, 3.4, 3.9, and 3.11, Director, Regulatory Audit Division (O:R), U.S. Customs Service, Room 2116, 1301 Constitution Avenue, Washington, DC 20229. Telephone: 202–566–2812.
Items 3.2, 3.4, 3.9, and 3.11, Director, Inspection, Room 4148, 1301 Constitution Avenue, Washington, DC 20229. Telephone: 202–566–2366.

Internal Revenue Service

NOTE: The following items refer to requirements issued under the Internal Revenue Code of 1939 and the Internal Revenue Code of 1954 which were in effect as of January 1, 1977. All regulations applicable under any provision of law in effect on August 16, 1954, the date of enactment of the 1954 Code, are applicable to the corresponding provisions of the 1954 Code insofar as such regulations are not inconsistent with the 1954 Code, and such regulations remain applicable to the 1954 Code until superseded by regulations under such Code. The Internal Revenue Service points out that the omission from this compilation of any record retention requirement provided for by law or regulation issued thereunder shall not be construed as authority to disregard any such requirement. The Service also points out that persons subject to income tax are bound by the retention requirement given in item 4.1 regardless of other requirements which for other purposes allow shorter retention periods.

The record retention requirements of the Internal Revenue Service are divided into the following categories: Income, Estate, Gift, Employment, and Excise Taxes.

---

*These records are required to be kept by manufacturers or producers, proprietors of bonded smelting and/or refining warehouses operating under section 312, Tariff Act of 1930, and importers.

Manufacturers of white phosphorus matches.

To maintain daily records showing material used, number of matches produced, and number of stamped packages and original packages in which packed; also the total number of stamped and original packages, together with total number of matches disposed of each day.
    Retention period: 3 years after due date of tax or date tax is paid, whichever is later, or after date claim is filed. 26 CFR 45.4804–10 (retention: 45.6001–1)

Manufacturers of sugar.

To maintain monthly record relating to quantity on hand, received, produced, sold, and other records relating to manufactured sugar.
    Retention period: At least 3 years after due date of tax or date tax is paid, whichever is later, or after date claim is filed. 26 CFR 46.6001–2 (retention: 46.6001–1)

Manufacturers, producers, or importers selling automobile tires and tread rubber.

To maintain records of tires sold with metal rims or rim bases attached to establish portion of finished product that represents weight of tire, of tax-free sales of tread rubber, and of exemption certificates with invoices and orders relating to such exemption:
    Retention period: Not specified. 26 CFR 48.4071–2, 48.4073–3, 144.1–2

Manufacturers of lubricating oil.

To maintain exemption certificates for oil seldom used as a lubricant and records of invoices, orders, statements, and documents substantiating claim for exemption or for credit or refund.
    Retention period: Not specified, 26 CFR 48.4091–6

Manufacturers, producers, or importers selling pistols, revolvers, other firearms, and shells and cartridges.

To maintain records to substantiate claim for exemption from tax imposed.
    Retention period: Not specified. 26 CFR CFR 48.4182–1

Persons transporting property by air.

To maintain exemption certificates, statements, documentary evidence of exportation and any other records as specified in section cited.
    Retention period: At least 3 years. 26 CFR 154.2–1

Persons acquiring secondhand civil aircraft.

To maintain evidence showing whether or not there was taxable use prior to acquisition, or evidence of reasons why unable to obtain such evidence.
    Retention period: Not specified. 26 CFR 154.3–1(d)(4)

Persons needing further information about listed record retention requirements should contact the following:
Mr. Jack L. Oleson, Chief, Bulletin Section, Technical Publications Branch (T:FP:P), Internal Revenue Service, 1111 Constitution Avenue N.W., Room 2571, Washington, DC 20224. Telephone: 202–566–3129.

Office of Law Enforcement

Persons needing further information about listed record retention requirements should contact the following:
Mr. Robert J. Stankey, Jr., Department of the Treasury, Office of Law Enforcement, 15th and Pennsylvania Avenue, N.W., Washington, DC 20220. Telephone: 202–566–5630.

Bureau of Alcohol, Tobacco and Firearms

Persons disposing of substances or articles of the character used in manufacturing distilled spirits, or disposing of containers of the character used for packaging distilled spirits.

To keep records pertaining to the disposition of such substances or articles or containers.
    Retention period: 3 years. 27 CFR 173.15

Persons manufacturing liquor bottles.

To keep records of the receipt, manufacture, and disposition of liquor bottles.
   Retention period: 3 years. 27 CFR 173.39 (retention: 173.15)

Manufacturers and vendors of distilling apparatus.

(1) In the case of any distilling apparatus removed for exportation without payment of tax, to keep a copy of each bill of lading covering exportation or consignment to a foreign-trade zone;
   (2) In the case of distilling apparatus for domestic use for purposes other than distilling (as defined in 26 CFR 196.10), to keep a record showing the apparatus manufactured, received, and removed or otherwise disposed of, the name and address of each purchaser, and the purpose for which each still is to be used.
   Retention period: Not less than 2 years. 27 CFR 196.62, 196.80, 196.82.

Scientific institutions and colleges of learning authorized to conduct experimental or research operations.

To keep records, daily, of quantities of spirits produced, received, and used.
   Retention period: Not less than 4 years. 27 CFR 201.72 (retention: 201.612)

Manufacturers of and dealers in proprietary anti-freeze made with completely denatured alcohol.

To keep such records as will enable an internal revenue officer to verify and trace the production, receipts, storage, and disposal of such products.
   Retention period: 3 to 6 years. 27 CFR 211.125, 211.262, 211.273, 211.274 (retention: 211.273)

Users of specially denatured spirits.

To keep records and copies of all applications, notices, and reports reflecting details of (a) specially denatured spirits received, used, recovered (including redenaturation), lost, and otherwise disposed of, and (b) products and articles manufactured and the disposition of such products and articles.
   Retention period: 3 to 6 years. 27 CFR 211.139, 211.168, 211.212, 211.214, 211.215, 211.218, 211.241–211.243, 211.251–211.253, 211.255, 211.265–211.267, 211.271–211.274 (retention: 211.273)

Dealers in and users of proprietary solvents and special industrial solvents.

To keep records of receipt, use, and disposition.
   Retention period: 3 to 6 years. 27 CFR 211.268, 211.272–211.274 (retention: 211.273)

Universities, colleges of learning, and institutions of scientific research authorized to conduct wine experimental or research operations.

To keep copies of approved applications and appropriate records of experiments and research.
   Retention period: 3 to 6 years. 27 CFR 240.546–249.549, 240.731, 240.732, 240.924 (retention: 240.924)

Manufacturers of tobacco products.

To keep authorizations to employ alternate methods or procedures, to employ emergency variations from requirements, to engage in another business within the factory, to use alternate means for marking packages of cigars or cigarettes, to repackage cigars or cigarettes, to remove cigars or cigarettes in bond for experimental purposes, to temporarily store cigars or cigarettes outside of factory, and to destroy cigars or cigarettes without supervision.
   Retention period: 3 years following close of calendar year in which operations under authorizations granted under Parts 270 and 295 are concluded. Not specified for authorizations granted under Part 290. 27 CFR 270.45–270.47, 270.212, 270.217, 270.232, 270.251, 270.253, 290.72, 290.73, 290.184, 295.21, 295.22 (retention under Part 270: 270.185)

Licensed firearms manufacturers, importers, dealers, and collectors. [Amended]

To maintain complete and adequate records and supporting documents reflecting the production, importation, receipt, and disposition of all firearms and ammunition produced, imported, received or disposed of in the course of licensed operations, except that no record need be kept of retail sales of shotgun ammunition, ammunition suitable for use only in rifles, or components for such shotgun and rifle ammunition.

Retention period: For ammunition 2 years from date transaction occurs. For firearms—permanent. Upon discontinuance of business, firearms and ammunition records must be delivered to successor, or, if discontinuance of the business is absolute, to the regional regulatory administrator. 27 CFR 178.122–178.127, Public Law 91–128 (83 Stat. 269)

Transferees of firearms. [Amended]

To maintain the application filed by the transferor and approved by the Director, Bureau of Alochol, Tobacco and Firearms, for the transfer of a firearm. This includes transfers exempt from, as well as subject to, the transfer tax.

Retention period: Transferee retains approved application for duration of his ownership of the related firearm. 27 CFR 179.84–179.93

Manufacturers, importers, or dealers in firearms (including pawnbrokers).

To keep records showing (a) the manufacture, receipt, transfer or other disposition of all firearms taxable under the Internal Revenue Code, (b) date of such manufacture, receipt, transfer or disposition, (c) the number, model, and trade name or other mark identifying each firearm, (d) the name and address of the person to whom any firearm is transferred.

Retention period: At least 4 years from date of disposition of the firearm. 27 CFR 179.131

Licensed explosives manufacturers, importers, limited-manufacturers, dealers and permittees.

To take true and accurate inventory of explosives material on hand as of February 12, 1971, or at time of commencing business. To maintain complete and adequate records and supporting documents reflecting the production, importation, receipt, and disposition of all explosives material.

Retention period: 5 years from date transaction occurs. Upon discontinuance of business, explosives records must be delivered to successor, or if discontinuance of business is absolute, to the regional regulatory administrator. 27 CFR 181.121–181.129

Registered importers of arms, ammunition, or implements of war, shown on the Import List.

Importers who are required to register under 27 CFR Part 47 shall maintain records of articles on the U.S. Munitions Import List that are imported, their acquisition and disposition.

Retention period: 6 years, The Director, Bureau of Alcohol, Tobacco and Firearms may prescribe a longer or shorter period in individual cases as he deems necessary. 27 CFR 47.34

Persons needing further information about listed record retention requirements should contact the following:
Mr. Jon S. Baker, Chief, Records and Reports Management Branch, Bureau of Alcohol, Tobacco, and Firearms, 1200 Pennsylvania Avenue N.W., Washington, DC 20226. Telephone: 202–566–7928.

CIVIL AERONAUTICS BOARD

Certificated route air carriers.

(h) To maintain complete file of papers and correspondence relating to each freight loss or damage claim.

Retention period: 3 years after settlement or rejection. 14 CFR 239.10 (retention: 249.13)

Certificated supplemental air carriers.

(i) To maintain complete file of papers and correspondence relating to each freight loss or damage claim.

Retention period: 3 years after settlement. 14 CFR 239.10 (retention: 249.8)

Persons needing further information about listed record retention requirements should contact the following:
Mr. Clifford Rand, Chief, Systems Development Sec., Accounting, Reporting System Division, Bureau of Accounts and Statistics, Civil Aeronautics Board, Room 603, Universal Building, 1825 Connecticut Avenue N.W., Washington, DC 20009 Telephone: 202–675–5113.

CONSUMER PRODUCT SAFETY COMMISSION

NOTE: CPSC Proposed general recordkeeping rules on November 3, 1977.

Persons marketing or handling certain fabrics intended or sold for interlinings or other covered or unexposed parts of wearing apparel and persons manufacturing wearing apparel containing such fabrics.

To maintain records which show the acquisition, disposition, and end use or intended end use of such fabrics.
   Retention period: Not specified. 16 CFR 1610.36(a), 1611.36(a)

Persons marketing or handling certain fabrics intended or sold for use in hats, gloves, and footwear and persons manufacturing hats, gloves, and footwear containing such fabrics.

To maintain records which show the acquisition, disposition, and end use or intended end use of such fabrics.
   Retention period: Not specified. 16 CFR 1610.36(b), 1611.36(b)

Persons guarantying as to flammable quality of fabrics in wearing apparel on basis of guaranties received by them.

To keep the guaranty received and identification of the fabric or fabrics contained in articles of wearing apparel guaranteed in turn by them.
   Retention period: 3 years after guaranty furnished. 16 CFR 1610.38(c) and (d), 1611.38(c) and (d)

Persons guarantying as to flammable quality of fabrics in wearing apparel on basis of class tests.

To maintain records showing identification of the class test; fiber composition, construction, and finish type of fabrics, or fabrics used or contained in articles of wearing apparel so guaranteed; and a swatch of each class of fabrics guaranteed.
   Retention period: 3 years after test. 16 CFR 1610.38(b) and (d), 1611.38(b) and (d)

Persons guarantying as to flammable quality of fabrics in wearing apparel who have made tests thereof. [Amended]

To keep records showing (a) style or range number, fiber composition, construction, and finish type of each fabric (including those with a nitrocellulose fiber, finish, or coating) used or contained in the article of wearing apparel, including a swatch of the fabric tested; (b) stock or formula number, color, thickness and general description of each fiber or film used in the article including a sample of the film; and (c) results of actual tests.
   Retention period: 3 years after test. 16 CFR 1610.38(a) and (d), 1611.38(a) and (d)

Persons shipping or delivering for shipment fabrics or articles of wearing apparel for processing.

To maintain records which establish that the textile fabrics or articles of wearing apparel have been shipped for appropriate flammability treatment and that such treatment has been completed, and records showing disposition of such fabrics or articles of wearing apparel subsequent to the completion of such treatment.
   Retention period: Not specified. 16 CFR 1610.39(b), 1611.39(b)

Importers of textile fabrics or articles of wearing apparel.

To maintain records which establish that the imported textile fabrics or articles or wearing apparel have been shipped for appropriate flammability treatment and that such treatment has been completed, and records showing disposition of such fabrics or articles of wearing apparel subsequent to the completion of such treatment.
   Retention period: Not specified. 16 CFR 1610.39(c), 1611.39(c)

Manufacturers of carpets and rugs subject to flammability standard FF 1-70 and small carpets and rugs subject to flammability standard FF 2-70.

To maintain records of (a) tests made to guarantee flammable quality including all identifying numbers, symbols, and manufacturing specifications, a sample of carpet or rug covered by guaranty, a copy of each test performed for purposes fo the guaranty which shall disclose the date of test, results, and sufficient information to clearly identify carpet or rug tested, and a record showing the yardage at which test was performed; and (b) the guaranty received and identification of carpet or rug or quality of carpet or rug guaranteed in turn by them.

Retention period: 3 years (a) from date tests performed; (b) from date guaranty furnished where applicable. 16 CFR 1630.31, 1631.31, 1631.32

Manufacturers, importers, or other persons initially introducing mattresses into commerce. [*Amended*]

To maintain records showing details, description, and identification of sampling and other plans; production units of all mattresses marketed or handled; test results and details of all tests performed, disposition of all failing and rejected mattresses; certain manufacturing specifications; certain test data; photographic evidence of test results; disposition and such other records as required in section cited.

Retention period: 3 years or longer as required in prototype testing. 16 CFR 1632.31 (c) and (i)

Manufacturers, importers, or other persons initially introducing children's sleepwear; sizes 0–6X and 7–14, into commerce. [*Transferred from 1.16 and amended*]

To maintain records necessary to establish line of continuity through manufacturing process of each production unit of items of children's sleepwear or fabrics or related materials intended or promoted for use in children's sleepwear to sale and delivery of finished items, and from specific finished items back to manufacturing records.

Retention period: 3 years, except records of prototype testing to be maintained as long as they are relied upon and for 3 years thereafter. 16 CFR 1615.31(e), 1616.31(d)

Persons shipping or delivering a hazardous substance in interstate commerce that is to be labeled in substantial quantity at an establishment other than that where originally manufactured or packed. [*Renumbered*]

To keep written agreements signed by and containing the post office address of the person and the operator, and containing whatever specifications for labeling of the hazardous substance that are necessary to insure that the hazardous substance will not be misbranded upon completion of such labeling.

Retention period: 2 years after final shipment or delivery of such hazardous substance from such establishment. 16 CFR 1500.84

Manufacturers and importers of clacker balls, baby bouncers and walkers, or similar articles. [*Renumbered*]

To maintain records of sale, distribution, and results of inspections and tests conducted.

Retention period: 3 years. 16 CFR 1500.86(a) (4)(vii) and (5)(v)

Manufacturers and importers of electrically operated toys and other articles intended for use by children. [*Renumbered*]

To maintain material and production specifications, description of quality assurance program, results of all inspections and tests conducted, and records of sales and distribution.

Retention period: 3 years after production or importation of each lot. 16 CFR 1505.4(a)(3)

Manufacturers or importers of baby cribs. [*Renumbered*]

To maintain records of sale, distribution, and results of all inspections and tests conducted.

Retention period: 3 years after production or importation of each lot. 16 CFR 1508.10

Manufacturers or importers of non-full size baby cribs. [*Added*]

To maintain records of sale and distribution and results of all inspections and tests conducted.

Retention period: 3 years after production or importation of each lot (effective 8–10–76). 16 CFR 1509.12

APPENDIX F   FEDERAL RECORD-RETENTION REQUIREMENTS   575

Manufacturers of poison prevention packaging. [Renumbered]

To maintain records of tests and results of both children and adults required under the Poison Prevention Packaging Act of 1970.
 Retention period: Not specified. 16 CFR 1700.20(a) (3) and (5)

Persons needing further information about listed record retention requirements should contact the following:
Edwin F. Tinsworth, Deputy Director, Bureau of Compliance, Consumer Product Safety Commission, Washington, DC 20207. Telephone: 301–492–6621.

ENVIRONMENTAL PROTECTION AGENCY

Persons awarded EPA grants, and contractors for all subagreements in excess of $10,000.

Grantee shall maintain books, records, documents, and other evidence and accounting procedures necessary to show (1) amount, receipt, and disposition of all assistance received for project, including non-Federal share, and (2) total costs of the project. Contractors of grantees shall maintain books, documents, papers, and records which are pertinent to specific EPA grants.
 Retention period: 3 years after date of final settlement, or after submission of annual financial report for grants which are awarded annually, or until appeal, litigation, claim, or exception is resolved. 40 CFR 30.805, App. A
 Retention period: 3 years. 40 CFR 52.1161

Persons obtaining an experimental permit for use of a pesticide chemical for which a temporary tolerance is established.

To maintain temporary tolerance records of production, distribution, and performance.
 Retention period: 2 years. 40 CFR 180.31(e)(4)

Owners or operators of any building, structure, facility, or installation emitting air pollutants.

To maintain records of the occurrence and duration of any startup, shutdown, or malfunction in operation of any affected facility, any malfunction of the air pollution control equipment, or any periods during which a continuous monitoring system or device is inoperative; a file of all measurements, including monitoring and performance testing measurements; and any other records which may be required by applicable subparts.
 Retention period: 2 years. 40 CFR 60.7

Owners and operators of stationary sources emitting air pollutants for which a national standard is in effect.

To maintain records of nature and amount of emission, air sampling data, and other information deemed necessary to determine compliance with applicable emission limitations or other control measures. (State Implementation Plans)
 Retention period: 2 years. 40 CFR 51.19 and Part 52 (see specific State plan)

Manufacturers of products subject to noise emission standards and labeling requirements of the Noise Control Act of 1972.

To maintain records relating to such products to determine compliance to the act.
 Retention period: Not specified. Public Law 92–574 (86 Stat. 1244)

State or interstate agency participating in the national pollutant discharge elimination program.

To maintain records of all information resulting from monitoring activities as indicated in section cited.
 Retention period: 3 years, or longer during period of unresolved litigation or when requested by Director or Regional Administrator. 40 CFR 124.62, 125.27

Persons holding permits to allow dumping of material into the ocean waters.

To maintain complete records of materials dumped, time and locations of dumping, and such other records as required in section cited.
   Retention period: Not specified. 40 CFR 224.1

Owners and operators of thermal processing facilities and land disposal sites.

To maintain records and monitoring data as required by regulations
   Retention period: Not specified. 40 CFR 240.211–240.211–3, 241.212–241.212–3

Producers of pesticides and devices, and producers of pesticides pursuant to an experimental use permit.

To maintain records of production, brand names, receipt, shipment, inventories, advertising, guarantees, disposal, tests, research, and such other orecords as specified in the section cited.
   Retention period: Various. 40 CFR 169.2, 172.5

State agencies using or applying pesticides pursuant to a quarantine-public health exemption.

To maintain records of all such treatments specifying records as contained in cited section.
   Retention period: Not specified. 40 CFR 166.6

Persons using or receiving pesticides and pesticide containers.

To maintain records to locate pesticides and pesticide containers within a designated landfill.
   Retention period: Not specified. 40 CFR 165.8, 165.9, 165.10

Owners or operators of public water systems.

To maintain records of (a) bacteriological analyses; (b) chemical analyses; (c) actions taken to correct violations of primary drinking water regulations; (d) copies of written reports, summaries or communications relating to sanitary surveys of the system; and (e) records concerning variances or exemptions granted to the system.
   Retention period: (a) 5 years; (b) 10 years; (c) 3 years after last action taken for each violation; (d) 10 years; and (e) 5 years after expiration of variance or exemption. 40 CFR 141.33

Persons who manufacture, process, or distribute in commerce any chemical substance or mixture subject to the Toxic Substances Control Act. [Added]

To maintain records of significant adverse reactions to health or the environment alleged to have been caused by the substance or mixture. Records required to be maintained include records of consumer allegations or personal injury or harm to health, reports of occupational disease or injury, and reports or complaints of injury to the environment.
   Retention period: For records related to adverse reactions to the health of employees, 30 years after such reactions are first reported to manufacturer. Five (5) years after first reporting for all other records of adverse reactions. Public Law 94–469 (15 U.S.C. 2601)

Manufacturers of new motor vehicles or new motor vehicle engines subject to air pollution control regulations. [Added]

To maintain general and specific records relating to such vehicles as specified in the sections cited.
   Retention period: 6 years after issuance of all related certificates of conformity. 40 CFR 85.006, 85.106 85.206, 85.306, 85.706, 85.806, 85.906, 85.077–7

Manufacturers of new motor vehicles or new motor vehicle engines who have been notified that such vehicles or engines are not in conformity with applicable emission standards and regulations. [Added]

To maintain records to permit the analysis of recall campaigns as specified in the section cited.
   Retention period: 5 years. 40 CFR 85.1806

Manufacturers of portable air compressors and medium and heavy duty trucks subject to the noise emission standards and controls for construction and transportation equipment. [Added]

To maintain general and individual records for test compressors and vehicles as specified in the sections cited.
   Retention period: 3 years from the date of production verification. 40 CFR 204.53, 205.53.

Manufacturers of new gasoline-fueled and diesel light-duty vehicles and new gasoline-fueled and diesel light-duty trucks subject to selective enforcement auditing procedures required by air pollution control regulations. [Added]

To maintain general and individual records relating to vehicle emission tests performed pursuant to test orders as specified in the section cited.
    Retention period: 1 year after completion of tests. 40 CFR 86.605

Persons needing further information about listed record retention requirements should contact the following:
Harold R. Masters, Chief, Administrative Management Branch, Management and Organization (PM-213), U.S. Environmental Protection Agency, 401 M Street, S.W., Washington, DC 20460. Telephone: 202-765-0840.

FEDERAL COMMUNICATIONS COMMISSION

Licensees of radio stations in the aviation services.

All stations at fixed locations, except radionavigation land test stations (MTF), to keep adequate records of operation; and stations whose antenna structure is required to be illuminated—a record of illumination; Aeronautical Public Service Stations—to keep a file of all record communications handled and all ground stations so licensed to keep a record of radiotelephone contacts either in the form of telephone traffic tickets or as a separate list.
    Retention period: 30 days; except those logs involving communications incident to a distress or disaster or involved in an investigation by the Commission—until written notification by the Commission to destroy; or logs incident to or involved in a claim or complaint—until satisfaction of such claim or complaint or until barred by statute limiting time for filing suit upon such claim. 47 CFR 87.99-87.109

Licensees of public safety, industrial, and land transportation radio services stations.

To keep records as follows: By all stations—transmitter measurements, service and maintenance records, the name, address, and license information of person or persons responsible for the foregoing and stations whose antenna or antenna supporting structure is required to be illuminated—a record of illumination.
    Retention period: 1 year. 47 CFR 89.175, 89.179, 91.160, 93.160

Owners or operators of industrial heating equipment.

To keep a log of inspections of industrial heating equipment.
    Retention period: Not specified. 47 CFR 18.105

Licensees of ship radiotelegraph stations provided for compliance with part II, title III of the Communications Act or the radio provisions of the Safety Convention.

To keep a record on board the ship of the direction finder calibrations, and check bearings made of their accuracy.
    Retention period: 1 year. 47 CFR 83.459, 83.462

Licensees of television broadcast stations.

To keep at each station a statement that transmitter and station performance measurements for any substitute transmitter have been made and that the data confirm that the station and transmitter performance are as certified by the licensee.
    Retention period: During utilization of the substitute transmitter. 47 CFR 73.640

Persons needing further information about listed record retention requirements should contact the following:
Upton K. Guthery, Federal Communications Commission, Washington, DC 20554. Telephone: 202-632-7024.

FEDERAL TRADE COMMISSION

Wool products manufacturers.

To keep records of the various fibers used in wool products. The records should show not only the fiber content of wool, reprocessed wool, and reused wool, but also any fibers used. Such records should contain sufficient information whereby each of the wool products manufactured can be identified with its respective record of fiber content including the source of the material used therein.

Retention period: 3 years. 16 CFR 300.31

Fur products manufacturers and dealers in furs and fur products.

To keep records showing all the information required under the Fur Products Labeling Act and under rules and regulations relating to such products or furs in a manner that will permit proper identification of each fur product or fur manufactured or handled. The item number required to be assigned to a fur product and to appear on the label and on the invoice relating to such product must appear in the records in such a manner as to identify the product through the various processes of manufacture, from whom purchased and the date of purchase; if exemption on basis of cost claimed, records of cost required.

Retention period: 3 years. 16 CFR 301.39, 301.41

Textile fiber products manufacturers and distributors substituting labels.

To keep records of the various fibers used in the manufacture of textile fiber products. Such records should contain sufficient information whereby each of the textile fiber products manufactured can be identified with its respective record of fiber content including the source of the material used therein.

Those substituting labels shall keep such records as will show the information set forth on the label removed and the name of the person from whom such textile fiber product was received.

Retention period: 3 years. 16 CFR 303.39

Informal dispute settlement mechanisms for warrantors of consumer products.

To keep records of the handling of warranty disputes by informal dispute settlement mechanisms, to compile and keep certain indices regarding the operation of such mechanisms and to compile and keep semi-annual statistical reports summarizing the records.

Retention period: 4 years. 16 CFR 703.6(f)

GENERAL ACCOUNTING OFFICE

Contracting parties under negotiated contracts for the construction, reconstruction, or improvement of facilities and equipment entered into in furtherance of any grant or loan made to a State or local public body under authority of the Urban Mass Transportation Act of 1964, as amended, 49 U.S.C. §§1601 et seq.

To keep any books, documents, papers, and records pertinent to operations and activities under the contract.

Retention period: Unspecified. 49 U.S.C. § 1608(b)

GENERAL SERVICES ADMINISTRATION

Contractors with fixed-price contracts in excess of $10,000 for (a) supplies, or (b) experimental, developmental, or research work where a profit is contemplated, when such contracts contain the standard longform Termination for Convenience of the Government clause.

Unless otherwise provided for in the contract, or by applicable statute, preserve and make available to the Government at all reasonable times at the office of the contractor but without direct charge to the Government, all his books, records, documents, and other evidence bearing on the costs and expenses of the contractor under the contract and relating to the work terminated thereunder, or, to the extent approved by the contracting officer, photographs, microphotographs, or other authentic reproductions thereof.

Retention period: 3 years after final settlement under the contract. 41 CFR 1–8.701

Contractors and subcontractors having certain cost-reimbursement type, time and material, labor-hour, incentive, research and development, or price redeterminable contracts in excess of $100,000.

To maintain books, records, documents, and other evidence and accounting procedures and practices, sufficient to reflect properly all direct and indirect costs of whatever nature claimed to have been incurred for the performance of the contract or subcontract.

Retention period: 3 years after final payment under the contract or subcontract or until expiration of the time periods for certain records specified in 41 CFR Part 1–20, whichever expires earlier; (2) if contract or subcontract is completely or partially terminated, the records relating to the work terminated shall be preserved for 3 years from the date of any resulting settlement; or (4) records which relate to appeals under the "Disputes" clause of the contract, litigation or the settlement of claims arising out of performance of the contract or subcontract, or costs and expenses of the contract or subcontract as to which exception has been taken by the contracting officer, shall be retained until disposition has been made of such appeals, litigation, claims, or exceptions. 41 CFR 1–3.814–2, 1–7.103–18, 1–7.402–7, 1–7.402–30, 1–7.602–5

Contractors with fixed-price or cost-reimbursement type research and development contracts containing the standard inspection clause.

Keep complete records of all inspection work by the contractor and make such records available to the Government.

Retention period: During performance of the contract and for such longer period as may be required by any other clause of the contract, subcontract, or applicable law or regulations. 41 CFR 1–7.302–4, 1–7.402–5

Contractor, educational or nonprofit institution having fixed-price or cost-reimbursement type research and development contracts without profit or fee.

To maintain records as are required to control, protect, preserve, and maintain all Government property delivered for use in connection with contract.

Retention period: Until relieved of responsibility therefor in accordance with written instructions of the contracting officer. 41 CFR 1–7.303–7, 1–7.402–25

INTERSTATE COMMERCE COMMISSION

Persons needing further information about listed record retention requirements should contact the following:
John Grady, Director, Bureau of Accounts, Room 6133, Interstate Commerce Commission, Washington, DC 20423. Telephone: 202–275–7565.

NATIONAL AERONAUTICS AND SPACE ADMINISTRATION

Contractors with negotiated fixed-price research and development contracts, in excess of $10,000.

To maintain books, documents, papers, and records involving transactions related to the contract.

Retention period: 3 years after final payment under the prime contract, or as specified in Appendix M of NASA Procurement Regulation. 41 CFR 18–7.104–15; 18–7.302–6; 1975 Edition of NASA Procurement Regulation (NHB 5100.2A) July 1975 Pub. L. 93–356

Contractors with cost-reimbursement type contract, including facilities contracts.

To maintain books, records, documents, and other evidence pertaining to the expenses for which reimbursement is claimed.

Retention period: 3 years after date of final payment, until settlement of litigation, or as specified by Appendix M of NASA Procurement Regulation. 41 CFR 18–7.203–7; 18–7.402–7; 18–7.451–7; 18–7.460–6; 18–7.702–13; 18–7.703–11; 18–7.704–5

Contractors with fixed-price contracts in excess of $10,000 or supplies or experimental, developmental or research work other than (a) construction, alterations or repair of buildings, bridges, roads, or other kinds of real property or (b) experimental, developmental or research work with educational or nonprofit institutions when no profit is contemplated.

To maintain books, records, documents and other evidence bearing on the cost and expenses of the contractor under the contract and relating to work terminated (may be kept in microfilm or other photographic form to the extent approved by the contracting officer).

Retention period: 3 years after final settlement. 41 CFR 18–8.701; 1975 Edition of NASA Procurement Regulation (NHB) 5100.2A) July 1975 Pub. L. 93–356

Contractors with construction and facilities contracts in excess of $2,000 (for work within the United States).

To keep payroll records showing name and address of each employee, classification, rate of pay, daily and weekly number of hours worked, deductions from pay and actual pay received.
  Retention period: 3 years after contract work completed. 41 CFR 18–12.403–1(d); 18–7.705–5

Contractors furnishing special tooling under fixed-price contracts.

To maintain property control records on all special tooling which they furnish.
  Retention period: Not specified. 41 CFR 18–13.704

Nonprofit contractors having Government furnished property under research and development contracts.

To maintain records of Government property, whether furnished to or acquired by them for the account of the Government, in accordance with the provisions of "Control of Government Property in Possession of Nonprofit Research and Development Contractors" (Appendix C, Subpart 3, NASA Procurement Regulation).
  Retention period: Not specified. 41 CFR 18–13.706, 18–13.707

Contractors with contracts containing the Small Business Subcontracting Program clause, and subcontractors with contracts containing provisions which conform substantially to the language of that clause.

To maintain records showing (a) whether each prospective subcontractor is a small business concern, (b) procedures which have been adopted to comply with the policies set forth in the contract clause entitled "Small Business Subcontracting Program", and (c) such other information required by the clause.
  Retention period: Not specified. 41 CFR 18–1.707–3(b)

Contractors with contracts containing an inspection clause.

To keep complete records of all inspection work by the contractor and make such records available to the Government.
  Retention period: During performance of the contract and for such longer period as may be specified elsewhere in the contract. 41 CFR 18–7.103–5; 18–7.203–5; 18–7.302–4; 18–7.402–5; 18–7.451–5; 18–7.702–6; 18–7.703–6; 18–7.704–8

Contractors with contracts containing the "Data Requirements" clause.

To maintain the following:
  (a) A set of engineering drawings sufficient to enable manufacture of any equipment or items furnished under the contract, or a set of flow sheets and engineering drawings sufficient to enable any performance of any process developed under the contract.
  (b) Any subject data which is necessary to explain or to help the Government technical personnel understand any equipment, items, or process developed under the contract and furnished to the Government.
  Retention period: 1 year after final payment under the contract. 41 CFR 18–9.202–1(e)

Persons needing further information about listed record retention requirements should contact the following:
Written inquiries:
Mr. Stuart J. Evans, Assistant Administrator for Procurement, NASA Headquarters, Washington, DC 20546
Telephone inquiries:
Mr. William T. Brown, Office of Procurement, 202–755–2262.

NATIONAL TRANSPORTATION SAFETY BOARD

Operators of aircraft involved in an accident or incident.

To preserve to the extent possible all records, including tapes of flight recorders and voice recorders, pertaining to the operation and maintenance of the aircraft and to the airmen involved in an accident or incident for which notification must be given to the Board.

Retention period: Until the Board takes custody thereof or a release is granted by an authorized representative of the Board. 49 CFR 830.10

Operators of aircraft involved in an accident or incident.

To retain all records and reports, including all internal documents and memoranda dealing with the accident or incident.
Retention period: Until authorized by the Board to the contrary. 49 CFR 830.10

Persons needing further information about listed record retention requirements should contact the following:
Mr. Frederick King, Chief, Operations & Facilities Division, Bureau of Administration, National Transportation Safety Board, 800 Independence Avenue, S.W., Washington, DC 20594. Telephone: 202–426–3807.

NUCLEAR REGULATORY COMMISSION

Licensees receiving, possessing, using, or transferring byproduct material, source material, or special nuclear material. [Amended]

To maintain records (a) used in preparing Form NRC–4, "Occupational External Radiation Exposure History"; (b) showing individual exposure to radiation and to radioactive material, including all the information required by Form NRC–5, and records of bio-assays, including results of whole body counting examinations; (c) showing the results of surveys made to evaluate the radiation hazards incident to the production, use, release, disposal or presence of radioactive materials or other sources or radiation; (d) showing the results of monitoring the external surfaces of packages received for radioactive contamination caused by leakage of the radioactive contents; (e) showing the results of monitoring the radiation level external to packages received containing quantities of radioactive material in excess of allowable Type A quantities, other than those transported by exclusive use vehicle; (f) relating to the disposal of licensed material by licensee or applicant; (g) relating to disposal of licensed material into a sanitary sewage system; and (h) relating to disposal of licensed material by burial in soil.
Retention period: (a) Until disposal is authorized by the Commission, 10 CFR 20.102; (b) until disposal is authorized by the Commission, 10 CFR 20.401; (c)–(e) for two years after completion of survey except that the following records shall be maintained until disposal is authorized by the Commission: (1) records of the results of surveys to determine compliance with 10 CFR 20.103(a); (2) in the absence of personnel monitoring data, records of the results of surveys to determine external radiation dose; (3) records of results of surveys used to evaluate release of radioactive effluents to environment, 10 CFR 20.401; (f)–(h) until disposal is authorized by the Commission, 10 CFR 20.401

Nonexempt licensees manufacturing, producing, transferring, receiving acquiring, owning, possessing, using, importing, or exporting byproduct material. [Amended]

To maintain (a) such records as may be determined by the Commission to be necessary or appropriate to effectuate the purposes of the Atomic Energy Act of 1954, as amended, and the regulations issued thereunder; (b) records of receipt of byproduct material; (c) records of export of byproduct material; (d) records of transfer of byproduct materials; and (e) records of disposal of byproduct material.
Retention period: (a) Unless otherwise specified by an appropriate regulation or license condition, until disposal is authorized by the Commission, 10 CFR 30.34 and 30.51(b); (b) as long as licensee retains possession of byproduct material and for two years following transfer, export or disposal of byproduct material. 10 CFR 30.51(c); (d) by licensee transferring byproduct material for five years after transfer, 10 CFR 30.51(c); (e) until disposal of records is authorized by the Commission, 10 CFR 30.51(c) and 20.401(c).

Licensees utilizing sealed sources of byproduct material for radiography. [Amended]

To maintain (a) records of the results and dates of calibration for each radiation survey instrument possessed by the licensee; (b) records of results of leak tests of sealed sources; (c) records of quarterly physical inventories of all sealed sources received and possessed under the license; (d) current utilization logs showing for each sealed source a description of the radiographic exposure device or storage container, the identity of the radiographer to whom assigned, and the plant or site where used and dates of use; (e) film badge and thermoluminescence dosimeter reports and records of pocket dosimeter readings; (f) records of physical radiation surveys.

Retention period: (a) For two years after the date of each calibration, 10 CFR 34.24; (b) for six months after performance of the next required leak test or until transfer or disposal of the sealed source, 10 CFR 34.25; (c) for two years after the date of each inventory, 10 CFR 34.26; (d) for two years after the date of each recorded event, 10 CFR 34.27; (e) until disposal is authorized by the Commission, 10 CFR 34.33; (f) for two years after completion of the survey, or for any survey used to determine an individual's exposure until disposal is authorized by the Commission, 10 CFR 34.43.

Licensees receiving, possessing, using, transferring, delivering, importing, or exporting source material. [Amended]

To maintain (a) such records as may be determined by the Commission to be necessary or appropriate to effectuate the purposes of the Atomic Energy Act of 1954, as amended, and the regulations issued thereunder; (b) records of receipt of source material; (c) records of export of source material; (d) records of transfer of source material; and (e) records of disposal of source material.

Retention period: (a) Unless otherwise specified by an appropriate regulation or license condition, until disposal is authorized by the Commission, 10 CFR 40.41 and 40.61(b); (b) as long as the licensee retains possession of the source material and for five years following transfer, export or disposition of the source material, 10 CFR 40.61(c)(1); (c) for five years after export of the source material, 10 CFR 40.61(c)(2); (d) until disposal is authorized by the Commission, 10 CFR 40.61(c)(3); (e) until disposal of records is authorized by the Commission, 10 CFR 40.61(c)(4) and 20.401(c)(3).

Licensees and holders of construction permits. [Amended]

To maintain (a) such records as may be required by conditions of the license or permit or by rules, regulations, and orders of the Commission (b) records of design, fabrication, erection, and testing of structure, systems, and components important to safety of a production or utilization facility; and (c) quality assurance records sufficient to furnish evidence of activities affecting quality, including operating logs, records showing results of reviews, inspections, tests, audits, work performance monitoring and material analyses, and records containing closely related data such as qualifications of personnel, procedures and equipment.

Retention period: (a) If not otherwise specified by regulation, license condition or technical specification, until disposal is authorized by the Commission, 10 CFR 50.71(c); (b) throughout life of facility, 10 CFR Part 50, App. A, Criterion 1; (c) not specified—to be established by applicant consistent with applicable regulatory requirements, 10 CFR Part 50, App. B, sec. XVII

Licensees receiving title to own, acquire, deliver, receive, possess, use, transfer, import, or export special nuclear material [Amended]

To keep (a) such records of ownership, receipt, possession, use, transfer, import, and export of special nuclear material as may be incorporated as a condition or requirement in any license; (b) records of changes to the material control and accounting program made without prior Commission approval; (c) records of changes to the physical security plan made without prior Commission approval; (d) records of receipt, acquisition, physical inventory or import of special nuclear material; (e) records of export of special nuclear material; (f) records of transfer of special nuclear material to other persons; (g) records of disposal of special nuclear material; (h) material balance records for each material balance showing the quantity of element and fissile isotope in each component of the material balance; (i) a record summarizing the quantities of element and fissile isotope for ending inventory of material in process and additions and removals of material in process during material balance interval; (j) a record summarizing the quantities of element and fissile isotope in unopened receipts and ultimate products maintained under tamper-safing or in the form of sealed sources; (k) records of results of review and audit of the nuclear material control system; (l) records of shipper-receiver difference evaluations, investigations, and corrective actions concerning special nuclear material received and shipped; (m) all data, information, reports, and documents generated by the measurement control program, including summary of error data utilized in limit of error calculations performed for each material balance period; and (n) records pertaining to training and qualification of personnel who perform measurement activities pursuant to 10 CFR 70.57(b)(7).

Retention period: (a) If not otherwise specified by regulation or license condition, until disposal is authorized by the Commission, 10 CFR 70.32(b)(5) and 70.51(b)(2); (b) five years from date of change 10 CFR 70.32(c); (c) two years from date of change, 10 CFR 70.32(e); (d) as long as licensee retains possession of special nuclear material and for five years following transfer or export of special nuclear material, 10 CFR 70.51(b)(3); six months for records of inventory of special nuclear material maintained to demonstrate compliance with requirements of 10 CFR 70.58(h) relating to establishment and maintenance of system of storage and internal handling controls, 10 CFR 70.51(b)(3); (e) five years after export of special nuclear material, 10 CFR 70.51(b)(4); (f) until disposal is authorized by the Commission, or for five years for records required by 10 CFR 70.51(e)(1)(v) to document transfers of special nuclear material between material balance areas, 10 CFR 70.51(b)(5); (g) until disposal is authorized by the Commission, 10 CFR 70.51(b)(6) and 20.401(c); (h) five years, 10 CFR 70.51(e)(4)(iii); (i) five years, 10 CFR 70.51(e)(4)(iv); (j) five years, 10 CFR 70.51(e)(4)(v); (k) five years, 10 CFR 70.58(c)(2); (l) five years, 10 CFR 70.58(g)(4); (m) five years, 10 CFR 70.57(b)(12); (n) two years, 10 CFR 70.57(b)(12).

Licensees and other persons subject to financial protection requirements and indemnity agreements.

To maintain records as deemed necessary by the Commission for the administration of the regulations concerning financial protection requirements and indemnity agreements.
  Retention period: Not specified, 10 CFR 140.6

Licensees packaging radioactive material for transport. [Amended]

To keep records of each shipment of fissile material or of more than a type A quantity of radioactive material as defined in 10 CFR 71.4(q), in a single package.
  Retention period: 2 years after generation of record, 10 CFR 71.62(a).

Licensees required to provide physical protection for special nuclear material in transit and at fixed sites. [Amended]

To maintain records of names and addresses of all authorized personnel, results of tests and inspctions of protected areas and security-related equipment shipments of special nuclear material, information to comply with requirements of this part, procedures for controlling access to protected areas, and such other records as indicated in 10 CFR 73.70.
  Retention period: Not specified, 10 CFR 73.70

Licensees manufacturing, distributing, or importing certain items containing byproduct material. [Amended]

To maintain (a) records of name and address of each person to whom material is transferred, and kinds and quantity of byproduct material transferred; and (b) records showing the name, address, and point of contact for each general licensee to whom he transfers byproduct material in devices, the date of each transfer, the isotope and quantity of radioactivity in each device transferred, the identity of any intermediate person through whom the transfer was made, and compliance with the report requirements of 10 CFR 32.52.
  Retention period: (a) for two years after each transfer, 10 CFR 32.20; (b) for five years from the date of each recorded event, 10 CFR 32.52(c).

Licensees authorized to possess at any one time and location more than 10,000 curies of tritium. [Amended]

To maintain records sufficient to enable the licensee to account for the tritium in his possession under specific license.
  Retention period: As long as licensee retains possession of tritium and for two years following transfer or export of tritium, 10 CFR 30.54(a), 150.18.

General licensees receiving, acquiring, possessing, using or transferring certain detecting, measuring, gauging, or controlling devices containing byproduct material [Amended]

To maintain (a) records of tests performed on such devices for leakage of radioactive material; (b) records of tests performed on such devices for proper operation of the on-off mechanism and indicator; (c) records showing compliance with requirements of 10 CFR 31.5(c)(3) relating to the performance on such devices of other testing, installation, servicing, and removal from installation involving the radioactive materials, shielding or containment.
  Retention period: (a) For one year after the next required leak test is performed or until the sealed source is transferred or disposed of, 10 CFR 31.5(c)(4); (b) for one year after the next

required test of the on-off mechanism and indicator is performed or until the sealed source is transferred or disposed of, 10 CFR 31.5 (c)(4); (c) for a period of two years from the date of the recorded event or until the device is transferred or disposed of, 10 CFR 31.5(c)(4).

Licensees authorized to operate nuclear production and utilization facilities. [Amended]

To maintain (a) records of changes to physical security plan made without prior Commission approval; (b) records of changes in the production or utilization facility as described in the safety analysis report made without prior Commission approval; (c) records of changes in facility procedures as described in the safety analysis report made without prior Commission approval; and (d) records of tests or experiments not described in the safety analysis report and made without prior Commission approval. The records described in paragraphs (b), (c) and (d) of this section shall include written safety evaluations which provide the bases for the determination that the change, test or experiment does not involve an unreviewed safety question.

Retention period: (a) For two years after date of change, 10 CFR 50.54(p); (b) until date of termination of license, 10 CFR 50.59(b); (c) for five years after each change in facility procedures, 10 CFR 50.59(b); (d) for five years after each test or experiment, 10 CFR 50.59(b).

Licensees authorized to operate nuclear production and utilization facilities. [Amended]

To maintain records to document each licensed operator's and senior operator's participation in the requalification program. The records shall contain copies of written examinations administered, answers given by the licensee, results of evaluations, and documentation of any additional training administered in areas in which an operator or senior operator has exhibited deficiencies.

Retention period: For two years after date of recorded event, 10 CFR Part 55, App. A, par. 5a.

Licensees for certain groups of medical uses of byproduct material.

To maintain records of (a) tests for contamination and/or leakage on certain sources or devices containing byproduct material; (b) quarterly physical inventories taken to account for all sources and devices received and possessed.

Retention period: Not specified. 10 CFR 35.14

Persons needing further information about listed record retention requirements should contact the following:
G. L. Hutton, Division of Rules and Records, Office of Administration, U.S. Nuclear Regulatory Commission, Washington, DC 20555. Telephone: 301–492–7211.

SPECIAL ACTION OFFICE FOR DRUG ABUSE PREVENTION

Federally funded drug treatment services and drug treatment central intake units.

To maintain system of patient records adequate to comply with all Federal and State reporting requirements.

Retention period: Not specified. 21 CFR 1402.12, 1403.12

Persons needing further information about listed record retention requirements should contact the following:
Mr. Robert A. Dormer, Special Action Office for Drug Abuse Prevention, Rockwell Building, Room 652, 11400 Rockville Pike, Rockville, MD. 20852. Telephone: 301–443–6697.

UNITED STATES POSTAL SERVICE

Persons needing further information about listed record retention requirements should contact the following:
John Finlay, U.S. Postal Service, 475 L'Enfant Plaza West, S.W., Washington, DC 20260. Telephone: 202–245–4142.

APPENDIX G
STANDARDS-SETTING AND SAFETY-INFORMATION ORGANIZATIONS

This listing is in two parts: (1) Voluntary standards-setting organizations and trade associations with some standards-setting functions, and (2) state purchasing offices which have developed or adopted standards of their own.

The bulk of the list is drawn from the *Directory of United States Standardization Activities,* Sophie J. Chumas, Editor, Institute for Applied Technology, National Bureau of Standards, Washington, DC 20234. This listing was last published in 1975. Every organization in the listing with any possible product-safety standardization function was contacted either by letter or telephone to confirm this function and to update the listed information.

The overwhelming majority of these organizations coordinate their standard-setting activities through the American National Standards Institute. An index of all safety-related ANSI standards is given in App. D. Organizations who publish their standards only through ANSI are not listed in this appendix. Organizations which publish their standards before ANSI finally approves them as American National Standards are listed here, however, because such approval frequently takes a year or more.

Some organizations that do not issue standards for product safety are listed, because they are judged to be particularly good sources of health and use-related data upon which safety design efforts can be based, or because their members may be available for consulting or for testimony as expert witnesses in liability cases.

Abrasive Grain Association, 2130 Keith Building, Cleveland, OH, 44115.   216-241-7333

Has published nine standards through ANSI.

Accrediting Bureau of Medical Laboratory Schools, Oak Manor Offices, 3038 West Lexington, Elkhart, IN 46514.   219-293-0124

Recognized by the U.S. Office of Education to accredit medical laboratory technician education programs below the baccalaureate degree.

Adhesive and Sealant Council, 2350 E. Devon Ave. Des Plaines, IL, 60018.   312-296-1166

Aerospace Industries Association, 1725 DeSales Street NW, Washington, DC 20036.   202-347-2315

Standardization activity comprises approximately 10 percent of the total AIA program, and is administered principally through the Technical Specifications Division of the Aerospace Technical Council, and its Standards Management Policy Group. The National Aerospace Standards Committee (NASC) is responsible for the development, maintenance, and promotion of the AIA standards document series of National Aerospace Standards (NAS). Standards in the NAS series are also developed under the Manufacturing Committee (machine tools) and the Transport Airworthiness Requirements Committee (transport and cargo).

National Aerospace Standards are published and distributed through the documentation services of: National Standards Association, Inc., 1321 Fourteenth Street, NW, Washington, DC 20005.

Air-Conditioning and Refrigeration Institute, 1815 North Fort Myer Drive, Arlington, VA 22209. 703-524-8800

The standardization activities of ARI include standards specifying acceptable installation criteria, including initial selection of equipment, and standards containing provisions intended to safeguard life, health, and property.

Air Diffusion Council, 435 North Michigan Avenue, Chicago, IL 60611. 312-527-5494

Members are manufacturers of grilles, registers, ceiling diffusers, high-velocity terminal control devices, and flexible ducts used in conjunction with air-conditioning systems in commercial construction.

Air Moving and Conditioning Association, 30 West University Drive, Arlington, Heights, IL 60004. 312-394-0150

Technical standards cover a wide variety of subjects including nomenclature and arrangements, standard sizes, spark-resistant construction, operating limits for centrifugal fans, and flue gas and air densities.

Air Pollution Control Association, 4400 Fifth Avenue, Pittsburgh, PA 15213. 412-621-1090

The Air Pollution Control Association contributes to the development of standards through representation in the following committees of standards-setting organizations: American National Standards Committee Z-21; Subcommittee on Standards for Domestic Gas-Fired Incinerators; American National Standard Z-105; Air Cleaning Equipment Committee; American National Standard Z-91; Committee of Installation Standards for Oil Burners and Oil Burning Equipment; American National Standard Z-228; Incinerator Committee; International Organization for Standardization; Technical Committee ISO/TC 146; Air Purity and Intersociety Committee *(Manual of Methods of Ambient Air Sampling Analysis).*

Air Transport Association of America, 1709 New York Avenue, N.W., Washington, DC 20006. 202-872-4000

The Association has published the industry standard specification for the preparation of aircraft manuals by manufacturers for the use of airline operators, the industry specification for the preparation of ground equipment manuals by manufacturers for the use of airline operators, the industry integrated data processing standard specification for the procurement of aircraft parts, the industry standard for packaging of parts and components of aircraft and aircraft systems, and case sizes and wiring for much of the radio communications and navigation and other electronics equipment installed in airline aircraft.

Alliance of American Insurers 20 North Wacker Drive, Chicago, IL 60606. 312-346-5190

The standardization work of this organization pertaining to occupational safety and health, and traffic safety, is carried on with ANSI. In fire safety, all standardization work is carried on with the National Fire Protection Association.

Aluminum Association, 818 Connecticut Avenue, N.W., Washington, DC 20006. 202-862-5100

Amateur Athletic Union of the United States, Inc., 3400 West 86th Street, Indianapolis, IN 46268. 317-283-5688

Besides the adoption of standard contest rules for various sports under its jurisdiction, the union also fixes standards on dimensions, weights, material, and shapes of the various implements, balls, etc. entering into athletic contests.

American Association of Bioanalysts, 411 North Seventh Street, 805 Ambassador Building, St. Louis, MO 63101.   314-241-1445

This association of bioanalyst laboratory directors is active in certification and accreditation of bioanalyst laboratory directors, laboratory supervisors, and clinical laboratories as a sponsoring organization of the American Board of Bioanalysis. AAB maintains a national program of external quality control known as The Proficiency Testing Service.

American Association of Cereal Chemists, 3340 Pilot Knob Road, St. Paul, MN 55121.   612-454-7250

Approved Methods of the AACC, now in loose-leaf format with replacements and additions appearing annually, is a two-volume, 872-page laboratory manual which includes 330 methods, over 90 pages of reference tables, and 45 full-color photos of insect fragments in its Extraneous Matter section.

American Association of Clinical Chemists, PO Box 15053, Winston-Salem, NC 27103.   919-725-0208

American Association of Motor Vehicle Administrators, 1828 L Street N.W.., Suite 500, Washington, DC 20036.   202-296-1955

This organization of state and provincial officials responsible for the administration and enforcement of motor vehicle and traffic laws in the United States and Canada includes committees on safety equipment and product safety.

The American Association of Petroleum Geologists, 1444 South Boulder, Tulsa, OK 74119.   918-584-2555

The American Association of Poison Control Centers, Childrens Memorial Hospital, 44th and Dewey Avenue, Omaha, NE 68105.   402-553-5400, extension 295

The Committee on Educational Activities has been active in efforts to develop materials that will be of value to poison-control and information centers in educating the lay public about the hazards of, and the prevention of acute poisoning in and about the home.

American Association of State Highway and Transportation Officials, 341 National Press Building, Washington, DC 20004.   202-624-5800

Committees include units on highway safety and environmental quality.

American Association of Textile Chemists and Colorists, PO Box 12215, Research Triangle Park, NC 22709.   919-549-8141

Practically all of the textile dyes, finishes, and many chemicals produced in the United States are controlled and checked by AATCC test methods.

American Automobile Association, 1712 G Street N.W., Washington, DC 20006.   703-222-6000

The AAA has developed a model safety-responsibility bill and a guide as to standards for state legislation on roadside development and control.

American Board for Certification in Orthotics and Prosthetics, 1440 N Street N.W., Washington, DC 20005.   202-234-8400

The American Board for Certification in Orthotics and Prosthetics was founded in 1948 in order to establish a credentials program for identifying orthotic and prosthetic practitioners, as well as facilities, qualified to render essential public health services related to artificial limbs and braces.

The American Boards of Examiners in Speech Pathology and Audiology, American Speech and Hearing Association, 10801 Rockville Pike, Rockville, MD 20852.   301-897-5700

Formulates standards and procedures for the determination of qualifications of individuals, organizations, and institutions applying for certificates of accreditation or clinical competence. Maintains and monitors boards of examiners responsible for arranging and conducting examinations to determine the qualifications of applicants for such certificates. Grants appropriate certificates. Maintains a registry of agencies, individuals, organizations, and institutions who have been issued such certificates.

American Boat and Yacht Council, Inc., 15 East 26th Street, Room 1603, New York, NY 10010. 212-532-9688

The Council's sole activity is the development of safety standards and recommended practices for the design, construction, equipage, and maintenance of boats and their related accessories. The Council has published about 60 standards in a large loose-leaf volume entitled *Safety Standards for Small Craft.*

American Boiler Manufacturers' Association, 1500 Wilson Boulevard, Arlington, VA 22209. 703-522-7298

This association, established in 1888, participates in the following standardization work: (1) publishes through the Technical Committee, Packaged Firetube Boiler Section, ratings standards entitled Packaged Firetube Boiler Ratings for Heating Boilers; (2) publishes a lexicon of industry terminology, coal analysis, and accessory product definitions; (3) acts as secretariat to the National Fire Protection Association's Committee on Boiler Furnace Explosions and to the Sectional Committees on Public Utility Units and Industrial Units.

American Bureau of Shipping, 45 Broad Street, New York, NY 10004. 212-785-9800

The Bureau's work includes (1) the preparation of standards, called "rules," for the construction of hulls and machinery of merchant ships, including material specifications and regulations for periodical surveys. The rules are published annually and are modified to keep pace with developments in shipbuilding and marine engineering; (2) the analysis of plans of vessels projected to be built, or conversions of existing vessels, to verify if they meet the standards set by the rules; (3) the verification of the building to approved plans of the new hull and its main machinery, boilers, and vital auxiliaries, and the conversion of existing vessels; (4) the witnessing of the testing of materials of construction for hull and machinery as required by the rules; (5) the carrying out of periodic and damage surveys as called for by the rules, (6) the carrying out of load-line surveys and the issuance of tonnage certificates, all under the authority of various governments and international conventions.

The American Ceramic Society, Inc., 65 Ceramic Drive, Columbus, OH 43213. 614-268-8645

American College of Surgeons, 55 East Erie Street, Chicago, IL 60611. 312-664-4050

The College is the only organization responsible at the national level for the standardization and approval of hospital cancer programs in the United States.

American Concrete Institute, 22400 West Seven Mile Road, Detroit, MI 48219. 313-532-2600

Since its organization in 1905, this institute has been devoted to the solution of technical problems related to the design, construction, and maintenance of concrete and reinforced-concrete structures and to the dissemination of information in this field.

American Concrete Paving Association, 1211 West 22nd Street, Oak Brook, Il 60523. 312-654-4330

Reviews concrete pavement specifications for Federal agencies such as the Federal Highway Administration, Federal Aviation Administration, U.S. Army Corps of Engineers, and U.S. Navy, plus state highway departments.

American Concrete Pipe Association, 1501 Wilson Boulevard, Arlington, VA 22209. 703-821-1990

American Conference of Governmental Industrial Hygienists, PO Box 1937, Cincinnati, OH 45201. 513-825-0312

This conference, founded in 1938, is a national professional association of practicing industrial hygiene personnel in Federal, state, and local agencies. Through its committees, the ACGIH assembles guides, recommended practices, and methods for the evaluation and control of the industrial environment.

The Conference publishes an annual listing, *Threshold Limit Values,* containing TLVs for over 500 substances (mostly chemicals and chemical compounds) in dusts, fumes, gases, vapors, mists, and physical agents. The values, which are under continuous review, are used as guides in the control of health hazards and should not be regarded as fine lines between safe and dangerous concentrations. (see Appendix B) Several states, the U.S. Department of Labor, and the British Ministry of Labour incorporate the TLVs in codes or regulations.

American Council of Independent Laboratories, Inc., 1725 K Street N.W., Washington, DC 20006.   202-659-3766

ACIL promotes standards of ethics employed by independent laboratories in special fields of interest and activity.

ACIL does not write standards for products or materials but its members participate in writing test procedures and methodology in other standards-writing organizations.

American Crystallographic Association, 335 East 45th Street, New York, NY 10017.   212-661-9404

American Defense Preparedness Association, Union Trust Building, 15th and H Streets N.W., Washington, DC 20005.   202-347-7250

Included within the technical divisions of the ADPA, in addition to divisions covering all types of armament systems, are the following: standards and metrology; materials; mobilization readiness; quality and reliability; technical documentation; value engineering; safety; and the packaging, handling, and transportation functions.

American Dental Association, 211 East Chicago Avenue, Chicago, IL 60611.   312-440-2500

Has had a specification and certification program for dental materials and devices since 1928. To date, 25 specifications and 5 standards have been adopted. In addition the ADA acts as proprietary sponsor on a project to handle standards for dental radiographic film, and operates two evaluation programs: a certification program based upon the physical standards, and an acceptance program based upon proof of biological and clinical safety and effectiveness.

American Die Casting Institute, 2340 Des Plaines Avenue, Des Plaines, IL 60018.   312-298-1220

This institute (ADCI) was founded in 1923, as a service to the customers of the die-casting industry. ADCI publishes product standards for die castings to guide designers and engineers to the most economical use of die castings. A quality control series was introduced in 1973.

American Dry Milk Institute, 130 North Franklin Street, Chicago, IL 60606.   312-782-4888

ADMI has issued standards on product definition and nomenclature, specifications and grade classifications, and promotes the use of its standards through publications and publicity.

American Electroencephalographic Society, 36391 Maple Grove Road, Willoughby Hills, OH 44094.   216-942-9267

Currently, the Society has 620 members. The membership is composed primarily of physicians and PhD scientists. The physician members are primarily neurologists and psychiatrists. The PhDs are primarily psychologists and neurophysiologists.

American Feed Manufacturers' Association, 1701 North Fort Myer Drive, Arlington, VA 22209.   703-524-0810

The Association is the national trade association of the animal feed manufacturing industry.

American Fishing Tackle Manufacturers' Association, 20 North Wacker Drive, Suite 2014, Chicago, IL 60606.   312-236-0565

American Footwear Industries Association, 1611 North Kent Street, Arlington, VA 22209. 703-522-8070

Has developed recommended manufacturing standards for the United States footwear industry. These standards relate to the lasts on which the shoes are produced and thus affect all related components.

American Foundrymen's Society, Golf and Wolf Roads, Des Plaines, IL 60016. 312-824-0181

With the exception of standards which the society has developed for the evaluation of foundry sands, standardization has been carried out in cooperation with ASTM and ANSI.

American Gas Association, Headquarters: 1515 Wilson Boulevard, Arlington, VA 22209; Standardization Laboratories: 8501 East Pleasant Valley Road, Cleveland, OH 44131. 216-524-4990 (Cleveland); 703-524-2000

This association of the gas distribution industry coordinates gas industry activities concerning research, standardization and information related to the production, distribution, and utilization of gas.

American Gear Manufacturers' Association, Suite 1000, 1901 North Fort Myer Drive, Arlington, VA 22209. 703-525-6000

Standards cover such areas as: gear industry nomenclature; gear specification drawings; application classification of gear motors and other types of speed reducers; tooth geometry; strength and durability formulas and inspection methods and practices.

American Home Economics Association, 2010 Massachusetts Avenue N.W., Washington, DC 20036. 202-833-3100

AHEA is the administrative secretariat of the American *National Standard Z61.1-1970 - Dimensions, Tolerances, and Terminology for Home Cooking and Baking Utensils.* In addition, the Association expresses its interest in standards through representation on the American National Standards Institute's Consumer Council. AHEA works closely with NBS and assisted in developing the *Voluntary Product Standard PS 54-72, Body Measurements for the Sizing of Girl's Apparel.*

American Home Lighting Institute, 230 North Michigan Avenue, Chicago, IL 60601. 312-236-3816

This institute is composed of manufacturers of residential lighting fixtures, distributor showrooms, and component parts manufacturers. The *AHLI Minimum Light for Living Standards* for houses and apartments are cited as a guide in the "Minimum Property Standards for One and Two Family Dwellings" of the U.S. Department of Housing and Urban Development.

American Hospital Association, 840 North Lake Shore Drive, Chicago, IL 60611. 312-645-9400

The Association provides education, research, and representation services for 7,000 institutional and 17,000 personal members. The Bureau of Management and Planning, through its Division of Design and Construction, has primary responsibility for standardization activities related to hospital supplies, equipment, and facilities. Concerns range from flammability, to structural integrity, to infection control—all those factors which pose a threat to the safety of hospital patients and employees.

American Hot Dip Galvanizers' Association, 1000 Vermont Avenue, Washington, DC 20005. 202-628-4634

The Association serves as the focal point for technically related inquiries from both the industry and from users of hot-dip galvanized products.

American Hotel and Motel Association, 888 Seventh Avenue, New York, NY 10019. 212-265-4506

This trade association representing the hotel and motel industry cooperated in the development of *USA Standard Safety Code for Elevators, Dumbwaiters, and Escalators;* and *USA Recommended Practice for the Inspection of Elevators.* It is also represented on ANSI sectional committees on standards and specifications for refrigerators, and on minimum requirements for plumbing and standardization of plumbing equipment.

American Industrial Hygiene Association, 66 South Miller Road, Akron, OH 44313.   216-836-9537

The Association was established in 1939 by leading industrial hygienists as a result of need for an association devoted exclusively to industrial hygiene.

The objectives of the Association are: (1) to increase the knowledge of industrial hygiene through interchange and dissemination of information; (2) to promote the study and control of environmental factors affecting the health and well-being of industrial workers; (3) to correlate such activities as are conducted by individuals and agencies throughout industrial, educational and governmental groups; and (4) to bring together persons interested in the various phases of industrial hygiene. The association publishes a monthly journal containing not only professional articles, but also guides for industrial health practices and procedures.

American Institute of Architects, Department of Professional Practice, AIA Codes and Regulations Center, 1735 New York Avenue NW, Washington, DC 20006.   202-785-7300

The nationally recognized society of over 24,000 licensed architects in the United States, the AIA maintains active liaison with over 80 national professional and Federal organizations involved in the art and science of building code and standards-writing as related to the practice of architecture.

American Institute of Chemical Engineers, 345 East 47th Street, New York, NY 10017.   212-644-8025

Equipment Testing Procedures Committee performs its work through seven equipment subcommittees: distillation columns, dryers, evaporators and crystallizers, heat exchangers, filters, fired heaters, mixers, and pumps; and one staff/service subcommittee, measurements. Twelve testing procedures have been published.

American Institute of Mining, Metallurgical, and Petroleum Engineers, 345 East 47th Street, New York, NY 10017.   212-644-7695

Composed of three constituent societies: the Society of Mining Engineers, The Metallurgical Society, and the Society of Petroleum Engineers.

American Institute of Steel Construction, Inc., 400 N. Michigan Ave., Chicago IL. 60011.

Nonprofit trade association representing the fabricated structural steel industry. The Institute provides a wide variety of services, including specifications, technical publications, computer design aids, regional engineering services, research and development, technical seminars, design award competitions, engineering fellowship awards, and programs of quality control and safety in both shop and field.

American Institute of Timber Construction, 333 West Hampden Avenue, Englewood, CO 80110.   303-761-3212

National trade association of the structural timber fabricating industry. The Institute maintains a quality control and inspection program for structural glued laminated timber based on PS 56-73 and the *Inspection Manual, AITC 200.*

American Insurance Association, 85 John Street, New York, NY 10038.   212-433-4400

Trade association created in 1964 by the merger of three organizations: the National Board of Fire Underwriters, the Association of Casualty and Surety Companies, and the former American Insurance Association. It is the largest business association serving property and casualty insurance companies and acts as spokesman for the industry.

American Iron and Steel Institute, 1000 16th Street NW, Washington, DC 20036.   202-452-7100

Does considerable work in classifying and defining products, collecting and compiling manufacturing tolerances and methods relative to standard methods of inspection, and reviewing existing specifications with a view toward standardizing those which are found to be most common.

American Ladder Institute, 111 East Wacker Drive, Chicago, IL 60601. 312-644-6610

Manufacturers of portable steel and extension ladders made from wood, metal, and fiberglass. A substantial part of the Association's activities is the cosponsorship of the American National Standards Institute's *Safety Code for Portable Wood Ladders, A14.1.*

American Leather Chemists' Association, c/o University of Cincinnati, Cincinnati, OH 45221. 513-475-2643

The technical society of the tanning and leather industry.

American Library Association, 50 East Huron Street, Chicago, IL 60611. 312-944-6780

Standards include *Measurement and Comparison of Physical Facilities for Libraries; Minimum Standards for Public Library Systems.*

American Lumber Standards Committee, 340 Hungerford Drive, Rockville, MD 20850. 301-972-1700

This committee consists of 23 representatives and 23 alternate representatives of groups of lumber manufacturers, lumber inspection agencies, engineers, architects, contractors, home builders, wholesalers, retailers, millwork manufacturers, and final consumers, as well as five *ex officio* nonvoting government agency representatives, all of which are appointed by the Secretary of Commerce.

American Lung Association, 1740 Broadway, New York, NY 10019. 212-245-8000

Devoted to the prevention and control of lung disease. The American Thoracic Society, as the medical section of this association, is a professional society dedicated to all aspects of respiratory disease. Both the ALA and the ATS publish standards, guidelines, and statements relating to all aspects of lung disease prevention, control, and patient care, including respiratory therapy and medical devices.

American Medical Association, 535 North Dearborn Street, Chicago, IL 60610. 312-751-6000

Many of its standards are advisory only: drug evaluation, medical terminology, guides to evaluation of physical impairment, physical fitness standards for industry, undergraduate medical education, hospital residency training programs, and continuing medical education.

American National Standards Institute, 1430 Broadway, New York, NY 10018. 212-354-3300

This is a nonprofit organization whose bylaws provide for membership from national trade, technical, professional, and labor groups; firms from commerce and industry; governmental agencies and departments; consumer groups; and similar organizations and individuals.

The Institute serves as the national clearinghouse for standards and provides the machinery for developing and approving standards which are supported by a national consensus.

Technical societies, trade associations, consumer groups, and the like make up the organizational members of the Institute. Other classes of members are governmental members (organizations not otherwise eligible for membership but interested in standards development or certification), individual members (persons interested in development of standards or in certification), and honorary members.

The American National Standards Institute is the United States member of the International Organization for Standardization (ISO).

American Nuclear Society, 244 East Ogden Avenue, Hinsdale, IL 60521. 312-325-1991

Three ANS standards and 12 American National Standards have been published. Some draft and trial standards are also available. In addition, the American Nuclear Society serves as secretariat for five American National Standards Committees of the Nuclear Technical Advisory Board.

American Oil Chemists' Society, 508 South Sixth Street, Champaign, IL 61820. 217-359-2344

Scientific organization concerned with basic research on animal, marine, and vegetable oils and fats;

their extraction, refining, and use in consumer and industrial products; and with safety, packaging, and quality control.

American Optometric Association, 7000 Chippewa Street, St. Louis, MO 63119 (Headquarters); 1730 M Street NW, Washington, DC 20036. (Washington Office). St. Louis - 314-832-5770, Washington, DC - 202-833-9890

Currently the Association has over 17,800 members. The Association and its members participate extensively in various American National Standards committees, including standards for safe use of lasers; occupational face and eye protection; as well as standards for lighting, color, etc.

American Paper Institute, 260 Madison Avenue, New York, NY 10016. 212-883-8000

Standards for testing certain physical characteristics, such as bursting strength, tear, brightness, opacity, etc., have been developed for many grades of paper. These specifications are officially published by the Technical Association of the Pulp and Paper Industry, One Dunwoody Park, Atlanta, GA 30341.

American Petroleum Institute, 1801 K Street NW, Washington, DC 20006. 202-457-7000

Over 300 standards formulated by API on engineering, operability, performance, and safety considerations.

American Pharmaceutical Association, 2215 Constitution Avenue N.W., Washington, DC 20037. 202-628-4410

Standardization programs administered by the Association pertain to drugs and drug products intended for medicinal use.

American Plywood Association, 1119 A Street, Tacoma, WA 98401. 206-272-2283

Industry trade association engaged in advertising, promotion, quality testing and inspection, product and applied research, and code and standards activities.

American Podiatry Association, 20 Chevy Chase Circle NW, Washington, DC 20015. 202-362-2700

American Psychiatric Association, 1700 18th Street NW, Washington, DC 20009. 202-797-4900

The American Psychoanalytic Association, One East Fifty-Seventh Street, New York, NY 10022. 212-PL 2-0450

American Public Health Association, 1015 18th Street N.W., Washington, DC 20036. 202-467-5000

Publishes *Standard Methods for the Examination of Dairy Products; Standard Methods for the Examination of Water and Wastewater;* and *Standards for Healthful Housing.* It publishes other works where standards are included; for example, Suggested Ordinance and Recommendations Covering Public Swimming Pools. It also publishes *Microbiological Examination of Foods* and *Recommended Methods for the Examination of Ambient Air.*

American Road Builders' Association, 525 School Street S.W., Washington, DC 20024. 202-488-2722

Committees study problems relating to highway legislation; finance, design, construction, maintenance, equipment, and operation.

American Society for Abrasive Methods, 1049 South Main Street, Plymouth, MI 48170. 313-455-7703

American Society for Artificial Internal Organs, National Office, Box 777, Boca Raton, FL 33432. 305-391-8589

Includes strong representation from both medical and engineering specialists. In recent years, major interests have focused upon work with artificial kidneys and artificial hearts, but research has been reported in a variety of other fields.

American Society for Medical Technology, Hermann Professional Building, Suite 1600, Houston, TX 77025. 713-664-8121

Approximately 18,000 members engaged in the supervision and performance of clinical laboratory tests.

American Society for Metals, Metals Park, OH 44073. 216-338-5151

This society, founded in 1920, publishes the *ASM Metals Handbook,* a multiple-volume series. Comprehensive coverage is given to properties, selection, heat-treating, cleaning, finishing, machining, forming, forging, casting and welding of metals, and to subjects of a more scientific nature such as metallography, crystal structures, and alloy constitutions.

American Society for Quality Control, 161 West Wisconsin Avenue, Milwaukee, WI 53203. 414-272-8575

As the professional organization in the quality control field, ASQC has actively developed and published standards since its organization in 1946.

American Society for Testing and Materials, 1916 Race Street, Philadelphia, PA 19103. 215-299-5400

As of July, 1978, some 5,000 standard specifications, methods of tests, and definitions were in effect and hundreds of research projects were underway, involving some 13,500 of the country's leading engineers, scientists, research workers and educators. Of the more than 20,000 regular members of the Society, about 2600 are corporate memberships, and the balance are individuals, universities, technical schools, technical societies, and libraries; 15 percent of which is from outside the United States.

American Society of Agricultural Engineers, 2950 Niles Road, St. Joseph, MI 49085. 616-429-0300

ASAE is a technical and professional society for engineers with interest relating to the production and processing of food, feed, and fiber.

The American Society of Anesthesiologists, 515 Busse Highway, Park Ridge, IL 60068. 312-825-5586.

This society, founded in 1905, is the sponsor of the American National Standards Sectional Committee Z79 on Standards for Anesthesia and Respiratory Equipment.

The Society has, in addition, a Committee on Mechanical Equipment which maintains liaison with the standardization work of other professional and technical bodies in the medical field.

American Society of Civil Engineers, 345 East 47th Street, New York, NY 10017. 212-644-7496

Participates through appointed representatives to standards-producing organizations, as well as through review of new standards and codes as they are formulated.

American Society of Electroplated Plastics, Inc., 1000 Vermont Avenue, N.W., Washington, DC 20005. 202-628-4634

Nonprofit organization devoted to improving the efficiency of its industry and to promoting the use of electroplated plastics. Standards and guidelines govern such considerations as: parts design, mold design, substrate fabrication requisites, plastic product quality, test procedures, and standards and performance capabilities.

American Society of Heating, Refrigerating and Air-Conditioning Engineers, 345 East 47th Street, New York, NY 10017. 212-644-7953.

ASHRAE standards are developed to assist industry and public by offering a uniform method of testing equipment for rating purposes and by suggesting safe practices in designing and installing such equipment.

American Society of Lubrication Engineers, 838 Busse Highway, Park Ridge, IL 60068.   312-825-5536

A total of 20 standards have been published to date.

The American Society of Mechanical Engineers, 345 East 47th Street, New York, NY 10017.   212-644-7722

The Society currently publishes 360 standards in all fields of mechanical engineering. The ASME Publications Catalog lists ASME publications as well as its standards. The boiler code is the most widely known.

American Society of Photogrammetry, 105 North Virginia Avenue, Falls Church, VA 22046.   804-534-6617

Its scope of interest includes the fields of aerial photography, photogrammetric surveys, photographic interpretation, and remote sensing.

American Society of Plumbing Engineers, 16161 Ventura Boulevard, Suite 105, Encino, CA 91316.   213-783-4845

Technical society organized to elevate the field of plumbing to professional status.

American Society of Safety Engineers, 850 Busse Highway, Park Ridge, IL 60068.   312-692-4121

Career safety specialists, organized to promote and foster the advancement of the profession and the well-being and professional development of its members.

In 1973 the Society adopted the position that as an organization it would no longer participate in the development of individual technical standards; however, it would continue to develop standards for the profession and/or the professional safety engineer and participate in standards policy bodies.

American Society of Sanitary Engineering, 960 Illuminating Building, Cleveland, OH 44113.   216-696-3228

This society was established in 1906 primarily for the purpose of promoting health, welfare, and safety of the public through better sanitary principles as related to plumbing.

American Sod Producers' Association, Garmo Inc., Association Building, 9th and Minnesota, Hastings, NE 68901.   402-463-5691

Membership consists of sod producers and associated interests such as equipment, seed, and chemical suppliers and landscapers.

American Vacuum Society, 335 East 45th Street, New York, NY 10017.   212-661-9404

American Water Works Association, 6666 West Quincy Avenue, Denver, CO 80235.   303-794-7711

American Welding Society, 2501 NW 7th Street, Miami, FL 33125.   305-642-7090

The technical committees of this society prepare standards such as codes, specifications, recommended practices, and technical reports. The standards emanating from these committees represent four broad categories: (1) welding fundamentals—including symbols, testing, definitions, filler metals, and safety and health; (2) welding processing—including, resistance welding, thermal spraying, brazing, and soldering; (3) inspection of welds, and qualification of welders and procedures; and (4) industrial applications of welding—pertaining to piping, buildings, bridges, ships, storage tanks, automobiles, and aerospace vehicles.

American Wood-Preservers' Association, 1625 Eye Street N.W., Washington, DC 20006.   202-331-1382

The Association has published 64 standards covering preservatives, treatment of commodities, analysis methods, conversion tables, and other miscellaneous standards.

American Wood-Preservers Bureau, PO Box 6085, 2772 S. Randolph Street, Arlington, VA 22206.   703-931-8180

Cooperating with the American Wood-Preservers' Association and the American Wood-Preservers Institute, the Association provides a nationally known quality mark that, when affixed to a piece of wood, certifies a definite preservative treatment.

Anti-Friction Bearing Manufacturers' Association, 2341 Jefferson Davis Highway, Suite 1015, Century Bldg., Arlington, VA 22202.   703-979-1261

Standards for ball and roller bearings and balls are published as a set of 13 booklets.

Architectural Precast Association, 825 East 64th Street, Indianapolis, IN 46220.   317-251-1214

Manufacturers of precast concrete panels and their suppliers.

Architectural Woodwork Institute, 5055 South Chesterfield Road, Arlington, VA 22206.   703-671-9100

Asbestos Textile Institute, PO Box 471, 131 North York Road, Willow Grove, PA 19090.   215-OL-9-5007

Works closely with the American Society for Testing and Materials Subcommittee DI3.14 (A-4 on Asbestos) concerning specifications, methods of test, and recommended practices for asbestos textiles.

The Asphalt Institute, Asphalt Institute Building, College, Park, MD 20740.   301-927-0422

The Institute has published construction specifications for a wide variety of asphalt applications in highway and airfield construction, uses of asphalt in hydraulic structures, asphalt protective coatings for pipelines, uses of asphalt in recreational areas, and others.

Asphalt Roofing Manufacturers' Association, 757 Third Avenue, New York, NY 10017.   212-HA-1-2690

Standards and specifications covering asphalt roofing products which are developed in cooperation with the Federal Government, the American Society for Testing and Materials, and the Underwriters' Laboratories.

Association for Education of the Visually Handicapped, 919 Walnut Street, 4th Flr., Philadelphia, PA 19107.   215-WA-3-7555

Association for the Advancement of Medical Instrumentation, 1500 Wilson Boulevard, Suite 417, Arlington, VA 22209.   703-525-4890

AAMI has a membership of over 3000 individuals, including physicians, engineers, scientists, other health professionals, researchers, educators, government representatives, and industry officials. In addition, AAMI has over 200 corporations and institutions as members. One of the primary coordination efforts of AAMI is to develop and promulgate medical device standards.

Association of American Railroads, American Railroads Building, 1920 L Street N.W., Washington, DC 20036.   202-293-4000

This association is the central coordinating and research agency of the American railroad industry. Safety and special services division is charged with responsibility for safety in all areas of railroading.

Association of Bedding and Furniture Law Officials, c/o State Chemists Office, Utah Department of Agriculture, Laboratory Bldg. State Capitol, Salt Lake City, UT 84114.   801-533-4131

Association of Edison Illuminating Companies, 51 East 42nd Street, New York, NY 10017.   212-OX-7-1336

The Association is officially represented on the following American National Standards Committees: B16, B31, B36, B49, C1, C8, C12, C29, C34, C37, C50, C55, C76, and 05; and on Committees A-1 and D22 of the American Society for Testing and Materials.

APPENDIX G STANDARDS-SETTING ORGANIZATIONS 597

Association of Engineering Geologists, PO Box 21-4164, Sacramento, CA 95821. 916-372-3800

Has committee on building codes.

Association of Home Appliance Manufacturers, 20 North Wacker Drive, Chicago, IL 60606. 312-984-5800

AHAM develops voluntary appliance performance standards and makes safety recommendations to Underwriters' Laboratories and American Gas Association, represents the industry in consumer and Government relations, compiles statistics, sponsors certification programs, and provides consumer appliance information, educational materials, and teaching aids.

Association of Iron and Steel Engineers, Suite 2350, Three Gateway Center, Pittsburgh, PA 15222. 412-281-6323

The Association has developed standards for the steel industry which include such items as motors, surface finish, cranes, wiring, brakes, bearings, mill buildings, etc.

Association of Official Analytical Chemists, Box 540 Benjamin Franklin Station, Washington, DC 20044. 202-245-1266

The Association, founded as the Association of Official Agricultural Chemists, is a professional organization of state and federal chemists devoted to developing, testing, and sponsoring standard methods for the analysis of fertilizers, foods, feeds, pesticides, drugs, cosmetics, hazardous substances, and other materials related to agriculture and public health.

Association of Official Seed Analysts, Federal Seed Laboratory, PO Box 1705, North Brunswick, NJ 08902 201-846-4500

Quality factors for which tests are made include: purity of sample, percentage of germination, rate of occurrence of noxious weed seeds, varietal purity, and assaying for fungicidal seed treatment.

Baking Industry Sanitation Standards Committee, 521 Fifth Avenue, New York, NY 10017. 212-MU-7-9071

A nonprofit organization dedicated to the achieving of sanitation in the baking industry.

Barre Granite Association, 51 Church Street, Barre, VT 05641. 802-476-4131

In 1937 this association created the first set of quality standards covering the physical properties of granite and quality standards of workmanship on granite monuments.

Bicycle Manufacturers' Association of America, Inc., 1101 15th Street N.W., Washington, DC 20005. 202-452-1166

Its member companies produce some 85 percent of all domestically manufactured bicycles.

Biological Stain Commission, Inc., Research and Assay Laboratories, The University of Rochester Medical Center, Rochester, NY 14642. 716-275-2751

The objectives of the Commission are the establishment of standard specifications for the identification, purity, performance, and labeling of the more important biological stains, in order that they may be relied upon as standard tools in biological and medical research.

Bituminous Pipe Institute, 8 South Michigan Avenue, Chicago, IL 60603. 312-356-1862

Inspection procedures have been established by the Research and Technical Committee to ensure high levels of manufacturing procedure.

Book Manufacturers' Institute, 904 Ethan Allen Highway, PO Box 368, Ridgefield, CT 06877. 203-438-0478

BMI is a trade association formed in 1933 for book manufacturers and suppliers of book materials and book manufacturing equipment.

Brass and Bronze Ingot Institute, Room 3500, One North La Salle Street, Chicago, IL 60602.   312-236-2715

The Brick Institute of America, 1750 Old Meadow Road, McLean, VA 22101.   703-893-4010

The national authority on brick construction.

Builders Hardware Manufacturers' Association, 60 East 42nd Street, New York, NY 10017.   212-682-8142

A certification program for the BHMA Cabinet Hardware Standard No. 201 has been operating since 1968. The testing and administration are performed by an independent third party, the Electrical Testing Laboratories, Inc. The program is open to all manufacturers whether or not they are members of BHMA.

Building Officials and Code Administrators International, Inc. 1313 East 60th Street, Chicago, IL 60637.   312-947-2580

Founded in 1915, Building Officials and Code Administrators International is a nonprofit municipal service organization involved in the field of building code administration and enforcement in particular, and community development in general. The association's goals encompass advocating the use of safe, suitable, modern construction techniques and materials through its BOCA model codes program.

Can Manufacturers' Institute, 1625 Massachusetts Avenue N.W., Washington, DC 20036.   202-232-4677

CMI has a standing Can Standards Committee which seeks to develop standards on sanitary cans for sizes in general demand.

Canvas Products Association International, 600 Endicott Building, St. Paul, MN 55101.   612-222-2508

CPAI, founded in 1912, is the trade association for the industrial fabric industry. Its members include fiber producers, weavers, fabric finishers, coaters, laminators, and manufacturers of industrial fabric products.

Carpet and Rug Institute, PO Box 2048, Dalton, GA 30720.   404-278-3176

The Institute is the national trade association for U.S. manufacturers of carpet and rugs.

Cast Iron Soil Pipe Institute, 2029 K Street, N.W., Washington, DC 20006.   202-223-4536

Provides a continuous program of pipe testing, evaluation, and development.

Caster and Floor Truck Manufacturers' Association, 1717 Howard Street, Evanston, IL 60202.   312-869-6963

Manufacturers in this association produce industrial casters, wheels, and manually operated materials handling equipment.

CFTMA has published a *Combined Industrial Wheel Standard,* and an *Industrial Caster Standard,* as well as standards for trailer trucks, platform trucks, and two-wheel hand trucks.

Ceilings and Interior Systems Contractors' Association, 1201 Waukegan Road, Glenview, IL 60025.   312-724-7700

An international organization consisting of major specialty subcontractors who, as a significant part of their business, sell and install ceiling systems as well as other related products and systems.

Cemented Carbide Producers Association, 2130 Keith Building, Cleveland, OH 44115.   216-241-7333

Manufacturers of cemented tungsten carbide cutting tools, dies and wear parts.

Chemical Specialties Manufacturers' Association, 1001 Connecticut Avenue N.W., Suite 1120, Washington, DC 20036. 202-872-8110

A national trade association representing 400 suppliers, manufacturers and marketers of aerosols, cleaning compounds, disinfectants, insecticides, transportation products, polishes, and floor finishes.

The Chlorine Institute, Inc., 342 Madison Avenue, New York, NY 10017. 212-MU-2-4324

Concerned with the safe manufacture, shipping, and handling of chlorine.

College of American Pathologists, Standards Committee, 230 North Michigan Avenue, Chicago, IL 60601. 312-677-3500

Concerned with standards useful in all phases of laboratory medicine, including anatomic and clinical pathology. These include: (1) national proficiency survey programs, now administered by a separate Surveys Committee; these go to about 8000 laboratories; (2) inspection and accreditation programs for clinical laboratories—administered by a separate CAP Committee; (3) batch certification of cyanmethemoglobin standards for the National Academy of Sciences—National Research Council; (4) distribution of pure primary standard solutions whose content has been verified; (5) standards for laboratory test reports and sample handling; (6) standards for medical usefulness needs and screening tests; and (7) product evaluation of laboratory products. Standards in other fields are ordinarily channeled through the National Committee for Clinical Laboratory Standards.

Commission on Accreditation of Rehabilitation Facilities, 6510 North Lincoln Avenue, Chicago, IL 60645. 312-282-8787

A national private, nonprofit organization setting standards for the operation of rehabilitation facilities.

Composite Can and Tube Institute, 1725 Eye Street N.W., Washington, DC 20006. 202-223-4840

CCTI publishes standard testing procedures to provide uniform methods for both manufacturers and users to measure and test the physical characteristics of composite cans, tubes, and cores.

Compressed Gas Association, Inc., 500 Fifth Avenue, New York, NY 10036. 212-354-1130

Major purpose is to provide, develop, and coordinate technical activities in the compressed gas industries, including end-uses of products, in the interest of safety and efficiency.

Concrete Reinforcing Steel Institute, 180 North La Salle Street, Chicago, IL 60601. 312-372-5059

Represents mill producers, fabricators, and suppliers of reinforcing bars. Associated members include producers and suppliers of other products used in concrete construction and manufacture of concrete fabricating equipment.

Construction Industry Manufacturers' Association, 111 East Wisconsin Avenue, Milwaukee, WI 53202. 414-272-0943

CIMA acts as a clearinghouse for the construction equipment manufacturing industry in the areas of safety, health, and environmental performance standards for construction machines.

The Construction Specifications Institute, 1150 17th Street NW, Suite 300, Washington, DC 20036. 202-833-2160

All segments of the construction industry including architects, engineers, contractors, material suppliers, students, educators, and others.

Contractor's Pump Bureau, 13975 Connecticut Avenue, Suite 310, Silver Spring, MD 20906. 301-871-8988

The organization is made up of 13 major manufacturers of pumps for the contracting industry.

Conveyor Equipment Manufacturers' Association, 1000 Vermont Avenue N.W., Washington, DC 20005.   202-628-4634

Cooling Tower Institute, Inc., 3003 Yale Street, Suite 107, Houston, TX 77018.   713-445-9431

Association of cooling tower manufacturers, owners, and suppliers of related chemicals and equipment.

Copper Development Association, Inc., 405 Lexington Avenue, New York, NY 10017.   212-953-7300

Primary efforts are in the development of new markets for copper and copper alloys; major emphasis is directed at creating new concepts, building prototypes, and proving commercial feasibility for these new applications for copper, brass, and bronze.

The Cordage Institute, 2300 Calvert Street N.W., Washington, DC 20008.   202-857-0001

The membership is composed of substantially all of the rope and twine manufacturers in the United States, with some Canadian manufacturers and Cordemex of Mexico as special members.

Corn Industries Research Foundation, 1001 Connecticut Avenue, N.W., Washington, DC 20036.   202-331-1634

Activities include the development of standardized procedures, terminology, instrumentation, and methods of measurement.

Crane Manufacturers' Association of America, Inc., 1326 Freeport Road, Pittsburgh, PA 15238.   412-782-1624

The organization of manufacturers of electric overhead traveling cranes; it promotes standardization and provides a basis for uniform quality and performance.

Crayon, Water Color and Craft Institute, Edean Hill Road, Newtown, CT 06470.   203-426-5958

The Certified Products Bureau of the Institute ensures the safety and quality of the products of subscribers to the bureau.

Dairy and Food Industries Supply Association, 5530 Wisconsin Avenue, Washington, DC 20015.   301-652-4420

Represents the manufacturers of supplies and equipment for the food industry.

Data Processing Management Association, 505 Busse Highway, Park Ridge, IL 60068.   312-825-8124

Encourages development of standards in data processing equipment, terminology, data codes, analysis, documentation, and computer programming languages. Formerly: National Accountants' Association (1965).

Diamond Wheel Manufacturers' Institute, 2130 Keith Building, Cleveland, OH 44115.   216-241-7333

Manufactures from basic raw materials of grinding wheels and blades in which the abrasive used is diamonds.

Distilled Spirits Council of the United States, Inc., 538 Pennsylvania Building, Washington, DC 20004.   202-628-3544

Typical projects include plant safety standards and metric size standards, both domestic and international. Other studies, with standards as a goal, involve the transportation and storage of hazardous materials, filtration processes, and containers.

Door Operator and Remote Controls Manufacturers' Association, 110 North Wacker Drive, Chicago, IL 60606.   312-321-1646

National trade association of manufacturers of vehicular door operators—residential, commercial, or industrial—and remote controls. The Association has cooperated with Underwriters Laboratories in its development of UL 325 Standard for Safety for Door, Drapery, Gate, and Window Operators and Systems.

Dry Color Manufacturers' Association, 561 Franklin Avenue, Nutley, NJ 07110.   201-667-3011

Composed of 33 United States producers of dry, flushed, and dispersed inorganic and organic pigments. The Association has an Ecology Committee, comprised of four subcommittees: Air and Water Pollution, Heavy Metals, Rhodamine Dyes and Pigments, and Toxicity.

Edison Electric Institute, 90 Park Avenue, New York, NY 10016.   212-573-8700

The national trade association of the investor-owned electric light and power companies. The major part of its standardization activities is carried out through representation on some 70 standards committees of the American National Standards Institute. Most of these are concerned with standards for electric utility equipment and customers' appliances and also codes involving industry practices, such as the National Electrical Safety Code.

Electrical Apparatus Service Association, Inc., 7710 Carondelet Avenue, St. Louis, MO 63105.   314-993-2220

A trade association of companies engaged in the repair of electrical apparatus. Most of the 1900 members are in the United States, Canada, or Mexico, and recently EASA added members in Europe, Asia, Australia, Central America, and Africa.

Electrical Generating Systems Marketing Association, Tribune Tower, 435 N. Michigan, Chicago, IL 60611.   312-644-0828

Electrical Testing Laboratories, Inc., 2 East End Avenue, New York, NY 10021.   212-288-2600

Electrical Testing Laboratories, Inc. is an employee-owned, independent testing, inspection, and certification agency. Operating as a multidisciplined organization, its divisions are acoustical, chemical, photometric, electrical/electronic, automotive/mechanical, air-conditioning, manufactured housing, and carpet certification.

Electronic Industries Association, 2001 Eye Street N.W., Washington, DC 20006.   202-457-4900

"EIA Engineering Standards are designed to serve the public interest by eliminating misunderstandings between manufacturers and purchasers, facilitating interchangeability and improvement of products, and assisting the purchaser in selecting and obtaining with minimum delay the proper product for his particular need."

Entomological Society of America, 4603 Calvert Road, College Park, MD 20740.   301-864-1334

Activities include standards on common names of insects, insecticide terminology, insecticide reference standards, insect survey and losses, professional training, standards and status, and special committee on insecticide resistance.

Essential Oil Association of U.S.A., Inc., 60 East 42nd Street, New York, NY 10017.   212-682-8142

Processors, importers, and dealers in essential oils and synthetic chemicals.

Expanded Shale Clay and Slate Institute, 1041 National Press Building, Washington, DC 20004.   202-783-1669

Producers of expanded shale, clay, and slate, which use rotary kilns.

Expansion Anchor Manufacturers Institute, 331 Madison Avenue, New York, NY 10017.   212-661-2050

The major U.S. manufacturers of expansion anchors for the construction industry. Its purposes are to further the development of the expansion anchor industry, to promote safe and effective application of expansion anchors, to encourage research, and to cooperate with organizations engaged in such work.

Expansion Joint Manufacturers' Association, 331 Madison Avenue, New York, NY 10017. 212-661-2050

This association was formed in April 1955 to foster and study the problems peculiar to expansion joints.

Factory Mutual Engineering and Research, 1151 Boston-Providence Turnpike, Norwood, MA 02062. 617-762-4300

Provides property and production loss-prevention engineering service to industrial organizations insured in the four companies of the Factory Mutual System. Numerous standards, including such subjects as installing automatic sprinklers, safeguards for flammable liquids, gases, dusts, industrial ovens and dryers, and protection of buildings against wind damage, are available to the public in data book form.

Farm and Industrial Equipment Institute, 410 North Michigan Avenue, Chicago, IL 60611. 312-321-1470

Manufacturers of farm and industrial equipment, representing over 90 percent of the North American business.

The Fertilizer Institute, 1015 18th Street NW Washington, DC 20036. 202-466-2700

Supports standardization through simplification and uniformity of Federal and state fertilizer regulatory laws as well as of chemical analytical methods. It also is involved in the safety standards activities at state and Federal levels.

Fibre Box Association, 224 South Michigan Avenue, Chicago, IL 60604. 312-663-0250

A trade association representing manufacturers of corrugated and solid fiberboard.

Fine Hardwoods–American Walnut Association, 666 North Lake Shore Drive, Chicago, IL 60611. 312-944-1252

Cooperates with the Hardwood Plywood Manufacturers Association in its *Rules for Measurement and Inspection of Veneers and Plywood.*

Finnish Plywood Development Association, 512 West Maple Avenue, Vienna, VA 22180. 703-281-6644

Represents member mills manufacturing birch plywood used in various interior and exterior applications.

Fir and Hemlock Door Association, Yeon Building, Portland, OR 97204. 503-224-3930

Flat Glass Marketing Association, 1325 Topeka Ave., Topeka, KS 66612. 913-266-7013

Fluid Controls Institute, 12 Bank Street, Summit, NJ 07901. 201-273-3909

Association of manufacturers of fluid control devices such as control valves, regulators, solenoid valves, steam traps, check valves, strainers and separators, and for space heaters.

Food Processing Machinery and Supplies Association, 7758 Wisconsin Avenue N.W., Washington, DC 20014. 202-833-5770

Forging Industry Association, 55 Public Square, Cleveland, OH 44113. 216-781-6260

The Association is the cosponsor, along with the National Safety Council, of the American National Standard B24.1-1971 *Safety Requirements for Forging.*

Friction Materials Standards Institute, Inc., Bergen Mall Office Center, East 210 Route 4, Paramus, NJ 07652. 201-845-0440

Gas Appliance Manufacturers' Association, 1901 North Fort Myer Drive, Arlington, VA 22209. 703-525-9565

Glass Container Manufacturers' Institute, Inc., 1800 K Street N.W., Washington, DC 20006. 202-872-1280

Glass Tempering Association, 1325 Topeka Ave., Topeka, KS 66612. 913-266-7064

The Association has technical committees involved in construction specifications and consumer safety-glazing legislation.

Graphic Communications Computer Association, Graphic Communications Center, 1730 North Lynn Street, Arlington, VA 22209. 703-527-6000

Gray and Ductile Iron Founders' Society, Cast Metals Federation Building, 20611 Center Ridge Road, Rocky River (Cleveland), OH 44116. 216-333-9600

Grinding Wheel Institute, 2130 Keith Building, Cleveland, OH 44115. 216-241-7333

This institute was joint sponsor with the International Association of Governmental Labor Officials in the development of *Safety Code for the Use, Care, and Protection of Abrasive Wheels,* which was approved and issued as American National Standard B7.1-1970.

Gummed Industries Association, Inc., The, 380 North Broadway, Jericho, NY 11753. 518-822-8948

Domestic manufacturers of water-activated gummed paper products and, through Association membershps, these manufacturers' raw material suppliers.

Gypsum Association, 1603 Oxington Avenue, Suite 1210, Evanston, IL 60201. 312-491-1744

Technical research programs are conducted in fire, sound, and structural testing of gypsum products and related accessories.

Gypsum Roof Deck Foundation, 5820 North Nagle Avenue, Chicago, IL 60646. 312-346-1826

Members of building contractors active in the promotion, sales, and installation of poured-in-place gypsum roof decks.

Hardwood Dimension Manufacturers' Association, 3813 Hillsboro Road, Nashville, TN 37215. 615-269-3254

Hardwood Plywood Manufacturers' Association, PO Box 6246, Arlington, VA 22206. 703-671-6262

Hoist Manufacturers' Institute, 1326 Freeport Road, Pittsburgh, PA 15238. 412-782-1624

Manufacturers of manual and electrically operated overhead handling hoists.

Home Ventilating Institute, 230 North Michigan Avenue, Chicago, IL 60601. 312-236-5822

HVI certified ratings for air delivery were introduced in 1960, and for sound emission, in 1971.

Illuminating Engineering Society, United Engineering Center, 345 East 47th Street, New York, NY 10017. 212-644-7926

Indiana Limestone Institute of America, Inc., Stone City National Bank Building, Suite 400, Bedford, IN 47421. 812-275-4426

Serves the construction industry, the architectural profession, and the limestone industry as a coordinating agency for the dissemination of information on limestone standards, recommended practices, grades, colors, finishes, and all technical data required for specifying, detailing, fabricating, and erecting Indiana limestone.

Industrial Fasteners' Institute, 1505 East Ohio Building, Cleveland, OH 44114.   216-241-1482

There are more than 500,000 standard and 3,000,000 special sizes, kinds, and shapes of fasteners and engineering components. In addition to maintaining its own standards-writing program, IFI publishes *Fastener Standards Book*.

Industrial Management Society, 570 Northwest Highway, Suite 4, Des Plaines, IL 60016.   312-296-7189

This society developed an occupational-rating plan for hourly and salaried occupations widely used throughout the country.

Industrial Medical Association, 150 N. Wacker Drive, Chicago, IL 60606.   312-782-2166

A professional organization for all physicians concerned with the relationship between health and work, and the work environment.

Industrial Safety Equipment Association, 2425 Wilson Boulevard, Arlington, VA 22201.   703-525-1695

The ISEA was founded in 1927 as a trade association for the manufacturers of personal protective equipment and those manufacturers of unit-type first aid kits and machinery guarding devices. The Association does not promulgate and publish its own standards but over a great many years has worked through the procedures of ANSI and the National Fire Protection Association.

The Industrial Truck Association, 1326 Freeport Road, Pittsburgh, PA 15238.   412-782-1624

This association has developed a *Manual of Recommended Practices;* these practices are used to advance safety and efficiency in the design, manufacture, and use of industrial trucks.

Industry Service Bureaus, 331 Madison Avenue, New York, NY 10017.   212-661-2050

Includes Aircraft Locknut Manufacturers' Association, the Electric Fuse Manufacturers' Guild, the Hand Tools Institute, the Socket Screw Products Bureau, the Tapping Screw Service Bureau, the United States Cap Screw Service Bureau, the United States Machine Screw Service Bureau, and the United States Wood Screw Service Bureau.

Institute of Electrical and Electronics Engineers, Standards Operations, 345 East 47th Street, New York, NY 10017.   212-644-7900

There are presently about 400 IEEE standards covering electrical and electronics equipment, test methods, units, symbols, definitions, and rating methods.

Institute for Interconnecting and Packaging Electronic Circuits (known as IPC, Inc.), 1717 Howard Street, Evanston, IL 60202.   312-491-1660

Members of this international trade association, formerly Institute of Printed Circuits, include producers and users of printed circuit boards.

Institute of Scrap Iron and Steel, 1729 H Street N.W., Washington, DC 20006.   202-298-7660

Institute of Transportation Engineers, Suite 905, 1815 North Fort Myer Drive, Arlington, VA 22209.   703-527-5277

Publishes recommended practices and technical reports for the safety and efficient movement of goods and people.

Instrument Society of America, 400 Stanwix Street, Pittsburgh, PA 15222.   412-281-3171

Individuals interested in the theory, design, manufacture, and use of instruments. Areas of technical activity include measurement, data acquisition, processing, display, telemetry, and automatic control in both industrial and laboratory applications.

APPENDIX G   STANDARDS-SETTING ORGANIZATIONS   **605**

Insulated Power Cable Engineers' Association, 192 Washington Street, Belmont, MA.   617-484-2819

Publishes standards jointly with National Electrical Manufacturers' Association and collaborates with other organizations.

Inter-Society Color Council, c/o F. W. Billmeyer, Department of Chemistry, Rensselaer Polytechnic Institute, Troy, NY 12181.   518-270-6000

Membership consists of 29 delegates from national societies and individual members, all with a common interest in color.

International Association of Electrical Inspectors, 802 Busse Highway, Park Ridge, IL 60068.   312-696-1455

This organization cooperates in the formulation of standards for the safe installation and use of electrical materials, devices, and appliances. IAEI also promotes the uniform understanding and application of the National Electrical Code, and other electrical codes and standards.

International Association of Milk, Food and Environmental Sanitarians, PO Box 701, Ames, IA 50010.   515-232-6699

International Association of Plumbing and Mechanical Officials. 5032 Alhambra Avenue, Los Angeles, CA 90032.   213-223-1471

IAPMO promulgates and sponsors the Uniform Plumbing Code that is used in over 2500 jurisdictions in the United States and is the mandatory code for 10 states.

International Association of Wall and Ceiling Contractors, 1775 Church Street NW, Washington, DC 20036.   202-667-8400

International Conference of Building Officials, 5360 South Workman Mill Road, Whittier, CA 90601.   213-699-0541

Publishes the *Uniform Building Code, Uniform Mechanical Code,* and *Uniform Fire Code* covering minimum requirements for safe construction in buildings or structures.

International Mobile Air Conditioning Association, Inc. 6116 North Central Expressway, Dallas, TX 75206.   214-361-7014

Serves system manufacturers, parts and service suppliers, distributors and dealers in mobile air conditioning applications, including: auto, heavy truck, recreational vehicle, farm and off-highway vehicle, boat, aircraft, bus, and railroad. Its program includes engineering standards and product certification.

International Municipal Signal Association, 1511 K St. N.W., Suite 430, Washington, DC 20005.   202-638-7283

Directly engaged in the engineering, construction, maintenance, and operation of electrical, electronic, and graphic communication systems used in the public safety services such as fire and police alarm, traffic controls, radio communication, street lighting, signs and markings, and related system.

International Nonwovens and Disposables Association, 10 East 40 Street, New York, NY 10016.   212-686-9170

Founded in June 1968 to represent the nonwoven fabrics and disposable soft goods industries.

Investment Casting Institute, 1717 Howard Street, Evanston, IL 60202.   312-869-6963

The ICI publishes the *Investment Casting Handbook.*

Joint Industrial Council, 7901 Westpark Drive, McLean, VA 22101.   703-893-2900

Organized in 1962 through the cooperative efforts of the National Machine Tool Builders' Association and large users of machine tools and the suppliers of accessory equipment to the industry. The purpose of the organization is to coordinate development of standards which will encourage the safe and reliable application of controls to equipment used in industrial applications.

Juvenile Products Manufacturers' Association, 59 East Main Street, Moorestown, NJ 08057. 609-234-0330

Most of the regular members manufacture products which can be broadly defined as juvenile furniture, as opposed to being toy manufacturers. The industry's activities for the development of juvenile product safety performance standards includes 12 individual subcommittees.

Lead Industries Association, 292 Madison Avenue, New York, NY 10017. 212-679-6020

This organization has available recommended specifications for lead roofing and flashing, sheet lead membranes for decorative pools and planters, lead-asbestos antivibration pads, lead plumbing, and other lead applications.

Linen Supply Association of America. PO Box 2427, 975 Arthur Godfrey Road, Miami Beach, FL 33140. 305-532-6371

Standards for washing and dry-cleaning cleanliness through test bundle reports measuring washing and dry-cleaning efficiency.

MTM Association for Standards and Research, 9–10 Saddle River Road, Fair Lawn, NJ 07410. 201-791-7720

Primary efforts are in the field of research and training in methods-time-measurement (MTM). It is basically devoted to the art and science of MTM in the area of "man at work." A wide variety of memberships include academicians, individual members, and corporate memberships that include various branches of the Government, insurance companies, and manufacturers.

Magnetic Materials Producers' Association, 1717 Howard Street, Evanston, IL 60202. 312-869-6963

Manufacturers in this association compound and process basic magnetic materials.

Malleable Founders' Society, 20611 Center Ridge Road, Rocky River, OH 44116. 216-333-9600

Concerned mainly with technical research and advisory services, assisting its members to maintain standard grades of products, and developing new applications and uses for malleable castings.

Manufacturers' Standardization Society of the Valve and Fittings Industry, 1815 North Fort Myer Drive, Arlington, VA 22209. 703-525-8526

Manufacturing Chemists' Association, 1825 Connecticut Avenue N.W., Washington, DC 20009. 202-483-6126

Represents U.S. and Canadian manufacturers of basic chemicals who sell to others a substantial portion of the chemicals which they produce. The Association sponsors a safety laboratory, ad numerous services. *Manual L-1, Guide to Precautionary Labeling of Hazardous Chemicals,* is widely used by industry and regulatory agencies.

Marking Device Association, 1611 Chicago Avenue, Evanston, IL 60201. 312-328-3540

This association prepares standards for various kinds of metal-marking tools and dies.

The Material Handling Institute, Inc., 1326 Freeport Road, Pittsburgh, PA 15238. 412-782-1624

The trade association representing manufacturers of industrial material handling equipment used in plants, plant-yards, piers, terminals, and warehouses.

Mechanical Contractors' Association of America, Inc., 5530 Wisconsin Avenue N.W., Suite 750, Washington, DC 20015. 301-654-7960

APPENDIX G STANDARDS-SETTING ORGANIZATIONS **607**

The Association is joint sponsor with the American Society of Mechanical Engineers and the Manufacturers Standardization Society of the Valve and Fittings Industry for American National Standards Committee B16 on Pipe Flanges and Fittings. In addition, it is represented on numerous American National Standards committees dealing with the following subjects: code for pipe threading; code for pressure piping; standardization of dimensions and materials of wrought iron and wrought steel pipe and tubing; standards for drawings and drafting room practice; approval and installation requirements for gas-burning appliances; graphical symbols and abbreviations for use on drawings; scheme for identification of piping systems, and safety in construction.

Mechanical Power Transmission Association, 1717 Howard Street, Evanston, IL 60202. 312-869-6963

Trade association concerned with the development of standards and other programs concerning V-belt drive systems and devices, variable speed drives, and transmission products including belt drives.

Metal Building Manufacturers' Association, 2130 Keith Building, Cleveland, OH 44115. 216-241-7333

The Association has published *Metal Building Systems Manual;* includes sections on recommended design practices, specifications, and nomenclature covering metal building systems.

Metal Cutting Tool Institute, 331 Madison Avenue, New York, NY 10017. 212-661-2050

One purpose of the Institute is to promote standardization of sizes, dimensions, and tolerances of rotary-type, multiple-point metal-cutting tools, such as twist drills, reamers, taps, milling cutters, and gear-generating tools, and to simplify these in cooperation with ANSI, American Society of Mechanical Engineers, and other organizations.

Metal Powder Industries Federation, PO Box 2054, Princeton, NJ 08540. 609-799-3300

Various trade associations operating within its structure include the Metal Powder Producers' Association, Powder Metallurgy Parts Association, In-Plant Powder Metallurgy Association, Powder Metallurgy Equipment Association, and Refractory and Reactive Metals Association.

Metal Tube Packaging Council of North America, 1414 Avenue of the Americas, New York NY 10019. 212-935-1290

Manufacturers of collapsible metal tubes in North America.

Milk Bottle Crate Manufacturers' Council, 2130 Keith Building, Cleveland, OH 44115. 216-241-7333

Mill Mutual Fire Prevention Bureau, 2 North Riverside Plaza, Chicago, IL 60606. 312-332-3912

Primary objective is to provide technical data to agri-processing plants for the reduction of loss to property by fire or wind and to personnel by injury within the plant.

Monorail Manufacturers' Association, 1326 Freeport Road, Pittsburgh, PA 15238. 412-782-1624

Monorail Manufacturer' Association Specifications For Underhung Cranes and Monorail Systems apply to underhung cranes operating on the lower flange of a track section, and to a single-track monorail system including all curves, switches, transfer devices, trolleys, lift-and-drop sections, and associated equipment. Provisions do not encompass all of the safety precautions and safeguards applicable to monorail systems primarily used for transportation of personnel.

Motor Vehicle Manufacturers' Association of the United States, Inc., New Center Building, Detroit, MI 48202. 313-872-4311

Practically all engineering standardization work arising in the industry represented by this organization is conducted through the Society of Automotive Engineers, financed in substantial part by grant from the Association.

National Academy of Sciences—National Academy of Engineering—Institute of Medicine—National Research Council, 2101 Constitution Avenue N.W., Washington, DC 20418. NAS & NAE & NCR—202-393-8100; Institute of Medicine—202-389-6891

The National Academy of Sciences is a private, nonprofit organization dedicated to the furtherance of science and its use for the general welfare, and required by its Congressional Charter of 1863 to act as an official advisor to the Federal Government, upon request, in all matters of science and technology. Its members, now numbering about 1000, are elected in recognition of their distinguished and continuing achievements in original research. The National Academy of Engineering was established in 1964 under the charter of the NAS. The Institute of Medicine was chartered by the NAS in 1970. The National Research Council was established by the Academy in 1916.

National Accreditation Council, 79 Madison Avenue, New York, NY 10016. 212-683-8581

NAC is the only nationally recognized standards-setting, accrediting organization for specialized services to the blind and visually handicapped.

National Association of Architectural Metal Manufacturers, 1033 South Boulevard, Oak Park, IL 60302. 312-383-7725

The following publications contain NAAMM's recommended practices and specifications and standards: *Metal Stairs Manual; Metal Bar Grating Manual; Metal Product Outline Manual; Metal Finishes Manual; Specifications for Custom Hollow Metal Doors and Frames—NAAMM Standard CHM-1-74; Fire-Rated Custom Metal Doors and Frames,* and *Glossary of Architectural Metal Terms Manual.*

National Association of Bedding Manufacturers, 1150 17th Street N.W., Suite 200, Washington, DC 20036. 202-872-0600

Represents manufacturers of mattresses, bedsprings, and dual-purpose sleep equipment as well as suppliers of machinery, raw and finished materials, and components and other supplies and services necessary to the manufacture of bedding.

National Association of Blue Shield Plans, 211 East Chicago Avenue, Chicago, IL 60611. 312-440-5500

National Association of Corrosion Engineers, PO Box 1499, Houston, TX 77001. 713-622-8980

NACE is engaged in preparing standards to promote the use of the best technical practices to reduce the cost of corrosion and to increase the safety of industrial, public, and private installations where corrosion damage could create hazards.

The National Association of Elevator Contractors, 4321 Hartwick Road, Suite 306, College Park, MD 20740. 301-927-3338

Independent elevator contractors and their suppliers. Some 30 percent of the Association's activities are devoted to the development, promulgation, and education of the industry of the *Safety Code for Elevators, Dumbwaiters, Escalators and Moving Walks* (American National Standard *A17.1-1971*).

National Association of Food Chains, 1725 I Street N.W., Washington, DC 20006. 202-452-8444

Standardization activities of this association include work in standardization of pallets, research on the shape and type of containers used to transport food products, and study of modularization of shipping containers for grocery products.

National Association of Food Equipment Manufacturers, 111 East Wacker Drive, Chicago, IL 60601. 312-644-6610

Standardization activities include research and educational programs in food-service layout, refrigeration, dishwashing, and dish-handling.

National Association of Furniture Manufacturers, Inc., 8401 Connecticut Avenue NW, Suite 911, Washington, DC 20015. 301-457-4442

National Association of Hosiery Manufacturers, 516 Charlottetown Mall, Charlotte, NC 28204. 704-372-4200

National Association of Hospital Purchasing Management, 1340 North Astor Street, Suite 1201, Chicago, IL 60610. 312-642-1082

National Association of Metal Name Plate Manufacturers, Inc., 1000 Vermont Avenue N.W., Washington, DC 20005. 202-628-4634

NAME publishes *Metal Name Plate Industry Standards and Practices.* This book is the only set of standards in existence for the industry in the United States.

National Association of Motor Bus Owners, 1025 Connecticut Avenue N.W., Washington, DC 20036. 202-293-5890

The national trade association for the intercity motor bus industry with membership of some 450 bus operating companies, 21 state and regional bus associations, and about 75 bus manufacturers, suppliers, and others with an interest in bus transportation.

National Association of Pipe Coating Applicators, 2504 Flournoy-Lucas Road, Shreveport, LA 71108. 318-686-4012

The National Association of Pipe Coating Applicators seeks to stimulate the use of plant-applied pipe coating and related materials, to standardize and improve specifications and materials, and to aid consumers and manufacturers in their coating material research.

National Association of Plastic Fabricators, 4720 Montgomery Lane, Suite 710, Washington, DC 20014. 301-656-8874

Suppliers of materials and machinery and manufacturers of decorative plastic laminated products for residential and commercial uses.

National Association of Plumbing-Heating-Cooling Contractors, 1016 20th Street N.W., Washington, DC 20036. 202-331-7675

National Association of Purchasing Management, Inc., 11 Park Place, New York, NY 10007. 212-267-3677

Representing 18,000 purchasing officials, both public and private.

National Association of Recycling Industries, Inc., 330 Madison Avenue, New York, NY 10017. 212-867-7330

National Audio-Visual Association, Inc., 3150 Spring Street, Fairfax, VA 22030. 703-273-7200

Dealers selling A-V equipment and materials, film rental libraries, manufacturers of A-V equipment, producers of films and other A-V materials, publishers, independent manufacturers' representatives, and A-V professional services members.

National Automatic Merchandising Association, 7 South Dearborn Street, Chicago, IL 60603. 312-346-0370

This is the national trade association representing vending and food-service management companies, vending machine manufacturers, and the suppliers of vendible products and component parts.

National Automatic Sprinkler and Fire Control Association, PO Box 719, Mt. Kisco, NY 10549. 914-241-2400

The primary objective of this association is the advancement of the art of automatic control of fire through automatic sprinklers, and the conservation of life and property from fire. This organization is a national trade association of automatic sprinkler manufacturers and installers.

National Automobile Theft Bureau, 17 John Street, New York, NY 10038. 212-233-1400

Although its primary purpose is to locate stolen cars, it is also a leader in the promotion of auto theft prevention activities.

National Board of Boiler and Pressure Vessel Inspectors, 1155 North High Street, Columbus, OH 43201. 614-888-8320

The Board confines its membership to persons charged with enforcement of the boiler and pressure vessel laws in various states, municipalities in the United States with a population of one million or over, and the Canadian provinces.

National Cable Television Association, Inc., 918 Sixteenth Street N.W., Washington, DC 20006.   202-457-6700

National Canners' Association, 1133 20th Street N.W., Washington, DC 20036.   202-331-5900

Commercial packers of food products in hermetically sealed containers, sterilized by heat. Develops improvements in the products, processes, quality control measures, spoilage prevention, and sanitation techniques used in the industry.

National Cargo Bureau, Inc., One World Trade Center, New York, NY 10048.   212-432-1280

Dedicated to the safe loading, stowing, securing, and unloading of cargo and cargo containers on all vessels, and for the design, strength, safety, and suitability of cargo-handling gear and cargo containers, including the security and integrity of containers. Membership is comprised mainly of persons who are prominently identified with steamship management or marine insurance underwriting organizations.

National Clay Pipe Institute, 350 West Terra Cotta Avenue, Crystal Lake, IL 60014.   815-459-3330

Association members are vitrified clay pipe manufacturers. The Institute maintains a research laboratory located at Crystal Lake, Illinois.

National Committee on Uniform Traffic Laws and Ordinances, 1776 Massachusetts Avenue N.W., Suite 430, Washington, DC 20036.   202-785-4066

The Committee, established in 1926, maintains the Uniform Vehicle Code and Model Traffic Ordinance as standards for quality and uniformity among state and local motor vehicle and traffic laws.

National Concrete Masonry Association, 6845 Elm Street, McLean, VA 22101.   703-790-8650

Trade association representing concrete masonry manufacturers throughout the United States, Canada, and 21 other countries.

National Cottonseed Products Association, 2400 Poplar Avenue, PO Box 12023, Memphis, TN 38112.   901-324-4417

This Association maintains, for members, trading rules which contain standards of quality, weight, and measurement of all cottonseed products.

National Crushed Stone Association, 1415 Elliot Place N.W., Washington, DC 20007.   202-333-1536

The National Easter Seal Society for Crippled Children and Adults, 2023 West Ogden Avenue, Chicago, IL 60612.   312-243-8400

Works toward the elimination of architectural barriers across the nation by: (1) increasing public awareness of the opportunities denied the handicapped for participation in community life because of architectural barriers; (2) stimulating community action to provide accessibility in public buildings, transportation, and housing to the disabled; and (3) assuring the elimination of architectural barriers by influencing legislation, building codes, and regulations.

National Electrical Contractors' Association, 7315 Wisconsin Avenue, Washington, DC 20014.   301-657-3110

The nationwide trade association representing the electrical contracting industry. A *NECA Standard of Installation* which defines good workmanship has been developed for inclusion in specifications for electrical installations. It is also used as an authoritative guide to determine the "neat and workmanlike manner" requirements of the National Electrical Code.

National Electrical Manufacturers' Association, 2101 L St. N.W., Washington, DC 20037. 202-457-8400

This is a trade association of manufacturers of almost every kind of equipment and apparatus used for the generation, transmission, distribution, and utilization of electric power. The membership of NEMA includes over 500 of the major electrical manufacturing companies in the country. NEMA has published over 200 separate standards publications for electrical apparatus and equipment in the following classifications: illuminating equipment, signalling and communication equipment, industrial apparatus, building equipment and supplies, insulating materials, insulated wire and cable, generation, transmission, and distribution equipment.

National Elevator Industry, Inc., 600 Third Avenue, New York, NY 10016. 212-986-1545

The Standards Committee has formulated standard layouts for the industry. These layouts give standard car sizes and hoistway and machine room dimensions for various types of elevators. The Central Code Committee is concerned with the preparations, interpretation, revision, and adoption of all safety codes for elevators, dumbwaiters, escalators, and moving walks.

National Environmental Health Association, 1600 Pennsylvania, Denver, CO 80203. 303-837-2879

Composed of 47 state associations with a coordinating national office in Denver.

National Environmental Systems Contractors' Association, 1501 Wilson Boulevard, Arlington, VA 22209. 703-527-0678

The main purpose of NESCA is to provide services to firms, or individuals who design, install, service, or repair heating, air-conditioning, and refrigeration systems. A major function of this association is the development of standards for the design and installation of warm-air heating and air-conditioning systems.

National Fire Protection Association, 470 Atlantic Avenue, Boston, MA 02210. 617-482-8755

This association includes 180 national and regional organizations, and approximately 28,500 individuals, firms, and corporations. One of the main functions of NFPA is in the standards-making field under which codes, standards, and recommended practices are developed as guides to engineered protection for reducing loss of life and property by fire. The other principal function is to educate the public in fire prevention to reduce human-caused fires. The standards are combined and published yearly as national fire codes.

National Fluid Power Association, Inc., 3333 North Mayfair Road, Milwaukee, WI 53222. 414-259-0990

Sponsors standards for the fluid power industry. It also sponsors the American National Standards Committee B93, Fluid Power Systems and Components, through which NFPA and other fluid power standards are processed to become American National Standards.

National Forest Products Association, 1619 Massachusetts Avenue, N.W., Washington, DC 20036. 202-797-5800

Represents more than 1200 producers of forest products.

National Hardwood Lumber Association, Suite 1450, 332 South Michigan Avenue, Chicago, IL 60605. 312-427-2810

The Association issues biennially a new edition of the *Rules for the Measurement and Inspection of Hardwood Lumber, Cypress, and Thin Lumber.*

National Knitwear Manufacturers' Association, 350 Fifth Avenue, New York, NY 10001. 212-947-1250

National Lime Association 5010 Wisconsin Avenue N.W., Washington, DC 20016. 202-966-3418

In order to assist lime consumers in the most efficient utilization of quick and hydrated lime, this association has developed construction guide specifications, materials specifications, and general recommendations in the mortar, plaster, stucco, highway, and water purification and pollution abatement fields.

National Lubricating Grease Institute, 4635 Wyandotte Street, Kansas City, MO 64112. 816-931-9480

A technical society whose objectives are the development of better lubricating greases.

National Machine Tool Builders' Association, 7901 Westpark Drive, McLean, VA 22101. 703-893-2900

Companies producing about 90 percent of the U.S. machine tool industry's total output. While the NMTBA formerly wrote an electrical standard, its committees now publish technical documents which are primarily informative in nature.

National Mineral Wool Insulation Association, Inc., 382 Springfield Avenue, Summit, NJ 07901. 201-277-1550

Promotes the welfare and development of mineral wool insulation products designed for installation in buildings utilized for human occupancy.

National Oak Flooring Manufacturers' Association, 814 Sterick Building, Memphis, TN 38103. 901-526-5016

The Association has adopted official rules on oak, birch, beech, hard maple, and pecan flooring, which cover in detail the grades and sizes of quartered and plain sawn stock.

National Paper Box Association, 231 Kings Highway East, Haddonfield, NJ 08033. 609-429-7377

Association which represents the rigid paper box industry.

National Particleboard Association, 2306 Perkins Place, Silver Spring, MD 20910. 301-587-2204

This association consists of manufacturers of wood particleboard and medium-density fiberboard.

National Printing Ink Research Institute, Lehigh University, Bethlehem, PA 18015. 215-691-7000, Extension 2220

Founded to engage in scientific research on printing inks, on the equipment and techniques involved in their production, and on the printing surfaces to which they are applied.

National Retail Merchants' Association, 100 W 31st Street, New York, NY 10001. 212-244-8780

This association takes an active part in the formulation of standards and specifications relative to retail store organization, retail systems, retail trade terminology, business practices, and specifications for commodities used in the trade.

National Rifle Association of America, 1600 Rhode Island Avenue N.W., Washington, DC 20036. 202-783-6505

Because some of its major programs include the supervision of markmanship instruction and competition and of safety education involving firearms, much of NRA standardization efforts are in these fields.

National Roofing Contractors' Association, 1515 North Harlem Avenue, Oak Park, IL 60302. 312-383-9513

Through the *NRCA Roofing Manual,* the Association provides to the roofing industry recommended procedures, practices, and evaluative comments on roofing specifications, construction details, and roofing materials.

National Safety Council, 425 North Michigan Avenue, Chicago, IL 60611. 312-527-4800

The mission of the National Safety Council, which was founded in 1913, is: to determine and evaluate methods and procedures that (1) prevent accidents, (2) mitigate injury and economic loss resulting from accidents, and (3) to provide leadership to expedite the adoption and use of those methods and procedures that best serve the public interest.

National Sand and Gravel Association, 900 Spring Street, Silver Spring, MD 20910. 301-587-1400

National Sanitation Foundation, 3475 Plymouth Road, Ann Arbor, MI 48105. 313-769-8010

The Foundation has published standards and criteria, under which testing and certification services are currently extended to over 1600 manufacturers who use the NSF Seal on over 25,000 items of equipment or products.

National Sash and Door Jobbers' Association, 20 North Wacker Drive, Chicago, IL 60606. 312-263-2670

NSDJA developed standards for wood interior hinged door units. NSDJA is also active in promoting standards for the use of safety-glazing materials in hazardous locations.

National School Supply and Equipment Association, 1500 Wilson Boulevard, Arlington, VA 22209. 703-524-8819

Manufacturers and distributors of school equipment and supplies and instructional materials. Standards produced by the Association include *Recommended Standards for Design of Interior Folding and Telescopic Seating.* Has worked on safety standards for heavy-duty playground equipment.

National Silo Association, 2310 Falls Avenue, Suite #2, Waterloo, IA 50701. 319-233-7631

NSA has developed an operator's safety manual.

National Slag Association, 300 South Washington Street, Alexandria, VA 22314. 703-549-3111

National Society for the Prevention of Blindness, Inc., 79 Madison Avenue, New York, NY 10016. 212-684-3505

The oldest voluntary health agency nationally engaged in the prevention of blindness through programs of community service, public and professional education, and research.

National Soft Drink Association, 1101 16th Street N.W., Washington, DC 20036. 202-833-2450

A party to several standards on bottles and contents.

The National Swimming Pool Institute, 2000 K Street NW, Washington, DC 20006. 202-331-8844

National trade association of approximately 1750 swimming pool builders, pool equipment manufacturers and suppliers, architects, engineers, public officials, and others allied with the pool industry.

National Water Well Association, 88 East Broad Street, Columbus, OH 43215. 614-846-9355

Organization of water well drilling contractors, manufacturers, wholesale suppliers, and professional geologists, hydrologists, and engineers.

National Wooden Pallet and Container Association, 1619 Massachusetts Avenue NW, Washington, DC 20036. 202-667-3670

Manufacturers and distributors of pallets, pallet containers, boxes, crates, and skids. The Association publishes standard specifications covering the construction of hardwood, softwood, and plywood pallets in nine quality grades.

National Woodwork Manufacturers' Association, 400 West Madison Street, Chicago, IL 60606. 312-782-6232

Sponsors many industry standards, through NBS.

Natural Gas Processors Association, 1812 First Place, 5th and Boston Ave., Tulsa, OK 74103. 918-582-5112

This association was founded in 1921 to develop standard tests and specifications for casinghead gasoline. Specifications, particularly for vapor pressure, were established for that and other petroleum products.

Northern Hardwood & Pine Manufacturers' Association, Inc., Suite 501 Northern Building, Green Bay, WI 54301. 414-432-9161

One of its objectives is to establish and maintain uniform standard grades for lumber and logs.

Optical Manufacturers' Association, 1730 North Lynn Street, Arlington, VA 22209. 703-525-3514

The Association is an active member of the American National Standards Committee Z80 that is concerned with standards for ophthalmic frames, lenses, contact lenses, and sunglasses.

Optical Society of America, 2100 Pennsylvania Avenue NW, Washington, DC 20037. 202-293-1420

Representatives on the ANSI Photographic Standards Board and on seven American National Standards sectional committees in photography, motion pictures, safety glass, and ophthalmic lenses.

Outdoor Power Equipment Institute, Inc., 1725 K Street N.W., Suite 903-905, Washington, DC 20006. 202-296-3484

Formerly: Lawn Mower Institute.

Packaging Machinery Manufacturers' Institute, 2000 K Street N.W., Washington, DC 20006. 202-331-8181

Working with the Occupational Safety and Health Administration, PMMI has published a safety standard for the care, use, and construction of packaging machinery.

Painting and Decorating Contractors of America, 7223 Lee Highway, Falls Church, VA 22046. 703-534-1201

One of the stated objectives of this organization is its efforts to maintain high standards of workmanship and safety in the painting, decorating, drywall, wallcovering, and coating industries.

Paperboard Packaging Council, 1800 K Street N.W., Washington, DC 20006. 202-872-0180

Trade association representing companies in the production and conversion of paperboard into folding cartons and packages. The Council's functions include marketing information and statistics, industrial relations and safety, technical and production, and Government relations.

Perlite Institute, 45 West 45th Street, New York, NY 10036. 212-CO5-2145

Publishes standards for perlite products used in the building, industrial, and horticultural industries.

Pharmaceutical Manufacturers' Association, 1155 Fifteenth Street N.W., Washington, DC 20005. 202-296-2440

Scientists of member firms constitute committees which work with the United States Pharmacopoeia and the National Formulary in developing methods of analysis and standards for drugs used by the medical and allied professions.

Photo Chemical Machining Institute, 1717 Howard Street, Evanston, IL 60202. 312-491-1661

Companies producing metal parts by photochemical machining.

Photographic Society of America, 2005 Walnut Street, Philadelphia, PA 19103. 215-563-1663

Members encompass experience in the uses of all types of photographic materials, the technology of their applications, and the characteristics and processes of their manufacture.

Pipe Fabrication Institute, 1326 Freeport Road, Pittsburgh, PA 15238. 412-782-1624

Standards and technical bulletins cover the design, fabrication, and erection of industrial and high-pressure–high-temperature piping to meet the most exacting requirements of power plant, chemical, petroleum, and process piping.

Pipe Line Contractors Association, 2800 Republic National Bank Building, Dallas, TX 75201. 214-655-2700

Contractors engaged in the main-line pipeline construction industry.

Polyurethane Manufacturers' Association, 600 South Michigan Avenue, Chicago, IL 60605. 312-332-5657

The Association, established in 1972, is a private, nonprofit trade association of companies involved in the manufacture of solid polyurethane thermosetting elastomers and their related chemical and equipment suppliers.

Powder Actuated Tool Manufacturers' Institute, Inc., 331 Madison Avenue, New York, NY 10017. 212-661-2050

All the major U.S. manufacturers of powder actuated fastening systems.

Pressure Sensitive Tape Council, 1201 Waukegan Road, Glenview, IL 60025. 312-724-7700

Manufacturers of self-sticking tapes.

Printing Industries of America, Inc., 1730 North Lynn Street, Arlington, VA 22209. 703-527-6000

Trade association representing the graphic arts industry.

Project Management Institute, PO Box 43, Drexel Hill, PA 19026. 215-622-5835

The Institute participates in national activities through the American National Standards Committee XK 36.3 and internationally, through liaison with an appointed observer to Internet.

Rack Manufacturers' Institute, 1326 Freeport Road, Pittsburgh, PA 15238. 412-782-1624

Firms engaged in the design and manufacture for sale of industrial steel storage racks.

Radio Technical Commission for Aeronautics, 1717 H Street N.W., Suite 655, Washington, DC 20006. 202-296-0484

RTCA is a medium through which the aviation community, industry, and Government, discuss and resolve common technical problems.

The Railway Tie Association, 314 North Broadway, St. Louis, MO 63102. 314-231-8099

Producers, pressure-treaters, and marketers of wood railroad crossties represented by purchasing officers and maintenance-of-way officers.

Red Cedar Shingle and Handsplit Shake Bureau, 515 116th Ave. N.E., Bellevue, WA 98009. 206-453-1323

Redwood Inspection Service, 617 Montgomery Street, San Francisco, CA 94111. 415-392-7880

The Service is the rules-promulgating agency for the redwood lumber industry.

The Refractories Institute, 1102 One Oliver Plaza, Pittsburgh, PA 15222. 412-281-6787

Association of refractories manufacturers.

Resistance Welder Manufacturers' Association, 1900 Arch Street, Philadelphia, PA 19103. 215-LO4-3484

RWMA has developed specifications for resistance-welding machines: spot, press, portable, seam, upset butt, flashbutt, etc. A standard classification of resistance-welding electrode alloys has been developed, stating minimum permissible physical and electrical qualities.

Rubber Manufacturers' Association, 1901 Pennsylvania Avenue N.W., Washington, DC 20006. 202-785-2602

Standards and specifications for all kinds of rubber and rubberlike products.

Scaffolding and Shoring Institute, 2130 Keith Building, Cleveland, OH 44115. 216-241-7333

Includes manufacturers of scaffolding and shoring. SSI establishes recommended criteria and inspection procedures for the proper and safe use of scaffolding and shoring to support formwork in concrete construction.

Scientific Apparatus Makers' Association, 1140 Connecticut Avenue N.W., Washington, DC 20036. 202-223-1360

Represents over 200 leading manufacturers and distributors of scientific instruments and laboratory apparatus.

Sheet Metal, and Air Conditioning Contractors' National Association, 8224 Old Courthouse Road, Vienna, VA 22180. 703-790-9890

Association of the sheet metal, heating, ventilating, air-conditioning, industrial sheet metal, and roofing industries.

Snell Memorial Foundation, Inc. 761 Laurel Drive, Sacramento, CA 95825. 916-453-2011

Primary purpose is to carry out research in brain trauma and protective headgear, and to develop and utilize advanced techniques for related critical measurements. Much of its work has been carried out under National Institutes of Health research grants.

The Soap and Detergent Association, 475 Park Avenue South, New York, NY 10016. 212-725-1260

Through its Technical and Materials Division, conducts research to determine the effect of industry product constituents in water and sewage treatment processes, on aquatic life and water resources, and on consumer safety.

Society for Information Display, 654 North Sepulveda Boulevard, Los Angeles, CA 90049. 213-472-3550

Primary efforts are in the field of computer-derived dynamic information display.

Society for Technical Communication, Inc., Suite 421, 1010 Vermont Avenue N.W., Washington, DC 20005. 202-737-0035

Educational membership organization whose purpose is to advance the theory and practice of technical communication in all media.

Society of Automotive Engineers, 400 Commonwealth Drive, Pittsburgh, PA 15096. 412-776-4841

Carries on technical standardization work for the motor vehicle, aircraft, airline, space vehicles, farm tractor, earth-moving and road-building machinery, and other manufacturing industries using internal combustion engines. With the exception of aerospace, safety, and environmental standards, which are published in loose-leaf form, the basic standards of the society are published annually in the *SAE Handbook.*

Society of Die Casting Engineers, 16007 West 8 Mile Road, Detroit, MI 48235. 313-273-2180

The society has a Technical Council with subcommittees working in several fields, including safety, machinery, alloys, process, dimensions, metrication, quality, die design, and coatings.

The Society of Manufacturing Engineers, 20501 Ford Road, Dearborn, MI 48128. 313-271-1500

SME's function is to follow and assess the trends and developments in manufacturing; then to interpret, publish, and distribute the information. It provides a common ground and focal point from which manufacturing engineers and corporate managers can share ideas, information, and accomplishments.

Society of Motion Picture and Television Engineers, 862 Scarsdale Avenue, Scarsdale, NY 10583.   914-472-6606

Concerned with the engineering aspects of motion pictures, television, instrumentation, high-speed photography, and the allied arts and sciences.

The Society of Naval Architects and Marine Engineers, 74 Trinity Place, New York, NY 10006.   212-WH3-8650

Standards, guidelines, and codes relating to the design, construction, maintenance, and operation of merchant marine ships, yachts, boats, offshore and ocean-bottom structures, hydrofoils, surface-effect ships, and submersibles.

Society of the Plastics Industry, Inc. 355 Lexington Avenue, New York, NY 10026.   212-573-9400

This is a trade and technical society of over 1200 companies in all branches of the plastics industry interested in quality standards, research, uniform accounting, traffic rates, wage-rate surveys, tariffs, codes, public relations, informative labeling, safety, fire prevention, food packaging, etc.

Southern Building Code Congress, International, 3617 Eighth Avenue, South, Birmingham, AL 35222.   205-252-8930

Private, quasi-legislative organization, dedicated to codification of minimum construction standards in a family of documents.

Southern Hardwood Lumber Manufacturers' Association, Sterick Building, Memphis, TN 38103.   901-525-8221

This organization cooperates with the National Hardwood Lumber Association in grade standardization of hardwood lumber; also with government agencies and all lumber associations in the development of American Lumber Standards fostered by the Department of Commerce.

Southern Pine Inspection Bureau, PO Box 846, Pensacola, FL 32594.   904-434-2611

The recognized organization in the southern pine industry for the formulation and maintenance of grading standards.

Specialty Wire Association, 1625 I Street N.W., Washington, DC 20006.   202-331-1611

Trade association of companies who manufacture from steel rod all forms of steel and alloy steel wire for industrial uses. Typical commodities are spring wire, stapling wire, rope wire, and tire bead wire.

Sporting Arms and Ammunition Manufacturers' Institute, 420 Lexington Avenue, New York, NY 10017.   212-986-6920

In terms of manpower and hours devoted by representatives of member companies who serve on SAAMI's several committees, study groups and task forces, most of the Institute's program is devoted to product safety and standardization.

Sport Car Club of America, Inc. PO Box 22476, Denver, CO 80222.   303-751-4900

SCCA has developed safety standards for competitions, and standards and procedures for speed events for automobiles which may take part in events, for issuance of competition licenses, and for the organization and conduct of its events.

Spring Manufacturers' Institute, 24 Stearns Street, PO Box 959, Bristol, CT 06010.   203-583-2403

Manufacturers of precision mechanical springs. SMI maintains standards in keeping with current technological requirements and works with material and equipment suppliers to improve industry capabilities. SMI develops materials such as the SMI spring design calculator and the SMI *Handbook of Spring Design,* a basic manual.

Standards Engineers Society, 2617 East Hennepin Avenue, Minneapolis, MN 55413.   612-861-4990

Individual members organized in 20 local sections throughout the United States and Canada. The objectives of this association include a forum for the interchange of information on standardization and standardization methods.

Steel Bar Mills Association, 1125 West Lake Street, Room 208, Oak Park, IL 60301.   312-848-0882

SBMA is involved with the solution of operational problems in electric furnace steelmaking and rolling of bar products to accepted standards from billet, rail, and axle steel. Standards activities, primarily in the development of bar standards in billet, rail, and axle steel, are undertaken in a dual cooperative basis with the American Society for Testing and Materials and other standards groups.

Steel Deck Institute, PO Box 3812, St. Louis, MO 63122.   314-965-1741

Manufacturers of steel roof deck, the Institute insures uniform industry standards for the engineering design, manufacture, and field usage of steel roof deck.

Steel Door Institute, c/o Thomas Associates, Inc., 2130 Keith Building, Cleveland, OH 44115.   216-241-7333

Manufacturers of swing type steel doors and frames used in commercial, industrial, and residential construction.

Steel Founders' Society of America, Cast Metals Federation Building, 20611 Center Ridge Road, Rocky River, OH 44116.   216-333-9600

Cooperates particularly with technical committees of the American Society for Testing and Materials in the development of standards and methods of test for steel and steel castings, metallography, radiographic and magnetic-particle testing, and other matters.

Steel Joist Institute, 1703 Parham Road, Suite 204, Richmond, VA 23229.   804-288-3071

Manufacturers engaged in the fabrication and distribution of open-web steel joists.

Steel Shipping Container Institute, 2204 Morris Avenue, Union, NJ 07083.   201-688-8750

Trade organization representing manufacturers of steel drums and pails.

Steel Structures Painting Council, 4400 Fifth Avenue, Pittsburgh, PA 15213.   412-621-1100

Steel Window Institute, c/o Thomas Associates, Inc., 2130 Keith Building, Cleveland, OH 44115.   216-241-7333

Trade association composed of a majority of American steel window manufacturers.

Sump Pump Manufacturers' Association, 221 North LaSalle Street, Chicago, IL 60601.   312-346-1862

Objectives and activities include: development and promulgation of quality standards and spelling out design and performance criteria for sump pumps used in homes.

Tanners' Council of America, 411 Fifth Avenue, New York, NY 10016.   212-686-7950

Trade association for the leather industry of the United States.

Technical Association of the Pulp and Paper Industry, One Dunwoody Park, Atlanta, GA 30341.   404-659-4313

The Association is divided into 11 divisions dealing with problems relating to pulp manufacture, paper and board manufacture, paper-synthetics, corrugated containers, coating and graphic arts, engineering, research and development, testing, environmental, management sciences, and finishing.

Telephone Group, American Telephone and Telegraph Company, 195 Broadway, New York, NY 10007. 212-394-4141

This group, which functions under the auspices of ANSI, consists of the American Telephone and Telegraph Company and the United States Independent Telephone Association and their member and associated companies. It is also represented on the following ANSI Technical Advisory Boards: Construction, Electrical and Electronics, Graphic, Information Systems, Mechanical, Miscellaneous, and Safety.

Thermal Insulation Manufacturers' Association, Inc., 7 Kirby Plaza, Mt. Kisco, NY 10549. 914-241-2284

Association representing manufacturers of insulation for thermal industrial uses.

The Thread Institute, Inc., 1133 Avenue of the Americas, New York, NY 10036. 212-575-1740

A national trade association for sewing thread manufacturers, converters, and jobbers.

Tin Research Institute, Inc., 483 West Sixth Avenue, Columbus, OH 43201. 614-424-6200

Members of the Institute participate widely in the development of standards and specifications for tin ingots, tinplate, tin alloys, bearings, solders, pewter and tin and tin alloy coatings.

Tire and Rim Association, 3200 West Market Street, Akron, OH 44313. 216-836-5553

The technical standardizing body of the tire, rim, and related parts manufacturers of the United States.

Transportation Data Coordinating Committee, 1101 Seventeenth Street N.W., Washington, DC 20036. 202-293-5514

Founded by leading shippers, carriers, and others interested in the need for standardization of transportation data, codes, formats, and systems that will permit computer-to-computer data exchange between parties involved in transportation, distribution, and trade activities.

Truck Body and Equipment Association, Inc., 5530 Wisconsin Avenue, Suite 1220, Washington, DC 20015. 301-699-5480

The Truck Trailer Manufacturers' Association, 2430 Pennsylvania Avenue N.W., Washington, DC 20037. 202-785-5833

Tubular Exchanger Manufacturers' Association, 331 Madison Avenue, New York, NY 10017. 212-661-2050

Standards cover various clarifications and expansions on material, thermal physical properties of fluids, and other general information relating to the various classes of exchangers.

Ultrasonic Industry Association, Inc., 271 North Avenue, New Rochelle, NY 10801. 914-235-4020

Underwriters Laboratories, Inc., 207 East Ohio Street, Chicago, IL 60611. 312-642-6969

This independent organization, devoted to testing for public safety, was established to maintain and operate laboratories for the examination and testing for safety of devices, systems, and materials. Founded in 1894, testing laboratories are maintained at Chicago, Illinois; Melville, L.I., New York; Northbrook, Illinois; Santa Clara, California; and Tampa, Florida. Headquarters scheduled to be moved to Northbrook in late 1979 or early 1980.

U.S. Pharmacopeia, Pharmacopeia of the United States of America, United States Pharmacopeial Convention, 12601 Twinbrook Parkway, Rockville, MD 20852. 301-881-0666

This convention is a nonprofit corporation which meets every five years to reorganize the revision program of the Pharmacopeia of the United States of America, established in 1820. It is made up mainly of representatives of the medical and pharmaceutical associations, the national trade associations, and the departments of the Federal Government most concerned with standards for medicinal preparations.

United States Testing Company, Inc., 1415 Park Avenue, Hoboken, NJ 07030.   201-792-2400

This independent commercial laboratory, established in 1880, plays an important role, generally on a fee basis, in assisting Government agencies, manufacturers, and trade associations in establishing national standards. The company is also known as Nationwide Consumer Testing Institute, Inc.

Vacuum Cleaner Manufacturers' Association, 1615 Collamer Street, Cleveland, OH 44110.   216-851-2400

Cooperates with ASTM Safety program.

Vehicle Equipment Safety Commission, 1030 15th Street N.W., Suite 536, Washington, DC 20005.   202-833-1596

The National Traffic and Motor Vehicle Safety Act of 1966 (Public Law 89-563) names the Vehicle Equipment Safety Commission specifically as consultant to the Department of Transportation in the promulgation of Federal Motor Vehicle Standards.

Water Pollution Control Federation, 3900 Wisconsin Avenue N.W., Washington, DC 20016.   202-337-2500

Technical membership organization.

Water Systems Council, 221 North LaSalle Street, Chicago, IL 60601.   312-346-1862

Manufacturers of domestic and farm-water equipment.

Welding Research Council, 345 East 47th Street, Room 801, New York, NY 10017.   212-644-7956

The Council is currently administering work in the following areas: interpretive reports, weldability, pressure, vessel research, resistance welding, structural steel, aluminum alloys, welding processes, high alloys, and reactive and refractory metals.

West Coast Lumber Inspection Bureau, 6980 SW Varns Road, PO Box 23145, Portland, OR 97223.   503-639-0651

Industry-owned, nonprofit corporation that provides lumber quality control services at cost.

Western Wood Moulding and Millwork Producers, PO Box 25278, Portland, Oregon 97255.   503-292-9288

Western Wood Products Association, 1500 Yeon Building, Portland, OR 96204.   503-224-3930

Its members process Douglas fir, larch, ponderosa pine, sugar pine, Idaho white pine, lodgepole pine, white fir, Engelmann spruce, Sitka spruce, mountain hemlock, western hemlock, western red cedar, incense cedar, red alder, and aspen.

Western Wooden Box Association, 430 Sherman Avenue, Suite 206, Palo Alto, CA 94306.   415-327-8200

Manufacturers and distributors of sawn wooden boxes, crates, lugs, veneer components, pallets, and loading material for interstate and export shipment of western fresh fruit, vegetables, and melons.

Wire Reinforcement Institute, 7900 Westpark Drive, McLean, VA 22101.   703-790-9790

United States and Canadian manufacturers of steel welded-wire fabric.

Wood and Synthetic Flooring Institute, 1201 Waukegan Road, Glenview, IL 60025.   312-724-7700

Zinc Institute, 292 Madison Avenue, New York, NY 10017.   212-679-6020

Specifications and standards in connection with the finished products of the zinc industry.

STATE GOVERNMENTS

Arizona, State of, Manager, Purchasing Office, Finance Division, Department of Administration, The Capitol Building, 1700 West Washington, Phoenix, AZ 85007. 602-271-5511

Colorado, State of, State Purchasing Director, Division of Purchasing, Department of Administration, Suite 232, State Services Building, Denver, CO 80203. 303-892-3261

Connecticut, State of, Director, Purchasing Division, Department of Finance and Control, PO Box 1141, 460 Silver Street, Middletown, CT 06457. 203-347-3361

Florida, State of, Director, Division of Purchasing, Bureau of Standards, Department of General Services, William D. Bloxham Building, Tallahassee, FL 32304. 904-488-2773.

The Division of Purchasing has published over 2000 standards.

Georgia, State of, Director, Purchasing and Supplies Division, Department of Administrative Services, 116 Mitchell Street SW, Atlanta, GA 30334. 404-656-3240

Illinois, State of, State Purchasing Agent, Procurement Division, Department of General Services, 801 State Office Building, Springfield, IL 62706. 217-782-2301

Kansas, State of, Director, Division of Purchases, Department of Administration, State Office Building, Topeka, KS 66612. 913-276-2376

Kentucky, Commonwealth of, Chief, Specification and Inspection, Division of Purchases, Department of Finance, New Capitol Annex, Frankfort, KY 40601. 502-564-4916

Maryland, State of, Chief of the Purchasing Bureau, Department of General Services, 301 West Preston Street, Baltimore, MD 21201. 301-383-3644

Michigan, State of, Standards Executive, Purchasing Division, Standards Section, Department of Management and Budget, Mason Building, Lansing, MI 48913. 517-373-0330

Minnesota, State of Director of Procurement, Standards and Engineering Unit, Procurement Division, Department of Administration, Saint Paul, MN 55101. 612-296-2600

Missouri, State of, Director, Contracting and Procurement Division, Office of Administration, Jefferson City, MO 65101. 314-751-2387

Montana, State of, Chief, State Purchasing Bureau, Department of Administration, State Capitol Building, Helena, MT 59601. 406-449-2575

New Jersey, State of, Director, Standards and Specifications Section, Division of Purchase and Property, State House, Trenton, NJ 08625. 609-292-4741

New York, State of, Division of Standards and Quality Control, Office of General Services, South Mall Tower, Albany, NY 12223. 518-474-7388

North Carolina, State of, State Purchasing Officer, Standards and Engineering Section, Purchase and Contract Division, Department of Administration, 116 West Jones Street, Raleigh, NC 27603. 919-733-7624

Oregon, State of, Administrator, Specification Section, Procurement Division, Department of General Services, 1225 Ferry Street SE, Salem, OR 97310. 503-378-4643

Pennsylvania, Commonwealth of, Secretary of Property and Supplies, Department of General Services, Room 602, North Office Building, Harrisburg, PA 17125. 717-787-5996

Rhode Island, State of, State Purchasing Agent, Division of Purchases, Department of Administration, 289 Promenade Street, Providence, RI 02908. 401-277-2321

Texas, State of, Executive Director, Texas State Board of Control, PO Box 13047, Capitol Station, Austin, TX 78711. 512-475-2211

Utah, State of, Purchasing Agent, Division of Purchasing, Department of Finance, State Capitol, Salt Lake City, UT 84114. 801-533-4620

Virginia, Commonwealth of, Director, Department of Purchases and Supply, PO Box 1199, Richmond, VA 23209. 804-786-3845

West Virginia, State of, Commissioner, Purchasing Division, Department of Finance and Administration, State Capitol Building, Charleston, WV 25305. 304-348-2300

Wisconsin, State of, Director, Bureau of Purchases and Services, Department of Administration, 1 West Wilson Street, Madison, WI 53702. 608-266-5612

Wyoming, State of, Purchasing Administrator, Purchasing and Property Control Division, Department of Administration and Fiscal Control, Cheyenne, WY 82002. 307-777-7253

APPENDIX H
INFORMATION SOURCES

The appendix includes the names, addresses, and functions of periodicals and other information sources not listed in Appendix G (Standards-Setting Organizations).

**GOVERNMENT SOURCES OF
SAFETY AND RELIABILITY DATA**

Aerospace Materials Information Center (AMIC), Air Force Materials Laboratory, Wright-Patterson AFB, OH 45433.

Materials covered include adhesives, coatings, lubricants, fibers, various manufacturing procedures, methods of materials evaluation—almost anything not specifically of interest to other Air Force research centers. May be used only by qualified DOD contractors.

Aerospace Safety Research and Data Institute, NASA-Lewis Research Center, 21000 Brook Park Rd., Cleveland, OH 44135.

Wide range of safety data, originally assembled for NASA research, but expanded into civilian areas as well.

Air Force Directorate of Aerospace Safety, Deputy Inspector General for Inspection and Safety, Norton AFB, San Bernardino, CA 92409.

Information on failures leading to accidents concerning the Air Force.

Air Force Engineering and Logistics Information System (AFELIS), Air Force Logistics Command, Wright-Patterson AFB, Dayton, OH 45433.

Compiles and disseminates data on the reliability of parts in the Air Force's inventory.

Army Board for Aviation Accident Research, Ft. Rucker, AL 36362.

Information on failures leading to accidents of concern to Army aviation and related equipment.

Coast Guard, Department of Transportation, 13th and E Streets, N.W., Washington, DC 20005.

Accident investigations and safety standards for shipping and ships.

Cryogenic Data Center, National Bureau of Standards, Institute for Materials Research, Boulder, CO 80301.

This lab, sponsored by NBS and by NASA, compiles data on fluid flow at low temperatures, and the effects of such flow on other materials.

Defense Ceramic Information Center, Battelle Memorial Institute, 505 King Avenue, Columbus, OH 43201.

Data on testing, fabrication, and performance of ceramic materials including borides, graphite, carbides, oxides, nitrides, silicides, sulfides, intermetallics, and glasses. Materials are evaluated for their behavior as coatings, fibers, composites, and foams.

Defense Metals Information Center (DMIC), Battelle Memorial Institute, 505 King Ave., Columbus, OH 43201.

Data on structural metals of interest to the Defense Department. Includes information on primary production, smelting, fabrication, and protection of the common (aluminum, steel alloys) and the exotic (rhenium, columbium), and everything in between.

Department of Energy, Argonne National Laboratory Code Center, Argonne, IL 60439.

Data bases include one for nuclear safety containing more than 35,000 entries and available through the Department's computer system, and one on physical and chemical compatibility of 2000 materials.

Department of Transportation, 800 Independence Avenue, S.W., Washington, DC 20590.

This address includes the Federal Aviation Administration and the main reference library (closed to the general public, but can be used through staff members there). National Transportation Safety Board (Washington, DC 20591) publishes findings through NTIS or GPO. FAA Flight Standards Service, P.O. Box 25082, Oklahoma City, OK 73125, accepts research requests, publishes monthly General Aviation Airworthiness Alerts, Aircraft Utilization & Propulsion Reliability Reports, and Special Study Reports.

Electronic Component Reliability Center (ECRC), Battelle Memorial Institute, 505 King Ave., Columbus, OH 43201.

Test results on electronic components.

Electronic Properties Information Center (EPIC), Air Force Materials Lab, Wright-Patterson AFB, Dayton, OH 45433, or Hughes Aircraft (E-175), Culver City, CA 90232.

Data are grouped by function: semiconductors, insulators, ferroelectrics, and so forth. Only materials information is available; circuit data and behavior of components in specific devices are generally not included in this data base.

Failure Rate Data System (FERADA), Navy Fleet Missile Systems Analysis and Evaluation Group, Corona, CA 91720.

Publishes failure-rate data on a wide variety of component types (see GIDEP below).

Fire Prevention and Control Administration, 2400 M St. N.W., P.O. Box 19518, Washington, DC 20036.

Established in 1976 by the Commerce Department; collects statistics on fire prevention.

Government-Industry Data Exchange Program (GIDEP), GIDEP Operations Center, Corona, CA 91720.

Coordinates numerous government data banks, including the Failure Rate Data Bank, the Metrology Data Bank, the Failure Experience Data Bank. These data can be accessed directly by remote terminal. Participants in the service are notified by mailed ALERTS of problems, or may be queried through an Urgent Data Request. Participants are primarily users of parts, materials, and subassemblies, rather than manufacturers of these items. Full participants may obtain and maintain full microfilmed files; partial participants may receive indexes to those files, and all ALERTS, UDRs, etc. Industry users may join free—they must only pledge to maintain the materials provided by GIDEP in usable condition, and should feed the data base with any problems they discover.

Lawrence Livermore Laboratories, Livermore, CA 94550.

In cooperation with the National Bureau of Standards, the Information Research group at LLL is developing a new data base containing properties of materials and various systems-analysis tools for energy-related projects.

APPENDIX H   INFORMATION SOURCES   625

Library of Congress, First St. and Independence Ave S.E., Washington, DC 20540.

The main stacks are for reference only—materials must be used at the library or obtained through inter-library loans. The library also coordinates the National Referral Center for Science and Technology, which attempts to link those who have problems with experts or recognized sources of suthoritative data.

Mechanical Component Reliability Center (MCRC), Battelle Memorial Institute, 505 King Ave., Columbus, OH 43201.

Tests mechanical components and summarizes data for publication.

NASA Scientific and Technical Information Office, Washington, DC 20546.

Publishes *Star,* an abstract journal with indexes. For document orders based on the system, use the following address: P.O. Box 33, College Park, MD 20740.

National Electronic Injury Surveillance System, Consumer Product Safety Commission, Washington, DC 20207.

Based on injuries reported at hospital emergency rooms. System is being revised at press time to improve quality of data and more closely define the scope of a "product-related" injury.

National Library of Medicine, National Institutes of Health, 9000 Rockville Pike, Bethesda, MD 20014.

NIH is developing a new data base of physical and chemical properties of various substances, with an emphasis on toxicity. Approximately 1000 items were scheduled to be on the data base by early 1978.

National Technical Information Service, U.S. Dept. of Commerce, Springfield, VA 22151.

Numerous government documents. Catalogs on request. Distributes Defense Documentation Center documents (indexed through U.S. Gov't R & D Reports).

Naval Publications and Forms Center, 5801 Tabor Ave., Philadelphia, PA 19120.

Stocks and distributes, free, the most commonly required military specifications and standards. Listings are recorded in the DOD Index of Specs and Standards, available from the U.S. Government Printing Office, Washington, DC 20402. Advantages of using this service, rather than GPO directly, are time (the Navy handles requests within a few days) and, of course, money. But users must demonstrate some government or public benefit to use the service.

Naval Safety Center, Attn.: Safety Education Office, U.S. Naval Air Station, Norfolk, VA 23511.

Distributes weekly summary of major aircraft accidents, flight surgeons' newsletter, and numerous other safety-related publications.

Nuclear Safety Information Center (NSIC), Oak Ridge National Laboratory, P.O. Box Y, Oak Ridge, TN 37831.

Safety and environmental standards, quality control, logs of experience on existing systems.

Oak Ridge National Laboratory, P.O. Box X, Oak Ridge, TN 37830.

Maintains, through publications and microfiche, compilations of federal data on mutagenicity and teratogenicity. The index is computer-based for searching.

Office of Naval Research (available through the National Academy of Science, 2101 Constitution Ave N.W., Washington, DC 20418).

Publications on toxicity of various materials on humans.

Office of Product Defect Identification, Consumer Product Safety Commission, 1750 K St. N.W., Washington, DC 20207.

Data on defect reports to the Commission.

Office of Toxic Substances, U.S. Environmental Protection Agency, 401 M St. S.W., Washington, DC 20460.

This office administers toxic substances legislation, as well as earlier pesticide laws. The office's listings of chemical compositions of various product mixtures (done under contract by the Chemical Abstracts Service and in cooperation with the Food and Drug Administration, the Occupational Safety and Health Administration, and the Consumer Product Safety Commission) and its Pesticide Episode Review System are particularly useful for firms trying to trace possible hidden chemical hazards.

Patent and Trademark Office, 2021 Jefferson Davis Highway, Arlington, VA (mailing address, Washington, DC 20231).

Useful to see if others have patented safety devices for your type of product. Patents may be searched most comprehensively through agents working in Washington, although most major cities have at least one library which keeps bound copies of patents.

Poison Control Clearinghouse, Food and Drug Administration, 5401 Westbard Ave., Bethesda, MD 20016.

EDUCATIONAL INSTITUTIONS

Carnegie-Mellon University
Pittsburgh, PA 15213

George Washington University
School of Engineering and Applied Science
Continuing Engineering Education
Washington, DC 20006

Harvard University
Cambridge, MA 02138

New Jersey Institute of Technology
333 High St.
Newark, NJ 07102

New York University
Washington Square
New York, NY 10019

North Carolina State University
Systems Safety Engineering Program
Raleigh, NC 27607

Notre Dame
Radiation Labs (Kinetic effects of radiation on chemical systems)
Notre Dame, IN 46556

Texas A & M
College Station
TX 77840

University of Arizona
College of Engineering
Tucson, AZ 85721

University of Missouri
Columbia MO 65201

University of Southern California
Institute of Aerospace Safety and Management
University Park
Los Angeles, CA 90007

University of Texas at Arlington
Arlington, TX 76010

University of Washington
Office of Short Courses and Conferences
336 Lewis Hall
Seattle, WA 98105

NONGOVERNMENTAL SAFETY AND LIABILITY SOURCES

American Chemical Society, 1155 Sixteenth St. N.W., Washington, DC 20036.

Association of Trial Lawyers of America, 1050 31st St. N.W., Washington, DC 20007.

Data for plaintiffs' attorneys. Newsletter and other publications.

Chemical Propulsion Information Agency, Applied Physics Laboratory, Johns Hopkins University, 8621 Georgia Ave., Silver Spring, MD 20910.

Sponsored by the Naval Air Systems Command. Will provide research data on request to solve specific problems.

Chemshare Corp., 2500 Transco Tower, Houston, TX 77027.

The CHEMTRAN computerized data base of 737 pure compounds and mixtures, particularly useful for chemical process plan designers. Available through United Computing System and through Tymshare.

Cindas, Purdue Industrial Research Park, West Lafayette, IN 47906.

Microfiche file of papers and abstracts, critically edited for thermophysical properties of more than 60,000 inorganic compounds. System is particularly strong on coatings, glasses, and ceramics. Separate microfiche files for electrical and basically chemical properties. A 13-volume handbook set summarizing the data is sold by Plenum Publishing Corp., 227 W 17th St., New York, NY 10011, and a computer-accessed data base is being developed.

Coblentz Society, P.O. Box 9952, Kirkwood, MO 63122.

Books and loose-leaf binders of infrared spectra of plasticizers, halogenated hydrocarbons, and other classes of materials.

Defense Research Institute, 1100 West Wells St., Milwaukee, WI 53233.

Data for defense attorneys.

Dyes Environmental and Toxicology Organization (DETO), 1075 Central Park Ave., Scarsdale, NY 10583.

Created in 1977 by the Synthetic Organic Chemicals Manufacturers' Association to gather information on problems associated with the manufacture, shipment, use, and disposal of dyes.

Flight Safety Foundation, 3120 Wilson Blvd., Arlington, VA 22209.

Provides consultants for government and industry. Conducts safety surveys.

Information Council on Fabric Flammability, 610 Texas Ave., Galveston, TX 77550.

Research data, injury statistics for the industry.

Information Handling Services, 15 Inverness Way East, P.O. Box 1154, Englewood, CO 80110.

Keeps track of government and industry standards and design specifications. Subscriptions available on microfiche or on microfilm.

Information Research Center, Battelle Memorial Institute, 505 King Ave., Columbus, OH 43201.

Collects data on information systems and scientific communication generally.

Lockheed Information Systems, 3251 Hanover St., Palo Alto, CA 94304.

On-line computer-accessed data bases. Available at many research libraries.

Manlabs, Inc. 21 Erie St., Cambridge, MA 02138.

Data bank of material properties, including vapor pressures, Gibbs free energy, solubility, etc. About 2000 items.

Mechanical Properties Data Center, Belfour Stulen, Inc., 13919 West Bay Shore Drive, Traverse City, MI 49684.

Structural design data, quality control, computer-aided design information.

Metcut Research Associates, 3980 Rosslyn Dr., Cincinnati, OH 45209.

The Machinability Data Center; over 30,000 documents available in microfiche; also useful handbook of data. The data base is computer-accessable.

National Board of Fire Underwriters, 85 John St., New York, NY 10038.

National Research Council, 2101 Constitution Ave., Washington, DC 20418.

This arm of the National Academy of Sciences does research in many areas, under contract to government and private organizations.

National Safety Council, 425 North Michigan Ave., Chicago, IL 60611.

Numerous publications, training aids, statistical studies.

National Security Industrial Association, Union Trust Bldg., 15th and H Streets N.W., Washington, DC 20005.

Practising Law Institute, 810 Seventh Ave., New York, NY 10019.

Numerous publications on product liability and related topics.

Sadtler Research Labs, 3316 Spring Garden St., Philadelphia, PA 19104.

Approximately 100,000 infrared spectra in the IRIS system, available through outlets of University Computing Corp.

Systems Development Corp., 2500 Colorado Ave., Santa Monica, CA 90406.

On-line computer-accessed data bases. Available at many research libraries.

SPECIALIZED PERIODICALS (Does not include publications of organizations listed in App. G or in earlier sections of this appendix.)

Federal Register, Superintendent of Documents, U.S. Government Printing Office, Washington, DC 20402.

Daily compilation of federal regulations, proposed regulations, executive orders, and notices.

NBS Publications Newsletter, National Bureau of Standards, Washington, DC 20234.

Indexes publications of the bureau.

Personal Injury Newsletter, M. Bender, 235 E 45 St., New York, NY 10017.

Company publishes several newsletters of interest to legal and managerial personnel concerned with product safety and liability.

Product Liability Letter, Washington Business Information, National Press Building, Washington, DC 20045.

Authoritative, interpretive information. Company also distributes special reports, studies of others.

Product Safety & Liability Reporter, Bureau of National Affairs, Inc., 1231 25th St. NW, Washington, DC 20037.

Weekly binder service, covers cases, regulatory standards, federal laws. Almost no interpretive information. Organization also publishes binder services on occupational safety and health, noise, and chemical toxicity.

Products Liability Reports, Commerce Clearing House, 4025 W. Peterson Ave., Chicago, IL 60645.

Biweekly newsletter and binder service. Includes state-by-state law summaries, court cases. Almost no interpretive information.

Verdict Reports, Jury Verdict Research Co., 5325 Naiman Pkwy., Suite B, Solon, OH 44139.

Reports mainly big settlements and court verdicts. Cases won by the defense are not reported.

FOREIGN DATA SOURCES

Aeronautical Research Institute of Sweden, Stockholm, Sweden.

Publishes memos and reports on these areas of application: man/machine relationships; airframe and structures; life support; escape, survival, and rescue; and crash/survival.

Defense Research Medical Laboratories, P.O. Box 62, Postal Station K, Toronto, Ontario, Canada.

Conducts studies and publishes reports in the following areas of application: man/machine relationships; airframe and structures; life support; escape, survival, and rescue; and crash/survival.

International Civil Aviation Organization, International Aviation Building, 1080 University Street, Montreal 3, P.Q., Canada.

The organization maintains specialization in the following areas of application: man/machine relationships; accident investigation; economic factors; operational considerations; maintenance concepts; navigation; and communications. Publishes the *ICAO Bulletin* monthly.

International Federation of Airline Pilots Associations, 1 Hyde Park Place, London, W. 2, England.

The association maintains proficiency in the following areas of application: data storage and retrieval; accident investigation; economic factors; operational considerations; maintenance concepts; crew station; life support; escape, survival and rescue; and crash/survival.

National Research Council of Canada, Ottawa, Canada.

Conducts studies and publishes bulletins and reports in the following areas of application: man/machine relationships; accident investigation; operational considerations; propulsion; fuels and lubricants; life support, escape, survival, and rescue, and crash/survival.

Royal Canadian Air Force, Institute of Aviation Medicine, 1107 Avenue Road, Toronto 12, Ontario, Canada.

Publishes memos and reports in the following areas of application: man/machine relationships; accident investigations; life support; escape, survival, and rescue, and crash/survival.

Technical Information and Library Services, Ministry of Aviation, Farnborough, Hants, England.

Maintains, stores, and provides information in the following areas of application: data storage and retrieval; man/machine relationships; propulsion; fuel/propellants; life support; escape, survival, and rescue; and crash/survival.

APPENDIX I
BIBLIOGRAPHY

For periodicals and other reference services, see App. H.

I Why Product Safety, and Why Now?

Beakley, George C., and **Ernest G. Chilton:** *Design: Serving the Needs of Man,* Macmillan, New York, 1974, 546 pages.

Berelson, B., and **G. A. Steiner:** *Human Behavior: An Inventory of Scientific Findings,* Harcourt, Brace, New York, 1964.

Blaxall, Martha, and **Barbara Readan:** *Women and the Workplace,* University of Chicago, Chicago, 1976, 325 pages.

Boley, Jack W.: *A Guide to Effective Industrial Safety,* Gulf Publishing Co., Houston, Texas, 1977, 120 pages.

Brown, James M.: *Probing the Law and Beyond; a Quest for Public Protection from Hazardous Product Catastrophies,* George Washington University, Washington, D.C., 1969.

Chumas, Sophie J. (ed.) *Directory of United States Standardization Activities,* U.S. Dept. of Commerce, Washington, D.C., 1975, 224 pages.

Coccia, Michael, John W. Dondanville, and **Thomas R. Nelson:** *Product Liability: Trends and Applications,* American Management Associations, New York, 1970.

Dickerson, F. Reed: *Products Liability and the Food Consumer,* Little, 1951.

Dickerson, F. Reed (ed.): *Product Safety in Household Goods,* Bobbs, New York, 1968.

Dixon, John R.: *Decision Engineering: Inventiveness, Analysis, and Decision Making,* McGraw-Hill, New York, 1966, 354 pages.

Doing Better and Feeling Worse, American Academy of Arts and Sciences, 1977, 281 pages.

Effects of CO on Vigilance Performance, National Institute of Occupational Safety and Health, Cincinnati, Ohio, 1977, 58 pages.

Elder, Rob and Sarah: *Crash,* Atheneum, New York, 1977, 253 pages.

Geiger, Gordon H. (ed.): *Supplementary Readings in Engineering Design,* McGraw-Hill, New York, 1975, 176 pages.

Gillam, Cornelius W.: *Products Liability in the Automobile Industry—A Study in Strict Liability and Social Control,* University of Minnesota, 1960.

Gray, Irwin: *Product Liability,* Amacom, New York, 1975, 239 pages.

A Guide to the Work-Relatedness of Disease, National Institute of Occupational Safety and Health, Cincinnati, Ohio, 1977, 115 pages.

Heinrich, H. W.: *Industrial Accident Prevention,* McGraw-Hill, New York, 1959, 480 pages.

Ishikawa, Kaoru: *Guide to Quality Control,* Asian Productivity Organization, Tokyo, Japan, 1976, 226 pages.

Keeton, Page, and **Marshall S. Shapo:** *Products and the Consumer: Defective and Dangerous Products,* Foundation, 1970.

Lowrance, William W.: *Of Acceptable Risk: Science and the Determination of Safety,* William Kaufmann, Inc., Los Altos, Calif., 1976, 180 pages.

More, Harry W.: *New Era of Public Safety,* C. C. Thomas, New York, 1970.

Nader, Ralph: *Unsafe at Any Speed,* Grossman Publishers, New York, 1972, 417 pages.

National Academy of Engineering: *Public Safety a Growing Factor in Modern Design,* Symposium, 1970.

National Commission on Product Safety: *Final Report,* Presented to the President and Congress, NTIS, Springfield, Va., 1970.

National Commission on Product Safety: *Hearings, Law, Arts,* NTIS, Springfield, Va., 1970.

Proceedings of Product Liability Prevention Conference, New Jersey Institute of Technology, Newark, N.J., 1971–1976 (5 volumes).

Redden, Martha Ross, Wayne Fortunato-Schwandt, and **Janet Welsh Brown:** *Barrier Free Meetings,* American Association for the Advancement of Science, Washington, D.C., 1976, 74 pages.

Spillers, William R.: *Basic Questions of Design Theory,* North-Holland, Amsterdam, Netherlands, 1974, 530 pages.

II The Regulatory Progress, Federal and Industrial

Epstein, Samuel S., and **Richard D. Grundy** (eds.): *Consumer Health and Product Hazards—Chemicals, Electronic Products, Radiation,* MIT, Cambridge, Mass., 1974, 342 pages.

——— *Consumer Health and Product Hazards—Cosmetics and Drugs, Pesiticides, Food Additives,* MIT, Cambridge, Mass., 1974, 389 pages.

Evaluation of Occupational Hazards from Industrial Radiation, National Institute of Occupational Safety and Health, Cincinnati, Ohio, 1977, 92 pages.

Guttman, Daniel, and **Barry Willner:** *The Shadow Government,* Pantheon, New York, 1976, 354 pages.

Hopf, Peter S.: *Designer's Guide to OSHA,* McGraw-Hill, New York, 1975, 304 pages.

International Labor Office, Geneva: *Encyclopedia of Occupational Health and Safety,* McGraw-Hill, New York, 1972, 1500 pages, 2 volumes.

International Vehicle Legislation—Order or Chaos?, Mechanical Engineering Publications, Suite 1210, 200 West 57 Street, New York, 1976, 180 pages.

MacAvoy, Paul W. (ed.): *OSHA Safety Regulation,* American Institute for Public Policy Research, Washington, D.C., 1977, 104 pages.

McGillan, James J., John E. Fiorini III, Charles A. O'Connor III, and **Michael A. Brown:** *Consumer Product Safety Law,* Government Institutes, Washington, D.C., 1977, 233 pages.

Miller, Marshall Lee: *Toxic Substances Law & Regulations,* Government Institutes, Washington, D.C., 1977, 220 pages.

National Commission on Product Safety: *Consumer Product Index,* NTIS, Springfield, Va., 1969–1970.

——— *Consumer Safety Legislation,* NTIS, Springfield, Va., 1970.

——— *Product and Injury Identification,* Supplemental Studies Vol. I, NTIS, Springfield, Va., 1970.

——— *Industry Self-Regulation,* Supplemental Studies Vol. II, NTIS, Springfield, Va., 1970.

―――― *Product Safety Law and Administration,* Supplemental Studies Vol. III, NTIS, Springfield, Va., 1970.

Product Liability in Europe, Kluwer-Harrap Handbooks, London, 1975, 155 pages.

Regulatory Policy Committee: *Toward Regulatory Reasonableness,* U.S. Department of Commerce, Washington, D.C., 1977, 260 pages.

Showalter, David R.: *How to Make OSHA-1970 Work For You,* Ann Arbor Science Publishers, Ann Arbor, Mich., 1972, 149 pages.

Sorenson, Howard C. (ed.): *Seminar on Products Liability and Structural Work Act,* Chicago Bar Association Committee on Continuing Legal Education, Chicago, 1966.

Vehicle Safety Legislation—Its Engineering and Social Implications, Mechanical Engineering Publications, Suite 1210, 200 West 57 Street, New York, 1975, 204 pages.

III Organizing and Operating Corporate and Departmental Product Safety Programs

Aljian, George W.: *Purchasing Handbook,* McGraw-Hill, New York, 1973, 1256 pages.

Anderson, C. Richard: *OSHA and Accident Control through Training,* Industrial Press, New York, 1975, 225 pages.

Barish, Norman N.: *Economic Analysis for Engineering and Managerial Decision Making,* McGraw-Hill, New York, 1962, 720 pages.

Best's Environmental Control and Safety Directory, A.M. Best, Morristown, N.J., 1970, 1028 pages.

Davis, Gordon B.: *Introduction to Management Information Systems,* McGraw-Hill, 1974, 492 pages.

de Neufville, Richard, and **Joseph H. Stafford:** *Systems Analysis for Engineers and Managers,* McGraw-Hill, New York, 1971, 368 pages.

Jenkins, J. P. (ed.): *Proceeding of the U.S. Navy Human Reliability Workshop 22–23 July 1970,* Naval Ship Systems Command, Office of Naval Research and Naval Air Development Center, Department of the Navy, Washington, D.C., 1971.

Juran, J. M., and **Frank M. Gryna, Jr.:** *Quality Planning and Analysis,* McGraw-Hill, New York, 1970, 684 pages.

Lucas, Henry C.: *The Analysis, Design and Implementation of Information Systems,* McGraw-Hill, New York, 1976, 416 pages.

Matwes, George J., and **Helen Matwes:** *Loss Control: A Safety Guidebook for Trades and Services,* Van Nostrand Reinhold, New York, 1973, 341 pages.

Meredith, Dale D., Kam W. Wong, Ronald W. Woodhead, and **Robert H. Wortman:** *Design and Planning of Engineering Systems,* Prentice-Hall, 1973, 393 pages.

Miles, Lawrence D.: *Techniques of Value Analysis and Engineering,* McGraw-Hill, New York, 1971, 320 pages.

Quality Costs Technical Committee: *Guide for Reducing Quality Costs,* American Society for Quality Control, Milwaukee, Wis., 46 pages.

Riggs, James L.: *Engineering Economics,* McGraw-Hill, New York, 1977, 554 pages.

Riordan, J. J. (ed.): *Zero Defects: The Quest for Quality,* Department of Defense, Washington, D.C., 1968.

Small Business Administration: *A Tested System for Achieving Quality Control,* Technical Aids No. 91 for Small Manufacturers, Washington, D.C., 1969.

Tarrants, W. E. (ed.): *A Selected Bibliography of Reference Materials in Safety Engineering and Related Fields,* American Society of Safety Engineers, Park Ridge, Ill., 1967.

United Nations Industrial Development Organization: *Guides to Information Sources No. 6, Information Sources in Industrial Quality Control,* United Nations, New York, 1973.

Wasson, Chester R.: *Product Management,* Challenge Books, St. Charles, Ill., 1971, 252 pages.

Wymore, A. Wayne: *Systems Engineering Methodology for Interdisciplinary Teams,* Wiley-Interscience, New York, 1976, 423 pp.

IV Development, Engineering, and Design of Minimum-Hazard Products: A—Mechanics, Materials, etc.

Aeronautical Systems Division: *Checklist of General Design,* Department of the Air Force, Wright-Patterson Air Force Base, Ohio, 1975.

———— *General Index and Reference,* Department of the Air Force, Wright-Patterson Air Force Base, Ohio, 1975.

———— *Systems Safety Design Handbook 1–6,* Department of the Air Force, Wright-Patterson Air Force Base, Ohio, 1975.

Amstadter, Bertram L.: *Reliability Mathematics,* McGraw-Hill, New York, 1970, 320 pages.

Au, Tung, Richard M. Shane, and **Lester A. Hoel:** *Fundamentals of Systems Engineering,* Addison-Wesley, Reading, Mass., 1972, 375 pages.

Beranek, Leo L.: *Noise and Vibration Control,* McGraw-Hill, New York, 1971, 864 pages.

Callender, John Hancock (ed.): *Time-Saver Standards for Architectural Design Data,* McGraw-Hill, New York, 1974, 1024 pages.

Clauss, Francis J.: *Engineer's Guide to High-Temperature Materials,* Addison-Wesley, Reading, Mass., 1969, 401 pages.

Crandall, Keith C., and **Robert W. Seabloom:** *Engineering Fundamentals in Measurement, Probability, Statistics and Dimensions,* McGraw-Hill, New York, 1970, 254 pages.

Davis, Charles A.: *Industrial Electronics,* Charles E. Merrill, Columbus, Ohio, 1973, 458 pages.

Denn, Morton M.: *Optimization by Variational Methods,* McGraw-Hill, New York, 1969, 300 pages.

Doughtie, Venton L., and **Alex Vallence:** *Design of Machine Members,* 4th ed., McGraw-Hill, New York, 1964, 564 pages.

Foster, Lowell W.: *Geometric Dimensioning and Tolerancing: Geometric Characteristics and Symbols,* Addison-Wesley, Reading, Mass., 1972, 24 pages.

Fox, Ricard L.: *Optimization Methods for Engineering Design,* Addison-Wesley, Reading, Mass., 1971, 270 pages.

Hall, Arthur D.: *A Methodology for Systems Engineering,* Van Nostrand, Princeton, N.J., 1962, 478 pages.

Ham, C. W., E. J. Crane, and **W. L. Rogers:** *Mechanics of Machinery,* McGraw-Hill, New York, 1958, 509 pages.

Hammer, Willie: *Handbook of System and Product Liability,* Prentice-Hall, Englewood Cliffs, N.J., 1972, 351 pages.

Improvement of Reliability in Engineering, Mechanical Engineering Publications, Suite 1210, 200 West 57th Street, New York, 1974, 130 pages.

Jones, J. Christopher: *Design Methods,* Wiley Interscience, New York, 1970, 407 pages.

Jones, Robert M.: *Mechanics of Composite Materials,* McGraw-Hill, New York, 1975, 350 pages.

Juvinall, Robert C.: *Engineering Considerations of Stress, Strain and Strength,* McGraw-Hill, New York, 1967, 464 pages.

Kapur, K. C., and **L. R. Lamberson:** *Reliability in Engineering Design,* Wiley, New York, 1977, 586 pages.

Kivenson, Gilbert: *Durability and Reliability in Engineering Design,* Hayden, New York, 1971, 186 pages.

Levy, Sidney, and **J. Harry DuBois:** *Plastics Product Design Engineering Handbook,* Van Nostrand Reinhold, New York, 1977, 332 pages.

McKinnon, Gordon P., and **Keith Tower** (eds.): *Fire Protection Handbook,* National Fire Protection Association, Boston, Mass., 1976, approx. 1000 pages.

Railroad Research Information Service: *Special Bibliography: Safety-Related Technology,* Highway Research Board, Washington, D.C., 1973.

Roe, L.: *Practices and Procedures of Industrial Electrical Design,* McGraw-Hill, New York, 1972, 320 pages.

Rogers, David F., and **J. Alan Adams:** *Mathematical Elements for Computer Graphics,* McGraw-Hill, New York, 1976, 256 pages.

Sandor, Bela I.: *Fundamentals of Cyclic Stress and Strain,* University of Wisconsin, Madison, 1972, 167 pages.

Scaling for Performance Prediction in Rotodynamic Machines, Mechanical Engineering Publications, Suite 1210, 200 West 57th Street, New York, 1977, 200 pages.

Swain, A. D.: *Safety as a Design Feature in Systems,* Sandia Laboratories, Albuquerque, New Mexico, 1965.

Tests of Glass Plano Safety Spectacles, National Institute of Occupational Safety and Health, Cincinnati, Ohio, 1977, 19 pages.

Thomann, Robert V.: *Systems Analysis and Water Quality Control,* McGraw-Hill, New York, 1972, 286 pages.

United States Department of Defense: *Quality and Reliability Handbook,* Office of the Assistant Secretary of Defense, Installations and Logistics, Washington, D.C., 1975.

Vibrations in Rotating Machinery, Mechanical Engineering Publications, Suite 1210, 200 West 57th Street, New York, 1977, 320 pages.

Waite, Harold H. (ed.): *Pressure Vessels and Piping: Design and Analysis,* American Society of Mechanical Engineers, New York, 1976, 601 pages.

The Wear of Non-Metallic Materials, Mechanical Engineering Publications, Suite 1210, 200 West 57th Street, New York, 1977.

Winter, George, L. C. Urquhart, C. E. O'Rourke and **Arthur H. Nilson:** *Design of Concrete Structures,* 8th ed., McGraw-Hill, New York, 1972, 640 pages.

Woodson, Thomas T.: *Introduction to Engineering Design,* McGraw-Hill, New York, 1966, 434 pages.

IV Design of Minimum-Hazard Products: B—Human Factors

Air Force Systems Command: *The Personnel Subsystems Design Handbook,* 1-3, Wright-Patterson AFB, OH 45433. (Updated continuously.)

Army Missile Command: *Human Engineering Design Data Digest,* Redstone Arsenal, AL 35809. (Updated continuously.)

Astrand, Per-Olof: *Textbook of Work Physiology,* McGraw-Hill, New York, 1977, 704 pages.

Barnes, Ralph M.: *Motion and Time Study,* Wiley, New York, 1963, 739 pages.

Bennett, Edward, James Degan, and **Joseph Spiegel** (eds.): *Human Factors in Technology,* McGraw-Hill, New York, 1963, 685 pages.

Blosser, William B.: *A Systems Approach to Biomedicine,* McGraw-Hill, New York, 1969, 544 pages.

Chapanis, Alphonse: *Ethnic Variables in Human Factors Engineering,* Johns Hopkins, Baltimore, 1975, 290 pages.

——— *Research Techniques in Human Engineering,* Johns Hopkins, Baltimore, 1959, 316 pages.

——— **Wendell R. Garner,** and **Clifford T. Morgan:** *Applied Experimental Psychology,* Wiley, New York, 1949, 434 pages.

Damon, Albert, Howard W. Stoudt, and **Ross A. McFarland:** *The Human Body in Equipment Design,* Harvard University, Cambridge, Mass., 1966, 360 pages.

Detail Design, Mechanical Engineering Publications, Suite 1210, 200 West 57th Street, New York, 1976, 140 pages.

Harkness, Sarah P., and **James N. Groom, Jr.:** *Building without Barriers for the Disabled,* Watson-Guptill, New York, 1976, 79 pages.

Human Engineering Guide to Equipment Design, Superintendent of Documents, Government Printing Office, Washington, D.C. 20402

Jensen, Clayne R., and **Gordon W. Schultz:** *Applied Kinesiology,* McGraw-Hill, New York, 1977, 368 pages.

Lenihan, John: *Human Engineering,* George Braziller, New York, 1974, 207 pages.

Maule, H. G., and **J. S. Weiner:** *Human Factors in Work, Design and Production,* Halsted Press, New York, 1977, 138 pages.

McCormick, Ernest J.: *Human Factors in Engineering and Design,* McGraw-Hill, New York, 1976, 504 pages.

Meister, David, and **Gerald F. Rabideau:** *Human Factors Evaluation in System Development,* Wiley, New York, 1965, 307 pages.

Morgan, Clifford T., Jesse S. Cook, III, Alphonse Chapanis, and **Max W. Lund** (eds.): *Human Engineering Guide to Equipment Design,* McGraw-Hill, New York, 1963, 615 pages.

Murrell, K. F. H.: *Human Performance in Industry,* Reinhold, New York, 1965.

Nertney, R. J.: *Human Factors in Design,* ERDA, Division of Operational Safety, Washington, D.C., 1976, 140 pages.

Proceedings of the Interprofessional Council on Environmental Design Conference on Application of Behavioral Sciences to Environmental Design, American Society of Civil Engineers, New York, 1970, 124 pages.

Proceedings of the Symposium on Human Performance Quantification in Systems Effectiveness, Naval Material Command and the National Academy of Engineering, Washington, D.C., 1967.

Smith, R. L., R. A. Westland, and **R. E. Blanchard:** *Technique for Establishing Personnel Performance Standards (TEPPS):* Technical Manual, Vol. 1, Man-Machine Systems Research Branch, Bureau of Naval Personnel, Washington, D.C., 1969.

Tobin, Charles E.: *Basic Human Anatomy,* McGraw-Hill, New York, 1973, 352 pages.

Vander, Arthur J., James H. Sherman, and **Dorothy Luciano:** *Human Physiology,* University of Michigan, Ann Arbor, 1975, 624 pages.

Webb, Paul (ed.): *Bioastronautics Data Book,* National Aeronautics and Space Administration, Washington, D.C., 1964, 400 pages.

Woodson, Wesley E., and **Donald W. Conover:** *Human Engineering Guide for Equipment Designers,* University of California, Berkeley, 1964, 473 pages.

V Production of Minimum-Hazard Products

Air Force Systems Command: *AFSC Zero Defects Program* (Supervisor's Handbook), AFSCP 11-2, U. S. Air Force, 1965, unpaginated.

Avitzur, Betzalel: *Metal Forming: Processes and Analysis,* McGraw-Hill, New York, 1968, 544 pages.

Becker, Peter W., and **Jensen Finn:** *Design of Systems and Circuits for Maximum Reliability of Maximum Production Yield:* McGraw-Hill, New York, 1977, 288 pages.

Clauser, H. R. (editor-in-chief): *The Encyclopedia of Engineering Materials and Process,* Reinhold, New York, 1963, 787 pages.

Considine, Douglas M. (ed.): *Process Instruments and Controls Handbook,* McGraw-Hill, New York, 1974, 1334 pages.

Cook, Nathan H.: *Manufacturing Analysis,* Addison-Wesley, Reading, Mass., 1966, 229 pages.

Coughanowr, Donald R., and **Lowell B. Koppell:** *Process Systems Analysis and Control,* McGraw-Hill, New York, 1965, 491 pages.

Davenport, Wilbur B., Jr.: *Probability and Random Processes,* McGraw-Hill, New York, 1970, 608 pages.

Davis, Harmer E., George Earl Troxell, and **Clement T. Wiskocil:** *The Testing and Inspection of Engineering Materials,* McGraw-Hill, New York, 1964, 475 pages.

Dempster, A. P.: *Elements of Continuous Multivariate Analysis,* Addison-Wesley, Reading, Mass., 1969, 388 pages.

Dodge, H. F., and **H. G. Romig:** *Sampling Inspection Tables—Single and Double Sampling,* Wiley, New York, 1959, unpaginated.

Drake, Alvin W.: *Fundamentals of Applied Probability Theory,* McGraw-Hill, New York, 1967, 256 pages.

Drury, D. G., and **J. G. Fox:** *Human Reliability in Quality Control,* Halsted Press, New York, 1975, 315 pages.

Duncan, A. J.: *Quality Control and Industrial Statistics,* Richard D. Irwin, 1974.

Feigenbaum, A. V.: *Total Quality Control: Engineering and Management,* McGraw-Hill, New York, 1961, 630 pages.

Ford, R. N.: *Motivation Through the Work Itself,* American Management Associations, New York, 1969.

Grant, Eugene L., and **Richard S. Leavenworth:** *Statistical Quality Control,* McGraw-Hill, New York 1972, 650 pages.

Guenther, William C.: *Concepts of Statistical Inference,* McGraw-Hill, New York, 1973, 432 pages.

Harris, D. H., and **F. B. Chaney:** *Human Factors in Quality Assurance,* Wiley, New York, 1969.

Herrick, Clyde N.: *Instruments and Measurements for Electronics,* McGraw-Hill, New York, 1972, 558 pages.

Hoelscher, Randolph P., Clifford H. Springer, and **Richard F. Pohle:** *Industrial Production Illustration,* McGraw-Hill, New York, 1946, 243 pages.

Japan's Quality Control Circle, Asian Productivity Organization, Tokyo, Japan, 1973.

Johnson, Curtis D.: *Process Control Instrumentation Technology,* Wiley, New York, 1977, 428 pages.

Johnson, Richard, A., William T. Newell, and **Roger C. Vergin:** *Production and Operations Management,* Houghton Mifflin, Boston, 1974, 500 pages.

Joint Automatic Control Conference: *Proceedings: Productivity,* The American Society of Mechanical Engineers, New York, 1976, 794 pages.

Juran, Joseph F., Frank M. Gryna, and **Richard Bingham, Jr.:** *Quality Control Handbook,* McGraw-Hill, New York, 1974, 1600 pages.

Knowler, Lloyd A., John M. Howell, Ben Gold, Edward P. Coleman, Obert B. Moan, and **William C. Knowler:** *Quality Control by Statistical Methods,* McGraw-Hill, New York, 1969, 128 pages.

Leslie, W.: *Numerical Control Users' Handbook,* McGraw-Hill, New York, 1970, 448 pages.

Lipson, Charles, and **Narendra J. Sheth:** *Statistical Design and Analysis of Engineering Experiments,* McGraw-Hill, New York, 1973, 522 pages.

McCormack, R. L.: *Inspector Accuracy: A Study of the Literature,* Sandia Laboratories, Albuquerque, New Mexico, 1961.

Mosteller, Frederick, and **John W. Turkey:** *Data Analysis and Regression: A Second Course in Statistics,* Addison-Wesley, Reading, Mass., 1977.

Nondestructive Testing, National Aeronautics and Space Administration, Washington, D.C., 1973, 282 pages.

O'Higgins, Patrick: *Basic Instrumentation–Industrial Measurement,* McGraw-Hill, New York, 1966, 512 pages.

Olsen, Eugene E.: *Modern Optical Methods of Analysis,* McGraw-Hill, New York, 1975, 544 pages.

Perone, Sam P., and **David O. Jones:** *Digital Computers in Scientific Instrumentation,* McGraw-Hill, New York, 1973, 448 pages.

Pfluger, Allan R., and **Richard E. Lewis:** *Weld Imperfections,* Addison-Wesley, Reading, Mass., 1968, 652 pages.

Pressman, Roger S., and **John E. Williams:** *Numerical Control and Computer-Aided Manufacturing,* Wiley, New York, 1977, 310 pages.

Riaz, M.: *Electrical Engineering Laboratory Manual:* McGraw-Hill, New York, 1966, 300 pages.

Roberts, Arthur D.: *Manufacturing Processes Fundamentals,* McGraw-Hill, New York, 1977, 480 pages.

Shooman, Martin L.: *Probabilistic Reliability: An Engineering Approach,* McGraw-Hill, New York, 1968, 448 pages.

Statistical Quality Control Handbook, Western Electric, Easton, Pennsylvania, 1964.

Thermal Analysis Techniques—Proceedings of a Roundtable, National Institute for Occupational Safety and Health, Cincinnati, Ohio, 1977, 255 pages.

Transactions of the First Pan American Congress on Quality Control and Statistics in Industry, Mexico City, 1965.

United States Department of Defense: *Military Standard, Sampling Procedures and Tables for Inspection by Attributes,* U.S. Government Printing Office, Washington, D.C., 1963.

——— *Military Standard, Sampling Procedures and Tables for Inspection by Variables for Percent Defective,* U.S. Government Printing Office, Washington, D.C., 1963.

Weber, Leonard J., and **Donald L. McLean:** *Electrical Measurement Systems for Biological and Physical Scientists,* Addison-Wesley, Reading, Mass., 1975, 416 pages.

Young, Hugh D.: *Statistical Treatment of Experimental Data,* McGraw-Hill, New York, 1962, 100 pages.

VI Marketing, Distribution, and Servicing

Aeronautical Systems Division: *Maintainability,* Department of the Air Force, Wright-Patterson Air Force Base, Ohio, 1975 (updated continuously.)

Blanchard, Benjamin S., and **E. Edward Lowry:** *Maintainability,* McGraw-Hill, New York, 1969, 352 pages.

Colburn, Robert E.: *Fire,* McGraw-Hill, New York, 1975, 342 pages.

Deutschman, Aaron D., Walter J. Michels, and **Charles E. Wilson:** *Machine Design,* Macmillan, New York, 1975, 932 pages.

Haddon, William, Jr., Edward A. Suchman, and **David Klein:** *Accident Research,* Harper & Row, New York, 1964, 752 pages.

Jardine, A. K. S.: *Maintainance, Replacement and Reliability,* Wiley, New York, 1973, 199 pages.

Krar, Stephen F., J. W. Oswald, and **J. E. St. Amand:** *Technology of Machine Tools,* McGraw-Hill, New York, 1977, 516 pages.

Lion, Kurt S.: *Elements of Electrical and Electronic Instrumentation,* McGraw-Hill, New York, 1975, 445 pages.

Lloyd, D. K., and **M. Lipow:** *Reliability: Management, Methods, and Mathematics,* Prentice-Hall, Englewood Cliffs, N.J., 1962.

Manual of Aircraft Accident Investigation, International Civil Aviation Organization, United Nations, New York, 1959, 256 pages.

Morbidity Patterns among Heavy Equipment Operators Exposed to Whole-Body Vibration—1975, National Institute of Occupationsl Safety and Health, Cincinnati, Ohio, 1977, 49 pages.

Philoppakis, Andreas S., and **Leonard J. Kazmier:** *Information Systems through Cobol,* McGraw-Hill, New York, 1974, 640 pages.

Smith, Charles O.: *Introduction to Reliability in Design,* McGraw-Hill, New York, 1976, 288 pages.

Smith, David J., and **Alex H. Babb:** *Maintainability Engineering,* Halsted Press, New York, 1973, 107 pages.

Thorndike, R. L.: *The Human Factor in Accidents,* U.S. Public Health Service, Division of Accident Prevention, Washington, D.C., 1965.

Windolz, Martha (ed.): *The Merck Index,* Merck and Co., Inc., Rahway, N.J., 1976, 1819 pages.

Working with Industrial Solvents, National Institute of Occupational Safety and Health, Cincinnati, Ohio, 1977, 6 pages.

VII Special Considerations for Chemical Products

Christensen, Herbert E., and **Edward J. Fairchild** (eds.): *Registry of Toxic Effects of Chemical Substances,* U.S. Department of Health, Education, and Welfare, Rockville, Maryland, 1976, 1245 pages.

Ewing, Galen W.: *Instrumental Methods of Chemical Analysis,* McGraw-Hill, New York, 1975, 672 pages.

Fleming, David G., and **Barry N. Feinberg:** *Handbook of Engineering in Medicine and Biology,* CRC Press, Cleveland, Ohio, 1976, 421 pages.

Irritant Effects of Industrial Chemicals: Formaldehyde, National Institute of Occupational Safety and Health, Cincinnati, Ohio, 1977, 124 pages.

LaFleur, Philip D.: *Accuracy in Trace Analysis: Sampling, Sample Handling, Analysis,* U. S. Department of Commerce, Washington, D.C., 1976, 1304 pages. Volumes I and II combined.

Laitinen, Herbert A., and **Walter E. Harris:** *Chemical Analysis,* McGraw-Hill, New York, 1975, 640 pages.

National Conference on Control of Hazardous Materials Spills: *Control of Hazardous Material Spills,* American Institute of Chemical Engineers, New York, 1974, 374 pages.

Proceedings of NIOSH Styrene-Butadiene Briefing, National Institute for Occupational Safety and Health, Cincinnati, Ohio, 1977, 176 pages.

Ruch, Walter E., and **Bruce J. Held:** *Respiratory Protection,* Ann Arbor Science Publishers, Ann Arbor, Michigan, 1975, 102 pages.

Sax, N. Irving: *Dangerous Properties of Industrial Materials,* Van Nostrand Reinhold, New York, 1968, 1258 pages.

Schieler, Leroy, and **Denis Pauze:** *Hazardous Materials,* Van Nostrand Reinhold, New York, 1976, 249 pages.

Selikoff, Irving J., and **E. Cuyler Hammond:** *Toxicity of Vinyl Chloride-Polyvinyl Chloride,* New York Academy of Sciences, New York, 1975, 337 pages.

Shift Work and Health, National Institute of Occupational Safety and Health, Cincinnati, Ohio, 1977, 283 pages.

VIII If All Else Fails—Going to Court

Cotchett, Joseph W., and **Robert E. Cartwright:** *California Products Liability Actions,* Bender, Chicago, 1970.

Godson, John: *The Rise and Fall of the DC-10,* David McKay, 1975, New York, 351 pages.

Goodman, Richard M., and **Paul D. Rheingold:** *Lawyers Drug Handbook,* Institute of Continuing Legal Education, Ann Arbor, Mich., 1967.

O'Brien, James L.: *Construction Delay,* Cahners Books, Boston, Mass., 1976, 367 pages.

Peters, George A.: *Product Liability and Safety,* Coiner Publications, Ltd., Washington, D.C., 1971, 334 pages.

Prosser, William E.: *Prosser on Torts,* West Publishing Co., Minneapolis, 1971.

Rheingold, Paul D., and **Sheila L. Birnbaum:** *Product Liability,* Practising Law Institute, New York, 1975, 1113 pages.

Robb, Dean A., Harry M. Philo, and **Richard M. Goodman:** *Lawyers Desk Reference,* Lawyers Cooperative Publishing Company, Rochester, N.Y., 1968, 1078 pages.

Roody, Peter, Robert E. Forman, and **Howard B. Schweitzer:** *Medical Abbreviations and Acronyms,* McGraw-Hill, New York, 1977, 240 pages.

Schwartz, William: *Products Liability Primer,* W. H. Anderson, Cincinnati, Ohio, 1970.

Thomas, William A.: *Scientists in the Legal System,* Ann Arbor Science, Ann Arbor, Mich., 1974, 141 pages.

IX Insurance: Rates, Claims, and New Directions

Heppell, E. A.: *Products Liability Insurance,* Pitman, Belmont, CA. 1967.

Interagency Task Force on Product Liability: *Insurance Report,* NTIS, 1977 (7 volumes).

National Commission on Fire Prevention and Control: *America Burning,* U. S. Government Printing Office, Washington, D.C., 1973, 177 pages.

Wincor, Richard: *Contracts in Plain English,* McGraw-Hill, New York, 1976, 143 pages.

APPENDIX J
USEFUL TERMS

This section was compiled mainly from definition lists incorporated in broadly used standards (especially military standards and specifications, and certain ASTM and ANSI standards), insurance rating manuals and policies, and human-factors guides. Jargon and specialized definitions relevant to specific fields of engineering were omitted, except where they directly involve safety-related or liability-related issues. Attention was paid to including legal terminology, human-factors definitions, and statistical terms bearing on product safety and liability.matters, for the authors feel the typical user of this book will be a design specialist or manager to whom those particular terms will be unfamiliar, yet must convey precise meanings where safety is concerned. Some terms are defined at length in the text and are not listed here. They are, however, referenced in the index.

A

Abduction. Movement of a limb away from the axis of the body. (See also *Adduction*.)

Absolute Visual Threshold. See *Threshold, Absolute Visual*

Acceleration. The time rate of change of velocity (speed or direction).

Accessibility. A measure of the ease of admission to various areas of a product.

Accessory. An item used in conjunction with or to supplement an assembly, contributing to its effectiveness without extending or varying basic function.

Accident. An event injurious to humans or property which springs from unknown or unexpected causes.

Accommodation, Sensory. The adjustment of a sense organ to receive an impression distinctly (adjustment of the eye to a given light level, for example).

Acoustic Reference Level. The common reference level for sound measurements; a sound pressure level of 0.0002 microbar, expressed as zero decibels.

Acoustic Tolerance. Ability to endure extreme auditory stimulation, defined by the maximum sound pressure level which can be experienced without pain. A sound of 120 decibels produces discomfort, and 140 decibels causes pain.

Adaptation, Sensory. Maintenance of sensory effectiveness under changing stimulation (positive adaptation) or reduction of sensory responsiveness with continued stimulation (negative adaptation).

Adduction. Movement of a limb toward the axis of the body. (See also *Abduction*.)

Advisory Light. A signal assembly to indicate safe or normal configuration, condition of performance, operation of essential equipment, or to attract attention and impart information for routine action purposes.

Aeroelasticity. Deformity of an airframe or vehicle surface brought on during flight by interaction between aerodynamic forces, elastic materials, and inertia. The quality of the material withstanding the deformity.

Afterimage. A visual impression which continues or recurs periodically for a short time after stimulation of the eye.

Allergy. An adverse reaction to a substance that is considered harmless to the majority of the population. An individual is normally sensitized by the first exposure to a substance, and reacts adversely to subsequent exposures.

Alternate System. A standby, redundant, or partially redundant system activated at the option of the operator in case a primary system fails.

Ames Test. See *Salmonella Test*.

Anoxia. Literally, the absence of oxygen in the blood, cells, or tissues.

Anthropometric Tables. Tables of body dimensions for use by designers in determining space and sizing requirements of equipment.

Anthropometry. Science of measuring the human body, its parts, and functional capacities. (See also *Photogrammetry*.)

Aptitude Relationship Principle. The principle of job design that all tasks assigned to one job should require the same or related aptitudes.

Articulation Index (AI). A predictive measure of the intelligibility of speech in the presence of background noise, ranging from 0.0 (voice communication nearly impossible) to 1.0 (communication excellent). The articulation index is generally based on the average peak-speech-to-root-mean-square-noise ratio obtained in selected frequency bands from 200 to 6000 hertz (i.e., peak amplitude of speech in relation to the root-mean-square amplitude of the background noise). If the speech peaks are at least 30 decibels (dB) above the ambient noise, the articulation index will be 1.0. If the difference is 0 dB the articulation index will be 0.0.

Assembly. A number of parts or subassemblies joined to perform a specific function and capable of disassembly. An assembly in one instance may be a subassembly in another where it forms a portion of the whole.

Associate Contractor. A prime contractor for the development or production of subsystems, equipment, or components meeting specifications furnished or approved by the procuring activity. An associate contractor can be one member of a group of contractors developing and producing a complete system.

Attitude, Psychological. An enduring learned predisposition to behave in a consistent way toward a given class of objects or activities, not necessarily as they are but as they are conceived to be.

Audit, Quality. See *Quality Audit*.

Auditory Threshold. See *Threshold, Absolute Auditory*.

Autokinesis. A sensation of movement initiated by internal stimuli, such as a shift in perception as a result of subjective factors (the apparent motion of a stationary point of light in a dark field, for example).

Automatic Testing Equipment. Devices that check two or more signals in sequence without intervention of a technician. The equipment may be programmed to stop when out-of-tolerance signal is detected.

Automatized Behavior. Stimulus-response associations which have become automatic, chiefly as a result of repetitive practice.

Availability. A measure of the degree to which a product is operable at any point in time.

"Average Man" Concept. A simplified method of describing the combined characteristics of a varied population, based upon "average" measurements. In many cases, design requirements are specified to include 90 percent of the population, the range between the 5th to 95th percentile for each body dimension considered.

B

Bioacoustics. The science of dealing with the interaction of sound fields or mechanical vibration with living organisms.

Bioassay. The application of chemical or biological agent(s) in controlled doses to test animals, in an attempt to develop data applicable to humans or other animals.

Bioconcentration. That property of certain chemicals to increase their concentration in organisms highest in the natural food chain.

Biomechanics. The study of mechanical forces on living bodies, and the resulting effects produced in them.

Biota. Living things.

Bit (Binary Digit). A single element of data; in information theory, that amount which, when put into a given assemblage consisting of a known number of alternative outcomes for a certain event, reduces the alternatives by one-half (bit = $\log_2 k$, where k is the number of alternatives).

Black Box. A term used loosely to refer to any component, usually electronic, that can be readily inserted into or removed from a larger system without knowledge of its internal structure.

Breadboard Model. An uncased assembly of a piece of equipment with the parts laid out on a flat surface and connected so as to permit checking its operation.

Brightness. The attribute of visual sensation determined by intensity of light reaching the eye, or the luminous intensity of any surface in a given direction per unit of projected area of the surface viewed from that direction.

Brightness Contrast. See *Contrast (Brightness)*.

Burn-In. The operation of a product to stabilize its characteristics through the "infant mortality" period.

C

California Bearing Ratio (CBR). This is a measure of the bearing capacity of soil, expressed in terms of a percentage of the bearing capacity of a standard crushed limestone.

Candle. A unit of luminous intensity of a source of light.

Capability. A measure of the ability of a product to perform satisfactorily.

Category I Tests. (Military) evaluation and necessary testing of individual components and subsystems. These tests are conducted primarily by the contractor with military participation, evaluation, and management control. Category I testing has as its objective the verification of engineering specifications of the individual hardware items.

Category II Tests. (Military) testing and evaluation of the integrated components and subsystems making up a complete system in as near an operational configuration as possible to determine that the system meets specifications.

Category III Tests. (Military) tests performed by the operating commands in operational environments to provide initial verification that the equipment will be suitable to meet requirements.

Caution Light. A signal assembly which alerts the operator to an impending dangerous condition requiring attention but not necessarily immediate action.

Center Frequency Octave Bands. Those octave bands specified by American National Standard S1.6-1960, *Preferred Frequencies for Acoustical Measurements*.

Channel Capacity. In information theory, the maximum transmission of information that a channel can provide; measured in "bits" by $\log_2 c$, where c is the number of classes of input messages that can be discriminated by the channel. (See also *Load, Sensory*.)

Checklist (Design). A list of minimum requirements based on experience and research. It may apply to a general class of problems or to a problem specific to a given product.

Circuit Analysis. Logical examination of circuit diagrams to locate a malfunctioning part or subassembly.

Circumduction. Continuous circular movement of a limb.

Climatization. Designing to provide for satisfactory functioning within a given climate.

Closed Loop. A family of automatic control units linked together with a process to form an endless chain. The effects of control action are constantly measured so that if the controlled quantity departs from the norm, the control units act to bring it back. (See *Feedback*.)

Coding. In human engineering, the design of controls and displays to facilitate their differentiation, identification, and efficient operation. (See also *Control Coding*.)

Colorimetry. Determining, measuring, or specifying color in numerical or other definite symbolic terms.

Common Tools. Items of tools and tool equipment which are found in common usage or which are applicable to a variety of operations or to a single operation on a variety of material. Screwdrivers, hammers, drill presses, and lathes are examples of common tools.

Compatibility. Capability of two or more components or materials to exist or function in the same system or environment without mutual interference. (See also *Interchangeability*.)

Component. An article manufactured for use in assemblies, subassemblies, or end products when such an article is listed in the blueprint, drawing, technical order, or specification of the respective product.

Computer, Analog. A computer in which numbers are converted into physically measurable quantities, such as continuously variable voltages or shaft rotations; these variables are then made to obey mathematical relations analogous to those of the problem to be solved.

Computer, Digital. A computer in which quantities are expressed in the form of digits which can assume only discrete values. Results are obtained by pure arithmetical operations.

Computer Programming. The process of expressing a problem in terms of a fixed set of operations so that it can be operated on by a computer.

Concept. A mental image or idea of the nature of something, or how a thing should be done.

Continuous Redundancy. Parallel and similar units, or circuits which are in continuous operation to ensure that failure of the primary item will permit continuous operation of the system at an adequate level of performance.

Continuous Tasks. See *Task*.

Contractor. An organization engaged to provide services or products within agreed limits.

Contrast. The difference in brightness between two portions of the visual field, usually expressed as the background luminance (B_1) minus the figure luminance (B_2), divided by the background luminance (B_1). Expressed in percent:

$$C = \frac{B_1 - B_2}{B_1} \times 100$$

Control. A lever, switch, pushbutton, or other device by means of which direction, or regulation, is exercised over something.

Control Coding. Designing controls for optimum tactile, kinesthetic, or visual identification, shape, size, color, or mode of operation.

Control-Display Compatibility. A harmonious relationship between a displayed condition and the corresponding control action; provides for compatibility between stimulus and response in a perceptual-motor task.

Control-Display Lag. Time between control movement and the resulting display of that movement.

Control Ratio. The relationship between the amount of movement of a control and the amount of movement of what is controlling.

Convergence. The coordinated movement of the eyes inward as a near object is viewed, to allow separate images to be formed on corresponding regions of the two retinas.

Correlation. The degree to which two or more variables are so related that change in one is accompanied by a corresponding change in the other; the degree of concomitance is measured by the correlation coefficient. (See also *Regression Analysis*.)

Correlation Coefficient. A number that indicates the strength and direction of the relationship between two or more variables. Perfect correspondence is expressed as +1.0; perfect inverse correspondence is −1.0; and complete independence of the variables is expressed as 0.0.

Correlation In Design. Correlation is the maintenance of the integrity of design parameters of interrelated system elements according to valid definition progresses. Typical examples are the integrity of reliability values between configuration items and subordinate system elements, maintenance of a valid weight budget, or the assignment of accuracy values to test equipment that correspond to the tolerances to which mission equipment must be calibrated.

Crashworthiness. The capacity of a vehicle to act as a protective container and energy absorber during potentially survivable impact conditions.

Creep. The property of a material which allows it to be permanently deformed when subjected to a stress.

Criterion. Any basis for judging the appropriateness of a method, measuring device, formula, and so forth.

Critical Incident. A man-machine event or occurrence which results in an accident or near-accident.

Criticality. The weight (usually numerical) assigned to subsystems or components based on the relative effects of malfunctions on system performance.

D

Dark Adaptation. The adjustment of the eye to low-intensity light.

Debugging. A process of detecting and fixing inadequacies, preferably prior to commercial sale.

Decibel (dB). One-tenth of a bel; a logarithmic ratio. Sound intensity is usually expressed in terms of the ratio between a given sound pressure level and a standard reference level of 0.0002 dyne/sq cm (the average threshold intensity for a tone of 1000 Hz). The number of bels is the $\log_{10}$ of the ratio.

Decision Time. The time required for an operator to reach a decision when presented with alternative choices.

Dependability. A measure of operating condition at one or more points in time, stated as the probability that a product will enter or occupy any of its required operational modes during a specified time.

Depth Perception. Optical awareness of the distance of objects from the observer, or of the distance from front to back of an object.

Design Adequacy. The probability that a product will successfully accomplish its task, provided it is operating within design specifications.

Design Criteria. The summation of all available knowledge about a product which defines to the maximum extent its nature, purpose, and limits so that it may be developed, manufactured, and marketed satisfactorily.

Design Load. See *Load, Ultimate*.

Detail Part. See *Part*.

Development Testing and Evaluation. Testing used to measure progress, verify accomplishment, and to determine if the product under development is technically sound, reliable, and safe.

Dichotic. Affecting the two ears differently as by conveying one sound to one ear simultaneously with a different sound to the other ear, or the presentation of the same signal alternately to each ear.

Difference Threshold. See *Threshold, Difference*.

Diotic. Pertaining to a stimulus affecting both ears alike.

Discrimination. The detection of differences among environmental stimuli.

Disorientation. Lack of normal orientation of one's usual ability to relate to space, time, and surrounding objects.

Display. A method of providing information, in symbolic form, of some condition or event in the real world; a device designed to present such information to the senses (e.g., an instrument panel).

Display Damping. Modifying display to minimize random fluctuations and facilitate accurate interpretation.

Dynamic Loading. Any loading during which the parts of a body or a system could not be considered in equilibrium.

Dynamic Stability. See *Stability, Dynamic*.

E

Electromagnetic Compatibility. See *Compatibility*.

Electronic Interference. Any electrical or electromagnetic disturbance that causes undesirable response in electronic equipment. The disturbance can arise inside or external to the equipment.

End Product. A finished product, complete within itself, whether a simple piece or made up of many pieces, ready for its intended use.

Engineering Psychology. The study of human behavior in using tools and machines, and of machine design in relation to human behavioral capacities, abilities, and motivation. (See also *Human Engineering*.)

Entropy. In information theory, an index of the number of possible outcomes an event can have; a measure of the amount of randomness in the state of a system; the amount of uncertainty in the categorization of items in a group, measured by the number of operations (statements, decisions, tests, manipulations, etc.) needed to select and categorize each one.

Environment. The sum of all influences (including physical location and operating characteristics of surrounding equipment and occupants, temperature, humidity, and contaminants of surrounding air, operational procedures, acceleration, shock, vibration, and radiation).

Equipment Relationship Principle. The principle of job design that all tasks assigned to one job should relate to the same equipment or subsystem.

Error-Probable Design. A design incorporating characteristics which increase the chances of errors by a human being in the system, including factors which violate population stereotypes, demand performance in excess of the user's capabilities, cause fatigue, do not provide adequate facilities or information, make the job unnecessarily difficult or unpleasant, or do not provide adequate safety features.

Evaluation, Test. Review and analysis of quantitative data produced during testing. or from operation and commercial experience.

Experience Data. The total available technical, manufacturing, and user experience on a product, expressed in terms of design principles, or guidance.

F

Facilities (in contract usage). A physical plant such as real estate and improvements thereto including building and equipment which provides the means for assisting or making easier the performance of a system function. The facilities to which this standard apply are those in which personnel perform system, operational, or maintenance duties.

Factor of Reliability. See *Reliability, Manufacturing*.

Failsafe Design. Failsafe design is one in which a failure will not adversely affect the safe operation of the system, equipment, or facility.

Failure. The inability of a product or system to perform within previously specified limits.

Failure Analysis. The logical, systematic examination of product or system (or its plans) to identify and analyze the probability, causes, and consequences of potential and real failures.

Failure, Dependent. One which is caused by the failure of an associated product or subsystem.

Failure, Independent. One which occurs without being related to the failure of associated products of subsystems. Not dependent.

Failure-Modes-and-Effects Analysis. An attempt to logically deduce the consequences of a failure in a product or system, or the effects of multiple failures in combination, and the odds of such failures and effects happening.

Failure, Random. Any failure whose occurrence is unpredictable in an absolute sense in any one sample of a product, but which can be predicted only in a probabilistic or statistical sense to occur among the product's population.

Failure Rate. The number of failures of a product or system per unit measure of life (cycles, time, miles, events, etc., as applicable).

Fatigue. Diminished ability to do work, as a consequence of previous and recent work; impairment of function of sense organs, nerves, or muscles due to continued recent stimulation and activity. In materials, loss of strength due to cycle stresses.

Fault Tree Analysis. A graphic representation of failure modes and effects, with failures at the top.

Feedback. The return of a portion of the output of a device to the input; positive feedback adds to the input, negative feedback subtracts from the input.

Feedback System. A system in which the difference between actual performance and desired performance is used as a basis for modifying inputs to the system so as to achieve or maintain the desired output (see *closed loop*).

Field Tests. Tests conducted in the field under conditions approximating those to be encountered in normal use.

Figure(s) of Merit. A measure of effectiveness through which quantitative requirements can be related to product objectives in optimizing design.

Fixation, Visual. The directing and focusing of the eye so that the object of regard, or fixation point, lies along a line drawn from the fovea through the pupil.

Flexion. Bending, especially of a joint.

Flow Chart (Flow Diagram). A diagram depicting the sequence of operations in the performance of a complex task or series of tasks; includes such functions as operator performance, the flow of communications and material, and the use of equipment.

Footcandle (fc). A unit of illuminance, incident light, or illumination equal to one lumen per square foot. This is the illuminance provided by a light source of a standard candle at a distance of one foot.

Footlambert (fL). A unit of luminance (or brightness) equal to $1/\pi$ candela per square foot or one lumen per square foot from a diffuse source. Sometimes known as "equivalent" footcandle.

Fovea. A small depression in the central region of the retina of the eye, containing only cone receptors, on which an image is focused for most acute vision.

Frequency-of-Use Principle. The most frequently used displays or controls should be placed in preferred locations, as in the center of the panel, with less frequently used items placed in less preferred locations, as around the fringes (see also *Functional Principle; Importance Principle*).

Function. The purpose of a product.

Functional Principle. The grouping of displays or controls according to their function, so that those having the same function are grouped together.

G

Ganged Controls. Controls which are grouped or "stacked" on a single axis so as to reduce crowding on panels of limited dimensions. For example, two control knobs attached to concentric shafts, or a double-pole, double-throw switch.

H

Hazard. Any real or potential condition that can cause injury or death to personnel, or damage to or loss of equipment or property.

Hazard Level. A qualitative measure of hazards stated in relative terms. For purposes of illustration the following hazard levels are defined and established: Conditions such that personnel error, environment, design characteristics, procedural deficiencies, or subsystem or component failure or malfunction:

(*a*) Category I—Negligible
. . . . will not result in personnel injury or system damage.

(*b*) Category II—Marginal
. . . . can be counteracted or controlled without injury to personnel or major system damage.

(*c*) Category III—Critical
. . . . will cause personnel injury or major system damage, or will require immediate corrective action for personnel or system survival.

(*d*) Category IV—Catastrophic
. . . . will cause death or severe injury to personnel, or system loss.

Hertz. The international unit of frequency (1 Hz = 1 cycle per second).

Human Engineering. The application of knowledge of man's capabilities and limitations to the development of systems, equipment, and facilities to achieve optimum personnel safety, comfort, and effectiveness.

Human Factors. A body of facts about human characteristics. The term covers all biomedical and psychosocial considerations; it includes, but is not limited to, principles and applications in the areas of engineering, personnel selection, training, life support, job performance aids, and human performance evaluation.

Human Transfer Function. The mathematical description of a human operator's outputs (control movements) in a task as a function of his inputs (display indications); usually described in terms of a linear differential equation.

Hypoxia. Oxygen deficiency in the blood, cells, or tissues so as to cause psychological and physiological disturbances; may result from scarcity of oxygen in the air being breathed, or by the inability of body tissues to absorb oxygen.

I

Illuminance. The total luminous flux received on a unit area of a given real (or imaginary) surface, expressed in such units as the footcandle, lux, or phot. Illuminance is analogous to irradiance, but illuminance refers only to light and contains the efficiency weighting factor necessitated by the nonlinear wavelength-response of the human eye. (The only difference between illuminance and illumination is that the latter always refers to light incident upon a material surface; see also *Brightness; Luminance*.)

Importance Principle. The principle of arranging the most important displays and controls in the most accessible locations for ease of reading or manipulation (see also *Frequency of Use Principle, Functional Principle*).

Impulse. The product of a force's average value and the duration in which it acts, equal to the change in momentum produced by the force.

Indicator.   A device for displaying information pertaining to position, location, or condition.

Information.   In information theory, a purely quantitative property of an ensemble of items that enables categorization or classification of some or all of them. The amount of information is measured by the average number of operations (statements, decisions, tests, etc.) needed to effect categorization of the items. (See also *Bit; Entropy.*)

Information Theory.   The transmission of messages or signals, or the communication of information. It draws upon communications theory, linguistics, psychology, and sociology.

Inherent.   Achievable under ideal conditions, generally derived by analysis, and potentially present in the design.

Integrating Contractor.   The contractor assigned responsibility by the procuring activity for overall scheduling and system interface of associate contractor activities and equipment, and for the furnishing of specified support services which are common to two or more of the contractors.

Interchangeability.   A condition which exists when two or more products or components possess such functional and physical characteristics as to be equivalent in performance and durability, and are capable of being exchanged one for the other without alteration of the items themselves or of adjoining items, except for adjustment, and without selection for fit and performance (see also *Compatibility*).

Interface.   A juncture of nonmaterial things, as two or more signal levels, power levels, impedance or the like, where matching is required.

Interference.   Any electrical or electromagnetic disturbance, phenomenon, signal, or emission that may cause undesired response, malfunctioning, or degradation of electrical or electronic equipment.

Item, Interchangeable.   One, which (1) possesses such functional and physical characteristics as to be equivalent in performance, reliability, and maintainability, to another item of similar or identical purpose; and (2) is capable of being exchanged for the other item (a) without selection for fit or performance, and (b) without alteration of the items themselves or of adjoining items, except for adjustment.

Item, Replaceable.   One which is interchangeable with another item, but which differs physically from the original item in that the installation of the replaceable item requires operations such as drilling, reaming, cutting, filing, shimming, etc., in addition to the normal application and methods of attachment.

Item, Substitute.   One which possesses such functional and physical characteristics as to be capable of being exchanged for another only under specified conditions or for particular applications and without alteration of the items themselves or of adjoining items.

J

Jerk.   The unit rate of change of acceleration.

Job.   The requirements, responsibilities, and tasks assigned to a given position in a work structure.

Job Aid.   A device, book, or other object designed to assist a worker in performing the duties and tasks of his position with greater accuracy, speed, reliability, or safety; these include troubleshooting checklists and manuals.

Job Analysis.   An analysis based upon observation, interviews, and study, to determine and identify the tasks and functions involved, together with the skills, abilities, knowledge, and responsibilities required.

Job Performance Evaluation.   Measuring the performance of personnel in terms of accuracy, speed, conformance to proper work habits, safety, and use of equipment, by means of a series of actual job activities (or work samples) performed under standard conditions.

Job Segment.   Any arbitrarily defined portion of a job being analyzed.

Just-Noticeable Difference.   The smallest perceivable difference between two stimuli.

K

Key Dimension. The dimension or dimensions used to establish size intervals, such as of bolts, wrenches, and other products.

Kinesthesis. The sense that yields knowledge of the movements of the body or of its members; awareness of movement due to the mechanical stimulation of special receptors in the muscular tissue, tendons, and joints.

Knowledge Relationship Principle. All tasks assigned to one position should be dependent on similar or related background knowledge, skill, or training.

L

Lambert. A unit of luminance equal to that of a perfectly diffusing and reflecting surface emitting or reflecting light at the rate of one lumen per square centimeter (see also *Lumen; Luminance*).

Learning. Any change in behavior that occurs as a result of training, practice, or experience.

Life Cycle Costs. Costs of acquisition plus operation and logistic support for the specified operational lifetime.

Life Support. That area of human factors which applies scientific knowledge to products requiring special provisions for health promotion, safety, protection, or sustenance.

Limited Substitute. A limited substitute is a component that can replace or be replaced by another only under certain conditions or in some particular applications.

Limit Load. See *Load, Limit*.

Link Analysis. A procedure for determining the frequency and importance of functional connections or interactions between various elements of a system (man-to-man, man-to-machine, machine-to-man, or machine-to-machine) and the types of communications involved.

Load. The force exerted upon an object under static or dynamic conditions, either by virtue of its own weight or by some imposed object or force. That which is placed upon a vehicle or person for conveyance or that which is held up or sustained. The power carried by an electric circuit; the impedance to which energy is being supplied.

Load Factor. The ratio of the weight or pressure of a specified load or force to a standard weight or pressure (see also *Ultimate Strength; Yield Strength*).

Load, Limit. The maximum allowable static or dynamic load that may be placed on or in a structure under normal operating conditions.

Load, Sensory. The variety of stimuli to which differential responses must be made. For example, if an operator must discriminate among several different visual stimuli, the load on the visual system is greater than if discrimination is of only one type or of limited types.

Load Stress, Psychological. The effects of excessive sensory inputs, decision requirements, or motor responses on all aspects of human behavior, including fatigue, anxiety, and loss of efficiency.

Load, Ultimate. The limit load multiplied by the ultimate safety factor (sometimes called "design load").

Load, Yield. The limit load multiplied by the yield safety factor.

Location Relationship Principle. All tasks assigned to one job should be performed in the same job location.

Loudness. The perceived intensity of a sound, related roughly to its physical intensity (sound pressure level) and its frequency and waveform (see also *Phon; Sone*).

Lumen. The luminous flux radiated into a unit solid angle (steradian) from a point source having a luminous intensity of one candela.

Luminance. Luminous flux emitted per unit solid angle (steradian) and unit projected area of source; sometimes called "photometric brightness." The footlambert and the millilambert are common units of luminance.

Luminous Flux. Luminous energy per unit time; the flux of visible radiation, weighted to account for the manner in which the response of the human eye varies with the wavelength of radiation. The lumen is the common unit of luminous flux.

M

Machine Dynamics. Changes in machine output resulting from a control movement made by the operator. Mathematically, equations showing the relationship between machine input and output, commonly called the "transfer function."

Man-Function. The function allocated to the human component of a system.

Maintainability. A characteristic of design and installation expressed as the probability that a product will be retained in or restored to a specified condition within a given period of time, when the maintenance is performed according to prescribed procedures and resources.

Maintainability Supports. Items which contribute to effective maintenance. Examples include tools, test equipment, maintenance checklists, personnel, and training.

Maintenance. All actions necessary for retaining product or system in (or restoring it to) a specified condition.

Maintenance, Corrective. The actions performed, as a result of failure, to restore a product or system to a specified condition.

Maintenance, Preventive. Actions performed in an attempt to retain product or system in a specified condition by providing systematic inspection and replacement of critical components.

Manufacturing Reliability. See *Reliability, Manufacturing*.

Masking. The interfering effect of one sensory stimulus upon another simultaneous stimulus.

Materials Factor. A factor included in design calculations because of uncertainty of material strength, detail design, inadaptability to accurate computations, or other reasons. Usually, any member affected by a materials factor will be analyzed by using as the allowable stress or load the normal allowable stress or load divided by the specified materials factor.

Mean Cycles to Failure. The average number of cycles between successive equipment failure; calculated as the total number of cycles under specified conditions, divided by the number of failures.

Mean Maintenance Time. The total preventive and corrective maintenance time divided by the total number of preventive and corrective maintenance actions during a specified period of time. This is not the mean time between scheduled maintenance points.

Mean Time Between Failures (MTBF). For a particular interval, the total functioning life of a population of product, component, or system divided by the total number of failures within the population during the measurement interval. The definition holds for time, miles, events, or other measures of life units. This is not the time by which half the units might be expected to fail. See chapter on production testing.

Mean Time Between Maintenance. The mean of the distribution of the time intervals between maintenance actions (either preventive, corrective, or both).

Mean Time to Failure (MTTF). The measured operating time of a single item divided by the total number of failures during that period of time. (The measurement is normally made during the period between the "infant mortality" and wear-out periods.)

Mean Time to First Failure (MTTFF). The average time to first failure of several products, used to determine the apparent approach of the equipment to its random failure rate. (The rate is usually calculated and observed in the prototype stage.)

Mean Time to Repair (MTTR). The total corrective maintenance time divided by the total number of corrective maintenance actions in a given period.

Mel. A measure of relative pitch sensation. A 1000-cycle-per-second tone of 40 decibels is used as a reference level and is arbitrarily declared to be 1000 mels; tones that subjectively sound twice as high are 2000 mels, and so forth.

Mental Set. A preparatory readiness for a particular kind of action or experience, usually as a result of instructions.

Milestone. An activity or action within the research, development, test, evaluation, production, and in-service life of a system. The milestone ideally will possess a distinct, identifiable point which can be used as a means of evaluating progress in terms of an estimated time schedule.

Military Specifications. Requirements, often generic, of a class of products for the military, but frequently used by civilian manufacturers.

Millilambert (mL). A common unit of luminance; one thousandth of a lambert.

Missile. An object thrown by a product, usually unintentionally, as a stone by a power mower, or piston rod from a reciprocating engine.

Mission. The objective, task, or purpose of a product or system.

Mission Analysis. The process of analyzing, on a time base, the projected missions which a system will be required to perform; usually used to identify human and machine functions and to estimate the probable effects of environmental variables and other constraints.

Mission Profile. A listing or graphic representation of the steps to be achieved by a system in the process of accomplishing its mission.

Mission Reliability. The probability that a system will operate as designed for the duration of a mission.

Mission Segment. A discrete portion of a mission; the time span between two milestones on a mission profile list.

Mock-Up. A model, often full-sized, of an aircraft, other product, or installation so devised as to expose its parts for study, training, or testing.

Mock-Up Inspection. Inspection of a mock-up to determine, so far as possible, its operational suitability.

Model. A physical or abstract representation of a part of the real world. Typical classes of models are working models, physical scale models, and computer models.

Modified Rhyme Test. A test used for measuring the adequacy of communication. A 50-word list is read by a talker, and a listener responds on a prepared multiple-choice format selecting one of six words as the item heard.

Module. A combination of components, contained in one package or arranged on a common mounting.

Monitor. To observe a project, without exercising direct supervision or control.

Motion Agreement Principle. Performance on a perceptual-motor task is superior when the display indicator moves in the same direction as the control, provided the subject perceives these movements to be in the same direction.

Motor. Pertaining to muscular movement or to that which causes movement. Mechanically, a device to convert outside energy into another form, as electric current to rotational energy.

Murphy's Law. If a part can be installed incorrectly, someone will install it that way. If something can go wrong, it will (and at the most inconvenient time).

N

Named Insured's Products. Goods or products, manufactured, sold, handled, or distributed by the named Insured or by others trading under his or her name, including any container thereof (other than a vehicle).

Noise. Any unintelligible signals in a communication system which tend to interfere with proper perception of the desired signals.

Normal Operating Range. The area in which an operator can easily perform a given task without undue reaching or bending. For equipment, the task for which it was designed and manufactured.

O

Occurrence. An accident, including continuous or repeated exposure to conditions, which results in bodily injury or property damage neither expected nor intended from the standpoint of the insured.

Operable. The state of being able to perform the intended function.

Operational Analysis. A technique for predicting the output of systems through analysis of the various inputs.

Operational Readiness. The condition or state of a system or piece of equipment that makes it ready and available for immediate action or use. Sometimes used to denote the probability that a system or product will perform satisfactorily at any point in time.

Operations Research. A fact-finding precedure aimed at discovering how, under the necessary requirements and constraints, a system can best accomplish what it is designed or expected to do. Especially useful in defining man-machine systems, it begins with a clear statement of objectives, it involves identifying the relevant variables, expressing them in quantitative terms, measuring their fluctuations in given situations, and discovering how they interact.

Operator Inputs. In a man-machine system, information sensed by the operator from instructions or displays, or directly from the environment.

Operator Outputs. In a man-machine system, actions taken by the operator.

Operator Overload. Occurs when an operator is required to perform more functions than he is able to handle effectively within given time limitations.

Optimum-Location Principle. Each display or control should be placed in its optimum location in terms of some criterion of use (convenience, accuracy, speed, force to be applied, etc.).

Organoleptic. Of, or relating to, the employment of sense organs, especially of subjective testing (as of odor or appearance of food products).

Orientation, Spatial. A highly integrated perception of the subjective vertical based on visual, postural, and muscular cues.

P

Packaging. The materials used for cleaning, preserving; inclosure by wrapping or encasing; application of cushioning; designing of shock and vibration systems; design and application of interior and exterior containers; and labeling to facilitate handling during transportation and storage.

Packing. The placement of a unit or intermediate container, or group of units or intermediate containers, in the exterior shipping container. It includes the necessary bracing, cushioning, weather-proofing, exterior strappings, and markings on the exterior shipping container.

Panic Button or Panic Bar. A control button or switch for use in an emergency.

Parallax. The apparent displacement of the position of an object in relation to a reference point, due to a change in the point of observation.

Parameter. A mathematical constant having a series of particular and arbitrary values, each value characterizing a member in a system or family of expressions, curves, surfaces, or functions. In human factors, any constant that estimates or defines the curve of the equation for some psychological function.

Part. One piece, or two or more pieces joined together which are not normally subject to disassembly without destruction of designed use.

Pathogen. Any disease-producing microorganism or material.

Peak-Clipping (Of Speech Signals). A technique for controlling the excursions of instantaneous peak-amplitudes to improve intelligibility of speech, usually followed by amplification of the signal to increase the amplitude of the clipped peaks to their original level, with proportional increase of the weaker speech sounds.

Peltier Effect. The production or absorption of heat at the junction of two metals upon the passage of an electrical current. Heat generated by current flowing in one direction will be absorbed if the current is reversed.

Perception. The awareness of objects or relations or qualities, by means of sensory processes.

Perception, Spatial. The direct awareness (primarily through sensory processes) of the spatial properties of an object, especially in relation to the observer.

Perceptual-Motor Task. A task involving an overt movement response to a nonverbal stimulus situation; the response is determined by the organization of sensory cues within the individual.

Perceptual Skill. Relative ability to detect and interpret information received through the sensory channels.

Perceptual Span. The amount of perceptual material which an individual is able to grasp at a single (usually brief) presentation.

Performance Decrement. A decrease in human proficiency often attributable to operator stress or fatigue, and characterized by increasing errors and misjudgements.

Performance Measures. Measures to evaluate personnel effectiveness; objective measures include job knowledge tests, performance samples, and checklists; subjective techniques include supervisor ratings.

Phenomenal Equivalence. Different but similar situations which are perceived as the same by a human, or evoke the same responses in an individual.

Phon. A measure of the subjective loudness level of sounds; sounds of various frequencies but of the same intensity do not necessarily create sensations of equal loudness. Tones of 1000 Hz are used as reference tones. The loudness level in phons is numerically equivalent to the decibel level of a tone of 1000 Hz, which is judged to be equivalent in loudness.

Photogrammetry. The science of obtaining reliable measurements by photography.

Photometry. The study of the measurement of the intensity of light. The science of obtaining reliable measurements by changes in light intensity.

Population Stereotype. A commonly anticipated behavioral sequence, of "the way most people expect something to be done." For example, when a control is rotated clockwise, it is expected that the value of the setting will increase.

Potable. Suitable, safe, or prepared for drinking.

Pre-Emphasis. Systematic distortion of the speech spectrum to improve intelligibility of speech sound by attenuating the low-frequency components of vowels (relatively unimportant for intelligibility) and proportionately increasing the amplitude of high-frequency vowel components and consonants (highly important for intelligible speech transmission).

Preload. The residual stress in the shank of a fastener after installation, but before external or joint stresses are applied.

Preproduction Model. See *Prototype*.

Preproduction Test. Test performed before full production to provide assurance that production items will comply with applicable specifications, and that the specifications are adequate to perform the designed task.

Preservation. Materials and processes required for protecting products against corrosion or other deterioration or contamination.

Primary High Explosives. Chemical compositions which nearly always detonate by simple ignition (spark, flame, impact, and other heat sources of appropriate magnitude).

Prime Contractor. One who enters into agreement directly with an organization to provide a product or service.

Probable Error (PE). A measure of the variability of a measure; the extent to which the obtained values deviate from the measure in question; a measure of the error of sampling; equal to 0.6745 of the Standard Error.

Producibility. Those inherent design characteristics of a product which determine the production factors having a bearing on its manufacture.

Production Model. The first completed object to be turned out by a particular method of production which serves as an example of the objects which will follow it (see also *Prototype*).

Products Hazard. Includes bodily injury and property damage arising out of the named insured's products or reliance upon a representation or warranty made at any time with respect thereto.

Proficiency. An individual's level of skill in performing a particular task at any given moment.

Proficiency Test. A test to measure an individual's level of development in the performance of a given task.

Pronation. Rotation of a joint or body part forward or toward the midline; movement of the forearm and hand so that the palm faces downward (see also *Supination*).

Proof Pressure. Test pressure to which a product is subjected without permanent deformation adversely affecting operation.

Property Damage. Physical injury to or destruction of tangible property, including the loss of use thereof at any time resulting therefrom, or loss of use of tangible property.

Proprioceptor. Any receptor sensitive to the position and movement of the body and its members, including receptors in the semicircular canals, and receptors in the muscles, tendons, and joints giving rise to kinesthetic sensations.

Prototype. A model suitable for evaluation of design and production potential.

Psychoacoustics. An intermediate discipline dealing with the physics of sound and physiology and psychology of sound reception.

Q

Qualitative. Indicative of the kind of response or reaction expected, but not the magnitude.

Quality Audit. An examination of the effectiveness of quality control measures.

Quantitative. Indicative of the kind and magnitude of the response or reaction being examined.

R

Radial Velocity. The velocity of approach or recession between two bodies. Frequently, the origin of the coordinate system in which an object's movement is measured is the observer.

Radio Frequency (RF). Frequency useful for communication; approximately 10 kilohertz to 300 gigahertz.

Radio Interference. Conducted or radiated electrical disturbances, including transients, which may interfere with the operation of electronic equipment.

Range. The difference between the maximum and minimum of a given set of numbers; in a simple harmonic process it is twice the amplitude, i.e., from positive peak to negative peak.

Rating. The value of a product or system parameter which can be attained under specified conditions.

Reaction Time, Complex. The time required to react when a discrimination needs to be made; e.g., a response is made to only one of two or more expected signals, or a different response is specified for each kind of stimulus. An estimate of reaction time can be obtained from the formula:

$$RT \text{ (in milliseconds)} = 270 \log_e(n + 1),$$

where n represents the number of discriminations required before reacting.

Reaction Time (RT). The interval between application of a stimulus and the beginning (sometimes the completion) of the subject's response.

Reaction Time, Simple. The time required to make a predetermined response to a prearranged signal; a combination of sensing time and response time.

Real Time. The absence of perceptible delay in acquisition, transmission, and reception of data.

Real-Time Processing. The processing of data rapidly enough so that results are available to influence the process being monitored or controlled. Even if the time available for solution is only slightly larger than the time required for computation, the system is said to be real-time.

Rebound. Deflection under transient load, such as hitting the floor in a fall.

Receptor. A sensory nerve ending or organ in a living organism that is sensitive to physical or chemical stimuli.

Redundancy. The existance of more than one means for accomplishing a given function. Each means of accomplishing the function need not necessarily be identical.

Redundancy, Active. All redundant items are operating simultaneously rather than being switched on when needed.

Redundancy, Standby. The alternative means of performing the function is inoperative until needed and is switched on upon failure of the primary means of performing the function.

Reflectance. The ratio of luminous flux reflected by a surface, to the incident flux (expressed as a percentage). "Selective reflectance" refers to the reflectance of particular wavelengths of light and the absorption of others, resulting in object color.

Regression Analysis. The computation of the most probable value of one variable from the known value of another variable, based on their correlation.

Reliability. The probability that a system will perform a required function under specified conditions for a specified period or at a given time.

Reliability, Computed. The calculated probability of a system's performing its purpose within specified limits based on estimates or tests of the reliability of its components.

Reliability, Manufacturing. The estimated reliability of equipment during the manufacturing process; it is based on the demonstrated failure rates of the subsystems and of the entire equipment during manufacturing tests. This is sometimes called "factory reliability."

Repair. The inspection, servicing, testing, and calibration, to restore a product to serviceable condition and extend its useful life.

Repairability Parameters. Quantitative factors which determine the repairability of a product, including time to diagnose and isolate malfunctions, time to repair them, manpower and skill levels required, and time the equipment is operating satisfactorily without requiring corrective maintenance.

Replaceability. The characteristics of a component or product that allow it to be substituted for another.

Resolving Power. The capacity of the human eye or a sensing system to see objects viewed simultaneously as distinct objects; the capacity to perceive as distinct objects, in close proximity, casting images on the sensor. Usually measured with a target of closely spaced lines.

Response Time. Time required for an operator to make a given response after a stimulus is perceived, including decision time.

Retinal Disparity. The difference between images on the two retinas resulting from the slightly different angle of the two eyes when viewing a solid object.

RF Power Density. The power per unit area on a surface normal to the propagation direction. The power density equals field intensity squared, divided by intrinsic impedance of free space, under ideal conditions. The common unit is watts per square meter.

S

Saccule. A sac in the vestibule of the inner ear having receptors for vibratory or low-tone auditory stimuli.

Safety. Freedom from conditions which can cause injury or death to humans and damage to property. The conservation of human life and its effectiveness, and the prevention of damage to property consistent with product or system requirements.

Safety Factor. The difference between the required capacity and the actual breaking point (limit load) of an item or structure. (**Ultimate**). The ratio of the ultimate strength of a structure to the limit load. (**Yield**). The ratio of the yield strength of a structure to the limit load.

Salmonella Test. A test of the mutagenicity of a chemical, from which possible carcinogenic potential can be deduced. Often called the Ames test after inventor Bruce Ames. Uses *Salmonella* bacteria *in vitro*.

Sandwich Construction. A composite consisting of dissimilar materials bonded together to provide strength with minimum weight. Usually these structures utilize lightweight core materials in foam, solid, or cellular form, with metal or wood facings.

Seat Reference Point. The point at which the center line of the seat back surface (depressed) and seat bottom surface (depressed) intersect. When the seat is positioned at the midpoint of the adjustment range(s), this intersection point is called the neutral seat reference point.

Seebeck Effect. The establishment of an electric potential difference tending to produce a flow of current in a circuit of two dissimilar metals the junctions of which are at different temperatures.

Semicircular Canals. Three tubes in the inner ear, set at nearly right angles to each other in three planes and containing the receptors for balance.

Sensing Time. The time required for an operator to become aware of a signal.

Sensitive Item. Any item which presents special transportation, packaging, or materials-handling problems because of vulnerability to shock and vibration, need for special environmental controls, or similar considerations.

Sequence-Of-Use Principle. Positioning controls and displays so that those used in sequence are physically arranged in order of operation.

Serviceability. A measure of the degree to which servicing of an item will be accomplished within a given time under specified conditions.

Servicing. The replenishment of consumables needed to keep a product in operating condition, not including any other preventive or corrective maintenance.

Shake Table. A laboratory device used for testing the effects of vibration on humans or on equipment.

Shelf Life. See *Storage Life*.

Somatotype. An overall classification of an individual's physique based on a comparative evaluation of his rotundity, muscularity, and linearity. The evaluation is indicated by a 3-digit formula giving a quantity for each component.

Sone. A measure of relative loudness sensation. A 1000-kHz tone of 40 decibels is used as a reference level and is arbitrarily declared to be 1 sone; tones that subjectively sound twice as loud are 2 sones, and so forth.

Sound Pressure Level. The intensity of a sound expressed in decibels based on a reference intensity or "zero" point of 0.0002 microbar.

Specification. An accurate description of the technical requirements for a material, a product, or a service, including the procedure by which it can be determined that the requirements have been met.

Spectrophotometry. The measurement of the relative radiant energy of the component wavelengths of a given sample of light; a "spectrophotometric curve" shows the breakdown of a light sample into its various wavelengths and indicates the energy intensities of the components.

Speech-To-Noise Ratio (Peak Speech to RMS Noise). The ratio between instantaneous peak amplitudes of speech and the root-mean-square (RMS) amplitude of background noise.

Speech Interference Level. The average, in dB, of the sound levels of masking noise in the three octave bands of frequency 600–1200, 1200–2400, and 2400–4800 cps.

Speech Spectrum. The frequency range over which normal voice sounds are generally distributed; from 100 to 8000 Hz.

Stability. That property of a system which causes it to return to its initial equilibrium condition after being disturbed by some outside force.

Stability, Dynamic. The property of a system which, when its equilibrium is disturbed, causes it to damp any oscillation and gradually return to its original state of equilibrium.

Stability, Static. The tendency of a system to return toward its equilibrium condition after being disturbed from its original state of equilibrium.

Standard Deviation. A measure of the dispersion of data points around their mean value. It is the positive square root of the arithmetic mean of the squares of the deviation from the arithmetic mean of the population:

$$s = \sqrt{\sum_{i=1}^{n} \frac{(x_i - \bar{x})^2}{n-1}}$$

where $\bar{x}$ is the arithmetic mean, x_i is the deviation, and n is the number of points.

Standard Error. An estimate of the sampling errors affecting a statistic; a measure of the amount the statistic may be expected to differ by chance from the true value; the standard deviation of the obtained values of the statistic on successive samples (see also *Probable Error*).

Stanine. A standard or derived score developed by the Air Force for reporting psychological test results. Raw scores are converted to standard units in a distribution whose mean is 5 and whose standard deviation is 2.

Statistical Significance. The degree of probability that, in an infinite series of measurements of the kind in question, the value or score actually obtained will not by chance alone occur with significant frequency, and hence can be attributed to something other than chance.

Stimulus. A physical event that causes physiological activity in a sense organ (receptor); if the energy is above threshold value, the stimulus is perceived (there is awareness of sensation).

Storage Life. The length of time a product can be stored under specified conditions and still meet specified requirements. Also called shelf life.

Stray Electrical Energy. Unwanted electrical energy.

Strength, Ultimate. See *Ultimate Strength*.

Strength, Yield. See *Yield Strength*.

Stress. The force per unit area of a body that tends to produce deformation. The effect of a physiological, psychological, or mental load on a human which causes fatigue and tends to degrade proficiency.

Subassembly. Two or more parts which form a portion of an assembly, or a unit replaceable as a whole, but having a part or parts which are individually replaceable.

Subordinate (sub)contractor. One who enters into agreement with a prime contractor or other subordinate contractor to provide a product or a service.

Subsystem. A combination of parts which performs an operational function within a system (and is usually a major subdivision of the system), such as the electrical subsystem of an automobile.

Suitable Substitute. A suitable substitute is a part or a product that can always replace another part or product in any application.

Supination. Rotation of a joint or body part backward and away from the midline; movement of limb that brings the palm or sole upward (see also *Pronation*).

System. Generally, a composite of equipment, capable of performing or supporting an operational role. A complete system includes all equipment, services, and personnel required for its operation and support to the degree that it can be considered a self-sufficient unit in its intended operational environment.

System Analysis. The discovery and identification of sources of error or variability in a system, the measurement of these errors, and then arrangement of elements to improve system performance.

System Engineering. The application of technology to the study and planning of a system so that the relationships of various parts of the system and the utilization of various subsystems are fully established before designs are committed.

System Error Analysis. An analysis of a system to determine the source of an error and to determine its effect on the performance of the system.

System Research. Investigation of general principles applicable to the design and development of new systems, including those of which humans are a part, and therefore including the characteristics of humans in relation to the instruments and machines utilized.

System Safety. The optimum degree of safety within the constraints of operational effectiveness, time, and cost, attained through specific application of system safety management and engineering principles throughout all phases of a system's life cycle.

System Safety Engineering. An element of systems engineering involving the application of scientific and engineering principles for the timely identification of hazards and initiation of those actions necessary to prevent or control hazards within the system. It draws upon professional knowledge and specialized skills in the mathematical, physical, and related scientific disciplines, together with the principles and methods of engineering design and analysis to specify, predict, and evaluate the safety of the system.

System Safety Management. An element of program management which insures the accomplishment of the system safety tasks, including identification of the system safety requirements; planning, organizing, and controlling those efforts which are directed toward achieving the safety goals; coordinating with other (system) program elements; and analyzing, reviewing, and evaluating the program to insure effective and timely realization of the system safety objectives.

T

Tactile. Of or relating to the sense of touch.

Task. A group of related job elements performed within a work cycle and directed toward a goal. A set of operationally similar tasks constitutes a "duty" in military parlance.

Task Element. A basic unit of behavior, made up of the smallest logically definable set of perceptions, decisions, and responses which the human being is required to perform in completing a task.

Technical Variance. Technical variance is the difference between a demonstrated value and the corresponding planned value (demonstrated variance), or between a specification requirement and the current estimate for the end product (predicted variance).

Temperature Tolerance. Ability of a product to endure extreme temperature, defined by the maximum and minimum temperatures beyond which efficiency is impaired.

Test Plan. A document which identifies in detail the test objectives, planned milestone schedules, and the reports required; established the concepts to be employed; and identifies the responsibilities of all participants.

Threshold, Absolute Auditory. The statistically determined intensity at which sound is perceived 50 percent of the time by the average human being. It varies with sound wave frequency; measured in terms of decibels relative to 0.0002 microbar, the threshold for a standard 1000-Hz tone is 0 dB, while the threshold for a 100-Hz tone is approximately 35 dB. Within the area of greatest sensitivity (2000–3000 Hz), a person with normal hearing may respond to sound pressure levels as small as 3×10^{-7} gram per square centimeter.

Threshold, Absolute Visual. The minimum intensity of light that can be seen by the human eye after complete dark adaptation, generally considered to be about 10^{-9} lambert in the periphery. Theoretically, as few as six quanta of light reaching the retina have a good probability of yielding a visual sensation.

Threshold, Difference. The minimum difference between two stimuli that can be perceived as different by the average person under optimum conditions; statistically, that difference which is perceptible 50 percent of the time.

Tolerance. The range within which equipment performance or dimensions may vary from a given standard because of state of the art, cost, or other limitation.

Traceability. The capability to track system requirements from a system function to all elements of the system which collectively or individually perform the function; an element of the system to all functions which it performs; and a specific requirement to the source analysis or contractual constraint which originated the requirement. Traceability includes tracking allocated design and technical program requirements through the work breakdown structure between the system level and the lowest level of assembly requiring logistic or maintenance consideration.

Training. The totality of instructions, planned circumstances, and directed activity by which personnel acquire or strengthen new skills which will enable them to perform assigned duties with maximum reliability, efficiency, and safety.

Transillumination. Illumination used on console panels or indicators utilizing edge and/or back lighting techniques on clear, flourescent, or sandwich-type plastic materials.

Troubleshooting. Locating and diagnosing malfunctions by means of systematic checking or analysis.

U

Ultimate Safety Factor. See *Safety Factor*.

Ultimate Strength. The maximum stress (tactile, compressive, or shear) that a material can withstand.

Utricle. A saclike structure in the vestibule of the inner ear which contains the receptors that are stimulated by the forces of gravity and provides information about body position in relation to the vertical.

V

Validity (Test). The degree to which a test measures what it was designed to measure, estimated by means of a coefficient of correlation between test scores and a criterion.

Vertigo. Sensation of dizziness or whirling in which objects, though stationary, appear to move in various directions, and a person finds it difficult to maintain an erect posture. It may result from overstimulation of the sense organs, from changes in the blood supply of the brain, or from disease. "Aviator's vertigo" is caused by a conflict between visual and gravitational cues.

Viewing Angle. The angle formed by a line from the eye with viewed surface.

Visual Acuity. The ability to perceive black and white detail at various distances. It can be expressed as the reciprocal of the visual angle, in minutes of arc, that is subtended by the smallest detail that can be visually discriminated. There are four types: minimum visible, minimum perceptible, minimum separable, and minimum distinguishable. (Also called visual resolution.)

Vulnerability. Susceptibility to damage from normal use.

W

Warning Light. A signal assembly which alerts the operator to a dangerous condition requiring immediate action.

Weber's Law. The least added difference of stimulus that can be noticed is a constant proportional part of the original stimulus. It may be expressed as $\Delta S/S$ (Weber Ratio or Weber Fraction), where ΔS is the change of stimulus that is just perceptibly different and S is the value of the stimulus; the fraction is a constant over the middle range of intensity.

White Noise. The noise that is heard when many sound waves of different lengths are combined so that they reinforce or cancel one another in haphazard fashion.

Workspace. The physical area in which an individual must perform some required task.

Y

Yield Safety Factor. See *Safety Factor*.

Yield Strength. The magnitude of the load or stress which must be applied to a given material in order to cause a permanent deformation of a specified amount; when a material does not have a specific yield point, the unit stress at which it exhibits a permanent deformation of some specified amount. A typical military requirement would be expressed in the amount of stress needed to deform a surface more than 0.002 inch per inch.

Z

Zero Defects Program. A military and aerospace quality control program begun in the mid-1960s. It attempted to voluntarily enlist the aid of all employees toward the zero defects goal.

GENERAL INDEX

A. K. Electric, 223
(a) rates, 290–293, 297, 300, 312–313
Abbreviations for standards-setting organizations (table), 58–59
Abinger, Lord, 7, 8
Abrasive wheels and products, insurance for, 18, 290, 294, 300, 314
Accident, defined, 641
Accidents, product-related:
    aircraft, 26, 246, 264, 285–286
    Apollo Project fire, 225, 226
    automobile, 4–5, 37–39
    bicycle, 38, 53
    cattle feed contamination, 225
    chemical products and, 225, 226, 246
    in chemical transportation (table), 270–273
    to children, 5, 53, 54, 59, 245–246
    explosions, 218, 279–280
    fires, 218, 225, 226, 246
    household products and, 4, 38–39, 53
    and incompatibility hazards *see* Compatibility
    injury-reporting systems, 52–53
    investigations and reports of, 52, 53, 139, 140, 218–221, 275–276
    with machine tools, 7, 11, 210, 213
    National Transportation Safety Board investigations of, 26
    NEISS reports on, 52, 53, 139, 140
    occupational, 4, 7, 11, 37, 210, 213, 242, 325–327
    oil heater explosions, 218, 223
    and product liability litigation *see* Court action; Litigation, product liability
    reports on, corporate, 218–221, 275
    severity classifications of, 138–140
    simulation of, 218, 220–221
    spills, 263–267
    statistics on, 3–4, 37, 270–273
    with toys, 5, 57
    and workers' compensation laws, 210, 322–327
Acetic acid, 382
Acetone, 274, 382, 398
Acetylene, 19, 382, 399
Acrylonitrile, 270–272
Administrative Procedure Act, 48
Advertising, 92, 102, 196, 203
    misleading on safety, 205, 206
Aerosol containers, 19, 39, 61
Aerospace Industries Association of America, 54

Aerospace industry, 16, 29
    accidents, 246, 264, 285–286
    Apollo Project fire, 225, 226
    compatibility data (tables), 247–256
    compatibility safeguards, 247–248
    and insurance, liability, 18, 19, 291, 295, 299
    space station, fire-extinguishing system for, 259
Aerospace Materials Specifications (AMS), 58
Agricultural equipment and supplies:
    cattle feed contamination, 225
    chipper-mulcher design development, 98
    pesticides and other chemicals, 19, 29, 32, 229, 291, 295
    tractor safety requirement, 37
Air bags, automobile, 24
Air Force, U.S., 247, 248
    Aviation Psychology Program, 105–106
    fire-suppression systems design, 258–263, 268
Air Force Systems Command Design Handbook I–X, Checklist of General Design Criteria, 329
Air Force Systems Safety Design Handbook, 1–6, 110, 112, 114, 122, 159, 175, 188, 198, 207, 217, 247–254, 262, 268
Air pollution, 3, 32
    concentration calculations, 267–269, 274
    lethal concentrations (LCs) of toxic substances, 235, 268
    toxic substances, exposure limits for, *see* Toxic substances, Appendix B, 379–399
Aircraft:
    accidents, 26, 246, 264, 285–286
    hazardous materials handling, federal regulations for, *see* Appendix C, 401–497
    (*See also* Aerospace industry)
Aircraft components industry insurance, 18, 291, 295, 299, 300, 314, 320
Alcohol, Tobacco, and Firearms Division, Treasury Department, 231
Alcohol compatibility data, 250–251, 255
Allergic reactions, 240–241
Allergy, defined, 642
Alloy Casting Institute (ACI), 58
Aluminum Association of America (AAA), 58
Aluminum compatibility data, 248, (table) 249
American Conference of Governmental Industrial Hygienists (ACGIH), 231, 235, 379
    Threshold Limit Values (TLVs) lists, 235, (tables) 379–399

663

American Cyanamid, 244
American Gas Association (AGA), 58
American Gas Association Laboratories, 54
American Law Institute (ALI), 9–11
　Restatement (second) of Torts, 6–22, 66–67
American National Standards, 54, 56, 64, 70, 499–523
American National Standards Institute (ANSI), 27, 58, 205, 373, 398
　and American National Standards, 54, 56
　coordinator of "consensus" standards, 50, 54, 56
　legal memorandum on liability of standards-setters, 64, (text) 65–72
　power press standard, 27
　Standards for Safety and Health, Appendix D, 499–523
American Society of Mechanical Engineers (ASME), 1, 54, 58, 65, 68
American Society for Testing and Materials (ASTM), 53, 54, 56, 58, 65
American Textile Machinery Association, 317
Ames, Bruce, 243, 246, 657
Ames test, 243–245, 657
Ammonia, 382
　compatibility data (tables), 249–251, 254
Ammonia, anhydrous, 270–272
　spill hazards, 267
Ammunition, 300
　exploding shell liability suit, 69, 72
Anderson, A. M., 56
Animal tests (bioassays), 274
　bioassay, defined, 643
　for carcinogenicity, 242–243, 245
　toxicity and lethal dose determination, 228, 231–235
Apollo Project fire, 225, 226
Army, U. S., 152
Arnold, Frank, 285–286
Arsenic, 229, 382, 396
Asbestos, 251, 382, 396
　compatibility data (table), 251
Asphyxiants, 381, 399
Assembly (product), defined, 642
Assembly (production operation):
　error minimization techniques, 147, 151, 155–156, 163
　error rates, 147, (table) 148, 155
　and fittings, incorrect, 159, 163
　incorrect, in carburetor case, 86
　worker substitutions in, 163
Association of Home Appliance Manufacturers, 54
Association of Trial Lawyers of America, The, 283
Assumption-of-risk, 20, 271
Atomic Energy Act, 29
Audio signals evaluation (table), 107
Audio-visual aids, 155–156
Auditory and visual warning signals, 352
Auto accessory stores, insurance of, 292, 296
Automobile components:
　industry insurance (tables), 18, 291–292, 295–296, 300, 314, 320
　standards for, 24
　tires *see* Tires, automobile
Automobile industry:
　and "infant mortality" period, 128
　in liability litigation, 7–12, 15, 49
Automobiles, 3–6, 128, 212
　accidents, 4–5, 37–39
　dashboard design, 149
　insurance, 5, 31, 321

Automobiles (*Cont.*):
　in liability litigation, 7–12, 15, 49
　MacPherson liability case, 8–11
　Nader vs. unsafe design of, 5
　recalls, 4, 26, 111, 223
　and safety design, 5, 24, 37, 111, 149
　safety devices for, 24
　standards for, 24, 26
　tires, *see* Tires, automobile
Automotive Parts and Accessories Association, Inc., 317
Aviation Psychology Program, 106

Babcock and Wilcox Co. v. Marsh Wood Products Co., 68
Backer-Loring Corp., 209
J.T. Baker Chemical Company, 211
Bans, product, 47, 50
　federal authority to impose, 28, 29, 35, 39
　on fluorocarbon aerosol propellants, 39, 61
　on food dye Red 2, 241
　on paint with gasoline solvent, 47
　on PCBs (polychlorinated biphenyls), 35
　on TRIS-treated fabric, 245
Barges:
　chemical transportation modes and mishaps (table), 271–272
Basic limit(s) rates, 289–294, 301, 312–313
　described, 302
　determination of, 309
　for product categories (tables), 290–293
"Bathtub" curve:
　product behavior model, 127–128, 170–172
　time zones in, 171
Batteries:
　auto, insurance for, 292, 296
　and hazardous industrial wastes (table), 229
Bay Area Rapid Transit (BART), 24
Bell Laboratories, 118
Bell Telephone Laboratories, Inc., 200
Benzene, 382, 397, 398
　transportation modes and mishaps (table), 271–273
Berkun, M. M., 152n.
Bermuda, 318
Beryllium, 382, 397
Best's Aggregates and Averages, 309n.
Bicycles:
　accidents and injuries involving, 38, 53
　standards for, 29, 53
Bioassays *see* Animal tests
Bioconcentration, 228, 230
　defined, 643
Biologic Limit Values (BLVs), described, 394
Birnbaum, Sheila L., 240n.
Birth control products, 16, 19
Blue Book, 7
Boats, regulation of, 25, 29
Boiler tube liability case, 68
Boilers, industrial, 1
Bolts, nuts, washers (checklist), 342–344
Bon Vivant Soups, 139
Booby-trap trip wires, 110–111
Boron trifluoride, 398
Boston Fire Department, 218, 223
Boston University, 21
Bottles, 208
　"crack map" court exhibit, 284
　explosion case, 10
Botulism, 139

Brazing (checklist), 346
Breach of warranty defenses (table), 278
Bromochlorodifluoromethane, 262, 268
Bromochloromethane, 260, 262, 268, 383
Bromotrifluoromethane, 261, 262, 268
Bronze compatibility data (table), 250
Buckley, J. L., 232
Buick Motor Company v. MacPherson, 8–10
Burn-in, 128, 172
    defined, 643
Butane, 383, 399

Cadmium, 229
Calgon, 266
Campbell's Soup, 139
Campo Doctrine, 20
Can openers, 39–40
Canadian Standards Association, 102*n*.
Cancer *see* Carcinogenic substances; Carcinogenicity
Carbon dioxide, 258, 261, 262, 268, 383
Carbon disulfide, 379, 383
Carbon steel compatibility data (table), 250
Carbon tetrachloride, 248
    toxicity, 244, 383, 397, 398
Carburetor failure case, 86
Carcinogenic substances, 231, 241–246
    and Ames test, 243–245, 657
    and cancer incidence, 396–397
        in children, 245–246
        in chimney sweeps, 242
        in females, 241, 245
        in males, 245
    coal tar substances, 242, 384
    diethylstilbestrol (DES), 241
    dioxin, 166–167
    food dye Red 2, 241
    in industrial processes, 396–397
    NIOSH listings of, 235
    profit and liability risks in, 241–242
    saccharin, 242–243
    tests, 241–245
    Threshold Limit Values (TLVs) of (tables), 396–397
    TRIS (2,3 dibromopropyl phosphate), 59, 242, 245–246
    vinyl chloride, 242–244, 395, 396
Carcinogenicity, 231, 241–246
    Ames test for, 243–245
    molecular structure clue to, 243
    mutagenicity as indicator of, 243–244
    tests for, 241–245
Cardozo, Benjamin, 7–10, 14
Carter v. Yardley and Company, 241
Casting industry insurance, 18, 290, 294, 300, 314, 320
Cattle feed contamination, 225
Caustic Poisons Act, 29
Caustic soda, 230
    transportation modes and mishaps, 270, 271, 273
Caution system, hazard, 100
Chamber of Commerce, U.S., 5, 6
Change control, production:
    checklist, 191
    documentation and record-retention, 189–191
Charschan, Sid, 205
Checker Motors, 59
Checklist, defined, 644
Checklists:
    basic considerations for, 330–331

Checklists (*Cont.*):
    bolts, nuts, washers, 342–344
    castings (fittings), 341
    change control, production, 191
    chemical hazards, 227
    combustible vapor detection, 351
    controls, 332
    corrosion, 348–349
    displays, 331
    electrical/electronic equipment and systems, 353–366
    electromagnetic compatibility, 356–357
    explosion detection, 351
    fasteners, 341–344
    fire extinguishing and suppression systems, 352–353
    fittings, 340–341
    fuel and storage systems, 370–372
    hazard detection, 349–352
    hazards identification, 99–100
    human factors, 331–332
    hydraulic equipment and systems, 366–368
    instructions, 334
    maintainability, 332–333
    material handling equipment, 372–377
    metals, structural, 339–340
    nonmetals, structural, 340
    on outside suppliers, use of, 167
    packaging, 334–338
    pins, 344
    pressurization and pneumatic equipment and systems, 368–370
    product safety system, 93
    production, 158
    rivets, 342
    screws, 344
    standards and standardization in, 330
    structural materials, 339–340
    toxic vapor detection, 352
    universal joints, 341
    warning signals, 352
    welding, 345–348
Chemical industry:
    and hazardous wastes (table), 229
    insurance, liability, for, 291
Chemicals, industrial, liability insurance for, 291, 294–295
Chemicals and chemical products, 225–274, 324
    and allergic reactions, 240–241
    carcinogenic, 225, 231, 235, 241–246, 396–397
        (*See also* Carcinogenic substances)
    compatibility of, 246–257
    concentration calculations, 267–269, 274
    documentation forms, 237, 238
    Dow "product stewardship" program for, 227, 230–231
    EPA "known chemicals" data bank, 35, 226–227
    and fire suppression, 257–263
        (*See also* Fire suppression)
    hazards checklist, 227
    hazards in industrial wastes, 228, (table) 229
    and insurance, liability (tables), 18, 19, 291, 294–295, 300, 314, 320
    in liability litigation, 240–241
    mutagenic, 243
    "new" chemical, defined, 35
    premarket notification procedure, 34–35
    spills, hazards in, (table) 232–233, 263–267, (table) 270–273

666 GENERAL INDEX

Chemicals and chemical products (*Cont.*):
   and third-party liability, 379
   toxicity hazards, 32–35, 231–239
   TOXLINE data bank, 227, 274
   transportation modes and mishaps (table), 270–273
   transportation regulations, federal (table) Appendix C, 401–497
   waste treatment processes for (table), 236–237
     (*See also* Carcinogenic substances; Hazardous materials; Toxic substances; and specific chemicals)
"Child-proof" containers, 36, 57, 208
Child Protection and Toy Safety Act, 29
Children:
   cancer incidence in, 245–246
   and containers, "child-proof," 36, 57, 208
   crib design regulations, 40
   and furnaces with open floor grills, 54
   highchair design for, 40
   NEISS injury data on, 53
   sleepwear for, carcinogenic, 59, 245–246
   sleepwear for, flammable, 59, 176, 245
   and toys, injurious, 5
   and toys, safety guidelines for, 57
Chipper-mulcher design development, 98
Chlorinated hydrocarbons, 226, 229, 244, 252–253
Chlorine: transportation modes and mishaps, 270–272
Chlorine trifluoride compatibility data, 249-251
Chloroform, 248
Christensen, Julien M., 4
Chromium, 229
Chrysler Corporation, 11, 281
Chumas, Sophie J., 585
Cigarettes, 240, 296*n*., 397*n*.
Circuit-board machine, 160, 161
Claims and complaints:
   accident investigation and reporting, 218–221, 275
   as feedback of product safety data, 196–200
   handling procedures, 196, 198
   insuror claims-handling procedures, 17, 315–316
Clean Air Act, 3, 29
Cleaning agents, 38, 53, 248
Cleary, Gottlieb, Steen and Hamilton, 33
Clothing *see* Wearing apparel
Coast Guard, U.S., 25, 26, 64, 264–266
   National Strike Force for spill emergencies, 264, 265
Coca Cola v. Escola, 10
Code of Federal Regulations (CFR), 60–62
   citations for major safety laws (table), 25
   organization of data in, 62
   titles (table), 60
Codes and coding:
   change control, 191
   coding, defined, 644
   color, 159, 247
   control, defined, 644
   packaging, 208
   trade association *see* specific standards-setting organizations, Appendix G, 585–621
Color, as warning device, 203
Colorado Captive Insurance Company Act, 319
Combustible vapor detection (checklist), 351
Communications:
   between design engineer and safety-related departments, 76, 193, 195
   emergency response procedures, 221–222, 264, 266
   feedback chain, 193, 195–202

Communications (*Cont.*):
   information flow in product safety systems (chart), 74
   in recalls, 221–224
   in spill emergencies, 264, 266
Communications industry, 44–45
Compatibility:
   and air cargo accident, 246, 264
   Air Force safety data on (tables), 247–256
   of chemicals, 246–257
   defined, 644
   electromagnetic (checklist), 356–357
   explosive reaction of solvents with nitrogen tetroxide (table), 248
   of fluids with metal and nonmetal lines and gaskets (tables), 249–251
   and hydraulic fluid selection (table), 252–253
   of propellants and oxidizing chemicals with various materials (table), 254–256
   segregation techniques, 247
Component, defined, 644
Components, 164
   electrical/electronic (checklist), 359
   in failure analysis, 99, 104–105, 118, 129, 131
   failure-rate assessments, 104–105
   in fuel and storage systems (checklist), 371–372
   in hydraulic equipment (checklist), 367
   and installation errors, 110, 175
   from outside suppliers, 30, 160, 167–170
   and repair and rework activities, 162
   storage of similar-looking, 159
   warranties on, 30
   (*See also* specific categories of components)
Computer Aided Manufacturing, Inc., 189–190
Computers, 111, 291, 295, 644
   analog and digital defined, 644
   for record-keeping, 189–190, 200, 201
Concentrations of hazardous substances:
   calculations of, 267, 269
   lethal *see* Exposure limits
Connectors, 247
   for electrical and electronic systems (checklists), 361–363
Constant (or normal operating) period, 127, 128, 170, 171
Consultants, outside, 85–90
   contract for, sample, 90
   liability of, 85–86
   use of, 87–89
Consumer, defined, 30
Consumer Federation of America, 37
Consumer movement, 3, 5–7, 23, 35–37
   and "class action" suits, 37
   evolution of, 5–6, 21, 23, 37
   Nader, Ralph, and, 5–7, 13, 21
   "regulators without portfolio," 37
   and standards, 21, 56, 57
   and toys, injurious, 5, 57
Consumer organizations, 37
Consumer Product Hazard Index, 53
Consumer product safety, 1–41, 56, 57
   Consumer Product Hazard Index, 53
   and court decisions, changing character of, 6–22
   how safe is "safe"?, 37–41
   "innocent bystander" liability protection, 13, 22
   major federal safety laws (table), 25
   (*See also* specific laws)
   Nader, Ralph, and, 5–7, 13, 21

Consumer Product Safety (*Cont.*):
  organized support for, 35–37
  pressures for, 1–6
  and statutory law, evolution of, 22–35
  (*See also* Consumer Product Safety Act; Government regulation; Regulatory process)
Consumer Product Safety Act, 3, 21, 25, 32, 37, 40, 46, 50, 277, 279
  described, 28–29
  record-retention provision (text), 193
  and stockpiling of suspect products, 49
  "substantial product hazard" notification requirement, 93, 169, 223
Consumer Product Safety Commission, 25, 28, 38, 40–41, 49–50, 61–64, 139, 158, 162, 169, 180, 191, 218–220, 223, 245
  checklist for product safety system, 93
  Consumer Product Hazard Index, 53
  established, 21, 28
  funds allocations (charts), 45, 46
  generic standard guidelines, 57
  Handbook and Standard for Manufacturing Safer Consumer Products, 101
  National Electronic Injury Surveillance System (NEISS), 52–53
  organizational structure of (chart), 51
  powers of, 28–29
  regulatory program structure (chart), 44
Consumer Product Safety Commission Standards, index to, Appendix E, 525–545
Consumer's Union of the United States, 37
Containers:
  aerosols, 19, 39, 61
  "child-proof," 36, 57
Contraceptives, 16, 19
Contracts:
  consultant, 90
  contract warranty doctrine, 10–12
  "hold harmless" clauses in, 322, 324
  implied, 10, 32, 206
  privity, 7–11, 13, 67
  purchasing, 166–167, 169
  "running," 10
  service, defined, 31
Contribution *see* Contributory negligence
Contributory negligence, 17, 323–327
  Campo Doctrine and, 20
  as defense argument, 277
  "Dole" rule on, 323–324
  in third-party suits, 323–327
  in worker compensation cases, 323–327
Control, defined, 644
Control instruments industry, 291, 295
Controls and control design, 57, 154
  crane crank, 150
  direction-of-movement indicators, 149–150
  human factors checklist, 332
  human factors principles and, 149–150
  missile, 149, 154
  "population stereotypes" and, 149–150
  and stress reactions, 149–151
  and user frame of reference, 148–150
Cooking units, mobile LPG, 258
Copper, 229, 248, 251
Corrosion, 253, 257
  checklists, 348–349, 364
  fire-extinguishing agents resistance to, 262

Corrosives delivery truck, 106
Cosmetics, 29, 240–241
Costs:
  and failure probabilities, 117, 198
  of recalls (table), 222
  of safety-conscious design versus liability claims, 102–103
Coupling, unsafe design for, 106
Court action, 275–286
  bottle-fracture case, 284
  and court decisions, evolution in, 6–22
  courtroom exhibits, 284–286
  defense arguments (tables), 277–279
    (*See also* specific arguments)
  discovery procedures, 276–278
    deposition, 277
    "interrogatory," 276
  engineer in pretrial proceedings, 276–278
  engineer on witness stand, 278–282, 286
  and ethics, professional, 279
  and evolution in court decisions, 6–22
  expert witnesses and, 14–15, 279, 280, 282–286
  "hold harmless" clauses and, 322, 324
  plane-propeller case presentation, 285–286
  preparation for, 275–276
  who should testify?, 278–282
  (*See also* Litigation, product liability; and specific lawsuit titles)
Court decisions, evolution in, 6–22
Cranes, 258
  control crank design, 150
  fire-extinguishers for, 258
Crest (Procter & Gamble) toothpaste case, 241
Cribs, baby, 40
Cronin v. J. B. E. Olson Corp., 23
Cryogenic fluids compatibility data (tables), 249–251
Cyanides, 229

Data Collection and Reaction (H.D. Hulme), 195*n*.
Data system, elements of (table), 195
"Death of Contract, The," (Gilmore), 8
Deere, John, 204
Defective products, disposal of, 162–163
Defects, product:
  failure duplication as clue to, 220–221
  repair and rework activities, 158, 162–163
  report forms, 196, 197, 199
  undetectable, as defense argument, 277
Defense Department, U.S., 58, 185, 186, 265
Defense Research Institute (DRI), 7, 13–14, 283
Defense Research Institute Newsletter, 281
Dental instruments and equipment, 293, 296
Design:
  checklists *see* Checklists
  compatibility considerations, 246–257
  of controls and displays, 149–151, 154
  and electrical shock hazards, 111–113
  and ethics, professional, 83–85, 279
  of fire-suppression systems, 257–263, 268
  human factors considerations and, 105–115, 151–152
  liability of designers and, 85–86
  of long-lived products, 210, 212–215
  and "population stereotypes," 149–150
  process (chart), 96
  records retention, 91–92

668 GENERAL INDEX

Design (Cont.):
  state-of-the-art defense argument, 277
  stress factors in, 149–152
  of tamperproofing devices, 209, 211, 213
  techniques for minimizing human error, 147–156
  and user expectations, 148–150
  of warnings, 202–206
  of workplaces, discomfort theory and, 151
Design engineers, 56, 95–97, 101, 104
  and autonomy, decision-making, 82
  in court:
    as expert witness, 15, 279
    pre-trial procedures and, 276–278
    on witness stand, 278–282, 286
  and ethics, professional, 83–85, 279
  liability of, 85–86
  and management abrogation of safety efforts, 83–85
  as prime mover for product safety, 75–78
  and records, safety design, 91–92, 193, 195
  regulatory procedures and, 48–50, 52–53
  responsibilities as product safety director, 79–80, 82, 193
  and responsibility to warn, 202–203, 206
  safety tasks of, 195, 202–203, 206
Design process (chart), 96
Design reviews, 97, 193, 206
  agendas for (table), 103
  and departmental design trade-offs, 102–103
  and failure rate estimation, 103–105
  formalization of, 100–105
  hazards reviews in (table), 102, 195
  initial considerations, 100–101
  management functions in, 102 (table), 104
  records of, 195, 201
  savings potential in (chart), 101
Design Techniques for Improving Human Performance in Production (Swain), 147n.
Detergents, 225, 263
Detoxification of hazardous wastes (table), 236–237
Dibromofluoromethane, 260, 262, 268
(2, 3 dibromopropyl) phosphate see TRIS
Dibromotetrafluoroethane, 262, 268
Dichloroethylene, 248
Dieldrin, 244
Dies, jigs, and fixtures industry insurance, 287, 290, 294
Diethylstilbestrol (DES), 241
Dimethyl hydrazine, 254, 256
Dinan, John, 105n.
Diodes, light-emitting (LED), 110
Dioxin, 166–167, 226
Direction-of-movement indicators, 149–150
Directory of United States Standardization Activities (S.J. Chumas, ed.), 585
Disclaimer, 279
"Discount" stores, 163
Displays:
  applications of types of (chart), 108–109
  design and user performance, 149, 151, 154
  fire control system, missile, 154
  human factors checklist, 331
Disposal, waste see Waste disposal; Waste treatment
Disposal of defective products, 162–163
DNA (deoxyribonucleic acid), 244
Documentation see Records and record retention
Dole v. Dow Chemical Co., 72n., 323
Dow Chemical Company, 169, 246
  Dole negligence suit, 72n., 323

Dow Chemical Company (Cont.):
  "product stewardship" safety program, 227, 230–231
  spills program, 263–264, 266
Dow Chemical Co. v. Dole, 72n., 323
Henry Dreyfuss Associates, 95
Drugs see Pharmaceuticals and drugs
Du Pont de Nemours and Co., Inc. v. Hall, 65–66, 72
Dusts, "nuisance," threshold limits for, 381, 397
Duty of care (due care), 7, 10–21, 65–68

Earth-moving equipment, 86, 246–247
Electic eye, 212
"Electric-heater failure":
  fault tree analysis of, 141–142
  FMEA exploration of, 132, 136, 139, 141–145
Electrical appliances (household), 29, 31, 40, 162
Electrical/electronic equipment and systems checklists, 353–366
  bonding, 363–364
  cable measurements, 361
  cable shielding, 360
  connectors, 361–363
  corrosion, 364
  coupling, 360–361
  discrete components, 365
  electromagnetic compatibility, 356–357
  filtering, 364–365
  general considerations, 353–356
  grounding, 354, 364
  installation and maintenance, 356
  interference-free component selection, 359
  power supplies, 366
  relays, 366
  shielding, 358–360
  spurious resonances elimination, 358
  spurious responses elimination, 357–359
  static charges, 365
  test equipment, 365
  testing, 366
  transmission lines, 361
Electrical/electronic industries:
  hazardous wastes (table), 229
Electrical hazards, 50, 111, 143, 151, 159
  "electrical widget" failure analysis, 118–121, 124
  light-bulb, explosion activator, 279–280
  shock hazards to adult males (chart), 112–113
"Electrical widget" failure analysis, 118–121, 124
Electricity equipment industry insurance, 290, 294
Electromagnetic compatibility (checklist), 356–357
Electronic products, 209
  "burn-in" test, 128, 172
  ground-support equipment failure, 170–171
  production error rates (table), 148
  and purchased components, 167–169
Electroplating and metal finishing industries, 229
Elkind, Arnold, 279
Emergency response procedures:
  for recalls, 221–224
  for spills, 264, (chart) 266
  "substantial product hazard" notification, 93, 169, 223
Engineering analyst, tasks of, 115, 117–120, 127
Engineers:
  design see Design engineers
  human factors, 106, 111, 115
  "test-development," 103

GENERAL INDEX **669**

Engineers Joint Council, 279
Engines and turbines industry insurance, 290, 292, 294, 296
Environmental Defense Fund, 245, 246
Environmental Protection Agency (EPA), 229
  bans, 35, 61
  chemicals data bank, 35, 226–227
  "new" chemical, defined, 35
  and premarket reporting and testing of chemicals, 32–35
  spills contingency plan, 264–266
  "target" substances list, 35, 234
  toxic substances control, 32–35
Escola v. Coca Cola, 10
Ethane, 386, 399, 439
Ethics, professional, 83–85, 87, 279
Ethylene, 387, 399, 440
Ethylene glycol, 270, 272, 273
Ethylene oxide, 250–251, 254
Expert witness, 14–15, 279, 280
  roles of, 282–286
Explosions, 68
  detection checklist, 351
  explosive reactions of solvents with N_2O_4 (table), 248
  light-bulb defect in plant explosion case, 279–280
  of oil-fueled space heaters, 218
Explosives, 151, 231, 258
Explosives industry:
  hazardous wastes in (table), 229
  liability case, 65
Exposure limits, 228, 231–235
  Biologic Limit Values (BLVs), 394
  chemical impacts and impact values in transportation accidents (table), 270–273
  concentration calculations, 267–269, 274
  and hazard levels of substances in spills (tables), 232–233
  lethal concentrations (LCs) in air, 235, 268
  lethal doses (LDs) *see* Lethal doses
  OSHA standards for sixteen compounds (table), 399
  Threshold Limit Values *see* Threshold Limit Values of toxic substances
  For specific toxic substances *see* alphabetical listings in Appendix B, 379–399

Failure analysis, 99, 115–147
  and "bathtub" curve model of product behavior, 127–128, 170–172
  of complex products, 119–120, 170–176
  defined, 647
  of "electrical widget," 118–121, 124
  Failure Modes and Effects Analysis (FMEA) technique, 118, 120–121, 129–147, 647
  failure rates, estimation and determination of, 103–105, 134–138
    (*See also* Failure rates)
  fault tree analysis technique, 99, 118–129, 131, 141–143, 176
  identifying and evaluating product hazards (chart), 116, 117
  and reliability (probability of survival) estimations, 172–174, 176
    (*See also* Hazards analysis)
Failure Modes and Effects Analysis (FMEA), 118, 120, 121, 129–147
  cost estimations, 137–138, 144–145
  defined, 647

Failure Modes and Effects Analysis (FMEA) (*Cont.*):
  "electric heater failure" example of, 131–134, 136, 139, 141–145
  failure classifications, 137
  failure rates and, 134–138, 140, 146
  and fault tree analysis, 118, 120–121, 129, 131, 141–143
  format and procedure for, 131–134
  frequency of failure occurrence and, 131–138, 144–147
  frequency classifications, 136–138
  hazard analysis matrix, 131, 134, 135
  and imperilment, degrees of, 131–135, 140–141, 144, 147
  imperilment categories, 141
  precautions in use of (table), 146
  and severity of effects, 131–133, 138–140, 144, 145, 147
  severity scales, 139–140
  steps in (table), 131
Failure rates, 99, 127–128, 140, 145, 146
  "burn-in" and, 128, 172, 643
  in constant (or normal operating) period, 127, 128, 170, 171
  determination of, 134–138
  estimation of, 103–105
  failure rate, defined, 647
  in "infant mortality" period, 127–128, 170, 171
  information sources for, 134
  and mean time between failures (MTBF), 99, 173, 174, 651
  and probability of survival (reliability estimates), 172–174, 176
  and time between failures (TBF) calculation, 172–174
  vs. time ("bathtub" curve), 127–128, 170, 172
  and warranty, 103–105, 137–138, 145
  in wearout or "old age" period, 127, 128, 140, 170, 171
  (*See also* Hazard rates)
Failure to warn, 14, 241
Failures:
  catastrophic, 141, 157, 176
  degradation, 141
  fatigue, 159, 248
  faults, categories of, 85, 117
  frequency classifications, 137–138
  primary, 99
  spontaneous, 141
Farm and Industrial Equipment Institute, 317
Fasteners, 208
  checklists, 341–344
  tamperproof, 211, 213
Fault tree analysis (FTA), 118–129, 131, 176
  branches, 99, 120
  calculations, 121–129
  complex example of, 122–123
  defined, 647
  of "electrical widget failure," 118–121, 124
  fault categories, 85, 117
  and FMEA, 118, 120–121, 129, 131, 141–143
  format examples, 119, 120
  hazard rate calculations, 121–129
  and hazards checklist preparation, 99
  precautions in use of (table), 146
  procedure, 118–121, 129
  symbols, 118, 119
Faults, product liability categories of, 85, 117

670 GENERAL INDEX

Federal Aviation Administration, 26, 44, 285
   airline pilot restrictions, 39
Federal Boat Safety Act, 25
Federal Coal Mine Health and Safety Act, 25
Federal Communications Commission, 44, 45, 48
Federal Food, Drug, and Cosmetic Act, 25
Federal Hazardous Substances Act, 25, 29, 32, 46
Federal Highway Administration, 23–24
Federal Metal and Nonmetallic Mine Safety Act, 25
Federal Pesticide Control Act, 32
Federal Railroad Administration, 24
Federal Railroad Safety Act, 25
Federal Record-Retention Requirements Related to Product Safety and Liability, 547–584
Federal Register, 33, 59, 61–64
   example from (text), 63
   organization of rulings in, 61–63
   record retention requirements, 89, 547–584
Federal Register, Office of, 89
Federal Tort Claims Act, 325
Federal Trade Commission, 25, 32, 61
   warranty regulation powers, 29–30, 32
Federal Trade Commission Act, 30
Federal Water Pollution Control Act, 264
Feedback chain, 97, 193–202
   participant responsibilities, 193, 195–196
   and product defects as safety data, 99, 196–202
   and records, 193, 195–202
   service reports and, 99, 196–200
Feld, Lipman, 86
Field engineering, 104
Filtering, electrical/electronic (checklist), 364–365
Fire-extinguishing agents, 260–263
   classifications and ratings of (table), 260–261
   lethal concentrations of (table), 268
   physical properties of (table), 262
   physiological properties of (table), 268
   standards for use on mobile equipment (table), 258
   toxicity hazards, 260–261, (table) 268
Fire suppression:
   Air Force experience with, 258–263, 268
   airport fire control standards, 519
   automatic missile fire-control system, 154
   checklist for extinguishing and suppression systems, 352–353
   combustible vapor detection (checklist), 351
   detection and sensing devices, 257–258, 263
   detection checklists, 350–352
   electrical controls for, 263
   extinguisher classifications and ratings (table), 260–261
   extinguisher design liability case, 67
   extinguisher standards for mobile equipment (table), 258
   extinguishing agents, 258, 260–263
   fire classifications and symbols (table), 260–261
   and products needing "outside" protection, 263
   sprinkler systems, 259, 263
   system design, 257–263
   system for space station, 259
   toxicity hazards, extinguishers and, 260–261, (table) 268
Fires, 246
   Apollo Project, 225, 226
   classifications of (table), 260–261
   oil heater explosions and, 218
Fittings, 110, 163, 257
   checklist, 340–341

Fittings (*Cont.*):
   fatigue failures of, 159, 248
   for segregating incompatible systems, 247
Flame retardants, 225
   TRIS, 59, 242, 245–246
Flammable and combustible materials, 228
   and Apollo Project fire, 225, 226
   combustible vapor detection (checklist), 351
   compatibility and, 246, 247
   flammability evaluation difficulties, 234
   Flammable Fabrics Act, 25, 29, 176
   TRIS controversy, 59, 242, 245–246
Flammable Fabrics Act, 25, 29, 176
Flanagan, John, 105–106
Florida, 325
Fluids:
   compatibility with metals (tables), 249–250
   compatibility with nonmetals (table), 251
   cryogenic (tables), 249–251
   fuel and storage systems (checklists), 370–372
   fuels (tables), 249–251
   hydraulic, non-flammable, 257
   hydraulic, selection of (table), 252-253, (checklist) 367
   oxidizers (tables), 249–251
   (*See also* specific fluids)
Fluorine compatibility data, 249–251, 255
Fluorocarbons, 39, 61, 398
Food and Drug Administration (FDA), 25, 46–47, 61, 205, 243
Food products, 11, 19, 29
   botulism cases, 139
   dye, Red 2, 241
   food and drug laws, 8, 9, 32
   Pure Food and Drug Act, 8
   saccharin controversy, 242
Footprints-on-bombs mystery, 156
Forbes, 21
Ford Motor Company, 202
"Forensic engineering," 283
Forgings (checklist), 347
Fortune, 318
Francis, John J., 11
Frasca v. Prudential-Grace Lines, Inc., 326, 327
Freon, 248, 261, 263
Fuels, fluid:
   checklist for fuel and storage systems, 370–372
   compatibility data (tables), 249–251
"Full" and "limited" warranties, 30–32
Furnaces with open floor grills, 54
Furniture for children, 40

Gas Appliance Manufacturers Association, 54
Gases, 234, 291, 295
   asphyxiants, 381, 399
   combustible vapor detection (checklist), 351
   compatibility data, 249–251
   hospital segregation techniques, 247
   "inert," 381
   ionized, detectors of, 257
   irritant, 380
   pressurization and pneumatic equipment (checklists), 368–370
   toxic, 380, 381, 399
      For specific toxic substances *see* alphabetical listings in Appendix B, 379–399
   welding fumes, 394, 398–399
   (*See also* Vapors)

Gasket materials, 247, 248
    compatibility with common fluids (table), 250–251
    for propellants and oxidizing chemicals (table), 254–256
Gasoline, 47
    compatibility data, 250–251, 254
    as inherently unsafe product, 39
    Threshold Limit Value determination, 398
General Fire Extinguisher Corp. v. Hempstead, 67, 72
General Motors, 5, 12, 16–17
Generic standards, 57
Gilmore, Grant, 8
Glassmaking plant safety program, 230
Good Housekeeping Seal of Approval, 66, 69
Gottfried, Paul, 115*n*.
Government-industry data bank (GIDEP), 134
Government regulation:
    of consumer safety *see* Consumer product safety; Consumer Product Safety Commisson; Consumer Product Safety Act
    evolution of statutory law, 22–35
    and exemptions, 59
    first action on products, 8
    of hazardous materials handling *see* alphabetical listing of specific materials and regulations in Appendix C, 400–497
    major federal laws, 23–26
    of occupational safety, 2, 26–28
    and registry of regulations *see* Code of Federal Regulations (CFR) and *Federal Register*
    Restatement (second) of Torts and, 6–22
    standards *see* Standards
    and stockpiling of suspect products, 49
    (*See also* Regulatory process; specific regulatory agencies and laws)
Grass, artificial, 28
Greenman case, 11, 12
Grinding and abrasive products *see* Abrasive wheels and products
Grinding Wheel Institute, 317
Gross National Product, 4
Gryna, F. M., and J. M. Juran, 182
    Quality Planning and Analysis, 170*n*., 177
Guards, machinery, 210, 212–216
    feeding devices (table), 212, 214, 215
    framework and filler materials for (table), 216
    interlocking devices (table), 212, 280
    liability case involving, 280–281
    OSHA recommendations (tables), 212, 216

Hagopian, J.H., 267
Hall v. E.I. du Pont de Nemours and Co., Inc., 65–66, 72
Hamburger machine liability case, 194
Hanberry v. Hearst Corp. 66, 69–70, 72
Hand, Learned, 21
Hand tools, powered, insurance and, 290, 294
Handbook & Standard for Manufacturing Safer Consumer Products (CPSC), 101
Harper, William, 284
Hazard, inherent, and responsibility to warn, 202–206
Hazard detection checklists, 349–352
    combustible vapor, 351
    explosion, 351–352
    fire, 350–351
    toxic vapor, 352
    warning signals, 352

Hazard levels, 228, 232, 233
    categorized, 648
    concentration limits, calculation of, 267–269, 274
    lethal doses, 228, 231–235
    (*See also* Lethal doses)
Hazardous materials, 169, 225–229
    chemical hazards checklist, 227
    cleaning agents, 53, 248
    compatibility considerations, 246–257
    concentration limits, calculation of, 267–269, 274
    delivery truck for, unsafe, 106
    FDA and, 46
    fire extinguisher standards for mobile equipment (table), 258
    flammable *see* Flammable and combustible materials
    mixtures of, and concentration limits, 267
    spills *see* Spills
    transportation modes and mishaps (table), 270–273
    transportation regulations for handling specific materials *see* alphabetical listing, by material, in Appendix C, 401–497
    transportation safety program at Dow, 264
    and warnings, packaging, 208
    in waste streams, industrial (chart), 229
    waste treatment processes (table), 236–237
    (*See also* Toxic substances)
Hazardous materials handling, federal regulations for *see* Appendix C, 401–497
Hazardous Substances Act, Federal, 25, 29, 32, 46
Hazards analysis:
    caution system, 100
    and design records, 195
    and design review process, 100–105
    and faults, categories of, 85, 117
    hazard, defined, 648
    hazard control checklist, preparation of, 95–100
    hazard rate, defined, 121
    hazard rate calculations, 121–129
    identification of product hazards, 75, 77, 95–100, (chart) 116
    matrix, 131, 134, 135
    reviews (chart), 102, 195
    and warning responsibilities and procedures, 202–206
    (*See also* Failure analysis)
Health, Education and Welfare Department (HEW), 27
Health Industry Manufacturers Association, 317
Hearst Corp v. Hanberry, 66, 69–70, 72
Heffron, Howard A., 46–48
Helium, 249
Hempstead v. General Fire Extinguisher Corp., 67, 72
Henderson, James, 22
Henningson v. Chrysler Corp., 11
Herbicides, 291, 294
Highchairs, infant, 40
Highway Safety Act, 23, 25
"Hold harmless" contract clauses, 322, 324
Holmes, Oliver Wendell, 8
Hooper, T.J., case, 21
Hoppe v. Midwest Conveyor Company Inc., 68*n*
Horwitz, Morton J., 10
Hospital equipment industry insurance, 17, 293, 296
Hospitals, 36
    nationwide injury-reporting system (NEISS), 52–53
    poison control centers, 36
    techniques for segregating materials, 247
Hotpoint, 56

672 GENERAL INDEX

Household products, 4, 38–40
Hulme, H. D., 195n.
Human factors, 83, 105–115
   audio signals evaluation (table), 107
   and control design, 149–150
   controls checklist, 332
   and design team effort, 111
   displays checklist, 331–332
   and electrical hazards circumvention, 111–113
   electrical shock hazard measurements (chart), 112–113
   foundations of, 105–106
   and production operations, 151–154
   stress reactions and performance, 151–152
   "subjective lowered standard" phenomenon, 151
   testing programs, 111
   in training-equipment design, 111, 114
   vibration tolerance (chart), 114
Human factors engineers, 106, 111, 115
Human performance:
   audio signals evaluation (table), 107
   design principles for improving, 147–156
   discomfort and, 151
   footprints-on-bombs mystery, 156
   and instructions, clarity of, 154–156
   in passive or repetitious tasks, 152–156
   "population stereotypes" and, 149–150
   stress and, 149–152
   "vigilance effect" in, 152–154
Hydraulic equipment and systems, 163
   checklists, 366–368
Hydraulic fluids, 246, 247
   nonflammable, 257
   selection of (table), 252–253, (checklist), 367
Hydrazine compatibility data (tables), 249–251, 254–256
Hydrogen, 388, 399
   compatibility data (tables), 249–251, 256
Hydrogen peroxide, 249–251, 254

Illinois Law Review, 9
Imperilment:
   categories of (table), 141
   defined, 133–134
   in FMEA, 131–135, 140–141, 144, 147
   and hazard analysis matrix, 134, 135
Implied warranty, 10, 32, 206
Indemnity, 323, 324, 327
Industrial hygiene:
   Dow "product stewardship" program, 227, 230–231
   and occupational exposure hazards, 231-235, 238, 239
   (*See also* Toxic substances)
Industrial machinery, 246
   and insurance, liability, 290, 294, 300, 314
   safety guards, 210, 212–216
"Infant mortality" period:
   burn-in, defined, 643
   burn-in test, 128
   described, 171
   and failure rate predictions, 127–128, 170, 171
Infrared radiation, 257
Inhibiting limit (IL), 228
Injury-reporting systems, 52–53
   NEISS, 52, 53, 139, 140
   severity classifications, 138–140

"Innocent bystander" liability rights, 13, 22, 75
Inspection, 159, 160, 167
   artificial defects as aid in, 154
   defect detection and errors in, 147, 153–154
   levels, 186
   vigilance effect in, 152–154
   (*See also* Sampling)
Installation, 38, 103, 104, 220
   of electrical/electronic equipment (checklist), 356
   incorrect, 110, 175, 194
   (*See also* Checklists for designers and installers, Appendix A, 329–377)
Institute of Electrical and Electronic Engineers (IEEE), 54, 58
Instructions, 38, 39, 103, 208
   audio-visual aids, 155–156
   checklist, 334
   manuals, effective, preparation of, 154–155
   package-handling, 208
   for production operations, 154–159
   (*See also* Warnings)
Instruments, medical, 293, 296
Insurance, product liability, 15–19, 81, 117, 275, 287–327
   (a) rates, 290–293, 297, 300, 312–313
   aggregate limits rates, 293, 297
   average rate as percentage of sales (table), 294–296
   basic limits rates, 289–294, 301–302, 309, 312–313
   "captive companies" and, 16, 316, 318–319
   "case reserve" funds, 315–316
   claims-handling, 17, 275, 315–316
   composite rating method, 301, 306, 307
   Comprehensive General Liability Policy (CGL), 292, 293, 297, 302, 303, 309
   costs (chart), 289
   and court action settlements, 275
   coverage and rating plans, by company size (table), 297
   credibility in rate-making, 304n., 306–307
   deductibles, 16, (table) 18, 298, 316–317
   "excess" or "umbrella" policies, 297, 298, 308, 317
   experience modification rating method, 297, 302–305
   high-risk industries, 299–300
   joint underwriting associations (JUAs), 321
   loss adjustment expenses (chart), 316
   loss control surveys, 313–315
   loss rating method, 301, 306–308
   manual rates, 290–293, 309, 312
   Monoline (CGL) policies, 297, 309, 312
   "not admitted" (surplus lines) insurors, 316, 319, 321
   package policies, 292–293, 302
   and plaintiff awards, rise in, 15–19
   "Plan D" retro rating plan, 307, 308
   premium volumes of major types of insurors (table), 288
   premiums and coverage, negotiation of, 287–313
   primary coverage policies, 292–293, 297–298, 316–317
   product categories under special scrutiny (table), 19
   product hazard premium (CGL) development, 303
   products recall coverage, 17
   professional engineer and, 85–86
   prospective (guaranteed cost) rating plan, 301, 307
   rate increases, 16–17, 287, 289–293, 300
   reinsurors and reinsurance transactions, 298, 299, 319, (table) 320
   retrospective rating plans, 301, 307–308, 310–311

GENERAL INDEX **673**

Insurance, product liability (*Cont.*):
  schedule modification rating method, 302–303, 306
  self-insurance programs, 16, 316–318
  self-insurance survey (table), 317
  "self-rating" accounts, 307
  "sistership exclusions," 17
  statute of limitations in, 298
  surplus lines insurors, 319, 321
  in target product classifications (tables), 18, 290–296, 299–300, 314, 320
  traditional rating method, 301–307
  "umbrella" or "excess" policies, 297, 298, 308, 317
  "unconventional" programs, 316–321
  underwriting decisions, factors in, 298–301
  when an insuror sues, 322–327
  workers' compensation and, 316, 322–327
Insurance Company of North America (INA), 17
Insurance industry, 4–5, 31–32, 36, 37, 275, 287–327
  "assigned risk" pools, 321
  captive companies, 16, 316, 318–319
  joint underwriting associations (JUA), 321
  medical malpractice policies, 17, 321
  New York City, "free trade zone," 321
  "not admitted" (surplus lines) insurors, 316, 319, 321
  product categories under special scrutiny (table), 19
  product liability insurance *see* Insurance, product liability
  products recall coverage, 17
  reinsurance transactions, 298, 319, (table) 320
  responses to rise in liability awards, 15–19
  Underwriters Laboratories, 54, 58, 67, 102, 143, 218, 260
  underwriting decisions, factors in, 298–301
Insurance Information Institute, 4–5, 36
Insurance Institute for Highway Safety, 36, 39
Insurance Services Office (ISO), 287, 289, 307, 309, 311*n*., 312, 316
  product code and liability rates, 294–296
Interagency Task Force on Product Liability surveys, 287*n*., 289–303, 314–320, 323*n*., 324–327
Interlocks, safety, 24, 98, 280
  for guarding machinery (table), 212
Internal Revenue Service, 318
International Standards Organization, 169
Interstate Commerce Commission, 24, 43–44
Ionized gas detectors, 257

Jacobs, Richard, 101, 206*n*.
Janata, Rudolph, 13–14
Jennings, William C., 44, 46–48
Jensen, Ralph A., 266
Julien, Alfred, 14, 280
Juran, J. M., and F.M. Gryna, 182
  Quality Planning and Analysis, 170*n*.
Juris Doctor, 6*n*., 15
Jury Verdict Research, Inc., 7, 17–18
Justice Department, U.S., 87

Kaiser, Henry J., 36
Kaitz, Edward M., 6
Kasel v. Remington Arms Co., Inc., 69, 72
Kerosene, 249, 251, 254
Kitchen tools, 39–40
Kohlmeier, Louis M., Jr., 43

Labels and labeling, 29, 38, 102, 246, 264
  direction-of-movement indicator, 149
  hazardous materials *see* transportation regulations, Appendix C, 401–497
  packaging, 167, 208
  of production materials, 159–160
  warnings, 159–160, 208
Labor Department, U.S., 25, 26
Labor unions:
  and occupational safety regulation, 26–27, 36–37
Law of Torts, The (Prosser), 65, 67, 68
Law-school courses in products law, 21–22
Lawn, synthetic, 28
Lawnmower hazards, 151, 212–213
Lawyer's Desk Reference, 21
Lead, 229
Leather, 229, 248
Legal implications:
  of contract warranty doctrine, 10–12
  in evolution of court decisions, 6–22
  of negligence issues, 7, 10, 20, 21, 65–68, 277, 323–327
  of privity, 7–11, 13, 67
  of Restatement (second) of Torts, 6–22, 66
  in statutory law, evolution of, 22–35
  of strict liability, 7, 8, 10–14, 23, 68–70, 278
  (*See also* Court action; Legislation; Litigation, product liability)
Legislation, 23–35
  "class action" suits and, 37
  consumer organizations and, 37
  on hazardous materials handling *see* Appendix C, 400–497
  major federal laws (table), 25
  organizational support for, 35–37
  and premarket notification procedure (chart), 34–35
  statutory law, evolution of, 22–35
  (*See also* Government regulation and specific laws)
Lethal doses (LDs), 228, 231–235
  defined, 231, 232*n*, 234–235
  exposure limit standards for specific substances, Appendix C, 370–399
  hazard and toxicity measurements (tables), 232–233
  inhalation, 234, 235
  oral, 234
  skin-absorption, 234, 381
    (*See also* tables of exposure limits, 382–395, 397)
  synergism and toxicity, 231, 235, 267, 274
Levitan, Sar, 36–37
Lewis, William Draper, 9
Liability and the Engineer: Responsibility to the Public (Feld), 86*n*.
Lifting and positioing equipment, (checklist), 373–377
Litigation, product liability, 50
  and accident investigations and reports, 218–221, 275–276
  assumption-of-risk argument, 20
  Bon Vivant Soups botulism case, 139
  bottle "crack map," courtroom exhibit, 284
  bottle-fracture case, 284
  Campo Doctrine and, 20
  carburetor failure case, 86
  "class action" suits, 37
  consumer movement and, 3, 7
  contract warranty doctrine and, 10–12
  "contributory negligence" in, 17, 20, 277, 323–327
  and court decisions, evolution in, 6–22
  Cronin v. J.B.E. Olson Corp., 23

Litigation, product liability (*Cont.*):
  defense arguments (table), 277–279
  delaying tactics, company, 49
  design engineer and, 85–86, 276–282, 286
  "Dole" rule, 323–324
  Dole v. Dow Chemical Co., 72n., 323
  and duty of (due) care, 7, 10–21, 65–68
  Escola v. Coca Cola, 10
  expert witnesses and, 14–15, 279, 280, 282–286
  Frasca v. Prudential-Grace Lines, Inc., 326, 327
  Greenman case, 11, 12
  Henningson v. Chrysler Corp., 11
  "hold harmless" clause, 322, 324
  indemnity and, 323, 324, 327
  "innocent bystander" liability rights, 13, 22, 75
  insurance and rise in plantiff awards, 15–19
  and insurance claims, 14, 275
    (*See also* Insurance industry; Insurance, product liability)
  liability settlements vs. safe design costs, 102–103
  light-bulb guilty in plant explosion case, 279–280
  loss potential due to (chart), 84
  and machine-tool safety-device rulings, 210, 212–213, 281
  MacPherson v. Buick Motor Co., 8–10
  negligence theories and, 7, 10, 14, 20, 64–68, 277, 279, 323–327
  plane propeller case, 285–286
  records retention and, 89, 91, 198, 200, 276, 277
  and Restatement (second) of Torts, 6–22
  settlements, out-of-court, 17–18
  state-of-the-art argument, 21, 277
  and statutory law, evolution of, 22–35
  strict liability defenses (table), 278
  strict liability interpretations, 7, 8, 10–14, 21, 23, 64, 68–70, 72, 241, 278
  Sunspan Engineering and Construction Co. v. Spring-Lock Scaffolding, 325
  third-party suits, 322–327
  against trademark licensor, 69–70, 72
  worker's compensation cases, 322–327
  (*See also* Court action; and specific cases)
Lloyds of London, 321
Lockheed, 189
Long-lived products, 196
  liability for, 22–23, 210, 212, 215
  product-safety approaches to, 210, 212–217
Longshoremen's and Harbor Workers' Compensation Act, 324–327
Lubricants:
  hydraulic fluids, lubricity of (table), 253
  for use with propellants and oxidizing chemicals (table), 254–256

McCarran-Ferguson Act, 31
Machine tool guards, 210, 212–216, 281
  feeding devices, (table) 212, 214, 215
  frame and filler materials for (table), 216
  interlocking devices, (table) 212, 280
  liability case involving, 280–281
  OSHA recommendations, (table) 212, (table) 216
Machine-tool industry insurance, 287
Machine tools:
  guards for, 7, 210, 212–216, 280–281
  tamperproofing, 210, 213
  and test facilities, built-in, 217

Machinery, industrial:
  and insurance, product liability, 18, 290, 294, 300, 314, 320
Machinery and Allied Products Institute (MAPI), 317
Machinery Dealers National Association, 317
McKenzie, R. M., 154n.
Mckinsey and Company, 287n., 319
MacPherson v. Buick Motor Company, 8–10
Magnuson-Moss Warranty Act, 25
  described, 29–32
  exemptions, 30–32
Magnuson-Moss Warranty–Federal Trade Commission Improvement Act (Title I), 25
Maintainability, 198
  checklist, 332–333
  defined, 651
Maintenance, 38, 103
  defined, 651
  of electrical/electronic equipment (checklist), 356
  and packaging choices (table), 207
Management:
  abrogation of safety efforts by, 83–85
  complaints and claims-handling, 196, 198, 218–221, 275
  and court action *see* Court action
  design review participants (table), 104
  maintainability, sectors involved in, (chart), 198
  and maintenance of safety program effectiveness, 82–83
  and outside consultant, use of, 87–89
  policy statement on safety, 73–76
  product-development roles of participating sectors (table), 81
  product safety system organization, 76–79, 93
  (*See also* Product safety system)
Manual rates, 290–293, 309, 312
Manufacturing Chemists Association, 226
Manufacturing department, 81, 104
Marketing:
  feedback chain and, 193, 195–202
  handling claims and complaints, 196, 198, 218–221, 275
  premarketing notification procedure for toxic substances (chart), 34
  and product development process, 81, 97, 103, 104
  and product recalls, 221–224
  (*See also* Recalls)
  records, 92, 193, 195–202
  reporting requirement for product hazards, 49
  responsibility to warn, 202–206
  stockpiling suspect products, 49
Marsh Wood Products Co. v. Babcock and Wilcox Co., 68
Maslow, Jonathan Evan, 6n.
Mass transit, 24
Massachusetts Area Council of Independent Testing Labs, Inc., 317
Massachusetts Institute of Technology (MIT), 226
Masselli, David, 176
Material handling, 159–160
  equipment (checklists), 372–377
  fire-extinguisher standards for mobile equipment (table), 258
  hazardous materials regulations, Appendix C, 401–497
Materials:
  compatibility considerations, 246–257
  hazardous *see* Hazardous materials; Toxic substances

Materials (*Cont.*):
  from outside suppliers, 160, 166–170, 226
  production, 158–160, 166–170
  quality control and (table), 164
  raw, 159–160
  records of incoming, 159, 167–168
  structural (checklist), 339–340
  (*See also* specific materials)
Materials technology department (chart), 161
Mayo, Elton, 105
Mean time between failures (MTBF), 173, 174
  defined, 651
Mean time to failure, 172
  defined, 651
Medical and health services professions, 36, 37
  malpractice insurance, 17, 321
Medical data sheet, 239
Medical devices, 25, 29
  and insurance, product liability (tables), 293, 296, 300, 314, 320
Medicine, preventive, 36
Mercury, 211, 229
Metal castings industry insurance, 18, 290, 294, 300, 314, 320
Metal-working machinery and equipment industry insurance, 290, 294
Metals:
  combustible, fire extinguisher for, 261
  compatibility with common fluids (table), 249–251
  ferrous and nonferrous castings industry, insurance data for, 18, 290, 294, 300, 314, 320
  processing industries insurance rates, 290, 294
  structural materials checklist, 339–340
  for use with propellants and oxidizing chemicals (table), 254–256
  (*See also* specific metals)
Methanol, 270–272
Methyl chloride, 231
Methylene chloride, 248
Michigan Chemical, 255
Midwest Conveyor Company, Inc. v. Hoppe, 68n.
Mihalasky, John, 206n.
Mining, 36, 229
Mists, toxic, 267
  (*See also* Vapors)
Misuse, as defense argument, 278
Mobile equipment, fire-extinguisher standards for (table), 258
Monel, 251
Monoline insurance policy, 297, 312
  defined, 309n.
Monomethylhydrazine, 256
Mosk, Stanley, 280
Motor vehicles, 50, 223
  industry insurance rates, 292, 296
  mandatory recall requirement, 26
  safety regulation of, 3, 23–24, 26, 29
  (*See also* Automobiles; and other specific vehicles)
Motorcycle helmets, 19
Motorcycles, 23
Mundel, August B., 129n.
Mutagenicity and mutations in Ames test, 243–245

Nader, Ralph, 5–7, 13, 21
National Aeronautics and Space Administration, 26
National Association of Fire Equipment Distributors, 258, 260
National Association of Manufacturers, 21
National Bureau of Standards (NBS), 27, 54, 58
  fire safety reports, 52
  organization of (chart), 55
National Business Council for Consumer Affairs, Sub-Council on Product Safety, 53, 54
National Cancer Institute, 245
National Commission on Product Safety, 4, 20, 21, 52, 279
National Conference on Control of Hazardous Material Spills, 232, 267, 270
National Electrical Code, 373, 605
National Electrical Manufacturers Association (NEMA), 54, 58
National Electronic Injury Surveillance System (NEISS), 52–53
  injury-reporting system (chart), 52–53
  severity of injury index, 139, (table) 140
National Fire Codes, 351, 352
National Fire Protection Association, 351, 352, 373
National Football League Players Association, 28
National Highway Traffic Adminstration:
  organizational structure (chart), 47
  safety functions, 24
  standards, 24
National Institute of Allergy and Infectious Diseases, 240
National Institute for Occupational Safety and Health (NIOSH), 27, 234–235
  "carcinogenic materials" list, 235
  "priority list" of toxic chemical standards, 235
  toxic substances listings, 234, 235
  workplace injury reports, 52–53
National Institutes of Health, 227, 242, 274
National Machine Tool Builders Association, 317
National Oil and Hazardous Substances Pollution Contingency Plan, 264–265
  "National Strike Force," 264
  organization of (chart), 265
National Society of Professional Engineers, 279
National Traffic and Motor Vehicle Safety Act, 3, 23, 25, 26
National Transportation Safety Board, 26
Negligence, 7, 10, 279
  contributory, 17, 20, 277, 323–327
  defense arguments (table), 277
  in duty of (due) care, 7, 10, 21, 65–68
  liability in standards-setting, 64–68, 70
Neon, 390, 399, 465
Neoprene, 248, 251
Nervous system disorders, PBBs and, 225
New York City, 321, 323–324
New York State Insurance Department, 17
Newport Air Park v. United States, 326
Nickel, 251
Nitric acid, compatibility of, 246, 249–251, 255
Nitrilotriacetic acid (NTA), 225
Nitrogen, 249–251
Nitrogen tetroxide, explosive reactions with solvents (table), 248
Nitromethane, 255
Noise as occupational hazard, 27–28, 97, 111
Nonmetals:
  compatibility with common fluids (table), 251
  as structural materials (checklist), 340

GENERAL INDEX

Normal (or constant) operating service period, 127, 128, 170
   defined, 171
Nuclear Regulatory Commission, 265
Nuisance particulates (dusts):
   listed, 397
   threshold limits for, 381

Occupational safety, 39
   accidents, 4, 7, 11, 37, 210, 213, 242, 325–327
   "black lung" disease, 36
   labor unions and, 26–27, 36–37
   machine-tool guards, 210, 212–216
   noise hazard, 27, 28, 97, 111
   and safety equipment design, 27–28
   and standards, "sweetheart," 27
   stressed and passive tasks and, 151–156
   and toxic substances, exposure to, 231–239
   (See also Toxic substances)
Occupational Safety and Health Act, 2, 24–27, 29, 32, 61, 235
Occupational Safety and Health Administration (OSHA), 4, 25–28, 64, 169–170, 203, 206, 231, 235
   fire-extinguisher standards (table), 258
   job restrictions, 39
   machinery guards, recommendations for, 212, 213, 216
   and safety equipment design, 26–28
   toxic substances exposure standards, 379, 380, (table) 399
   tractor safety requirement, 37
   vapor concentration limits, 267, 269
Office of Engineering Standards Services, 54
Office of the Federal Register, 62
Oil see Petroleum
Oil heater accidents, 218, 223
Olson, J.B.E., Corp. v. Cronin, 23
On the Accuracy of Inspectors (McKenzie), 154n.
Opatow, Lorna, 207
Operator performance see Human performance
Otis, Arthur, 105
Outside consultants, 85–90
Outside suppliers, use of, 166–170, 226
   checklist for, 167
   and contracts, purchasing, 166–167, 169
   flow of materials to stock from (chart), 168
   foreign, 169
   policy statement and, 73–74
   quality assurance requirements, 166–167
   and quality control, 169
   records and, 167
   and "second sourcing," 169
   and specifications, 166–168
   standards and, 166, 167, 169
   and "substantial product hazards" notifications, 167, 169
   testing and, 166–168
Oxidizer fluids, compatibility of (tables), 249–251
Oxidizing chemicals, materials for use with (table), 254–256
Oxygen, 255
   and Apollo Project fire, 225, 226
   and asphyxiant hazards, 381
   compatibility data, 249–251
   high-pressure (checklist), 369
Ozone, 61, 257

Packaging, 38, 167, 206–210, 246
   "child-proof" closures, 36, 57, 208
   defined, 653
   described, 206–207
   environmental factors and (checklist), 336–337
   goals, 207–208
   hazardous materials regulations see alphabetical listing, by material, Appendix C, 401–497
   identification and marking, 208, (checklist), 337–338
   maintenance factors in choice of (table), 207
   mercury spills kit, 211
   Poison Prevention Packaging Act, 25, 29, 36, 63
   safety techniques for, 208–211
   sheet-metal housings, 209, 210
   storage considerations, 208
   tamperproofing devices, 209, 211, 213
   transportability (checklist), 337
   warnings and instructions, 208–209
"Packaging—Handling and Products Safety" (Jacobs and Mihalasky), 206n.
Packaging Impact: It's What They Think They See That Counts (Opatow), 207n.
Packing, 246, 253
   defined, 653
   for use with propellants and oxidizing chemicals (table), 254–256
Paint and dye industries, 229
Paints and coatings, 47, 253
Pan American World Airways, 246, 264
Parts see Components
Pawlak, Ronald, 281
Pennsylvania, 325–326
   Department of Health, 380n.
Pentaborane compatibility data, 249–251
Pentagon, 231
Perchloroethylene, 248
Performance Decrement Under Psychological Stress (Berkun), 152
Performance measures, 111
"Performance" standards, 56–57
Pesticide industry:
   and hazardous wastes (table), 229
   product liability insurance rates, 291, 295
Pesticides, 19, 29, 471
   Federal Pesticide Control Act, 32
Peters, George, 282–283
Petroleum, 257
   and hazardous industrial waste (table), 229
   and hydraulic fluid selection (table), 252–253
   processing-plant explosion case, 279–280
   spills, contingency plan for, 264, 265
Pharmaceuticals and drugs:
   allergic reactions and liability claims, 240–241
   and hazardous industrial wastes (table), 229
   and insurance, product liability, 15–16, (tables) 18, 19, 293, 296, 300, 314, 320
Phosphate esters, hydraulic fluid selection and (table), 252–253
Phosphates, 225
   TRIS (2,3 dibromopropyl) phosphate, 59, 242, 245–246
Pins (checklist), 344
Pipe, galvanized, 248
Pipelines, gas and liquid, 24, 26, 50
Plane propeller case, 285–286
Pneumatic equipment and systems (checklist), 369–379
Poison control centers, 36
Poison Prevention Packaging Act, 25, 29, 36, 63

Poisonous gases *see* Gases
Poisons, "child-proof" containers for, 36, 57
Policy statement on product safety, corporate, 73–76, 91
Polybrominated biphenyls (PBBs), 225
Polychlorinated biphenyls (PCBs), banned, 35
Polytetrafluoroethylene decomposition products, 398
Polyurethane, 234, 247
Polyvinyl chloride (PVC), 4, 19
"Population stereotypes," 149–150
Potts, Percival, 242
Power press standard, 27
Pratt and Whitney, 189
Prediction techniques, 115–147
  "bathtub" curve model of product behavior, 127–128, 170–172
  and engineering analyst, tasks of, 115, 117
  failure modes and effects analysis (FMEA), 118, 120, 121, 129–147
  fault categories as liability indicators, 85, 117
  fault tree analysis, 99, 118–129, 131, 141–143, 176
  hazards identification and evaluation (chart), 116
  testing, 115, 117, 124, 127–128, 176
Premarket notification procedure (chart), 34–35
Pressure vessels (checklist), 369
Pressurization and pneumatic equipment and systems (checklists), 368–370
Preventive medicine, 36
Pricing and safe-product considerations, 50, 54
Printing and duplicating industries, and hazardous wastes (table), 229
Privity, 7–11, 67
  as "citidel" against liability, 7–10, 13
Probability, 115, 117
Probability-of-occurrence, 117
  calculations, in fault tree form, 121–129
Procter and Gamble, 241
Procurement *see* Purchasing
Product analysis program, INA, 17
Product attributes, 38
  and liability, potential, 12
Product behavior prediction *see* Prediction techniques
Product defect as liability defense, 13, 14, 18
Product development, 95–156
  corporate safety group participation in, 95–96, 99
  departmental roles in (table) 81, (table) 104
  design process (chart), 96
  design review and, 100–105, 193, 206
  engineering analyst tasks in, 115, 117–121, 127
  evolution of product (chart), 97
  example (chipper-mulcher) of, 98
  fault categories and potential liability, 117
  hazard analysis as first need, 95–100
  hazard analysis checklist, preparation of, 99–100
  hazard caution system and, 100
  hazard reviews (table), 102
  human factors considerations, 105–115
  prediction techniques, 115–147
    (*See also* Prediction techniques)
  profitability: safety-related costs vs. liability claims, 101–103
  records, 91–92, 195, 198, 200
  and techniques to minimize human error, 147–156
  "test development engineer" and, 103
  (*See also* Product safety)
Product liability:
  assumption-of-risk arguments, 20
  Campo Doctrine and, 20

Product liability (*Cont.*):
  contract warranty and, 10–12
  costs, 102–103, 313
  culpable product characteristics (table), 12
  defect as defense, 13, 14, 18
  of design engineers, 85–86
  and "economically" safe presumptions, 138
  extensions of, 13
  "failure to warn" argument, 14, 241
  fault categories and, 81, 117
  "innocent bystander" and, 13, 22, 75
  insurance industry and rise in plaintiff awards, 15–19
    (*See also* Insurance industry; Insurance, product liability)
  litigation *see* Litigation, product liability
  for long-lived products, 22–23, 210, 212, 215
  and loss control surveys, insurance, 313–315
  and loss potential (chart), 84
  and machine tool safety devices, 210, 212–216, 281
  negligence principles and, 7, 10, 14, 20, 21, 64–68, 277, 279, 323–327
  and organized pressures for safer products, 35–37
  of outside consultant, 85–86
  outside suppliers and, 160, 166–170, 226
  potential, criteria for (table), 12
  products under special scrutiny by insurors (table), 19
  records retention and, 89–92, 198, 200
  and Restatement (second) of Torts, 6–22
  and standards, voluntary, 20–21
  of standards-setters, ANSI memorandum on, 64–72
  state-of-the-art argument, 21, 277
  strict liability interpretations, 7, 8, 10–14, 21, 23, 64, 68–70, 72, 241, 278
  third-party, 322–327, 379
  of trademark licensor, 69–70, 72
  "unreasonably dangerous" concept in, 18, 20, 22, 35
  and worker's compensation cases, 322–327
Product Liability and Safety (Peters), 282–283
Product Risks: Prediction Techniques (Gottfried), 115*n*.
"Product rule," 176
Product safety, 1–41
  and change control, production, 189–191
  consumer acceptance of risk and, 20, 38–41, 278
  consumer movement and, 3, 5–7, 21, 23, 36, 37, 57
  and court decisions, evolution in, 6–22
  government regulation of *see* Government regulation; Regulatory process
  health professions support for, 35–37
  how safe is "safe"?, 37–41, 50
  insurance interests and, 36
  labor unions and, 36–37
  organized support for, growth of, 35–37
  outside suppliers and, 160, 166–170, 226
  pressures for, 1–6, 35–37
  in product development process *see* Product development
  profitability: safety-related costs vs. liability claims, 101–103
  records, 89–92, 193, 195, 198, 200–202
  regulation *see* Government regulation; Regulatory process; Standards
  Restatement (second) of Torts and, 6–22
  and standards, industry, 20–21, 52–54, 56–59
  and statutory law, evolution of, 22–35
    (*See also* specific laws)

Product safety (*Cont.*):
　"substantial product hazard," defined, 28
　"substantial product hazard" notification, 169, 223
　and warnings, manufacturer, 14, 20, 50, 65, 75, 202–206, 208, 241, 279
　　(*See also* Checklists for designers and installers, Appendix A, 329–377)
Product safety program:
　claims and complaints as safety data, 196–199
　design engineer, tasks of, 195, 202–203, 206
　design engineer as prime mover, 75–78
　director, 75, 78–80, 82, 193
　feedback chain and, 193, 195–202
　and insuror loss control surveys, 313–315
　management contravention of, 83–85
　policy statement, corporate, 73–76, 91
　profitability, 101–103
　records, 193, 195, 198, 200–202
　responsibility to warn, 75, 202–206
Product safety system, 73–93
　and autonomy of designer, 82
　checklist for, 93
　claims and complaints as problem indicators, 196–199
　design engineer, responsibilities of, 75, 195, 202, 206
　design engineer as prime mover in, 75–78
　and design review process, 100–105
　director: qualifications and responsibilities of, 75, 78–80, 82, 193
　emergency response documents and procedures, 92, 221–224
　feedback chain and, 193, 195–202
　hazard detection checklists, 349–352
　information flow (chart), 74, 76
　liability of designer and, 85–86
　and loss potential areas in liability (chart), 84
　maintaining effectiveness of, 82–83
　management contravention of designer and, 83–85
　organization of, 76–78
　and outside consultant, use of, 73–74, 87–89
　policy statement, corporate, 73–76, 91
　recall procedures, 221–224
　records and records retention, 89–92, 193, 195, 198, 200–202
　safety team organization (chart), 79
　(*See also* Product development; Product safety; Product safety program; Product safety team)
Product safety team:
　design engineer, responsibilities of, 75, 195, 202, 206
　feedback chain and, 193, 195–202
　organization of (chart), 79
　and product development, 95–96
　recall procedures, 221–224
　and records, standardization of, 201–202
　responsibility to warn, 75, 202–206
Production, 157–191
　assembly errors, 147, 148, 155, 159
　assembly substitutions, as hazards, 163, 196, 198
　change control, 189–191
　checklist, 158
　defect detection in inspection, 147, 153–154
　defects, chronic and sporadic (table), 177
　defects, service records as clue to, 196–198
　disposal of defective products, 162–163
　and failure patterns for complex products, 170–176
　　(*See also* Failure analysis)
　identifying causes of chronic defects, 161–162

Production (*Cont.*):
　inspection operations, 147, 153–154, 160, 161
　instructions, effective, preparation of, 154–159
　materials and material handling, 158–161, 168
　materials flow, 168
　minimizing human error, 147–156, 163
　and outside suppliers, use of, 160, 166–170, 226
　　(*See also* Purchasing)
　processes, 158, 160–163
　quality control tasks (table), 164–165
　records, 92, 159, 162, 166–168, 189–191
　repair and rework activities, 158, 162–163
　safety-related activities in, 157–160, 165–170
　sampling program, 176–188
　storage and, 158, 159, 162
　tests, planning guides for (table), 178
Productivity, 105
Products, long-lived, 22–23, 196, 210, 212, 215
Products Liability Comes of Age (Maslow), 6n.
"Products Liability of Members of Standards Writing Committees" (ANSI), 65n.
Professional Insurance Company, 17
Professional societies, 83–84, 279
　and ethics, 87, 279
　as standards-setters, 53, 54
　and standards-setting liability, 65–72
　(*See also* specific societies)
Propellants:
　fluorocarbon for aerosols, 39, 61
　materials for use with (table), 254–256
Propyl nitrate, 255
Propylene, 391, 399
Prosser, William, 8
　Horwitz on, 10
　Law of Torts, 65, 67, 68
　and Restatement (second) of Torts, 7, 10–12, 20
Prototype, 103
　birth of, 81
　defined, 655
　hazard reviews of, 102
Prudential-Grace Lines, Inc. v. Frasca, 326, 327
Psychology:
　Aviation Psychology Program, 106
　and human factors engineering, 105–106
Pulp and paper industries, 229
Purchasing, 74, 81, 161–162
　contracts, 166–167, 169
　outside suppliers, use of, 166–170, 226
Pure Food and Drug Act, 8

Quality assurance, 215
　and outside supplier, 166–167
　sporadic and chronic quality problems (table), 177
　tasks, 164–165
　(*See also* Sampling)
Quality control, 15, 77, 81, 104, 169
　and defects, sporadic and chronic (table), 177
　and mandatory recall legislation, 26
　sampling and *see* Sampling
　tasks in three basic areas (table), 164–165
　(*See also* Quality assurance)
Quality Planning and Analysis (Juran and Gryna), 170n., 177

Radio, 291, 295
Radioactivity, 228

GENERAL INDEX 679

Railroads, 264
   chemical transportation modes and mishaps (table), 270–271
   government regulation of, 24, 25, 43–44
   hazardous materials transportation regulations (table), 401–497
   and mass transit, 24
   worker protection, 24
Railway Program Institute, 317
Raj, P.P.K., 267
Reardon, Roy, 12, 13
Recalls, product, 176, 218
   of automobiles, 4, 26, 111, 223
   of Campbell's Soup, 139
   costs (table), 222
   "emergency response" documents and procedures, 92, 221–224
   insurance, 17
   records, 162, 221–222
   of toasters, 162
   and TRIS-treated fabrics, 245
   of trouble lights, 4, 223
Record-Retention Requirements Related to Product Safety and Liability, Federal, 547–584
Records and record retention, 89–92, 159, 213
   basic organizational documents, 91
   categories of corporate safety data, 201–202
   change control, 189–191
   computers and, 92, 189–190, 200, 201
   of design data, 91–92, 189–191, 193, 195–201
   documentation guidelines, 93, 201
   drawings and specifications filing plan (chart), 189
   elements of data system (table), 195
   emergency response documents, 92, 221, 222
   federal retention requirements, 89, 193, 547–584
   feedback chain and, 193, 195–202
   and liability problems, 92, 200, 276, 277
   on marketing and shipping, 92
   on outside suppliers, purchases from, 166–168
   on product safety policy, 91
   on production operations, 92, 159, 162, 166–168, 189–191
   and recalls, 162, 221–222
   on repair and rework activities, 162
   servicing, 99, 196–200
   standardization of, 201
   on toxicity, format examples of, 238, 239
Refrigerator Safety Act, 25, 29
Regulators, The (Kohlmeier), 43
Regulators Handbook, The (Jennings), 44
Regulatory agencies *see* Regulatory process; and names of specific agencies
Regulatory process, 43–72
   agency rulemaking procedures, formal and informal, 48–49
   Code of Federal Regulations (CFR), 25, 60–62
   Federal Register, 59, 61–64
   how agencies are captured, 43–49
   how commissioners are appointed, 45–46
   how regulators actually regulate, 43–53
   how regulators delay regulation, 46–49
   and industry career opportunities, 44–46
   industry standards and, 53–54, 56–59
   procedures for implementing legislation, 59–64
   registry of regulations *see Code of Federal Regualtions; Federal Register*
   regulation text, example of, 63
   regulations, issuance of, 61–64

Regulatory process (*Cont.*):
   regulations, unpublicized, 47–48
   and safety guidelines for design engineers, 50, 52–53
   and standards-setters, liability of, 64–72
   and "yak butter" petition, 43
   (*See also* Government regulation; and specific regulatory agencies)
Reliability, 57, 99, 100, 104–105, 147, 220
   defined, 656
   hazard rate calculations, 121–129
   probability-of-survival estimates, 172–174, 176
   "product rule," 176
   and quality control tasks (table), 164–165
   risk of malfunction concept, 121
Remington Arms Co., Inc. v. Kasel, 69, 72
Repair and rework activities, 162–163
   checklist, 158
Responsibility to warn, 75, 202–206
Restatement (second) of Torts, 6–22, 66–67
   and negligence liability theories, 66–67
   and strict liability doctrine, 7, 10–14
   on "unreasonably dangerous" defects, 18, 20, (text) 22
Review Commission, 64
Rheingold, Paul D., 13, 14, 240*n*.
Rhode Island, 326
Risk, 65–67, 102
   assumption-of-risk concept, 20
   assumption-of-risk as defense, 278
   social acceptance of, 38–41
   unreasonable, 26, 32–35, 50, 75
River, Gordon, 283
Rivets (checklist), 342
Rock crusher, 2
Ronan, W. W., 152*n*.
Root, Elihu, 9
Rubber, natural, 248
Rubber and plastics industries, 229
Rust, Edward B., 5–6

Saccharin, 242–243
Safe Drinking Water Act, 32
Safety belts, auto, 24, 292, 295
Sales personnel, 97
Salmonella bacteria in Ames test, 243, 244, 657
Sampling:
   attributes and variables tests compared (table), 189
   comparison of plans (table), 187
   and defects, sporadic and chronic (table), 177
   designing program for, 176–188
   and outside suppliers, use of, 166, 167
   stratified and random, compared (table), 188
Sampling Procedures and Tables for Inspection by Attributes, 180
Sampling Procedures for Inspection by Variables for Percent Defective, 185
Scaffold failure case, 325
Scaffolding, portable, 206
Screws (checklist), 344
Seals and sealing, 248
   for shielding electrical/electronic equipment (checklist), 358–359
Selenium, 229
Service, 81, 99, 217
   contracts, 31, 213, 215

Service (*Cont.*):
    and feedback on product performance, 193, 196–200, 202
    record forms, 197, 199, 200
    safety program and, 196–200, 202
Service contracts:
    defined, 31
    distinguished from written warranties, 31
    on long-lived products, 213, 215
Severity:
    of failure effects in FMEA, 131–133, 138–140, 144, 145, 147
    levels, 139–140
    NEISS index of injuries (table), 140
    scales (tables), 139–140
    and warranty, 103–104
Shipping, 102, 104
    hazardous materials, federal regulations for, Appendix C, 401–497
Shoes, 27, 66
Silicone, 252–253
Simpson, Richard O., 28
Sinclair, Upton, 8
Skin absorption of toxic substances, 234, 381
    (*See also* Toxic substances)
Smoke sensors, 257
Society of Automotive Engineers (SAE), 54, 58
Soldering, 148
Solvents, 169
    explosive reactions with nitrogen tetroxide (table), 248
    flammable, in paint, 47
Sound:
    audio signals evaluation (table), 107
    noise as hazard, 27–28, 97, 111
Sound systems, 291, 295
Space heater, oil-fueled, 218, 223
Space station, fire-extinguishing system for, 259
Specification, defined, 657
"Specification" standards, 57
Specifications:
    government purchasing-contract categories, 166–168
    for outside suppliers, 166–168
    substitution hazard, 196, 198
Spills, 263–267
    airborne hazards from (chart), 267
    cleanup and disposal, 264–266
    emergency response procedures, 264, (chart) 266
    hazard and toxicity levels (tables), 232–233
    National Contingency Plan for, 264–265
    of oil, 264, 265
    safety measures at Dow, 264
    transportation modes, impacts and impact values (table), 270–273
Sports Car Club of America, 39
Sports equipment, 19, 56
    as injury producer, 38, 53
Spot welder, 205
Spring-Lock Scaffolding v. Sunspan Engineering and Construction Co., 325
Sprinkler systems, 259, 263
Stability:
    defined, 638
    of hydraulic fluids (table), 252
Stainless steel compatibility data, 248, (table) 250
Standards, 21, 23–29, 50, 100
    for bicycle design, 53

Standards (*Cont.*):
    in checklist preparation, 330
    compliance with, as defense argument, 277
    consumer movement and, 21, 57
    Consumer Product Safety Act and, 21, 28, 29
    Consumer Product Safety Commission Standards, index to, 525–545
    as designer guides, 50, 52, 99–100, 102, 330
    as evidence of due care, 21
    for fire extinguishers on mobile equipment (table), 258
    and foreign suppliers, 169
    industry *see* Standards, industry
    for occupational safety and health, 2, 26–27, 235
    and outside supplier, use of, 166, 167, 169
    power press, 27
    pressures for, 1–6, 21, 57
    for sampling procedures, 185, 186
    "sweetheart," 27
    for toxic substances exposure limits, 379, 399
    toxicity "priority list," 235
    (*See also* Standards-setting organizations)
Standards, industry, 53–59, 106
    "American National Standard," 54
    for boilers, industrial, 1
    courts and, 21, 52
    "generic," 57
    limitations of, 20–21, 52
    "performance," 56–57
    and regulatory process, 53–59
    "specification," 57
    and standards-setters, liability of, 65–72
    standards-setting organizations *see* Standards-setting organizations
    strengthening of safety aspects, 56
    voluntary, 2, 20–21
Standards for specific products, (*see* Index of Standards for Specific Products and Practices)
Standards-setters, liability of:
    ANSI memorandum on, 64, (text) 65–72
    causes for action, 65–70
    parties subject to, 70–71
Standards-setting organizations, 53–59, 585–621
    abbreviation codes for American and foreign, 58–59
    consumer-oriented, 54
    liability of, 64–72
    public participation in, 56, 57
    safety attitudes in, 54, 56
    state government purchasing offices, 585, 621–622
    testing and certifying laboratories, 54
    trade associations, 53–54, 585–621
    types of standards used, 56–57
    voluntary, 54, 585–621
    (*See also* specific organizations)
Standards-setting process:
    ANSI and, 54, 56
    federal regulatory process and, 59–64
Stannous fluoride, 241
Starr, Chauncey, 38
State of the art (in design):
    defense plea, 21, 277
    defined, 277
Statute of limitations, 22–23
    as defense argument, 277–278
    in insurance, product liability, 298
Statutory law, evolution of, 22–35
Steel, carbon, compatibility data (table), 250

GENERAL INDEX 681

Steel alloys compatibility data (table), 250
Stieglitz, William I., 279
Storage, 168
    and fuel systems (checklist), 370–372
    packaging and, 208
    of production materials and parts, 158–160, 162
    records, 159
    of wastes, hazardous (table), 237
Stress:
    defined, 658
    design techniques and, 149–152
    emergency behavior studies, 152
    and human performance, 149–152
    noise hazards, 27, 97, 111
    and "subjective lowered standard" phenomenon, 151
Strict liability:
    defenses (table), 278
    defined, 68
    Prosser and, 10–12
    and standards-setters, legal liability of, 64, 68–70, 72
    in tort, evolution of, 7, 8, 10–14, 21, 23
Structural materials (checklist), 339–340
    (*See also* specific materials)
Styrene, 270–272
"Subjective lowered standard" phenomenon, 151
"Substantial product hazard":
    defined, 28
    government notification of, 167, 169, 223
Sulfuric acid, 270, 271, 273
Sunspan Engineering and Construction Co. v. Spring-Lock Scaffolding, 325
Surplus lines ("not admitted") insurors, 319, 321
Swain, Alan D., 147, 150, 151, 155
Switches, 110, 149–150
Symbols:
    in fault tree analysis, 118, 119
    for fires, classes of, 260–261
Synergism and toxicity, 231, 235, 267, 274
Systems Safety Society, 283

Tamperproofing devices, 209, 211, 213
Teflon, 248, 251, 254–256
Television:
    banned antenna device, 50
    industry liability insurance rates, 291, 295
Temperature:
    and hydraulic fluid selection (table), 252
    sensors, 257
"Test development engineer," 103
Testing and certifying laboratories, 54
Tests and testing, 102, 115, 117, 226
    Ames carcinogenicity test, 243–245, 657
    bioassays, 228, 231–235, 242–243, 245, 643
    built-in facilities for (table), 217
    for carcinogenicity, 241–245, 657
    human factors programs, 111
    and liability, 215
    long-lived products and, 215, 217
    and outside suppliers, use of, 166–168
    planning product tests (table), 178
    as predictive technique, 115, 117, 124, 127–128, 176
    premarket, 32–34, 240–241
    protocols and imprecise regulations, 49–50
    psychological, 105
    of safety equipment, 27
    sampling *see* Sampling

Tests and testing (*Cont.*):
    testing department responsibilities (chart), 186
    of toxic chemicals, federal reporting requirements for, 32–34
    Toxic Substances Control Act requirements (chart), 33
    for toxicity, 231, 234
Tetrachloroethane, 248
Textile industry, 229
Threshold, lethal (TLm), 228
Threshold Limit Values (TLVs), 231, 235, 379–399
    American Conference of Governmental Industrial Hygienists (ACGIH) listings of, Appendix B, 379–399
    of asphyxiants, 381
    calculating concentrations of, 267, 269, 274
    for carcinogens and suspect carcinogenic substances, 396–397
    categories of, 379–380
    Ceiling (TLV-C), defined, 380
    Ceiling (C) vs. Time-Weighted Average (TWA) limits, 380–381
    definitions of, 379–380
    and environmental factors, 381
    lethal doses *see* Lethal doses
    of mixtures of substances, 267, 269, 381
    of nuisance particulates, 381, 397
    OSHA exposure limits, 379, (table) 399
    Short Term Exposure Limit (STEL), defined, 379
    for skin exposure, 381
        (*See also* notations on skin in tables of toxic substances)
    for substances of variable composition, 398
    tests for individual susceptibility, 379
    Time-Weighted Average (TWA), defined, 379
    Time-Weighted Average (TWA) limits and permissible excursions, 380, 397–398
    of toxic substances, 379–381, (tables) 382–399
    for welding fumes, 398–399
    (*See also* Biologic Limit Values)
Thresholds, vibration (chart), 114
Tilley, A.I., 95
Tires, automobile:
    industry liability insurance and, 19, 30, 287, (tables) 291–292, 295, (table) 296
    standards, 24
Toasters, recalled, 162
Toluene, 274
Tooling, 104
Torque-wrenching demonstration, courtroom, 285–286
Torts, 323, 325, 326
    as defined in Restatement (second) of Torts (text), 22
    and Restatement (second) of Torts, 6–22
Toxic substances, 32–35, 231–237, 379–399
    and allergic reactions, 240–241
    asphyxiants, 381, 399
    Biologic Limit Values (BLVs), 394
    carcinogenic *see* Carcinogenic substances
    cattle feed contamination, 225
    chemical hazards (checklist), 227
    definition difficulties, 231
    dioxin, 166–167, 266
    EPA list of target substances, 35
    exposure-limit calculations, 267, 269, 274
    exposure limit standards, 274
        from ACGIH, 379–399
        from ANSI, 398

Toxic substances (*Cont.*):
    from OSHA, 267, 379, 380, (table) 399
  fire-extinguishing agents, 260–261, (table) 268
  gasoline, 398
  government regulation of *see* Toxic Substances Control Act
  inhalation doses, 234, 235
  lethal concentrations (LCs), 235, 268
  lethal doses (LDs), 228, 231–235
    defined, 231, 232, 234–235
  NIOSH listings of, 234–235
  nuisance particulates (dusts), 381, 397
  PBBs (polybrominated biphenyls), 225
  PCBs (polychlorinated biphenyls) banned by EPA, 35
  polytetrafluoroethylene decomposition products, 398
  premarketing notification procedure, 34–35
  "priority list" (NIOSH), 235
  skin (cutaneous absorption) susceptibility to, 234, 381
    (*See also* skin designations in tables of exposure limits)
  spills, toxicity and hazard levels in (tables), 232–233
  synergism and, 231, 235, 267, 274
  testing requirements, premarketing, 32–35
  Threshold Limit Values (TLVs) *see* Threshold Limit Values
  Toxic Substances Control Act, 25, 32–35, 226–227, 234
  TOXLINE, data bank, 227, 274
  TRIS (2,3-dibromopropyl phosphate), 59, 242, 245–246
  vapors, concentration calculations for, 267, 269, 274
  vapors, detection of (checklist), 352
    (*See also* Vapors)
  in wastes, 236–237
  welding fumes, 394, 398–399
Toxic Substances Control Act, 25, 266–227, 234
  described, 32–35
  premarket notification procedure (chart), 34
  premarket testing requirements, 32–34
Toxicity, 231–239
  documentation forms, 238, 239
  fire-extinguishing agents and, 260–261, (table) 268
  hazard determination (chart), 228
  by inhalation, 234, 235
  lethal dose (LD$_{50}$), 231, 232, 234
  lethal doses, 231–235
  by skin absorption, 234, 381
    (*See also* skin designations in tables of exposure limits)
  spills, hazard levels in (tables), 232–233
  synergism and, 231, 235, 267, 274
  tests, 231, 234
  Threshold Limit Values (TLVs), 231, 267, 269, 274, 379–399
  (*See also* Toxic substances)
TOXLINE, 227, 274
Toys, 19
  Child Protection and Toy Safety Act, 29
  injurious, 5, 57
  and standards, safety, 57, 523
Tracing, 162, 191
Tracking, 107, 109
Tractors, 37

Trade associations:
  self-insurance survey (table), 317
  as standards-setters, 53–54, 56
Trademark licensor liability, 69–70, 72
Trailers, 19, 23, 292, 296
Training equipment design, 111, 114
Training for Emergency Procedures in Multiengine Aircraft (Ronan), 152*n*.
Transportation, 246, 264
  of chemicals: modes and mishaps in (table), 270–273
  fire-extinguisher standards for mobile equipment (table), 258
  hazardous materials handling, federal regulations for *see* Appendix C, 401–497
  ICC early regulation of, 43–44
  mass transit and urban systems safety, 24, 26
  material-handling equipment (checklists), 372–377
  packaging (checklists), 334–338
  safety laws and regulations, 23–26
    (*See also* specific laws and regulatory agencies)
  and spills, 232–233, 263–267, 270–273
  trucklines, interstate, 44
Transportation Department, U.S. (DOT), 47, 59, 61, 223, 231, 246, 265
  hazardous materials handling regulations, Appendix C, 401–497
  safety functions, 23–24, 26
Traynor, Roger, 10, 11, 14
  on strict liability, 11
Trichloroethylene, 248
TRIS (2,3-dibromopropyl phosphate), 59, 242, 245–246
Trouble lights, recalled, 4, 223
Trucks:
  chemical transportation: modes and mishaps (table), 272–273
  coupling hazard, 106
  fire-extinguisher standards for (table), 258
  trucklines, 44

Underwriters Laboratories (UL), 54, 58, 67, 102, 143, 218, 260
Uniform Commercial Code, 11, 12, 29
Uniform Sales Act, 11, 12
United Mine Workers, 36–37
United States Code, 25
United States v. Newport Air Park, 326
Universal joints (checklist), 341
Unsafe at Any Speed (Nader), 5
Urban Mass Transportation Administration, 24, 26

Vapors:
  airborne spill hazards (chart), 267
  asphyxiants, 381, 399
  calculating hazardous concentration limits in, 267, 269, 274
  combustible, detection of (checklist), 351
  exposure limits for toxic substances in, 267–269, 274
    (*See also* alphabetical listings of toxic substances, Appendix B, 379–399)
  and fire-extinguishing agents, toxic properties of (table), 268
  lethal concentrations (LCs) in, 235, 268
  toxic vapor detection (checklist), 352
Vibrations, human tolerance of (chart), 114
"Vigilance effect," 152–154
Vinyl chloride, 242–244

"Voluntary legislature," 9
Voluntary standards, 54
   (*See also* Standards, industry)

Warnings, 20, 38, 50, 159–160, 208, 279
   and advertising, misleading, 206
   color used for, 203
   as design funcion, 202–203, 206
   "failure to warn" argument, 14, 65, 241
   on hazardous materials, 208
      (*See also* transportation regulations for specific materials, Appendix C, 401–497)
   responsibility to warn, 75, 202–206
   signals, audio and visual (checklist), 352
   signs, labels, messages, 38, 98, 202–206
Warranty:
   breach of warranty defense arguments (table), 278
   consumer protection (written), 29–32
   contract warranty doctrine, 10–12
   failure rate data and, 103–105, 117, 137–138, 145
   implied, 10, 32, 206
   Magnuson-Moss Warranty Act, 29–32
   registration card return and, 30–31
   "running," 10
   Uniform Commercial Code, 29
   written, distinguished from "service contract," 31
Washer-and-spacer installation, 110
Waste disposal, 237, 266
Waste treatment processes (table), 236–237
Wastes, industrial:
   hazardous substances in, (table) 228, (table) 229, 236–237, 264–267
   spills cleanup and disposal, 264–266
Water, safe, 32
Water and Wastewater Equipment Manufacturers, 317
Water glycol, 252–253

Wear-out or "old-age" period, 127, 128, 140, 170, 171
Wearing apparel:
   care labeling, 29
   for children, 59, 176, 245
   shoes, 27, 66
Welding, 157, 258
   fumes, exposure limits for, 394, 398–399
   spot welder advertisement, 205
Western Electric, 105
Western-Willamette Corporation, Western Environmental Services Division, 265
Wiener, S. A., 232
Wilkinson, R.T., 154n.
Women, 16
   carcinogenic substances and cancer in, 167, 241, 245
   toxicity sensitivity of, 231
Woodworking Machinery Manufacturers Association, 317
Workers' compensation laws:
   and product liability cases, 322–327
Workplace, defined, 661
Workplaces, 2, 4, 242
   discomfort theory and, 151
   footprints-on-bombs mystery, 156
   labor unions and safety of, 36–37
   and toxic substances, exposure to, 242
      (*See also* Toxic substances)
Wrench, impact, air-driven, 40
Written (consumer protection) warranty, 29–32

"Yak butter" petition, 43
Yardley and Company v. Carter, 241
Yerkes, R.M., 105

Zinc, 229, 397

INDEX OF STANDARDS FOR SPECIFIC PRODUCTS AND PRACTICES
From Standards Setting Organizations

Abrasive equipment, products, methods, 503–504, 593, 600, 603
Accident-prevention signs, 514–515
Accident recording methods, 514, 518
Acetylene cylinder charging plants, 522
Adhesives and sealants, 526, 585
Aerial passenger tramways, 507
Aerospace industries, 583–586
Agricultural equipment, supplies, products, 507, 513–514, 594, 597, 602
Air and gas cleaning equipment, 518
Air-conditioning and refrigeration equipment, 586, 594, 605, 611, 616
Air pollution control, 586, 601
Air-purifying cartridges and canisters, 510
Air quality, 593
Air tools, portable, 509
Aircraft:
   breathing systems, 520
   fuel systems, 518
   manuals and equipment, 586
Airport fire control and prevention, 519
Aluminum, 586
Anchors, expansion, 601
Anesthesia, 594
Anhydrous ammonia handling, 510
Animal feeds, 589, 594, 597
Appliances, home electrical, 597
Architecture, 591, 610
Armament systems, 589
Arms and ammunition, 617
Asbestos, 513, 527, 596
Asphalt, 500, 596
Athletic apparatus (*see* Sports equipment)
Audio-visual equipment, 609
Automobile safety, 587
Automobiles (*See* motor vehicles)
Automotive lifts, 508

Bakery:
   equipment, 516
   industry, 516, 597
   sanitation, 597
Batteries, 527
Bearings, 597
Bedding, 596, 608
Belts, safety, 500

Benzene, 527, 528
Beverages, 600, 613
Bicycles, 597
Boats, 518, 588, 617
Boilers, 609
Books, 597
Bottles, 613
Boxes:
   fiberboard, 602
   wooden, 620
Brass and bronze, 598
Bricks, 598
Brushing tools, 508
Building codes, 597, 598, 605, 610, 617
Building construction, 500, 598, 605
Buses, 509, 609

Cable, 605
Cableways, 506
Canning of food, 610
Cans, tubes, and cores, 520, 598, 599
Canvas products, 598
Cargo handling, 610
Carpets and rugs, 598
Casters, industrial, 598
Casting:
   die, *see* Die casting
   investment, 605
Casting:
   die, 589
   malleable, 606
   steel, 618
Ceilings, 598, 605
Cemented carbide tools and dies, 598
Ceramics, 588
Cereals, 587
Chemical equipment testing, 591
Chemical specialties, 599
Chemicals, hazardous, labeling of, 518, 606
Children, products for, 516, 523, 606
Chlorine, 599
Circuit boards, printed, 604
Civil engineering, 594
Clothing, 611
   protective, 509–511
Coating, pipe, 609
Coatings (*see* Paints and coatings)

INDEX OF STANDARDS FOR SPECIFIC PRODUCTS AND PRACTICES 685

Color, 604
Color code for physical hazards, 516
Communications, 603, 605, 616
Compressed gas, 599
    cylinder identification, 515
Compressor systems, 505
Computers and computer equipment, 603, 616, 619
Concrete construction and products, 500, 596, 599, 616
Concrete structures, 588
Construction industry and equipment, 599, 605, 617
Construction operations, 499–500, 598, 599
Controls:
    door, 600
    fluid, 602
    for mechanical tools, 605-606
    remote, 600
Conveyors and conveying systems, 505, 600
Cooling towers, 600
Copper marketing, 600
Cordage, 600
Corn, 600
Corrosion, 608
Cosmetics, 597
Cottonseed products, 610
Cranes, 506, 600, 607
Crayons and watercolors, 600
Crushed stone, 610
Crystallography, 589

Dairy equipment and products, 593, 600, 605
Data processing equipment, 600
Demolition, 500
Dental materials and devices, 589
Derricks, 506
Diamond (abrasive) wheels, 600
Die casting engineering, 616
Die casting machines, 508
Die castings, 589
Dispensers, flammable liquid, 520
Display, information, 616
Disposable soft goods, 605
Distilled spirits, 600
Diving equipment and operations, 516, 519
Doors, 602, 613, 618
Drafting room practice, 607
Dredging, marine, 500
Drive systems and devices, 601
Dumbwaiters, 501, 590, 608
Dust explosion prevention, 513–514
Dyes and finishes, textile, 587
Dyes and pigments, 601

Earth moving and grading, 500
Electrical appliances, 601–605
Electrical Code, National, 605, 610
Electrical equipment, 604, 611
Electrical generating systems, 601, 611
Electrical industry practices, 601
Electrical installations, 610
Electrical materials, 605
Electrical testing, 601, 604, 619
Electrical utility equipment, 601
Electronic industries and equipment, 601, 604
Elevator door locking devices, 503
Elevators, 501, 590, 608, 611

Envelope manufacturing equipment, 508
Environmental health, 611
Epoxy resin labeling, 510
Escalators, 501, 590, 608
Excavation, 500
Exchangers, tabular, 619
Exhaust systems, 513
Explosion prevention, 513–514, 523
Explosive materials, 522
Explosives and blasting agents, use of, 522
Eye protection, 516, 593, 596, 613

Fabrics, nonwoven, 605
Factory safeguards, 602
Farm equipment, 602
Fasteners, 604
Fastening tools, explosive-actuated, 500, 615
Ferrous metals, 591
Fertilizers, 597, 602
Fiberboard, 602, 612
Fire codes, 605
Fire detection thermostats, 520
Fire extinguishers, 502, 522, 523, 609
Fire-extinguishing systems, 502, 522, 523, 609
Fire-fighting at airports, 519
Fire protection, 518, 522, 602, 607, 609, 611
Fire pumps, 522
Fire suppression, 520, 609
Firearms, 612
Fireworks, 522
First aid kits, 523
Fittings, 606
Flame arresters, 520
Flammability of liquids, 521
Flammable-liquid dispensers, 520
Floor and wall openings, railings, toe boards, 506
Flooring, 612, 620
Fluid controls, 602
Fluid power systems, 611
Fluids, metalworking, 509
Food, 593, 597, 605, 608
Food, drug, and beverage equipment, 509
Food industry equipment, 600, 602, 608–610
Football helmets, 517, 523
Footwear, 590
    occupational, 505, 515
Forest products, 611
Forging and forming operations, 505, 602
Foundry operations, 521, 603, 606
Foundry sands, 590
Friction mats, 603
Fumigation, 523
Furniture, 596, 606, 608

Garden power equipment, 507
Gas:
    compressed, 515, 599
    fuel, 590
Gas appliances, 520, 603, 607
Gasoline, 614
Gears, 590
Geology, 587, 597
Glass, safety, 514
Glass containers, 603
Glass marketing, 602

686 INDEX OF STANDARDS FOR SPECIFIC PRODUCTS AND PRACTICES

Glazing materials:
   architectural, 517
   safety, 514, 603, 613, 614
Grain-industry explosion prevention, 513
Granite, 597
Graphic communications, 603
Graphical symbols, 509
Grinding, polishing, and buffing equipment, 608
Grinding fluids, 509
Grinding machines, 503–504, 600, 603
Grocery-handling equipment, 608
Gummed paper products, 603
Gypsum, 603

Hammers, nail, 508
Hardboard, 512
Hardware, 598
Hardwoods, 602, 611, 614, 617
Hazardous substances handling, 401–497, 518
Hearing protection, 519
Heating and cooling, 594, 609, 611
Helmets and headgear, 517, 523, 616
Highways, 587, 593, 610
Hoists, 500, 506, 603
Home economics, 590
Home playground equipment, 523
Hosiery, 608
Hospital equipment and supplies, 590, 609
Hot-dip galvanized products, 590
Housing, 593
Hydraulic power presses, 504

Industrial equipment, 602
Industrial hygiene, 591
Injection molding machines, 508
Instruments, industrial and laboratory, 604, 616
Insulation:
   mineral wool, 612
   thermal, 69
Insurance, 591
Internal combustion engines, products using, 616
Iron and steel production and products, 591, 597, 603, 604

Joints, expansion, 601
Joists, steel, 618

Knitwear, 611

Labeling, hazardous materials, 518
Laboratory products, 599, 604
Ladders, 501, 592
Lasers, 519, 593
Laundry and dry cleaning equipment, 512, 606
Lawnmowers, 507, 615
Lead products, 606
Leather, 592, 618
Lenses, 614
Library equipment, 592
Lifting devices, 506, 508
Lighting, 593, 596, 603
   home, 570

Lighting (*Cont.*)
   school, 501
   workplace, 500
Lime, 611–612
Limestone, 603–604
Lockout protection, 521
Locks, elevator door, 503
Lubrication, 595, 612
Lumber, 592, 602, 603, 611, 614, 615, 617, 620
Lung disease prevention, 592

Machine tools, 504, 605–606, 612
Magnetic materials, 606
Management, 604, 606, 614, 616–617
Manlifts, 502
Manufacturing, general, 616–617
Marine fittings, 521
Marine terminal operations, 511
Marine vessels and structures, 617
Marking devices (for metal), 606
Masonry work, 500
Materials handling equipment, 598, 603, 606
Materials testing, 594
Meat processing saws, 509
Mechanical Code, Uniform, 605
Mechanical engineering, 595, 605–609
Mechanical power transmission apparatus, 504–505, 607
Medical advisory information, 592, 608
Medical equipment, 594
Medical instrumentation, 596
Medical specialties, 593-594
Medicine:
   industrial, 604
   laboratory, 599
Metal, sheet, 616
Metal building systems, 607
Metal-cutting tools, 607
Metal extrusion equipment, 504
Metal name plates, 609
Metal powder industry, 504, 607
Metal products, architectural, 608
Metal technology information, 594
Motor vehicles, 607

National Electrical Code, 605
Nets, safety, 500
Nonwoven fabrics, 605
Nuclear industry, 592

Occupational safety and health, 586
Oils, essential, 601
Oils and fats, 592–593
Optical goods, 614
Optometric products, 593
Outdoor power equipment, 507, 614

Packaging machinery, 508, 614
Paints and coatings, 516, 522, 618
   hazard prevention for children, 516
Pallets, 613, 620
Paper bags and sacks, 521
Paper boxes, 612
Paper manufacturing, 512, 593

INDEX OF STANDARDS FOR SPECIFIC PRODUCTS AND PRACTICES 687

Paperboard packaging, 614
Parking garage equipment, 503
Particleboard, 512, 612
Paving, 500, 588, 596
Perlite, 614
Pesticides, 597, 601
Petroleum, 614
    exploration, 587
    operations, 591, 593
Pewter, 619
Pharmaceuticals and drugs, 593, 597, 614, 619–620
Photochemical machining, 614
Photogrammetry, 595
Photography, photographic materials, 614, 617
Pile driving, 500
Pine, southern, 617
Pipe:
    bituminous, 597
    cast-iron, 598
    clay, 610
    coating of, 609
    concrete, 588
    fabrication of, 614
Pipeline construction, 615
Pipes, metal, and piping, 607
Piping systems identification, 500–501, 607
Plastics, 594, 609, 615, 617
Platforms, work, 500, 502, 503
Plumbing and plumbing equipment, 591, 595, 605, 609
Plumbing Code, Uniform, 605
Plywood, 512, 593, 602, 603
Poison-control centers, 587
Polyurethane, 615
Power presses, 504
Pressure vessels, 609–610
Printed circuit boards, 604
Printing industry, 615
Printing inks and equipment, 509, 612
Printing press controls, 507
Project management, 615
Pulp and paper industries, 512, 618–619
Pumps, 599, 618
Purchasing, 609

Quality control, 594

Racks, storage, 615
Radio technology, 615
Railroad ties, 615
Railroads, 596
Record-keeping methods, 514
Recycling, 609
Redwood lumber, 615
Refractories, 615
Refrigeration, 594
Refrigerators, commercial, 591
Refuse collection, 521
Rehabilitation facilities, 599
Research, 597, 608
Respiratory equipment (medical), 594
Respiratory protection, 516, 517, 520, 592
Retailing, 612
Rhodamine dyes, 601
Rivet setting, 508
Road-building, 593

Roof decks, 603, 618
Roofing, 500, 596, 612
Rope, 600
    wire, 511
Rubber goods machinery and products, 505–506, 616
Rubber protective equipment for workers, 508–509

Safety, public, 612–613
Safety belts, 500
Safety engineering, 595
Safety equipment, industrial, 604
Safety nets, 500
Sand and gravel, 613
Sanitary engineering, 595
Sanitation, industrial and commercial, 512, 597, 605, 613
Saw mills, 511–512
Saws:
    chain, 509
    meat-processing, 509
Scaffolds and scaffolding, 500, 502, 616
Scales and weighing machines, 508
School supplies and equipment, 613
Science and technology information, 608
Scrap metal, 604
Scrap processing equipment, 521
Scuba diving equipment, 516
Seeds, 597
Service bureaus, industrial, 604
Sewage treatment, 616
Shale, clay and slate, 601
Sheet metal, 616
Shingles and shakes, red cedar, 615
Shipbuilding, 588, 617
Silo safety, 613
Ski lifts, 507
Slag, 613
Snow throwers, 507
Soaps and detergents, 616
Sod, 595
Soft drinks, 613
Solvent extraction plants, 522
Space heaters, temporary, 500
Sports car speed events, 617
Sports equipment, 516, 517, 587, 589, 617
Springs, 617–618
Stairs, industrial, 502
Standardization methods, 618
Standpipe and hose systems, 522
Steel bars, 618
Steel construction and construction products, 500, 591, 618
Steel fuel tanks, 507
Steel plate shops, 520
Steel shipping containers, 618
Steelmaking, 618
Stone, crushed, 610
Sump pumps, 618
Sweeping compounds, 520
Swimming pools, 593, 613
Symbols, graphic, 607

Tanks, steel, for fuel, 507
Tape, pressure-sensitive, 613
Telephones, 619

688 INDEX OF STANDARDS FOR SPECIFIC PRODUCTS AND PRACTICES

Television, 617
  cable, 610
Testing, 594, 620
  electrical, 601
  laboratory products for, 599, 604
  materials, 594
  seeds, 597
  steel and steel castings, 618
Textile dyes and finishes, 587
Textile industry operations, 510–511
Thread, 619
Threshold Limit Values (TLVs) for toxic substances, 589
Tile work, 500
Timber construction, 591
Tin, 619
Tire and tire manufacturing, 24, 505–506, 619
Towers, mobile, 502
Toxic substances exposure limits, 589
Toys, 523
Traffic laws, 610
Trailers, 509
Transportation data, 619
Transportation engineering, 604
Tricycles, 523
Trucks, 598, 619
  industrial, 506, 598, 604
Tubes and tubing, metal, 607
Tunnel and shaft construction, 500

Ultrasonic industry, 69
Uniform Building Code, 605
Uniform Fire Code, 605
Uniform Mechanical Code, 605

Uniform Plumbing Code, 605
Uniform Vehicle Code, 610

Vacuum cleaners, 620
Vacuum equipment, 595
Valves, 606
Vehicle Code, Uniform, 610
Vending machines, 609
Veneers, 512, 602
Ventilating equipment, 513, 603

Warning signs and symbols, 514–515
Waste (effluent) treatment equipment, 518
Wastewater, 593
Water, 593, 595, 613
Water pollution control, 601, 616, 620
Water safety buoyant devices, 521
Water systems, 620
Welding and cutting equipment, 515, 615
Welding technology, 595, 620
Windows, steel, 618
Wire, steel, 617, 620
Wire machinery, 508
Wire rope for mines, 511
Wiring, 500
Wood materials manufacturing, 512, 602, 603, 612, 615, 620
Wood preservation, 595–596
Woodwork, 596, 613, 620
Woodworking machinery, 511

Zinc products, 620